Routledge Revivals

The Quest for a Science of Accounting

Originally published in 1997, the principal object of the editors in compiling this collection of Robert R. Sterling's work was to make more of his publications accessible in a convenient form to the academic and professional accounting communities, and to current and future generations of accounting students. While it is not a complete portfolio of his published work to date, this anthology contains all of Sterling's major articles.

Through his long-term quest for a science of accounting, Sterling sought to bring together accounting educators, practitioners, regulators, and researchers in order to identify credible advancements in accounting knowledge, authoritative changes to accounting practice, and transforming improvements to accounting education.

The Quest for a Science of Accounting

An Anthology of the Research of Robert R. Sterling

Edited by
Thomas A. Lee
Peter W. Wolnizer

Routledge Revivals
Routledge
Taylor & Francis Group

First published in 1997
by Garland Publishing, Inc

This edition first published in 2021 by Routledge
2 Park Square, Milton Park, Abingdon, Oxon OX14 4RN

and by Routledge
605 Third Avenue, New York, NY 10017

Routledge is an imprint of the Taylor & Francis Group, an informa business

Publisher's Note
The publisher has gone to great lengths to ensure the quality of this reprint but points out that some imperfections in the original copies may be apparent.

Disclaimer
The publisher has made every effort to trace copyright holders and welcomes correspondence from those they have been unable to contact.

A Library of Congress record exists under ISBN: 081533026X

ISBN: 978-0-367-69819-5 (hbk)
ISBN: 978-1-003-14341-3 (ebk)
ISBN: 978-0-367-69826-3 (pbk)

THE QUEST FOR A SCIENCE OF ACCOUNTING

An Anthology of the Research of Robert R. Sterling

Edited by

THOMAS A. LEE
PETER W. WOLNIZER

GARLAND PUBLISHING, Inc.
New York & London / 1997

Library of Congress Cataloging-in-Publication Data

Sterling, Robert R.
The quest for a science of accounting : an anthology of research / by Robert R. Sterling ; edited by Thomas A. Lee, Peter W. Wolnizer.
p. cm. — (New works in accounting history)
Includes bibliographical references.
ISBN 0-8153-3026-X (alk. paper)
1. Accounting. 2. Accounting—Research. 3. Sterling, Robert R.
I. Lee, T.A. (Thomas Alexander) II. Wolnizer, P.W. III. Title. IV. Series.
HF5625.S79 1997
657—dc21

97-26158

CONTENTS

Accounting Theory and Practice

Accounting Education and Research

PREFACE

T. A. Lee and P. W. Wolnizer

Robert R. Sterling graduated from the University of Florida in 1965 with a doctorate in economics. His dissertation, later published as *Theory of the Measurement of Enterprise Income* (University of Kansas Press, 1970), sought to explicate the notion of income in the context of a single wheat trader, and to prescribe the most appropriate manner in which it could be measured. By analyzing the wheat trader's activities, Sterling determined what financial information the trader needed in order to make informed financial decisions.

While his doctorate is in economics, Bob Sterling's scholarship is greatly influenced and enriched by his avid reading and intelligent understanding of the literatures of fields other than accounting and economics - most noticeably those of the history and philosophy of science. When elucidating the application of measurement theory to the determination of the income of a firm, he explains with meticulous care and clarity that measurement is an empirical process, and the related elements of income and wealth are observable commercial and economic phenomena. The numerical representation of these elements, being dated market prices and price-level changes, are empirically testable. The "verity" of statements about them can be independently authenticated. Being concerned with measurement, Sterling takes pains to explain the commonsense and scientific requirement that numerals must correspond with the empirical phenomena they purport to represent (the "correspondence concept") and the essential (empirical) element of additivity. In so doing, he shows that conventional accounting is "calculational-nonempirical," and not measurement.

As an accounting scholar and educator, Sterling is also vitally concerned with problem-solving; appraising conventional accounting, and eradicating errors, inconsistencies and contradictions therein; discovering a more serviceable form of financial reporting; and improving the state of accounting practice, education and research. A rigorous theorist, he is inquisitive, interested in any inquiry that may improve the state of accounting, and unwilling to restrict either the scope of "research questions" or limit the variety of "research methods." Analytical questions, he says, call for analytical modes of inquiry, and empirical questions call for empirical modes of inquiry.

An effective and lively facilitator of and participant in debate and discourse, Sterling organized and chaired many colloquia over twenty years. Several of the proceedings of those conferences were published by the Scholars Book Company, of which he is editor. Under his editorship, the Scholars Book Company has published some thirty-two scholarly works in accounting, including original works and reproductions of accounting classics.

Sterling's published scholarship is characterized by carefully constructed and rigorous argumentation; a concern with the empirical nature of the "subject matters" of accounting and process of measurement; an emphasis on the necessity for products of the accounting process to be compatible with and relevant to decision models rather than with decision makers; and by the analysis of simple cases before moving to complex situations. His quest to develop a "fruitful" (scientific) theory of accounting is encapsulated in *Toward a Science of Accounting* (Scholars Book Company, 1979).

Our principal object in compiling this collection of Bob Sterling's work, is to make more of his publications accessible in a convenient form to the academic and professional accounting communities, and to current and future generations of accounting students. He is also the author of two books (cited above), one monograph (reproduced in this collection as item 32), and editor of or contributer to eight books. Twice he has been the honoured recipient of the AICPA Gold Medal - the US accountancy profession's highest award for notable contributions to the accounting literature (items 16 and 39 reproduced in this collection).

While not a complete portfolio of his published work to date, this anthology contains all of Sterling's major articles. Forty-one pieces are reproduced herein. Only duplications and minor articles have been excluded. Five are co-authored. Many of the articles have been published in leading accounting journals over thirty years: nine in *Abacus*; eight in *The Accounting Review*; four, including his two award-winning articles, in *The Journal of Accountancy*; three in the *Journal of Accounting Research*. Of the articles included in this collection, eleven were published in the 1960s, nineteen in the 1970s, eight in the 1980s, and three in the 1990s.

We have arranged the articles under four separate, but related, subject headings: (1) The Nature of Science, Theory and Practice; (2)

Accounting Theory and Practice; (3) Appraising Conventional Accounting; and (4) Accounting Education and Research. Each section is preceded by a brief (editorial) introduction that outlines the major drifts of argument contained in the articles included in the section.

In addition to reproducing his outstanding contributions to the journal literature, Sterling's professional talents and contributions in related areas are recognized in a series of commissioned short essays - as teacher and mentor (Kevin McBeth); as administrator (Duane Windsor); and as a Senior Fellow at the FASB (Todd Johnson). While his excellence in each of those areas is widely acknowledged and much appreciated, it is his excellence in scholarship that we extol most highly in these pages. Accordingly, we thought it most appropriate and desirable that the eminent accounting scholar, Ray Chambers, write the leading and major (contributed) essay for this anthology, titled "Sterling as Scholar," and we are delighted that he agreed to do so. Working independently, Chambers and Sterling have been concerned with the theoretical foundations of accounting over three decades, and both advocate that assets be valued at current market selling prices, and that income be determined in dated real terms. They argue that these prescriptions go a long way to overcoming the fundamental flaws in conventional accounting practice. Chambers and Sterling were honoured as the first AAA Distinguished International Lecturers in 1976: Chambers, from the University of Sydney, Australia, visited the USA, while Sterling, then at Rice University, visited Europe. To all of these contributors we owe a considerable debt, and to each we express our sincerest gratitude.

By compiling this anthology, we acknowledge our special debt to Bob Sterling. Over the many years that it has been our privilege and pleasure to know Bob as a friend and colleague, his conversations, lectures and writings have greatly influenced and stimulated our intellectual ideals and pursuits. We hope that all who read his published discourses will share in the benefits, insights and instruction to be gained from the dedicated scholarship of Robert R Sterling.

T. A. Lee (Tuscaloosa, Alabama) and
P. W. Wolnizer (Geelong, Victoria)

ACKNOWLEDGMENTS

The editors, the series editor, and the publisher of this volume wish to thank the following authors, institutions, journals, and publishers for their kind permission to reproduce the copyright materials in this volume. Every effort has been made to trace authors and publishers. The items reproduced are indicated by the numbers by which they are listed in the contents page.

2. American Accounting Association, (c) 1970.
3. R. R. Sterling, (c) 1973.
4. Reprinted with permission from the *Financial Analysts Journal*, September-October 1975. Copyright 1975, Financial Analysts Federation, Charlottesville, VA. All rights reserved.
5. School of Accountancy, University of Alabama, (c) 1975.
6. Reprinted with permission from *The Journal of Accountancy*, copyright (c) 1976 by the American Institute of Certified Public Accountants, Inc. Opinions of the authors are their own and do not necessarily reflect policies of the AICPA.
8. *Abacus*, Blackwell Publishers, (c) 1966.
9. American Accounting Association, (c) 1967.
10. Institute of Professional Accounting, University of Chicago, (c) 1967.
11. Reprinted with the permission of the University Press of Florida, (c) 1971.
12. *Abacus*, Blackwell Publishers, (c) 1971.
13. *Journal of Business Administration*, (c) 1972.
14. *Abacus*, Blackwell Publishers, (c) 1972.
15. *Abacus*, Blackwell Publishers, (c) 1972.
16. Reprinted with permission from *The Journal of Accountancy*, copyright (c) 1975 by the American Institute of Certified Public Accountants, Inc. Opinions of the authors are their own and do not necessarily reflect policies of the AICPA.
17. *Abacus*, Blackwell Publishers, (c) 1981.
18. Reprinted with permission from *The Journal of Accountancy*, copyright (c) 1982 by the American Institute of Certified Public Accountants, Inc. Opinions of the authors are their own and do not necessarily reflect policies of the AICPA.
19. Scholars Book Company, (c) 1982.
20. *Accounting and Business Research*, (c) 1985.

22. *Abacus*, Blackwell Publishers, (c) 1966.
23. *Abacus*, Blackwell Publishers, (c) 1967.
24. American Accounting Association, (c) 1968.
25. The Institute of Chartered Accountants of Scotland, (c) 1968.
26. Institute of Professional Accounting, University of Chicago, (c) 1969.
27. *Abacus*, Blackwell Publishers, (c) 1969.
28. American Accounting Association, (c) 1971.
29. American Accounting Association, (c) 1972.
30. Reprinted with permission from *The Journal of Accountancy*, copyright (c) 1973 by the American Institute of Certified Public Accountants, Inc. Opinions of the authors are their own and do not necessarily reflect policies of the AICPA.
31. Reproduced with the permission of Ernst & Young, LLP, (c) 1977.
32. Accounting Research Centre, University of Sydney, (c) 1985.
33. *Advances in Accounting*, JAI Press Inc., (c) 1988.
34. Reprinted with permission from International Thomson Publishing Services, M. Mumford and K. V. Peasnell (eds.), *Philosophical Perspectives on Accounting*, Routledge Press, 1993.
36. American Accounting Association, (c) 1962.
37. American Accounting Association, (c) 1967.
38. American Accounting Association, (c) 1972.
39. Reprinted with permission from *The Journal of Accountancy*, copyright (c) 1973 by the American Institute of Certified Public Accountants, Inc. Opinions of the authors are their own and do not necessarily reflect policies of the AICPA.
40. Institute of Professional Accounting, University of Chicago, (c) 1974.
41. Reprinted with permission from *The Journal of Accountancy*, copyright (c) 1976 by the American Institute of Certified Public Accountants, Inc.
42. Clarkson Gordon Foundation, (c) 1982.
43. American Accounting Association, (c) 1989.
44. Permission from *Journal of Accounting Education*, September 1990, R. R. Sterling, 'Teacher, Educate Thyself,' Elsevier Science Ltd, Oxford, England.
45. *Abacus*, Blackwell Publishers, (c) 1990.

1. Sterling as Scholar

R. J. Chambers

And gladly wolde he learne, and gladly teche.
(of the Clerk, Chaucer, *The Canterbury Tales*)

One of the keenest pleasures of a dedicated teacher is to explain to inquisitive minds how things work - how things observable and experienced are systematically related to other things - and to give dependable warrant for those explanations. It is also an obligation or duty; for the teacher assumes the responsibility for shaping others' minds in ways that will in future shape the course of events not yet dreamed of. It would be utterly false to that duty to perpetuate ignorance, false belief and misunderstanding. One who would so teach must, first and continually, learn - as was the wont of Chaucer's clerk.

Sterling has been such a teacher. Over years of grappling with what seemed to be a mixture of tenable and questionable ideas - "hard labor", as he said - he confessed: "I enjoy wrestling with these ideas .... I do it for fun." (Sterling, 1979, p.xii). Another had said: "There is only one paramount reason for studying anything but the multiplication table. Either you are so interested in a subject that you cannot let it alone, or you are not. In the end it is a matter of intellectual passion" (Homans, 1951/1959, p.2). Sterling's labours and utterances are the expression of a sustained, but temperate, passion.

A genial and easy demeanour have been the beguiling accompaniment of an inquisitive disposition to learn alike from the legacy of scholarly antecedents, events of the past and the immediate present, and the countless engagements with the varied acquaintance that circumstances provided. Sterling would challenge obscurity, inconsistency and unreason with argument and example from what sometimes seemed an inexhaustible armoury. He would engage freely with professionals and academics, in and beyond the accounting domain, enriching his judgment and molding and strengthening his convictions. In exposition and debate alike, he has been governed by the patience and care that are the hallmarks of disciplined inquiry and artful instruction.

Sterling has concerned himself dominantly with the theory of accounting. But not "theory" in the loose sense of cataloguing prevalent rules and their justifications; rather in the sense of understanding the conditions under which effective practices may be developed - a sense common to all expert technologies. In all such fields, the aim of thought is to improve the product of practice in a world filled with physical, biological and social objects and circumstances and constraints of bewildering variety. The limited human mind copes with that variety by observation, imagination and reasoning. Where similar events are observed to have similar consequences, those uniformities (laws of causation or succession) are guides to action in subsequent settings of similar kind. But wants, expectations and preferences are idiosyncratic products of sentiment and imagination; “there is no accounting for tastes.” In practical affairs, however, imagination is subservient to the observables - what we can see or discover to be the case at or near the time of choice. It is futile to imagine what we might do next if we do not now know what means we have of doing anything. This commonsense idea lies at the root of all deliberate action, all judgments about the past, all speculations about the future, all counting, measuring and instrumentation systems, whether they relate to physical, biological, economic or financial affairs. The dominant importance of getting at the facts from time to time has been the key element distinguishing Sterling's work from that of most others, the element on which he would base the contention that accounting is, or should be, constructed on the pattern of empirical science.

Of persons, things and accounts

Whether any specific set of experiences or circumstances prompted Sterling to challenge the prevalent corpus of accounting doctrine and practice is unknown. But clearly he had wider acquaintance with disciplined discourse than many of his contemporaries. In undergraduate and graduate work in the late 1950s and early 1960s, he studied and taught economics and accounting. The concerns of both have an apparent affinity. Both deal with the income and wealth of persons and firms, with property (money and other goods) and claims to property, with transactions between competent parties at money prices. The common elements of the human condition are the diversity of wants, the scarcity of means for their satisfaction, and the necessity of choice in the face of changing wants and changing supplies of means. In an interdependent society, people seek to satisfy wants principally by exchanges of goods for money. Goods have diverse capacities for satisfying wants or for the production of other goods - diverse utilities, as it is said. However, what passes between the parties to an exchange is not utilities, but goods on the one hand and money on the other. The course of commerce, then, in a manner of speaking, is the circulation of money and money's worth. Economists had woven together these ideas into a systematic description of these interactions and interchanges. Perhaps the same could be done for the subject matter of accounting - the financial interactions of one person or firm with the rest of the community.

The engagement of any party in the circulation of money and money's worth depends on the command of money and money's worth, money being the common and most versatile medium of exchange. That is the case whether or not a person or firm keeps accounts of property and debts. But wise and prudent dealing is aided by systematic bookkeeping. From such accounts "... at any time the merchant can be resolved what he gaineth or loseth by every particular person he dealeth with, or merchandise he dealeth in, and consequently what he is worth to a farthing" (Hatton, 1695, p.137). In a nutshell, bookkeeping, like economics, would be concerned with income and wealth; but of individual persons or firms, not with the community aggregates of economics.

The deployment and management of the wealth at the command of firms in the pursuit of income was always a risky but never a haphazard affair. Merchants and their agents may plan trading operations with particular ends in view. But the actions of customers, suppliers, competitors, creditors and others may thwart their expectations, obliging them to modify plans, by much or little, in the light of changes in buying and selling prices, interest rates and trade conditions generally. They would seek more profitable lines of trade; diversify to reduce risks; eliminate technical inefficiencies; reduce holdings of idle resources, and so on. But all would depend on access to money and money's worth. They would monitor the relationship of cash inflows to cash outflows, the ratio of short term debt to liquid assets, the relationship of debt to equity, the rate of profit on capital invested. These relationships are simply aspects of the interlocked amounts of capital, debt and property (assets) constituting the financial position or state of affairs of a firm from time to time. An adverse drift in any of these relationships may imperil the survival of the firm, calling for remedial measures; a favourable drift would signal the possibility of growth. The value of systematic records indicative of the state of affairs and changes in that state should be apparent.

Sterling regarded the firm clinically; as a complex system of linked variables of which its accounts are analogous to the instrumentation of other complex systems. The idea had been advanced as long ago as the 17th century; but it had become submerged in practice, over the intervening years, by a vast array of invented "valuation rules" and "opinions" by which states of affairs could be made, by book entries, to appear better or worse than in fact they were. The function of an instrument is the representation of some feature or features of the object or operation under scrutiny. The principle may be described as correspondence; the instrument is required to be so constructed that changes in the "readings" it yields correspond with changes in the real variables monitored. On this principle, the accounting record is made to correspond with the financial engagements of the firm with the rest of the world; if necessary, by adjustments from time to time based on observation of the dated money equivalents (values in exchange, or resale prices) of the property in its legitimate possession and the debts it owes or is owed. Recourse to observation of the amounts of these variables makes the representations in financial statements an empirical matter, not a matter of opinion as accountants had widely claimed that they could be. Carnap (1934, p.34) had said: "Statements having content, i.e. statements, as is usually said, expressing some state of affairs, belong to the field of empirical science." Sterling has aimed to establish accounting as part of that field. Only thus could financial affairs be managed or kept under discriminating scrutiny by officers of a firm, or the creditors and other parties who rely on the skill and good faith of those officers.

Isolates and systems

Buying and selling, borrowing and lending, give rise to determinate legal-financial rights and obligations which are settled in due course by transfers of money and money's worth. But they may be required to be settled at any time by the exigencies of creditors, death, bankruptcy, termination of partnerships and liquidation of companies.

It seems a matter of common sense, then, that accounts of firms should represent in detail and in total the up-to-date money's worths of property and debts. Further, the periodical profit or loss from trade would indicate whether a firm was or was not worthy of the continued financial support of investors and creditors. The legal-financial nexus of firms, expressed in periodical accounts, would thus provide a set of checks and balances on the management of the mercantile and financial engagements of firms. But the integrity of the whole system would depend on the integrity of the accounting which linked its parts.

By the end of the 19th century accountants had come to regard firms as committed to predetermined policies and programs in a stable environment into an indefinite future. On that ("going concern") supposition, there would be no need to adapt to changing states of the firm or its environment; no need for accounts representing affairs in up-to-date prices. Assets could be valued at the discretion of principals, made to show better or poorer results and positions than achieved. Imagination and invention would yield "valuation bases" that had no counterpart in commercial dealing. It would be said: "Every balance sheet must be largely a matter of opinion..." (Dickinson, 1908, p.422). Balance sheets had become incomprehensible complexes of past facts, present guesswork and future expectations - useless as instrumentation that might aid in the management of solvency, financial flexibility and profitability. From time to time there would occur disastrous failures, bankruptcies, corporate reconstructions, when immediately prior balance sheets indicated success, not impending doom.

The isolationist notion of the firm and the isolationist nature of accounting doctrine and practice were in marked contrast to the systematic features of commercial interaction as economists represented them. For generations accounting manuals and textbooks had fostered the isolationist attitude. They offered no analysis of the conditions of reasoned choice, of the information pertinent to choice and judgment, of the conditions of informative communication, of the necessary conditions of valid measurement, aggregation and relation. These matters had long been the object of inquiry and the subject matter of conclusions well established both in discourse and practical affairs in other fields. They could, thought Sterling, provide the elements of a coherent set of propositions yielding a realistic, verifiable, continually up-dated accounting. The course to be followed would be the same as in the development of other reliable knowledge.

"The method of scientific investigation is nothing but the expression of the necessary working of the human mind," said Huxley (1894, p.363). Sterling would examine the setting, the choices and the actions, "the necessary working of the mind," of a wheat trader as an example (Sterling, 1970).

He described his *Theory of the Measurement of Enterprise Income* (Sterling, 1970, p. xii) as a polemic. But it was disputatious only to clarify and make way for the positive drift of the work. Treating the products of accounting as messages from the source to the users of information, it was stipulated that information is useful to the extent that it is true ("veritable"), relevant to the problems confronting the receiver, and intelligible to the receiver (Chapter IV). Two further chapters (V and VI) examined the features of measurements and predictions, the conditions of valid cumulation, and the problems of dealing with heterotemporal measurements - all in a fashion not previously attempted in the literature. Only after these preliminaries were the thought-processes of the trader examined. Taking the pursuit of profit and the maintenance of solvency as principal aims and constraints of the trader, it was shown that presently dated money's worths (values in exchange, selling or exit prices) of assets are relevant to every choice available to the trader, and to the decisions of other parties financially related to the trader (Chapter VII).

This theory systematically links the firm to the circumstances of the commercial environment as the merchant (or any person) faces them. Under it, balance sheets would be dependable representations of the financial relationships of firms with the rest of the world, rather than the prevalent incompatible mixtures of presently verifiable, hypothetical and imaginary magnitudes. Many have held that accounting cannot be governed by firm principles or laws, such as the laws of nature. Such opinions betray neglect (or ignorance) of the fact that the "laws" of the natural and other sciences are not "given in nature," "immutable," but are deliberate constructions of people anxious to cope with the vagaries of nature. However, there are "laws" governing financial arrangements that are analogous to the laws of the physical sciences. "The more a firm is in debt, the less is its prospect of further borrowing" is, in principle, no different from the physical laws of expansion and contraction under changes in temperature. That accounting is a deliberately constructed device for coping with the vagaries of commercial and financial affairs was among the driving beliefs of Sterling.

Qualities and quantities

We commonly add, subtract and relate money amounts in daily short-run settings, treating numbers of money units as we treat simple numbers. And in the short-run we are seldom misled. Perhaps for that reason, accountants came to treat the singular money amounts associated with diverse commodities and debts as similar in kind, freely aggregable in balance sheets and income accounts regardless of the dates of the transactions which generated them. But, over time, business firms are confronted with changes in the composition and prices of commodity and durables holdings, and changes in the general purchasing power of the money unit. Both are of importance in the calculation of periodical income, if income is to be regarded, as it is ordinarily expected to be, as a genuine increment in general purchasing or spending power. These two problems - "a change in the ratio of exchange [price] and a change in the numeraire," as Sterling (1970, p.331) described them - and their effects on aggregation and relation were scarcely noticed under "the accounting tradition." Some of the amounts appearing in financial statements would be purchase prices at widely different dates, some would be selling prices at different dates, some would be money transfers at different dates, and many would be "synthetic" amounts derived by any of the numerous "valuation" options in common use. It should have been clear that aggregates of such heterogeneous and heterotemporal amounts could have nothing to do with dated financial positions and results. But mathematical (and practical) propriety was set aside. Dicksee (1905, p.147) had said: "Accounting is not a matter of arithmetic, or of mathematics of any kind." And Gilman (1939, p.257) had warned against "trying to justify a proposition as a principle of accounting because it is based on a principle of mathematics ..." Such a cavalier attitude would isolate accounting from the disciplinary principles of mathematics and measurement widely respected in other technologies.

Sterling was not the first to decry the folly of heterogeneous aggregation. But he has been one of the few to deal with the matter systematically. Dated sums of money and similarly dated values in exchange can be validly added, the sum representing for all items so quantified the same quality as each individual amount represents for each item. This cannot be said of any of the qualities - utility, service potential, future services, physical capital - proposed by others as the focus of attention; for none of them is observable, and none is quantifiable in a common and known scale. However, of no commodity does the dated value in exchange vary according to any known mathematical law. It is not an intrinsic quality, but must be found from time to time by observation at the point where buyers confront sellers, or from the numerous price lists, catalogues, trade journals and announcements in the public press which serve to facilitate buying and selling. Differences between discovered prices at successive dates enter into the calculation of income no less than differences (net revenues) between the prices paid and the prices received from any purchase and sale.

As for a change in the general purchasing power of the money unit, its effect falls on every unit representing wealth at the beginning of a period. Its amount is obtained by applying to the opening wealth a "coefficient" of variation in the general purchasing power of the unit. Call it a "purchasing power scale adjustment." The genuine increment in wealth, the increment in general purchasing power, is then the algebraic sum of recorded revenues, price variations and the scale adjustment.

In essence, then, Sterling's "market value" accounting would rely on dated observations of transactions and other events (as does prevalent day-to-day accounting practice), dated observations of selling prices, and dated official indexes of the change in the general purchasing power of money (or dated inflation rates). Before and since Sterling expounded his scheme, accountants have held that accounting is quite unlike other disciplined pursuits. The contention cannot properly be sustained. The variables of engineering, of chemistry, of biology, are brought under scrutiny by the application of the same general principles as Sterling applied to the scrutiny of financial affairs, by dated observations coupled with intertemporal adjustments for changes in the significance of the unit.

Of things and theories

Notice has been taken of the derivation of systematic knowledge by the selection and relation of statements (propositions) dealing with particular objects and ideas. Some statements are descriptive, positive, describing what is or is not the case. Some are evaluative, stating what is desired or desirable. Some are prescriptive, imperative (or normative), stating what shall or should or must be done to attain desired ends. By the conjunction of all or some of such statements we may derive other statements by inference. The sets of initial statements and derived statements we call theories. Theories, said Pareto (1916/1963, p.2024), "are merely what people say about the things they do or experience." They are verbal or other symbolic expressions of what are believed to be the connections between objects and events, and their antecedents and consequents. It is a common folly to suppose that theories are not, or not necessarily, related to things, events and occurrences, that theory and practice are, or may be, or should be, divorced. There are, for example, theories about how books of account should be kept and summaries derived. But books of account do not aid in earning profits or securing solvency unless bookkeeping rules are linked to the full set of events of which profits and solvency, in the common meaning of those terms, are the outcome. If that linkage is not established, there can be no assurance that businessmen and their agents, at an intellectual and spatial distance from the events, will be able to respond appropriately to the real circumstances of their firms.

A theory is, in effect, a message. Its object is to inform the judgments and choices of those engaged in the application or advancement of reliable knowledge of what, on the basis of disciplined observation and argument, is believed to be the case - generally or universally. We say of a statement that corresponds with "what is the case" that it is a true statement, to whomsoever it is addressed.. The search for true statements underlies all inquiry directed to the discovery or propagation of reliable knowledge. That, at least, is how Sterling has seemed to view the prevalent knowledge of the time over a daunting range of disciplines and technologies. The notion of correspondence pervades them all - except accounting.

Yet the products of accounting are likewise messages. They purport to be, and are widely expected to be, informative of what was the case and what is the case at stated dates. It follows from "informative" that the symbols used shall correspond in all significant particulars with what is or was experienced or observed; and that whatever "processing" is done shall do no violence to the substance of what was experienced or observed. That Sterling made use of "truth" (verity) as a prime feature of communications has already been noticed. The wholesale disregard of truth as correspondence by accounting teachers, both in general discourse and in the research output of recent decades, gave him cause for an across-the-board foray against the consequences of its neglect (Sterling, 1988). Citing

Huxley, Santayana, Quine and Popper on the commonsense character of scientific knowledge, he deplored what he saw as the obscurity and pretentiousness of those who would disregard the commonsense language and everyday usages of commerce and turn to ideas that have no counterpart in the very things and processes to which accounting relates. Item by item and piece by piece he would show the particulars of conventional dicta and practice to offend common sense and common reason.

Innovation, and consolidation?

Many persons and ideas have risen to prominence in academic, scientific and business life in an already supportive milieu. Professional and academic establishments develop codes and criteria of recognition and advancement that, generally, are protective of their habits and orthodoxies. The path of an innovator has long, perhaps always, been thorny. "...there is nothing more difficult to carry out, nor more doubtful of success, nor more dangerous to handle, than to initiate a new order of things. For the reformer has enemies in all those who profit by the old order, and only lukewarm defenders in all those who would profit by the new order.... Thus it arises that on every opportunity for attacking the reformer, his opponents do so with the zeal of partisans, the others only defend him half-heartedly, so that between them he runs great danger." (Machiavelli, c1519/1952, p.55). Especially hazardous is the promotion of ideas that entail a serious shift in mode or style of practice and thought. The shift from entry price accounting to exit price accounting was such a serious shift. So also was the derivation of principles and rules by systematic observation and inference, in place of the prevalent traditions and their apologetics. There was in the 1960s no centre of inquiry or teaching which would make common cause with these novelties. Sterling's pungent style and incisive argument were, it seems, intended to arouse rather than to shock. For, though he reached his conclusions by clear steps and stated his positions categorically, he was tolerant, even charitable towards critics. Of an opposing contention, rather than say "that is wrong," he would say "I have no experience of that," or "I know of no case of that." Where he found entrenched ideas that confronted his own, he would seek, and often find, that both could be accommodated in a comprehensive, self-consistent scheme. Thus, although he argued meticulously for exit prices as the only appropriate periodical values for financial position statements, he showed that entry prices, purchase (replacement) prices, and discounted values entered, each in its proper place, in his decision-making scheme.

But writing alone would not further the reformation he sought. He had specifically acknowledged his debts to an institutional economist, a neoclassical economist, a philosopher-metrician, a philosopher-sociologist, a physicist-philosopher, and a philosopher of science (1970, p.xii) - all, let it be noted, cross-disciplinary scholars. The colloquia he organized, first in the University of Kansas in 1969, and later elsewhere, would bring together such people and academic and practising accountants of diverse persuasions. He hoped that these interchanges would be beneficial both to the development of theory and the development of practice (Sterling, 1971, p.v). With the aid and sponsorship of professional firms, the proceedings were published by his company, Scholars Book Company; reprints by that company of a number of accounting "classics" would make more readily available some of the best 20th century writing in the field. In the 1970s he brought to the Rice University faculty a number of the more prolific writers on accounting, notwithstanding their disagreement with him on many points of doctrine. In 1974, he launched the Accounting Researchers International Association, a small self-elected group of teachers and researchers. In other fields such associations had served to strengthen the community of interest in the ideals of scholarship and the pursuit of reliable knowledge. By these means he hoped, it seems, to replace conflict and debate with collaborative striving for excellence in doctrine and practice.

In 1981-83, he was engaged as a Senior Fellow in the US Financial Accounting Standards Board. Here, perhaps, at the centre of professional standard setting, in the middle years of the Board's "conceptual framework" project, there would be an opportunity to develop principles and standards along the lines of disciplined practice in other technologies. However, the pattern of the project had already been laid down. The term "conceptual framework" had been appropriated from the literatures of science, where it meant the set of ideas descriptive of the objects and events which would be the concern of theories explaining their associations. Such theories would indicate what could and what could not be done in the present state of knowledge. What kinds of financial information relate to real world states of affairs; what distinguishes information from opinion; what distinguishes measurement from speculation and prediction; what magnitudes are aggregable, and what are not; what messages are intelligible, and relevant to judgment and choice - these are elements of the framework on which Sterling had based his work on income measurement. But the FASB had redefined conceptual framework as a "constitution" regulating practice by fiat, not by reference to features of the real world with which the products of accounting practice should be made to correspond. Ruminating on some features of the FASB's utterances, Sterling (1982, p.104 ff) was pessimistic about the outcome. It would turn out that, instead of eliminating optional valuations, the Board expected that the use of five named valuation schemes (renamed "attributes") would continue (FASB, 1984). The ideas that Sterling fostered might one day influence thought and technique; but that day was not yet.

Art, and Science

Whether accounting is or should be called an art or a science may seem to be a verbal quibble, for the choice turns on what is meant by art and by science. The two terms are prodigally used in debate about accounting with little concern about what either may mean. Inevitably it came under the notice of Sterling. To some, "art" seems to mean the process and product of creative imagination, directed perhaps dominantly to the pleasurable experience of aesthetic satisfaction. To some, "science" seems to mean the process and product of disciplined inquiry into the general and necessary relations between the observables of experience, directed perhaps predominantly to the exploitation of those observables. These are not definitive descriptions. They hint vaguely at some distinctive features; but there are also similarities. Leonardo's "Mona Lisa," Michelangelo's "David," Vivaldi's "Four Seasons" and Shakespeare's sonnets, are products of creative imagination. But each has an identifiable form to which each artist paid respect, and which enable others to classify and treat them as examples of other works. But no less the products of creative imagination are the geometry of Euclid, the cosmology of Galileo, the laws of Newton or Mendel, - and the accounting of Sterling. Mathematicians and scientists are confronted, not with ready made laws, theories or frameworks, but with masses of raw observables or artifacts which they seek to describe and arrange in readily intelligible, coherent and satisfying sets of identified properties of objects and relationships. Scientists have, indeed, explicitly avowed the similarities and conjunctions of science and art. "Our aesthetic judgment demands harmony between the representation and the represented, and in this sense science is often more artistic than modern art" (Pearson, 1911, p.17). "Nothing could be more absurd than the attempt to distinguish between science and art. Science is the noblest of the arts and men of science the most artistic of all artists. For science, like art, seeks to attain aesthetic satisfaction through the perceptions of the senses; and science, like art, is limited by the impositions of the material world on which it works" (Campbell, 1919/1957, p.227). On this latter ground, conventional accounting could be said to resemble neither art nor science.

But, what of science? The 19th century was rich in discovery, invention, and political and social change. It saw the beginnings of the accountancy profession and of preparation for it by the educational establishment. But that preparation was limited to bookkeeping and some special aspects of law; and, though adolescents may have had some elementary instruction in the natural, physical and social sciences, it virtually ceased where professional studies began. There was therefore no continuing association with the disciplined inquiry, the careful observation and experimentation, and the rigorous argument that marked advances in fields that dealt with matters physical and biological. The laws they learned were socially endorsed edicts. Almost naturally they would come to believe that the rules of accounting were of the same kind - endorsed rules or conventions. Those who taught would propagate that belief; and, later, as practitioners they would hold to it, though the consequences would repeatedly and sometimes grievously be apparent.

Sterling's task was to shake at least some free from the bonds of tradition and convention, by demonstrating that the advances of the sciences could be emulated. The abundance and variety of his illustrations and examples might, he hoped, convince the teachers and legislators that the modes and models of the empirical sciences would lead to unequivocal conclusions, in place of the "incomprehensible mixtures of present facts, historical data and accounting conventions" (MacNeal, 1939) that interfere with the reasoned conduct of financial affairs. He had no illusions about the difficulty of getting others "to think anew" (Sterling, 1979, p.ix). Of twenty years of diligent inquiry, debate and exposition, in the face of tolerance on the part of some and intransigence on the part of many, he could say "I did it for fun" - meaning of course the deep satisfaction of making order out of what once was chaos. But, with becoming modesty, he would say that his ideas "need to be tested against reason as well as against nature. I invite you to test the ideas, correct my errors, extend any ideas that survive the tests, and join in the fun" (Sterling, 1979, p.xii). Thus spake a dedicated artist, scientist, scholar.

References

N. R. Campbell, *Physics, the Elements,* 1919 (reprinted as *Foundations of Science*, Dover, 1957).

R. Carnap, *The Unity of Science*, Kegan Paul, 1934.

A. L. Dickinson, "Accounting Practice and Procedure," *Journal of Accountancy*, October 1908, pp.415-25.

L. R. Dicksee, "Importance of Accurate and Adequate Accounting," *The Accountant*, 4 February, 1905, pp.146-51.

Financial Accounting Standards Board (FASB), *Statement of Financial Accounting Concepts No.5*, 1984.

S. Gilman, *Accounting Concepts of Profit*, Ronald Press, 1939.

E. Hatton, in J. Hawkins, *Clavis Commercii*, or *The Key of Commerce*, Passinger, 1689.

G. C. Homans, *The Human Group*, Routledge & Kegan Paul, 1951/1959.

T. H. Huxley, *Darwiniana*, Macmillan, 1894.

N. Machiavelli, *The Prince*, Mentor, c1519/1952.

K. MacNeal, *Truth in Accounting*, University of Philadelphia Press, 1939.

V. Pareto, *The Mind and Society* (translated by A Bongiorno and A Livingston), Dover, 1916/1963.

K. Pearson, *The Grammar of Science*, Black, 1911.

R. R. Sterling, *Theory of the Measurement of Enterprise Income*, University Press of Kansas, 1970

R. R. Sterling, (ed.) *Asset Valuation and Income Determination*, Scholars Book Company, 1971.

R. R. Sterling, "Relevant Financial Reporting in an Age of Price Changes," *Journal of Accountancy*, September 1975, pp.42-51.

R. R. Sterling, *Toward a Science of Accounting*, Scholars Book Company, 1979.

R. R. Sterling, "The Conceptual Framework: An Assessment," *Journal of Accountancy*, November 1982, pp.104-7.

R. R. Sterling, "Confessions of a Failed Empiricist," *Advances in Accounting*, Volume 6, 1988, pp.3-35.

2. Sterling as Teacher and Mentor

K. H. McBeth

It was the summer of 1986. I was attending a social for accounting doctoral students in the College of Business prior to commencing my PhD program at the University of Utah. This environment seemed quite alien after spending several years as a CPA in both public accounting and private industry. As I made my way through the crowd, introducing myself and becoming acquainted with my new peers, I wondered if this mid-career change had been a wise choice. Before long, however, I found myself reliving the experience of every student past elementary or grammar school who faces a new academic year with multiple, unknown teachers. I was eagerly involved in numerous discussions about courses and instructors with both new and continuing students.

Much of the talk was what I had expected - some liked certain courses and faculty better than others, but there was little unanimity or passion in any of it. With one exception. More than once I was warned about a Dr Sterling, from whom I would be required to take two doctoral seminars. I made inquiries. Was he a poor teacher? Perhaps he was ill-tempered? Did he have a pact with the administration to limit the number of successful PhD candidates? None of these was answered affirmatively. I gathered only that Sterling was a scholar of international renown whose purposes seemed to be those of enhancing the image of the College through his research and immersing students in a dialogue of difficult and peculiar ideas from which few would emerge unscathed. As someone who had been told that a PhD program was a "union card," an experience to endure and be done with, I was not looking forward to being on the losing side of the intellectual battle which I expected to ensue in a few short weeks.

On the first day of Sterling's seminar on the philosophy of science and research methodology, the three new doctoral students were asked to share briefly their educational and employment histories. It turned out that I was the only one who had spent much time in the practice of accounting, particularly public accounting. Sterling thereupon made a prediction (one of the few I ever heard him utter) to the effect that the ingrained habits of thought which I had undoubtedly acquired during my practice of accounting would likely prevent me from truly grasping the ideas that I would encounter during the course. What could I say? The battle had scarcely commenced, and I had lost.

Happily, both Sterling and I were wrong - utterly wrong. His classroom was not a battleground where the mentally inferior were doomed to perish, but rather a nursery for the developing doctoral intellect. And despite my years of practice as an accountant, I had not forgotten the questions and concerns about accounting that had arisen during my earlier education and remained unanswered. As the weeks passed, an awareness grew within me that Sterling would help answer those questions.

Sterling taught two other doctoral seminars while I was a student. One was on financial accounting theory - where he expounded his scientific approach to accounting theory and exit value accounting - and the other on other accounting theories and accounting research paradigms. Each of the three seminars was intellectually challenging and stimulating. Each contained jewels of thought which helped me then and have guided me since. In the philosophy of science seminars Sterling taught an interdisciplinary attitude towards the acquisition, dissemination, and creation of knowledge. Accounting was not to be regarded as an isolationist discipline with the right to ask all its own questions and give all its own answers. He taught a broad approach to research methodology as well, legitimizing tools in addition to those of statistics. It is thanks to Sterling that I made the almost startling discovery that the act of writing is itself a research tool which can lead to new ideas.

Sterling's seminar on financial accounting theory was the highlight of my classroom experience with him. His 1979 work *Toward a Science of Accounting*, together with his personal explanation of the same, provided not only a clear voice to the unarticulated dissatisfaction I had long felt with accounting principles, but also a reasoned and eloquent expression of the solution to the problems of financial accounting. Sterling used other readings and discussions to shed light on the relationship of financial accounting to its subdisciplines of managerial accounting, auditing, accounting information systems, and income taxation, and taught the dependence of these subdisciplines on the quality of the financial accounting product.

In his third seminar, Sterling shifted the focus to concepts of accounting theory and programs of research that were frequently in opposition to his view of theory and research. There I learned about efficient markets research and positive accounting theory. In addition I learned important lessons about research and academic criticism. Sterling taught respect for the right of a researcher to pursue any path of inquiry that he believes will be fruitful, whether or not anyone else believes such research to be important. With respect to criticism of others' research, he taught two important principles. First, that comprehension is prerequisite to analysis, and second that ideas - not people - are the proper object of academic criticism.

Sterling's influence as a teacher extended beyond the classroom. On an informal basis, he regularly spent his lunch hour in the faculty lounge of the student union cafeteria with doctoral students. All topics of conversation were permissible as long as they were accounting-related. Sterling often introduced ideas from disciplines such as philosophy, history, economics, physics, and literature into the discussions, making them as valuable and interesting as any classroom experience. Sterling enlarged the classroom experience on a more formal basis as well. With funds from his endowed professorship and a global network of colleagues, he occasionally invited notable members of accounting academia to campus to speak to the doctoral students. From time to time he also arranged for accounting scholars to visit the university for part or all of an academic year. Abraham Briloff, Tom Lee, and George Staubus were among those who enlivened and enriched the learning environment during my years in the doctoral program. To Sterling's credit, these interactions between professors and students did not end in the seminar room. Each of Sterling's guests was honored either at a luncheon on campus or at a dinner buffet at Sterling's home. Always an engaging and gracious host, Sterling made the doctoral students an integral part of his social functions on these and many other occasions.

In my particular case, Sterling served not only as a teacher, but also as a mentor. For much of my doctoral experience I was assigned to be his research assistant. In addition, he was on my course work committee and supervised my dissertation. Each of these relationships provided valuable insights and contributed to the successful completion of my degree.

As his research assistant, I was impressed both by the breadth and depth of Sterling's scholarship, and the meticulous manner in which he crafted a piece of writing. Sterling regularly quoted authors in fields seemingly unrelated to accounting without omitting references to relevant accounting authorities. He approached academic inquiry with a certain humility, saying that he read widely from other disciplines because he never knew but that what he read might relate to his accounting research. Yet within the accounting discipline, his insight and analysis were sharp and focused. For all this, or perhaps because of these traits, each writing effort that Sterling undertook was a painstaking process of examination and reexamination, drafting and redrafting.

In his role as course work advisor and dissertation supervisor, Sterling continued to encourage a broad intellectual perspective. He encouraged me to take courses outside the accounting department and business college beyond those required. As a result, I enjoyed experiences in graduate philosophy and economics courses that I would otherwise have missed. When I reached the dissertation stage, my topic was a union of accounting theory, tax policy, and a certain amount of philosophy. In keeping with the eclectic nature of my doctoral experience to that point, Sterling formed a dissertation committee which included an economics professor and a philosophy professor. Thanks to Sterling's unfailing interest and aid, I completed the dissertation and the degree. And in that ending I recognized threads of the beginning, when Sterling drew me into his world of accounting thought in that first doctoral seminar.

I look back on these experience with a mixture of awe and gratitude. It still amazes me that very ordinary expectations about my PhD program were transformed into what I regard as an extraordinary reality by Sterling's ability and concern as a teacher and mentor. I remain grateful too that he expended such time and effort on one with such an unlikely background and with such modest post-doctoral plans. Truly, Sterling is one of the great accounting educators of our times.

3. Sterling as Administrator

D. Windsor

Bob Sterling was founding dean of the Jesse H. Jones Graduate School of Administration at Rice University from April 1, 1976 until Summer 1980, when he went to the University of Alberta. I worked for Bob from Summer 1977 as assistant to the dean (and subsequently assistant dean), while holding a faculty appointment in public management. Todd Johnson (subsequently dean of the School of Business and Public Administration at the University of Houston at Clear Lake) had responsibility for the accounting programs. As I was not at Rice during the seminal events of 1974-76, I am reconstructing that earlier history from discussions I had with Bob and others after my arrival.

Bob was at the University of Kansas when he received a 1974 appointment in the then Rice Department of Economics and Accounting (which offered a PhD in economics) as Jesse H. Jones Professor of Management and Professor of Accounting. (Bob's PhD and BS were in economics.) He was the senior professor of an accounting group within the department.

Originally opened in 1912 as the William Marsh Rice Institute, Rice University (from 1960) granted PhD degrees in some 28 fields. There were also professional programs in architecture and engineering. Accounting instruction had been offered at Rice for many years. As a result of Rice's origin as a science and engineering institute, there was in place an unusual degree structure reflecting a long tradition of liberal education before professional education. Students could take a BA or a BS degree in science and engineering fields. Professional master's degrees in the engineering fields functioned as a fifth-year program. As a result, students interested in accounting careers took a BA in appropriate fields, including specified prerequisite courses, followed by a specialized fifth-year BS in accounting.

There rapidly occurred in 1974-76 two important organizational changes at Rice, in which Bob was a key figure. A separate Department of Accounting was established with Bob as the founding chairman. The fifth-year BS became a professional Master of

Accounting (MAcco) degree. A separate PhD in accounting degree was also established. The Jesse H. Jones Graduate School of Administration was established on paper in 1974, being organized in 1976 with Bob's appointment as first dean. Rice also established a Shepherd School of Music at about the same time. There was thus a movement toward an expansion of professional education in selected areas. Subsequently separate buildings were constructed for the Jones (1984) and Shepherd (1991) schools. In 1993, the James A. Baker III Institute for Public Policy was established, also with a designated building.

The key donor to the Jones School was the Houston Endowment, Inc., which had earlier provided the Jones Professorship already held by Bob. This charitable foundation, which has provided untold benefits for the people of Texas, had been established to carry out the philanthropic activities of Jesse H. and Mary Gibbs Jones. Jesse H. Jones, for whom the school was named, was a prominent business and civic leader responsible in large measure for Houston's early growth before World War II. He brought the 1928 Democratic convention to Houston and built the Houston Ship Channel (making Houston an inland port). During the Great Depression he served as chairman of the Reconstruction Finance Corporation and as Secretary of Commerce. He was considered for the US Vice-Presidency in the 1940 election.

The Jones School's governing philosophy resulted from a faculty committee in which there were several notable Rice professors from interested departments, including Sterling. Three main themes guided the early development of the school. Firstly, it was to be Rice's only purely graduate professional school, offering separate management and accounting degrees. While the accounting faculty continued to offer some undergraduate courses, the school had no operational responsibility for undergraduate management education. An undergraduate BA program in managerial studies was directed by an interdepartmental and interschool committee reporting to the Provost (subsequently to the Dean of Social Sciences), although the program was administered through the Jones School. Secondly, the Jones School was to be a school of administration embracing accounting, business management, and public management. Thirdly, graduate management education took a broad social sciences approach to integrating accounting with business and public management. The original management degree approved by the university faculty was a two-year Master of Business and Public Management (MBPM). Yale University began offering a similar Master of Private and Public Management (MPPM) at about the same time, but the similarity of title and curriculum was coincidental rather than imitative. The MBPM degree was built around a strong required core of typically two semester courses each in accounting, economics, quantitative methods, organizational theory, communications, legal and governmental processes, and management policy. (George Bush served as a lecturer in the organizational theory course for a year before running for the vice presidency.) In a substantial departure from the conventional MBA approach, there were initially no functional courses in the core. This approach reflected partly an intellectual view concerning the future of management education and partly the reality that in a startup situation with no undergraduate management faculty in place there were no functional specialist other than accountants.

The university turned to Bob as first dean. Bob had chief responsibility for getting the new Jones School up and operating, and for representing the school to the university and the business community. There were a thousand-and-one things to do requiring strategic vision, enormous energy, and painstaking attention to detail. The new school shifted physical location from part of one building to part of another building across campus. Bob personally handled design and supervised construction of classroom facilities and school offices, and acquired necessary equipment. He personally recruited the first 1977 entering class of two-year management students (13 MBPM's graduated in 1979). When I arrived at Rice in summer 1977, he handed me the application files of the entering class and gave instructions for getting the permanent admissions and placement processes going. (Subsequently, professional officers for admissions and placement were added.) A Council of Overseers, consisting of prominent Houston-area business leaders, was created to provide advice concerning the development of the school. Bob initiated what is now the school's Office of Executive Development for delivery of special educational programs to the business community.

Bob personally recruited the new school's faculty. The Department of Accounting was absorbed into the school. Faculty were appointed in either accounting or administrative science. Courses were then and are still today listed as either accounting or administration, the latter a shortening of the similar longer title for management faculty. The Rice university catalogue and administrative process are organized by department within school. The three purely professional schools - administration, architecture, music - have no formal departmental structure. Bob assembled a distinguished senior accounting faculty during this early period, with emphasis on well-known names in accounting theory: Philip Bell, Edward Edwards, Arthur Thomas, and Stephen Zeff. Sterling also began the process of developing an administrative science faculty. There were then and subsequently a number of important cross-appointments from other departments at Rice, most notably English, economics, mathematical sciences, political science, and psychology.

Bob recruited Francis D. Tuggle, a former colleague at the University of Kansas, as associate dean and professor of business policy in 1977-78 to build the MBPM program. Subsequently, Tuggle took over as acting dean and then became second dean of the school after Bob's departure. (Tuggle was succeeded in 1987 by the third and present dean Benjamin F. Bailar, who had been postmaster general of the US during the Ford and Carter administrations.) In 1984, the school occupied a newly constructed building named in honor of Robert R. Herring, a prominent businessman and chairman of the Rice Board of Trustees. In 1985, the school changed the degree title from MBPM to the more conventional MBA. The principal and substantial evolution of both the curriculum and the faculty was the addition of finance and marketing functions.

The foundations of the Jones School's subsequent development were built by Bob Sterling two decades ago. He created the basic organizational structure and administrative process that, although certainly greatly modified over time, still exist in the present Jones School. The school has to a very substantial extent followed the general path marked out during his deanship. Today, the Jones School admits a class of typically 100 or so MBA students in addition to a select number of MAcco students. It has alumni numbering well in excess of 1,000. The faculty comprises in excess of 50 full and part-time appointees providing instruction in accounting, entrepreneurship, finance, international management, marketing, operations management, organizational behavior and human resource management, strategic management and planning.

4. Sterling at the FASB

L. T. Johnson

Bob Sterling's two-year tour at the Financial Accounting Standards Board (FASB or Board) began in July 1981. The position to which he was appointed, "senior fellow," was a new one that had been created expressly for him. "Senior" not only acknowledged his standing in the academic community but also indicated the role he was to play on the research and technical activities (RTA) staff; "fellow" denoted that his appointment was a secondment, similar to the Board's extant two-year "practice fellow," "industry fellow," and "academic fellow" positions.[1]

Although both FASB Chairman Don Kirk and RTA Director Mike Alexander knew of some of Bob's writings, they had not yet met him at the time I joined the RTA staff in 1979 as a project manager. At my suggestion, Bob was invited to Stamford to lead a "PD" (professional development) session for members of the Board and staff and to give a paper at the Conceptual Framework Symposium that the FASB sponsored in June 1980 in New York City. Those presentations gave Don and Mike (as well as others) an opportunity to see Bob in action, and they asked him to come to the FASB specifically to work on the conceptual framework project.

For Bob, working on the conceptual framework was an offer he could not refuse. He had, after all, spent most of his academic career addressing conceptual issues, and the chance to help shape concepts and the accounting standards that ultimately would be based on them was a once-in-a-lifetime opportunity. In a sense, it was analogous to an economic theorist being offered the opportunity to join the staff of the President's Council of Economic Advisors.

I looked forward to the prospect of working with Bob again, because I knew him well, having worked closely with him since 1974 when he came to Rice University as the first Jesse H. Jones Professor. A lot had happened during those years: a master's degree and a doctoral degree in accounting were approved and implemented, the Department of Accounting was formed, which later became the core of the new Jesse H. Jones Graduate School of Administration, and Ed Edwards, Phil Bell, Art Thomas, and Steve Zeff all had been enticed to join the faculty. Most of that would not have happened without Bob. He clearly was someone who had the stature and ability to make things happen.

The Board needed someone like Bob at the stage it had reached in its conceptual framework project. Earlier phases of the project had focused on the more fundamental aspects, namely the objectives of financial reporting, the qualitative characteristics of accounting information, and the elements of financial statements, all of which had been concluded with the issuance of concepts statements. However, the elements phase had required the issuance of a second exposure draft, a sign of more difficulties to come as the result of changes in the Board's membership. Moreover, the Board had set the goal for itself of achieving unanimous Board votes for the issuance of each of the concepts statements, which became more problematic as the Board moved from the more abstract to the more concrete issues (which were the ones remaining to be done when Bob arrived on the scene). And certain members of the Conceptual Framework Task Force were already becoming restive about the possibility that the Board might move away from the traditional "defer and match" approach to accounting.

The next phase of the project to be completed was labeled as "accounting recognition criteria," which the Board had envisioned as consisting of two parts, one focusing on the initial recognition of assets and liabilities, and the other on the recognition of revenues, expenses, gains, and losses. The Board had commissioned a research report for each part. *Recognition of Contractual Rights and Obligations*, by Yuji Ijiri, was published in December 1980, and *Survey of Present Practices in Recognizing Revenues, Expenses, Gains, and Losses*, by Hank Jaenicke, was published in January 1981. The plan had been to issue for public comment a neutral discussion memorandum based on those reports. That phase of the project was to focus solely on issues of recognition. Issues of measurement, which were sure to be contentious, were to be addressed in a later phase, pending what was learned from the experimental disclosures mandated by FASB Statement No. 33, *Financial Reporting and Changing Prices*, issued in September 1979.

The Statement 33 effort had been led by Bryan Carsberg,[2] who originally had come to the FASB as an academic fellow and who subsequently had moved into the role of one of Mike Alexander's assistant directors. As a follow-on to his work on Statement 33, Bryan had been assigned responsibility for the phase of the conceptual framework project that included income reporting. Work on that phase resulted in the issuance of the FASB Exposure Draft, *Reporting Income, Cash Flows, and Financial Position of Business Enterprises*, in November 1981, shortly after Bob's arrival. Because Bryan also was overseeing research on Statement 33, he implicitly was responsible for the measurement phase of the Conceptual Framework project.

Bob, however, soon concluded that it would be futile to try to address recognition without considering measurement as well. In particular, he argued that the primary recognition issues involved income recognition, which could not be meaningfully addressed without also addressing measurement. While he acknowledged that there were some free-standing issues associated with the recognition of assets and liabilities (such as those addressed in Ijiri's research report), he believed they paled in comparison to those associated with income recognition. He eventually was able to develop support from the Board to undertake a more ambitious set of goals than those that had been established for recognition at the time that phase of the project got under way and to broaden the scope of the recognition phase to include measurement.

Those familiar with Bob's writings should not be surprised that he would want to pursue measurement because most of his work has been on measurement rather than recognition (indeed, there is little in the academic or authoritative literature on recognition per se, which is why the Board commissioned the Ijiri and Jaenicke research reports). Moreover, Bob was concerned that the measurement phase might result in something akin to Statement 33, which he viewed as inconsistent and lacking a clear underlying philosophy. He believed that Statement 33 had accommodated too many differing viewpoints and effectively "papered over" real differences in views of Board members in order to obtain agreement. In addition, Bryan Carsberg's views about measurement, which tended to focus more heavily on predictive ability, were not entirely in line with Bob's. Thus, Bob's efforts to link measurement to recognition could be viewed as a preemptive strike.

It is not clear that all of the Board members initially understood where Bob stood on measurement, but it was not long before they realized that he advocated not only current values over historical costs but also a particular form of current value. The Board soon split into two camps, with one generally supporting his positions and the other opposing them. However, even some of those who favored replacing historical costs with current or fair values were not comfortable using current exit values in all - or even many - instances.

Because of the Board split, a three-pronged strategy was adopted. (1) Bob would develop the text of what was to be an exposure draft of a concepts statement on recognition and measurement, (2) Reed Storey and I would develop a research report on recognition concepts and conventions generally, and (3) Bob, Paul Miller, and I would develop a set of simple, concrete cases to illustrate the concepts involved and discuss them with the Board at its regular weekly meetings.[3] Collectively, those three prongs were intended to educate the Board and help them think through the issues.

Although that approach enjoyed the general support of the RTA director and four of the seven Board members, the other three Board members became increasingly resistant. Eventually, their resistance led to calls for a separate effort to forward their views, and Bob Mautz was asked to consult with the Board and oversee that effort. That approach ultimately did not fare any better, however, and the Board was still at an impasse when Bob's term as senior fellow ended in June 1983. The Board finally brought the recognition and measurement phase of the project to a close in December 1984 with the issuance of Concepts Statement No. 5, *Recognition and Measurement in Financial Statements of Business Enterprises*, a document that many have criticized as being little more than a recapitulation of concepts adopted in earlier concepts statements coupled with general acceptance of the status quo in practice. It is not a document with which Bob would have wanted to be associated.

Although Bob subsequently has called his efforts with the Board his "greatest failure," it is doubtful that anyone else would have done better at that time, given the ambitious goals that had been set and the divisions within the Board. The times had changed since the conceptual framework project's inception, as had the Board's membership, with both having become more protective of the status quo.

But Bob's efforts may well have helped pave the way for some of the Board's more recent movements toward greater use of current or fair values, especially in the context of accounting for financial instruments, a topic that had not yet loomed large when the conceptual framework project was under way, but which now consumes much of the Board's (and the financial community's) attention. Those instruments now dominate many balance sheets, and it is becoming increasingly understood and accepted that the most relevant - and often the most reliable - measurement of those instruments is fair value. I think Bob would approve.

Footnotes

1. The only other senior fellow has been Ray Perry, who joined the RTA staff in 1992 upon his retirement as a senior partner of Deloitte & Touche.
2. After returning to the UK and serving in the government, in recognition of which he was knighted, Sir Bryan is now Secretary-General of the International Accounting Standards Committee.
3. The results of all three prongs ultimately saw the light of day, however. Bob's *An Essay on Recognition* was published by the University of Sydney's Accounting Research Centre in 1985. Reed's and my research report, *Recognition in Financial Statements: Underlying Concepts and Practical Conventions*, was published by the FASB in July 1982. *The FASB Cases on Recognition and Measurement* was jointly published by the FASB and Richard D. Irwin, Inc., in 1991 (the second edition of the *FASB Cases* was published in 1995 by John Wiley & Sons, Inc.).

BIOGRAPHICAL NOTES

Raymond J. Chambers

Ray Chambers is retired and living in Sydney, Australia. Regarded as one of the most distinguished accounting theorists, Professor Chambers served the University of Sydney throughout most of his academic career (1953-82), and was the founding editor of the leading journal, *Abacus*. He earned the degree of Doctor of Science in Economics from the University of Sydney (1973), was awarded the AAA/AICPA's Gold Medal for Notable Contributions to the Accounting Literature (1966), and the AAA's Outstanding Educator Award in 1991. He was the AAA's Distinguished International Lecturer in the US in 1976, the national President of the Australian Society of CPAs (1978), and was elected to the Accounting Hall of Fame (1991). He was named an Officer of the Order of Australia (1978).

L. Todd Johnson

Todd Johnson is a doctoral graduate of the University of Michigan, a former faculty member at Rice University, and currently Research Manager at the FASB. He worked with Bob Sterling at Rice University and at the FASB.

Thomas A. Lee

Tom Lee is a doctoral graduate of the University of Strathclyde, and currently Hugh Culverhouse Endowed Chair of Accountancy at the University of Alabama. Professor Lee was previously Professor of Accountancy and Finance at the University of Edinburgh; and a Visiting Professor of Accounting at the University of Utah during Bob Sterling's tenure there.

Kevin H. McBeth

Kevin McBeth is a doctoral graduate of the University of Utah, where he studied under Bob Sterling, and currently an associate professor at Weber State University.

Robert R. Sterling

Bob Sterling is retired and living in Houston, Texas. During his distinguished academic career, he held faculty positions at the Universities of Denver (1955-7), Florida (1957-62), Southern California (1962-3), New York at Binghamton (1963-6), Yale (1996-7), Kansas (1967-74), Rice (1974-80) (including founding Dean of the Graduate School of Administration for 1976-80), Alberta (1980-1, and Utah (1983-92). He was Senior Fellow at FASB from 1981 to 1983. Twice winner of the AAA/AICPA's Gold Medal for Notable Contributions to the Accounting Literature (1968 and 1973), Professor Sterling held numerous honorary positions and awards from academic and professional bodies. He was six times a distinguished faculty at the AAA's doctoral consortium, and was the AAA's distinguished bicentennial international lecturer (1976). Professor Sterling has served the AAA in numerous positions, including as Director of Research (1972-4).

Duane Windsor

Duane Windsor is a doctoral graduate of Harvard University and is currently Lynette S. Autrey Professor of Management and Associate Dean of the Jesse H. Jones Graduate School of Administration, Rice University.

Peter W. Wolnizer

Peter Wolnizer is a doctoral graduate of the University of Sydney, where he studied under Ray Chambers and taught from 1976-87. He is Professor of Accounting and Dean of the Faculty of Business and Law at Deakin University, Australia. He worked with Bob Sterling as the Kendall D. Garff Research Associate at the University of Utah in 1986.

The Quest for a Science of Accounting

NATURE OF SCIENCE, THEORY AND PRACTICE

INTRODUCTION

Sterling on Theory and Practice

T. A. Lee

Bob Sterling is primarily a philosopher of science whose main focus is on accounting. Because of this background, Bob differs from other accounting theorists of the 1960s and 1970s who were and are accountants first and foremost. Bob's doctoral dissertation is based on scientific economic argument and, following, its completion, he extended his education as a philosopher of science in the Departments of Philosophy and Physics at Yale University (1966-7). Unsurprisingly, most of his subsequent research reflects this training, and some of his portfolio of writings specifically deals with theory as a basis for observing accounting. A selection of these items is contained in this section of the text.

Readers of Bob's writings on theory receive a thorough grounding in the nature and importance of theory. Much of what he writes about in the five items reproduced here is related to accounting, but reflects Bob's awareness that, to fully understand theoretical prescriptions on accounting, accountants require to comprehend the role of theory in scientific inquiry. He lucidly explains the place of theory in scientific thinking, and outlines the main components of a theory. In particular, he reveals the place of signs in theory, and the relationships between signs and observable events. From this particular stance, it is relatively easy to see how much of Bob's research, exemplified in all sections of this text, is concerned with accounting as a measurement process.

Much of this section of the text relates to accounting measurement, and specifically to scientific measurement. Bob perceives accounting as a science because of its focus on measurement of empirical phenomena, and he argues persistently for accountants to adopt an accounting model in which the objective is to scientifically measure properties of relevant events and objects. For this reason, he clearly advocates a scientific rather than a legalistic approach to accounting measurement. He argues for the use of accounting laws of measurement which are empirically testable in a way which arbitrary accounting conventions are not. His appeal to accountants is that accounting measurement should rely on scientific truths rather than a legalistic authority and precedent. By using scientific theories, accountants should be better able to challenge the anomalies of conventional accounting calculations, resolve the inherent measurement problems of contemporary accounting statements, and advocate lasting accounting solutions to meet the decision needs of financial statement users.

The five writings reproduced in this section are presented in chronological order, but reflect a logical sequencing of Bob's thoughts on accounting theory over the years - i.e., from descriptions and explanations of theory and measurement generally, to specific applications to accounting, and then to the most specific issue of convincing accounting practitioners, educators and researchers to think about accounting problems in a scientific way - which is the object of the next section of the text.

On Theory Construction and Verification

Robert R. Sterling

I. Introduction

THERE are many disputes over the way in which theories are constructed. It seems that many theories come about by "intuitive flashes." There are "laws of nature" (observed regularities) which are discovered by induction. However seldom are the theories—which connect and explain these laws in a coherent and general way—discovered by induction. Thus, the process of theory construction is imperfectly understood. Clues for this lack of understanding are given by the language used to describe the process. For example, we characterize a great theoretician as a "genius," which implies that his intellect is beyond our understanding or that we could not have duplicated the process. The "intuitive flash" description implies a lack of understanding of the mental processes by which the discovery is made.

Even though we don't know how theories are constructed, we can note that a new theory usually arises as a result of "anomalies" in the old theory.[1] Scientific theories provide certain "expectations" or "predictions" about phenomena and when these expectations occur, they are said to "confirm" the theory.[2] When unexpected results occur, they are considered to be anomalies which eventually require a modification of the theory or the construction of a new theory. The purpose of the new theory or the modified theory is to make the unexpected expected, to convert the anomalous occurrence into an expected and explained occurrence.

Although the process of theory construction is imperfectly understood, it has been noted that the theories of empirical science have some common properties and that they share a structure. This paper will present a brief review of the nature of empirical theories for the purpose of providing a relief for some current and proposed theories of accounting.[3] Selected alternative interpretations of accounting

This paper was prepared for submission to the American Accounting Association Committee on Theory Construction and Verification. The views expressed are those of the author and do not necessarily represent the views of the Committee or the Association.

Helpful comments from the members of the Ohio State University Accounting Colloquium and financial support from the Fourth National Bank of Wichita Foundation is gratefully acknowledged.

[1] Thomas S. Kuhn, *The Structure of Scientific Revolutions* (The University of Chicago Press, 1962), Ch. VI.

[2] Several different terms are used for this process. Rudolf Carnap, "Testability and Meaning," *Philosophy of Science*, Vol. 4, (1937), distinguishes between testable, verifiable and confirmable. I will use "verifiable" to refer to the intersubjective perception of observers concerning a proposition which specifies an individual occurrence. I will use "confirmable" to refer to a collection of propositions (a theory). It is the "verification" of the singular propositions which is taken to be the "confirmation" of the theory which contains those propositions.

[3] For a particularly lucid discussion of the nature of theories in accounting, see Thomas H. Williams and Charles H. Griffin, "On the Nature of Empirical Verification in Accounting," Working Paper 68–37, (The University of Texas, 1968).

Robert R. Sterling is the Arthur Young Distinguished Professor of Accounting at The University of Kansas.

theory will be examined and critiqued. An outline for a program for the construction of a theory of relevant measurements will then be suggested.

II. The Nature of Theories

A "theory" is, first of all, a set of sentences. Theories are expressed in a language, and therefore the study of language is pertinent to the study of theories. Indeed, much of the philosophy of science is nothing but a study of language, although it is a study of the language peculiar to the scientist. Morris,[4] Carnap[5] and others have distinguished three areas in the study of language: Syntactics, Semantics and Pragmatics.

Syntactics is the study of the relations of signs to signs. By themselves syntactical propositions have no empirical content. The disciplines of mathematics and logic are syntactical in that a mathematical or logical proposition says nothing whatsoever about the real world. Such propositions are often referred to as "analytic propositions" and are characterized by being logically true, as opposed to being empirically true. For example, "If all electrons have magnetic moments and particle x has no magnetic moment, then particle x is not an electron" is an analytic proposition. One does not need to know the meaning of "electron" or "magnetic moment" to see that this proposition is true. It is true by virtue of the form of the sentence and the agreed upon way in which the logical constants (if-then, and, not) are used. One could replace the descriptive terms with nonsense words without altering the truth value, e.g., "If all bzrs have wales and x has no wale, then x is not a bzr."[6] The proposition "$(a+b)^2 = a^2+2ab+b^2$" is analytic. It is true by virtue of the agreed upon rules of algebra which specify the way in which the signs of algebra may be arranged and manipulated.

Also, statements which are true by virtue of the meanings of their constituent terms are analytic, e.g., "a bachelor is an unmarried adult male" is true by virtue of the meanings of "bachelor," "unmarried," etc.[7] Note that analytic propositions require a prior commitment to a set of rules or definitions. "A bachelor is an unmarried adult male" is analytically true because of the prior linguistic commitment to define "bachelor" in a particular way. "Fifteen is one-half of thirty" is analytically true because of a prior commitment to the rules of arithmetic.

Semantics is the study of the relation of signs to objects or events. If signs are to have referents in the real world, it is necessary to have rules or understandings as to the linkage between a particular sign and a particular object or event. These are called "semantical rules," and it is these rules that give empirical meaning to the signs. It is possible, of course, to define a particular sign by showing how it relates to other signs, but it is impossible to define all signs in this way. More precisely, the definition of signs by reference to other signs can be done only on pain of circularity and lack of empirical meaning.[8]

[4] Charles Morris, *Foundations of the Theory of Signs* (University of Chicago, 1938).

[5] Rudolf Carnap, *Introduction to Semantics* (Harvard University Press, 1942).

[6] See Rudolf Carnap, *Philosophical Foundations of Physics* (Basic Books, Inc., 1966), Chs. 26–28 for a more complete discussion. The electron example appears on p. 266.

[7] Arthur Pap, *An Introduction to the Philosophy of Science* (The Free Press of Glencoe, 1962) distinguishes between "broadly analytic" and "strictly analytic" propositions. He argues that broadly analytic propositions like "a bachelor is an unmarried male" can be reduced to strictly analytic propositions with the help of appropriate definitions (p. 97). The distinction and the disagreement about the possibility of reduction is not pertinent to this study.

[8] "Definitions of terms by reference to other terms belonging to the same language system (for example, the language of physics) are *internal* definitions, and one might, by using this kind of definition alone, build a whole ingrown language whose terms referred to each other but to nothing else. Definitions which go outside the language system to something else—perception, for instance—are *external* definitions, and they are required if the whole system is to mean anything." Peter Caws, *The Philosophy of Science* (D. Van Nostrand Company, Inc., 1965), p. 46.

It is generally agreed, especially in connection with metrical notions, that the semantical rules should be in the nature of *operational* definitions. The selection of a particular sign to refer to a particular object or event is quite arbitrary initially, but subsequent use of that sign requires careful specification of the operations by which we link the sign to the object or event.

Given the semantical rules for linking signs to objects or events and the syntactical rules for linking signs to signs, propositions with empirical content can be formed. In contrast to the analytic propositions discussed above, these "empirical propositions" are intended to say something about the real world and therefore their truth value is contingent upon observation.[9] For example, the proposition "John is a bachelor" is intended to say something about a thing in the real world, and "John" is the sign for that thing. The truth value of that proposition can be either true or false without contradiction.

Thus, the truth value of analytic and empirical propositions is discovered by different procedures. Analytic propositions are *proved* by the use of syntactical rules. They are either true (valid) or contradictory. Empirical propositions are *verified* by operations of observation. They are either true (conform with the observations) or false.

Pragmatics is the study of the relation of signs to the users of those signs. Different signs invoke different responses from a particular user even though those signs are intended to have the same referent. Different users may interpret the same sign in different ways.

This three-part division of the study of language provides the basis for a two-part division of the sciences. In general, sciences may be classified as empirical or nonempirical. Examples of the latter are logic and mathematics. These sciences are composed exclusively of analytic propositions and therefore do not depend upon empirical findings for their truth value. The empirical sciences have for their purpose the explanation and prediction of occurrences in the real world. The propositions of empirical science, therefore, are said to be true only if they correctly explain or predict some empirical phenomena.

Despite the empirical test for the assignment of truth value, the theories of empirical science are not composed entirely of propositions which can be verified by observations. Instead, a theory in empirical science is composed of a combination of analytic and empirical propositions. The syntactical or logical part of a theory can be abstracted and studied in isolation from the empirical part of that theory. This process is usually called the "axiomatization" or "formalization" of a theory and the result is called an "axiomatic" or "formal" system. Of course, the formal system per se is not an empirical theory. In order for the formal system to function as a theory of empirical science the semantical rules must be added.

These ideas are often illustrated by using geometry as an example. Geometry qua mathematics is a formal system. It says nothing about the real world and its theorems can be deductively derived from its axioms. It has a set of primitive terms—e.g., "point," "straight line"—which have no empirical meaning. By semantical rules these primitive terms are given empirical meaning, e.g., a point is taken to mean the intersection of cross-hairs or the tip of a surveyor's stake, a straight line is taken to mean a taut string or the path of light rays. In this way geometry becomes an

[9] There are several different names for the contrasting propositions. Since they are contingent upon observations, what I have called "empirical propositions" are called "contingent propositions" by some philosophers. Others contrast "a priori statements" with "empirical statements." Followers of Kant contrast "analytic" with "synthetic." Earlier writers were making the same distinction when they spoke of "necessary" and "accidental" truth. In this paper I will generally use the terms "analytic" and "empirical" to make the distinction.

empirical theory. It is now a theory of physics and as such it says some things about the real world. The outputs of geometry qua physics are intended to be empirical propositions and their truth value can be verified by observations. For example, the length of a hypotenuse can be calculated from the theory. The theory specifies the relevant empirical inputs (length of the two sides) and it specifies the way in which those inputs are manipulated. The output is the length of the hypotenuse and that output can be verified, within the limits of measurement error, by a separate empirical operation.

The last step, the verification of the output, is indispensable if the theory is intended to be empirical. It is not required that every proposition in an empirical theory be verifiable; there are many terms which operate within the formal system that are not subject to observation. (These are often called "theoretical terms" in contrast to "observational terms.") However, an empirical theory must have *some* propositions that are verifiable. The verification of these individual propositions is taken as a test of the theory. If the propositions are found to be true, then the theory is said to be "validated" or "confirmed."[10]

Hempel[11] presents all of this in a simple diagram:

The arrow represents a deductive inference and the number above the arrow refers to a particular sentence by which the deduction is effected. These sentences are:

"(3.2) Def. $s(x_i) = v(x_i)/w(x_i)$"

which is the definition of the specific

[10] Carl Hempel, *Philosophy of Natural Science* (Prentice-Hall, Inc., 1966), p. 30, makes this point as follows:

> But if a statement or set of statements is not testable at least in principle, in other words, if it has no test implications at all, then it cannot be significantly proposed or entertained as a scientific hypothesis or theory, for no conceivable empirical finding can then accord or conflict with it. In this case, it has no bearing whatever on empirical phenomena, or as we will also say, it lacks *empirical import.*

He then discussed an article entitled "Gravity and Love as Unifying Principles" and characterizes the view that physical bodies are attracted by love as a "pseudo-hypothesis" because:

> No specific empirical findings of any kind are called for by this interpretation; no conceivable observational or experimental data can confirm or disconfirm it. In particular, therefore, it has no implications concerning gravitational phenomena; consequently, it cannot possibly explain those phenomena or render them "intelligible." To illustrate this further, let us suppose someone were to offer the alternative thesis that physical bodies gravitationally attract each other and tend to move toward each other from a natural tendency akin to hatred, from a natural inclination to collide with and destroy other physical objects. Would there by any conceivable way of adjudicating these conflicting views? Clearly not. Neither of them yields any testable implications; no empirical discrimination between them is possible. *Ibid.*, p. 31.

[11] Carl Hempel, *Aspects of Scientific Explanation* (The Free Press, 1965), p. 181. Minor changes were made in the symbols for clarity and to correct a typographical error.

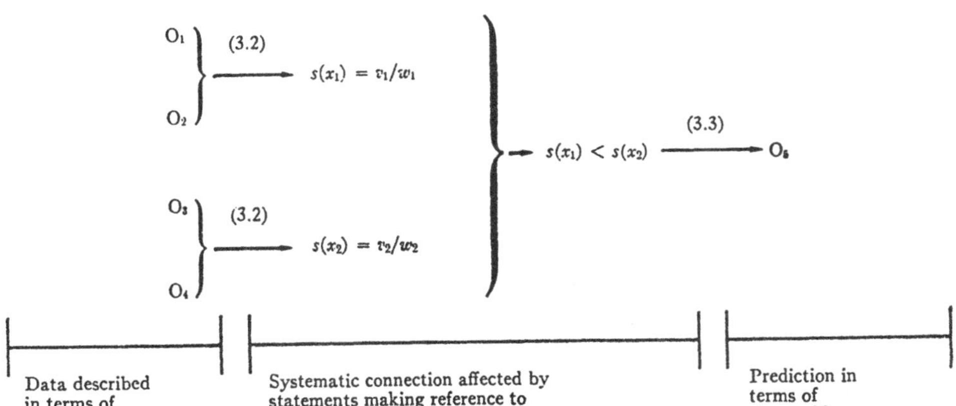

gravity of a body x_i where w_i and v_i refer to the weight and volume of that body; and

> "(3.3) A solid body floats on a liquid if its specific gravity is less than that of the liquid,"

which refers to the expression $s(x_1) < s(x_2)$ in the diagram, i.e., (3.3) can be restated as "If $s(x_1) < s(x_2)$, then x_1 floats on x_2."

The particular values of weight and volume are obtained by "appropriate operational procedures," i.e., "in terms of the directly observable outcomes of specified measuring procedures," and the symbols O_1, O_2, O_3, O_4 are observation terms connecting O_1 to w_1, O_2 to v_1, etc. O_1 through O_4 are the observational inputs to the formal system. O_5 is the observational output. It is also necessary that the output be operationally defined so that it can be verified or falsified.

This diagram of an empirical theory, albeit an overly simple theory, is thought to capture the essentials of any empirical theory. Hempel intends it to be general and shows how more complex theories (Newtonian physics) can be cast in a similar schematic.[12] Margenau's "construct" and "percept" diagrams are almost identical. He says that theories "attain validity through empirical confirmation. This process represents a circuit, traceable in either sense, from perception (observation) via rules of correspondence to constructs and back along some other route to perception."[13]

In summary, a theory of empirical science may be divided into two parts: (1) A Formal System which is composed of abstract symbols and a set of syntactical rules for manipulating those symbols; and (2) An Interpretation of the formal system which connects certain symbols to observations via semantical rules. The propositions in the formal system are analytic in the sense that they are deduced from axioms or definitions. The propositions of the interpreted theory are intended to be empirical and they must be tested by observations. The semantical rules are concerned with two different kinds of observations: (1) Inputs and (2) Outputs. In order for a theory to be complete the kinds of observations to be made and the measurement rules must be specified. These are the empirical inputs to the formal system. Those inputs are then manipulated according to the syntactical rules. The outputs of the formal system are connected via semantical rules to observations. If the observations are as specified by the formal system, then that particular proposition is said to be verified.

This may be diagrammed as follows:

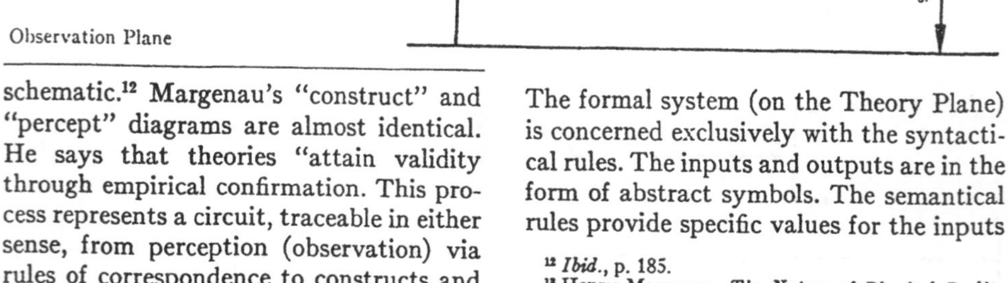

The formal system (on the Theory Plane) is concerned exclusively with the syntactical rules. The inputs and outputs are in the form of abstract symbols. The semantical rules provide specific values for the inputs

[12] *Ibid.*, p. 185.

[13] Henry Margenau, *The Nature of Physical Reality* (McGraw-Hill Book Company, Inc., 1950). The diagrams appear on pp. 85, 93 and 106. The quotation appears on p. 121.

in a particular case, i.e., numerals are inserted in place of the abstract symbols. These numerals are manipulated in the same way as the abstract symbols are manipulated, i.e., in accordance with the syntactical rules. Then the outputs are also specific numerals instead of symbols and they provide, via semantical rules, an expectation or prediction of an observable occurrence. If the occurrence is in fact observed then that particular case is said to be verified. If enough cases are verified the theory is said to be confirmed.

III. Some Accounting Interpretations

Theories are restricted to certain subjects or certain kinds of phenomena. Although generality is desirable, there is no general theory of the general scheme of things; instead each theory is limited to a particular subject matter. One of the difficulties encountered in accounting theory construction and verification is that different accounting theories are often theories about different subject matters. The problem is not so much that there are conflicting theories about the same subject matter as it is that the various theories are concerned with different subject matters. It is to be expected that different subject matters will produce different theories. Perhaps a review of some of these theories would be helpful.

An Anthropological Interpretation

Probably the most ancient and pervasive method of accounting theory construction is to observe accountants' actions and then rationalize those actions by subsuming them under generalized principles. The result is not a theory about accounting or a theory about the things to be accounted for; instead it is a theory about accountants. The "principles of acounting" then is a theory that says that under such and such conditions the accountant will act in such and such a way. The input is the condition and the output is the accountants' action.

This is quite similar to, say, the theory that "the essence of primitive religion is animism."[14] This theory allows anthropologists to predict that under certain conditions, primitive man will act in a certain way. The test of the theory is the observations of the actions of primitive man. In the same fashion, the test of an anthropological theory of accounting is the observations of the actions of accounting man. For example, if the accounting anthropologist has observed that accounting man normally records a "conservative" figure and generalizes this as the "principle of conservatism," then we can test this principle by observing whether or not accounting man does in fact record a conservative figure. If the accounting anthropologist sets forth the "principle of diversity," then we can test this principle by observing whether or not accounting man does in fact record similar occurrences in different ways. And so forth.

There are several difficulties with this kind of theorizing. First, it is not necessarily true that accounting man acts in the manner in which he ought to act. It is an error to conclude that because *x is* the case, then *x ought* to be the case. There is no way to arrive at the way accounting man ought to act from observing and generalizing how he in fact does act. Thus, this kind of theorizing may provide us with an explanation of why accountants act in a certain way and it may provide us with the ability to predict their actions, but it does not yield a judgment about the goodness of their actions. To judge the goodness of their actions requires other criteria. Second, the process does not permit change. By requiring the present generation of accountants to act in accordance with generally accepted principles of accounting—which principles were derived

[14] Bronislaw Malinowski, *Magic, Science and Religion* (Doubleday & Company, Inc., 1948), p. 18.

by observing the actions of the previous generation of accountants—change has been prohibited. If the requirement were strictly enforced, each generation would act just like the previous generation and this could be traced back to the first generation. Of course, changes have been made in accounting theory, but these changes are not explained or provided for by the anthropological interpretation. Third, subsequent to the first generation, the process is circular. We observe accountants' actions to discover what to teach, then we teach them how to act, then we observe accountants' actions to discover what to teach, etc. Fourth, and most importantly, is my value judgment that the theory of accounting ought to be concerned with accounting phenomena, not practicing accountants, in the same way that theories of physics are concerned with physical phenomena, not practicing physicists. The anthropological investigations provide useful information. It is important for us to know how practicing accountants act and to understand why they act that way. Comprehension of those actions is aided if they can be generalized under "principles of accounting." However, such knowledge does not provide a basis for a theory of accounting, as opposed to a theory of accountants' actions, and therefore the anthropological interpretation is not appropriate.

A Model-of-the-Firm Interpretation

The process of accounting may be cast in the form of the above schema as follows: There are observable occurrences (transactions, exchanges) which are inputs (entries) to the formal system. These are manipulated (partitioned or classified and summed) according to certain rules. The outputs (the financial statements or the balance of any particular account) are verified (audited). The formal system—the manipulation process—can be stated quite generally. Elsewhere[15] I have attempted to demonstrate that, given the inputs, the accounting outputs can be generated by an analytically defined process.

This interpretation indicates that the financial statements or the individual balances say something about the state of the firm. The accounting system under this interpretation is taken as a "model" of the firm in much the same way that a planetarium is a model of the sky. One can look at the financial statements and be able to determine the position of the firm in the same way that one can look at a planetarium and determine the position of a star. The individual propositions are verified every time the statements are audited and thus the theory has been confirmed many times.

The difficulty with this interpretation springs from the peculiar nature of the verification process in auditing. With minor exceptions, none of the outputs of an accounting system are *separately* verifiable. That is, there is no independent empirical operation which one can perform in order to verify the figures that were calculated from the inputs. Neither "net income" nor "total assets" are observable or separately measurable; instead they are summations of account balances. Account balances are not observable or separately measurable; instead they are summations of the entries.[16] The auditing process is not a verifi-

[15] Robert R. Sterling, "Elements of Pure Accounting Theory," The Accounting Review, Vol. XLII, No. 1, (January 1967).

[16] Contrast the verification of the quantity of inventory with the verification of the book value of that inventory. For quantities there is a well-defined formal system (perpetual inventory system) which specifies the relevant empirical inputs (receipts and issues) and the output provides an expectation or prediction of the quantity on hand. The physical count is a separate verification of that output.

For book values there is disagreement about the formal system (lifo or fifo) and disagreement about the relevant inputs (which costs are to be attached and which are to be expensed). The output provides no expectation and is not separately verifiable. It is the lack of verifiability of the output which prohibits resolution of the disagreement about the formal system and the inputs.

cation of the outputs; instead it is, in essence, a *recalculation* of the outputs and an "examination" of the underlying business documents in order to check on the accuracy or verity of the inputs. Thus, the auditing process focuses on the inputs to the system and the way in which those inputs are manipulated. It does not verify the outputs of the system.

The inadequacy of this procedure to confirm a theory is immediately apparent. If one were to attempt to confirm a theory of astronomy, as exemplified by a particular planetarium, then one might begin by checking on the accuracy of the observational inputs and one might also check for errors in computation. However, at some point the outputs of the system would be verified. One would look at the sky to see if the stars were in fact in the position indicated by the planetarium. In the absence of this last step, several absurdities could result. First, the set of equations could describe any situation whatsoever, e.g., a rectangular orbit. If one restricted the "verification" procedure to a check on the accuracy of the inputs and a recalculation, then one would certify that this planetarium presents fairly the position of the stars. The only way to discover that the orbit ought or ought not to be rectangular is to perform a separate operation and compare the results of that operation with the outputs of the system. If enough of these outputs were subjected to independent verification, the theory of rectangular orbits would be either confirmed or disconfirmed. Second, if there were two planetariums concerned with the same phenomena but with different sets of equations resulting in contradictory outputs, then the auditing procedure would require that both of them be certified as correct when at least one of them is necessarily wrong. Finally, the number of different sets of equations with different outputs is limitless.

The above example is similar to the problems currently faced in accounting. At the present time there are several different sets of equations for the allocation of cost. No matter how carefully one checks the accuracy of the inputs and the calculation, this process does not provide a method of confirming or disconfirming any of those sets of equations. As a consequence, any of those sets of equations are acceptable and the auditor has no way to choose among them. Two different sets of equations may be applied to the same inputs (in different firms) and the auditor will certify that the outputs of both present fairly when one must necessarily be wrong. Additional sets of equations can be added at will. For example, Thomas[17] has mentioned a sum-of-the-lunar-months method; Ijiri[18] has shown how the sum-of-the-year's-digits equation can be applied to inventory. The only reason that these suggestions appear to be odd is that they are unfamiliar. In the absence of the verification of the outputs of these equations, they are equally as good (or bad) a method of cost allocation as those equations presently in use.

Consider the depreciation equation. It says, in effect, a magnitude called "depreciation expense" is a function of time and the original cost. In some sense this is probably true; the market value of an asset normally declines over time. The difficulty is that the precise form of that function is open to question as is evidenced by the fact that there are several acceptable depreciation methods. Compare this situation to the problem of determining the function for a free falling body. The distance travelled by a free falling body is also a function of time, viz.,

[17] Arthur L. Thomas, "The Amortization Problem: A Simplified Model and Some Unanswered Questions," *Journal of Accounting Research*, Vol. 3, No. 1, (Spring 1965), p. 110.

[18] Yuji Ijiri, "Logic and Sanctions in Accounting," unpublished paper presented at Accounting Colloquium I, (University of Kansas, April 1969).

$$d = 1/2\ gt^2.$$

Suppose I argued that the above is wrong and that the correct function is

$$d = 2\ gt^{1/2}.$$

The only way to resolve the dispute is to observe the position of the body and the distance travelled and compare that observation to the calculated *d*'s.[19] The same is true in regard to the depreciation equation.

Note, however, that current accounting practice ***prohibits*** separate verification. Auditors have substituted the word "examination" for "verification" because the latter is not "an accurate portrayal of the independent auditor's function."[20] Depreciation is an "allocation," not a "valuation," and that allocation is not "a measurement, expressed in monetary terms, of the physical deterioration within the year, or of the decline in monetary value within the year, or, indeed of anything that actually occurs within the year."[21] Therefore, independent observations of market prices or the physical state are not relevant to the examination of depreciation expense.[22]

In summary, the outputs of present accounting theory are not separately verifiable. From the pronouncements in the literature, it appears that they are not intended to be a description of an empirical state and are not intended to be separately verifiable. Therefore, we must conclude that the model-of-the-firm interpretation is not an appropriate interpretation of present accounting theory.

A Psychological Interpretation

The model-of-the-firm interpretation can be broadened to include the receivers of the accounting reports. Under this interpretation the financial statements are not the final output of the theory; instead they are inputs to the receivers. The receiver's reactions to the financial statements are the observable outputs of the system.

[19] Another method of selection is to subsume the particular function under a more general theory. In this case, the former function "fits into" the general scheme of the Newtonian Laws of Motion and can be deduced therefrom. Thus, we could accept the former and reject the latter on that basis even if the distance travelled were not separately verifiable. However, in order to accept the theory into which this function fits, that theory would have to be confirmed by having some of its outputs verified. Otherwise, disputes about the theory are unresolvable. If the theory were well confirmed and this function could be deduced therefrom, we could claim that *d* was "indirectly verified." See James W. Cornman, "Indirectly Verifiable: Everything or Nothing," *Philosophical Studies*, Vol. XVIII, No. 4, (June 1967), and the literature he cites for a more complete discussion of indirect verification.

[20] *Auditing Standards and Procedures, No. 33* (American Institute of Certified Public Accountants, 1963), p. 94.

[21] *Accounting Research and Terminology Bulletins*, Final Edition, Terminology Bulletin 1 (American Institute of Certified Public Accountants, 1961), p. 24.

[22] The irrelevance of market prices to the examination of depreciation expense raises some questions about the original justification for the recording of that expense. If it were not for the prediction that the market price of the asset was going to decline from its purchase price to its salvage value, there would be no justification for recording an expense. If the salvage value were expected to be greater than or equal to the purchase price, then there would be no cost expiration to be allocated. Yet interim observations of prices are thought to be irrelevant to the allocation.

Of course it can be argued that the pattern of the cost allocation need not be the same as the pattern of price movements, but this raises the very question that has remained unresolvable: What should the pattern be? Moreover, in the absence of a verification, it is not certain that the expense should be a function of time. Making it a function of revenue would also result in a "rational" allocation. The usual objection to making depreciation a function of revenue is that it results in an undesirable smoothing of income. However, a function can be defined in which depreciation varies inversely with revenue. Such a function would result in less smoothing than the presently used straight-line method. That is, since income is the difference between revenue and expense, the smoothing of the expense results, cet. par., in the smoothing of the income. Thus, if smoothing is undesirable then the presently used depreciation method can be criticized on the same grounds that was used in the original justification given for instituting the present depreciation method.

In short, both the form that the depreciation equation should take and the kind of variables that should go into the depreciation equation are unresolvable issues in the context of current accounting theory because there is no separate verification of the output of that equation. If the objective of the depreciation equation were to describe or predict the path of some observable phenomena (such as price change or physical deterioration) then there would be some chance of deciding which equation is best. That objective seems reasonable in light of the fact that the very existence of the calculation depends upon the prediction of a price decline.

Thus, this interpretation is identical with the above model-of-the-firm interpretation except for the verification of the outputs. The inputs are the observable transactions or exchanges which are manipulated according to the syntactical rules of accounting. These rules produce financial statements (or other accounting figures) which are sent to the receivers. The receivers then react (or fail to react) and this is the observable output of the system. If the receivers react, it is taken as evidence that the financial statements are "useful" or that they contain "information."

Although usefulness has long been a tenet of accounting, it is only recently that the receivers' use or lack of use of the reports has been tested. There are some inconclusive results, but the tests that have been performed indicate that accounting reports are in fact used by the receivers. These results are important and continued research needs to be done in this area.[23] However, there are several lines of criticism that can be directed against this interpretation.

First, the subject matter of this interpretation is the reactions of people. This is the reason I call it a psychological interpretation. It follows the methodology of the stimulus-response school of psychology. The financial statements are the stimuli and the response is the receivers' decisions. The evidence has been gathered in respect to the effect of the frequency of the stimuli, the correlation of changes in the stimuli to changes in securities prices, the effects of different stimuli on investors and managers, the effect of the receipt of the stimuli upon price change and volume change, etc. This is quite similar to observing the effects of frequency, intensity, etc. of, say, electric shock upon people or laboratory animals. The resulting theory will also be quite similar. That is, it will be a theory which will explain or predict the reactions of people to stimuli. It is not clear that a theory of accounting should take on this character.

Second, if the response of receivers to accounting stimuli is to be taken as evidence that certain kinds of accounting practices are justified, then we must not overlook the possibility that those responses were conditioned. Accounting reports have been issued for a long time, and their issuance has been accompanied by a rather impressive ceremony performed by the managers and accountants who issue them. The receivers are likely to have gained the impression that they ought to react, and have noted that others react, and thereby have become conditioned to react. The fact that Pavlov's dog reacted to the sound of a bell does not provide justification for the existence of the bell.

Third, is the vital distinction between pragmatic informational content and semantic informational content. The study of pragmatics is concerned with the relation of signs to the users of signs. The study of semantics is concerned with the relation of signs to objects or events. If a person reacts to a sign, then that sign has pragmatic informational content. However, that reaction has nothing to do with the semantic informational content of that sign. People may react to a sign which we call a "lie." What we mean by the term "lie" is that it has negative semantic informational content, or, as we also say, it is "misinformation." The same is true with accounting reports. They are signs to which people react. However, the signs may or may not be connected to real world phenomena and the receivers may or may not be aware of the connection or lack of connection. The receivers may be interested in certain real world phenomena and may rightly or wrongly think that the signs al-

[23] The importance of the results can be most vividly illustrated by considering the effects of the converse results. If it had been discovered that the receivers do not use accounting reports, the raison d' être of accounting would be open to question.

low them to discriminate that phenomena. Thus, the fact that receivers react to accounting reports does not necessarily mean that they ought to react.[24,25]

The final point of criticism can best be presented by an analogy. A physician will strike the knee of a patient and note the reaction. The phycician does not conclude from this reaction that the patient has received information; instead the reaction is information to the physician. The physician then decides whether or not that reaction is pathological. The reaction is an observable input to the theory of medicine. It is my value judgment that the accounting profession ought to take a similar stance in regard to the reaction of the receivers. The fact that the receivers react is information to us and it is up to us to decide whether or not that reaction is pathological.

IV. A Program for Constructing a Theory of Relevant Measurements

In my view, accounting ought to be a measurement-communication process. Accountants ought to measure something and then communicate that measurement to the people who will make the decisions. Under this interpretation, the outputs of the accounting system are the inputs to decision theories. This interpretation focuses on decision *theories,* in contrast to the psychological interpretation which focuses on decision *makers.*

If there exists a well-defined decision theory, then that theory will specify what observations are to be made or what properties are to be measured. This provides a definition of relevance: All properties that are specified by a decision theory are relevant to that theory. All properties that are not specified by a decision theory are irrelevant to that theory. Consider Hempel's example of specific gravity. The most obvious thing about this theory, so obvious that it remains tacit, is that somebody wants to know whether or not x_1 will float on x_2. The motivation for acquiring this knowledge in general form may have been idle curiosity. However, in any particular application of the theory, it is likely that the motivation is provided by a problematic situation. That is, someone must act; someone must decide between two or more courses of action and let us assume that the property of floating on is the basis for the decision. Therefore, this theory is applicable to that problematic situation. The theory clearly specifies that weight and volume are the relevant properties and that color, electrical resistance, and a host of other properties are irrelevant.

The reason for focusing on decision theories instead of decision makers is now apparent. Some or all of the decision makers may believe that the floating on property can be predicted by color or electrical resistance, i.e., their decision theories are wrong. If there were a large number of different decision makers with a large number of different erroneous decision theories, then it would be impossible to supply the data for all of them. More important is the fact that the erroneous decision theories are likely to produce erroneous decisions, i.e., decisions which do not produce the objectives desired by the decision makers. For these reasons, among others, I believe that accounting ought to supply the data specified by decision theories rather than the data desired by decision makers.[26]

[24] Beaver has carefully made this point in reporting his results. He says that his test is of the "investor *reaction* to earnings reports" and his "paper empirically examines the extent to which common stock investors *perceive* earnings to possess informational value." William H. Beaver, "The Information Content of Annual Earnings Announcements," *Empirical Research in Accounting: Selected Studies 1968* (Institute of Professional Accounting, 1969) p. 67, italics supplied.

[25] In his discussion of pragmatics, S. S. Stevens, *Handbook of Experimental Psychology* (John Wiley & Sons, Inc., 1951) p. 4, reminds us of the reaction of Diderot to the mathematical signs presented by Euler. In an attempt to win a debate about the existence of God, Euler presented a symbolic expression which had nothing to do with the existence or nonexistence of God but which, nevertheless, routed Diderot.

[26] My critics sometimes attack this approach on

In one sense, under this interpretation, there is no separate theory of accounting. Every theory calls for measurements, and accounting is simply the measurement activity for certain kinds of theories. In the physical sciences the development of measurements is inextricably entwined with the construction of theories. After the theory has been established and the measurement operations are well defined, then the measurement activity can be turned over to technicians. During the development stage, however, the very concepts that one seeks to measure are strongly influenced by the theory that one is trying to establish. Sometimes this is expressed by noting that the very act of measurement requires a commitment to a particular theory. Compare, for example, the measurements in relativistic time and space to the measurements "of the same phenomena" in absolute time and space. It is for this reason that I have previously argued that accountants qua metricians must become involved in the construction, refinement and elaboration of the decision theories.[27] Churchman has taken another tack. For similar reasons he has argued that operations researchers qua theoreticians must become involved with the development of measurements.[28] Whether it is the metricians who ought to become theoreticians or the theoreticians who ought to become metricians is not important. What is important is that theory construction and measurement development must be fused. Part of our previous problems have been the result of conceiving of them as separable activities.

Theory without measurement is mere speculation. We noted above that one can construct a theory of love to replace the theory of gravity. Such theories can be constructed in any number. Measurement without theory is aimless wandering. Hempel's "hage" example makes this clear:

Concepts with empirical import can be readily defined in any number, but most of them will be of no use for systematic purposes. Thus, we might define the

grounds similar to the notion of consumer sovereignty. In their view, information is like any other good or service, and they argue that the accounting profession ought to give the decision maker the information he wants in the same way that any other producer ought to respond to the wants of consumers. The free play of market forces will then be the instrument that decides which information should be supplied. There is merit in this view but it depends upon some questionable assumptions.

First, the group that directly pays for the preparation of accounting reports, and influences their preparation, is only a part of the group of consumers. Investors receive the reports free of any direct payment. Thus, the value of the reports, in the sense of the price that people would be willing to pay for them, has not been tested in the open market. Second, the notion of consumer sovereignty depends upon the pristine will of the people. Joseph A. Schumpeter, *Capitalism, Socialism and Democracy* (Harper & Row, 1947), Ch. XXII, has pointed out that it makes little sense to justify one's actions on the basis of responding to the will of the people if that will has been manufactured. John K. Galbraith, *The Affluent Society* (Houghton Mifflin Company, 1958), Ch. XI, has made the same point more recently in what he calls the "dependence effect." Supra I made the same point by wondering whether or not the receivers have been conditioned to respond to accounting reports. Third, the efficacy of consumer sovereignty depends upon competition and free entry into the market so that alternatives can be provided. The provision of alternative kinds of accounting information is prohibited by requiring that it be in accord with generally accepted accounting principles. Entry into the accounting profession is limited by a licensing procedure. Of course, the consumer can choose different sources of information, e.g., he can choose between financial analysts and accountants, but this is like the consumer being able to choose between the local electric and gas companies (both of which are monopolies in many instances) for his source of power. It hardly meets the requirements of free competition which is so necessary to the defense of consumer sovereignty.

Finally is my value judgment that the notion is inapplicable in this instance. In my view, the accounting profession ought to devote some of its effort and resources to the education of the receivers. The profession ought to tell the receivers which decision theories are correct and then supply the data specified by those theories. Other professions have done this, e.g., the medical profession has gone to some lengths to convince the population that the germ theory of medicine is correct and that the demon theory of medicine is incorrect. In one sense this is a normative, as opposed to a positive, position. It results in an ought statement. The medical profession is saying, in effect, that the population ought to apply the germ theory. However, in another sense it is a positive position. The medical profession is not dictating the goal that the population ought to seek; instead it is informing them of the best method of achieving *any* health goal. If one seeks illness, then the germ theory is the most efficient method of achieving that goal in the same way that it is the most efficient method of achieving the goal of avoiding illness. The demon theory will not allow one to achieve either goal. Accounting can take a similar position. A

> hage of a person as the product of his height in millimeters and his age in years. This definition is operationally adequate and the term 'hage' thus introduced would have relatively high precision and uniformity of usage; but it lacks theoretical import, for we have no general laws connecting the hage of a person with other characteristics.[29]

This example is particularly pertinent to many accounting arguments. Regardless of many other *desirable* features—such as uniformity, precision, feasibility, objectivity, verifiability, freedom from bias, etc.—hage is a curiousity because it does not meet the *indispensable* requirement of being specified by some theory. The full disclosure of the method of calculation does not make the concept understandable or useful. That it is a fact or the truth does not make it meaningful. The same is true for the figures we generate in accounting. The theoretical import of accounting figures is the first question to be considered. Without a decision in regard to this question, the considerations of feasibility, objectivity, etc. are beside the point.

In short, theory construction and measurement development are inseparable. The theory specifies what is to be measured, how the measurements are to be manipulated and what measurable outcomes one can expect. This implies that the theory is constrained by what can be measured. It also implies that the measurements interact with the theory in that the predicted occurrences will be either verified or falsified by separate measurements. Some of the measurements may be considered anomalous and result in the modification or rejection of the theory. Thus, if accounting is to be a measurement-communication process, then the "theory of accounting" is only a part of the more general decision theories. Under this view it is the decision theories that need confirmation. Accounting figures are simply measurement inputs to the decision theories and we may want to verify those figures in the same way that we would verify any other measurement, but there is no separate theory of accounting to be confirmed.

The above is a long run proposal. If it were accepted, it would take years for it to be implemented. For the interim period I will briefly outline a short run program. First, decision theories that exist in the economics, operations research, etc. literature can be taken as givens. Instead of trying to construct our own decision theories we can search the literature for the extant decision theories. Thus, the "empirical research" that is required is a literature search. Second, the decision theories that are found in the literature can be classified and summarized in various ways. Perhaps the decision theories within a given class can be stated in a general form. It may be that some decision theories share a structure and the number of different theories can be reduced to manageable proportions by considering those with a common structure to be one theory. Third, an examination of the decision theories will reveal the relevant properties. There will be some properties that are specified by a number of the-

theory that allows one to maximize profits can also be used to minimize profits, satisfice profits, earn a certain rate or amount, etc. On the other hand, an erroneous theory will not permit the achievement of any of those goals. For example, if one bases his decision upon sunk costs, then it is likely that he will not achieve his goal, regardless of whether that goal is to maximize or minimize. Thus, my normative position is that the accounting profession ought to assist in the achievement of efficient decisions and to let the decision makers choose their goals.

[27] Robert R. Sterling, *Theory of the Measurement of Enterprise Income* (The University Press of Kansas, 1970), p. 59.

[28] C. West Churchman, "A Systems Approach to Measurement in Business Firms," unpublished paper presented at Accounting Colloquium I, (University of Kansas, April 1969).

[29] Carl G. Hempel, *Fundamentals of Concept Formation in Empirical Science* (The University of Chicago Press, 1967), p. 46.

ories. This may provide a basis for deciding which properties should be measured if we find that we cannot measure all of them.

This program is concerned with the discovery of the relevant properties. It appears that much of the previous accounting literature has not been concerned with that problem. Instead it has been concerned with *how* one measures and *what* one measures has been taken as a given. My concern is with the discovery of what one ought to measure, i.e., what properties are relevant. *After* that has been established, then the question of how one goes about the measurement activity should be considered. Undoubtedly there will be a good many measurement problems, some of which may be unresolvable, but in regard to this interim program the measurement problems are of secondary concern.

Even the short run program is a formidable task. It is not, however, an insuperable task. Elsewhere[30] I have used this method in an analysis of the decisions regarding an oversimplified firm. Although the analysis was tedious, I was encouraged by the fact that it was possible to generalize the decision theories. If one were forced to examine each of the many decision theories and interpretations, the task might be well nigh impossible. The generalization of the decision theories allowed the task to be reduced to reasonable proportions. I was also encouraged by the findings. There were in fact some properties that were specified by all the decision theories, some properties that were specified by some of the decision theories, and some properties that were not specified by any of the decision theories. On this basis one can choose which properties to measure and communicate. Thus, a theory of accounting, in the sense of it being a theory of what to measure or account for, can be constructed from the specifications of the broader theories of economic decisions. The subject matter of accounting theory is, under this program, the broad theories of economic decisions. Thus, the observation plane of accounting is the theoretical plane of economics and related disciplines. The economic decision theories will have a separate set of confirmation procedures and problems.

The above is a cursory review of one possible method of constructing a theory of accounting. It is entirely programmatic and, like any other program, there will be many difficulties in its implementation.[31] I am not sure that these difficulties can be overcome, but I believe that this approach is more promising than the others that have been tried.

[30] Sterling, *Enterprise Income*.

[31] Beaver, Kennelly and Voss argue that the predictive ability of accounting figures is a more feasible approach because of the difficulty in determining the decision theories used and because the predictive ability approach requires a lower level of specificity regarding the decision theory. Their idea is appealing if one accepts the proposition that the decision theories are impossible to specify, and their discussion is most thorough and enlightening. However, I am not convinced that it is impossible to specify the decision theories. William H. Beaver, John W. Kennelly and William M. Voss, "Predictive Ability as a Criterion for the Evaluation of Accounting Data," The Accounting Review, Vol. XLIII, No. 4, (October 1968).

THE MOTIVATION OF THE MEASURER

by

Robert R. Sterling
Arthur Young Distinguished Professor
School of Business Administration
University of Kansas

Darrell Harden
Associate Professor
School of Aerospace, Mechanical
and Nuclear Engineering
University of Oklahoma

Prepared for

presentation at the

Annual Meeting

of the

American Society of Engineering

June 17, 1973

I often say that when you can measure what you are speaking about and express it in numbers, you know something about it, but when you cannot measure it, your knowledge is of a meager and unsatisfactory kind. -- Lord Kelvin

The object of metrics has been well put by Lord Kelvin. We can all agree that our knowledge is richer, more satisfactory, when we can express it in numbers. Or saying it another way, our information is more informative if it can be expressed as a measurement. The motivations of the measurer is to make measurements which make information more informative. The measurer is interested in the characteristics of measurement that give it this higher status.

The purpose of this paper is to discuss the measurement of perceptions as practiced in the laboratory. We will present some propositions of measurement from Sterling (1) which most metricians will accept in spirit if not in detail. At first glance these basic propositions may seem simple-minded but they are the foundation from which we build a science of measurement. Metricians who have read this discussion have accepted the propositions as necessary but have criticized the set of propositions as being incomplete. The broad school (to be described later) would consider it incomplete because of the absence of the nominal scale; the narrow school because of the absence of sharp delineation between measurements and nonmeasurements.

Perceptions to be measured may be objective such as encountered in the "physical" sciences or psychic as encountered in the "social" sciences. In either case the impetus of the measurement is a desire for information of a certain "informational content". Informational content can be "qualitative" rather than "quantitative" and there exists no a priori reason for deciding on the measurement type. In general, the engineer purports to be skilled at eliciting and using quantitative information. Thus he will be interested in measurement procedures that generate numerical information.

Anyone who expects to find a single, well-established definition of measurement is due for a disappointment. One cannot search the literature and find a system of measurement principles that is not disputed. For this reason we will briefly review the dispute among metricians.

Opinion on measurements may be roughly divided into two categories. Following Stevens (2), we will call these the "broad" and the "normal" schools (Definitions, p. 19). These are shorthand descriptions and should not be interpreted in any pejorative sense. The narrow school looks closely at the measurement procedures and distinguishes between "fundamental" and "derived" measurements. For example, Campbell (3) says that length is fundamental because it does not depend upon any previous measurements, while density is derived because it is dependent upon the measurement of weight and volume. The broad school looks to the mathematical properties of numerical assignment and distinguishes between various scales on that basis. For example, Stevens lists the statistical procedures that are appropriate to the four scales: norminal, ordinal, interval, and ratio. Another difference is that the narrow view is inclined to think of objects as "possessing" a certain pre-existing property or characteristic that can be measured. The broad view, mainly the operationists, believe that there are only well-defined operations of measurements and that to attribute pre-existing properties to objects commits one to an untenable metaphysical position.

As is true of all developing systems of description there is some merit in both positions. The narrow school's focus on the empirical attributes of measurement emphasizes the restraints given in nature. The broad school's focus on mathematics emphasizes what we can do with the numbers once they have been generated. The "pre-existing property" idea is hard to defend a priori, but once a scale or dimension has been defined, then it is eminently reasonable to speak of objects possessing that property, whether or not it is measured. Thus, there is a pre-existing property of objects, given a previously defined scale or dimension. The importance of a well-defined operation can scarcely be overemphasized; but the operation itself does not yield conceptual import.

To continue with our introductory remarks concerning the "informativeness" of information we note that Churchman (4) states, "The contrast between quantitative and nonquantitative seems to imply a contrast between "precise" and "vague" information. Precise information is information that enables one to distinguish objects and their properties to some arbitrarily assigned degree of refinement. . .the reason that precision information can be used in a wide variety of problems."

Churchman's concern appears to be with precision. Notice, however, that precision is a concern of the second order. More fundamental is enabling "one to distinguish objects and their properties". Obviously, if there was no need to distinguish, there would be no need to distinguish precisely. Thus, the more fundamental aspect of measurement is its concern with the distinction between properties or characteristics of objects.

In more general terms, measurement is a process of comparison. We say that objects are longer, heavier, more resistant, etc., than other objects. We use the comparative form of the words in order to distinguish certain properties of objects. This basic and simple-minded fact is sometimes overlooked because the results of measurement are ordinarily stated in a positive form of speech. The very fact that we tend to forget that it is a comparison is testimony to its conceptual significance. "Three feet long" brings forth an image that is so definite that we think of it as a positive, black or white, description. Upon reflection, however, it is obvious that the statement is a comparison. It means that this object is longer than all objects that are less than three feet, equal to all objects that are exactly three feet, and shorter than all objects that are greater than three feet. Thus, the fundamental purpose of measurement is to allow us to distinguish or discriminate in respect to some property. We thus state, the first of five measurement propositions.

Measurement Proposition 1: The purpose of measurement is to order or compare objects or events to other objects or events.

Comparison of objects can be achieved in many different ways. The examination of any particular object will reveal a multitude of properties or characteristics that can be utilized to discriminate between that object and others. It will have length, volume, color, density, hardness, sweetness, shape, etc., any one or all of which can be utilized to compare. Even the simplest of objects possesses a bewildering array of different characteristics, and the complete description of all these characteristics may be well-nigh impossible. An attempt to describe all the characteristics of even the simplest object would require an enormous amount of time and effort, if it were possible at all.

Ordinarily, however, we do not want to know all of the characteristics of any particular object. The comparison is made between only certain selected characteristics of the objects. The purpose of the comparison will determine which characteristics should be measured and which should be ignored. Crusoe's problem (Churchman, Definitions, p.84) of finding a flagstone to fit his hearth specified the characteristics that were relevant. Shape, length, and perhaps smoothness were relevant characteristics. Sweetness, specific gravity, carbon half-life, and perhaps color were not. But, our discussion overlaps. The selection of the characteristics to be measured employs the same relevancy criterion as the selection of the information to be transmitted. The metrician has a problem and that problem, along with the theory for its solution, specifies which characteristic should be measured.

The primacy of the theory (some say "construct" or "conception") is stated by almost all investigators of the subject of measurement. It becomes even clearer here than in the writings on information. Churchman refers to the efficient use of the information in "any problem-situation"[1] and in another context the generation of "a class of information that will be useful in a wide variety of problems" (Definitions, p. 18). Stevens asks the question as "What purposes are we trying to serve?"[2] instead of referring to the solution of problems; but the difference is only in the choice of words. The "purpose served" is clearly the solution of a problematic situation even if that problematic situation be entirely theoretical. In measurement theory the theory performs the indispensable service of describing or explaining the dimension (property, characteristic) that is to be measured. As Cassirer puts it, all measurements must be "conceived and sought".[3] That is, we do not discover

[1] "The scaling of a property of an object provides information as to the most efficient use of that property in any problem-situation." (Ref. 5, Churchman, "Materialist", p. 490).

[2] "As I see this issue, there can surely be no objection to anyone computing any statistic that suits his fancy, regardless of where the numbers came from in the first place. Our freedom to calculate that remain as firm as our freedom to speak. The only question of substantial interest concerns the use to which the calculated statistic is intended. "What purposes are we trying to serve?" (Stevens, Definitions, p. 29).

[3] Caws (6) quotes Cassirer and then presents a cogent argument for the prior conception notion: "This [operationism] is a neat solution to the problem of the identity of the measured and the defined, since the same operation serves for both processes. But it leaves the problem of the nature of what is measured and defined untouched. Suppose we measure a length by the familiar device of putting a standard measuring rod against it, and obtain a numerical result; does this tell us anything about length as such? What it does yield is something that may be called a 'specific length', by analogy with specific gravity; but when the process is complete we know nothing about length as it applies to the case in question that we did not know about it as it applied to the standard measuring rod that we used. We would know something about length operationally only if the measuring rod itself had no length....one first has a concept of some quality and looks afterwards for quantitative expressions of it." (Caws, p. 8).

dimensions; we mentally conceive them and then seek to perform an operation that allows us to express that conception as a measurement.[4] The conception of the dimension is fundamental. One cannot measure an unconceived dimension. The juxtaposition of a meter stick to an object in the absence of a conception of the dimension of length would be pointless. There are philosophical disputes over the existence of a dimension prior to its conception, but this is not germane. It is plain that one cannot seek an expression of something that he has not conceived.

Of course numbers can be generated for a wide variety of things, some of which may be quite abstract and difficult to describe. Length is a conception common to almost everyone, and thus "two yards" brings forth an immediate mental image. Entropy is not so common, and therefore a measurement of entropy would be totally meaningless to many people. It requires extended explanation of the constructs of physics before measurements of entropy bring forth a meaningful mental image.

---

[4]Guild refers to a creation of a magnitude instead of a conception: "It is probably usual to regard the experimental processes of determining equality and of adding as something which we have just found to be convenient method of determining quantitative relations inherent in the nature of the magnitudes, whereas the processes are the necessary connecting links between phenomena and number without which there would be no basis of comparison between the laws of the former and those of the latter. The experimental criteria do not merely enable us to measure a magnitude, they create the magnitude by defining the fundamental relations which are to be the basis of the classification." (In Ferguson (7), p. 298).

The "definition of the fundamental relation" is a mental conception which must come prior to the operation. "Create" seems to be tantamount to "conceive".

Measurement is concerned with a process of comparing or ranking objects in respect to some specific property. Obviously, that property must be amenable to comparison or we cannot measure it. More fundamental is the conception and the definition of the scale or dimension. "Dimension" is a convenient name for the concept of a particular property and the notion of scaling that property.

Measurement Proposition 2: The construction and definition of a dimension is a prerequisite to the operation of measurement.

Given the conceived dimension we can then relate or compare objects to other objects with respect to that dimension. We can align one object to another and discover which is longer without further refinements. This is a crude form of comparison, however, and further, it is only a specific relation of one object to another. In order to make the comparison general, we need a unit of measurement; in order to refine the degree of discrimination, we need to make use of numbers.

The operation of measurement involves the comparison of the object with a unit of measure. The purpose is to facilitate the comparison of the object to other objects in the specified dimension. In other words, the use of a unit makes the comparison general. By going through the medium of a unit, by expressing the relevant dimension in terms of units, we can relate an object to all other objects that have been, or will be, measured. Units allow one to make what appears to be a positive, purely descriptive statement but one which is, in reality, a comparative statement that can be used in a wide variety of circumstances. An ordinal scale of measurement without the units can be established for a class of objects; but this type of scale has the deficiency of the noncomparability of a particular object in one class with an object from another class. For example, we can create an ordinal scale by saying that A is greater than B in some dimension. Likewise, we can say that X is greater than Y in the same dimensions. However, this does not permit the comparison of X to A. We have no idea of the relation of X to A without a further operation. By contrast, if both X and A are described in some kind of units, comparison can be made even though they belong to different classes. Thus, the benefit of utilizing a unit is that it generalizes the results of measurements.

One requirement of a unit is that it "possess" the same dimension as the object. (For example, an inch has the dimension of length, a pound the dimension of weight, etc.) Without this characteristic, it would be impossible to compare the object to the unit. The possession of the dimension, however, implies nothing about the interval of that unit. The original establishment of a unit is quite arbitrary, and no particular unit has any claim to being more proper or correct than any other. The origin of the length unit may have been a King's nose, or a light wave, and although the latter may appear to be more scientific, because it is more esoteric, and the former more humorous, both have equal claim to the title "unit".

Moreover, the different units may be used interchangeably by the process of measuring one in terms of the other. The resulting relationship is called, in metrics theory, a "transformation function"[5]. For example, the transformation function of yards to feet is the numberal "three"; from inches to centimeters, "2.54"; etc. It is true that one unit system may be easier to work with, such as metric versus English, but this easiness is due to the decimal base of the number system rather than to a property of the units.

Although the origin of a unit is arbitrary, the subsequent selection must be made with some care if the use of the measurement is to be generalized. Wide use of a measurement by different people requires familiarity with the unit in which the measurement is expressed. For example, most English-speaking people use the English system of foot-pound-second. To these people a measurement expressed in meters is meaningless. They must discover the length of a meter before such expressions are meaningful. That is, until they relate meters to something in their own experience (inches or yards), the informational value of the measurement is nil.

---

[5] Suppes distinguishes three separate transformations: "A real-valued function ϕ is a similarity transformation if there is a positive number α such that for every real number x

$$\phi(x) = \alpha x.$$

In transforming from pounds to grams, for instance, the multiplicative factor α is 453.6.
A real-valued function ϕ is a linear transformation if there are numbers α and β with $\alpha > \phi$ such that for every x

$$\phi(x) = \alpha x + \beta.$$

In transforming from Centigrade to Fahrenheit degrees of temperature, for instance, $\alpha = 9/5$ and $\beta = 32$.
A real-valued function ϕ is a monotone increasing transformation if, for any two numbers x and y, if $x < y$, then $\phi(x) < \phi(y)$.
Such transformations are also called order-preserving." (Suppes, Definitions, p. 131n.) We utilize the general notion of similarity transformation without distinguishing the different kinds.

The purpose of units is to make the objects comparable to all other objects in the specified dimension, i.e. to make the measurement general. If we want to expand the generality of measurements to different classes of users of the data, the unit selected must be one that is familiar to those users.

Measurement Proposition 3: Units allow a general comparison of objects. A familiar unit allows a general use of measurements by different people.

The comparison of the object to the unit usually results in a statement of numerosity. The reasons for the use of numbers are (1) to gain a greater degree of refinement in discriminating between objects and (2) convenience.

Parts of speech contain only three classifications--positive, comparative, and superlative--which permit only the crudest of comparisons. Using only these classifications we could only positively identify the two extremes. For example, we could point out only the shortest and the longest in a given set of rods. All the others could be described only in the comparative form--longer than the shortest, next to the longest, shorter than the longest--which permits little discrimination and is cumbersome.

By setting up a verbal classification, it is possible to make finer distinctions. The Beaufort scale is an example. "Gentle breeze" is less than "moderate breeze", which is less than "fresh breeze", etc. Such verbal classifications have several unfortunate characteristics[6]. First,

[6]Other writers describe the advantages of quantitative concepts in more detail. See, e.g., Hempel, pp.56-57. The Beaufort scale example is from Hempel (8).

each dimension measured requires the establishment and definition of a new classification. Not only does this require time and effort on the part of the metrician, it also limits the users of the measurements to those who have taken the trouble to learn the classifications. Second, any refinement of the classification scheme requires the introduction of new terms. Very fine gradations become cumbersome. Third, each classification fails to discriminate between items within that classification, although there may be a relatively large deviation, and at the same time it makes very fine distinctions at the boundaries of each classification, often without adequate criteria for making those distinctions.

Numerosity of units does not have such limitations. Only one classification--the unit--is necessary. Beyond that, the general number scheme can be utilized for all units in all dimensions. Thus, one attribute of numerosity is its convenience. Another attribute is the infinitely fine gradation available in the number scheme. Numbers can be fractionalized to any desired degree. If the unit is subject to fractionalization, a measurement expressed in numbers can be carried to any degree of precision. The limitations of precision, when numbers are used, is a result of the limited perception of the metrician and/or the limitation of the instrument; it is not due to any characteristic of numbers.

Measurement Proposition 4: The use of numbers is more convenient and permits a higher degree of percision than a verbal classification scheme.

The operation or procedure of measurement has for its purpose the placement of a given object in a dimensional scale. The purpose of the operation has nothing to do with instrumentation, precision, or specification of procedure. There may be a variety of different instruments and procedures available to measure any particular object, but the selection of the instrument is not germane to the purpose. Weight may be measured by the use of several different kinds of insturments each of which require a different procedure. However, in each case the desired end is to discover, by means of the procedure and instrument, the number of pounds, grams, etc., that the object possesses. Once the numerosity of units has been discovered, the object has then been related to all other objects of this dimensional scale through the medium of the numbers of units.

This is a fundamental disagreement with the rather common statement that measurement is the assignment of numbers to an object. Assignment is much too broad a term in describing operations of measurement. One can mentally project any number to any object in a capricious and arbitrary fashion. Such a projection or assignment cannot be called a measurement, because it does not discriminate among objects in respect to a property. We do not deny that the dimension is a mental conception and that the units are arbitrary. However, once this dimension has been conceived and the units defined, the objects then possess a certain number of those dimension units; and the purpose of the operation is to discover that number.

We have a well-defined conception of the dimension of length and several (arbitrary) units of length. Given the conception and the unit, it makes no sense to speak of "assigning" numbers to a rod unless we agree to use the word in a rather peculiar fashion. Discovery is a much more appropriate term, because that is what the operation accomplishes; it discovers, or reveals, the numerosity of the dimension units in that rod. Of course, we could agree to use "assign" in conjunction with the word operation--"assign numbers in accordance with a specified operation" --and this would mean the same thing. For example, we could say "assign the number to this object equal to that number of weights that is required to make this scale balance". However, the purpose of this operation is abundantly clear. It is to discover the number of weights that are required to make the scale balance. The object has the dimension of weight; there is an extant condition of that object; and the operation reveals a numerosity of units that allows us to compare it to other objects.

Precisely the same thing is true in an ordinal scale. For example, in Moh's scale of hardness certain minerals have been selected as basic referents and have been assigned numbers. We assign numbers to a scale; we discover the numerosity of units in an object. These minerals and their corresponding (assigned) numbers constitute a scale of the dimension of hardness. The units in such a scale lack certain attributes that other units possess; but that is not pertinent at the moment. Given the preconceived notion of hardness and the arbitrarily constructed units, the purpose of an operation of a measure of hardness by Moh's test is to discover the proper placement of an object in a preassigned numerical scale. Suppose that objects X and Y have been assigned the numerals 1 and 2 in Moh's scale. If we measure minerals Z by the operation of scratching and find that it scratches X and is scratched by Y, we have discovered its place on Moh's scale: it belongs between 1 and 2. The exact point between 1 and 2 is not known; but the operation discovered, albeit imprecisely, the place in the scale where the object belonged.

Of course, one can point out that letters of the alphabet could have been used instead of numbers. Because of that fact some metricians argue that Moh's scale is not properly called a measurement. We will not join in this dispute; our point is much less subtle: given the fact that numbers are used, the operation discovers the particular number (or range of numbers) that describes the object's place in the scale. The object has an existing condition, the operation discovers that condition.

Measurement Proposition 5: The purpose of the operation of measurement is to discover the proper placement of a given object in a given scale. The general statement of placement is in terms of numerosity of units.

SUMMARY

The purpose of measurement is to make information more informative. We noted that measurements were "conceived and sought"; and the reason they are sought is precisely because they are relevant. An irrelevant measurement is not "information" as we have defined it. Given the requisite of relevance, the question remains: Why are relevant measurements more informative than relevant nonmeasurements?

A review of measurement theory reveals two apparently self-contradictory attributes which make measurements more informative: they are both more general and more precise at the same time--more general because we can relate any object to all other objects by utilizing the medium of units; more precise because we can refine our discriminatory powers by expressing the units in degree numerically.

The concept of measurement may be outlined as four temporally ordered steps:

1. The conception of a dimension (because this dimension is relevant to some problematic situation).

2. Definition of the units and scale of the dimension.

3. Agreement to express the units numerically.

4. Description and application of an operation that discovers the numerosity of units in a given object.

The operation of measurement occurs in the reverse order. Two objects, A and B, are not ranked or related when found in experience. The application of the operation discovers the placement of these objects on a scale and expresses that placement in numerosity of units. This expression permits the conceptual ranking of those two objects in the dimension and also, because of the generality of the units and numbers, the potential ranking of those two objects to all other objects. We can now say that A is greater than, less than, or equal to, B in respect to some property which we call a dimension. Also A is greater than, less than, or equal to, C, D, E,...., which have been, or will be, expressed in the same units by the same operation. This ranking, presumably, is not an idle exercise; instead it is a deliberate attempt to obtain that information because that dimension is considered to be relevant to some theory and that theory is considered to be applicable to some problematic situation.

Of course, the two objects, A and B, could be ordered one to the other without going through the units. However, if at a later time we wanted to add C to our conceptual order, we would be forced to compare it to both A and B before placing it on the scale. Then if D were added, the same process would be required, and perhaps one of the earlier placements would have to be shifted. In a very short time this would become cumbersome. Thus, the units perform the function of generalizing the relationship of objects to objects. They relate all objects to all other objects with respect to a particular property.

In addition, units generalize the comparison in another direction. To communicate the fact that "A is greater than B" presupposes that the receiver knows the size of B; "A is greater than B and less than C" presupposes that he knows the sizes of both B and C. If the receiver does not know the sizes of the referent objects, there can be no conceptual ordering. The use of a unit permits all receivers who have knowledge of the size of the unit to make the generalized comparison.

The use of numbers is a convenient method of ordering magnitudes that is common to almost all members of the community. Moreover, if the unit is subject to fractionalization, the use of numbers allows us to state the magnitude in a degree of precision that is limited only by our perception or instrumentation. Thus, under ideal conditions of measurement, each object would have a unique place on the scale.

REFERENCES

1. Sterling, Robert R., Theory of the Measurement of Enterprise Income, Lawrence, Kansas: The University Press of Kansas, 1970.
2. Stevens, S. S., "Measurement, Psychophysics, and Utility", in Measurement: Definitions and Theories, eds. C. West Churchman and Philburn Ratoosh, pp. 18-63. New York: John Wiley & Sons, 1959.
3. Campbell, Norman R., Account of the Principles of Measurement and Calculations. London: Longmans, 1928.
4. Churchman, C. W., "Why Measure?" in Measurement: Definitions and Theories, eds. Charles West Churchman and Philburn Ratoosh, pp. 83-94 New York: John Wiley & Sons, 1959.
5. Churchman, Charles West, "A Materialist Theory of Measurement", in Philosophy for The Future, eds. Roy Wood Sellars, V. J. McGill, and Marvin Farber, pp. 476-94. New York: Macmillan Co., 1949.
6. Caws, Peter, "Definition and Measurement in Physics", in Measurement: Definitions and Theories, eds. C. West Churchman and Philburn Ratoosh, pp. 3-17. New York: John Wiley & Sons, Inc., 1959.
7. Ferguson, A., etal. "Quantitative Estimates of Sensory Events", British Association for the Advancement of Science, 1938, pp. 277-334; January 1940, pp. 331-49.
8. Hempel, Carl G., "Fundamentals of Concept Formation in Empirical Science" (International Encyclopedia of Unified Science, II, No. 7) Chicago: The University of Chicago Press, 1952.

by Robert R. Sterling

Toward a Science of Accounting

We accountants do not resolve issues, we abandon them. I do not mean to imply that we ignore issues. Quite the contrary, we debate them long and loud. However, the debate, instead of coming to a resolution, continues until another issue comes along that is more current and more controversial, and then we forget the former issue. Consider the LIFO-FIFO debate that occupied so much of our attention and journal space a few years ago. Currently LIFO versus FIFO is a dead issue. Note that I said "dead issue"; I did not say "resolved issue." Despite the fact that it is not resolved, at the present time there is no attention or journal space devoted to it. The reason for this is that other more pressing issues came along to divert our attention. One can run through the list of unresolved issues and discover much the same thing: tax allocation, accelerated versus straight-line depreciation, pooling versus purchasing treatment of business combinations, full versus direct costing, etc. For example, the reason we quit debating full versus direct costing was not because the issue was resolved but rather because the merger movement caused us to divert our attention to the more pressing issue of purchases versus pooling.

Further evidence of our inability to resolve issues is the fact that we periodically resurrect dead issues. The classification of bad debts and the treatment of interest as a cost were controversial issues when I was a student. Conclusive evidence that these issues were not resolved at that time is provided by the fact that they are once again being debated in the literature.[1] Such issues are periodically brought up for debate, abandoned for a while and then resurrected and debated again. Accountants anticipated the ecology movement by some years; instead of disposing of issues, we recycle them.

Instead of resolving issues in accounting, we move from one unresolved issue to another unresolved issue. Our inventory of unresolved issues grows larger and larger. Additions to the stock of unresolved issues arise in the natural course of events, but it has been virtually impossible for us to subtract from the stock. Why can't we resolve these issues?

The explanation for our inability to resolve issues is to be found in the way we conceive of the issues. We conceive of the issues in such a way that they are *in principle* unresolvable. The reason we cannot answer our questions is because we phrase the questions in a way that *prohibits* obtaining answers. We define our problems so that the very definition *precludes* the possibility of a solution.

Art versus Science

Our misconceptions start with the broadest of issues—the definition of accounting. In the official pronouncements of our societies,[2] in journal articles,[3] as well as in textbooks,[4] we find accounting defined as an "art" as opposed to a "science." These authors contrast the methods of accounting with those of science and claim that accounting is necessarily based upon *conventions,* as opposed to the *laws* that form the basis of a science.

The definition of accounting is based upon two misconceptions. First, the authors have a misconception of the nature of science. They seem to be-

Robert R. Sterling is Jesse H. Jones Professor, Department of Economics and Accounting, Rice University. *This article is based on a presentation at the Price Waterhouse Distinguished Lecture Series, Stanford University, April 11, 1975.*

1. Footnotes appear at end of article.

lieve that in order for a discipline to be scientific it must consist of immutable laws and absolute truths. The fact is that in even the most exact sciences laws are mutable. Witness the recent overturn of the Newtonian laws of physics by Einstein. To a scientist, laws are generalizations that must be continually subject to empirical challenge. If they were immutable, scientists would call them "definitions," not "laws."[5]

In direct contrast to scientists, accountants conceive of laws as immutable and seem to believe there are no uncertainties in science. For example, Lawler writes:[6]

> If, in truth, a practitioner of the accounting art is a truthseeker, he is confronted by a host of uncertainties. There are no natural laws of accounting which he can employ, only conventions validated by experience, estimates born of human judgments, guidelines developed by his professional societies.

We can all agree that there is a "host of uncertainties" in accounting. I believe it is the existence of such uncertainties that causes accountants to define accounting as an art. If one conceives of science as consisting of absolute truths, then one must conclude that accounting is not a science since there is so much uncertainty in accounting. However, that conclusion is based upon a misconception of the nature of science. There is also uncertainty in science, else there would be no reason for scientists to continue their research. Thus, when accountants define accounting as an art because of its uncertainty, they are basing their definition upon a misconception of science.

The second misconception is that there is something about accounting that makes it inherently unscientific. That accounting is based upon conventions instead of laws is the present condition of accounting, but it is not a necessary condition. Compare the primitive medicine man to the modern medical scientist. Both study illness—they have the same subject matter—but they differ in their approach to that subject matter. One performs artistic rituals designed to exorcise demons. The other performs the arduous scientific task of looking for empirical generalizations or laws. Thus the difference between them is not the nature of the subject but rather their approach to that subject. Once the medicine man *defines* illness as the product of the inexplicable caprice of demons, he is trapped. His problems will remain unresolved because he has defined them in such a way as to make them in principle unresolvable. The first step toward science is to change the definition of the problem. The modern medical scientist faces a host of uncertainties, e.g., the cause of cancer, but he does not fall into the trap of defining the problems so that they are in principle unresolvable.

I think the analogy fits accounting. There is nothing about our subject matter that requires that it be based upon conventions instead of laws. It is based upon conventions for the simple reason that we define it that way. It is possible to define it in some other way. There is nothing inherently unscientific about accounting; it is our approach to accounting that has been unscientific. It is possible for us to adopt a scientific approach.

Objectives: Artistic versus Scientific

Although I have never found the notion of accounting associated with science in accounting texts, I often find such associations in science and philosophy texts. In fact, many definitions of science include "account for" or "account of" as an integral part of the definition of science. For example, Torgerson writes:[7]

> The principal objective of a science, other than the description of empirical phenomena, is to establish, through laws and theories, general principles by means of which the empirical phenomena can be explained, *accounted for*, and predicted. (emphasis added)

Insofar as I am concerned, this is also the objective of accounting. Certainly we want to account for empirical phenomena. Hopefully, our financial statements provide explanations to the reader. I also believe that we should seek laws which will allow us to predict in the scientific sense. (Whether or not we want to predict in the sense of forecasting is one of those current unresolved issues I want to avoid in this article.)

Let us contrast the objectives of art to those of science. The purpose of an artist is to present his personal "interpretation" of an object, not to present an accurate representation of that object. Thus the picture that shows up on the canvas is due more to the imagination of the artist than to the object he is painting. Artists (at least post-Renaissance artists) strive to be different—to present *different* depictions of the *same* object. For example, if Picasso had painted a picture of Madame Matisse, he may have depicted her with only one eye since there are in fact Picasso paintings showing one-eyed women. On the other hand, as you will recall, Matisse depicted her with two eyes—and a green nose. It is unlikely that Picasso would have chosen green as the color of her nose. Both Picasso and Matisse would be looking at the same object, but the representations that would show up on the canvas would be quite different. In art, different representations of the same object are not only acceptable, they are highly desirable. The representations are intended to depend upon the imaginations of the artists, not upon the object.

By contrast, scientists strive to avoid such differences. If two scientists were to count the number of Madame Matisse's eyes or determine the color of her nose, differences between them would be cause for alarm. The same is true if they were to count her white blood cells or weigh her or diagnose her ailment. A basic tenet of science is that there be agreement among independent observers. The representations are intended to depend upon the object, not upon the imagination of the scientists.

Defining accounting as an art is, unfortunately, a fairly accurate description of the current condition. There is that infamous memo in the Penn Central Case that says that one person's "imaginative accounting is adding millions of dollars annually to our reported income."[8] Certainly in that case the representation depended more upon the imagination of the accountant than upon the financial position of Penn Central. I fear that there are a good many such instances. In the present unscientific state of accounting, I fear that the representation may depend more upon the imaginations of the accountants than upon the firms being accounted for. In this sense accounting may be in fact more like an art than a science.

This is not the way that things *ought* to be, however. If two accountants were to count Madame Matisse's eyes, a difference in the count should be cause for alarm. The same is true if they were to measure her income or assets or liabilities. A basic tenet of accounting ought to be agreement among independent observers. In accounting the measure ought to depend upon the condition of the firm, not upon the imagination of the accountant. In short, the objectives of accounting ought to be identical to the objectives of any of the sciences.

Instructions to Artists

Perhaps the danger of defining accounting as an art can be more vividly illustrated by considering Oliver Cromwell's instructions to his portrait painter:[9]

> Mr. Lely, . . . , I desire you would use all your skill to paint my picture truly like me and not flatter me at all; but remark all these roughnesses, pimples, warts and everything, otherwise I never will pay a farthing for it.

The very fact that Cromwell could give these instructions to his painter is significant. It means that he could have given instructions to do the opposite. I suspect that it is an almost universal human trait to want to be flattered, to be shown in the most favorable light. Since managements are human, I cannot imagine that they instruct their accountants to "paint me as I am, warts and all." I suspect that they give opposite instructions:

> Flatter me just a little—a 10 per cent increase in earnings per share would be about right. Conceal my warts and pimples with cosmetically phrased footnotes.

Since most of us are not as blunt as Cromwell, I omitted the threat to never pay a farthing if the instructions were not followed. Nonetheless, I expect that the threat is there, albeit tacit. The controller or auditor is keen enough to recognize that he is likely to be replaced if he does not follow instructions.

The danger is that, if we define accounting as an art, then we leave ourselves open to receiving such instructions and threats. If we defined accounting as a science, we would be considerably less vulnerable.

Conventions versus Laws

If accounting is to be an empirical science, then we must redefine our discipline so that it is based upon laws instead of conventions.[10] Of course, all sciences have need for some conventions, but these are relatively unimportant matters. For example, an inch is defined by convention to be a certain length. It could have just as easily been defined as some other length, and that fact is what makes it a relatively unimportant matter. The selection of a particular convention is an arbitrary choice. Therefore, conventions are things that are decreed, not debated.

We have need for conventions in accounting, but we must be clear on the distinction between conventions and laws. At the present time the texts define accounting as being based upon conventions in general and then talk about various "cost conventions" in specific cases. For example, in regard to inventory valuation, LIFO is described as one convention and FIFO as another. In regard to depreciation, declining balance is described as one convention and straight line as another. Despite the fact that these are described as conventions, the texts present arguments about the relative merits of each and then say that the choice in a particular case "depends upon the circumstances."

Although arbitrary, conventions, once decreed, must be followed consistently. Thus it is contradictory to say that the selection of a particular convention depends upon circumstances.[11] Consider the convention of driving on the right side of the road in this country. That this is truly a convention is evidenced by the fact that they drive on the left in England. Since it is a convention, there is no need to continue the debate about which is best—either is equally as good as the other. We simply need to make a decision and then forget about it. A similar convention exists in accounting. We put the credits on the right. Since putting the credits on the left would be equally as good, it is easily recognized to be a convention. There is no need to debate the issue.

Conventions are decided by decree, by fiat. To drive on the right side of the road was decided by a legislative body. If these various cost allocations are truly conventional, then we need to do the same thing in accounting. Let Marshall go up to Mount Stamford and fast for 40 days and 40 nights and at the end of that time return with stone tablets that say:

1. THOU SHALT USE LIFO;
2. THOU SHALT USE STRAIGHT LINE;
3. THOU SHALT FLOW THROUGH;

and so forth. If Marshall has any difficulty in deciding on which conventions to choose, I would be glad to loan him my solid-state binary decision-maker—he can flip my coin.

In choosing conventions the important thing is to select one and then be consistent—*which* convention is selected is not important. Consider again the convention of driving on the right side of the road. If the legislative body let each individual choose which side of the road to drive on, the result would be chaos. If we let each individual choose which side to put the credits on, the result would be chaos. We *have* let each individual choose between LIFO and FIFO, accelerated and straight line, etc., and the result *has been* chaos.

The point is that selection of any particular convention is arbitrary. It does not make any difference which convention is selected, but it is important to be consistent. In accounting we have defined the problem as the choice among alternative conventions, but then we have confounded ourselves by making the selection of conventions depend upon unspecified circumstances, thereby precluding resolution of the problem.

Measurements versus Allocations

In addition to defining the problem of determining costs and income as a choice among conventions, we also define it so that a *present* magnitude depends upon a future magnitude. For example, we say that the "true depreciation" cannot be known until the asset has been sold. We say that the "true income" cannot be determined until the firm has been liquidated. The problem here is that we have *by definition* made the determination of income or depreciation impossible until a future event occurs. This wreaks havoc with the system. The definition prohibits resolution of disagreements. If one conceptually makes a present magnitude depend upon subsequent events, then the present magnitude can never be known because subsequent events always lie in the future and the future can never be known—it can only be estimated or forecast. This notion is particularly pernicious because it commits one to a continual correction of past magnitudes or else an admission that all past magnitudes are wrong.

Suppose we were to calculate my weight in the same way that we depreciate an asset. We know that at acquisition (birth) Sterling weighed 10 pounds. I estimate that his salvage weight at time of disposal (death) will be 210 pounds and that his useful life will be 50 years. On the basis of a straight-line allocation, I would report his present weight, at age 42, as 178 pounds. If another accountant were to estimate that Sterling's useful life will be 100 years, then he would report his present weight as 94 pounds. There is no way to resolve this disagreement. The disagreement is in principle unresolvable because we have defined it so that his *present* weight depends upon his *future* life. Since we cannot resolve disagreements regarding his future, we cannot resolve disagreements about his present weight.

This definition causes additional problems. Suppose that we have been reporting Sterling's weight (on the past balance sheets) and his weight change (on the past income statements) on the basis of a 50-year life estimate. Suppose that present events now cause us to believe that Sterling's useful life estimate should be changed from 50 to 100 years. What do we do? Do we correct all the past balance sheets and income statements or do we admit that all the past statements were wrong? If we decide to correct all of the past statements, what good does it do? That is, how much does it benefit a reader to discover in the 1970's that the financial statements of the 1940's are wrong? Although we can change our past statements, the reader cannot change the past decisions made on the basis of those statements. Also, if we adopt the policy of correcting past statements, then we will need to correct all the past statements again next year when next year's events cause us to change our estimates of his future life or salvage value again.

Given these considerations, we will likely decide that correcting past statements is not a desirable policy. But what is the alternative? Changing the estimate of my useful life from 50 to 100 years means that there is a change in my recorded weight of 84 pounds, a write down from 178 to 94 pounds. Do we report that 84-pound weight loss on the 1975 income statement? It seems odd, to say the least, to report an 84 pound loss in 1975 when one thing that we know for certain is that my weight did not decrease by 84 pounds in that year. Given these considerations, we will likely reject this alternative. But we have already rejected the other alternative. We have only two alternatives and we have rejected both: a classic example of the horns of a dilemma.

The dilemma is due to the way we define the problem. One is not required to forecast the future in order to make a present measurement. In fact, that is a contradiction of terms. Measurement is the process of discovering a present existing magnitude. It is not a process of allocating past magnitudes to time periods on the basis of forecast future magnitudes. In science, the determination of my present weight would be defined as a measurement, not as an allocation. Defining it as a measurement does not automatically solve the problem, but it does make it possible to solve it. Defining the problem as an allocation makes it in principle unresolvable.[12]

When I was a student this definition resulted in an issue known as "all inclusive income versus dirty surplus." That the problem was never resolved is evidenced by the fact that we are still debating it under the name of "extraordinary items." Today's controversial "big bath accounting" issue is the same problem with a different name. When a firm's management takes a "big bath," it changes past overly optimistic estimates of the firm's future to a present more pessimistic estimate. This change of *past* optimistic estimates of the *future* to *present* pessimistic estimates of the *future* results in changing *past* reported profits to losses, permitting management to change *future* losses to reported profits. As long as we define past and present measures to be based upon future magnitudes, such problems will remain unresolved.

The Challenge of Measurement

Somebody is sure to tell me that the situation is unfortunate, but there is nothing that can be done about it. The problem, they say, is that it is impossible to make the measurements that I suggest and, therefore, we must resign ourselves to conventional allocations of past expenditures on the basis of estimates of the future. People have, in fact, told me that. That may be an appropriate artistic or accounting response, but it would not be considered an appropriate scientific response.

Consider the following bit of (apocryphal) history: At one time in the past it was impossible to measure the distance traveled by a free falling body until it came to rest. That is, if I dropped an object, then you would have to wait until it hit the floor before you could measure the distance traveled. My accounting ancestors just shrugged that off and said it was too bad, but there was nothing that could be done about it.

Luckily, I had other ancestors who decided to take that as a challenge instead of resigning themselves to the problem. They tried to *develop* methods of making observations of the object while it was still falling. In the early days these methods were crude observations of balls rolling down inclined planes. By continuing to work on the problem, scientists developed means of making precise measures. They now measure the distance traveled by falling objects in evacuated tubes with high speed photography.

We must admit that our present measurement problems are formidable. In the same way that the ancients could not measure the distance traveled until the body came to rest, we cannot (so it is alleged) measure the cost of a depreciable asset until it is sold. The difference is that we seem to have resigned ourselves to our inability to measure, while the scientists viewed their inability as a challenge. The point is that we could also view our measurement problems as a challenge instead of resigning ourselves to unresolvable problems.

An Example of an Accounting Law

In the previous discussion I said that we accountants have defined various cost allocation methods as being conventional. It is possible to define them as scientific laws—as testable empirical generalizations. Consider depreciation. In their discussion of the definition of depreciation, the Committee on Terminology says:[13]

> The term [depreciation] is broadly descriptive of a type of process, not of an individual process, and only the characteristics which are common to all processes of the type can properly be reflected in a definition thereof. These common characteristics are that a cost or other basic value is allocated to accounting periods by a rational and systematic method and that this method does not attempt to determine the sum allocated to an accounting period solely by relation to occurrences within the period which affect either the length of life or the monetary value of the property. Definitions are unacceptable which imply that *depreciation for the year* is a measurement, expressed in monetary terms, of the physical deterioration within the year, or of the decline in monetary value within the year, or, indeed, of anything that actually occurs within the year.

Let me repeat: "*Definitions* are unacceptable which imply that *depreciation*...is a measurement...of the physical deterioration...or the decline of monetary value..., or, indeed, of anything that actually occurs within the year." This definition precludes empirical tests because depreciation is defined as a convention instead of some empirical measure of a testable phenomenon.

Let me redefine the problem. I want to propose an empirically testable generalization. That is, I want to propose a scientific law. First, in order for it to be empirically testable, I must define an observable.

Sterling's Definition: Depreciation is the decline in the exit value of productive assets.

Second, the law (actually a hypothesis until it is well confirmed) is stated in such a manner that it can be subjected to empirical tests:

Sterling's Law: The depreciation of automotive equipment is described by applying the declining balance method at 1.5 the straight-line rate.

You may not like my law since it deals with values instead of costs. Please forget about that for a moment. Let us focus only on the *structure* of the law: It has all the attributes of any scientific law, the main one being that it is an empirically testable generalization. This means that, if an issue arose, we could resolve it. Suppose that an opponent offered the following law:

Opponent's Law: The depreciation of automotive equipment is described by the straight line method.

To choose between the two laws the only thing we would have to do is make a sufficient number of observations of exit values to decide whether Sterling's Law or Opponent's Law is correct.

Note the contrast. If depreciation is defined as a conventional allocation of costs, there is no possibility of deciding between accelerated and straight line—the issue will remain unresolved because it is in principle unresolvable. If present depreciation is defined to depend upon estimations of future lives and salvage values, then we can never know the present depreciation because we can never know the future. The proposed redefinition has the advantage of being a resolvable issue.

Defining Concepts without Theoretical Import

Many of you will not like the law proposed in the previous section. You may say that my law is concerned with values and that accounting is concerned with costs. I have been told this before.[14] I do not want to debate the merits of that issue here, but rather merely to point out that accounting's concern with costs is a consequence of the *definition* of accounting. We could define it some other way.

A more potentially damaging criticism of the proposed law is that historical cost depreciation may be a concept that has theoretical import even though it lacks empirical import. In science there are two basic kinds of concepts: empirical and theoretical. The empirical concepts must be subjected to empirical test. Theoretical concepts, on the other hand, are subjected to logical test—the demonstration that the concept has some logical connections, via laws, with other concepts. In accounting terms this means that a theoretical concept must be relevant—at least, in the way that I define relevant.[15]

The reason for this requirement is set forth most clearly by Hempel when he defines "hage" as the product of man's height and age.[16] As Hempel points out, the concept of hage has many qualities. In his terms, it "...would have relatively high precision and uniformity of usage..." In accounting terms hage would be "objective, verifiable and free from bias." However, it lacks the quality of theoretical import or relevance. Hage is irrelevant to everything or, as Hempel says, "...we have no general laws connecting the hage of a person with other characteristics." Since it fails the test of theoretical import, no scientist bothers to calculate or report hage.

Hempel's example was fictional. If you want a real example, consider the concept of the cephalic index. At one time many scientists were busy calculating and reporting cephalic indices in the belief that they were theoretically important. Brodbeck, using "useful" as a synonym for "theoretical import," writes:[17]

> ...the concept cephalic index can be quite adequately defined in terms of the ratio of the width of a person's head to its length, with the method of measurement precisely stated. Yet, for the psychologist at least, a person's cephalic index is an uninteresting fact. It is not interesting because a person's cephalic index has no connection, as far as we know, with any of his behavior. There are, in other words, no laws connecting it with behavioral concepts. It is, therefore, not a *useful* concept. Because cephalic index does not enter into laws, the concept is *useless* for predicting or explaining behavior. It lacks "meaning" in the sense of significance.

Since the cephalic indices were irrelevant, since

they failed the test of theoretical import, scientists quit calculating and reporting them. Thus irrelevance in science is sufficient reason for abandoning a concept.

It may be that the concept of historical cost depreciation passes the test of theoretical import. However, I have not been able to discover any instances where it is connected to other concepts or, to put it another way, any decision models that specify the concept, despite a diligent search for such laws or decision models. While doing the research for *Enterprise Income*, I examined a number of economic decision models. In no case did the examined decision models specify such concepts as "depreciation" (as we accountants define it). Since such concepts were not specified, the inevitable conclusion is that they were irrelevant to *those* decision models.

I wrote and talked about that conclusion for some years. However, since it is impossible for me to examine *all* laws or decision models, it is impossible for me to *prove* that historical cost depreciation does not pass the test of relevance or theoretical import. That is, the fact that I have failed to prove its relevance does not mean that it *is* irrelevant, since I may have overlooked something. For this reason, I published a challenge for someone to prove that such concepts were relevant to *one* decision model.[18] Eight years have now elapsed since that challenge and no one has yet published a reply. If accounting were a science, one of two things would have occurred: (1) someone would have rushed into print with a proof of the relevance of such concepts or (2) the discipline would have quit calculating and reporting such concepts. Again, consider the cephalic index. If someone could have demonstrated its relevance to just one law, scientists would have continued to calculate and report those indices; in the absence of such a demonstration, scientists ceased calculating and reporting those indices.

Until someone accepts my challenge, I will continue to wonder about the relevance of such concepts. I will wonder why we define such concepts as cost allocations instead of value measures. Since historical cost depreciation is not empirically testable and since, insofar as I know, it fails to pass the test of theoretical import or relevance, why do we continue to define depreciation as a cost allocation? That is, why do we define it so that it is in principle unresolvable?

Summary

It is my contention that we do not resolve issues in accounting. Instead we move from one unresolved issue to another, while the stock of unresolved issues continues to increase. The purpose of this article was to examine the reason for our inability to resolve issues.

It seems to me that our inability to resolve issues stems from the way in which we define our problems. The definition of accounting problems precludes resolution of those problems. Most accounting issues are not "researchable" in the scientific sense of subjecting them to tests of empirical and theoretical import. Instead, accounting issues are defined so that they are matters of taste as in art and the "research" consists of arguments whether one person's taste is better than another's.

I conclude that a prerequisite for the resolution of accounting issues is the redefinition of those issues. Specifically, the issues must be defined so that they are subject to scientific tests. Redefinition of the issues will not provide us with easy solutions to our problems. On the contrary, there are many unresolved issues in science. There are disputes among scientists just as there are disputes among accountants. The difference is that scientific issues and disputes are subject to resolution by the application of scientific tests. At the present time, accounting issues and disputes are defined so that their resolution is in principle impossible. Resolution of the issues is a long way off, but the first step toward that resolution is to redefine the issues so that they are testable. ■

Footnotes

1. The exchange among Cramer, Peterson and Scott concerns bad debts. Anthony and Defleise are recent proponents of treating interest as a cost.
2. Accounting is the art of recording, classifying and summarizing in a significant manner and in terms of money, transactions and events which are, in part at least, of a financial character, and interpreting the results thereof.

   If accounting were called a science, attention would be directed (and perhaps limited) to the ordered classifications used as the accountant's framework, and to the known body of facts which in a given case are fitted into this framework. See, Committee on Terminology, "Accounting Research and Terminology Bulletins, Number 1, Review and Resume," *Accounting Research and Terminology Bulletins*, Final Edition (New York: AICPA, 1969), p. 9.
3. Marvin L. Stone, "Public Confidence in Private Enterprise—Let's Keep It," *Journal of Accountancy* (April 1968), p. 53. "But I must point out that accounting principles are intellectual concepts. They are not subject to the kinds of proof that are applied to laws of physical science. So legitimate differences of opinion within the profession itself are virtually inevitable."

   See also, John Lawler, "The Quest for Accounting Philosophers," *Empirical Research in Accounting: Selected Studies 1967* (Chicago: Institute of Professional Accounting, 1968), p.88.

4. H. A. Finney and Herbert E. Miller, *Principles of Accounting Intermediate,* 5th ed. (Englewood Cliffs, N.J.: Prentice-Hall, Inc., 1964), pp. 165-166. "It would be incorrect to suggest that the rules which establish whether a given accounting procedure is acceptable or unacceptable are in the nature of principles like those found in physics or chemistry. Accounting principles are more properly associated with such terms as concepts, conventions and standards. It is important to remember that accounting principles are man-made, in contrast to natural law.

   Principles cannot be established in accounting, as they are in the realm of natural sciences, by experimentation; nor have they been determined, as in the law, by authoritative pronouncement, . . ."

5. Peter Caws, *The Philosophy of Science* (Princeton, N.J.: D. Van Nostrand Co., Inc., 1966), pp. 85-86. The author draws the distinction: "The same statement can at different times and under different circumstances be a principle, a definition, or a law. If its truth is *asserted* and not considered liable to empirical challenge, it is a definition; if not—that is, if it is taken to be empirically significant—then it is a principle if it contains theoretical terms, otherwise a law. A principle turns into a law if what before could not be observed becomes observable by virtue of some advance in experimental technique."

   See also, Karl R. Popper, *The Logic of Scientific Discovery* (New York: Science Editions, Inc., 1961), pp. 40-42, for an extensive discussion of the falsifiability requirement in science.

6. Lawler, p. 88.
7. Warren S. Torgerson, *Theory and Methods of Scaling* (New York: John Wiley & Sons, Inc., 1967), p. 1.
8. Joseph R. Daughen and Peter Binzen, *The Wreck of the Penn Central* (Boston: Little Brown and Co., 1971), p. 224.
9. C. H. Firth, *Oliver Cromwell and the Rule of the Puritans in England* (London: Putnam, 1938), p. 453.
10. See Robert R. Sterling, "On Theory Construction and Verification," *Accounting Review* (July 1970), p. 446, for a brief discussion of the distinction between the empirical and nonempirical sciences. For a more extended discussion see Caws or Popper.
11. In addition, consider the fact that the circumstances upon which the selection is supposed to be based have never been specified. See, Lanny G. Chasteen, "An Empirical Study of Differences in Economic Circumstances as a Justification for Alternative Inventory Pricing Methods," *Accounting Review* (July 1971), p. 508. The author attempted to discover the circumstances which correspond to different inventory methods being applied in practice. He concluded, "Generally, no significant differences in economic circumstances were consistently found among firms which use different methods of inventory pricing . . ."

    See also, Gary M. Cadenhead, " 'Differences in Circumstances': Fact or Fantasy?" *Abacus* (September 1970). The author arrived at a similar conclusion.

    I have previously expressed doubt about the existence of such circumstances: "The disputes are empirically unresolvable since there are no observations which could be used to confirm or disconfirm either convention. It is sometimes said that the 'appropriate' inventory or depreciation method 'depends upon the circumstances' but I am unable to discover any particular circumstances which imply any particular method. My inability to discover the circumstances does not prove that they do not exist but the fact that no one has yet made them explicit, even though the problem is a pressing one, casts some doubt upon their existence." See, Sterling, "An Explication and Analysis of the Structure of Accounting Part Two," *Abacus* (December 1971), p. 160n.

12. See, Arthur L. Thomas, *The Allocation Problem in Financial Accounting Theory,* Studies in Accounting Research #3 (Menashaw, Wisconsin: American Accounting Association, 1969), for an extended analysis of the unresolvability of allocation problems.

    See also, Sterling, *The Theory of the Measurement of Enterprise Income* (Lawrence: University Press of Kansas, 1970), Ch. V-VI, for a discussion of measurement.

    See also, Sterling, "The Going Concern: An Examination," *Accounting Review* (July 1968), pp. 479-499. The author discusses the confusion of temporal locations in accounting.

13. Committee on Terminology, p. 24.
14. Sterling, *Enterprise Income,* p. vii.
15. Sterling, *Enterprise Income,* p. 50. "The theory concerning the solution of the problem specifies the relevant information."

    If a property is specified by a decision model, then a measure of that property is relevant (to that decision model). If a property is not specified by a decision model, then a measure of that property is irrelevant (to that decision model). See, Sterling, "Decision Oriented Financial Accounting," *Accounting and Business Research* (Summer 1972), p. 199.

16. Carl G. Hempel, *Fundamentals of Concept Formation in Empirical Science,* International Encyclopedia of Unified Science, Vol. I & II (Chicago: University of Chicago Press, 1952), p. 46.
17. May Brodbeck, ed., *Readings in the Philosophy of the Social Sciences* (New York: The MacMillan Co., 1968), p. 8.
18. What is historical cost relevant to?

    Since this is a polemic, I will state the proposition positively so that the reader can demolish it:

    (1) "Relevance is the primary standard . . ." and ". . . all information that does not meet the

standards should be excluded."

(2) Historical cost is irrelevant to all economic decisions (Sterling's allegation).

(3) Ergo, historical cost should be excluded. The quarrel will probably be with (2) and, again being deliberately polemical, I challenge any one to demonstrate that historical costs are relevant to economic decisions. Since (2) includes a universal quantifier it will take only one counter case to falsify it. See, Sterling, "ASOBAT Review," pp. 110-111.

References

Anthony, Robert. "Accounting for the Cost of Equity." *Harvard Business Review* (November-December 1973), pp. 88-102.

Brodbeck, May, ed. *Readings in the Philosophy of the Social Sciences*. New York: The Macmillan Co., 1968.

Cadenhead, Gary M. " 'Differences in Circumstances': Fact or Fantasy?" *Abacus* (September 1970), pp. 71-80.

Caws, Peter. *The Philosophy of Science*. Princeton, N. J.: D. Van Nostrand Co., Inc., 1966.

Chasteen, Lanny G. "An Empirical Study of Differences in Economic Circumstances as a Justification for Alternative Inventory Pricing Methods." *Accounting Review* (July 1971), pp. 504-508.

Committee on Terminology. "Accounting Terminology Bulletins, Number 1, Review and Resume." *Accounting Research and Terminology Bulletins*, Final Edition. New York: AICPA, 1969, pp. 1-32.

Cramer, Joe J., Jr. "Bad Debt 'Expense': Not a Member of the Class of Data for Measuring Operating Income: A Reply." *Accounting Review* (October 1973), pp. 779-784.

_________. "Incompatibility of Bad Debt 'Expense' with Contemporary Accounting Theory." *Accounting Review* (July 1972), pp. 596-598.

Daughen, Joseph R. and Peter Binzen. *The Wreck of the Penn Central*. Boston: Little, Brown and Co., 1971.

DeFleise, Philip L. "The Economic Case against Capitalization of Leases—A New Look at Facility Accounting." *Institutional Issues in Public Accounting*. Edited by Robert R. Sterling. Scholars Book Co., 1974.

Finney, H. A. and Herbert E. Miller. *Principles of Accounting Intermediate*. 5th ed. Englewood Cliffs, N. J.: Prentice-Hall, Inc., 1964.

Firth, C. H. *Oliver Cromwell and the Rule of the Puritans in England*. Black and White Library Edition. London: Putnam, 1938.

Hempel, Carl. G. *Fundamentals of Concept Formation in Empirical Science*. International Encyclopedia of Unified Science, Vo. I & II. Chicago: University of Chicago Press, 1952.

Lawler, John. "The Quest for Accounting Philosophers." *Empirical Research in Accounting: Selected Studies 1967*. Chicago: Institute of Professional Accounting, 1968, pp. 86-92.

Petersen, Russell J. "Incompatibility of Bad Debt 'Expense' with Contemporary Accounting Theory: A Comment." *Accounting Review* (October, 1973), pp. 777-778.

Popper, Karl R. *The Logic of Scientific Discovery*. New York: Science Editions, Inc., 1961.

Scott, Edward R. "Bad Debts: Take Two: A Comment." *Accounting Review* (October 1973), pp. 775-776.

Sterling, Robert R. "An Explication and Analysis of the Structure of Accounting Part Two." *Abacus* (December 1972), pp. 145-162.

_________. "Decision Oriented Financial Accounting." *Accounting and Business Research* (Summer 1972), pp. 198-208.

_________. "The Going Concern: An Examination." *Accounting Review* (July 1968), pp. 481-502.

_________. "On Theory Construction and Verification." *Accounting Review* (July 1970), pp. 444-457.

_________. "A Statement of Basic Accounting Theory: A Review Article." *Journal of Accounting Research* (Spring 1967), pp. 95-112.

_________. *The Theory of the Measurement of Enterprise Income*. Lawrence: University Press of Kansas, 1970.

Stone, Marvin L. "Public Confidence in Private Enterprise—Let's Keep It." *Journal of Accountancy* (April 1968), pp. 52-57.

Thomas, Arthur L. *The Allocation Problem in Financial Accounting Theory*. Studies in Accounting Research #3. Menashaw, Wisconsin: American Accounting Association, 1969.

Torgerson, Warren S. *Theory and Methods of Scaling*. New York: John Wiley & Sons, Inc., 1967.

THE NATURE AND VERIFICATION OF THEORIES

Robert R. Sterling
Jesse H. Jones Professor, Rice University

I start with the premise that accounting ought to be a science. I have often been told, both in the literature and in person, that this is impossible—that for various reasons accounting cannot be a science. Perhaps accounting will never become a science. If it does not, I think that the reason will be not that people have tried to make accounting a science and found it to be impossible but rather that people have defined it as inherently unscientific. It may be that we will never be able to make accounting a science. In my view, we have never tried. I urge that we begin to try it at this time. If we fail, then we will have some evidence for the inherent nonscientific nature of our discipline. If we never try, we will never know whether the nonscientific nature is due to our subject matter or due to our failure to make the effort.

If accounting is to become a science, then we will have to devise a theory about some empirical phenomena. To put it another way, we will have to devise a method of modelling a class of empirical phenomena. Then we can apply that general method of modelling a class of empirical phenomena to a particular case. The long run goal is to make a particular accounting system a model of a particular empirical system. Thus, the theory of accounting ought to be concerned with the general properties of the model and the general properties of the class of empirical phenomena. The application will be the devising of a particular accounting system which will be a model of a particular empirical system which may be called a "firm" or "entity." Thus, we will apply the general method to various firms in which their accounting system models the empirical phenomena of that firm.

In order to accomplish this long range goal—in order to do scientific research—we must have a general idea of the nature of theories and their verification. The purpose of this paper is to make the first step towards becoming a science of accounting by explaining the nature and verification of scientific theories. Once we get a general idea of the nature of theories perhaps we can devise a theory of accounting.

1. Purpose of models: Explanation and Prediction

The purpose of a model is to explain and predict empirical phenomena.[1] By means of a model we conceptually move from observed empirical phenomena to an expectation of unobserved empirical phenomena. We move from known empirical facts to an expectation of unknown empirical facts. The process is diagrammed in Figure 1.

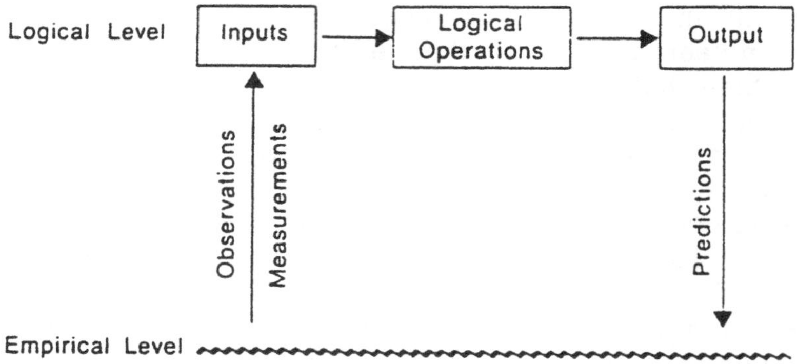

Figure 1

Starting at the empirical level one makes certain observations or measurements. These become the inputs to the model. Logical (includes mathematical) operations are performed on these observations and certain outputs emerge on the logical level. These outputs are intended to refer back to the empirical level. They are intended to allow us to anticipate observations. Thus, they are called "predictions." For example, Euclidean geometry is a model of flat surfaces which allows us to conceptually move from measured attri-

---

[1]Indeed, to explain and predict empirical phenomena is the purpose of science in general: "The principal objective of science, other than the description of empirical phenomena, is to establish, through laws and theories, general principles by means of which the empirical phenomena can be explained, accounted for, and predicted." (Torgerson, p. 1.) Note that Torgerson adds "account for" to the purpose of science. Many scientists and philosophers of science use the phrases "account for" and "account of" when discussing the purpose of science. Caws (p. vii) writes about "the account of the world" which is presented by models. He defines "scientific explanation" as "accounting for particular events by reference to general laws, together with the actual conditions under which those laws act, or accounting for laws by reference to principles still more general (p. 91)." Thus, "account of" or "account for" and "scientific explanation" are synonymous in this context.

butes to a prediction of the magnitude of unmeasured attributes. The familiar Pythagorean theorem

$$\text{(Eq. 1)}\quad h = (a^2 + b^2)^{1/2}$$

specifies the inputs (independent variables a and b), the logical operations or method of calculation (squaring, summing, extracting the square root) and the output (dependent variable h) which will emerge. Equation (1) is in its general form—it refers exclusively to the logical level. For a specific case the symbols representing the inputs are replaced by measurements. If you want to put a diagonal brace on a bookcase, you can predict the required length of that brace by measuring the two sides and then inserting those measurements in the form of Equation (1). Suppose the length of the two sides is 3 and 4 feet. Inserting the measurements yields

$$h = (3^2 + 4^2)^{1/2}$$

and by logical operations you predict

$$h = 5.$$

Thus, you have conceptually moved from measured empirical phenomena ($a = 3$, $b = 4$) to a prediction of unmeasured empirical phenomena ($h = 5$).

In ordinary usage "prediction" normally refers to a future state. In scientific usage it refers to any unknown state regardless of the temporal location of that state. Thus, "prediction" may refer to the past or the present, as well as to the future. In the above example the prediction referred to an existing or present state. The bookcase presently exists but the length of the diagonal (hypotenuse) is unknown. We predicted that its hypotenuse *is* 5 feet. If we know that George Washington had a bookcase with sides of 3 and 4 feet then we could predict that its hypotenuse *was* 5 feet. If we plan to build a bookcase with sides of 3 and 4 feet then we can predict that its hypotenuse *will be* 5 feet. Thus, "prediction" is timeless—it may refer to the past, present or future.

The process of explaining is the reverse of the process of predicting. In predicting we observe inputs and infer outputs. In explaining we observe outputs and infer inputs. In general, predictive statements are in the form "If X, then Y" and explanatory statements are in the reverse form "Y because X." Consider the following examples:

Prediction	Explanation
If a = 3 and b = 4, then h = 5.	h = 5 because a = 3 and b = 4.
If wages go up, then prices will rise.	Prices rose because wages went up.
If you get your feet wet, then you will catch a cold.	You have a cold because you got your feet wet.
If Penelope is a swan, then Penelope is white.	Penelope is white because she is a swan.

In each case the explanation is the reverse of the prediction. In general that is what we mean by "explanation." We observe some empirical state, such as h = 5 or that you have a cold, and then we look for a statement which would have allowed us to predict that empirical state. The predictive statement contains an input or "antecedent" and citing that antecedent is an explanation of the output or "consequent."

You may not be satisfied with the kind of explanations given above. If you ask, "Why is h = 5?" you may intend to inquire about something other than the relationship given in the Pythagorean theorem. If so, "h = 5 because a = 3 and b = 4" will not satisfy you. However, this is the only kind of explanation that is available *within Euclidean geometry.* If you are asking why George Washington built a bookcase of that size, then you are not asking a question that can be answered within the context of geometry. You may be asking about the motivation of George Washington and this is a psychological question, not a geometrical question. Obviously, psychological explanations require psychological models and it is unreasonable to expect a geometrical model to provide psychological explanations. The point is, however, that the psychological explanation would be of the form "Y because X" where X refers to a, perhaps complex, psychological attribute. Turning this around to "If X then Y" would permit us to make psychological predictions. Even this psychological explanation may not satisfy you. You may not feel that you have received a complete explanation. The problem is that there is no such thing as a "complete explanation." No matter how many explanations are provided, someone can always ask "why?" one more time. In a well developed field one can provide a large number of "becauses" but that number is always less than the possible number of "whys?" Scientists are also dissatisfied with explanations like those given above and they continue to seek "better" explanations in the sense of seeking more general laws. Thus, if you are dissatisfied with the above explanations, it is just a symptom of a healthy case of scientific curiosity. One word of warning however; no model can or is intended to explain everything. All models are restricted to a certain "empirical domain." The fact that a geometrical model does not explain psychological motiviations is not a legitimate criticism of the geometrical model.

In summary, the purpose of a model is to explain and predict empirical phenomena. In prediction, certain antecedent conditions are observed and the model, via logical operations, allows us to conceptually move to an expectation of certain consequences. In explaining, certain consequences are observed and the model, via logical operations, allows us to conceptually move to an expectation of certain antecedent conditions. Thus, the model connects different empirical facts and it allows us to conceptually move from one set of facts to another.

An accounting system ought to be a model of certain aspects of an empirical system. Hence, its purpose ought to be to explain and predict certain empirical phenomena. This means that via the accounting system we ought to be able to conceptually move from one set of empirical facts to an expectation of another set of empirical facts.

2. Empirical Testing of Models

Since the purpose of a model is to explain and predict empirical phenomena, the ultimate test of a model is how well it explains and predicts. This is called "empirical testing." The process of empirical testing a model is the *comparison* of the model's *predictions* to *separate measurements* of the empirical phenomena.

In the previous section, the length of the diagonal of the bookcase was predicted to be 5 feet. If a tape measure is laid along the diagonal, a separate measurement is obtained. Denoting $\hat{h}$ as the separate measurement and h as the prediction, the question is: Does $\hat{h}$ equal h? If $\hat{h} = h$, then that *individual prediction* is said to be "empirically verified." If $\hat{h} \neq h$, then the *model* is said to be "empirically falsified."

The difference is that the model is intended to refer to *all* hypotenuses. If we ever find *one* hypotenuse in which $\hat{h} \neq h$, then the model is falsified. On the other hand, the finding of one case where $\hat{h} = h$ does not guarantee that $\hat{h} = h$ in all cases. In fact, the finding that $\hat{h} = h$ in 1,000 cases or even in 1,000,000 cases does not guarantee that it is true in all cases.

Models are devices for predicting and explaining empirical phenomena. By definition, "prediction" refers to empirical phenomena that are *not yet observed.* There is no point in predicting empirical phenomena that have already been observed. Thus, models always refer to unobserved empirical phenomena and, therefore, the model itself can never be completely verified. The statement, "All swans are white," can be used for predicting the color of unobserved birds.

Axiom: All swans are white.
Input: Penelope is a swan.
Output: Penelope is white.

The statement is useful for predicting the color of swans only if there are unobserved swans. But as long as there are unobserved swans, there is the chance that one might be found that is non-white. If a non-white swan is found, then "All swans are white" is false. By contrast, no matter how many white swans are observed—no matter how many individual predictions are empirically verified—the statement "All swans are white" still refers to unobserved swans and, therefore, that statement is not completely verified.

The same is true of the Pythagorean Theorem. In words it says "All hypotenuses of right triangles are equal to the square root of the sum of the sequence of the sides." The input is "This bookcase is a right triangle with sides of 3 and 4 feet." Thus, the calculation of the length of a hypotenuse is the same process as the prediction of the color of a swan. It also suffers the same limitation: it refers to *all* hypotenuses, some of which have not been observed, and, therefore, the model has not been completely verified.

The lack of ability to completely verify models causes scientists to deliberately try to falsify them. They know that the verification of another 1,000 cases will not prove that the model is correct. For this reason, they subject their models to the harsher test of falsification—they deliberately search for counter cases. If they fail to find counter cases, if they fail to falsify it, then the model is accepted as true. Speaking loosely we sometimes say that a particular model "has been verified" or that it is "well verified." However, what we mean is that the model has *not* been falsified. We mean that we have confidence in the model because a number of its predictions have been subjected to empirical testing and so far none of them have been found to be false.

No model is applicable to all kinds of empirical phenomena. The phenomena to which a model is applicable is called its "empirical domain." Obviously, the domain of a model must be explicit befor it can be tested. However, sometimes we are unsure of the boundaries of the domain. Often empirical testing, particularly the search for counter cases, aids in defining the boundaries of the domain. In testing a model it may be found to be false in some applications but not found to be false in other applications. When this happens, modifiers are added to the model to indicate its domain. For example, when black swans were found in Australia, the statement "All swans are white" was falsified. However, the statement can be modified to "All European swans are white" and, insofar as we know, this statement is true. Thus, the domain was reduced from all swans to all European swans. Euclidean geometry is also restricted to the domain of flat surfaces. It is easy to show that $\hat{h} \neq h$ on curved surfaces. Thus, when a model is falsified, it does not necessarily mean that it is discarded. The falsification may result in modifying the model to indicate that its domain is more restricted than originally thought.

The more times individual predictions are empirically verified, the greater our confidence in the model from which those predictions emerge. We have great confidence in Euclidean geometry because its individual predictions have been empirically verified time and time again. Our confidence is so great that we regard $h = 5$ (given $a = 3$, $b = 4$) as empirically true without bothering to verify it by a separate measurement.

There are many models in which we are not so confident. They are not so well verified as Euclidean geometry. We continue to subject individual predictions of these models to empirical tests in an attempt to gain the desired confidence or to reject or modify them if a prediction is found to be false. Empirical testing is at its height of activity when new models are being proposed. When moving into new areas, different scientists are likely to propose different models of the same phenomena. Disputes among scientists arise as to which model is correct. Such disputes are adjudicated by subjecting the models to empirical tests.

Consider the fictional, but illustrative, test that Galileo was supposed to have performed at the Leaning Tower of Pisa. Galileo had proposed

$$\text{(Eq.2)} \quad d_G = \tfrac{1}{2} gt^2$$

as the model of free falling bodies where d_G = distance travelled, g = gravitational constant and t = elapsed time. Galileo's model is one of accelerated motion—the longer a body falls, the faster it goes. Suppose that Sterling proposed a model of uniform motion as in Eq. (3)—the body travels at the same speed throughout its fall.

$$\text{(Eq. 3)} \quad d_S = \tfrac{1}{2}\, gt$$

No matter how many people Sterling has on his side, no matter how good his arguments, the dispute would be settled in favor of Galileo because when the balls are dropped and the distance is measured it is found that $\hat{d} = d_G$ and $\hat{d} \neq d_S$.

In retrospect, the testing of Galileo's model seems overly simple. At the time, however, there were many people who tried to settle such disputes with logic. They would *argue* about which model was the correct one. The problem is that such disputes are *in principle* unresolvable by argumentation. It is an empirical question—a question of fact—and such questions can be settled only by observation. Thus, the principle is clear: models must be *empirically* tested—the predicted outcome must be compared to a *separate* measurement.

Over the years there have been many disputes in accounting. Undoubtedly as accounting progresses, and particularly as it is applied to new areas, many more disputes will arise. Unfortunately, in accounting, as in science in general, empirical questions have sometimes been confused with logical questions. We have tried, and failed, to settle questions of fact by argumentation. Since an accounting system is a model of an empirical system, the ultimate test of an accounting system is to promote its predictions to separate measurements of the empirical phenomena.

3. Logical Testing of Models

In the previous section empirical testing was emphasized because the purpose of a model is to explain and predict empirical phenomena. The ultimate test of a model is how well it fulfills its purpose. However, logic also plays a crucial role in both the construction and operation of models. It is the logical operations that allow us to conceptually move from one set of empirical facts to an expectation of another set of empirical facts. On the logical level the model consists of nothing but abstract symbols and logical operations. Predictions and explanations are made when these symbols are replaced by measurements. Thus, both logic and empirics perform crucial functions in models. They do, however, perform very different functions.

Logic is concerned with the relation of symbols to symbols. Empirics is concerned with the relation of symbols to observations for measurements. A "logical question" is one that is answered by examining the *form* and *meaning* of the *symbols*. An "empirical question" is one that is answered by examining the real world—by making observations or measurements. An example will clarify the distinction. Consider the symbols (words) of the English language. The statement "A bachelor is an unmarried adult male" is logically true. It does not require observations to determine its truth or falsity. The statement is concerned only with the relation of symbols to symbols. "All bachelors are happily married" is logically false for the same reasons. The statement is *contradictory* in that "bachelor" *means* unmarried. If we tried to apply this statement to a particular person, Al, we would be saying in effect, "Al is married and Al is unmarried." We do not need to observe Al's marital status in order to determine that this statement is logically false or contradictory. We need only to examine the meaning and form of the symbols. Hence, its truth or falsity is a logical question. By contrast, the simple statement "Al is a bachelor" requires that we observe Al's marital status in order to determine its truth or falsity. Examination of its symbols alone will not tell us anything at all about its truth. Hence, its truth is an empirical question.

In order to facilitate the study of logical truth, logicians and mathematicians use more abstract symbols. They strip away the content of the statements and concentrate on their form by replacing the words with letters. Denoting X as a statement and $\tilde{X}$ as the negation of that statement (i.e., not-X) makes it easy to see that "X and $\tilde{X}$" is logically false regardless of its content. If X stands for "Al is married," then "X and $\tilde{X}$" says "Al is married and Al is unmarried." If X stands for "It is raining" then "X and $\tilde{X}$" says "It is raining and it is not raining." All statements of this form are logically false regardless of what X stands for. In the same fashion all statements of the form "X or $\tilde{X}$" are logically true. It must necessarily be the case that Al is married or not married and that it is raining or not raining. "If X, then X" is also logically true since "If Al is married, then Al is married" is somewhat less than controversial. The truth of these statements can be determined by examining the form and meaning of their symbols. Determination of their truth does not require observations. Hence, their truth is a logical question, not an empirical question.

By contrast, statements like "X and Y," "X or $\tilde{Y}$" and "If X, then Y" require that we replace X and Y with descriptive words before we can determine their truth. They could mean "Al is a bachelor and he is happy," "Al is a bachelor or he is unhappy," and "If Al is a bachelor, then he is happy," respectively. Each of these statements could be true or false without contradiction. We must observe Al in order to determine their truth. Hence, their truth is an empirical question, not a logical question.

One important class of logical truths is that of mathematics. Simple statements of arithmetic like "7 = 2 + 5" as well as the more unfamiliar statements of higher mathematics are true by virtue of the form and meaning of their symbols. "7" is a symbol whose meaning makes it equal to the symbols "2 + 5" just as "bachelor" is a symbol whose meaning makes it equal to "unmarried adult male." Similarly "9 = 2 + 5" is logically false or contradictory just as "Al is married and unmarried" is contradictory. Of course, there are many mathematical statements which, when interpreted, are also empirically true. However, mathematics per se or pure mathematics is concerned only with the relation of symbols to symbols and, therefore, all of its statements are either logically true or contradictory.

Models are often stripped of their content in order to lay bare their form and to study the logical truth of their statements. As such, they are called "uninterpreted" models because they consist of nothing but uninterpreted symbols. Such models are also called "axiomatized" because they focus on the axioms (also called "postulates," "laws," "premises" and, in some cases, "assumptions" or "definitions") and what can be deduced (a logical operation) from those axioms. An "axiom" is a statement that is taken for granted for the purpose of seeing what logically follows from it. A "theorem" is a logical truth that is deduced from the axioms. An uninterpreted or axiomatized model is a collection of these two kinds of logical statements together with a demonstration (proof) that the theorems follow from the axioms.

One example of an axiomatized model is Euclidean geometry. When you studied geometry, you were probably required to prove the Pythagorean Theorem. That is, you started with Euclid's axioms and then, by logical operations alone, you were required to deduce the Pythagorean Theorem. As an additional step, you probably interpreted Euclidean geometry as marks on graph paper. Note the difference between the *empirical test* of *measuring* the hypotenuse on the graph paper and *comparing* it to the prediction as opposed to the *logical test* of *proving* the Pythagorean Theorem. The same kind of difference exists outside the classroom: Mathematicians prove theorems of Euclidean geometry and care little about interpretations. Surveyors have interpreted Euclidean geometry so that they can use it to make predictions of unobserved lengths, areas, etc. They care little about proving theorems.

Another example of a model that has been axiomatized is the Newtonian laws of motion. (It is a historical accident that we refer to Newton's "laws" and Euclid's "axioms." They serve the same purpose and mean the same thing.) Galileo's law of free falling bodies can be deduced from Newton's laws. Thus, "$d = \frac{1}{2} gt^2$" is logically true in that it follows from Newton's laws. It is a theorem of Newtonian physics. An empirical test requires an interpretation. If "d" and "t" are interpreted as distance and time, it will be found to be empirically true. However, if "d" and "t" were interpreted as density and temperature, it would be found to be empirically false.

The important thing to note is the difference between logical truth and empirical truth. In addition to empirical tests, a model must pass a logical test. These are two different kinds of tests and both must be performed. If a model fails to pass its logical test, it must be altered or discarded in the same way that it must be altered or discarded if it fails its empirical test.

Contradictions constitute failure of the logical test. If the outputs of a model are contradictory, then there is no possible way for the model to be an accurate replica. Suppose, for example, that Sterling proposed a geometry such that we could validly deduce both "$h = (a^2 + b^2)^{1/2}$" and "$h = a + b$" from his axioms. This is a contradiction—one of the individual statements must necessarily be false because together they say "$h = (a^2 + b^2)^{1/2}$ and $h \neq (a^2 + b^2)^{1/2}$." The full statement is of the form "X and $\tilde{X}$" because one says "equal" and the other "not equal." In Sterling's geometry, a bookcase with sides of 3 and 4 feet would be predicted to have a diagonal of both 5 and 7 feet. Since the diagonal cannot be both 5 and 7 feet, Sterling's geometry must necessarily be false. The failure of the logical test guarantees the failure of the empirical test.

The converse does not hold. Although logical falsity guarantees empirical falsity, logical truth does not guarantee empirical truth. Even if the outputs of a model are logically true, they still must be subjected to empirical tests. Arithmetic provides an example. From the axioms of arithmetic, such statement as "$7 = 5 + 2$" can be shown to be logically true. Under certain interpretations, such statements are also empirically true. Length and weight are two such interpretations. That is,

(Eq. 4) 7 (feet) = 5 (feet) + 2 (feet)

and

(Eq. 5) 7 (pounds) = 5 (pounds) + 2 (pounds)

are empirically true statements. A 5 foot object joined end to end with a 2 foot object results in a length of 7 feet for the combined objects. We know this because it has been empirically tested. The "7 (feet)" in Eq. (4) is a prediction that can be compared to a separate measurement. In general, such comparisons will reveal $\hat{L} = L$ where $\hat{L}$ denotes the separate length measurements and L denotes the predicted lengths. The same is true for Eq. (5). However, there are other interpretations where the logically true statements of arithmetic are empirically false. Temperature is one such interpretation. Arithmetic would lead us to believe that Eq. (6) is a true statement.

(Eq. 6) 7 (degrees) = 5 (degrees) + 2 (degrees)

It turns out that (6) is empirically false. If one liquid of 2 degrees is poured together with another liquid of 5 degrees, the temperature of the combined liquids is not 7 degrees. That is, the empirical test reveals that $\hat{T} \neq T$. Despite the fact that "7 = 5 + 2" is logically true, the interpretation in (6) is empirically false. Thus, logical testing allows us to falsify a model, but it does not allow us to verify it. Contradictions guarantee empirical falsity but logical truths do not guarantee empirical truths.

The subject discussed in the previous paragraph is known as "additivity" in the measurement theory literature. Some attributes, such as length or weight, are said to be additive and others, such as temperature or color, are not additive. The important thing to note is that additivity is an empirical, as opposed to a logical, question. Addition of numerals is a logical operation. The statement "7 = 5 + 2" is logically true in all cases because we are referring exclusively to symbols on the logical level. Thus, numerals are always additive. However, if we interpret those numerals, if we intend for those numerals to represent empirical phenomena, then whether or not that interpretation or representation is additive is an empirical question. In other words, Equations (4), (5), and (6) are in fact models of empirical phenomena and, like all other models, they must be empirically tested by comparing their predictions to separate measurements. Past empirical tests have shown $\hat{L} = L$ and $\hat{W} = W$, so that these attributes are said to be additive while $\hat{T} \neq T$ and, therefore, temperature is not additive.

The study of accounting can be divided into its logical and empirical components. It can be studied as an uninterpreted logical system and subjected to logical testing. If contradictions are found, then it must be altered or discarded. It can also be given several interpretations. That is, there are several applications of the logical system. Once the system has been interpreted, it can be subjected to empirical tests to see if the logically true statements are also empirically true statements.

4. Complete Models

A model is a device which allows us to conceptually move, via logical operations, from one set of observed empirical facts to an expectation of another set of empirical facts. It must pass both an empirical and a logical test. Thus, there is an interplay of logic and empirics in a model. Logic is concerned with the relation of symbols to symbols and empirics with the relation of symbols to observations. All of the symbols must be connected to other symbols by logic and some of the symbols must also be connected to empirical phenomena by observations. For a model to be *complete* it must have *both* kinds of connections and there must be *more than one* of each kind of connection. If any of these connections are missing, then the model is *incomplete* or *deficient.*

A complete model may be visualized in Figure 2.

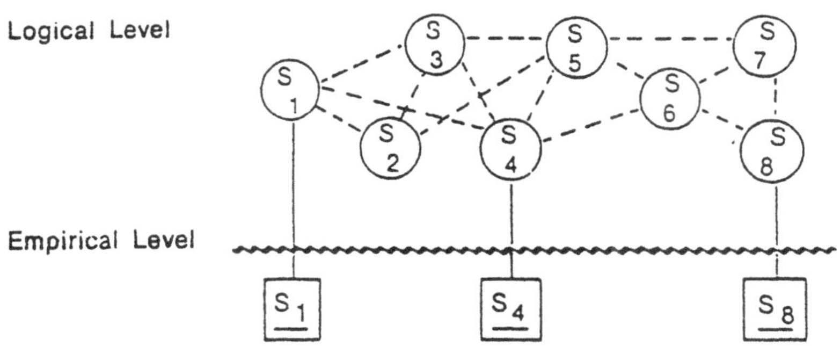

Figure 2

The circles containing S_i indicate symbols and the squares containing $\hat{S}_i$ indicate observations. The dashed lines are intended to show the logical connections among the symbols and the solid lines show the empirical connection of a symbol to an observation. Some of the observations are inputs and the other (expected) observations are outputs. Which of the observations are inputs depends upon what we want to predict or explain. It may be possible to predict S_8 by inputting S_1 and S_4 or to predict S_1 by inputting S_4 and S_8.

All of the symbols are logically connected. If a symbol has no logical connections, then it is of no use in logical operations and it is eliminated. However, not all of the symbols are empirically connected. The purpose of empirically unconnected symbols is to provide an *intermediate* logical step that eventually leads to a prediction. The empirically unconnected symbols are an essential part of the model despite the fact that they have no empirical referant—despite the fact that they are not observable.

We can again use the Pythagorean Theorem to illustrate the empirically unconnected symbols. Figure 3 shows the detailed logical and empirical connections of the Pythagorean Theorem.

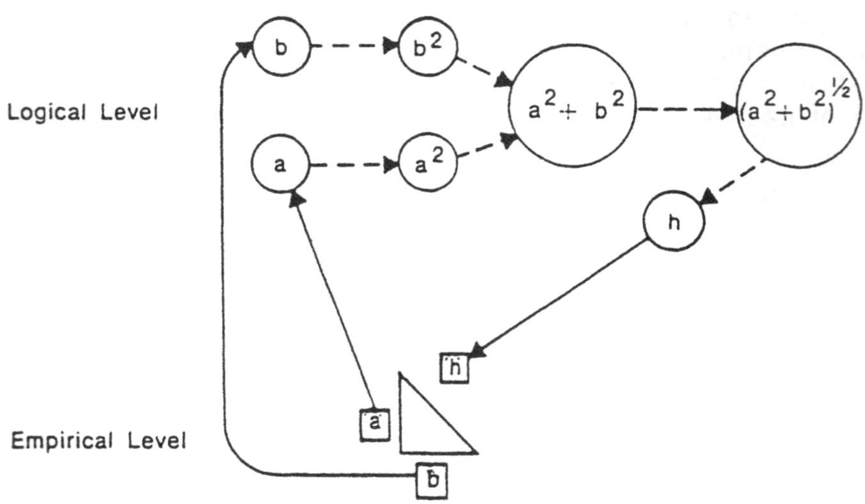

Figure 3

Assume that the right triangle is the only thing we can observe. Then several of the symbols have no empirical connections (no solid lines) because there is nothing on the empirical level that corresponds to them. The symbols a^2, for example, has no empirical referent—there is nothing in the triangle that is represented by a^2. Instead, it is an intermediate logical step that is necessary for the prediction of h.

Although not all of the symbols are empirically connected *some* of them must be so connected. If there are no empirical connections, then the model is incomplete because it lacks an interpretation—it is a study in pure mathematics or pure logic instead of a model of empirical phenomena. Moreover, the empirical connection must go in two directions—there must be *both* inputs and outputs that refer to the empirical level. There are many statements which have empirical inputs but no empirical outputs. Sometimes such statements are confused with models. An arithmetic mean (average) is an example.

$$\text{(Eq. 7)} \quad M = \sum_{i=1}^{n} x_i \,(1/n)$$

According to this equation, if Al weighs 160 pounds and Betty weighs 100 pounds, then their mean weight is 130 pounds. The equation is like the Pythagorean Theorem in that measurements are inputted, logical operations performed and the magnitude of the dependent variable emerges. However, there is a vital difference. We can empirically test the Pythagorean Theorem by comparing $\hat{h}$ to h. In this case there is no $\hat{M}$ to compare to M. There are empirical inputs, but there are no empirical outputs. Therefore, (Eq. (7) is not empirically testable. "The mean weight of Al and Betty is 130 pounds" is neither empirically true nor empirically false, it is simply not empirically testable. Having no empirical output, (7) is incomplete.

Although not empirically testable, (7) is logically testable. In words it says "An arithmetic mean is the sum of the magnitudes of the observations divided by the number of observations" and this statement is logically true in the same way that "A bachelor is an unmarried adult male" is logically true. The specific case of the mean weight of Al and Betty is also logically testable. That is,

$$\text{(Eq. 8)} \quad 130 = (100 + 160)\tfrac{1}{2}$$

is a logically true statement. It is logically true in that there are no arithmetic errors and also in that it is in the same form as (7). If someone were to calculate the mean weight of Al and Betty as

$$140 = (100 + 160)\tfrac{1}{2}$$

they have made a logically false statement—they are claiming that 140 = 130 which is contradiction occasioned by an arithmetical error. Other possibilities are

$$800 = (100 \cdot 160)^{1/2}$$

and

$$180 = 100 + 160\ (1/2)$$

which are logically false in that they are not in the same *form* as (7).

In addition to this logical testing, the inputs of (8) can be empirically tested by the simple procedure of reweighing Al and Betty. There is the possibility of measurement errors and the repetition of the measurements constitutes an empirical verification (or falsification) of the inputs. However, the empirical testing of the *inputs* does not constitute empirical testing of the *model*. Empirical testing of the model requires that the *outputs* be separately measurable. When the model is incomplete in the sense that the outputs are not separately measurable, there is no way to settle disputes. Suppose, for example, that there was a dispute about whether the arithmetic or the geometric mean is the "true" mean. The formula for the geometric mean is

$$\text{(Eq. 9)} \quad G = \left(\prod_{i=1}^{n} x_i\right)^{1/2}$$

and, therefore, the mean (geometric) weight of Al and Betty is

$$\text{(Eq. 10)} \quad 126.5 \cong (100 \cdot 160)^{1/2}$$

How would one settle this dispute? Equations (9) and (10) can be subjected to the same kinds of logical tests as (7) and (8) but this is of no help since both are logically true. Empirically testing the inputs is also of no help since the accuracy of the inputs is irrelevant to the dispute. There is no way to settle this dispute. In general, the difficulty with incomplete models whose outputs are not separately measurable is that there is no way to settle disputes as to which one is correct or true. The question "Which is the true mean?" is meaningless in this context.

The way to settle such disputes is to complete the model. The two means are not complete models; instead, they are usually used as intermediate logical steps in a complete model. If we examine the complete model, there will be outputs which are separately measurable. Then we can decide which mean to use on the basis of what it is that we wish to predict or explain. That is, we can settle the dispute on the basis of the specific logical connections. M may be an intermediate logical step to predicting X but not connected at all to the prediction Y. Hence, if we wish to predict X, then M is selected on the basis of its logical connections.[2]

Means were used in the example because they often have many logical connections in models. Symbols with many logical connections are said to be *significant.* Isolated symbols are of little use and, therefore, are *insignificant.* The cephalic index is an example of an insignificant concept. It is defined as

(Eq. 11) $C = W/L$

where W is the width and L is the length of a person's head. The cephalic index is like a mean in that it is not separately measurable; hence, (11) is not a complete model because it cannot be empirically tested. The difference is that, insofar as we know, C has no logical connections. It doesn't lead anywhere. At one time it was thought that intelligence and certain aspects of behavior were connected to the cephalic index. However, no such connections have been found and, therefore, C is an insignificant concept. Being insignificant, having no logical connections, there is no way to complete a model containing C.

The problem is that incomplete models are sometimes constructed by arbitrarily defining and connecting a number of insignificant concepts. For example, someone may define "hage" (H) as the product of a person's height (h) and age (a).

(Eq. 12) $H = ha$

Now H is neither separately measurable nor significant. There is nothing that can be done to make it separately measurable, but one

[2]Sometimes this criterion is stated imprecisely as "depending upon the purpose" or "depending upon the circumstances." This imprecision has resulted in some misuse of the criterion. Sometimes people select on the basis of what they want to show or how they want to appear. For example, if Al and Betty are trying to give the appearance of having lost weight, they might report the geometric mean because $G < M$. Conversely, if they are trying to give the appearance of having gained weight, they might report the arithmetic mean because $M > G$. Applying the criterion in this fashion is at best misleading and at worst dishonest. Unfortunately, this situation is sometimes encountered in accounting. Sometimes people attempt to select a particular accounting method on the basis of how they *want* to appear. I hope it is obvious that this is not what I mean when I say that they must be selected on the basis of logical connections.

can attempt to make it significant by combining it with the cephalic index. An alpha concept can be defined as

$$(\text{Eq. } 13) \quad \gamma = (H + C)^{1/2}.$$

Such concepts can be defined in any number. Thus, one can create a vast superstructure of logical connections in this fashion. Although we now have logical connections and, therefore, the concepts are significant in a technical sense, the model is incomplete because its outputs have no empirical connections. There is no way to separately measure α and, therefore, the model is not empirically testable.

Although the example may seem frivolous, there have been several instances of this kind of thing in the history of science. When the subject matter is complex it is possible to inadvertently set up an incomplete model and then fail to recognize that it is incomplete. In such situations, disputes are in principle unresolvable. If someone defines hage as a quotient instead of a product, there is no way to decide which is the correct definition. Since there is no way to settle such disputes, there is no point in arguing about them.

At the present stage of the development of accounting, most applications of accounting systems are incomplete. Thus, there are a number of unanswered questions and unresolved disputes in accounting. Some of these disputes are in principle unresolvable because the model is not complete. In these cases the only way to settle the disputes is to complete the model.

5. Observer Agreement

In the previous sections we have examined the empirical and logical truth of various statements. The question that we now turn to is: how do we know when a statement is true? The answer to this question is that we cannot know in some absolute sense that something is true, but we can accept it as true when independent, qualified observers *agree* that it is true. The scientific test for truth is *corroboration* of the findings of one scientist by other scientists. If other scientists corroborate the findings, if they agree with the findings, then they will be accepted as true and said to be "verified."

That something is merely accepted as true, instead of being "really true," is not very satisfactory upon first encounter. However, once you think about it you will realize that there is no other test for truth available to us. The lack of other tests forces us to use agreement among independent, qualified observers in everyday affairs, as well as in science. Consider the cover of this paper. How do you know that it is "really true" that its color is blue? Of course, it is obvious that its color *is* blue, but *how do you know?* At some time in the past, there was an agreement that the symbols "red," "grey," and "blue" would be used as names for the attribute of color. This agreement was purely conventional originally as can be seen by the fact that we could have agreed to use the symbols "hobgoblin," "gremlin" and "elf" instead of those mentioned above. However, given the agreement on symbols, you can correctly say that "The color of this book is elf" is a false statement. It contains a logical mistake. To test the truth of the statement requires that you call upon independent, qualified observers. When they agree that "elf" is not the name of a color, you will have proved your point. Note, however, that the only thing that you have proved is that independent observers *agree* with your understanding of the meaning of these symbols. You haven't proved anything about the color of the paper. Now suppose someone said, "The color of this paper is grey." Since you know that the color is blue, you can also correctly say that the statement is false. It contains a perceptual or empirical mistake. It is an error in observation. The test for empirical truth is the same as for logical truth: agreement among independent, qualified observers. To test the truth of the statement requires that you call upon other qualified observers and when they agree that it is blue you will have proved your point. But you haven't proved anything about the "real" color; you have only proved that other observers *agree* with your perceptions.

To see the importance of observer agreement, imagine that everyone in the world, except you, is color blind. Although the paper is "really" blue, everyone else perceives it to be grey. What kind of arguments or tests could you present that would convince other people that the book is really blue? In such a situation, it would be you who would be classified as color blind, and you would probably accept the classification. That is, you would agree that it is grey. This is exactly the situation of color blind people in our society. They perceive this paper to be grey, but they agree that it is "really blue."

Scientists would neither agree nor disagree with the proposition that this paper is "really blue." Agreement among independent, qualified observers is the accepted scientific test for truth. Since "really blue" is not subject to the accepted scientific test, scientists would simply classify the proposition as unanswerable. In general, questions about what is "really true" are not considered to be scientific questions because they are not answerable by the accepted scientific tests.

The observers who perform the tests must be independent as well as qualified. "Independent" means two different things in this context. First, it means there must be different observers. A scientist may test his own work by repeating both his empirical observations and his logical operations. However, corroboration requires that different observers perform these tests. Second, it means that the observers must be free of vested interests in the outcome of the tests. If an observer wants a test to come out a certain way (either positive or negative), then he is not independent in this sense. There is, of course, the possibility of dishonesty if an observer is not independent. A more prevalent problem, however, is that a non-independent observer's perceptions may be affected by his desires or expectations. Sometimes *what* we see is affected by what we *want* or *expect* to see. Even if a coach is absolutly honest, he is more apt to see a foul committed by the opposing team than one committed by his team. For this reason, a coach is not allowed to be the referee. For the same reason, a judge is disqualified if the case involves one of his relatives or if it involves a corporation in which he holds stock. Thus, independence in the second sense means that the observer must be indifferent as to the outcome of the tests.

Color blind people provide an example of unqualified observers. Of course, they are unqualified only in regard to perceiving color. In science observers are trained to be alert for certain attributes. A botanist and a geologist can walk through a wood and each perceive things that the other overlooked. The geologist is not qualifid to observe the structure of the plants and the botanist is not qualified to observe the structure of the terrain. The same distinction can be drawn in regard to logical errors. If a person does not speak English, he is not qualified to make judgment about whether or not "elf" is a name of a color. If a person does not speak mathematics, he is not qualified to judge the logical correctness of "$a^2 = a \cdot a$." However, science is intended to be public, not private, as is indicated by the word "agreement" in the test, and, therefore, in the absence of some inherent limitation (such as color blindness), it is intended that anyone can become a qualified observer. A botanist can learn to observe geological structures, a person can learn to speak English or mathematics, and, if they do, they will become qualified observers. Thus, science is, in principle, open to all who wish to participate.

Although science is open to all who take the trouble to become qualified observers, not all statements are open to corroboration by empirical observation. Lack of ability to corroborate a statement may be due to either its content or form. Although "this paper is blue" is in the same form as "this unicorn has one horn," the former is subject to empirical test and the latter is not because of the difference in content. "This unicorn has one horn" is neither empirically true or false because there is no observation whatsoever that would establish its truth or falsity. That is, there can be no agreement among observers if there is nothing to observe.

A class of statements that are not corroborable by virtue of their form are first person reports. The statement, "I perceive this paper to be grey" is different in form from "this paper is grey." The color can not be corroborated because there is no way for you to get inside my head and check what *I* perceive. *You* may perceive it to be blue, and everyone else may agree with you, but your perception cannot possibly refute the report that *I* perceive it to be grey. There are a large number of such statements. "I intend to write a book," "I plan to go into business for myself," and "I am going to major in accounting," are other examples. Since they cannot be corroborated, statements of this form—first person reports—are excluded from statements of science. The exclusion of such statements is just another way of saying that science is concerned with public knowledge and first person reports are private knowledge.

In short, the test for the truth of a statement is agreement among independent, qualified observers. Logical testing requires agreement as to the form and meaning of the symbols. Empirical testing requires agreement as to perceptions or measurements of empirical phenomena. There are many statements which are not empirically testable either because they do not refer to empirical phenomena or because they are personal perceptions or intentions which cannot be independently observed.

6. Summary

The purpose of a model is to explain and predict empirical phenomena. Some empirical phenomena are observed and, via logical operations, we move to an expectation of different empirical phenomena. In predicting we observe some empirical state, input that into the model and then expect to observe a different empirical state. Explanations are similar in that we observe some empirical state and then look for a statement which would have allowed us to predict that empirical state. Citing that statement constitutes an explanation of the observed empirical state.

Scientific models are subjected to two kinds of tests: empirical and logical. Empirical testing of a model consists of comparing the output of the model (prediction) to a separate measurement of the empirical phenomena. Thus, empirical testing has to do with the relation between the symbols and the empirical phenomena. Logical testing, by contrast, has to do with the relationships among the symbols. In logical testing we look at the form and meaning of the symbols in contrast to empirical testing where we must look at the empirical phenomena. The discovery of a contradiction constitutes a failure of the logical test. Statements which are contradictory assert that two different empirical states exist and this guarantees a failure of the empirical test. Although failure of a logical test guarantees failure of the empirical test, the reverse does not hold. The absence of contradictions does not guarantee that a model will accurately predict an empirical state.

For a model to be complete at least two different empirical states must be connected by the logic of the model. That is, we must be able to move from one observed empirical state to an expectation of another empirical state through the logic of the model. In the absence of such predictions, the model is incomplete or deficient—it does not qualify as a scientific model.

The ultimate test of truth in science is the agreement among independent, qualified observers. There is no way to determine "reality" other than by making observations and comparing them. If independent, qualified observers agree, then we accept the observations as true. This means that science is a public enterprise and, therefore, it excludes all personal reports of perceptions or personal opinions. Sometimes these personal reports or opinions are referred to as "subjective" because they depend upon the subject. Science attempts to be objective in the sense that it wants to rely on the object, rather than the subject, and the test for objectivity is agreement among independent, qualified observers.

WORKS CITED

Caws, Peter. *The Philosophy of Science: A Systematic Account.* Princeton, N.J.: D. Van Nostrand Company Inc., 1965.

Torgerson, Warren S. *Theory and Methods of Scaling.* New York: John Wiley & Sons, Inc., 1958.

ADDITIONAL REFERENCES

Brodbeck, May, ed. *Readings in the Philosophy of the Social Sciences.* New York: MacMillan Co., 1968, pp. 6-11.

Hempel, Carl G. *Fundamentals of Concept Formation in Empirical Sciences.* International Encyclopedia of Unified Science, edited by Otto Neurath, Rudolf Carnap, and Charles W. Morris, Vol. II, No. 7. Chicago: University of Chicago Press, 1952, pp. 1, 32-37.

———. *Philosophy of Natural Science.* Englewood Cliffs, N.J.: Prentice-Hall, Inc., 1966, pp. 30-32.

Kemeny, John G. *A Philosopher Looks at Science.* Princeton, N.J.: D. Van Nostrand Co., Inc., 1954, pp. 14-35.

Margenau, Henry. *The Nature of Physical Reality: A Philosophy of Modern Physics.* New York: McGraw-Hill Book Co., Inc., 1950, pp. 75-122.

Accounting at the crossroads

Robert R. Sterling, *Jesse H. Jones Distinguished Professor, Department of Economics and Accounting, Rice University, Houston, Texas, urges the profession to adopt a more scientific and less legalistic approach to help avert government control. This article is reprinted from the Spring 1976 issue of* World, *published by Peat, Marwick, Mitchell & Co.*

Accounting is always at the crossroads; there are always alternative routes that we can take. The alternatives that we currently face are more critical than most. Which route we choose will certainly determine the nature of our profession in the future. The choice may even determine whether or not our profession will survive. Those alternatives are two different methodologies.

Perhaps the methodological alternatives can best be explained as a historical comparison. Ever since we began to try to become a profession we have compared ourselves to the professions of medicine and law. In the past that comparison has been made at the professional level concerning such things as public service, codes of ethics, etc. The question was whether we were going to become a profession like medicine and law or follow an alternative route. That question is now settled. We deliberately set about emulating the professional characteristics of medicine and law. As a consequence, we are now a profession.

Although medicine and law are similar in regard to their professional characteristics, they differ greatly in regard to the method that each profession employs: The method of authority vs. the method of science. Now that we have settled the question in regard to the professional similarity of accounting to medicine and law, perhaps we can move to the next question—the question of method. Should we emulate law or medicine in regard to the method that we employ in accounting? That is the question that I will address in this article.

Medicine and law address different types of questions. Accordingly, they employ different types of methods to answer those questions. I will consider the two methods in turn.

The legal method: authority

The law is concerned with justice and equity but it ultimately relies on raw power. This is not to denigrate the law but rather to recognize its nature. Although each legislator and jurist will try to be fair, will try to do the right thing, the question is not so much right or wrong as it is a question of deciding and enforcing.

"Postive law . . . consists only of that thinking, right or wrong, which has received the express approval of the decision making authority of the state. . . . Authority, rather than right reason, is the primary characteristic of this concept.[1]"

Thus, the primary characteristic of the law is authority, not right reason. When one considers the kinds of question that the law addresses, this primary characteristic is rather easy to understand.

The questions that legislatures must decide are quite disputatious.

[1] Carlton C. Rodee et al., *Introduction to Political Science*, 3rd ed. (New York: McGraw-Hill Book Co., 1976), pp.50-51.

Whether the rich should pay more taxes than the poor, whether possession of marijuana should be a misdemeanor or a felony, whether we should drive on the right or left side of the road are questions that have no inherent rightness or wrongness. Nonetheless they are questions that must be decided. For this reason, the government has given various legislatures the power to make laws and the power to enforce compliance.

The same is true of the courts. By their very nature, courts are concerned with disputes. Both of the litigants think that they are "right," but they differ in their idea of what is right and this leads to a dispute. They ask the court to adjudicate the dispute. We expect the court to do it wisely, to do it in accordance with the law and in accordance with justice, but we cannot expect the loser to agree that the court is right in its decision. Therefore, the court is also an instrument of power.

"When we recognize that the law is the primary power instrument of the nation-state, the study of law rather naturally shades off into a study of politics. Political science has been defined as . . . the study of power relationships between individuals and groups, i.e., what we call 'politics.' . . ."[2]

Other evidence for this is given in the title of political science books. For example, *Politics and Power* is an entire book devoted to the way in which different kinds of power, including law, are obtained, wielded and muted in our system. Thus, law and politics are related in an essential way. The body politic is the ultimate source of power. It deputizes certain groups of individuals, such as legislatures and judges, to make laws and enforce them. It is for this reason that when we consider the legal method we cannot avoid the method of politics. Both are subsumed under the method of authority.

The medical method: science

Medicine utilizes the method of science. Physicians do not legislate that penicillin will cure pneumonia; instead, they prove it by scientific methods. The essential difference in method is that medicine appeals to truth rather than authority.

To put the distinction another way, medicine relies on research while law relies on deliberation. If a question needs to be decided in the law, certain people will be appointed—given authority—to decide the issue. By contrast, if a question needs to be decided in medicine, certain people will do research on the issue. They will attempt to provide empirical evidence bearing on the issue.

To put the distinction still another way, one can look to the status of the person who utters a legal or medical verdict. In law, the status of the person is of utmost importance. My legal opinion is of no consequence while the chief justice's legal opinion is the law. In medicine it matters not a whit who utters a medical finding. The question is not who utters it but whether it can be corroborated by other researchers. For example, Linus Pauling, one of the most highly respected scientists in the world and a Nobel Laureat, recently broached some claims about the efficacy of vitamin C to cure the common cold. Despite his fame and respected position, his claim was not accepted because it could not be corroborated by other researchers. The reverse is also true.

Adjudicating disputes. All of us know that the law is disputatious. However, many of us nonscientists tend to think that science is cut and dried, that there are no disputes among scientists. Nothing could be further from the truth. The disputes among scientists are legion. They are engaged in almost constant arguments, some of which are protracted.

Empirical tests. The disputes among scientists are in regard to alternative hypotheses concerning the same phenomenon. One scientist will entertain a hypothesis that is different from the one entertained by another scientist. In the context of a general discussion of the contrast between the method of authority and the method of science, Cohen and Nagel[3] write

"When thus faced with alternative hypotheses, logic develops their consequences, so that when these consequences are compared with observable phenomena we have a means of testing which hypothesis is to be eliminated and which is most in harmony with the facts of observation."

In essence, that is what science is all about: An attempt to see which view is most in harmony with the facts. The rather rebarbative term "empirical test" simply means that one looks at real things in the real world to find out what is true.

Empirical base. Many nonscientists, particularly accountants, seem to think that there is something mysterious about science. The exact opposite is the case. Scientific findings must be subject to *public* test. For this reason the findings cannot be mysterious. The evidence cannot be private for the same reason.

This requirement delimits the subject matter of science. In order to perform an empirical test there must be an empirical base. Scientific knowledge is intended to refer to real things in the real world. Thus, disputes about nonempirical things are not within the realm of science.

A common counterexample—one that we sometimes laugh at—is the question of how many angels can dance on the head of a pin or whether angels copulate. At one time these were serious questions.[4] The problem is that they are not concerned with real things in the real world. (Whether or not they are concerned with real things in the next world will not detain us here.)

By contrast, our most abstract, theoretical discipline—mathematics—is quite useful and practical. Indeed, it was developed to meet specific, practical problems.

We now tend to think of mathematics as being abstruse and theoretical which we use as antonyms for useful and practical. Quite the opposite is the case. There is nothing more useful and practical than,

[2] Ibid., p.17.

[3] Morris R. Cohen and Ernest Nagel, *An Introduction to Logic and Scientific Method* (New York: Harcourt, Brace & World, 1934), p.196.

[4] For an extended discussion, see Thomas Aquinas, *Basic Writings of Saint Thomas Aquinas*, edited and annotated by Anton C. Pegis, vol. I (New York: Random House, 1945), pp.480-608.

say, geometry, despite its abstract, theoretical nature.[5]

Geometry is most useful, as is evidenced by the fact that without it it would be difficult to conceive of building a house or a bridge, surveying land, navigating or even reading a map. The reason it is useful and practical is because it helps us to explain, predict and understand certain empirical phenomena.

Legalistic accounting

I think that we must agree that accounting is much more legalistic than scientific. It is easy to find parallels between accounting and the law; it is exceptionally difficult to find parallels between accounting and science.

One parallel is the source of our accounting rules. In the legal profession, there are two sources of law: precedents and statutes. In the accounting profession there are two sources of generally accepted accounting principles: precedents and statutes. We accountants don't normally call them "precedents and statutes" but that is in fact what they are.

Precedents. In the law a precedent is a past decision which, under the doctrine of *stare decisis*, is one source of law. In accounting one source of GAAP is past practices. That is, past decisions by other practitioners form precedents which we follow and then they become generally accepted. Originally this was an informal procedure. More recently it has become formalized. We have adopted the legalistic doctrine of "substantial authoritative support" and one element of obtaining substantial authoritative support is the "surveying of practices."[6] In addition to formalizing the method of following precedents, we have become more efficient at their retrieval.

Statutes. The second source of the law is statutes. Various legislatures have been empowered by the government to enact statutes. We also have various legislatures enacting statutes in accounting. The committee on accounting procedure, Accounting Principles Board and Financial Accounting Standards Board were/are de facto legislators of accounting statutes. That they were/are *private* legislative bodies—not specifically empowered by the government to write statutes—does not negate the fact that they perform a legislative function.

Although we accountants may be hesitant to recognize the legal nature of GAAP, Commerce Clearing House treats our accounting statutes in exactly the same way as it treats any other legal statutes. Those statutes have been classified and cross-indexed. We even have a looseleaf service to update changes in accounting statutes. These publications have all the trappings of any other set of laws and regulations. I find it difficult to discern the difference between financial accounting statutes and, say, tax statutes. In short, legislation of accounting statutes has become more formal and its retrieval has become more efficient.

Politics. Another parallel is the increasingly political nature of accounting. One of the major reasons for the demise of the APB was the political pressure put upon it. Evidently this pressure is continuing. Marshall S. Armstrong has just given a speech in which he deplores the political pressure put upon the FASB.[7] As we noted above, such political pressure is part and parcel of the method of authority—it is to be expected of any legalistic system.

There are many other parallels between the law and accounting that could be drawn. Since I think that we would all agree that accounting is legalistic, I will not draw any further parallels. Instead, I will turn to the reasons for its legalistic nature.

Lack of empirical base. Very early in our history—when we were still bookkeepers—we developed the idea that accounting is a calculational, nonempirical discipline. We have no evidence that the early bookkeepers ever left their high stools to observe and measure empirical phenomena. Instead, they footed columns, balanced accounts, took averages, etc. Their entries were supposed to reflect exchanges but they never observed exchanges; instead they made their entries from documents supplied by managements. Their balances were supposed to reflect empirical phenomena but they never observed those phenomena and compared them to their balances. The bookkeepers in our early development had no authority or responsibility for the accounting system or the financial statements. Managements designed the accounting system, supplied the inputs and decided wha was to be recorded and reported. The bookkeeper was a human calculator, not an empiricist.

When bookkeepers became auditors (in about 1850) they continued this idea. The early auditors thought that it was their duty to tick and cast, not to observe or measure the empirical phenomena. Auditing became a process of reexamining the basic business documents, retracing the entries and recalculating the balances and averages. Auditors examined the accounts, not the empirical phenomena.

There have been many developments in accounting and auditing. However, the basic idea that accounting and auditing is a calcula-

[5] Recently at four separate conferences I have heard practitioners complain about the impracticality and uselessness of the abstract, theoretical, academic literature. I think what they mean is that they find it unintelligible. On that basis, they have a point. We academics haven't done as good a job as we ought to do in regard to communicating our theoretical findings to practitioners. We ought to use plain language insofar as we can. However, when practitioners complain about abstract theory being "impractical and useless" they miss the mark.

[6] Marshall S. Armstrong, "Some Thoughts on Substantial Authoritative Support," JofA, Apr.69, pp.44-50.

[7] Marshall S. Armstrong, "The Politics of Establishing Accounting Standards," speech before the Third Annual Securities Regulation Institute in San Diego, California, on January 16, 1976.

tional, nonempirical discipline has continued.[8]

Since we were not concerned with empirical phenomena, we couldn't adopt the scientific method. Since we couldn't adopt the scientific method, we adopted the alternative —the legalistic authoritative method. We now rely almost exclusively on authority, not truth. This reliance has been expressed in many different ways. One way is the common theme in accounting literature that it is impossible to discover principles of accounting in the same way that one discovers principles of science. Another way is the oft-heard pronouncement that accounting is an art, not a science. A third way of saying the same thing is to stress the conventional nature of accounting.[9]

By definition, conventions do not refer to empirical phenomena. That is, in this context, "convention" is defined as an agreement arrived at either informally by custom and usage or formally by the vote of a legislature.[10] For example, a convention arrived at by custom and usage is to wear black at a funeral.

The idea that accounting is a process of allocating costs crystallized in the 1930s. We made the concept of "asset" synonymous with "unexpired cost" and the concept of "expense" synonymous with "expired cost." There were various methods of calculating expired and unexpired cost; we could allocate the costs by different conventional methods. This cost allocation idea is now firmly entrenched. Our textbooks talk about little else than "matching costs and revenues."

These concepts are not concerned with real things in the real world. In the same way that we cannot observe angels, either copulating or not copulating, we cannot observe costs, either expired or unexpired. There is no way to empirically determine whether a cost is properly or improperly matched. For this reason we cannot adjudicate our disputes. We can *argue* about straight line versus accelerated depreciation and Lifo versus Fifo inventories, just as Aquinas argued about angels, but we cannot settle the dispute by appealing to the facts.

Usefulness. The lack of empirical base puts us in an awkward position. Accounting has always been a practical discipline. We have prided ourselves in the usefulness of our activities. The problem was, and is, that nonempirical concepts are not useful and are not practical. That is, if one wants to make a decision about an asset there are many things that are relevant to that decision but its "unexpired cost" is *not* relevant to any decisions that I know of.[11]

Scientific accounting

I think that adopting a scientific method would be wholly beneficial to the accounting profession. However, my beliefs are of little consequence. The more important thing is that the profession ought to be able to make a rational decision.

The lack of recognition of a scientific alternative is the first obstacle that must be overcome. If we continue to define accounting as an art, as necessarily conventional, as inherently unscientific, then we cannot make progress toward becoming a science. It will continue to be a self-fulfilling prophecy.

The second obstacle to overcome is the idea that there is something mysterious about science. The exact opposite is the case. Unscientific concepts are quite mysterious. Scientific findings must be subject to public test. Compare the notion of angels copulating to the area of a rectangle. I find the former to be quite mysterious and the latter to have a complete absence of mystery. Similarly, I find the concept of unexpired costs to be quite arcane and mysterious.

The third obstacle to overcome is the notion that there is something inherently unscientific about the subject matter of accounting. It is not the subject matter of accounting that is unscientific; it is the approach that is unscientific.

What I am calling for here is an empirical base for accounting. Instead of defining accounting as a process of allocating unobservable costs, we must define it as a process of keeping track of real things in the real world. Until we do that it will remain legalistic instead of scientific.

An example. I chose the example of depreciation of fixed assets because it is thought to be one of the most difficult problems in accounting. Its difficulty is evidenced by the fact that we have been arguing about it for more than 100 years without reaching a solution. Another reason for choosing depreciation is that we have officially and explicitly defined it as a nonempirical concept:

> *"Definitions are unacceptable which imply that* [depreciation] . . . *is a measurement . . . of the physical deterioration . . . or of the decline in monetary value . . . or, indeed, of anything that actually occurs within the year."*[12]

---

[8] It has continued in regard to the dollar figures but not in regard to quantities. McKesson-Robbins required us to perform empirical tests on quantities. I think McKesson-Robbins is the most significant theoretical advance in accounting in the 20th century because it partially transformed accounting from a calculational discipline to an empirical science. My argument, in a nutshell, is that we ought to go all the way; we ought to empirically test the dollar figures as well as the quantities.

[9] See Reed K. Storey, *The Search for Accounting Principles: Today's Problems in Perspective* (New York: AICPA, 1964), p.9ff, for the history of this idea. He traces the idea back to the influential committee on cooperation with stock exchanges. He says that that committee "laid the foundation" for our subsequent ideas and that most of our GAAP "is dependent in one way or another on the report of this committee." He then goes on to say that "the committee . . . emphasize[d] the necessarily conventional . . . nature of accounting."

[10] See senses 4 and 5, *Webster's New World Dictionary of the American Language*, college ed. (Cleveland: World Publishing Company, 1959).

[11] Of course, we can *legislate* the relevance of unexpired cost. We do that in regard to income taxes. The law sometimes requires that taxes be based upon our accounting method of calculating unexpired cost. (At other times the law requires a different basis.) Since the payment of taxes is a real world phenomenon, it is relevant to decisions. This makes unexpired cost indirectly relevant because the tax law sometimes specifies that it is to be used to calculate the tax liability. Other than taxes, insofar as I know, unexpired costs are irrelevant to all decisions.

I have previously made that statement with the accompanying challenge to readers to demonstrate just one case where the unexpired cost is relevant to a decision. No one has provided such a demonstration so I will repeat that challenge here. (See Robert R. Sterling, "A Statement of Basic Accounting Theory: A Review Article," *Journal of Accounting Research*, Spring 1967, pp.110-11.

[12] Committee on Terminology, "Accounting Terminology Bulletin No. 1, 'Review and Resume,'" in *Accounting Research and Terminology Bulletins*, final ed., pp. 1-32 (New York: AICPA, 1969), p.24.

Thus, depreciation is explicitly defined as *not* being a measurement of *any* empirical phenomena. Instead, it is an allocation—a calculation. That is, it is a purely mental construct, a fiction. In the apt phraseology of Thomas,[13] depreciation is a part of the furniture of accountants' minds.

It is for this reason that disputes over the proper method of calculating depreciation cannot be resolved by scientific test. As long as depreciation does not refer to empirical phenomena, then no scientific test can shed light on the matter. It is for this very reason that disputes about depreciation have remained unresolved for so long a time. The only way to resolve a dispute about the furniture of our minds is to enact a statute that says "thou shalt use straight line" or "thou shalt use accelerated."

Worse, depreciation suffers from being useless. In a decision context, we regularly teach our students that they must ignore the amount of depreciation that has been "matched" against the revenues. If they don't ignore it, they are likely to make the wrong decision. Similarly, we teach them to ignore the unmatched portion of the cost—the "unexpired cost" or "book value"—of a fixed asset when making a decision. If they don't ignore it, they will err in their decision.

In order to overcome these problems, we must redefine depreciation as something that is observable. My candidate, on grounds of usefulness, is exit value. I mean by "exit value" the amount of dollars that one could receive by an almost immediate sale in the marketplace. Such market prices are observable. We can go to the marketplace and observe people exchanging dollar bills or checks for assets. Thus, I offer the following definition: Depreciation is the decline in the exit value of productive assets.

Once we have defined an observable, then we can adjudicate disputes. We will have to make some distinctions between classes of assets before we can adjudicate the disputes because it is not likely that we will find one equation that will describe the decline in exit value of all kinds of productive assets. For one class of assets, automotive equipment, the decline in exit value—the average wholesale price of automobiles as shown in the "blue book"—is fairly well described by applying the 1.5 declining balance method. Thus, I offer the following empirical generalization or "scientific hypothesis": Depreciation of automotive equipment is described by applying the 1.5 declining balance method.

The first and most immediate advantage of this redefinition is that if another accountant were to propose an alternative hypothesis—a different method of calculating the decline in exit value of automotive equipment—we could resolve the dispute. Suppose that someone else were to say that the decline in exit value of automotive equipment can be predicted by applying the straight line method. The only thing that we would have to do is to observe enough exchanges to see which, if either, of these alternative hypotheses is correct.

More importantly, as is usually true when we are speaking of empirical phenomena, we have now defined a concept that is useful. The exit value of a productive asset is relevant to a great many decisions. For example, if one is thinking about replacing the productive asset with one that is technologically superior, then the exit value of the old asset is relevant to the decision. If one is thinking about leasing or renting such productive assets instead of owning them, then the exit values of the old productive assets are relevant. Moreover, the decline in the exit value of productive assets represents a real world phenomenon. The exit value of an asset represents the ability to command real goods at a point in time. When the exit value of an asset declines over time, it means that there has been a decline in the command over goods.

In summary, the old legalistic definition of depreciation is (1) useless and (2) seemingly unresolvable. The only way to resolve disputes about fictional concepts of this kind is to legislate more and more statutes in more and more detail. Although we enacted a great many statutes, we haven't dealt with depreciation. As a result, we have the chaotic situation of permitting the same asset to be assigned different numbers and different assets to be assigned the same numbers. We recognize the problem but we have failed to recognize the unscientific nature of the definition of depreciation. Our failure to recognize that fact has caused us to argue about the proper method of calculating depreciation for the last 100 years. If we don't redefine it, I expect that we will continue the argument for another 100 years.

The new definition has the advantage of being (1) useful and (2) empirically resolvable. To my mind, those are compelling reasons for adopting the new definition.

A program. Depreciation is just one example of the kinds of redefinitions that are needed. We need to do the same thing for other kinds of assets and expenses. Obviously, this cannot be done overnight. It will have to come about incrementally. The eventual goal is to transform accounting into an empirical science. Such a transformation will be truly revolutionary. However, that revolution must be brought about in a slow, orderly, evolutionary manner.

Perhaps we can parallel the development of geometry. In pre-Egyptian times, knowledge of geometry could only be obtained by direct measurements. There were no equations or hypotheses available. Then thinkers began to propose various equations or alternative hypotheses.

[13] Arthur L. Thomas, *The Allocation Problem: Part Two,* Studies in Accounting Research No. 9 (Sarasota, Florida: American Accounting Association, 1974), p.114.

Many of these proposals were wrong and most were at best crude approximations. Since the Egyptian priests had the authority, they could have decided to legislate statutes regarding the alternative geometrical hypotheses. If they had followed that route, geometry would be a nonempirical useless activity today. Luckily, they chose the scientific, empirical route. Instead of legislating statutes, they began to perform empirical tests. These empirical tests permitted the wrong equations to be discarded and the others to be refined.

Eventually, geometry became a collection of disconnected equations. There was no logical connection between, say, the area of a rectangle and the length of a hypotenuse. Other thinkers began to see logical connections between the various equations. It was Euclid who provided a general theory that logically connected all of the previously disconnected equations. He reduced geometry to an elegant logical system from which one could deduce certain consequences. These consequences also referred to empirical phenomena—they also were subject to empirical test. The final outcome was a logical-empirical theory of great usefulness and practicality.

If we accountants choose the empirical route, then we will probably have to rely on direct measurements for many assets and expenses. We will not have equations available to calculate the value of many assets and expenses. The results of these direct measurements will facilitate the development of specific disconnected equations about various kinds of assets and expenses. Since these equations will refer to empirical phenomena, we will be able to subject them to empirical tests and to adjudicate our disputes. Each individual equation will also be useful. However, initially they will not be logically connected. We can expect that sooner or later an accounting Euclid will come along to provide the logical connections. Eventually we can hope for a logical-empirical theory of accounting of great usefulness and practicality.

Summary

Accounting is at the crossroads. We can emulate the law and continue to employ the method of authority. If we do, then we will become more and more legalistic. This will result in more statutes, in more detail, from more legislative bodies. Accounting will become more and more political. The law rather naturally shades off into a consideration of politics. Thus, we can expect more and more political pressure from various interest groups being applied to the FASB. We can also expect those interest groups to appeal to higher legislative authorities when they don't get their way with the FASB. We have already seen some of this when interest groups have appealed to the Congress, the SEC and the Executive Branch. We can expect more of it. Eventually, I suspect that accounting legislation will become exclusively a governmental activity. Law making and law enforcement are usually reserved to the government—it usually maintains its monopoly of the law.

The alternative is to adopt the method of science. If we are to do this, then the first thing that we must do is to quit reinforcing the notion that accounting is inherently unscientific. We must cease lamenting our unscientific subject matter and begin to look for ways of making it scientific. The most important thing that we must do in this direction is to redefine our subject matter. We have previously defined our subject matter as unobservable fictions. Unobservable fictions are not subject to scientific tests. My candidate for a new subject matter is exit values. My main reason for selecting exit values is that they are useful to a great many decisions.[14]

My second reason is that since they are subject to empirical test, we will be able to resolve disputes about them.

Several thoughtful nonaccountants have defined accounting as a "ritual."[15] In its present state I must reluctantly concur. We have defined mysterious, nonempirical concepts. I can find no uses for those concepts. Thus, when we calculate such concepts we must be engaged in a ritual. We can continue performing these rituals and we can even enact statutes to regulate the way in which we perform them. Alternatively, we can redefine our subject matter so that we once again become a useful, practical discipline. I hope we choose the latter course. ■

---

[14] I have considered many different decision models and decision makers in Robert S. Sterling, *The Theory of the Measurement of Enterprise Income* (Lawrence, Kansas: University Press of Kansas, 1970). In that volume I found exit values to be relevant to more decisions than any other kinds of values. It is for that reason that my candidate is exit values instead of, say, replacement cost.

[15] K. E. Boulding, "Economics and Accounting: The Uncongenial Twins," in *Studies in Accounting Theory*, edited by W. T. Baxter and Sidney Davidson (Homewood, Illinois: Richard D. Irwin, Inc., 1962), p.53.

ACCOUNTING THEORY AND PRACTICE

INTRODUCTION

Sterling on Accounting Theory

T. A. Lee

This second section of the text contains thirteen items covering a twenty-year period of publication. Most of the writings are reproduced from leading accounting journals of the day. They each reflect Bob Sterling's attempts to communicate his view of what accounting theory should look like, particularly in the related areas of income determination and asset valuation. As in the first section, the items are offered chronologically, and reflect Bob's desire to start with basics and then move to more complex matters.

What is most evident from these writings is Bob's development of his primary message that accounting is a measurement process which has a focus on physical properties - i.e., it is concerned with representing various economic stocks and flows in business. He therefore builds his ideas about accounting theory, not by reference to costs or values, but by observation of quantities in exchange relationships. The valuation process is perceived by Bob to be an important but secondary process in accounting measurement. What is of fundamental significance is the identification of physical properties and quantities of relevance to defined decision models. Accounting measurement is a process of measuring decision relevant quantities and quantity changes. These ideas have only recently been accepted in principle by accounting standard-setters using the criterion of representational faithfulness.

Much of the early work in this section is devoted primarily to the issue of relevant quantities. Later research by Bob then focuses on the valuation of these quantities. Again, the essential principle is relevance to a defined decision model. Unlike other accounting theorists, Bob denies the utility of reporting in different value terms and, instead, by means of carefully constructed scientific argument, identifies the valuation alternative best suited to provide a relevant informational input to the specified decision model. In this respect, several of the writings in this section consider a variety of valuation alternatives (including conventional historical cost) by reference to a number of criteria. However, behind each valuation argument lies Bob's reminder that accounting is dealing with physical properties which can be measured realistically for the benefit of decisions which require to be made in that physical world. In this sense, he is consistently concerned with decision models rather than decision makers.

What is most clear from this selection of Bob Sterling's writings is that he perceives accounting theory to be about accounting rather than accounting preparers or users. He sees accounting as a measurement of things in the real world that are of interest when decisions have to be made. What is crucial in the process is that accountants select the physical properties that are likely to impact decisions and that can also be measured meaningfully. In particular, he reveals that accounting is, first and foremost, about recognition of relevant phenomena. It is then about relevant representations of the recognized phenomena. To undertake these tasks, accountants require to understand that conventional accounting is not designed to complete these tasks meaningfully. Indeed, they are not educated to have that understanding. These issues are addressed in the writings in the next two sections.

ROBERT R. STERLING

An Operational Analysis of Traditional Accounting

I. Introduction

C. D. Broad drew a distinction between 'speculative' and 'critical or analytical' philosophy. He described critical philosophy as 'the analysis and definition of our fundamental concepts, and the clear statement and resolute criticism of our fundamental beliefs'.[1] If we may be permitted to use the same distinction in accounting, then this paper is of the critical, analytical variety. I intend to (1) analyse accounting into various parts, and (2) critically examine those parts.

Sections I and II are devoted to analysis. A physical analogue and some simplified valuation rules are presented. This will be taken as a model of accounting, as a system, which requires specifiable data inputs and, after some manipulation, which comes forth with data outputs.

Under this view the accountant's function is to supply the data inputs and the system's function is to manipulate those inputs and come forth with data outputs.

[Accountant] —Inputs→ [System] —Outputs→

Section III will be devoted to an analysis of the inputs, a listing of the kinds of human judgment required of the accountant, and a discussion of the operational adequacy of those judgments.

II. Physical Accounting

The accountant works with *stocks* and *flows*. I will take these terms to be primitive and assume that they can be located in time and space.

Definition:

(1) q_{ij} = a quantity stock at the ith moment at location j.

(1.1) $\Delta q_{ij} = q_{ij} - q_{i-1,j}$

A flow is *from* one location *to* a different location. Thus, a flow affects at least two stocks. The stocks so affected will be said to be *related* and denoted by $\circledR$. Thus, the expression

(1.2) $\Delta q_{ij} \circledR \Delta q_{ik}$

indicates the flow from location j to k or vice versa. When such an expression is written it will be assumed that all of the stocks affected by a single flow are included. It is possible for a flow to affect more than two stocks but, for ease of exposition and also to reflect accurately the accountant's thinking, I will speak of these flows as if they affected only two stocks unless specified otherwise.

1. C. D. Broad, *Scientific Thought*, New York, 1927, p 18.

Robert R. Sterling is Visiting Research Fellow, Yale University.
The author gratefully acknowledges the criticism of Arthur L. Thomas and is indebted in a more general way to Henry Margenau and Sid B. Thomas.

Assuming that the flow is conservative (that nothing is lost in the flow), and that both the increment and decrement are measured in the same units, the flow can be represented by a zero sum equation.

(1.3) $\Delta q_{ij} + \Delta q_{ik} = 0$ (Δq_{ij} ® Δq_{ik})

That is, the increment is equal absolutely to the decrement. Hence, double entry or the equality of debits and credits.

All of the above holds for the universe. We can partition this universe into *entities*. Let us take a collection of stocks, say, those that we can directly observe, and call these observables the *real* stocks. However, let us maintain the same system that we have above by writing a zero sum equation (1.3) for each flow into or out of the entity. In this way we can record the *source* of each flow and stock in the entity.

Given this convention, in each entity matrix we have two classes of stocks: real and source. At the formation of each entity we will assume that all stocks are zero. Thus, for any entity

(1.4) $$\sum_{j=1}^{n} q_{ij} = 0; q_{ij} = 0$$

We can rearrange the terms of (1.4) by sign.

(1.5) $a_{ij} = q_{ij}$; $q_{ij} > 0$

(1.6) $\epsilon_{ij} = q_{ij}$; $q_{ij} < 0$

An array of a_{ij} ($j = 1 \ldots . n$) and ϵ_{ij} ($j = 1 \ldots . r$) and their sums is called a 'quantity balance sheet'. Obviously

(1.7) $$\sum_{j=1}^{n} a_{ij} = -\sum_{j=1}^{r} \epsilon_{ij}$$

or the quantity assets equal the quantity equities.

Note that the source stocks can have either positive or negative signs. Flows out of a given entity to locations other than those from which there have been inflows (or from which there have been smaller inflows) will result in source stocks with a positive sign. The converse will result in source stocks with a negative sign. Three stocks have been identified:

1. Real stocks (Positive sign)
2. Source stocks
    a. Positive sign.
    b. Negative sign.

These can be arrayed in various ways to form an equation but the ordinary way is given in (1.7) or

(1.8) Positive source stocks & Real stocks = — Negative source stocks.

It should be emphasized that the above is concerned exclusively with quantities. Values are deferred until the next section. Nevertheless quantities bear a striking resemblance to value — price aggregate, initial cost — accounting. The positive sources may be likened to monetary assets, the real stocks to non-monetary assets and the negative sources to equities. Of course, it does not yield all the implications of value accounting but its *structure* is almost identical. For example, any two entities can be 'consolidated'. The summation of the matrices of any two entities would result in the flows between those two entities cancelling out or, to say the same thing differently, the sources from j to k plus the sources from k to j would add to zero. The resulting quantities would consist of the sum of the real stocks of both entities and the sources from and to all locations other than those contained in the two entities.

In addition, it is possible to group sources in various ways. We could, for example, define a subset of extra-entity locations as customers and call this collection 'retained earnings', the flows could be called 'income transactions' and those transactions divided by direction of flow, or sign, into 'revenue' and 'expense'[2] and these could be subclassified as desired. The same is true for the flow of funds.

An implication inherent in value accounting that is not implied by physical flows and stocks is the notion of debt or obligation. Inflows in accounting oblige the entity to make an outflow at some future time or event; debt sources are to be returned at some future time, ownership sources at the event of liquidation. Conversely, outflows are expected to be collected at a future time or event. In physical accounting one can have continuous unidirectional flows without the expectation or obligation that they be reversed.[3]

In addition, physical accounting has no counterpart for cash. Cash may be thought of as 'markers' for flows from various locations which are generalized in their command over all other locations. It will be convenient here, however, to treat cash as a physical quantity for reasons which will become apparent.[4]

The important point in the above presentation is that it reflects a rather

2. Fisher's older terms — in-come and out-go — are even more descriptive. He also distinguishes entities and the direction of flow between them, e.g., 'Smith's income is the farm's outcome'. (Irving Fisher, *The Nature of Capital and Income,* New York, Macmillan Co., 1906, p 122). John B. Canning (*The Economics of Accountancy,* New York, The Ronald Press Company, 1929), followed Fisher rather closely and used similar language. The concepts and language continue to the present time. See, e.g., Maurice Moonitz and Louis H. Jordan, *Accounting: An Analysis of Its Problems,* rev. ed, Vol I, New York, Holt, Rinehart and Winston Inc., 1963; George J. Staubus, 'Alternative Asset Flow Concepts', *Accounting Review,* July 1966, and compare the above to Hector R. Anton, *Accounting for the Flow of Funds,* Boston, Houghton Mifflin Company, 1962, p 11-12.

3. Boulding's biological analogy of homeostasis includes this implication. (Kenneth Boulding, *A Reconstruction of Economics,* New York, John Wiley & Sons Inc., 1950, p 26). Biologists reciprocate by using our terms. Roger Bannister speaks of 'the oxygen debt' of the human body after sustained exertion. 'The Punishment of the Long-Distance Runner', *New York Times Magazine,* 18 September 1966, p 76.

4. I am treating cash — coins and currency — as a real stock. Alternatively, a more abstract *numeraire*-commodity could be used. Peter Newman, (*The Theory of Exchange,* Englewood Cliffs, Prentice-Hall Inc., p 79), does this by using a guinea for which there is no physical marker. Use of such a unit would do no violence to what follows but it would require an extension of the discussion on obligations to transfers of obligations. This would be peripheral to my main purpose so I will invite the reader to think of cash as a real stock.

surprising amount of accounting. Leading accounting theorists have always presented a *physical base* for accounting. They say accounting is concerned with quantities of some kind — service potentialities, units of capacity — and that these are the 'significant elements' of accounting. After the physical presentation they turn to the problem of *valuation.* Dollar valuations are thought to be 'only convenient' and 'not synonymous' with the physical base.[5] It is rather interesting and not insignificant to demonstrate that the basic mechanics of accounting can be stated exclusively as quantities and their locations without mentioning the valuation problem.

III. Historical Cost Valuation

In dealing with physical accounting I stipulated that the related increment and decrement be measured in the same units. In this way we can get equal debits and credits and a balance sheet that balances. Note that this requirement does not imply that the balance sheet will be in homogeneous units. That is, we could have increments of ten tons of coal and five gallons of oil. Both would have decrements, sources, in the same units. Thus, the sum of the quantity assets would be '15' and the sources sum would be '-15'. It balances, but one wonders about the *meaning* of the number 15 in this connection.

A necessary condition for a sum to have meaning is that the units be homogeneous. Homogeneity of units could be accomplished by measuring all stocks and flows in the same units. Another method in the physical sciences is to know the conversion coefficient, e.g., one gram equals one cubic centimetre of distilled water or the change in energy, in ergs, is equal to the change in mass, in grams, times $(3 \times 10^{10})^2$ or, more simply, one foot equals 12 inches.

Contemporary accounting follows a procedure similar to the conversion coefficient method. Each quantity stock and flow is multiplied by a *valuation coefficient* denoted here by p_{ij}. The rules for assigning valuation coefficients in pure 'historical cost-realization convention' accounting are quite simple and straightforward.

First, we stipulate that the valuation coefficient of a dollar is unity. Second, we stipulate that all flows either (a) have an inflow or an outflow of dollars, or (b) have a previously assigned valuation coefficient. Third, the sum of each flow is zero. That is, p_{ij} is a positive real number assigned to each term in each flow such that

$$(2) \quad p_{ij}\,\Delta q_{ij} + p_{ik}\,\Delta q_{ik} = 0; \quad (\Delta q_{ij} \circledR \Delta q_{ik})$$

Fourth, the quantities are independently determined. Fifth, a valuation coefficient, once assigned, remains constant.

Note that three of the four variables are given when there is an inflow or outflow of dollars and thus the unknown valuation coefficient can be calculated. A dollar flow is necessary for the original assignation of a valuation coefficient.

5. These references are to Paton and Littleton, *An Introduction to Corporate Accounting Standards* (American Accounting Association, 1940) and Vatter, *The Fund Theory of Accounting* (Chicago, University of Chicago Press, 1947), but I think that the physical base pervades accounting thought.

In subsequent flows the previously calculated valuation coefficient is used and again three of the four variables are known and the fourth can be calculated.

The above rules can be applied to all of the ordinary transactions in accounting. For example,

a. Investment

$$\text{Book value per share} = \frac{\text{Inflow of dollars*}}{\text{Number of shares*}}$$

b. Purchase (of inventory or any asset subject to amortization, depreciation or depletion)

$$\text{Cost per unit} = \frac{\text{Outflow of dollars*}}{\text{Number of units*}}$$

c. Internal Transformation

$$\text{Cost per product} = \frac{\text{Previously assigned p times quantities used*}}{\text{Number of products*}}$$

d. Sale

$$\text{Increase in book value per share or income per share} = \frac{\text{Inflow of dollars* minus outflow of quantity* of products times previously assigned p.}}{\text{Number of shares*}}$$

The above examples do not exhaust the entries of historical cost accounting and thus they do not prove the fidelity of the valuation rules. However, they are highly suggestive. Of course, there are exceptions but I wish to concentrate on the ordinary cases, on the general rules instead of the exceptions.[6]

The important point is that the quantities are always the independent variables (starred), the valuation coefficients are the *dependent variables*. Valuation coefficients are a well-defined function of related quantity flows, they are routine calculations that can be relegated to a computer.[7] Quantities, on the other hand, have to be independently determined and the increments and decrements must be related. The computer cannot do this, these are required inputs, data.

Given this I conclude that accountants account for quantities, not 'costs'. That is, cost to an accountant means a specific mathematical calculation based upon

6. The exceptions are of three kinds: (1) a flow where cash (or near-cash) is not involved and there is an independent valuation, e.g., a trade of real assets or stock issuance for property; (2) revaluations in the absence of a flow, e.g., market in lower of cost or market or quasi-reorganizations; and (3) standard costs.

7. Mr. Arnold Koweek (Harpur College, Binghamton, N.Y.) has written a programme based on these rules with rather good results for simple problems. A more elaborate programme incorporating a valuation preference array and exception routines is in process. I am indebted to Peter Vukasin and Harpur College for support of this project.

quantities and their relations. Inventory is the paradigm case and ought to make this intuitively clear:

$$\left[\frac{\text{dollars outflow}}{\text{units inflow}}\right] (\text{units inflow} - \text{units outflow}) = \text{Inventory}$$

By the distributive law we can write

$$\left[\frac{\text{dollars outflow}}{\text{units inflow}}\right] \text{units inflow} - \left[\frac{\text{dollars outflow}}{\text{units inflow}}\right] \text{units outflow} = \text{Inventory}$$

or

Purchases — Cost of Goods Sold = Inventory

and these are the three terms for our financial statements:
Purchases is a use of funds, cost of goods sold an expense and inventory an asset. The only thing required for calculating these costs is to be able to *count* and *relate* the outflows to the inflows. We count the units purchased and the related dollars expended. We then count the units sold (or the units remaining or both), multiply and relate the product to Retained Earnings.

The above is somewhat over-simplified because it excludes the fact that we usually make these calculations by purchase *lot* and set up a beginning inventory. To take account of this mathematically all that is needed is a term for each lot but, as we shall see, it complicates the relation task. Let

X_i = dollars outflow for lot i.
Y_i = units inflow for lot i.
Z_i = units outflow from lot i.

Then

$$(2.1) \quad \left[\frac{X_1}{Y_1}\right](Y_1 - Z_1) + \left[\frac{X_2}{Y_2}\right](Y_2 - Z_2) + \dots + \left[\frac{X_n}{Y_n}\right](Y_n - Z_n)$$

$$= \text{Inventory for all lots up to n.}$$

When $Y_i = Z_i$ the value of lot i is zero. The terms can be collected and a set of them defined as the beginning inventory. Say, lots 1 to j-1. Then $\left[\frac{X_i}{Y_j}\right] y_j + \dots + \left[\frac{X_n}{Y_n}\right] Y_n$ are the 'purchases'. Mathematically this is trivial but it imposes a difficult (often impossible) task on the accountant. He must *identify* each unit by lot.

This extended example has been given because it can be generalized to other assets. Fixed assets is an inventory of services, a quantity, which is kept by the perpetual inventory method. Prepayments is an inventory of services of various kinds, wasting resources is an inventory of extractable units, cash is an inventory of dollars and so forth. In fact, equation (2.1) can be interpreted as total assets. Let each term represent an inventory of different kinds of units, an asset account, and the sum is total assets.

IV. The Inputs

Sections II and III were an attempt to lay an intuitive base for the construction of an abstract model of accounting. A model, by definition, is an over-simplification of reality and this model is no exception. However, it seems to me that it captures the essential elements of present accounting. These elements are all contained in equation (2). Given this equation and the usual operators of arithmetic, the outputs of accounting — the financial statements — can be defined *mathematically*. I have done this elsewhere.[8] It is true that the financial statements are not simply mathematical formulations, arrangement and reclassification are also important, but the mathematical formulation will provide the *figures* necessary for the preparation of the statements. Thus, equation (2) is the fundamental equation for deriving the figures, cost-values, of financial accounting and therefore it deserves close analysis.

Equation (2) has only two elements: quantities and relations. These are the independent determinations that the accountant must make. Stated another way, if we were to programme accounting on a computer only two kinds of inputs would be required:

a. Quantity increments and decrements.

b. Relations between the increments and decrements.[9]

Everything else can be defined mathematically, built into the programme. For example, we can stipulate that dollars be assigned a valuation coefficient of unity and thereby have the machine calculate all other valuation coefficients.

8. 'Elements of Pure Accounting Theory', *Accounting Review*, January 1967.

9. Two of Ijiri's three axioms are similar: Quantities and Exchanges. He also lists 'Ownership' as an axiom but that seems unnecessary to me. If we can determine the relationship between two quantities at different locations then we have already determined the *source* and it is possible to account by source instead of ownership. The only place where it differs in any significant respect is where income is from customers but owned by shareholders. Even there we maintain a distinction by source when we keep retained earnings in a separate account.

Moreover, it seems to me that we define an entity as a collection of assets for a common purpose and (secondarily) their sources, not the other way around. We are careful to distinguish between business assets and personal assets, both *owned* by the same individual. It seems to me that a notion of obligation, reversal of source flows, is more pertinent than ownership.

Notice that this disagreement is not crucial. I would say that one of Ijiri's axioms is unnecessary and he would probably say that my two requirements are insufficient. For two investigators independently to arrive at agreement on two axioms or requirements is a corroboration. I find this highly encouraging since I have been trying to argue this point for a number of years without any noticeable effect. My colleagues wanted to argue points (e.g., Lifo versus Fifo) which, under this framework, are in principle unresolvable.

However, Ijiri and I differ in other more important respects, the main one being the approach to the problem. He *assumes* that the accountant has 'the amazing ability' to do these things. I am sceptical. See Yuji Ijiri, 'Axioms and Structures of Conventional Accounting Measurement', *Accounting Review*, January 1965, p 36-53.

We can have the machine sum the increments and decrements, distinguish between positive and negative numbers, recall which increments and decrements were related and which were not related, and print out various arrays of these figures in different combinations, e.g., decrements related to retained earnings (expenses), increments related to cash (uses of funds), sum of increments and decrements in the unit category 'tons of coal' (balance of the coal inventory account) and so forth.

This simplifies accounting a great deal and allows us to focus our attention on human judgments and ignore the routine, the mechanical. We can ask what is *involved* in the two inputs.

First, the accountant must *decide what kind of units* he is going to use. Second, he must *determine the number of units* in both the increment and decrement. Third, he must *make the relation*. Let us take these in turn.

Decisions on the kind of units.

This is rarely discussed as a decision problem. Almost all texts list the kinds of units that are in use but they leave the selection up to the reader. The difficulty with this procedure is that it permits different cost-values to be calculated. Depreciation by units of output will be equal to depreciation by years of service if and only if units of output is a linear function of time. Whether or not this is the case is an empirical question. But that question is not given as a criterion for the selection of units. Sometimes it is pointed out that they will give the same results if units of output vary proportionally with time but the sameness of result is not set forth as a requirement for the selection of units.

The decision on units is important because of another consideration. The kinds of units we use are closely related to our conception of 'account'. We need a separate account for each different kind of units. 'Inventory' may contain both tables and chairs but in some place there must be an account for both. If we did not have a separate account we could not value the inventory because the valuation coefficients are different. This may be nothing more than a line on the periodic inventory sheet but it is a *subclass* based on different kinds of units and therefore, to my mind, a different account. Thus, I define an account as a homogeneous collection of units.

This raises what is sometimes called the 'unit of account' problem. Should we conceive of a fleet of trucks as total collection of service-life as in group depreciation or as a collection of individual trucks each with a service-life (in years or miles or ton-miles?) or as a collection of tyres (expensed as discarded or group depreciation?) plus a collection of motors (are new spark plugs maintenance or betterments or a separate inventory?) plus a collection of chassis etc. Of course, an opponent will be quick to point out that a 'truck' is greater than the sum of its parts because of their arrangement. This is true but it starts another chain. A fleet is greater than the sum of individual trucks . . . the firm is greater than the sum of the individual assets. Thus, we might set up one account for the firm by deciding to use 'services to customers' as the quantity.

All of the above may be observed in practice. Roofs are depreciated separately from the building, master valuation accounts are set up (when purchased) to take account of the difference between the whole of the firm and the sum of the assets, material repairs are amortized and reserves for deferred maintenance are created, some units of inventory are thought to be base quantities and others circulating, and so forth.

Another way of viewing this problem is to ask what we ought to *average* over. The valuation coefficient, in all cases except for dollars, is an average. The difference is that sometimes we average over different kinds of units and other times over a smaller or larger number of the same kind of units. The Lifo and Fifo inventory methods average the dollar outflow over a single purchased lot. The so-called moving-average method averages over all the goods on hand. Another difference is what is included in the numerator, what is taken to be the dollar outflow for a specified quantity. For example, in straight-line depreciation we include the dollar outflow for the machine, the purchase price, in calculating the average. The theoretical justification for accelerated depreciation is that maintenance costs are also necessary for the services and if they are not included in the numerator we will not get a true average.

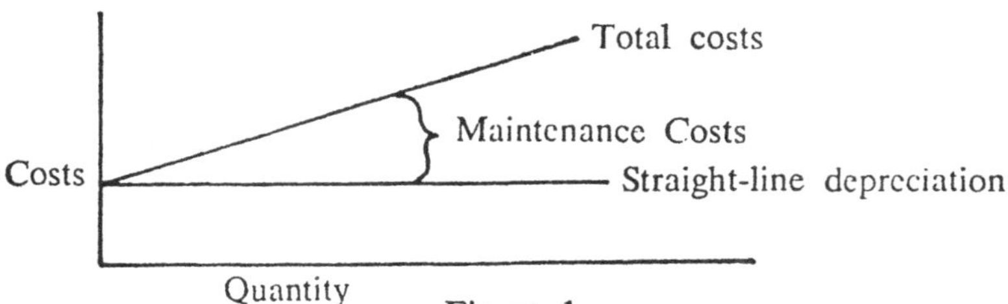

Figure 1

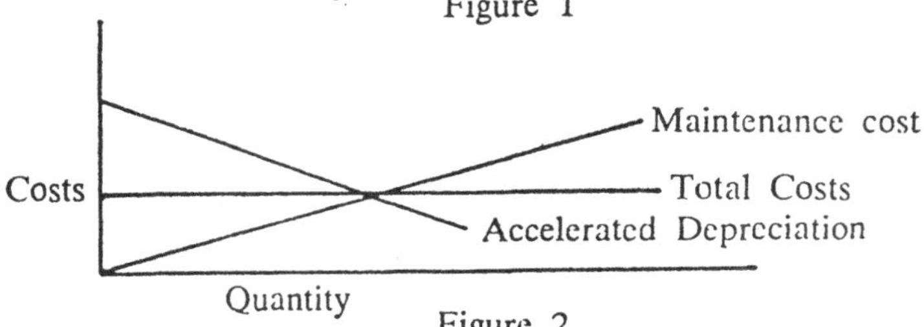

Figure 2

The total costs line in figure 2 gives a 'true' average of all the costs associated with this quantity. A similar type of reasoning is employed in the argument over whether the direct costs or the full costs ought to be averaged over the units produced.

What is included in the numerator is more pertinent to the relationship problem discussed below. For the moment I want to concentrate on the denominator and ask what should be included there. The recent debates over

Lifo versus Fifo have simply assumed that we ought to average by lot. One could argue that, since the units of inventory are homogeneous, the 'true' average is that one obtained by dividing all the goods purchased into all the dollar outflows (weighted-average method) or that the 'true' average is obtained by the moving-average method. Such an argument would be absurd because averages are definitional. For me to say 'the average height is 6 feet' would make no sense because the reader does not know whether I am averaging over adult males in the U.S. or adult males in the Australian bush or adult male toadstools.

We continually calculate averages in accounting, every valuation coefficient is one. Usually we average over different kinds of units but we do not specify what kinds of units are to be used. Sometimes we average over subsets of a given kind of units but we do not specify what that subset ought to be.

The reader may think that this is just the age-old classification problem in a new guise. Classification is of course included in this problem but I am not here interested in functional versus organizational classes. Instead I am trying to ask a fundamental question: What ought we to account for? In the previous sections I tried to demonstrate that we account for quantities. Here I want to know what kinds of units ought to be used and to demonstrate that the question is non-trivial.[10]

Determination of Quantities

Suppose that we settle on the kinds of units to be used and move to the problem of determining their numerosity. The problem is important because the cost-values are dependent upon the quantities.

Unfortunately, the operation by which these quantities are determined is usually discussed only in the easiest cases, i.e., in the cases where the discussion is probably unnecessary. Almost any auditing text will give explicit rules for counting cash and inventory. The degree of uniformity on the quantities in these accounts is near-perfect because the operation is so well understood. Every accountant knows how to count cash and any disagreement between two counts can be eliminated by repeating the operation.

Moving down the balance sheet however, the description of the operation becomes quite vague and finally dismissed as an estimate or assumption. Textbook problems invariably state the years of life of a fixed asset as a datum. The life of an intangible can be found by looking back in the chapter for the proper assumption. What happens in practice? How are we supposed to determine the life of an asset when there is no text to state it as a datum?

We could rely on the foreman, engineer or manager to supply the quantities but, given the rules for valuation coefficients, accounting would be reduced to multiplication and auditing reduced to checking the accuracy of the product.

10. The non-triviality of this question would be granted without argument in the physical sciences. The typical elementary text in Physics will begin with a discussion of units and dimensions. But the discussion does not stop there. Einstein was careful to specify ergs and grams in his famous equation. If he had not, one could use joules and stones and demonstrate that the equation is false.

In a previous age we allowed management to certify to the quantities and the auditor went through the documents to check the accuracy of the product. Since McKesson-Robbins we have been reluctant to do this for inventory. The possibility of similar situations arising ought to make us reluctant to accept managements' determination of other quantities.

Thus, if accounting is to be something more than arithmetical manipulation, and auditing something more than checking arithmetical accuracy, and if we are to avoid further scandals, we must develop a method of determining the quantities. This, however, is a very large order. The acceptable kinds of units are 'future benefits'. Since these are in the future they require a *prediction.*

To a Humean sceptic prediction is a precarious business. Predictions are based on what Keynes has called an unwarranted assumption about the uniformity of nature. Russell has addressed himself to the problem with similar conclusions.[11] The accountant has also been sceptical when the prediction concerns prices or valuation. He asserts that he records what has *actually* occurred. By this he means he records the exchange that occurred but he *values* the assets on the basis of a prediction of the quantity of future benefits.[12]

11. John M. Keynes (*Treatise on Probability,* London, Macmillan and Co. Ltd., 1948, Ch. I), and Bertrand Russell (*Human Knowledge: Its Scope and Limits,* New York, Simon and Shuster, 1948, passim). For an excellent and unanswered short piece see Russell 'On Induction' in *A Modern Introduction to Philosophy,* eds Paul Edwards and Arthur Pap, Glencoe, Illinois, The Free Press, 1959.

12. Assets are things which benefit the *future* and are valued in the *present* at their *past* cost. This is, to say the least, an odd juxtaposition of temporal locations. Temporal confusion is not uncommon in accounting. Even Ijiri is not immune. He says '. . . the basis for historical cost measurement is phenomena that *have* occurred, whereas the basis for market value measurement is phenomena that *could have occurred,* or *can occur* or *will occur*'. (p 51 op cit). Yesterday's market prices were phenomena that did in fact occur at a specific past temporal location. One might argue that yesterday's market price is not relevant to our valuation because we did not exchange but that does not deny its existence. Moreover, the lack of relevance requires exogenous justification because historical cost valuation is, by definition, based on an exchange. To say that it is not relevant because we did not exchange would beg the question.

He goes on in footnote 26 to say 'Nobody reads tomorrow's weather forecast the day after tomorrow, whereas historical records on weather are permanent'. Notice that the quantities of future benefits are forecasts and cost-values are dependent upon those forecasts and thus cost-values are historical records *of forecasts.* On the other hand, historical records of market prices, printed daily in the newspaper along with temperature readings, are 'permanent'.

Pursuit of these differences would probably be fruitful but space prohibits it here. For Ijiri's reply to the above see his footnote 27 which I think commits him to the 'intended use doctrine' which I develop in Chapter VIII of *The Theory of the Measurement of the Income of Trading Enterprises* (forthcoming). Phenomena that did 'in fact' occur is a more difficult problem which I discuss briefly in Chapter III. For more extended discussion see e.g., N. R. Hanson, *Patterns of Discovery* (Cambridge, The University Press, 1958, pp 11-19 et passim), Thomas Kuhn, *The Structure of Scientific Revolutions,* (Chicago, University of Chicago Press, 1962, passim but esp. Ch. 10, 'Revolutions as Changes of World View'), and Henry Margenau, *The Nature of Physical Reality* (New York, McGraw-Hill Book Co., 1950, Sec. 4.2). The Gestalt experiments are also highly illuminating. Professor Hanson's forthcoming *Scientific Observations* addresses the problem in a more systematic fashion.

Predictions of physical processes are difficult enough. A forest ranger, for example, may wish to predict the growth, in board feet, of a collection of trees. In so doing he must, either implicitly or explicitly, predict sunshine, rainfall, insect behaviour, fires, or, in short, all those things that could possibly affect the growth of the trees. In addition, the size of the collection is important. He may refuse to predict for one tree but be willing to do so for a large number. The accountant's prediction contains an equally lengthy array of variables. It is more difficult, however, because his prediction often concerns only one asset and, more importantly, it concerns the accuracy or constancy of human judgment, a notoriously fickle variable.

Human judgment is the primary factor in determining the life of many assets. Hatfield tells us:

> All machinery is on an irresistible march to the junk heap, and its progress, while it may be delayed, cannot be prevented by repairs.

but an antique automobile owner might disagree with this statement. The life of a machine is a function of, depends upon, repairs to that machine. Otherwise the life of the machine is equal to the life of the necessary part which fails first. The Army is well aware of this fact. The life of a truck in combat is very short, not because it is destroyed, but because it is rather difficult to get anyone to do repairs in a combat situation. Thus, a flat tyre or an empty gasoline tank ends the life.

Antique automobiles and army trucks are extreme cases but they serve to emphasize the point. The life of a machine is bounded by the life of the necessary part which fails first and infinity. One can operate at any point between these boundaries by varying the inputs.[13] Management *decides* what 'the life' of an asset is when it decides its input policy. Thus, *in principle* there is no way of determining this kind of quantity. Instead there is a way of deciding what that quantity will be.

If accountants accept 'the life' on the basis of managements' decisions, they must be predicting or assuming (1) that managements' decision, based on a predictive model, is 'correct' and (2) that the decision will remain constant.

13. The inputs to an antique automobile bring up the unit of account problem again. The owners want all the component parts to be original and thus they will repair things that are normally replaced, lamp bulbs for example. In one sense all repairs are replacements. We replace the tungsten element or the piston rod or even the grease and gasoline. The level at which we replace depends on the relative prices of the various inputs and complexes of inputs. It also depends on some elemental physical properties such as metal fatigue or irreversible chemical actions but 'the asset' is never at this elemental level. Hatfield's statement has caused accountants to focus on the wrong things. It was the telling point in the argument for depreciation but it has become a shibboleth used to exclude the *possibility* of appreciation or constant value. If things were truly on an irresistible march to the junk heap then their value would depreciate until it got to the value of junk. Even then the value change need not be regular or unidirectional over any given period of time. There are too many logical problems and counter-examples to permit one to make a priori judgments about de- or ap-preciation. Of course many assets do decline in value over time but that is an empirical generalization and may or may not apply to a particular asset.

These are heroic assumptions for the accountant to make. If the decisions are not correct, say, because of an unpredicted technological or consumer taste change, then the costs will be misallocated. If the management changes its mind about the input policy, the life will vary and thus the costs will be misallocated.[14]

Determination of Relationships

The determination of related increments and decrements is necessary for valuation coefficient calculation. Every journal entry is such a relation, i.e., we make a debit and a related credit, we relate an increase in inventory to a decrease in cash, an increase in cash to a decrease in notes payable,[15] etc. Most texts call this an 'analysis' of transactions. This is a misnomer. We do not analyse (separate) anything, we *relate* two (or more) accounts.

The problem is to *identify* the relationships. Suppose that Z exchanges occur simultaneously. Thus there are Z increments and Z decrements and we know that there is a one-to-one correspondence. How do we identify the related pairs? The benefit theory gives us a criterion for capitalizing some of the increments but does not give a criterion for relating any particular increment to a particular decrement. The attaching concept tells us to attach the costs to the related quantities but does not tell us how to identify that quantity.

According to the textbooks it is possible to determine net income by constructing a balance sheet at two different dates. This is mathematically true but the difficulty lies in determining the values on the balance sheet. The balance sheets can be constructed only if complete data on all exchanges involving asset acquisition is given. Consider the following:

Balance Sheet 31 December 1964

Cash	\$1000	Net Worth	\$1000

Balance Sheet 31 December 1965

Inventory (1000 widgets)	\$x	Net Worth	\$x

By following historical cost valuation rules the value of x cannot be calculated because it is the product of 1000 and an unknown valuation coefficient. That is, the *cost* of the inventory can never be determined unless we know the related cash decrement.[16]

14. Note the character of the argument for historical cost valuation of fixed assets. Market values are said to be irrelevant because the asset is intended for use, not sale. The going concern 'basic concept' assumes that the business will continue long enough 'to use up the assets according to the plans and expectation presently held'. (Paul Grady, *Inventory of Generally Accepted Accounting Principles for Business Enterprises*, New York, American Institute of Certified Public Accountants, 1965, p 28.) This leads other observers to claim that 'the future is known to the firm for certain' is a necessary assumption for validity of accounting values. Edgar O. Edwards and Philip W. Bell, *The Theory and Measurement of Business Income*, Berkeley and Los Angeles, University of California Press, 1961, p 7.

15. Credits and credit balances have a negative sign in this framework.

16. Of course the inventory can be independently valued by various methods. None of these methods, however, will yield historical cost-value except by accident.

Thus, the identification of related quantities is crucial to the operation of accounting but the question of how this identification is made remains. The usual textbook method is to use a series of synonyms. We have certain words that imply the identity of the related quantities, e.g., purchase, sale, collection, debt retirement, put in process, etc. All of these terms describe an exchange. The only difference between them is that they describe exchanges between particular quantities or classes of quantities.

We tell our students to 'record the purchase of 500 widgets for $1000 on account'. The following associations are made:

Purchase = asset debit; cash or monetary equity credit.
Widgets = the unit category of inventory, therefore the asset 'inventory'.
On Account = accounts payable, a specific monetary equity; therefore, not cash.

This is an exercise in synonym association. 'Purchase' *means* asset, not expense or any other class of accounts. 'Widget' *means* a unit of inventory and thus narrows it to a particular asset account. Given the general constraint of equal debits and credits, the entry reduces to the simplest of logical associations. At a later time we will tell him to 'record the sale of 200 widgets for $500'. 'Sale' *means* asset debit, revenue credit. '$500' (without further specification) *means* cash, and so forth.

The difficulty with this method of identification is that the student must know all the words. Without a general criterion the student cannot determine the related quantities by reason. It is like learning vocabulary. Either you have looked it up in the dictionary or you do not know the meaning. Unfamiliar words—unless you can infer from the context, i.e., know all the surrounding words and have a good grasp of the topic—have no meaning. The same is true with unfamiliar exchanges.

In the intermediate course the student is told in bold type 'Depreciation is an expense' and this means that Retained Earnings is related to a value decrement in a fixed asset. 'Depreciation of factory equipment' appears analogous but if the student reasons this way, he errs. The student must *know,* he cannot reason, that depreciation of factory equipment is related to Factory Overhead.

Unfamiliar exchanges present exactly the same problem to the experienced accountant. Witness the flap over stock options, leased equipment, pension plans, etc. It may be argued that the fact that these are new and unfamiliar exchanges is the reason for the debate on the relationships. This will not hold, however, because there are many ancient and familiar exchanges which are still debated. Direct costing is a recent example. Whether or not fixed factory costs are related (ought to be attached) to the units produced is not any nearer settlement than the investment credit controversy. For that matter, the mundane problems of freight, material handling costs, scrap, by-products, packaging costs, storage costs, etc., are still open questions. It just does not happen to be fashionable to debate them at this time. The N.A.A. survey reveals that about half the companies relate storage costs, for example, to the inventory and the other half relates them to retained earnings as a selling expense. When there is this much diversity in recording an activity that is as old as accounting, one must conclude that there is some difficulty in perceiving the relationship.

The reason for this difficulty is that accountants look for *causal* connections.[17] The literature on direct costing is pervaded with causal arguments. Costs that vary with, are caused by, production ought to be attached to the products. The full costers reply that fixed costs are also *necessary* for production. Thus, they apply the same argument but use different cut-off points. The same is true in the general rule to 'capitalize all costs reasonably necessary to acquire this asset'. 'Necessary to acquire' can be translated into 'costs caused by this acquisition' with little distortion. Again the cut-off point is different; some cut off at freight, others at handling charges and so forth. Of course, causal tracing must be cut off at some point on pain of infinite regress. Aristotle cut it off at the first mover, Aquinas at God and modern scientists cut it off at the laws of nature.[18] Accountants also have to cut it off but the question is: Where?

This question is impossible to answer in accounting because, in one sense, the causal relations are *circular*. The usual examples in philosophy are linear, e.g., Abraham begat Isaac who begat Jacob who begat Joseph . . . which permits Aquinas to reverse directions to Terah . . . Shem . . . Adam and stop at God.

If this were a circle in which, say, Joseph begat Adam the genealogy becomes repetitive and there is no unassailable starting or stopping point. Compare this to a going concern. We often find diagrams such as:

[cash] —purchases→ [merchandise] —sale→ [cash] —repeat→

These may be made more complex by including collections, internal conversions, etc., but the important point is that they repeat, they form a circle. Thus, purchases are necessary for sales but if the firm is to continue going it must replenish its stock. In order to replenish its stock it must have cash which necessitates a sale. Thus, all purchasing expenses are selling expenses and all selling expenses are purchasing expenses and so forth indefinitely. The circle can be

17. In *The Theory of the Measurement of the Income of Trading Enterprises* I present three inductively derived principles of accounting: Conservatism, Causality and Convenience. I argue that conservatism is the fundamental reason for historical costs (as opposed to other valuation schemes), causality is the rationale used for manipulating the figures and convenience is appealed to when it is too troublesome to trace all the causes. Thus, I think that causal tracing is fundamental in traditional accounting thought. This is conjecture about how other people think and subject to all the frailties of doing that sort of thing. Many of my colleagues deny that they use any notion of causality and I accept their word. However, their substitutes mystify me. For example, 'fairness', 'truthfulness', 'rational allocation' are all desirable but I am unable to relate two accounts by their application.

18. See T. Patterson Brown, 'Infinite Causal Regression', forthcoming in *The Philosophical Review*, for an excellent summary and analysis of various causal arguments.

arbitrarily chopped up and certain activities *defined* as selling, manufacturing, purchasing, etc. This reverts to the synonym method. Storage costs would mean debit inventory or debit expense depending upon the way we defined it. However, a definition is different from a determination or an identification. Given the circularity of a going concern in which all actions are necessary for all other actions, determination of the cause is, in principle, impossible.

The circular view of the firm is often used for freshmen but it is much too simple. Suppose we neglect the going concern circle or agree that cash is at the apex of all causal tracing. Everyone agrees that cash affects people's behaviour. There is, in a pecuniary economy, a directly perceivable effect of a monetary outlay: a dime on the counter is both necessary and sufficient to acquire a cup of coffee, cream, sugar, a place to sit, heat, light, shelter and perhaps a smile from the waitress. However, we have known since, at least, Mill that 'a principle is wanting to apportion' that cost to the various services provided.[19] That is, even when the connection can be established there is, in principle, no way to allocate joint costs. Of course, we do allocate joint costs, usually on the basis of sales value. This is justified as a search for 'a cost that is an index of the products' ability to generate [cause] revenue'[20] and we have completed the circle again. If the selling price is a mark-up on cost the circle is vicious.

The joint cost problem is too well known to belabour here but the pervasiveness of joint costs is perhaps not so well known. Above I asked what we would average over. Here I would like to ask: Why average? Accountants are probably more satisfied with the valuation coefficient for inventory than with any other. But this is a joint cost of a sort also. 'The cost' is of a lot, a car load, of inventory and the calculated valuation coefficient is almost certain to be different from the price per unit.[21] Thus, there is no descriptive correlate or empirical verification for this valuation coefficient. That would lead some philosophers of science to claim that this dimension is not extensive or additive.[22] Averages probably satisfy our sense of fairness but there is no unassailable method of allocating a dollar outflow to 100 different inventory units any more than there is to allocating a dollar outflow to a beef and beef hide.

19. John Stuart Mill, *Principles of Political Economy*, edited by W. J. Ashley, 1921, p 570.
20. Charles T. Horngren, *Cost Accounting, A Managerial Emphasis*, Englewood Cliffs, Prentice-Hall Inc., 1962, p 447.
21. See also Arthur L. Thomas, 'The Amortization Problem: A Simplified Model and Some Unanswered Questions', *Journal of Accounting Research*, Spring 1965, pp 103-114.
22. These terms are those of Bergmann, and he would probably argue that valuation coefficients are not additive. For a dimension to be extensive there needs to be a physical operation of combination which, when a measurement operation is performed on the combination, results in a number that is equal to the sum of the numbers obtained from the operation performed on the parts. Thus, if the price per unit is different from the valuation coefficient the sum of the individual prices would not equal the price of a lot. Therefore, valuation coefficients have no descriptive correlates but note that this problem applies with equal force to those who wish to value the assets at market. The sum of the prices of the assets is likely to be different from the price of the combination and thus the sum has no descriptive correlate. Gustav Bergmann, 'The Logic of Measurement', *State University of Iowa Studies in Engineering*, 1956.

Even if there were an unassailable way of allocating joint costs, the fact that they exist would present us with a network of causal connections of almost unbelievable complexity. These multiple connections and/or the sheer number of connections leads me to agree with Chambers' characterization of a firm as a 'black box'.[23] I also agree that the connections are in principle definable or, to put it another way, the necessary conditions for any given operation are enumerable. Businessmen do, in fact, enumerate the necessary conditions for producing products, making sales, etc. In general, this enumeration encompasses all of the other activities of the firm and the circle is again complete.

VI. Summary and Concluding Remarks

Accounting can be represented by a rather simple physical analogue. This analogue will yield 'financial' statements that exhibit all the mathematical features of accounting. However, such statements lack meaning because they may be operations on heterogeneous units.

There is a set of valuation rules which permit the calculation of a valuation coefficient. This closely resembles a conversion coefficient and, presumably, its application converts the units into a homogeneous set so that arithmetical operations can be legitimately performed.

Such a procedure requires the accountant to determine quantities and relations between quantity changes. These requirements were examined from an operationalist's point of view. The weakest conclusion to be drawn is that the accountant is required to do things that are operationally undefined. The strongest conclusion is that they are, in principle, impossible to perform.

If one settles for the weak conclusion, the obvious corollary is that we ought to get busy and *operationally* define these requirements. Until this is done there can be no uniformity or comparability of cost-values. The lack of uniformity that I am talking about does not spring from the current hot issues. These have been well documented and the divergency calculated. Bows, for example, calculates an income variation of a factor of three because of Lifo versus Fifo, accelerated versus straight-line, etc., and urges reform on *method*.[24] My concern is not with these issues. Instead it is with the fundamental requirements of determining quantities and relationships. The divergence here can be empirically tested. One simple way is to select an elementary problem and delete all references to the life of the assets. Another way is to present an exchange for which there is no synonym, e.g., an ordinance which requires the installation of a fire escape. (This clearly does not add to the existing capacity but it is necessary for any capacity.) Some CPA friends have worked problems of this kind. The cost-value varies from a factor of about two to ten even after they have been adjusted to the same method.

I prefer the strong conclusion. The fact that these requirements have not yet been operationally defined is additional, albeit weak, evidence for this conclusion.

23. R. J. Chambers, *Accounting, Evaluation and Economic Behavior*, Englewood Cliffs, Prentice-Hall Inc, 1966, p 252.

24. Albert J. Bows, 'The Urgent Need for Accounting Reforms', *N.A.A. Bulletin*, September 1960, p 44.

If the strong conclusion is valid, then we must resign ourselves to lack of uniformity and comparability. No court or principles board could possibly adjudicate upon all the disputes, or define all the quantities and relationships.

An alternative to resignation is to modify or abandon the traditional theory. Previous arguments for this alternative have been singularly unsuccessful. There are many reasons why accountants reject proposed theories or schemes of valuation. However, there is one in particular that appears in almost every argument, viz., historical costs are supposed to be objective and verifiable while other methods of valuation are not. Many observers have denied that historical costs are objective under any reasonable definition of that term. Yet, objectivity as justification for retaining historical costs persists.[25] If nothing else, I hope that this paper casts some doubt on the objectivity of the fundamental operations of accounting. Goldstein[26] has written:

> The more I think about it, the stronger becomes my feeling that it would be entirely beneficial if the words 'subjective' and 'objective' could be expunged from the vocabulary of philosophy.

This is doubly true for accounting.

Finally, the limited scope of this paper should be noted. I have concentrated on what might be called the internal workings of accounting. I have said nothing about the outputs of the system or their recipients, but that is another story.

September 1966

25. 'Accountants . . . argue that cost can be measured with greater accuracy and objectivity than a more relevant concept . . .' (George J. Staubus, op cit, p 412). I agree that they do argue this way but I think 'objectivity' in such contexts has, at most, emotive content.

26. Leon J. Goldstein, book review, *The Journal of Philosophy*, Spring 1965, p 191.

Elements of Pure Accounting Theory

Robert R. Sterling

THE purpose of this paper is to abstract a general statement of present accounting theory. It is an attempt to describe, in quasi-formal fashion, what accountants do when they account. It is an attempt to connect what previous theorists have said about accounting. It is not an attempt to present a new theory of accounting. Most of what follows could be stated much more formally in either the notation of symbolic logic or mathematics. Such a presentation would have the advantages of brevity and rigor. It would also have the disadvantage of being unintelligible to a large segment of accountants. For this reason, I have used only the bare minimum of symbols. Nevertheless it is hoped that the result is sufficiently formal so that this statement can (1) be used to test the present theory, and (2) be used as a relief for proposed theories of accounting.

Unexpired and Expired Costs.

Much of the accounting theory in recent years has been stated in terms of expired and unexpired costs. The recent *Inventory of Generally Accepted Accounting Principles* makes repeated reference to the notion.[1] Costs are said to "benefit" and the distinction between them is temporal: costs that are expected to benefit the future are defined as "unexpired," and those that have no future benefit are defined as "expired."

This notion plays a basic role in Paton and Littleton's *Standards*. They list "Costs Attach" and "Effort and Accomplishment" as "basic concepts" of accounting.[2] These are now known as the "matching" and "attaching" concepts. The present literature, however, errs in combining and confusing two things which Paton and Littleton separated. "Costs Attach" has an understood prepositional phrase. It must mean that they attach *to something*. Thus, when we match costs with revenues we must also be matching the something-to-which-they-attach with revenues. Costs, per se, cannot benefit the future; it is the something to which the costs attach which brings about the benefit. "Initially, cost incurrence produces an asset or provides a service, the benefits of which are expected to produce present or future revenues."[3] I think that the correct interpretation is that the "*assets or services* produce revenue" and that the costs attach to those assets or services. Paton and Littleton, although not always as clear and consistent

[1] Paul Grady, *Accounting Research Study No. 7* (American Institute of Certified Public Accountants; 1965), pp. 99 and 228.

[2] W. A. Patton and A. C. Littleton, *An Introduction to Corporate Accounting Standards* (American Accounting Association, Monograph No. 3, 1940).

[3] Paul Grady, p. 99.

Robert R. Sterling is a Visiting Research Fellow in the Economics Department, Yale University.

on this point as one would prefer, state it explicitly when they write: " . . . all costs incurred should be viewed as ultimately clinging to definite items of goods sold or service rendered."[4] When speaking of the concept of "measured consideration," e.g., when they are arguing for the "price-aggregate" (cost) method of valuation they write: "Accounting uses money-price only because it is a convenient common denominator by which diverse objects and services are expressed homogenously and because it is the common mode of expressing bargained exchanges. It is not "money" that is significant; it is not "price" that is significant. "Service" is the significant element behind the accounts, that is, service-potentialities . . . "[5]

Thus, service-potentialities are the *significant elements;* money-price is used only because it is *convenient.* Vatter develops this concept further and makes service-potentials the basis for his definition of assets. He carefully draws the distinction between assets and the method of valuing them.[6] Many other writers have drawn the same, or a similar, distinction. "Costs benefit" is a confusing phrase which neither describes what accountants do nor how they think. Conversely, a sharp distinction between (1) service potential and (2) valuation of service potentials facilitates the development of a model which reflects the current state of accounting theory and explains a great deal of accounting practice. For this reason I emphasize the distinction and will discuss the two concepts seriatim.

Units and Definitions

The concept of service-potentialities is well established in accounting. They are thought to be the "homogeneous substance" and the "significant elements" of assets. Thus, assets may be thought of as a *set,* the elements of which are service-potentialities (for brevity, "potens" henceforth). A characteristic common to all potens is that they "have the ability to satisfy human wants." Economists use "utility" to describe want satisfaction and "util" to describe a unit of utility. Thus, a poten may be described as a unit of potential utility, a potential util.

(1) x = a poten, a unit of potential utility.

There is a universal set, X, which contains all potens.

(1.1) $$X = \{x: x \text{ is a poten}\}$$

The universal set may be partitioned in any convenient manner and the subsets identified and named. One such method of partitioning results in "objects."

(1.2) $$X_i \subset X; \quad i = 1 \cdots r$$

Although this conception has theoretical usefulness, the number of potens contained in any object has not been operationally defined. The difficulties encountered in the attempts to measure utility are well known. There is at least equal, and probably greater, difficulty in the measurement of potential utility. In all likelihood, this difficulty is the explanation for the virtual abandonment of "potens" and the development of the "concept of capacity."

The concept of capacity, although only relatively recently named, has been used in accounting since, at least, the advent of depreciation. Assets are thought of as "bundles of services" and the number of services in most assets declines over time or use. This is ordinarily expressed as

(1.3) $$\frac{\text{Net cost of total services}}{\text{Number of services}}$$

$$= \text{Amortization or value per unit of service}$$

This is a ubiquitous expression. It is used for amortization of all kinds of assets, e.g., depreciation of fixed assets, depletion of

[4] Paton and Littleton, p. 15.
[5] Paton and Littleton, p. 13.
[6] William J. Vatter, *The Fund Theory of Accounting* (University of Chicago Press; 1947), pp. 16–17.

wasting assets, assigning unit costs to inventory lots whether by purchase or manufacture, interest amortization, expense accruals of various kinds, etc. It can be expanded to include many other accounts if it is restated as

$$(1.4) \quad \frac{\text{Value of things}}{\text{Number of things}} = \text{Value per thing}$$

This now includes income accruals, equity averages such as income per share, book value per share, etc.

Given the omnipresent nature of this expression, it is obvious that the "things" are an important part of accounting. I prefer to call these things "caps," representing an abbreviation for "units of capacity." Thus, "cap" is the generic term for all the various units of measure that are used in accounting. For example, ton-miles for delivery equipment, space-time for buildings, units of output or hours used for equipment depreciated on a use basis, units of time for equipment depreciated on time, units of time for interest, insurance, etc., shares of stock for net worth, and so forth.

A cap, then, is any "physical" unit that is utilized in accounting. It is used as a substitute for potens since the quantity of caps, presumably, can be determined and the number of potens cannot. Thus, a cap is a representation of an undefined number of potens.

Each object possesses at least one "physical" dimension. Let μ_i denote the appropriate measure function for X_i. It may be that X_i possesses more than one dimension, e.g., both weight and volume. However, when it is measured by the jth measure function it will be considered as belonging to the jth class of objects. That is, the measure function applied to an object or set of objects determines the class within which that object falls. The application of a measure function to an object or set of objects results in a quantity denoted by q_i.

(1.5) q_i = a quantity of caps of the ith category representing a collection of potens contained in an object.

(1.6) $q_i = \mu_i(X_i)$

The concept of "account" is best described as a homogeneous collection of caps. Different accounts will contain different kinds of caps and the accounts may contain different physical representations of the caps, but each account will contain only one kind of cap. For example, the account "Delivery Equipment" may contain pickups, stakes, semi-trailers, panel trucks, etc. The element common to all is the caps—ton-miles—that each contains. "Buildings" may contain many structures of various shapes and sizes but the common element is space-time caps that they furnish. Reclassification and combination of accounts is similar. "Work-in-process" is a collection of fractional units of product which was transferred from "materials," a collection of, say, board feet; labor, a collection of hours of effort; and overhead, a collection of ancillary services to the factory. That is, "materials" is transferred into work-in-process by changing the conception of the caps from board feet to units of product.

The quantity of caps in an account may vary over time. The temporal location of the quantities will be indicated by adding a second subscript and the following symbols used.

(1.7) q_{it} = the quantity of caps in the ith account at the tth moment.

(1.8) $\Delta q_{it} = q_{it} - q_{it-1}$; the change in the number of caps in the ith account from $t-1$ to t.

(1.9) $\Delta^+ q_{it} = \Delta q_{it}; \Delta q_{it} > 0$; a cap increment in q_i.

(1.10) $\Delta^- q_{it} = \Delta q_{it}; \Delta q_{it} < 0$; a cap decrement in q_i.

The process by which the quantities change is a *transfer* of objects from one account class to another. That is, an object in the ith account, and therefore measured in ith caps, may be put in the jth account and measured in jth caps. This may be viewed from two directions: as a cap increment in the jth account or a cap decrement in the ith account. This process is called an exchange and is here denoted by Ⓡ.

(1.11) $\Delta^{+}q_{it}$ Ⓡ $\Delta^{-}q_{jt}$

The exchange is the only way in which quantities of caps can change. Thus, for every decrement there is an increment. Occasionally the exchange relationship may be between more than two accounts, e.g.,

(1.12) $\Delta^{+}q_{it}$ Ⓡ $\Delta^{-}q_{jt}, \Delta^{-}q_{kt}$

That is, there may be a simultaneous transfer from the jth and kth accounts to the ith account. Ordinarily it is possible to segregate such transfers and consider them as two separate exchanges. For this reason, and also for ease of exposition, the exchange relationship will be spoken of as if it involves only two accounts unless specified otherwise.

The transfer in (1.11) above is from the jth account to the ith account and therefore involves the transformation of caps of the jth category to caps of the ith category. Such a transformation, however, does not necessarily require a change in physical form. It may be accomplished by applying a different measure function. For example, the caps in the jth account may be in volume units and the caps in the ith account in weight units.

The functional relationship between the quantities of caps in an exchange may be determined by a measurement operation or by a similarity transformation. We may independently measure both the increment and decrement and thus determine the function. It may be that this function is unique, and therefore an independent measurement for each exchange is required. Conversely, the function may be constant for all exchanges between two given accounts. If the latter is true, this is a similarity transformation, and the number of caps in either account, but not both, may be determined by a mathematical operation. A homely example is the similarity transformation of feet to inches. A transfer from an account in which the caps are inches to an account in which the caps are feet may be accomplished by measuring either the increment or decrement and then multiplying by 12 or 1/12 and then assigning the product to the other account. In this case 12 or 1/12, as appropriate, is the similarity transformation.

Homogeneity of units is a necessary, although not a sufficient, condition for arithmetical operations. In order for the sum of the numbers assigned to two accounts to have descriptive correlates, meaning, the units must be homogeneous. The simplest way of accomplishing this is by use of a similarity transformation. The similarity transformation appropriate to accounting will be called a "valuation coefficient." It should be emphasized, however, that valuation coefficient (for brevity, "valco" henceforth) in this context is purely a mathematical operation and has nothing to do with axiology or prices.

A valco, p, is defined as a positive real number that is assigned to each term in each exchange such that

(1.13) $p_{it}\Delta^{+}q_{it} + p_{jt}\Delta^{-}q_{jt} = 0$
($\Delta^{+}q_{it}$ Ⓡ $\Delta^{-}q_{jt}$)

The zero sum of (1.13) is implied by the accounting axiom that debits equal credits. Of course, there are an infinite number of valcos which will meet the zero sum requirement. The rules for selecting a particular pair of valcos will be discussed below.

It is obvious that the valcos of accounting will eventually be given a dollar sign.

Note, however, that (1.13) is common to similarity transformations in general, and thus there is nothing peculiar about dollar valuation in this context. The essential characteristic is the *exchange*. For example, suppose that 36 inches of material is transferred from one pile to another. In the second pile the material is measured in feet.

$$(1.14) \quad \Delta^+(x \text{ feet}) + \Delta^-(36 \text{ inches}) = 0$$

Solving for x yields

$$(1.15) \quad 3 + (1/12)(-36) = 0,$$

which confirms our previous knowledge about the similarity transformation of inches to feet. The term "exchange" implies a zero sum. It is, in essence, a "conservation law" and may be likened to the conservation laws (energy, mass, momentum) of physics.

A situation more analogous to dollar-cost valuation follows. Suppose that we have a bar of metal that is now being measured in both cubic inches and pounds. That is, we know that there are 36 cubic inches and that there are 2 pounds per cubic inch. Suppose we transfer this bar to an oven, melt it down, and independently determine that we have 4 gallons of molten metal. The caps are the cubic inches and gallons; the valcos are the pounds per cubic inch and the pounds per gallon.

$$(1.16) \quad p_g(\Delta^+ \text{ 4 gallons}) + 2(\Delta^- \text{ 36 cubic inches}) = 0$$

Solving for p_g yields

$$(1.17) \quad (18)(4) + 2(-36) = 0$$

This is more analogous because almost all accounting exchanges are stated as *dollars per cap*. In fact, this example is the logical isomorph of the ubiquitous expression given in (1) above. This example also emphasizes the conservation assumption. The pounds per gallon figure could be determined independently and it may or may not equal 18. (Perhaps some evaporated and thus in order to apply the law of conservation of mass, the experiment would have to be in a closed, isolated system in which the vapor could be accounted for.) On the other hand, in accounting the *caps are independently determined* but the *valcos are always treated as similarity transformations*, i.e., the valcos are determined in precisely the same way as the pounds per gallon in the above example.

The point of this discussion is to indicate that valcos—similarity transformations—are not peculiar to accounting and that they may be viewed as a physical device or a logical concept. In this way disputes over valuation methods may be segregated from the body of the theory. The "cost" valco presently in use is discussed below.

The number of caps in an account has been referred to as a "quantity," the valco as a "coefficient" of that quantity. The product will be called a "value."

(1.18) $\Delta v_{it} = p_{it}\Delta q_{it}$; a value increment(decrement) in the ith account at the tth moment.

(1.19) $v_{it} = \sum_{j=1}^{t} \Delta v_{ij}$; the value of the ith account at the tth moment.

Matrices

The above definitions may be viewed as five $m \times n$ matrices. Each row is the account classification and each column is the temporal location.

$$(2.1) \quad \Delta Q = (\Delta q_{it})$$

$$(2.2) \quad Q = (q_{it})$$

$$(2.3) \quad P = (p_{it})$$

$$(2.4) \quad \Delta V = (\Delta v_{it})$$

$$(2.5) \quad V = (v_{it})$$

The five matrices are related in the following ways: each element of Q is equal to the row sum of ΔQ.

(2.6) $$q_{it} = \sum_{j=1}^{t} \Delta q_{ij}$$

Each element of ΔV is the product of the elements of ΔQ and P.

(2.7) $$\Delta v_{it} = p_{it}\Delta q_{it}$$

Each element of V is equal to the row sum of ΔV.

(2.8) $$v_{it} = \sum_{j=1}^{t} \Delta v_{ij}$$

Since the caps are heterogeneous, the column sums of ΔQ and Q have no descriptive correlates.

(2.9) $$\sum_{i=1}^{m} \Delta q_{it} = \text{undefined}$$

(2.10) $$\sum_{i=1}^{m} q_{it} = \text{undefined}$$

And because the sum of each exchange is zero, each Δv_{it} is offset by an equal value change. These can be paired off and summed. Therefore,

(2.11) $$\sum_{i=1}^{m} \Delta v_{it} = 0$$

(2.12) $$\sum_{i=1}^{m} v_{it} = 0$$

In other words, values are created (recorded) only at exchange and since the sum of each exchange is zero, the sum of all values is zero.

Balance Sheet

The financial statements may be formed by various operations on the value matrices. A balance sheet is an array of values at a point in time. Thus, it is simply a column vector of V.

(3.1) $$V_t = \begin{bmatrix} v_1 \\ v_2 \\ \cdot \\ \cdot \\ \cdot \\ v_m \end{bmatrix}$$

V_t contains all the elements of a balance sheet at time t. However, the elements with opposite signs are segregated. Each element with a value greater than zero will be defined as the value of an asset account. These asset accounts are quantities of homogeneous caps with a positive sign (and thus potens with a positive sign) which have been assigned a valco at the time of exchange in accordance with (1.13). They may be interpreted as a class of things which have the ability, either directly or indirectly, to satisfy human wants.

(3.2) $$a_{it} = v_{it}; \qquad v_{it} > 0$$

(3.3) $$A_t = \begin{bmatrix} a_1 \\ a_2 \\ \cdot \\ \cdot \\ \cdot \\ a_s \end{bmatrix}$$

Each element with a value less than zero will be defined as the value of an equity account. These are quantities of caps with a negative sign (and thus negative potens) which were previously assigned a valco in accordance with (1.13). Negative caps may be interpreted as some person's or group of people's claim on, restriction of, or ownership in the asset accounts.[7]

(3.4) $$e_{it} = v_{it}; \qquad v_{it} < 0$$

[7] An account was previously defined as a homogeneous collection of caps. This is a necessary, but not a sufficient, condition for the definition of equity accounts. Different people have different kinds of claims (usually legally defined) on the assets. These different claims are collected into homogeneous sets and this forms the basis for classifying the negative caps into different equity accounts. Compare John B. Canning, *The Economics of Accountancy* (Ronald Press Co.; 1929).

(3.5) $$E_t = \begin{bmatrix} e_1 \\ e_2 \\ \cdot \\ \cdot \\ e_w \end{bmatrix}$$

The formal balance sheet is the juxtaposition of A_t and E_t. Since the sum of V_t is zero it is obvious that the sums of A_t and E_t are equal in absolute value.

(3.6) $$\sum A_t = -\sum E_t$$

Flow of Funds Statement

The flow of funds statement summarizes an array of value changes that are related by exchange to a group of accounts for a given period of time. The pertinent accounts depend upon the definition of "funds." Sometimes it includes only the cash account, sometimes net quick assets; most often it is net working capital. Let these accounts be denoted by f_i.

(3.7) $f_{it} = v_{it}$; v_{it} is a fund account.

(3.8) $\Delta f_{it} = \Delta v_{it}$; v_{it} is a fund account.

Only the value changes related by an exchange to a fund account are pertinent. Thus, ΔV must be examined and the fund exchanges or the non-fund exchanges identified. That is, the statement may be formed by including all fund exchanges or excluding all non-fund exchanges. Following the usual procedure, I will define it by exclusion. Let

(3.9) $$\Delta\theta_{it} = \sum_{j=s}^{t} \Delta v_{ij}; \qquad \Delta v_{ij} \sim Ⓡ\, \Delta f_{ij};$$
$$\Delta v_{ij} \sim \Delta f_{ij}$$

(3.10) $$\theta_t = \begin{bmatrix} \Delta\theta_1 \\ \Delta\theta_2 \\ \cdot \\ \cdot \\ \Delta\theta_m \end{bmatrix}$$

Then,

(3.11) $$V_t - V_s + \theta_t = \Delta G_t.$$

The column vector ΔG_t contains all the values, Δg_t, necessary for a funds statement. However, the elements are rearranged as follows:

(3.12) $$F_t = \begin{bmatrix} f_1 \\ f_2 \\ \cdot \\ \cdot \\ f_r \end{bmatrix}$$

(3.13) $s_t = \Delta g_t$; $\Delta g_t > 0$; source of funds

(3.14) $u_t = \Delta g_t$; $\Delta g_t < 0$; use of funds

(3.15) $$S_t = \begin{bmatrix} s_1 \\ s_2 \\ \cdot \\ \cdot \\ s_r \end{bmatrix}$$

(3.16) $$U_t = \begin{bmatrix} u_1 \\ u_2 \\ \cdot \\ \cdot \\ u_r \end{bmatrix}$$

The formal flow of funds statement is a juxtapositon of F_t, F_s, S_t, and U_t. It is obvious that

(3.17) $$\sum S_t + \sum U_t = \sum F_t - \sum F_s$$

Income Statement

The income statement is also concerned with value changes related by exchanges to a certain account. Thus, it is similar to the funds statement. The pertinent account in this case is retained earnings. Let y_{it} denote the value of the retained earnings account and Δy_{it} denote changes in its value (dividends are excluded).

The income statement from time s to t may be defined as follows:

(3.18) $\Delta h_{it} = \sum_{j=s}^{t} \Delta v_{ij}$; Δv_{ij} Ⓡ Δy_{ij};

$\Delta v_{ij} \sim \Delta y_{ij}$

(3.19) $$H_t = \begin{bmatrix} \Delta h_1 \\ \Delta h_2 \\ \cdot \\ \cdot \\ \Delta h_m \end{bmatrix}$$

The column vector H_t contains all the values necessary for the income statement. Again, however, they need to be segregated by sign.

(3.20) $r_i = \Delta h_i$; $\Delta h_i > 0$; revenues

(3.21) $c_i = \Delta h_i$; $\Delta h_i < 0$; expenses

(3.22) $$R_t = \begin{bmatrix} r_1 \\ r_2 \\ \cdot \\ \cdot \\ r_a \end{bmatrix}$$

(3.23) $$C_t = \begin{bmatrix} c_1 \\ c_2 \\ \cdot \\ \cdot \\ c_b \end{bmatrix}$$

The income statement is the juxtaposition of R and C and their sums. It is obvious that

(3.24) $\sum R_t + \sum C_t = y_{it} - y_{is}$

Entities

The above remarks should be construed as pertaining to one "entity." There is a collection of entities which have the same or similar account classes. Thus, when the entities are added the various matrices take on a third dimension. That is, the *elements* of the universal matrix are partitioned to form the entity matrices. The entity will be indicated by adding a third subscript. For example, v_{ijk} represents the value of the ith account, at the jth moment in the kth entity.

The method of segregating accounts into entities is accomplished by identifying the purpose of the accounts. They are then collected by common purpose. Thus, an entity may be defined as (1) a collection of asset accounts that have been gathered together for a common purpose and (2) the related equity accounts.

Market and Internal Exchanges

The transfer of caps from one entity to another is defined as a "market-exchange." The transfer of caps from one account to another within the same entity is defined as an "internal-exchange." The previous definition of an exchange can now be restated by entity.

(4.0) $\Delta^+ q_{itk}$ Ⓡ $\Delta^- q_{jtk}$

(4.1) $\Delta^+ q_{itk}$ Ⓡ $\Delta^- q_{itg}$

(4.0) is an internal exchange involving the ith and jth accounts in the kth entity. (4.1) is a market exchange between the kth and gth entities involving a transfer of caps of the ith category. Note that this exchange is of homogeneous caps and thus, since it is a transfer,

(4.2) $\Delta^+ q_{itk} + \Delta^- q_{itg} = 0$

That is, a transfer of caps which does not involve a change in the measure function is, by its very nature, summed to zero. However, this is a reciprocal exchange in which both entities receive something and both give up something. Thus, the complete expression of a market exchange is

(4.3) $\Delta^+ q_{itk} + \Delta^- q_{itg} = \Delta^+ q_{jtg} + \Delta^- q_{jtk}$

These are recorded within each entity in the same form as an internal exchange.

(4.4) $\Delta^+ q_{itk}$ Ⓡ $\Delta^- q_{jtk}$; $\Delta^+ q_{jtg}$ Ⓡ $\Delta^- q_{itg}$

Each entity now needs to assign a valco to both terms. In short, a market exchange involves two different account classes and two different entities.

Cash, Monetary, and Real Accounts

There is a set of asset accounts that have the ability to satisfy human wants directly by the process of *consumption*. There is another set of asset accounts that have the ability to satisfy human wants indirectly by the process of *producing* consumer goods. These two sets will be defined as "real accounts."

Real accounts also have the ability to satisfy human wants indirectly by the process of *exchange*. Both producer and consumer goods can be exchanged for other producer and/or consumer goods which have the attributes mentioned above. However, it is usually inconvenient to exchange real accounts for real accounts. For this reason, an artificial good—cash and monetary accounts—has been created. The ordinary market exchange will consist of one entity receiving real accounts and giving up cash or monetary accounts and vice versa for the other entity.

Cash, in addition to its convenience as a medium of exchange, has the attribute of being a non-temporally determined, general command over all goods offered in the market. That is, cash can be used in exchange for any good offered in the market at any time. Thus, it may be thought of as a "store of value" in the sense that one can delay the exchange into the indefinite future. In addition, it may be thought of as a "standard of value" since the ratio of exchange between all goods offered in the market is stated in cash units (dollars). The latter attribute is defined as "price."

Of course, the price of cash is unity. The prices of other accounts are determined by forces which are not relevant here. It should be emphasized, however, that these forces change over time and therefore the prices are temporally variable. Cash has the ability to satisfy human wants *only* through exchange. It has desirability only by virtue of its command over goods. Since the prices change over time, a constant amount of cash does not ensure a command over a constant number of caps.

Monetary accounts are claims against or promises to pay cash at a future time. Thus, cash is a claim against goods, and monetary asset accounts are one step further removed from goods by being a claim against cash. Monetary equity accounts are promises to pay cash. Thus, monetary assets and monetary equities in the economy are equal in magnitude but have opposite signs. There is another significant distinction between cash and monetary accounts: the monetary assets are claims against *specific* entities, while cash is a *general* claim in the market.

The distinction between monetary equities is usually the temporal location of the cash settlement. Monetary equities are exchanged for cash at a specific time; other equities are exchanged for cash or other caps at the time of a specified event, e.g., income for dividends or liquidation of the entity.

Monetary accounts may be exchanged for cash prior to the due date although it is relatively uncommon to do so. They are usually "collected," i.e., cash is exchanged for the monetary account at the due date with the specific entity that has the claim. However, there is a money market in which the claims may be exchanged.

Valuation Rules

It was pointed out above that cash has a price of unity. It is also assigned a valco of unity. The caps of the cash account are known as "dollars" and the unity valco is assigned to each dollar independently of other considerations. The caps of monetary accounts are also dollars but they are usually stated as the number of dollars that will be paid or received in the future. The number of dollars which they can be exchanged for in the present is normally less than the agreed number of future dollars. The valco assigned to monetary accounts is also unity. However, the value of monetary accounts is the valco of unity times the *present* number of dollars, not the future number of dollars.

Thus, both cash and monetary accounts are independently valued by the assignation of unity to each dollar. As noted above the usual market exchange involves cash or a monetary account. Given the requirement that the value of each exchange must sum to zero, the valco assigned to the real account is determined. That is, given that

$$p_{it}\Delta^{+}q_{it} + p_{jt}\Delta^{-}q_{jt} = 0 \tag{4.5}$$

and that, say, q_j is cash, then

$$p_{it} = \frac{-\Delta^{-}q_{jt}}{\Delta^{+}q_{it}} \tag{4.6}$$

The valcos of all accounts that are acquired by market exchanges are assigned in this manner.[8] Once the valco has been assigned, it remains constant.

Accounts so valued may now be exchanged internally. In all internal exchanges, one account will have a previously assigned value. Thus, the value and valco of the other account is determined.

This rather abstract statement of accounting valuation may be clarified by an example in more familiar notation. Suppose that a "thing," an "object," is acquired by an entity in exchange for cash. This thing will be called an "asset." There is no reason to acquire an "expense." Thus, any acquisition could be first recorded as an asset and then, by internal exchanges, recorded as an expense. The same is true for an equity "payment." The creation of an equity was originally by acquisition of an asset by promising to pay cash. Thus, the acquisition of an asset in exchange for cash may be considered a general case. The recording is

Dr. Asset.............	$10,000	
Cr. Cash..................		$10,000

This entry may be broken down into six distinct operations:

1. A cash decrement is observed.
2. The amount of the cash decrement is determined. The dollars are valued by a valco of unity.
3. The thing acquired because of the cash sacrifice is identified. The quantities are related.
4. The total value of the asset is set equal to the value of the cash decrement. This is the assumption of a dead-level exchange.
5. The quantity of caps contained in the asset is independently determined.
6. The value assigned in (4) is divided by the quantity determined in (5) to determine the valco ("cost per cap").

The valco determined in (6), assumed to remain constant, is important to all future exchanges involving this particular asset. If this is a depreciable asset, the value or unexpired cost declines with the decline in q. Suppose the asset is determined to have a five ($=q$) year life. The depreciation schedule would show the unexpired costs as $p(5)$, $p(4)$, $p(3)$, and so forth for each succeeding year. The same is true for inventories. The number of units ($=q$) would be determined periodically and multiplied by the constant p to get the value of the inventory account.[9] This p is also

[8] Some of the readers of the preliminary draft of this paper have objected to the use of valco. They have suggested that "valco" is the same as "price." In some cases this is true, but in the vast majority of cases there is no "price" for the caps that we use in accounting. For example, inventory is usually purchased by lot; we gather the costs of the lot and then divide by the number of units to get the valco. It would be a rare case for the price of a unit of inventory to equal the valco. In many other cases a valco is determined for a cap that is not traded in the market. In cost accounting we assign a valco by dividing total costs by equivalent units—something seldom traded in the market. In general, the valco per cap is different from the price, or there is no market for caps and hence no price.

[9] This method yields an average and assigns an equal valco to each cap. However, it should not be interpreted that this restricts the method to straight-line depreciation or the "average" cost method for inventory. Gellein has called this the "constant-charge" method and says that it "assumes that the same cost factor should be

used for the transferred portion of the asset. The value increment in Cost of Goods Sold, Depreciation Expense, Work-in-Process, etc., is the constant p times the $\Delta^{+}q$.

For acquisitions of cash in exchange for another asset, the same process is used. We still assign a unity valco to cash, keep any previous valco constant, and set the value of the other account(s) equal. For example, in the following entry

Dr. Cash.................	$25,000	
Cr. Asset.........................		$20,000
Cr. Retained Earnings.............		5,000

the difference between the independent valuation of cash and the previous valuation of the asset is taken to Retained Earnings where the caps are shares and the valco is earnings per share (on this exchange).

These examples have been an attempt to demonstrate the fidelity of the valuation rules. The demonstration is admittedly incomplete and there are many exceptions. Exceptions include lower of cost or market, values for gold and certain agricultural products, donated assets, the accounting rule for trade-ins, discovery values, quasi-reorganizations, and standard costs. The characteristic common to all these exceptions is that they are independently valued. All, except standards, are valued at market and obviously historical cost valuation is not present market valuation. Thus, these exceptions to the valuation rules are also exceptions to historical cost accounting.

Summary and Conclusion

There exists a set of service potentials which are units of potential want satisfaction. These service potentials are impossible to measure but they may be represented by various units of capacity called caps. Dollars are defined as one category of caps.

Caps of one category are collected to form an account. Asset accounts with a common purpose and their related equities are collected to form an entity.

Caps may be transferred from one account to another. This process is called an exchange and, when the caps are of the same category, it has a natural zero sum.

There are rules by which heterogeneous caps may be stated in homogeneous units. However, the caps do not lose their identity. Instead, a coefficient called a valco is attached to caps.

Values are the product of a quantity of caps and a valco. These values may be arrayed in various ways to form financial statements.

The elements of present accounting theory are three: caps, exchanges, and

---

assigned to every like unit (whether a unit of time, product, or some other factor) in the series with which benefits from the use of an asset or service can be identified. Straight-line and units-of-production methods of depreciation are two obvious examples of this concept."

He also shows that interest methods of depreciation are based on a constant-charge concept. And more important, he notes that the so-called decreasing charge methods are constant-charges with a more inclusive numerator. Gellein writes: "A common theoretical justification for such methods is found in the argument that, since the repair and maintenance costs for some depreciable assets will rise in later years of their life, it is logical to offset such increases with decreasing depreciation charges and thus achieve the approximate results of straight-line apportionment (constant charge concept) of combined maintenance and depreciation costs." Oscar S. Gellein, "The Decreasing Charge Concept," *Journal of Accountancy*, August 1959, p. 57.

The quantity of caps is still used as a divisor, but the dividend has been expanded to include maintenance costs in addition to the original outlay.

The same is true for inventories. Total inventory costs of a specific quantity are divided to find the valco. If the total inventory costs for a specific quantity vary then the valcos will vary. These different valcos are segregated by Fifo and Lifo methods of costing. The moving-average method expands the numerator to include more than one inventory lot.

The fact that valcos vary over inventory lots presents a problem. There is a certain valco assigned to each q. Presumably these q's are homogeneous else they would not be in the same account. However, the valcos vary and thus the *values* of q's in different lots vary. That is, there are different values for identical items, this is an enigma. Some accountants try to solve it by indentfying the caps that were sold and insisting that the originally assigned valcos be used. Specific identification is the most obvious example. Thos who reason from a cost-flow basis evidently conceive of the valcos as being interchangeable among the caps.

valcos. The isolation of these elements provides a rather natural division of the unresolved areas of accounting.

The process of determining the quantity of caps and the choice between different categories of caps. It is trivial in most cases to determine the quantity of inventory or cash but unfortunately our textbooks discuss only these trivial cases. The more difficult problems of *deciding* what kind of caps (say, the choice between units of output or years of life) and then *determining* the quantity are usually left to "professional judgment." Perhaps estimates and assumptions are inevitable in the face of uncertainty. On the other hand, exploration in this direction might lead to some guidelines or a set of alternatives, some of which are more applicable to a given situation than others.

The process of determining the accounts related by exchange. Our textbooks usually make this relation for us by a statement like "Purchase of 1,000 widgets for $2,000." This relates inventory to cash but it does not say anything about ancillary costs. We know, from previously being told, that transportation outlays are also related to inventory but that purchasing outlays are not. However, there is no way to reason to that conclusion; we must *know*. Each unfamiliar exchange presents us with a problem. Witness the flap over stock options, leases, pension plans, and investment credit. Occasionally, settled relations are reexamined such as the direct coster's claim that fixed factory overhead is related to retained earnings instead of inventory. So far as I can determine, there is nothing in the extant theory that would allow us to resolve these disputes. Up until now we have relied on authority but this is intellectually unsatisfactory. Perhaps exploration in this direction would yield some criteria for making relations.

The rules for assigning valcos. Valuation disputes are beyond the scope of this paper. The rules presented above were an attempt to describe, without prejudice, the extant historical cost rules. Whether or not these ought to be the rules is another question. However, in this framework, these disputes can be sharply segregated from the other problems. Heterogeneous units require valcos of some kind. Current costs or exit prices have to be assigned to something and we need to be clear on what that something is. Cost of the factors to reproduce an asset is likely to be different from the cost of replacing the asset in a secondhand market. The sum of the selling prices for each part of an asset is likely to be different from the selling price of the asset. Thus, the cap problems are pertinent in other valuation schemes. Selection of a particular valuation scheme requires criteria that have not yet been established.

A Statement of Basic Accounting Theory: A Review Article

ROBERT R. STERLING*

The Committee to Prepare a Statement of Basic Accounting Theory[1] was charged "to develop an integrated statement of basic accounting theory which will serve as a guide to educators, practitioners, and others interested in accounting. The statement should include adequate support for any position taken and sufficient explanation to provide clarity, yet be as concise as feasible." (p. v) This is indeed a large order, so large that hardly anyone would be surprised if the committee failed.

The ideas presented in the *Statement* can readily be traced to the literature but this is not a criticism; instead it is the nature of a committee effort. A committee will report only what is "generally accepted" by its members and often general acceptance of ideas requires previous exposure. We are told that the committee met eight times for a total of twenty days (p. vi) and this lends further support to the previous exposure hypothesis. Radically new ideas would have probably required much longer. Thus, the accounting theorist will find little that is new in the *Statement*. He may disagree with parts or all of it but he will find nothing to shock or stimulate.

Nevertheless, this document is a revolutionary one when its contents are compared to contemporary practice and education. The differences are not only in the specific suggestions on valuation, e.g., current cost, non-transaction data, but also in two more important respects: (1) methodology and (2) world-view.

---

* Visiting Research Fellow, Sloane Physics Laboratory, Yale University.

[1] *A Statement of Basic Accounting Theory,* American Accounting Association (Evanston, Ill., 1966); hereafter the *"Statement"* and the "committee." Page numbers for quotations without further reference are from the *Statement.*

Methodology

The committee's methodology is self-consciously antithetical to the previous inductive or empirical methods. They imply that such methods do not yield a theory: "... many accountants ... equate 'accounting theory' with the sum total of all accounting practices currently in use." (p. 6) The function of a theory to them is prescriptive, not descriptive. Their standards "... provide means of *accepting or rejecting accounting methods....*" (p. 6) "Not only should information that meets the standards be included in accounting; all information that does not meet the standards should be excluded." (p. 3)

This is diametrically opposed to the Paton and Littleton method of weaving together current practices into a coherent whole and to Grady's method of inventorying practices and then justifying them. Also it is a decisive break with the AICPA method of issuing bulletins on current controversial issues which arise in practice.

I agree with this break; I think that the "inductive" approach commits the elementary fallacy of getting *ought* from *is:* to conclude that what *is* is what ought to be. The enthymeme is that there is some natural law or divine hand that makes the *is* good, or perhaps unalterable. I know of no modern science that takes this view. In mechanics, friction *is,* but no one concludes that it ought to be. On the contrary, the physicist continually tries to lessen or avoid it. Sociology and anthropology observe human behavior and generalize about it but no one concludes that it ought to be the way it is. On the contrary, "value judgments" about what people ought to do are carefully avoided. Except for some theologies, I know of no discipline other than accounting which induces what ought to be from what is.

The AICPA bulletins follow a method which has been described as the "crisis" or "fire truck" methodology. They wait for a fire and then rush in to put it out. Often the previous set of generally accepted principles proves to be insufficient for the resolution of the crisis. In such cases a new principle is introduced ad hoc, i.e., the practices cannot be explained by the existing principles and thus a new principle is introduced for the specific purpose of explaining the practice. For example, *Bulletin No. 43* states that cost is the principle (presumably because it fulfils the objective of measuring income by matching appropriate *cost* against revenues). But several different flows are generally accepted and therefore an ad hoc principle needs to be introduced which permits several "costs"; lower of cost or market is justified by introducing costs which "lose their utility"; market higher than cost is generally accepted for some products and thus the ad hoc principle of "immediate marketability at quoted prices" is introduced.[2] It is a commonplace observation

[2] *Accounting Research and Terminology Bulletins,* American Institute of Certified Public Accountants, 1961. It is enlightening to compare the depreciation defi-

that any theory can be saved by the simple expedient of introducing ad hoc principles every time a crisis arises.[3] However, the question is not whether it *can* be saved but whether it *should* be saved. With the introduction of a number of ad hoc principles, soon the theory denies nothing. A proposition which denies nothing affirms nothing. The cost principle for inventory denies very little since it permits net realizable values, replacement prices, standards, and a host of costs. More importantly, if another unknown value were to become generally accepted, we could add another principle to cover it. Thus the theory cannot, in principle, deny anything and, therefore, it is totally useless except as an apology for what is or was.

The committee disclaims this approach, but there is no discussion of why they rejected it nor is there any explicit presentation of the method they employed. I think I know what method they employed but it would have been preferable had they stated it.

The committee redefined accounting and then deductively reasoned to the standards, guidelines, and specific recommendations. "The committee defines accounting as the process of identifying, measuring, and communicating economic information to permit informed judgments and decisions by users of the information." (p. 1) To them accounting is a measurement-communication system. Such a definition is often referred to as "invitational," i.e., a writer or speaker invites the audience to think of the word as he defines it. I will indicate below how readily the standards follow if one accepts the definition.

The committee has invited us to accept a definition of accounting and deductive reasoning, both of which are radical changes from previous official publications (the Moonitz mutation excepted) without justification for either. The deductive method is not new in science, but it is new and radical in accounting and this change requires some persuasive arguments. So does their definition. It might be said that the new

---

nition (p. 76) with the lower of cost or market discussion. (p. 30) Assets lose their utility by using up service potential and costs are used to allocate (not value) that loss; but inventory loses its utility because the market declines. "Although the *cost basis* ordinarily achieves the objective of a proper matching of *costs* and revenues, under certain circumstances *cost* may not be the amount properly chargeable against the revenues of future periods." (p. 30) I hardly see how anything other than cost can be appropriate to the objective of properly matching costs and revenues.

Also, compare the Mason dissent on valuing marketable securities (p. 23) with the discussion of inventories valued at market higher than cost. (p. 34) Below I refer to this as "cognitive insulation." Elsewhere I have called it "apologetics" in the strict sense of that term. (*The Theory of the Measurement of Enterprise Income*, Chapter VI, forthcoming.)

[3] Philosophers of science sometimes play a parlor game in which someone interprets the new scientific discoveries by use of the older, abandoned constructs, e.g., Aristotle's elements of air, earth, fire, and water or the phlogiston theory. It can always be done if ad hoc principles are permitted.

definition is "self-evident" and thus needs no justification. It is not self-evident to Mr. Morrison, who thinks that the *Statement* is only "...of certain aspects of...accounting.... But it offers little in the way of basic accounting theory as a foundation for a body of sound accounting principles...." (p. 97) Knowing Mr. Morrison's propensity to "fairness" one could have predicted this reaction. But that is precisely the point: knowing others' propensity to "conservatism," "matching and attaching," etc., one can predict their reaction. Eventually the battle will have to be fought at this level of abstraction. One will have to present well-formed arguments about what accounting ought to be. Until then one can either accept or reject the committee's definition and deductions. Since they did not make the argument and one practitioner has already reacted, it is doubtful that they have fulfilled the charge to guide practitioners.

It is more difficult to judge how the *Statement* will fare in guiding educators. A long tradition of accounting education has developed from the inductive approach. (Recall that Littleton presented the coherent theory as an aid to education so that students need not memorize rules.[4]) Most undergraduate accounting curricula seem designed solely to prepare the student for accounting practice. The popular textbook trilogies point almost exclusively toward the CPA exam and often the success of a school is judged by the percentage of students who pass. This means training the student for contemporary practice by teaching him what is now done. Thus, the changes in curricula come from changes in practice as do changes in theory. Changes in practice are likely to be cognitively insulated—two practitioners solving the same problem in different ways and both practices becoming accepted—and thus it comes as no surprise that the texts are cognitively insulated, e.g., rejecting appraisal values because they vary in the theory chapter and then laboriously explaining the variations in costs in the rest of the chapters. Students and teachers have done fairly well in accepting this much insulation, but I doubt if they could accept a redefinition. It will take a master weaver to weave "accounting is matching and attaching" together with "accounting is a measurement-communication system."

If educators and textbook authors continue to emphasize practice, the *Statement* will have little impact. I suspect that they will continue because the students need jobs. Thus practice will continue to dominate education and the committee will have failed in its charge.

The committee has, however, fulfilled the less ambitious function of providing an "official" collection of ideas generally accepted by theorists.

[4] "Teachers of bookkeeping and later of accounting and auditing found it necessary to supplement the accumulated rules and descriptions of procedure by explanations and justifications. This was done in order that study should be something more than memorizing of rules." A. E. Littleton, *Structure of Accounting Theory* (American Accounting Association Monograph No. 5, 1953), p. 185.

Previous individual efforts by theorists have not been successful. For the most part, they have not been refuted—just ignored and forgotten. It may be more difficult to ignore a committee's official pronouncements, and this might be a first step in reversing the direction of accounting change. Perhaps it will go from theory to practice instead of the previous direction. If so, it will be the most significant development since Pacioli.

Like most developments, it will create new problems. The first is the implementation of new ideas from theorists. An analogy can be drawn from technology. At some point the theory needs to be frozen so that an instrument can be built and debugged. The next instrument will embody further theoretical advances, some of which result from the discoveries in the previous one. Accounting is more difficult because it is continually practiced and consistency is desirable, i.e., the time-series needs to be linked. More important, accounting is an institution in the Veblenian sense—a habit of thought by a large group of people—and as such it is inevitably slow to change and Veblen (but not Marx) would argue that it is completely invulnerable to revolution. Under this view, the theory of accounting is subject to revolutionary change but the practice of accounting must be evolutionary. The education of practicing accountants is the connecting link and requires some hard thought and choices from among rather unattractive alternatives.

A final point on methodology springs from the following: "These techniques include generally accepted accounting principles and practices, as well as alternatives which may not meet the criterion of 'general acceptance' but for which there is substantial authoritative support." (p. 6) "Techniques" is not well defined but it includes things "... used by accountants in measuring, describing. . . ." (p. 6) I find this an odd proposition in the context of the *Statement,* although it would not be odd under the Paton and Littleton, Grady, or Bulletin 43 methodology. "General acceptance" is a necessary and sufficient condition for the inclusion of a technique under the inductive method, but the committee's proposition indicates that *either* "general acceptance" or "substantial authoritative support" is sufficient. This permits more latitude in selecting techniques and therefore less uniformity of practices. Moreover, reversion to "general acceptance" seems to contradict the committee's position that a theory should be prescriptive. A prescriptive theory implies a criterion of theoretical validity, and neither general acceptance nor authoritative support guarantees theoretical validity.

World-View

The committee has invited us to view accounting as a measurement-information system. This new view precludes some questions but poses others. In their reference frame, it is no longer appropriate to argue simple observation that someone must read the pointer and this is, *ipso facto*, a subjective perception. Even more damaging is the ultimate test of the instrument. We might all agree that the butcher's scale points to 50 pounds when one wiener is placed on it but I suspect that we would prefer our "subjective" estimation, i.e., we would claim that the objective reading was *wrong* and revert to some subjective basis such as hefting. In accounting, objectivity is even more confused, so the force of, e.g., Mr. Morrison's comment is lost to me. He denies current cost because no objective method of determining it has been found. (p. 98) I do not know what he had in mind but I suggest the following procedure: (1) Set out the tests of objectivity in as precise a form as possible. (2) Apply those tests with equal vigor to both historical and current costs. (3) Report the results in comparative form.

I suspect that "objectivity" to accountants is nothing more than an emotional response to suggestions for other (non-cost) valuation schemes, and we would do well to abandon the term. This may have been the motivation of the committee. However, abandoning the term does not solve the problem that gives rise to the term. Perhaps verifiability and freedom from bias are attempts to clarify so that meaningful propositions can be formed. If so, it is a beginning but a woefully weak one. If we are to conceive of ourselves as metricians, there is a lot of epistemological spade work to be done before we can proceed.

The last standard of quantifiability is rather puzzling, given the measurement view. There are many different meanings attached to measurement but insofar as I know they all have to do with numerals and/or numbers.

The elaboration (pp. 11–13) of quantifiability seems directed to two ends: (1) Accounting need not be restricted to "value" quantities and (2) "The quantification of data adds usefulness." I agree with the first point since relevant quantities are not necessarily value quantities. The second point is followed by a brief outline of the famous S. S. Stevens school of measurement. In some circles this school is considered infamous because in some instances it negates the usefulness of quantification. The best known case is the numbering-of-football-players question. Stevens would claim that the numbering of football players is a "Measurement" (under the nominal scale) while others claim that this does violence to a well established linguistic fact and it adds nothing to the names of the players. This violation may cause confusion instead of adding usefulness. An example more germane to accounting is any asset to which a number has been assigned. Stevens would claim that the "assignment of numerals according to a rule—any rule—" is a measurement[7] and *then* he would concern himself with what one could legiti-

[7] S. S. Stevens, "Measurement, Psycho-physics and Utility" idem. p. 19. The chief architect of the physics view says: "Measurement is the process of assigning numbers to represent quantities. . . ." Norman R. Campbell, *Physics: The Elements*

about which convention or assumption comes closest to the "actual" cost or income; it is not appropriate to assume that if we carefully describe (fully disclose) the methods used, then the figures will be meaningful, or that only invested costs or transaction data are the subject matter of accounting or that by its very name accounting reflects costs. Under the new view, measurements in accounting are a function of some end.

This is a change in "world-view" and is the stuff that revolutions[5] are made of. Given this view, the standards, particularly the relevance standard, are almost too obvious. This is not a detraction; instead it is in the nature of the change in world-view.

To raise the question of measurement is to raise the question of relevance. One never measures all the properties of an object; instead one measures those properties that are relevant to him. Churchman's Crusoe example makes this abundantly clear.[6] When Crusoe sets out to find a flagstone to fit his hearth, the length is obviously relevant. It is equally obvious that the carbon half-life and a host of other properties are irrelevant. However, it is obvious only under this view. Under some other view, one could argue that the carbon half-life was the appropriate measure because it was, say, the truth or perhaps more objective than length.

To raise the question of measurement is to raise the question of communications. Measurement is a process of comparison; one measures the same object at different times to make an inter-temporal comparison, or different objects at the same time to make an instantaneous inter-object comparison. This means that one communicates inter-spatially or inter-temporally. The communication can be inter-personal or with one's self. (The object of Churchman's example was to show that Crusoe had to communicate with his past.) This is commensurate with information theory since self-information is included.

Verifiability and freedom from bias are desiderata of all measurements and thus, they follow readily from the new view. The surprise is not that these are included as standards but that "objectivity" is *excluded*. In one sense, the committee is to be commended for avoiding this quagmire. What is "objective"—the real properties as opposed to our perception of them—has gone through several reversals in philosophy and, as a consequence, it is highly confused. From the measurement literature of the physical sciences one would assume that instrumentation is the requisite for an objective measurement. A pointer reading that all would agree to is considered objective. This view can be confuted by the

[5] This is a construct about the formation of constructs and the disputes are legion. For my bias as well as the phrase, see Thomas Kuhn, *Structure of Scientific Revolution* (Chicago: University of Chicago Press, 1962), p. 90 *et passim*.

[6] C. West Churchman, "Why Measure," in *Measurement: Definitions and Theories*, eds. C. West Churchman and Philburn Ratoosh (New York: John Wiley & Sons, Inc. 1959), p. 89.

mately do with that number. Thus, to Stevens all of our current methods—LIFO, SYD, lower, discounted—and any others would be measurements. Bergmann, for example, and most metricians of physics orientation would deny that it is a measurement unless it is additive and the property of additivity requires some descriptive correlate or empirical meaning. Thus, to Bergmann our current methods would not be measurements unless we could stipulate the descriptive correlates.

The Stevens position makes one question the verifiability standard. Suppose my rule was different from yours. Could you then "verify" my figure? The auditor does verify but it is in the peculiar fashion of accepting management's estimate of the life and salvage value, management's decision on which ancillary costs should be attached to the asset and which should be expensed, and finally management's decision on which depreciation equation should be used. All of these are bounded but they vary widely and thus the auditor has "verified," come up with the same figure, only after the odd procedure of accepting all the decisions which *necessarily* (analytically) lead to that figure. Bergmann would probably say that this is neither a measurement nor a verification. My reading of the *Statement* leads me to believe that the committee would consider a quantity so derived to be a measurement and a verification. If so, I note an exception.

This problem is crucial to the *Statement* because Mr. Morrison has rejected current costs because they are not objective and verifiable; and because the majority of the committee continually concede that historical cost is more verifiable than current cost. "Historical transaction-based information has been verified by a market transaction, and hence is of great usefulness when verifiability is emphasized." (p. 30) This is a contradiction of the primary standard of relevance. A figure may be verifiable but irrelevant and therefore completely useless. On the other hand, an unverified guess at a relevant figure may be quite useful. If the guess is erroneous it may lead to erroneous decisions but that is the category mistake that the committee is making. Different degrees of accuracy, different tolerances of errors, are required for different decisions, but this is covered by the relevance standard. Verification may make us more confident of the accuracy of the figure because the measurement has been repeated and it makes deliberate misrepresentation more difficult. Verifiability is therefore highly desirable but relevance is indispensible.

For these reasons, I do not understand why "... the original-transaction data or other valuation will continue to be reported in the current-

(Cambridge: Cambridge University Press, 1920), p. 267. In addition to all the other differences in these definitions, the numeral-number distinction causes some difficulty. Cf. C. G. Hempel, "Fundamentals of Concept Formation in Empirical Science," *International Encyclopedia of Unified Science,* Vol. II, No. 7 (Chicago: The University of Chicago Press, 1952), pp. 55 and 85.

cost column where current cost is unverifiable because there is no other evidence which meets the minimum requirement of the verifiability standard." (p. 28) Presumably the reason for reporting current cost is that it is relevant, and historical cost, in this context or column, is not. But the above proposition shifts criteria and reports an irrelevancy. This irrelevancy is reported in the current-cost column and added in so that the problem of summing inconsistent figures—figures which represent different dimensions—arises again. Further, it assumes that the original-transaction data or other valuation does meet the verifiability standard. Some of the peculiarities of historical-cost verification were outlined above, but note here that this verification requires a shift in operations. Current cost measurements require a set of operations quite different from those of historical cost measurement. Thus, in principle, one cannot verify historical cost with current cost operations or vice versa. If there are current costs which cannot be measured and verified, then I would opt for presenting non-quantative information in accordance with the quantifiability standard. "When accountants present non-quantitative information in compliance with the other standards they should not imply its measurability." (p. 7) If current cost is relevant but not measurable, we should not imply its measurability by substituting historical cost.

Finally I think the committee concedes too much to the verifiability of historical cost. Elsewhere I have reviewed the operational requirements for determining historical cost.[8] It is sufficient here to note the resemblance between incorrigible statements and some of the things an auditor is asked to verify. An incorrigible statement is a first-person present-tense report of a sensation, e.g., "I feel pain" or "I see blue dots." It is readily seen that such statements are impossible to verify or falsify. Compare these incorrigible statements to statements of estimation or intention. For example, "I estimate that boulder to weigh 50 tons." If you weigh it, you can falsify the predicate "50 tons" but you can never falsify the fact that my estimation was 50 tons. If you estimate its weight without measuring it, you have neither verified nor falsified either the 50 tons or my estimation. Consider "I estimate the life of that machine to be 50 years" or worse "I intend to maintain and use that machine so that it will last 50 years." Ex post there is a way to find out how long it did last but that is too late. Ex ante one might make a separate estimate but that does not help. These statements, particularly the latter report of intentions, are in principle unverifiable and unfalsifiable. Current costs, in many instances, are also estimates, but there is no reason to concede that one kind of estimate is more verifiable than another.

The guidelines presented are also extensions of the measurement no-

[8] Robert R. Sterling, "Operational Analysis of Traditional Accounting," *Abacus*, December, 1966.

tion. The first three may be considered an elaboration of the relevance standard. The last two recognize that measurements are comparisons and that comparisons in two directions are possible and desirable. If one wants inter-firm comparisons, then there must be "uniformity of practices", and we can stop all this nonsense about diversity being good. If one wants to argue for "flexibility" one must deny inter-firm comparisons and replace it with some other desideratum. Accountants have long accepted guideline 5—"Consistency of practices through time"—because it is obvious that one cannot compare or link time-series without consistency. Guideline 4 is simply an application of consistency to different firms for the same reasons.

The View Extended

The measurement-communication system presented by the committee may be diagramed as follows:

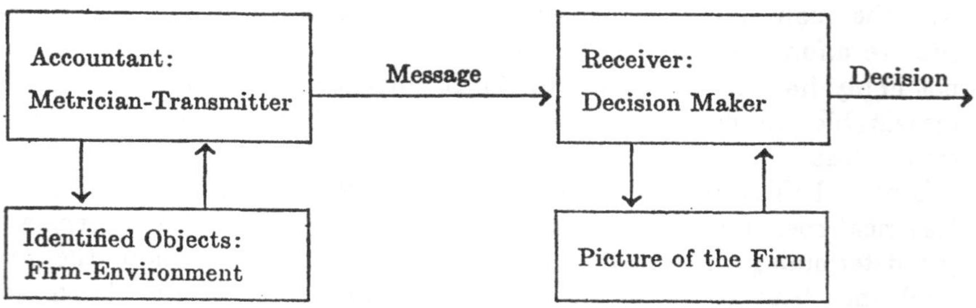

This conforms to the definition of "accounting as the process of identifying, measuring, and communicating economic information to permit informed judgments and decisions by users of the information." (p. 1) The firm or other entity and its environment are identified and measured and then a message is prepared and communicated to the receivers.

The diagram again emphasizes the notion of relevance. Everything about the firm cannot be reported—the modifier "economic" limits the scope—nor should everything be reported. The information to be reported must be relevant to some "decision model." (p. 31 *et passim*). More important, this diagram locates the decision model: it is at the destination that the receiver possesses the decision model.

The diagram also emphasizes the omissions. The model originated by Shannon and Weaver includes a channel with a finite capacity. This omission, I think, is a serious defect in the committee's work. They imply that the advent and increased use of computers obviate this consideration. While it is true that the computer has and probably will continue to increase capacity for gathering and processing information it still has a finite capacity. Even if it did not, we would still want to limit the capacity. Anyone on the mailing list of U.S. Government documents knows very well that it is possible to be inundated with relevant information.

This communication system is a solution to a prior economic decision. Scarce resources have been allocated to the system and it must operate within that constraint. In fact, one could say that information or communication theory is an "economic" problem. It is an attempt to maximize the quantity of information with a given constraint. Without the constraint the problem is trivial. Redundancy would provide a complete solution.

My reaction to the "different incomes for different purposes" proposal is in the same vein. The motivation for this proposal is quite correct: no single statistic is relevant to all purposes. However, to propose that a different statistic be prepared for each purpose overlooks the constraint. It is the trivial solution to the problem and solves nothing.

The committee has not made this proposal but it has proposed that we transmit *more*. Both historical and current costs are recommended and "...the committee advocates the reporting of all information that is believed to be relevant to the judgments and decisions of any substantial group of users." (p. 22) In my view, more is certainly needed but the crucial question has not been broached: within a given constraint how do we select the statistics so that we maximize[9] the information?

Reference to the relevance standard will not solve this problem. There are many receivers with a wide variety of purposes, and different receivers with the same purpose may have different decision models. At the formal level of analysis, relevance is an either-or proposition. Either

[9] I mean by "maximize information" considerably more than the information or communication theorists mean. They are concerned with "...the *choice*, the range of possible messages..." and exclude "...moral import, scientific significance, artistic quality, even speculative value in business.... Not one of these concepts, essential though they are to the usual meaning of 'information' come within the ambit of our definition...." G. T. Guilbaud, *What is Cybernetics?* (New York: Criterion Books, 1959), p. 59. Guilbaud is quoting Brillouin in part of the above.

Almost all information theorists emphasize this distinction. Goldman, for example, says information theory measures "the *quantity* of information, not its value" (p. 300) and then makes the distinction clear by the following example:

> The quantity theory of information which we have been developing may appear incomplete and perhaps disappointing to the reader because it does not treat the *value* of information. There are just as many binits in the information which tells whether John Smith's wife had a boy or girl, as in the information which tells whether your own wife had a boy or girl. Stanford Goldman, *Information Theory* (New York: Prentice-Hall, 1953), p. 63.

In accounting we are primarily concerned with the "value" of the information, not in the choices or the number of binits. Thus, formal information theory has little to contribute to accounting except insofar as the *general* concepts help us to organize our thinking. But this emphasizes the seriousness of the omission of the general concept of a limited capacity.

a given statistic is specified by the decision model or it is not, and therefore it is either relevant or irrelevant. Given the variety of purposes and the variety of models for the same purpose, the channel capacity begins to bind at the outset.

This immediately suggests a binary measure of relevance. We could poll the receivers to find out which binits were (1) relevant and which were (0) irrelevant to them. Then we could transmit the binits with the largest value. Suggestions for this sort of thing have been advanced previously, but some rather important problems result from this approach.

Suppose we convince ourselves that any decision model which specifies historical cost is an invalid model, i.e., it will yield decisions consonant with the specified purpose only by chance. Further, suppose that the poll of the receivers showed historical cost to be relevant to most receivers. Should we transmit historical cost?

The force of this question will not be lost on those who have taught decision-making courses. We have known since Jevons that "in commerce, bygones are bygones" but our students rarely know this. In fact, exclusion of *the* cost from a decision seems to be counter-intuitive. I suspect that this is true for the general population as well as our students. Of course, if we have enough capacity we can transmit this data along with others.

The concern of the committee with socio-economic matters or with the "correct" allocation of resources opens this position to question. If we are convinced that the receivers are using the wrong decision model, we have a dilemma. (1) We can transmit the information specified by their wrong model which will yield right decisions only by chance. (2) We can transmit the information specified by the right model which will be irrelevant to their model, and hence right decisions will result only by chance.

Neither alternative is attractive but I would argue for the second, largely on the grounds that communications are not neutral; instead they are educational. Comparative sociologists have often pointed out that our taste in "news," "literature," "music," etc. is largely determined by what was previously communicated to us. If the newscasters poll the populace today they will find that present tastes place football scores high on the list and cricket scores low. However, the very transmission of football scores reinforces this taste and is a major factor in determining the tastes of the coming generation. The accountant is in the same position. He cannot be neutral because his transmissions will be a major factor in determining what the future generations consider relevant. The very definition of information is dependent upon previous information; it is a cause of desires in an on-going process as well as an effect of the present desires.

For this reason I am suspicious of the simplistic idea of polling the receivers. In the present state of accounting, I have no doubt that a poll would improve our current reporting but it does not even approach a satisfactory solution. In my view there is no "final" solution for the following reasons.

The major problem of accounting is to develop a *general* information system. By this I mean a system that supplies relevant data to both specific and unspecific decision models. The point can best be illustrated by the committee's programmed-unprogrammed matrix. (p. 44) If we have a production process with a variable material mix, there is a unique solution by a linear programming model. The capital budgeting model will provide a yes-no solution to simple investment problems. These models clearly specify the relevant data. Therefore, they can be automatized—hooked to the information-computer system—and the output, the "information" that is received by humans, is already a decision. The relevance problem is trivial in such cases. In fact, the computer can be programmed to *ask* for the relevant data.

It is in the unprogrammed areas that difficulties are encountered. There the decision models are not well defined; indeed the problems are often unknown. It is this area of internal reporting that intersects with external reporting. External reporting also has programmed data requirements, e.g., the revenue code specifies the relevant data in tedious detail and thus there is no relevance problem. The difficult task is to make measurements that are relevant to the unprogrammed decisions. Since the problems which give rise to unprogrammed decisions are likely to change over time and since the perceived problems are (partially at least) a function of the information received, it is unlikely that a final solution can ever be found.

This is not a note of despair. On the contrary, I think it is a realistic view of the difficult and exciting problems which face us. They have always faced us, we have just failed to recognize them. That is, the change in world-view both permits and forces us to look at a different set of problems. In my opinion, the new view is the correct one and it has the potential to change accounting from a ritualistic and dogmatic tradition to a vital part of the economic process and an academic discipline with problems that would challenge the greatest intellects.

Historical and Current Costs

The committee asserts: "A case was built, on the grounds of relevance, for the communication of a current expression in the form of replacement cost of the economic significance of the resources acquired, utilized, and held by an accounting entity." (p. 73) A perusal of Chapter III does not support this assertion. There is no systematic case presented for current cost although there are a number of individual allegations that it is relevant. The committee summarizes the argument on p. 19: "Evidence of dissatisfaction with extant accounting practices abounds. A principal criticism relates to the deficiencies of historical cost as a basis of predicting future earnings . . . ," and "we find historical cost information not adequate for all purposes." "We accordingly recommend that current-cost information as well as historical-cost information should be reported." Thus, the primary support for current cost comes from dissatisfaction with historical cost. This does not follow. Not-p does not necessarily imply q. That is, the rejection of or dissatisfaction with one alternative does not lead to the acceptance of another without further argument. The second point is that historical cost is deficient in *predicting* future earnings. There is no assurance that current cost will be any better for purposes of prediction. Measurement is commonly confused with prediction. Measurement is a process of discovering an *extant* condition, and prediction is concerned with a future condition. Thus, prediction requires some kind of law connecting the past and present with the future. Measurement does not require the additional step of applying the law. Goodman's simplistic example[10] is "if butter is placed in a 300° degree oven, it will melt." One can measure the temperature of the oven without making the prediction. As a second step the prediction can be made if the effects of temperature on butter is known, i.e., if the law connecting the measurement of the extant state with a future state is known. Temperature is said to be relevant to this law and tensile strength is not. However, the fact that tensile strength is not relevant does not imply that temperature is. The deficiencies of historical cost in predicting the future does not imply that current cost is any less deficient. Unless one can demonstrate the existence of some law-like conditional which specifies current cost, the point is moot.

Given these considerations, I am puzzled by the conclusion that ". . . accordingly we recommend that current-cost information as well as historical cost information should be reported." Nothing the committee has said leads me to that conclusion. It may be that they are trying the shotgun approach: by presenting *more* statistics accountants will satisfy more receivers. But the suggestion for *more* neglects the standard of relevance.

It is possible to be just as dogmatic about current cost as about historical cost. It is possible for everybody to jump on the relevance-current-cost bandwagon in the same uncritical way that we attached ourselves to the matching-historical-cost construct. If the new world-view is to be accepted and acceptable, it needs to be applied with rigor and precision. All the details cannot be worked out immediately, perhaps all of them can never be completely worked out. But current cost is not a de-

[10] Leonard Linsky, *Semantics and the Philosophy of Language* (Urbana, Ill., University of Illinois Press, 1952), pp. 162–65. In this book Goodman uses the butter example in an exposition of counter-factual conditionals, not predictions. However, the same law-like process holds.

tail, it is an entire scheme of valuation. Therefore, it deserves and requires more justification than the committee gave it.

In short, my plea is for a demonstration that current cost is relevant. Without the demonstration there is the danger that relevance and irrelevance can be tossed about as "appropriately match" has been in the past. There is already some evidence of this in the cost accounting literature. Direct cost is said to be relevant to managerial decisions and therefore goods ought to be valued that way on the balance sheet and income statement. It is obvious that the historical cost, however defined, of those units already produced is sunk and therefore irrelevant to all decisions about those units. Direct cost may be used as a guide in projecting what the future marginal cost will be but it is only a guide since we may expect various changes and adjust for them. These adjusted costs are the expected marginal costs in the short or intermediate run and are relevant to some short run decisions. The direct costs are relevant only insofar as they furnish a guide to future marginal costs. Moreover, they are a guide to only part of the picture because it is likely that at least part of the "fixed costs" will become variable within the firm's target horizon, i.e., it will be necessary to replace part of the plant. These expectations of indirect costs are also relevant; these future expected outlays are relevant to whether the firm will continue or not. They must be netted against expected future revenue, discounted, and then compared to the present exit value to decide whether to continue or liquidate.

This illustrates the economic decision process, albeit in an oversimplified way. The historical costs are never relevant except as one uses them in a projection. Even in a projection, a series of several past prices is desirable; a single cost is not likely to be used for projecting future behavior. Also, current costs, meaning present replacement prices, are not relevant. All replacements, except those already made, lie in the future and therefore the (discounted) future price is relevant. That is, the time adjusted predicted prices are compared in order to select one of the available alternatives but the present replacement price is, at best, only one price in a trend that will be used to predict the future.

The present replacement price may be stated thus: if I were to replace now, then X is the amount I would have to pay. But we never replace *now*. It may be that the committee is working under the tacit assumption of going concern. If so, one can derive a physical capacity or opportunity cost argument. This works best for inventories where the operations are repetitive and there is some discretion over price, i.e., a markup-turnover model. Under this view one must replace (because going concern is interpreted that way), and therefore a unit of inventory has an opportunity cost equal to its replacement price. If the markup is based on the historical cost and prices are rising, *cet. par.*, then the number of units in inventory will decline.

I think there are many things wrong with the going concern view but it is not appropriate to review them here. The pertinent point is that if the committee made the going concern assumption, it was not stated. Instead they simply alleged that current cost "*is* a relevant variable." (p. 34) It may be relevant to some model, like going concern, but that model needs to be exhibited before we can make a judgment.

The committee makes few assertions about the relevance of historical cost. Perhaps the only general claim made is that it is "of great usefulness when verifiability is emphasized" which was discussed above. Otherwise justification of historical cost is limited to fulfilling specific demands such as those from tax authorities and regulatory commissions. Such agencies "... not only have special needs but also the power to specify the information to be submitted...." (p. 21) These special needs could be fulfilled by reference to some general ethic such as a Hobbsian edict—one ought to obey the law—instead of a principle peculiar to accounting.

The committee recommends that special needs should be fulfilled but labeled as "not in conformity with generally accepted accounting principles." (p. 16) I am in complete accord with this and also with the proposition that such requirements should not influence accounting principles. One can prepare tax returns without it affecting his theory of accounting.[11]

The committee takes note of the marginal analysis for internal management. (p. 60) There would be little distortion if one asserted that the whole of the marginal analysis can be directed to proving that historical cost is irrelevant to economic decisions. Given this, and the committee's position on legal authority, and the lack of cogency of historical cost's claim to verifiability, then one may wonder why there is a historical cost column in Appendix II. What is historical cost relevant to?

Since this is a polemic, I will state the proposition positively so that the reader can demolish it.

(1) "*Relevance* is the primary standard ..." (p. 7) and "... all information that does not meet the standards should be excluded." (p. 3)

---

[11] The tax law is a good example of the non-neutrality of information. In my view, the chief determinant of tax law has been extant accounting practices; that is, the information previously prepared by accountants has determined, to a very large extent, the kind of information specified by the tax authorities. Negative support for this view comes from the almost total lack of effect of the cogent "command over goods" arguments from Simons, Haig *et al.* Positive support is harder to come by but it can be observed that tax law, in the main, has closely conformed to generally accepted accounting principles. It would be circular to now argue that we ought to supply historical costs to taxing authorities because "they want them." To base accounting principles on the tax code makes the circle vicious. As information processors, accountants occupy a crucial position. We can stop beating our breasts about being a profession and quietly accept the almost awesome power and responsibility that is thrust upon us by the very nature of an information system. Another alternative is to let our instrumental function be usurped by another group (statisticians perhaps) while we become a priesthood with nothing but an empty ceremony to perform.

(2) Historical cost is irrelevant to all economic decisions (Sterling's allegation).

(3) Ergo, historical cost should be excluded.

The quarrel will probably be with (2) and, again being deliberately polemical, I challenge any one to demonstrate that historical costs are relevant to economic decisions. Since (2) includes a universal quantifier it will take only one counter case to falsify it.[12]

Perhaps the committee intended the *Statement* to be transitional. If so, I have no quarrel with the inclusion of historical cost. The difficult problems of transition were noted above and I can sympathize with the committee's dilemma.

Summary and Conclusion

My reaction to the *Statement* is on two levels. First, I agree with the new methodology and world-view. My criticism on this level is directed to the absence of explicitness and persuasive argument. This gap makes general acceptance less likely.

Second, given the new world-view and methodology, there are errors and omissions. The capacity constraint is the most serious omission because this obscures the crucial problem of developing criteria for the selection of data; it permits the trivial solution of transmitting everything and rejecting nothing. The effect of information, the non-neutrality notion, was also omitted and this is serious because it neglects the importance of the information transmitter's role and allows for the possibility of forming a vicious circle.

The standards and guidelines readily follow from the new view, and the relevance standard is correctly considered to be primary. There are some difficulties, however, with the verifiability and quantifiability standards, particularly when they are vis-à-vis.

The specific valuation recommendations do not immediately follow from the relevance standard. The model in which current cost is relevant was not exhibited. Historical cost seemed to spring from tradition and transitional consideration instead of a deduction from the relevance standard. This is compounded when the committee, erroneously I think, concedes greater verifiability to historical cost and then, on these grounds, permits its inclusion in an additive column where it had previously been excluded on the grounds that it was irrelevant.

---

[12] In order to avoid Plutarch's criticism of critics, I will state my suggestion for the replacement of the criticized ideas. I think the current exit value of a held asset is relevant to almost all economic decisions. Further, it has the additional informative characteristic of indicating the direction, but not the magnitude, of the expectations of those in control. Convincing argument for this proposition is too lengthy for this review. In fact, attempts to be definitive, even under simplifying assumptions, are apt to become tedious. However, tedium is sometimes necessary and I go through the exercise in *The Theory of the Measurement of Enterprise Income.*

There is some evidence that the committee suffered from indecisiveness as to what the *Statement* ought to be. In some places it is pure theory, in other places it takes specific positions on contemporary practices[13] and in other places it is concerned with transition and the future.[14] I would have preferred that it concentrate on theory and would argue that the "basic accounting theory" and "fundamental research" phrases in the charge support my preference. Others have taken the opposite position and are disappointed because the committee did not set out a long series of allocation rules. All of which only proves that it is impossible to please everybody; that different receivers have different constructs and that no single *Statement* is relevant to all.

Most of my criticism can be summed up under the "adequate support" charge. My plea was for more: more support, development, explicitness, rigor, precision. Note however, that the committee was also charged to be as "concise as feasible"; it also had a capacity constraint. Given this constraint, a historical perspective, the fact that it was a committee and so forth, perhaps this *Statement* is all that one could reasonably expect. In addition, as Kuhn puts it:

> ... that commitment [to the new world-view or paradigm] must extend to areas and to degrees of precision for which there is no full precedent. If it did not, the paradigm could provide no puzzles that had not already been solved.[15]

Or, if the committee had done everything, there would be nothing left for the rest of us to do.

---

[13] For example on pooling versus purchasing (p. 23) they recommend the latter because the former carries forward the historical cost which is irrelevant to "investment decisions." They want to record the new exchange values caused by this "new market transaction" of merging. Why? Current cost as of the date of each succeeding balance sheet is going to be reported anyway. They are quarreling about what goes in the historical cost column and argue for a historical cost as of the date of merger instead of as of the date of original purchase. Is there something inherently more relevant in, say, a 1960 cost than in a 1950 cost?

[14] "Scope of Future Accounting" (pp. 64–65) expresses their belief in a trend toward multiple valuations and multi-dimensional reporting. "The committee has taken a first step by recommending two-column reports emphasizing historical cost and current cost."

[15] Kuhn, *op. cit.* p. 99.

A Response

Robert R. Sterling

PROFESSOR DEINZER begins with his characteristic thoroughness by citing some fifty-eight articles which have discussed ASOBAT.[1] The purpose of this commendable literature search is to demonstrate that there are many diverse interpretations of ASOBAT. I agree. I, too, have been struck by the number of different, sometimes contradictory, interpretations of the report. If one were to view ASOBAT as a completed theory which is supposed to provide *answers* to questions, then this would be a disturbing situation. I do not find these diverse interpretations disturbing or even surprising because I do not view ASOBAT as providing answers. Instead, I view it as asking new and different kinds of questions. In Kuhn's language, the message of ASOBAT is a new paradigm or a commitment to a new world-view. He says, "that commitment must extend to areas and to degrees of precision for which there is no full precedent. If it did not, the paradigm could provide no answers to puzzles that had not already been solved."[2] In my view, ASOBAT opens up a new line of inquiry. Like any other new line of inquiry, there are plenty of puzzles that need to be solved.

1. Harvey T. Deinzer, *Development of Accounting Thought* (New York: Holt, Rinehart and Winston, 1965).
2. Thomas S. Kuhn, *The Structure of Scientific Revolutions* (Chicago: University of Chicago Press, 1962), p. 99.

Prior to ASOBAT, there were many diverse interpretations in the literature. Since ASOBAT, there have been many diverse interpretations in the literature. The difference is only in what we are trying to interpret. Prior to ASOBAT, we were trying to define such concepts as "income," "financial position," and "unexpired cost." The literature prior to ASOBAT took the concept of, say, income as a given and then argued about how we ought to measure that concept. You will recall the lengthy and still unresolved arguments about whether LIFO or FIFO resulted in the best measure of income. You will also recall the equally lengthy and equally unresolved arguments over accelerated versus straight-line depreciation. Thus, in those days we knew *what* it was that we wanted to measure, and the arguments were concerned with *how* we were to measure the given concept. ASOBAT suggests a different line of inquiry. The relevance standard is concerned with *what* we ought to measure. If we knew which attributes were relevant, there would be no need to set up a relevance standard. Thus, the relevance standard is a question instead of an answer. It doesn't solve any problems; instead, it asks a new and different question. Given the newness of the question, I am not surprised that there are many different answers.

The notion of relevance is not new. Prior to ASOBAT, several scholars had suggested, in one form or another, that we should consider the question of relevance prior to the consideration of other questions. The thing that was new about ASOBAT was that this standard was stated *ex cathedra*. It was an official committee of the AAA that proposed this standard. Previously, the official committees of the AAA studied such specific concepts as "realization." They suggested rules for when one should realize revenue, i.e., they came up with specific measurement rules. The reasoning behind the suggested rules did not appear to be based upon relevance. ASOBAT has suggested a new line of inquiry. If we were to re-examine such questions and follow the ASOBAT suggestions, then, we would start with the question of relevance and the concept to be measured would be derived therefrom. Given that starting point, we might find that we did not need to measure realized revenue. If so, the question of how to measure it would be beside the point.

"Relevance" is an underdeveloped notion in accounting and, as we have already seen, there will be many problems in its application. However, in its general form, it seems to me that relevance is a simple and straightforward notion. All disciplines apply a standard of relevance, either implicitly or explicitly. All of the empirical sciences measure some attributes and do not measure others. Psychologists measure psychological attributes and physicists measure physical attributes. It would be odd to find a physicist administering an I.Q. test. It is not that the physicist considers I.Q. tests to be worthless or unimportant. It is simply that he finds them to be irrelevant to the problems he is concerned with. In developing his physical theories, he finds weight, volume, velocity, etc., to be relevant attributes, and he finds such things as intelligence and income measures to be irrelevant. Accountants must make the same kind of discrimination. We must decide what kinds of problems we are going to be concerned with, develop some theories for the solution of these problems, and then measure the attributes that are relevant to these theories.

In short, I think that the main message of ASOBAT is the relevance standard. To segregate attributes into relevant and irrelevant categories requires the existence of a theory. Even for a simple object, there is almost an infinite number of attributes that one could measure. Therefore, one cannot hope to measure all the attributes of any given object, and to just capriciously select certain attributes would serve no purpose. The function of a theory is, in part, to specify the attributes that are relevant. But then, there are a great many theories about a great many things. If we were to attempt to measure all the attributes specified by all the theories, we would again have an impossible task. Thus, we must select a problem area with which we wish to be concerned, and this will serve to limit the number of theories that we need be concerned with.

Perhaps an analogy would be helpful. Physicians are concerned with a great many things. The things that they are concerned with can be classified only in very general terms, i.e., "health problems." Under this general rubric, they propose and test various theories. To come upon a theory which solves a health problem is an arduous task which sometimes appears to depend as much on luck as it does on insight and intelligence. An example of this is Semmelweis' discovery of the cure for childbed fever.[3] Semmelweis tested a number of things—from the ringing of the priest's bell to vaguely defined atmospheric-cosmic-telluric changes—before he discovered the cause and cure for childbed fever. The discovery was made when one of his colleagues was accidentally nicked by a scalpel while performing an autopsy. The col-

3. Carl G. Hempel, *Philosophy of Natural Science* (Englewood Cliffs, N.J.: Prentice-Hall, 1966), pp. 3 ff.

league became ill and displayed the same kind of symptoms that were displayed by the women who had childbed fever. Semmelweis then leaped to the conclusion that there was something that got into the bloodstream that caused the malady. That is, he proposed a hypothesis or a theory which he subsequently tested and confirmed. By today's standards, his tests were crude. His measurements were even cruder. Nevertheless, his theory specified what it was that ought to be measured and controlled, albeit it was specified only in overly general terms such as "cadaveric matter." Subsequent advances in measurement methods have resulted in refinements in the theory. Conversely, subsequent advances in the theory have resulted in more specific attributes to be measured. Nowadays, measurements of such attributes are routinely made. The principle still holds: the pathologist or his laboratory technician normally measures such things as the percentage of red blood cells, but he does not normally measure the viscosity of the blood. The theory specifies that the percentage of red blood cells is relevant and that viscosity is not. These relevant attributes are then communicated to a practicing physician who makes a decision—diagnosis—based upon this information.

I propose the same kind of procedure for accounting. We can characterize the problems that we are concerned with only in the most general terms, e.g., "economic decisions." Then, we academic accountants can do research on economic decisions. We can propose theories and test them. In our quest, I expect that we will stumble and falter as much as Semmelweis did. The task is arduous. Once we have proposed and confirmed a theory, that theory will specify the relevant attributes to be measured. Then we can work on refinement of the measurement methods, which will affect the theory, and also work on refinements of the theory, which will affect what things are to be measured. The measurements routinely made by practicing accountants would be based upon the best theory available at the time.

The difficulties of this procedure are immense. In addition to the problems of research, there are political problems. If the researchers happen upon a theory which specifies a difficult measurement, they are almost certain to be told that they cannot make the measurement, because it is not objective and verifiable, or worse, because it is not generally accepted. This view inhibits progress. If medical researchers had taken this view, they could still be arguing how to measure atmospheric-cosmic-telluric changes, despite the fact that this measure is not specified by any theory. That is, it is irrelevant to everything even though it may have been generally accepted by the physicians at the time, and the measurement may have been considered objective and verifiable. For this reason, I agree with ASOBAT when it labels relevance as the *primary* standard. We must first propose and test a theory and then try to refine our method of measuring those properties that are specified by the theory. Quantifiability, freedom-from-bias, and other such standards are *secondary* considerations. General acceptance by practicing accountants is beside the point. Can you imagine a medical researcher discarding a confirmed theory because it is not generally accepted by practicing physicians? By definition, a new theory is new and therefore unknown. Therefore, the test of a new theory cannot be general acceptance.

To continue the analogy, I view the practicing accountant in the same light as the pathologist and his laboratory technicians. They routinely make the measurements that are specified by the extant theories. This does not, as some people claim, reduce the professional status of the pathologist and make him a mere bookkeeper. Difficult measurements require difficult professional judgments. This view does, however, prevent him from treating each case as if it were unique. He cannot use different measurement methods because of "differing circumstances." Each case differs in some respects, and the purpose of measurement is to discover the differences in the relevant attributes. The pathologist is not prohibited from doing research on his cases. However, he is *first* required to make the routine measurements specified by the extant theory.

The practicing physician is the receiver of the information. To communicate the relevant information to the practicing physician is not the same as making the diagnosis for him. The relevant information permits him to make a better or more-informed diagnosis. It does not guarantee that he will make the right diagnosis. The more precise the theory, the more evident the diagnosis, but, even with the relevant information, there are still a large number of judgmental diagnoses. The same is true with the receivers of accounting information. Receipt of the relevant information does not relieve the decision-maker of the task of making the decision, nor does it guarantee the right decision. Some decision models are so well specified that they can be programmed, but, even with the relevant information, most economic decisions require judgment, as well as personal preferences.

The medical researcher does not survey the practicing physicians to find out what information they want. Instead, he tries to communicate to them the advances in medical research, i.e., the confirmed new theories or the refinements in the old theories, and he tries to persuade them to use such advancements. To do otherwise would require that advances in medical theory come from the practice of medicine instead of from medical research. If medical researchers had followed this path, they would probably still be letting blood in the same way that we are still reporting sunk costs. If, as I believe, sunk costs are demonstrably irrelevant, then the fact that some decision-makers use them is not sufficient justification to continue to report them.

The above implies, and I make explicit, that I believe that there is no separate theory of accounting. Instead, there is a problem area which I prefer to call economic decisions. Researchers concerned with such problems should propose and test theories and work on refining the measurement and communication methods. Practicing accountants should routinely make the measurements that are specified by the best theory available at the time, in accordance with the best measurement methods available at the time. Then they should communicate these measurements to economic decision-makers. Thus, the practice of accounting is simply the measurement-communication function of the discipline concerned with economic decision problems. If there were a theory of accounting, it would be a theory of that function.

The impact of the message of ASOBAT is to place the burden for accounting advancements squarely where it belongs, i.e., upon the shoulders of you and me. We can no longer inventory accounting practices and then teach those practices. We can no longer try to determine the needs of the receivers by surveying them, nor can we try to justify the figures that we report by noticing that receivers use those figures. We cannot expect the APB to do the research. They are too busy with their own practice and with putting out brush fires. We academics must do the research and then try to communicate the results of that research to both practicing accountants and users of accounting information. For accounting, this is a revolutionary line of inquiry. Since it is a line of inquiry or a question instead of an answer, I am not surprised or disturbed by the diversity of opinion about the message of ASOBAT. I am only disappointed that we have, as yet, made so little progress.

ROBERT R. STERLING

An Explication and Analysis of the Structure of Accounting Part One

Introduction

> Some years ago there arose doubt as to whether the United States Army did indeed possess a large number of a certain type of tanks and if so, where they were! Yet the Army is an establishment with a highly developed, bureaucratic recording system and most thorough accounting procedures. This incident, whatever the facts in the case, shows the type of difficulty also encountered, without doubt, by large businesses. It would be interesting to learn how often similar instances occur, as they undoubtedly do, in our largest industrial enterprises. These firms also have great difficulties in finding out where their inventories are and what they consist of.[1]

A recent visit to one of the world's largest oil companies brought Morgenstern's point home to me with some force. The company was having considerable difficulty in keeping track of its inventory — crude oil and oil products — as well as keeping track of its railroad tank cars and other mobile equipment. Keeping track of its stationary and semi-stationary capital assets was less of a problem but there were still some difficulties.

The source of the difficulty, at least partly, seemed to be that the accounts were kept in value (cost) terms in accordance with time-honored accounting principles, but the information most often needed concerned the quantity of the assets. For example, it was easy to determine that there was a $100,000 inventory of crude oil at location *x* but it was difficult to determine how many barrels of crude oil were at that location. Yet the decisions about transporting, converting, ability to meet needs, etc., almost invariably required that the decision-maker know the quantity at that location, but seldom if ever was he required to know its cost.

This paper will outline a method of accounting for physical quantities. One of the meanings of 'to account' is 'to keep track of' things. I propose to show how the double-entry system can be used to keep track of physical quantities as well as to keep track of costs or values.

Although the 'practical' problems of keeping track of the physical quantities are interesting in and of themselves, the 'theoretical' problems of financial accounting are my main concern in this paper. I will argue that the quantity accounting system

1. Oskar Morgenstern, *On the Accuracy of Economic Observations*, 2nd edition, Princeton University, 1963, p. 73.

ROBERT R. STERLING is Professor of Business Administration in the University of Kansas.

An earlier draft of this paper was presented at the Spring Seminars Programme of the Université de Laval and benefited from the criticism received.

has exactly the same structure as the financial accounting system, i.e. they are logical isomorphs. Except for valuation, which can be discussed in similar terms, the two systems are identical. The quantity system is much simpler than the financial system and the experiential (or phenomenological) reduction is obvious. Thus, the physical world provides a simple and intuitively obvious interpretation of the quantity accounting system. The financial accounting system will be cast in relief against the quantity system and an attempt will be made to clarify some problems, expose some errors, and gain some insights.

Description of the physical system

Consider a space which is partitioned into *n* discrete locations. These locations can be denoted, classified and sub-classified in various ways. For example, some of the locations may be called 'oil wells' and a certain collection of the wells is called 'oil field *x*' while another collection is called 'oil field *y*'. Other locations may be called 'tanks' and a certain collection of those tanks may be called 'storage plant *x*'. Some minor difficulties arise with such things as 'railroad tank cars' which may be labelled as locations for convenience but the spatial location is a variable. Multi-classification is necessary in such cases in order to be able to sum over the collection of tank cars in transit as well as the collection of tank cars within a given geographical area. Obviously, one can attach as many classification subscripts as is desired, but for convenience we will use only one and speak of it as a 'location'.

At any given moment in time each of these locations will contain a non-negative physical quantity. Define

q_{ij} = The numeral representing the physical quantity at the ith location at time j.

The term 'numeral representing the physical quantity' is included in the definition to emphasize the distinction between the physical world and the recording system which is intended to replicate certain properties of that world. That is, we will build a 'model' of a physical system. The set of accounts that will be described is the model, and the goal is to be able to look at the accounts in order to know the magnitude and location of a quantity in much the same way that an astronomer can look at a planetarium in order to know the location of a star.

The distinction is important for several reasons. The actual quantity at location *i* at time *j* may be different from the numeral representing that quantity. It is cumbersome to measure independently the quantities each time one wants information about them and thus, it is more convenient to keep track of the 'transfers' and calculate q_{ij} from those transfers. Define

Δq_{ij} = the signed numeral representing an increment ($\Delta^{+}q_{ij}$) or decrement ($\Delta^{-}q_{ij}$) at location i at time j.

Assuming that the original quantity at each location is zero we can calculate q_{it} as:

$$q_{it} = \sum_{j=1}^{t} \Delta q_{ij}$$

Since a receipt at one location is an issue at another location any transfer can be represented by a zero sum equation.

$$\Delta^{+}q_{ij} + \Delta^{-}q_{kj} = 0$$

This equation indicates that location *i* received Δq quantity from location *k* at time *j*. I am assuming simultaneity of transfers. Obviously it requires some time period to effect the transfer in a real system. However, this is because we are usually interested in the transfer between spatially separated locations. For contiguous locations the transfer is simultaneous. For example, what comes out of a tank simultaneously goes into a pipeline and what comes out of a pipeline simultaneously goes into a tank. Since we are usually concerned with the oil in the different tanks, we conceive of the transfer as requiring a time period instead of being simultaneous. The period required is an important datum because of the opportunity cost of a stock out. An alternative is to keep the pipeline full and connected, which permits simultaneous transfers between tanks, but this procedure requires a large inventory and the additional costs thereof.

Given the fact that the original quantity at each location is zero, that each transfer sums to zero, and that the quantity at each location is calculated from the transfers, it follows that the sum of the quantities at all locations is zero:

$$\sum_{i=1}^{n} q_{ij} = 0$$

That is, every increment at one location is offset by a decrement at another location; the quantity stock at each location is defined as the sum of the increments and decrements to that location; therefore, the sum of all the quantity stocks is zero. Although this may be counter-intuitive, it is nothing more than a conservation law. You may recall that one way of expressing the various (e.g. mass, momentum, energy) conservation laws of physics is to note that within any given closed, isolated system the sum of the changes is zero.

The notion of a 'closed, isolated system' is the key to the conservation laws. There may be a positive amount of, say, energy within a closed, isolated system, but the sum of the changes within that system is zero. If we shift our focus to a larger system, then we can explain where the energy in the smaller system came from, but the sum of the changes is still zero in respect to the larger system. Now we can shift our focus to an even larger system but, no matter how large the system, the changes still sum to zero. The same is true in regard to oil in any particular location. That oil came from some source location but that source location had a previous source location. Thus, there is a chain of source locations and each quantity can be traced all the way back to the deposit in ground. But that deposit also came from somewhere and the source of the deposit also had a source, and so forth. A decision must be made as to how far back the tracing will be carried or else suffer an infinite regress. For this reason physicists restrict their attention to some part of the universe. In some circumstances they are concerned with closed, isolated systems which are some segment of the universe. In respect of closed isolated systems they enunciate conservation laws. In other cases they are concerned with closed but not isolated systems, systems to which there are admitted inputs (say, heat) from the larger system of which the system under examination is a part, and from which outputs (say, work) are given off to the larger system.

We have introduced our analysis by reference to a closed isolated system of locations.[2] But the entity we shall consider hence forward will be a closed but not isolated entity, analogous to the usage in physics. We will work with transfers between various locations within the entity as well as transfers between the entity of interest and entities which are parts of the larger system. Thus, the universe of locations is classified as:

(A) entity locations and (B) extra-entity locations.

Given the above classification of locations we can also classify the transfers. From the point of view of any particular entity there are three kinds of transfers:

(1) transfers which affect two locations within the entity of interest will be called 'intra-entity transfers';

(2) transfers which affect one location in the entity of interest and one extra-entity location will be called 'inter-entity transfers'; and

(3) transfers which affect two extra-entity locations will be called 'extra-entity transfers'.

The inter-entity transfers may be sub-classified by direction:

(i) extra-entity locations which receive quantities will be called 'recipient locations' from the point of view of the issuing entity;

(ii) extra-entity locations which give up quantities will be called 'source locations' from the point of view of the receiving entity; and

(iii) the locations within the entity of interest will be called 'real locations'.

Since extra-entity transfers do not affect the entity of interest they will normally be disregarded.[3]

Thus, the combination of the transfer and location classification yields three classes of locations for any given entity: Recipient, Source and Real. One can keep track of the transfers and thereby know the quantities at each location within the entity as well as the quantities that have been issued to and received from extra-entity locations.

This section has been an attempt to describe a simple physical system. The characteristics of that system are familiar and intuitively obvious. This system will serve as the referrent for the interpretation of the formalized system which will be described in the next section. That is, this section was intended to be a description of a particular 'real world' as opposed to the 'constructed' formal system of the next section. The distinction is important. A formalized system can be set up and its properties investigated without any reference to the application of that system to the real world. Much of mathematics is developed in this way. On the other hand, one may try to set up a formalized system which will serve as a model for the real

2. We also account for only a specified subset of the events that occur at those locations. For example, in the case of the oil tanks we account for changes in volume but we do not account for a host of other events such as changes in color or viscosity.

3. Extra-entity transfers may be relevant to the valuation question but they do not affect the quantities in the entity of interest and therefore the discussion of them is deferred.

world. In the latter case one of the tests of the model is how well it replicates the real world; in the former case that test is irrelevant.

In summary, the described physical system obeys a conservation law in regard to the quantities in which we are interested and therefore all the changes sum to zero. The space of the system is partitioned into locations and a particular set of locations is called an entity. One can represent the quantities by numerals and one can calculate the quantities at the various locations by summing the increments and decrements to that location. This physical system will serve as the referrent for the formal system which is described in the next section.

Definition of the accounting system

This section will *define* an accounting system. The purpose of the accounting system is to keep track of something and some possible interpretations will be given as we proceed but it is important to remember that this is a *formal* system. Whether or not the defined accounting system will accurately reflect the physical system is a separate question.

Definition 1—*Transfer*: $(\Delta q_{ij})\,(\exists \Delta q_{kj})\,[\Delta q_{ij}\ \mathbf{R}\ \Delta q_{kj}]$

For every Δq_{ij} there exists a Δq_{kj} such that they are related. The related pair will be called a 'transfer' and denoted $\Delta q_{ij}\ \mathbf{R}\ \Delta q_{kj}$. The relation **R** is asymmetric (and therefore irreflexive), one-one and transitive. That is,

$$(\Delta q_{ij})\,(\Delta q_{kj})\,[(\Delta q_{ij}\ \mathbf{R}\ \Delta q_{kj}) \rightarrow \sim(\Delta q_{kj}\ \mathbf{R}\ \Delta q_{ij})].$$

However, there is a converse relation, $\mathbf{R}^{\cup}$, such that

$$(\Delta q_{ij})\,(\Delta q_{kj})\,[(\Delta q_{ij}\ \mathbf{R}\ \Delta q_{kj}) \rightarrow (\Delta q_{kj}\ \mathbf{R}^{\cup}\ \Delta q_{ij})].$$

The transitivity of the relation permits one to drop a term

$$(\Delta q_{ij})\,(\Delta q_{kj})\,(\Delta q_{mj})\,\{[(\Delta q_{ij}\ \mathbf{R}\ \Delta q_{kj})\ \&\ (\Delta q_{mj}\ \mathbf{R}\ \Delta q_{ij})] \rightarrow (\Delta q_{mj}\ \mathbf{R}\ \Delta q_{kj})\}.$$

There are many interpretations of this definition, i.e. there are many relations which are like the one defined. For example, the relation 'husband of' is asymmetric and one-one. If *a* is the husband of *b*, then *b* cannot be the husband of *a* and therefore the relation is said to be asymmetric. The relation 'wife of' is the converse of 'husband of'. (The relation 'spouse of' by contrast is said to be symmetric since if *a* is the spouse of *b*, then *b* is the spouse of *a*.) Likewise if one transfers quantity *q* to tank *i* from tank *k*, then the relation between the tanks is asymmetric for that particular transfer. The converse relation is simply a reversal of the terms — 'from tank *k* to tank *i*'. Thus the relation 'transfer from' is the converse of 'transfer to' in this instance in the same way as 'wife of' is the converse of 'husband of'.

'Husband of' is also a one-one relation in monogamous cultures, as opposed to one-many in polygamous cultures and many-one in polyandrous cultures. If all pipelines connect two, and only two, tanks then any transfer between tanks is a one-one relation. If the pipeline branches, then the transfer could be one-many or many-one or many-many. If the latter were the case, then we would need some method of decomposing the transfer so that it could be treated as if it were one-one. That is, the system being described *requires* that the relation be one-one or be decomposable so that it can be treated as if it were one-one.[4]

There are many familiar transitive relations, e.g. greater than, ancestor of, equal to, and successor to. If a is the ancestor of b and b is the ancestor of c, then a is the ancestor of c. If $a > b$ and $b > c$, then $a > c$, etc. The transfer relation is transitive in that it is meaningful to say that if quantity q went to location i from location k and then went to location m from location i, then quantity q went to location m from location k. It may become necessary to refine the relation in the same way that Russell[5] refines 'successor', i.e. by distinguishing between 'immediate successor' and 'successor', but this refinement is not necessary for the present purpose.

Definition 1.1—*Zero-sum*: $(\Delta q_{ij}\ \mathbf{R}\ \Delta q_{ij})\ [\Delta q_{ij} + \Delta q_{kj} = 0]$

The related quantities are signed numerals such that each transfer sums to zero.

There are several possible interpretations of the zero-sum definition. The most obvious one is that in any conservative system the changes sum to zero provided, of course, that both quantities in any given transfer are expressed in the same units. That is, if one quantity is expressed in grams and the other is expressed in ounces, then the transfer will not sum to zero even though the system conserves mass. Thus, both quantities in any transfer must be expressed in the same units. Of course, the original measurement of the two quantities need not have been expressed in the same units or even the same dimension. One can convert ounces to grams by a simple mathematical operation. By use of the appropriate 'conversion coefficient', ounces can be converted to grams (or vice versa). Even more complex conversions can be made; one can convert the measure of one property to the measure of another property of the same object if there is a known and fixed relationship between the measures of the two properties. For example, a weight measurement could be converted to a volume measurement because we know that one gram of distilled water at 4° C. is equal to one cubic centimeter and therefore one can convert volume to weight or vice versa.

Likewise it is possible physically to convert crude into gasoline and therefore one could make the measurement in terms of crude but then mathematically convert it to the gasoline that it will (or did) yield.

4. Surprisingly, this seemingly simple aspect is a rather difficult hurdle in the formalization of accounting. Simple entries (one debit — one credit) are rather easily formalized but compound entries (many debits — many credits) present problems. *See* Mattessich's discussion of duality — Richard Mattessich, *Accounting and Analytical Methods*, Richard D. Irwin, Inc., 1964, p. 34 — and Ijiri's discussion of multiple causal networks — Yuji Ijiri, *The Foundations of Accounting Measurement*, Prentice-Hall, Inc., 1967, pp. 58ff. *See also* Section IV Part Two of this paper for a discussion of some operational problems caused by non-one-one relations.

5. Bertrand Russell, *Introduction to Mathematical Philosophy*, George Allen & Unwin, Ltd, 1948, p. 23.

The interpretation of the conversion process is more appropriate to the valuation question and a more detailed discussion is deferred. It is sufficient to note at this point that we are discussing a formal system and that it is quite easy formally to define a coefficient which will make each transfer sum to zero. If $\Delta q_{ij} + \Delta q_{kj} \neq 0$, because the two are expressed in different units or for any other reason, then a coefficient,

P_{ij} (or P_{kj}) is defined as $\dfrac{-\Delta q_{kj}}{\Delta q_{ij}} \left(\text{or } \dfrac{-\Delta q_{ij}}{\Delta q_{kj}}\right)$. Note that

$$\left(\frac{-\Delta q_{kj}}{\Delta q_{ij}}\right) \Delta q_{ij} + \Delta q_{kj} = 0 \text{ or } \Delta q_{ij} + \left(\frac{-\Delta q_{ij}}{\Delta q_{kj}}\right) \Delta q_{kj} = 0.$$

The defined coefficient can be used to convert any transfer into a zero-sum equation and therefore make all transfers meet the requirement of Definition 1.1.

Definition 2—*Entity*: $I = \{i : i = 1, 2, \ldots, m\}$
The entity I is a well-defined set of locations. Entities J, K, ... are defined similarly such that the sets are disjoint, i.e., $I \cap J \cap K \ldots = \phi$.

The above definitions are the fundamental ones for the accounting system to be described. They could be called axioms or postulates if one chose to do so. The primitive or undefined terms include 'quantity', 'relation', 'location', and 'time'. All of the above definitions made use of at least one of those primitives. 'Transfer' was defined as a 'relation' with certain properties. One of those properties was that the 'related' 'quantities' summed to zero. 'Entity' was defined as a collection of 'locations'. The primitive 'time' will be used in the definitions that follow. All of these are intuitively simple terms and all of the rest of the accounting system can be defined with these primitives alone. It will not be necessary to introduce new primitive terms from this point on. These primitives are the descriptive terms of the defined system. Certain other terms (and operators) from mathematics and logic are also left undefined. These include the logical constants 'or', 'and', 'If . . . then . . .', 'not', and such notions as 'set', 'element of', etc. The operators are 'summation' and 'partition'.

Definition 2.1—*Entry*: $(\Delta q_{ij}\ \mathbf{R}\ \Delta q_{kj})\ [(i \in I) \vee (k \in I) \rightarrow \Delta q_{ij}\ \mathbf{R}\ \Delta q_{kj}$ is an entry for I]

For every transfer if one or both of the locations is contained in entity I, then that transfer is defined as an entry for entity I. Entries for entities J, K, . . . are defined similarly.

Balance sheet definition. From the above set of definitions it is possible to define a quantity balance sheet that has the same structure and some of the same interpretations as the financial balance sheet. The balance sheet will be defined for entity I and it should be understood that all the definitions refer only to the transfers that have been classified as entries in entity I. Balance sheets for entities J, K, . . . are defined similarly.

Definition 3.1—*Balance of account i*: $q_{it} = \sum_{j=1}^{t} \Delta q_{ij}$

The balance of account *i* at time *t* is the sum of all the changes to that account from time 1 to time *t* and is denoted q_{it}.

The above definition uses the word 'account', instead of 'location', because we are defining an accounting system and the physical system so far discussed is only one possible interpretation (or application) of that accounting system. It is important to distinguish between the accounting system and the system which is being accounted for. An account contains a collection of numerals; a location contains a quantity. Obviously, under the quantity interpretation the account balances are intended to reflect the quantity flows and stocks at the various locations.[6]

Another reason for using the word 'account' is that there will be more accounts than locations in a given entity. Definition 2.1 specifies that an entry will be made any time that either of the locations is contained in the entity. Since the entry is a pair of numerals, an account balance will be defined for some extra-entity locations. Since account balances will exist if and only if that location appears in an entry, the set (or chart) of accounts is implicitly defined by Definitions 2 and 2.1.

Definition 3.2—*Source accounts*: $(q_{ij})\ [(i \notin I)\ \&\ (q_{ij} < 0) \rightarrow q_{ij}^{-}]$

For all account balances if *i* is not an element of I and q_{ij} is negative then classify as a source account and denote as q_{ij}^{-}.

Definition 3.3—*Recipient accounts:* $(q_{ij})\ [(i \notin I)\ \&\ (q_{ij} > 0) \rightarrow q_{ij}^{+}]$

For all account balances if *i* is not an element of I and q_{ij} is positive then classify as a recipient account and denote as q_{ij}^{+}.

Definition 3.4—*Real accounts*: $(q_{ij})\ [i \in I \rightarrow q_{ij}]$

6. Of equal importance is the distinction between an interpreted and an uninterpreted formal system. An uninterpreted system can only be tested for logical consistency. Since it is uninterpreted, it is not intended to refer to anything other than itself and therefore reference to empirical phenomena is irrelevant. An interpreted system, on the other hand, is intended to refer to some empirical phenomena and therefore it can be empirically tested.

In reference to the uninterpreted accounting system, the definition of the 'balance of account *i*' can only be challenged on the grounds that it contradicts some other part of the system. But when the accounting system is interpreted, it can be challenged on the grounds that it does not accurately model the empirical phenomena. For example, it could be empirically demonstrated that the system being defined accurately models volume stocks and flows under conditions of constant temperatures, but it does not under conditions of varying temperatures.

The same two tests are applicable to value accounting. If traditional accounting is intended to be an uninterpreted system, then the definition of, say, 'unexpired cost' can be challenged only on logical grounds. If traditional accounting is intended to be an interpreted system, then at least some of its terms must refer to some empirical phenomena and be subject to empirical test. For example, it might be found that traditional accounting accurately models the firm under conditions of constant prices but that it does not under conditions of varying prices.

For all account balances if i is an element of I then classify as a real account and denote as $\hat{q}_{ij}$.

All real account balances will be non-negative and all zero balances will be disregarded. The quantity balance sheet can be displayed in the following form in as much detail as is desired:

Entity I
Quantity Balance Sheet
Time t

Recipient accounts:	q_{it}^{+}	Source accounts:	q_{it}^{-}
Real accounts:	$\hat{q}_{it}$		
Total 'assets':	$\sum_i q_{it}^{+} + \sum_i \hat{q}_{it}$	Total 'equities':	$\sum q_{it}^{-}$

And of course the total 'assets' equal the total 'equities' (in absolute values) because each transfer sums to zero and therefore the sum of all transfers is zero.[7]

The interpretation of the balance sheet is straightforward. The real accounts should reflect the quantities at the various locations within the entity. The recipient accounts should reflect the net outflows of quantities, classified by destination, from this entity to extra-entity locations. The source accounts should reflect the net inflows of quantities from extra-entity locations. That this is the case is indicated by an even more intuitive arrangement of the accounts.

$$\sum_i \hat{q}_{it} = |\sum_i q_{it}^{-}| - \sum_i q_{it}^{+}$$

or

Quantity Balances = Quantity Inflows less Quantity Outflows.

The recipient accounts are like monetary assets on the financial balance sheet. Whenever an entity has a receivable outstanding it means that something is due from someone but it also means that someone has been a recipient of something from the entity. The real stocks are like the tangible assets on the financial balance sheet; the main difference is that the quantities are not valued. The sources are like the equities (liabilities and proprietorship). Some people now argue that the financial equities should be thought of as sources of assets.

Flow statements definition. Quantity statements with the same structure as the statements of sources and applications of funds and the income statement can also be defined. Consider first the funds statement. The purpose of the state-

7.Since, by Definition 1.1 $\Delta q_{ij} + \Delta q_{kj} = 0$ for each transfer, it follows that $\sum_i \Delta q_{ij} = 0$. The account balances are sums of the changes over time $q_{it} = \sum_{j=1}^{t} \Delta q_{ij}$ by Definition 3.1 and therefore it follows that $\sum_i q_{it} = 0$. Definitions 3.2, 3.3 and 3.4 serve to partition the account balances into three mutually exclusive and exhaustive sets. Therefore $\sum_i q_{it}^{+} + \sum_i \hat{q}_{it} + \sum_i q_{it}^{-} = 0$. Subtracting $\sum q_{it}^{-}$ from both sides yields $\sum_i q_{it}^{+} + \sum_i \hat{q}_{it} = -\sum_i q_{it}^{-}$.
which is the form of quantity balance sheet presented above. However, this changes the sign of the source account balances from negative to positive and it is important to retain the negative sign for future processing.

ment is to isolate the inflow and outflow of 'funds'. Those funds are contained in one account if 'funds' is defined as cash or in a set of accounts if it is defined as net quick assets or net working capital. Thus, the 'funds accounts' are just a well-defined proper subset of the set of accounts for a particular entity. The most direct way to define a funds statement is to use the same definitions as presented above for real, source and recipient accounts. For purposes of illustration we will use similar notation. Again all references are to the transfers that have been classified as entries in entity I.

Definition 4.1—*Fund accounts:* $F = \{i : i \text{ is a fund account}\}$

The fund accounts are a well-defined subset of the set of accounts in entity I. It is usually, but not necessarily, a proper subset.

Definition 4.2—*Fund transfers*: $(\triangle q_{ij}\ \mathbf{R}\ \triangle q_{kj})\ [(i \in F) \vee (k \in F) \rightarrow (\triangle \dot{q}_{ij}\ \mathbf{R}\ \triangle \dot{q}_{kj})]$

For every transfer if *i* or *k* or both is a fund account then classify as a fund transfer and denote as $\triangle \dot{q}_{ij}$.

Definition 4.3—*Sum of fund transfers*: $\dot{q}_{it} = \sum_{j=t-1}^{t} \triangle \dot{q}_{ij}$

The net effect on account *i* of the fund transfers from time *t*—1 to *t* is the sum of the changes and is denoted $\dot{q}_{it}$.

Definition 4.4—*Sources of funds*: $(\dot{q}_{it})\ [(i \notin F)\ \&\ (\dot{q}_{it} < 0) \rightarrow \dot{q}_{it}^{-}]$

For every $\dot{q}_{it}$ if *i* is not a fund account and $\dot{q}_{it}$ is negative then classify as a source of funds and denote as $\dot{q}_{it}^{-}$.

Definition 4.5—*Recipient of funds*: $(\dot{q}_{it})\ [(i \notin F)\ \&\ (\dot{q}_{it} > 0) \rightarrow \dot{q}_{it}^{+}]$

For every $\dot{q}_{it}$ if *i* is not a fund account and $\dot{q}_{it}$ is positive then classify as a recipient (or use or application) of funds and denote as $\dot{q}_{it}^{+}$.

The funds statement would be displayed in the following form in as much detail as desired.

Entity I
Quantity Funds Statement
Time *t*—1 to *t*

Sources of funds:	$\sum_{i} \dot{q}_{it}^{-}$
Recipients (applications) of funds:	$\sum_{i} \dot{q}_{it}^{+}$
Change in funds:	$\sum_{i \in F} \dot{q}_{it}$

This statement has exactly the same structure as the balance sheet presented above. That is,

$$\sum_{i \in F} \dot{q}_{it} = |\Sigma \dot{q}_{it}^{-}| - \Sigma \dot{q}_{it}^{+} \qquad \text{or,}$$

Quantity balance changes from *t*—1 to *t* = Quantity Inflows from *t*—1 to *t* less Quantity Outflows from *t*—1 to *t*.[8]

The only difference between the two statements is the set of accounts which they focus on and the time period covered. The balance sheet displays the net changes in quantities that has occurred at a given set of locations (the entity) from time 1 to time *t* and the recipients and sources of those quantity changes. The funds statement displays the net changes that have occurred at a given set of locations (the funds set) from time *t*—1 to *t* and the recipients and sources of those quantity changes. The difference lies in the focus. In both cases one focuses on a set of locations and then focuses on the transfers which have affected those locations during a specified time interval. Then one calculates the net changes in those locations and their sources and recipients.

Of course the funds statement is not ordinarily prepared by inclusion as we have done above; instead it is prepared by exclusion. Obviously the two should achieve the same results. That is, since

$$q_{1t-1} + \sum_{j=t-1}^{t} \Delta q_{1j} = q_{1t}$$

and

$$\sum_{j=t-1}^{t} \Delta q_{1j} = \sum_{j=t-1}^{t} \Delta \dot{q}_{1j} + \sum_{j=t-1}^{t} \Delta \tilde{q}_{1j}$$

where the dot designates fund transfers and the tilde non-fund transfers, then

$$q_{1t} - q_{1t-1} - \sum_{j=t-1}^{t} \Delta \tilde{q}_{1j} = \sum_{j=t-1}^{t} \Delta \dot{q}_{1j}$$

and the sign of $\sum_{j=t-1}^{t} \Delta \dot{q}_{1j}$ indicates whether it is a source (—) or an application (+).

Definition of the income statement is similar but a little more complicated. Both statements require partitioning the set of transfers. The fund statement

8. The simplest interpretation is that the funds accounts are a subset of the real accounts. This would mean that the funds statement explains the changes in certain physical quantities within the entity. This in turn might be taken to mean that cash is a physical quantity. However, that interpretation is not necessary. One can interpret cash — coins and currency — as simply a convenient token of an undefined recipient (and also as a token of a claim against an undefined source). This would place cash in the form of coins and currency in the same class as cash in the form of bank deposits. Economic activity can be characterized as the transfer of real goods and services from one location (or person) to another. Cash may be thought of as a generalized recipient location that is used when we are not interested in recording the specific location, e.g. cash sales as opposed to sales to customer *x*. Of course, cash is also a generalized claim against real goods and services offered in the market and for this reason we usually call the activity an 'exchange' instead of a 'transfer'.

However, in non-barter exchanges the transfer of real goods and services causes one to be obligated to transfer real goods and services in the reverse direction and cash, in whatever form, is simply a token of, or a marker for, that obligation. The transitivity of the transfer relation permits the reverse transfer to be circuitous. The existence of cash simplifies the bookkeeping. One is not required to trace and record all the real transfers in order to know who has received (and is obligated for) what. Thus, in a sense the transfer of real goods and services is the more fundamental economic activity and the notion of an 'exchange' (for cash) is derived from the fundamental activity of transferring real goods and services. In this sense cash in the form of coins and currency serves the same function as cash in the form of bank deposits, i.e. cash is merely a bookkeeping device representing a non-specific recipient of (and a non-specific claim against) real goods and services.

This latter interpretation does not invalidate the funds statement presented in the text. One can isolate a set of recipient locations and explain its changes by noting what quantities went to and came from those locations.

distinguishes fund from non-fund transactions and the income statement distinguishes income from non-income transactions. The basis for distinction is to classify a certain set of extra-entity locations as 'customers'. Again for purposes of illustrating the similarity of the structure we will use similar notation.

Definition 5.1—*Customer accounts*: $C = \{i : i = \text{a customer account}\}$

Definition 5.2—*Sources from customers*: $q_{Ct}^{-} = \sum_{\substack{i \varepsilon C \\ j=t-1}}^{t} \Delta^{-} q_{ij}$

Definition 5.3—*Issues to customers*: $q_{Ct}^{+} = \sum_{\substack{i \varepsilon C \\ j=t-1}}^{t} \Delta^{+} q_{ij}$

The income statement is displayed in the following form in as much detail as desired.

Entity I
Income Statement
Time $t-1$ to k

Revenues (sources from customers):	q_{Ct}^{-}
Expenses (issues to customers):	q_{Ct}^{+}
Net income:	Y

The quantity interpretation is again straightforward. There has been an inflow of quantities from customers and an outflow of quantities to customers. The sum is the net inflow or outflow of quantities to or from a particular set of (customer) locations. This is even clearer if the signs are reversed.[9]

$$Y = |q_{Ct}^{-}| - q_{Ct}^{+}$$

or

Net Quantity Income = Quantity Inflows from customers less Quantity Outflows to customers.

Of course, the income statement may also be defined by exclusion as was the fund statement. Sometimes we do this when solving problems called 'statements from incomplete data'.

Consolidations. The most direct method of 'consolidation' is to redefine the

9. The interpretation of the above quantity income statement that is closest to the interpretation of the financial income statement is to think of cash as a real account. The revenues on the financial income statement are the offset to the receipts of cash or near-cash from customers. The expenses on the financial income statement are the offsets to the issues of assets to customers. This is clear in the case of inventory but it is also a possible interpretation of other expenses. Under traditional theory, a depreciable asset is conceived of as a quantity of service potentials or units of capacity. These units have a valuation coefficient (cost per unit) 'attached' in the same way that a unit of inventory has an attached valuation coefficient. Thus, one may think of depreciation expense as representing an issue of part of a year of service life to customers in the same way that one thinks of cost of goods sold as representing an issue of a unit of inventory to customers. All of these issues to customers are 'matched' against the receipts from customers. However, these assets which are issued to customers are the offset to a previous cash or near-cash issue, which is the basis for the attachment (of the cost) to the asset. They are just deferred cash issues and therefore, the financial income statement, in one sense, is a statement of cash receipts and cash disbursements *from* and *to customers*. The excess of the cash receipts over the disbursements is the net income.

The same interpretation is possible for any quantity. We can define a set of locations and consider the quantity received from those locations less the quantity issued to those locations as income.

entity and select the transfers which affect that entity. We originally defined entity I as

$$I = (i:i = 1, 2, \ldots, m)$$

and we can define entity J as

$$J = (i:i = m+1, m+2, \ldots, n)$$

Then we could instantiate $I \cup J$ in Definition 2 and this would change our set of entries in Definition 2.1. The statements would then be prepared in exactly the same way as before. However, it is not ordinarily possible to prepare consolidated reports in this way because each entity has already recorded its entries and summed them. For this reason consolidated statements are prepared by a method of exclusion or elimination.

Any transfer between the entities I and J will be recorded on both sets of books as an increment and decrement to a real location with an offset to a source and recipient account. For example, the transfer to location *m* in entity I from location *n* in entity J would be recorded as

$$\Delta^+q_{mj} + \Delta^-q_{nj} = 0$$

on the books of entity I and Δ^-q_{nj} will be summed to q^-_{nj}, i.e. a source account. On the books of entity J it would be recorded in exactly the same way except that Δ^+q_{mj} would be summed to q^+_{mj} i.e. a recipient account. Obviously we cannot simply sum these by location because the balance would include $2\Delta^+q_{mj}$ as the increment to location *m*. There would be 'double counting'. The solution is equally obvious: all q_{ij} on the books of entity I which have been classified as source or recipient accounts and $i \in J$ are to be added to all q_{ij} on the books of entity J which have been classified as source or recipient accounts and $i \in I$. This sum is zero, of course, if no errors in recording have been made.

There are several alternative ways of formulating the consolidation procedure. One method would be to scan all Δq_{ij} **R** Δq_{kj} and select those which $i \in I$ and $k \in J$ or $i \in J$ and $k \in I$. Since there would be two Δq_{ij} **R** Δq_{kj} (one as an entry for each entity) then we could subtract out one of the Δq_{ij} **R** Δq_{kj}. Another way would be to sum the inter-entity balances. On the books of I, define

$$q_{Jt} = \sum_{i \in J} q_{it}$$

and, on the books of J, define

$$q_{It} = \sum_{i \in I} q_{it}$$

and sum

$$q_{It} + q_{Jt} = 0$$

and report only the non-zero balances. Any of these methods has the effect of eliminating the source and recipient accounts between I and J and leaving only the transfers between the real locations.[10]

10. The above consolidation procedure eliminates only the inter-company balances. In traditional financial accounting we also eliminate the inter-company profits or mark-up. That is, historical cost is defined as the cost *to the entity* in question. At the initial recording the entity is considered to be I (or J) and therefore the quantities are valued as if the transfer were inter-entity. Upon consolidation the entity is considered to be $I \cup J$ and therefore the transfer is intra-entity and the quantities need to be revalued at the cost to $I \cup J$. Revaluing at the cost to $I \cup J$ is the same as eliminating inter-company profits.

Practical applications

There are many parallels between the quantity accounting system and the financial accounting system. One can keep track of or account for quantities in debits and credits in much the same way as we account for costs, e.g.,

Tank i	q bbls	
Well i		q bbls
Railroad tank car j	q bbls	
Tank i		q bbls
Tank k	q bbls	
Railroad tank car j		q bbls
Refinery m	q bbls	
Tank k		q bbls

and so forth. One can collect all the tanks at a given location and consider that collection to be an entity and then calculate the recipient and source locations of the transfers for that entity, i.e. prepare a balance sheet. One can take a subset of those tanks and calculate the recipient and source locations of the transfers for a given period, i.e. prepare an oil flow statement. One can take a particular set of extra-entity locations and calculate the inflows and outflows of the entity of interest from and to those locations, i.e. prepare an oil income and outgo statement. One can consolidate any two or more entities and prepare the same kind of statements.

The above scheme can be readily cast into an input-output matrix. The interdependence coefficients calculated from the matrix can then be used to see what is likely to happen to the total system when certain exogenous events occur. Assigning probabilities to the exogenous events permits one to calculate various optimal strategies, e.g. the optimal inventory at each location. The data is also readily cast into a transportation tableau and one can calculate the optimal transportation network and, since the above system will have recorded the actual transportation network, the optimal can be compared to the actual. Connecting the inventory problem to the transportation problem sometimes shows that the 'optimal' inventory level at a particular location is not truly optimal because one can lower the total costs by using a faster transportation method (at a higher freight rate) to supply that particular location in case of a stock-out. One can play around with graph theory and critical path analysis since the locations are nodes and the times of receipt and issue are available. Such analyses can be extended in many directions. For example, it is possible to estimate the inventory level of the gasoline tanks in the automobiles of the ultimate consumers and include those locations in the matrix. Since it is quite costly to vary the production of a refinery beyond certain limits, it is sometimes less costly to try to vary the quantity demanded by 'gas wars'. Such wars are more effective in areas where the gasoline tanks are relatively empty and the demand schedule elastic, i.e. areas with relatively low income and a high number of automobiles per capita.

Note that some of the information necessary for the above analyses may be obscured if the quantities are valued as they are transferred. This is particularly true if the quantities are valued at actual, as opposed to standard, cost. Of course, the perpetual inventory cards will contain both the quantities and unit values but sometimes summary reports do not specify the quantities. Yet I found only one case where the cost-value figures are relevant to 'rational' decisions. Sometimes one can lessen the income tax by selecting certain quantities that have a higher cost-value. In the case observed, I made a rough estimate of the possible tax savings and compared it to an equally rough estimate of the incremental cost in the bookkeeping system occasioned by keeping track of the cost-values and the incremental cost of selling the selected quantities. The evidence is not clear because one must estimate the future cost-values of the inventory in order to know how long the tax payment will be deferred. However, there is some doubt as to whether the tax saving is greater than the incremental costs necessary to garner that saving. In any event the bookkeeping convenience and other advantages of standard costing is well recognized and its advantages would probably outweigh the possible tax savings in the case observed. However, since the standard cost is a constant the variations in total inventory cost are occasioned solely by variations in quantities. One wonders if it wouldn't be simpler and more economical to keep the accounts in terms of quantities and multiply by the constant when needed rather than multiplying by the constant for each entry.

In short the explicated system is a 'practical' and 'workable' one. It is at least possible to conceive of an entire accounting system based upon quantities alone.

Required operations

Although the quantity system has some practical uses, I am more concerned with the theoretical issues. The attempts at interpretation above have been for the purpose of trying to convince the reader that the quantity accounting system has the same structure as the financial accounting system. If one looks at the structure, one is struck by the fact that the following operations are required:

First, it has to be decided what constitutes the class of events that are to be recorded. There are some events that are recorded and others that are not. To put it another way, one has to decide what the inputs of the system will be. In the physical system we decided that volume changes would be an input and that color changes would not. In financial accounting we do the same thing — some events are 'transactions' and some are not — but it is difficult to state a general definition of those events that are recorded, i.e. it is difficult to define precisely a 'transaction' in such a way that it in fact includes all the things that we record and excludes all the things we do not record. Nevertheless, it is clear that the events classified as transactions are only a proper subset of the universal set of events.

Second, it has to be decided what constitutes an 'entity'. Entity definition is a prerequisite for 'entry' definition. The entries are a proper subset of the events that are recorded. We selected this subset by defining a collection of locations as an entity and then defining an entry as those events-to-be-recorded that affect that entity. The same process is followed in financial accounting. For example, 'purchases' is a general term describing a *kind* of event to be recorded but only the purchases made by a particular entry are recorded on the books of that entity.

Third, entries are cast into a particular form. In the quantity accounting system we defined the form as a two term zero-sum equation—$\Delta^{+}q_{ij} + \Delta^{-}q_{kj} = 0$. In financial accounting we define the form as

Date	(=j)	Dr. Account Name	(=i)	Amount	$(=\Delta^{+}q)$
		Cr. Account Name	(=k)	Amount	$(=-\Delta^{-}q)$

and we note that Debits = Credits or that $\Delta^{+}q_{ij} = -\Delta^{-}q_{kj}$.

Fourth, the entries are processed in various ways. For example, we calculate the balance of an account by summing all the increments (debits) and decrements (credits) to that account. We partition the entries into income and non-income, fund and non-fund subsets and calculate the funds flow and income for a period of time.[11]

Fifth, the processed entries are cast in certain specified forms and issued as financial statements. These are the outputs of the system.

There are several alternative ways to classify the above process. However, enough has been said to serve my purpose. I merely wanted to try to convince the reader that one could account for quantities in exactly the same way that we account for dollars or costs. If the isomorphism of the two systems is accepted we can use the quantity accounting system as a relief in discussing the financial system. The required operations will be examined in Part Two of this paper.

11. The so-called 'nominal' accounts are well named. We could establish nominal accounts for the funds statement or we could prepare the income statement by excluding the non-income transactions. The two statements are quite similar in that both focus on a particular subset of transactions for a particular period of time. I think that the argument over which statement is most important is rather sterile and therefore I don't want to get involved. However, it can be noted that the balance sheet is a summary of all the transactions from the inception of the entity until the date of preparation. By contrast the fund and income statements are schedules of a *proper* subset of the transactions for a shorter period of time.

Journal of Business Administration Vol. 3 #2 (Spring, 1972) p.3–23

Measuring Income and Wealth: An Application of the Relevance Criterion*

*Robert R. Sterling***

I. Introduction

The purpose of this paper is to consider the various measures (valuation methods) of wealth and income that have been proposed in the recent literature. A prerequisite to the consideration of that issue is the development of criteria by which the various measures are to be judged. I will review some of the major conflicts that have arisen about the criteria, state my reasons for selecting an overriding criterion and then attempt to show how that criterion can be applied.

II. Conflicting Objectives

There are conflicting viewpoints about the objective of accounting reports. This conflict is rather difficult to detect. One must look closely for it. Almost all of the literature on accounting states that accounting reports must be "useful" or that accounting is a "utilitarian art." It seems that we all agree that the objective of accounting is to provide useful information. However, we discover conflicts when we examine the remainder of the "basic concepts" of accounting. Consider the requirement that accounting data be objective and verifiable. It is possible for a measure to be useful even though it is not objective and verifiable. Thus, a conflict arises: Should we accountants provide useful data even if it is not objective, or should we provide objective data even if it is not useful?

There are many other conflicts. The particular terms that are used depend upon the author that one is reading. In regard to income, many

* An earlier draft of this paper was presented to the accounting workshops at the Universities of Washington and British Columbia. I am grateful for the criticism received from the participants in those workshops. Special thanks is due to Professor Hutton Barron for his detailed criticism.

** Arthur Young Distinguished Professor, University of Kansas.

authors begin their discussion with a remark about the need for providing useful information, but then they switch their attention to the realization convention. It is possible that realized income is not the most useful measure of income. Thus, there is a conflict between realization and usefulness. Other authors speak of the need to be conservative, and since it is possible for the most useful measure to be liberal, there is a conflict between conservatism and usefulness. Other authors note that a particular measure would violate the going concern assumption and reject the measure on those grounds without regard to the usefulness of that measure. And so forth for most of the other concepts of accounting. Each one of them may be set off against the notion of usefulness and be seen to be in conflict with it at some point.

Given the conflicts, we must decide which of the concepts is to be the overriding criterion. If we simply pay lip service to the notion of usefulness by allowing it to be constrained by all of these other concepts, then we are in fact denying the criterion of usefulness. Of course, if we can have our measures meet all of these requirements, then we are in the happy position of having no conflicts. The unfortunate fact is that they often are conflicting and we must decide which is the overriding criterion.

I think the overriding criterion should be usefulness. The other concepts are important but they are secondary. If, in order to make a decision, someone needs a measure of a particular property, then a rough guess at the magnitude of that property is useful. Of course, a precise, objective measure of that property is *more* useful, but the converse does not hold. If one does not need to know the magnitude of a particular property, then a measure of that property is useless no matter how precise and objective it may be.

Thus, I view accounting as a measurement-communication activity with the objective of providing useful information. Once we have discovered which properties are useful, then we must devise methods of measuring those properties. Hopefully, we can devise measurement methods which fulfill the requirements of objectivity, verifiability, etc. However, these requirements are secondary. They are desirable, but usefulness is indispensable. Therefore, providing useful information must be the primary objective of accounting.

III. Conflicting Definitions of Usefulness

Problems arise whenever we attempt to define the concept of usefulness. Like other hortatory concepts (e.g., truth, justice, fairness) everyone is in favor of usefulness in the abstract. All of us agree with Spacek's postulate of fairness. Who could speak out in favor of being unfair? The difficulty is in defining fairness. In the same way, the difficulty with "usefulness" is in making its meaning precise enough to be applicable to a concrete situation. In an attempt to be more precise, I have in previous works[1] replaced "usefulness" with "relevance."

The dictionary defines "relevant" as "bearing upon or relating to the matter in hand." This is what I mean by "relevant information," except that I substitute "decision model" for "matter in hand." In the same way that one cannot determine what is relevant to the matter in hand without being aware of the matter in hand, I cannot determine what is relevant information without being aware of the decision model. One of the characteristics of a well defined decision model is that it will specify the measurement (or estimation) of certain properties. This allows my definition of relevance to be simple and straightforward:

> If a property is specified by a decision model, then a measure of that property is relevant (to that decision model). If a property is not specified by a decision model, then a measure of that property is irrelevant (to that decision model).

One conflict that has arisen is concerned with that definition. Several people have argued that we should focus on decision *makers* instead of decision *models*. They say that if decision makers want to know the measure of a particular property, then that property is relevant or useful. Some of them have run tests designed to determine whether or not people (decision makers) use certain kinds of accounting data. When they found a certain kind of data being *used*, they concluded that this data was *useful*. They argue that we should supply the decision makers with the kind of data that they want and that this is the end of question of relevance.

At first glance this view is rather appealing. In the same way that we give the voter and consumer a free choice, so the argument goes, we should give the decision maker a free choice. Thus, the argument is stated in terms of democracy or consumer sovereignty, and it is difficult for anyone to be against democracy. At the risk of making you think that I am a dictator, let me briefly outline my reasons for being opposed to this view.

1. In the present system, the decision maker can either use the accounting reports that we give him or make his decision in the absence of that information. His choice is to use or not use our data. There is no third alternative.[2] If we were to adopt my

---

1 Robert R. Sterling, *Theory of the Measurement of Enterprise Income* (The University Press of Kansas, 1970), pp. 50, 132, 354, et passim and "On Theory Construction and Verification." *The Accounting Review* (July 1970), p. 454.

2 This is the basis for a technical criticism of the tests that have been run to see if decision makers use accounting data. Most experiments require a "control" of some kind. The tests would have more force if the decision makers were offered a choice between using accounting data and using some kind of control data. To put it another way, suppose we ran a test in which decision makers could choose either (1) zero information or (2) x information. I suspect that the decision makers would choose x information. A more powerful test would be to offer them the choice between x and y information.

suggestions for changing the kind of data to be included in accounting reports, the decision maker would have the same choice. Therefore, the adoption of my suggestions would be equally as "democratic" as the present system. The only difference would be in the kind of data being reported.

2. Decision makers are a diverse lot. They make their decisions on a wide variety of different bases. We have all heard about people who trade the market on the basis of astrological signs or arthritic pain. "Technical analysts" on Wall Street trade the market on the basis of the "flags," "heads and shoulders" and "double bottoms" they see in their charts. Given this diversity, it is an economic, if not a physical, impossibility for us to supply *all* the information that *all* decision makers want. Therefore, we must select and in the process of selection, we will fail to satisfy the wants of some decicion makers. What we are arguing about then is the *basis* for selection.[3]
3. The basis for selection that I prefer is to supply information for rational decision models. The modifier "rational" is defined to mean those decision models that are most likely to allow decision makers to achieve their goals. Since I don't believe that astrology allows people to achieve their stated goals, I am not interested in supplying them with an astrology report even though they use that kind of information in trading the market. For the same reason, I am not interested in supplying decision makers with some of the kinds of data now being included in accounting reports even though they use that data.

The above is only a rough sketch of the conflict. I have gone into some other aspects of the problem elsewhere.[4] Although there are a good many scattered remarks in opposition to this view, insofar as I know, there is only one article devoted exclusively to the problem.[5] As I have said before,[6] I believe that the proponents of the decision maker view have overlooked the distinction between pragmatic and semantic information. Pragmatic information is defined by the receivers' reaction

---

[3] Section II was, in effect, an argument about the basis for selection. That is, it was an argument against excluding data on grounds of objectivity, realization, etc. Thus, accountants are *now* being selective in the kind of data that they report. Indeed, they must be selective since no information system can report everything. The pertinent grounds for argument then must be the basis for selection and it is impertinent–the commission of the fallacy of alleging a non-existant difference–to argue on the grounds that one information system is selective (dictatorial) and another is not.

[4] Sterling, *Enterprise Income*, pp. 54-61.

[5] A. Rashad Abdel-khalik, "User Preference Ordering Value: A Model," *The Accounting Review* (July 1971), pp. 457-71.

[6] Sterling, "Theory Construction," p. 453.

to the report. For example, if I yelled "Fire" and all of you ran to the exits, my report would be said to contain pragmatic informational content. Semantic informational content is concerned with the connection of reports to objects and events. For example, if there were a fire, my report would be said to contain semantic informational content. If there were no fire, it is semantic misinformation, or in plain English, a lie. Note that the two kinds of information are separable and that one kind does not imply anything about the other. Of course, we accountants know this from harsh experience. Everybody agrees that decision makers used the McKesson-Robbins financial statements and therefore there was pragmatic informational content. The problem was the absence of the inventory and therefore the presence of semantic misinformation.

Although many of my critics agree in principle with the decision model approach, they throw up their hands in despair at the prospect of trying to apply it. There are a great many different kinds of decision models, e.g., EOQ, PERT, Linear Programming, Capital Budgeting, etc. Such decision models are applicable to only certain kinds of decisions, e.g., inventory ordering, scheduling, allocations, investments, etc. In addition, there are a great many choice criteria that are used in reaching decisions, e.g., minimax, maximin, Hurwicz, least regret, etc. Thus, we have a great variety of decision models applicable to a variety of decision situations with a variety of proposed criteria. It appears to be impossible to set up a general information system or to design a set of general purpose financial statements which would meet the requirements of all these models. An even more difficult problem arises whenever we encounter decision situations for which there is no well defined decision model.[7]

The trick is to generalize—to try to capture the elements that are common to all decisions. Although such a generalization, like all other generalizations, leaves out many important details, it allows us to get a handle on the problem. Let me attempt such a generalization. All decision models require information about:

1. Alternatives $= A = \{a_1, a_2, \ldots, a_n\}$
2. Consequences $= C = \{c_1, c_2, \ldots, c_n\}$
3. Preferences $= P =$ a function for ordering consequences

Alternatives (or possible courses of action) must be presently feasible. There is no point in choosing a course of action that is not feasible. One may plan what he will do if and when an alternative becomes feasible or he may ruminate about past alternatives, but the choice is always re-

---

[7] See Robert R. Sterling, "A Statement of Basic Accounting Theory: A Review Article," *Journal of Accounting Research* (Spring 1967), p. 107.

stricted to the alternatives that are feasible at the time of the decision—the present. The alternatives must be competing in the sense that the selection of one obviates the selection of the other, and hopefully, the list would completely specify all alternatives. If alternatives are not competing, then no decision is required. One need not choose between x and y if one can select both x and y. If the list is not complete, then one may not know about the existence of a preferred alternative. Thus, a decision maker is faced with a set of alternatives, the elements of which are mutually exclusive and exhaustive. The decision maker may contemplate a broad range of possible courses of action but he must select from "alternatives"—those courses of action that are available to the decision makers at the moment of choice.

Consequences (or outcomes or payoffs) of the alternatives lie in the future. They must be predicted. The consequences may be stated in terms of certain uncontrollable events, and then probabilities assigned to the uncontrollable events. For example, one can predict that if a_i is selected the consequence will be c_i^1 if event x_1 occurs, c_i^2 if event x_2 occurs, etc. By assigning probabilities to events, $x_1, x_2, \ldots$ and aggregating $c_i^1, c_i^2, \ldots$ one can speak of "the" consequence, c_i, associated with a_i.

Preferences are personal. Even though different decision makers are faced with the same alternatives and they predict the same consequences, they may make different decisions. This may come about from different assignments of probabilities or different choice criteria or different utility functions or simply the inexplicable choice of the decision maker. I include such things under the category of "preferences" and in the present state of the art they are "matters of taste" that are personal to the decision maker. Given the one to one correspondence of alternatives and consequences, the preference for a given consequence uniquely determines the alternative to be selected.

A summary of the decision process is shown in Figure 1.

Figure 1
The Decision Process

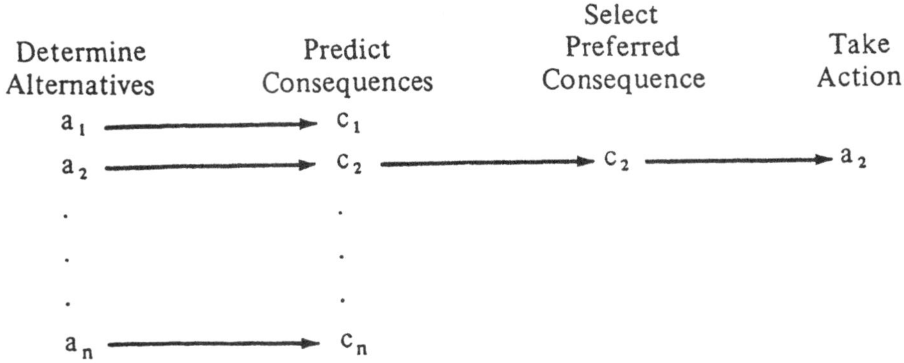

Decision models are abstractions which are separate and apart from decision makers. For example, the EOQ model is an idea which can be thought about separately from the persons who hold or use that idea. It is the decision *model* that requires information about alternatives, consequences and preferences. The decision maker can be thought of as a supplier of information to the decision model. Consider Figure 2.

Figure 2

Information System

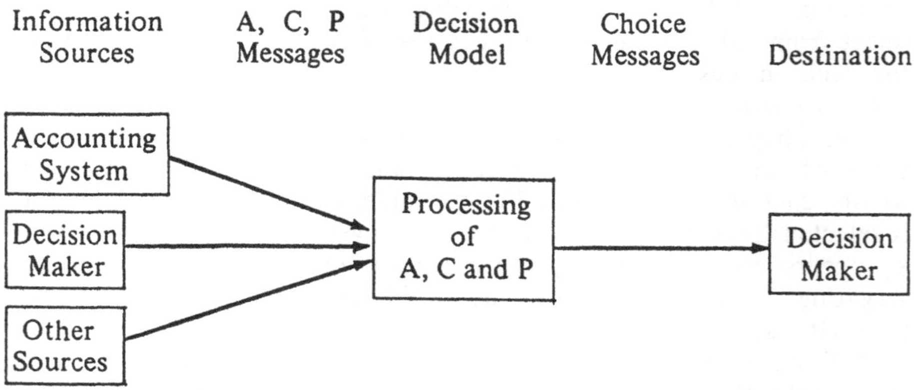

The accounting system is also a supplier of information, but it is not necessary for it to supply all of the information required by the model. In non-feedback situations, such as providing financial statements to investors, it is impossible for the accounting system to provide information about the preferences of the decision makers. Since the decision makers already know their preferences, the point may seem to be unimportant. However, there are many accountants who have become bogged down in their efforts to design an information system because they were unable to specify the decision maker's utility function or because there were several different decision makers with different utility functions. If we view the decision maker as the supplier of this kind of information to the decision model, then this problem is bypassed, if not solved. The accounting system could then concentrate on supplying information which would aid in defining alternatives and predicting consequences.

In summary, an accounting system should be designed to provide relevant information to rational decision models. The accounting system cannot supply all of the information desired by all decision makers and therefore, we must decide to exclude some kinds of information and to include other kinds. Restricting the decision models to rational ones permits the exclusion of a raft of data based upon the whims of decision makers. It permits us to concentrate on those models that have been demonstrated to be effective in achieving the decision makers' goals. Information specified by decision models may be classified as alternatives, consequences and preferences. Excluding information about preferences, on the grounds that the decision makers already possess this information, permits us to concentrate on supplying information concerning the definition of feasible alternatives and the prediction of consequences.

IV. Conflicting Valuation Methods

Although we sometimes attempt to separate the question of how to value assets from the question of how to measure income, the two are, in fact, inextricably entwined. This is indicated by the fact that we often say that our financial statements "articulate." It is even clearer whenever we consider the basic accounting equation.

$$A = L + P \tag{1}$$

Almost every elementary accounting textbook has a problem which is concerned with the determination of income by utilizing this equation. They assign a time index (t_i) and state the proprietorship as a residual.

$$A(t_i) - L(t_i) = P(t_i) \tag{2}$$

Then the income (neglecting investment and disinvestment) for the period t_i to t_{i+1} is given by (3).

$$P(t_{i+1}) - P(t_i) = Y \tag{3}$$

It is obvious that if the assets take on different values, then the income for the period will take on different values. For example, a switch from straight-line to accelerated depreciation or from FIFO to LIFO will affect both the reported asset values and the reported income. The same is true if we state the assets at their historical cost as opposed to, say, current market value. Thus, when one talks about different methods of valuation, and the conflicts between them, then one is also at the same time talking about conflicts in income measurement.

There are four major valuation methods that have been proposed in the literature:

(1) historical cost (HC),

(2) replacement cost (RC),

(3) exit values (EV), and

(4) discounted cash flows (DCF).

Some people have argued that price-level adjusted historical costs should be listed as a fifth valuation method. However, one could adjust each of the above methods for changes in price-levels and thereby add a total of four more methods. I am in favor of price-level adjustments, but I think that the selection of a valuation method is a separate problem. We must first select the valuation method(s) and *then* we can consider the necessary adjustment for price-level changes. Therefore, I will neglect the problems of price-level adjustments in this paper and concentrate on specific price changes.

The incomes that result from applying these valuation methods have been called

(1) realized income,
(2) business income,
(3) realizable income, and
(4) economic income.

All of these names are somewhat inaccurate. Some economists would say that "realizable income" is "economic income" and therefore, they would object to the names that we have used. "Historical cost" is somewhat inaccurate in that there are many assets on the balance sheet that are not valued at cost, e.g., cash and accounts receivable. "Realized income" is somewhat inaccurate as, for example, when the percentage of completion method of revenue realization is used. In addition, these methods sometimes borrow from one another. For example, HC sometimes uses DCF in accounting for bonds or notes. In the same way, some of the authors who propose, say, EV will occasionally revert to either RC or HC. Thus, none of the methods are pure. Finally, there are different procedures within each of the methods. Just as income may be calculated by using either LIFO or FIFO, and both of them referred to as "realized income," there are different procedures within the other methods. I will not attempt to discuss all of these exceptions and differences; instead, I will concentrate on describing the major differences among the methods.

All four valuation methods use a price of some kind as the basis for valuing, but each method endorses a different price. The endorsed prices differ by their temporal location and by the market in which they are found. Both HC and RC use the prices found in the purchasing market. They differ only in the temporal location of those prices. A past (time of purchase) price is used in HC while a present (time of statement preparation) price is used in RC. Thus, except for the temporal location of the prices, RC is identical to HC. EV, by contrast, focuses on the present (time of statement preparation) prices in the selling market. EV is similar, but not identical, to the "net realizable values" used in HC in applying the lower of cost or market rule to inventories.

DCF uses both purchase and selling prices, but it focuses on the future—the prices that will be in effect at the time of future exchanges. DCF is similar to the "present value method" of accounting for bonds used in HC. In DCF the cash receipts from the future sale of the products and the cash expenditures for the future purchase of the factors of production are predicted and then discounted to get "present value" or "present worth." Hereafter, I will substitute "discounted value" for "present worth" to avoid confusion.

These differences are summarized in the following matrix.

Time / Market	Past (Purchase)	Present (Statement Preparation)	Future (Exchange)
Purchasing	HC	RC	DCF
Selling		EV	DCF

The differences in income may also be described in general terms. The revenues (asset inflows from sales) would be the same for all four methods, but the amount charged to expense would differ considerably. We all know how the allocations are made in HC. RC uses the same allocation techniques, but it costs out the quantities at their current purchase prices. The argument is that we should match current costs with current revenues and thus the line of reasoning is the same as that of many LIFO proponents. However, unlike LIFO, RC also uses current purchase prices on the balance sheet which results in including "holding gains" (also called "cost savings") in income. EV looks to the market to determine the expenses. Initially, the expense is the difference between the purchase price and the exit value at the date of statement preparation. Subsequently, it is the difference in the exit values at two statement preparation dates. Both HC and RC are *allocations* (amortizations) of a purchase price on the basis of use or sale or passage of time. EV attempts to avoid the allocation problem by going to the market to determine how much the asset could be sold for. The decrease (increase) in the amount it could be sold for is the amount of the cost (gain) of using or holding that asset.

DCF recognizes a gain at purchase equal to the difference between the discounted value of the products produced by the acquired asset and the face value of the cash sacrificed. The amount of the subsequent income is simply the interest earned (the interest rate times the discounted value) in exactly the same way that interest income is the yield rate times the discounted value of bonds receivable in HC. Adjustments are required in DCF whenever events are different from those predicted. These adjustments present problems similar to those encountered in HC when, say, the actual life of an asset is different from its predicted life.

There are many arguments in favor of and in opposition to all of these valuation methods. However, the proponents of the various schools rely most heavily on the usefulness or relevance criterion. Each school claims that its particular valuation method would be more useful than the others. For this reason, and also because I believe that usefulness should be the overriding criterion, I will ignore the other criteria and try to select the appropriate valuation method by applying the criterion of relevance.

V. Application of the Relevance Criterion to Market Decisions

Although there are a good many decisions that do not involve a market exchange, in a market economy such as ours probably a majority of decisions are concerned with whether or not to make an exchange in the market. The market operates with prices, and since the conflicting valuation methods differ mainly in their endorsement of certain prices, a general consideration of prices and market decisions is pertinent to the conflict.

Market Alternatives

The market alternatives that are available to any person or any firm depend upon two factors:

(1) The funds that are currently available to invest in the contemplated project.

(2) The magnitude of the investment required to engage in the contemplated project.

Specifically, the funds available for a given project must be greater than or equal to the investment required for that project. Otherwise, that project is not a feasible market alternative.

Although this point is obvious, I wanted to make it explicit in order to demonstrate that "profitability" is *not* the first nor the sole criterion for selecting projects. There are many projects which I think would be very profitable, but I cannot undertake them because my available funds are less than the required investment. For example, I would like to purchase General Motors, but since my available funds are less than the purchase price this is not a feasible alternative for me.

Market Consequences

The market consequences of undertaking a given project are the future cash flows that result from that project. There may be non-market consequences which the decision maker should consider (e.g., one may be sent to jail for engaging in an illegal project or one may get satisfaction from beating the competition), but I will concentrate on the market consequences. Since these cash flows lie in the future, they must be predicted.

Preferences

The decision maker is faced with an array of future cash flow magnitudes. He must select one of those magnitudes by applying his personal preference function. He may do this by converting the money magnitudes to utility magnitudes, assigning subjective probabilities to the flows under varying conditions, and utilizing one of the various choice criteria. Such information is to be supplied to the decision model by the decision maker because it is a matter of personal preference.

In addition, the discount rate should be supplied by the decision maker because each decision maker is likely to have different needs for liquidity and different views on the time value of money. That is, people are likely to have different "reservation rates" and these rates are likely to be different from the cost of capital rate of the firm. For this reason, I will distinguish "future cash flows" (FCF) and "discounted cash flows" (DCF) henceforth.

After appropriate adjustment for risk, I would select the project with the largest cash flows. That is, I am a maximizer. However, that is a personal preference and there may be some who have different preferences. The above discussion does *not* depend upon the assumption of profit or wealth maximization for its validity. If one wants to minimize he can be a more efficient minimizer by following this general outline for decisions.[8]

The main point about preferences is that, as before, they are to be supplied to the decision model by the decision maker. Therefore, in the following discussion I will concentrate on supplying information about alternatives and consequences.

Price Interpretation

The market alternatives and consequences have been defined and the preferences have been left to the decision makers. It is now necessary to give these alternatives and consequences a price interpretation. Recall that the market alternatives depend upon the available funds and the required investment. In turn, the available funds depend upon:

(1) The present selling prices of all assets held, including the "selling price" of cash.

(2) The ability to borrow.

(3) The ability to raise equity capital.

---

8 This point should be underscored because several people have criticized my previous works for assuming profit maximization or postulating an economic man. In the above classification scheme, the goal of the decision maker is included in the category of preferences. A maximizer's preferences will cause him to select a consequence different from the one selected by a minimizer. A satisficer will cease searching for additional alternatives whenever he has found a satisfactory consequence. Regardless of the goal, an accounting system which provided information about alternatives and consequences would aid the decision maker in achieving that goal. Of course, decision models are not usually designed to minimize, but that is simply an indication that few people are minimizers and that most minimization problems are trivial. For example, a linear programming model could be used to search for the lowest profit-highest cost solution by simply altering the objective function, but a minimizer could more easily achieve his goal by considering the consequences of selling his product at a negative price or by burning his plant.

I will consider (2) and (3) infra. In regard to (1), note that the present selling prices are the only prices relevant to defining the available funds. Past prices are irrelevant, because they are no longer obtainable and future prices will be relevant to defining future alternatives, but they are irrelevant to defining the current alternatives. Purchase prices are obviously irrelevant if one is trying to determine how much cash he can get if he sells.

The required investment is given by:

(1) The present purchase prices of assets *not* held.

(2) The present selling prices of assets held.

Obviously, if one is contemplating the purchase of an asset, then the present purchase price of that asset is relevant to the determination of whether or not the alternative is feasible. The investment required for maintaining the status quo, however, is given by the selling prices of the assets held. Since the individual or firm already holds the assets necessary to maintain the status quo, then there is no need to contemplate their purchase. Instead, the (implicit) required investment is the amount of cash that one could get if one sold those assets. That is, the decision not to disinvest is structurally identical to the decision to invest, and therefore, the required investment for continuing the status quo is the amount of cash that was not received by not disinvesting.

The future cash flows require a prediction of the future selling prices of the outputs of the project as well as the quantities that will be sold. The future selling prices of the inputs are also relevant. That is, the salvage values of productive assets at the termination or abandonment of a project are future cash inflows and are, therefore, relevant. If a project requires future replacement of productive assets or the purchase of the factors of production, then the future purchasing prices of the inputs are also relevant.

The decision requires the comparison of the future cash flows of each project. Other things equal, the decision maker can make his selection by scanning the array of future cash flows and applying his preference function. However, in this case other things are seldom equal. Usually the required investments are not of equal magnitude. If the projects have unequal required investments, it is not possible to make a rational decision by considering only their future cash flows. One project may have large cash flows but an even larger required investment. A common method of overcoming this difficulty is to calculate the rate of return on the required investment and then compare the rates of return. Note that this method is a comparison of the required investment to the future cash flows, i.e., rate of return is the time adjusted quotient of the future cash flows and required investment. In general, whenever required investments are not equal one needs to compare the required investment to the future cash flows.

The above is simply a generalization of the capital budgeting model, absent an explicit consideration of discounting. The capital budgeting model specifies the prediction of future cash inflows and outflows, and then the time adjusted net flows of the various projects are compared to one another or to the required investment. Since the capital budgeting model is usually applied to new projects, we tend to forget that it is also applicable to existing projects. Sometimes our predictions are wrong and sometimes we change our predictions after initiating a project. For this reason, existing projects should be re-evaluated periodically. In this re-evaluation, the decision model specifies a comparison of the *updated* prediction of cash flows to the *present* required investment. That required investment is given by the selling prices of assets held. Obviously, if one wishes to maximize, he should discontinue a project and sell the assets if the future cash flows are less than the sum of the selling prices. Just as in the case of a new project, a maximizer should not commit the required investment if it is greater than the predicted cash flows. In the case of an existing project, the required investment is the sum of the present selling prices of the assets.

In summary, a rational market decision model specifies the following prices:

(1) The present selling prices of all assets held because
  (a) when compared to (2), they define the feasible market alternatives, and
  (b) they completely define the investment required to maintain the status quo.

(2) The present purchase prices of all assets not held because
  (a) when compared to (1), they define the feasible alternatives, and
  (b) they completely define the investment required for new projects.

(3) The future purchase and selling prices associated with a given alternative because when compared to the required investment [(1b) or (2b)], they permit a rational decision.

Creditor and Investor Market Decision Models

The above analysis is general. In addition to managerial decision models it is also applicable to creditor and investor decision models. Each creditor and investor must determine the feasible alternatives by comparing the available funds to the required investments. The available funds are defined, as before, by the selling prices of the assets held (by the creditor-investor) and the ability to borrow or raise equity capital.

That is, investors borrow and creditors issue equity shares, and therefore, the funds available to them are determined in exactly the same way as outlined above. The required investment for new projects is the amount of the loan application or the present purchase price of the stock. For existing projects, the required investment is the present selling price of the debt or equity instrument.

The creditor-investor decision model also calls for a comparison of the required investment to the future cash flows. In this case, the future "selling prices" of the "output" is the interest or dividends. The "salvage value" is the maturity or liquidation value of the instrument. Since the project may be abandoned or aborted prior to the maturation of the debt or liquidation of the firm, the salvage value may be a future selling price of the instrument.

In short, the investor-creditor decision model specifies exactly the same prices as those given above. However, these prices refer to assets held *by the creditor-investor* and to the various prices *of the debt-equity instrument*. Strictly speaking, this is *all* that the creditor-investor needs to know. That is, after an investor has narrowed the stocks down to those that are feasible alternatives, the only thing he needs to know is their purchase prices and their future selling prices (including dividends) *in the stock market*. He can then compare and make his choice(s).

If the creditor-investor can predict these future prices without regard to the operations of the individual or firm to whom he is lending-investing, then we need go no further with this analysis. Many investors do not look beyond the securities market when they make such predictions. They act as if the price fluctuations in the stock market were completely independent of the economic fluctuations of the firms that issue the stock. If this is true, then the stock market is simply a lottery with no underlying economic meaning, and we accountants should quit wasting our time and paper by issuing financial statements. Instead, we should draw the income numbers out of a hat and thereby determine who has won and lost. However, I, personally, am not interested in the stock market qua lottery. I believe that stock prices (as well as dividends, interest and ability to repay loans) do in fact depend upon the economic conditions of the firms. Moreover, I believe that stock prices *ought* to depend upon the economic conditions of the firms and that if we accountants supplied better information about the firms, the stock prices would conform more closely to those conditions. In short, I believe that a well designed investor-creditor decision model should specify information about the states and operations of the firms. I am not trying to dictate to investors. If they want to trade the market by "reading the tape," then that is their business. If they can be successful on that basis, then more power to them. However, I believe that information about the firms should be available to investors, whether they use it or not.

For all these reasons, I will concentrate upon the information specified by a rational creditor-investor decision model and assume that other information about the market will be supplied from non-accounting sources.

Future Cash Flows of the Firm. The ability of a firm to service a debt, pay dividends or simply to survive depend upon its future cash flows. Thus, the future cash flows of a debt-equity instrument depend upon the future cash flows of the firm. It follows that the future cash flows of the firm are relevant to the creditor-investor.[9] The creditor-investor may make his own predictions of the flows or be supplied those predictions by someone else. The predictor may assign probabilities to the completion of the project and the abandonment of the project and predict the cash flows under both conditions. Many other refinements of this kind could be listed. The only point that I want to make is that the future cash flows of the firm are relevant to the investor-creditor, because the future flows of debt-equity instruments depend upon them.

I would urge that the prediction of the future cash flows used by the creditor-investor be independent of the prediction made by the management. This is not to impugn the honesty of managements, but rather to note that managements are likely to be optimistic about their own projects. If they were not, they would not have proposed them. Thus, an independent prediction is called for. This means that, as a minimum, the creditor-investor needs to know *which* projects are planned by management. Then, the creditor-investor (or his agent) can independently assess the probability of success and independently predict the future purchase and selling prices of the project, as well as applying his personal discount rate.

Selling Prices of Firm Assets. Whenever someone lends, invests or purchases, he is acquiring some value that exists now as well as some values that are predicted to exist in the near and distant future. The presently existing values can vary from zero to one hundred per cent of the purchase price. For example, if I "purchase" a ten dollar bill with two fives, then the presently existing value of the ten is 100% of the purchase price. Moreover, the ten will not increase in value in the future. On the other hand, if I grubstake a miner in return for a share of his find, then the presently existing value is zero—*all* of the value that I have purchased lies in the future. That future value may be much greater than $10, or it may be zero. Obviously, grubstaking a miner is much riskier than purchasing a ten dollar bill. This risk relationship of the presently existing value to the purchase price is true in general. The smaller the presently existing value in relation to the purchase price, other things equal, the higher the risk.

[9] Again, there are many other factors that are relevant, such as the "character" of debtors and the "resilience" and "ingenuity" of management. However, I will focus on the more immediate market factors.

This means that the present selling prices of the assets held (and the selling prices that will exist immediately after purchase) are relevant to the decision. Perhaps the point in regard to an investor can be made clear by considering mutual funds. Suppose you have the option to purchase one share of either the L or the N fund for $100. Now the managers of both funds would promise you the moon if the SEC would let them get by with it. Therefore, you ought to make an independent prediction of the future "performance" of both funds. Suppose you predict that the selling prices x years from now will be $140 and $120 for the shares of the L and N funds, respectively. Without further analysis, you can make your selection. If you are a maximizer, you will select the L fund. However, let me add two facts and then see if you agree that these facts should be specified by a well designed decision model.

The L fund is a load fund and the amount of the load is $90. The N fund is a no-load fund. That is, the per share exit value[10] is $10 for the L fund and $100 for the N fund. Therefore, the value of the assets held by L must increase by 1,300% to reach the predicted price while the increase required by N is only 20%. Almost all of the value of L lies in the future while most of the value of N exists presently. Other things equal, L is a much riskier investment.

As many people have correctly pointed out, one should go ahead and buy a load fund if one thinks that it will out-perform a no-load fund by more than the amount of the load. However, the amount of the load is relevant to a well designed decision model. This amount is determinable if the present selling prices of the assets held are disclosed.

There is also a "load" or "premium" on the price of the stock of industrial firms. The price of some stock is several hundred times its per share exit value. In such cases the purchased value lies almost wholly in the future. Other things equal, the greater the portion of the value that lies in the future the higher the risk. That is, if the firm does not perform in accordance with expectations the price of the stock is likely to drop drastically. By contrast, some stocks sell at a "discount"–the price of the stock is less than its per share exit value. Closed-end funds, for example, often sell at a discount. The future price and dividends of discounted stock still depend upon the future cash flows of the firm, but, other things equal, it is much less risky. The value presently exists and therefore even if the firm liquidated immediately the investor would not lose. Indeed, he would profit.

Therefore, I conclude that the magnitude of the discount or premium is relevant to a well designed decision model. That accountants know this is evidenced by their lower of cost or market rule. Although formally

---

[10] The sum of the present selling prices of the assets held by the fund less the liabilities divided by the number of shares outstanding.

applicable only to inventories, it is also applied to a great many other assets. For example, I know of a case where the auditors insisted upon writing the value of land down to "fair market value," even though they knew that this write-down would be likely to result in the liquidation of the firm. The land had been purchased at a price which reflected the expectation of mineral deposits which had failed to materialize. The auditors evidently thought that the "fair market value" (exit value?) of this land was relevant to investors and creditors.

The problem is that this is a one-way rule. I know of another case where the stock of a retail chain is selling at about $10.00 per share. Based on its poor earnings, this is a reasonable price. That is, if it continues in the future as in the past, its future cash flows will be meager and its reported income even less. However, this firm owns the land upon which its stores are built and the per share exit value of the land alone is conservatively estimated to be $40.00 per share. This land is carried on the balance sheet at its ancient historical cost of about 20¢ per share. I believe that the exit value of that land is equally as relevant in this case as in the above case.[11] If the Gerstle vs. Gamble case[12] is taken as evidence, it appears that the SEC also believes that exit values are relevant to investors.

Although these cases are extreme, they illustrate the fact that the price of stock ought to depend upon the presently existing exit values of the firm as well as depending upon the future cash flows of the firm.

I have spoken only of investors above because creditors have long recognized the relevance of the selling prices of assets. They are usually willing to loan only at a discount. That is, if a particular asset is pledged, they are willing to loan only a fraction of that asset's selling price. If they are general creditors, they are willing to loan only a fraction of the conservative (lower of cost or market) value of the total assets. Of course, creditors also look to the future cash flows of firms, if for no other reason than that they would prefer to avoid the expense of foreclosure. However, the selling prices are also relevant to them and they explicitly recognize the risk relationship when they speak of the amount of the discount or the amount of the net worth as providing a "cushion of safety."

VI. Implications for Wealth and Income Measurement

If the above analysis is correct and complete, then the implications are fairly straightforward. We noticed that

(a) Present selling prices (EV) of assets held by the firm,

---

[11] The only reason why I don't buy all the stock and liquidate the firm is that I lack the required investment of $10.00 per share for over 2 million shares.

[12] *Gerstle v. Gamble-Skogmo*, 298 Federal Supplement 66 (1969).

(b) Present purchase prices (RC) of assets not held, and

(c) Future cash flows (FCF) of the firm

are relevant to well designed market decision models of managers, investors and creditors.

Conspicuous by their absence from this list are past purchase prices (HC). I do not find them specified by any market decision model, and therefore, I conclude that they are irrelevant. This is a conclusion that I have held for many years and one that I have spoken about and written about many times. On one occasion, I challenged all readers to demonstrate just one case where historical costs were relevant to economic decisions.[13] It has now been four years since that challenge was made, and no one has published a direct reply. Since then, several people have argued for historical cost on the grounds of objectivity, feasibility, etc. This is the reason why I said in Section II that there were conflicting views on the objectives of accounting. Other people have argued for historical costs because managers, creditors and investors do, in fact, use the financial statements that we give them. However, the fact that they use HC does not indicate that they would use HC if other information were supplied or that they ought to use them, in the sense that other information may be more likely to allow them to achieve their goals. This is the reason why I discussed the conflict between decision makers and decision models in Section III. If we really mean it when we say that accounting data should be useful or relevant, then we should demonstrate the relevance of HC or the superiority of HC to other valuation methods, and if we cannot do that, then we should abandon HC as a valuation method.

I exclude present purchase prices (RC) for a different reason. Present purchase prices of the assets *not* held are relevant to market decision models. The source of information about these prices is the market itself, and they are already being supplied to management by the purchasing department. Financial statements report on assets held, and since present purchase prices are not relevant to assets held, they should not be used as a basis for the valuation of assets on financial statements.[14]

---

[13] Sterling, "ASOBAT Review," p. 111

[14] Future purchase prices of planned replacements and additions are also relevant since they are a component of FCF. Many people argue that income should be calculated on the basis of RC because it is a good predictor of FCF. This may or may not be true. It is an empirical question that cannot be settled here. It is important to note, however, that the claim of this argument is not that RC are relevant per se but rather that RC are good predictors of FCF. Note that this is my interpretation of the argument It is usually stated that RC income is superior to other income concepts because it is a better predictor of future *RC income*. Using this reasoning, one could argue that straight-line depreciation is the superior depreciation concept because it is a perfect predictor of future straight-line depreciation. Obviously, this is not what the RC proponents mean. I think they mean that business income is the superior concept because it is a good predictor of a relevant property (FCF), not that it is superior because it is a good predictor of itself.

Every decision requires a prediction of the future consequences of various alternatives. For this reason, if I thought it were possible, I would urge that accountants report future cash flows. Knowledge of the future is always the most valuable kind of information. The reason it is so valuable is that it is so scarce. We have no way of knowing what the future holds, and there are many conflicting views about it. The existence of these conflicting views of the future partially makes the market operate. Except for specialization and liquidity requirements, there would be no market if buyers held the same view of the future as sellers. This is most obvious in the commodity markets, where there is a long for every short. The speculators hold diametrically opposed views of the future—the long (buyer) expects a price increase and the short (seller) expects a price decrease. One of them must be wrong. The same thing happens in varying degrees in other markets. Thus, differing predictions of the future are an inherent part of the operation of a market.

It is this difficulty which causes me to reject the notion that accountants ought to report FCF. First, we cannot report FCF, we can only report predictions of FCF. If we were perfect predictors, we would destroy the market, i.e., prices would be set equal to the discounted value of the future cash flows and, except for liquidity requirements and specialization, no exchanges would occur. For example, if we all had access to future issues of the *Wall Street Journal*, the price of every stock would be bid so as to equal the discounted value of the known future prices and dividends.[15]

Of course, we really needn't worry about destroying the market because it is not very likely that we will be perfect predictors. That is, accountants are, in the present state of the art, about as prone to err in predicting FCF as are decision makers. Thus, we have the choice of (1) not predicting or (2) presenting erroneous predictions. Erroneous predictions are not relevant to decision models. Indeed, they are likely to be harmful and, given the attitude of the courts about accountants' legal liability, this harm is likely to redound to accountants. For these reasons, I don't think that accountants should at this time report their predictions of FCF.[16] Since DCF is simply FCF discounted by a rate and since different rates are appropriate for different decision makers,

---

[15] Supra I said that the reason that knowledge of the future is so valuable is that it is so scarce. Note that in this case, it would not be valuable because it is not scarce. That is, the price of exclusive access to future issues of the *Wall Street Journal* would be extremely high. However, when everyone has equal access, the price would probably be about the same as the price of today's issue.

[16] This leaves the predictions of FCF up to the decision makers. This presents no problem insofar as managements are concerned. A major part of managements' function is to try to peer into the future in order to select the preferred consequence. The problem is that the managements' decisions, based upon *their* predictions, affect the well being of the creditor-investor. Unless the creditor-investor is willing to rely solely upon the managements' predictions, he

it follows a fortiori that DCF is not an acceptable method of measuring income and wealth.

We noted that selling prices (EV) were relevant to all three market decision models. They are necessary to define market alternatives, they express the investment required to hold assets and they are a component of a risk indicator. For all of these reasons, I conclude that the items on the balance sheet should be valued at their present selling prices. Since income is defined as the difference between wealth (net worth) at two points in time, it follows that the income statement would be an explanation of the changes in the exit values on two successive balance sheets.

---

must make independent predictions. In order for the creditor-investor to make an independent prediction, he must know, at least in broad outline, the managements' plans. The budget is the most likely source of information about managerial plans. The creditor-investor can peruse this budget and then make (or have his agent make) a prediction of the future cash flows that will result. Therefore, I would urge that we include a partially audited management budget in our reports because it provides the basis for an independent prediction of the future cash flows.

Thus, I am not opposed to expanding the accounting function so that it includes information about expected futures. On the contrary, I think that we should provide all the relevant information that we can. However, I don't think that erroneous predictions are relevant. (This includes those erroneous predictions which are disguised as "past" cost allocations in HC. Recall those costs capitalized because of the "future benefits" expected from the Edsel, Cleopatra, TFX, super sonic transports, etc.) If we get to the point where our ability to predict is better than that of the decision makers, then I will argue that we ought to report our predictions. In the meantime, I think the best we can do is to supply information to decision makers which will aid them in making their predictions.

ROBERT R. STERLING

'The Market Value Method According to Sterling': A Reply

I am flattered that Professor Mattessich would take the time to write a critique[1] of *Enterprise Income*.[2] From the language used and from the repetition of the points, it appears that Mattessich is mainly concerned with (1) the approach taken for constructing the theory and (2) the boundaries of the theory. I will consider these in turn.

1. APPROACH

Mattessich's first major point of criticism is that the approach followed by *Enterprise Income* is incorrect. He states the approach (teleological) that he considers to be correct, draws a conclusion (different-incomes-for-different-purposes) that he thinks results from following that approach and presents an example of following that approach which is asserted to be a refutation of *Enterprise Income*.

Teleology

Mattessich contrasts the 'market value' with the 'teleologic' approach (p. 177) and criticizes *Enterprise Income* for taking the former approach. Since I have often used the term 'teleological' to describe the approach to accounting theory that I prefer and since I consciously attempted to apply that approach[3] in *Enterprise Income,* I was surprised as this line of criticism.

Teleology is the study of ends or purposes. It is often opposed to Mechanism. In biology, for example, a mechanistic theory would attempt to explain and predict the actions of an organism by reference only to the parts of that organism, while a teleological theory would refer to the purposes or goals of the organism. Thus, as I use the phrase, a 'teleological approach' to constructing an accounting theory would begin with a consideration of the purpose(s) of accounting.[4]

1. Richard Mattessich, 'The Market Value Method According to Sterling: A Review Article', *Abacus,* Vol. 7, No. 2, pp. 176-93.
2. Robert R. Sterling, *The Theory of the Measurement of Enterprise Income,* University Press of Kansas, Lawrence, Kansas 1970.
3. Note, however, that the approach was applied in an attempt to construct a theory of income measurement, not a general theory of accounting.
4. This is spelled out in more detail in Robert R. Sterling, 'On Theory Construction and Verification'. *The Accounting Review,* July 1970, pp. 444-57.

ROBERT R. STERLING is Arthur Young Distinguished Professor, University of Kansas.

Enterprise Income follows this approach. As the preface indicates (p. viii), the approach is to consider the purpose of supplying useful information and then deduce the data requirements from that consideration. Now it may be that this approach was applied imperfectly and I could understand a criticism of that kind, but I cannot understand the criticism that it does not follow the teleological approach.

The problem seems to be that Mattessich has confused an approach with a conclusion. 'Market value' is evidently considered to be an *approach* to theory construction by Mattessich (as evidenced by his contrasting it with the teleologic approach), but in *Enterprise Income* the superiority of market (exit) values is a *conclusion* drawn by applying the teleologic *approach*. A clue to this confusion is given when after using the phrase 'teleologic approach' several times he switches to 'teleologic (purpose-oriented) theory of valuation' which 'asserts that for certain purposes the correct value basis is the acquisition cost, for others the market value, for others the present value, etc. . . .' (p. 182). This must be a conclusion (surely it is not a premise) of Mattessich's teleological theory.

Thus, the net result of these contrasted approaches is the juxtaposition of two contradictory conclusions. That is, the only thing Mattessich is telling us is that he disagrees with what he takes to be the conclusions of *Enterprise Income*, but this is hardly news since he states (p. 177) that his 'opposition to the exclusive market value method is only too well known'.

Different incomes for different purposes

Mattessich's teleological conclusion, quoted above, is reasserted in several other places in his critique. In *Enterprise Income* his conclusion was referred to as the 'different incomes for different purposes' notion. This notion is of utmost importance to Mattessich's criticism as is evidenced by the statement that *Enterprise Income's* 'fatal flaw [is] underrating' this notion (p. 178) and its 'decisive flaw' is dealing with it only in its extreme form (p. 182). He says that the notion was disparaged, side-stepped, brushed off, etc. (p. 178). Therefore, let us consider it.

First, to note that there are different purposes and then to conclude that measures of different properties are needed to meet those purposes is a trivial exercise. For example, suppose I decided to consider measuring the properties of my desk. I could note that for decorating purposes the properties of shape and colour are relevant, for moving purposes the properties of weight and volume are relevant, and for writing purposes the properties of height and hardness are relevant. It is trivial to draw the conclusion that for different purposes different property measures are relevant. The same is true in regard to measuring the properties of the firm. For Mattessich to present three different purposes (p. 179) and then state that this is 'obvious evidence of the need for different valuation methods and income definitions for different purposes' (p. 181) is a conclusion that I find neither startling nor significant. To my mind, different-incomes-for-different-purposes is a statement of a problem, not a conclusion to be taken as the solution of a problem.

Second, the proposal to prepare and report all of these different income figures overlooks what *Enterprise Income* refers to as the 'capacity constraint.'

> The author's criticism of the 'different incomes for different purposes' notion stems from these considerations. If it is feasible for each receiver to feedback his particular purpose and then for the transmitter to prepare and transmit all of the information requested, there is no problem. If the channel has such a large capacity, and the corollary large costs, the non-problem has been solved. It is only when a limitation on transmissions has been set that we are required to select some data and reject some. Without this limitation *all* of the data could conceivably be transmitted, and the receiver could filter out the relevant bits. With the limitation the transmitter must filter the data; and how that is done is the problem. (*Enterprise Income*, p. 52n.)

Another aspect of the capacity constraint is that even if we could afford to incur the large costs of preparing and reporting all of these income figures, the receiver would be overwhelmed. As I said before, 'anyone on the mailing list of U.S. Government documents knows very well that it is possible to be inundated with relevant information'.[5] (Subsequently this has come to be known as the 'information overload' problem instead of the 'capacity constraint.') Thus, the different-incomes-for-different-purposes notion overlooks the possibility of the limited capacity of the communication system and the limited capacity of the receiver to digest the information received.

Third, Mattessich is in favour of different definitions for the same term. He says: 'every possible evaluation method provides a different interpretation and thus strictly speaking a different definition (sub-definition)' (p. 179). In order to avoid confusion I would prefer that each of these definitions refer to different terms. When writing *Enterprise Income,* I toyed with the idea of inventing different terms to refer to each valuation method, e.g., COG for command over goods, DEP for discounted expected prices, PAPP for past allocated purchase prices, and CARP for current allocated replacement prices. To my mind each of these measure a different property and therefore they ought to be labelled with different terms.[6] To use the same term for each of these properties invites the kind of confusion that would result if we used 'weight' to refer to both the reading of a balance scale and the reading of a thermometer. Thus, I am opposed to different-incomes-for-different-purposes because it entrenches the use of the same term to describe different properties and confusion is almost inevitable.

Finally, in one sense the major thrust of the book is devoted to this issue. The book started by noting that different income measures (valuation methods) exist. Then it tried to find commonalties among user's needs and to use this as a basis for eliminating some measures and for ranking those measures that remained. Had

5. Robert R. Sterling, 'A Statement of Basic Accounting Theory: A Review Article,' *Journal of Accounting Research*, Spring 1967, pp. 104-5.

6. I was dissuaded by the force of customary usage and by the resistance to technical jargon in accounting. I think that this is a mistake. Our communication can be no more precise than our language and, worse, precision in thinking is inhibited by imprecise language. See Robert R. Sterling, 'An Explication of the Structure of Accounting', in Kermit Larson (ed.), *The Accounting Colloquium 1969-70*, University of Texas, p. 35n.

no commonalties been found, then the different-incomes-for-different-purposes conclusion would have been drawn.

But this would have been a defeat. The book's conclusion would have been identical with its introduction.

Mattessich's 'refutation'

Mattessich lists three purposes for measuring income: (1) reports to creditors and public investors; (2) minimization of taxes; and (3) reports to management (p. 179). By considering an example he derives evidence which is 'sufficient to refute the thesis that the market value method is the only correct method for measuring entrepreneurial income' (p. 180). Although this 'refutation' is central to Mattessich's criticism, I find it most difficult to reply because I am unaware of exactly what it is that he is criticizing.

From the tone it appears that his criticism is based on his belief that *Enterprise Income* did not consider these three purposes. He speaks of the 'obvious evidence' generated by such a consideration and wonders how I could 'fail to recognize this evidence' (p. 181). If this is the basis of his criticism, it is easy to rebut. In general, the major thrust of the book is to look to these ends or purposes in order to decide what kind of information to report. Specifically, pages 133-55 of *Enterprise Income* consider the three purposes listed by Mattessich in some detail. If his criticism is based on the absence of consideration of these three purposes, it is patently false. Since his piece is a critique of *Enterprise Income,* it would seem appropriate for him to point out the errors on those pages which led to the wrong conclusion. Instead he invented his own case and drew the different-incomes-for-different-purposes conclusion. Let us consider his case.

'For the first purpose [reporting to creditors and public investors] we have already agreed to the market value method and no dispute is necessary' (p. 180). This passage is quoted not only to indicate that no further discussion is needed in regard to the first purpose, but also to permit the reader to join with me in admiration of Mattessich's acumen.

Unfortunately, however, he seems to be unable to distinguish between measuring income and minimizing taxes. He writes: ' . . . any consultant advising that the market value is the only correct way of measuring income for this [tax minimization] purpose has hardly much chance of being called upon again, since this advice would lead to unnecessary tax payments on an additional amount of $70,000' (p. 180). Once again Mattessich and I are in agreement—market value income is not the appropriate basis for minimizing taxes in his example.

However, I disagree when he says 'Obviously the income concept IA [historical cost] and not IM [market value] should be chosen here' (p. 181). His example contains three income figures:

IM [market value] = 100,000
IA [historical cost] = 30,000
IP [discounted value] = —100,000

It is clear that IP would yield a smaller tax payment and therefore it ought to be selected. That is, for purposes of income tax minimization, the principle is clear: select the smallest income figure. Therefore, Mattessich erred by selecting IA.

But, Mattessich will reply, IP is not permitted by law. That is precisely the point. Taxable income is a legal concept—the ways in which it can be calculated are specified by law. Thus, if we add some sort of ethical precept, such as 'One ought to obey the law,' then the principle is modified to: select the smallest income figure permitted by law.

Now that the principle is clearly stated, we can turn to the question of the relation of the legal definition of taxable income to the construction of a theory of income measurement. Perhaps it would be helpful to consider the experiences of other fields. At one time a state statute defined the value of π as 3.0. Thus, according to the law in that state $3r^2$ defined the area of a circle and all of the law-abiding geometry students, surveyors, etc., calculated it that way. Should this law have a bearing on the theory of geometry? The infamous 'monkey trial' was the result of the legal definition of man's ancestry. Should this law have a bearing on the theory of evolution? Ancient law specified that the earth is the centre of the universe. Should this law have a bearing on the theory of astronomy?

Of course, my answer to all of these questions is 'no'. For the same reasons, I do not think that a legal definition of taxable income should have any bearing on the theory of income measurement. I concede Mattessich's claim to have 'demonstrated . . . that the exclusive market valuation model . . . does not give a measure of income which leads to the minimization of income tax obligations . . .' (p. 183). Indeed, I would have conceded the point without the demonstration. I will also concede that the market value method does not necessarily[7] lead to the minimization of property tax obligations, sales tax obligations, excise tax obligations, etc. However, I do not understand how this can be used as a criticism of the market value method. Would anybody consider it a criticism of, say, historical cost if it was pointed out that it did not necessarily lead to a minimization of legally payable dividends?

Linguists sometimes refer to the 'tyranny of words' and I believe that the source of this confusion is that we are tyrannized by the fact that it is called an *income* tax. If it were called by some other name, perhaps it would be easier for us to separate the problem of measuring income from the problem of paying taxes. As it is, I often encounter the argument that market values are not an appropriate way of measuring income because it would result in a larger income than that obtained from historical costs and therefore a larger tax payment. The same

7. Mattessich alleges that the phrase 'not necessarily' is used as an 'escape clause' in *Enterprise Income* and that such locution is a 'trick for eluding empirical test [by] maximiz[ing] vagueness' (p. 179 n.5). My intent is exactly the opposite. I am trying to be more precise. I mean that the market value method could accidentally lead to minimization, but it does not inevitably lead to minimization. The statement he complains about in *Enterprise Income* is ' . . . income definition derived for different purposes do not necessarily vary' and I intended this to be in contrast to the proposition that different purposes necessarily (or inevitably) lead to different income definitions.

argument can be used against historical cost, e.g., the method of accruing historical cost is not an appropriate way of measuring income because it results in an income figure larger than that obtained from the cash basis of accounting and therefore a larger tax payment. There are many instances in which the historical cost income reported on financial statements is greater than the income reported on the tax return as is evidenced by the controversy over tax allocation. Thus, it has been conclusively demonstrated that it is possible for the reported income figure to be different from the taxable income figure. Yet the argument persists. The only explanation that I can think of is that the word 'income' is being used in two different ways and this clouds our thinking.[8]

In spite of my belief that there is no necessary connection between the legal definition of taxable income and the theory of income measurement, the problem of income taxation was explicitly considered in *Enterprise Income* (pp. 151-4). In general, the occurrence of any event which placed the enterprise in an obligatory position was classified as a relevant bit of information. These were called 'particular factual conditions'. The occurrence of some events result in a tax obligation and therefore the events specified by the tax law are included in the class of 'particular factual conditions'. Throughout the subsequent analysis 'particular factual conditions' were included in the listing of relevant information. (See, e.g., pp. 156, 165, 166, 170, 173, 188.) In addition, see p. 154 for a summary of the reasons for not allowing the present tax law to influence the conclusions of a theory of income measurement.

I do not understand the basis of Mattessich's criticism regarding the purpose of minimizing tax. If it is that income taxation was not considered in *Enterprise Income* it can be rebutted by simply opening the book. If it is that the analysis errs at some point, then he failed to point out the errors. If it is that the tax law has some relation to the theory of income measurement, then it is up to him to point out that relationship or at least confront the arguments presented in *Enterprise Income*. His demonstration consists of nothing more than positing an example in which $IA < IM$ and proving that since the tax rate, r, is positive, then $r(IA) < r(IM)$. By simply changing the figures in his example, I could prove that $r(IM) < r(IA)$ and thereby 'demonstrate that the historical cost valuation model does not give a measure of income which leads to the minimization of taxes'. However, since that demonstration does not contribute to the construction of a theory of income measurement, it is not pertinent to this discussion.

In regard to the third purpose, Mattessich concludes:

> If the purpose of income measurement or valuation is a managerial investment (including disinvestment) decision, then a dual valuation juxtaposing the current objective evaluation

8. In accordance with my suggestion for differrent names for different concepts, I offer LID for legal income definitions in general and then to emphasize that there are many different legal definitions, it can be modified to FLID, SLID, CLID when referring to federal, state, and city statutes, respectively. Perhaps these terms would even aid in resolving the tax allocation dispute. It appears to me that much of that dispute is caused by the failure to clearly distinguish FLID from PAPP and the making of implicit assumptions about relations between them.

of the market with the subjective valuation of the investor is required. If the (complete) subjective evaluation yields a higher value than the market value the investment object should be acquired or kept, if it yields a lower subjective value than the market value, it should be sold or not acquired. (p. 183)

I am in complete agreement with the statement. *Enterprise Income* stressed the need to compare these two values, albeit the phrases 'present prices' and 'expected future prices' are used in place of the words 'objective' and 'subjective.'

What is Mattessich criticizing? It cannot be that he thinks that consideration of this purpose was omitted, because in another connection he refers to the section which contains the discussion and says 'Sterling is here rather concerned with information needed by managers . . . ' (p. 191). It cannot be that he disagrees with the specification of the relevant information because it is exactly the same as he specified. He says that he has 'demonstrated . . . that the exclusive market valuation model . . . does not enable correct investment decisions to be made' (p. 183). But this cannot be the source of his criticism because *Enterprise Income* not only agrees, it emphasizes, the need for a comparison of the two values. *Enterprise Income* goes on to conclude that, given a choice of the two values, the market value ought to be reported. Mattessich draws the same conclusion, albeit for different reasons.[9]

In regard to this purpose, Mattessich's 'demonstration' reduces to the consideration of a decision which was also considered in *Enterprise Income,* specifying the two values relevant to that decision which is the same as the two values specified in *Enterprise Income,* drawing the same conclusion as to which value should be reported, and claiming that all of this 'demonstrated' that *Enterprise Income* erred. I am bewildered.

2. BOUNDARIES

Mattessich's second major point of criticism concerns the boundaries of accounting theory. He writes:

there looms the more incisive question as to the appropriateness of the boundaries set explicitly and implicitly by Professor Sterling to accounting theory. Sterling seems to stake the boundaries of accounting theory in such a narrow way that at best it would serve only the investor, or potential investor, interested in buying, selling or keeping shares of the pertinent enterprise. (p. 186)

He complains about my 'narrow brand of financial accounting' and states that I have fallen into a 'trap' by claiming 'to be concerned with financial accounting only, but . . . behav[ing] as if accounting consisted of nothing else but financial accounting. The passages quoted above and many other passages of Sterling's book are evidence of this.' (p. 182.)

9. He states that he agrees with the market value approach for reporting to creditors and investors (p. 180) and that subjective values should not be reported because they would give away too much confidential information (p. 186).

Since I was unaware that I had fallen into this trap, I examined the 'passages quoted above' that were 'evidence of this'. The reader may easily verify that the passages quoted have nothing whatsoever to do with the boundaries of accounting theory. In fact, neither the word 'accounting' nor the word 'theory' was ever used in any of the passages referred to by Mattessich. I invite the reader to peruse all of the passages which Mattessich quoted and judge for himself whether or not there was any explicit or implicit attempt to narrow the boundaries of accounting theory. I invite Mattessich to disclose those 'many other passages [which] are evidence of this'.[10]

The point of his criticism seems to be that *Enterprise Income* 'deals neither with tax accounting nor managerial accounting but exclusively with financial accounting' and that this has a 'dangerous psychological impact' because 'it suggests that all other non-financial accounting is a side-issue of no or very little relevance to accounting' (p. 182).

In regard to tax accounting he says he 'cannot accept the argument . . . that it is not the task of financial accounting to generate financial statements (within the confines of the tax law) that would minimize the corporations' tax obligation' (p. 186). I, too, cannot accept that argument. If Mattessich will show me a book or an article that makes that argument, I will gladly write a rejoinder to it. Tax accounting is a lucrative source of revenue and it would be foolish for us to give it up. However, I do not understand this comment in the context of a critique of *Enterprise Income*. It is true that *Enterprise Income* does not contain an explicit statement to the effect that accountants ought to prepare tax returns. However, the absence of such a statement does not imply an argument that the preparation of tax returns is not the task of accounting. A statement that one ought to use double entry was also omitted from *Enterprise Income*. Does anyone take that omission as an argument that double entry ought not to be used?

In regard to managerial accounting, his criticisms are contradictory. In one place he says that the book 'deals neither with tax accounting nor managerial accounting but exclusively with financial accounting' (p. 181). But to make another point of criticism he says 'Sterling is here rather concerned with information needed by managers and 'other interested receivers' relevant to their problems, hence with what traditionally is called managerial accounting in the broad sense' (p. 191). He can't have it both ways: either the book dealt with managerial accounting or it did not. I don't know how to reply to a critique that claims that both are true.

10. Recall that *Enterprise Income* was written several years ago when such topics as user needs and alternative valuation methods were thought to be outside the boundaries of accounting. At that time I was called a 'radical' on several occasions, and *Enterprise Income* was criticized because it attempted to broaden the scope of accounting theory. Mattessich now refers to me as a 'conservative' (p. 189) and criticizes *Enterprise Income* for attempting to narrow the boundaries of accounting theory. I find this particularly amusing because it almost precisely parallels my change in political views from 'communist' (because of my non-violent *opposition* to the Viet Nam war) to 'reactionary' (because of my *non-violent* opposition to the Viet Nam war).

In the sense that *Enterprise Income* concludes that market (exit) values ought to be reported [on financial statements], it is true that *Enterprise Income* is concerned with financial accounting instead of tax or managerial accounting. However, the process by which this conclusion was reached was to consider the needs of various users, including managers and taxing authorities. Thus, Mattessich misinterprets the aim of the book when he alleges that it attempts to narrow the boundaries of accounting theory to where it 'would serve only the investor' (p. 186). He also misinterprets the result of the conclusion. By his own example, exit values are relevant to managers and therefore if they are reported, then managers as well as investors are served. Finally, he misinterprets the conclusion itself. He refers to it as the 'exclusive market value method' and implies that the goal is 'to banish other valuation methods' (p. 176). The fact is that *Enterprise Income* ranked the various valuation methods and drew the conclusion that the use of market (exit) prices is the 'superior valuation method' (*Enterprise Income*, p. 361; quoted by Mattessich, p. 178). Nowhere does it claim that it is the *only* value relevant to decisions or that *all* other valuation methods should be banished. If it ever made such a claim it would be a gross contradiction to its own analysis. For example, it notes that managers are required to compare the present exit prices with the future predicted prices. Since a comparison is required, it would be foolish to claim that only present exist prices are relevant to this decision—what would one compare them with? In this context 'superior' can be taken literally as 'higher in rank'. That market (exit) values are relevant to more decision models than any other single valuation method and that they meet the stated criteria better than any other valuation method does not mean that they are the only relevant values nor does it mean that other values should not be determined.

Enterprise Income is a book concerned with income and valuation problems, not a book on accounting theory, financial or otherwise. In this sense the focus of the book was quite narrow. In the kind of firm it analyzed it was even narrower. Only in the attempt to consider a number of different kinds of users and several different valuation methods could it be considered broad. As the Introduction states, the book was narrowly focused because: 'It was felt that it would be more beneficial to try to settle one issue, however small, than to continue the global argument for another century' (p. 4). Thus the book can be legitimately criticized for being narrowly focused. However, to criticize it for not being a general theory of accounting is going a bit far. It was not intended to be a general theory of accounting.

This does not mean that a general theory of accounting is unneeded. On the contrary, I share Mattessich's hankerings for such a theory. However, given the way he has defined the task, I despair at accomplishment. If, as he states, the general theory must include all legal definitions of income, it seems to me, *a priori*, to be impossible. Consider how one would include the legal definition of the area of a circle as $3r^2$ in a general theory of geometry or the legal definition of the earth as the centre of the universe in a general theory of astronomy. Such a theory would either be internally inconsistent or empirically false or both. I fear the same fate for a general theory of accounting if that general theory is required to encompass the various legal definitions of income.

I think Mattessich has defined an impossible task. On the other hand, I believe that tax theory, as opposed to tax law, could easily be included in a general theory of accounting. A recent book on tax theory contains many propositions that would easily fit into such a theory and, in my opinion, they ought to be included. For example, it says:

> Equity demands that the income concept on which such taxation is based accurately reflect differences in the ability to pay of different taxpayers. Examining various alternatives leads to an accretion definition of income defined in money terms. . . .
>
> The definition of income used here . . . [is] conceptually . . . the same as the well-known Haig-Simons definition—consumption enjoyed during a particular period, plus any accretion (less any diminution) to net worth.[11]

As I said before, income definitions derived for different purposes do not necessarily vary.

3. A CHALLENGE

Enterprise Income opened with the statement that it was a polemic and that the attempt was to set down the reasoning in enough detail to allow the reader to know precisely where it erred. It closed with a challenge to demonstrate that the conclusions were invalid. The reason for this (in addition to the fact that I relish a good argument) was that I believe that public debate is a good way to clarify ideas. The focus of *Enterprise Income* was quite narrow because I thought that the narrower the focus the better the chance of resolving the issue. Thus, I had hoped that through public debate we could clarify our ideas and by focusing narrowly we could resolve a small issue. After that we could go on to bigger issues.

I am aware of many imperfections in *Enterprise Income*. There are probably many more of which I am ignorant. I would be delighted (albeit embarrassed) for its errors to be pointed out clearly and publicly. Such a critique would be of benefit to me, but more importantly it would help others avoid these errors. In this spirit, I again challenge Professor Mattessich (and the reader) to demonstrate that its conclusions are invalid.

Mattessich makes a number of assertions which I find intriguing, but of no benefit to me. For example, he says that the classification of the various states, positions, prices, and values as information bits is a worthy method but the conclusion was biased because of a one-sided and partial application of that method (p. 191). Perhaps I was biased in the application of that method. However, after re-reading the section, I was unable to discover that bias, although I did discover an error.[12] Since his criticism merely asserted the existence of a bias

11. Martin David, *Alternative Approaches to Capital Gains Taxation*, Studies of Government Finance, The Brookings Institution, Washington D.C. 1968, pp. 51, 49.

12. Table VIII-2 omitted the price P_3 at time t_3. This is a serious error, but I do not think it biased the conclusions.

and since I was unable to discover that bias, it was of no benefit to me. I would have preferred that he point out how the analysis was biased. Mattessich's critique contains many other assertions of this kind. In the same spirit, I challenge Professor Mattessich (and the reader) to point out those errors instead of merely asserting their existence.

4. CONCLUSION

Professor Mattessich has made many valuable contributions to the literature of accounting. Unfortunately, his critique is not one of them. He criticized *Enterprise Income* for

1. not taking an approach (teleological) that it in fact took;
2. not considering three users (creditors and stockholders, taxing authorities, and managers) that it in fact considered;
3. not drawing a conclusion (different-incomes-for-different-purposes) that was identical to its statement of the problem;
4. placing boundaries (to serve only stockholders) on the theory of accounting that it did not place;
5. drawing a conclusion (exclusive market values) that it did not draw; and
6. not being a general theory of accounting when it was explicitly stated to be (and entitled) a theory of income measurement.

Mattessich concludes by likening the structure of *Enterprise Income* to a building in the baroque architectural style. I am sorry that I cannot extend the simile. Mattessich's critique was so amorphous that I was unable to determine its architectural style, but I did note an architectural flaw—it was without foundation.

ROBERT R. STERLING

An Explication and Analysis of the Structure of Accounting Part Two

Introduction

In Part One of this paper a system of accounting was formally defined and a quantity interpretation given to the formal system. It was argued that accounting for quantities has the same structure as accounting for dollars or costs. Since quantity accounting is simpler, in the sense that the experiential reduction is obvious, it can be used as a relief in discussing the theoretical issues of financial accounting. Some such issues will be examined in this Part.

Event selection

In the quantity accounting system certain events were recorded and others were not. The same is true for the financial accounting system. Thus, in both systems some criteria must be employed for segregating those events to be recorded from those which are not recorded. Usually these criteria are tacit; they are assumed to be understood. There are many examples of this. In the description of the physical system we simply assumed that changes in volume would be recorded and that changes in energy would not be recorded. It is important to note, however, that one cannot deduce this from the definitions given in Section III of Part One. There is nothing in the set of definitions that would permit one to conclude that volume changes ought to be recorded or that energy changes ought not. There are several quantities that would 'work' in the explicated system, e.g., since energy is in fact conserved we could record energy transfers without altering the structure of the accounting system. Thus, exogenous criteria are required to segregate the events into those that are recorded and those that are not.

In financial accounting we are faced with the same problem. There are some events that are recorded and others that are not. These have changed over time, e.g., depreciation is now recorded. There is now a major dispute over the recording of some events, e.g., the signing of a lease. There are several differents kinds of valuation methods that would 'work' in the present structure. Often the arguments over what events are to be recorded do not employ exogenous criteria. Some of the arguments can be reduced to simple definitional tautologies. For example,

Major Premise:	Accounting is (read: is identical with) a record of historical costs.
Minor Premise:	Price-level changes do not affect the historical cost of an item.
Conclusion:	Price-level changes should not be recorded.

ROBERT R. STERLING is Professor of Business Administration in the University of Kansas.
Part One of this paper was published in *Abacus*, Vol. 7, pp. 137-52.

Such arguments are valid. They have the same form as

Major Premise:	A horse is an animal with four legs.
Minor Premise:	John does not have four legs.
Conclusion:	Therefore, John is not a horse.

The problem is that the major premise contains a prescription for the inclusion of some events and the exclusion of others. Thus, the quarrel over which events ought to be recorded cannot be resolved by appealing to the major premise; it is precisely the thing in dispute.[1] The acceptance or rejection of the major premise is a matter that requires other criteria.

Consider the valuation dispute. It has been argued that accounting 'by its nature' implies the historical cost method of valuation. Ijiri presents the most sophisticated argument of this kind. He writes:

> . . . we shall show that the double-entry system is closely related to historical cost valuation and that actually the former was devised to suit the latter. . . . We may note here that the three factors described above are an expression of the cost principle, which imputes the value of the increment from the value of the decrement. Therefore, what makes the double-entry system double is not the double classification (Assets = Equity) that is often described in accounting literature but rather the cost principle, which recognizes the casual relationship between an asset required and an asset foregone. In this sense, the double-entry system and the historical cost principle . . . have a logical connection since one is a form developed to express the other.[2]

In my view, double-entry is not unique to accounting. It is simply a special case of the more general conservation laws. Note that the imputations that Ijiri mentions in the quoted passage follow directly from a conservation assumption. The measure of an increment (or decrement) at one location can be used to impute the measure of the decrement (or increment) at a connected location if the system is conservative. This is a common and highly useful assumption. The housewife who pours a cup of milk into a mixing bowl is imputing the measure of the increment in the bowl from the measure of the decrement in the cup. She could also impute the measure of the decrement in the milk bottle from the measure of the increment in the cup. All such actions can be cast into a double-entry accounting system and the measure can be imputed.

In traditional financial accounting the value of the non-cash item is imputed from the value of the related cash item. In a purchase, for example, the cash or near-cash sacrificed is valued independently and the value of the debit is set equal.

1. Some price-level adjustment proponents take a different tack. They accept the major premise and challenge the minor premise, i.e., they say that price-level adjustments result in a 'restatement' of historical costs. This is an argument over what ought to be included in a class for which the definition has been accepted. It has the same form as the argument over whether apes ought to be included in the class of bipeds or quadrupeds. The definition of the class is accepted but the front appendages of apes have some characteristics of both hands and feet and therefore it is not clear whether they are bipeds or quadrupeds.

2. Yuji Ijiri, *The Foundations of Accounting Measurement*, Englewood Cliffs, N.J. 1967, pp. 101–8.

In a sale the cash or near-cash acquired is valued independently and the value of the credit is set equal. In structure this is quite similar to the physical imputation described in the preceding paragraph. Thus, the imputation of the initial value seems quite reasonable. For subsequent valuation an additional operation is required. We normally divide the quantified non-cash item into the quantity of cash and use the quotient as a valuation coefficient. Non-cash assets are conceived of as collections of service potentials. These service potentials are expressed in a variety of units, e.g., years of service life, units of inventory, number of outputs, etc. The quotient is called depreciation per year, cost per unit, amortization per unit, etc. The value of the non-cash asset varies as the number of units varies.[3] This can be expressed more compactly as follows.

Let X_{ij} = number of service potentials of the ith class received at time j.
X_{kj} = number of dollars (service potentials of the kth class) sacrificed at time j.

$$p_{ij} = \frac{X_{kj}}{X_{ij}}$$

Then the entry is

Date	j	Account i		$p_{ij}X_{ij}$	
			Account k		X_{kj}

or the initial valuation of X_{ij} is $p_{ij}X_{ij}$ which is equal to X_{kj}.

This process also has a physical interpretation. Assume, for example, that X_{ij} is the quantity received at the ith location where the measure is in volume units and X_{kj} is the quantity issued from the kth location where the measure is in weight units. Then p_{ij} would be interpreted as volume units per weight unit,

3. It would facilitate communications, and perhaps understanding, if we had general terms for such things. It is awkward to continue to refer specifically to years of service life, units of inventory, depreciation per year, cost per unit, etc., when all of these things are structurally alike. In general there are *quantities* and *valuation coefficients* for those quantities, including an understood valuation coefficient of unity for cash or near-cash. These are the two elements of 'value' whether it be historical cost or some other value. Recognition of the generality of this procedure might be facilitated if general terms were adopted, in addition to making the exposition easier. Other fields normally use a 'technical jargon' for both the above reasons. Another reason for inventing new technical terms is to avoid the confusion that arises when a special meaning is given to an existing term. This has happened in accounting with the term 'depreciation', for example. Depreciation in ordinary usage means a decrease in the valuation coefficient with a constant quantity. We say that an automobile or a building depreciates, for example, and what we mean is that there is *one* automobile or building that declines in value. Since the quantity is conceived as being constant at unity it is the decrease in the valuation coefficient (price) that occasions the decrease in value. In accounting, however, we mean by depreciation that the quantity declines while the valuation coefficient is held constant. This is also true of inventory, supplies, depletable assets, prepayments, etc. It is even true of cash and near-cash. The stable price level assumption means that the value of cash varies only as the quantity varies; the valuation coefficient for cash is held constant at unity instead of being multiplied by a particular valuation coefficient called a price index. Despite their similarity we continue to talk about these things in separate categories. I think that both conceptualization and communication would be enhanced if accounting adopted a technical jargon which expressed the generality of these procedures.

e.g., gallons per pound. Thus, both the imputation of the value of the increment (or decrement) from the value of the decrement (or increment) and the calculation of the valuation coefficient are similar to purely physical processes. This similarity should add to our confidence in the procedures that we employ but it should also make us doubt the uniqueness of the methodology. In my view, 'for every debit there is an equal credit' is but a substitution instance of 'to every action there is always opposed an equal reaction'.

In the valuation process described above the *initial* value of the increment was imputed from the decrement. At a later time, say *t*, the value of the asset and expense is calculated as follows.

$p_{ij} X_{it}$ = asset value at time *t*
$P_{ij} (X_{ij} - X_{it})$ = expense from time *j* to *t*

Thus, the asset value varies as the quantity varies. The valuation coefficient is held constant over time. Whether or not this ought to be the case depends upon what events one decides to take into account.

Compare this valuation process to the physical example. If X_{ij} is the number of volume units and X_{kj} is the related number of weight units then p_{ij} is in fact the volume units per weight unit for this particular transfer at this particular time. This is a reasonable procedure. However, it does not follow from that fact that p_{ij} remains constant over time. It does not follow that $p_{ij}X_{it}$ is the correct expression of the weight at time *t* even though it is correct at time *j*. On the contrary, in this example we know that if the temperature of the item has changed, then p_{ij} is *not* the correct ratio at time *t*. However, in order to know this we have to expand our set of events to include temperature changes. We could decide, if we choose, to restrict our set of events so that temperature changes were not taken into account.

Note that there is a similar imputation process available in such cases. If there is another transfer at time *t* and we calculate the ratio of that transfer and find it to be p_{it}, and we know that the quantity received from a previous transfer is similar in all relevant respects, then it is reasonable to impute p_{it} to the quantity of the previous transfer. This is common process. For example, if one has a flask of liquid that was originally at temperature *j* but it is now known that it is at temperature *t*, and one has another flask of the same liquid at temperature *t*, then one can calculate the volume-weight ratio of the second flask and impute that same ratio to the first flask. On the other hand, we could decide to restrict our observations to the first flask and refuse to take the second flask into account. However, there is nothing within the process that permits one to validly deduce that he ought to restrict his observations in this fashion. Such decisions require exogenous criteria.

This example is analogous to historical cost accounting. The historical cost method of valuation is particularistic. The cost is attached to a particular quantity on the basis of the transaction involving *that* quantity. Other transactions involving identical quantities are not considered to be evidence of a change in the valuation coefficient of the original quantity. We could, if we choose, decide to expand the set of events to include transactions other than the original one. For example, we could use the valuation coefficient of the most recent transaction within the entity of interest to value the quantity still on hand from a previous transaction. Or we could use the valuation coefficient of the most recent transactions between other entities to value the quantity held in the entity of interest. These are imputations that are quite similar to the physical example given above. Whether we should or should not make such imputations in financial accounting cannot be validly deduced from the double-entry process.

The accounting system that was explicated above is neutral with respect to valuation. We could keep track of the quantities without ever bothering to value them or we could value them in any one of several ways. That is, it has been demonstrated that quantity statements can be prepared that have the same structure as the financial statements. We could now consider the valuation of the quantities to be a *separate* process. We could multiply the quantities by any valuation coefficient we choose—historical costs, standard costs, entry prices, exit prices, discounted expectations, etc. We could even mix them if we choose. For example, we could value the quantities at their acquisition price initially and then value them at their current cost (or other value) at a subsequent date. This would permit one to 'analyze the variance' in each asset classification in the same way that we analyze the difference between standard and actual costs. The difference in the value at two points in time could be attributed to the 'price variance' (difference between acquisition cost and current cost), 'quantity variance', and 'joint variance'. We could then show the 'sources' of these variances in any one of several ways, e.g., we could show a unrealized appreciation account as the source of the price variance of those items still on hand.

Which particular valuation method we ought to select will not be considered in this paper. My present interest is in the structure of the system and the things that can and cannot be deduced from that structure. I think that the events that ought to be taken into account cannot be deduced from the structure. Obviously the events that we take into account must be restricted in some fashion. Every field of inquiry must set up such restrictions since no field can examine everything. Psychology restricts its considerations to psychological events, physics to physical events, etc. Accounting must also restrict itself. Thus, it is not the act of restriction that I object to; instead it is the process that we have been using to make the restriction. I think that the selection of events to be recorded requires criteria exogenous to the structure.

These exogenous criteria should include:

1. Teleological considerations—the purpose or objective of the reports.
2. Operational considerations—the feasibility, objectivity, verifiability, etc., of the measurement of the events.

At the present time the operational considerations are often given much greater weight than the teleological considerations. Many suggestions for the 'improvement' of accounting (expanding or changing the set of events to be accounted for) that are made on teleological grounds are rejected on operational grounds. It is often admitted that it would be desirable to present the suggested events, but it is said that it is not feasible, or that such figures are not obtainable, or they are not objective, etc. In my opinion too much weight has been given to the operational considerations. Of course, the suggested events must be measurable since accounting is a 'practical' discipline. We cannot theorize on teleological grounds alone. There are many useful concepts (e.g., utility) that are not, in the present state of the arts, measurable and therefore they have no place on accounting reports. Likewise, however, it is possible to measure many events that serve no purpose and these measurements also have no place on accounting reports. The teleological considerations ought to be given higher status than they have been given in the past. If one needs to know a particular magnitude because it serves some purpose or is relevant to some end, then a rough estimate of that magnitude is of some use. The opposite is not true. A precise and objective measure of an irrelevant magnitude is, at best, a curiosity. Thus, both teleological and operational considerations are necessary criteria to decide which events are to be recorded.[4]

In summary, the double-entry notion is applicable to a great many different kinds of quantities. It is not unique to accounting. Recording historical costs as an initial value is connected to double-entry, as Ijiri points out, in the sense that it is reasonable to impute the value (or quantity) of an increment (or decrement) from the value of a related decrement (or increment). However, it does not follow that the initial value should be held constant. Subsequent non-cost values can be imputed by a procedure not too different from the original imputation procedure. What imputations one should make is not given by the structure of the system. It depends upon the events one decides to take into account. The selection of the events to be taken into account requires exogenous criteria. These criteria ought to include both teleological and operational considerations.

Entity definition

I have previously proposed that we define an entity in financial accounting as a set of assets collected for a common purpose and their related equities.[5] Consideration of the physical system reveals the same sort of process. We partitioned the universe of locations and decided to call a certain subset of locations an entity. We also partitioned the universal set of events and decided to record some and not to record others. Accounting is chock full of such partitioning. We partition the subset further by fund versus non-fund transactions, income versus non-income

4. I suspect that many of the arguments that are stated on operational grounds in fact stem from other considerations. Many proposals are rejected because they are not feasible even though it is admitted that they would be useful. If one compares the operational requirements of the measurement of the proposed events to the operational requirements of the traditional accounting system, it is not clear that the determinations required by traditional accounting are any more feasible or objective than the determinations required by the proposed systems. It would seem, therefore, that tacit criteria are being employed and it would be helpful if those criteria were made explicit.

5. Robert R. Sterling, 'An Abstract of Accounting Theory', *Annals of Economics and Management Science*, No. 5, Kobe 1968, p. 88.

transactions, capital versus expense, account 1 versus accounts 2, 3, . . ., m, and so forth.

All of these are classifications. In my view, entity definition is the same kind of classification process as account definition. It has been said that classification is an 'arbitrary business' and this is true.[6] One can define a set in any way he chooses. However, purposeful classification usually involves collecting items with some common property. This requires careful specification of the particular property and an operation for determining the existence or non-existence of that property in a specific instance.

Classification is a problem of large dimension and pervasive effect for accounting. I don't propose to treat it here. Fortunately I can plead space limitations and thereby conceal my ignorance. Let me just say that the information retrieval people, particularly in connection with library cataloguing, have had some interesting things to say about the problem and these things seem to be applicable to accounting, although I am unsure of precisely how they could be applied.[7]

In regard to the particular classification process that distinguishes an entity, my major complaint is that the criterion that is usually given is too narrow. Typically one finds a discussion about a *business* entity coupled with some remarks about private property and profit maximation.[8] Now if these discussions are intended to describe fully what accountants actually account for, then they are false. There are a great many non-business applications of accounting. The Red Cross is an accounting entity, for example. Socialist countries apply the same accounting methodology and they need a concept of an entity; yet the notion of ownership or profit is an anathema. Thus, the typical discussions of entities are inadequate in that they do not encompass all of the entities that accountants account for. In addition, some of the expressed views are rather parochial. A few years ago there was a spate of articles urging that accounting be used to defend free private enterprise. In my view accounting is (or ought to be) apolitical in the same way that mathematics and chemistry are apolitical. There may be differences in accounting theory or practice but there are also common elements that transcend political boundaries or particular institutional arrangements.

The entity is a classification and that classification depends on one's purpose. We could account for any set of things in which we are interested. Thus, what is included and excluded from an entity depends on our interests of purposes, i.e., teleological considerations. The physicist's system can range from a particular heat oven in a particular lab to the entire solar system, depending on his purpose. An accounting entity can have a similar range for similar reasons. Of course, this is the easy way out. My notion of an entity is like the notion of a set—it can be anything one wants to focus on. In one sense this is entirely appropriate because

6. Cf. S. S. Stevens, *Handbook of Experimental Psychology*, New York 1951, p. 27.
7. *See* Yehoshua Bar-Hillel, *Language and Information*, Reading, Mass. 1964, Part V for a critical summary of some of the research on information retrieval.
8. *See*, e.g., Paul Grady, *Inventory of Generally Accepted Accounting Principles for Business Enterprises*, 1965, pp. 24–7.

it indicates the range over which accounting can be applied. In another sense it is inappropriate because it does not describe the kinds of things which we currently account for.

If I were to axiomatize accounting in a completely general way (and take the easy way out) then I would find it necessary to include an entity axiom to the effect that it be a 'well-defined set'. Ijiri has taken the more difficult route. In his earlier work he included the axiom of ownership.[9] The objects 'owned by' the subject was the criterion used to define the entity. This was both too narrow and too broad. Too narrow because it excluded all accounting entities in socialist countries. Too broad because we often account for the business assets but not the personal assets, even though both are owned by the subject. His more recent work[10] includes the axiom of control for the purpose of defining an entity. The control axiom more accurately describes what we currently account for because it is broad enough to include non-profit organizations, leased assets and the like. Ijiri is willing to expand the criteria to include 'other factors such as location, possession and physical attachment' and he notes that the 'syntax of accounting language is not affected by the control criteria that are used'.[11] In my view he is on the right track. He recognizes the necessity of defining an entity and the necessity for providing *criteria* so that we can know what is and is not included in a particular entity and he also attempts to *describe* in a general way the kinds of entities that we currently account for. However, I would caution against taking the description as a prescription. A division of a firm could also be accounted for as a separate entity even though it is not under the control of a separate management. Such flexibility is desirable. We can, and do, apply the accounting methodology to a great many diverse things running all the way from a few accounts for an individual to the highly consolidated accounts for the income of nation states. It depends solely upon what one is interested in or what one wants to focus on.

The entity, under the quantity interpretation, is a set of locations in which we are interested. There is also a set of events in which we are interested. The intersection of these two sets gives us the things that an accountant accounts for. If one is willing to accept the above explication as an appropriate description of the accounting methodology, then this set of locations and events can be almost anything. When the physicist says '. . . it will be seen that this lost work can be traced and strictly accounted for . . .'[12] or 'This simple-account-keeping rule—total Mv after collision is the same as total Mv before . . .'[13] the similarity of language is not accidental. One can account for the changes in physical measures in a well-defined

9. Yuji Ijiri, 'Axioms and Structures of Conventional Accounting Measurement', *Accounting Review*, Vol. XL, No. 1, January 1965, p. 39.
10. Ijiri, *Foundations*, p. 69.
11. Ijiri, *Foundations*, p. 70.
12. G. R. Noakes, *A Text Book of General Physics: An Introduction to Mechanics, Properties of Matter and Wave Motion*, 1950, p. 116.
13. Eric M. Rogers, *Physics for the Inquiring Mind*, Princeton 1960, p. 141.

system in exactly the same way as we account for certain events in a well-defined entity. One can change the focus without affecting the structure. A funds statement which defines funds as cash focuses on only one account. A balance sheet focuses on a collection of accounts. Both statements have the same structure. Both present the changes in a set of accounts and their sources and recipients for a particular period of time. Thus, in one case we focused on one account and, in a sense, this became an 'entity', while in the other case we focused on a set containing more than one element and it was 'the entity'. Thus, our interest is the controlling factor in classifying something as an entity. It is futile to try to define *the* entity as if it had an existence separate and apart from our interests. The reason why I find the axiom of control appealing is that we usually are in fact interested in the assets under the control of some person or some group. However, if our interests shift we should not rule out other entities defined by a different criterion.

Closely connected to entity definition is the long-standing argument over the nature of equities. Are they 'sources' or 'claims'? In the physical system it is clear that they are sources. Two locations are *related* by noting that what came *from* one location went *to* another location. The same is true in financial accounting. One entity receives something from another.

When one is speaking of a relation then one can also speak of the converse of that relation. The converse of 'ancestor of' is 'descendant of'. If 'John is the ancestor of Mary' is true, then it is also true that 'Mary is the descendent of John'. In matters economic it is usually true that when some real good or service comes from John then it is also true that some real good or service is due to John. Thus, 'received from' is the converse of the relation 'due to' in respect to real goods in the ordinary economic case. Money sometimes clouds this relation because the receipt of money for a good is considered a final settlement of the transaction. However, money is not desirable for its own properties; instead it is a generalized claim on the real goods that are offered in the market. Thus whenever we supply somebody with a real good then he is the recipient of that good but he is also the source of some other good, i.e., recipients are also receivables. Whenever we receive a real good from somebody it is usually the case that a real good is due to that person, i.e., sources are also payables.

The monetary unit serves as a bookkeeping device, among other things. It is a unit of measure for which no unit object need exist. The unit 'Guinea' illustrates this point and the fact that we consider a cheque to be money provides further illustration. The advent of the cheque-less society will make it even more evident. Thus, cash is a marker indicating a claim on good which was received because goods were supplied. The transitivity of the relation sometimes obscures the point. If $a < b$ and $b < c$ then $a < c$. If something went from location *a* to location *b* and then went from *b* to *c* then we could meaningfully say that it went from *a* to *c*. Commerce is a series of transitive relations when the 'monetary veil' is removed. If *a* supplies *b* with a real good then *a* is due a real good from *b*. If *b* now supplies *c* with a real good then *b* is due a real good from *c*. It is possible to keep the obligatory relations specific as to both person and goods, as in a barter transaction, or it is possible to keep them specific as to person only, as in exchanges on account. In the latter case *b* has a receivable from *c* and a payable to *a*. We can now generalize this further by dropping the *b* term and say that *a* has (indirectly) supplied *c* with a real good and *a* is due a real good from *c*. In effect this is what the bank does when *b* deposits his cheque from *c* and *a* deposits his cheque from *b*. A major function of banking is to keep track of such transitions. Money is a general claim on goods that goes in the opposite direction to the flow of real goods and its purpose is to keep track of the obligations for the opposite (converse) flow of real goods.

Given these considerations the argument over whether equities are either sources or claims can be resolved. Usually it is the case that if 'X is a source' is true then it is also true that 'X is a claim' and vice versa. Thus, equities are usually sources *and* claims. Unfortunately, we have to include the word 'usually' in the definition because there are a few odd cases. We have to be content at this point in time, if we want to be completely general, to say that equities are sources or (in the inclusive sense) claims. That is, equities are either sources or claims or both.

I suspect that the argument over the proprietorship versus the entity theory can be reconciled in a similar fashion. It has always seemed to me that the two theories are simply different ways of looking at the same thing. The difference between the two schools is usually discussed in terms of the algebraic transformation of $A - L = P$ to $A = L + P$ (or vice versa). Sometimes it is expressed as the difference between $A = E$ and $A - L = P$. The $A = E$ expression is supposed to emphasize the similarity of liabilities and proprietorship. I agree that they are similar but I also agree that it is desirable to subclassify them into the two categories and then to subclassify them further.

I am not sure what theoretical or practical differences are derived from the two theories. One could, I suppose, claim that 'entity income' is the net change in *total* assets. Paton and Littleton came close to defining income that way in their discussion of the business entity. They write:

> Gains and losses are changes in enterprise assets, not in proprietors' assets or in stockholders' assets. [It is more rational] to conceive of business property as belonging to the entity, and of income as asset-increment.[14]

Under this view all asset increments would be revenues to the entity, including debt creation and owner's investment, and all asset decrements would be expenses, including debt retirement and dividends.

Of course this is not the intent of Paton and Littleton as is clear from their discussion of revenues, costs and income. Revenues, they say, are 'new assets received from customers'[15] and this makes 'income' the net asset increment *from customers*. This is quite different from the net increment in entity assets. Yet either could be used as a definition of income. Whether interest payments are 'expenses'

14. W. A. Paton and A. C. Littleton, *An Introduction to Corporate Accounting Standards*, p. 9.
15. Paton and Littleton, *Introduction*, p. 46.

or 'distribution of income' depends upon our focus, not upon anything inherent in the definition of income or the nature of the entity.

Net receipts from customers, in our legal system, are peculiar in that there is no converse relation. Receipts from creditors or owners usually implies a 'due to' obligation which is not present in a finalized transaction with a customer. Instead, the net receipts from customers are due to the owners. Thus, it is the owner's or proprietor's income that is in fact reported, not the entity's income. This does not seem to me to imply a contradiction. It simply makes the income figure the result of a subset of the transactions of an entity. The funds statement also consists of only a subset of the transactions of an entity. We could label the figure on the last line of the funds statement 'income' if we so desired.

In summary, the notion of an entity is indispensable to accounting. We cannot account for all events that affect all objects and the entity is a general term used to delimit the objects that we focus on. Exactly what we ought to focus on depends on our interests and purposes. The sources versus claims argument over the interpretation of equities is a false issue. A physical system can be described in which they are sources and not claims. It is possible to imagine an institutional arrangement of obligations in which they are claims and not sources. In our legal system equities are usually both claims and sources. The notions that are held in opposition to the entity concept, such as the proprietorship theory, can be subsumed by the entity concept. We can account for proprietorship income as a part of a given entity or we could define a particular entity as all (business and personal) assets of a given proprietor.

Perhaps the entity dispute can best be laid to rest by comparing it to the physicist's notion of a 'system'. Physicists sometimes contemplate the entire solar system and consider it to be a closed, isolated system in which energy is transmitted from the sun to plants to animals, etc., and is conserved. At other times a system is a small apparatus in the laboratory. Their definitions are tautological. Energy is said to be conserved if and only if the system is closed and isolated. But then a closed, isolated system is defined as one in which energy is conserved. Accountants can also contemplate the entire universe or a very small corner of that universe. Perhaps we ought to define an entity as anything we wish to focus on and to which we apply the accounting methodology. Thus, an entity would be anything which is accounted for by a self-balancing set of accounts.

The entry

Once it is decided which events are to be recorded and the entity has been defined, then each selected event is cast into a specified form called an 'entry'. In financial accounting the entry has four essential elements: (1) It is dated so that one may sum over a particular period of time; (2) It is classified by sign (debit or credit) so that one knows whether to add or subtract; (3) It is classified by account name (or number) so that one may sum over a particular classification;

and (4) It is doubly classified in such a way that the effects are of opposite signs and equal magnitude.[16]

The zero-sum equation in Definition 1.1[17] contains the same elements. Each transfer is classified by (1) temporal location, (2) spatial location or account class, (3) sign, and (4) dual effect so that it sums to zero. Other classifications may be added as desired. Thus, except for valuation, the entries of the quantity accounting system are the same as the entries of the financial accounting system.

These entries are the inputs of the accounting system. Once the event has been quantified and classified the other operations necessary for the preparation of reports are rather routine. An examination of the quantity balance sheet and flow statements definitions reveals that the preparation of these reports can be relegated to the computer. Those reports are simply summations and partitions of the entries. Since the entries are already classified and indexed by subscript, the partitioning process is a routine selection of a defined set of subscripts. The same is true in financial accounting. The entries are classified by account as the event occurs. Then the preparation of the financial statements is simply the summation of the entries by account and the segregation of those accounts into various classes.

Thus, it is the entry equation, not the balance sheet equation, that is the 'fundamental equation' of accounting. In the formulation presented in this paper the balance sheet equation is derived from the entry equation. Of course it is possible to validly derive Dr = Cr from A = E and it is often done. This is simply an instance of the fact that an axiom in one formulation can be a theorem in another formulation and vice versa. Thus, what is and is not an axiom of any given formulation is, with some restrictions, a matter of choice. I chose the entry equation as a starting point because it more accurately reflects current accounting practice and the theory supporting that practice.

In financial accounting, as it is currently practised, it is impossible to determine independently the values of the assets, equities, revenues and expenses. If it is thought that A = E is the fundamental equation, and that Dr = Cr is derived therefrom, then it would be reasonable to assume that the values of A and E could be determined independently of the values of the debits and credits. But this is not the case. The cost-value of any particular asset or equity (or revenue or expense) is the 'algebraic' sum of the debits and credits, and that sum cannot be directly determined.[18] It is possible, of course, to determine independently the

16. These are the elements contained in each entry. There may be other subclassifications. For example, the purchase of inventory on account may be classified by inventory part number, invoice number and name of supplier. The 'inventory' classification then is a set which is the union of several subsets. The same is true for the supplier. There are a number of suppliers to whom money is owed and these are collected in various sets according to whether it is an 'account' or 'note' payable, etc. However, all of these additional classifications can be handled by adding subscripts or by adding further instructions as to which elements are contained in which subsets. The above list states the *essential* elements of every entry. Other things *may* be added as desired.

17. *See Abacus*, December 1971, p. 142.

18. Support is provided by the definition of an asset as anything with a debit balance after the books are closed: *Accounting Research and Terminology Bulletins*, Final Edition, New York

quantity of the assets but it is not possible to determine independently the historical cost of those assets. Thus, the venerable notion of 'marshalling the assets' and *then* valuing them is not applicable to historical cost accounting. One cannot in fact begin with the A = E notion and prepare a historical cost balance sheet; one must begin with the Dr = Cr notion.

The A = E notion is a possible starting place for non-cost valuation methods. One could marshall the assets and then value them at their replacement cost, current cash equivalent, etc., because those methods *require* independent valuation from observations in the market. Historical cost *prohibits* independent valuation; it requires that the valuation coefficient for an asset be calculated from the amount of cash that was sacrificed for that *particular* asset. This means that one can know the historical cost of an asset if and only if he traces through the debits and credits to that asset.

The point in the preceding paragraph is not intended to be a commentary on the valuation dispute. Whether we ought to value the quantities dependently or independently is not at issue here. I merely want to draw the distinction. There are several analogous physical processes. Sometimes one can directly measure the state of a system; sometimes one can only infer the state of a system from the events of that system. A common example of the inference method runs as follows: Suppose there is a lake, a five-gallon container, an eight-gallon container and no other instrument of any kind. Is it possible to segregate 1, 2, . . . , 13 gallons of water? To anyone familiar with double-entry this problem is easily solved, e.g., to segregate three gallons:

Dr. 8-gallon container	8	
Cr. lake		8
Dr. 5-gallon container	5	
Cr. 8-gallon container		5

and the balance in the eight-gallon container is three gallons. Assuming the eight-gallon container to be the only location in the entity, the balance sheet is as follows:

Recipients:		Sources:	
5-gallon container	5	Lake	8
Real:			
8-gallon container	3		
Total Assets	8	Total Equities	8

The flows statement (income or fund) is as follows:

Sources of water or revenues:	
Lake	8
Applications of water or expenses:	
5-gallon container	5
Net Change in Water or Net Income	3

1961, p. 13. That is, an asset is defined as the sum of the flows (debits and credits). No separate definition of an asset is given and a separate operation for determining the cost-values is not available.

The magnitudes on the two statements cannot be measured directly if we confine our observations to the entity and to the instruments given in the statement of the problem. For this reason, it would be odd to claim that the statement equations were fundamental and the increment-decrement equations were derived. The same is true for historical cost accounting. It is in fact the case that the magnitudes on historical cost financial statements are derived from an array of debit-credit equations.

The argument over which equation is fundamental is more important to the operation of the accounting system than it is to the formalization of that system. As noted above one can formally derive either one of the equations from the other. Operationally, however, the statement magnitudes are derived from the debit-credit magnitudes. The debit-credit magnitudes are measured or estimated or determined. They are the *inputs* to the system and are the *only empirical* operations that are required. The *outputs* of the system are *calculated* from the inputs. Therefore, the accuracy of the outputs depends solely upon the accuracy of the inputs, assuming no calculational errors.

Given that the outputs depend on the inputs, an examination of the empirical operations necessary to the system reduces to an examination of $\triangle^{+}q_{ij}\ \mathbf{R}\ \triangle^{-}q_{kj}$ in the quantity accounting system. An operator of the system must be able to determine

(1) the time that the event occurs;
(2) the magnitude of the increment or decrement; and
(3) the related locations so that he can impute the increment from the decrement or vice versa.

In previous works I have claimed that these same determinations (plus others) must be made in financial accounting.[19] To my surprise this claim has met considerable resistance. It seems to me that when an accountant makes an entry he must determine the magnitude of an increment (debit) and a decrement (credit) and the two accounts which are affected. In the described quantity accounting system this is incontrovertible. Since the two systems are isomorphic, except for valuation, the same empirical determinations are required. Why this point is in dispute is not clear to me.

The import of precisely specifying the empirical determinations necessary to operate the system is the same in accounting as it is in any other discipline: one can examine the operational adequacy of the required determinations and one can sharply segregate the types of arguments about the system.

Recall that q_{it} is defined as $\sum_{j=1}^{t} \triangle q_{ij}$. Thus, if $\overline{\triangle q_{ij}}$ is the true magnitude and $\overline{\triangle q_{ij}} \neq \triangle q_{ij}$, then $\bar{q}_{it} \neq q_{it}$ unless the errors offset. For example, if the true life of an asset is different from the estimated life then the recorded cost-value of

19. Robert R. Sterling, 'Elements of Pure Accounting Theory', *Accounting Review*, Vol. XLII, No. 1, January 1967, p. 73.

the asset (and the related expense) will be different from the true cost-value. This is *not* the 'uniformity problem'. That dispute is over which way one ought to calculate a cost-value; it is debate over the functional form into which the empirical determinations are cast. It is an argument different in *kind* from the point I am raising. Even if the functional forms were standardized, the problem of the estimate being different from the true magnitude would remain. That is, if there were only one acceptable depreciation method the cost-values would still vary among accountants if the life estimates varied. The recorded cost-value would still be different from the true cost-value if the life estimates were different from the true life.

The importance of this problem can hardly be overemphasized. The accuracy of the outputs depends upon the accuracy of the inputs. Yet the operations necessary to measure the magnitude of the inputs are seldom, if ever, discussed in the accounting literature. It is surprising that such a fundamental and pervasive aspect of accounting should be so neglected.

The determination of the relation is equally important and even more problematic. If a transfer goes from location k to location i but the operator of the accounting system misperceives the transfer as being from location k to location m then the records will be in error. In financial accounting this is known as debiting (or crediting) the wrong account. However, a problem arises whenever we try to specify the empirical operation(s) necessary to determine which accounts are related. For example, in the transfer of raw materials from inventory to work-in-process (or to a customer) one can observe the two locations and measure the *quantity* of the increment or decrement. However, the determination of the cost-value of the decrement requires a finer discrimination. Usually inventory items of the same class are partitioned by purchase lot because the different lots were purchased at different prices. Thus, there are sub-accounts in the inventory account and the relation that must be determined is between work-in-process and *one* of those sub-accounts. The only observable is the quantity and therefore the relation between work-in-process and the particular sub-account can be determined only conventionally, i.e., we can decide to use lifo or fifo and credit the sub-account specified by that convention but we cannot observe that that particular account is the one that is in fact related to work-in-process.

An analogous problem would arise in a quantity accounting system if we relaxed the one-one relation assumption. Suppose that liquid is being pumped from tanks 1 and 2 to tanks 3 and 4 in the following configuration:

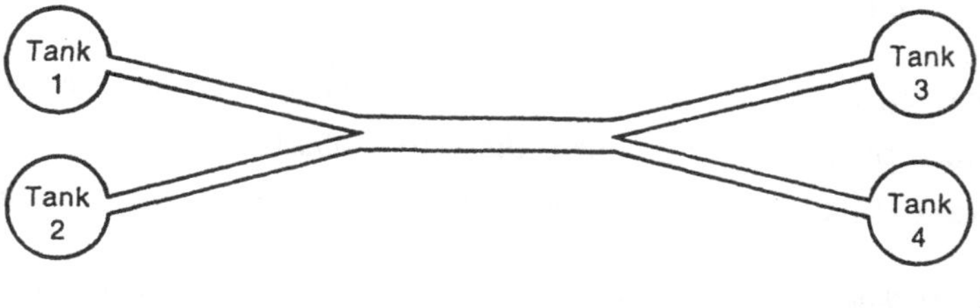

Suppose also that we can measure the decrements to tanks 1 and 2 but we cannot measure the increments to tanks 3 and 4. There is no way to impute the increments to tanks 3 and 4. We could establish the convention that tank 1 is related (connected directly) to tank 3 and that tank 2 is related to tank 4. This would allow us to calculate the quantities, e.g., the balance in tank 3 is, by convention, equal to the absolute value of the sum of the decrements to tank 1.

The difficulties with this procedure are easy to see in this example. We have forced a two-two relation into a one-one relation framework. From a teleological viewpoint the calculated 'quantities' are close to nonsense. It is difficult to imagine a use for the figures which is not productive of error. From an operational viewpoint it is clear that there is no empirical operation for the determination of the relation. This is evidenced by the fact that instead of conventionally relating tank 1 to tank 3 we could conventionally relate tank 1 to tank 4 for equally good or bad reasons. There is no way to settle a dispute over which tanks ought to be considered to be related. Compare this example to the inventory conventions. Under one convention we relate lot 1 to work-in-process and lot 2 to final raw material inventory and vice versa under another convention. Under the historical cost method of valuation it is impossible to determine independently the cost-value increment to work-in-process; it must be imputed from the decrement to the inventory. Thus, the two problems are analogous. We are forcing a many-many relation into a one-one relation framework. The figures that result from using that procedure in financial accounting are just as questionable as they are in quantity accounting. We are required to 'determine' a relation for which no empirical operation is specified. Therefore, the disputes that arise (lifo versus fifo or accelerated versus straight-line) are unresolvable.[20]

One solution to the branching pipeline system is to measure the state of the system, if that is possible, and then infer the events from the difference in the state at two points in time. In the lake-container system presented above the opposite approach was required. In that system it was impossible to measure the state; instead the state had to be inferred from the measured events. In the branching pipeline system it is impossible to infer the state from the events; instead the events must be inferred from the measured states. Which approach is appropriate cannot be established *a priori*. It depends on the nature of the system.

The same two approaches are available to financial accounting and differences of opinion about which approach is appropriate provide the basis for divergent views on valuation. Chambers, for example, views the firm as a 'black box' in which it is impossible to trace and record all the events.[21] He argues that '. . .

20. The disputes are empirically unresolvable since there are no observations which could be used to confirm or disconfirm either convention. It is sometimes said that the 'appropriate' inventory or depreciation method 'depends upon the circumstances' but I am unable to discover any particular circumstances which imply any particular method. My inability to discover the circumstances does not prove that they do not exist but the fact that no one has yet made them explicit, even though the problem is a pressing one, casts some doubt upon their existence.

21. Raymond J. Chambers, *Accounting, Evaluation and Economic Behavior*, Englewood Cliffs, N.J. 1966, p. 252.

financial positions at successive points are the primary data from which income is but inference',[22] i.e., the state (stocks of value) ought to be independently measured and the events (flows of value) inferred therefrom. As we noted above it is impossible to independently value assets at their historical cost. Therefore, Chambers is *necessarily* in favor of a non-cost valuation method. *Per contra* the proponents of historical cost argue that it is impossible to value the stocks independently; instead the stocks must be inferred from the flows. The distinction was drawn early and clearly by Montgomery.

> If an absolutely accurate balance sheet could be prepared at the beginning and the end of a period, the difference would represent the net profits or the net loss for the term.

Thus, he grants the approach in principle but he rejects it on practical grounds: '. . . the valuation and revaluation of capital assets involves too much speculation'.[23]

The point at issue in the preceding paragraph is an *operational* one. It is asserted by one side that it is impossible to measure the state and the other side asserts that it is impossible to measure the events. Independent valuation of the assets and equities at market is said to be impossible (impractical, subjective, infeasible) by the proponents of historical cost. Dependent valuation at historical cost is said to be impossible by the proponents of market value.

This is not a theoretical dispute over what *ought* to be measured. It is an operational dispute over what *can* be measured. The resolution of the dispute depends upon the nature of the thing to be accounted for. It cannot be resolved by theoretical argument. That is, the inference of the events from the measurement of the state is as theoretically valid as the inference of the state from the measurement of the events. In some physical systems either approach is possible and both approaches yield the same figures. In other systems one is forced to use one approach because the other is impossible. The same possibilities exist in financial accounting. Thus, what is needed is an examination of the accounting entity. If that examination reveals that the jointness of the business process makes the relation many-many, as some people claim, then this finding would imply that the event approach is not applicable to business entities and vice versa for the state approach. Thus, we should direct our investigations to the nature of the entity, not the nature of accounting, in order to settle the dispute over which approach is appropriate.

In summary, the entries are the inputs to the accounting system. The balances of the accounts are simply summations of those inputs. The financial statements are simply partitionings of those balances. Thus, the entries are the only empirical determinations required by the accounting system. The outputs of the system are only as good as the inputs and therefore, the improvement of the outputs requires an improvement of the inputs.

Examination of the entry reveals that an operator of the system must be able to measure the increment (or decrement) and determine the two accounts (or

22. Chambers, *Accounting . . .*, p. 342.
23. Robert A. Montgomery, *Auditing*, New York 1916, p. 206.

locations) that are related. Past researchers have paid little attention to these operations and there is some question as to whether or not they are, or can be, adequately performed. Disagreement as to the possibility of performing these operations leads to divergent views on valuation.

Summary

The decision as to which events are to be recorded and the definition of the entity are concerned with *what* is to be accounted for. This decision and definition serve to delineate the inputs to the accounting system. These inputs are then manipulated according to some agreed upon rules. The manipulation rules are concerned with *how* we account for things. The process of deciding what is to be accounted for has been discussed in some detail and some operational problems have been pointed out. The process of deciding how we account for things has not been discussed. That is a task for another occasion.

relevant financial eporting in an age of price changes

by Robert R. Sterling

This article has the modest goal of clarifying the concept of price level adjustments. Since price level adjustments have been debated for a great many years, it may seem that the concept has previously been made quite clear. Perhaps so, but my reading of the recent literature, especially the testimony presented to the Financial Accounting Standards Board, persuades me that concept clarification is needed rather desperately. To put it negatively, I fear that if we take action on price levels —establish a standard—prior to further clarification of the concept, we may make things worse instead of better.

A highly simplified case will be considered in this article. The advantages of simplified cases are that they are easily understood by both the reader and the author and they are more easily solved. If we cannot solve the simplified cases, then we can be fairly certain that we also cannot solve the complex cases. Thus, if a particular approach fails to provide a solution for simplified cases, then we can avoid wasting effort by trying that approach on complex cases. The main disadvantage of simplified cases is that even if we can solve them, there is no guarantee that the obtained solution can be extended to realistic cases. But the problem with realistic cases is that they are too complex to be easily understood or solved. I chose the simplified case in this article in the

Robert R. Sterling, *Ph.D., is currently Jesse H. Jones Distinguished Professor at Rice University's Department of Economics and Accounting in Houston. Among the numerous academic honors he has received is the AICPA accounting literature award for his article "Accounting Research, Education and Practice," which appeared in the September 1973* Journal of Accountancy. *He has been involved in much committee work for the American Accounting Association and has been a prolific contributor of books, articles and papers to the field of accounting. This article has been adapted from a speech given on Accounting Day at the University of California at Berkeley, May 30, 1974.*

Author's Note: I am grateful for the support of Arthur Young & Company in the preparation of this article. The conclusions, however, are mine and do not necessarily reflect the views of Arthur Young & Company.

Only price level adjusted current value financial statements fully meet the primary objectives of accounting—relevance and interpretability.

hope that the concept, once clarified, can be extended to more complex cases.[1]

The necessity of choosing attributes and the criteria for choosing

A measurement requires that one consciously decide which attribute is to be measured. Consider a physical object. It is impossible to measure that object; instead, one must decide which attribute (e.g., length, weight, hardness, color, density, carbon half-life, etc.) of that object is to be measured. The same is true for accounting measurements: we must decide which attribute is to be measured.[2]

The decision as to which attribute ought to be measured cannot be made on the basis of one's being "wrong" and the other's being "right." In regard to measuring a physical object, for example, one cannot say that it is wrong to measure the attribute of, say, length and right to measure the attribute of, say, weight. For some purposes,

[1] The choice of a simplified case reflects my general feeling that we accountants often err by immediately tackling the complex cases. I think that one of the reasons we can't get more solutions (or more agreement) is that we try to run before learning to crawl. Compare the procedure in the sciences where they first study highly simple cases. As Nelson Goodman (*Fact, Fiction, and Forecast* (New York: Bobbs-Merrill, 1965), p. xii) puts it:

"... science has to isolate a few simple aspects of the world. ... This, admittedly, is over-simplification. But conscious and cautious over-simplification, far from being an intellectual sin, is a prerequisite for investigation. We can hardly study at once all the ways in which everything is related to everything else."

By contrast, in accounting we seem to think that simplification is an intellectual sin. I think we would make more progress more rapidly if we took the roundabout route of examining simple cases before going on to the complex cases.

[2] Unfortunately, a single accounting term is often used to describe different attributes. It is clear, for example, that the income figure derived by using Fifo is different from the one derived by using Lifo, yet we refer to both as "income." Similarly, "price-level adjusted income" and "unadjusted income" are measures of different attributes despite the fact that both are called "income." The point is that it does not help to simply state that the attribute sought is "income" because that single term is used to refer to different attributes. Precise distinction of these attributes requires the use of different names —jargon—in this article.

length is the relevant attribute and, for other purposes, weight is relevant. The same is true in accounting. We cannot say that unadjusted figures are wrong and adjusted figures are right. Instead, we must provide interpretations of the attributes that are being measured and then decide which one we ought to measure. The decision as to which attribute we ought to measure must be based on the relevance of the attributes, not on one's being wrong and the other's being right.

Consideration of what we ought to measure requires that we focus on the appropriate criterion — relevance.

The interpretation of an attribute is related, but not identical, to its relevance. A thorough discussion of interpretation and relevance requires distinctions that cannot be drawn here. The reader interested in pursuing these notions should see May Brodbeck, especially the discussion of the significance of concepts,[3] or Carl G. Hempel, especially the discussion of the theoretical import of concepts.[4] For the purpose of this article, the following brief discussion will suffice.

Interpretation

When an attribute involves an arithmetical calculation, the "empirical interpretation" of that attribute requires that it be placed in an "if . . . then . . ." statement. For example, the attribute "area" is defined as the product of the length and width of a plane, i.e., A=LW. To repeat the definition of that attribute is not an empirical interpretation. Instead, an empirical interpretation would require a statement such as "if this space were to be covered with tiles of this size, then it would require x tiles." This "if . . . then . . ." statement provides the listener with an understanding of the meaning of "area" as well as demonstrating one of the uses of the concept.

A counter example will show that the repetition of the definition does not aid in understanding the meaning of an attribute. I hereby define the attribute "ster" as the quotient of the length and width of a plane, i.e., S=L/W. If you were to ask me the meaning of that attribute, you would be justly disappointed if I simply repeated that it is the quotient of the length and width of a plane. Since "ster" cannot be inserted in an "if . . . then . . ." statement, it is not empirically interpretable and, therefore, it should be regarded with suspicion. We don't have any idea of the meaning or use of "ster" because we haven't been able to interpret it. We should be highly suspicious of attributes if we don't understand their meaning or use. We therefore arrive at Criterion 1: *Attributes must be interpretable.*

Relevance

Everyone agrees that accounting information should be useful. As with other abstractions (e.g., truth, justice, fairness), however, we run into difficulty when we try to apply the concept. In an attempt to be more precise, to make the concept more concrete, in previous works I have replaced the term "usefulness" with the term "relevance."[5] I define relevance as follows:

"If a decision model specifies an attribute as an input or as a calculation, then that attribute is relevant to that decision model."

The negation, of course, is that if the attribute is not specified by the model, then that attribute is not relevant to that model.

Consider, for example, the decision about which object one should select as a life raft. One needs to know which, if any, of the available objects will float on water. The decision model specifies two attributes (weight and volume) as inputs and one attribute (density, the quotient of weight and volume) as a calculation. Then it specifies that one compare the density of the object to the density of water. Indeed, the interpretation of the calculated attribute of density is "if object x is less dense than fluid y, then x will float on y." Thus, three attributes—weight, volume and density—are relevant to the model. All other attributes are irrelevant.[6]

---

[3] May Brodbeck, ed., *Readings in the Philosophy of the Social Sciences* (New York: Macmillan, 1968), pp. 6-9.

[4] Carl G. Hempel, *Fundamentals of Concept Formation in Empirical Science* (Chicago: University of Chicago Press, 1952), p. 46.

[5] For example, see Robert R. Sterling, "Decision Oriented Financial Accounting," *Accounting and Business Research*, Summer 1973.

[6] Note the distinction between relevant to the decision *model* and relevant to the decision *maker*. Some decision makers may think that, say, area (instead of volume) is relevant to the decision. Others may think that color is relevant. Still others may think that a third attribute is relevant. Given a large number of decision makers, it would be impossible to supply measures of all of the attributes that all of them think are relevant. Moreover, all attributes other than weight, volume and density are of no help to the decision maker, despite the beliefs to the contrary.

The analogy fits accounting. We service a large number of decision makers (e.g., investors and potential investors), many of whom have demonstrably erroneous ideas about which attributes are relevant to their decisions. For example, despite the fact that the efficient market research has demonstrated that "technical analysis" (price charting) is of no use in trading the market, many investors and financial analysts still use it. Others use other attributes. It is impossible for us to supply measures of *all* the attributes that *all* investors think are relevant. Worse, such attributes are of no help in making the decision despite the fact that decision makers use them and think that they are relevant. Hence, we must define relevance in relation to decision models, not decision makers.

As the example makes clear, relevance is concerned with what ought to be measured. If someone were to measure the area of the object, it would not be wrong—it would simply be irrelevant to the decision. The area attribute meets the interpretability criterion, but it does not meet the relevance criterion. Applying this to accounting means that the selection of the attributes that we ought to measure and report requires that we examine the decision models and determine which attributes are specified by those models. Therefore we arrive at Criterion 2: *Attributes must be relevant.*

Complete exchange case

Description of the case

Consider the highly simplified problem of accounting for a trader on the New York Stock Exchange. The only activities of this simplified firm are the purchase and sale of securities in a near perfect market. To further simplify, assume that there are zero transaction (e.g., commission) costs and that all exchanges are for cash. There are no liabilities, which means that the total assets figure is equal to that of total owner's equity. In addition, assume that at the time of statement preparation all of the inventory has been sold so that the only asset on hand is cash.[7] Hence, there is only one asset—cash—to account for.

To simplify even further, assume that the only good that the trader consumes is bread, so that the Consumer Price Index is just the ratio of the prices of bread at two dates. Thus, there are only two real (nonmonetary) goods in this economy: securities (measured in shares) are the only producers' goods, and bread (measured in loaves) is the only consumers' good.

The facts of the case are that at January 1 the firm had $1,000 in cash. At the same date it purchased 100 shares for $10 per share. At February 1 the price has increased to $15 per share, and the entire inventory is sold. During the same period the price of bread increased from $.50 to $.60 per loaf, resulting in a Consumer Price Index of 1.2 (= $.60/$.50).

Measuring NOD

Exhibit 1, this page, shows the standard (unadjusted) financials for this firm. The interpretation is straightforward. The attribute being measured is number of dollars (NOD). The balance sheets report the stocks of NOD at two dates, and the income statement reports the increment in NOD during the period.

Exhibit 1

Measuring number of dollars

Complete exchange case

	Comparative balance sheets	
	January 1	February 1
Cash	$1,000	$1,500
Invested capital	$1,000	$1,000
Retained earnings	-0-	500
Total owner's equity	$1,000	$1,500

	Income statement Month of January
Revenues	$1,500
Cost of securities sold	1,000
Net income	$ 500

Many people assert that unadjusted financials, such as those in Exhibit 1, are "wrong." Accompanying this assertion are a variety of comments about "changing purchasing power," "changing value of the dollar," etc. Although many different terms are used to make the criticism, they all refer to the ability of dollars to command goods and services. It is true that the financials in Exhibit 1 do not measure command over goods (COG). However, it is equally true that those financials accurately measure NOD. Thus, the criticism cannot possibly be that the financials are "wrong," because they are quite correct. I believe that the critics intend to say that the financials do not measure the relevant attribute—the COG attribute.

I don't mean to quibble over words. However, I do want to be clear as to the source of the difficulty. If the objective is to measure NOD, then auditors must certify the financials in Exhibit 1. However, if we decide that the objective is to measure COG, then it is easy to demonstrate that those financials do not meet that objective. This is an important distinction. It shifts the basis of the argument from wrong vs. right to what we ought to measure and report. Consideration of what we ought to measure requires that we focus on the appropriate criterion—relevance.

It is axiomatic that money per se is not desirable. Rather, it is the ability of money to command real goods that is desired. Witness Confederate money. Measuring the stocks of or incre-

[7] This is what I mean by a "complete exchange." See Robert R. Sterling, *Theory of the Measurement of Enterprise Income* (Lawrence: University Press of Kansas, 1970), pp. 27-28, for further discussion. For a discussion of the related notion of "complete cycles," see *Objectives of Financial Statements*, a report of the Accounting Objectives Study Group, Robert M. Trueblood, chairman (New York: AICPA, 1973).

Exhibit 2

Measuring command over goods in price level adjusted dollars

Complete exchange case

	Comparative balance sheets	
	Jan. 1	Feb. 1
Cash (January 1=$1,000 x 1.2)	1,200	$1,500
Invested capital ($1,000 x 1.2)	$1,200	$1,200
Retained earnings	-0-	300
Total owner's equity	$1,200	$1,500

	Income statement Month of January
Revenues	$1,500
Cost of securities sold ($1,000 x 1.2)	1,200
Net income	$ 300

ments in Confederate money is irrelevant—no one is interested in the results of such measurements—precisely because that money has no ability to command goods. As the extreme case of Confederate money makes clear, measurements of NOD are not specified by decision models; hence, NOD is irrelevant. Instead, decision models specify the measurement of COG; thus, Proposition 1: *COG is the relevant attribute.*

Measuring COG

As the name makes clear, the command over goods (COG) attribute is a measure of the number of goods that could be commanded in the market. Since the goods that could be commanded are physical objects, COG is a physical measure. The measurement is accomplished by multiplying the monetary units by a price index. The purpose of such price level adjustments is to permit the adjusted monetary units to be interpreted as physical units. Economics and statistics textbooks state this point explicitly. Wallace C. Peterson, for example, writes, "If we adjust by the above price index, the result will be a measure of *physical output*. . . ."[8] To put it another way, if price level adjustments are done properly, then the resulting figures can be interpreted as a measure of physical units.

Recall that there is only one consumer good in this simple case and therefore the Consumer Price Index is the ratio of the prices of that good at the two dates. The price of bread was $.50 and $.60 at January 1 and February 1, respectively. Hence, the Consumer Price Index is 1.2 (= $.60/$.50). In order to convert the NOD attribute in Exhibit 1 to the COG attribute, we need only multiply each of the January 1 figures by 1.2. The result is shown in Exhibit 2, this page.

The point to be stressed is not the procedure, however, but rather the ability to interpret those figures. We can divide all of the figures in Exhibit 2 by the $.60 per loaf price of bread at February 1 and obtain the following interpretation:

- ☐ If all of the assets of the firm had been used to purchase bread at January 1, then 2,000 loaves (= $1,200/$.60) could have been purchased.
- ☐ If all of the assets of the firm had been used to purchase bread at February 1, then 2,500 loaves (=$1,500/$.60) could have been purchased.
- ☐ Hence, the increment (income) in COG is 500 loaves (= $300/$.60).

The figures can be interpreted; therefore, they meet the interpretability criterion. Indeed, in this simple case we could prepare financials in physical units as shown in Exhibit 3, this page. One can check the accuracy of these financials by using the unadjusted January 1 figures and dividing by the price per loaf at January 1. For example, the unadjusted cash on hand at January 1 was $1,000 and the price per loaf was $.50. Therefore, the firm could have commanded 2,000 loaves (= $1,000/$.50) at January 1. In addition, note that all of the ratios of the figures in Exhibit 3 are the same as those in Exhibit 2. For example, Exhibit 2 shows a $300 net income on sales of $1,500, a return on sales of 20 percent. Exhibit 3

Exhibit 3

Measuring command over goods in physical units

Complete exchange case

	Comparative balance sheets	
	January 1	February 1
Cash	2,000 loaves	2,500 loaves
Invested capital	2,000 loaves	2,000 loaves
Retained income	0 loaves	500 loaves
Total owner's equity	2,000 loaves	2,500 loaves

	Income statement Month of January
Revenues	2,500 loaves
Cost of securities sold	2,000 loaves
Net income	500 loaves

[8] Wallace C. Peterson, *Income, Employment, and Economic Growth* (New York: W. W. Norton & Co., 1962), p. 68.

shows a 500 loaf net income on sales of 2,500 loaves, a return of 20 percent.

Market basket interpretation. Interpretation of price level adjusted figures is usually more difficult because the price index is made up of a collection ("market basket") of goods. However, the concept is identical to the one-good index used in this simple case. To illustrate, consider a two-good, equally weighted index composed of bread and milk.

> ... price level adjusted historical costs do not fully meet the criteria. The cash figures are interpretable and are measures of the relevant COG attribute. However, the securities and total asset figures are not interpretable (by me), are not specified by any decision model that I know of and are not measures of COG.

Assume prices of \$.50 per loaf and \$1 per gallon at January 1 and \$.60 per loaf and \$1.20 per gallon at Febuary 1. Thus, the index is the same: (\$.60 + \$1.20)/(\$.50 + \$1) = 1.2.

The January 1 cash figure of \$1,000 would be adjusted to the same \$1,200 (= \$1,000 x 1.2). The interpretation, however, requires the use of both goods with equal budget allocations. One-half of the adjusted \$1,200 divided by \$.60 per loaf and by \$1.20 per gallon yields 1,000 loaves (= \$600/\$.60) and 500 gallons (= \$600/\$1.20). Thus the interpretation is:

☐ If all of the assets of the firm had been used to purchase bread and milk with equal budget allocations at January 1, then the firm would have been able to buy 1,000 loaves of bread and 500 gallons of milk.

With a two-good index the preparation of financials in physical units would be cumbersome. The addition of more goods to the index would make it even more cumbersome. However, the concept is the same. The price level adjustment converts a monetary measure into a physical measure. It allows one to interpret the figures as the number of physical units that could have been bought.

Incomplete exchange case

Description of case

The difference between the "incomplete exchange" and the "complete exchange" cases is that, in the former, some noncash assets are held; hence, some securities have been bought but, since they have not yet been sold, the exchange (or cycle from cash to cash) is said to be "incomplete." Assume that on January 1 the firm purchased 70 shares at \$10 per share, leaving a cash balance of \$300. No other transactions occur. The price of the securities has increased, as before, to \$15 per share. Also, as before, the price of bread has increased from \$.50 to \$.60, resulting in a Consumer Price Index of 1.2.

Although this case is highly simplified, its consideration is complicated because there are four different proposed methods of accounting for it:

1 Historical cost.
2 Price level adjusted historical cost.
3 Current value.
4 Price level adjusted current value.

Historical cost. The familiar historical cost financials are presented in Exhibit 4, this page. Despite the increase in the prices of both bread and securities, the February 1 figures are exactly the same as those at January 1. It seems to me that these financials do not meet the criteria.

First, I am unable to interpret the figures. I don't know how to place them in an "if . . . then . . ." statement. Thus, I don't think they meet the interpretability criterion. However, my inability to interpret them may be due to a deficiency in my thinking rather than a deficiency in the figures. Therefore, instead of concluding that they are not interpretable, I will challenge the readers to provide an interpretation.

Second, I have not been able to find decision models that specify the figures. Thus, I don't think they meet the relevance (or usefulness) criterion.

Exhibit 4

Unadjusted historical cost

Incomplete exchange case

	Comparative balance sheets	
	January 1	February 1
Cash	\$300	\$300
Securities	700	700
Total assets	\$1,000	\$1,000
Invested capital	\$1,000	\$1,000
Retained earnings	-0-	-0-
Total owner's equity	\$1,000	\$1,000

	Income statement Month of January
Revenues	\$ -0-
Cost of securities sold	-0-
Net income	\$ -0-

Exhibit 5

Price level adjusted historical cost

Incomplete exchange case

	Comparative balance sheets	
	Jan. 1	Feb. 1
Cash (January 1 = $300 x 1.2)	$360	$300
Securities ($700 x 1.2)	840	840
Total assets	$1,200	$1,140
Invested capital ($1,000 x 1.2)	$1,200	$1,200
Retained earnings (deficit)	-0-	(60)
Total owner's equity	$1,200	$1,140

	Income statement Month of January
Revenues	$ -0-
Cost of securities sold	-0-
	-0-
Loss in COG from holding cash ($360-$300)	60
Net income (loss)	$(60)

Again, however, since I may have overlooked the decision models that specify these figures, I will challenge the readers to demonstrate their relevance rather than concluding that they are irrelevant.

Third, the figures clearly do not measure the COG attribute. There is no way to interpret them —prepare financials in physical units such as Exhibit 3—as measures of the ability to command goods.

Price level adjusted historical cost. A number of people have suggested—e.g., see Accounting Research Study No. 6[9]—that historical cost financials be adjusted by the following procedure:

1 Multiply the January 1 cash balance by the price index and take the difference between the adjusted January 1 balance and the unadjusted February 1 balance as a loss.

2 Multiply the January 1 securities cost by the price index and carry that adjusted figure forward to the February 1 balance sheet.

Financials adjusted by this procedure are shown in Exhibit 5, this page. The cash figures can be interpreted as follows:

☐ If the firm had used its cash at January 1 to purchase bread, then it could have purchased 600 loaves. (Adjusted cash of $360 divided by February 1 price per loaf of $.60 equals 600 loaves. Alternatively, the unadjusted cash of $300 divided by the January 1 price per loaf of $.50 equals 600 loaves.)

☐ If the firm had used its cash at February 1 to purchase bread, then it could have purchased 500 loaves (= $300/$.60).

☐ Hence, the loss from holding cash is $60 (= $360 − 300), which is equivalent to 100 loaves (= $60/$.60 and = 600 − 500).

Thus, the cash figures are (1) interpretable and (2) measurements of the relevant COG attribute. This is a major improvement over the unadjusted historical cost financials.

The problem lies with the figure for securities at February 1. First, I cannot find a true interpretation of the figure. I am not able to place it in an "if . . . then . . ." statement. Perhaps the figure is interpretable. Perhaps it is just that I don't know how to do it. For that reason, I will again challenge the readers to provide an interpretation rather than concluding that it is not interpretable.

Although I am not certain of the proper interpretation, I am certain that the figure cannot be interpreted as either NOD or COG:[10]

☐ If the securities were sold (or replaced) at February 1, then the NOD received (or required) would *not* be $840.

Thus, NOD cannot be the proper interpretation.

☐ If the securities were sold at February 1 and the cash proceeds used to purchase bread, then

[9] Accounting Research Study No. 6 *Reporting the Financial Effects of Price Level Changes* (New York: AICPA, 1963), p. 11.

[10] It is possible to interpret the figures as a measure of both NOD and COG by making the contrary to fact assumption of proportional price changes.

☐ If the securities were sold (or replaced) at February 1 and *if price changes were proportional,* then the NOD received (or required) would be $840, which is equivalent to COG of 1,400 loaves (= $840/$.60).

The statement is false. Price changes were not proportional in the case under consideration. More importantly, they are not proportional in the real world. In fact, many changes are in opposite directions. For example, last year refined petroleum products went up 79.5 percent while animal feeds went down 26.5 percent, both of which are components of the Wholesale Price Index which went up 16.4 percent. Clearly then, we cannot assume proportional price changes any more than we can assume a stable measuring unit.

When writing *Enterprise Income* (p. 347), it occurred to me that since price level adjusted historical costs were interpretable if all price changes were proportional, perhaps the proponents had implicitly assumed proportional price changes. I rejected the idea, however, because the assumption was contrary to fact. That the proponents were implicitly assuming proportional price changes now seems more plausible because several authors mention what would be the case if it were true. For example, in "Problems of Implementing the Trueblood Objectives Report," *Empirical Research in Accounting: Selected Studies* (Chicago: Institute of Professional Accounting, 1974), Richard M. Cyert and Yuji Ijiri correctly claim that "[price level adjusted historical costs] are exactly the same as current values if all prices move up or down in the same proportion." The problem is that price changes have not been proportional in the past and they are not likely to be proportional in the future.

the number of loaves that could be purchased (i.e., the COG) is *not* 1,400 (= $840/$.60).

Thus, COG cannot be the proper interpretation. This makes it difficult to interpret the total assets figure. As demonstrated earlier, the cash figures can be interpreted as COG and it seems clear that the intent of ARS No. 6, among others, is to measure COG. So, the cash figure is a COG measure, and the securities figure is not a COG measure. Since the total assets figure is the sum of a measure of COG and a measure of not-COG, what is its interpretation? For the reasons given above, I again challenge the readers to provide an interpretation.

Second, I do not know of any decision model that specifies the securities or the total assets figure; therefore, I will tentatively (until the readers demonstrate otherwise) conclude that these figures are irrelevant. I can firmly conclude that they are irrelevant in regard to Proposition 1 since they do not measure COG.

In summary, price level adjusted historical costs do not fully meet the criteria. The cash figures are interpretable and are measures of the relevant COG attribute. However, the securities and total asset figures are not interpretable (by me), are not specified by any decision model that I know of and are not measures of COG.

> We should not be arguing that one set of figures is right and another is wrong; instead we should be arguing about which attribute we ought to measure and report. Selection of the attribute that ought to be measured requires precise criteria, rigorously applied.

Current value. The current value financials are shown in Exhibit 6, this page. Recall that 70 shares were purchased at January 1 for $10 per share. Hence, the current value of securities at January 1 was $700 as shown. At February 1 the price has increased to $15 per share for 70 shares or $1,050 current value.

The figures can be interpreted as measures of NOD:

☐ If the securities were sold at February 1, then $1,050 would be received.

The total assets figure can be interpreted similarly:

☐ If all of the assets of the firm were converted into cash at February 1, then the firm would hold $1,350.

Exhibit 6

Current value

Incomplete exchange case

	Comparative balance sheets January 1	February 1
Cash	$300	$300
Securities	700	1,050
Total assets	$1,000	$1,350
Invested capital	$1,000	$1,000
Retained earnings	-0-	350
Total owner's equity	$1,000	$1,350

	Income statement Month of January
Revenues	$ -0-
Cost of securities sold	-0-
	-0-
Gain on price increase of securities	350
Net income	$350

That is, there is no difficulty in adding the $300 on hand to the number of dollars that could be acquired if the securities were sold. The sum is a straightforward interpretation of the number of dollars that would be held if the securities were sold.[11] The income statement shows the increment in NOD due to the $5 per share price increase for 70 shares. If desired, this increment could be labeled "unrealized" since the securities haven't been sold.

The figures for individual and total assets can also be interpreted as measures of COG. For example:

☐ If the firm had used all of its assets at February 1 to purchase bread, then it could have purchased 2,250 loaves (= $1,350/$.60).

This is a major improvement over the price level adjusted historical cost financials.

The problem lies with the income figure. The $350 NOD increment (net income) does not reflect the increment in COG. COG at January 1 was 2,000 loaves (= $1,000/$.50) and, at Febru-

[11] Technically, there is a difference between this figure and the NOD figure in the complete exchange case. Perhaps they should be distinguished by calling the above figure COD (command over dollars) instead of NOD. However, since the difference is slight and since I have already tried the readers' patience by introducing new jargon, I didn't make the distinction. Interested readers should consult Raymond J. Chambers (*Accounting, Evaluation, and Economic Behavior* (Englewood Cliffs, N.J.: Prentice-Hall, 1966)) for a description of current cash equivalents (CCE) which is, as I read it, identical to COD. Chambers also provides for a price level adjustment of CCE.

Exhibit 7

Price level adjusted current value (measuring command over goods in price level adjusted dollars)

Incomplete exchange case

	Comparative balance sheets Jan. 1	Feb. 1
Cash (January 1 = $300 x 1.2)	$360	$300
Securities (January 1 = $700 x 1.2)	840	1050
Total assets	$1,200	$1,350
Invested capital ($1,000 x 1.2)	$1,200	$1,200
Retained earnings	-0-	150
Total owner's equity	$1,200	$1,350

	Income statement Month of January
Revenues	$ -0-
Cost of securities sold	-0-
	-0-
Gain from holding securities ($1,050-$840)	210
Loss from holding cash ($360-$300)	(60)
Net income	$150

Exhibit 8

Interpretation of price level adjusted values (measuring command over goods in physical units)

Incomplete exchange case

	Comparative balance sheets January 1	February 1
Cash	600 loaves	500 loaves
Securities	1,400	1,750
Total assets	2,000 loaves	2,250 loaves
Invested capital	2,000 loaves	2,000 loaves
Retained earnings	-0-	250
Total owner's equity	2,000 loaves	2,250 loaves

	Income statement Month of January
Revenues	-0- loaves
Cost	-0-
	-0-
Gain from holding securities	350
Loss from holding cash	(100)
Net income	$250 loaves

ary 1, it was 2,250 loaves (= $1,350/$.60), an increment of 250 loaves. Division of the $350 NOD increment by the January 1 price per loaf of $.50 yields 700 loaves. Division by the February 1 price per loaf of $.60 yields 583⅓ loaves. Since neither division yields the actual 250 loaf increment, the current value income statement does not measure the COG increment.

In summary, current values do not fully meet the criteria. All of the figures are interpretable as measures of NOD, but only the assets figures are interpretable as measures of COG. The income figure can only be interpreted as NOD. Since COG is the relevant attribute, current value income does not meet the relevance criterion.

Price level adjusted current values. In order to "price level adjust" the current value financials in Exhibit 6, we need only multiply each of the January 1 figures by the Consumer Price Index of 1.2[12] The adjusted financials are shown in Exhibit 7, this page.

All of the individual figures as well as the sums and differences in Exhibit 7 can be interpreted:

☐ If all of the assets of the firm had been used to purchase bread at January 1, then 2,000 loaves (=$1,200/$.60) could have been purchased.

☐ If all of the assets of the firm had been used to purchase bread at February 1, then 2,250 loaves (=$1,350/$.60) could have been purchased.

☐ Hence, the increment (income) in COG is 250 loaves (= $150/$.60), which is the net of a gain of 350 loaves (= $210/$.60) from holding securities and a loss of 100 loaves (= $60/$.60) from holding cash.

The complete interpretation is given in Exhibit 8, this page. As before, note that the ratios of all the figures in Exhibit 8 are the same as those in Exhibit 7. For example, the increase in total assets is 12.5 percent in both exhibits.

The figures can be interpreted. Moreover, they are interpreted as measures of the relevant COG attribute. Therefore, price level adjusted current values meet both criteria.

Summary and conclusion

The modest objective of this article was to clarify the concept of price level adjustments. The first clarification was concerned with what we ought to be arguing about. We should not be arguing that one set of figures is right and another is wrong; instead we should be arguing about which attribute we ought to measure and report. Selection of the attribute that ought to be measured requires

[12] This is "inflating" the past financials. It is possible to "deflate" the current financials without destroying the interpretability. The reasons for preferring to adjust the past financials is given in Sterling, *Enterprise Income*, p. 339. For the same reasons, I prefer the "roll-forward" procedure.

precise criteria, rigorously applied. I agree fully with the Trueblood Committee that the primary objective (or criterion) of accounting is usefulness. The substitution of "interpretability" and "relevance" for "usefulness" was an attempt to make that criterion more precise and more concrete, not a disagreement.

The criterion of interpretability is that a given attribute be capable of being placed in a true "if . . . then . . ." statement. The failure of an attribute to meet that criterion should cause us to be skeptical of that attribute. The criterion of relevance is that an attribute be specified by a decision model. This must be what is meant by "usefulness," since if an attribute is not specified by any decision model, then I can't imagine how it could be useful.

These criteria were utilized in the examination of the simple problem of accounting for a trader on the New York Stock Exchange under the two cases of a complete and an incomplete exchange. The examination of the first case—complete exchange—revealed that although the NOD attribute is interpretable, it is irrelevant. COG is the relevant attribute. The conclusion that COG is the relevant attribute permitted a more precise application of the relevance criterion in examining the incomplete exchange case, i.e., determination of whether or not the attribute could be interpreted as COG.

When accounting for an incomplete exchange, there are four competing methods. Each of these methods was subjected to the criteria. Some methods partially meet the criteria but only one method —price level adjusted current values—fully meet them. The results are summarized in Exhibit 9, this page. Since the cells that contain "no" may be due to a deficiency in my examination rather than a deficiency in the figures, the readers were challenged to demonstrate their interpretability and relevance. Until such a demonstration is provided, I will maintain that only price level adjusted current value financials fully meet both criteria.

It follows that the appropriate procedure is to (1) adjust the present statement to current values and (2) adjust the previous statement by a price index. It is important to recognize that *both* adjustments are necessary and that neither is a substitute for the other. Confusion on this point is widespread. For example, a business executive recently announced that his firm had converted to current value accounting when, in fact, the firm had done nothing but make price level adjustments to historical costs. In addition, several CPAs seem to be saying that current value accounting is a substitute for price level adjustments. Also, although I am not entirely clear on the Securities and Exchange Commission's position on this issue, it seems that it is leaning toward current replacement costs as a substitute for price level adjustments. Finally, the phrasing of the FASB's questions seemed to indicate that it thought of current values and price level adjustments as competing methods, only *one* of which should be selected.

I hope that the consideration of this simple case demonstrates that both are required. ■

Exhibit 9

Method \ Criteria	Interpretable	Relevant
Historical cost	No	No
Price level adjusted historical cost	No	No
Current value	Yes	No
Price level adjusted current value	Yes	Yes

ABACUS, Vol. 17, No. 2, 1981

ROBERT R. STERLING

Costs (Historical versus Current) versus Exit Values

The three alternative methods of accounting are sharply distinguished, the questions regarding those methods are segregated, a criterion — relevance — that will discriminate the methods is identified, and that criterion is applied to the alternatives. The relevance criterion is applied initially in the context of a simple case and subsequently in the context of more complex cases. The exit value system is supported because the exit value of an owned asset is demonstrably relevant to exchange decisions and because it fares no worse than other systems when other criteria such as additivity, are considered.

Key words: Accounting theory; Assets; Financial reporting.

INTRODUCTION

Those whose conceits are seated in popular opinions need only but to prove or dispute, but those whose conceits are beyond popular opinions have a double labour; the one to make themselves conceived and the other to prove and demonstrate.

Francis Bacon

This essay is intended to be a contribution to the continuing quest for improved methods of accounting. It has three separable but related goals which are addressed to three problems. The primary goal is to differentiate clearly three alternative methods of accounting. The primary problem is that in previous discussions we have not sharply distinguished the alternatives and we have combined separable questions. The secondary goal is to consider a specific, simple case and try to demonstrate that one of the alternative methods is superior to the others. The secondary problem is that past discussions have utilized criteria that do not discriminate the alternatives and therefore do not aid in making a rational choice. The selection of the preferred alternative requires the identification and application of a criterion that will discriminate. The tertiary goal is to extend the application of the identified criterion to other specific cases. The tertiary problem is that there are many different kinds of firms and different kinds of assets for which the method of accounting is in dispute. The overall goal is to reach for the chalice of more general principles that has eluded us for so long. The overall problem is that we have too many specific, *ad hoc* principles.

The three related goals and problems constitute the three sections of this essay. A highly simplified case will be utilized to explain the nature of the alternatives in Section 1 and to identify and apply the criterion in Section 2. The advantage of simplified cases is that they are easily understood by both author and reader. The idea is to strip away the complexities so that we can concentrate on the conceptual differences and see which one

---

ROBERT R. STERLING is Winspear Distinguished Professor, University of Alberta.

best achieves the objectives of reporting. If we can be clear on the concepts and objectives, it should aid in the analysis of more complex cases which is the goal of Section 3.

Since this essay considers exit values that are beyond popular opinion, it has the double labour: first, making them understood and, second, proving and demonstrating. The sequence is important to my aspirations. I would be pleased if I could clear up the many misunderstandings which surround exit valuations whether or not the demonstrations withstand the readers' tests. Of course, I think that the demonstrations are correct, else I would not present them, but I would rather have them shown to be incorrect than to be misunderstood.

1. EXPLICATION

To form an intelligible theory we ought to absolutely identify the sense of the word *wealth* with that which is presented to us by the words *exchangeable values*. In the act of exchange, as in the transmission of power by machinery, there is friction to be overcome, losses which must be borne, and limits which cannot be exceeded. Our part is to observe, and not to criticize, the irresistible laws of nature.

Augustin Cournot

The purpose of this section is to explicate the two different kinds of exchangeable values which vie for inclusion in the accounts. The differences arise from frictions which cannot be avoided. A second source of differences is the temporal location of the two kinds of exchangeable values. In this section our purpose is to observe — to explain precisely and neutrally — and not to criticize.

1.1 *The Problem*

Rapidly changing prices caused many clients (users) and accountants to seek improvements to historical cost accounting. Many proposed that we begin to report current prices rather than (or in addition to) historical costs. At first the focus was on timing, on *current* prices versus *historical* costs, as was evidenced by the recurring theme that we should report more up-to-date information. It seems that almost all accountants, perhaps primarily because we are accustomed to recording costs, perceived the only alternative to historical costs to be current costs. For this reason, the focus narrowed, almost unnoticed, from current *prices* to current *costs*. The overwhelming majority of the research and discussion has been directed toward the question of current costs versus historical costs.

The narrowed focus caused us to overlook two important points: (1) there are two different kinds of current prices — current costs and exit values — as will be explained below, and (2) the pros and cons of reporting current information versus historical information are different from the pros and cons of the kind of information that should be reported. Overlooking these two points has caused much mischief.

First, it has prohibited the widespread recognition of the *existence* of an alternative. Most of the past discussion has been about the merits of alternative methods of accounting for costs, and the use of exit values has not been perceived as an alternative. Recognition of the existence of an alternative is a prerequisite for the rational choice of the preferred alternative. We may know that we prefer vanilla to strawberry but we cannot know that we prefer vanilla to chocolate if we do not know that chocolate exists.

Second, it has prohibited the widespread recognition of the *conceptual differences* between the two. Many have thought that since both are current prices, and since the difference in magnitude is often immaterial, the conceptual difference is immaterial. The fact is that the difference in magnitude is sometimes material and the conceptual difference is always material. The equality of the two has hindered resolution of the question of current costs versus historical costs because it has often been debated on the basis of the characteristics of exit values. In effect, such arguments say that we should adopt (reject) current costs and abandon (retain) historical costs because exit values are good (bad).[1] We may know that we like vanilla but we cannot know that we prefer vanilla to strawberry by tasting chocolate.

Third, it has prohibited the widespread recognition of the *nature* of the two alternatives. As a result, arguments are often based on a misunderstanding. We have witnessed spirited arguments that current costs are superior (inferior) to exit values because exit values are based on past (future) prices when in fact exit values are one kind of current price. We may know we like vanilla but we cannot know that we prefer vanilla to chocolate if we mistake pistachio for chocolate.

Fourth, current costs versus historical costs *combines* two separable questions. It is quite possible, for example, to favour reporting current prices but to oppose reporting costs, or vice versa. The dissenters' views in relation to Financial Accounting Standard 33 provides an example of a case where current information is favoured but a particular kind of current information is opposed. This suggests that we might make more progress if the question were divided. A menu that lists only vanilla ice cream and strawberry pie combines the choice of vanilla versus strawberry with the choice of ice cream versus pie. We may decide to forgo dessert even though we might have selected strawberry ice cream had it been offered.

1.2 *The Price Distinction*

Consider a marketable security with a price of $1,000 per share. If one were to purchase a share, one would pay $1,000 plus the commission of, say, $100 for a total of $1,100. If one owned a share and were to sell it, one would receive $1,000 minus the commission,

[1] I must take my share of the blame for this. Many of my past efforts (see, for example, Sterling [1970]) have been primarily concerned with the current versus historical question and, in order to avoid becoming embroiled in the combined issues, I made some assumptions which equated current costs and exit values. As a result, my past work is interpreted as support for current costs about equally as often as it is for exit values. For example, Vancil and Weil [1976] introduced a reprint of my 'Relevant Financial Reporting' with some very kind words which concluded: 'He proved that using replacement costs to measure income produces a result which is interpretable and relevant' (p. 2). I appreciate what I consider to be a very high compliment since it is so difficult to prove anything in accounting, but I hasten to confess that I was trying to prove that exit values, not replacement costs, met those criteria.

It is enlightening to compare the interpretation of the works of others in similar situations. Revsine [1973], for example, presents an analysis of a perfectly competitive, frictionless market for the purpose of demonstrating some characteristics of replacement costs. In such a market the frictions of transaction costs are nonexistent and therefore replacement costs and exit values are identical. For this reason, every conclusion regarding replacement costs also applies to exit values yet no one interprets Revsine's work as support for exit values. I believe that the cost paradigm is so ingrained that we seldom perceive the existence of an alternative.

or $900. The $1,000 is, of course, the familiar 'cost' which is 'historical' if it refers to the past date of purchase, 'current' if it refers to the present, or 'future'. The $900 is the unfamiliar 'exit value', which can also be modified by adding 'historical', 'current', or 'future'. Thus, there are figures representing three concepts:

Definition 1: Cost = cash paid or payable if purchased ($1,100).
Definition 2: Price = reference figure ($1,000).
Definition 3: Exit value = cash received or receivable if sold ($900).

The concepts refer to the same moment in time — the figures exist simultaneously. The ranking is important and constant. The historical cost was greater than the historical exit value, the current cost is greater than the current exit value, and the future cost will be greater than the future exit value. The difference is *always* twice the commission.[2]

1.3 *The Questions*

Now that we have drawn the distinction we can ask the first question.

Question 1: Should we adopt costs or exit values as the basis for reporting assets and income?

The question arises at purchase as well as at all interim balance sheet dates.

1.31 *Purchase* The question initially arises at the moment of purchase. To record the cost we would write

1 Jan.	Marketable Securities	$1,100	
	Cash		$1,100

on the basis that the cost is determined by setting it equal to the amount of cash *paid*. By contrast, to record the exit value we would write

1 Jan.	Marketable Securities	$900	
	Loss on Purchase	200	
	Cash		$1,100

[2] Terminology is difficult because the desire for precision conflicts with the desire for communication. Precision demands that different words be used for different referents and that often requires the use of jargon; but jargon requires that readers learn the new terms and that inhibits communication. The problem first arises here in the meaning of 'cost'. The way that I am using the term conforms with the instructions to capitalize all costs necessary to acquire the asset. Since commissions are necessary, $1,100 would be recorded as the cost. An alternative is to expense the commission on the basis of properly classifying costs or conservatism or tax considerations. This would result in recording the price of $1,000 as the cost. The lower of cost or market rule, if applied strictly, would require that it be recorded at the net realizable value of $900 and in subsequent years this would also be referred to as the cost. Thus, even in this simple case there are three possible meanings of 'cost'. For this reason, I toyed with the idea of using a more precise but less familiar jargon, such as 'entry value', to refer to the $1,100 but rejected it since 'current cost' is widely used and was recently distinguished from 'replacement cost' in FAS 33 [1979].

The same problem plagues 'exit value'. Some refer to the $900 as the 'sale price' and that terminology has the advantage of being widely known since all accountants deal with sales but it has the disadvantage of being widely misunderstood. In my experience most accountants associate sale price with the unknown price that will exist in the future when the sale is made. This differs from exit value both because it refers to the price — $1,100 instead of $900 — and it refers to the future instead of the present. 'Net realizable value' would require deducting the commission and therefore refers to the $900 but it too is often associated with the future instead of the present as well as being part of the lexicon of 'historical cost'. Some define exit values, especially in regard to inventories, as the future proceeds from sale (cf., e.g., Edwards [1975], p. 240). For that reason, I toyed with the idea of using an even more unfamiliar term than 'exit value' but decided instead to try to define precisely what *I* mean when I use the term.

on the basis that the exit value is determined by setting it equal to the value of the cash *receivable.* Of course, we could record the cost of the share at $1,100 and then draft another entry to write it down to $900 and we could call the $200 'commission expense'. I drafted the entry in the form that would contrast the conceptual difference and I called the $200 'loss on purchase' for the same reason.

In the cost literature assets are defined as things that are expected to *benefit* the *future.* This immediately raises a question about the above entries. If assets benefit the future, why record the present price instead of the future price?

Question 2: Should we record the present price or the future price (and future dividends)?

This question will not detain us long. I raise it for two reasons. First, to point out that it is separate from Question 1. To decide to record costs does not *ipso facto* answer the question of whether we should record present or future costs. And the same is true for exit values. The reason we do not record future prices is obvious: the future is unknown. We would be accused of hubris or worse if we attempted to record the future price since the best we could do is to record somebody's forecast of the future price. There have been a number of people who have recommended that we report forecasts because they would be useful. *If* we decide to accept those recommendations, we would still be faced with the question of the kind of forecasted future price that we should report. In this essay, I will consider the relevance of forecasted prices (and dividends) to decisions but I will not delve into the problems of reporting them.

Second, the response to the unknown future is a primary conceptual difference between costs and exit values. Assets are often defined as '*costs* that will benefit the future'. To put it negatively, if a cost will not benefit the future, then it should not be capitalized, should not be recorded as an asset, should be expensed. The reason for the recording of cost is that the benefit is expected to be greater than the cost. The sacrifice, cash paid, is measured and the value of the share is set *equal* to that *sacrifice* because the *benefit* is expected to be *greater* than the sacrifice. Setting the value equal to the sacrifice precludes recording a gain or loss at purchase. By contrast, exit values focus on the *present benefit of the cash receivable.* The idea is that if the share were sold one moment after the purchase, the cash balance would be $900 which is compared to the cash balance of $1,100 one moment prior to purchase. The decline in the benefits of the cash balance is the $200 loss on purchase. To put the same idea in more familiar terms, the $1,100 is an expenditure and in that sense it is a cost; the $900 is a receivable and in the sense of debiting receivables and crediting revenues, it is a revenue; the 'matching of costs and revenues' yields a $200 loss.

1.32 *Interim dates* Question 1 arises again at each balance sheet date. Assuming the price to have increased to $1,050 at 31 January, adding and subtracting the commission yields a cost of $1,150 and an exit value of $950 at that date.

Historical cost accounting prohibits making an entry to record the price increase on the basis of conservatism or the realization convention or both. We could institute a similar prohibition in regard to exit values and call it 'historical exit value accounting'. Then we could return to Question 1 because the alternatives are to report the $1,100 historical cost or the $900 historical exit value on the 31 January balance sheet. The point is that deciding to report historical prices does not *ipso facto* answer the question of what kind of prices to report. Likewise deciding to report costs or exit values does not *ipso facto* answer the question of historical versus current. There is a third, separate question.

Question 3: Should we report the current price or the historical price at each balance sheet date?

It seems that the combination of Questions 1 and 3 has hindered progress toward resolution of both questions and I have separated them for that reason. Of course, no one has ever suggested that we report historical exit values but that is merely additional evidence of the fact that almost all accountants think in terms of costs. Since I, too, do not want to put it forward as a serious contender, I will not discuss it further except to say that 'exit value' means 'current exit value' unless specifically indicated otherwise. This leaves us with the three alternatives of historical cost, current cost and exit value.

The adjusting entry to record both the current cost and the exit value is:

31 Jan.	Marketable Securities	$50	
	Gain		$50

Although the adjusting entry records the same amount for both, the concept is different. For current costs the idea is to write the share up to the amount payable at 31 January, i.e., to record the cash that would be required to be paid if it were purchased on that date. Since the amount payable is now $1,150 and the amount paid was $1,100, there is a 'holding gain' of $50.[3] By contrast, for exit values the idea is to write the share up to the receivable amount at 31 January, i.e., to record the amount of cash that would be received if it were sold on that date. Since the amount receivable is now $950 and it was $900, there is a 'value gain' of $50. Thus, there are two different concepts:

Definition 4: Holding Gain = sacrifice change = cash payable − prior cash payable (paid).

Definition 5: Value Gain = benefit change = cash receivable − prior cash receivable (paid).

The conceptual difference is the same as at purchase. The future benefits were expected to be greater than the sacrifice, cash paid, at purchase, and therefore the value of the share was set equal to that sacrifice. At interim dates the increase in future benefits is expected to be greater than (or equal to) the increase in the sacrifice, cash payable, and therefore the value of the share is set equal to the present sacrifice and the difference is a holding gain. By contrast, exit value is an attempt to record the present benefit and it is considered to be a gain because that present benefit is greater than the past benefit. Thus, the gains (or losses) are based on two quite different concepts.

In the case at hand the difference in amount reported is $200. Current cost would report net income of $50 consisting of the holding gain of that amount. Exit value would report a net loss of $150 consisting of the value gain of $50 and the loss on purchase of $200. Of course, historical cost would report a zero gain.

In subsequent months the same type of adjusting entry would be required to record the change in the cash payable or cash receivable. Dividends would be recorded in the usual way and therefore the net income for both current costs and exit values would be the dividends plus or minus the holding gains or value gains, respectively. The net

[3] I am aware that a number of professional versions of CCA do not recognize the $50 as a 'gain'. The notion used here is that developed by Edwards and Bell [1964].

income for historical cost would be equal to the amount of the dividends since it records neither holding gains nor value gains. Since dividends have the same effect on all three options, they are not pertinent to the distinction.

1.33 *Sale* The questions do not arise at time of sale. Instead, all three methods debit the cash for the amount received, credit the share for its recorded value and take the difference to be a gain. For example, if the share were sold on 1 February and there had been no changes from 31 January, we would write

1 Feb.	Cash	$950	
	Loss on Sale	150	
	Marketable Securities		$1,100

for historical costs, or

1 Feb.	Cash	$950	
	Loss on Sale	200	
	Marketable Securities		$1,150

for current cost, or

1 Feb.	Cash	$950	
	Marketable Securities		$ 950

for exit values.

As usual when the cycle of cash to cash is complete, there is no difference in valuations or in reported income for the entire period. In this case the net loss is $150 for the two months for all three options.

For costs, both historical and current, the idea is the familiar matching of costs and revenues. Since the future has now become the present, the benefits — cash receipts — are known and therefore it is no longer necessary to focus on the sacrifice. Instead, the benefits can be matched with the sacrifice. Both match the $950 with a past cost. The difference is that historical cost matches it with cash paid at purchase of $1,100 while current cost matches it with the cash payable of $1,150 at the last balance sheet date. Exit values, by contrast, continue to focus on the benefits by taking the difference between the cash received and the prior cash receivable.[4]

1.4 *Summary*

The case reveals that there are both similarities and differences. One similarity is that all three report the same total gain from purchase to sale. The major difference between current prices and historical costs is that a past amount is reported on the present balance sheet under historical costs while current prices report an amount of cash equivalents at the balance sheet date. Current costs and exit values are similar in that they both measure at the balance sheet date and in that they both measure cash equivalents. They differ only in that current cost measures the cash equivalents payable if purchased while exit values measure the cash equivalents receivable if sold.

Since all three report the same amount of cash received and paid, as well as the ultimate gain after sale, the only deviation in reported values and gains occurs on interim financial statements. Exhibit 1 summarizes the characteristics of the three options.

[4] In an unfortunately neglected article, Bedford and McKeown [1972] stated the distinction clearly in points (1) and (2), p. 337.

EXHIBIT 1

Interim Balance Sheet

Focus		Time	Numeraire	Flow Direction		Event		Accounting Method
Sacrifice	of	Past	Dollars	Paid	at	Past purchase	is	Historical cost
Sacrifice	of	Present	Dollars	Payable	for	Immediate purchase	is	Current cost
Benefit	of	Present	Dollars	Receivable	from	Immediate sale	is	Exit value

Interim Income Statement

Time Period	Accounting Method		Gain
Past — Past	Historical cost	is	Zero
Present — Previous	Current cost	is	Holding gain
Present — Previous	Exit value	is	Value gain

Depending upon the predisposition, one will be struck by either the similarities or the differences. In the interim, when differences exist, I would characterize the differences in two ways: first, the measurement of a sacrifice attribute versus a benefit attribute, and, second, the measurement at a point in time versus measurement at purchase. Recognition that they are measurements of different attributes should dispel much confusion and assist in the analysis.

2. THE SPECIAL CASE

Most people argue as though they are passive observers on the side lines, as it were. They talk as though someone else, someone none too bright, some disembodied character, were the decision maker. Since there is no point in your getting prematurely embroiled in the psychological foibles of others, let us first concentrate on what choice *you*, the reader, would want to make in a given situation. Therefore let us discuss a concrete decision problem under uncertainty with *you* cast in the role of the decision maker, a decision problem in which *you* are asked to make the choice.

Howard Raiffa

Now that the alternative methods have been distinguished and defined, we can attempt to answer the questions, to decide which method is best and on what grounds. As suggested in the quotation by Raiffa, I ask the reader to get involved in the decision instead of worrying about what information some unknown users may or may not want or understand.

2.1 *The Problem*

Recognition that the alternatives are different attributes and understanding the nature of each is a prerequisite to selection. An additional prerequisite is the specification of the criteria that are to be used in the selection. Understanding the nature of the alternatives will not permit selection in the absence of criteria but such understanding will permit us to recognize inappropriate criteria. The criteria (sometimes called 'principles', 'basic concepts', 'conventions', etc.) that have been used in the past were inappropriate either because they did not discriminate among the alternatives or they confused definitions with criteria. To illustrate the nature of the problem I will present a few, but only a few, examples.

2.11 *Undiscriminating criteria* Much of the criticism that has been levelled against the alternatives in the past was based on various criteria that did not discriminate. When all alternatives satisfy a criterion or all fail to satisfy it, the criterion does not discriminate, does not aid in making a choice.

One prevalent criterion is 'economic reality' which has been used at one time or another to defend *and* to criticize *all* accounting practices and proposals. Such a broad and contradictory usage is ample evidence that the criterion is intolerably vague yet it continues to be used.[5] Historical cost proponents often criticize current price accounting because it records cash equivalents instead of the economic reality of cash. The argument is that we should record actual cash as opposed to the recording of hypothetical, unreal cash equivalents. The fact is that historical cost also records cash equivalents for all non-cash exchanges. If the share had been purchased on account, for example, the cost would have been set equal to the cash equivalent of the account payable. If the share had been sold for a note, for example, the cash equivalents of that note receivable would have been matched with the past cash equivalents of the account payable to determine the 'actual' cash realized. Receivables and payables are not concepts foreign to historical cost accounting. The only difference is that historical cost records such cash equivalents at the event of exchange instead of at the balance date but that difference concerns the timing of the measurement, not its reality. The opposite is also true. Cash or cash equivalents paid at purchase are as economically real as cash equivalents receivable or payable at the balance sheet date. The only distinction is that one is past and the other is present, not that historical costs are unreal. Thus, the criterion of economic reality fails to discriminate.

It has often been said that both historical costs and current costs are consistent with the going concern assumption while exit values violate that assumption. Many say that exit valuation requires a liquidation assumption or that it implies that the firm is liquidating because it records 'liquidation values'. The fact is that a going concern both purchases and sells. In the case of marketable securities it is abundantly clear that from time to time the firm will sell some shares for their exit value as well as purchase some shares for their cost. To assign interim values on either basis does not imply anything at all about continuity or liquidation of the firm. To argue that we should adopt historical or current costs because a going concern purchases at cost has as little force as arguing that we should adopt exit values because it sells at exit value. Thus, the going concern criterion fails to discriminate. The criterion of management intent is similar. We often hear that the fact that management does not intend to sell proves that exit values are absurd. That criterion can be reversed. The fact that management does not intend, indeed cannot, purchase an asset that it already owns provides as much proof that costs are absurd. Thus, the criterion of management intent fails to discriminate.

It has been said that historical costs 'provide a permanent record' of the activities of

[5] One reason that I have proposed the criterion of empirical testability in other works is to try to make 'economic reality' operational. In the specific sense of empirical testability I think economic reality is a useful criterion that will discriminate alternatives but in its general sense it does not discriminate.

the firm while current prices 'destroy that permanent record'. A variant is that exit values destroy the permanent record but current costs do not because they are a 'natural extension' of historical costs. It is difficult to know what this means but it must be based on some sort of misunderstanding. Current price accounting reports the amount paid as a use on the funds statement, the current prices on the balance sheets or statement of financial position, and the differences on the income statements. Historical cost accounting reports the amount paid as a use on the funds statement *and* as an asset on the balance sheet *and* it continues to report that amount on interim balance sheets, with the consequence of reporting a zero gain on interim income statements. The argument seems to be about what statement the amount paid should be reported on and how often it should be reported rather than about permanent records. The 'natural extension' variant must mean that current costs are updated historical costs but that is an argument about what to put in the record, not its permanence. Since all three write the journal entries in indelible ink, the criterion of providing a permanent record fails to discriminate.

2.12 *Definitions vs criteria* Many of the past debates have mistaken definitions for criteria. In effect, such debates have defined a rectangle as consisting of straight lines, pointed out that circles have curved lines and then concluded that rectangles are preferable to circles because rectangles meet the criterion of straight lines and circles do not. If the original question concerned straight versus curved lines, such arguments are restatements of the question, not criteria.

The conservatism principle has often been invoked in such debates. Since exit values are always less than current costs, we can say that exit values have the virtue of being more conservative. Although conservatism discriminates in this sense, it is merely a synonym for 'less than' and therefore the argument reduces to a consideration of whether less than is preferable to greater than. Since we have not resolved that issue, to argue that exit values should be reported because they are more conservative than current costs is merely a restatement of Definitions 1 and 3, not a criterion. We cannot say whether current prices are more or less conservative than historical costs since prices could go up or down. We can define 'historical costs' as the lower of historical cost or current price and then say that 'historical costs' have the virtue of being conservative. But to argue that 'historical costs' are more conservative than current prices is merely a restatement of the definition of lower of cost or market, not a criterion. Hence, conservatism is a definition of a difference, not a criterion.

The realization convention is similar. The criticism that exit values record a gain at purchase is based on a misunderstanding since, as illustrated above, exit values record a loss on purchase. By contrast, both historical costs and current costs defer recognition of that loss until sale. Thus, the first question is whether the realization convention applies to losses as well as gains and, if so, do exit values violate that convention by recording a loss at purchase or do costs violate that convention by not recording a loss until sale? But this is merely a restatement of Question 1 since the definition of exit values requires recording a loss at purchase, and vice versa for costs. It is true that current price accounting violates the realization convention by recording gains prior to sale while historical cost accounting does not violate that convention. But this is merely a restatement of Question 3 since the definition of historical cost prohibits recording a gain prior to sale and vice versa for current prices. Hence, realization is a definition of a difference, not a criterion.

The stewardship or accountability objective is similar. What should the steward be accountable for? For example, we could make the steward accountable for dollars and adopt financial capital or make him accountable for physical units and adopt physical capital. What we make the steward accountable for determines what we account for. In this sense it is a criterion that does not discriminate. Sometimes those who employ stewardship implicitly define what the steward should be accountable for and therefore it is a definition, not a criterion. The objective of accounting for economic events is also similar. What events should we account for? Historical cost defines exchanges as accountable events and defines a price increase in the absence of an exchange a nonaccountable event. Current price defines a price increase as an accountable event. It is either a criterion that does not discriminate or those who employ it have some implicit events in mind and therefore it is a definition instead of a criterion.

There are a great many such criteria that have been utilized in the past. Space limitations, as well as tedium, prevent a consideration of all such criteria. The above examples should be sufficient to make the point: the criteria that have been utilized in the past do not aid in a rational choice and therefore we must seek other criteria.

2.2 *The Criterion*

Recognition that the alternatives are measurements of different attributes immediately suggests the criterion of relevance. Just as my height and weight are different attributes of the same object, the cost and exit value of the share are different attributes of the same object. Merely stating an objective permits a selection of the attribute. If my objective is to gain or lose weight, then I must measure my weight to see whether, and by how much, I have achieved that objective. Of course measurement of height is a perfectly legitimate activity and it will be relevant to decisions regarding other objectives but it is irrelevant to decisions regarding weight gains. That is, height and weight are both 'useful' in the sense that height will be relevant to some decisions but not to others and the same is true for weight. The point is that 'usefulness' in the absence of a specific decision context is too general to allow us to decide which attribute should be measured: it is a criterion that will not discriminate among attributes.

The same is true for costs and exit values. If we can be clear on the objectives and the decisions regarding those objectives, it will allow us to decide which attribute(s) to measure and report. 'Usefulness' is too general since costs will be relevant to some decisions but not to others and the same is true of exit values. It is this reason that causes me to state the relevance criterion in relation to a specified decision model.

Criterion 1: An attribute is relevant to a decision model if that attribute is specified by that decision model.

The corollary, of course, is that if an attribute is not specified by a decision model, it is irrelevant to that decision model.

2.3 *Application of the Criterion*

The objective of economic activity is said to be 'profit maximization' but that begs the question since we are exploring alternative ways to measure profits. However, it is clear that humans prefer more net cash flows to less net cash flows. Thus, we can say that the objective of economic activity is to maximize future net cash flows. Since the cash balance is a summary measure of the cash inflows (debits) and outflows (credits), we can express the same idea by saying that the objective is to increase the cash balance, to obtain a future cash balance that is greater than the present cash balance. The task is to identify the decision model that is pertinent to that objective and then to examine that decision model to see which attributes are specified by that decision model, to see which attributes are relevant.

2.31 *Exchange decisions* One advantage of considering the simple case of marketable securities is that the decision model is well known. As every accountant and financial analyst knows, the decision to exchange requires the comparison of the current price with the future cash flows. Of course the future cash flows may require various adjustments, primarily for the time differences by discounting and also perhaps a separate adjustment for risk differences, but those are refinements which are explored in great depth in many finance and accounting textbooks and need not detain us here. The future cash flows consist of the future dividends and the terminal price, i.e., the price when the share is sold in the future. Thus, this well-known decision model specifies two attributes:

(1) Future Cash Flows which consist of
  (a) Future Dividends, and
  (b) Future Terminal Price.
(2) Current Price.

Some shares are bought for growth or 'capital gains' rather than 'current income' and this provides a convenient way to divide the question.

First, consider a growth share in which future dividends are expected to be zero. This reduces the relevant attributes to the (lb) future terminal price and (2) current price. If the future terminal price is expected to be less than the current price then a cash maximizer will not purchase an unowned share for the obvious reason that his future cash balance will be less than his present cash balance if he does purchase. A cash maximizer will sell an owned share under those conditions for the equally obvious reason that his present cash balance will be greater than his future cash balance if he does sell. There is *no* reason to purchase or not sell in this situation because it is, in effect, the exchange of, say, 1,000 present dollars for, say, 700 expected future dollars and that is not a cash maximizing decision even with zero discount rate, zero time differential, zero risk, etc. When the future terminal price is greater than the current price we can only say that a cash maximizer will *tend* to purchase or not sell because the decision also depends upon the date of the future price, the discount rate, and the existence of other alternatives which may be more cash maximizing.

It is rare to find universal agreement about anything, especially in accounting, but it does appear that the above decision model and its specified (relevant) attributes are undisputed.[6] The relevance of the two prices requires that we reconsider Question 2:

[6] I have tried very hard to state it in a form that is undisputed but perhaps I should explicitly disclaim normative decision models, intrinsic values, abnormal returns and the like. First, the decision model is not normative in that it can be applied to the objective of minimizing cash by reversing all the inequalities and

should we report the current or the future price? As noted above, we cannot report the future price because it is unknown. The recommendations to report forecasts of future prices have been based on general 'usefulness' and they often conclude that we should report forecasted prices (or discounted cash flows) *instead of* current prices. The relevance criterion, by contrast, clearly indicates that *if* we could accurately forecast future prices, we should report the forecasted prices *in addition* to current prices. That is, the relevance criterion does not discriminate future from current prices because both are specified by the decision model and therefore both are equally relevant. However, it does discriminate current from past prices because the decision model does not specify any past price, neither at a past event, such as purchase, nor at a past time. This does not mean that past prices are 'useless' nor does it mean that they were not relevant to past decisions but it does mean that they are not relevant to present exchange decisions.

The decision model was stated above in terms of prices because it is usually stated that way. In the usual statement of the decision model the distinction between costs and exit values is either implicit or thought to be 'negligible' in economic terminology or 'immaterial' in accounting terminology. The demonstration of the conceptual difference requires that the distinction be explicit regardless of materiality. Thus, we must refine the decision model by substituting current cost or exit value as appropriate.

In deciding to purchase or not purchase, one must compare the current cost to the terminal exit value. To use the same figures as those in the journal entries, the current price at 1 January was $1,000 and the terminal price was $1,050 and therefore a cash maximizer would tend to purchase if the decision were based on prices. But that would be an error since the cash outflow would be the $1,100 current cost and the cash inflow would be the $950 terminal exit value. Thus, one must compare the current *cost,* not the current *price,* to the terminal *exit value,* not the terminal *price,* in making cash maximizing purchase decisions.

In deciding to sell or not sell, one must compare the current exit value to the terminal exit value. In terms of the journal entry figures, the $900 1 January exit value needs to be compared to the $950 terminal exit value. A cash maximizer would tend to not sell since the future cash balance is expected to be $50 greater than the present cash balance. Comparing the current price of $1,000 to the terminal exit value of $950 would indicate a sale that is an error.

The terminal exit value is relevant to both decisions but the current cost is relevant to the purchase or not purchase decision and the current exit value is relevant to the sell or not sell decision. To put it another way, the current cost is relevant to decisions regarding

---

defining 'better off' as a smaller cash balance. It is difficult to think of examples where that objective would be in force but perhaps a misanthropic manager of a philanthropic foundation illustrates the case. Since the tax regulations generally require that income be distributed in grants, the misanthrope can avoid such distributions by avoiding income and therefore the above decision model applies. Second, it does not matter whether the cash maximizer uses intrinsic value, inside information or a Ouija board to form the expectations. The basis for forming the expectations is not pertinent to my purpose. Third, the cash maximizer may earn abnormal returns from inside information or those returns may be due to accepting a high risk or it may not be possible to earn abnormal returns. The only thing required is that the cash maximizer be trying to earn some returns. Some of my past work has been misinterpreted and I apologize for not having been more explicit but I find it difficult to disclaim everything that I do not mean so I will ask the reader to take note of what I do not say as well as what I do say.

EXHIBIT 2

	GM	GE
Current Cost	$1,100	$1,100
Price	1,000	1,000
Exit Value	900	900
Dividends	55	66
Rate of Return		
on Current Cost		
$55/$1,100	5%	
$66/$1,100		6%
on Exit Value		
$55/$900	6.1%	
$66/$900		7.3%
Position	owned	unowned

exchanges of *unowned* shares and the current exit value is relevant to decisions regarding exchanges of *owned* shares.

The current exit value of an owned share is relevant in another way that seems to be both obvious and difficult to grasp. (Perhaps the problem with grasping it is that it is too obvious.) Decisions are the choice between *mutually exclusive* alternatives. If one can own one share of GM and one share of GE, then one need not choose between them, no decision is required. Current exit values of owned shares, in comparison to current costs of unowned shares, specify the *available* mutually exclusive alternatives. Consider Exhibit 2. Since one must sell one share of GM for $900 and purchase one share of GE for $1,100, the purchase of one share of GE is *not* an available alternative. The available alternative to owning one share of GM is to own 900/1,100 or about 82 per cent of one share of GE. Of course one could add $200 cash to the exit value of GM and then purchase GE but that emphasizes the point since one cannot purchase GE without having the additional $200 cash.

Consideration of the second — current income — type of share will further clarify the point. Assume that the cash maximizer expects the future dividends to be as shown in Exhibit 2 in perpetuity. The effect of this assumption is to eliminate the terminal exit value as a future cash flow and reduce the relevant attributes to the (1a) future dividends and (2) current price. This again brings up Question 3 about reporting future dividends versus current prices and the answer is the same: both are relevant but the best we can do in regard to future dividends is to report somebody's forecast. It also again brings up the need to distinguish the kind of current price. In this case the decision is usually based on comparing rates of return. It has been vigorously argued that since we compute the rate of return on the current cost of unowned shares, we must also compute the rate of return on the current cost of owned shares in order to be consistent. Otherwise, so the argument goes, we will be comparing apples and oranges. On the basis of that consistent comparison, we should sell GM and purchase GE in order to earn 6 per cent instead of 5 per cent. But the purchase requires additional financing of $200 which, at the same interest rate of 6 per cent, would cost $12. The dividends from GE of $66 less the interest of $12 yields a net of $54 as compared to the $55 from GM. Thus, the result of a decision based on the consistent comparison is a decline in cash flows of $1. The $54 is, of course, 900/1,100 times the dividend of $66 which is another way of saying that the alternative to owning one share of GM is to own 900/1,100 shares of GE.

Another way to illustrate the point is to assume that the cash maximizer could invest any amount in a bank time deposit at 6 per cent. Since he now earns only 5 per cent on GM, he should sell GM and put the money in the bank in order to earn 6 per cent. But the result is the same since 6 per cent of the $900 exit value is $54. The difference, of course, is that GM is now earning 6.1 per cent *on exit value* and in order to make cash maximizing decisions one must compare that rate to the rates of return on the current cost of alternatives. Since the 6.1 per cent return on exit value for GM is greater than the 6 per cent return on current cost for either GE or a time deposit, the cash maximizing decision is to not sell GM. The 5 per cent return on current cost for GM may be consistent but it is also not relevant to cash maximizing decisions.

In summary, exit values are demonstrably relevant to exchange decisions of owned assets in regard to straightforward cash magnitude comparisons as well as in regard to rate of return comparisons. Since owned shares are listed on the balance sheet (and unowned shares are not listed), I conclude that, on the basis of relevance, exit values should be reported.

2.32 *Previous exchange decisions* At various times in the past it was decided to purchase or not purchase or sell or not sell. This was made on the basis of the decision model identified above and required the forecasting of either future dividends or the terminal exit value. The future, or at least part of it, has now become the present and we want to look backward to see whether, and by how much, the cash maximizer has achieved the objective. In other words, we want to *evaluate* past decisions.

If the share has been sold, then all cash flows from this share have already occurred and the only thing required is to compare the present cash balance with the past cash balance. Since the original decision was made on the basis of a forecasted cash balance greater than the current cash balance, since the cash maximizer prefers larger to smaller cash balances, if the present cash balance is greater than the past cash balance, then the cash maximizer has achieved the objective of being 'better off', the difference in magnitude is a measure of how much better off and the corresponding accounting term is 'gain'. The problem arises at interim dates when we need to make some sort of determination of whether, and by how much, the cash maximizer is better off than he was at some prior date. The choices are to report the historical cost and a zero gain, the current cost and a holding gain, or the exit value and a value gain.

Historical cost accounting does not address the problem. It repeats the report of the past cost on the present balance sheet with the consequent of a zero gain. Thus, in the best interpretation it does not provide an evaluation of the past decision at interim dates and in the worst interpretation it provides an erroneous evaluation since a zero gain is reported regardless of subsequent events. (The lower of cost or market version of historical cost provides an asymmetric evaluation.) By contrast, current price accounting does address the problem but it presents the choice of two attributes.

Current costs focus on cash outflow differences, sacrifice differences, and assert that one is better off from cost increases because future cash inflows parallel cost increases. Thus, a current cost increase heralds a future cash balance greater than the present cost. Exit values focus on cash inflow differences, the benefit difference, and assert that one is better off from exit value increases because the present cash balance if sold will be greater than a past cash balance. In the above case the price increased from $1,000 to $1,050 which resulted in reporting a holding gain and a value gain of $50. Since both current costs and exit values report that the cash maximizer is better off by the same amount, it appears that the distinction is semantic and of no consequence. Further inquiry, however, reveals that the two different concepts can lead to different amounts.

It is possible for current costs and exit values to change while the price remains constant. The occasional restructuring of commission rates is a real-world case of such a situation. Suppose that a share was owned when the commission increased from $100 to $150 but the price remained constant. Exhibit 3 contrasts the two cases.

EXHIBIT 3

	(a) 1 Jan.	(b) 31 Jan.	(c) 31 Jan.	(d) (b) − (a)	(e) (c) − (a)
Current Cost	1,100	1,150	1,150	50	50
Price	1,000	1,050	1,000	50	−0−
Exit Value	900	950	850	50	−50

When the price increases, column (b), the reported gain is the same under both options as shown in column (d). Whether we label that $50 gain a holding gain or value gain is of no consequence. However, when the commission increases, column (c), the amount of the reported gain differs by $100, a holding gain of $50 versus a value loss of $50 as shown in column (e). The simplicity of the case permits us to see that there are different kinds of holding gains. I will divide the growth (zero dividend) share from the current income (zero terminal exit value) share to distinguish the kinds of holding gains.

First, consider the current income share. This reduces the problem to the relation of increases in current costs to increases in future dividends. It is agreed that an increase in expected future dividends will result in an increase in the present price. If we reverse this reasoning and say that an increase in the present price will result in, and therefore is evidence of, an increase in future dividends, we have erred. All that we can legitimately conclude from an increase in the present price is that it is evidence of an increase in expectations. Since those expectations may or may not be realized, a holding gain based on a price increase is *conjectural*. If the current cost increase is due to a commission increase, it has no relation to expected future dividends, much less to actual future dividends. There is no evidence, neither logical nor empirical, that would allow us to conclude that either expected or actual future dividends parallel commission increases. It is unlikely that such a parallel would exist and therefore we can say that a holding gain based on a commission increase is *dubious*.

Second, consider the growth share with zero expected dividends. This reduces the problem to the relation of increases in current costs to increases in terminal exit values. Since prices can go up or down, the effect of a present price increase on the terminal exit value is unknown. Thus, holding gains based on price increases are *conjectural*. On the other hand, we can be certain that the effect of a commission increase is to decrease the terminal exit value. Whatever the terminal exit value turns out to be, it will be less by the amount of the commission increase. Thus, in regard to the future cash flows from the terminal exit value, a holding gain based on a commission increase is *detrimental.*

In summary, when we look at cost increases that are expected to benefit the future, we find that in regard to dividends they are at best conjectural and at worst dubious and in regard to terminal exit values they are at best conjectural and at worst detrimental. When we divide the question the other way, we find that the benefit from a price increase on both types of cash flows is conjectural and the benefit from a commission increase is at best dubious and at worst contradictory. It is contradictory because it is a benefit that is detrimental, i.e., not beneficial.[7]

Current cost analysts recognize the existence of cost increases that are not beneficial but their proposed solution is 'a selective elimination from income of those price [current cost] changes that do not reflect expected changes in [future cash] operating flows while including those that do correspond to expected flow changes' (Revsine [1973], p. 144). Implementation of this solution will present a dilemma: either inconsistent reporting of assets — some at current cost and others at historical cost — or the disposition of a deferred credit for those current cost increases that are not beneficial. But the more important question is if the objective is to measure benefits, why not measure benefits? Why measure the sacrifice and use it as a surrogate for benefits? My hypothesis is that we are so steeped in measuring costs or sacrifices that we do not perceive the alternative of measuring benefits. That is, Question 1 — costs versus exit values — is never addressed because it is taken for granted that we will report costs and the only question is current versus historical costs. This *combines* Question 1 with Question 3 — current versus historical — but it also *confuses* Question 1 with Question 2 — future versus current — because the reason for measuring the current sacrifice is that it is expected to benefit the future.

The confusion of temporal locations has plagued accountants for a very long time. Earlier we were told that it was impossible to measure the present but that we could measure past costs and that we should report them because they will benefit the future. Now we are told that it is possible to measure current costs and that we should report them because they will benefit the future. Since current costs benefit the future, changes in current costs — holding gains — indicate changes in future benefits. But when it is discovered that some changes in current costs will not benefit the future, we are told to segregate them and report only those that will benefit the future. If the objective is to report forecasts of future benefits, why not report forecasts of future benefits? The usual answer is that the future is unknown and that forecasts are unreliable. But the proposed

My conjecture is that all cash maximizers would consider themselves worse off from a commission increase and therefore would think that it is contradictory to report it as a gain. I discussed the justification in its future benefit form rather than the past cost saving form because my conjecture is that most accountants, having been brought up in the historical cost tradition, look at current cost increases as future benefits. Those brought up in the economic tradition, such as Edwards and Bell [1974], think of it as a cost saving and explicitly disclaim it being a benefit increase or, in their terminology, an addition to 'realizable income' (p. 93). My conjecture is that all cash maximizers would consider a commission increase to be a cost dissaving and therefore would think that it is contradictory to report is as a gain. See Rosenfield [1969] for an excellent discussion in general as well as a specific conclusion that holding gains are 'unintelligible', which is similar to my conjecture. See Samuelson [1980] for a lucid exposition in general as well as a specific conclusion that cost savings have no natural zero point. See Revsine [1973] for a thorough analysis in general as well as the specific conclusion that some types of holding gains are not beneficial.

solution requires that we forecast the future in order to segregate those cost increases that benefit the future from those that do not. Thus, reporting the segregated cost increases as holding gains because they benefit the future is, in fact, a report of a forecast, albeit disguised. If forecasts are too unreliable to report, then the segregated holding gains are also too unreliable to report. That is, holding gains are at best conjectural.

Even if holding gains were reliable indicators of future benefits, it would not relieve us of the task of measuring the present. As noted above (Section 2.31), the decision model specifies *both* the present price and the future price (or future dividends). One cannot decide to purchase or not purchase from knowledge of the future exit value alone; it requires a comparison of the current cost with the future exit value. One cannot decide to sell or not sell on the basis of knowledge of the future exit value alone; it requires a comparison of the present exit value with the future exit value. Thus, if current costs were reliable forecasts of future exit values or holding gains were reliable forecasts of changes in future exit values, the relevance criterion would require that *both* be reported. The reason is that decisions require that the present be distinguished from the future. A cash maximizer purchases because he expects his future cash balance to be greater than his present cash balance. In the evaluation of previous exchanges the present must be distinguished from the past for the same reason. Reporting holding gains because they benefit the future mixes future expectations with past gains. In order to *decide* one must compare the *present* with the *future* and confusing the two will produce decision errors. In order to *evaluate* past decisions one must compare the *present* with the *past* and confusing the two will produce evaluation errors. We do distinguish the future, present and past at the event of sale. When the cash is collected, the present cash balance is compared with the past cash balance to determine the past gain and there is no notice taken of what the future cash balance may be. The present cash balance is likely to be used to purchase another share and therefore we could confound ourselves with questions about whether the present cash balance will benefit the future or not. But we do not so confound ourselves; we simply and straightforwardly measure the present benefits of the present cash balance, recognizing that it is both decision relevant (in comparison with future balances) and evaluation relevant (in comparison with previous balances).

Exit valuation is an attempt to measure the present benefits without regard to the future benefits or present or past sacrifices. Exit values are measures of what the present cash balance would be if the share were sold in the present. It is an attempt to determine the equivalent cash balance. Thus, exit values are simply an extension of the idea that humans are better off when their cash balances increase and worse off when they decrease. A value change *is* the difference between equivalent cash balances. For that reason, I conclude that value changes should be reported on the income statement.

2.4 *Summary and Conclusions*

A major impediment to resolving questions about alternative accounting methods has been the utilization of criteria (or principles) that either do not discriminate or mistake definitions for criteria. For this reason, we must seek other criteria. It is generally agreed that accounting reports should be useful but that criterion is too general to be of much help in choosing accounting methods. The criterion of relevance, by contrast, refers to a specific decision context and a specific decision model. Identification of the decision context and the decision model permit an unequivocal specification of the relevant attributes.

A well-known, universally accepted decision model regarding exchanges of shares was identified. It was assumed that the objective is to maximize net cash flows or balances. (Strictly speaking, that assumption is unnecessary because the identified decision model could also be used to minimize cash flows or balances.) Since that decision model and the specified attributes are undisputed it permits three unequivocal conclusions:

Conclusion 1: Future cash flows are relevant to cash maximizing decisions regarding exchanges of shares.

Conclusion 2: Costs are relevant to cash maximizing decisions regarding purchases of unowned shares.

Conclusion 3: Exit values are relevant to cash maximizing decisions regarding selling of owned shares.

Since previously purchased — owned — shares are reported on the financial statements, the conclusions permit the elimination of costs, both current and historical. Only future cash flows and exit values are relevant to cash maximizing decisions regarding owned shares. Since the future is unknown, only forecasts of future cash flows can be reported. The problem of reporting forecasts is beyond the scope of this essay but if accurate forecasts can be made, the relevance criterion indicates that both should be reported. Until that issue is settled, exit values should be reported because they are necessary, but not sufficient, to cash-maximizing decisions regarding owned shares.

Conclusion 4: Exit values of owned shares should be reported on the balance sheet.

The forward-looking decisions require the distinction of the present cash balance from the expected future cash balance. Backward-looking evaluations of past decisions require the distinctions of the present cash balance from the past cash balance. When the share is owned, when the cash has not been collected, the forward-looking decisions require the comparison of the present cash equivalent balance with a future cash balance. Backward-looking evaluations require the comparison of the present cash equivalent balance with the past cash balance. Thus, interim gains for owned shares should be measured as the difference between the present cash equivalent balance and the previous cash balance.

Conclusion 5: Exit values of owned shares should be utilized as the basis for measuring past gains and those value gains should be reported on the income statement.

2.41 *Irrelevance* I cannot extend the conclusions to say that costs should *not* be reported on the basis of irrelevance because there may be other decision models which specify costs. I cannot think of anything that one can do with owned shares except sell or not sell them so I do not believe that other decision models exist. But that is a test of a joint hypothesis since it is at least equally likely that my failure to find such a decision model is due to my limitations as it is to the nonexistence of such decision models. In either event, I cannot prove the nonexistence of such decision models. As every auditor knows, it is much easier to prove the existence of an asset than it is to prove the nonexistence of a liability. For this reason, the onus is on others to prove the relevance of costs. In order to stimulate the provision of that proof, I will offer a conjecture that goes much beyond what has been demonstrated.

Conjecture 1: The cost of an owned share is irrelevant to all cash maximizing decisions regarding that share.

Note that it takes only *one* case of demonstrated relevance to prove that conjecture wrong since I have been so bold (or foolish) to say that costs are irrelevant to *all* cash maximizing decisions regarding an owned share. I challenge the reader to prove Conjecture 1 wrong.

2.42 *Ranking* In previous works I have attempted to rank the various alternatives on the basis of relevance. The reason for that attempt was to allow other criteria to influence the decision. For example, a characteristic of relevance is timeliness which would permit a finer partioning — a distinction between current costs and historical costs — resulting in the following:

(1) Exit values
(2) Current costs
(3) Historical costs.

One other criterion has already influenced that array, namely, the unknown future eliminated the future terminal exit value and future dividends. Where forecasts should be ranked is an open question. But note that such questions need not conflict with this ranking. For example, Staubus [1977] has presented a well-reasoned case for the reporting of evidence of future cash flows. I happen to be sceptical of our ability to accomplish that but I would be the last to deny the relevance of evidence of future cash flows. Thus, Staubus's work is complementary to the ranking, not conflicting.

The proposal for additional disclosure is also not in conflict. We could decide to adopt two of the methods, use multi-column reports or supplementary statements, and this would require that other criteria be utilized to decide which of the two. For example, Bedford and McKeown [1972] present a well-balanced case for reporting both (1) and (2). It is conceivable that such a combination would be more relevant than any single category. I am sceptical of that but I have not done enough work on combinations to permit me to draw a conclusion one way or the other. Another version of disclosure is to present any one or a combination of the above at lower levels of aggregation or in more detail. Others want to report all three methods plus anything else that seems useful. But at some point other criteria must come into play. Unbridled disclosure cannot be the answer because constraints such as the marginal cost of producing the marginal information exceeding its marginal benefits or information overload must come into force at some point. (See Revsine [1973], pp. 14-18 for a clear, concise statement of the problem.) Perhaps the relevance criterion would allow us to eliminate the lower ranked methods as those constraints become binding. In addition, there may be other conflicting criteria that would result in different rankings which would force us to consider trade-offs. At one time the criterion of objectivity was thought to conflict with the ranking but the redefinition of objectivity by Ijiri and Jaedicke [1966] permitted empirical tests, e.g. by McDonald [1968], which indicate that the criterion of objectivity is not in conflict with the above ranking and therefore trade-offs are not required.

Some studies on user wants conflict with the ranking. For example, Benston and

Krasney [1978] have reported that sophisticated users have a strong demand for historical costs. Other studies complement the ranking. For example, Tweedie [1977] has reported that naive users have a strong demand for cash flows and exit values. The combined test results serve only to refine the question: should we supply the information demanded by sophisticated users or naive users or both? In this sense, tests on user wants do not conflict with the ranking.[8] Since it is widely recognized that a market is efficient with respect to a given information set, then the market would still be efficient with respect to (1) or (2) or (1) and (2) etc. so that the ranking does not conflict with the efficient market tests. There is nothing that I am aware of in any of the behavioural studies, information economics, or agency theory, that conflicts.

For all these reasons, I would like to say Q.E.D. in regard to the relevance of the exit value of an owned share. That is a small achievement but my aspirations are small. I would like to see us solve one problem in accounting, however trivial, instead of continuing to move from one unsolved problem to another, instead of continuing to accumulate unresolved issues.

3. EXTENSIONS

> This new tinge to modern minds is a vehement and passionate interest in the relation of general principles to irreducible and stubborn facts. All the world over and at all times there have been practical men, absorbed in 'irreducible and stubborn facts': all the world over and at all times there have been men of philosophic temperament who have been absorbed in the weaving of general principles. It is this union of passionate interest in the detailed facts with equal devotion to abstract generalization which forms the novelty of our present society.
>
> Alfred North Whitehead

The reason for considering the special case in detail was the hope that it will provide insights into other special cases. The purpose of analysis — the breaking apart — is to discover commonalities which will permit a synthesis — the putting together — so that

[8] Of course, we could answer the question on the basis that sophisticated users know more than naive users, by definition, but I think that there is a more fundamental question involved. Namely, are we accountants passive suppliers of neutral information or are we a part of a milieu in which the kind of information that we supply influences the demand of the users? I have previously offered the conjecture ('hypothesis' overstates my feeble offering) that the latter is the case. Specifically, I conjectured that if we surveyed users the results would be that naive users would demand exit values and that sophisticated users would demand historical costs (Sterling [1970], pp. 54 and 343). The combined results of Benston and Krasney [1978] and Tweedie [1977] confirm that conjecture. Indeed the Benston and Krasney results show that less sophisticated users have a weaker demand for historical costs than do more sophisticated users. Tweedie's results show that naive users have a near zero demand for historical costs. Thus, the three data points suggest that demand for historical costs varies directly with sophistication.

In an attempt to explain the first conjecture, I offered a second conjecture that the issuance of a particular kind of information has a tendency to influence the users to demand that information. That conjecture was a *priori* with a smattering of anecdotal evidence. In an attempt to be clear on my meaning I used the analogy of a conditioned response in psychology and phrased the conjecture in terms of users being conditioned to respond to our reports. As subsequent events proved, that was unfortunate phraseology because it set off a firestorm of protest. Regardless of what it is called, however, it is clear that the combined test results are not a falsification of the second conjecture. In my mind at least, the combined results support the second conjecture and this causes me to worry about us being in a vicious circle in which supplying historical costs strengthens the demand for historical costs and the measurement of the demand strengthens our resolve to supply historical costs. Perhaps a reader can convert this vague conjecture into a testable hypothesis which will shed some light on the issues.

we have an understanding of all special cases. The ultimate goal is to weave a general principle that is founded on irreducible and stubborn facts.

3.1 *The Problem*

It often seems to me that we tend to view each type of exchange and each type of asset in isolation with the result that each type requires the application of a special principle. The problem with Generally Accepted Accounting Principles is that general refers to accepted instead of principles. Instead of there being a few general principles, there are a myriad of special principles. This, I believe, is what people mean when they say that there are *no* principles of accounting. What I think they are expressing is a desire for more general principles. I share that desire.

All general principles have limited application. That apparent paradox is illustrated by the general principles of plane geometry being limited to applications to flat surfaces. To show that a principle has a limited range of application is not sufficient reason to reject it since that is a characteristic of all principles. However, we prefer more general principles to less general principles for such reasons as simplicity, elegance and parsimony. The practical aspect of such a preference is that it aids in learning, reduces confusion and promotes consistency. A general principle is a powerful, practical tool in dealing with stubborn facts. Compare pre-Euclidean with post-Euclidean surveying and construction to see the practical power of the general principles of geometry. Thus, we continue to seek more general principles initially for theoretical reasons but utlimately for practical reasons. We seek fewer principles with broader ranges of application. To put it negatively, we would like to avoid inconsistencies due to the confusion stemming from too many special principles or from incompleteness in principles which require additional *ad hoc* principles. It is my contention that the very nature of the cost principle severely limits its range of application. To illustrate that the limitations are fundamental and pervasive, let us consider a few simple cases.

3.11 *Exchanges* A basic element of accounting is an exchange which, in general form, is symbolically represented by the following entry:

Time t	Account i	Dr	
	Account j		Cr

The entries that we deal with are of two basic types:

(a) Measure the debit and set the credit equal.
(b) Measure the credit and set the debit equal.

An example of a type (b) entry is a purchase in which we measure the cash sacrificed, set the debit to the asset equal and call it a cost. An example of a type (a) entry is borrowing funds in which we measure the cash received, set the credit to the payable equal and do *not* call it a cost. The cost principle is silent in regard to type (a) entries. Its range of application has been exceeded because neither the cash nor the payable is a cost. When we sell inventory we normally break the compound entry down into a type (b) entry for cost of goods sold and a type (a) entry for revenue. All compound entries can be decomposed in that fashion so that if we look to the elementary or simple (not compound) entries we can say that the cost principle does not apply to type (a) entries. Sometimes it does not apply to type (b) entries. For example, if we lend money, we measure the cash credit and set the receivable equal but seldom if ever do we speak of the receivable as a cost; instead we call it a loan or investment.

The point is that whether or not we apply the cost principle depends upon the *type of exchange*. Sometimes the cost principle applies and sometimes it does not. In order to know how to account we must know how to classify exchanges by type and then either apply the cost principle or apply some other special principle. If we are looking for a hierarchy of principles, we must seek the more general principle which allows us to classify exchanges because the type of exchange determines which special principle applies. In so far as I am aware, no such general principle exists.[9] We can distinguish the types of entries with ease in the majority of cases but in the absence of a general principle which classifies exchanges we will encounter difficulties as illustrated by barters.

3.12 *Barters* Recall that the cost principle requires that the purchased share be set equal to the cash paid and no gain or loss is recognized at the event of purchase. At sale the cash received is matched with the cost, either historical or current, and a gain or loss is recognized. The concepts are clear and easily applied when the exchanges are for cash but they provide no guidance when the share is exchanged for a non-cash asset. The first question that arises is whether the exchange is a purchase or a sale, a type (a) or type (b) entry. The question is important because different concepts are utilized. In terms of realization, historical cost prohibits the recognition of a gain until sale so that the sale is sometimes referred to as the 'crucial event'. The event of a sale is also crucial in current costing since it utilizes the same concept of matching costs and revenues at the event of sale.

Suppose that the cash maximizer acquired a share with a price of $1,000 by sacrificing land that had a historical cost of $500. This simple exchange is a quandary for historical costs since one cannot determine whether it is a purchase or sale because cash was not exchanged. If it is considered a sale, then the value of the share must be determined and the difference recorded as a gain. But that means that a gain is recognized upon acquisition of the share whereas previously a gain was prohibited upon acquisition of the share. If it is considered a purchase, then the value of the share is set equal to the sacrifice. That sacrifice could be taken to be the $500 historical cost but in a purchase the sacrifice is usually independently valued and the $500 is a previous sacrifice, not a current sacrifice. Setting the value of the share equal to $500 is utilizing the sacrifice of the cash for land instead of the current sacrifice for the share. But if we want to set the share equal to the current sacrifice it would require writing up the land to the current cost or exit value and such write-ups are prohibited by historical costs. That it is a quandary, that the cost principle does not extend to barters, is evidenced by two factors. First, it has required the issuance of a special principle based on the relative case of determination of the acquisition or the sacrifice. Second, an empirical test of how practitioners would record this simple exchange revealed that there were considerable differences of interpretation. (See Sterling, Tollefson and Flaherty [1979].)

[9] In Sterling and Flaherty [1971] the hypothesis was offered that the general principle was the relative liquidity of the exchanged assets. The test in Sterling, Tollefson and Flaherty [1979] revealed that the classification of barters by type (a) or (b) was more complicated since both conservatism and acquisition influenced the classification. Thus, the general principle, if it exists, eluded that test.

In this simple case the share can be recorded at any one of the following amounts:

(1) Current cost of the share.
(2) Exit value of the share.
(3) Current cost of the land.
(4) Exit value of the land.
(5) Historical cost of the land.

That the cost principle does not extend to this case (or that the practitioners were confused by too many special principles) is evidenced by the fact that each of the five values was selected by some practitioners. That the cost principle does not aid in distinguishing purchases from sales is evidenced by the fact that some practitioners recorded the difference as a realized gain and some as an unrealized gain.

Current costing results in less variation but it also requires that purchases be distinguished from sales because a different value is recorded at sale. Edwards [1975], one of the pioneers of current costing, states the question clearly and succinctly: 'The point at issue, of course, is not *whether* to value by current entry or exit prices, but *when* to shift from entry to exit values' (p. 240). After stating the alternative points at which one can shift, he says: 'The realization principle normally rests on the sale event to signal the displacement of entry values by exit values' (p. 240). Unfortunately, that answer does not extend to barters where the very question is whether it is a purchase or a sale.

To illustrate the problem, assume that the current cost of the land is $800. If this is a purchase we would set the share equal to the sacrifice.

1 Jan.	Marketable Securities	$800	
	Land		$800

If this is a sale, that would be the event at which we displace current costs with exit values.

1 Jan.	Marketable Securities	$900	
	Land		$800
	Gain on Sale		$100

Apparently current cost concepts do not extend to this case because we do not know which of the entries is appropriate, we do not know whether the exchange is a purchase or a sale. There is another issue involved because when an identical share was purchased in Section 2 it was recorded at $1,100 rather than either the $800 or $900 in the above entries. Thus, we must report different amounts for identical assets if we adopt either of the above entries. Of course, we can record the exchange either way and then write the share up to the $1,100 current cost. But if we do that we have made the determination on the type of asset, not on the type of exchange.

3.13 *Assets* Although it is often said that *all* assets are valued at cost, in fact only *some* assets are valued at cost. The exit value of an account receivable is measured at the time of sale and it continues to be reported at its exit value until collection. We do not write up accounts receivable to current cost as was a possibility when we acquired a share in the barter. But the acquisition of an account receivable and the sacrifice of land is, in fact, a barter since cash was not exchanged.

The point is that some types of assets are reported at their exit value and others at their cost. In the phylum of assets there are two classes:

(α) those at exit value such as cash and accounts receivable;

(β) those at cost such as inventory and equipment.

It seems to me that the argument of cost versus exit value reflects a significant difference in assets so that in classifying them we should take the first cut there. It is a much more significant difference than the current versus fixed classification that we now use. In addition, it is this classification that permits us to distinguish a purchase from a sale. A purchase is a type (b) exchange *because* the acquired asset is in class (β) and the sacrifice comes from class (α). The confusion about barters is *because* both the acquired share and the sacrificed land are in class (β). As a consequence it is neither a purchase nor a sale: one can look at it as purchasing a share as easily as selling land. For this reason, *ad hoc* principles are required and have in fact been used but the principle of ease of determination still does not resolve the question of whether the exchange should be treated like a type (a) or type (b) or some other special type.

As indicated by its name, the cost principle applies to those assets in class (β) but is silent in regard to those assets in class (α). The problem in regard to the barter then, is whether the share belongs in class (β) and should be reported at cost regardless of how acquired or whether its method of acquisition makes it a type (a) entry and therefore should be reported at exit value regardless of its class. I fear that the two concepts will be in perpetual opposition.

3.14 *Summary* Classification of assets and exchanges by type is a prerequisite to applying the cost principle. The range of application of the cost principle is limited to those assets that are stated at their sacrifice value and those exchanges that are classified as purchases. For all other types of assets and exchanges, other special principles are required.

Many recent controversies stem from the limited range of application of the cost principle. Purchase-pooling, for example, is in essence a barter question and the argument was over what type of exchange occurred. If it was a purchase, we got one kind of answer and if it was not a purchase, we got another. Front-end loading is, in essence, a barter question and the argument was about what type of exchange occurred. If it was a sale, we could realize income but if it was not a sale, we should not realize income. R + D, for example, is an asset classification question. If we try to measure its present benefits we get one type of answer but if we set it equal to its sacrifice value on the basis of expected future benefits, we get another answer. R + D is the same type of question as whether the acquired share should be treated like a receivable and valued at its exit value or treated like inventory and valued at its cost.

This indicates that the cost principle is a special principle and that a prerequisite is the provision of a general principle that will permit unambiguous classification of exchanges by type and assets by class. Exit values are fundamentally different. The concept is that all assets are, in essence, the same in regard to the measured attribute. The objective is to measure the benefit value of all assets. The exchange is a relatively unimportant event since it is conceived of as merely changing the form of benefit values, not a signal for switching from one kind of value to another. It is for these reasons that I believe that exit values have the potential of providing a much more general principle of valuation.

3.2 *Restatement*

Prior to extending the analysis to other special cases, I will restate the marketable security case in a more general and compact form. The elements of all three accounting methods are displayed in Exhibit 4. Column A is the future cash receipts from the terminal exit value. The future and past dividends, if any, are not displayed since they affect all accounting methods, decisions and income in exactly the same way. Since the terminal exit value lies in the future, I have entered a U for unknown in the pertinent cells. Columns B and C refer to the present, the date of the financial report, but B refers to the benefit of the cash receivable if sold while C refers to the sacrifice of the cash payable if purchased. Since the present price and commission are known I have entered a K in the pertinent cells. Column D is the sacrifice of the past cash paid at purchase and it is also known.

EXHIBIT 4

	Attribute	A	B	C	D
		Exit Value		Cost	
Accounting Method		Terminal	Current	Current	Historical
1	Historical Cost	U			K
2	Current Cost	U		K	K
3	Exit Value	U	K		K

Historical cost, row one, can be stated in terms of the ultimate gain, G.

$$A - D = G \qquad (1)$$

Since A is unknown, G cannot be reported on the income statement nor can A be reported on the present balance sheet. It is often said that the principal problem of accounting is that the future is unknown. In my view that is a misstatement of the problem. I would state the problem as the need to divide the total gain into the future expected gain versus the past gain, which requires the measurement of the present. To make the same point in different words, the present needs to be measured in order to make forward-looking decisions *and* to make backward-looking measurements of past gains.

That statement of the problem deserves emphasis. I used 'ultimate gain' because 'ultimate income' has been used by Canning [1929] and others to refer to the net cash receipts after liquidation of the firm. The ultimate income is what was reported in venture accounting and it referred to the cash receipts of the venture at liquidation minus the cash paid at formation. The switch to periodic reporting was undertaken because there was need for interim information between formation and liquidation of the firm. The same concept can be applied to individual assets. The ultimate gain from an asset is venture accounting and it refers to the cash received at sale minus the cash paid at purchase. We need to switch to periodic reporting because there is a need for interim information between purchase and sale of the asset. Thus, current price accounting is simply an extension of the idea of periodic reporting.

Historical cost accounting does not address the problem of periodic reporting of assets. It does not attempt to measure the present. Instead, it reports D on the present balance sheet, which is not relevant to present exchange decisions, and it reports a zero gain on the present income statement, which is a failure to attempt the measurement of past gains.

Both current cost and exit value address the problem of periodic reporting for assets, of measuring the present, but they measure different attributes. Current costs, row 2, divides the future from the past on the basis of the sacrifice from a present purchase.

$$(A - C) + (C - D) = G \tag{2}$$

The first term, A − C, is the expected future gain and the second term, C − D, is the past holding gain. The first term is relevant to the purchase versus not-purchase decisions since, in the absence of expected future dividends, a cash maximizer would not purchase the asset if $A < C$. However, since the asset is owned, the purchase versus not-purchase decision has already been made and therefore the current cost of owned assets is irrelevant to exchange decisions regarding owned assets. The past holding gain depends upon the cause of the current cost increase as to whether its benefit is conjectural, dubious or detrimental and therefore it is not a reliable measure.

Exit values, row 3, divide the future from the present on the basis of an immediate sale.

$$(A - B) + (B - D) = G \tag{3}$$

The first term, A − B, is the expected future gain and the second term, B − D, is the past value gain. The first term is relevant to the sell versus not-sell decision since, in the absence of expected future dividends, a cash maximizer would sell the asset if $A < B$. The second term, B − D, indicates the amount of the increase in the cash balance there would be if the asset were sold. Hence, it is a measurement of the incremental equivalent cash balance.

Therefore, I conclude that exit values should be reported on the present balance sheet since they are necessary, but not sufficient, for exchange decisions regarding owned assets; and that they be used to measure past gains since they are measures of incremental equivalent cash balances. I will leave open the question of the reporting of forecasts of A, the terminal exit value, since A is undeniably relevant but the forecast of A presents other problems.

3.3 *Extension to Other Assets*

Using Exhibit 4 and the three equations as the basis let us explore the measurement and reporting problems of three other types of assets. In effect, these are different types of firms. The marketable security case is what I have previously called a 'trading firm' which buys and sells in the same market. The inventory case is concerned with a 'merchandising firm' which buys in one market, e.g. wholesale, and sells in another market, e.g. retail. The firm does not change the form of the goods but merely holds them for sale, i.e., it adds time and place utility. The depreciables case is a 'producing firm' which is characterized by buying in the factor market and producing a product which it sells in a different market. In this case the firm produces a service, i.e., a perishable product. Receivables is a special case.

3.31 *Inventory* To separate the issues, consider a firm that holds no depreciables so that we can concentrate on inventory. The only activity of this firm is to purchase in one market for the wholesale price and sell at a later time in another market for the retail price. To hold the practical problem of determining the current cost or exit value in abeyance, let us consider goods where the wholesale market is fairly active and therefore the prices are fairly easy to observe. A real-world example is a retail coin dealer. In such a company there is no analogue for dividends. The inventory is analogous to the growth share with zero dividends.

Column A is the unknown future retail price. Of course the firm can mark up the cost and thereby *offer* the unit at any retail price that it chooses but whether it can sell for the offering retail price is problematical. It may be forced to mark down the retail price in order to sell. Another way to state the problem is that there is a delay, sometimes lengthy, between purchase and sale so that even if the firm is adamant about the retail price, the time period between purchase and sale is problematical. Viewing the future and the present as the same is the cause of the confusion about exit values recognizing a gain on purchase. Retail prices are exit values in the sense that they are selling prices but they are future exit values, not current exit values. For the same reason that we cannot report the terminal exit value of a marketable security, we cannot report the terminal exit value — retail price when sold — of a unit of inventory. The best we could do would be to report the forecasted retail price.

The current exit value, column B, is the wholesaler's purchase price less ancillary costs such as freight. The wholesaler also attempts to buy cheap and sell dear so that the wholesale purchase price is less than the wholesale selling price. The current cost, column C, is the wholesaler's selling price plus ancillary costs. Thus, the current cost of the retailer is greater than the exit value by the amount of wholesaler's margin plus twice the ancillary costs. The historical cost, column D, is the wholesaler's selling price plus ancillary costs at the event of purchase.

Given that interpretation, $A - D$ is the total gain, G, or in more familiar terminology A is the revenue, D is the historical cost of goods sold and G is the gross margin. The historical cost method would wait until the sale is consummated before recording a gain. Current cost and exit value would record interim gains as shown in equations (2) and (3).

The relevance of the exit value can be demonstrated in the same fashion as in Section 3.2. The expected future gain is $A - B$ and a cash maximizer will sell now for B if $A < B$. Alternatively, if the firm sets the price at A, then the time period until sale is the variable to be forecasted. The interest on B is forgone from holding the inventory until it can be sold for A and if that interest is greater than $A - B$, then a cash maximizer will sell now for B. For the same reasons, B is a measure of the present equivalent cash balance and therefore $B - D$ is a measure of the incremental equivalent cash balance.

One reason I selected a retail coin dealer as the prototype firm is that the wholesale price, and the wholesaler's margin, is fairly well known and therefore there is not much of a problem in determining the retailer's current cost or exit value. Another reason is that in recent years it has often been the case that $A < B$ and the retailer has, in fact, sold for the exit value. The sharp price increases of gold and silver resulted in sharp price increases in the wholesale price for common gold and silver coins because they had passed the melt-down point. The retail price was less responsive to the price of gold and silver resulting in many retailers deciding to sell their common coins to the wholesalers for the exit value. That is, deciding to sell for B because A < B was not a rare occurrence. Those who did not sell expected A > B. Some expected the retail price to become more responsive while others expected the price of gold and silver to continue to increase and therefore the wholesaler's purchase price would continue to increase. Thus, the terminal exit value was either the future retail price or the future wholesale price and we do not know which it was for any given retailer but we do know that they forecasted an A such that A > B. The point is that B was relevant to the decision regardless of whether their expected future gains were from retail sales or from, in effect, speculating in gold and silver. Their past gain, B − D, was the incremental equivalent cash balance at the time of the decision.[10]

The expected gain from purchase is A − C because a retailer would not purchase if A < C but since the inventory is owned, the current cost is irrelevant to exchange decisions. The past holding gain, C − D, depends upon future events. The fact that retail prices were not responsive to wholesale prices in this case is another example of the same kind of problem discussed in Section 2 regarding price increases and commission increases. Thus, C − D is at best conjectural, it may be dubious and perhaps it is detrimental.

Historical cost, D, was relevant to the purchase decision but since the purchase has been made it is no longer relevant. Reporting D or G = O is irrelevant to present exchange decisions, both purchase versus not purchase and sell versus not sell. If the inventory has been allocated by LIFO, FIFO, moving average or whatever then it is not relevant to any decision — past, present or future — that I have been able to identify.

For the same reasons as given in Section 2.4, I cannot prove the irrelevance of current costs or historical costs. I can only rephrase Conjecture 1 by substituting 'inventory' for 'share' and offer the same challenge. One caveat is that extending the time period beyond the sale of the inventory now on hand requires the forecast of the future cost so that even if one assumes continued replacement of identical units, it is the future cost, not the current cost, that is relevant to the decision. The long-run decisions require the forecast of the long-run net cash flows which in this case consist of the inflows from future retail prices and outflows for future wholesale prices plus ancillaries as well as the quantities purchased and sold and the dates of purchase and sale. Once all those forecasts have been made, then we can discount the net cash flows to make long-run decisions. In

[10] Subsequent events, particularly silver prices, have shown that those who expected A > B were wrong. The retail price never did move up to parallel the earlier higher current cost and the wholesale price of silver coins declined precipitously. Exit values would report that subsequent decline as a loss in subsequent periods. Some would say that the subsequent loss proved that the previous reported gain was 'wrong' and 'misleading'. The search is for irrevocable profits which subsequent events cannot erase. I fear that the search is doomed to fail because the realized gains that were in fact reported by coin dealers were in fact erased by subsequent events when they reported realized losses. Thus, the criterion of irrevocable gains does not discriminate. The same is true for the criterion of 'yo yo profits'. Value gains would in fact yo yo in this case as would holding gains. Those dealers who did not sell would report a zero realized gain which did not yo yo. But the difference then is concerned with the *report* of the phenomena, not the phenomena. I could measure my past weight and continue to report that magnitude so that the result would be a *reported* zero weight gain. If my weight did yo yo then we have a choice of the report faithfully representing that yo yo gain or reporting a zero gain. The notion of yo yo profits is a definition of a different method of reporting, not a criterion. In addition, the realized profits did in fact yo yo so that the notion does not discriminate.

the meantime we must remember the ancient economic axiom that the long run consists of a series of short runs.

3.32 *Depreciables* To separate the issues, let us consider a firm that holds no inventory so that we can concentrate on depreciables. To hold the practical problems of determining current cost or exit value in abeyance, let us consider the depreciation of an automobile since the active market for used automobiles will allow us to concentrate on the concept rather than the magnitude. A real-world counterpart is a taxi company. In such a company the analogue for dividends is the cash inflows from fares less the cash outflows for fuel, repairs, etc. Since these net cash flows, both past and future, are the same for all three accounting methods, they are omitted from Exhibit 4.

Column A is the unknown future salvage value. The magnitudes for columns B and C would be obtained from the current listings of used car prices, with B obtained from the 'wholesale price' column and C from the 'retail price' column. That is, if the automobile were to be purchased, one would have to pay the retail price to the automobile dealer and hence that is its current cost while if it were sold, one would receive the wholesale price and hence that is its exit value.

Given that interpretation, A − D is the ultimate gain, G, which is expected to be negative in this case and therefore it is an expected ultimate loss. In more familiar terminology, it is the expected total depreciation. The historical cost method would amortize or allocate that amount to each time period. Current cost and exit values would record interim losses (depreciation expense) as shown in equations (2) and (3).

The relevance of the exit value can be demonstrated in the same fashion as in Section 3.2. The expected future value loss is A − B and a cash maximizer would sell now for B if the future net cash flow from fares is less than the forecasted value loss. If the opposite is true, then we can only say that the cash maximizer would tend to not sell. In addition, since the terminal exit value is likely to be far in the future and relatively insignificant, it will be more convenient to include it as one of the future cash inflows. Then all future cash flows would be discounted and compared to B in order to decide to sell or not sell. Similarly B − D is the decline in the equivalent cash balance and therefore B − D is a measure of decremental cash to date.

Current cost would be relevant if one were deciding to purchase or not purchase an identical automobile but it is not relevant if the automobile is already owned. If the time horizon goes to or beyond replacing, then the future replacement cost, not the current cost, is relevant because it is one component of the forecasted future cash outflows. In regard to the holding loss, C − D, we face similar problems to those discussed above. If Detroit-built taxis increase in price and Japanese-built taxis decrease in price with concomitant increases and decreases in current costs, will the owners of Detroit taxis be better off and the owners of Japanese taxis be worse off? The effect on the future cash flows from fares due to such current cost changes is at best conjectural. The analogue for a commission increase is a sales tax increase or the imposition of a transaction tax which would increase the current cost and decrease the exit value of the automobile. The effect of such a tax on the future cash flows from the terminal exit value is detrimental. Therefore, C − D is not a reliable measure of past gains.

Historical cost depreciation is defined as an allocation and (A − D)/L is a straight line where L is the life, 2[(A − D)/L] is first year double declining balance, and so forth.

Some have proposed that 'current cost depreciation' be defined as the cost of a *new identical* asset which is then allocated in the same fashion as historical cost. Others have proposed 'replacement cost depreciation' which is an allocation of the cost of a *new non-identical* asset. The characteristic common to all such proposals is that they are allocations, not measurements, and such allocations are not relevant to any decisions that I have been able to identify. Current cost is relevant to the present purchase decision and historical cost — past cash paid — was relevant to the past purchase decision but I have never found one instance of decision relevance for an allocated cost, neither current, historical nor replacement.

For the same reasons as given in Section 2.4, I cannot prove the irrelevance of current costs, historical costs or allocated costs. I can only rephrase Conjecture 1 and offer the same challenge. The same caveat applies regarding the future costs versus the current costs.

3.31 *Receivables* It is rare to find mention of receivables in the context of costs, either historical or current. I include this discussion for precisely that reason. Consider a firm that holds an interest bearing note receivable. The interest is the analogue for dividends and is excluded from Exhibit 4. Since notes are traded we could determine the amount of cash that would be paid if purchased or received if sold (factored or discounted without recourse) and we could enter these amounts in columns B and C.

It would appear that under GAAP notes receivable are in class (α) — stated at exit value — having been acquired in a sale or type (a) exchange. But the provision for doubtful accounts makes it appear that we are forecasting a terminal exit value instead of measuring a current exit value. Thus, there is a question of whether GAAP would place notes in column A, the terminal exit value, or in column B, the current exit value. The literature is of little help. First, it is exceptionally sparse. Second, it is exceptionally terse and far from explicit. It seems that the tight focus on costs, on type (b) exchanges and class (β) assets, has resulted in a benign neglect of type (a) exchanges and class (α) assets. Since the cost principle does not extend to notes and since the literature is sparse and terse, I cannot determine exactly what it is that we have been trying to measure in this case.

I think that others share my confusion. The problem is exemplified by the following entries:

Type (a)	Notes Receivable	Face	
	Revenue		Face
Type (b)	Cost of Land Sold	Cost	
	Land		Cost

That the cost principle does not extend to the type (a) entry and the class (α) notes is evidenced by two factors.

First, accountants were rocked by the bad press resulting from disclosures about land dealings, especially 'front end loading'. The problem was that the notes issued in payment for development land were very long term, with interest rates much below the market, with miniscule down payments and, as subsequent events proved, they had an enormous default rate. Why did the auditors issue a clean opinion on the financial reports of land development companies and their financiers? One hypothesis that was advanced in the press is that they were immoral or grossly negligent. My hypothesis is that they did not have an adequate theory to guide them, that the theory they applied was based on costs so that they focused on the second entry almost to the exclusion of the first entry.

Second, consider our reaction to the bad press. In its surprise and dismay, the AICPA issued some very specific principles regarding when a sale is a sale, that is, when we should apply accrual methods as opposed to cost recovery or instalment methods. Many of the tests for the distinction are based on future events. My hypothesis is that the reason the AICPA had to issue such specific and complex rules is that there was no general concept that could be used as guidance, that the concepts at hand were so focused on costs that the standard setters could not do much other than what they did. Consider their words: '*Implicit* in the realization principle is the assumption that consideration received in the exchanges can be valued with reasonable certainty' (AICPA [1973], p. 4, emphasis added). Whether or not my hypothesis is correct, the principles issued are (1) so specific that they are not likely to be applicable to the next, unknown problem which will result in a bad press; (2) so detailed that they almost invite compliance with the letter instead of the spirit; (3) so complex that they are difficult to apply; and (4) require that the auditor forecast the future.

That description is too brief to cover such an important topic but it provides a broad outline. My proposed solution is to insert the notes receivable in column B. That is, to ask what is the amount that they would fetch in an immediate sale, i.e., factored or discounted without recourse. Column A is the unknown amount of cash that will be collected in the future just as the terminal exit value of a share is unknown. Columns C and D are not applicable since receivables are not costs.

The relevance analysis is the same. A cash maximizer would sell the notes for B if $A < B$. If $A > B$ the maximizer would tend to keep them for collection and $A - B$ is the expected future gain. Note that $(A - B)/B$ *is* the market rate of interest for notes of *this* risk class. That is, in the same way that the market rate of interest for a bond is determined by observing its current price, the market rate for the notes is determined by observing their current exit values. Thus, B is relevant to exchange decisions for notes in the same way as it was relevant for marketable securities.

The use of B to determine the revenues is consistent with the idea of using cash to determine the revenues when the sale is for cash. That is, B is an attempt to determine how much cash would be received if the notes were sold. Note, incidentally, B would be much less than the face value of the notes and would be much closer to, perhaps even less than, the cost of the land which would prohibit front-end loading.

No one can deny that it will be difficult to determine the amount that the notes would fetch in an immediate sale. But is it reasonable to think that it is easier to forecast the future collections via forecasting the uncollectables? I think not. Is it more practical to apply the specific, complex rules which require determining such things as whether the property will be useful for residential purposes at the end of the payment period, i.e., what the developer will do in the future? I think not. In short, I think that determining the exit value is more practical and less difficult than the application of the specific rules. In considering that issue we should distinguish the difficulty of determination from the determination of a zero amount. Sometimes we say that it is impossible to factor the notes without recourse and therefore they have *no* exit value. If that statement refers to the fact that there is an inactive market, it is an expression of a difficult measurement problem. If it refers to the fact that no one would purchase the notes, it is an expression of a zero exit value. If the latter, then we should record the notes at zero, recognizing a loss, and wait for future collections before recording a gain. That is not an application of a specific instalment-sales-method-of-realization rule but rather the application of the general concept of measuring the amount that would be received from an immediate sale of *any* asset.

3.4 *Extension to Multiple Assets*

The previous cases may be characterized as single asset firms. The question is whether we can extend the analysis and conclusions to firms with multiple assets. My answer is: I am not sure. To illustrate the nature of the problem, I will return to considering marketable securities since their simplicity aids in understanding as well as exposition. The question is whether the analysis and conclusions regarding a single share can be extended to a block of several shares. If the decision context is to purchase or sell the block, it is clear that it can be extended. But a problem arises if we do not know the decision context because the sum of the exit value of each share is likely to be different from the exit value of the block.

This has become known as the 'additivity' or the 'aggregation' problem and has received considerable attention. The problem can easily be explained in this simple case. An extra commission, called an 'odd lot differential' is charged for sales of single shares. For shares traded in blocks of 100, called 'round lots', no odd lot differential is charged. If the odd lot differential is $0.25, then the exit value of a round lot is $25 greater than the exit value of 100 single shares. To use the same figures as in the journal entries, if there were 100 shares at a price of $10 each, instead of one share at a price of $1,000, the exit value of the round lot is $900 but it is $875 for the single shares. The question is whether we should report the $900 or the $875 as the exit value.

Examination of the various proposed solutions to the problem would lead us too far afield. Suffice it to say that many think that the problem is intractable (see Vickrey [1970]) and it has often been used as a criterion in criticizing exit values. I, too, am not completely satisfied that the problem in all its ramifications has been solved. Notice, however, that the problem is symmetrical. It affects current costs in exactly the same way. Since current cost is the amount of cash paid if purchased, then the amount paid for 100 single shares would be $1,125 instead of $1,100 for the round lot. Thus, the criterion of additivity fails to discriminate.

In regard to historical costs, it is the same problem but it is called aggregation or disaggregation. If we have 100 shares at a price of $10 each, we multiply 100 times $11.25 (or $8.75) and call the product of $1,125 (or $875) the current cost (or exit value) of the 100 shares when the current cost (or exit value) of a round lot of $1,100 (or $900). If we have $1,100 historical cost of the round lot, we divide $1,100 by 100 shares and call the quotient of $11 the historical cost per unit when the cost per unit is $11.25. Any questions raised about the multiplication must also be raised about the division. If there is a problem of aggregation there will be a problem of disaggregation stemming from the same cause. Thus, the criterion of aggregation fails to discriminate.

The problem can be divided. First, is the question of whether cash receivable or payable can be added. There is general agreement that it can. (See Vickrey's [1970] discussion of 'numerosity'.) Second, is the question of the category we should use to measure the cash receivable or payable. For example, one category is the single share and another is the round lot. Given a categorization, additivity can be demonstrated. (See Trowell [1978] for a rigorous mathematical demonstration, or Sterling [1979], Section 10.3 for a verbal demonstration.) But that leaves open the question of what categories should be used. Should we use the category of single shares, of round lots, of all shares of the same kind (e.g., all GM in one category and all GE in another) or all shares in the portfolio? The problem has me stumped. I had hoped that separating additivity from categorization would make it more tractable but it has not. Perhaps the reader can provide a solution. In the meantime, note that the problem is applicable to both current costs and exit values. Thus, categorization does not discriminate current costs from exit values.

The problem also extends to historical costs. We must decide on account categories when we make the entry for purchases. When prices have fluctuated we set up sub-categories by time of purchase. Then at sale we must decide which of these sub-categories should be used to make the entry. In more familiar terminology, we must choose between FIFO and LIFO. Thomas [1974] has demonstrated that the selection of the category — LIFO versus FIFO — is arbitrary. But the same can be said for the choice of categories in current costs or exit values. They are equally arbitrary and therefore the criterion of arbitrary categories does not discriminate.

However, the criterion of relevance does discriminate. The current cost of any given category is relevant to decisions regarding purchases of *that* category. The exit value of any given category is relevant to decisions regarding sales of *that* category. By contrast, the historical cost categories are not relevant to any decision model that I have been able to identify.

To put it another way, the historical cost categories do not have an empirical referent. To add different past costs of shares does not result in a sum that refers to anything in the real world that I have been able to identify. Until that empirical referent has been identified, we must say that allocated historical costs are not additive and therefore the additivity criterion discriminates allocated historical costs from current prices. For the same reason, they are not empirically testable. In previous works I have proposed a sub-criterion of empirical testability because that is a necessary, but not a sufficient, condition for relevance.[11]

The above analysis can be extended to other assets with the same results. For example, the additivity of GM plus GE shares is the same type of problem of adding inventory and a depreciable asset. Choosing the category of the entire portfolio versus the categories of GM plus GE is the same type of problem as deciding to value the firm

[11] In addition, in a fundamental sense it is a necessary, but not a sufficient, condition for auditability. Except in the sense of recalculation, historical cost categories are not auditable because they are not additive, not empirically testable. Contrast the method of auditing the quantity of the inventory to the book value of the inventory. That quantities are additive, empirically testable, is evidenced by separate physical count which confirms the sum of the quantity numerals in the accounts. That historical costs are not additive is evidenced by the fact that there is no way to measure separately the book value which would either confirm or deny the sum of cost numerals in the accounts.

as a whole versus summing the assets. However, there is no analogue for adding class (α) and (β) assets. In adding the shares we were always adding either costs or exit values but in adding the assets of the firm the cost principle requires that we add costs to exit values. That concerns me since it is the summation of different attributes. Exit valuation does not face that problem since all assets are measured by the same attribute. For that reason I would give exit valuation the edge in determining total assets by summing various asset categories.

3.5 *Summary and Conclusions*

Application of the cost principle requires that assets be divided into classes (α) and (β). When the exchange is interclass it permits the distinction between type (a) and (b) entries but when the exchange is intraclass we cannot make the distinction. A requirement of application of the cost principle is a separate principle for all intraclass exchanges. To date we have not identified a general principle for intraclass exchanges so that each new exchange requires a principle specific to that exchange. For this reason, we have witnessed controversies as new exchanges are invented and it has required the issuance of *ad hoc* principles to resolve each controversy. We can expect new exchanges to continue to be invented and each to bring a new controversy.

The criterion of relevance can be extended to other types of assets. Each type of asset is similar to the simple marketable security case and there is an analogue for dividends, either zero as in inventory or positive as in depreciables, and an analogue for the various values. Therefore, the conclusions drawn in Section 2 are applicable to each type of asset by simply substituting different names of assets. The conjecture and challenge is also applicable with the same substitution of names.

The criterion of relevance can also be extended to multiple assets but with less definitive conclusions. The problems of additivity and categorization plague all three accounting methods and therefore we cannot use those problems as criteria for choosing a method. Since exit values do not have two classes of assets based on measuring different attributes, they suffer less from this problem than does cost. For the same reason, exit value is a more general principle and therefore should require fewer *ad hoc* principles.

4. GENERALIZATION

> It has been said that democracy is the worst form of government except all those other forms that have been tried from time to time.
>
> Winston Churchill

The ways in which assets vary are almost infinite. One general variation is that some assets produce a dividend or analogue which we call by various names such as interest, rent, net proceeds from sale of the outputs less the cost of purchasing the inputs. Other assets do not produce a dividend; the only future cash inflow comes from the terminal exit value or analogue. Examples are growth (zero dividend) shares, non-interest-bearing notes, unrented land, and inventory.

Asset commonalities are few but significant. Exhibit 5 displays the commonalities that have been discussed in this essay.

EXHIBIT 5

Price \ Temporal Location	Past	Present	Future
Purchase	Historical Cost	Current Cost	Replacement Cost
Sale	Historical Exit Value	Current Exit Value	Terminal Exit Value

There are two prices — purchase and sale — for any given asset at any given moment in time. Except for rare and temporary conditions, such as arbitraging, the cost of purchasing any asset is greater than the exit value from the sale of that asset at all moments in time. We have a choice of prices, of reporting the cost or the exit value. In addition, we have a choice of temporal locations, of reporting a past, present, or forecasted future price. Thus, we have a choice of six values to report. Of course, there are many other variations. Past prices could be allocated, for example, and forecasted future prices could be discounted but, at base, the six values displayed in Exhibit 5 are the choices that we face.

Since six values are undoubtedly too many to report, we must select which one(s) to report. The criterion for selection proposed in this essay is relevance to specific decision models as opposed to unspecific usefulness or as opposed to criteria that do not discriminate. I believe that the decision model examined in this essay is applicable to all assets. That is, one must decide to own or not to own any given asset, to purchase or not purchase if unowned or to sell or not to sell if owned. That decision model specifies the current exit value and terminal exit value, as well as the future dividends or analogue if any, of all owned assets. That decision model does not specify the cost, neither historical nor current, of owned assets.

Since the terminal exit value and future dividend is unknown, the only relevant value that we can report, as opposed to reporting somebody's forecast of a future value, is the current exit value. Therefore, I conclude that at a minimum we should report the current exit value of all owned assets.

There are many problems in reporting exit values. One is additivity or categorization but since all valuation methods are equally vexed by that problem, it fails to discriminate.

Another is measurement when markets are incomplete or thin but that problem also effects all valuation methods equally and therefore does not discriminate. Such problems have been sufficient to cause many accountants to reject the conclusion that we report exit values. I agree that exit valuation presents problems but I think that it presents fewer problems than the alternatives that have been tried or proposed.

It often seems to me that those who reject reporting exit values because of additivity, incomplete markets, social welfare effects and similar reasons are looking for perfection, for a valuation method that will be problem free. Until such a perfect method is discovered, until the millennium arrives, we must report something even if imperfect. Therefore, it seems clear that we must compare the alternatives, apply the criteria with equal force to all alternatives, and then select the alternative that best meets the criteria, to choose the one that is least imperfect. When I follow that procedure in seeking a generalized method of reporting, I reach the same conclusion as Churchill in regard to democracy: exit valuation is the worst form of reporting except for all those other forms that have been tried or proposed from time to time.

REFERENCES

American Institute of Certified Public Accountants, *Accounting for Retail Land Sales* (An AICPA Accounting Guide), AICPA, 1973.

Bedford, N. M. and J. C. McKeown, 'Comparative Analysis of Net Realizable Value and Replacement Costing', *The Accounting Review,* April 1972.

Benston, G. J. and M. A. Krasney, 'DAAM: The Demand for Alternative Accounting Measurements", *Journal of Accounting Research,* Supplement, 1978.

Canning, J. B., *The Economics of Accountancy,* Roland Press, 1929.

Edwards, E. O., 'The State of Current Value Accounting', *The Accounting Review,* April 1975.

Edwards, E. O. and P. W. Bell, *The Theory and Measurement of Business Income,* University of California Press, Berkeley 1964.

Financial Accounting Standards Board, Statement of Financial Accounting Standards No. 33, *Financial Reporting and Changing Prices,* FASB, September 1979.

Ijiri, Y. and R. K. Jaedicke, 'Reliability and Objectivity of Accounting Measurements", *The Accounting Review,* July 1966.

McDonald, D. L., 'A Test Application of the Feasibility of Market Based Measures of Accounting", *Journal of Accounting Research,* Spring 1968.

Revsine, L., *Replacement Cost Accounting,* Prentice-Hall, Englewood Cliffs, N.J. 1973.

Rosenfield, P., 'Reporting Subjunctive Gains and Losses', *The Accounting Review,* October 1969.

Samuelson, R. A., 'Should Replacement-Cost Changes be Included in Income?', *The Accounting Review,* April 1980.

Staubus, G. J., *Making Accounting Decisions,* Scholars Book Co., Houston 1977.

Sterling, R. R., *Theory of the Measurement of Enterprise Income,* The University Press of Kansas, 1970.

———, *Toward a Science of Accounting,* Scholars Book Co., Houston 1979.

Sterling, R. R. and R. E. Flaherty, 'The Role of Liquidity in Exchange Valuation', *The Accounting Review,* July 1971.

Sterling, R. R., J. O. Tollefson and R. E. Flaherty, 'Exchange Valuation: An Empirical Test', *The Accounting Review,* October 1979.

Thomas, A. L., Studies in Accounting Research No. 9, *The Allocation Problem: Part Two,* American Accounting Association, 1974.

Trowell, J., 'A Study of the Additivity of CCE with Respect to Assets', unpublished Master's thesis, University of New England, Armidale, N.S.W. 1978.

Tweedie, D. P., 'Cash Flows and Realisable Values: the Intuitive Accounting Concepts? An Empirical Test', *Accounting and Business Research,* Winter 1977.

Vancil, R. F. and R. L. Weil, *Replacement Cost Accounting: Readings on Concepts, Uses & Methods,* Thomas Horton & Daughters, 1976.

Vickrey, D. W., 'Is Accounting a Measurement Discipline?', *The Accounting Review,* October 1970.

The conceptual framework: an assessment

Robert R. Sterling, *Ph.D., senior fellow of the Financial Accounting Standards Board, Stamford, Connecticut, says he is both optimistic and pessimistic about the board's progress in constructing a conceptual framework for financial accounting and reporting. The following article is an adaptation of his presentation at a 1980 FASB-sponsored symposium in New York City on the framework when Dr. Sterling was Winspear Distinguished Professor at the University of Alberta, Edmonton, Alberta, Canada.*

In reflecting on the Financial Accounting Standards Board's project on the conceptual framework for financial accounting and reporting, I was reminded of the old saying that an optimist is one who sees a glass as half full, while a pessimist is one who sees the same glass as half empty. In regard to the conceptual framework, I am both an optimist and a pessimist.

The framework in general

Looking backward, I am an optimist. When comparing the framework to the previous attempts (e.g., Accounting Research Bulletin no. 43, *Restatement and Revision of Accounting Research Bulletins*,[1] and Accounting Principles Board Statement no. 4, *Basic Concepts and Accounting Principles Underlying Financial Statements of Business Enterprises*[2]), I am much impressed by the significant accomplishments of the FASB. The board is to be congratulated on how far it has come. It is to be congratulated for what it has eliminated from as well as for what it has included in the framework. The fact that it has eliminated some of those recurring, tired, demonstrably invalid concepts from the framework is equally as important as the fact that it has included some much-needed new perspectives from the research literature.

Looking forward, I am a pessimist. The half-empty portion needs to be filled rather urgently, but the obstacles to be overcome are even more formidable than those encountered in filling the first half. The problem is that the portion of the framework that has been completed is more general and more abstract than the portion yet to come. When the board begins to tackle the more specific, more concrete portion—e.g., the statements on recognition, measurement and income—interest in the project is certain to increase. Few managers and practitioners are interested in abstract theory, but nearly all will be most interested in a change in recognizing revenue or valuing assets or adjusting for inflation. As the framework gets nearer completion the likely changes will

[1] Accounting Research Bulletin no. 43, *Restatement and Revision of Accounting Research Bulletins* (New York: American Institute of Accountants, 1953).

[2] Accounting Principles Board Statement no. 4, *Basic Concepts and Accounting Principles Underlying Financial Statements of Business Enterprises* (New York: AICPA, 1970).

be more easily anticipated, and therefore it will be easier to anticipate real or imagined adversely affected vested interests. Thus, progress toward completion will be accompanied by a crescendo of perceived adversely affected vested interests, which in turn will be accompanied by a crescendo of resistance and criticism. The resistance may become so great that the board will find it impossible to complete the framework. If so, it may be forced to return to the procedure of putting out brush fires and abandon the project. I am not forecasting that outcome, but I do think that it is a possibility that shouldn't be lightly dismissed.

In short, in looking at the history I see the glass to be half full in that the board has made much more progress than its predecessors, but in forecasting the future I see the glass to be half empty in that each step in filling it is going to be increasingly difficult.

The concepts in particular

I am also both an optimist and a pessimist when I examine the individual concepts. In comparing the previous concepts to the ones the board has defined, I see great progress. Consider, for example, the previous definition of an asset as anything with a debit balance after the books are closed. The board recognized the deficiency of this definition—that it provided no guidance in deciding what was or was not an asset. As a result of this recognition, a much superior definition of an asset was developed in Concepts Statement no. 3, *Elements of Financial Statements of Business Enterprises*.[3] The definition is superior because it does provide guidance, stating three characteristics that a thing must possess in order to qualify as an asset. The glass is half full because the board recognized the deficiency. The glass is half empty because the board didn't recognize the basic nature of the deficiency and therefore only partially rectified it.

In my view the basic nature of the deficiency of the previous definition is that it is an internal definition—a word being defined by other words without reference to empirical phenomena.[4] It doesn't tell you what real-world phenomena the debit balances refer to so that you can see whether those phenomena exist and thereby determine whether there should be debit balances, much less the magnitude of those balances. In other words, it wasn't an empirical concept and therefore

[3] Financial Accounting Standards Board Concepts Statement no. 3, *Elements of Financial Statements of Business Enterprises* (Stamford, Conn.: FASB, 1980).

[4] For a general discussion of the nature of definitions, see, e.g., Peter Caws, *The Philosophy of Science* (D. Van Nostrand Co., Inc., 1966), ch. 7. Specifically in regard to internal definitions, he says (p.46): "Definitions of terms by reference to other terms belonging to the same language systems (for example, the language of physics) are *internal* definitions, and one might, by using this kind of definition alone, build a whole ingrown language whose terms refer to each other but to nothing else. Definitions which go outside the language system to something else—perception, for instance—are external definitions and they are required if the whole system is to mean anything."

I think this is an uncomfortably accurate description of traditional accounting. It is an ingrown system whose terms refer to each other but to nothing else. As such it is meaningless. To its great credit, the board is trying to provide meaning to accounting terms, but I fear it doesn't fully recognize that the requisite for meaning is that the major terms of a language system have empirical referents.

Caws goes on to warn that "one useful but dangerous property of intensional definitions—and of internal definitions in general—is that names for nonexistent objects may be created by means of them" and illustrates that danger by relating physicists' experience with ether. Reasoning led physicists to believe in a substance which they named ether, and they defined it by stating two characteristics (low density and high rigidity) that a thing must possess in order to qualify as ether. Up to this point, the paths of physics and accounting are parallel. The board has provided intensional or internal definitions, based on reasoning, that state the characteristics of the thing they are defining. My fear is that at this point the paths will diverge. In the physics case careful empirical testing failed to reveal the existence of ether. Since the term had no empirical referent, it was expunged from the vocabulary of physics. In the accounting case we aren't yet fully aware of the requirement that terms have empirical referents, and therefore we aren't likely to even recognize that we have defined nonexistent things and that those terms lack meaning, much less to expunge them from our vocabulary.

wasn't subject to empirical test. In the terminology of the board, it couldn't have the quality of representational faithfulness because it didn't specify what it was supposed to represent, if anything.

The new definition, albeit much superior to the old, doesn't exhibit recognition of the basic nature of the deficiency because it permits some nonempirical things to qualify as assets. As a consequence, the definition won't eliminate as many alternatives as the board evidently desires. Even more deleterious is the confusion that this will cause in completing the framework. The measurement project, for example, may founder in this confusion because it will be required to specify methods of measuring things that don't exist—a contradiction of the meaning of measurement.

I think that the failure to be clear about requiring our figures to be empirically testable is a fundamental flaw that is certain to weaken the entire project, perhaps causing it to collapse. Empirical testability is crucial, being among other things a necessary but not sufficient condition for relevance. The placement of representational faithfulness in the hierarchy of concepts and the discussion of that concept indicate confusion about its meaning and lack of appreciation of its crucial nature.

In short, the board has made commendable improvements in the concepts, but the root cause of the previous deficiencies hasn't been identified, and therefore the concepts will need rather substantial refinement in the near future. I am an optimist because of the improvements. I am a pessimist because I fear that neither the board nor its constituencies will have the stomach for a near-term substantial refinement of the concepts, and therefore the basic deficiency will continue to plague us.

Connections between concepts and conclusions

Those who see the framework as providing immediate solutions to specific practice alternatives are bound to be disappointed. Those who see the framework as a first step toward better financial reporting (i.e., reporting relevant, comparable figures) are less likely to be disappointed.

I am optimistic because the first step has been taken, but I am pessimistic about the next step because, if history is used as a guide, it is likely to be a misstep. In my view the next essential step is to display replicable logical connections between the concepts and the conclusions about specific practices. Provision of such connections is likely to require honing the concepts to make them logically fertile. In the rush to get to conclusions about specific practices, the board may decide, or be pressured into deciding, to try to use the concepts as premises for reasoning to specific practice standards without providing the logical connections. That is, it may skip the second step in an attempt to show that the framework will bear fruit.

I think that skipping the second step would be a serious mistake. I would urge the board to continue the dual effort: continue work on the concepts, accompanied by ad hoc pronouncements on troublesome issues. If this isn't done, if the concepts aren't honed to the point where the logical connections are at least plausible, preferably replicable, the framework is likely to be at best useless and at worst used to rationalize preconceived positions that are likely to be contradictory. This has been the outcome of past attempts at conceptual frameworks. Everybody knew that such things as conservatism and going concern were "basic concepts," but nobody was able to provide even plausible connections between those concepts and, say, Lifo versus Fifo or historical versus current costs. Without the connections, the concepts were useless and therefore were ignored except when they could be used to bolster preconceived positions that were often contradictory.[5] I fear that the framework will suffer the same fate, unless the danger is recognized and a concerted effort is made to provide the logical connections.

In short, the board has taken an important first step, but it hasn't explicitly addressed the essential second step of providing logical connections between the concepts and conclusions about specific practices. I am an optimist because a first giant step has been taken. I am a pessimist because the board may overlook the second step or, perhaps more likely, be pressured into skipping the second step.

Benefits

I don't see much in the way of short-run, direct, practical benefits from the framework. One can't posit the concepts that have been provided for the purpose of deciding whether to capitalize research and development; that continues to require reference to a specific standard. Since practitioners—both preparers and auditors—want that kind of direct guidance, I don't think that they will find the framework helpful, and I expect they will ignore it. Even when the concepts are honed to the point that such conclusions can be reached, I don't expect them to be of much direct benefit to the present generation of practitioners. Rigorous logic hasn't been a tool of

[5]One example was the positing of the going concern concept in order to conclude that assets were intended for use instead of for sale, from which it is "obvious" that present market values are irrelevant and historical costs are relevant. That was (and in some circles still is) the most prevalent and telling argument for historical costs in general, and it was often referenced in discussions of valuing plant and equipment. However, it was conveniently forgotten when discussing marketable securities and inventories intended for sale instead of for use, from which it is equally "obvious" that historical costs are irrelevant and market values are relevant. But this didn't deter those with strong preconceptions; they posited the going concern in order to conclude that the company would be able to sell the inventory in the normal course of business and therefore have a future sales price, from which it is "obvious" that its past purchase price is relevant and its present market value is irrelevant. Unfortunately, contradictions such as these were rampant when the basic concepts were used. Fortunately, those concepts were rarely used.

accounting in the past, and we professors haven't taught the past generation of students (the current generation of practitioners) how to do it. The habits of thought established by education and years of experience won't be easily changed. For this reason, it will be up to the board, not the practitioners, to reach the conclusions and continue to issue statements on specific practices. The increased quality of the statements by the board will provide short-run, indirect benefits to practitioners, and there are likely to be long-run, direct benefits as habits of thought change and, if we educators do our job, as future generations of practitioners come on-line.

I do expect the framework to bring important educational benefits. The primary recipient of those benefits is likely to be the board itself, as well as its staff. One thing is clear: much effort and thought have been put into the project. In the process, the board has educated itself, and that education augurs well for future development. The intellectual capital accumulated in the minds of board members and staff will permit them to think more clearly in completing the framework and in drawing conclusions about specific practices from that framework. Even if the most pessimistic scenario comes about and completion of the framework is abandoned, that intellectual capital will greatly improve the output of case-by-case deliberations.

Secondary recipients of the educational benefits are likely to be academics. The board has done a good job of exhibiting its reasoning, of eliminating demonstrably invalid concepts and of avoiding the more obvious non sequiturs, and therefore it has provided academics with potentially valuable teaching and research material.

The main benefit to teaching will come from the hoped-for logical connections between concepts and conclusions. At present, the typical textbook contains one chapter on theory or concepts that has no discernible connection to the other chapters on inventories, fixed assets and the like. If the framework is completed so that a coherent system is created in which the connections between concepts and conclusions are at least plausible, even if not rigorously demonstrable, then we will have provided an enormous benefit to the educational process, both in the content and the efficiency of transmission. In turn, this will have significant long-run benefits for practice, since today's students are tomorrow's practitioners.

Research in accounting suffers from the same problem as theory—it is an isolated activity having no connection to either education or practice. Research had remarkably little impact on the deliberations of the American Institute of CPAs committee on accounting procedure and the APB. Part of the reason for the lack of impact lies with the researchers' choices of subject matter, but part of the reason also lies with the practical man's disdain for research and theory. Another reason is that the part-time status of the APB and the inadequate size of its staff didn't provide the time to read and digest the research literature. To its great credit, the present full-time FASB, with its much larger staff, hasn't exhibited such disdain. The FASB statements and exposure drafts reveal considerable reliance on and influence of the research literature. I am convinced that a major reason that the board's output is much superior to that of its predecessors is that it has had both the time and the inclination to review that literature. Equally as important as the research literature's improving the output of the board is that the inclination to rely on that literature has gone some distance toward filling the gap between research and practice. If we can foster the connection between research and practice via the bridge of the board, it is likely to bring vast benefits to the profession. Indeed, the potential benefits are so great that they may overshadow the considerable benefits of the framework.

Note also that fostering this connection will provide immediate benefits to the board. There are thousands of capable, impartial researchers out there who will turn their attention to subjects pertinent to the board, if they know that their efforts will be seriously considered by the board and perhaps even be incorporated in a statement. This means that the board will in effect acquire thousands of additional workers at zero cost.

Conclusion

These kinds of considerations cause me to entertain a number of scenarios when I speculate about the future. The most pessimistic one is that the board meets so much resistance that it fails to complete the task and reverts to "ad hocery." The most optimistic scenario, indeed wildly optimistic, is that I can convince everyone that it is possible for accounting to become a scientific discipline and thereby rely more on the method of science—empirical and logical testing—and less on the method of authority. The most likely scenario is that the board will complete its task, albeit faced with increasing resistance, and will therefore be forced to slow it down or water it down or both. Thus, the most likely scenario is that the board will continue to make progress, continue to improve accounting, but that this will occur by inching along and not by a quantum leap. ■

1. LIMITATIONS OF PHYSICAL CAPITAL

Robert R. Sterling
Winspear Distinguished Professor
University of Alberta

1. INTRODUCTION

There is no less merit in keeping what we have got, than in first acquiring it. Chance has something to do with the one, while the other will always be the effect of skill. (Ovid)

Keeping what we have got requires skill in any circumstances. Inflation makes it difficult and double-digit inflation makes it doubly difficult. In a commendable attempt to aid users by reflecting inflationary effects, accountants have been honing their skills. Many accountants have noted that in times of increasing prices, if historical cost income is paid in dividends, it does not provide the firm with adequate funds to keep what we have got—the ability to replace physical units declines—and therefore historical costs produce "false profits." The proposed solution is to use current costs. The argument is that "true profits" are those figures that reflect an increase in physical capital because that is the amount that can be paid in dividends without reducing the number of physical units of the firm.

1.1 Purpose

The primary goal of this essay is to clarify the concept of physical capital. Evidence of the need for clarification is provided by FASB's indecision in FAS 33 (1979). The alternatives of (1) maintaining financial capital versus (2) maintaining physical capital were clearly stated (para 97b) but it "concluded that it should express no preference for either concept at this time" (para 104). Instead, FAS 33 (paras 124, 131) refers to the views of *some* Board members and such statements in conjunction with the failure to make a choice provide ample evidence that the Board is split on this issue.

The basic difference between financial and physical capital is that the former seeks to measure a monetary or value attribute and the latter a physical attribute. This is a crucial distinction: the choice of financial versus physical capital requires that we address the fundamental question of *what attribute* we should account for. Obviously the question of the attribute that we account for goes to the very foundation of accounting thought and practice.

A corollary of the difference in attributes is a difference in reported income: the write-up to current cost is credited to income in the financial option but that write-up is credited to equity in the physical option. That is, *both* options adjust the *assets* to current cost but the *former* takes that adjustment to *income* and the *latter* to *equity*. Physical capital proponents insist that the write-up to current cost should be taken to equity, not income, for the straightforward reason that the write-up does not reflect a change in physical capacity. Thus, some Board members would take the write-ups directly to shareholders' equity, bypassing the income statement. Financial capital proponents insist that the write-up is income for the equally straightforward reason that it is an increase in monetary capacity. Thus, some Board members would term the write-ups "holding gains" and take them to the income statement. Obviously the two options will result in significant differences in reported income.[1]

It is not my purpose to review or critique FAS 33. Instead, my primary purpose is to clarify the concept of physical capital by casting it in a simple and easily understandable context. My secondary purpose is to state the arguments that I use in choosing between financial and physical capital. If I achieve the primary purpose, it should advance accounting thought in general, as well as advancing the deliberations of FASB, regardless of the ultimate choice. A choice, however, is imperative both for the well-being of accounting

1. FAS 33, in fact, compromised the two positions. In brief, it changed the name of "holding gains" to "increase in current cost" (para 135) and then employed the financial capital concept by *placing* it on the income statement, but employed the physical capital concept by *not adding* it to income (para 70). The idea is to allow users to decide whether or not it should be an addend in the calculation of income. Both dissenters point to the proliferation of income numbers which reflects "the range of views [of] respondents" (p. 25) and "offers a smorgasbord of data [which has] something for everybody" (p. 28).

This outcome confirms my long held view that the FASB is a legislative body and that the function of a legislature is to record the compromises that it can effect among its constituencies. It also confirms my view that such compromises do not achieve their intended objective: instead of reaching a middle ground that satisfies everyone, it reaches a muddle that dissatisfies everyone. I fear that this describes the compromise adopted in FAS 33: even though it reflects the range of views of all respondents, it dissatisfies all respondents. The process of reaching a compromise resembles "the prisoners' dilemma" which has caused my captive students to dub it "Sterling's prisoners' dilemma." It goes like this:

- — no group is fully satisfied unless its endorsed position is adopted;
- — each group is highly dissatisfied if an opposing position is adopted;
- — FASB records a compromise to avoid a high level of dissatisfaction in all, save one, groups;

and for the well-being of FASB. For the well-being of accounting, indecision results in a proliferation of income numbers which can exist only on pain of vast confusion. In regard to the well-being of FASB, recall that a major criticism of its predecessors, perhaps a major factor in their demise, was the inability to make a choice when presented with alternatives.

1.2 Outline

In this essay I will focus exclusively on the physical capital version of current costing. I will not consider the financial capital version or, except incidentally, the more general question of current costs versus other valuation proposals. The essay may be divided into two major parts: first is an *explication* of physical capital (Section 2) and second is an *examination* of physical capital (Sections 3 and 4). The sparse literature necessitates the explication in order to know more precisely what is being examined. The examination is subdivided into two separable questions which also roughly divide the proponents of physical capital into two camps. First, there are those who argue that maintenance of physical capital is the objective and therefore it should be measured (Section 3). Second, there are those who argue that the maintenance of future cash flows is the objective but that physical capital is a means to the end of maintaining and forecasting cash flows and that is the reason physical capital should be measured (Section 4). Each section is further subdivided into two main questions. Section 3.1 examines the measurement of physical capital while Section 3.2 examines the objective of maintaining physical capital. Section 4.1 examines the forecasting of cash flows from physical capital measures while Section 4.2 examines the objective of maintaining cash flows.

— ergo, no group is fully satisfied and all groups are partially dissatisfied.
The point is that compromising is not a process of achieving satisfaction, it is a process of lessening the level of dissatisfaction. This explains why all groups, even strong supporters of the establishment and continuation of FASB, are critical of FASB's pronouncements.

To avoid the muddle, the internal inconsistencies of compromise, and the attendant criticism, FASB must select one of the positions. It must "exercise strong leadership" and decide what is right rather than trying, and failing, to satisfy everyone by compromise. But the adoption of this strategy requires sufficient power to enforce its decisions as well as sufficient power to gain immunity from retaliation by those constituencies whose endorsed positions were rejected. FASB has not been granted that power. Thus, both the problem and the contradiction are evident: we established FASB for the purpose of deciding on accounting principles and procedures but we did not grant it sufficient power to make such decisions. We now criticize it for not deciding just as we criticized and eventually abolished its predecessors for not deciding. It is certain that if FASB is to fulfil its purpose and, in my view, it is probable that if it is to survive, then it must make the hard decisions. A requisite is that its constituents allow it to make the hard decisions. To paraphrase Shakespeare:

> Accountants are sometimes masters of their fates: the fault, dear colleague, is not in our FASB but in ourselves. *We* are the constituents.

2. EXPLICATION

The purpose of an explication, as that word is used in the philosophy of science, is to describe something precisely and neutrally. It differs from decision or argumentation in that it is neutral and it comes prior to decision or argumentation in that the choice is facilitated by precisely delineating the alternatives or knowing precisely what it is the argument is about. The primary purpose of this section is to explicate in that sense. First, I will briefly review the background to see how we arrived at the present juncture. Second, I will attempt to provide a precise, easily understandable, and neutral description of the notions of physical and financial capital. (I apologize in advance for introducing neologisms in that description since I know that they bother some readers and I am not fond of them either, but my quest for precision and neutrality demands neologisms since the common terms have several meanings and they often evoke a positive or negative response.) Third, I will state the advantages of physical capital as they are seen by some or all proponents of physical capital.

2.1 Background

The proposal to measure physical capital has been with us, in one form or another, for a very long time. It was a major factor in the ancient LIFO-FIFO debate. Proponents of LIFO coined the terms "false profits" and "fool's profits" because if LIFO income was paid in dividends, it resulted in a decline of physical capital. Since the argument for LIFO was based on physical capital, the natural progression was to NIFO—next in-first out—which was permitted in some cases. NIFO is, of course, merely another name for current cost of inventory. Another form of the proposal arose in the equally ancient debate over price level adjustments. Although there was fairly widespread agreement that price level adjustments were needed, there was disagreement about the kind of price index that should be used: some favored a general index and others a specific index. Those who favored a specific index argued that a general index did not reflect the pattern of purchases of the firm being accounted for and therefore it was inappropriate to use a general index. A firm-specific index was more appropriate and the natural progression was to an asset-specific index. Adjusting historical costs by an asset-specific index is, of course, merely another way of reflecting current costs.[2]

2. For inventory, the proposal was to define the index, I, as p_1/p_0 where p_0 is the purchase price at date of purchase (i.e., historical cost) and p_1 is the purchase price at date of sale (i.e., current cost), and then "price level adjust" the historical cost figures by multiplying by I. Obviously $Ip_0 = (p_1/p_0)\, p_0 = p_1$. Thus, this kind of price level adjustment is merely current costing by another name.

In 1961 the theory of replacement costing was presented by Edwards-Bell. They proposed to value assets at replacement cost and to bifurcate income into "current operating profits" (revenues less current costs) and "holding gains" (the increase in costs). Their argument against historical cost income was that it deferred the reporting of holding gains until they were realized instead of reporting them when they occurred or accrued, thereby reporting false profits. The work gradually gained supporters, mainly from academe, but it also met strong resistance, mainly from practice, primarily because it violated the realization convention. Some of the holding gains were write-ups of assets that were unsold or unused and therefore unrealized. There were precedents in practice for writing up assets to current costs but the credit had been to appraisal surplus, not income.

Several debates ensued. Some debated the merits of replacement costing while others debated the proper interpretation of replacement costing. Rosenfield (1969, 1972, 1975), for example, presented cogent criticism of replacement costing as well as lucid expositions of the distinction between price level adjustments and replacement costing. There were many who debated the proper interpretation of replacement costing culminating in Revsine's (1973) provision of a theoretical base different from Edwards-Bell (1961) but with similar conclusions. But these were theoretical debates which had no effect on practice. The APB had already rejected the Moonitz (1961) and Sprouse-Moonitz (1962) research studies and therefore it appeared that practice was safely insulated from replacement costing. The SEC broke through that insulation in 1976 with the issuance of ASR 190 requiring disclosure of replacement costs. This brought many practitioners into the debate, most of whom were opposed. It also resurrected the academic debates about the proper interpretation. One notable reaction to ASR 190 was the Johnson-Bell (1976) charge that it was a misinterpretation of replacement costing. It was notable both because of its cogency and because Bell was a co-author of the seminal book—Edwards-Bell—and was the former professor of Sandy Burton, the architect of ASR 190. In effect, Professor Bell graded student Burton's paper and found it wanting. In short, many practitioners resisted ASR 190 because it was replacement costing and academics resisted it because it was not the proper interpretation of replacement costing.

In the debate over the proper interpretation of replacement costing many refinements were proposed. One recurring theme was that holding gains are not income because they are not realized. For a recent argument that holding gains are not income for other reasons see Samuelson (1980). In effect, these proponents of replacement costing wanted to truncate the income statement at current operating profit, eliminating the holding gains. The elimination of holding gains allows one to avoid violation of the realization convention or, to put it positively, reporting only current operating profit allows one to embrace both replacement costing *and* the realization convention. In addition, it is even more conservative than historical cost income because it eliminates realized holding gains as well as unrealized holding gains.

By more than mere coincidence current operating profit is exactly the same as "operating income" in the physical capital proposal. Operating income is the amount that can be distributed without impairing physical capital and therefore it is also known as "distributable income" or, in Revsine's terminology, "distributable operating flows."

Thus, the two proposals converged. Replacement cost income less holding gains is exactly the same as physical capital income. The confluence of the adherents of these two proposals swells the support for reporting operating income as well as undermining the opposition based on the violation of the realization convention. Additional opposition was dissipated when the idea of data expansion via multi-column financial statements was introduced in the academic literature and interpreted as supplementary statements in practice. Recognition that physical capital statements could supplement instead of supplant historical cost statements subsumed the proposal under the hoary concept of additional disclosure. In short, the effect of the refinements was to add supporters from other camps and to quiet the opposition. The trend was one of increasing support and decreasing resistance and that trend seems to be continuing.

The present widespread support is evidenced by Standard Setters in Australia, Canada and the U.K., all opting for current cost/physical capital methods of reporting, at least in the Exposure Draft stage. In the U.S., as noted above, FASB is divided on this issue and has presented a compromise. Those Board members who support physical capital present their case in FAS 33:

> Erosion of physical capital (or erosion of operating capability) may be regarded as the failure to retain sufficient financial resources to acquire assets needed to maintain the capacity of the enterprise to provide a constant supply of goods and services. The concept of physical capital erosion may be linked to a concept of distributable income where distributable income is defined as the amount of cash that may be distributed without reducing the operating capability of the enterprise. (para 124).
>
> [C]osts must be measured at current cost in order to provide for the maintenance of operating capability. Assume, for example, that inventory is purchased for $1,000 and sold for $1,500 at a time when current cost is $1,200. Although historical cost/nominal dollar income is $500 ($1,500 less $1,000), distributions may be limited to $300 ($1,500 less $1,200) to maintain operating capability. Costs are measured at $1,200 in order to provide for the replacement of inventory out of revenues. An increase of $200 ($1,200 less

> $1,000) in *current costs would not be regarded as part of income* under concepts that address maintenance of physical operating capability. (para 125, emphasis supplied.)

In brief, the argument is that historical cost/nominal dollar accounting produces false profits because of the need to replace the inventory at its current cost and that the difference between current cost and historical cost is not income for the same reason.

In summary, the proposal to measure physical capital has a very long history. It has roots in practice—LIFO and appraisal surplus—as well as in theory—specific price indices and replacement costing. Support is growing, having become sufficient to be adopted or exposed in other English speaking countries, and having become sufficient to cause FASB to retract its choice in the Exposure Draft (1978) and to compromise in FAS 33.

Given the history and the widespread support, it is most curious that the literature on physical capital is exceptionally sparse. The quotation from FAS 33 above is a typical statement of the case for physical capital both in regard to content and brevity.[3] It seems that the widespread support for physical capital is based on the intuitive appeal of such brief statements. Surely the fundamental nature of the question of what attribute we account for requires a much more intensive and extensive analysis. The trend toward adopting physical capital in all English speaking countries, including the promise to review and revise FAS 33 (para 15) in not more than five years, makes the provision of such an analysis especially urgent. My hope is that the following remarks will motivate others to enter into the debate and thereby aid in the provision of the more intensive and extensive analysis, so that physical capital will either rest on a bedrock foundation or be abandoned if its intuitive appeal does not withstand such analysis.

2.2 False Profits

The argument that historical cost income results in false profits can be clearly seen by considering a simple merchandising firm. Assume that the firm starts with $100 cash on January 1 and buys 100 units for $1.00 each on

3. There has been much literature on replacement costs but little on maintenance of physical capital. Edwards-Bell (1961) focuses on current costs versus historical costs instead of financial capital versus physical capital. Revsine (1973) focuses on forecasting future distributable operating flows and physical capital is merely a means to that end. The case for physical capital is stated by Revsine (1973, p. 70n) in a fashion very similar to the quotation from FAS 33 both in regard to content and brevity. That the case is incidental to his primary purpose is evidenced by the fact that he placed it in a footnote.

I am using "current cost" instead of "replacement cost" to conform to the distinction drawn in FAS 33 (para 99).

January 2. On January 31 it sells all the units for $1.60 each and pays its income in dividends. The combined financial statements appear in Exhibit I.

Exhibit I

MEASURING NOD

MERCHANDISING FIRM
COMBINED FINANCIAL STATEMENTS

	Jan 1	*Month of Jan*	*Feb 1*
Cash	$100		$100
Shareholders' Equity	$100		$100
Beginning Retained Earnings	-0-		-0-
Sales		$160	
Cost of Goods Sold		100	
Net Income		60	
Less Dividends		60	
Change in Retained Earnings	-0-		-0-
Ending Retained Earnings	-0-		-0-
Total Equity	$100		$100

Examination of Exhibit I reveals that there is absolutely nothing false about any of the figures. It accurately reflects the easily measurable attribute of *N*umber *o*f *D*ollars (NOD). The NOD on hand at January 1 and February 1 was in fact $100 and that could be readily tested empirically, or, as we also say, readily audited. The increment (net income) in NOD during January was $60 which is also readily auditable. Since the figures conform to empirically testable facts, they must be characterized as true and those who claim them to be false are mistaken.

The basis of the mistaken claim that the figures are false is that they do not reflect physical capital. Proponents of physical capital want to measure *S*pecific *U*nits *P*urchasable (SUP), not NOD. To obtain a direct measurement of SUP the only thing required is to divide the February 1 NOD figures by $1.25, the current cost on that date. This division restates the dollars as equivalent units purchasable, i.e., $100 would purchase 100 units on January 1 but $100 will purchase only 80 units on February 1. Thus, there is a decline in physical capital of 20 units. In the same fashion, the sales of $160 is divided by $1.25 to obtain the equivalent units purchasable of 128 from which is deducted the 100 units sold to yield the "true profit" of 28 units. The problem is that the $60 NOD profit was paid in dividends which is equivalent to 48 units (=$60/$1.25) resulting in the decline of 20 units in physical capital. (Cf. FAS 33, paras 100b, 125.) Exhibit II displays all of these SUP Figures.

Exhibit II

MEASURING SUP IN UNITS

MERCHANDISING FIRM
COMBINED FINANCIAL STATEMENTS

	Jan 1	*Month of Jan*	*Feb 1*
Cash	100 units		80 units
Shareholders' Equity	100 units		100 units
Beginning Retained Earnings	-0-		-0-
Sales		128 units	
Cost of Goods Sold		100	
Net Income		28	
Less Dividends		48	
Change in Retained Earnings	-0-		(20)
Ending Retained Earnings	-0-		(20)
Total Equity	100 units		80 units

All of the figures in Exhibit II are also true in that they conform to empirically testable facts.[4] Thus, both exhibits are true. The distinction is that they measure different attributes, not that one is true and the other false.

Of course, it cannot be denied that Exhibit I gives a false measure of SUP. It overstates SUP profit by 20 units. As a result 20 units of SUP capital was paid out and therefore SUP assets declined by 20 units. If this trend continues, so the argument goes, the firm will dwindle and eventually die. If income taxes are levied on the basis of NOD, it is possible for those taxes to be greater than SUP profit and therefore confiscatory, i.e., a tax on SUP capital. It is on the basis of these evils that NOD profit is said to be false.

4. Those who object to specific units purchas*able* because it refers to "hypothetical, not actual, transactions" can achieve the same results by shifting the accounting period ahead by one day and having the firm repurchase the units on February 2. This allows one to interpret SUP as specific units purchas*ed* instead of purchas*able*. SUP Financial Statements from January 2 to February 2 will contain exactly the same figures as those in Exhibit II.

Many accountants criticize physical capital and other proposals on grounds that hypothetical transactions are *ipso facto* illegitimate or false and therefore should not be reported; others on grounds that it is impossible to measure things that didn't actually happen. A moment's reflection will reveal the error: scientists often measure the potential instead of the actual. There is a whole class of scientific concepts, called "dispositional terms," that end in "ble" such as flexible, soluble and flammable. If we prohibit such concepts in science, then we will artificially deprive ourselves of an enormous number of useful scientific measurements. For example, we won't be able to say "there are x Btu's in that coal pile," both because it is potential, not actual, energy and because it is flamm*able* or burn*able*, not burn*ed*. For the same reason that we shouldn't prohibit such concepts in science, we shouldn't prohibit them in accounting. Thus, purchasable is both legitimate and measurable and therefore shouldn't be prohibited on those grounds.

2.3 True Profits

Physical capital proponents want to avoid the aforementioned évils by measuring SUP. They propose to measure SUP by adjusting the historical costs to current costs in the following entry:

Inventory	$25	
Shareholders' Equity		$25

This entry writes up the 100 units from the $1.00 per unit historical cost to the $1.25 per unit current cost. All—both physical and financial capital—current cost proponents are agreed that the asset accounts should reflect the current cost. Hence the most general proposition of current cost accounting is:

Proposition 1: Asset accounts should reflect the current cost, not the historical cost, of the assets.

All physical capital proponents agree that the adjustment should be taken to equity, not income. The argument is that the original capital invested was 100 units and that this has not changed. It is incidental that the 100 units was expressed as $100 originally and is now expressed as $125. Since the only thing that has changed is the dollar expression, since the underlying physical capital has not changed, the adjustment cannot be considered income—it is an equity adjustment. Thus, the second proposition of physical capital current costing is:

Proposition 2: Differences between current costs and historic costs are equity adjustments, not income.

After the adjustment to inventory, as given in the above entry, the recording of cost of goods sold is straightforward:

Cost of Goods Sold	$125	
Inventory		$125

The purpose of charging the current cost against revenues is to get the net income to reflect the change in units. This idea may also be stated as a general proposition:

Proposition 3: Income is the change in physical capital and is determined by deducting current costs from revenues.

The above adjustment to inventory can be backed up to an adjustment to cash. The $100 cash was used to purchase 100 units of inventory but it would now require $125 to purchase the same number of units. Thus, the January 1 cash should be stated at $125 to reflect the fact that it would require that amount on February 1 to purchase the 100 units. The effect of these propositions and entries is displayed in the combined financials in Exhibit III.

Exhibit III

MEASURING SUP IN DOLLARS

MERCHANDISING FIRM
COMBINED FINANCIAL STATEMENTS

	Jan 1	*Month of Jan*	*Feb 1*
Cash	$125		$125
Shareholders' Equity	$125		$125
Beginning Retained Earnings	-0-		-0-
Sales		$160	
Cost of Goods Sold		125	
Net Income		35	
Less Dividends		35	
Change in Retained Earnings	-0-		-0-
Ending Retained Earnings	-0-		-0-
Total Equity	$125		$125

The January 1 figures are stated at the current cost as of February 1.[5] The Cost of Goods Sold is also stated at the current cost resulting in a $35 SUP net income as contrasted to the $60 NOD net income. The smaller net income results in smaller dividends being paid and hence more cash retained in the firm. (Cf. FAS 33, para 124.)

These dollar figures are intended to reflect physical capital—the objective is to measure SUP, not NOD. That this objective has been achieved can be seen by dividing all the figures in Exhibit III by $1.25. The quotients of such divisions are displayed in Exhibit IV. This is said to prove that the true profit is $35 since that is the dollar expression of the increase in units purchasable arising from sales.

5. If there is an objection to adjusting the January 1 cash from $100 to $125, one can shift the accounting period forward by one day and adjust the January 2 inventory from $100 to $125. Some prepublication readers objected to adjusting cash but did not object to adjusting inventory. I do not understand the distinction: to my mind there is no difference between writing up cash to more than was actually in the till and writing up inventory to more than it actually cost, especially when that cash is used to purchase the inventory and the value of the cash is imputed to the cost of inventory.

Exhibit IV

MEASURING SUP IN UNITS

MERCHANDISING FIRM
COMBINED FINANCIAL STATEMENTS

	Jan 1	*Month of Jan*	*Feb 1*
Cash	100 units		100 units
Shareholders' Equity	100		100
Beginning Retained Earnings	-0-		-0-
Sales		128 units	
Cost of Goods Sold		100	
Net Income		28	
Less Dividends		28	
Change in Retained Earnings	-0-		-0-
Ending Retained Earnings	-0-		-0-
Total Equity	100 units		100 units

2.4 Advantages

The proponents of physical capital claim that measuring SUP produces a number of advantages. First, it aids *dividend policy.* As we have seen, if dividends of more than $35 are paid, the physical capital is reduced. SUP income is sometimes called "distributable income" to indicate that it is the amount that can be distributed in dividends without reducing physical capital. (Cf. FAS 33, para 124.) Second, it aids *tax policy.* (Cf. FAS 33, para 94b.) If income taxes were based on SUP income, it would prevent taxation of capital under the guise of taxing income. For example, in the case at hand, if an income tax rate of 60% or greater were based on NOD income, it would reduce the specific units purchasable thereby, in fact, being a tax on physical capital.

All proponents are agreed on the above advantages. Many go further and argue that it also aids *price policy.* Some argue that selling prices track or parallel current costs. FAS 33 (para 117), for example, alludes to the possibility of selling prices being closely related to current costs. Others argue that management should establish a policy of setting selling prices on the basis of current costs. The suggestion is to apply the markup rate to current cost instead of historical cost in order to gain the same increase in physical capital that would have been had there been no change in purchase price. In this case the markup rate of 60% is applied to the $1.25 current cost to yield a sales price of $2.00. See Exhibit V.

Exhibit V

MARKUP APPLIED TO CURRENT COST

MERCHANDISING FIRM
COMPARATIVE INCOME STATEMENTS

MONTH OF JANUARY

	Constant Cost		*Increasing Cost*	
	(1) Dollars	(2) Units	(3) Dollars	(4) Units
Sales	160	160	200	160
Cost of Goods Sold	100	100	125	100
Net Income	60	60	75	60

If purchase prices had remained at $1.00, as in column (1), the SUP income would have been $60 which is equivalent to 60 units as shown in column (2). In order to obtain the same increase in units, as shown in column (4), we must base the markup on the increased purchase price and thereby increase the revenue to $200. To put it negatively, if the markup of 60% is based on historical cost, the result is an increase of 28 units, as shown in Exhibit IV, instead of the increase of 60 units originally planned. Applying the same markup rate to current cost allows the firm to earn the same SUP income as it would have earned had there been no increase in purchase price.

Those who make this suggestion argue that such an increase in sales price is likely to be possible because competitors who purchase at a later time will incur the increased cost and therefore will want to mark up on that basis. In this case competitors will purchase the units at $1.25 each and therefore will be forced to sell at $2.00 in order to earn a 60% gross margin. Thus, in general, firms can be competitive with the sales price based on current cost.[6]

Up to this point the discussion has focused on the advantages of this pricing policy that would accrue to the *firm.* Note also that it has advantages for the *owners* of the firm. The distributable income—dividends payable without decreasing physical capital—would have been $60 had purchase prices remained constant. With the selling price based on the current cost the

6. Physical capital proponents assume, either implicitly or explicitly, that the firms can be competitive under these conditions. Specifically, the assumptions are: (1) the same number of units will be sold at the new selling price as at the old selling price; (2) the new selling price is based on the application of a constant markup rate to the current cost. Revsine (1973, p. 71n) is one of the few who explicitly recognizes the necessity of the assumptions: "(1) operating levels are unchanged, and (2) input costs and output prices move in parallel fashion." (See the Revsine-Weygandt quotation later in this section and the Revsine quotation in section 4.13 for a repetition of the same point in different words.) In order to be consistent with the proponents, I am making the same assumptions even though I think they are likely to be violated more often than they are met.

distributable income is $75. Thus, if the profit is in fact distributed the owners will receive an additional $15. Since owners do not purchase the specific units of inventory from their dividends, since owners are likely to be interested in their capacity to purchase consumer goods from their dividends, the fact that $60 and $75 are equivalent in terms of SUP is not relevant to them. Instead, the consumer price index is relevant to determining the owners' relative well-offness, but regardless of where the consumer price index stands at the time of the receipt of dividends, $75 will always purchase more than $60 and therefore the owners are always better-off from constant markups on increasing purchase prices. The situation is truly Utopian: the *firm* is *equally* as much better-off and the *owners* are *more* better-off from using this method of accounting and the attendant pricing policy. For this reason, many managers and owners are strong supporters of the physical capital proposal.[7]

Another advantage to owners and others is the *predictive power* of SUP profit. (Cf. FAS 33, paras 116-123.) Many proponents base their entire argument on the ability of present SUP profits to predict future SUP profits. Since SUP profit is distributable income—the maximum amount that can be paid in dividends without reducing physical capital—then dividends equal to SUP profit will allow physical capital to be maintained at the same level and therefore allow SUP profits to continue at the same level.

Since share prices are the discounted value of future dividends, this aids owners in the valuation of their share prices. For example, we noted above that dividends increased from $60 to $75 due to the constant markup being applied to the increased current cost. This means that share prices would increase 25% to reflect the discounted value of the 25% increase in dividends since present SUP profits are good predictors of future SUP profits and SUP profits can be distributed without impairing physical capital.

7. They are particularly enthusiastic in price regulated industries such as public utilities. The managers and owners of such industries want to write-up the assets to current cost because the public utility commissions allow them to earn a "fair rate of return" and the application of that rate to an increased asset base permits higher selling prices. Since the write-up is taken to equity instead of income, the same result is achieved if the public utility commission figures the return on equity rather than on assets.

Since the expenses deducted are the higher current costs, they can still report an acceptable profit to the public and the public utility commissions. In addition, they and other non-regulated firms hope to eventually convince taxing authorities to levy the income tax (but not the property tax) on the basis of current costs.

This would make almost everybody happy. Managers would be happy because they could increase their reported assets without an accompanying sacrifice and they could increase their selling prices and revenues. Owners would be happy because they could increase their reported equity without an accompanying reported or taxed profit and they could increase their dividends. Both managers and owners would be happy with the prospect of paying lower income taxes. Accounting practitioners would be happy because they have pleased their clients. Accounting academicians would be happy with the rarely received support of owners, managers, and practitioners for their theoretical proposals. Perhaps consumers and other taxpayers would not be happy with this system, but then you cannot please everyone.

One of the more straightforward arguments for the predictive power of SUP measures was presented by Revsine-Weygandt (1974, p. 75):

(1) "[T]he value [present price] of a firm's ownership shares is determined by the level of its cash operating flows."

(2) "[A]t a minimum mangement can be assumed to be constantly striving to maintain existing share prices."

(3) "[I]n order to maintain existing share prices management must maintain operating flows at their current level."

(4) "[M]anagement's primary controllable variable in attempting to maintain operating flow levels is to maintain the prevailing physical level of operations on the assumption that the margin between input and output prices will remain constant."

(5) "[Adopting as the objective of accounting] the primacy of cash flow predictions . . . whichever inflation accounting method generates an income figure that best reflects the maintenance of the physical operating level of the firm ought to be preferred."

Therefore, SUP measures are preferred. Not only can they be used to predict cash operating flows of the firm, they can also be used to predict dividends of the owners, thereby meeting the objective of providing information useful to investors for predicting, comparing and evaluating potential cash flows.

In addition, current costs are said to be a *surrogate* for the present value of future cash flows and SUP profits a *surrogate* for "economic income" (change in present values). Since many consider net present value to be the "ideal measure" that cannot be obtained for practical reasons, a surrogate is almost ideal. (Cf. FAS 33, paras 132-133.) *Assessing managerial effectiveness* is also aided by SUP measures because management has control over the quantity of physical units but does not have control over prices. Therefore owners can judge the quality of managerial decisions by focusing on what they can make decisions about. For the same reason managers should be considered stewards of the physical units and therefore SUP measures best meet the *stewardship* objective.

In summary, SUP measures are said to be true because they reflect the physical capital of the firm. In addition, such measures are said to provide advantages for formulation of dividend policy, tax policy and price policy, as well as having predictive power, being a surrogate for ideal measures, aiding in assessing management and providing the best report on stewardship. For these reasons, the proposal has rather wide appeal and support from influential groups.

3. MAINTAINING AND MEASURING PHYSICAL CAPITAL

The objective is to maintain physical capital. SUP measures contribute to that objective by limiting distribution to SUP profits which permits SUP capital to be maintained. In addition, SUP measures allow us to see whether, and by how much, the objective has been achieved. In this section I will first examine the measurement problems and then turn to the question of the objective.

3.1 Measurement Problems

Examination reveals that there are four conditions of the firm which must be met in order for SUP measures to be applicable. Namely, the firm

(1) continues to replace *identical units;*
(2) faces continuously *increasing costs;*
(3) buys and sells in *different markets;* and
(4) is *fully invested* in the physical unit.

If a firm fails to meet any one of these conditions, serious problems with SUP measures are encountered. To demonstrate the nature of the problems, the negation of each condition will be considered seriatim. Namely, the firm

(1) replaces *different units;*
(2) faces *decreasing costs;*
(3) buys and sells in the *same market;* and
(4) is *partially invested* in the physical unit.

3.11 Different Units.

As long as a firm replaces identical units, we can report empirically testable SUP measures as demonstrated above. But what happens if the firm changes the kind of units that it purchases? Such changes do not violate the going concern assumption; indeed they are regular occurrences in long-established firms. Macy's and Gimbels, for example, purchase and sell mini-skirts one season and then purchase and sell maxi-skirts the next season. How does one employ a measure of physical capital when the units change from minis to maxis?

To make the problem concrete, assume that Macy's starts with $100 on January 1, purchases 100 minis at $1.00 each on January 2, sells 100 minis at $1.60 each on January 31 when the current cost of minis is $2.00, and replenishes its inventory on February 2 with maxis at a cost of $1.25 each, that cost having increased from $1.20 each on January 2. Even though the case is simple there are several different asset and income figures that can be derived. Two of the more obvious arguments are:

(1) The firm actually sold minis and therefore the current cost of minis should be utilized as the basis for accounting. This results in a $40 loss as shown in Exhibit VI.

Exhibit VI

MEASURING S_nUP

MACY'S
COMBINED FINANCIAL STATEMENTS

	Jan 1		Month of Jan		Feb 1	
	Dollars	*Units*	*Dollars*	*Units*	*Dollars*	*Units*
Cash	$200	100n			$160	80n
Shareholders' Equity	$200	100n			$200	100n
Beginning Retained Earnings	-0-	-0-			-0-	-0-
Sales			$160	80n		
Cost of Goods Sold			200	100		
Net Income (Loss)			($40)	(20)n		
Less Dividends			-0-	-0-		
Change in Retained Earnings	-0-	-0-			(40)	(20)
Ending Retained Earnings	-0-	-0-			(40)	(20)
Total Equity	$200	100n			$160	80n

Exhibit VII

MEASURING S_xUP

MACY'S
COMBINED FINANCIAL STATEMENTS

	Jan 1		Month of Jan		Feb 1	
	Dollars	*Units*	*Dollars*	*Units*	*Dollars*	*Units*
Cash	$104.16	83.33x			$104.16	83.33x
Shareholders' Equity	$104.16	83.33x			$104.16	83.33x
Beginning Retained Earnings	-0-	-0-			-0-	-0-
Sales			$160.00	128.00x		
Cost of Goods Sold			104.16	83.33		
Net Income			$ 55.84	44.67x		
Less Dividends			55.84	44.67		
Change in Retained Earnings	-0-	-0-			-0-	-0-
Total Equity	$104.16	83.33x			$104.16	83.33x

(2) The firm actually replaced maxis and therefore the current cost of maxis should be utilized as the basis for accounting. This results in a $55.84 profit as shown in Exhibit VII.

We have a choice of reporting a substantial profit or a substantial loss from the same set of facts. Which figure do we report? The criterion used by physical capacity proponents is truth, but examination reveals that the alternatives are equally true. The choice is S_nUP (for mi*n*is as the basis) versus S_xUP (for ma*x*is as the basis), not truth versus falsehood. S_nUP is true in that 100 minis were purchased on January 2 and 80 minis could have been (but were not) purchased on February 2. S_xUP is true in that 128 maxis were purchased on February 2 and 83.33 maxis could have been (but were not) purchased on January 2. Thus, any defense or criticism of one applies with equal force to the other: either both are true or both are false since both contain one factual purchase and one counterfactual purchase. Thus, we have returned to the fundamental question: what attribute should we account for? The only difference is that we now face the choice of S_nUP versus S_xUP instead of NOD versus SUP. I confess that I do not know the answer. I fear that physical capital proponents also do not know the answer because insofar as I am aware the question is never addressed.

A digression to discover how FAS 33 would answer the question will illustrate the difficulty of the answer as well as the concealment of the question. Based on the definition of current cost it appears that FAS 33 would prefer option (1). It emphasizes that current cost refers to the asset *owned* (para 99f) as opposed to replacement cost which is defined as the current purchase price of "the best available asset to undertake the function of the asset owned" (para 99c). In this case the assets owned at time of sale were minis, and maxis are the best available asset to undertake their function. It is not at all clear what "function" means in this context but it does appear that "current cost" is the present purchase price of minis ($2.00) and "replacement cost" is the present purchase price of maxis ($1.25). That is, current cost is S_nUP. Therefore, the correct report is a $40 loss.

This would clear it up were it not for the lack of explanation as to the reason for the distinction. It appears to be purely definitional: the "current cost income" is a $40 loss and the "replacement cost income" is a $55.84 profit and there is nothing to distinguish them except the words. Mr. Walters evidently shares my confusion (FAS 33, p. 28, emphasis supplied): "In most cases, it [distributable income] is a result of subtracting the estimated cost of the *next purchase* from the revenue of the *last sale.*" This supports reporting a $55.84 profit by subtracting the cost of maxis from the revenue of minis. That is, S_xUP is the correct measure. As a member of the Board, Mr. Walters was a party to the deliberations and therefore it seems likely that if the question had been raised, he would know the answer given by the proponents even though he disagreed. My conjecture is that the question was never answered because it was never raised.

Thus, FAS 33 either answers the question by definition or it fails to answer the question. If the former, it merely rephrases the question: should we account for current cost or replacement cost? If the latter, we return directly to the original question of S_xUP versus S_nUP. Was the "current income from continuing operations" a \$40 loss or a \$55.84 profit? Should the firm pay its "distributable income" of \$55.84 in dividends or should it seek additional financing of \$40 to restore its physical capital position which was diminished by a \$40 loss? Perhaps the proponents can answer, I cannot.[8]

Extension of the time period reveals that both S_nUP and S_xUP result in conceptual as well as practical problems. If we choose S_nUP we must apply it consistently in February in order to achieve comparable figures. The conceptual problem is apparent: maxis are being purchased and sold in February and therefore the presumed objective is to *maintain* the physical capital of maxis but we are *measuring* the physical capital of minis. Of what use to either managers or owners is information about minis when the firm is dealing in maxis? The practical problem is also apparent: since minis are out of style, they are no longer being manufactured in February and therefore we cannot observe their current cost because we cannot observe others purchasing for the purchase price. It would be possible to either estimate that purchase price or determine the reproduction cost but one wonders whether this would be cost beneficial in view of the conceptual problems. Both the conceptual and practical problems are highlighted by further extensions of the time period. Not only could we consider such problems in March when midis will be in style, we could also assume that Macy's adopted physical capacity measures in 1880 when bustles were in style and confound ourselves with the 1980 conceptual

8. A third possible interpretation of FAS 33 would result in reporting a zero current cost income. The Board (para 126) decided to use "current cost or lower recoverable amount" when replacement is not "worthwhile" which is defined as when "recoverable amounts [selling prices for inventories] are lower than current costs." Applying the illustration presented and the example discussed to the mini-maxi case yields the following income statement:

Sales Revenue	\$160
Cost of Goods Sold	160
Income from continuing operations	-0-
Cost at date of sale	\$200
Cost at date of acquisition	100
Increase in current cost	\$100

I am not sure that the illustration applies to the mini-maxi case but if it does, the confusion is compounded. The above cannot be interpreted as SUP even though the objective is to measure SUP. The reader is invited to try to cast the above in the form of Exhibits III and IV. To put the problem in more familiar terms, the books do not balance. The debit to inventory (or cost of goods sold) necessary to reflect the "recoverable amount" is \$60 while the credit to

and practical problems of measuring minis, maxis and midis on the basis of bustles.

The problems of S_xUP are parallel. In order to achieve comparability we must restate the December figures on the basis of maxis. But the firm was dealing in hot pants in December and this raises the conceptual problem of usefulness as well as the practical problem of observing the current cost of maxis before they were being manufactured and sold. For the same consistency-comparability reason, we would need to restate the past figures, going back at least five years if not all the way back to bustles, on the basis of minis in January, maxis in February, midis in March and so forth every time the style changed. Not only would frequent restatements be confusing, they would also be very costly and the benefits would be minimal.

Given these considerations we must reject both S_xUP and S_nUP. A third approach is to define a more abstract unit. The argument is:

(3) The firm actually bought and replaced skirts and therefore the current cost of skirts should be used as the basis for accounting. This results in a \$35 profit as was previously shown in Exhibits III and IV.

This measures S_sUP (for *s*kirts) as opposed to the rejected S_xUP and S_nUP. The criterion of truth is met since S_sUP conforms to empirically testable facts.

In essence, S_sUP is an application of the solution to the well-known problem of adding (or subtracting) apples and oranges. The proposed solution is to call the sum (or difference) units of "fruit" instead of "apples" and "oranges." Here we call the difference "skirts" instead of "minis" and "maxis." If one had 128 apples on February 1 and 100 oranges on January 1, it is reasonable to say that one is better off by 28 pieces of fruit just as it is reasonable to say that one is better off by 28 skirts.

Extension of this approach to more dissimilar units, however, yields absurd results. For example, it would be absurd to say that if one had 2 pineapples on February 1 and 100 grapes on January 1, then one is worse off by 98 pieces of fruit. The reason we consider the result to be absurd is that pineapples and grapes are not sufficiently similar to permit us to ignore the difference in, say, food value. To put it positively, the reason we consider the difference between apples and oranges to be reasonable is that, at least implicitly, we *equate* one apple to one orange in some sense such as food value. Since we are not willing to equate one pineapple to one grape, we consider sums and differences of pineapples and grapes to be absurd.

---

shareholders' equity necessary to reflect the "increase in current cost" is \$100. The debits do not equal the credits; the February 1 balance sheet shows total assets of \$160 and total equities of \$200.

The limited objective of this article as well as limited space prohibits me from exploring the perceived ambiguities of this application despite my itch to do so. Since I cannot see how this application measures SUP, it is irrelevant to the main thrust of this article.

The same applies to measuring the profit of Macy's. It is reasonable to say that the firm is better off by 28 skirts only if we are willing to equate, in some sense, minis to maxis. The question is: in *what* sense is one mini equal to one maxi? The fact that both are skirts does not answer the question unless we are willing to ignore differences in workmanship, design, quantity of material, kind of material, and so forth. A cotton mini is not equal to a wool maxi in several senses not the least of which is market value.

To make the point, consider the extreme example of Macy's deciding to compete with Neiman-Marcus by replacing its cotton mini skirts with ermine maxi skirts at a cost of $80 each. The $160 cash will purchase 2 ermine maxis at $80 each on February 1; the $100 cash will purchase 100 minis at $1.00 each on January 1; the decrease in the ability to purchase skirts is 98, which, at $80 each, is a $7,840 loss. The consequent is absurd. Just as we cannot equate pineapples to grapes because of differences in food value, we cannot equate cotton to ermine because of differences in market value.

Once again we have come full circle to the fundamental question: what attribute should we account for? To be able to equate different units requires that we measure the same attributes in both to see whether they are equal in regard to that attribute. The unanswered question is: what attribute should we measure to determine that equality? I confess that I do not know the answer if value measures are excluded. I fear that physical capital proponents also do not know the answer. Worse, I fear that they do not know the question. Instead of addressing the question it seems that they assume, often tacitly, that the firm replaces with identical units.[9]

In summary, adopting SUP instead of NOD does not resolve the question. If we decide to account for specific units, we must decide *which* specific units we should account for. If we assume replacement with identical units, no decision is required but if we make the more realistic assumption of, at least eventually, replacing with different units, we must choose the unit that we use as the numeraire. This simple case reveals three plausible choices—minis, maxis and skirts—with no apparent reason for preferring any one over the

9. There is another dimension to the problem of identical units. The above discussion was concerned exclusively with making comparisons over time within the same firm. We also need to make comparisons among firms at a point in time. We would like to be able to compare the assets and income of Macy's to those of Gimbels. If Macy's used S_xUP and Gimbels used S_nUP, it prohibits such comparisons for the same reasons that switching from S_xUP to S_nUP within Macy's prohibits comparisons over time. It would be very difficult to formulate a standard which would require Macy's and Gimbels to use the same unit because of differences in the timing of purchases and sales.

I mention this problem in a footnote because it seems to me that the objective of physical capital proponents is to account for each firm individually without regard to comparisons to other firms. Since I do not think that they can achieve their chosen objective when they encounter different units over time, I have not delved into the problem of different units among firms.

others. Extension of the time period or extension to more dissimilar units reveals that all three result in such severe conceptual and practical problems that all three must be rejected.

Therefore, I conclude that physical capital measures are not applicable to firms that replace with different units. This excludes a large number of firms. Car dealers replenish their inventory of luxury cars with compact cars and appliance dealers replenish their inventory of black and white televisions with color televisions. Toy dealers purchase and sell hula hoops one year, while they purchase and sell skateboards the next year. Last year's propellers are this year's jet fans in firms that sell airplane parts, and last year's slide rules are this year's hand-held electronic calculators in firms that sell office and engineering supplies. Last week's fresh strawberries are this week's fresh cherries at the grocery. And so on for a great number of firms. In time all firms must either adapt to changing tastes and changing technology by replacing with different units or fail to adapt and die. Thus, physical capital measures eventually become inapplicable to all living firms, to all going concerns.

3.12 Decreasing Costs.

Arguments for measuring physical capital are almost invariably couched in terms of increasing current costs. In times of inflation it is natural to think about increasing prices but even in times of inflation, some prices decrease. Dealers in electronic calculators provide a ready example since their prices have decreased dramatically in the recent past.

Let us consider the case. Assume that Radio Shack purchased 100 calculators at $1.00 each on January 2 and the current cost is $0.50 each on January 31. According to Propositions 1 and 2 we need to make the following entry:

Shareholders' Equity	$50	
Inventory		$50

The arguments are the same: (1) the inventory account now reflects the current cost of the units; and (2) the adjustment is to equity, not income since the 100 units has remained constant and the only thing that has changed is the incidental dollar expression of these units. Upon sale of the units the entry is:

Cost of Goods Sold	$50	
Inventory		$50

This is in compliance with Proposition 3 that the income is the change in physical capital and this is determined by deducting the current costs from revenues.

The pricing policy arguments are also applicable. Radio Shack can place itself in the same physical capital position by basing its markup on the current cost. That is, if the current cost had remained constant, it would have earned $60 on a 60% markup which would have allowed it to pay the equivalent of 60 units in dividends after provision for replacing the 100 units. Basing the markup on current costs the firm will earn $30 which will allow it to pay the equivalent of 60 units (=$30/$0.50) in dividends after provision for replacing the 100 units. Of course, Radio Shack would prefer to sell the units at $1.60 each instead of $0.80 each, but its competitors who have purchased later at the decreased current cost will set their prices at $0.80 and therefore it will be forced to sell at $0.80 in order to meet the competition.

Exhibit VIII displays these figures.

Exhibit VIII

MEASURING SUP

RADIO SHACK
COMBINED FINANCIAL STATEMENTS

	Jan 1		*Month of Jan*		*Feb 1*	
	Dollars	*Units*	*Dollars*	*Units*	*Dollars*	*Units*
Cash	$50	100c			$50	100c
Shareholders' Equity	$50	100c			$50	100c
Beginning Retained Earnings	-0-	-0-			-0-	-0-
Sales			$80	160c		
Cost of Goods Sold			50	100		
Net Income			$30	60c		
Less Dividends			30	60		
Change in Retained Earnings	-0-	-0-			-0-	-0-
Ending Retained Earnings	-0-	-0-			-0-	-0-
Total Equity	$50	100c			$50	100c

The unit figures reveal that the firm started with 100 units and ended with the ability to replace 100 units and therefore physical capital has been maintained. The income statement figures are the same as they would have been if current cost had been constant—their equivalent units are exactly the same as those in Exhibit V. Thus, in regard to SUP, the firm is the same in all respects.

But something is not quite right. The firm purchased units for $100, sold them for $80, and yet it reported a $30 profit. This is a very curious statement. One reason it is curious is that the well-offness of the firm and the owners have diverged. In the increasing cost case the firm was equally as much better-off, having earned the same SUP profit in units, and the owners were more better-off, having increased their dividends. In this decreasing cost case the firm is equally as much better-off, having earned the same SUP profit in units, but the owners are worse-off, having suffered a decrease in dividends. The owners' ability to purchase consumer goods has been halved—dividends decreased from $60 to $30—and they would find small comfort in the fact that their ability to purchase calculators has been maintained. That $30 will purchase the same number of calculators now as $60 would have purchased before is irrelevant to the owners. From the owners' point of view, there has been a $20 loss—a decline from $100 to $80—not a $30 profit. Therefore, owners would object to receiving a distribution of profit, a dividend, when, from their point of view, there was no profit to distribute.

The halving of dividends and the $20 loss is likely to incur the wrath of owners. But when assessing management they will be forced to give them good marks because the managers have achieved the objective of maintaining physical capital. Note the contradiction of the owners being unhappy with the results of management's actions and yet being required to conclude that they have been good stewards since their only controllable variable is the number of physical units and since they have achieved the objective of ending with the same number as they started with.

Even managers are unhappy with themselves since they have not achieved the minimum objective of maintaining share prices. (See point 2 of the Revsine-Weygandt quotation in Section 2.1.) Since the share price is the discounted value of the dividend, the halving of the dividend results in the halving of the share price. In order to maintain the same dividend and the same share prices, managers should double the physical capital, not maintain it. But the need to double physical capital means that the SUP profit must be retained and therefore SUP profit is not distributable income. The owners must invest an additional $20 to permit the doubling of physical capital, as well as forgoing the dividends. That required investment is an alternative explanation of the reason that the owners think that the firm has suffered a $20 loss instead of earning a $30 profit.

The cruelest blow comes when we find that our efforts to convince the IRS to base the income tax on SUP profits have been successful and therefore they levy a 50% tax on the $30 profit. This requires the owners to invest $45 in order to maintain share prices and dividends and therefore causes them to complain that the tax is confiscatory, i.e., a tax on capital, not income.

The world has gone haywire. All of those wonderful advantages of SUP measures are now catastrophes. And the only thing that has changed is the direction of the price movements. All of the other facts and assumptions in this decreasing cost case are exactly the same as in the increasing cost case.[10]

10. The critical assumptions are those mentioned in footnote 6 supra, namely: (1) the same number of units will be sold at the new selling price as at the old; (2) the same markup rate is applied to the current cost as was applied to historical cost.

The basic problem is that SUP measures of units do not coincide with SUP measures of dollars. When prices are increasing, the physical capital measures enhance the owners' well-offness since SUP profits in units remain constant but SUP profits in dollars increase which permits a dividend increase. When prices are declining the opposite happens—SUP profits in units remain constant but SUP profits in dollars decrease which requires a dividend decrease.

The magnitude of the divergence increases as the price declines. Consider the extreme case of zero current cost. Although rare, there are actual cases of zero prices. Recall the sharp decline in prices of hula hoops after that fad had peaked. At the end of that fad, hula hoops could not be sold at a positive price—they were free—and therefore wholesalers offered them to retailers at a zero current cost. Consider a retailer who held an inventory of hula hoops at the time the current cost went to zero. Since the retailer had previously paid for the inventory and since it cannot sell that inventory, a monetary measure would show a loss equal to the cost of the inventory. But a physical measure will not show a loss since the number of units has not changed. On the contrary, it will show a SUP profit in units since it can now acquire, say, 1,000,000 additional units—its specific units purchasable has increased since it requires no dollars to purchase at a zero price. Thus, with no further action, by the sole fact that current cost has gone to zero, the retailer would report a SUP profit of 1,000,000 units. The SUP profit in dollars is zero since the multiplicand of the units is zero. The adjustment of the asset to current cost with the offset taken to shareholders' equity means that the firm started with zero dollar capital and ended with zero dollar capital, hence a zero loss.

Such a report is not merely curious, it is absurd. If prices are truly of no consequence, if physical units are the only thing of interest, then we must allow any firm that traffics in free goods to report an infinite SUP profit in units and a zero SUP loss in dollars. The reason such reports are absurd is that the owners invested dollars with the expectation of receiving a dollar return in dividends. They are worse-off, having lost their original dollar investment and having no prospect of receiving dollar dividends. Therefore, the owners would certainly consider such reports to be absurd.

In summary, when prices are declining SUP measures are, at worst, contradictory in that they permit the firm to show a profit when the owners have suffered a loss and, at best, asymmetrical in that all the advantages when prices increase are disadvantages when prices decrease. The reason for adopting SUP measures was to avoid the evils of NOD profits when prices are increasing but SUP profits produce equally as many evils when prices are decreasing. Therefore, physical capital proponents must reject SUP measures when prices are decreasing for the same reasons they reject NOD measures when prices are increasing.

I therefore conclude that SUP measures are not applicable when prices decline. This excludes a fair number of firms. In the recent past we have experienced substantial, albeit short-term, price decreases (or "rebates") in television sets, automobiles, beef, poultry, airframes, electronics and so forth. Even if inflation continues we can expect price declines in other goods from time to time. For this reason we can expect SUP measures to eventually become inapplicable to most firms.

3.13 Same Market

Arguments for current costing are invariably couched in terms of merchandising or manufacturing firms. The thing that characterizes such firms is that they operate in two markets: the market in which they purchase is different from the market in which they sell. For example, a retailer purchases in the wholesale market and sells in the retail market. There is another class of firms, called "trading firms," that purchase and sell in the same market.

Consider a trading firm, e.g., a mutual fund, that purchased 100 shares of General Motors on January 1 for $1.00 per share and sold them on February 1 for $1.60 per share. This firm will report a zero SUP profit for the month. To put it in terms of the balance sheet, the firm started with $100 which would purchase 100 shares and it ended with $160 which will purchase 100 shares. Thus, it is equally as well-off in physical capital since 100 shares is equal to 100 shares. To put it in income statement terms, the revenues are $160, the current cost of goods sold is $160 and the difference is zero.

Now compare this firm to another one that purchased 100 shares of General Electric on January 1 for $1.00 per share and sold them on February 1 for $0.75 per share. For the same reasons as given above, the firm will report a zero SUP profit for the month. Thus, the same SUP profit will be reported for both firms despite the fact that one had a price increase and the other a price decrease. The same holds for the gold speculator who bought for $35 and sold for $700 per ounce and for the silver speculator who bought for $50 and sold for $10 per ounce. Both will report a zero SUP profit.

In general, *any* firm that buys and sells in the same market will *always* report a zero SUP profit on its exchanges for the obvious reason that the selling price always equals the current cost of the identical units.[11] The con-

11. To be slightly more technical, a price greater than zero will always result in reporting a zero SUP profit. A zero price will allow the firm to increase its physical capital and hence report a positive SUP profit in units. A second technical assumption is that the firm does not hold cash. If cash is held and prices increase (decrease) SUP measures could show a loss (profit) because the units purchasable from the cash balance decrease (increase). This assumption will be relaxed and discussed infra (Section 3.14). A third technical assumption is zero transaction costs. If such costs were taken into account, all such firms would always report a loss equal to the transaction costs.

sequent of a zero profit for *all trading firms,* for *all exchanges* for *all price changes* is absurd. There is no point in measuring profit if one knows a priori that its magnitude will always be zero. There is no point in reporting profit if the recipients of the report know beforehand that the reported amount will always be zero.[12]

For these reasons we must conclude that SUP measures are not applicable to trading firms. This excludes a large number of firms and an even larger segment of the economy. The most apparent exclusions are those firms whose major assets are marketable securities. There are a large number of financial institutions who would thus be excluded. In addition, SUP measures would not be applicable to the marketable securities held by merchandising or manufacturing firms. Thus, there would be inconsistencies in the method of accounting for different assets in such firms. All commodity traders—wheat, soybeans, oil, copper, etc.—would also be excluded, as well as all real estate traders.

3.14 Partial Investment

The arguments for physical capital focus on the income statement. The deduction of current costs from revenues is thought to measure distributable income and thereby maintain physical capital. This is true if the firm is fully invested in the physical unit as was demonstrated in Exhibits III and IV. However, if the firm is not fully invested, additional adjustments are required.

The problem and the nature of the required adjustments can be demonstrated by a slight alteration of the simple case. Assume that the firm started with \$100 on January 1 when the purchase price was \$1.00 per unit and it purchased 80 units, leaving a \$20 cash balance. It sold the units for \$1.60 each on January 31 when the current cost is \$1.25. According to Proposition 3 the current cost of \$100 (=80 units @ \$1.25) would be deducted from the revenues of \$128 (=80 units @ \$1.60) to obtain the distributable income of \$28. But if

12. Some prepublication readers were of the view that a zero profit for all exchanges in trading firms was so obviously absurd that I should omit this section. They implied that the fault was in my interpretation of physical capital rather than a logical consequence of physical capital. Perhaps my interpretation is faulty, but a reexamination failed to reveal the flaw. On the contrary, the reexamination provided some evidence that reporting a zero profit for such exchanges is precisely the objective of physical capital proponents. Note that merchandising and manufacturing firms operate in two markets for their inventory, but they buy and sell plant and equipment in the same market. Thus, the treatment of plant and equipment is an instance of exchanges in the same market. Some physical capital proponents are quite explicit in their view that sales of plant and equipment do not result in a profit or loss:

> During the year, plant and equipment having a net book value in the historical cost financial statements of \$1,200,000 was sold for \$2,000,000. The sale proceeds are assumed to provide an appropriate measure of the current cost of the assets at the date of sale. The \$800,000 gain on disposal reflected in the historical cost income statement represents the realization of an increase in the current cost of a productive asset and is eliminated from current cost income of the enterprise. The

\$28 is distributed, the physical capital has not been maintained; it is diminished by 4 units. The firm has \$120 cash on February 1 (\$20 cash balance plus \$128 revenues minus \$28 dividends) which will purchase 96 units (=\$120/1.25) as compared to the initial cash of \$100 which would purchase 100 units. Thus, physical capital proponents must characterize the profit obtained from this procedure as false for the same reason that they characterize NOD profits as false.

The problem, of course, is the \$20 cash balance. It would purchase 20 units on January 1 when the purchase price was \$1.00 but it will purchase only 16 units on February 1 when the purchase price is \$1.25. Thus, there is a loss from holding cash, a loss from not purchasing, of 4 units or \$5.00. In order to obtain the "true profit" we must add the following line on the Income Statement: Loss from not purchasing \$5.00. Although the problem is easily rectified in this simple case, it is often overlooked. The endorsed procedure of deducting current costs from revenues does not achieve the objective of reporting distributable income, of maintaining physical capital. Proposition 3 is inaccurate. The argument that holding gains are equity adjustments is inaccurately stated for the same reason: taking holding gains to equity will not, by itself, accurately measure SUP profits.

In general, focusing exclusively on the income statement will not provide an accurate measure of SUP. Instead, a balance sheet approach is required. In order to achieve the objective of accurately measuring and maintaining SUP, *all* of the balance sheet accounts must be restated as SUP and the gain or loss for each account calculated and reported. Recognition that a balance sheet approach is required reveals another, more serious, problem. In essence, the problem is the same as discussed in the mini-maxi case: *which* specific unit should be used as the basis for SUP measures?

To illustrate, consider a multi-product firm. Assume that the firm holds \$20 cash and that it sells both mini-skirts and calculators. The purchase price of the former went from \$1.00 to \$1.25 resulting in a \$5 loss from holding cash on the basis of minis. The purchase price of the latter went from \$1.00 to \$0.50 resulting in a \$10 gain from holding cash on the basis of calculators. The question

amount of the increase in current cost is disclosed as part of the change in the amount required to maintain the operating capability of the enterprise. (CICA Exposure Draft, 1979, para D.13.)

Thus, if one purchases plant and equipment for \$x and then sells it for \$y, the procedure is to consider \$y to be the current cost and then deduct the current cost from the sale proceeds, i.e., \$y from \$y which yields zero in all cases.

The reasoning for plant and equipment in the quotation is the same as that used in the text for marketable securities and commodities. If readers find zero reported profits for all exchanges in the same market to be absurd, perhaps the fault lies in the concept of maintaining physical capital.

is: Do we report a $5 loss from not purchasing minis or a $10 gain from not purchasing calculators?[13] What is the distributable income? After we have deducted the current cost of both the minis and the calculators from the revenues, do we add a $10 gain or subtract a $5 loss to obtain the distributable income? In general the question is: which specific unit is it that we should measure and maintain? I confess that I do not know the answer. Until the question is answered one could select either unit, or any combination, with equal justification, permitting other criteria (such as the desire to maximize, minimize or smooth income) to dominate. I fear that physical capital proponents also do not know the answer. Worse, I fear they do not know the question because of the focus on the income statement.

Another reason that I fear that physical capital proponents do not know the question is their criticism of the use of price indices. They have correctly pointed out that price indices are based on a specific pattern of purchases ("market basket") which is not likely to describe the actual pattern of purchases of the firm. The consumer price index has come under heavy attack because the firm does not conform to the pattern of purchases upon which that index is based. To use the consumer price index would base accounting measures on hypothetical transactions which could never occur since the firm never purchases consumer goods and therefore the consumer price index is obviously inappropriate. A firm-specific index is better but suffers from similar deficiencies since it is also based upon some sort of assumed, hypothetical transactions as to the pattern of purchases. The selection of the particular pattern of purchases or particular index, so the argument goes, is totally arbitrary and therefore we should eschew price indices and adopt current costs. I agree with physical capital proponents when they describe the problems of price indices, but I part company with them when they allege that the adoption of current costs permits us to avoid the arbitrary selection of a particular index.[14] The question stated in the previous paragraph is, in essence, a price index question and can be restated thus: which price index should be used to adjust the cash? The question arises *anytime* that cash is held. A single product firm merely conceals the question. This can be illustrated by considering trading firms. We noted in the previous section that trading firms would always report a zero SUP profit on exchanges. We can now note that trading firms will report a non-zero SUP profit from holding cash, from not purchasing. If a mutual fund held $20

13. The same question can be asked in regard to depreciable assets. Does one report the gain or loss from holding cash on the basis of not purchasing the inventory or of not purchasing the depreciable asset?

14. The problem of price indices was discussed in more detail in Sterling, 1970, pp. 331-50. One prominent current cost advocate has cited that discussion in several places to bolster his arguments that price indices lead us to a quagmire which current costs avoid. I have been amused by that because, in my view, current cost *is* a price index with a market basket that contains only one good.

in cash when the price of GM stock went from $1.00 to $1.60 per share it could report a $12 loss from not purchasing GM. Alternatively, it could report a $5 gain from not purchasing GE when the price went from $1.00 to $0.75 per share. We can note in passing that a trading firm is a good place to start the consideration of physical versus monetary capital because switching attributes reverses *all* processes and definitions. NOD gains occur *only* when *stock* is held and the price *increases* while SUP gains occur *only* when *cash* is held and the price decreases.[15]

In such firms the central question is which price index should be used to calculate the gains from holding cash since that is the only way that gains can occur. To make the point, consider the extreme case of Sterling who has kept $100 on deposit with his broker for the last several years but has not made any trades. When silver went from $50 to $10 per ounce, Sterling reported a SUP profit of $80 since his ounces purchasable went from 2 to 10 by not purchasing. By contrast, King Faisol bought gold for $40 and sold it for $200 per ounce and reported a zero SUP profit for the same time period. Thus, according to SUP measures Sterling became better-off during the period while King Faisol did not, the exact reverse of the usual definition of "better-off." But note that Sterling could have declared that if he had traded he would have traded gold and thereby report a SUP loss from not purchasing gold at $200 since his ounces purchasable went from 2 to ½ by not purchasing. By contrast, Bunker Hunt bought silver for $50 and sold it for $10 per ounce during the same time period and reported a zero SUP profit since his ounces purchasable remained constant. Thus, according to SUP measures Sterling became worse-off during this period while Mr. Hunt did not. The question that physical capital proponents must address is whether Sterling became better-off or worse-off during the time period and also whether he became more or less better-off than King Faisol and Mr. Hunt. And the question must be faced each year. If the price of Chrysler stock continues downward, Sterling can declare that he has switched to being a trader in Chrysler stock and report a tidy SUP profit from not purchasing Chrysler. Alternatively, if the price of soybeans continues upward, Sterling can report a substantial loss from not purchasing soybeans and then use that loss to offset other SUP profits when filing his tax return, after we have convinced the IRS to base taxes on SUP profits to avoid taxing capital.

Of course the case is extreme but it is not without real world analogs. The most celebrated analog was when Sewall Avery began to accumulate cash in

15. The entire problem is displayed in the simple model of the trading firm presented by Boulding (1955, Ch. 26, and 1977). He succinctly discusses the "apparent paradoxes" which, in this context, we would say result from switching from measuring NOD to measuring SUP. I commend the Boulding references to the reader because those apparent paradoxes are in fact a simple, succinct statement of the question of physical versus monetary measures which demand an unequivocal answer. I present my answer to that question in detail in Sterling, 1970, Ch. IX.

Montgomery Ward in anticipation of a post-war depression. As I recall, at the time he was deposed the cash balance was greater than the sum of all the other assets and therefore the gain or loss from not purchasing would have overshadowed the profits or losses from operations. If we allowed Mr. Avery to select a specific price index he could have shown a tremendous gain because some prices declined. If we allowed Mr. Avery's opponents to select a specific price index they could have shown a tremendous loss because some prices increased. That is, S_iUP and S_jUP yield vastly different answers and we must be prepared to certify to one or the other, to attest that Mr. Avery was right (wrong) and Montgomery Ward became better- (worse-) off during the period and that it became more (less) better-off than Sears which did not accumulate cash. Was the opponents' charge of poor stewardship true or false? And so forth for all of the questions regarding distributable income, taxes, managerial effectiveness, . . .

Again the world has gone haywire. All of these answers that seemed so clear in Section 2 are now enigmas. And the only thing that has happened is that the firm holds cash. All of the techniques for measuring SUP that were described in Section 2 have been faithfully applied to this case. The basic problem is that everything is reversed. When measuring monetary attributes we face problems when the assets are in non-monetary, i.e., physical, form. When measuring physical attributes we face problems when assets are in non-physical, i.e., monetary, form. SUP measures do not solve the measurement problems, they substitute one kind of problem for another. SUP measures do not avoid the price index problem, they conceal it. Such problems must be addressed not only to prevent rogues like Sterling from manipulating income, but also to allow sincere businessmen like Mr. Avery and his opponents to determine income.

In summary, consideration of firms partially invested reveals that deducting current costs from revenues is not an accurate measure of SUP profits. An additional adjustment for each balance sheet account is required to calculate the SUP gain or loss from not purchasing the specific unit. It is not at all clear which unit should be used in multi-product firms. Extending the question to cash-rich companies reveals that SUP measures run into serious conceptual problems regarding the measurement of monetary assets. Until these problems are solved, I must conclude that SUP measures are not applicable to firms that hold a material amount of monetary assets. This excludes virtually all firms since almost all firms hold a material amount of monetary assets at all times.

3.15 Summary

SUP measures assume, albeit tacitly, that the firm continually replaces identical units, faces continuously increasing costs, operates in two markets and is fully invested in a single kind of unit. For firms that do not meet any one of these four conditions, SUP measures encounter serious conceptual and practical problems. Until these problems are solved, SUP measures cannot be applied to firms that do not meet all four conditions. Therefore, measuring physical capital is, at best, a special case. It can be utilized only after determining that the firm meets the conditions. It may be that no firm can meet all four conditions. Therefore, measuring physical capital is, at worst, inapplicable to all firms.

3.2 Objectives

A question that should arise prior to, and is more fundamental than, consideration of the problems of measurement is: why set the objective to be the maintenance of the physical capital of the firm? In the typical argument for adopting physical capital the question of objectives is never examined. Instead, it is proved that NOD profits do not maintain physical capital, that SUP profits do maintain physical capital, and these proofs are considered to be sufficient to conclude that we should measure SUP and not measure NOD. But note that the conclusion is reversible. It is equally valid to conclude that we should measure NOD profits because the same proofs show that SUP profits do not maintain NOD capital and that NOD profits do maintain NOD capital. Thus, such proofs do not discriminate. The question of objectives is separate from the question of measurement.

One problem that was encountered when considering measurement was that in some cases the well-offness of the firm diverged from the well-offness of the owners. For this reason, we could address the objectives question in terms of the objectives of the firm versus the objectives of the owners.

3.21 Firms vs. Owners

Should we account for the objectives of the firm or the objectives of the owners of the firm? This choice is sometimes phrased as the entity versus the proprietorship concept.[16] It can be more simply and starkly phrased as: whose income and wealth should we measure? The concepts of income and wealth must refer to something quite specific. This is indicated in ordinary language when we speak of the wealth and income *of* the nation or the wealth and income *of* General Motors or the wealth and income *of* Sterling. Until we

16. See Lee (1980) for an insightful discussion of how neglecting this choice has confused the U.K. standard setting process. I suspect that an examination of the U.S. standard-setting process would reveal a similar neglect, and that much of our difficulties could be traced to that neglect. As Lee points out, the different concepts lead to different standards, and therefore vacillation in the choice of concepts leads to vacillation in standards and confusion of the concepts leads to confused standards.

supply the object for that preposition, we cannot begin to measure wealth and income. The choice considered here is the firm versus the owner.

The firm, at least in its corporate form, is known to be a fictitious person. We can postulate that this fictitious person's objective is to maintain or maximize physical capital. Since this fictitious person is not a consumer, we can conclude that ability to command consumer goods is irrelevant. Since it does not consume the goods that it deals in, it has no declining marginal utility for those goods. Its utility is a linear function of the quantity of goods. The prices of those goods are not pertinent except insofar as the purchase prices affect the quantity that it can command when it holds cash. It is indifferent to price changes of goods that it holds in inventory since those changes do not affect the quantity. Its pertinent price index is the price relative to the good that it deals in since it is only interested in its ability to command that particular good.

By contrast, the owner is a real person, a consumer. For any particular good, the marginal utility declines with the quantity owned. The first calculator provides more satisfaction than the second so that even if the owner qua consumer were not willing to exchange the first for a pound of meat, he may be quite willing to exchange the second for a pound of meat. The third provides less satisfaction and so on to the hundredth calculator which provides such minimal marginal utility that he would be eager to exchange it for almost anything. The point is that utility is enhanced by a variety of goods. The way to obtain a variety of goods in a market economy is via exchange. The medium of exchange is money, and the ratio of exchange is price. Thus, prices and price changes are of utmost importance to owners qua consumers.

Just as the firm is indifferent to price changes (under the assumed objective), the owner is indifferent to quantity changes given constant value. It makes no difference to the owner whether the firm owns 100 units that can be sold for $1.00 each or 2 units that can be sold for $50.00 each since both yield $100. The value is equal, the command over the variety of other goods is equal, and therefore the owner is indifferent to the quantities.

If the owner qua consumer owns a good and its selling price goes up relative to the purchase prices of other goods, the owner is better-off because he can command a greater quantity of *other* goods, and vice versa if the selling price of an owned good declines. By extension, if the firm owns goods and the owner owns the firm, then the owner is better-off when the selling prices go up relative to the purchase prices and is worse-off when the selling prices go down. It matters not to the owner whether the firm can replace the same quantity as long as the value is maintained. Thus, the owner prefers a monetary measure of the firm to a physical measure of the firm because the monetary measure better reflects his ability to command a variety of goods. Of course, if the price *level*, as opposed to the *specific* price, changes, then we need to adjust the monetary measure to more accurately reflect the changes in his ability to command the variety of goods. But since it is a variety of goods that is of interest, it is clear that the pertinent index is not the price relative to the assets owned by the firm but rather a general index that more nearly reflects the owner's pattern of purchases, e.g., the Consumer Price Index.

3.22 Conclusion

My primary purpose here is to try to clearly reveal that the fundamental question of what attribute we should account for involves the equally fundamental question of who we should account for. The reason that the question of who we account for is fundamental is that there may be different objectives and the decision of who we account for will determine what objective is to be pursued and in turn the objective will determine what attribute is to be measured. My secondary purpose is to try to point out that the entity per se has no objective. Just as we cannot say whether a building's objective is to be taller or wider, we cannot say that an entity's objective is to maintain physical or monetary capital. Invoking the entity concept obscures the question instead of answering it. The entity is a creation of humans and as such it pursues the objective that humans set for it, not its own objective. If there is a conflict in objectives, it is a conflict among humans—customers, creditors, employees, owners—not a conflict between the firm and the owners. Employees, including managers, may have the objective of maintaining their jobs or of maximizing their income from the entity. Customers may have the objective of maintaining their source of supply or of minimizing the cost of the goods purchased from the entity. If we recognize these different, sometimes conflicting, objectives, then we may be able to measure various attributes that will tell the various humans whether they have achieved their objectives. If we envelop all of these various objectives in the entity concept, we may so confuse the issue that we cannot even determine whether the objective is to minimize or maximize, let alone what attribute to measure. My tertiary purpose is to cast the choice of firm versus owner in such stark relief that it will clearly reveal that although it is possible to account for fictitious persons with assumed objectives of maintaining or maximizing physical capital, the results of such an accounting so diverge from the objectives of human owners that those owners consider those results to be absurd. No human owner would ever agree that he earned the same zero profit from purchasing and selling gold and silver. No one can deny that the ounces purchasable were maintained but that is not what humans mean by "profit." No human owner would ever agree that starting with $100 and ending with $80 results in $30 profit. No one can deny that the calculators purchasable were maintained, but that is not the objective of humans. Since we do, in fact, account for humans and one group of humans is owners, I conclude that we should reject the measurement of SUP because it does not reveal whether the owners' objectives were achieved.

4. MAINTAINING AND FORECASTING CASH FLOWS

Up to this point we have focused exclusively on the maintenance and measurement of physical capital. The maintenance of physical capital was the objective and the measurement of SUP was to see whether or not that objective was achieved. Many proponents set the maintenance of cash flows as the objective and see the maintenance of physical capital as a means to that end. Maintenance of physical capital is merely an intermediate objective which is thought to be necessary to achieve the ultimate objective of maintaining cash flows. Likewise, the *measurement* of physical capital is but a means to the end of *forecasting* cash flows. As pointed out in Section 2.4, two of the alleged advantages of SUP measures are their predictive power and their surrogation of discounted ("economic") value and income. The two advantages are related since discounted values are time adjusted forecasts of cash flows and therefore both will be examined in this section.

The maintenance of cash flows coincides with the objectives of owners and therefore the discussion of firms vs owners (Section 3.21) is not pertinent to the forecasting and maintenance of cash flows argument for physical capital. In an attempt to separate the issues, I will also assume that none of the problems discussed in Section 3.1 are pertinent. That is, in this section it will be assumed that SUP measures can be unambiguously obtained. Thus, the first question to be addressed in this section is the connection of the measurement and maintenance of physical capital to the forecasting and maintenance of cash flows. The second question concerns the objective of maintaining cash flows instead of maintaining physical capital.

4.1 Forecasting

The question of forecasting can be divided into four parts. It depends upon the connection of

(1) present physical stocks to future physical flows;

(2) physical flows to cash flows;

(3) present SUP profit to future SUP profits; and

(4) present purchase prices to future cash flows.

Each relation will be examined seriatim.

4.11 Physical Stocks vs. Flows.

The argument for SUP profits is usually stated in a negative form: if NOD profits are distributed, physical capital will decline. That is bad not because maintenance of physical capital is the objective but because it causes future SUP profits to decline. That is bad not because maintenance of future SUP profits is the objective but because it causes future cash flows to decline. That is bad for two reasons: (1) maintenance of future cash flows *is* the objective, and (2) it inhibits the forecasting of future cash flows.

The second point does not follow from the first. The forecasting of a declining magnitude is not inherently more difficult than the forecasting of an increasing magnitude. If we can discover a connection between present physical capital and future cash flows, then that will enable us to forecast future cash flows regardless of the direction of change. A decrease in physical capital will herald a decrease in future cash flows and vice versa for an increase in physical capital. Thus, the problem of forecasting is to discover the connection.

When the argument is put positively it seems to say simply that maintenance of physical capital maintains future SUP profits, which maintains future cash flows. Maintenance suggests constancy and it is easy to forecast a constant magnitude but the problem is to discover the connection between the maintained physical capital and the maintained cash flows. Physical capital is a stock that exists a moment in time, which is clearly different from flows that occur over time. The future cash flows are a function of the future physical flows, so if we can discover a connection of physical stocks to future physical flows, we have answered the question.

In regard to inventory, the distinction is between the quantity *on hand* (a stock of physical capital) and the quantity *sold* (a flow of physical units). Although the distinction is elementary, it is often blurred in arguments for physical capital. In such arguments we often see the substitution of terms that refer to flows for terms that refer to stocks with no intervening explanation. For example, Revsine (1973, pp. 70-71, 71n, emphasis supplied) is one of the most careful and incisive analysts, yet he blurs the distinction:

> If the entire $500 [NOD profit] were to be distributed to owners as a dividend, the firm would find itself unable to reestablish its previous physical inventory level at prevailing replacement prices. The importance of this decline in asset levels is that it may affect the ability of the firm to generate future operating [cash] inflows. Notice, however, that by maintaining physical asset levels, the firm does not necessarily maintain total operating [cash] flows at their previous level. Total operating [cash] flows will remain constant only if (1) operating levels are unchanged, and (2) input

> costs and output prices move in parallel fashion. Thus, by ***maintaining physical asset levels intact,*** the firm ***satisfies*** one condition ***necessary to maintain total operating*** [cash] ***flows.*** Whether total [cash] flows remain at the previous level is a function of the second condition as well.

The quotation begins with reference to asset levels, quantity *on hand.* It switches to a reference to operating levels, quantity *sold.* Then it switches back to a reference to asset levels, quantity *on hand.* Distinguishing the terms yields the following restatement of the argument:

(a) If NOD profits are paid in dividends, quantity *on hand* will decline. Dividends limited to SUP profits permits quantity *on hand* to be maintained.

(b) Future operating cash inflow, revenue, will remain constant only if (1) quantity *sold* and (2) selling price remain constant since revenue is the product of the quantity *sold* and the selling price.

(c) Maintenance of quantity *on hand* satisfies condition (1) of maintaining quantity *sold* but not condition (2) of maintaining the selling price.

The restatement of the argument with the terms distinguished reveals the error: maintenance of quantity on hand does *not* satisfy the condition of maintaining quantity sold. The commonplace notion of "turnover" illustrates the point. Increased turnover means that the quantity sold is increased without increasing the quantity on hand. Managers often strive to increase turnover in order to reduce carrying costs. When they succeed it proves the point that it is not necessary to maintain the quantity on hand to maintain the quantity sold.

Indeed, managers would prefer not to hold any inventory to avoid all carrying costs. The reason they hold inventory is to avoid the lost revenues from stockouts. Managers compare carrying costs to losses from stockouts in deciding how much inventory to hold. Thus, there is a connection between quantity on hand and quantity sold in regard to stockouts, but that is a negative connection. The future quantity sold depends upon a host of factors that are combined in the word "demand." We must first forecast the demand and then deduct the quantity not sold from stockouts. In the absence of future demand a zero quantity will be sold and therefore the stockout question is irrelevant. Of course, a zero future quantity sold is an extreme case but it does make the point that it is possible for a large quantity on hand to have no connection to the future quantity sold. At the other extreme are drop-shippers who maintain no quantity on hand but sell large quantities. Therefore, with little, if any, distortion we can conclude that quantity on hand is independent of quantity sold.

Future quantity purchased, by contrast, is dependent upon the quantity on hand in the short-run. One can obviate the need to purchase a unit if there is a unit on hand but once the quantity on hand is depleted, purchases will have to be made if sales are to continue. Eventually, therefore, quantity purchased depends upon quantity sold rather than quantity on hand. Thus, short-run quantity purchased is dependent upon quantity on hand but long-run quantity purchased is dependent upon quantity sold. But the short-run dependence is based on the depletion of the quantity on hand which is another way of saying that physical capital was not maintained. If the physical capital is maintained, then short-run quantity purchased is also dependent on quantity sold. Since quantity sold is independent of quantity on hand and quantity purchased is dependent upon quantity sold, quantity purchased is independent of quantity on hand.

For these reasons, I conclude that the connection of physical capital to physical flows has not been demonstrated. Since SUP profits are dependent upon physical flows, the connection of the maintenance of physical capital to the maintenance of SUP profits has not been demonstrated. The reverse has been demonstrated by many physical capital proponents as well as in Section 2.3. Limiting distribution to SUP profits maintains physical capital. But the question is whether "maintains" is reflexive or irreflexive, whether it is a one way or two way connection. To say that Mary is the spouse of John is different from saying that Mary is the wife of John because "spouse of" is reflexive and "wife of" is irreflexive. My conjecture is that physical capital proponents have assumed that "maintains" is reflexive so that demonstrating that SUP profit maintains physical capital is tantamount to demonstrating that physical capital maintains SUP profits. My claim is that "maintains" is likely to be irreflexive for the reasons given above and therefore a separate demonstration is required. Until that demonstration is provided we cannot conclude that maintenance of physical capital maintains SUP profits. For the same reason, the connection of the maintenance of physical capital to the ability to forecast SUP profits and, in turn, to forecast dividends, has not been demonstrated. And the same holds for the maintenance and forecasting of the cash flows of the firm since those cash flows also depend upon physical flows.

4.12 Physical vs. Cash Flows

Since SUP profits and cash flows are both a function of physical flows, we now turn to the question of their relationship. Instead of examining the maintenance of physical capital, quantity on hand, we will examine the maintenance of physical flows, quantity purchased and sold. Revsine (1973, p. 34, emphasis supplied) presents the case succinctly:

> Future operating [cash] flow levels are determined by (1) the physical level of future operations and (2) future input [purchase]

> and output [selling] prices. Future price levels are usually a function of events external to the firm. Accordingly, in striving to maintain net operating [cash] flow levels, management's real controllable variable is to *maintain the existing physical level of operations.*

Revsine's purpose is to distinguish the controllable physical flows from the uncontrollable prices. Since management cannot control prices, they should concentrate on the maintenance of physical flows. The focus has shifted from maintaining physical capital to maintaining physical flows. Apparently the reason for the shift in focus is to argue that the control over and maintenance of physical flows aids in the achievement of the objectives of maintaining and forecasting cash flows.

In this simple case the cash flows, F, are easily modelled:

(eq. 1) $$F = sq_s - cq_p$$

where

s = selling price
q_s = quantity sold
c = purchase price
q_p = quantity purchased.

Inspection of (eq. 1) reveals that the argument makes some tacit assumptions about s and c. Once again it seems that the case for SUP measures and forecasts assumes continuously increasing prices. If the selling price declines, maintenance of the physical flows will not maintain cash flows.[17]

In the decreasing cost case (Section 3.12) management did in fact maintain the quantity sold (as well as the quantity on hand) but the cash flows decreased because the selling price decreased. In order to maintain the cash flows, management would have been required to double the quantity sold. But doubling the quantity sold would violate the assumption of constant volume which was necessary to the demonstration of the advantages when prices were increasing. Alternatively management could have maintained the cash flows by increasing the markup rate. But that would violate the assumption that

17. It is my conjecture that the tacit assumption is increasing prices since we are in inflationary times and since decreasing costs are seldom discussed. More generally, the maintenance of cash flows would be maintained by the maintenance of physical flows if the difference between s and c is constant. A constant difference may be what is meant by the assumption that purchase and selling prices move in a "parallel fashion." I have interpreted that assumption as meaning a constant markup rate. Either is unrealistic but it seemed to me that a constant markup rate is less unrealistic because a constant difference would yield a continually decreasing (increasing) markup rate in times of increasing (decreasing) prices. For example, if price changes were extreme, it would mean that an item bought for $1.00 and sold for $1.60 would be sold for $100.60 if the purchase price increased to $100.00 or sold for $0.61 if the purchase price decreased to $0.01.

such rates are constant which was necessary to demonstrate the advantages when prices were increasing as well as violating the statement in the argument that the firm is a price taker—that prices are a function of events external to the firm. In addition, if we allow markup rates to vary, the cash flows could be maintained even if physical flows declined. That is, if management's controllable variables include the markup rate, then it may achieve the objective of maintaining cash flows by *decreasing* (not maintaining) the physical flows and *increasing* the markup rate regardless of whether purchase prices increase, decrease or remain constant.

Even if management's only controllable variable is the physical flows, the maintenance of those flows is not the best way to achieve the maintenance of cash flows. In the decreasing cost case, management could have come closer to maintaining cash flows by decreasing the physical flows. The maintenance of physical flows resulted in a negative cash flow but decreasing the physical flows to zero would have increased the cash flows to zero. That is, if management had purchased a zero quantity, decreased its physical flows, the firm would have better achieved the objective of maintaining its cash flows.

In general, *maintenance* of physical flows does not achieve the maintenance of cash flows. Managements should *vary* physical flows in striving to achieve the maintenance of cash flows. When the firm is a price taker, when the prices are a function of events external to the firm, then the physical flows are management's only controllable variable. In perfect markets they can purchase or sell any quantity at the given price. A trading firm is an example of a price taker in a near perfect market in which the decision process can be easily outlined. The management can decide to purchase or not purchase particular shares. Assuming zero dividends, if the present entry value (given price plus commission) is greater than the forecasted exit value (future price less commission) management will not purchase. It can also decide to sell or not sell. If the present exit value (given price less commission) is greater than the forecasted exit value, then management will sell. Both decisions turn on the relation of the forecasted exit value to the present sacrifice (entry value if unowned, exit value if owned). In such cases the decision to not purchase or not sell, to decrease the physical flows, is equally as important to the maintenance of the cash flows as is the decision to purchase or sell. For example, if GM is owned and has a present exit value of $100 and a forecasted exit value of $160 and if GE is the next best alternative with a present entry value of $100 and a forecasted exit value of $125, then the forecasted cash flows will be enhanced by not selling GM and not purchasing GE.

A similar decision process is applicable to merchandising firms that are price takers. Retail prices lie in the future and must be forecast. If the present purchase price of the lot is greater than the sum of the forecasted retail prices of the individual units, management will not purchase. If the present exit value (i.e., wholesale selling price) of the lot is greater than the sum of the forecasted retail prices, management will sell now for the exit value. Again as a price taker the objective of maintaining cash flows requires management to vary the physical flows, not maintain them. More important, if the firm is truly a price taker in the retail market, then the quantity sold is problematic. Being a price taker in the retail market usually means that the price is regulated and the maintenance of quantity sold requires cash outflows for service or marketing, i.e., "cost competition." This was the case when retail prices were controlled by fair trade laws. A more familiar and recent example was the airlines prior to deregulation. They attempted to increase quantity of tickets sold by providing more service. Obviously, however, management would not provide an additional service if the incremental cash outflow from providing that service was greater than the incremental cash inflow from the incremental quantity sold. The obverse is that management may decrease the cash outflows from providing a service even if that results in a decrease in quantity sold, if the decremental cash inflow is less than the decremental cash outflows. Recognition of that truism means that management will vary its cash outflows in an attempt to maintain (or increase) its net cash flows without regard to the effect on quantity sold.

In most cases merchandising and manufacturing firms are not price takers. In such cases the prices and physical flows are interdependent and the management may attempt to increase the quantity sold by decreasing the sales price. Or it may increase the sales price and accept a decrease in the quantity sold. Which course management will elect depends upon the forecasted effect on cash inflows, revenue. We cannot say that management should strive to maintain quantity sold or maintain selling prices: we can only say that management should strive to maintain cash inflows. We cannot say that management has control over quantity sold or control over selling prices: we can only say that management should strive to control cash inflows. Of course management does have control over cash outflows, quantity purchased or produced, but that does not solve the problem. The recent slump in automobile sales is a vivid example. The management did have control over the quantity produced but the maintenance of that physical flow resulted in a buildup of quantity on hand, not quantity sold, and a decrease in net cash flows. Management has tried to increase quantity sold by price reductions (rebates) but it seems that it would require further reductions to bring the quantity sold back to where they were, i.e., to maintain them. Evidently management forecasts that the price reduction would have to be so deep that the maintenance of quantity sold would not be worth it, i.e., net cash flows would be further reduced. Such analysis leads me to conclude that the most we can say is that in striving to maintain cash flows management should strive to maintain cash flows.

For these reasons, I conclude that even if the maintenance of physical capital maintained future physical flows, it would not necessarily maintain future cash flows. For the same reasons, even if present physical capital (or past or present physical flows) was a perfect forecaster of future physical flows, it would not necessarily forecast future cash flows. I say "not necessarily" in both cases because it is possible to posit certain conditions which would result in net cash flows being perfectly correlated with physical flows. To use older terminology, it is possible for certain "firm models" to have those characteristics, and it is for that reason that I have been urging for a long time that we examine various specific firm models because we can draw different conclusions from different firm models and because it requires that the firm model be made explicit. My conjecture is that the physical capital proponents have a specific, tacit firm model in mind in which net cash flows covary with physical flows. Until that firm model is made explicit, I conclude that the connection of the maintenance of physical flows to the maintenance of cash flows has not been demonstrated.

4.13 Present vs. Future SUP Profits

It is possible for SUP profits to be sufficiently stable to permit one to project them into the future. Revsine (1973, pp. 120-21) called this the "extrapolation method" of forecasting, and pointed out that its validity depended on some stringent assumptions about the stability of the underlying factors.

Two such assumptions are: (1) constant volume, and (2) constant markup rate which have been mentioned several times supra. These are heroic assumptions yet they are not sufficient to permit extrapolation, as will be demonstrated. SUP profit, Y, is defined in equation (2).

$$\text{(eq. 2)} \qquad Y = sq - cq$$

where

s = selling price per unit
c = current cost per unit
q = quantity of units sold.

Since s = cm by assumption (2), where m is the markup factor, we can eliminate s as in equation (3).

$$\text{(eq. 3)} \qquad (m - 1)\,cq = Y$$

Since m is constant by assumption (2) and q is constant by assumption (1), variations in Y depend solely upon variations in c. Thus, equation 4.

$$\text{(eq. 4)} \qquad Y_{t+1} = (c_{t+1}/c_t)\,Y_t$$

The discerning reader will have noticed the sole dependence of SUP profit changes upon current cost changes in the previous discussion. When the current cost increased by a factor of 1.25, from $1.00 to $1.25, the SUP profit increased by the same factor from $60 to $75. When the current cost decreased by a factor of .5, from $1.00 to $0.50, SUP profit decreased by the same factor, from $60 to $30. The discerning reader will also notice that in such cases the SUP profit cannot be extrapolated. The SUP profit of $60 was not a good forecaster of the $75 SUP profit when current costs increased nor was the $60 a good forecaster of the $30 when current costs decreased.

Therefore, the stability of the quantity sold and the markup rate is not sufficient to permit extrapolation. The net effect of the two assumptions is to reduce the problem to forecasting c. If we can forecast c_{t+1} at time t, then we can forecast SUP profits via equation (4). But forecasting future purchase prices is difficult at best and the problem here is to determine which additional underlying factors need to be stable to permit extrapolation. Revsine (1973, p. 137, emphasis supplied) provides the answer: "The reasoning is that current operating [SUP] profit of one year is—*in the absence of price and volume changes*—an indicator of the succeeding period's current operating [SUP] profit." The emphasized phrase reiterates assumption (1) of constant volume, and it also extends assumption (2) of constant markup rates to (3) constant future prices. The effect of all three assumptions is:

(a) q_t is constant for t, t+1, t+2 . . .
by assumption (1);

(b) s_t is constant for t+1, t+2, t+3 . . .
by assumptions (2) and (3); and

(c) c_t is constant for t+1, t+2, t+3 . . .
by assumption (3)

Under these conditions Y_{t+1} is a perfect forecaster of Y_{t+2} and all subsequent years. However, it does not resolve the problem of forecasting Y_{t+1} from Y_t. The effect of the assumption is to make Y constant for t+1, t+2, t+3 . . . and also for t−1, t−2, t−3 . . . with the only change occurring at t. Thus, we forecast Y to be constant for all periods prior to t and then experience an abrupt change at t, after which we resume forecasting Y to be constant for periods subsequent to t. Forecasting is a difficult task and it often turns out that the best available forecast of a future magnitude is a present magnitude. Thus, the assumption may be quite reasonable for purposes of forecasting. However, my purpose is to examine various accounting methods, not forecasting methods.

In examining the various accounting methods, I find the assumption of constant prices to be ironic for two reasons. First, the raison d'etre of the physical capital proposal is to provide a better method of accounting when prices are changing, and one of the alleged betterments is that it aids in forecasting, but the demonstration of that betterment assumes constant prices. Second, the assumptions do not discriminate SUP from NOD. When all of the underlying factors are constant, NOD profits are also constant and therefore present NOD profits are perfect forecasters of future NOD profits. Maintaining NOD capital is the same as maintaining SUP capital and even the financial versus physical capital distinction between current costs disappears since there are no holding gains when prices are constant.

Vancil-Weil (1976, p. 58) state the argument in its most general form: "If the world does not change, the company can maintain its physical capacity next year and have the same amount of distributable income [SUP profit] that it had this year." I agree, but I hasten to add that the same is true of NOD profit. The problem as I see it is not how to account when the world does not change but rather how to account when the world does change.

For these reasons, I conclude that the ability of present SUP profits to forecast future SUP profits has not been demonstrated. Even if we assume that the maintenance of physical capital maintains physical flows, that the maintenance of physical flows maintains cash flows, and that physical flows and markups are constant, it does not permit SUP profits to be extrapolated. The demonstration of that extrapolation is accomplished by also assuming that prices are constant. This assumes all independent variables to be constant which makes forecasting trivial but the probability of all independent variables being constant is vanishingly small and therefore forecastability has not been demonstrated. The assumptions also eliminate the distinction between NOD and SUP and therefore the superiority of the forecastability of SUP has also not been demonstrated.

4.14 Present Costs vs. Future Cash Flows

Many accountants consider the discounting of future cash flows to be the ideal method of measuring value and income. Since this ideal cannot be achieved because the future is unknown, they continue to seek a surrogate and current cost is thought to provide such a surrogate. The argument is straightforward: profit maximizing managements will not purchase an asset unless its current cost is less than the discounted cash flows emanating from that asset. (See FAS 33, para 133 for a statement of that view and further discussion.) From this premise the conclusion is drawn that the current cost of a given asset is a conservative (lower limit) indicator of its discounted value.

This argument is utilized as a major justification for reporting current costs in both the financial and physical capital versions. For some proponents the surrogation of discounted value is sufficient justification since discounted value produces the true or ideal income. For others the justification is based on the relevance of future cash flows. Since discounted value is the (time adjusted) future cash flows and current cost is a surrogate for that discounted value, the reporting of current costs aids users in assessing the amounts, timing and uncertainty of future cash flows. It does not provide much aid in assessing the specific amounts, timing and uncertainty, but it does provide aid in comparisons since a firm that owns assets with greater current costs will have greater future cash flows than a firm that owns assets with lesser current costs.

Although there is much to be said for the relationship of current costs to discounted values in general, the application of the notion requires four distinctions. First, the market price of an asset is the result of the consensus of all market participants who assign different discounted values to the asset and have alternative uses for the asset. A given participant will not purchase unless his specific discounted value from his specific use of the asset is greater than the current cost. The difference is sometimes called "producer's surplus" and its magnitude varies among firms for a number of different reasons. It will also vary with the scale of production within a given firm even for identical assets. The second asset is likely to have a different producer's surplus from the first because of economies or diseconomies of scale. The point is that the relationship of current costs to discounted values is quite specific and it cannot be generalized.

Second, a specific firm will not purchase unless the current cost is less than *management's forecast* of the future cash flows. The distinction is between future cash flows and management's forecast of future cash flows. Since management may err in its forecast and incur a current cost on the basis of that erroneous forecast, current cost may provide an erroneous indicator of future cash flows. For example, Ford Motor Company incurred abnormally high current costs when it produced the Edsel. General Motors, on the other hand, incurred normal current costs by retooling for a new model Chevrolet. The management of both firms forecast that the cash flows would be greater than the current cost. Both firms erred. The cash flows from the Edsel were significantly overestimated while the cash flows from the Chevrolet were significantly understimated. If users had compared the current costs and used them as an indicator of future cash flows, they would have been misled. Thus, current costs are not surrogates for discounted values or indicators of future cash flows. Instead, they are at best surrogates for management's estimates or forecasts. The distinction is crucial since management may err.

Third, even if management were omniscient, current costs do not necessarily provide a surrogate for discounted value. Current cost is a conservative surrogate for management's estimates only if management would replace with an identical unit. To prove the point consider the case of different units. If the firm now owns minis but decides to replace with maxis, then the current cost of minis is not a reliable surrogate for management's estimated discounted value. The decision to replace may be outlined as follows: (1) the current cost of minis is subtracted from the estimated discounted value of minis; (2) the current cost of maxis is subtracted from the estimated discounted value of maxis; (3) the differences are compared and the larger difference is selected. We have assumed that the decision was to purchase maxis and therefore we can infer that the difference in (2) is greater than the difference in (1). We can also infer that the difference in (2) is positive. It is these inferences that permit the conclusion that the current cost of maxis is a conservative indicator of management's estimated discounted value of maxis. But there are no inferences that permit the conclusion that the current cost of minis provides such an indicator for minis. The problem is that the difference in (1) could be either positive or negative. Therefore, the current cost of minis could either be a conservative indicator of the management's estimated discounted value of minis or it could be greater than said discounted value. Since we do not know which is the case, we must conclude that current costs do not in general provide a conservative indicator of management's estimated discounted value. They provide such an indicator only when management would replace the identical units.[18]

Fourth, it may be desirable to provide an indication of management's expectations even though we fully recognize that they may err.[19] If so, we must distinguish two different kinds of decisions. The decision process is such that we can confidently infer that current cost is less than management's estimated discounted value when the decision to purchase is being made. It is only at the moment of purchase that the inference can be drawn. Financial statements are prepared subsequent to the purchase and therefore we need to value assets that were previously purchased. To put it another way, we need to value *owned* assets and the decision process from which the inference is drawn is applicable to *unowned* assets. For owned assets a similar managerial decision process is utilized and similar inferences can be drawn. The only difference is that management must now decide to sell or not sell the owned asset instead of deciding to purchase or not purchase the unowned asset. The decision to sell requires the comparison of the estimated discounted value from not selling to the cash that would be obtained from an immediate sale, i.e., the exit value. In the absence of more profitable alternatives, management will decide to keep plant assets only if the forecasted cash flows from use are greater than its exit value. Management will decide to keep inventory only if the forecasted cash flows from keeping (i.e., the sum of the forecasted retail prices of the

18. It may have been this problem that caused FASB to provide for an exception. When the difference in (1) is negative it is not "worthwhile" to replace the identical unit and therefore it is valued at the "recoverable amount" instead of at the current cost. (See FAS 33, para 126.)

19. For further discussion of the reasons for providing the information and the related decision process see Sterling (1970, pp. 133 ff).

units) are greater than its exit value (i.e., the immediate sale price of the entire inventory in the wholesale market). Current costs are not relevant to these decisions and therefore current costs are not a reliable surrogate for management's forecasts of future cash flows of owned assets.

In summary, the claim that current costs are surrogates for discounted values or for future cash flows has not been demonstrated. Drawing the distinctions reveals that the best we can report are surrogates for management's forecasts or estimations in very specific situations. Since management may or may not decide to purchase and we cannot know which until the decision is made, we are limited to inferences about owned assets. Since management has already decided not to sell its owned assets at the time the report is prepared, we can infer that exit values are surrogates for management's expectations.

4.15 Changes in Present Costs vs. Future Cash Flows

Some make the case on the basis of changes in purchase prices instead of the magnitude of purchase prices. One reason for the distinction is to justify including such changes in income in the financial capital version. Another reason is to justify using such changes as indicators of changes in the amount of future cash flows. My reconstruction of the argument follows:

(1) an increase in current costs results in an upward shift of the marginal cost curve of all firms;

(2) this results in an upward shift in the industry supply curve and therefore an increased selling price;

(3) this results in increased revenues, increased cash inflows, to each firm;

(4) this results in increased net cash flows to each firm;

(5) if we knew the timing and magnitude of the increased net cash flows, we could discount them and thereby determine the increase in discounted value;

(6) since we do not know the future, we can take the increase in current costs as an indicator of the increase in discounted value;

(7) therefore increases in current cost are a surrogate for increases in discounted value.

In general, the argument suffers from the failure to make the distinctions drawn in the previous section. For example, if management were faced with the purchase decision at the increased current cost it could decide to not purchase and perhaps substitute some other kind of asset. That is, for the specific use of the asset in a specific firm, the increase in current cost does not necessarily indicate an increase in either cash flows or management's expectations. (Cf. Revsine's Type A, B and C price changes for a similar point—1973, pp. 108-116.)

More specifically, the argument pivots on an enthymeme regarding quantity sold in point (3). Revenue is the product of the quantity sold and the selling price but in general the higher the selling price the lower the quantity sold and vice versa. Thus, the multiplier and multiplicand vary in opposite directions and whether revenue increases or decreases when the selling price increases depends upon the magnitude of the decrease in quantity sold. It could be that the quantity sold decreases sufficiently to decrease the future revenue in which case a current cost increase is a surrogate for a discounted value decrease. In other words, it depends upon the elasticity of demand. Until we know the elasticity of demand, an increase in current cost may indicate either an increase or a decrease in discounted value.

There is another enthymeme in point (4): the selling price increases by an amount equal to or greater than the increase in current costs. Even assuming constant quantity sold, since the future current costs are future cash outflows, the net cash flows will be greater only if the selling price increase is equal to or greater than the current cost increase. That depends upon the shape of the firm's marginal cost and marginal revenue curves and may or may not be true. Since the increase in current costs could be greater than the increase in selling prices, an increase in current cost could be an indicator of a decrease in discounted value.

The enthymemes in the argument are tacit reiterations of those assumptions of constant volume and constant markup rate that have been mentioned repeatedly. The argument holds if and only if the assumptions hold, and whether or not they hold depends upon specific questions about the nature of specific firms and cannot be generalized. For this reason, I conclude that the allegation that changes in current cost are surrogates for changes in discounted values or future cash flows has not been demonstrated.

4.16 Summary

The argument that SUP measures forecast cash flows is flawed. First, it has not been demonstrated that there is a connection between physical stocks and physical flows. Therefore, the maintenance of physical capital does not necessarily maintain physical flows. Second, the maintenance of physical flows does not necessarily maintain cash flows. Management should vary physical flows to achieve the objective of maintaining cash flows. Third, the claim that SUP profits can be extrapolated has not been demonstrated. The assumption that all independent variables are constant is dubious in the extreme, and, if it were to hold, it would not discriminate SUP from NOD. Fourth, the claim that current costs are surrogates for discounted values or future cash flows overlooks some crucial distinctions. Drawing the distinctions reveals that at best current costs are surrogates for management's expectations, not surrogates for future cash flows, and that they are surrogates for management's expectations only when management would replace with an identical unit. Exit values provide a generalized surrogate for management's expectations while current costs do not. Fifth, the claim that changes in current cost are surrogates for changes in discounted values overlooks the same distinctions as well as distinction in the specific firms' demand and cost curves. It rests on the assumption of constant volume and constant markup rate which cannot be expected to hold in all cases, probably not even in a majority of cases.

In general, I conclude that the ability of SUP measures to forecast themselves or to forecast cash flows has not been demonstrated. That is not to say that it cannot be demonstrated. The ultimate test, as Revsine repeatedly emphasizes, is empirical.[20] We can discover empirical relations when the *a priori* argument is flawed or even in the absence of an *a priori* argument. Physicists often refer to "phenomenological laws" to indicate a relation that is based on observed phenomena but is not explained by a theory. Moreover, there have been many instances which historians of science call "jumping the logical gap" or making "happy guesses" to describe researchers who have discovered important relationships on the basis of incomplete logic or inadequate evidence. For that reason, I try to find ways to encourage researchers to test what they believe rather than to require them to test what I believe. Perhaps the best way to encourage researchers in this case is to draw an exaggerated conclusion: I conclude that there is no relationship between present SUP measures and future cash flows.

It has now been eight years since Revsine's hypothesis was presented in expanded form and, insofar as I am aware, no one has attempted to prove him right. Perhaps my exaggerated conclusion will motivate someone to prove me wrong, which will prove him right, and then we can call it Revsine's law. In the meantime, the issue is moot.

4.2 Objectives

The objective under consideration is to maintain and forecast cash flows. In Section 3 the objective considered was to maintain and measure physical capital. In Section 3.2 I concluded that we should not measure physical capital because it was not a human objective. In Section 4.1 I concluded that

20. He is also most careful to state the assumptions and limitations of his analysis. It was that scholarly characteristic that allowed me to use quotations from his work to illustrate the points. A careful reading of Revsine (1973) reveals that his *only* conclusion is that it all depends on empirical tests. With that I am in complete accord.

the ability of physical measures to forecast cash flows has not been demonstrated. The careful reader will have noted a curious omission. Why did we go directly from measuring to forecasting? If the ultimate objective is to maintain cash flows, why do physical capital proponents fail to propose that we measure cash flows? Perhaps the answer is that our zeal to aid users in assessing the amounts, timing and uncertainty of future cash flows has caused us to overlook the distinction between forecasts and measurements.

4.21 Forecasts vs. Measurements

The confusion of temporal locations has plagued us for a long time. The arguments for historical cost often contained allegations that it was impossible to measure the present, and therefore we had to be satisfied with reporting allocations of past measures. Such arguments are less common now. They have been replaced by arguments that we should forecast instead of measure. From the correct observation that all decisions require forecasts, the erroneous conclusion has been drawn that measures of present states are irrelevant. A variant is that we must find a present measure that will also forecast the future. To put it negatively, if the only thing that a measure reveals is the present state, it is deficient.

The fact is that forecasting and measuring are different processes. Measurement is the process of discovering a present state. It requires an operation of some kind and that operation can only be performed at the present moment. The operation for measuring my weight is to step on the bathroom scale. I cannot step on that scale yesterday or tomorrow but I can step on it now. I could have stepped on it yesterday and recorded the reading but I cannot go back in time to measure yesterday's weight. I can forecast tomorrow's weight and I can step on the scale when tomorrow becomes today, but I cannot go forward in time to measure tomorrow's weight.

By contrast, forecasting is the process of mentally projecting a future state. There is no measurement that I know of which *ipso facto* reveals the future. Even in astronomy, where forecasts are near perfect and relatively simple, the measurement of the present spatial location of a planet does not reveal anything at all about its future location. No astronomer disparages the measurement for that reason. No astronomer argues that since decisions require forecasts, measurements of present locations are irrelevant. Accountants who hold such beliefs about accounting measures have set standards for accounting that are beyond the reach of astronomy, the paradigm of forecasting.

In forecasting, one usually starts with a law which specifies the relation of two or more measures. In astronomy, for example, the law states that spatial location is a function of time and that orbits are elliptical. Given the law, one can forecast a future spatial location by, in effect, "forecasting" a future temporal location. In other pursuits the relation is less precise. For example, rum imports are a function of population. Given the relation, one can forecast rum imports by forecasting population. One may err in the forecast of the future population or the relation between rum imports and population may change, or both, resulting in an error in the forecast of rum imports, but the process is the same as for astronomy.

In both cases the forecast is separate from the measurement. More important, the measurements precede the law which enables the forecast to be made. It was Tycho Brae's accumulation of accurate measurements of present planetary locations which Johannes Kepler used as the basis for formulating his three laws of planetary motion which now enable us to forecast future locations of planets. It seems that we accountants want to skip the measurement step and go directly to forecasting. We have not measured previously because we told ourselves it was impossible and therefore we have no accumulation of measurements upon which to base a possible law. Instead, our data bank consists of allocations which depend as much on the accountant's mind as on the object measured. We do not want to measure now because we tell ourselves it is more important to forecast and therefore we seek to report numerals which will foretell the future. I am afraid that the goal is overly ambitious and that we would make more progress more rapidly by measuring now and waiting for an accounting Kepler to use our accumulated accurate measurements to try to formulate laws which will enable subsequent generations to forecast.

4.22 Implications of the Objective

To say that the *maintenance* of cash flows is the objective is a slight misstatement. It should be said that the objective is to *at least* maintain cash flows. Of course if cash flows are maintained at a *constant* level, then they can easily be forecast, but that gives the forecasting of the objective a higher priority than the objective. The choice between difficult to forecast positive cash flows and perfectly forecastable negative cash flows is obvious. Thus, the primary objective is to maximize cash flows and the objective of forecasting future cash flows is of lower priority.

Any measurement system should reveal whether or not the objective has been achieved. Since maximizing cash flows is the objective, then past cash flows must be measured in order to reveal how well the objective has been achieved. Since future cash flows is the object of the forecast, past cash flows must be measured and compared to past forecasts in order to reveal forecast errors. Even if SUP measures could be unambiguously obtained and even if they were perfect indicators of future cash flows, it would not negate the need to measure past NOD flows. We could not know that distant past SUP measures had been perfect indicators of near past NOD flows in the absence of measuring near past NOD flows. Thus, the objective of maximizing future NOD flows entails the measurement of past NOD flows.

For the same reasons that humans prefer a larger to a smaller amount of future cash flows, they prefer a larger to a smaller present cash balance. Thus the present cash balance is an object of interest in its own right. In addition, the present cash balance is the sum of all cash flows, and the change in the cash balance for an interval of time is equal to the sum of the cash flows for that interval of time. Thus, the present cash balance and changes in cash balances provide summary measures of past cash flows. That is, there is the usual relationship between NOD stocks or capital and NOD flows. The objective of maximizing future NOD flows is tantamount to maximizing future NOD capital (neglecting dividends) and therefore present NOD capital should be measured to check on how well the objective has been achieved.[21]

SUP and NOD are different attributes. The choice of which one (or both) to measure depends upon the objective. Truth will not permit a choice. Just as my height and weight are both true, SUP and NOD are both true. Covariability, or lack thereof, will not permit a choice. Just as my height and weight may vary in the same or opposite directions, SUP and NOD may vary in the same or opposite directions. Forecastability will not permit a choice. I might assume certain things to be constant and then argue that present height forecasts future height or that present height forecasts future weight. The first requires past measures of height and the second requires past measures of height and weight to experimentally (empirically) test the relationship. The same is true of SUP and NOD. However, setting an objective will permit a choice. If my objective is to maximize future weight increments (flows) or, to say the same thing, to maximize future weight (stocks), then I must measure my past weight increments and my present weight to check on the progress. And that holds even if my past weight increments and present weight provide no aid in forecasting future weight or in achieving the objective. The same is true for NOD. That is, the objective of maximizing NOD entails the measurement of NOD.

21. Undoubtedly the relationship is so obvious that stating it tries the reader's patience. I include the discussion for three reasons. First, some have proposed systems of measuring cash flows in which they have come perilously close to deducing that present cash stocks are irrelevant from the premise that cash flows are relevant. Second, some have focused on the *maintenance* of capital and correctly noted that since firms contract and expand, the notion does not model the firm. From this correct observation, they conclude that the notion should be abandoned, overlooking the fact that it simply means that income is the increment in the "maintained" initial capital. Third, is the recurring argument that we should measure flows and forget about stocks, often stated as articulation being an artificial constraint that impedes progress, overlooking the relationship between stocks and flows.

4.23 Extended Implications

In the simple cases examined herein all assets are in cash at the beginning and end of the period. The cycle from cash to cash is complete. For untold years this was considered to be accountants' heaven. It was the place where income could be determined with complete accuracy and there were no problems in valuing assets. In such cases the only thing that one has to do is to count the NOD. The problems arise when the cycle is incomplete, when noncash assets are held at the balance sheet date. The proposal for SUP has now come along and reversed all processes. The completed SUP cycle is from physical units to physical units instead of from cash to cash. The problems with SUP arise when its cycle is incomplete, when cash is held at the balance sheet date. If it started and ended each period with the same physical units, the only thing that one would have to do is count the number of physical units in order to unambiguously determine assets and income. The SUP proposal is to measure cash as the *present equivalent number of units purchasable.* The reverse is to measure noncash assets as the *present equivalent number of dollars receivable* , i.e., NOD equivalents.

It seems to me that the objective of maximizing NOD flows also entails the measurement of NOD equivalents. As we saw above, the objective entails measuring past NOD flows and present NOD stocks both to check on the achievement of the objective and because NOD flows and stocks are objects of interest in their own right. At any moment in time a noncash asset can be sold which converts it to an immediate NOD inflow and an increment to present NOD stocks. Thus, each asset can be stated as its NOD equivalent. For the same reasons that humans prefer larger to smaller future NOD flows and larger to smaller present NOD stocks, they prefer larger to smaller present NOD equivalents. Thus, the present NOD equivalent is an object of interest in its own right. It is also a measure of achievement of the objective. The reason for not selling an asset is that its future NOD flows are expected to be greater than its present NOD equivalent. If the asset has been sold when the future becomes the present, we must measure the intervening NOD flows and compare them to the past NOD equivalent to see if the expectations were fulfilled, to see if the objective was achieved. If the asset has not been sold when the future becomes the present, we must measure its present NOD equivalent and compare it to the past NOD equivalent to see how well the objective has been achieved so far. The reason for not selling is that the NOD flows that still lie in the future are expected to be greater than the now present NOD equivalent. We cannot measure the NOD flows because they still lie in the future, but we can measure the present NOD equivalent and compare it to the past NOD equivalent.

For these reasons, I conclude that NOD equivalents should be measured and reported when the cycle is incomplete. Of course, "NOD equivalents" is simply another name for "exit values" or for "current cash equivalents" in Chambers' apt terminology. Another reason for measuring exit values is their relevance to decisions, as was pointed out above on several occasions, when the decision process was outlined. Other reasons are given in detail in Sterling (1979) and (1970), and overviews in Sterling (1972) and (1975). The various works of Chambers reach almost identical conclusions for sometimes the same, sometimes different, reasons.

5. CONCLUSION

And many false prophets shall rise, and shall deceive many.
(Matthew 24:11)

Physical capital proponents have correctly identified serious deficiencies in historical cost accounting. We are indebted to them for pointing out those deficiencies in particular and for helping us to peer through the monetary veil in general. However, they have not identified the correct remedy for the deficiencies. Their proffered solution is intuitively appealing and has attracted many disciples, but they have been deceived by an incomplete analysis. Further analysis reveals that:

(1) physical capital measurement is at best a special case which is only applicable to firms that meet severely restricted conditions, and at worst is inapplicable to all firms;

(2) the maintenance or maximization of physical capital does not coincide with and is often contrary to the cash flow objectives of owners;

(3) the ability of physical capital measures to forecast themselves or to forecast cash flows has not been demonstrated; and

(4) the objective of maximizing cash flows entails the measurement of cash flows and stocks as well as the measurement of cash equivalents of noncash assets.

Therefore, at the present time, the need to beware the false prophets of physical capital is equally as pressing as the need to beware the false profits of historical cost.

6. REFERENCES

Boulding,K.E., *Economic Analysis* (Harper & Brothers, 1955).

__________,"Economics and Accounting: The Uncongenial Twins," in W.T. Baxter and S. Davidson (eds.), *Studies in Accounting* (Institute of Chartered Accountants in England and Wales, 1977).

Canadian Institute of Chartered Accountants (CICA), "Current Cost Accounting," Exposure Draft (December 1979).

Edwards, E.O. and P.W. Bell, *The Theory and Measurement of Business Income* (University of California Press, 1961).

Financial Accounting Standards Board (FASB), "Financial Reporting and Changing Prices," Exposure Draft (December 1978).

__________, *Financial Reporting and Changing Prices,* Statement of Financial Accounting Standards No. 33 (September 1979).

Johnson, L.T. and P.W. Bell, "Current Replacement Costs: A Qualified Opinion," *Journal of Accountancy* (November 1976), pp. 63-70.

Lee, T.A., "The Accounting Entity Concept, Accounting Standards and Inflation Accounting," *Accounting and Business Research* , No. 38 (Spring 1980), pp. 176-186.

Moonitz, M., "The Basic Postulates of Accounting," American Institute of Certified Public Accountants, *Accounting Research Study 1* (1961).

Revsine, L., *Replacement Cost Accounting* (Prentice-Hall, Inc., 1973).

__________ and J.J. Weygandt, "Accounting for Inflation: The Controversy," *Journal of Accountancy* (October 1974), pp. 72-78.

Rosenfield, P. "Reporting Subjunctive Gains and Losses," *The Accounting Review* (October 1969), pp. 788-797.

__________, "The Confusion Between Price-Level and Value Accounting," *Journal of Accountancy* (October 1972), pp. 56-62.

__________, "Current Replacement Value Accounting—A Dead End," *Journal of Accountancy* (September 1975), pp. 63-73.

Samuelson, R.A., "Should Replacement-Cost Changes be Included in Income?" *The Accounting Review* (April 1980), pp. 254-268.

Securities and Exchange Commission, "Notice of Adoption of Amendments to Regulation S-X Requiring Disclosure of Certain Replacement Cost Data," *Accounting Series Release No. 190* (1976).

Sprouse, R.T. and M. Moonitz, "A Tentative Set of Broad Accounting Principles for Business Enterprises," American Institute of Certified Public Accountants, *Accounting Research Study 3* (1962).

Sterling, R.R., *Theory of the Measurement of Enterprise Income* (Scholars Book Co., 1970).

____________, "Decision Oriented Financial Accounting," *Accounting and Business Research* (Summer 1972), pp. 198-208.

____________, "Relevant Financial Reporting in an Age of Price Changes," *Journal of Accountancy* (February 1975), pp. 42-51.

____________, *Toward a Science of Accounting* (Scholars Book Co., 1979).

Vancil, R.F. and R.L. Weil, "Current Replacement Cost Accounting, Depreciable Assets, and Distributable Income," in Vancil and Weil (eds.), *Replacement Cost Accounting* (Thomas Horton and Daughters, 1976).

On Identification of Users and Firms

Robert R. Sterling*

Fraser and Nobes (F & N) make the important point that the users of information need to be clearly specified prior to deciding what information is relevant to them. Although I think that the point is important, even crucial, and I am delighted they have made it, I believe that they overlooked some other important points.

Identification of users

The general conclusion of F & N is that 'each of these [Chambers, Edwards & Bell, and Sterling] three theories is based upon the identification of management as ... *main* users of financial statements. In ... Chambers and Sterling ... [this] is an inescapable conclusion from the decisions being considered ...' (F & N, p. 146). I would not presume to speak for Chambers or Edwards & Bell, but I certainly did not intend to make management the prime or main user of financial statements. However, it is clear that F & N read my works—at least the three of my works that they cited—as being based exclusively (or perhaps overwhelmingly) on management decisions. Since it is at least equally as probable that I miswrote as that they misread, there is no reason to argue that here. Instead I will try to explain what I meant rather than defend what I wrote.

Single Owners

The basis for F & N's 'inescapable conclusion' is that it is management, not owners, 'who normally make decisions about buying and selling the business' assets' (F & N, p. 145). I made the same point when I introduced the discussion of other external users in *Enterprise Income* (1970, p. 142):

> The trader [manager] may decide on a position and then exchange in order to obtain that position. The other interested receivers [external users] have no such control; they are observers of the trader's decisions.

Later I realised that I had been thinking about multiple owners when I wrote that sentence: a single or sole owner of a firm does in fact have the option to sell the assets of the firm. Therefore, I drew another distinction when I wrote *Toward a Science* by including a section entitled 'Relevance to Single Owners and Creditors' (p. 174–75) and said that a single '... owner faces three alternatives: (1) Keep the firm. (2) Sell the firm. (3) Sell the assets (liquidate).' Thus if I were to criticise *Enterprise Income*, I would say that the distinction drawn between management and owners was too sharp rather than not being sharp enough, as F & N would have it. I readily accept F & N's point that there is often separation of ownership and control but I hasten to add that such separation is a special case, albeit an important case, and when that case is not in effect, owners can and do decide to buy and sell the firm's assets.

Multiple Owners

The option to sell the firm's assets is also available to multiple owners (of a partnership, corporation, joint venture, cooperative, etc.) if the other owners agree to sell those assets. Shareholders may (1) sell their shares, or (2) keep their shares *and* (2a) vote to keep (or sell and replace) all or part of the firm's assets and continue operations, or (2b) vote to sell (or abandon) and not replace the firm's assets and cease operations. It seems to me that the decision of a single owner to sell or not sell the firm's assets is almost identical to the decision of a multiple owner to *vote* to sell or not sell the firm's assets. Therefore, it seems to me that the information needed to make that decision is the same for both single and multiple owners.

With minor, but indispensable, bracketed insertions I can fully agree with F & N's oft repeated comment that (minority) shareholders are not (individually) able to buy or sell a company's assets. However, there is incontrovertible evidence that minority shareholders can and do make collective decisions by voting, including the decision to sell or not sell the assets. If we could agree on that preliminary point, we could turn to the important question of what kind of information, if any, should be supplied to multiple owners who need to decide how to vote.

Evaluators

In addition to the individual decisions of single

*I am grateful to the members of the Brown Bag Seminar at the University of Utah—particularly Larry Deppee, Roy Faeber, and Paul Miller—for their comment and criticism, to the editor for inviting these comments, and especially to F & N for raising important issues.

owners and the collective decisions of multiple owners, it seems to me that external users need a grounding in decision models, such as asset buy-sell models, to be able properly to evaluate the goodness and outcomes of decisions. The comments about 'Costs vs Values' caused me to realise that I had not made that point explicit in that piece. Let me now apologise for and attempt to rectify that lacuna. The main purpose of discussing the asset buy-sell decision model in 'Costs vs Values' (pp. 104–07) and elsewhere was to enable everybody—managers, owners, creditors, and especially accountants—to understand the model and the information that is relevant to it. The discussion of the model preceded the discussion of the evaluation of the decisions (pp. 107–10), because an understanding of the decision model is, in my view, a prerequisite to such an evaluation.

I think that evaluators have the right to evaluate decisions on the basis of the decision model that the evaluators believe to be correct even if the decision makers do not use that model when making their decisions. Perhaps the case is strongest in regard to the principal-agent relationship of owners and managers: even if managers *qua* agents make their asset sell-hold decisions on the basis of comparing costs, either historical or current, to forecasted future net cash inflows, I think that owners *qua* principals have a perfect right to judge the goodness of those decisions on the basis of comparing present exit values to forecasted future net cash inflows if they believe that to be the correct decision model.

Consider, for example, a manager who makes the decision to sell an asset that does not produce periodic cash inflows—e.g., unrented land, zero coupon bonds, growth (zero dividend) shares, a unit of inventory—by comparing its cost, either historical or current, of $1,100 to *his* forecast of its future terminal exit value of $950. If the present exit value of that asset is $900, then that is a bad decision (assuming a better alternative use of the funds) arising from the use of a demonstrably wrong decision model. If I were an owner, I would decide to replace, or vote to replace, managers who made such bad decisions by using such wrong decision models. Note that F & N's deep concern about being clear that it was the manager, not the owners, who made that asset-sell decision has no bearing whatsoever on the isssue of the owners' use of the asset-sell decision model to evaluate the goodness of that decision and the resultant decision to replace or not replace the manager.

In addition to evaluating the goodness of decisions, the outcomes of decisions can also be evaluated—separately evaluated. Indeed it will often be the case that the only thing multiple owners and other external users can evaluate is outcomes of decisions to purchase and not sell because they will not have access to information about managers' forecasts nor to foregone opportunities. Again, I think that evaluators have the right to evaluate outcomes of decisions on the basis of the decision model that the evaluators believe to be correct even if the decision makers do not use that model when making their decisions.

Suppose, for example, that at 1 January the manager had decided not to sell the asset described above. It is now 31 January and the owners and other external users want to evaluate the outcome of that decision. Due to an increase in transaction costs, at 31 January the current cost is $1,150 and the exit value is $850. There are three main candidates for expressing the to-date outcome: (1) *zero* using historical cost, (2) $50 *gain* using current costs, and (3) $50 *loss* using exit values. It is not my purpose here to address the merits of those three candidates but rather to point out that external users need to address those merits in order to decide which one they want to use to evaluate the to-date outcome of the decision. In turn, it seems to me that the way for external users to address those merits is for them to examine asset buy-sell decision models. Again note that although F & N are correct when they point out that it was the manager who made the decision not to sell the asset, that has nothing to do with external users' examination of asset buy-sell decision models for the purpose of deciding how to evaluate the outcome of that decision.

To try to make the decision process and the identity of the decision makers crystal clear, I posit that Fraser, Nobes and Sterling are minority shareholders. In making my general decisions about this firm—how to vote, whether to sell or keep my shares—I would use the outcomes of previous managerial decisions as an input. This requires that I decide how to evaluate those outcomes. I have decided to evaluate the to-date outcome of the example as bad (even though it resulted from a good decision with an erroneous forecast) and therefore I want it reported as a $50 loss. I base that evaluation on my previous examination of asset buy-sell decision models. F & N also need to make general decisions about the firm and the specific decision about how to evaluate outcomes, including what they want reported about this particular outcome. They also need to establish the basis for their evaluation. Whether they agree or disagree with my evaluation is not the immediate issue: the point is that as minority shareholders they must decide how to evaluate managerial decisions. I again invite F & N to get involved in this evaluation decision rather than worrying about what some unknown users may or may not want or understand.

The reason for issuing invitations to accountants to get involved in the decisions is that I believe that the seriatim assumption of the roles of various decision makers will allow accountants to make better decisions about what information to report. Thus I would like F & N to get involved in the evaluation decision in their role as accountants because it is accountants, in the main, who make decisions about what to report to shareholders. Once we have cleared up all these preliminaries, we can return to the original question of whether to report zero, $50 gain, or $50 loss in the example and then to the question of the extension of that method to other cases.

Summary

F & N (i) note that I discuss asset buy-sell decision models at some length, (ii) observe that managers, not owners, normally make asset buy-sell decisions, and (iii) draw the conclusion that '... Sterling's theory too has management as the prime users' (p. 145). I disagree only with the conclusion. I intended (whether I succeeded is another question) to treat all users equally in regard to their information requirements while keeping in mind that some users, such as management and government, have access advantages. The basic point of disagreement seems to stem from my views: (i) that in considering what information is relevant we should take into account that owners and other external users sometimes, under some conditions, make 'managerial' decisions and (ii) that what can be learned from 'managerial' decision models forms the basis for the determination of what information is relevant to external uses, especially in regard to their evaluations of the goodness and outcomes of decisions.

Identification of firms

I believe that the clear specification of the characteristics of the type of firm under consideration is of great importance in gaining understanding and agreement about accounting issues. To put it negatively, I think that one cause of the continuing disagreement among some accountants is that they focus on different types of firms—they have tacitly adopted different firm models. Although F & N rightly concentrate on identifying users, they also make comments about firm models that lead me to believe that we have different firms in mind and that this is one cause of the divergence of our views.

The Going Concern Model

Some version of the firm as a 'going concern' served as a firm model in accounting for a very long time. At one extreme, the firm as a going concern has been viewed as one that must continue to replace its currently owned assets with exactly the same kind of assets until it liquidates. At the other extreme, the only requirement for a firm to be a going concern is that it has not formally wound up its affairs. What most accountants have in mind when they speak of a going concern undoubtedly lies at various points on the continuum between these two extremes. Nonetheless, the vast difference between the extremes troubled me because it presented a potential for vast misunderstanding among accountants when they invoked the going concern concept. As a result, I examined the going concern concept in some detail. One conclusion of that examination (Sterling, 1968, p. 497) was that the concept should be purged from accounting thought because it is ill-defined and confused. Fremgen (1968) independently reached almost indentical conclusions.

Another result of that examination was that the conclusions, particularly the valuation conclusions, which used the going concern concept as a premise were invalid or unsound or both. At that time it was almost universally believed that a conclusive proof of the wisdom of historical cost reporting was to simply say that they are going concern values. At the same time it was equally widely believed, and often uttered in the same breath, that a conclusive proof of the error of exit value reporting was to simply say that they are liquidating values and therefore not relevant to a going concern. My inability to corroborate such 'proofs' strengthened my conviction that the concept was excess baggage and should be purged.

I am happy to report that the mention of a going concern in the learned journals has become increasingly rare in recent years. Even the laggard authoritative literature, e.g., FASB Concepts Statements, no longer lists it as a basic concept of accounting. Nonetheless, F & N (p. 145) resurrect that hoary notion for the purpose of making the unexplained suggestion that '...*for going concerns*, exit values should not form the main valuation basis, but would be useful as notes.' I have only the vaguest idea of what they mean by 'going concern', even less idea of the logical connections they have discovered between that concept and the conclusion that exit values should not form the main valuation basis, still less idea as to how they arrive at the conclusion that exit values would be useful as notes, and no idea whatsoever of the criteria they use to segregate the main valuation basis from notes.

In addition, it seems to me that being a going concern vs a liquidating concern are options that are available to owners and they individually or collectively need to *decide* which option they prefer. Thus, it seems to me that we put the cart before the horse: instead of the going concern being a preliminary condition to be used by accountants to decide what information to report to owners (or where to report it), being a going concern is the result of a decision by owners to whom accountants need to supply information relevant to the decision. If I am right about that, perhaps we can amuse ourselves in the midst of all this seriousness by contemplating the conundrum of the accountant who was required to prepare a report for owners before the decision was made (because the owners needed information to decide whether to be a going concern or a liquidating concern) but was also required to wait for the decision to be made before preparing the report (because the accountant needed to know which option was selected in order to decide what to report, i.e., report going concern values if it was a going concern and liquidating values if it was a liquidating concern).

The Trader Model

My conviction that a major cause of disagreement among accountants stemmed from differences in tacit firm models caused me to want to be quite explicit about the characteristics of the firm that I considered. In addition, I believed that it was more productive and efficient to move from the simple to the complex. For both reasons, I posited a trader in commodity futures in *Enterprise Income* and gave a rather detailed description of the pertinent characteristics of that firm and its setting. Almost all of the received criticism has been directed at the firm rather than the reasoning or conclusions.[1] F & N continue that tradition. They are evidently quite troubled by the firm and its setting.

Although I readily admit that commodity trading firms are relatively rare and unimportant, I believe that they are worth considering. First, it has always seemed to me that the contrast should be between the posited firm model and other types of firms rather than between unreal and real firms because there are, in fact, real firms that trade futures contracts and the question of how to account for them is both real and disputatious, having been addressed by FASB as well as in the learned journals, e.g., Bar-Yosef and Livnat (1984). Second, some of them are single commodity trading firms that operate in almost perfectly competitive markets, such as wheat and soybeans, and all available evidence indicates that they do in fact attempt to maximise profits. (At least there is no evidence that any of them attempt to minimise profits.) Thus, the posited firm is real, albeit simple, and the described setting is also real, albeit rare.

For these reasons, it seems to me that the primary question to be addressed is whether the conclusions drawn in regard to that firm in that setting are or are not valid. Some critics, perhaps including F & N, bypass the validity issue *because* they have doubts about extensibility:

> The accounting entity . . . [considered] is a single commodity trading venture which is attempting to maximise profits in a perfectly competitive market. Clearly these assumptions are sufficiently material to make the extension of Sterling's developed theory, from his simple model to other types of firms, at best a hazardous venture. (F & N, p. 145)

I have long been disappointed by critics who express such doubts rather than address the validity of the conclusions because I fully agree that extensibility is an open question. Indeed, the very last words in *Enterprise Income* express the restricted applicability of the conclusions and characterise beliefs about their extensibility as 'unsupported conjectures.'

In any event, the question of extending those conclusions to other types of firms must be secondary because if the conclusions are not valid, then the extensibility question would not be broached.[2] Surely no one would want to extend invalid conclusions and therefore concern about extensibility must indicate belief that the conclusions are valid. Since F & N raise the extensibility issue, perhaps I should take that as evidence of their tacit agreement with all the reasoning and conclusions in *Enterprise Income*. If so, I congratulate them on their rare perspicacity.

Mainstream Firms

F & N (p. 145) note that '. . . one of the obvious drawbacks of Sterling's work . . . [is his failure] to adapt his theory to cover mainstream commercial and industrial companies.' I think this is a legitimate criticism of *Enterprise Income* and I would fully agree with raising it if their review had been restricted to that work. However, F & N brought under their purview two other works that are in fact attempts to adapt or extend the theory to cover mainstream firms. The firm model considered in *Toward a Science* was said to be exemplified by airlines, car rental companies, and the like, and was specifically intended to cover the accounting issues of such mainstream companies as Hertz, Avis, PanAm, TWA, and so forth. 'Costs vs Values' attempted to bring additional types of firms and assets, such as merchandise and receivables, into its ambit.

Now that mainstream firms have been

[1]A common criticism has been to contrast the *simple* firm to *real* firms and the *restrictive* setting to *real world* settings, thereby implicitly or explicitly relegating the subject matter to unreal firms in an unreal world.

[2]Some accountants, not F & N, think that extensibility is the primary question and that validity is dependent on a yes answer to that question. I encountered that reversal of logic in discussions with three FASB members who alleged that it would be *incorrect* to account for the market value (undifferentiated between current cost and exit value) of shares owned by closed end mutual funds (as recommended in 'Costs vs Values') *because* accounting for the market value of the assets of General Motors would be impossible, inappropriate, ridiculous, etc.

examined—extension or adaption has been attempted—perhaps we can turn our attention away from criticism of the types of firms and focus on the question of what kind of information such firms should report.

Summary

I am not clear about exactly how F & N view firm models and their place in the process of deciding what to report. However, it seems apparent that our views differ. F & N evidently believe that invoking the going concern firm model allows accountants to decide what values to report while I believe that reporting values allows owners to decide whether to be a going concern. F & N criticise one work because they fear the hazardous venture of extending its theory from a simple firm model to other more complex firm models yet they get no comfort when other works attempt the venture and survive the hazards, albeit scathed. F & N are pained by one work because its firm model is not a mainstream company yet they do not seem to get relief from other works whose firms models are mainstream companies.

References

Bar-Yosef, Sasson and Joshua Livnat, 'Investment in Commodities Futures—The Accounting Implications', *Abacus*, June, 1984.

Chambers, Raymond J., *Accounting, Evaluation and Economic Behavior*, Englewood Cliffs: Prentice-Hall, 1966. Reprinted Scholars Book Co., Houston.

Edwards, Edgar O. and Phillip W. Bell, *The Theory and Measurement of Business Income*, Berkeley: University of California Press, 1961.

Fraser, I. A. M. and C. W. Nobes, 'The Assumed Users in Three Accounting Theories', *Accounting and Business Research*, Spring, 1985.

Fremgen, James, 'The Going Concern Assumption: A Critical Appraisal', *Accounting Review*, October, 1968.

Sterling, Robert R; 'The Going Concern: An Examination,' *Accounting Review*, July, 1968.

Sterling, Robert R., *The Theory of the Measurement of Enterprise Income*, Lawrence: University Press of Kansas, 1970. Reprinted Scholars Book Co., Houston.

Sterling, Robert R., *Toward a Science of Accounting*, Houston: Scholars Book Co., 1979.

Sterling, Robert R., 'Costs (Historical vs Current) vs Exit Values', *Abacus*, December, 1981.

CONVENTIONAL ACCOUNTING

INTRODUCTION

Sterling on Conventional Accounting

P. W. Wolnizer

From his earliest writings, Sterling acknowledges that, in relation to conventional accounting doctrine and practice, he takes "a critic's stance." In so doing, he makes plain that "... the purpose of the critic is the improvement of the system by elimination of inconsistency and error. ... One criticises only that which one cares about and only when one cares enough to try to improve it" (1968b, p.589).

Sterling's criticisms of conventional accounting over thirty years reduce to one fundamental point: "... that with rare exceptions accounting numerals do not represent [real world] phenomena ... and that making numerals represent or not represent phenomena is a matter of choice" (1988, p.4). Because "the subject matter of accounting is numerals, not magnitudes of wealth and profit," he argues that conventional accounting practice is "numerology," a "calculational activity" the results of which "have no empirical referent"' (1993, pp.133, 139). This, he declares, is "the most serious problem" of accounting practice: "Accounting practice numerals need to be made meaningful by making them empirically verifiable, demonstrating that they are decision-useful (not merely used), and defining them operationally" (1993, p. 139).

This leads Sterling to be critical of conventional auditing practices. "The verification of book values is a problem of vast consequences. Usually the verification of a figure requires that an empirical operation be specified which can be repeated by the verifier. We seem to be moving toward the mistaken idea that verification is the repetition of an arithmetical operation and that it is management's responsibility to estimate the variables and select the functional form in which the variables are related. This notion of verification makes management responsible for the determination of quantities and the selection of accounting methods" (1968b, p594).

As a scientist, Sterling (1973, 1977) ponders how such a "mistaken idea" developed among accountants and why it has endured. He provides several clues. "In the absence of a cohesive theory, in the absence of police power, in the presence of ignorance and apathy of the community, [the accountant's] only defence was precedent and persuasion. Precedent soon became rule and rigid application of rules was [the accountant's] primary weapon" (1973, p.61). Since accountants could not increase their authority, Sterling argues that they have sought to decrease their responsibility; for example, by substituting the word "examination" for the word "verification" in the auditing literature, and by weakening the wording (and purport) of the audit opinion (1973, pp.64-5).

An historical explanation of how and why this habit of thought has developed, and a prediction that "accounting will become more and more legalistic" are also offered by Sterling (1977). "The lack of ability to empirically test the alternative calculational methods resulted in accountants denying that there was such a thing as truth in accounting. ... The auditors' lack of power and lack of a concept of truth caused them to develop the habit of thought of relying upon rules" (1977, p.250).

Although a critic of conventional accounting, Sterling has sought to explicate some aspects of it (with Flaherty, 1971; and Flaherty and Tollefson 1972). With meticulous care he has also dissected conventional accounting doctrine. And with flawless logic and cogent argumentation, he lays bare the egregious errors, inconsistencies and contradictions of accounting lore. He claims that the notion of conservatism is "the fundamental principle of valuation in [conventional] accounting" and "the premise ... from which the historical cost-realization rule is derived" (1967, p.112). He concludes that "Since verity is a sine qua non of information, ...conservatism yields, not only zero information, but also, misinformation" (1967, p.131). "Going concern", which he describes as "the accountant's firm model", is shown to be "one of the most important concepts in [conventional] accounting" (1968a, p. 481). However, after arguing that "... the allegation that the going concern is necessary to accounting has not been proven and there are strong arguments to the contrary" (1968a, p.484), he shows that the conventional notion of going concern "... implicitly contains the conditions necessary for a firm in a stationary state'' as against a firm that is a going concern in a volatile state (1968a, p.489).

The uniformity versus flexibility question has also been dealt with, analytically and empirically by Sterling (e.g., in 1966, 1969a [with Radosevich], 1969b). As a consequence of traditional accounting being "conventional" and "calculational-nonempirical", "the perceived alternative to determining truth [in accounting] was the adoption of rules" (1977, p.250). Observing the flexibility of accounting practices allowed by accounting rules, he concludes that "Calculation is a much safer activity than determination of the [empirical] factors" (1969b, p. 47). However, after noting that "To let management or the taxing authority make the determinations is a good way to avoid responsibility," he warns that "... if we continue to define the accounting process so as to make it safe and so as to avoid responsibility, we may define it so narrowly that it withers and dies" (1969b, p.47).

Against the background of that warning, his experiences as Senior Fellow at the Financial Accounting Standards Board, and the critical concern he has for the future of accounting, Sterling presents *An Essay on Recognition* - published as the first R. J. Chambers Research Lecture in the University of Sydney in 1985. A capstone essay, it deals "... with the fundamental question of which words and numerals should appear on *all* financial statements and what those words and numerals should represent" (p.2). Drawing upon cartography as an analogy, Sterling argues that "... the first task of recognition is to select the phenomena that are relevant to rational investment, credit and similar decisions. The second task of recognition is to faithfully represent the relevant phenomena and to provide assurance, via verification, that they are faithfully represented" (1985, p.85). In keeping with his scholarly motivation as a critic of conventional accounting practice, Sterling states that his objective in developing "concepts to guide decisions on recognition" is "to improve [accounting] practice" (1985, p.4).

R. R. STERLING

In Defence of Accounting in the United States*

In 'Financial Information and the Securities Market' (*Abacus* Vol I, No. 1) Professor Chambers presented some figures which reflected unfavourably on U.S. accounting relative to U.K. accounting. Specifically, he asserted that there are 124,416 different ways of getting cost in the U.K. but only 9,100 different ways in the U.S. No direct comparisons were made but the figures are there for all to see and the clear implication is that U.K. accounting is richer in variety than that of the U.S. That is a slander of U.S. accounting and cannot be left unchallenged. This note will demonstrate that the figures are wrong and that the opposite is true: U.S. accounting is much richer than that of the U.K.

Two separate types of errors may be identified in Mr. Chambers's figures: (1) logical fallacies[1] and (2) inadequate research.

Logical Fallacies

Chambers listed the possibilities of valuing only inventory in the U.S. but he listed commodity stocks, fixed assets (three classes) and security investments (three classes) for the U.K. Obviously, a larger number of classes will yield a larger number of combinations, other things being equal. Thus, the comparison is grossly unfair because the U.K. figure was calculated from a larger number of classes.

Second, he erred in calculating the number of different costs to be derived from inventory methods. He is talking about a manufacturing operation in which there are four different classes of inventory: materials, supplies, work-in-process and finished goods. Even a modest firm will have several different kinds of materials, etc. Any one of the ten methods may be used for each inventory and the order of using them is important. For example, Lifo for finished goods

* The author would like to thank Mr. Duns Scotus for reading this manuscript. Unfortunately, under some theories at least, that is impossible.

1. A recent article showed that logical consistency is a symptom of an illness called valuitis. It is well known that Chambers has been suffering from valuitis for a long time. This fallacy is evidence of the absence of the symptom and therefore we may hope that he is recovering his health. However, I do not wish to draw that conclusion since it might be logically valid and therefore it would indicate that I am ill. For the same reason, I do not wish to conclude that a valid conclusion of mine would indicate that I was ill because that might be valid and therefore it would indicate that I was ill. Thus, I must conclude a contradiction but then the conclusion that I must conclude a contradiction might be valid. This is a question I intend to research further at a later time.

R. R. STERLING is Visiting Research Fellow at Yale University.

and Fifo for materials will produce a cost different from Fifo for finished goods and Lifo for materials.

Thus, under the conservative assumption that there are only ten inventories in a given firm, the number of different costs is 10! not 10. This yields 3,628,000 different costs from a consideration of different *rules for inventory alone.* If we now take account of the other factors listed by Chambers we have 10! x 7 x 13 x 3 x 3 = 2,971,332,000. The U.K. figure of 124,416 pales in comparison.

Inadequate Research[2]

Evidently in getting the '10 rules' for inventory valuation, Chambers took a cursory look at the *Accountants' Handbook.* Had he bothered to look further he would have found that this is a highly abstract list and that each category contains a rich variety of methods. Neuner[3] for example, lists five different kinds of Lifo:

1. Lifo — perpetual
2. Lifo — periodic

Increases in inventory under 2. may be valued at

3. earliest purchase price
4. latest purchase price
5. average purchase price.

Later he lists six areas 'on which there is no uniform practice'. Freight-in is one category for which there are three different methods, for example. Each of these six categories has at least three different methods.

Next, there is a list of four categories of 'Debatable inventory costs' and each of these four has at least three different methods. There are others but I will conclude with the 3 x 3 cost-or-market rule which Chambers mentions. Thus, there are 5 x (3x6) x (3x4) x (3x3) = 9,720 different costs for *Lifo alone.*

We could go through each of the ten methods with similar results. However, one case is sufficient to demonstrate the inadequate research upon which Chambers bases his figures. In the U.S. we have more different methods for Lifo alone than he gives us credit for in total!

2. The results of the following are part of a two-stage study on accounting which is forthcoming. First, I am preparing a complete inventory of accounting practices. The second stage will be to weave together the practices into a coherent body of principles. In this way, the principles can be inductively derived out of the facts of accounting action in practice without relying on assumptions and premises except where assumptions are necessary because the data are not perceptible facts.

The study will take a little longer than originally planned because I have not yet finished with Lifo inventories. So far, I have observed 1984 different methods of Lifo. It is too early to draw distinctions or perceive objectives or sense relevance but I can tentatively report a corroboration of the A.I.C.P.A. definition of assets. All accounts with a debit balance after the books are closed except those that are contra liabilities are *in fact assets.* The reader is cautioned that this corroboration pertains only to Lifo inventories in only 1984 cases.

3. John W. Neuner, *Cost Accounting Principles and Practice,* 6th ed, p 136ff.

These calculations have dealt only with actual costs. There are 9,720 different *actual costs* under the Lifo method. In the U.S. there is a regrettable trend toward recording standard costs in the accounts. 'Standards' are useful for comparison purposes but they are *fictitious* and therefore they should not be entered in the accounts.[4] The accounts must be records of events that have actually occurred, not what might have occurred or what will occur. There is, of course, no objection to putting standard costs in a footnote.

The inclusion of standard costs would strengthen our case against Chambers since there are different times for isolating the variance, different methods of calculation and different methods of disposition. Thus, standards would extend the richness of U.S. accounting but this would be an unfair tactic since they are not actual costs.

Of course, the *actual* actual costs can be obtained only by the method of specific identification.[5] This is the only way to measure the actual income but unfortunately it is sometimes impossible to use. This method would also have strengthened the richness case. Observe that if we have a large number of items in an inventory at different actual costs, there are almost an infinite number of combinations and hence almost an *infinite number of actual actual costs* and actual incomes. I did not use this method in making the calculations for this note because it would have required an estimate of the bias introduced by the shipping clerk or an assumption of randomness and I wanted my figures to be objective and verifiable.

But, I digress. Theoretical issues are not pertinent here. The important point is that I have shown that U.S. accounting is much richer than Chambers has

4. In addition to being fictitious, standards are based solely on someone's projections and are not actual facts of economic experience. I can see no reason why anyone would want to put standards in the accounts when 9,720 different objective Lifo costs are available. Variance analysis is helpful to management but managerial desires should not be confused with sound financial accounting. Moreover, accountants have completely overlooked a fertile source of variance. We could calculate the difference between the costs of the particular method in use and the costs of the alternative methods. Thus, for Lifo we could calculate 9,719 variances and then we could extend the analysis to Fifo, averages and so forth. In this way we could generate an almost infinite number of variances without ever referring to standards. Such variances would be completely *objective* since they are differences in *actual* costs.

5. Specific identification avoids the subjectivity of assuming a flow and accounts for the *real* flow of the goods. Many people have noted this and the fact that accounting for the real flow prevents management from manipulating their profits by assuming an unrealistic flow. It is true that some managers might instruct their shipping clerks to ship the goods on a highest-in-first-out basis in order to reduce taxes. This is not a valid objection to the method because if the goods were shipped in this order, then this would be the real flow (hence the actual costs and actual income) but it does present an auditing problem. The auditor must insist that the goods be indelibly marked with their actual costs. Some managers may object to the added expense of this procedure and they are often too obtuse to understand the subtleties of actual costs and income. The auditor can then explain that the expenses incurred in marking the goods will further reduce the income and thus further reduce taxes in accord with the original goal. This can also be applied to the managers who ship their goods on a lowest-in-first-out basis in order to increase their income. The expense of marking the goods is a small price to pay for the increase in actual income.

given us credit for and, using the figure of 124,416, it is richer than U.K. accounting. The actual facts demand an immediate retraction and apology.

October 1966

RETRACTION AND APOLOGY

I grant Mr. Sterling's point, and apologize to all who may have been misled or misrepresented by my conservatism. We have it on the highest authorities that conservatism is virtuous, and gives a fair representation. Perhaps it is not, and does not. I have since raised the estimate ('A Matter of Principle', *The Accounting Review,* July 1966) but even then in the same wantonly cursory manner. My apologies on that score too.

R. J. CHAMBERS

ROBERT R. STERLING

Conservatism: The Fundamental Principle of Valuation in Traditional Accounting*

I. Conservatism

Accounting has always been a highly practical discipline. Accountants have been faced with the problem of making immediate decisions in order to meet the exigencies of practice. They have not had the luxury of unlimited reflection before taking a position. In addition, they were not much more than specialized craftsmen when an almost overwhelming responsibility was thrust upon them. They were asked to become stewards of a community's wealth in a period of financial piracy. They were required to have integrity when deceit was not uncommon.

As a consequence of these factors, there were twin developments: problems were solved in isolation; and the solutions became accepted and rather rigid. Accountants met problems and solved them on the basis of their best judgments about the particulars of those specific problems. Very likely the cognition of a particular problem was completely insulated from a similar problem that they had previously solved. The resulting cognitive dissonance probably did not bother any single accountant because his main concern was with the ethical effects of his decision. Meanwhile, another practitioner in another firm was solving a problem that was only slightly different and often coming up with a vastly different solution. Thus, there developed intra- and inter-practitioner inconsistencies. At the same time, the accountant needed a strong defence against sometimes simply optimistic, occasionally dishonest, financiers. He was placed in the precarious position of being subject to the pecuniary discretion of the person he was obliged to keep honest. In the absence of a cohesive theory, in the absence of police power, in the presence of ignorance and apathy of the community, his only defence was precedent and persuasion. Precedent soon became rule and the rigid application of rules was his only weapon in the face of a powerful adversary.

The accountant passed through the era of swashbuckling manipulation; the era of watered stock and financial bubbles; in short, the era of chicanery by financial overstatement. In addition, he has always been faced with the effervescent optimism of the entrepreneur. The entrepreneur is naturally optimistic about his project. If he were not, he would not be engaged in it. This optimism is exhibited by a tendency to overvalue the enterprise. Faced with the universal tendency to overstate, the accountant conceived his role to be one of temperance.

* The author gratefully acknowledges the criticism of Ralph Blodgett and the support of Dean Joseph McGuire of the University of Kansas.

ROBERT R. STERLING is Visiting Research Fellow, Yale University, and Associate Professor, University of Kansas.

As a steward, he needed to be the ultimate in solidarity and stability. He wanted to insure that the value was *at least* the amount he reported. Often, to combat overstatement, he proposed understatement, perhaps with the hope of striking a balance.[1]

Thus, the most ancient and probably the most pervasive principle of accounting valuation is conservatism. Recently this rule has come under attack. The Finney and Miller texts, which mirror the mainstream of accounting thought, referred to conservatism as a 'principle of accounting' through four editions. In the fifth edition, however, they complain about the 'fetish of conservatism'.

We recognize that conservatism has lost favour in accounting circles, that it is not applied in practice as much as it once was, and that the academics challenge it. Nevertheless, the author considers conservatism to be the most influential principle of valuation in traditional accounting. Other principles, e.g. cost, consistency, realization, going concern, etc., are often given higher (always no less than equal) status. We regard such lists as erroneous and consider conservatism to be a much more fundamental and pervasive principle of practice or behaviour than the others usually listed.

Evidence for this assertion comes more from the accountant's deeds than his words. Accountants violate the historical cost principle when they value at the *lower* of cost or market. The realization convention is violated in the case of instalment sales and the writing *down* of obsolete inventory. The going concern assumption is abrogated when it results in a value *greater* than market. If the consistent application of a valuation rule becomes unconservative, accountants usually become inconsistent. The basic 'benefit theory' is violated in favour of conservatism in several instances, e.g. advertising and research expenditures.

In addition to these examples, evidence comes from justifications presented in the literature. Many authors take a moderately conservative or even anti-conservative position when they are writing under the head of 'Principles'. However, when they are discussing the valuation of a specific asset, the recurrent phrase that something 'is or is not conservative' is almost inevitable.

For example, Johnson and Kreigman take an 'anti-ultraconservative' view in their chapter on accounting theory.

> Misrepresentation was often injected in the balance sheets of businesses by policies involving the deliberate understatement of asset values in order to achieve so-called 'conservative' values for these assets. . . . By these practices, 'conservative' values became 'ultra-conservative' values *not* fairly presenting the net income and financial position of a given business.[2]

The tone is clearly anti-ultraconservative. Perhaps it is anti-conservative when we juxtapose a statement from an earlier discussion of principles. 'The statement of

1. It is interesting that one of the consequences of the U.S. Federal Income Tax has been a tendency to reverse the roles. The accountant has had to resist the entrepreneur's desire to avoid taxes by financial understatement.
2. A. W. Johnson and O. M. Kreigman, *Intermediate Accounting*, 3rd ed, New York, Holt, Rinehart and Winston, 1964, p 740.

income and the balance sheet, therefore, must be built upon the cornerstone of *truth*.' (p 5.) Yet when they discuss the valuation of stocks, they write:

> The valuation at current market of stocks and bonds held for short-term investment purposes, when market is higher than cost, is a practice not generally approved by accountants. This disapproval rests on the fact that the practice not only involves a departure from original cost as the time-honored yardstick of accounting valuation but also involves accounting recognition of appreciated values. *The practice is obviously not conservative*; and accountants generally have been loth to place an unrealized surplus account on the balance sheet. What support has been given the practice has been defended on the grounds of showing the financial position of the business on a realistic basis. (p 129. Emphasis supplied.)

It is not clear whether these are the authors' arguments or whether they are reporting the predominant view of the profession. Either case supports our point.

The above quotation sets out two conflicting concepts, conservatism versus realism. Without further argument—the above quotation is the *entire* discussion of the pros and cons of market valuation of securities—they draw a conclusion. They point out that valuation at market 'is not generally approved' by the accounting profession and then they support a cost valuation.

> The authors believe that profits and losses on marketable securities should be recognized *only* at the date of their sale. On the balance sheet, marketable securities should be valued at cost. (p 129.)

Obviously, conservatism takes precedence over realism for both the profession at large and these authors. We suspect that the authors would abandon their strict cost position in a period of deflation.

Moreover, they state explicitly the connection of the realization convention to conservatism.

> Today, the doctrine of conservatism is essentially a policy of caution. Revenue, for example, will receive accounting recognition only after it has been realized. . . . (p 740.)

That is, the realization convention has its roots in the principle of conservatism.

Another widely used text supports this thesis:

> The doctrine of conservatism is illustrated in the application of practices such as the following: increases in the values of assets and anticipated gains are normally ignored until realized by means of sale; declines in asset values and anticipated losses, however, are normally recognized . . . certain expenditures are charged in full against current revenue despite the possibility of future benefits.[3]

This text then takes a moderately conservative position: 'A conservative approach in the measurement process is desirable.' (p 49.)

Later, the arguments for valuation at market are briefly surveyed and then rejected. The reasons for the rejection in their *entirety* follow:

> Little tendency to accept valuation at market has been shown by the accounting

3. W. E. Karrenbrock and H. Simons, *Intermediate Accounting*, 4th ed, Cincinnati, South-Western Publishing Co, 1964, p 49.

> profession. Such procedure has been challenged chiefly on the grounds that it represents a departure from the cost concept and would *violate accounting conservatism*. (p 248. Emphasis supplied.)

In view of the authors' previous statement, which justifies departure from the cost concept in favour of conservatism, we could infer that the violation of accounting conservatism is the fundamental argument against valuation at market.

One additional reason for our thesis—that conservatism is the fundamental principle—is the odd character of the attacks on it. Much of the literature opposes conservatism because it is not conservative! A common argument against conservatism in one period is that it produces unconservative values in another period. Paton argues that 'cost or market is not truly conservative' because:

> A low inventory at the end of one year is reflected in the cost of sales of the ensuing period, and as a result the income of the second period is increased (or the loss reduced) by precisely the amount by which the opening inventory was reduced through the operation of the 'conservative' rule.[4]

That is, intertemporally, an apparently conservative procedure is not truly conservative.

A slight variation of this argument is presented in an official pronouncement of the AICPA:

> The argument advanced in favor of immediately writing off discount was that it extinguished an asset that was only nominal in character and that it resulted in a conservative balance sheet. The weight attached to this argument has steadily diminished, and increasing weight has been given to the arguments that all such charges should be reflected under the proper head in the income account, *and that conservatism in the balance sheet is of dubious value if attained at the expense of a lack of conservatism in the income account, which is far more significant*.[5]

That is, the fundamental principle is conservatism, and, therefore, a conservative value on the more important statement is more desirable than a conservative value on a less important statement.

In sum, our primary hypothesis is: *Conservatism is the fundamental principle of valuation in accounting.*

Our secondary hypothesis is: *Conservatism is the premise, often tacit, from which the historical cost-realization rule is derived.*

There is some support for our secondary hypothesis in the accounting literature. We gave some examples above. Some authors freely admit that certain valuation rules are applications of the conservative principle. These are usually authors with a 'liberal' bent. Other authors, the most conservative, in fact, if not in statement, strain to justify valuation rules on grounds other than conservatism.

We should not leave this discussion without indicating that we think there are principles of valuation other than conservatism, viz., causality and convenience.

4. W. A. Paton and W. A. Paton, Jr, *Asset Accounting*, New York, The Macmillan Company, 1952, p 84.

5. American Institute of Certified Public Accountants, *Accounting Research and Terminology Bulletins*, Final edition, New York, AICPA, 1961, p 129. Emphasis supplied.

Briefly, the notion of convenience is that throughout the history of accounting there has been an unyielding pressure to get *some* statistic out in the shortest possible time, at a low cost, with the least chance of being challenged. This has resulted in valuation rules which are convenient. For example, 'cost' (purchase price) is a readily available statistic; 'realization at point of sale' is a fairly clean-cut, easy-to-apply rule; 'materiality' is a justification for breaking the rules if it is much more convenient to do so. Standard costs are an aberration and, without the notion of convenience, it is difficult to explain their acceptance.

The third principle—causality—is a relatively recent addition, coming from academics who attempted to apply causal reasoning to existing accounting practices. Cost accountants were in the forefront of this process, arguing that cost should be attached to the unit that 'caused' the cost to be incurred. They became involved in long arguments over the allocation of overhead, culminating in the recent controversy over direct costing. Another example is 'cost-benefit theory' which charges costs to the periods which they benefit, i.e. periods in which those costs 'cause' revenue. The 'matching' and 'attaching' concepts spring directly from causality arguments.

We think that these three principles, singularly or in mixed-weight combinations, are sufficient to explain virtually all accounting valuations. However, the last two principles are not as germane to this paper as the first.

II. Historical Cost

As many people have previously pointed out, 'cost' has many variations in application and thus it is difficult to analyse the rule in the abstract. We think that the explanation for the variations is contained in our hypothesis. Cost is not a fundamental tenet of accounting; instead it is a derivative of the conservatism principle of valuation. First, and most importantly, the rule almost always yields a conservative value. Cost, particularly of assets which have been amortized, i.e. valued *below* cost, is virtually certain to be below market. If not, it is written down, i.e., when the cost rule is not conservative, it is violated. Second, cost figures are usually far more convenient to obtain than any other value. Ordinarily there is easy access to documents, invoices, cheques which yield a cost of an item.[6] Occasionally, there is some difficulty in obtaining the cost figures and the accountant reverts to conservatism by making a rather low estimate or, if the amount is 'immaterial', by assigning a zero value. Third, costs are attached to products or periods by some causally derived rules. Some costs 'benefit future periods'—cause revenue in the future—and some value is maintained on the books. Other costs have 'benefited past periods'—caused past revenue—and are valued at zero. If a cost produces a product which is 'expected to benefit future periods', the cost attaches to the product until it is sold (causes revenue). If the product 'loses utility' (loses part of its capability to cause revenue) there is a

6. We say 'a' cost instead of 'the' cost because, as several people have pointed out, ten different accountants are likely to get twelve different costs. Cf Charles T. Horngren, *Cost Accounting: A Managerial Emphasis*, Englewood Cliffs, Prentice-Hall, Inc, 1963, p 315.

reversion to conservatism as it is written down. Of course, values other than cost could 'attach' so that causality is not a necessary principle for the cost rule. Instead it seems that cost came first and there was a need for some rationale for making the allocations. Causality provided the rationale.

In short, cost is both conservative and convenient, and thus it fits our general hypothesis. Our secondary hypothesis—that cost is a derivative of the general principle of conservatism—is supported by the fact that when cost and conservatism conflict, conservatism prevails. Additional evidence, albeit indirect, for both hypotheses is the manifestly specious character of the arguments for the cost rule. We think that the explanation for this is that the arguments are essentially apologetics for accounting practice. The practice is governed by conservatism, but the authors deny the principle of conservatism and thus are left in the untenable position of defending what they deny. As a consequence, the arguments become strained in attempting to defend the rule.

III. Arguments for the Cost Rule

For our purposes it will be convenient to distinguish two broad categories of arguments for the cost rule. The distinguishing factor is the temporal location of the valuation; valuations are made at

1. the time of acquisition (initial valuation)
2. times subsequent to acquisition (subsequent valuation).

Initial valuation is accomplished by setting the acquired asset equal to the cash (or cash equivalent) sacrificed and with this we have no quarrel. We usually find ourselves in disagreement with the arguments but, since the conclusions are identical, we omit the criticism.[7]

Our quarrel is with subsequent valuation. Subsequent valuation at historical cost is a measure of past sacrifice which we think is irrelevant to the present valuation. We will analyse only those arguments which are most pertinent to this quarrel.

Finney's Argument

Finney begins his argument with reference to marketable securities and specifically raises the question of subsequent valuation in terms of 'revenue realization'. Essentially the question is, 'Should securities be valued at original cost or at present market price?' There are some accountants who would value at present market price but would not allow the value increment to affect income. Finney does not make the distinction. He is concerned with both valuation and income at the same time.

His argument has appeared in texts and learned journals. For ease of reference, we present it in its entirety with marginal indications of the progress of the argument.

(Question) Is unrealized appreciation revenue? Let us consider this ques-

7. For a striking exception, cf Russell Bowers, 'Tests of Income Realization', *The Accounting Review*, June 1941, p 142.

> tion first with respect to marketable securities, as to which it is possible to make the strongest case for an affirmative answer.
>
> (Example) If marketable securities were purchased for $50,000, were worth $60,000 at the end of the year of purchase, and were sold for $70,000 in the following year, was there a $20,000 profit in the second year or a $10,000 profit each year? While it possibly may be said that $10,000 of the profit accrued each year, and while it certainly can be said that a $10,000 profit could have been realized the first year, it nevertheless is true that realization did not occur until the second year.
>
> (Principle, Premise) The requirements of the accounting principle relative to revenue realization were not met during the first year because, when the management elected not to sell at the end of the first year but preferred to take the hazards of market fluctuation, (Conclusion) there was no realization of profit nor any reasonable assurance that a profit would be realized.
>
> If readily marketable securities cannot properly be valued at a price in excess of cost, although a profit could be immediately realized by a sale at the market price, the valuation of inven- (Generalization) tories at market prices in excess of cost is under ordinary conditions, even less proper.[8]

In order to understand the argument we must reproduce the principle:

> The governing accounting principle is: *Revenue* should not be regarded as *earned* until an asset increment has been *realized* or until its realization is reasonably assured. (p 364. Emphasis supplied.)

Before we can utilize the principle, we need definitions for revenue, earned and realized.

> *Revenue* consists of an *inflow of assets*, in the form of cash, receivables, or other property, *from customers and clients*, and as related to the *disposal of product* in the form of goods or to the *rendering of services*. (p 363. Emphasis supplied.)

'Consists' and 'related to' are not sharp words, but the meaning is clear:

> *Definition 1.* Revenue is the receipt of cash or near-cash from sales.

'Realized', in the Fisher tradition, is unequivocally the receipt of cash. However, when the cash basis of accounting was modified, the terms were retained; some confusion resulted. Finney says:

> Realization of revenue does not necessarily require a collection in cash, since a valid receivable from a solvent debtor is an asset in as good standing as cash.

8. H. A. Finney, 'Principles and Conventions', *The Accounting Review*, October 1944, pp 365-366. The argument has also been reprinted with minor changes in the texts. See H. A. Finney and H. Miller, *Principles of Accounting Intermediate*, 5th ed, Englewood Cliffs, Prentice-Hall, Inc, 1963, p 176.

> The point of sale, therefore, is the step in the series of activities at which the revenue generally is regarded as realized. This point has been generally adopted because (1) it is the point at which a conversion takes place—an exchange of one asset for another—and conversion is regarded as evidence of realization; and (2) it is the point at which the amount of the revenue is objectively determinable from the sale price acceptable to both parties. (p 363.)

Realization is concerned with the occurrence of an act—a sale—and with the form of assets—cash or near-cash—that can be included as 'realized'. It is a trifle obscure in light of the phrase about 'conversion *being evidence* of realization', because realization is defined as occurring at conversion. Nevertheless, in view of the rest of the literature and Finney's other works,[9] we can define it explicitly:

Definition 2. Realization occurs when cash or near-cash is received from sales.

Earned is simply a synonym. 'As used in accounting, however, "earned" and "realized" are generally regarded as synonymous.'[10] Again 'generally regarded' prohibits sharpness, but in light of the above quotation the definition is clear:

Definition 3. Earned equals realized.

Since one cannot have receipts from sales without the occurrence of a sale, it appears that revenue is the more general term. Substitution of 'revenue' for 'realization' in Definition 2 does not distort the meaning:

Definition 2. [Revenue] occurs when cash or near-cash is received from sales.

Revenue is defined as receipts-from-sales; therefore, revenue occurs when the sale is made. There can be no lapse of time as there might be on a cash basis because receivables are included in the 'realization'. Thus, 'revenue' and 'realization' are synonyms and 'realized revenue' is redundant. Receipts-from-sales is the basic concept. At the very most, the distinction is that realization refers to the *timing* of the receipt while revenue refers to the receipt (inflow) per se. With very little, if any, distortion the general definition may be stated as:

$$\begin{aligned}\text{Receipts-from-sales} &= \text{revenue}\\ &= \text{realization}\\ &= \text{earnings}\\ &= \text{realized revenue}\\ &= \text{earned revenue}\end{aligned}$$

We can now restate and understand the governing principle:

> [Receipts-from-sales] should not be regarded as [receipts-from-sales] until an asset increment has been [received-

9. The latest edition of the Finney and Miller introductory book answers the question in slightly more direct fashion.

> 'When is revenue earned? Revenue is earned when goods are disposed of or when services are rendered. A transfer or exchange occurs. The business gives up goods or renders services and acquires other assets in exchange. There is a performance accompanied by a concurrent acquisition of an asset.'

H. A. Finney and H. Miller, *Principles of Accounting, Introductory*, 6th ed, Englewood Cliffs, Prentice-Hall, Inc, 1963, p 241. As we note in the text, Finney equates earnings with realization.

10. H. A. Finney, 'Principles and Conventions', p 363.

> from-sales] or until its [receipt-from-sales] is reasonably assured.

A 'principle' of this kind needs no commentary.

We can now restate Finney's argument.

> Is [not-receipts-from-sales] [receipts-from-sales]? While it possibly may be said that $10,000 of the profit accrued each year, and while it certainly can be said that a $10,000 profit could have been [received-from-sales] the first year, it nevertheless is true that [receipts-from-sales] *did not occur* until the second year.
>
> The requirements of the accounting principle relative to [receipts-from-sales] [receipts-from-sales] were not met during the first year because, when the management *elected not to sell* at the end of the first year but preferred to take the hazards of market fluctuation, there was no [receipts-from-sales] nor any reasonable assurance that a profit would be [received-from-sales].

No one would deny that 'realization did not occur'. By assumption, no sale was made and by definition, realization occurs at sale. His conclusion is of the same order. In effect he says 'when management elected not to sell there was no sale', i.e. 'when there was no sale there was no sale'. A more exquisite example of *petitio principii* is impossible to imagine.

Two minor points remain. First, the tense of the last statement is important. It is said there was no 'reasonable assurance that a profit *would be* realized'. Finney is concerned with the future, with the ultimate profit to be realized from sale, not with the measurement of past events. He says 'it certainly can be said that a $10,000 profit *could have been* realized'. He does not deny that he could measure the amount that could have been realized, but he refuses to do so because that may not be the amount that will ultimately be realized. That is, the fact that the future price is unknown leads him to reject a known present price. We do not follow this reasoning and in addition we do not understand how it leads to the acceptance of a past price.

Second, the word 'certainly' implies *sureness of the amount* that 'could have been realized'. Could this be interpreted as admission of an objective measurement prior to sale? His second justification of realization is that the sale 'is the point at which the amount . . . *is* objectively determinable . . .', not is *more* objective; yet he seems to imply that there may be other points when the amount is objective. Both of these points will come up again in the sequel.

Finney's argument must be rejected as circular, repetitious and ambiguous. Many explanations for this circularity could be advanced, but in light of the report that he has sold over a million copies to a rather conservative audience, we prefer the hypothesis of a tacit assumption of conservatism.

May's Assumption and Argument

May's argument is presented in an AICPA research study because it is 'pertinent for the light it throws on the reasoning behind this guide [realization convention]'.[11] We consider it for the same reason.

> Manifestly, when a laborious process of manufacture and sale culminates in the delivery of the product at a profit, that profit is not attributable, except conventionally, to the moment when the sale or delivery occurred. The accounting convention which makes such an attribution is justified only by its demonstrated practical utility.
>
> It is instructive to consider how it happens that a rule which is violative of fact produces results that are practically useful and reliable. The explanation is that in the normal business there are at any one moment transactions at every stage of the production of profit, from beginning to end. *If the distribution were exactly uniform*, an allocation of income according to the proportion of completion of each unit would *produce the same result* as the attribution of the entire profit to a single stage.[12]

The general thesis is correct under the assumption given. If a firm engages in a repetitive process of purchasing and selling at constant prices in constant quantities with constant time lapses, the recognition of income at sale will yield a valid figure. More precisely, it will yield a constant income figure for all temporal instants except the first and the last.

If we take May's assumption of exact uniformity and assign t_0 to the instant of the first purchase (at the inception of the business), which is to be sold at t_1, and another purchase at t_1 to be sold at t_2, etc., and the last sale (at the cessation of the business) at t_n, we can represent the transactions in full as in Figure 1. At t_0 a product is acquired costing, say, \$100 and is sold for, say, \$125 at t_1. Another purchase for \$100 is made at t_1 and sold at t_2 for \$125 and so forth until the firm makes its final sale at t_n and closes down.

The accounting rules require that the cost of the merchandise be deferred until sold, at which time the cost expires and is matched against the revenue. There is an asset of \$100 from t_0 to t_n. The first revenue occurs at t_1 and the asset acquired at t_0 then becomes an expense. Revenue remains constant from t_1 to t_n at \$125 and expenses remain constant at \$100 and thus a profit of \$25 per instant. In short, the accountant shifts the purchase curve one instant to the right and changes its name.

Under these assumptions, the virtues ascribed to the rule are perfectly correct. As May pointed out, the rule would produce the same result as an allocation according to the 'proportion of completion'. We agree. Our criticism is that he did not go far enough. *Precisely the same result would be achieved by recognizing*

11. Robert T. Sprouse and Maurice Moonitz, *A Tentative Set of Broad Accounting Principles for Business Enterprises, Accounting Research Study, No 3*, New York, American Institute of Certified Public Accountants, 1962, p 13.

12. George O. May, *Financial Accounting*, New York, The Macmillan Company, 1943, p 30. Emphasis supplied.

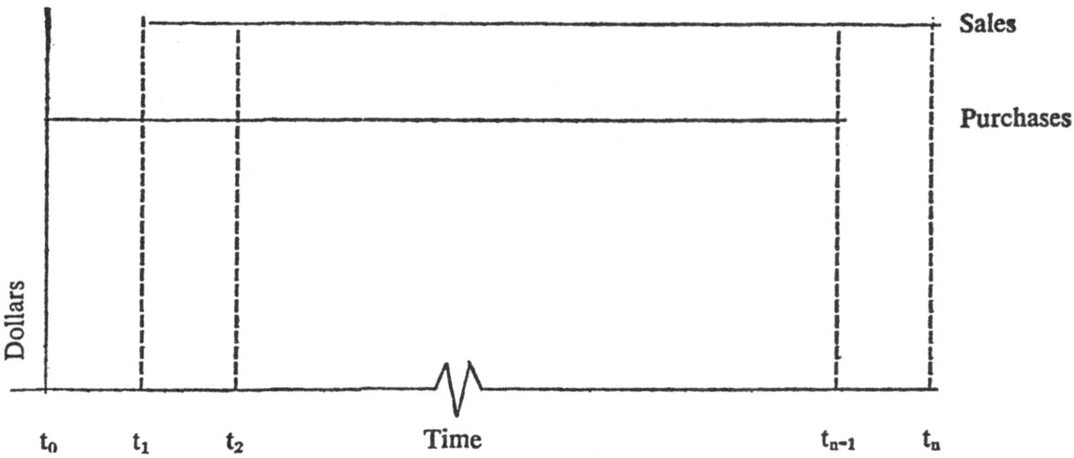

FIGURE 1

income on the cash basis, the sale basis, the purchase basis, or more simply by recognizing it on Tuesdays, equinoxes, or phases of the moon. Except for the first and last instants, *any* temporally uniform basis would produce the same result if the distribution were exactly uniform. Thus, we could ask what is special about the sale basis that would cause us to select it as the only point for revaluations. Unfortunately, May does not address this question. His argument for a sale basis of recognition is equally applicable to all other temporally uniform bases.

May goes on to say that the realization convention should be violated when the stable-firm assumptions are not met and gives construction contracts as an example. With this we can agree, but note that the assumption requires constant prices and constant quantities at all instants in time. Since these requirements are

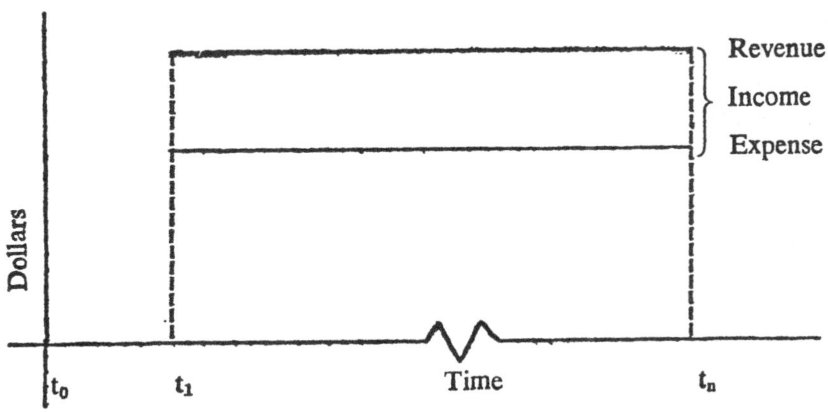

FIGURE 2

seldom, if ever, met we could conclude that the realization convention should be violated in almost all valuation situations.

May's argument is enlightening because the assumptions are made explicit. As far as we know this is the only place where an accountant has explicitly stated these assumptions in defence of the convention, although others have claimed that the stationary state is a necessary condition for validity. It is tempting to speculate about the relationship of the notions of the stable firm and the stationary state to the notion of the going concern. Some of the arguments for going concern values seem implicitly to assume the stable firm and it may be that the two assumptions are identical. In addition, the argument is enlightening because it requires a future. The purchased good has a value because it *will be sold* in the succeeding time period. However, the fact that the good has a value does not necessarily lead to a cost valuation. Instead the argument seems to turn on convenience and conservatism. It is likely that the convenient-conservative practice existed and May hit upon the stable-firm assumption as a means of justifying the practice. Other observations of May lend some credence to this view; for example, 'To me, conservatism is still the first virtue of accounting. . . .' (Ibid, p 44.)

Paton and Littleton

About thirty years ago the American Accounting Association became increasingly disturbed about the lack of theory in accounting. It formed committees and study groups in order to remedy the deficiency and 'to bring order out of this chaos of conflicting ideas and practices'.[13] The result of this concern was the publication of *An Introduction to Corporate Accounting Standards* which, it was hoped, would 'be one of the really significant contributions to accounting literature' (p vi). If acceptance, use, and citation are the criteria, their hopes were realized. *Standards* has had a tremendous influence on accounting thought and has since become a classic. It has been accurately described as the 'accountants' theoretical bible'. For this reason, we feel obliged to analyse the authors' argument for the cost rule.

Our consideration of *Standards* is much more difficult than that of either Finney or May because we are unable to locate a concise valuation argument that we could analyse. The discussion is somewhat diffuse and the reader will have to depend upon our outline of the argument instead of a complete direct quotation. That is the source of our first criticism. One would hope that such a basic treatise would present a rather full argument for the endorsed valuation method. Unfortunately this is not the case; its lack is a major defect in an otherwise noble effort.

Paton and Littleton's approach is to derive 'standards' (norms for behaviour)[14] from 'concepts'.

> The circumstances surrounding the use of accounting clearly indicate the need for accounting standards. But such standards cannot be determined by an appeal

13. W. A. Paton and A. C. Littleton, *An Introduction to Corporate Accounting Standards*, Chicago, American Accounting Association, 1940, p vi.

14. 'Accounting standards therefore become responsible for furnishing guideposts to fair dealing in the midst of flexible rules and techniques.' Ibid, p 2.

> to authority or to common opinion. The doctrines supported by writers and the practices accepted by professional accountants need to be subjected to analysis and coordination, with a consequent sifting out of inconsistencies and unessentials and an integration of essentials. The approach to standards should be by way of the broad function of accounting so that the standards formulated may be relevant thereto, and by way of the *basic concepts or assumptions* underlying accounting so that the standards formulated may be well grounded. To be relevant, a standard needs to be clearly related to the essential purposes of accounting; to be well grounded, a standard needs to be recognized as resting upon known and accepted assumptions.
>
> The *basic concepts, or assumptions,* here summarized constitute a suitable foundation for the discussion of accounting standards which follows. (p 7. Emphasis supplied.)

Thus, the behavioural norms (standards) spring directly from the *assumptions.* There are several headings in the chapter, which presumably are a list of these basic assumptions. Under each of the headings there is some statement about *cost,* with no consideration of any competing method of valuation.

Under the caption 'The Business Entity', they write:

> With the entity concept as a basis, there is no difficulty in accepting the proposition that all costs legitimately incurred by the enterprise are properly included, in the first instance, in the total of assets. Thus organization expenditures, costs of raising capital, and related charges are elements of enterprise assets and capital. (p 9.)

Their analysis is concerned with the segregation of business from personal affairs and with the *items* which can be properly included as assets. After they justify the inclusion of certain items, the term 'cost' is used as a general description. They do not give reasons for their selection of cost as opposed to another value.

Under the caption 'Continuity of Activity', they write:

> To the courts, concerned with the problem of determining immediate equities and restoring rights if damage has been suffered, assumptions with respect to future activity seem largely irrelevant. Hence the stress on 'values' and 'valuations' rather than on costs and the processes of accounting for costs. *The accountant,* on the other hand, deals primarily with the administration of the affairs of the continuing business institution and *accordingly emphasizes* the flow of costs and the interpretation of assets as balances of unamortized costs. (pp 10-11. Emphasis supplied.)

They never say *why* he 'accordingly emphasizes the flow of *costs*', simply that he does emphasize it. In fact, they say that 'earning power—not price . . . is the significant basis of enterprise value'. But they then switch to a discussion of income statements, and they define income as the resultant of the proper matching of *costs* and revenues.

Under the caption 'Measured Consideration', they introduce the term 'price-aggregate'; and then in the summary they conclude that 'price-aggregates involved in the exchanges . . . constitute the basic subject matter of accounting'. The word 'consideration' is being used here in the same way as it is used in the law of contracts, i.e. it means the amount given in exchange. Thus 'consideration' appears to be both one of the basic assumptions of accounting and 'the basic subject matter of accounting'. The next assumption is that '*costs* attach'. Then, '*costs are considered* as measuring effort' under the caption 'Efforts and Accomplishments'. Under the caption 'Verifiable, Objective Evidence', they *never mention* price-aggregates or cost (except the cost of obtaining evidence); yet in the summary, the reasons given for costs being the basic data is that they are 'objective'.

The full statement in the summary is:

> In general, the only definite facts available to represent exchange transactions objectively and to express them homogeneously are the price-aggregates involved in the exchanges; hence such data constitute the basic subject matter of accounting. (p 7.)

Their concern is only with exchange transactions; purchase prices are proper for the valuation at time of exchange. But they do not say why they are proper for *subsequent* valuations. One could speculate about the reasons for their conclusions but it would be preferable if they had stated them.

Perhaps the explanation for the use of cost without justification lies under the last heading. Under the caption 'Assumptions', they write:

> The fundamental concepts or propositions of accounting, like those of other fields, are in themselves assumptions in considerable measure or are predicated upon assumptions which are not subject to conclusive demonstration or proof. (p 21.)

It appears that cost is one of the basic assumptions which is not subject to proof. Upon this basic assumption they build their superstructure of concepts.

Stout evidence that they assume the cost rule comes from the peculiar character of their methodology. Their approach is tersely stated in the preface. 'We have attempted to *weave together* the fundamental ideas of accounting rather than to state standards as such.' (p ix. Emphasis supplied.) That is, they have taken the fundamental ideas that they have found in practice and woven them together.[15] One idea that they found was cost. 'The assumption that recorded dollar cost continues to represent actual cost permeates accounting thought and practice, as it does the law'. (p 23.) Upon finding this permeation, and without explicit critical analysis of the effects of using cost, they wove cost in as a basic assumption. It is hardly surprising, therefore, that the final chapter of *Standards* concludes that cost is the proper value for use in accounting.

It would be unkind to accuse them of circular reasoning. Their arguments turn out to be circular but this is because of their methodology. They conceive their role to be one of rationalizing (making rational) the extant practice of accounting. Thus, they are not guilty of circular reasoning because they do not attempt to reason from premise *to* conclusion. They take the existing ideas and try to

15. In a later work Littleton makes the process more explicit. He devotes an entire chapter to 'Inductively Derived Principles', i.e., principles derived from observing the practices of accountants. A. C. Littleton, *Structure of Accounting Theory,* Menasha, Wisconsin, George Banta Publishing Company, 1953.

connect them; they are apologists in the strict sense of the term. As it turns out, they are apologists for a practice that is conservative.

The Liquidity Argument

A number of authors have argued that income should not be recognized until the asset that it represents is in liquid form, a form that is distributable, available to pay dividends. The most readily available (liquid) asset is cash and this may be one of the reasons underlying the preoccupation with exchanges and money.

We do not know exactly why this position is taken. There has been little analysis in the literature since the *Eisner* v. *Macomber* case. The profession seems to have believed that the court settled the 'separation' issue and nothing was left to be said. Bowers has pointed out that this is based upon a misunderstanding of the court's decision.

> This decision seems to have been misunderstood by many practitioners and textbook writers. The court did not hold, as is often supposed, that a stock dividend in the same class of stock is not income. The earlier Macomber decision had merely denied that the receipt of common stock constituted effective realization if received as a dividend on common stock, that is, if it were merely capitalized surplus which was already a common stock equity.[16]

The court held that the receipt of stock did not effectively change the position of the recipient since it was simply a different form of the equity which he had previously owned. Thus, it could be interpreted to mean that the 'income' arose *before* the issuance of the stock dividend.

Because of this misunderstanding, the separation notion seems to be an *assumption* of accountants. This hypothesis is strengthened by the absence of analysis and the occasional explicit statement that it is an assumption. For example, Bowers discards the economic power theory on measurement grounds and then *assumes* availability.

> If the economic-power theory has any conceptual superiority the possibility of applying new measuring devices should be studied more carefully. In the remainder of this article it will be *assumed* that the efficacy of any realization criterion lies in two essential attributes, first, measurability, and second, *availability*. (pp 91-92. Emphasis supplied.)

The reason behind the assumption is that income is not available to pay dividends until it is in liquid form. Accountants 'help' management by restricting income (receipts) to assets that are in distributable form. From this they assume that income cannot arise until the availability criterion is met. The argument is confused and unsound.

First, there is the possibility of paying dividends in kind. This has been done, particularly during the Great Depression, but it is cumbersome. It is more convenient to pay cash dividends and, of course, this requires possession of cash

16. Russell Bowers, 'Tests of Income Realization', in S. Davidson, D. Green, C. Horngren, G. Sorter (eds), *An Income Approach to Accounting Theory*, Englewood Cliffs, Prentice-Hall, Inc, 1964, pp 90-91.

before they can be paid. Usually a corporation has several sources of cash. It could, for example, pledge a non-liquid asset on a loan and obtain sufficient cash to pay a dividend.

More important, however, is the confusion of two separate concepts. The possession of cash is a question of fact about the *form* of the assets at a given *moment in time*. The income question is concerned with *changes* in wealth *over time*. If the ability to pay cash dividends is the sole criterion, the income question becomes the ultimate in simplicity. Either the company has cash or it does not, and that is the end of the problem.

In their writings on earned surplus and retained income, accountants not only recognize, they emphasize, the difference between the two questions. They lament the confusion resulting from the equation of retained income to 'ability to pay dividends'. In an effort to prevent this confusion, they carefully point out that the final determinant of dividend payments is the *availability of cash*, not income.

Hill and Gordon present a fairly typical statement.

> This order gives recognition to the fact that dividends are legally paid out of accumulated, rather than current, earnings. In this connection, it should be noted that while dividends are declared 'out of earnings', they are paid 'out of cash'. Consequently, insofar as past retained earnings have been invested in productive assets, they are not available for distribution.[17]

That is, dividends are distributions of income, but a *separate requirement* is that the assets must be in distributable form.

When the increment in assets which represents income is reinvested in productive facilities, it is no longer in distributable form, and this is exactly what has happened in the majority of corporations in America. It is very common to find the retained earnings figure to be several times the amount of cash and it is not uncommon for it to be larger than total current assets. It is clear that such a situation prohibits the immediate payment of cash dividends equal to the retained income, and it is clear that accountants recognize this. Their cognizance somehow leads them to the conclusion that liquidity should be the deciding factor in the recognition of current income.

A consistent application of the liquidity argument would require that income could never be more than cash on hand. Thus, even if income were realized upon receipt, it would have to be 'dis-realized' upon the transformation of cash to a non-liquid asset. Since most corporations have an aversion to holding idle cash, income would be realized only momentarily.

For example, suppose that a trader started with \$100 cash at t_1 and had \$150 cash at t_2. This meets the distribution requirement and the unequivocal amount of income is \$50. If one instant later he makes a purchase, the distribution requirement is not met. Should we dis-realize the income? If so, has he suffered a loss? Of course the accountant would not dis-realize the income. He would

17. T. Hill and M. Gordon, *Accounting: A Management Approach*, rev ed, Homewood, Richard D. Irwin, Inc, 1959, p 51.

value the purchased asset at $150 (cost) and the difference ($50) would remain in the retained income account.

If the price of this latter asset rose between the date of purchase and a balancing date t_3, a report at t_3 will show a current income of zero regardless of how high the price has gone because the amount of the rise in price is not in distributable form. However, the t_3 report will show $50 of retained income which also is not in distributable form. The only difference between current and retained income is the period of time that is covered. Retained income includes all income from t_1 to t_3 and current income is only that income from t_2 to t_3. Thus, the inclusive income concept, the longer period income, does not meet the distribution requirement, but the requirement must be met before the shorter period income can be realized. Something is not quite right here.

If Devine's notion of administering working capital is taken literally, we can be more insistent that income be dis-realized. He writes:

> For our present purposes the important aspect of income realization is that accountants usually *insist on helping* management administer its working capital by *recognizing income only when working capital is available to permit withdrawal* (if desired) without impairing the current position of the firm.[18]

The accountant restricts the amount of legally payable dividends by not recognizing income until it is liquid. Leaving aside the ethical question of the accountant taking it upon himself to do this, it is clear that the accountant could be of even more 'help' if he dis-realized income when there was no cash available. If he thinks that management needs help on financial matters, it would be eminently reasonable to reduce income at least to the cash on hand, and perhaps he should even deduct planned disbursements.

We are not seriously suggesting such a procedure. Instead we are trying to emphasize that the problems should be separated by showing that the connection leads to absurdity. We think that the liquidity argument is nothing more than conservatism—Devine's article is an attack on the notion that *losses* need to be 'realized'—in evidence again.

The Going-Concern Concept

The going-concern assumption is common to almost all accountants. Textbooks seldom fail to list it as a 'standard', 'convention', etc. The following is fairly representative:

> When the future is unpredictable, one can only assume a continuity of existence and a business environment to follow that is similar to that in which the enterprise finds itself currently. The business unit, thus, is viewed as a 'going concern' in the absence of evidence to the contrary. The continuity assumption is support for the preparation of a balance sheet that reports costs that are assignable to future activities rather than realizable values that would attach to properties in the event of voluntary liquidation or forced sale.[19]

18. C. T. Devine, 'Loss Recognition', in *An Income Approach to Accounting Theory,* op cit, p 163.
19. Karrenbrock and Simons, op cit.

The assertion that one 'can *only* assume a continuity of existence' is absurd. One *can* assume anything he pleases about the future. There is a continuing philosophical debate about what one *should* (logically) assume, but we have found no philosopher who prescribes one assumption. Even the most future-minded of the philosophers insist on an evidentially (historically) based *projection*, not an assumption. The high rate of business failures would make it difficult to build an evidential case for a projection of continuity. No business has ever continued 'indefinitely' into the future. All businesses, except those presently in existence, have ceased operations. Thus, it would seem more reasonable to assume cessation instead of continuity.

A case could be built for a mean life-expectancy of businesses and this, like other statistical generalizations, would have some conceptual use. However, the generalization is about a universe and to apply it blindly to any particular element in that universe would be a gross misuse of statistical projection. Surely no one would *assume* that a leukemia patient is expected to reach the mean life expectancy of the population.

It is difficult to come to grips with this assumption. There seems to be little reasoning behind it and even less evidence. Another investigator had similar difficulties:

> *The continuity (or permanence) of the business enterprise.* Relatively little can be found explaining this concept other than (a) the postulate itself—that in the absence of actual evidence to the contrary, the prospective life of the enterprise may be deemed to be indefinitely long, and (2) [sic] the statement that it is an accepted postulate because continuity is typical of all entities.[20]

Our reading leads us to the same conclusion. We think that the reason why relatively little is said about it is because there is relatively little that can be said about it. We have a propensity to be suspicious of bald assertions and, therefore, we reject (a). A perusal of *Dun's Review of Business Failures* leads us to deny that 'continuity is typical'.

For purposes of discussion, however, let us make the continuity assumption and examine the valuation consequences.

Futurity is an overriding concern of the accountants. For example, we found it in both Finney and May supra. This is apparently contradictory because accounting is generally thought to be purely historical. Further, most accountants think of themselves as recorders of past facts. Yet benefit theory, the matching process, attaching notions, etc., are clearly futurity concepts. A typical statement of the criterion for distinguishing between a positive and a zero carrying value follows:

> (1) . . . any acquisition cost or portion thereof which is productive of *current period* revenue is an expense [zero value], and
>
> (2) . . . any acquisition cost or portion thereof which is to be productive of *future* revenue is an asset [positive value].[21]

20. Arthur Andersen & Co, *The Postulate of Accounting*, Chicago, September 1960, p 18.
21. Hill and Gordon, op cit, p 168.

Thus, to follow these rules, the accountant assumes the continuity of the firm and then *projects* the benefits from each individual expenditure.

From this, he reasons that the proper value of these projected benefits is always equal to the historical cost. This reasoning normally takes the form of concentrating on the intended use and disallowing alternatives and/or sacrifices. The following is typical:

> Even when a disparity exists between old costs shown in the balance sheet and current values, the usefulness of the balance sheet is not destroyed, because in most cases the assets in question will have been acquired to be used and not to be resold. In such cases current values often are of slight significance to a 'going concern' (an established business which is being conducted with the expectation of continuing indefinitely), because in most cases, assets with current values differing materially from cost would be such things as buildings, machinery, and equipment that were acquired to be used and not to be resold.[22]

We fail to follow the reasoning that connects intended use and value. We can understand how the expected net revenue from an intended use affects the valuation decision of a given entrepreneur, but since those expectations are certain to change over time,[23] the value would also change. Only if one assumed that the expectations remained constant could the intended use have a one-to-one relationship with value. If one takes this view, the intended use notion is additional evidence for the existence of the 'stable-firm stable-economy' assumption.

Moonitz and Jordan explicitly deny the stable economy assumption by introducing uncertainty, and defend the use of cost as an initial value. 'The choice of cost as the basis of *initial* valuation is, in most cases, reasonable.'[24] However, in a refreshingly candid statement, they point out that cost is a conservative value, initially, and further that the subsequent valuation at cost is solely on the basis of conservatism.

> In terms of the basic accounting problem, the cost rule is apparently conservative. Initial entry at cost results in no change in the difference between assets and liabilities; the acquisition of merchandise or of a fixed asset is treated as a 'dead-level' transaction without effect on profits or proprietorship. . . . At dates subsequent to purchase, the reasons for adherence to cost differ. Here the *rationale is frankly on conservative grounds.* (pp 168-9. Emphasis supplied.)

We are in complete agreement with this assessment. Note, however, that their justifications of the cost rule are based on futurity considerations. The theoretical framework is very close to that of Irving Fisher, although the conclusions vary.

Moonitz and Jordan's notion of value is grounded firmly in expected future receipts of *cash*. They make this explicit in several places.

> . . . for only through a carefully prepared projection of *estimated* cash receipts and cash disbursements, based on past experience corrected for anticipated

22. Finney and Miller, *Introductory*, p 10.
23. Except perhaps in the very limited case of a government perpetuity.
24. M. Moonitz and L. Jordan, *Accounting: An Analysis of its Problems*, rev ed, New York, Holt, Rinehart and Winston, Inc, 1963, Vol I, p 168.

> variations, can the value amounts assignable to any of the items that become reflected in the financial picture of an enterprise be even approximately determined. (p 126.)

Moreover, and this is crucial, these cash receipts must come from the intended use of the assets. In neither of the cases—complete certainty and complete uncertainty—do they ever consider any alternative use of the assets; presumably because they think that only the intended use is relevant to valuation problems. But under complete uncertainty the cash receipts from the intended use are unknown and, therefore, no valuation can be made.

> When the future is presumed to be completely unknown, our accounting must deal entirely with the past. We can prepare, for example, a schedule of cash received to date and from whom, and of cash paid out to date and for what. But we cannot prepare a balance sheet, because each asset in a balance sheet *represents something applicable to the future*, and each liability likewise indicates a commitment to do something in the future. (p 127. Emphasis supplied.)

The underlying assumption must be of the 'locked-in' variety, i.e. the firm is locked in the market with no alternatives. Otherwise the receipts from an immediate *sale* of the asset would yield some recordable value. We can think of no justification for the intended use valuation other than the locked-in assumption. If this be the authors' assumption, we are basically in agreement with the conclusions, i.e., zero value. However, we do not see why the locked-in assumption should be made.

Because of this futurity notion most accountants claim that income cannot be measured until the enterprise ceases operations. Robnett, Hill and Beckett describe this as an 'inherent limitation' in accounting.

> *Business earnings are fundamentally indeterminate short of the total life of the business venture.* Any interim calculation of earnings is, therefore, an estimate. . . . In the first place, potential difficulty stems from the necessity, noted earlier in this chapter, for forecasting the future in order to interpret the past. *Underlying all interim valuation estimates is the general assumption that the business unit will continue as a going concern*, i.e., that it will function in the future in much the same manner as it has in the past.[25]

Note the odd twist in the juxtaposition of the emphasized statements. All valuations, at all instants in time, are made on the basis of the going-concern assumption. This would include the 'last' valuation when the business has ceased operations. Thus, the earnings are *always* indeterminate. Of course this is not their intent. They mean that income is indeterminate until all assets are converted into cash. At that time one can take the difference in the cash magnitudes and determine the income finally and unequivocally.

This again points up the accountant's preoccupation with cash. He conceives income almost exclusively in terms of cash receipts and disbursements but, facing uncertainty, he cannot forecast the cash movements and, therefore, denies his

25. R. H. Robnett, T. Hill and J. Beckett, *Accounting: A Management Approach*, Chicago, Richard D. Irwin, Inc, 1951, pp 509-10.

ability to measure income. This is an uncomfortable position. He claims to measure income on the accrual basis but conceives of it on the cash basis and then denies that he can measure it. It is patently impossible to *measure* the future and we could sympathize with the accountants' dilemma if it were not for the fact that it is self-imposed.

We do not understand the going-concern assumption. First, we do not know why the assumption is made and second, we do not understand how it leads to the cost rule. The assumption seems to have sprung from Dicksee's[26] consideration of parliamentary companies (public utilities) which were *required* to continue operations. Thus, the intended use of the asset was the only source of receipts and price fluctuations were irrelevant except at replacement. However, Dicksee did not apply it to private enterprises; instead he suggested a net worth accretion measurement. Perhaps the reason why the specific has become general is that in the periods of rising prices, the net worth accretion rule was unconservative.

This is a point of fundamental disagreement among accountants. We believe that income ought to be *measured* and that measurement is the operation of discovering the numerosity of units descriptive of an *existing condition,* not a prognostication of the future.

Objectivity

The assertion that cost is objective is probably used more often to defend the cost rule than any other single argument. There are several lines of reply, any one of which is sufficient grounds for rejecting this argument.

First, the construct criticism. What is or is not objective depends to some degree upon the perceiver's preformed theoretical construct.[27] One cannot get intersubjective agreement from those whose constructs vary. Thus, if the question is on ontological reality, we must first have some method of choosing from among the competing constructs. Perception of reality is an epistemological question of vast consequences. Accountants have been extremely cavalier in their treatment of the problem. Usually they do no more than make an unsupported assertion that cost is objective and that other values are not. We consider that assertion unwarranted and have presented some evidence elsewhere.[28]

Second, the defensive criticism. We agree that cash receipts and disbursements are convenient and univocal. However, that is not the question. Every basic text lists widely varying alternatives for the *initial* recording of cash outflows. The problem of determining which cash outlays should be treated as of a 'capital'

26. Lawrence Robert Dicksee, *Auditing,* London, 1892.

27. Chambers implicitly uses the construct criticism when he writes:

> It is no defense to argue that all accountants or auditors would agree that the method of accounting and reporting used is a method acceptable to them. This would be equivalent to asking the flat-earthists whether the earth is flat.

R. J. Chambers, 'Measurement and Objectivity in Accounting', *The Accounting Review,* April 1964, p 270.

28. Robert R. Sterling, 'An Operational Analysis of Traditional Accounting', *Abacus,* December 1966.

nature and which as expenses is one of the most difficult problems in accounting. The continuing valuation problems are subject to even wider deviations. Lifo and depreciation disputes are well known, but the myriad of lesser 'attaching' alternatives are relatively unfamiliar. The author once amazed himself by setting up a game tree which revealed over a thousand valuation alternatives in a very simple enterprise. The degree of divergence is astounding. A glance at the literature discloses that the most discussed and hotly-debated issue is the lack of uniformity in valuation concepts, in theory as well as practice. For the accountant to reject present values because they are 'subjective' is the pot calling the kettle black. Like Paton,[29] we 'marvel' at accountants who consider cost to be objective. I suspect, but I cannot prove, that present values would vary less as between firms than historical costs, and thus they would be more objective in the inter-observer agreement sense.

Third, the conservative argument. This has been detailed above. The telling point is that accountants are always willing to record a subjective (other than cost) value if it is *lower* than the objective (cash cost) value. No asset on the balance sheet is valued at its cash cost with perhaps the single exception of land, and land is likely to be valued at cost only if the market price is above or equal to the cost. Almost all assets are valued at less than their cost because they have been subjected to amortization, allowances, lower of cost or market, or some other procedure which results in lowering the value. The result is that the assets are valued at something other than their 'objective' cost; they are almost all valued subjectively.

The Study Group on Business Income, in understatement more characteristic of the British, has written:

> Those who have favored adherence to present practice have commonly talked in terms of 'factual' and 'objective' determinations and 'uniformity'. They perhaps have not given adequate recognition to the extent to which accounting is necessarily characterized by 'postulates', 'estimates', 'subjective choice of method', and 'variety in methods'.[30]

This may be true. Perhaps accountants, although they work with the materials daily, have not given adequate recognition to their own subjectivity. We think that a more reasonable hypothesis might be that they resist change, which is simply another aspect of conservatism.

Fourth, the information criticism. The final point is the strongest; yet it is most often misunderstood. Many writers outside the field of accounting continually refer to the precision and objectivity of accounting data. They lament the lack of theoretical validity but excuse it on practical grounds. We believe that the cost figures are neither precise nor objective. However, even if they were, they are irrelevant.

There are a number of management decision models in the current literature

29. Paton and Paton, *Asset Accounting*, p 54.
30. Report of Study Group on Business Income, *Changing Concepts of Business Income*, New York, Macmillan and Co, 1951, p 50.

which specify the relevant data. The marginal analysis also specifies the relevant data. There is a noticeable absence of historical cost data on any of those lists. A guess at a relevant figure is infinitely more valuable than a precise and objective irrelevancy. If one's decision model prescribes that length is relevant and radioactivity is not, then radioactivity is useless regardless of its precision or objectivity. A rough estimate of length is of some use, no matter how imprecise or unobjective.

IV. Summary and Conclusions

Accounting is a discipline without any cohesive, unified theory of valuation. The extant valuation methods vary widely for a wide variety of reasons. The result is a confusing array of combinational possibilities of valuation.

We submitted the hypothesis that conservatism was the fundamental principle of valuation. Evidence in support of this hypothesis comes from the following.

1. The history of accounting development produces a natural propensity toward conservatism.
2. Conservatism prevails when there is a conflict between it and other principles.
3. Writers in the field ordinarily justify a specific valuation procedure by appealing to conservatism even though they profess to be anti-conservative.
4. Criticism of conservatism often takes the form of using conservatism as the basic criterion.
5. Arguments for the historical cost-realization convention are manifestly specious when removed from the context of conservatism.

Because of the last point, we submitted the secondary hypothesis that the cost rule is, in fact, nothing more than a manifestation of conservatism. We examined several representative arguments for the cost rule and found them to be neither valid nor sound. We think that this supports both the primary and secondary hypotheses.

Criticism of conservatism as a principle tends to take on a moral tone. Conservative accountants consider it a virtue; anti-conservatives consider it unethical. We would like to avoid moral controversies. Perhaps Hill and Gordon hit on the explanation when they described it as an 'inborn tendency'. We were not born with the tendency and, therefore, find ourselves in sharp disagreement with the principle.

In terms of measurement-information criteria, it is clear that conservative measurements are not veritable. The final result of a deliberate understatement is deception, no matter how laudable the objective may be. It is clear that the *intent* is to deceive. It is also clear that the desired ends of the conservative are commendable, but we disagree with the means they choose to achieve that end. Since verity is a sine qua non of information, we must conclude that conservatism yields, not only zero information, but also, misinformation.

Historical costs, when they are used, are conservative and we think they are justified if and only if conservatism is justified.[31] Thus, we must also conclude that historical costs yield misinformation. Perhaps the most convincing evidence of this comes not from the above considerations but instead from the real world. In the last Presidential election the candidates revealed their wealth to the electorate. *Life* magazine reported President Johnson's wealth at about $14 million. Previously the figure of $3.5 million had been reported. A reader noticed the discrepancy and inquired about it. The editor replied:

> The accounting firm retained by the President said, in explaining how they arrived at their low $3.5 million estimate: 'The investments . . . are carried at cost, less allowance for depreciation. . . .' *Life* considers it more realistic to give the amounts these properties would bring in a sale today rather than what they originally cost.[32]

We agree that the present exit values were more realistic and further that this is what people generally mean when they speak of wealth. To report historical costs was misleading because the electorate did not want or expect that kind of valuation. In addition, it misled the electorate in another direction because the wealthier (based on present values) candidate had a smaller original cost. This particular incident may or may not have been a factor in the election. What is pertinent here is that the journalist, a confessed novice in matters of valuation, was forced to supply the desired, realistic information because the expert would not or (if we are to believe his protestations) could not.

June 1967

31. Historical costs are also convenient; it is much easier to check off an invoice than to find a present price. But, since values are the product of a valuation coefficient and a quantity, the invoice price procedure merely shifts the problem to one of determining the quantity of future benefits. Since these benefits lie in the future their magnitude is in principle unmeasurable and hence the convenience of historical cost is an illusion. Of course, we can avoid the problem altogether by accepting management's estimate of the quantity. Under those circumstances historical costs are very convenient: the only thing the accountant has to do is divide and multiply.

32. *Life*, 18 September 1964, p 32.

The Going Concern: An Examination

Robert R. Sterling

I. Introduction

The "going concern" is the accountant's "firm model." It seems to be universally accepted,[1] is believed to be a *necessary* axiom, and thought to have a direct *connection* to historical cost valuation. Thus, the going concern is one of the most important concepts in accounting. Such status would lead one to believe that the concept would be well defined, its necessity as an axiom thoroughly discussed, and its connection to historical cost demonstrated. Anyone with such expectations is due for disappointment. Although Paton and Littleton, Moonitz, Grady, various AAA Statements, the *Accountants' Handbook* and practically all texts list it as a postulate, concept,[2] etc., there is very little elaboration, justification, or development. The *Index to the Accounting Review* shows only one article[3] devoted to the subject, although many articles mention it or appeal to it in argument. Even the heterodox literature accepts the going concern concept without discussion.[4]

The purpose of this paper is to make some exploratory probes into the going concern concept. I will raise questions about precisely what is meant by the concept and what follows from it, paying particular attention to its connection to historical cost and its necessity as an axiom. In addition, I will explore its temporal dimension.

II. Necessity

It is difficult to know what is meant by the assertion that the going concern is necessary to accounting. Paton and Littleton simply state that "the possibility of abrupt cessation of activity cannot afford

This research was supported in part by a grant from the Ford Foundation. Acknowledgement is due to the members of the Accounting Colloquia of The University of Kansas, especially Professor Howard Stettler, for helpful comment and criticism.

[1] The *Accountants' Handbook* says "... it is generally agreed that ... it is entirely reasonable to regard the business entity as continuing ..." and I know of no one who explicitly rejects it although there are some who fail to mention it. For example, the recent *Statement of Basic Accounting Theory* does not list it as a concept, but I have argued elsewhere that they have tacitly assumed a kind of going concern model. Rufus Wixon, ed., *Accountants' Handbook* (Ronald Press Co., 1965), Sec. 1, p. 15. American Accounting Association, *A Statement of Basic Accounting Theory* (AAA, 1966). Robert R. Sterling, "A Statement of Basic Accounting Theory: A Review Article," *Journal of Accounting Research* (Spring 1967), pp. 109–110.

[2] The most prevalent term is "concept" although "assumption" is not uncommon. See W. A. Paton and A. C. Littleton, *An Introduction to Corporate Accounting Standards* (AAA, 1940), pp. 9–11; Maurice Moonitz, *The Basic Postulates of Accounting* (AICPA, 1961), pp. 38–39; Wixon, *Handbook, loc. cit*; Paul Grady *An Inventory of Generally Accepted Accounting Principles for Business Enterprises* (AICPA, 1965), p. 27; *Accounting and Reporting Standards for Corporate Financial Statements and Preceding Statements and Supplements* (AAA, 1957), p. 2.

[3] Reed K. Storey, "Revenue Realization, Going Concern and Measurement of Income," The Accounting Review (April 1959). This piece provides an excellent history of the going concern concept and argues (successfully, I think) that the concept does not provide justification for valuing inventories at cost.

[4] Edwards and Bell, for example, accept it without elaboration. They refer the reader to Paton and Littleton (*op. cit.*) for "an excellent discussion." Edgar O. Edwards and Philip W. Bell, *The Theory and Measurement of Business Income* (University of California Press, 1964), p. 7.

Robert R. Sterling is Associate Professor of Business Administration at the University of Kansas.

a foundation for accounting."[5] Exactly why this is true is not explained. On the surface it would seem that this is contradicted by the fact that accountants do account for firms that are in various stages of liquidation. Significant portions of the textbooks are devoted to accounting for firms in dissolution and preparation of statements of affairs, etc. Of course, these accounts are kept under different valuation methods, but the fact that they are kept at all is conclusive evidence that it is possible to do so. Moreover, it is alleged that the "true" income of the firm cannot be calculated until the firm is dissolved.[6] This is an odd state of affairs: The going concern is thought to be necessary to accounting and to be the normal case, yet all of the statements prepared under normal conditions are only "provisional." It requires the abnormal case before the final, accurate statements can be prepared. The going concern is thought to have a direct connection to historical cost valuation yet it requires the liquidated concern (with the attendant liquidation values) before the true values can be calculated. To state it negatively: Since income is fundamentally indeterminant prior to final dissolution, under normal conditions—the going concern—income can *never* be determined. If the object of accounting is to measure the true income and position of a firm, then the *liquidated firm is necessary* to accounting. The going concern is an obstacle that cannot be overcome, under this theory.

Paton and Littleton's argument is that the going concern concept is necessary to accounting. Others argue that the concept is necessary to management, and then identify managerial expectations with accounting concepts. For example, Grady says: "Corporate managements must view the operations as a continuing process."[7] Taken literally, this is unfortunate wording. Corporate managers *can* view their operations any way they like, and I am sure that some of them do not view it as a continuing process. At the extreme, there are "pirates" who "milk" the company and then liquidate. Less extreme are the one-man operations which begin to liquidate as the driving force approaches retirement. Finally, there is the quite common case of planned liquidation when it becomes clear that the original expectations are not going to be realized. Nonetheless, Grady is correct in the sense that managements are required to peer into the future and often do, in fact, view their operations as continuous. However, the connection between the view of management and accounting concepts is not apparent. Managers and entrepreneurs have always been optimistic about their operations. Traditionally it has been the independent accountant's function to put a check on this optimism insofar as it concerns valuation, i.e., to be conservative. The accountant has been careful to insulate himself from this optimism in order to make an independent, unbiased appraisal of the situation. It would seem that the accountant ought to take the same position on management's view of continuity for the same reasons.

In short, even if management views the firm as continuous, there is no *a priori* reason for accounting to take the same view, and there are good reasons for accounting to take an independent view. Thus, man-

[5] Paton and Littleton, *op. cit.*, p. 9.

[6] "Throughout Volume One, the point has been stressed that the calculation of periodic profit is beset with uncertainties, that the ultimate final profit or loss of an enterprise cannot usually be known until that enterprise is completely wound up. As a result, so-called liquidation gains or losses are in large part corrections of errors made in previous years in the valuations attached to assets and liabilities;" Maurice Moonitz and Louis H. Jordan, *Accounting: An Analysis of its Problems*, Vol. II (Holt, Rinehart and Winston, 1964), p. 72. This statement is typical. Almost all texts imply the proposition and many state it explicitly. Recall Paton and Littleton's (*op. cit.*, p. 10) statement about the "provisional character" of financial statements "even under the most favorable circumstances" and the "complete picture of an enterprise is never entirely discernible prior to final liquidation."

[7] Grady, *op. cit.*, p. 27.

agement's view of the firm is irrelevant to the view of the firm that accountants should take.

The notion of "future benefits" gives accounting a forward-looking direction and thus it may be argued that the existence of the firm in the future is necessary to the benefit theory. There are a number of difficulties with this argument. First, it makes accounting coterminous with the benefit theory. The benefit theory currently is widely accepted but it is (1) a relatively recent theory and (2) not accepted by all accountants. Thus, there were and are theories of accounting which reject the benefit theory and therefore may or may not find the going concern concept necessary. Second, strictly speaking, one only needs to know something about the future in order to utilize the benefit theory. If the benefits are time dependent (as is the usual conception and as is implied by the phrase "future benefit") then one needs only to know the "amount" of the future. For example, if the future is five years (the life of the firm or asset is five years) and x equals the amount of benefits per year, then $5x$ equals the amount of future benefits. In general, if y is the number of future periods, then yx equals the amount of future benefits. It is possible for y to range over the set of all positive real numbers and zero and thus $yx=0$ if $y=0$. This is a possible interpretation of our dissolution statements under the benefit theory. In that case, the future benefits are zero because the amount of the future is zero. Therefore, strictly speaking, a future or a going concern concept is not necessary to the benefit theory. It is only that the amount of future be *known* in order to calculate the future benefits.

This reveals a more fundamental aspect of the going concern concept. It is necessary to have a going concern for the benefits to be realized by the firm. If we purchase a machine "with a ten-year life" then it is necessary for the firm to have a life of ten years in order to garner all ten years of benefits. Thus, the going concern is necessary (but not sufficient) for the correctness of our predictions about positive future benefits of individual assets. This is an important distinction. The benefit theory requires only that the future be known. Since the future cannot be known, we must predict or assume something about the future. If we predict that a particular asset will benefit the firm in the future, it is possible for that prediction to be either right or wrong. A necessary condition for it to be right is that the firm continue. Thus, if we assume a going concern, we are in effect assuming that our individual predictions have the possibility of being correct. However, this does not mean that the going concern assumption is necessary to account. It is only necessary for us to be right when we account. All of us would prefer to be right when we account, but it is precious little comfort to know that a going concern is necessary to be right and then *assume* a going concern.

In order for us to be right when we account, the firm must continue; but in order for the firm to continue, it must be successful. Continuity *per se* is a form of success, albeit minimal. It is not likely that a firm will continue if it continuously suffers losses. Thus, it can be argued that the going concern assumption is an assumption which entails a successful firm. Many authors recognize this and state it directly. For example, Grady writes:

> In the second place, any depreciation formula which employs an estimate of useful life is based upon the concept of a going concern (among other concepts) which will operate at least as long as this useful life and, furthermore, will be able to recover the undepreciated cost of the assets from future revenues.[8]

Being able to *recover* the costs from future revenues requires that the revenues be

[8] Grady, *op. cit.*, p. 29.

greater than or equal to the costs, i.e., the minimum requirement for a going concern is non-negative income.[9] Therefore, it appears that the assumption of a going concern is tantamount to assuming a successful firm. Juxtapose this to the fact that the major purpose of accounting is to measure the income of the firm and that the going concern assumption is alleged to be necessary to accounting. This means that it is necessary to *assume* non-negative income in order to *measure* income.

In summary, (1) the liquidated firm is necessary to measure the true income and position. Under conditions of a going concern the income and position can only be estimated and all statements are provisional. (2) Management's view of the future of the firm may or may not be one of a going concern, but regardless of the view held by management, there are good reasons for accountants to take an independent view. (3) The going concern assumption is not necessary to the benefit theory; instead, the going concern is necessary for positive future benefits to be realized. (4) The going concern is necessary for predictions about positive future benefits to be correct but not necessary to make those predictions. (5) Continuity entails success and it is an error to assume success when that is what was set out to be measured.

For these reasons, I conclude that the allegation that the going concern is necessary to accounting has not been proven and that there are strong arguments to the contrary. The fact that we do account for firms in liquidation is persuasive evidence that the going concern is not necessary to account. It would seem instead that the going concern model is merely one of several models of the firm. From the different models, different methods of accounting are deduced. Then it may be said that a "liquidating concern concept is necessary to account on a liquidation basis" in the same way that a "going concern concept is necessary to account on a going concern basis," but such statements are clearly vacuous. The liquidating firm concept could, and sometimes does, serve as a foundation for accounting. There are other models that also could serve. At best the going concern is a choice from among alternative models.[10] The important questions are: Why did we choose that model instead of another one? What are the consequences and implications of the chosen model?

III. Connection

As noted *supra* the going concern is thought to have a connection to historical cost valuation. The argument almost invariably takes the form of contrasting liquidation values and historical cost:[11] If

[9] ". . . unless 'continuity' implies continued operation *at a profit*, it fails to justify fully the carrying of any assets at values that can be fully realized only by the earning of future net income." Williard J. Graham, "Allocation of Income Taxes," *The Journal of Accountancy* (January 1959), p. 59.

[10] The final answer to the question of the necessity of the going concern as an axiom will have to await agreement upon what accounting theory is and the formalization of that theory. Moonitz' list of postulates (*Postulates, op. cit.* and R. T. Sprouse and Maurice Moonitz, *A Tentative Set of Broad Accounting Principles for Business Enterprises* (AICPA, 1962)) contains the going concern concept, but this system was not adopted and it was not sufficiently formal to test the independence, necessity, and sufficiency of the postulates. Richard Mattessich, *Accounting and Analytical Methods* (Richard D. Irwin, Inc., 1964), p. 44 presents an axiom of "Duration" which is concerned with "the expected life of the entity" but this is quite different from the going concern because it allows for any expected life, including zero. Yuji Ijiri, "Axioms and Structures of Conventional Accounting Measurement," The Accounting Review (January 1965), p. 36 argues that his axioms "are not only *necessary* but also *sufficient* to explain the majority of the principles and practices in conventional accounting." The going concern is not included in his set of axioms. In my previous efforts in this direction, I have not found it necessary or desirable to include the going concern concept. Robert R. Sterling, "Elements of Pure Accounting Theory," The Accounting Review, (January 1967) and "A Formal Statement of Present Accounting Theory," (Working Paper, Harpur College, June 1964).

[11] "To the courts, concerned with the problem of determining immediate equities and restoring rights if damage has been suffered, assumptions with respect to future activity seem largely irrelevant. Hence the stress on 'values' and 'valuations' rather than on costs and

the firm were in liquidation, then liquidation values would be appropriate; in a going concern liquidation values are not appropriate; therefore, historical cost valuation is appropriate. There are several things wrong with this argument. First, it takes account of only two valuation alternatives. Since there are *several* valuation alternatives the *exclusion* of *one* of those alternatives does not permit the *selection* of *one* from the remainder. Even if we were to grant that liquidation values are not appropriate for the going concern, it would not lead to the conclusion that historical costs are appropriate.[12] Second, the fact that a firm is not in liquidation does not automatically exclude liquidation values. On the contrary, there is a "command over goods" school of income and wealth[13] that argues for liquidation values even if the firm is a going concern. In the face of this, the assertion that liquidation values are not appropriate simply because the firm is not liquidating is not very convincing. Third, the argument makes the valuation method dependent upon the state of the firm: (1) If the firm is liquidating, then use liquidation values. (2) If the firm is a going concern, then use historical cost. In order to apply these criteria, the state of the firm must be *determined*, not *assumed*, for to assume a going concern under these conditions is tantamount to assuming historical cost. In actuality, however, the state of the firm may be a consequence of the valuation method instead of the other way around. The following case will illustrate this point.[14]

C.P.A. firm X had been auditing the ABC Corporation for a number of years under the assumption that it was going to continue to have business life. On this basis a small income had been shown yearly. The rate of return on assets was small because certain land had been bought at a price which reflected the expectation of mineral deposits that had failed to materialize. On the basis of the going concern assumption, this land was kept at its "going concern value" (cost) instead of its "liquidation value" (exit price). The management did not intend to liquidate. When C.P.A. firm Y took over the audit and insisted that the land be written down to "fair market value" (?) the firm was shown to have a large deficit instead of retained "income." As a consequence, the management was replaced and the firm went into an orderly liquidation.

This was a difficult case. If the ABC Corporation is assumed to be a going concern and valued accordingly then it will *in*

the processes of accounting for costs. The accountant, on the other hand, deals primarily with the administration of the affairs of the continuing business institution and accordingly emphasizes the flow of costs and the interpretation of assets as balances of unamortized costs." Paton and Littleton, *op. cit.*, pp. 10–11.

"The importance of this assumption [going concern] can be indicated by contrasting it with a possible alternative; namely, that the business is about to be liquidated or sold. Under the latter assumption, accounting would attempt to measure at all times what the business *is currently worth* to a buyer, but under the going-concern assumption there is no need to do this, and it is in fact not done. Instead, a business is viewed as a mechanism for adding value to the resources it uses, and its success is measured by the difference between the value of its output (sales of goods and services) and the cost of the resources used in creating that output." Robert N. Anthony, *Management Accounting Principles* (Richard D. Irwin, Inc., 1965), p. 19.

"Here are some of the consequences of the going concern convention in the valuation of certain accounts, in contrast to those which would prevail if accounting had adopted, instead, a liquidation concept." The consequences they present are historical cost or lower of cost or market for all accounts listed. Benjamin Newman and Martin Mellman, *Accounting Theory—A CPA Review* (John Wiley and Sons, Inc., 1967), p. 35.

[12] Meigs and Johnson recognize this and argue that the "... going concern concept justifies ignoring immediate liquidating values ..." but this assumption "... does *not*, as is sometimes claimed, represent the accountant's justification for reporting assets at cost." Walter Meigs and Charles E. Johnson, *Accounting: The Basis for Business Decisions* (McGraw-Hill, 1967), p. 646. I agree with the second proposition, but not with the first.

[13] See, for example, Robert M. Haig, "The Concept of Income—Economic and Legal Aspects" in Richard A. Musgrave and Carl S. Shoup, eds., *Readings in the Economics of Taxation* (Richard D. Irwin, Inc., 1959) and Henry Simons, *Personal Income Taxation* (The University of Chicago Press, 1938).

[14] This case was related to me on a confidential basis and therefore it is disguised, but the essentials are factual.

fact be a going concern. Therefore, it may be argued that the auditors who wrote the land down were logically at fault. They *caused* the firm to be liquidated by violating an assumption that is a canon of accounting. (The management did make the argument.)[15] The previous auditors, on the other hand, had caused the firm to continue by valuing in accordance with the assumption that it was going to continue.

In cases like this it is impossible to use the state of the firm as a criterion for selecting a valuation method. The logical antecedent is the empirical consequent, and the empirical antecedent is the logical consequent. Thus, if one assumes a going concern and values accordingly, then one is in effect assuming a valuation method which has the going concern as a consequent, and vice versa.

The above has been concerned with the general argument as it is applied to the firm. The argument for valuing individual assets within the going concern is usually couched in terms of the intended use[16] of the assets. This is merely the non-liquidation argument applied to specific assets instead of to the firm. *Supra* we noted that since the firm is not in liquidation—the assets are not being sold—the liquidation values are said to be improper. The intended use argument takes precisely the same form: The assets are intended for use, not sale; therefore liquidation values are not proper; therefore historical cost is the proper valuation method. This argument suffers from all the defects pointed out above, the main one being that only two alternative valuation methods are considered. There is nothing inherent in the fact that an asset is to be used that permits one to conclude that liquidation values are not proper or that historical cost is proper. In addition, this argument has some defects which are peculiar to it. The general argument presented two possibilities for the antecedent—liquidating or going concern—and two consequents—liquidation or cost values. The individual asset argument has two possibilities in the antecedent—use or sale—but it has only *one* consequent. Compare these: This machine is intended for use, not sale; therefore, historical cost. This inventory is intended for sale, not use; therefore, historical cost. Since the consequents are the same it is obvious that the condition stated in the antecedents is not the discriminable factor.[17] Use versus sale, then, is irrelevant and the intended use argument does not hold.

[15] The auditors who wrote down the land justified their actions by "tell the truth [about fair market value] and let the chips fall where they may." That is, the land was valued on the basis of some higher criterion (truth) and the continuation or liquidation of the firm was the consequence (the falling chips) of that higher criterion. But this will not hold. Both firms are truthful; the historical cost of the land was the truth and both firms regularly certify to statements based on historical cost. Perhaps it was cases like these that prompted Arthur Andersen & Co. (*The Postulate of Accounting* (Arthur Andersen & Co., 1960), p. 19) to state that "The so-called postulate of the assumed continuity of business entity is often used to justify ignoring facts . . ." but I don't see that the ABC Corp. case is quite that clear cut. On the contrary, it was clear that the ABC Corp. could have lasted a few more years; it had already lasted several years beyond the disappointment on the deposits and perhaps it could have lasted "indefinitely." Of course, one could argue that it would have been liquidated eventually regardless of the valuation procedure, but maybe eventually isn't soon enough, especially in view of the fact that in all likelihood all firms will be liquidated eventually. Just what the "facts" are in the case of ABC Corp. is open to question. Both historical cost and fair market value were "facts" in this case. Indeed, both historical cost and fair market value as well as present entry price, exit price, discounted expectations, and many other valuation procedures are "facts" for all firms. But different sets of facts lead to different actions, including actions which directly affect the life of the firm.

[16] "It [going concern] merely rules out liquidation and requires asset valuation according to intended use." Storey, *op. cit.*, p. 237. See also Grady, *op. cit.*, p. 29 and almost any text.

[17] This point seems to be the main thrust of Storey's (*op. cit.*) article. Since the going concern concept will not support the valuation of both inventory and fixed assets at cost, he argues that some other concept or convention must be employed. His suggestion is the realization convention, but this shifts the argument to the appropriateness of that convention. For an extension of that argument, see Arthur L. Thomas, *Revenue Recognition* (University of Michigan Press, 1966).

A more important point is the difference between the argument applied to the firm and its application to individual assets. The firm can be thought of as an on-going process and like any other on-going process the components require replacement. A living organism continually replaces its cells in the same way that a going concern continually replaces its assets (and debts). The replacement process in the firm is by purchase and sale, i.e., liquidation of the individual assets. In other words, all assets are sold eventually, if only for scrap.[18] Thus all assets are intended for sale and the distinction between them is the time lag. This makes it difficult to apply a *non*-liquidation argument to assets. Under conditions of a going concern, the firm is not going to be liquidated but all the assets are liquidated; therefore the consequent of the non-liquidation argument is applicable to the firm, but not the components—assets—of that firm. But the value of the firm is the sum of the values of the assets under the present theory, and therefore the non-liquidation argument will have no effect on the valuation of the firm. If the firm were to be valued as a whole, independent of the value of the assets, the non-liquidation argument might have some effect; but as it is now, the effect is via the valuation of the assets and therefore the argument applied to the firm is only as good as its application to the assets.

The application of the argument to assets is similar to its application to the firm in another respect. It is often lamented that the values of assets are only estimates prior to the liquidation of those assets in the same way that the financial statements of the firm are only provisional prior to the final liquidation of the firm. Here again, this makes liquidation a necessary condition for the final, accurate determination of the value of an asset as well as the value of the firm. The reason given for this is that future activities may be different from our expectations and thus the valuations (allocations) based on those expectations may be wrong.[19] There is however, a vital difference: The liquidated firm is thought to be a final stopping place with no future activities about which to worry. The liquidated asset is simply a quantity of cash that must be used to replace those ". . . things we must continue to own in order to be a going concern."[20] Thus, cash under the going concern view, is awaiting conversion into some other asset. If it is impossible to accurately value a machine because of something that may happen in the future, it is likewise impossible to value cash that is required to be used to replace that machine in order to be a going concern. If future activities can make present valuations of non-cash assets inaccurate, then future activities can also make present valuations of cash inaccurate since cash is merely a prelude to a non-cash asset. It is possible to make an unfortunate purchase with cash and then argue that subsequent events proved the cash to be overvalued in the same way that subsequent events proved that the machine bought with that cash was overvalued.

[18] Alexander in an argument with May said: "Capital assets are just like an inventory that lasts a lot longer." *Five Monographs on Business Income* (AICPA, 1950), p. 207. Arthur L. Thomas, "The Amortization Problem: A Simplified Model and Some Unanswered Question," *Journal of Accounting Research* (Spring 1965), views inventory costing as an amortization procedure very similar to that procedure used for fixed assets. Mathematically the two procedures are identical. Sterling, "Elements," *op. cit.*, p. 64.

[19] "The future is uncertain; and yet the validity of the statement of asset values as of December 31, 1920, for example, depend in large measure upon the future course of events." W. A. Paton in *Paton on Accounting*, Herbert F. Taggert, ed. (University of Michigan Press, 1964), p. 129. "To measure expense or revenue for a period necessarily involves leaving some part of the data for future resolution." William J. Vatter, "Postulates and Principles," *Journal of Accounting Research*, (Spring 1963), p. 189.

[20] H. T. McAnly, "The Case for Lifo: It Realistically States Income and is Applicable to Any Industry," *The Journal of Accountancy* (June 1953), p. 691.

Thus, the liquidation argument—the argument that values can be determined at liquidation—is applicable only to the firm under this view.[21] But if we grant this argument, it has far reaching effects. Among other things, the realization convention falls. The essential point of the realization convention is the conversion of the inventory into cash or near-cash because revenue cannot be determined prior to that point. Sometimes it is said that it cannot be accurately or objectively determined, sometimes, that the point of sale is when the revenue and profit are irreversible, i.e., subsequent events cannot change the amount. But in a going concern, subsequent events can prove the valuation of cash to be wrong and therefore the revenue and income figure is reversible and subjective in the same way that any other valuation is subject to correction because of subsequent events.[22] Another way to make this point is to note that the original recognition of revenue and income requires cash or near-cash. Thus, current income is supported by the receipt of cash and this is justified by the assertion that one " . . . important aspect of income realization is that accountants usually insist on helping management administer its working capital by recognizing income only when working capital is available to permit withdrawal (if desired) without impairing the current position to the firm."[23] Neglecting dividends and adjustments, the only difference between current income and retained income is the time period covered. However, in fact as well as in conception under the going concern assumption, the cash received from sales is often used for further acquisitions. Thus, an argument for *dis*realization of income upon further acquisition can be made on the same grounds as the argument for the original realization.

In summary, the connection of the going concern concept to historical cost valuation is via the non-liquidation argument. This argument must be rejected because (1) it is invalid (technically, it commits the fallacy of denying the antecedent); (2) it considers only two valuation alternatives; and (3) in some cases it is a self-fulfilling prophecy. When this argument is applied to assets instead of the firm, it suffers from the same defects. In addition, it is irrelevant because it does not discriminate between various classes of assets.

The component-whole distinction leads to several difficulties. (1) If the whole is thought to be continuing but the components liquidating, then the non-liquidation argument is applicable to the whole but not to the components. Then the non-liquidation argument would seem to apply to the components, but it cannot since the value of the whole (total assets) is the sum of the values of the components. (2) If the components are thought to be circulating and that circulation is necessary to the continuation of the whole, then the non-liquidation argument would apply to the components as well as the whole. The paradox arises when we juxtapose the notion that values cannot be determined prior to *final* liquidation because there is no final liquidation of the whole or the components as long as the firm is a going concern. Thus, the values of the whole and the components are indeterminant as long as the assumption (going concern) upon

[21] "One wonders, however, about the meaning of 'provisional' reports in a situation where *no* liquidation date for the enterprise is assumed. . . . Possibly the term 'final liquidation' should refer to the exhaustion of specific items of real capital." Harvey Deinzer, *Development of Accounting Thought* (Holt, Rinehart and Winston, Inc., 1965), p. 90.

[22] The irreversible concept has always puzzled me. We seem to have shifted from a venture to a continuity concept in respect to the firm, but retained the venture concept in respect to assets. The sale of an asset is treated as a completed venture without regard to the fact that if no further purchases were made the firm would be in *de facto* liquidation. The going concern concept requires another purchase to be made and, therefore, there is no irreversible, completed venture in respect to assets.

[23] Carl T. Devine, "Loss Recognition," *Accounting Research* (October 1955), pp. 310–311.

which those values are based is true. (3) If it is thought that the present valuations of some of the components are susceptible to correction by future events, and the assumption of continuity of the whole entails continuity of the circulation of the components, then the valuation of all the components (including cash) is susceptible to correction because all circulate. Thus, the components can never be correctly valued if the assumption upon which the valuations are based is true.

In short, the arguments for historical cost valuation are confused and unsound *when put in the context of a going concern.* It seems to me that contrary to the going concern assumption providing support for historical cost, it provides a framework for criticizing the arguments for valuing at cost. I think that the reason for the confusion is to be found in the failure to distinguish between benefits and the valuation of benefits. We talk about *assets* having future benefits or service potentials. Then we immediately leap to statements about *costs* which benefit the future. Costs cannot benefit the future or have service potential (as anyone who has ever made an unfortunate purchase knows). Instead, cost is a method of valuing those benefits or potentials. The incurrence of a cost does not guarantee the existence of benefits, nor does the existence of benefits require the incurrence of a cost. They are independent concepts. The benefit theory is concerned with the determination of when something is *of* value, not with *how* to value it. There is a connection between the benefit theory and the going concern in the sense that they are both future oriented, but there is no connection that I have been able to discover between the going concern concept and historical cost valuation.

IV. The Firm Model

Exactly what accountants mean when they speak of a going concern is difficult to determine. Contrast the going concern model to the pure competition model, for example. A number of conditions are carefully specified, which together define what is meant by a purely competitive firm, and these conditions also serve to delineate the applicability of the model. Plainly, this precision is needed before the implications of a purely competitive system can be deduced. The going concern model, by contrast, is loosely defined as a firm "that will continue in much the same manner as in the past." Exactly what conditions that implies is not spelled out. It certainly implies more than continuity *per se.* It was previously noted that there is at least one implicit condition of the going concern, namely, success or non-negative income. Further implicit conditions of the going concern model are the subject of this section. Specifically, I will present the hypothesis that the going concern model implicitly contains the conditions necessary for a firm in a "stationary state." I will not argue that the stationary state is necessary for the "validity" of historical cost as do Edwards and Bell.[24] Instead, I will argue that the stationary state is what many accountants have in mind when they speak of a going concern, particularly when they make valuation arguments.

There are several clues that suggest the stationary state. First, the phrase "continue in the *same manner*" suggests a certain stability of the firm and the economy.

Second, the concept states that the firm will continue long enough to carry out *present* plans and expectations. It does not provide for a change in plans. Future events could be better *or* worse than expected and either is likely to cause a change in plans. Only when things remain the same are the plans likely to remain unchanged. The concrete meaning of this is

[24] "To summarize, present accounting practices would be fully valid only if . . . [there were a] . . . stationary state." Edwards and Bell, *op. cit.*, p. 9.

that favorable subsequent events may cause one to expect more future benefits than were originally planned and therefore too much cost will have been allocated. The opposite is true for unfavorable subsequent events—too little cost will have been allocated. Thus, only when the events are as expected will the plans remain constant and the allocation be correct.

Third, carrying out any given plan will almost certainly require stability of the firm and may require growth or success. The plan to refund a debt will require a certain minimum net worth-debt ratio and/or current ratio as well as income earned and income propspects. The plan to use an asset for ten years requires some minimum market for the product produced by that asset at some minimum price, as well as the replacement of all of the raw materials, supplies, complementary assets, and a continuing supply of labor. The price ratios of all of those factors must remain fairly stable to prevent substitution for the original asset. Technology must remain fairly stable for the same reason. And so on indefinitely. The mere assumption of continuity long enough to carry out present plans, then, assumes stability of the firm and economy.

Fourth, there is the widespread use of the it-doesn't-make-any-difference argument. This argument is applied in many areas but most often to the difficult capital versus expense decision. For example, in deciding how to treat research and development expenditures, it is often said that "it-doesn't-make-any-difference because the amount of the amoritization will tend to equal the amount of the expenditure after a suitable time lapse." It can be demonstrated that this is true. If the expenditure each year is constant and each year's expenditure is amortized over n years, then at the end of n years the expense will equal the outlay.[24a] For this to be true, it requires a *constant* expenditure each year, and that each year's expenditure yield a *constant* benefit. In turn, this requires *constant* prices of the factors that go into research and development. If the prices were to go up and the total expenditures remain constant, then *ceteris paribus* the quantity of benefits would decline. Thus, the it-doesn't-make-any-difference argument is quite true if everything is constant.

The it-doesn't-make-any-difference argument has been applied to many assets. It is all right to expense the hand tools because it doesn't make any difference since the replacement expenditures will tend to equal the amortization.[25] Many accountants make this kind of argument when speaking of individual assets but few have followed it through to its logical conclusion as did George O. May. When arguing for the "validity" of the realization convention, May wrote:

> It is instructive to consider how it happens that a rule [realization] which is violative of fact produces results that are practically useful and reliable. The explanation is that in the normal business there are, at any one moment, transactions at every stage of the production of profit, from beginning to end. If the distribution were exactly uniform, an allocation of income according to the proportion of completion of each unit would produce the same results as the attribution of the entire profit to a single stage.[26]

Three points need to be emphasized. (1)

[24a] My thanks to an unknown referee for pointing out that the total unexpired cost after n years will be $(n/2)c$ if the expenditures, c, are made at midyear; $[(n-1)/2]c$ if the expenditures are made at the beginning of the year; and $[(n+1)/2]c$ if the expenditures are made at the end of the year.

[25] "We may refrain from computing depreciation on small tools (thus violating a major principle as applied to a specific item) because the *difference* between strict accrual accounting and the 'expenditure' basis of assigning small tools cost to expense may be *slight*." Vatter, *op. cit.*, p. 184, [emphasis supplied]. This discussion is concerned with "materiality," but note that in order to know that the difference is going to be slight or immaterial, we must assume stability. The stationary state notion (or, as Vatter names it, "status quo extension") comes *prior* to the application of the concept of materiality.

[26] George O. May, *Financial Accounting* (Macmillian Company, 1943), p. 30.

The "proportion of completion" method of measuring profits is accepted as the correct method and thus as the standard by which other methods can be judged. (2) The historical cost-realization method is justified because it will "produce the same result" as the correct method, i.e., it doesn't make any difference. (3) This will be true only in a "normal business" because a normal business is one where "there are at any one moment transactions at every stage of the production of profit." In addition, the business must *continue* to be "normal" as is clearly implied by the statement.

May's statement is quite true, given the conditions. He views each unit as gradually increasing in value at a *constant* rate. If the number of units at each stage of production is constant at each point in time, the total increase in value is constant at each point in time. Therefore, the increase can be ignored because it will always be the same and will also be equal to the realized profits for all time periods except the first and last.[26a] However, the conditions necessary for this to happen are numerous: The production process cannot change over time; the quantity of raw materials purchased and put in process must be constant and at constant time intervals; the prices must be constant because if the selling price changes, then the rate of value increase changes. The same is true for a change in purchase price. (A constant markup rate will not produce the same profits nor will a constant profit per unit with fluctuating prices produce the same value of the inventory.) In general, if everything is constant—a stationary state—then the historical cost-realization method will produce the same result as the proportion of completion method. These conditions are referred to as the "normal business" and perhaps that is what is meant by a going concern.[27]

Under the conditions specified, the only variable in the model is time. Since everything else remains constant the only thing needed to measure income is a clock. Also, the process can be reversed; by measuring the income one could measure the elapsed time in the same way that the position of the stars permits one to tell time or a clock permits one to tell the position of the stars.

May recognized the importance of time in his model. One of his exceptions was when the time period covered by the income statement was shorter than the time period covered by the complete transaction, e.g., ship building or highway construction contracts. Under those conditions he argued for the proportion of the completion method because it would *not* produce the same results as the historical cost-realization method. This argument is valid and it can be extended to other

[26a] This assumes that the time period over which the value increment of each unit accrues is significantly shorter than the accounting period. Otherwise there will be a difference between the realized income and proportion of completion income for the first several accounting periods and the last several accounting periods. For example, if the value increment for each unit is V and it requires n periods for this increment to accrue then the value increment that has accrued for the ith unit is $V_i(t/n)$ where t ranges from 0 to n. Then the total value increment for the period t_i to t_{i+1} is:

$$\Delta V(t_0) = V_1(0/n)$$
$$\Delta V(t_1) = V_1(1/n)$$
$$\Delta V(t_2) = V_1(1/n) + V_2(1/n)$$
$$\Delta V(t_n) = V_1(1/n) + V_2(1/n) + \cdots + V_n(1/n)$$
$$\Delta V(t_{n+1}) = V_2(1/n) + V_3(1/n) + \cdots + V_{n+1}(1/n)$$

Since there are n terms in the equation at t_n and beyond, the total value increment for each period is V. One term drops off at the end of each period as it is realized. Thus, if we define the accounting period as t_i to t_j such that $i \geq n$ and $j > i$ then the number realized in the accounting period is $t_j - t_i$ and the realized profit is $(t_j - t_i)V$. The number of periods in the accounting period is likewise $t_j - t_i$ and the proportion of completion profit is $(t_j - t_i)V$. For periods 0 to n the realized profit will differ from the proportion of completion profit by $\Delta V(t_i)$.

[27] The identification of the "normal business" with the going concern in a stationary state is not unique to May, but he makes it more explicit than anyone else. In the discussion in *Five Monographs* (*op. cit.*, passim) he continues to come back to the "postulate of continuity or permanence" and uses this as the foundation for his arguments. Alexander detects the identification of this postulate with the stationary state and says: "You can assume continuity without considering perfect stability." (p. 207).

cases. Consider a firm which normally completes a contract every year and starts another. For example, the contracted revenues are \$100,000 and the total cost per contract is \$60,000 and that \$40,000 cost is incurred finishing a contract each year and \$20,000 cost is incurred beginning another contract each year. Then the proportion of completion method will yield \$40,000 profit each year:

$$\left(\frac{100,000}{60,000}\right)\$40,000+\left(\frac{100,000}{60,000}\right)\$20,000 - (\$40,000+\$20,000)=\$40,000$$

which is the same as the historical cost-realization method:

$$\$100,000 - \$60,000 = \$40,000.$$

But now suppose the number of contracts changed, or the time to complete a contract changed, or the total cost changed, or one contract was different from the other, or the costs incurred on next year's contract changed, etc. If anything changes, the historical cost-realization method will *not* produce the same result as the proportion of completion method. Therefore, so the argument goes, the proportion of completion method should be used.

The consequences of change are easy to see in the example because there is only one product being produced each year. In such cases we are willing to make an "exception" to the realization convention. But the example is exactly like a firm that manufactures many products in all relevant respects. The main difference is that the time required to produce the product is shorter and the cost and revenue per product is smaller. The same figures can be used by assuming that we complete and sell at one dollar 100,000 units which cost \$.60 each during the year. The realized profit is:

$$100,000(\$1) - 100,000(\$.60) = \$40,000$$

as before. And the proportion of completion method is the same.

$$\left(\frac{1}{.6}\right)\$40,000 + \left(\frac{1}{.6}\right)\$20,000 - (\$40,000 + \$20,000) = \$40,000$$

Or, in terms of quantities instead of dollars:

$$\$1[(66,666\ 2/3 \text{ completed}) + (33,333\ 1/3 \text{ equivalent units})] - [.6(66,666\ 2/3 \text{ completed}) + .6(33,333\ 1/3 \text{ equivalent units})] = \$40,000.$$

Thus, the manufacture and sale of 1 unit at \$100,000 is the same as manufacturing and selling 100,000 units at \$1 as far as the proportion of completion versus the realization method is concerned. The two methods will produce the same results only if everything remains constant.[28]

Sprouse and Moonitz recognize this feature when they write:

> . . . realization is a statistical generalization, an assertion about the validity of a convenient method of measurement . . . and can accordingly be applied or not, depending on whether it fits the situation under review.[29]

Thus, the historical cost-realization method is a *convenient* method of achieving *valid* results (proportion of completion) but it will achieve those results only when the firm is operating under conditions of a stationary state. It would seem that the fulfillment of these conditions would be so rare that the method would never be used.

More pertinent is the fact that this is a weak criterion even if the firm meets the conditions. Under conditions of a stationary state the recognition of profits at purchase would "produce the same results." Therefore, an argument can be made for recognition at purchase on the same

[28] The two methods could also produce the same results with a series of accidental offsets, but this is unlikely.

[29] Sprouse and Moonitz, *op. cit.*, p. 14.

ground and with the same force as the argument for recognition at sale.[30]

In summary, the phraseology of the going concern concept implies stability of the firm and the economy. Upon examination, the carrying out of present plans requires that future events be much the same as expected, i.e., costs, prices, technology, etc. remain fairly stable. This point is buttressed by the existence of the it-doesn't-make-any-difference argument. It will not make any difference only if everything is constant. Extending this argument to the firm clearly reveals the stationary state as a necessary condition for the validity of the historical cost-realization method under the criterion of it-doesn't-make-any-difference. The rarity of the stationary state makes this argument fall of its own weight: every case ought to be an exception. It is also a weak criterion since it does not differentiate between recognition at purchase and recognition at sale. Therefore, if the going concern model implies the conditions of a stationary state, then the model would rarely, if ever, be applicable and if it were applicable the historical-cost realization method would not uniquely follow from the model.

V. The Problem of Futurity

The futurity problem has long been with us and is peculiarly recalcitrant to solution. Hume[31] stated the problem most clearly and it has become known as "Humean Skepticism" as a result. More recently Russell and others have argued that we need to sharply separate the *cause* of our beliefs about the future from the *logical connection* of the past to the future. That event *a* has followed event *b* on all past observed occasions does in fact cause us to expect *a* when *b* occurs. Everyone expects the sun to rise tomorrow because it "always" has risen. However, the fact that it has always done so does not logically lead to the conclusion that it will tomorrow. Russell,[32] in an example that remains unanswered, describes a chicken which has been led to expect a life of tranquility because its life has always been tranquil. Unexpectedly, it has its head chopped off.

The problem extends beyond past and future and is one of generalizing from a limited number of observations. It goes by the name of "the problem of induction" and the classic example is: All swans that I have observed are white; therefore all swans are white. This is a classic because some black swans were discovered. The future takes the same form: On all past occasions *x* has occurred; therefore *x* will occur on all future occasions.

Despite these difficulties people continue to make this assumption, albeit most often tacitly. The physicist makes it when he predicts that if a body is dropped it will fall. The full statement of such a prediction is: If nature is uniform in all relevant respects and a body is dropped, it will fall. But the uniformity of nature is almost always left as an enthymeme. It is an umbrella assumption under which all predictions are made and if it were false in any relevant respect then all predictions would be false. This seems to be tantamount to our operations in accounting. We talk about future benefits under the umbrella assumption that the firm will exist in the future in order to receive those benefits. It makes it much easier to predict the benefits from a particular asset if we can assume that the complex into which the asset fits will continue in the same fashion as it has in the past.

Thus, the going concern concept becomes a kind of *celeris paribus* condition or umbrella assumption for our predictions

[30] In fact, recognition at *any* event will produce the same results since there are constant time intervals between all events in a stationary state.

[31] See David Hume, *An Inquiry Concerning Human Understanding* and *A Treatise of Human Nature*, especially Book I, Part III.

[32] Bertrand Russell, *The Problems of Philosophy* (Oxford University Press, 1956), p. 63.

about individual assets within the firm. Under this interpretation, the concept seems quite reasonable but there are still a number of unresolved questions.

One arguable point is the *level* at which the assumption ought to be made. We could raise the assumption to the economy level, for example, and then predict the future of the firm under the assumption of a "going economy."[33] Or, we could predict the changes in the economy under some more general assumption about the future and then let the effects of this prediction filter down to the sector, industry, firm, and assets of that firm. I see no *a priori* reason for any of these levels as it depends on the purpose for which the reports are being prepared. A strong case can be made that the accounting reports ought to show something about the likelihood of the firms continuing instead of the reports being prepared under the assumption that it will continue. If one accepts this as a proper function of accounting, then the status of the going concern concept ought to be changed from an *assumption* to a *prediction.*

Support for the proposition that the reports ought to reflect the predicted future of the firm can be garnered from the various statements about the going concern "assumption." Grady says that "in the presence of evidence that the entity has a limited life, it should not be viewed as remaining in operation indefinitely. Under these circumstances the . . . financial reports should make clear this characteristic of limited life."[34] From this statement two points can be adduced: (1) The reports ought to show expectations about the life of the firm, and (2) the *assumption* is abrogated when there is *evidence* against it. It is odd to speak of an evidentially based assumption in this context. A more suitable term would be "prediction."

However, if the going concern concept is construed as a prediction, it is a peculiar one because it calls for "*absence* of evidence to the contrary." As every auditor knows, it is much easier to prove the existence of an asset than it is to check out all the possibilities necessary to prove the nonexistence of a liability. Analogously, it would seem to be much easier to convince oneself of continuity on the basis of evidence *for* continuity than on the basis of *absence* of evidence for liquidation.

It may be that the "absence of evidence" qualifier was added to prohibit the absurd assumption of continuity when it was clear that liquidation was imminent. But note that there are three possibilities: (1) evidence for continuity; (2) evidence against continuity, or evidence for liquidation; and (3) zero evidence. In many cases there will be a mixture of (1) and (2). If so, and if the "absence of evidence" phraseology is taken literally, then one could arrive at the equally absurd conclusion of liquidation simply because there was not a *complete* lack of evidence of liquidation.

Of course, the proper procedure for a prediction is to gather all the evidence, both pro and con, and weigh it before arriving at a conclusion. But the term "assumption" and the "absence of evidence" phraseology obscures this fact. When there is evidence of liquidation, we are told not to make the assumption, but

[33] In essence, Moonitz does this when he writes of the "orderly society in which the potential consequences of actions can be predicted with some degree of success." (*Postulates, op. cit.*, p. 21.) This is quite reasonable and it raises the assumption to the society level, but this does not give us license to assume that the components (firms) of that society will continue. The physical world is also "orderly" but we expect death and decay of the extant components and the "order" is in the rate of death and decay and their replacement. In some cases the physical world is orderly only at certain macro levels. One cannot predict the position of any single particle, and thus the famous "Heisenberg uncertainty principle." Vatter (*op. cit.*, pp. 189–90) argues that continuity is "a fact of life" and a "verifiable attribute of the business system" and that the assumption "is that *this particular concern* will remain in operation." I grant that the system continues, but I would like to propose an uncertainty principle in regard to each firm within that system.

[34] Grady, *op. cit.*, p. 28.

when there is no evidence of liquidation, we are told to assume continuity. Taken literally this omits evidence for continuity altogether. Under the more reasonable construction that all the evidence is taken into account, we don't need an assumption; we can predict. The only cases where the assumption rule would apply is where there is zero evidence or where the evidence is offsetting. In that event it would be difficult to justify assuming either continuity or liquidation.

A second arguable point is the justification for the assumption. The most common justification is that "continuity is typical of business enterprise." If this were true then we could make a case for *assuming* continuity, despite the problem of induction. However, I have never seen any formal evidence in support of that justification and *Dun's Review*[35] provides many counter instances. In fact, an argument from induction would lead to the opposite conclusion: "All businesses, except those currently in existence, have ceased operations." One would expect that this truism would cause us to believe that cessation is more likely than continuity in the same way that "All men, except those now living, have died" causes us to expect death, not immortality.

The comparison illuminates two points. First, relative frequency does not help. If 90% of all the people who have ever lived are now living, it would not be proper for us to assign a .9 probability to immortality, and the same is true for firms. Second, the calculation of a mean life expectancy for the general population is not applicable to an individual. Each firm is peculiar in some respects, and these peculiarities may be relevant to its continuity. An attempt to justify that x_1 will continue on the basis of statistical generalizations about the continuation of $x_2, x_3, \cdots, x_n$ requires that x_1 be similar in all relevant respects. That is, even if continuity were typical, it would not be evidence for the continuity of a particular firm unless that firm were typical.

Given the vast differences among firms, it is difficult to conceive of *one* assumption that would be applicable to *all* firms. The local service station is quite different from the local automobile dealer and both are quite different from Standard Oil and General Motors. The number of firms in the former category is much larger than in the latter and thus the number of applications of the going concern assumption is much larger in the former than in the latter. Yet the number of business failures in the former is so large that they are labeled "sick industries" in economics. Probably all of us expect Standard Oil and General Motors to continue, but the basis for this judgment is the difference between firms. We stratify the population and are confident of the continuation of certain strata, but chary about others. Within the stratum we make further distinctions. Presently, there is considerably more question about the future of American Motors than of General Motors.[36]

If the going concern concept entails success, the lack of justification for the assumption is even more striking. Successful firms continue and failures disappear. Perhaps the visibility of success is what causes us to expect success. It is difficult to recall Packard, Studebaker, Hudson, Kaiser, and Willys much less the Tucker and Stutz

[35] "Commercial and industrial bankruptcies since 1957 have varied within a narrow range, running between 12,000 and 17,000 annually." *Dun's Review and Modern Industry* (November 1967), p. 127. See also *Dun's Quarterly Failure Report.*

[36] My critics rightly point out that the 500 listed in *Fortune* control a large percentage of the nation's assets and earn a large percentage of its business income. However, the going concern assumption is applied to firms, not assets or income. If accounting principles are intended to be applicable only to the 500, then we should so state and provide other principles for other firms. If futurity assumptions are intended to be applicable to assets, then we need to re-examine the basis of those assumptions, especially in view of the costs capitalized for the Edsel, TFX, new products at Chock Full O'Nuts, etc.

Bearcat. Since they are gone we forget them and forget that their managements expected continuity and the accountants assumed them to be a going concern. Perhaps there is good reason to expect General Motors, Ford, and Chrysler to continue and even be successful, but the basis of that expectation must be that the firms are *different* from those firms that have ceased. They are atypical and that is the reason why their future cannot be assumed.

It may be that "all firms, except those currently in existence, have ceased operations" will be thought to be unrealistic because it takes in a time span that is too long. Probably no one expects a firm to continue *forever* "in much the same fashion as it has in the past." But if this is the case, what we expect is cessation—eventually—and what we are arguing about is *when* the firm will cease. However, if we take the going concern concept literally we will assume a going concern at all points in time, including all future points in time, from which it follows that we are assuming an infinite life of the business. In order to avoid this absurdity, we must make a *prediction* for a finite time span. (An assumption of continuity for a finite time span, however short, will revert to an infinite life if that assumption is made at all points in time.)

Under present conditions each asset is valued on the basis of (its life expectancy is based on) considerations of that particular asset under the umbrella assumption of a going concern. That is, an asset's life is predicted on factors inherent in that asset without regard to the possibility of the firm being liquidated (or otherwise changing) prior to the asset being used up. Given the jointness of the production process, the use of any asset depends upon the existence of other assets. A lathe needs a building to house it and a conveyor belt to supply inputs and remove outputs. Since the assets have different life spans, "the life" of any asset requires the replacement of complementary or supporting assets. Then the replacement of the complementary assets requires the replacement of the original asset and so on indefinitely. Therefore, "the life" of any asset implies an infinite life of the firm except in the unlikely coincidence of all assets wearing out at the same time.

Thus, if it is true that the going concern is used as an umbrella assumption, as was alleged *supra*, for the purpose of making it easier to predict the life of particular assets, then the effect of the particular finite predictions is to make the life of the firm infinitely long—which consequent is absurd. Also it is circular: Different life spans of complementary assets implies (requires) an infinite life of the firm and an infinite life of the firm implies (requires) continual replacement of the assets.

In summary, it seems that the best construction of the going concern concept is that it is an umbrella assumption under which predictions about assets are made. One unresolved question is the level of the assumption. Perhaps the accountant ought to report the future prospects of the firm instead of assuming them. If so, then the going concern concept is a prediction and ought to be reworded to so indicate. Also, the phraseology about evidence should be altered to make it clear that all evidence is to be gathered and weighted. The second unresolved question is the justification for the assumption. If we interpret the concept as an assumption, then we ought to be able to justify that assumption as a reasonable one. The "continuity is typical" justification is dependent upon the time span taken into account, the kind of firm, peculiarities of the particular firm and other factors. An infinite life is not typical and is contrary to our expectations. Some kinds of firms have a history of a high rate of failures. Most industries have some "marginal" firms. Therefore, again, the concept needs to be reinterpreted as a prediction. The third unresolved question is the time span of the prediction. This question is important because it directly affects the life of the individual asset. The present situation is to predict the life of the assets without considering the life of the firm, which implies an infinite life and is contrary to our expectations and therefore unreasonable.

VI. An Alternative to Prediction

Given the accountant's penchant to record "past facts" and eschew predictions, the conclusion that the going concern concept ought to be reinterpreted as a prediction is not likely to meet with acclaim. It is admittedly difficult to make predictions, especially predictions about firms. But this difficulty is the very reason why an assumption is inappropriate. This conclusion is predicated on the fact that most accountants are convinced that the future has something to do with present measurements. Thus, my conclusion is conditional. If the future state of the firm needs to be known in order to account, then that future state ought to be predicted, not assumed.

The valuation implications of this conclusion are a separate question. There is a carefully worked out valuation scheme that is based entirely on the future, viz., the discounted expectations theory of Irving Fisher and his followers. Accountants have rejected this theory because it is future oriented and because the future is uncertain. In fact, certification to predictions is currently considered unethical.[37] Yet the future benefits notion and the assumption that the firm will continue in the future is an integral part of traditional theory. Is it ethical to certify to an (unwarranted, in my opinion) assumption about the future and unethical to certify to a prediction? I think there is a fundamental confusion here. We cling to historical cost because the purchase price is a past fact and therefore "objective and verifiable." Yet we allocate that purchase price on the basis of what the *future* holds. Therefore, accounting *is now* a future oriented valuation system. In light of this, my suggestion for predicting the future state of the firm seems less radical.

Whether or not accounting ought to be a future oriented valuation system is a third question. I think that the general inclination of accountants to avoid the problems of the future is a healthy one. This inclination is based on the sound observation that the future, particularly in matters of commerce, is unknown and unknowable to any reasonable degree of precision. If this is accepted, then there is another alternative for the disposition of the going concern concept: purge it. It is a futurity concept and if we wish to avoid problems of the future, then it ought to be purged.

Since the concept is not necessary to account and has no connection to historical cost valuation, it could be purged without any effect on present practices. I see no theoretical obstacles to purging it. Indeed, I think it would be wholly beneficial. Such purging, however, extends beyond the going concern concept. The fundamental confusion is a temporal one. The literature continues to speak of accounting as if it were entirely historical, but this is simply not true as is evidenced by the same literature lamenting the fact that future events have to be considered before present valuations can be made. Consider this: An asset is an asset because it will benefit the *future* and is valued on the *present* balance sheet on the basis of a *past* price; the firm will have to continue in the *future* in the manner expected at the *present* in order for the *present* allocations of *past* expendi-

[37] Rule 2.04, AICPA *Code of Professional Ethics*.

tures to be correct while the *past* allocations made on the basis of the *past* expectations of *future* events now need to be corrected to reflect *present* expectations of *future* events.[38]

This confusion is *entirely* conceptual and it is inhibiting theoretical as well as practical progress. It causes us to set up problems for ourselves which are in principle unresolvable. The proposition that the true value of the firm is indeterminate prior to final liquidation is not an "inherent limitation" of accounting. It is correct only if one *defines* the "true value" as the liquidation value at the time of liquidation, i.e., as the cash on hand after everything is converted to cash.[39] If one conceptually makes a present measurement dependent upon subsequent events, then the present magnitude can never be known because subsequent events always lie in the future and can never be known. This notion is particularly insidious because it commits one to a continual correction of past magnitudes or an admission that all past magnitudes are wrong. That is, it makes that "permanent record" of the past impossible because as the subsequent events occur, the record needs to be changed or else remain a false permanent record. Berkeley's oft-quoted comment is apposite: "they raise a dust and then complain that they cannot see."[40] The confusion of temporal locations is a cloud of dust that is impairing our vision. One is not *required* to peer into the future in order to make a present measurement. In fact, that is a contradiction in terms: Measurement is the discovery of an extant condition and requires a present act. One cannot measure a magnitude that lies in the future. Instead, one predicts such magnitudes and *verifies* them by a measurement operation when the future becomes the present.

Of course, the future consequences of business decisions are important information, but this problem is not unique to accounting or economics. The future consequences of the selection of route A over route B is important information but that

[38] Statements by Grady (*op. cit.*) provide many specific instances of temporal mixtures. On revenue recognition, for example, it is said that conservatism requires that "revenues and income are not to be anticipated." (p. 36). Thus, revenues appear to lie in the past but under the going concern discussion it is noted that revenues are measured by the amount of the receivable and "we ordinarily recognize an account receivable (and the related revenue) whenever future cash receipts from customers are definitely expected. . . . The size of the receivable is geared to the size of the anticipated future cash receipts, not to the present realizable (liquidation) value of the receivable in the market." (p. 28). Thus,

Receivable Dr = Revenue Cr
Receivable Dr = Anticipated Cash Receipts.

Therefore,

Revenue Cr = Anticipated Cash Receipts

which is a contradiction of the edict that revenues are not to be anticipated. Grady recognizes this as is indicated by his discussion on page 76. His statement that revenues are not to be anticipated refers to proper cut-off. That is, revenues are not to be recognized prior to the event of sale (except for the exceptions) and the meaning of the statement is that the event of sale is not to be anticipated. However, this needs to be clarified further because the value of the receivable is based on the future sale of the receivable for cash. Thus, in the simplest situation we have a past exchange (cash for inventory), a present exchange (inventory for receivable), and a future exchange (receivable for cash) all combined in one entry.

[39] There are also current controversies which suffer form this problem. The tax allocation arguments, both pro and con, depend upon what the future holds. (The arguments also depend upon the component—whole distinction.) In its simplest form, those in favor of allocation assert that the tax payment is merely postponed because the firm will continue in business and continue to earn taxable income. Those opposed argue that the postponement is permanent because the firm will continue to replace its assets in the future. Since the two arguments start with different premises about the future, they can never be resolved. Even if evidence is gathered in support of the permanent hypothesis, *a la* Price Waterhouse, an opponent can still reply that the deferments have only been "permanent" up until the present and the tax payments will catch up with them in the future. That is, it is in the nature of evidence that it is always about the past and reasonable men can still disagree about the future. In addition, that evidence may not provide a rule for all firms. Ralph S. Johns ("Allocation of Income Taxes," *The Journal of Accountancy* (September, 1958), p. 46) presents the case of Servel, Inc. which is an exception. Therefore, we again have the problem of determining the future course of the particular firm regardless of what the general experience of all firms has been.

The introduction to Johns' article (p. 41) notes that "tax-effect accounting has been a subject of lively controversy for many years." Graham's reply (*op. cit.*, p. 57) refers to the "period of transition" in tax allocations. The lively controversy and period of transition con-does not prohibit one from measuring his present location.[41] The future consequences of driving at 40 versus 80 mph is important information, but that does not prohibit one from reading the speedometer now. Nor does one have to assume that the automobile will continue along the planned route at the planned speed in order to make those measurements. One does not have to assume that it will continue at all. Whether it continues or stops is irrelevant to the present measurement. Alternatively one can, if he wishes, predict where he will be at some future time and then manipulate that prediction in various ways. For example, he could "discount" it back to the present, as in the Fisher Tradition, or he could take the "effort" he expended in order to reach some previous location and "amortize" (average) that effort over the total predicted time or distance, as in the Accounting Tradition. The point common to both of these methods is that they require a prediction and, therefore, both are limited by our ability to foresee the future. But this is not the nature of things; one *decides* to use or not to use these methods. That is, one decides to predict or measure (or both) and the failure to sharply separate the two encumbers our thinking.

Because of the problems of the future (and other reasons), I think that accounting ought to be a measurement system. Thus, all values would be assigned on the basis of *present* (the immediate past) prices instead of on the basis of manipulated predictions or assumptions. I am aware of the many practical difficulties in implementing this suggestion. I am not sure that all of the problems can be solved. The only thing of which I am sure is that they will not be solved if no effort is made to solve them. At present we conceive of our problems in such a way that they are in principle unresolvable, and this causes us to resign ourselves to inherent limitations instead of searching for better measurement methods. At one time, speed was indeterminate until the object came to rest in the same way that income is now said to be indeterminate prior to liquidation. If physicists had resigned themselves to this limitation, speedometers would not have been built.

But the cause of the resignation in accounting is conceptual, not practical, problems. Already there is a considerable backlog of experience in preparing values based on present prices occasioned by the lower of cost or market rule. Although the rule is formally applicable only to inventories, in fact it has been applied to a great many assets under the influence of conservatism. The inclination to write things down to market has been strong enough to cause practitioners to overcome the practical problems. To write things up would be no more difficult, and thus the only thing lacking is the inclination to do so.

Pricing of fixed assets is thought to be particularly difficult, but compare the current depreciation procedure, which requires the accountant to predict a future price—salvage value—for those assets. Surely it is easier to discover the present price than the future price of the *same* asset.

Such considerations lead me to believe that there are fewer practical problems in the discovery of present prices than in the determination of historical cost.[42] This is

tinues at present—almost 10 years since the articles appeared—and I fear that it will continue to continue as long as the future remains unknown.

[40] Bishop Berkeley, *A Treatise Concerning the Principles of Human Knowledge*, Part I.

[41] The present location is also important information. Among other things, it delineates the alternatives available. Thus, one must start with his present location in order to perceive his available alternatives. *Then* he predicts the future consequences of the alternatives and chooses one. Ask any navigator. The same is true in business. One decides to continue in business if the discounted expected net revenues are greater than the sum of the present liquidation values. But one must know those liquidation values in order to make that decision.

[42] See also Robert R. Sterling, "An Operational Analysis of Traditional Accounting Theory," *Abacus* (December 1966), for a further discussion of the difficulties in obtaining historical cost.

the reason that I claim the resistance is due to conceptual problems and, therefore, those problems need to be cleared up prior to attacking the practical problems.

One such conceptual problem is the going concern. The change from the venture to the going concern concept is one of the most heralded advancements in accounting. Insofar as the change raised the specter of the future, it was not an advancement. In another sense, it was a most significant advancement and one that needs to be extended further. The essence of this advancement is that it caused the measurement of the income and wealth of the firm to be made at a point in *time* instead of at the *event* of liquidation. Information was needed prior to the event and reports were prepared periodically to meet this need. Remnants of the venture concept remain, however, in that we value the components on the basis of an event—transaction—and value the whole at a point in time. The sum of the component event-values is thought to yield a correct temporal value for the whole. We have seen that this is true only in the very special circumstances of a stationary state.

Consider a firm which has only one asset, say, land. That land is valued at the event of purchase and that value remains constant until the event of sale. Such a firm is on the venture basis of accounting because the total asset value remains constant until the event of liquidation, yet the financial statements are prepared periodically. There is no point in preparing periodic statements unless the magnitude varies over time. Therefore, we can reasonably assume that the temporal variability of wealth (and therefore income) is granted and the purpose of periodic reports is to show the amount of variation. But, the report in effect denies the temporal variability of the wealth because it is held constant until an event occurs.

The incompatibility of the event and temporal approach is shown clearly in that simple example because there is only one asset and, more importantly, that asset has a constant quantity. Most assets have variable quantities, and this variation is what causes the change in the value of assets. That is, a quantity of something is received in exchange for a quantity of cash. At the *event* of this exchange the quotient of the two quantities is calculated and that quotient is used to value future quantity variations and quantity stocks. Let C be the cash (or cost outlay) given in exchange, $q(t_1)$ be the quantity received and $p(t_1)$ be the valuation coefficient (cost per unit).

$$(1) \qquad p(t_1) = \frac{C}{q(t_1)}$$

Then the quantity varies as it is sold, as in inventory, or put in process, as in raw materials, or used, as in equipment depreciated on an output basis, or as time passes, as in buildings depreciated over the service life, etc. Then at a later time (t_2) the quantity is again determined.

$$(2) \qquad p(t_1)q(t_2) = \text{asset value at } t_2$$

$$(3) \qquad p(t_1)[q(t_1) - q(t_2)] = \text{expense from } t_1 \text{ to } t_2$$

Viewed in this way it is clear that the only difference between the land case and other assets is the quantity variation. The difficulty is that the quantities are determined at a point in *time* in order to prepare periodic reports, and properly so, but the valuation coefficient is determined at the *event* of purchase and thought to remain constant over time. This results in a past valuation coefficient being multiplied by a present quantity in order to determine the present value. If the present quantity is conceived to be future benefits, the confusion is even greater.

The point is that the disavowal of the venture concept necessitated periodic reporting and accountants (sometimes reluctantly) began to account for variations in value over time instead of waiting for an event. The switch was not complete, however, in that only the variation in quantities was accounted for. The next step is to extend the concept to apply to the valuation coefficient. Value in accounting is a product of a p and a q, and they ought to be temporally consistent.

In summary, I think accountants are correct in attempting to avoid the problems of the future. The difficulty is that contemporary accounting is partially a future oriented system and partially a past oriented system. It is an error to think that future events must be known in order to make present measurements. Therefore, the going concern concept is irrelevant insofar as it concerns the future state of the firm. However, insofar as the concept focuses on making measurements at a point in time instead of at an event, it is a good thing. To date, the temporal measurement has been applied to the whole but not the components. Since the value of the whole is the sum of the values of the components, the concept has not been fully applied and should be extended. Since the value of the components is a product of two coefficients, the concept should be extended to cover the valuation coefficient as well as the quantities.

VII. Summary

The notion that the going concern concept is necessary for us to account is erroneous. Vatter[43] has pointed out, and rightly, that "we could assume noncontinuity if we wanted to." Thus, there is a free choice to be made.

If one chooses to assume a going concern, then that assumption ought to be justifiable and its consequences ought to be carefully worked out. It is thought that one such consequence is historical cost valuation. That consequence is derived by either the non-liquidation or the it-doesn't-make-any-difference argument. It has been demonstrated that the non-liquidation argument is invalid and unsound, and that the it-doesn't-make-any-difference argument is true only in a stationary state. Therefore, the alleged consequence of historical cost is erroneous.

It is difficult to justify the assumption of a going concern because of uncertainty about what the future holds, particularly in matters of commerce. Therefore, if the going concern concept is to be retained, it ought to be reinterpreted as a prediction. Another alternative is to purge the going concern concept insofar as it applies to the future of the firm. The change from the venture concept to a going concern concept does not necessitate that the future be predicted or assumed. Instead, it requires only that the measurement be made at a point in time because information is needed prior to a future event. One can measure the change that has occurred in a continuing process without knowledge of how that process will change in the future. Perhaps we could call this the temporal concept in contrast to the venture or event concept. This concept ought to be extended to the valuation of the components of the firm as well as to the firm, and to the valuation coefficients of assets as well as to the quantities of assets.

Appendix

The Non-Liquidation Argument

Definitions:

p = the state of being liquidated
q = liquidation values
r = historical cost values
$\supset$ = material implication ("if . . . then . . .")
$\sim$ = negation ("not")
$\vee$ = disjunction ("or")
$\cdot$ = conjunction ("and")
$\therefore$ = deduction ("therefore")

[43] Vatter, *op. cit.*, p. 190.

The structure of the argument when applied to the firm is:

(1) $p \supset q$ Premise (If liquidating then liquidation values)
(2) $\sim p$ Assumption (Going concern or not-liquidating)
(3) $\therefore \sim q$ Deduction (Therefore, not liquidation values)
(4) $\therefore r$ Deduction (Therefore, historical cost values)

The deduction in (3) is invalid.[44] The deduction in (4) is also invalid since it follows from (3). (4) could be valid in the following form:

(1) $q \vee r$ Premise
(2) $\sim q$
(3) $\therefore r$

This still leaves the problem of deriving $\sim q$ from some premise, but more importantly, it shows the enthymeme of only two valuation methods—$q \vee r$. The quarrel is that the premise ought to be $q \vee r \vee s \vee t$ . . . e.g., liquidation values or current costs or current entry prices or discounted expectations, etc. Under this premise $\sim q$ would allow one to deduce $r \vee s \vee t$ . . . but not *r alone*. This is an important point because it is often overlooked by both sides. For example, *A Statement of Basic Accounting Theory* argues that historical cost is inadequate and then concludes that current cost ought to be presented without considering the other alternatives.

The similarity to the intended use argument is apparent. Let p be the intention to not-use or sell, q the liquidation values, and r the historical cost values.

(1) $p \supset q$
(2) $\sim p$
(3) $\therefore \sim q$
(4) $\therefore r$

The argument is identical and therefore suffers the same defects. But when this argument is applied to inventory, temporary investments and the like, it takes the following form:

(1) $p \supset q$
(2) p
(3) $\therefore \sim q$
(4) $\therefore r$

(3) is a contradiction of Modus Ponens and invalid. (4) still suffers from the enthymeme of $q \vee r$ and from the fact that it is deduced from (3) which is invalid.

If we grant the premises

(1) $p \supset q$
(2) $\sim p \supset r$

we are still faced with the problem of the self-fulfilling prophecy. In some cases the empirical results are

(3) $r \supset \sim p$
(4) $q \supset p$

which yields

$$[(p \supset q) \cdot (q \supset p)] \vee [(\sim p \supset r) \cdot (r \supset \sim p)]$$

which is perfectly valid logically but impossible to apply.

[44] See any standard work on logic, for example, Irving M. Copi, *Symbolic Logic*, 2nd ed. (The Macmillan Company, 1965), p. 23.

A Glimpse of the Forest

ROBERT R. STERLING, B.S., M.B.A., PH.D.

Associate Professor of Business Administration, University of Kansas

Over the past several years I have been privileged to attend a number of participant-observer programmes of various accounting firms. This has been a very valuable experience for me: insight into practical as well as theoretical questions was gleaned; I accumulated a file of actual cases that have been used in my classes with great success; I understand better the vast problems of the practitioner, in addition to the fact that the programmes and discussions were enjoyable in and of themselves.

The stated reason for these programmes was to give academics like me a chance to get some practical experience. I am one of those who, as my friends are fond of pointing out, has never met a payroll. This is admitted and I appreciate the distinction. I have the luxury of unlimited reflection before I take a position. The practitioner is forced to sign, or not sign, this year's certificate *this year*. He cannot wait, as I can, for more research or more data. In view of the lack of research and sparse data upon which he must make his decision, my position is indeed luxurious.

Even after extended reflection, however, there are a number of cases that I have observed which still trouble me. In a feeble attempt to reciprocate the kindness shown me, I would like to present three of those cases and ask some " academic " questions about them. If you will, I would like to try to catch a glimpse of the forest; I went on an excursion with the practitioner through the trees and now I invite the practitioner to go with me.

Since I take a critic's stance here and since this stance has been misunderstood in the past, I refer the listener to Caws,[1] among others, who notes that the purpose of the critic is the improvement of the system by the elimination of inconsistency and error. Progress can be made by elimination of error as well as by constructing systems. The Michelson-Morley argument that the ether-drag theory was in error was a significant step toward relativity, albeit they were " only " critics. I do not want to imply that my criticisms are of that stature or significance, just that critics also perform a useful rôle even if they don't replace the criticised parts. Also note the psychologists' antonym for love is indifference, not hate. One criticises only that which one cares about and only when one cares enough to try to improve it.

[1] PETER CAWS: " The Philosophy of Science " *Princeton: D. Van Nostrand Co., Inc.*, 1965, page 1.

Case 1: An Error Discovered

In a routine check of the land account the junior had discovered that parcel *a* had been sold but the cost of parcel *b* had been charged to expense. He had traced back several incidental costs to ensure that they were proper charges to capital and had found, of course, that the tax-minded management had expensed most of the costs. In tracing the credits he found that the description of the parcel sold did not agree with the book entry and thereby discovered the error.

A brief history of the transaction follows. Several acres had been purchased over 20 years earlier. Only a small portion was put into use by the firm. Another portion was contiguous to a rail spur and was sold shortly after purchase. Over 60% of the purchase price was allocated to the portion sold. The remaining land was made up of some worthless sand dunes and the site of the firm. Over the years there were a number—I couldn't determine how many or how much exactly—of cash outlays in connection with the land. Almost all of these were expensed and that treatment was not questioned by the previous auditors although some were clearly improvements that should have been capitalised and amortised under present theory and tax regulations. One connected outlay was a recent tax assessment which was greater than the original purchase price. Several other parcels were sold sporadically. The original cost and the subsequent capitalised costs were apportioned as the parcels were sold on two different bases; area for the earlier, and relative market value for the latter, sales.

Several years earlier it had become apparent that the worthless sand dunes were becoming very valuable for use as near-beach and beach-front resorts. Accordingly, the management had the land plotted and the accountants allocated the remaining costs between the site and beach land on the basis of the then existing relative market prices. The costs of plotting and other incidentals were then added to the beach property and allocated to each plot on relative market value. The management held the land for about another five years and watched its value grow as the houses and motels built up along the beach.

After they started selling, the bookkeeper erred by expensing parcel *b* which had a recorded cost of £1,700, instead of parcel *a* which cost £1,100.

Case 2: Inventory Observation

On one occasion I observed the observation of the physical inventory count. The firm had a large number of re-usable containers which were charged to inventory when purchased and to expense on a LIFO basis upon initial use. The containers that had been used at least once were physically segregated from the unused containers. Since the used containers were charged to expense, they were ignored by the auditors. The unused containers were carefully counted by the warehouse crew and the auditors verified their count in some rather ingenious ways. Then they made sample tracings of the original cash outlays to ensure that the containers were properly valued.

The used containers outnumbered the unused ones by about 20 to 1. Converting to equivalent new units, the ratio was about 10 to 1. The company was on a LIFO basis and was expanding. As a consequence, all the unit costs in the unused inventory were at least four years old and some were much older.

Case 3: A Theoretical Question

I was invited to consider the following problem. A bond issue with a book value of £4·4 million had been converted into common stock. The date of conversion was between interest payment dates and some £70,000 of interest had been accrued. Should the expense be reversed against the accrued payable or should it stand as it is? Another way to state the problem is to ask whether £4,400,000 or £4,470,000 is the proper credit to the capital stock account.

Acceptable Variations and the Notion of Error

A point common to these cases is the permissible variation in the cost. The cost of the parcel of land in Case 1 could have varied between £400 and £5,300, approximately. The recorded cost of the parcel that was sold was £1,100; the cost of the unsold parcel was £1,700. Thus, the magnitude of the "error" was £600 or about one-eighth of the *acceptable* variation. Since both £1,100 and £1,700 lie within the range of £400 to £5,300, it could be said that either is "correct". Since the £1,100 correct figure is about three times larger than the lowest acceptable figure and about one-fourth of the highest acceptable figure, there is a question of materiality here. The most unusual or careless error is not likely to have produced a figure that lay outside this range and therefore one wonders about the necessity of auditing the figure and making the correction.

In Case 2 the cost of the inventory could have been greater by a factor of ten if the containers had been depreciated over their useful life. The reason the used containers were not depreciated was that, like many other items such as hand tools, the difference between the expenditures approach and amortisation approach was said to be immaterial. This same concept could easily be extended to the unused containers, however, especially in view of the fact that the used containers outnumbered the unused by about ten to one on an equivalent unit basis. If this concept had been applied to the unused containers (and the auditors indicated that such a procedure would be acceptable if it were followed consistently) then the book value of the entire inventory would have been zero. Thus, the acceptable variation in unexpired cost was from zero to about ten times larger than that figure shown on the books. This variation is due entirely to quantities, *i.e.* the books would show a zero quantity to be accounted for if all had been expensed and would show both the used and unused if all had been capitalised and amortised. The grossest error in the inventory count would not have produced a figure outside this range and therefore one wonders about the necessity of observing the count. Any error would have been immaterial in the sense that it lay in the acceptable range.

Case 3 was similar in that different amortisation procedures could have produced an acceptable variation in the book value that was several times larger than the £70,000 dispute. In fact, the call price of the bonds was £5 million and thus there was a £600,000 difference that could have been recorded if the call price had been taken as the evidence of value at the date of the exchange. The £70,000 interest seems to be immaterial since it is considerably less than the acceptable variation and since either method will produce a figure that lies within the acceptable range.

These figures are summarised in Exhibit I.

Exhibit I

Acceptable Variations in Recorded Cost

	A *Minimum Accept-able*	B *Maximum Accept-able*	C *Accept-able Variation*	D *Error or Disputed Item*	E D÷C
Case 1:					
Land	£400	£5,300	£4,900	£600	12%
Case 2:					
Inventory					
Quantity	0	10*q*	10*q*	none	..
Cost per unit	*p*	10*p*	10*p*	none	..
Book value	*pq*	100*pq*	100*pq*	none	..
Case 3:					
Accrued Interest	4·4	5·0	·6	·07	12%

In cases like these it would seem that a cursory check of the book values and a quick physical examination of the property would be all that is required. Instead, however, the auditors spent a significant amount of time carefully tracing the transactions, observing the count and pondering about the correct method of handling the accrued interest. I wonder about the wisdom of such procedures.

If a safety inspector had set up a tolerance limit—acceptable variation—of, say, three feet, we would question the wisdom of using a micrometer to see if a particular item met the specifications. It seems to me that the same concept ought to be applicable to auditing. In the inventory case, for example, several man-hours were used observing the count and taking samples and then several more man-hours were used to make inferences about the size of the population from the sample. Yet the size of the population could have been ten times greater than it was or zero. Aren't we using a micrometer when a yardstick would do?

If the safety inspector said that the length of a beam was within the acceptable range but that there was error in the length that needed to be corrected, we might think that he had contradicted himself. If he found an error in the recorded length of four inches (12% of the tolerance limit) and bothered to correct it, we might say that he was concerned with trifles or immaterial amounts. Aren't we doing the same thing when we search out and correct errors when the figures lie in the acceptable range and the error is only 12% of the acceptable variation?

Materiality

The word "material" has been used in the above discussion in a way that is not common in accounting. A pre-publication receiver of this paper objected to the usage and said—

> "The magnitude of the effect of using different accounting methods is therefore not relevant to the materiality of an error, or item in dispute, uncovered by an audit." [2]

I think that this is a correct report of the way in which we now view the concept of materiality. My point is that this is too narrow a view of a very important concept. If different acceptable accounting methods permit a variation in cost values of £4,900, as in Case 1, then it seems that it would be impossible for a variation of less than £4,900 to be considered material.

This is supported by Grady.[3] His notion of materiality rests, ultimately, upon the effect that a difference in value would have on a reasonable or prudent man. Current generally acceptable accounting principles would permit the book value of the land in Case 1, for example, to vary from £400 to £5,300. We must, therefore, take the position that this variation would *not* affect the conduct of a prudent man, if we are taking the concept of materiality seriously. If this much variation would not affect his conduct, then a £600 variation would not affect his conduct and therefore the £600 is immaterial. Generalising, we could say that any error or item in dispute is immaterial if it is less than the variation permitted by applying different generally accepted accounting principles. Since all of the errors that I witnessed were less than the acceptable variations, all of them could be said to be immaterial. The prerequisite to the discovery of material errors, in the prudent man sense, is to narrow the acceptable variations, or, to state the same thing another way, to more precisely define what is correct.

It is true that an accounting method, once selected, must be applied consistently over time. However, the consistency concept is of little help in this problem because the initial selection can be made from a variety of methods which result in large variations in book values. Consistency over time is defended on the basis of comparability,

[2] The quote is taken from a letter from a reviewer of this paper. The reviewer refers me to "Statements of Auditing Procedure No. 33" *New York: AICPA*, 1963 page 16, to support his point.

[3] "A statement, fact, or item is material, if giving full consideration to the surrounding circumstances, as they exist at the time, it is of such a nature that its disclosure, or the method of treating it, would be likely to influence or to 'make a difference' in the judgment and conduct of a reasonable person." PAUL GRADY: "Inventory of Generally Accepted Accounting Principles for Business Enterprises" *New York: AICPA*, 1965 page 40.

and with this I am in full accord. Consistency is a requisite for the comparability of any time-series.[4] Because of this, changes in method are permitted only in unusual circumstances, and the *magnitude* of the effect must be disclosed. In simplified form we report something like this:—

> If LIFO had been used consistently instead of changing to FIFO, then the income (inventory) would have been greater (less) by x dollars.

But precisely the same concept can be applied to a firm at any given moment:—

> If LIFO instead of FIFO had been originally selected, then the income (inventory) would be greater (less) by y dollars.

The reasons for reporting the y dollar variation in the second case are the same as those for reporting the x dollar variation in the first case. One reason is contained in the materiality concept: either variation may affect the conduct of a prudent man. Of course, it is impossible to make the comparison in the second case because there are so many different figures that could be calculated.[5] However, the impossibility of making the comparisons does not negate the principle; instead it emphasises the need to narrow the alternatives in order to narrow the variation.

Justifications given by the Partners

In essence I am asking about the purpose of auditing. Given that the discovery of defalcations is no longer considered to be the major objective of auditing, serious questions can be raised about carefully auditing something when the grossest error would produce a variation less than the acceptable one. This point, in connection with the above cases (and others), was discussed at some length with the partners of the various firms. The rationale given by the partners was that the purpose of auditing was to ensure that the accounting system was working as intended. It was management's duty to set up the accounting system and decide which methods were to be used. It was the auditor's duty to check for errors in that system. There was no concept of fairness, truthfulness, correctness or the like being employed; only a concept of fidelity to the established system. When pressed on this issue the partners invariably defended their actions by appealing to the fact that they were management's statements.

The management's statement proposition raises serious questions about the independence of the auditors. After all, the internal auditors can check on the fidelity to the established system. To differentiate himself, the independent auditor needs to have some higher goal in mind.

Another point discussed with the partners (and another reason for selecting these particular cases) was the large difference between the recorded cost and market value. The land in Case 1 was sold for £73,000 and had a recorded cost of £1,100. The other parcel with a recorded cost of £1,700 could have been sold for approximately the same amount. The £600 " error " seems even less material in light of this. The market value of the stock in Case 3 at the date of conversion was £5·6 million (according to the auditors) but its book value was £4·4 million. In view of this £1·2 million difference, the £70,000 seems less material. The re-usable containers in Case 2 are more difficult. Exactly what the used containers could be sold for or what their replacement cost would have been is difficult to determine. But even the most conservative estimate would have been much greater than the zero value at which they were recorded. The new containers replacement cost was easy to determine. It was about twelve times the recorded cost.

When pressed on this issue the partners responded that cost, not market, was the generally accepted valuation method. Reasons given for its acceptance were that it was objective and verifiable, *i.e.* there was a *single* cost figure which could be traced back to the basic business documents. The single cost proposition is rather odd in light of the acceptable variation in the book values in the above cases. It is true that often there is a single purchase price but auditors do not certify to purchase prices; they certify to book values which have large variations.

The verifiability of cost is another question. Look at it this way: in every purchase there is an expenditure for a quantity of something, $q(t_1)$, which is divided into the cost outlay, C, to get the cost per unit p.

$$(1)\ p = \frac{C}{q(t_1)}$$

Subsequently $q(t_1)$ is segregated into units still on hand or unexpired, $q(t_2)$, and units that have been sold or expired, $q(t_1) - q(t_2)$. Then the book values are:

$$(2)\ p\,q(t_2) = \text{asset book value at time } t_2$$
$$(3)\ p[q(t_1) - q(t_2)] = \text{expense from } t_1 \text{ to } t_2$$

Let us grant that C can be verified by referring back to the check, invoice, receiving report, etc. In some cases $q(t_1)$ can be verified by physical count, as in inventory, but in other cases it cannot, as in the life of equipment. There-

[4] Diversity on the other hand is defended mainly on the grounds that it is a fact of life. No one can deny that diverse accounting methods exist but I think it is a mistake to elevate something to the status of a basic concept simply because it exists. Comparability is the basic concept, in my view, because consistency is a necessary (but not sufficient) condition for comparability. But comparability is desirable among firms as well as over time and thus consistency among firms follows from the same premise that is used to defend consistency over time. Another argument for diversity is that firms "... find it necessary to develop their own systems to fulfil better their particular requirements for management information and control." GRADY: *op. cit.*, page 34. This is the primary support for the management's statements proposition which is discussed *infra.*

[5] Once in a frivolous moment I calculated that there were 2,971,332,000 different book values that could be reported for inventory. Obviously we could not report a comparison for all of these methods. To report a comparison for only major categories would also be cumbersome since there are about ten different major methods of inventory valuation. For the calculation see ROBERT R. STERLING: " In Defense of Accounting in the United States ", ABACUS December 1966, page 181.

fore, in some cases p cannot be verified in any meaningful way because it is the quotient of an expression whose divisor cannot be verified.

Even in the inventory cases where $q(t_1)$ can be verified, we have a problem in verifying $q(t_2)$ and the difference between them. The question is: *which* units are to be considered to make up $q(t_2)$? In the re-usable container case it was not apparent to me that only the unused containers should be inventoried and valued. How does one verify the *decision* to include only unused containers in $q(t_2)$? After this decision is made then another decision is required concerning whether $q(t_2)$ should be conceived of as the last units received (therefore FIFO) or the first units received (therefore LIFO). The question is: how does one verify a FIFO inventory *as opposed* to a LIFO inventory? What are the differing "circumstances" that make it appropriate for one firm to select LIFO and another similar firm in the same industry to select FIFO? Until these kinds of questions can be answered, the book value of inventories cannot be verified in any meaningful sense of that term.

Of course, we all know this since we all know that there are large variations possible in book values. All accountants would get an unequivocal value for cash *because* it can be verified by a simple, well-understood operation. When the verification operation cannot be specified, then large variations can be expected. This is precisely the case for many non-cash assets. There is no way to verify that the book value of the container inventory "presented fairly" because there is no standard against which to compare the figure and no empirical operation which the auditor can go through to come up with a figure. Yet the container inventory was clearly valued on the basis of historical cost, which was defended because that valuation method is verifiable. I think the problem here is in confusing purchase prices, which can be verified, with book values, which in many cases cannot be verified.

When pressed on these issues the partners again fell back to the management's statements proposition. The management knew what it intended to do and what information it wanted; therefore, management was in the best position to estimate the quantities in the case of equipment and select the method in the case of inventories.

Management's Statements

The trail always led back to management. The consequences of this are most disturbing. Note that if management is allowed to determine the quantities and select the accounting method, then all the accountant has to do is divide as in equation (1) and multiply as in equations (2) and (3). Then all the auditor has to do is to check the *arithmetical* accuracy of those calculations and be sure that they are consistent over time. That is, if management is allowed to make the significant decisions (quantities and methods) and the accountant accepts these decisions because they are management's statements, then accounting will be reduced to mechanical bookkeeping and auditing to column footing. Of course, the profession hasn't been reduced to this level but the management's statements proposition is leading in that direction.

At one time we allowed management to certify to all quantities and auditing was restricted to reviewing the documents. Now we go out and empirically test the physical existence of quantities. This was a significant expansion of the auditor's responsibility and most of us would agree that that expansion was desirable. Unfortunately however, it took the *McKesson-Robbins* case to bring that expansion about. The defence that generally accepted auditing procedures did not include empirical verification of the quantities was of little use in that case. The public's confidence in accounting was shaken, even though technically we were not at fault. Let us hope that it won't require a similar scandal to get the profession to expand its responsibilities to include which quantities are to be inventoried and valued, the reasonableness of the estimates of quantities that are not inventoriable, and the appropriateness of the accounting method being applied.

An even more disturbing aspect of the management's statements proposition is that it contains an embryonic tendency to escape responsibility. The profession has been characterised by a fierce devotion to integrity and a jealously guarded independence. It was once claimed that the function of accounting was to tell the Truth. To rely on management's statements is far removed from that attitude. If carried much further, management could serve the same function as Christopher Robin's friend Pooh. You may recall that, when asked a difficult question, Christopher would consult Pooh before answering because—

> "Then it doesn't matter what the answer ought to be
> Cause if he's right, I'm right and if he's wrong, it isn't me." [6]

I fear that the public would not be willing to accept such an attitude and will blame the accounting profession even though, technically, it may have been management's error.

Summary and Conclusions

I was struck by three things in my exposure to practice. First, the auditors were intelligent, dedicated and industrious. They were better educated on the average and seemed to have a better overall grasp of the situation than the managements of the firms they were auditing.[7] Second, the auditing procedures were concerned with

[6] A. A. Milne: "Now We Are Six", *New York: E. P. Dutton & Co., Inc.*, 1927, page 65. *London: Methuen & Co.*

[7] Often the accountant came up with important suggestions for improving the operations of the firm. In such cases, it was not uncommon for them to be required to explain the *present* operations to the management in order for the management to understand the benefits of the suggested changes. As an outside observer, I found it odd that the accountants who visited the firm once a year could see the operations more clearly than the management who worked with the operations daily. One of the partners advanced the hypothesis that the management was too close to the trees to see the forest. It seemed to me that the same malady affected the accountant's view of his daily operations, particularly in the discovery of errors of less magnitude than the acceptable variation. Hence the title of this paper.

" immaterial " amounts in the sense that the errors and disputed points were always within the acceptable range of variation. The concept of materiality needs to be reinterpreted to apply to this problem. Surely there is no point in searching for errors if the acceptable variation is greater than the grossest error. The reduction of the acceptable variation is a prerequisite to making sense out of the notions of " error " and " correct ". Third, the justifications for these practices were specious and shortsighted. The claim that there is a single cost figure is simply not true and I fail to understand why it continues to be used as a justification. There may be a single purchase price but the purchase price is only *one* of the factors used to determine the book value, and book values, not purchase prices, appear on the statements. The verifiability of book values is a problem of vast consequences. Usually the verification of a figure requires that an empirical operation be specified which can be repeated by the verifier. We seem to be moving toward the mistaken idea that verification is the repetition of an arithmetical operation and that it is management's responsibility to estimate the variables and select the functional form in which those variables are related.

This notion of verification makes management responsible for the determination of quantities and the selection of accounting methods. Since the variations in quantities and different methods cause large variations in book values, this procedure, in effect, permits management to make the significant decisions and reduces auditing to a concern with trifles. The most disturbing thing I found was that the partners were not resisting this erosion of their function. Instead they were embracing it and justifying their actions on the basis of the management's statement proposition. This attitude is limiting accounting's function instead of expanding it. I would like to see the trend reversed and the accountant take more and more responsibility for the determination of quantities and the selection of appropriate accounting methods. After all, it is the accountant who says that the statements " present fairly ", not the management.

A Valuation Experiment

ROBERT R. STERLING and RAYMOND RADOSEVICH*

In a previous issue of this journal, McDonald investigated the feasibility of measuring current cost depreciation for a fleet of trucks.[1] His findings indicated that on the basis of the minimum variance test proposed by Ijiri and Jaedicke,[2] current cost depreciation was at least as feasible as historical cost depreciation. This paper reports a similar test of feasibility, but uses an alternative asset as the basis for comparison. As McDonald, we will concentrate on the practical aspect of the current versus historical cost issue, ignoring the theoretical justifications of each.[3]

The Study

A questionnaire was prepared in which the installment purchase of a depreciable asset was described as follows:

A CPA purchased a ten-key Monroe Printing Calculator on September 1, 1965. The calculator had a price tag of $900 but it was agreed that it could be bought

* Associate Professor and Assistant Professor, respectively, of Business Administration, University of Kansas.

[1] Daniel L. McDonald, "A Test Application of the Feasibility of Market Based Measures in Accounting," *Journal of Accounting Research*, 6 (Spring, 1968), 38–49.

[2] Yuji Ijiri and Robert K. Jaedicke, "Reliability and Objectivity of Accounting Measurements," *The Accounting Review*, XLI (July, 1966), 474–83.

[3] The theoretical issues are discussed extensively by Raymond J. Chambers [*Accounting, Evaluation and Economic Behavior* (Englewood Cliffs, N.J.: Prentice-Hall, Inc., 1966)], Maurice Moonitz ["The Basic Postulates of Accounting," *Accounting Research Study No. 1* (New York: AICPA, 1961)], Robert T. Sprouse and Maurice Moonitz ["A Tentative Set of Broad Accounting Principles for Business Enterprises," *Accounting Research Study No. 3* (New York: AICPA, 1962)], and Edgar O. Edwards and Philip W. Bell [*The Theory and Measurements of Business Income* (Berkeley: University of California Press, 1961)], to list just a few. The practical issue is set out clearly by Morrison in his dissent to *A Statement of Basic Accounting Theory* (Evanston: AAA, 1966), pp. 97–98.

for $100 down and $100 per month for seven months for a total of $800. The installment contract was accepted and no cash price was determined.

This was the only tangible asset the accountant owned. He rented a furnished office and bought supplies in small quantities.

The respondents were asked to supply information on (1) the depreciation method, (2) capitalized cost, (3) salvage value, and (4) years of life that was "best for book [as opposed to tax] purposes." In addition, they were asked for minimum and maximum figures for capitalized cost, salvage value, and life to which they would "certify." Finally, they were asked to "take a guess at the fair market value as of today."

The questionnaire was sent to a random sample of 500 CPAs in the United States. The overall return was 26%. However, 15 responses which contained ambiguities or inconsistencies were discarded, leaving a final sample size of 115 usable returns.

A ten-key printing calculator was selected as the asset because it is an asset that all accountants use and with which all would be familiar. The problem was stated in such a fashion that this asset was material to the firm. Nonetheless, the relatively low cost of the item probably caused some bias in the returns. This problem was recognized prior to the design of the questionnaire, but it was decided that the familiarity aspect was more important than materiality. Each accountant would be expected to have had considerable experience with this type of asset and therefore have some knowledge about its life, salvage value, and resale value.

The notion of "fair market value" was left undefined. The respondent was free to interpret the question any way he desired—e.g., as net realizable value, replacement cost of the same machine, replacement cost of the same services, etc. The respondent could then choose any number or kind of factors he desired as a basis for determining his estimate of the fair market value. Thus, the experiment allowed the respondent about the same degree of freedom in deciding upon the appropriate procedures and information that he would use in determining both the book and the current values. The phrase "take a guess" was inserted after the pretest of the questionnaire indicated a reluctance to estimate the fair market value. Nevertheless, only 99 estimated the market value, whereas all of the respondents estimated the factors that were required for the determination of the historical cost.

The Hypotheses

From the preceding discussion of the assumed merits and disadvantages of the alternative valuation schemes, three obvious hypotheses can be drawn:

Ho_1: Book values are univocal while current (market) values are not.

Ho_2: Book values are more objective than current values.

Ho_3: Book values are verifiable while current values are not.

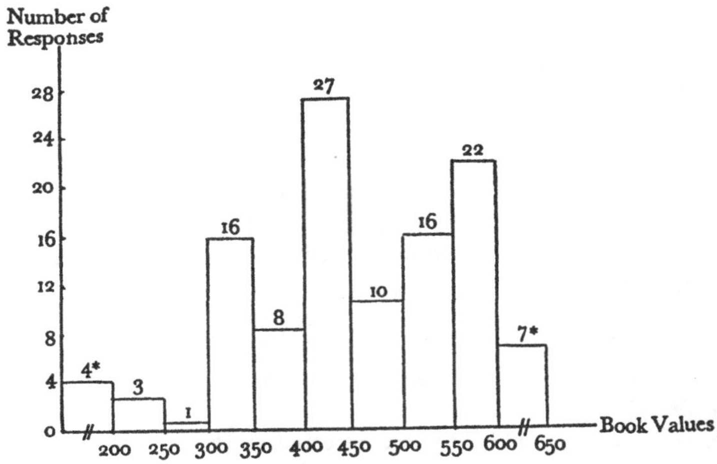

FIG. 1. The Distribution of "Best" Book Values

The Results

An end-of-year book value was calculated for each respondent from the depreciation method, cost, life, and salvage value that he chose. These values were calculated as of the end of the third year to be consistent with the elapsed period of time between the purchase of the asset as described in the questionnaire and the request for the estimate of the market value. These book values were calculated on the basis of the "best" method and factor values given by each respondent.

Examination of the distributions for the book value and the market value rejects the first hypothesis. Although the 99 estimates of market value contain 26 different values, the 115 book values contain 35 different values.

The objectivity of the measures was based on the inter-observer variance suggested by Ijiri and Jaedicke.[4] Histograms of the two distributions are shown in Figures 1 and 2. The mean of the distribution of book values was \$454.98 and the variance was $(\$121.07)^2$ or 14,658. The mean of the distribution of market values was \$441.28 and the variance was $(\$179.40)^2$ or 32,184. Although the average historical and current values derived from this study are quite close, the variances are significantly different. Therefore, Hypothesis 2 would be accepted since the historical values are more objective (have a significantly lower variance).

To test the verifiability of the historical valuation scheme, we used a measure of intra-observer range. For each respondent we calculated the maximum and the minimum acceptable book values by using the extreme values for life, cost, and salvage value to which he would certify. We then

[4] Ijiri and Jaedicke, *op. cit.*

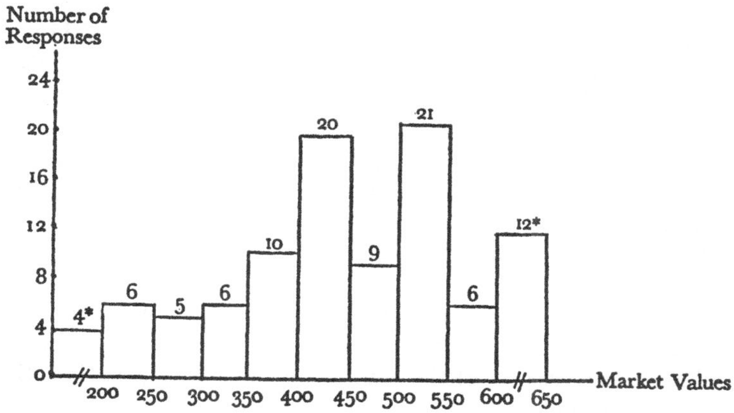

* The left-most and right-most categories represent, respectively, all responses less than $200 and all responses over $600. The book values actually ranged from $50.00 to $687.50. The market values ranged from $100.00 to $1,200.00.

FIG. 2. The Distribution of Market Values

TABLE 1

The Distribution of Extreme Acceptable Book Values for All Respondents

	High	Low	Mean	Standard deviation
Maximum acceptable book value	$755.00	$350.00	$540.79	$121.04
Minimum acceptable book value	590.00	0	282.18	165.64
Difference for each respondent	755.00	0	258.61	156.61

calculated for each respondent the difference between his maximum acceptable book value and his minimum acceptable book value. Characteristics of the distributions of these values and their differences for the 115 respondents are shown in Table 1.

The auditor attests or certifies to book values and he looks for means of verifying those values. This usually means tracing the figures back to the "basic business documents." In this case, where the basic documents are identical, the large acceptable variations indicate that this kind of verification is inadequate. The notion of verification in accounting is ill-defined. With respect to depreciable assets, it sometimes seems to mean that the auditor simply recalculates the book value and depreciation for the year after having accepted management's decisions as to which depreciation method to use and management's estimates of useful life and salvage value. However, the auditor should check these factors for "reasonableness." The purpose of our test was to see what the range of reasonableness was or, to borrow a term from engineering, to test the "tolerance limits." In this case, one auditor would have tolerated a book value ranging from zero to $755 at the end of year three. On the average, the acceptable variation per respondent was $258.61 with a standard deviation of $156.61, so that the mean acceptable variation plus three standard deviations is $728.44 or about 91% of the total cash outlay for this asset. Comparing the mean maximum and minimum acceptable book values with the mean best book value shows that, on the average, the best book value could have varied by 19% on the upside and 38% on the downside.[5] Usually, verification has to do with the discovery of errors, and it is difficult to see how an error could be discovered when the tolerance limits are so broad.[6]

Unfortunately, there was no way that we could think of to devise a test to compare the verifiability of fair market values with the verifiability of book values. Nonetheless, we would tend to reject Hypothesis 3 by questioning the characterization of book values as "verifiable" when the acceptable variation is as large as it is in this case.

Conclusions

From the results of this study, we would conclude that historical costs are more objective but are not univocal or verifiable. Current values are probably no worse with regard to these latter two characteristics. Moreover, the greater objectivity of historical costs should be accepted with two reservations. First, objectivity usually refers to agreement among *qualified* or *competent* observers.[7] Accountants profess to be competent to

[5] As large as these acceptable variations are, they are probably understated for two reasons: (1) They are calculated on the basis of factor variations only. That is, the figures in Table 1 were calculated by using the maximum acceptable lives, salvage values, and capitalized costs while holding the endorsed depreciation method constant. Presumably, each respondent would also have certified to book values calculated by any of the other depreciation methods. Had we allowed the depreciation method to vary, the acceptable variation would have been greater, particularly on the downside. (2) We suspect that some of the respondents would have permitted more variation than their responses indicate. For example, as shown in Table 1, one respondent indicated that his acceptable difference was zero, i.e., he would not have certified to any book value different from the one he considered best. This means that he would have denied a clean certificate to all the other respondents if we are to take his response literally. Another respondent indicated that he would not have accepted a book value of less than $590. Thus, over 85 of the other CPAs would have been denied a clean certificate by that auditor. The same is true of the auditor who indicated that the maximum acceptable book value was $350. He would have denied a clean certificate to over 90 respondents if we take his response literally.

[6] See Robert R. Sterling, "A Glimpse of the Forest" (Working Paper #8, University of Kansas), forthcoming in *The Accountants' Magazine* (Scotland) for a report of "errors" uncovered in audits when the errors were smaller than the acceptable variation.

[7] Most methodologists imply that the observer should be competent or qualified, and many state it directly. There are problems, of course, in providing a precise general definition of "qualified" or "competent." Nonetheless, it is necessary to make the restriction because it is impossible to obtain observer agreement without it.

establish book values but deny any expertise in matters of market values. Perhaps different results would be obtained had expert appraisers been asked to estimate the market values.[8]

A second reservation is necessary in light of the findings reported on this topic by McDonald. He provided two samples of CPAs with different supplementary information regarding a fleet of automobiles. The variance of the book values provided by one group was greater than the variance of the market values chosen by the other group, a result which is antithetical to the results of this study. The different results are probably explainable in terms of the type of information available to the respondents. In general, we would expect current values to be more objective for types of assets which have well established market price indicators, such as automobiles. For a class of other assets, with markets that are not so well defined, the current values would be less objective.

Finally, we should point out the possibility that there exists a "uniformity problem" in current values as well as in historical costs. It seems clear, for example, that some of our respondents were interpreting "fair market value" as replacement cost new because their estimates were several hundred dollars above the purchase price. Others seemed to interpret it as the exit value in the second-hand market. We have no way to test it from the data we have, but it would be interesting to know the relative variation between, say, exit values and book values calculated on a straight-line basis.[9]

[8] There are two variables involved here: expertise and information available on market activities. Unfortunately, the two variables also interact. There are expert appraisers available for appraising automobiles, for example, and their availability affects the availability of market information about automobiles, which in turn affects (if it does not determine) the prices of automobiles. For other classes of assets, there are no experts and little information. Thus, market values generated by appraisers may vary more or less than book values generated by accountants and the degree of variation in both market and book values is likely to be different for different classes of assets regardless of who makes the valuation.

[9] This last point was consciously accepted because of the previously mentioned reluctance to estimate. We were afraid that our response rate would be lowered if we specified more precisely the kind of market values. In addition, we were concerned that we would bias the results if we specified a particular kind of market value, especially since there is a continuing quarrel among current value proponents as to which current value is appropriate.

ROBERT R. STERLING

A Test of the Uniformity Hypothesis

There is a large body of literature on both sides of the debate over uniformity versus flexibility. An entire issue, for example, of *Law and Contemporary Problems* was devoted to the subject.[1] Although the opinions of the authors who write on this subject are varied, there is one recurrent theme presented by those who favour uniformity, namely,

1. different methods or principles result in different accounting figures on the financial statements,
2. these different figures for like items are undesirable,
3. therefore, the methods or principles should be standardized or made uniform.

The reason why different figures for like items are undesirable has not always been explicit. There seems to have been a shift in emphasis from mere uniformity to comparability of the results of uniform practices.

> One significant change in attitude took place almost imperceptibly. The arguments for a code of accounting principles changed between the first and second 'boom' in interest in statements of accounting principles. This change was not one that can be pinpointed to specific articles or even to a specific brief period (rather, a reader proceeding through the literature becomes increasingly conscious of it), but by the mid-'fifties accountants were talking about *comparability* of accounting *statements* rather than *uniformity* of accounting *principles.* The writers of the 'thirties had been vague about why 'uniformity' of accounting principles was desirable and were often wont to defend or condemn uniformity *per se.* In the post-war period, accountants were quite specific in identifying comparability of statements as the major factor requiring standardized principles, terminology, methods, etc.[2]

The present view therefore seems to be that different figures for like items are undesirable because they vitiate interfirm comparisons.

Although it is not often stated explicitly, one gets the clear impression that if the accounting principles or methods were uniform then the accounting figures for

1. *See also* Reed K. Storey, *The Search for Accounting Principles*, AICPA, New York 1964, for further evidence of the amount of concern over this subject. He indicates that concern over uniformity, although waxing and waning, has preoccupied accountants for over 30 years. In one place he describes the problem as 'a superabundance of accepted alternative practices', p. 32. A request to Arthur Andersen & Co. for their file on this subject brought references to about 750 books and articles which were indexed under 'Need for principles producing comparability' and related titles. For a representative cross-section of this literature *see* the works cited by Storey and the articles in *Law and Contemporary Problems,* Autumn 1965.
2. Storey, *Search*, p. 38.

ROBERT R. STERLING is Professor of Business Administration in the University of Kansas. The author acknowledges the helpful comment and criticism of Richard Pollay and Raymond Radosevich.

like items would be the same. For example, Bows[3] calculates the different income and asset figures that could be presented by contrasting straight-line with accelerated depreciation, lifo with fifo, etc. He deplores this situation and pleads for uniformity of method, presumably because uniformity of method would yield identical figures for identical situations.

A problem that has received little or no attention by those who favour uniformity is that the variation in accounting principles or methods is not the only cause of variation in the figures that appear on accounting reports. The situation is clearest in regard to depreciable assets.

The book value of a depreciable asset (and the related depreciation expense) is a function of three factors—capitalized cost (i.e., invoice price plus or minus adjustments for discounts, freight, etc.), life and salvage value. Obviously book values will vary if the estimates of those factors vary, i.e., if two accountants in different firms were to estimate different lives for an identical asset, then different book values would be reported. In addition, the book value will vary as the functional form in which the factors are related varies. This functional form is the 'depreciation method', and the 'uniformity problem' is that different methods are used for identical assets.

Thus, there are *two* sources of variation—different estimates of the *factors* and different *methods* of depreciation. The purpose of the research presented in this article was to test the variation in book values and the sources of that variation in respect of one depreciable asset.

Hypotheses

One might frame the uniformity hypothesis in regard to depreciable assets in one of the following ways:

A. If the method of depreciation were standardized then identical book values would be reported for identical assets.

B. If the method of depreciation were standardized then the variations in reported book values would be negligible or immaterial.

C. The major cause of variations in reported book values for identical assets is that different depreciation methods are used.

The Study

A questionnaire was designed in which a depreciable asset was described as follows:

> A CPA purchased a ten-key Monroe Printing Calculator on September 1, 1965. The calculator had a price tag of $900 but it was agreed that it could be bought for $100 down and $100 per month for seven months for a total of $800. The installment contract was accepted and no cash price was determined.
>
> This was the only asset that the accountant owned. He rented a furnished office and bought supplies in small quantities.

The questionnaire was mailed to 500 randomly selected CPAs in the United States and 134 provided usable responses. The respondents were asked to supply information on the depreciation method, capitalized cost, life and salvage value

3. Albert J. Bows, 'The Urgent need for Accounting Reforms', *N.A.A. Bulletin*, September 1960, p. 44.

that they would use if they were accounting for this asset.[4]

The Results

Although there are several other acceptable depreciation methods, the respondents listed only the three that are most commonly used: 62%, 31%, and 7% selected straight-line, double-declining balance and sum of the year's digits, respectively. The distribution of the factor estimates for all respondents is shown in Table I.

In response to another question some respondents indicated that an immediate write-off of the expenditure was an acceptable procedure. In effect they would have assigned a zero life to this asset. However, in answer to the direct question, What life would you use if you were accounting for this asset? there were no zeros given. Thus, there is an ambiguity in the lower end of the range of lives that would or could be used in accounting for this asset. Also at the upper end of the life range there were some non-specific responses that could have been interpreted as an estimate of more than 20 years. It was decided that only specific figures given in response to the direct question would be used in these and the following calculations.

TABLE I

Distribution Characteristics of the Factor Estimates for All Respondents

	High	Low	Mean	Standard deviation
Capitalized cost	900	731	800	15.10
Salvage value	200	0	44	44.50
Life	20	3	8	2.24

Table II shows the book values that could have been obtained had the different depreciation methods been applied to the mean factor estimates.

TABLE II

Variation in Book Values Due to Different Depreciation Methods with the Factor Estimates Held Constant at their Mean Values

Year	Straight-line	Sum of the year's digits	Double-declining balance	Mean	Range	Standard deviation
1	706	632	600	646	106	44.17
2	611	485	450	515	161	69.14
3	517	359	338	404	178	79.80
4	422	254	253	310	169	79.41
5	328	170	190	229	158	70.04
6	233	107	142	107	126	53.06
7	139	65	107	103	73	30.10
8	44	44	0	29	44	20.74

4. They were also asked to supply information on the minimum and maximum lives, salvage values and capitalized costs which they would 'certify to'. That is, two types of questions were asked: (1) What life (salvage value, capitalized cost) would you use if you were accounting for this asset? (2) What minimum and maximum life (salvage value, capitalized cost) would you certify to if you were auditing this firm? The data used in this study were taken from Type (1) questions. Had the minimum and maximum figures from Type (2) questions been used the variations in factor estimates would have been larger. The data from Type (2) questions were used to test the verifiability of book values. *See* Robert R. Sterling and Raymond Radosevich, 'A Valuation Experiment', *Journal of Accounting Research* (Spring 1969) for the results of that test.

Table III shows the book values that could have been obtained had the depreciation method been held constant and the factors allowed to vary. In making the calculations in Table III, all book values were calculated on the basis of an $800 capitalized cost. There were problems in handling the contents of the responses. First, it was impossible to determine exactly how the respondents would have treated the difference between the figure they set forth and the $800 outlay. Presumably they would have treated the difference as an income item. If so, the procedure used has the effect of understating the possible variations in total assets and expenses, as well as the possible variation in the particular asset. Second, one would expect, other things being equal, that the life and salvage value would vary inversely—the shorter the life estimate, the higher the salvage value estimate—but this was not the case. The life and salvage value estimates had a Pearson Product Moment correlation coefficient of —.149 which is not significantly different from zero at a .05 confidence level. Thus, the idea of calculating the possible variations by associating the highest salvage with the shortest life and the lowest salvage with the longest life was rejected. Instead, these two factors were taken in pairs as they were found on the responses.

Third, there were no significant differences in the factor estimates of the respondents grouped by different methods. That is, those who selected straight-line had about the same pattern of factor estimates as those who selected an accelerated method. Although differences in the number of respondents who selected each method made it difficult to be certain, it appears that factor estimates are independent of depreciation method selection. By a Kolmogorov-Smirnov test the factor estimates could be said to come from the same population at a .30 confidence level. In the author's opinion the theoretical argument for independence is more important. In accounting theory one is supposed to select the best depreciation method and that selection has nothing to do with estimating the life of the asset. Critics of an earlier draft of this paper have suggested that the practising accountant may have a specific depreciation figure or pattern of figures in mind and then he selects the method and factors that will yield that figure or pattern of figures. Under this argument the factor estimates are not independent of the selected method. If this is the case then the depreciation calculation is redundant. That is, if it is possible to estimate directly the depreciation expense or book value then the estimation of the factors and the calculation is a ritual. It would be much simpler just to record the direct estimate. Nevertheless, the independence hypothesis is an interesting one and it should be tested more rigorously than the data of this study allow.

For these reasons, the entire sample of factor estimates was used in calculating the book values for each of the depreciation methods in Table III.

TABLE III
Variations in Book Values Due to Differences
in Factor Estimate with the Depreciation Method
Held Constant
(Assuming independence of method selection and factor estimates)

A. Straight-line (n = 134)

Year	High	Low	Mean	Range	Standard deviation
1	760	550	704	210	33.39
2	720	300	613	320	65.94
3	680	50	523	630	98.90
4	640	0	434	640	125.77
5	600	0	347	600	148.41
6	560	0	271	560	151.17
7	520	0	207	520	136.56
8	480	0	147	480	125.28

B. Double-declining balance (n = 134)

Year	High	Low	Mean	Range	Standard deviation
1	720	267	601	453	69.38
2	648	89	461	559	95.78
3	583	50	357	533	101.85
4	524	0	278	524	100.41
5	472	0	218	472	95.01
6	425	0	165	425	94.72
7	383	0	127	383	84.33
8	343	0	93	343	78.85

C. Sum of year's digits (n = 134)

Year	High	Low	Mean	Range	Standard deviation
1	724	425	634	299	49.63
2	651	175	497	476	83.84
3	583	50	381	533	102.35
4	518	0	286	518	107.32
5	457	0	211	457	100.03
6	400	0	150	400	93.59
7	347	0	108	347	77.92
8	297	0	78	297	63.88

Table IV shows the book values calculated on the basis of the specific responses by each respondent. That is, the data were taken from the questionnaires in quadruples—method, capitalized cost, salvage value and life—and there was no interchange by method. Table IV could be interpreted as the actual range of book values that would have been reported by the respondents as opposed to the possible range of book values presented in Table III. The small number of respondents who selected sum of year's digits makes Table IV difficult to interpret and this is the reason for presenting the two tables calculated under different assumptions.

A comparison of Table II with Tables III and IV leads to a rejection of hypothesis A. Book values of identical assets are not necessarily identical even if the depreciation method is held constant. Acceptance or rejection of hypothesis B depends upon what one means by 'materiality'. An attempt was made to make the respondents think that the book value of this asset was likely to be material

TABLE IV

Variations in Book Values Due to Differences in Factor Estimates

(Assuming factor estimates are not independent of method selection)

A. Straight-line (n = 83)

Year	High	Low	Mean	Range	Standard deviation
1	819	550	705	269	40.52
2	738	300	608	438	73.86
3	688	50	512	638	108.93
4	650	0	419	650	131.48
5	612	0	328	612	149.63
6	575	0	261	575	130.39
7	538	0	201	538	106.34
8	500	0	140	500	89.89

B. Double-declining balance (n = 42)

Year	High	Low	Mean	Range	Standard deviation
1	681	480	616	201	42.48
2	590	288	477	302	61.81
3	512	173	370	339	67.95
4	443	104	289	339	67.04
5	384	0	222	384	72.47
6	333	0	173	333	66.35
7	289	0	135	289	59.59
8	250	0	83	250	71.95

C. Sum of year's digits (n = 9)

Year	High	Low	Mean	Range	Standard deviation
1	661	533	612	128	50.00
2	549	320	456	229	83.28
3	449	160	326	289	102.82
4	362	53	222	309	108.63
5	287	0	144	287	101.30
6	225	0	92	225	82.65
7	175	0	58	175	65.27
8	137	0	37	137	53.94

by indicating that this was the only asset owned by the firm. Nonetheless, the variations may still be considered immaterial if the revenue or cash balance were large. However, if one views materiality as the variations in book value relative to the mean book value, then hypothesis B would be rejected.

Hypothesis C is more difficult. If one accepts the ranges of book values as an appropriate test, then hypothesis C would be rejected since the ranges in Table III and IV are greater in all years than the ranges in Table II. If one accepts the standard deviation as an appropriate test, similar conclusions would be drawn. The standard deviations in Table II, Part A are greater than those in Table II in six of the eight years. In Parts B and C of Table III the standard deviations are greater in all years than those in Table II. Comparison of Parts A and C of Table IV with Table II yields similar conclusions. Part B of Table IV does not permit the conclusion since the standard deviations in the first four years due to factor differences are less than the standard deviations due to different methods. However, it does seem safe to say that the differences in factor estimates causes at least as much variation in book values as do the differences in methods, and therefore hypothesis C should be rejected.

The Importance of the Life Estimate

Analysing the factor estimates individually reveals that the life estimate is the most important factor in that it causes more variation in book values than the other factors. This is due to the functional form of the depreciation equations and the size of the salvage value relative to the capitalized cost. The salvage value estimates varied most, having a coefficient of variation of 101%.[5] The coefficient of variation for life estimates was much smaller—28%—but it caused much more variation in book values. This can be illustrated by the same method used to calculate standard cost deviations. Using the maximum and minimum lives and salvage values shown in Table I and assuming a straight-line method, the first year's depreciation expense can be analysed as follows:

	Life	Capitalized cost	Salvage value	First depreciation expense
	3	$800	$200	$200.00
	20	800	0	40.00
Difference	17	$ 0	$200	$160.00

Depreciation variance due to difference in life estimates	$(170.00)
Depreciation variance due to difference in salvage value estimates	66.66
Depreciation variance due to the joint effect	(56.66)
Net	$ 160.00

Of course, after three years the difference in depreciation expense drops to $40 but that difference is due entirely to the difference in life estimates. Under double-declining balance the first year depreciation expense is even greater ($453.33) and that difference is also due entirely to the difference in life estimates. Thus, the factor that caused the greatest variation in the book values was the difference in life estimates. The second greatest cause was the differences in salvage value estimates and the factor that caused minimal variation was the capitalized cost.

Limitations of the Results

It would not be proper to attempt to generalize these findings. It may be that other kinds of assets would yield smaller differences in factor estimates. These differences might be small enough to make the variations in accounting figures due to factor estimates significantly less than the variations due to depreciation methods. Whether or not this is the case will have to await further research. However, it should be noted that the asset selected for this study is one that almost all accounting firms own and therefore one with which all respondents are likely to be familiar. One would expect that variations in factor estimates

5. Capitalized cost varied least with a coefficient of variation of less than 2%. This had little effect on book values and was another reason for making all calculations on the basis of $800 in Table III.

concerning this asset would be less than variations concerning an asset with which the accountants were less familiar. To put it negatively: had a manufacturing machine been selected it is likely that extreme estimates would have been received from respondents who had specialized in banking or retailing. Thus, one might reasonably assume that a different asset would have resulted in greater differences in factor estimates.[6]

There are, of course, many other limitations on the generality of the results of this test even if the above supposition is correct. For example, this test concerned only one asset. Perhaps there is an offsetting effect in the life estimates of multiple assets. If so, the different depreciation methods may cause more variation in total assets than the different life estimates. Another obvious limitation is that this was a (singular) test of the uniformity hypothesis in regard to a depreciable asset. Tests of inventory variations, for example, are likely to reveal that the different methods contribute more to the variation than differences in the count. In short, the test reported is only one data point and many other tests must be conducted before any general conclusions can be drawn. This test was intended to suggest the existence of a problem; it was not intended to be a definitive test of the general problem of uniformity.

Conclusions

If the above results are representative, the implications for accounting research are vast. Taking the amount of literature devoted to the subject as evidence, it appears that accountants think that the existence of different depreciation methods is a problem of major proportions and they do not recognize that differences in factor estimates exist or they think that such differences are negligible. If the objective is to represent identical items with identical book values, then the results of this test would indicate that much more effort should be directed toward finding a method for estimating factors, particularly life, than toward eliminating different depreciation methods.

Another example of this same situation occurs in the tax allocation dispute. If one used these data to calculate the income effects of allocation and non-allocation relative to the income effect of different life estimates, the allocation effect would be miniscule relative to the life effect. However, the amount of literature devoted to the two subjects would lead one to believe that the exact opposite is true. If the objective is to make income statements more comparable, then narrowing life estimates is a much more pressing problem that the existence of different methods of treating taxes.

In short, accountants have been addressing themselves to only a partial cause of the variation in accounting figures. It appears that there would be less variation in accounting figures if the factor estimates were standardized than there would

6. Along the same lines one might expect that different kinds of accountants would have had different patterns of estimates. This was tested by grouping the respondents in various ways, e.g., public v. industrial accountants, members of national firms v. members of local firms, partners of firms v. their juniors. We were unable to discover any significant differences in factor estimates among the groups.

be if the methods or principles were made uniform. Thus, at least a portion of future research on uniformity or comparability should be directed toward narrowing the differences in factor estimates.

The Problem in Perspective

Despite the fact that this test was concerned with one depreciable asset and therefore the *conclusions* must be restricted to that asset, the *problem* of making factor estimates or measurements can be generalized. Accounting values can be generally characterized as a function of some underlying factors. The value of inventory is a function of the quantity of units purchased, the quantity of cash expended, the date of purchase, and the quantity sold. The book value of a depreciable (or depletable) asset is a function of the quantity of service life or output purchased, the quantity of cash expended, the date of purchase, the present date or the quantity of output used. And so forth for each asset or expense. Thus, in general an accounting value, V_i, is a function of some specific quantity, q_i.

(1) $V_i = f(q_1, q_2, \ldots)$

Some people argue that a particular value ought to be calculated in a different way.

(2) $V_j = g(q_1, q_2, \ldots)$

Thus, two different accountants or two different firms could report either V_i or V_j as a description of the same object or event. This is the uniformity problem. In addition, two different accountants or two different firms could estimate different q's.

(3) $V_i' = f(q_1', q_2', \ldots)$

We now have four possible accounting values—V_i, V_j, V_i', V_j'—that could be used to describe the same object or event.

From a structural point of view it is obvious that possible differences in the q's are just as important as the differences in the functions. In this one test the differences in the q's are also equally as important from an empirical point of view. That is, in the case tested the range from V_i' to V_i or from V_j' to V_j was greater than the range from V_i to V_j. Whether or not the differences in the q's are empirically important in other cases will have to await further research. Regardless of the empirical importance of the differences in the q's, they will remain quite an important problem from a structural point of view. Note that the functional form is a method of *calculating* a figure but the determination of the q's is an *empirical* operation—either an estimation or a measurement. Now the calculation of a magnitude is quite a different process from the measurement of a magnitude. Among other things the arguments concerning the two take different forms and the resolution of the arguments require different operations. That is, the argument over whether $f(q_1, q_2, \ldots)$ or $g(q_1, q_2, \ldots)$ is the 'best method' is different in kind from the argument over whether q_i or q_i' is 'more accurate'.

Note also that highlighting the fact that factor estimates are required may be helpful in analysing some of the current disputes. For example, it is now considered to be theoretically correct to capitalize only the discounted value of the payments on an instalment contract and treat the discount as interest expense. Finney and Miller[7] present that argument but conclude that ' . . . this is rarely done—partly because of the necessity of arbitrarily deciding on an interest rate'. This test confirms the rarity of the procedures and the debriefing of a sub-set of the respondents to the pre-test confirms the reasons given by Finney and Miller. The respondents did not discount because they said they did not know what interest rate to use. The interesting point is to compare the difficulty of determining what interest rate to use with difficulty of determining the life or salvage value of the asset. It is not immediately apparent that the life or salvage value is any less arbitrary or difficult to determine than the interest rate. Yet all of the respondents were willing to estimate a life and salvage value while less than 2% indicated that they would discount and less than ½% specified a rate. As one other example, one might want to compare the difficulty of determining the life or salvage value of the asset with the difficulty of determining its replacement cost or current cash equivalent. It is not immediately apparent that the life and, particularly, the salvage value are that much easier to determine.

In summary, the process of accounting for something may be broken down into three parts:

(1) a particular functional form is selected from a set of generally accepted functional forms,
(2) the factors that go into the selected function are determined,
(3) the accounting figure is calculated.

A good deal of effort has been expended on Part (1), and Part (2) has been neglected. From a structural, and perhaps from an empirical, point of view Part (2) is as important as Part (1). Arguments about Part (1) are different in kind from arguments about Part (2) and they will require different kinds of research to resolve them. Comparing the determinations required in Part (2) to some suggested determinations raises some questions about the justifications given in the literature.

Critics of an earlier draft of this paper have objected to the above generalization of the problem. Some of them objected to the specific test. The grounds for objection were that it was not the accountant's duty to determine the factors. Instead it was alleged that this was management's duty and therefore the questionnaire should have been mailed to managers, not accountants. The argument presented above, that the familiarity of the asset was likely to lessen the variation in factor estimates, was countered on similar grounds. It was alleged that, if a completely unfamiliar asset had been selected for the test, then the variation in life estimates would have been small because the respondents would have gone to the income tax guidelines and used whatever life they found there. Perhaps the critics are correct. It may be that it is not the accountant's duty to determine the factors. However, the consequences of this view are most disturbing. If one

7. H. A. Finney and Herbert E. Miller, *Principles of Accounting Intermediate*, Englewood Cliffs, N.J. 1958, p. 335.

accepts the above three-part view of the process of accounting then it will be noted that Part (1) is supposed to be performed by management because the '. . . responsibility for financial statements of corporations (a) rests primarily on management, who has the duty to employ [select] methods of accounting best suited to the needs and purposes of the corporation, . . . '.[8] The critics are claiming that Part (2) also ought to be performed by management or by the taxing authority. This leaves only Part (3)—the calculation—to be performed by the accountant.

Perhaps these considerations are the most important findings of this simple little test. It appears that a significant number of accountants view accounting as exclusively a calculational process. The literature lends some support to this view. In the textbooks the students are taught how to calculate depreciation, work-in-process, etc., but they are not taught how to determine the service life or the number of equivalent units. Journals are full of discussions about which way one ought to calculate depreciation, cost of goods sold, etc., but seldom does one find a discussion of how one determines the salvage value or the number of units in the inventory. If this conjecture is true—that accounting is viewed as a calculational process with the factors supplied by somebody else—it would partially explain why some suggestions have become accepted accounting practices and others have not. It would also permit some predictions as to which suggestions will become accepted and which will not. For example, price-level adjusted historical costs will become an accepted accounting practice because one can calculate those figures and the index used for the calculation is supplied by somebody else. Non-cost valuation proposals will not become accepted accounting practices because one cannot normally calculate replacement costs or current cash equivalents.

This conjecture seems to fall under the more general point made by Alexander:[9]

> Another very powerful factor operating on the development of accounting methods has been the attempt to reduce the accountant's responsibility for the human judgments which must be made in passing from a consideration of the accounts to the conduct of business affairs. This attempted avoidance of responsibility has led accountants to set up two requirements for sound accounting that somewhat limit the choice of methods. These are the requirements of objectivity and conservatism. To the extent that accountants have achieved objectivity and conservatism they have transformed the measurement of income into a safer activity but one which yields a result that only partially achieves the end sought.

Calculation is a much safer activity than determination of the factors. To let management or the taxing authority make the determinations is a good way to avoid responsibility. However, if we continue to define the accounting process so as to make it safe and so as to avoid responsibility, we may define it so narrowly that it withers and dies.

8. Paul Grady, *Inventory of Generally Accepted Accounting Principles for Business Enterprises*, AICPA, New York 1965, p. 31.

9. Sidney S. Alexander, 'Income Measurement in a Dynamic Economy' in *Five Monographs on Business Income*, The Study Group on Business Income of the American Institute of Accountants, New York 1950, p. 2.

The Role of Liquidity in Exchange Valuation

Robert R. Sterling and Richard E. Flaherty

THE purpose of this paper is to describe the method of assigning values to goods at the event of exchange under the historical cost system. It is *not* an attempt to evaluate the historical cost system. That is, in this paper we will not judge the historical cost system in regard to some higher level criteria concerning the goals or objectives of accounting nor will we compare historical costs to current costs or present values. Instead, we will take the historical cost system as a given and attempt to generalize the exchange valuation rules of that system. Thus, the historical cost system is the frame of reference of this paper and any judgments that we make will be within that reference frame.

To put it another way, this paper will attempt to explicate a part of the traditional (historical cost) theory of accounting. Kemeny defines explication as the process of "making an intuitive concept precise."[1] Precision in thinking and communication is a worthwhile end in itself; in addition, it is a means to an end. As Kemeny says "... the great merit of explications is that they serve to clarify such disputes, and even get us to admit that we have made a mistake."[2]

We believe that the explication of traditional accounting theory is at least a desirable, and perhaps a necessary, prerequisite to the evaluation of that theory. Note, however, that the explication process, per se, is neutral; making a theory more precise could result in *either* the retention or rejection of that theory. In this paper, we are concerned exclusively with explication and therefore, we have endeavored to be completely neutral in regard to the evaluation of the traditional theory.

Accounting for Exchanges

An exchange is a two-way flow of goods: An acquisition is accompanied by a sacrifice. Thus, an exchange has a "double effect"—an increment in one good and a decrement in another—which requires a "double entry" on the books of account. We increment (debit) an account and decrement (credit) another to reflect the changes in the two goods.

The operations necessary to make the entry may be analysed in general terms.

This paper was presented to the faculty and students of the University of Syracuse and benefited from the comments received.

[1] John G. Kemeny, *A Philosopher Looks at Science* (D. Van Nostrand Company, Inc., 1959), p. 106.
[2] Kemeny, p. 108.

Robert R. Sterling is Arthur Young Distinguished Professor at The University of Kansas and Richard E. Flaherty is Assistant Professor of Accounting at Oklahoma State University.

Let

G_i = good i such as cash, inventory, equipment, promises, etc. ($i=1, 2, \ldots, m$);

A_i = account i such as "cash," "inventory," etc. "Accounts" are marks on paper which are meant to reflect certain attributes of the things called "goods." ($i=1, 2, \ldots, m, m+1, m+2, \ldots, n$)[3];

Δ = an increment (Δ^+) or decrement (Δ^-).

Consider the following partial entry ($i \neq j$):

Dr. A_i
  Cr. A_j

The entry is meant to reflect the underlying flow of goods. Therefore, we must be able to make the following associations (or perform the following operations) in order to make the entry:

1. Associate a particular ΔG_i with a particular ΔG_j. For example, if we exchanged $1,000 for inventory and at the same time exchanged $1,500 for equipment, it would be an error to debit inventory $1,500. Thus, we must be able to associate particular increments with particular decrements.
2. Associate G_i with A_i and G_j with A_j. For example, if we exchanged a $1,000 check for things called "widgets," it would be an error to debit buildings and credit petty cash. Thus, we must be able to associate particular goods with particular accounts.
3. Associate increments in goods with debits to accounts and decrements in goods with credits to accounts. Obviously, if we credit inventory upon the receipt of goods, we have erred.

Some of the problems in performing these operations have been discussed elsewhere.[4] For purposes of this paper, we will assume the performance of the operations and concentrate on the valuation process.

An exchange is an increment in one good accompanied by a decrement in another good. Neither of these *goods* necessarily has a value attached; instead we *assign* a value to them. In most cases this assignation of a value is done intuitively, i.e., without an explicit consideration of the process. The simplest cases are cash exchanges in which the value of cash is set equal to the quantity of cash.[5] Then, the value of the offset (associated good or associated account) is set equal to the value of cash.

Although it seems odd to speak of "valuing cash," it is necessary to do so if we are to describe the process generally and precisely. In the abstract, we are presented with a Δ^+G_i associated with a Δ^-G_j and their values are not apparent. We must determine those values. That is, we must have an operation that will allow us to move from a "good" to a "value" of that good. In general, we determine the value of one (or both) of the goods and then, to use Ijiri's language,[6] we "impute" that value to the offset. Thus, one good is "independently valued" and the offset is "dependently valued" by being imputed from, or set equal to, the independently valued good.

The valuation operations may be generalized as follows:

Given Δ^+G_i associated with Δ^-G_j,
(1) select G_i or G_j,
(2) independently value the selected good, and
(3) dependently value the offset.

Two examples of cash exchanges will il-

[3] From a strict entity point of view, one could argue that there is a one to one correspondence of goods to accounts. Liabilities could be considered to be negative goods or negative assets and owner's equities considered to be just another liability. Others would argue that there are more accounts than goods, as in the above definition. The dispute is not pertinent to this paper. The same results will be achieved by either definition.

[4] Robert R. Sterling, "An Operational Analysis of Traditional Accounting," *Abacus* (December 1966), pp. 119–36.

[5] More generally, the valuation coefficient of cash is set equal to one. See Robert R. Sterling, "Elements of Pure Accounting Theory," The Accounting Review (January 1967), pp. 62–73.

[6] Yuji Ijiri, *The Foundations of Accounting Measurement* (Prentice-Hall, Inc., 1967), p. 95.

lustrate the process. First, consider the acquisition of inventory in exchange for \$1,000 in cash. It would be an error to select the inventory for independent valuation. If it were valued independently at, say, \$1,200, then it would be recorded as

Dr. Inventory........................\$1,200
  Cr. Cash............................\$1,000
  Cr. Gain..............................\$200

which is obviously an error (i.e., not in accordance with standard practice). The correct entry in general form is:

Dr. Inventory....................Dependent
  Cr. Cash........................Independent

Second, consider the acquisition of cash in exchange for inventory which is valued at \$1,000 (cost). If the cash were dependently valued and the inventory independently valued, the exchange would be recorded as

Dr. Cash............................\$1,000
  Cr. Inventory.......................\$1,000

which is an error. The correct entry in general form is:

Dr. Cash.......................Independent
  Cr. Revenue....................Dependent

and

Dr. Cost of Goods Sold............Dependent
  Cr. Inventory....................Independent

The erroneous as well as the correct entries illustrate the fact that in both cases (1) the cash is selected for independent valuation, (2) the value of the cash is determined, and (3) the value of the associated good (or account) is set equal. The Cost of Goods Sold-Inventory entry provides another illustration. The inventory is selected for independent valuation,[7] its value is determined, and the offset is set equal.[8]

The Valuation Preference Array

The previous examples were of cash exchanges, the simplest case. If the theory is to be complete and unambiguous, a rule must be provided for all possible exchanges. All possible simple[9] exchanges are the combinations of all the goods taken two at a time, i.e., (G_1, G_2), (G_1, G_3), . . . , (G_1, G_n), (G_2, G_3), (G_2, G_4), . . . , (G_{n-1}, G_n). Given any of the possible exchanges, the accountant must select (at least) one of the goods for independent valuation.

We know that such selections are now being made. We can observe that when an accountant is faced with the exchange of inventory for an account payable, he will independently value the payable, not the inventory. When faced with an exchange of an account receivable for inventory, we can observe the independent valuation of the receivable. Since selections are now being made in the practice of accounting, a decision rule must now exist, albeit tacitly. The present theory is incomplete in the absence of an explicit statement of that rule.

It may be the case that there are many different decision rules. Each combination

[7] "Dependent" and "independent" valuation is intended to refer to a single exchange. The inventory is dependently valued at acquisition—its value is imputed from the independently valued sacrifice—but it is independently valued at disposition. Note that in both the sacrifice of cash and the sacrifice of inventory, the amount of the "independent value" is equal to the "book value." However, when a payable is sacrificed, no book value exists and, therefore, the equality does not hold and the value of the payable must be directly determined.

[8] For ease of exposition, the cash sale was presented in simple entry form. The compound entry form is more difficult to describe. That is, if the sale is recorded as

Dr. Cash......................Independent
  Cr. Inventory.................Independent
  Cr. Gain......................Dependent

then we cannot specify the direction of the inputation because of the possibility of a loss. The zero-sum method of analysis would permit the generalization of these kinds of cases, i.e., specify that the values of each exchange must sum to zero and treat debits as positive values and credits as negative values. See Sterling, "Elements" for a discussion of entries cast in the zero-sum form.

Note also that both goods are independently valued under the definition given. The imputation is to the gain account instead of to an account representing a good. Such a procedure is covered by Rule A2 stated below.

[9] By analogy with simple and compound entries, "simple exchange" is used to mean the acquisition of one good for the sacrifice of one other good. A "compound exchange" would be the acquisition of more than one good or the sacrifice of more than one good.

of goods may have a unique rule. In addition, different accountants may have different decision rules. If so, in an exchange of G_i for G_j, one accountant might select G_i for independent valuation and another accountant might select G_j. Both sources of differences are undesirable. Different rules for different combinations would be cumbersome and difficult to apply. "Simplicity" and "elegance" are said to be desiderata of theories, and a set of unique rules would be neither simple nor elegant. Different rules by different accountants would result in inconsistency and lack of comparability.

It would be desirable if the goods or accounts could be arrayed in accordance with accountants' preferences for valuation. The good to be independently valued could be selected by determining its relative position on the array. That is, given the exchange of G_i for G_j, if $i<j$, then value G_i independently; if $j<i$, then value G_j independently. (If $i=j$, it is a "trade-in" which presents special problems. See section below on "Barter.") This rule would be simple and easy to communicate. If the array were communicated and became common to all accountants, it would avoid inter-practitioner inconsistencies in selection of the good to be independently valued. The transitivity of the array would obviate the necessity of stating specific rules for specific combinations of goods.

We offer the hypothesis that such an array is implicit in the traditional theory and practice of accounting. Since the array is intended to reflect the accountants' preferences for valuation, it will be called the "Valuation Preference Array." The basis for that preference is the next question.

The Liquidity Hypothesis

We offer the hypothesis that the valuation preference array is based on the relative liquidity of the goods, i.e., if G_i is more liquid than G_j, then G_i is selected for independent valuation. Evidence in support of that hypothesis is adduced from the way in which accountants normally record exchanges.

In any exchange in which cash is acquired or sacrificed, the cash is always independently valued and the value of the offset is imputed therefrom. Most of accounting theory is stated as if all exchanges were for cash or "cash equivalents." Paton and Littleton provide a clear example:

> In cash transactions cost is measured by the amount of the immediate cash consideration; in credit transactions cost is the amount of money which would be required to effect immediate settlement of the obligation incurred.[10]

The quotation is taken from their chapter on "costs," and it seems clear that they mean the acquisition of an illiquid good and the sacrifice of a liquid good. When the flow is reversed, they are even more explicit:

> Revenue is the product of the enterprise, measured by the amount of new assets received from customers. . . . .
>
> . . . .
>
> [Revenue is realized when] . . . it is evidenced by cash receipts or receivables, or *other new liquid* assets. Implicit here are two tests: (1) conversion through legal sale or similar process; (2) validation through the acquisition of *liquid* assets.[11] (Italics supplied.)

In both cases the illiquid good (or account) is "measured by" or imputed from the independently valued cash or equivalent. The direction of the flow is of no consequence in deciding which good to value; only the liquidity of the goods is pertinent.

The rule extends beyond exchanging cash and cash equivalents. If a firm were to issue bonds in exchange for land, it is almost certain that the accountant would independently value the bonds and dependently value the land, i.e., set it equal to

[10] W. A. Paton and A. C. Littleton, ***An Introduction to Corporate Accounting Standards*** (American Accounting Association, 1940), p. 24.
[11] Paton and Littleton, pp. 46, 49.

the value of the bonds. However, if the bonds were issued in exchange for cash, it is equally certain that the accountant would independently value the cash—determine the net proceeds—and set the value of the bonds equal. Thus, the description of the good (or account) by itself gives us no indication of how to value that good. Bonds payable are not valued in isolation; instead, their valuation depends on their relation to the good received in exchange. If the bonds are less liquid than the other good, then they are dependently valued; if they are more liquid than the other good, then they are independently valued. For the three items mentioned, the valuation preference array is: Cash, Bonds Payable, and Land. This array appears to be based on liquidity.

In the inventory-cash and cash-inventory exchanges discussed above, the valuation preference array was: Cash, Inventory, and Retained Earnings subaccounts. This array is consistent with the liquidity hypothesis. In the receivable-inventory and inventory-payable exchange examples, the more liquid receivable and payable were independently valued.

Other examples could be related at length. However, enough has been said to suggest that the goods are arrayed on the basis of liquidity, and that the more liquid good is valued independently and the less liquid good (or account) is dependently valued. There is no conclusive proof, but there seems to be enough evidence to warrant further investigation.

The Purchase-Sale Distinction

"Exchange" is a generic term, species of which are "purchases" and "sales." A "sale" results in "recognition" or "realization" of gains or revenue. Conversely, a "purchase" results in a "cost." No cost is incurred at sale and no gain or revenue is permitted at purchase.[12] Because of these differences, the ability to distinguish between purchases and sales is crucial to the accounting process. Without such a distinction, we would be unable to determine whether we have incurred a cost or realized a gain. Thus, there must exist a rule for making the distinction.

The rule for distinguishing purchases and sales is not given in the literature. Instead, it seems to be assumed that all of us can make the distinction. For most exchanges, this is a reasonable assumption, but, as will be demonstrated, there are some exchanges which present problems. For completeness of the theory, as well as for guidance in the troublesome cases, it is necessary to make the rule explicit.

We offer the hypothesis that the distinction is based on the direction of the flow of liquidity. Whenever the acquisition is more liquid than the sacrifice, the exchange is considered to be a sale and gains can be realized. Whenever the sacrifice is more liquid than the acquisition, the exchange is considered to be a purchase and a cost is incurred. Although there are some species of exchanges in which this rule does not

[12] "Accountants are correct in holding to the general rule that income should not result from the recording of acquisitions." [Eldon S. Hendriksen, *Accounting Theory* (Richard D. Irwin, Inc., 1965), p. 288.] This quotation is presented in support of the rule that gains are not permitted at purchase. Undoubtedly, all of us understand Hendriksen's meaning, but it is interesting to note that if we take his statement literally, it would prohibit recognition of all gains. An exchange, by definition, is an acquisition accompanied by a sacrifice. Therefore, the literal interpretation of Hendriksen's statement would prohibit the recognition of income or gains at any exchange, including sales. Of course, that is not Hendriksen's intent, as is made clear from the context—acquiring plant and equipment—of his statement. However, it does illustrate the ambiguity in our theoretical language as well as the necessity for classifying exchanges into purchases and sales.

A similar ambiguity occurs in Lim's discussion of the "purchase" of accounts receivable [Ronald S. Lim, "The Mathematical Propriety of Accounting Measurements and Calculations," The Accounting Review (October 1966), p. 647n]. Although it is possible to think of purchasing accounts receivable instead of selling inventory, the valuation procedure is different and such locution is apt to lead to confusion. For example, if we conceive of the acquisition of accounts receivable associated with the sacrifice of inventory as a purchase, then we would not be permitted to record a gain on that exchange.

apply,[13] it seems that when the choice is between classifying a particular exchange as a purchase or a sale, the rule provides us with a basis for making the distinction. Consider the two Paton and Littleton quotations (above) in which two different concepts—cost and realization—are explained. The only difference between the two exchanges described in those quotations is the direction of the flow of liquidity. In regard to realization, they say that there are two tests: (1) sale and (2) acquisition of liquid assets. It seems that test (1) is contained in test (2). How would one recognize that a sale had occurred if one did not know that liquid assets had been acquired in exchange for illiquid assets? In the abstract, an exchange is a $\Delta^{+}G_i$ accompanied by a $\Delta^{-}G_j$. There is some characteristic of the exchange that allows us to decide whether it is a purchase or a sale or some other species of exchange. We believe that the characteristic that permits the distinction is the direction of the flow of liquidity.

Although different authors use different terms, the literature seems to be fairly consistent on this point. Thomas[14] distinguishes monetary from nonmonetary items. His definition of "monetary items" is apparently identical to Paton and Littleton's implied definition of "cash and cash equivalents." Thomas[15] then uses the monetary/nonmonetary distinction as a basis for various approximations to the realization rule. After stating the realization rule, he derives the historical cost rule as a "consequence" of realization.[16] He states the realization rule as follows:

> Revenue is to be recognized when, and only when (1) a sale or similar transaction occurs between the company and a solvent, independent external party; or (2) net assets of known worth, such as current net claims against solvent, independent external parties, are increased, either to the conversion of nonmonetary into monetary items or by other external action.[17]

We believe that the "conversion of nonmonetary into monetary items" in part (2) of his definition is the basis for deciding that the exchange is a sale as required by part (1) of his definition.

Instead of "monetary" and "nonmonetary," Ijiri sets up the classes of "basic" and "nonbasic." When selecting cash for the basic class, he includes "cash to be received or paid in the future,"[18] i.e., receivables and payables. This distinction seems to be equivalent to the classifications of Thomas and Paton and Littleton. Ijiri then states the rule directly. He says that value gains and losses should not be recognized until the "cycle ends with the basic class [i.e., the receipt of an item in the basic class]. Before that time, the values of the resources are always recorded as being equal to the values of their predecessors in the cycle."[19] In other words, when the acquisition is in the nonbasic class and the sacrifice is in the basic class, the exchange is classified as a purchase and results in a cost. An exchange in the reverse direction is a sale, and gains are permitted to be realized.

These and other authors seem to be making the same point: If the acquisition is in the *class* of liquid goods, the exchange is classified as a sale; if the acquisition is in the *class* of illiquid goods, the exchange is classified as a purchase. The problem is that this rule applies only to inter-class exchanges. It does not apply to exchanges when both goods are in the basic or mone-

[13] For example, the classification of an exchange as an "investment" results in the strict prohibition of realization regardless of any other characteristics of the exchange. In addition, in such exchanges, the acquisition of a non-monetary asset would be considered an (unexpired) cost regardless of whether it was dependently or independently valued.

[14] Arthur L. Thomas, "Revenue Recognition," *Michigan Business Reports Number 49* (The University of Michigan, 1966), p. 9.

[15] Thomas, pp. 10–12.

[16] Thomas, pp. 12–13.

[17] Thomas, p. 12.

[18] Ijiri, p. 92.

[19] Ijiri, p. 94.

tary class or when both goods are in a nonbasic or nonmonetary class. Yet, there are many intra-class exchanges. Consider exchanges within the monetary class; for example, the exchange of cash for an account receivable. This exchange is like a sale in that the cash will be valued independently and a gain or loss may be recognized. It is common for a receivable to be recorded net of discount and gains to be recognized if the gross amount is paid, and vice versa. An alternative is to treat the exchange like a purchase and impute the book value of the receivable to the cash account, regardless of the amount of cash collected—which is contrary to standard practice. As another example, consider the acquisition of cash in exchange for a note payable. This is also valued like a sale in that the value of the acquisition is imputed to the sacrifice. That is, the entry is the same, in structure, as a debit to cash and a credit to revenue. Although we would have no difficulty in valuing the described exchanges, the rule, as stated, does not cover them. In both cases, the two goods are within the monetary or basic class, and there is no explicit provision for imputing values from one monetary good to another. (Cf. Ijiri's rules.)[20]

Thus, the problem is that goods or accounts are segregated into classes and a rule is provided for exchanges between those two classes, but no rule is provided for exchanges within the classes. The problem is similar to the problem of selecting a good for independent valuation. A rule is needed which would cover all possible simple exchanges. That is, for all combinations of all the goods taken two at a time, a rule is needed to permit one to recognize whether the exchange is to be valued like a purchase or a sale. In the way in which exchanges are now recorded, it appears that the implicit rule conforms to the liquidity hypothesis. Instead of goods being simply segregated into two classes, it appears that they are ranked according to their relative liquidity. Therefore, we offer the hypothesis that the criterion for distinguishing purchases and sales is: When the acquisition is more liquid than the sacrifice, the exchange is valued like a sale; when the sacrifice is more liquid than the acquisition, it is valued like a purchase.

Summary

The present practice of accounting requires that in every exchange one (or both) of the goods be independently valued and the other good (or account) be dependently valued. The rule for selecting the good to be independently valued is not stated and the traditional theory is incomplete in the absence of an explicit rule for selection. The present practice also requires that purchases be distinguished from sales. The traditional theory provides a rule for making the distinction for inter-class exchanges, but it does not provide a stated rule for intra-class exchanges. Since intra-class exchanges occur, the traditional theory is incomplete.

From informal observations of accounting practice and from hints in the literature, the hypothesis was adduced that the relative liquidity of the good provides the basis for both of the omitted rules. The more liquid good is selected for independent valuation, and the direction of the flow of liquidity is used for distinguishing purchases from sales. The combined rules may be stated generally as follows:

A. If the acquisition is more liquid than the sacrifice, then value the acquisition independently.
  - A1. If the sacrifice has no value assigned, then impute to it the value of the acquisition.
  - A2. If the sacrifice has a previously assigned (book) value, then the difference between the values is called the "realized gain" (or loss), and that difference is imputed to a retained earnings sub-

[20] Ijiri, p. 95.

account. Alternatively, the independent value of the acquisition is called "realized revenue" and imputed to a retained earnings subaccount, as in Al. The independent value of the sacrifice is called an "expense" and imputed to a retained earnings subaccount, as in B.

B. If the sacrifice is more liquid than the acquisition, then value the sacrifice independently. ("Value independently" is defined to mean the book value if a book value exists.) Impute the value of the sacrifice to the acquisition and call it the "cost" of the acquisition.

Since it is possible to exchange any two goods, it is necessary to rank all the goods (and accounts) in order to apply the above rules. Such a ranking has been named the "Valuation Preference Array." Although it is impossible to completely specify this array at the present time, it seems apparent that cash would be at the top and retained earnings and its subaccounts would be at the bottom. Receivables, payables, and marketable securities, followed by inventory would be near the top, while plant, equipment, and contributed capital would be near the bottom. Combining the array with the rules would permit unambiguous treatment of inter-entity exchanges.[21]

The presentation of these hypotheses is an attempt to make the theory of historical cost valuation more complete by making a minor logical extension of the stated theory. The presentation is also an attempt to make explicit what seems, from informal observation, to be the present practice of accounting. There are, however, certain kinds of exchanges whose suggested treatment in the literature is in conflict with the hypotheses.

Barter

"Barter" is another species of the genus "exchange." It is difficult to provide a general definition which precisely delineates barter from nonbarter exchanges. However, a rough definition is sufficient for the purpose at hand. Exchanges of one nonmonetary good for another nonmonetary good will be called a "barter."

When faced with a barter, the accountant must make the same decisions that he makes when faced with other exchanges. First, he must select one or both of the goods for independent valuation. Second, he must decide whether the exchange is to be valued as a purchase or a sale. To be consistent with the hypotheses presented in the previous section, the more liquid good would be valued independently. If a more liquid good were acquired, it would be considered a sale and a gain could be realized. If the more liquid good were sacrificed, it would be considered a purchase and no gain would be permitted.

The authors who present rules for barters and trade-ins do not explicitly recognize the necessity of making the second decision, and most of them make the first decision without explaining their criteria. As a result, at least partly, the literature is conflicting. Different rules are presented by different authors.[22] More importantly,

[21] Intra-entity exchanges are not intended to be covered by the rules. Such exchanges are normally treated as purchases, even though the entity is acquiring a more liquid good. For example, finished goods is more liquid than work-in-process, but the exchange is valued like a purchase in that the value of finished goods is imputed from the value of work-in-process and gains are normally prohibited.

[22] The following alternatives are presented in the literature: (1) Set the value of the acquisition equal to the "selling [exit] value" of the sacrifice. (Paton and Littleton, p. 27.) This may or may not be the same as the "market value" proposed by Paul Grady, "Inventory of Generally Accepted Accounting Principles for Business Enterprises," *Accounting Research Study No. 7* (American Institute of Certified Public Accountants, 1965), p. 254; or the "fair market value" proposed by Walter B. Meigs, Charles E. Johnson and Thomas F. Keller, *Intermediate Accounting* (McGraw-Hill Book Company, 1963), p. 522. They may, for example, be thinking of entry values. (2) Set the value of the acquisition equal to the book value of the sacrifice. [Norman J. Lenhart and Philip L. Defliese, *Montgomery's Auditing* (The Ronald Press Company, 1957), p. 244.] (3) Independently value the acquisition at its "replacement cost." (Ijiri, p. 97. Ijiri is describing "the most likely treatment in conventional accounting," not advocating it.) (4) Value "whichever is the more clearly evident" at "fair value." [*Accounting Research and Terminology Bulletins*, Final Edition, Accounting Research Bulletin

the specific rules for barters and trade-ins given by the majority of the authors conflict with the more general rules of historical cost valuation.

The Majority View

Those authors who explicitly consider barters or trade-ins almost invariably state a preference for independently valuing the sacrifice, and most of them permit the realization of a gain. Grady's statement is typical:

> If property other than cash is the consideration in a transaction, a fair measure of the actual cash cost is the amount of money which would have been realized if such property had first been directly converted into cash. If the property has no determinable fair market value, the market value of the properties received in the exchange may be used. A gain or loss will occur when fair market value differs from the book value of the property given up.[23]

When put in the context of the general framework of historical cost valuation, this is a most peculiar rule. It violates the spirit, and in many cases the letter, of the more general rules of historical cost valuation.

The Realization Criteria. Davidson says "... it appears that present accepted tests for realization require receipt of a current (or liquid) asset capable of objective measurement of a market transaction for services rendered."[24] From this, and the other literature on realization, three criteria can be adduced:

(1) Acquisition of a liquid asset,
(2) Ability to objectively measure the acquisition, and
(3) An exchange.

A barter, by definition, does not result in the acquisition of a liquid or monetary asset.[25] If it did, it would not be classified as a barter. Therefore, criterion (1) is not satisfied. The acquisition is likely to be no more objectively measurable than the sacrifice. Even if the acquisition is objectively measurable, the majority rule states a preference for valuing the sacrifice. Therefore, criterion (2) is either not satisfied or irrelevant or both. An exchange has

---

No. 43 (American Institute of Certified Public Accountants, 1961), p. 38.] (5) Value both at their "fair market value." [Maurice Moonitz and Louis H. Jordan, *Accounting: An Analysis of its Problems*, Volume One (Holt, Rinehart and Winston, Inc., 1963), p. 361.]

In regard to alternative (5), an interesting question arises if the fair value of the acquisition is different from the fair value of the sacrifice. Moonitz and Jordan's assumption is the sale of the old for hypothetical cash and then the purchase of the new for hypothetical cash. If there is a difference in fair values, a balance is left in the hypothetical cash account. Do we show the balance as an asset, like goodwill, if a debit, or as an equity, like consolidated surplus, if a credit? If we write-off the balance, this reverts to valuing only one of the goods and setting the other equal. Therefore, there would be no need to independently value both.

Although retaining the balance of hypothetical cash seems odd from an accounting point of view, it would not be odd from an economic point of view. In exchanges, one normally gains a "producer's (or consumer's) surplus" above the purchase price. Thus, the exchanges could be recorded to show an intangible asset in the amount of the producer's surplus, which would not be too dissimilar from showing a balance in hypothetical cash. However, in accounting we usually inpute the value of one good to another and thereby rule out such intangibles. For this reason, there is no reason to independently determine the fair market value of both goods in a barter.

Note that although the five alternatives are the only ones suggested in the literature, they do not exhaust the logical possibilities. We could value the acquisition at its book value to the other entity, as we sometimes do in poolings, and any of the fair market value proposals permit the possibility of showing the difference as an unrealized gain.

[23] Grady, p. 254. For similar rules, see e.g., Rufus Wixon (ed.), *Accountants' Handbook* (The Ronald Press Company, 1965), Sec. 16, p. 4; Carl T. Devine, "Asset Cost and Expiration," *Modern Accounting Theory*, Morton Backer (ed.) (Prentice-Hall, Inc., 1966), pp. 146–47; H. A. Finney and Herbert E. Miller, *Principles of Accounting: Intermediate* (Prentice-Hall, Inc., 1965), p. 332; Meigs, Johnson and Keller, p. 523; Paton and Littleton, p. 27.

[24] Sidney Davidson, "The Realization Concept," *Modern Accounting Theory*, Morton Backer (ed.) (Prentice-Hall, Inc., 1966), p. 102.

[25] It could, of course, result in the acquisition of a current asset. However, we have selected the term "liquid" from Davidson's "current (or liquid)" phrase for two reasons: (1) The current classification is itself based on liquidity as is evidenced by the criterion of "being converted into cash within a year." Therefore, liquidity seems to be the fundamental criterion and the current classification is but an application of that criterion. (2) The current classification contains goods which are considered to be "costs" because, in normal circumstances, a more liquid good is sacrificed in order to acquire them. If we decided to use the current classification as one of the realization criteria, then we could

occurred and, therefore, criterion (3) is satisfied. Since two of the three criteria are not satisfied, the recognition of a gain on a barter transaction violates the realization requirements.

The Prohibition of Write-ups. Following the majority rule, a barter would be recorded in general form as follows:

Dr. Acquisition........Fair Market Value of Sacrifice
  Cr. Sacrifice.............Book Value
  Cr. Gain................Fair Market Value of Sacrifice less Book Value

This compound entry may be broken down into two simple entries. Just prior to the exchange, the following entry could be made:

Dr. Sacrifice.............Fair Market Value less Book Value
  Cr. Gain......................Fair Market Value less Book Value

Then at the moment of the exchange, the acquisition would be recorded as

Dr. Acquisition............New Book Value
  Cr. Sacrifice...................New Book Value

The first of the two simple entries is a write-up of an existing asset and is a clear violation of APB Opinion No. 6.[26] Even when write-ups were permitted, the amount was not classified as realized. Therefore, the entry errs on two counts.

The Prohibition of Hypothetical Transactions. Evidently Grady is thinking of the sale of the sacrifice for cash and then the purchase of the acquisition for the cash acquired. Moonitz and Jordan agree with the rule presented by Grady and make their assumption more explicit. They write: ". . . the difficulty [of valuing barters] may be overcome by assuming a sale of the old unit for cash, followed by the immediate use of that cash in the purchase of a new unit."[27] It is often said that one of the virtues of historical cost accounting is that it records "actual transactions" and does not permit hypothetical transactions to enter the books of account. This rule is crucial to the prohibition of current values and the retaining of historical cost. If hypothetical transactions are allowed, there is nothing to prevent the hypothetical sale and re-purchase of all the assets, thereby recording all of them at their current values. The majority rule permits hypothetical transactions and, therefore, it violates one of the more important rules of historical cost accounting.

The Prohibition of Recording Gains at Purchase. Writers who present the majority rule are evidently thinking of barters as purchases. A clue to their thinking is given by the language they use. Almost invariably they speak of the "consideration" and the "cost" of the acquisition. (See the quotation by Grady above.) Since cost is incurred at purchase, not at sale, it appears that they have classified the exchange as a purchase. Another clue is given by the fact that they independently value the sacrifice instead of the acquisition. As Devine explains, "The usual definition of 'cost' is in terms of sacrifice." [28] That is, we focus on the sacrifice when incurring a cost and we focus on the acquisition when realizing a gain.[29,30] For

---

consider such things as prepayments and inventories as "realizations" instead of "cost incurrences." For example, we could record a gain upon the acquisition of inventory in exchange for cash. This was done in the now discredited method of recording purchase discounts as realized income. The current classification as a criterion would not rule out the realization of purchase discounts. The acquisition (inventory) is in the current classification, it is capable of objective measurement (assumed), and it is a market transaction for services (cash) rendered. Therefore, the following entry would be allowed:

Dr. Inventory..................Independent
  Cr. Cash......................Independent
  Cr. Gain (Discount)............Dependent

[26] Accounting Principles Board, "Status of Accounting Research Bulletins," *Opinion No. 6* (American Institute of Certified Public Accountants, Inc., 1965), p. 42

[27] Moonitz and Jordan, p. 361.

[28] Devine, p. 143.

[29] Devine, p. 143, clearly makes the distinction between cost-sacrifice and accomplishment-realization. The full quote is:

The usual definition of "cost" is in terms of sacrifice.

these reasons, it seems apparent that the majority writers have classified barters as purchases. The problem is that the majority rule contradicts the general rule that specifically prohibits gains from being realized at purchase. (See the Hendriksen quotation in Footnote 12 above.) Therefore, if they have classified the exchange as a purchase, they have erred by recording a gain.

In short, the majority rule for valuing barters violates virtually all of the more general and more basic rules of historical cost valuation. Therefore, the majority rule is in error and should be rejected.

An Alternative Rule

The majority view states a preference for independently valuing the sacrifice. The reasons for that preference are not made explicit. Sometimes textbooks discuss barters or trade-ins without considering the possibility of independently valuing the acquisition.[31] Bulletin 43, on the other hand, says to independently value either the acquisition or the sacrifice "whichever is more clearly evident."[32] On the face of it, it seems more reasonable to select the good whose value is more clearly evident than to state a preference for valuing either the acquisition or the sacrifice. Grady provides for the case when the sacrifice has "*no* determinable fair market value" and permits the independent valuation of the acquisition in that case. We see no reason to select the sacrifice for independent valuation if its value is *more* difficult to determine than the value of the acquisition. Thus, we would argue for the ease of determination of the value as the criterion for selecting the good to be independently valued. Selection by this criterion would be consistent with the liquidity hypothesis. It is usually the case that the liquidity of a good varies directly with the ease of determination of the value of that good. The most liquid good is cash and its value is also the easiest to determine. A receivable is highly liquid and its value is also relatively easy to determine. A marketable security is both more liquid and easier to value than equipment or buildings. In general, the good whose value is more clearly evident will also be the good which is more liquid.

Once the selection of the good for independent valuation is made, it is then necessary to decide whether the transaction is a purchase or a sale. That is, we must decide whether the exchange is of the character that would permit the recognition of a gain. The direction of the flow of liquidity would also provide a criterion for mak-

The cost of attaining a particular goal is said to be the sacrifice from the necessity for giving up or compromising other objectives. Thus, the measurement of accomplishment is in terms of goal attainment, and the cost of such accomplishment is the sacrifice of other goal-accomplishing potential. Rules and procedures for recognizing goal attainment belong to the area of revenue recognition, and corresponding guidelines for recording objectives compromised or sacrificed belong to cost recognition and accounting.

[30] Further evidence that this is considered a purchase can be garnered by comparing the two rules given in the *Accountants' Handbook*. When considering the trade-in of used equipment for new equipment (Sec. 16, p. 4), they say that ". . . the cost of the new asset would be the *market value* (not book value) of the asset given up." By contrast, when considering the acquisition of used inventory and the sacrifice of new inventory (Sec. 12, p. 60), it is suggested that the acquisition be valued at its ". . . estimated cash purchase price." Thus, when the item being traded is "inventory" to the firm, the acquisition is independently valued, but when it is "equipment," the sacrifice is independently valued. It appears, then, that equipment acquisitions are purchases and inventory dispositions are sales.

These rules are either contradictory or incomplete. The problem may be most vividly demonstrated by considering an exchange in which equipment is acquired and inventory is sacrificed. If the two rules are intended to apply to this case, then the exchange is both a purchase and a sale. Therefore, the independent valuation of the equipment is both required and prohibited, the valuation of the inventory at market is both required and prohibited, and, under one interpretation, the realization of a gain is both required and prohibited. If the two rules are not intended to apply to this exchange, then the set of rules is incomplete because no other rule is provided to cover this exchange.

[31] For example, Meigs, Johnson and Keller, pp. 521–24, in their discussion entitled "Trade-ins and Exchanges" present three different ways of valuing the sacrifice, but they do not consider the possibility of independently valuing the acquisition.

[32] Bulletin 43, p. 38.

ing this distinction. The application of this criterion, however, requires the resolution of two subsidiary questions.

Book Value vs. Fair Market Value. If the sacrifice is selected for independent valuation, we must choose between book value and fair market value. The reader will note that in the examples given in the previous sections, the book value of the sacrifice in a purchase was equal to the fair market value, or, in the case of liability creation, there was no previous book value and the independent valuation created the book value. For example, when cash is sacrificed, its book value is equal to its fair market value and no choice is required. In barters, the book value of the sacrifice is likely to be different from the fair market value. When there is a difference, we are forced to choose between the book value and the fair market value as the "independent value" of the sacrifice.

The majority view is that the cost of the acquisition is equal to the fair market value of the sacrifice. The reasons given for selecting the fair market value are, at best, cursory. As indicated above, we think that selecting the fair market value of the sacrifice violates the more general and the more basic rules of historical cost valuation. Thomas has surveyed the literature and presented twenty arguments ". . . in favor of the realization rule and against the recognition of unrealized appreciation. . . . "[33] The reader is invited to compare those twenty rules to the practice of valuing the sacrifice at fair market. To do so violates virtually every one of the arguments in favor of the realization rule. For this reason, we conclude that the decision to value the sacrifice at its fair market value is in error. Within the general framework of historical cost accounting, we would agree with *Montgomery's Auditing* when it says that setting the value of the acquisition equal to the "carrying [book] value" of the sacrifice is "sound practice."[34]

Relative vs. Absolute Liquidity. Following the rules given in the previous section, any time the acquisition was more liquid than the sacrifice, the exchange would be valued like a sale and a gain would be permitted. Another view is that the acquisition must pass a certain threshold of liquidity prior to a gain being permitted. Thomas' summarizations of the realization rules contain the phrase "conversion of nonmonetary items into monetary items."[35] Following this rule, the acquisition must be in the monetary class before a gain could be realized. Ijiri states it directly when he says that in exchanges of goods in the nonbasic class, the acquisition shall be set equal to the value of the predecessor.[36] The acquisition must be in the basic class before a gain could be realized. Thus, the choice of criteria is between the *relative* liquidity of the two goods involved in the exchange and the *absolute* level of liquidity of the acquisition. If the relative liquidity rule were adopted, there could be an exchange of two illiquid goods and the accountant would be forced to independently value the acquisition at its fair market value if it were less illiquid than the sacrifice. For example, if a building were acquired in exchange for land, the relative liquidity rule would require that the accountant independently value the building (assuming that it is more liquid than the land) at its fair market value. A gain would be realized if the fair market value of the building were greater than the book value of the land. This procedure does not seem to be in the spirit of the realization notion, although it is not so conspicuous a violation as the majority rule.

If the absolute liquidity rule were followed, there could be an exchange in which the liquidity of the two goods was significantly different but no gain would be

[33] Thomas, p. 30.
[34] *Montgomery's Auditing*, p. 244.
[35] Thomas, pp. 10–12.
[36] Ijiri, p. 94.

recognized. Consider the acquisition of marketable securities in exchange for land. Since marketable securities are usually dependently valued at their cost, they are not in the monetary or basic class. Thus, the value of the marketable securities would be set equal to the book value of the land. This also does not seem to be in the spirit of the realization notion.

Another difficulty would be encountered in trade-ins. If the firm were trading old for new delivery equipment, the absolute liquidity rule would require that it be recorded as a purchase. Since the firm as a whole is becoming less liquid to the extent of the boot, we think this is proper. That is, we think the "tax method" of recording trade-ins is consistent with the general rules of historical cost valuation, and the "accounting method" violates those rules. However, when we consider recording the exchange on the books of the firm which deals in delivery equipment, there are problems. From the viewpoint of that firm, it looks more like a sale than a purchase, since the firm is becoming more liquid to the extent of the boot and since the firm is disposing of its inventory. Yet, the absolute liquidity rule would prohibit gains and require that this also be recorded like a purchase. That is, since the used equipment is not in the monetary or basic class, it could not be valued independently. Instead, it would be valued at the difference between the cash received and the book value of the new equipment. If trade-ins on used equipment were common, this procedure could result in zero values for the used units and therefore, in effect, the "cash basis" of accounting.[37]

Summary

In recording barters, there are three possibilities for selecting the good to be independently valued:

(A) always value the acquisition,
(B) always value the sacrifice, or
(C) select the (C_1) acquisition or (C_2) sacrifice for independent valuation on some grounds, such as ease of determination or liquidity.

In cases (B) and (C_2) there is the possibility of independently valuing at either

(1) book value or
(2) fair market value.

In cases (A) and (C_1) no book value exists and therefore independent valuation is at fair market.

In cases (B, 1) and (C_2, 1) there is no difference in values and therefore no concern about realization. In cases (A), (C_1), (B, 2) and (C_2, 2), there may be a difference and we have the choice of recording that difference as

(α) realized, or
(β) unrealized.

The majority view is (B, 2, α), or, the valuation of the sacrifice at its fair market value and the realization of a gain. Since this treatment violates the general rules of historical cost-realization accounting, we believe that it is in error. In any of the cases where there is a difference between the book and fair market values, it is possible to treat the difference as unrealized. However, we did not find anyone who suggested that treatment and there-

[37] For example, if $1,500 cash and used unit A were acquired in exchange for a new unit with a cost (book value) of $2,000, the entry would be:

Cash	1,500	
Used Unit A	500	
New Unit		2,000

Since used unit A is not in the monetary or basic class, it could not be independently valued. It would be dependently valued as the difference between the independent values of the cash and the new unit. Now, if $500 cash and used unit B were acquired in exchange for used unit A, the entry would be:

Cash	500	
Used Unit B	-0-	
Used Unit A		500

For the same reasons, used unit B would be valued at the difference. Then, on all subsequent exchanges, the gain would be equal to the cash received, i.e., the cash basis of accounting with zero book values assigned to used units C, D, . . . , N.

fore, we will neglect consideration of that possibility.[38]

For monetary-monetary and interclass exchanges, the general rules are $(C_1, 2, \alpha)$ and $(C_2, 1)$. It is possible to extend this rule to barters and thereby recognize a gain any time the acquisition is more liquid than the sacrifice—the relative liquidity rule. An alternative is to require that the acquisition attain a certain level of liquidity—the absolute liquidity rule. Thus, we have a choice. We can extend the relative liquidity rule to barters or we can treat all barters as purchases, i.e., $(B, 1)$.

Both rules present problems. The relative liquidity rule may result in a gain being realized upon the acquisition of the highly illiquid good. The absolute liquidity rule would prohibit gains upon the acquisition of a highly liquid good and, in some cases, it would revert to the cash basis of accounting. Neither of the rules is strictly implied by the principles of historical cost valuation. In extreme cases, both seem to violate the spirit of those principles, even though neither violates the letter of those principles.

Regardless of which rule is selected, there is still a need for the valuation preference array. We still need a rule which would allow us to recognize a gain when cash is acquired in exchange for an account receivable. We still need a rule which would specify that cash be independently valued and the value of a note payable be set equal whenever cash is acquired in exchange for a note. Thus, the monetary or basic items still need to be arrayed by the accountant's preference for valuation. However, if the absolute liquidity rule is accepted, the valuation preference array would be truncated after arraying the monetary or basic items. All nonmonetary or nonbasic items would be considered equal in liquidity. Whichever rule is selected, there needs to be an explicit listing of the valuation preference array. In the absence of that listing and in the absence of the explicit statement of the rule, the theory is incomplete.

Conclusions

The explicit theory of historical cost accounting is stated as if all exchanges involved a monetary and a nonmonetary good. Given the evolution from the cash basis to the accural basis, this is understandable. The cash basis theory provided rules for cash exchanges. The accrual basis is simply an extension of the cash basis in that near-cash is included in the class of monetary or basic goods and rules are provided for exchanges of monetary and nonmonetary goods. In the same way that the cash basis did not provide rules for exchanges which did not involve cash, the accrual basis does not provide rules for intra-class exchanges. Since intra-class exchanges occur, the explicit theory is incomplete.

Exchanges within the monetary class cause few problems because they usually involve cash, i.e., they are species of exchanges such as "collections" (of receivables) or "payments" (of payables). One can simply apply the cash basis rules to exchanges of this type. In barters, however, confusion reigns. Different authors present different rules and the majority rule violates the more fundamental rules of historical cost accounting.

From the fact that on the cash basis the cash is independently valued and that on the accrual basis the monetary goods are

[38] Note that when write-ups were permitted, they were considered to be unrealized and were usually titled something like "appraisal surplus." Since the independent valuation of the sacrifice at its fair market value may be thought of as a write-up, we were surprised when we did not find anyone who even considered the possibility of recording the difference as unrealized. It would seem that $(B, 2, \beta)$ would be "more consistent" with the general valuation rules of accounting, in that it would violate the notion of historical cost but would not violate the notion of realization. The majority view $(B, 2, \alpha)$ violates both.

independently valued, the hypothesis was adduced that the accountant preferred to independently value the more liquid good and to dependently value the less liquid good. The direction of the flow provides a basis for distinguishing purchases from sales. This distinction also provides definitions for "cost incurrence" and "revenue realization."

In regard to barters, however, we were unable to decide whether the criterion should be the relative liquidity of the two goods involved in the exchange or the absolute liquidity of the acquisition. Our inability to choose between these criteria on theoretical grounds should not come as a surprise. The choice requires a precise definition of realization, and therefore it raises all of the long unresolved questions about separation of income from capital, distributability of the acquisition, and objectivity. Our inability to choose between the criteria lends support to Sprouse and Moonitz's observation that the "concept [of realization] lacks analytical precision."[39] We would only add that, since the concept of cost is inextricably entwined with the concept of realization, the concept of cost also lacks analytical precision.

We think that the implicit ranking of goods by liquidity pervades accounting thought and practice. For example, in the species of exchanges called "investments," the normal rule is to independently value the assets and set the capital account equal. In most examples of investment transactions, the assets invested are in the monetary class. However, if the securities of the firm are publicly traded and the acquisition is nonmonetary, it is likely that the more liquid securities would be independently valued and the value of the less liquid acquisition set equal. Thus, the selection for independent valuation is made on the basis of liquidity. In acquiring shares of another firm in exchange for cash, the treatment is, upon consolidation, to independently value both the acquisition (at book value) and the sacrifice (at face value). Since the exchange is a purchase, i.e., the sacrifice is more liquid than the acquisition, the difference between the values is classified as "consolidated surplus" (not a realization) or "goodwill." Thus, in structure, the entry is identical to the compound form of the entry to record the acquisition of cash in exchange for inventory. The treatment is to independently value both the acquisition (at face value) and the sacrifice (at book value). Since this is a sale, the difference in values is classified as a realized "gain" or "loss." The only structural difference in the two entries is the direction of the flow of liquidity.

The current controversy over business combinations provides another example. "Purchase" accounting is an apposite name for the proponents of one school because they focus on the value of the "consideration" as the appropriate measure of the "cost." Such terms as "funny money" indicate that they are implicitly applying a liquidity criterion. They believe that the types of securities sacrificed are close substitutes for money, and *therefore* the exchange ought to be treated as a purchase, i.e., the value of the acquisition ought to be set equal to the independently determined value of the sacrifice. The pooling proponents take the view that the acquisition ought to be independently valued and the capital account set equal. The similarity of purchase-pooling to barters even extends to the controversy over fair market value versus book value. Since Catlett and Olson[40] deduct the goodwill

[39] Robert T. Sprouse and Maurice Moonitz, "A Tentative Set of Broad Accounting Principles for Business Enterprises," *Accounting Research Study No. 3* (American Institute of Certified Public Accountants, 1962), p. 15.

[40] George R. Catlett and Norman O. Olson, "Accounting for Goodwill," *Accounting Research Study No. 10* (American Institute of Certified Public Accountants, 1968), p. 90.

from net worth, they are, in effect, independently valuing the acquisition at fair market and setting the net worth equal. Others would independently value the acquisition at book value.

Thus, we believe that the *concept* of the valuation preference array is now being implicitly applied to all types of interentity exchanges. This is, in part, an empirical hypothesis concerning the way that accountants act. A test of this hypothesis is now being conducted by Richard E. Flaherty. However, this paper has been concerned more with the logic of the historical cost system than with the way in which accountants act. It has been demonstrated that some decision rule is necessary to the system. We believe that a valuation preference array based on liquidity is consistent with that system and that it captures and generalizes the property common to several individual rules.

Note that these points are separable in the sense that the validation or invalidation of one point does not necessarily validate or invalidate the others. For example, one could accept the idea of a valuation preference array but reject the idea that it is based on liquidity, or one could accept the logical necessity and consistency of an array based on liquidity but reject the hypothesis that accountants implicitly or explicitly make their decisions on the basis of such an array.

Finally, it should be reiterated that the purpose of this paper was to discover and describe the rules of historical cost valuation and to cast those rules in a logically consistent system. It was *not* an attempt to evaluate the system *vis a vis* other valuation systems. One could argue that fair market values should be recorded at barter regardless of the flow of liquidity. We have avoided this argument because it immediately leads into an evaluation of historical costs and the controversy over current values versus historical costs. The goal of this paper has been to make the historical cost system more explicit and precise, not to defend or criticize that system.

Exchange Valuation: An Empirical Test

Robert R. Sterling, John O. Tollefson and Richard E. Flaherty

THIS paper presents the results of an empirical test of hypotheses which were developed in a previous paper.[1] The hypotheses are concerned with describing certain aspects of the conventional (historical cost) theory, as opposed to evaluating that theory vis à vis competing theories. The purpose of this test is to discover how practicing accountants would record particular situations and thereby attempt to infer the de facto, as opposed to the de jure, generally accepted accounting principles.

In the following section, we will summarize the considerations which led to the hypotheses.[2] The remainder of the paper will be devoted to describing the test and the results.

Background

The conventional theory is stated as if all exchanges resulted in the acquisition or sacrifice of cash or near-cash. It dichotomizes accounts as monetary versus nonmonetary and provides explicit rules for two general types of exchanges:

Type A: Acquire monetary and sacrifice nonmonetary.
Type B: Acquire nonmonetary and sacrifice monetary.

Type *A* exchanges are referred to as "sales" and type *B* exchanges are referred to as "purchases." The associated valuation rules are:

Sale Rule: Independently value the acquisition and impute the difference between that value and the book value of the sacrifice to a realized gain (loss) account.
Purchase Rule: Independently value the sacrifice and impute that value to the acquisition.

For example, if cash or a receivable is acquired, it is "independently valued" (at or near market or face value) and the difference between that market value and the book value of the sacrifice is the realized gain. The rule for exchanges in the opposite direction is symmetrical, except that gains are not permitted. If cash or a payable is sacrificed it is "independently valued" (at or near market or face value) and that value is imputed to the acquisition. For asset/asset exchanges of type *B*, the market value of the sacrifice is equal to its book value and therefore the purchase rule may be restated as:

We wish to express our thanks to the American Institute of CPAs for a grant to cover the survey costs, to the University of Kansas Computation Center for computer services and to Oklahoma State University Research Foundation for released time for Richard E. Flaherty.

[1] Robert R. Sterling and Richard E. Flaherty, "The Role of Liquidity in Exchange Valuation," THE ACCOUNTING REVIEW (July 1971), pp. 441–56.

[2] For a more complete description of these considerations, see Sterling and Flaherty; and Robert R. Sterling, *Theory of the Measurement of Enterprise Income* (University Press of Kansas, 1970), Chapters XI and XII.

Robert R. Sterling is Arthur Young Distinguished Professor and John O. Tollefson is Associate Professor of Business Administration at the University of Kansas. Richard E. Flaherty is Assistant Professor of Accounting at Oklahoma State University.

> *Purchase Rule:* Impute the book value of the sacrifice to the acquisition.

Since we will be concerned with only asset/asset exchanges in this paper, we will refer to this restatement as the purchase rule henceforth.

These rules are consistently applied when type *A* and type *B* exchanges occur. These exchanges may be referred to as "interclass exchanges." The problem is that the conventional theory does not explicitly provide the premises necessary to deduce a rule for valuing "intraclass exchanges." That is, within the confines of the conventional explicit theory there is no way to determine whether an intraclass exchange should be classified as a purchase or a sale and therefore there is no way to determine which valuation rule is applicable. Thus, we believe that the conventional explicit theory is incomplete. For this reason, we expect to observe a greater variation in the recording of intraclass exchanges than in the recording of interclass exchanges or no-exchange situations.

Despite the absence of explicit criteria in the conventional theory, accountants do in fact record intra-class exchanges. Thus, implicit criteria must exist. It would be desirable to discover these criteria and make them explicit. An explicit statement of the conventional system is a necessary prerequisite to an informed evaluation of that system. Thus, this study should assist in an evaluation of the current system, in addition to furthering theory development. In Sterling and Flaherty it was argued that one such implicit criteria is the liquidity of the two goods being exchanged. Specifically, it was argued that accountants prefer to independently value the more liquid good and to impute this value to the less liquid good or account. In addition, it was argued that the direction of the flow of liquidity provided the implicit criteria for distinguishing purchases and sales. Two possible interpretations of the purchase/sale distinction were considered: (1) when the acquisition reaches some *absolute* level of liquidity, classify the exchange as a sale, otherwise classify it as a purchase; (2) whenever the acquisition is *relatively* more liquid than the sacrifice, classify the exchange as a sale, and when the flow of liquidity is reversed, classify it as a purchase. For barters we were unable to decide which interpretation was correct.

Both the preference for independently valuing the more liquid good and the relative liquidity criterion for distinguishing purchases and sales seem to be consistently, albeit tacitly, applied in monetary/monetary and interclass exchanges. However for barters (nonmonetary/nonmonetary exchanges) a majority of accounting authorities[3] endorse the following mixed rule:

> *Majority Rule:* Value sacrifice at market and impute that market value to the acquisition. Impute the difference between the market value and the book value of the sacrifice to a realized gain account.

We call this rule "mixed" because it resembles the purchase rule in that it imputes from sacrifice to acquisition, but it resembles the sale rule in that it results in an upward revaluation of total assets and a realized gain.

A minority of authorities have endorsed the purchase rule. None have endorsed the sale rule. Also none of the authorities have endorsed a rule which classified the gain as unrealized.

Both the majority and minority considered their endorsed rule to be applicable to *all* barters. That is, they did not allow for the selection of different rules in different situations. We believe that this is an error in the sense that it does not describe generally accepted accounting principles. We think that the liquidity criterion per-

[3] For references to these authorities see Sterling and Flaherty.

vades the conventional theory, despite the fact that it is not explicit, and therefore we expect to observe a "liquidity effect" in the valuation of barters.

We hypothesize that the liquidity effect will manifest itself in two ways: First, the direction of the flow of liquidity will affect practitioners' selections of the valuation rule to be applied. Second, given a choice of recording the market value of two assets of unequal liquidity, there will be a tendency for practitioners to select the market value of the more liquid asset.

Note that both of these hypotheses are in direct opposition to the pronouncements of both the majority and minority of accounting authorities. That is, the authorities endorse one rule for all barters without regard to the direction of the flow of liquidity, and the majority rule specifies that the sacrifice shall be valued at market without regard to the relative liquidity of the two assets.

In addition, we believe that purchase and sale are the fundamental classifications for valuation purposes in the conventional theory and that practitioners will attempt to fit barters into these classifications by analogy. If this is true, the characteristics of the valuation rules will allow us to predict tendencies of practitioners. Specifically, the characteristics of the sale rule are upward revaluation, realization of a gain and independent valuation of acquisition at market. Thus, revaluation and realization are associated with the independent valuation of the acquisition at market in the sale rule, as opposed to being associated with the valuation of the sacrifice at market in the majority rule. We expect to observe an "acquisition effect" in barters in that when revaluations or gains occur, there will be a tendency to independently value the acquisition instead of the sacrifice.

Finally, conservatism is often listed as one of the basic concepts of accounting. Its effect seems to pervade the whole of the present theory and some authors believe that the historical cost method of valuation is, in the main, an outcome of conservatism.[4] For this reason, we believe that, given the choice between two values to be recorded for a particular asset, there will be a tendency to select the smaller value. Thus, we expect to observe a "conservatism effect" in the valuation of barters.

In summary, from an a priori examination of the conventional theory we offer the following hypotheses:

1. Incompleteness: the explicit theory is incomplete in regard to intraclass exchanges and therefore we expect to observe variation among practitioners in recording those exchanges.
2. Liquidity Effect: the classification of the exchange and the selection of the asset to be valued at market, other things being equal, will be affected by the relative liquidity of the two assets.
3. Acquisition Effect: if revaluation or realization of a gain occurs, other things being equal, accountants will tend to independently value the acquired asset.
4. Conservatism Effect: given the choice of assigning two values to an asset, other things being equal, accountants will tend to choose the lower of the two values.

Questionnaire Design

Seventeen different questionnaires, describing three different cases (and different situations in two of the cases), were designed and mailed to a random sample of CPAs. The cases described may be outlined as follows:

Case A Interclass exchange

Case B Intraclass exchanges:

Situation B_1 Land acquired/stock sacrificed:

[4] See Sterling, *Enterprise Income*, Chapter XI.

Questionnaires B_{11}–B_{15} Market value of stock varied
Situation B_2 Stock acquired/land sacrificed:
Questionnaires B_{21}–B_{25} Market value of stock varied
Case C No exchange:
Situation C_1 Stock held:
Questionnaires C_{11}–C_{13} Market value of stock varied
Situation C_2 Land held:
Questionnaires C_{21}–C_{23} Market value of land varied

Each questionnaire presented the respondent with a choice of several values. They were asked to select the value that is "in accordance with generally accepted accounting principles." When the selected value permitted the possibility of a gain they were asked to classify it as realized or unrealized.

Case A questionnaire described a simple stock for cash exchange. The five values presented were: (1) high; (2) close (middle) and (3) low prices of stock on the day of the exchange; (4) quoted price and (5) quoted price plus the commission.

Case B described an exchange of stock and land. Seven value choices were presented: (1) original cost; (2) high, (3) close (middle) and (4) low price of stock on the date of exchange; and (5) high, (6) middle and (7) low appraised value of land near the date of exchange. In order to test the effect of the direction of the exchange, half the questionnaires (B_1) in Case B described the acquisition of land and the sacrifice of stock, and the other half (B_2) reversed the asset acquired and the asset sacrificed. The original cost of the sacrificed asset (stock or land) and the appraised value of the land were held constant in all questionnaires in this group. In order to test the effect of the magnitude of the values on the response, the market values of the stock were varied by the same amounts in B_1 and B_2.

Thus, all values in B_{1i} are the same as those in B_{2i}; the only difference is the reversal of the sacrifice and acquisition. All conditions in B_{i1} are the same as $B_{i2}, \cdots, B_{i5}$ except for the variation in the market values of the stock. The specific values are given in Table 1.

Table 1

Questionnaire Values for the Intraclass Exchange Case
(000 omitted)

Values			*Applicable Questionnaires*
Book value of sacrifice (stock or land):		$5	B_{11}–B_{25}
Appraised value of land:			
High	*Low*	*Middle Value*	
$485	$475	$465	B_{11}–B_{25}
Market value of stock:			
High	*Low*	*Close*	
$453	$447	$450	B_{11}, B_{21}
463	457	460	B_{12}, B_{22}
477	472	476	B_{13}, B_{23}
493	487	490	B_{14}, B_{24}
503	497	500	B_{15}, B_{25}

In a pilot run of the questionnaires 25 CPAs who were recruiting on campus were asked whether stock or land "is more liquid." Of these, 23 replied that stock is more liquid. The other two said, in effect, that it depends on the circumstances. When put in the context of stock traded on the New York Stock Exchange, as described in the questionnaires, 24 classified stock as "significantly more liquid" than land and one replied that it is "probably more liquid." From these results, it appears that practitioners share our perception of which asset is more liquid and therefore we classify stock as more liquid than land in testing the liquidity effect. Despite the fact that the practitioners consider the stock to be more liquid, when we asked them why they had selected a particular valuation rule none of them mentioned liquidity or any related concept.

Case C described the holding of an asset where the original cost is less than the market value. Four value choices were presented: (1) high, (2) middle (closing price for stock) or (3) low market value, and (4) original cost. In an attempt to determine if the kind of asset held had any effect on the value selected, half of the questionnaires described the holding of stock (C_1) and the other half the holding of land (C_2). In order to determine if the magnitude of the difference between market and cost affected the responses, the market values were varied by the same amounts in C_1 and C_2.

One hundred of each questionnaire were mailed. The mean effective response rate was 53.9 percent with a low of 39.4 percent and a high of 68.8 percent.

Variation Among Cases

We believe that the present theory is complete in regard to interclass exchanges and no-exchange situations. As a consequence, we expect to observe little variation in the responses to questionnaires describing Cases A and C. By contrast, we believe that the theory is incomplete in regard to barters and therefore we expect to observe significantly more variation in the responses to the questionnaires describing Case B.

Table 2 displays the percentage of respondents, by case, who selected a market value (as opposed to those who selected a cost or book value) and the percentage who classified the gain as realized.

Table 2

Variation in Responses

Cases	*Selected Market Value*	*Realized Gain*	*Total Number of Respondents*
A (interclass)	0%	0%	57
B (barter)	77%	69%	464
C (no-exchange)	2%	0%	335

None of the respondents selected a market value in Case A and thus there was no possibility of recording a gain, either realized or unrealized. The only variation in the responses to Case A was occasioned by the capital versus expense decision for ancillary costs. Of 57 respondents, 5 (9%) selected the quoted price (implicitly expensing the commission) and 52 (91%) selected the quoted price plus the commission. Both of these values would be classified as a "cost method of valuation," but the variation does indicate a need for more precisely defining "cost."

Of the 335 respondents to Case C, 329 (98%) selected the original cost of the asset and 6 (2%) selected a market value. Of the 6, all classified the gain as unrealized. The small number of respondents who revalued makes it impossible to test the effects of the asset held and the difference between market and cost. However, it appears that neither had any effect: three revalued land and three revalued stock; two revalued (stock) in the smallest difference case, one revalued (land) in the middle difference case, and three revalued (1 stock, 2 land) in the greatest difference case.[5]

By contrast, in Case B the respondents were divided on both the value selection and the gain realization. Of the 464 respondents, 356 (77%) were agreed on a market value (either stock or land) as compared to almost 100 percent who were agreed on a cost in Cases A and C. Of the total respondents to Case B, 69 percent would show a realized gain, as opposed to 100 percent who would not in Case C.[6]

We interpret the small variation in responses to Cases A and C as evidence that

[5] Out of curiosity we asked the respondents to indicate whether or not they personally agreed with the GAAP covering this situation. Of the 328 respondents who answered this question, 266 (81%) expressed agreement and 62 (19%) expressed disagreement. Thus, it appears that although virtual unanimity exists concerning the applicable GAAP, a substantial minority (19%) disagrees with those GAAP.

[6] The unrealized group consisted of 38 respondents who selected a market value but classified the gain as unrealized, plus the 108 respondents who selected a book value and therefore precluded the possibility of a gain. Thus, only 11 percent of the market value group did not realize a gain. Those who did not realize were evenly distributed among the various questionnaires and therefore no distinction is made between realized and unrealized in the subsequent analyses.

both the interclass and no-exchange cases are relatively well defined in the conventional theory. The greater variation in Case B may be due to incompleteness of the theory, or to differences in the situations described. We consider this question in the next section.

Barter Analysis

The variation in the responses to the barter questionnaires could be the result of two things: differences in the implicit criteria being applied and/differences in the situations described. That is, different practitioners could, in effect, hold different conventional theories. If so, we would expect response variation from the application of *different* criteria. On the other hand, all practitioners could hold the same theory but this theory could specify that barters be recorded in different ways in different situations. If so, we would expect response variation from the application of the *same* criteria. In either event, it would be desirable to make these criteria explicit.

In an attempt to determine the cause of the response variation and to identify the criteria, discriminant analyses[7] were performed on the data from the barter questionnaire. The objective of these analyses was to measure the degree to which the valuation rule selected by an individual depends upon the situational variables. If we find that we can perfectly predict a practitioner's valuation treatment from the situation, then we can conclude that the situational variables (e.g., direction of flow of liquidity) are the sole cause of the response variation. That is, the practitioners are applying the same criteria but these criteria specify different valuation rules in different situations. If, on the other hand, the valuation rule cannot be perfectly predicted from the situation, then the degree of failure to predict is a measure of the extent to which different criteria are being employed by different practitioers.[8]

The Test

In the analyses responding practitioners were placed into "response groups" depending upon their valuation of the transaction. We attempted to predict valuation response, or "group membership," from the variables reflecting differences in the situation. The three variables employed to reflect differences in situations are: (1) I/O, (2) $P_S - P_L$, and (3) $P_O - P_I$. The variable I/O is a dichotomous variable indicating the direction of flow of the items involved in the exchange. It has the value 0 when land is sacrificed and stock is acquired and the value 1 when stock is sacrificed and land is acquired. $(P_S - P_L)$ is the average market price of the stock less the average appraisal value of the land. $(P_O - P_I)$ is the average market value of the sacrificed (outgoing) asset less the average market value of the acquired (incoming) asset. Table 3 summarizes the number of valuation responses observed for each combination of these situational variables.

Some of the discriminant analyses were addressed to three valuation response groups and others considered only two valuation response groups. A valuation re-

[7] Two standard references on discriminant analysis are T. W. Anderson, *An Introduction to Multivariate Statistical Analysis* (John Wiley & Sons, Inc., 1958) and C. R. Rao, *Advanced Statistical Methods in Biometric Research* (John Wiley & Sons, Inc., 1952). A somewhat less mathematically demanding, yet thorough, discussion may be found in H. C. Fryer, *Concepts and Methods of Experimental Statistics* (Allyn & Bacon, Inc., 1966). The analyses were performed using programs described in W. J. Dixon, ed., *BMD Biomedical Computer Programs* (University of California Press, 1970), and available through the program library of the University of Kansas Computation Center.

[8] This test has a direct bearing on the incompleteness hypothesis. If we find that we can perfectly predict from the situation, then we can conclude that the de facto theory is complete and the problem lies wholly within the realm of the de jure theory. Following the anthropological method of accounting theory construction, we could rectify the incompleteness of the de jure theory by simply codifying the predictive relationships. See Robert R. Sterling, "On Theory Construction and Verification," The Accounting Review (July 1970), pp. 444–57, for a discussion of the anthropological method of accounting theory construction.

TABLE 3
NUMBER OF VALUATION RESPONSES OBSERVED FOR EACH SITUATION

	Situational Variables		
I/O	P_S-P_L (000)	P_O-P_I (000)	*Number of Observations*
1	−25	−25	37
1	−15	−15	45
1	0	0	42
1	15	15	46
1	25	25	57
0	−25	25	46
0	−15	15	48
0	0	0	48
0	15	−15	45
0	25	−25	50

sponse group consists of all respondents who utilized a particular valuation method (e.g., imputation of book value of the asset sacrificed to that acquired). Each of the analyses proceeded in generally the same way. First, we attempted to determine whether the different valuation groups occupy significantly different positions in a multidimensional space, the axes of which correspond to the situational variables. The null hypothesis in each test was that each group constitutes an independent random sample from one underlying population. That is, we hypothesized that differences in the situation do not significantly affect the valuation method employed (group membership). If this hypothesis is not true, of course, we would expect to find the valuation groups at significantly different locations when plotted against the situational variables.

The second part of each analysis was concerned with measuring the extent to which valuation response group membership can be predicted from the situational variables. That is, given a particular situation, how accurately can we predict which valuation method will be employed? In the three-group analyses, this was accomplished through the development of classification functions which compute the posterior probability of group membership from the prior probability (the relative frequency of membership in that group for the sample) and the situational variables. In the two-group analyses, this was done through the development of a linear discriminant function of the situational variables.

In all analyses, a split-sample method was used to determine the predictive power of the situational variables. Half of the observations in each group were utilized as an analysis sample, from which the coefficients for the appropriate functions were estimated. The functions were then tested on a validation sample consisting of the other half of the observations. This split-sample procedure was necessary because the ability of discriminant functions to predict group membership within the body of data from which the functions are developed tends to overstate the true predictive power. Thus, subsequent statements about the fraction of respondents correctly classified are based upon the performance of the functions when applied to the "fresh" data of a validation sample.

The Results

Initially, two three-group analyses were performed, viz., (1) book value versus market value of land versus market value of stock, and (2) book value versus market value of acquisition versus market value of sacrifice. In both analyses we found that we could reject the null hypothesis of no situational difference between groups. Consistent with that result, we also found that we could predict overall group membership significantly better than chance. However, the predictive ability varied considerably within the groups. In the first analysis, we would expect to predict group membership correctly by chance for 38.8 percent and the classification functions performed significantly better ($\alpha < .01$), correctly predicting for 50.2 percent of the entire sample. But, only 26 percent of the Book Value group were correctly classified, whereas

64.4 percent of the Market Values Land group and 56.4 percent of the Market Value Stock group were correctly classified. In the second analysis, we would expect to predict group membership correctly by chance for 36 percent; and here too the classification functions performed significantly better than chance ($\alpha<.01$), correctly predicting for 54.1 percent of the entire sample. But again, only 11.1 percent of the Book Value group were correctly classified whereas 85.4 percent of the Market Value Sacrifice group and 56 percent of the Market Value Acquisition group were correctly classified.[9] Thus, it appeared that the predictive ability lay wholly within the Market Value group and that the Book Value group was not responsive to the situational variables.

To determine whether this was the case, we discontinued the three-group analyses and split the respondents into two groups consisting of those who chose a book value versus those who chose a market value (regardless of whether it was stock or land, acquired or sacrificed).

A test for separation was performed on, and classification functions developed from, an analysis sample of 54 book value and 177 market value responses. The null hypothesis that these two valuation groups are independent random samples from the same underlying population cannot be rejected ($F_{2,228}=0.3688$, for which $\alpha>0.5$). This lack of separation is confirmed by application of the classification functions to the validation sample in an attempt to predict group membership. The results are given in the confusion matrix in Table 4.

The classification functions correctly predict group membership for 121 (51.9 percent) of the 233-respondent validation sample. If the respondents were randomly classified, we would expect to correctly classify 114.7 (49.2 percent). Thus, the classification functions do not predict significantly better than chance ($\alpha=.18$).

TABLE 4
BV, MV VALIDATION SAMPLE CONFUSION MATRIX[a]

Actual Group Membership	Predicted Group Membership:		
	Book Value	*Market Value*	*Total*
Book value	31	23	54
Market value	89	90	179
Total	120	113	233

[a] The number of respondents who actually occupied a particular group is given in the total column. The number of respondents who were predicted by the classification function to select a valuation method is given in the respective cells. Thus, in regard to Table 4 54 respondents actually selected a book value and the classification predicted 31. A total of 121 (31+90) were correctly predicted in this table.

We conclude from these analyses that the tendency to apply the Purchase Rule (impute book value sacrificed to the asset acquired) does not depend upon the situational variables that we have considered. That is, a minority of the respondents classified the described barter as a purchase without regard to the relative liquidity of the two assets, which asset was acquired or sacrificed, or the differences between the market values of the assets. In the same way that a minority of accounting authorities classify all barters as purchases, it appears that a minority of practitioners record all barters as purchases.

This means that the response variation noted in the previous three-group analyses is due to different practitioners applying different criteria. In effect, there is more than one conventional theory. It also means that for the Book Value group we did not observe the liquidity, acquisition and conservatism effects that we hypothesized.

MARKET VALUE GROUP ANALYSIS

The previous analyses indicated that the Market Value group was highly responsive

[9] The test used to determine whether group membership was predicted significantly better than chance across all three groups is that given by Frederick Mosteller and Robert R. Bush, "Selected Quantitative Techniques," in *Handbook of Social Psychology*, ed. by Gardner Lindzey (Addison Wesley, 1954), pp. 307–11.

to the situational variables but that the Book Value group was not. For this reason, we decided to exclude the Book Value group and concentrate on the role played by the situational variables in the choice of valuation rule within the Market Value group. Discriminant analyses, as described in the previous section, were utilized for this purpose.

Market Value of Stock versus Market Value of Land

A test for separation was performed for two groups, consisting of 85 responses showing a preference for market value of land and 271 indicating a preference for market value of stock responses. The null hypothesis is that these two groups are independent random samples from the same underlying population. A generalized measure of the distance between the two groups, which reflects the degree to which they are separated, is provided by the Mahalonobis D^2 statistic. For these groups, located in a space having the variables I/O and $(P_S - P_L)$ as axes, $D^2 = 0.811$, which is significantly different from zero ($F_{2,223} = 26.16$, for which $\alpha < .01$). Thus, we may reject the null hypothesis. Preference for either valuing land or stock at market definitely depends, at least in part, upon the situation surrounding the exchange.

In measuring the predictive power of the situational variables, a linear discriminant function was developed from the analysis sample and applied to the validation sample to provide an unbiased measure of the ability to predict valuation response (group membership). This procedure yielded the confusion matrix shown in Table 5. Application of the discriminant function enabled us to correctly classify 133 (75.1 percent) of the 177-respondent validation sample. If the 177 respondents were randomly classified, we could expect 113 (63.8 percent) correct classifications. Thus,

TABLE 5

MARKET VALUE OF LAND, MARKET VALUE OF STOCK CONFUSION MATRIX
(Number of respondents)

Actual Group Membership	*Predicted Group Membership*		
	Market Value of Land	*Market Value of Stock*	*Total*
Market value of land	20	22	42
Market value of stock	22	113	135
Total	42	135	177

the discriminant function allows us to predict significantly better than chance ($\alpha < .01$).

Another means of gauging the predictive power of the situational variables is provided by regression of a dummy variable for group membership on I/O and $(P_S - P_L)$. This regression yields a multiple correlation coefficient $R = .3593$, which is significantly different from zero. Thus, about 13 percent (R^2) of the variability in group membership is "explained" by a linear relationship with I/O and $(P_S - P_L)$.

Since the choice of valuation rule does depend in part upon the situation, there is value in examining the role played by each variable. The linear discriminant function is:

$$Z = .00396(I/O) + .0000928(P_S - P_L).$$

This function was developed from the entire sample, since, in considering the relative importance of each variable, more reliable results may be achieved by utilizing all of the data. Higher values of Z are associated with membership in the "market value of land" group ($\bar{Z}_1 = .00616$) and lower values of Z are associated with membership in the "market value of stock" group ($\bar{Z}_2 = .00387$). The positive coefficient for I/O indicates a tendency to value the acquisition instead of the sacrifice. The positive coefficient for $(P_S - P_L)$ indicates a tendency to value conservatively.[10]

The magnitude of the coefficient b_j, in the discriminant function above of the form $Z=b_1(I/O)+b_2(P_S-P_L)$, does not reflect the importance of the jth variable in discriminating between the two groups. We favor a measure of relative importance, used by Mosteller and Wallace,[11] given by:

$$b_j(\overline{X}_{j1}-\overline{X}_{j2}),$$

where $\overline{X}_{jk}$ is the mean of the jth variable for the kth group. This quantity is the portion of the discriminant score separation between the two groups, $\overline{Z}_1-\overline{Z}_2$, which is attributable to the jth variable. These are presented in Table 6.

Although they do not indicate relative discriminating power, the discriminant function coefficients in standardized form are included in Table 6 for the interested reader. For the jth variable, the standardized coefficient is:

$$b_j^* = b_j\sigma_j,$$

the change in the linear discriminant function score, Z, produced by a one standard deviation change in the jth variable.

TABLE 6

RELATIVE IMPORTANCE OF I/O AND (P_S-P_L) IN DISCRIMINATING BETWEEN THE MARKET VALUE OF LAND AND THE MARKET VALUE OF STOCK

Variable	*Coefficient*	*Standardized Coefficient*	*Relative Importance*
I/O	.00396	.001982	.00129 (56%)
P_S-P_L	.0000928	.001736	.00100 (44%)
			.00229*

* $(\overline{Z}_1-\overline{Z}_2)$.

It does not appear that the variables differ greatly in relative importance. About 56 percent of the separation achieved between the two groups may be attributed to the I/O variable and about 44 percent may be attributed to the (P_S-P_L) variable. In summary, it appears that a tendency to value the acquisition and a tendency to value conservatively play nearly co-equal roles as partial determinants of a valuation procedure.

Market Value of Sacrifice versus Market Value of Acquisition

A test for separation was also performed on the two groups consisting of 137 who imputed the market value of the sacrifice to the asset acquired and 219 who valued the acquisition directly at its market value. As to be expected from the grouping, the (P_O-P_I) variable was the more effective situational variable. In fact the (P_S-P_L) variable was completely ineffective in discriminating between these two groups.

The degree of separation was determined by testing the null hypothesis that these two groups are independent random samples from the same underlying population. The generalized Mahalonobis distance between the two groups in a space having the variables I/O and (P_O-P_I) as axes is $D^2=2.08$, which is significantly different from zero ($F_{2,353}=87.46$, for which $\alpha\doteq 0$). Thus, the null can be rejected. These two groups are apparently more distinct, situationally, than are the market value of stock and the market value of land groups.

Development of a linear discriminant function from an analysis sample and application of the function to a validation sample yielded the confusion matrix shown in Table 7. Application of the discriminant function to the validation sample of 177 respondents led to the correct classification of 135 (76.3 percent). If respondents were randomly classified, we would expect to correctly classify either 88.1 (49.8 percent) or 93.5 (52.8 percent), depending upon our detailed assumptions about what is meant

[10] "Value conservatively" means to select the lower market value in this context. It would be much more conservative to use the book value.

[11] Frederick Mosteller and David L. Wallace, "Inference in an Authorship Problem," *Journal of the American Statistical Association* (June 1963), pp. 275–309.

by "randomly classified." The performance of the discriminant function is significantly better than either ($\alpha \doteq 0$).

To provide another indication of the predictive power of the situational variables,

TABLE 7
MARKET VALUE SACRIFICE, MARKET VALUE OF ASSET ACQUIRED CONFUSION MATRIX
(Number of respondents)

Actual Group Membership	Predicted Group Membership		
	Market Value of Sacrifice	*Market Value of Asset Acquired*	*Total*
Market value of sacrifice	58	10	68
Market value of asset acquired	32	77	109
Total	90	87	177

a dummy group membership variable was regressed on I/O and $(P_O - P_I)$. This regression yielded a multiple correlation coefficient $R = .5756$, which is significantly different from zero. Thus, about 33 percent (R^2) of the variability in group membership is "explained" by a linear relationship with I/O and $(P_O - P_I)$.

Turning our attention to the role played by each of the situational variables, the linear discriminant function is:

$$Z = .0095(I/O) - .0000928(P_O - P_I),$$

where higher values of Z are associated with membership in the market value of the sacrifice group ($\bar{Z}_1 = .00589$) and lower values of Z are associated with membership in the market value of the acquisition group ($\bar{Z}_2 = .00001$). The positive coefficient for I/O indicates a tendency to value the more liquid asset instead of the less liquid asset, since use of the market value of the sacrifice becomes more likely when stock is the sacrifice ($I/O = 1$). The negative coefficient for $(P_O - P_I)$ indicates a tendency to value conservatively.

Measures of relative importance like those employed previously and standardized forms of the coefficients are presented in Table 8. Liquidity (I/O) is a much more important factor than is conservatism ($P_O - P_I$). Nearly 90 percent of the discriminant score difference between the two groups is attributable to the liquidity variable. Stated another way, of the 33 percent variability which can be "explained" by a linear relationship with I/O and $(P_O - P_I)$,

TABLE 8
RELATIVE IMPORTANCE OF I/O AND $(P_O - P_I)$ IN DISCRIMINATING BETWEEN THE MARKET VALUE OF THE SACRIFICE AND THE MARKET VALUE OF THE ASSET ACQUIRED

Variable	*Coefficient*	*Standardized Coefficient*	*Relative Importance*
I/O	.00950	.004756	.00527 (90%)
$P_O - P_I$	−.0000928	−.001734	.00061 (10%)
			.00588*

* $(\bar{Z}_1 - \bar{Z}_2)$.

about 29 percent is attributable to the liquidity variable (I/O). The other 4 percent which is "explainable" can be attributed to the conservatism variable ($P_O - P_I$).

Interaction of Effects

The questionnaires can be grouped in various ways to indicate the interaction of the liquidity, acquisition and conservatism effects. In some questionnaires all of these effects are working in concert while in others they are counteracting. An examination of these effects provides evidence complementary to and aids in the interpretation of the results of the discriminant analyses.

Questionnaires B_{21} and B_{22} describe the acquisition of stock when the market value of the stock is less than the market value of the land. Thus, the liquidity (L), acquisition (A) and conservatism (C) effects are all working in concert toward the selection of the market value of the stock. Of the market value respondents to these two questionnaires, 97 percent chose the market value of the stock. In Figure 1 we label these effects "LAC."

Questionnaires B_{11} and B_{12} describe the acquisition of land when the market value of the stock is less than the market value of the land. Thus, the liquidity and conservatism effects point toward the selection of the market value of the stock but the acquisition effect is contrary. Of the market value respondents to these two questionnaires, 87 percent selected the market value of the stock. In Figure 1 we label these effects "LÃC."

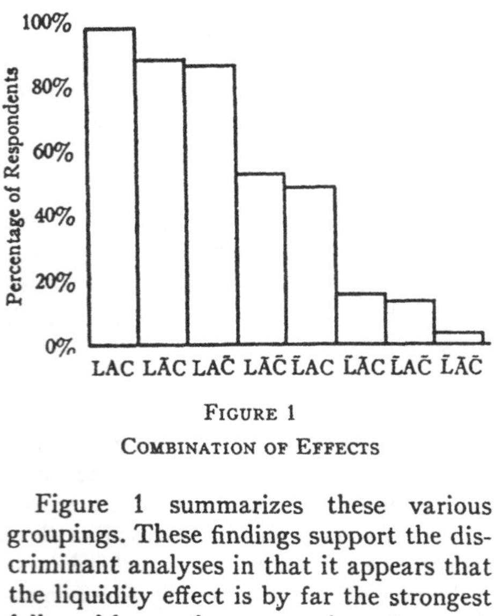

FIGURE 1
COMBINATION OF EFFECTS

Figure 1 summarizes these various groupings. These findings support the discriminant analyses in that it appears that the liquidity effect is by far the strongest followed by weaker, approximately equal, conservatism and acquisition effects. More importantly, when all three effects are working in concert we observe 97 percent agreement which is about equal to the agreement that we observed in the no exchange case. In addition, of the 72 market value respondents to these two questionnaires, 67 selected the middle (equal to the closing price) value of the stock. Thus 93 percent are agreed on the particular market value which is about equal to the 91 percent agreement on a particular cost value observed in the cash exchange case.

SUMMARY AND CONCLUSIONS

The comparison of the responses in the barter case to those in the cash exchange and no exchange cases revealed significantly more variation in the barter case. This could be interpreted as evidence that the conventional theory is incomplete. The discriminant analyses provided more direct evidence. First, in the book value versus market value analysis we were unable to predict group membership from the situational variables. It appears that a minority (23 percent) of practitioners hold that the purchase rule (Book Value group) should be applied to barters without regard to the situation. A majority (77 percent) hold that either a sale or majority rule (Market Value group) should be applied to barters. This division may be interpreted as the existence of two different conventional theories. Second, although we were able to identify a liquidity, acquisition and conservatism effect, the majority of the total variance remained unexplained.[12] This may be interpreted as indicating that other implicit criteria exist which we have not identified.

Within the Market Value group, liquidity, acquisition and conservatism had a marked effect, particularly when all three were working in concert. In that case we observed virtual unanimity in the re-

[12] It might be suspected that more variance could be explained, or the predictive power of the situational variables could be more completely manifested, by the use of nonlinear functions. To explore this possibility we performed analyses parallel to all the foregoing, introducing additional variables corresponding to several transformations of (P_S-P_L) and (P_O-P_I) (e.g., square, reciprocal, square root, logarithm). There is no opportunity to improve fit by utilizing nonlinear transformations of I/O since it is a dichotomous variable. None of the analyses utilizing transformations yielded more predictive relationships. Thus, we are reasonably confident that the linear functions reported above embody virtually all of the predictive power of the situational variables.

sponses. However, when the variables were counteracting there was more variation in the responses. This may be interpreted as evidence that different weights are being assigned to the three variables by different practitioners. That is, assuming that there are only three variables, then the summation of the three should yield approximately 100 percent agreement, regardless of the weight attached to each. However, when the variables are counteracting, different assignments of weights will yield different sums. Apparently this is what we observed in the Market Value group. If so, we can conclude that we have identified all of the variables which affect practitioners' responses, but that different practitioners assign different weights to these variables.

Thus, all of the evidence supports the incompleteness hypothesis, either in the sense of more variation in responses or different theories or different weights. In one theory (Market Value group) the evidence indicates that we have identified all the relevant situational variables and the variation is due to the assignment of weights.

In both Sterling and Flaherty and this paper we have endeavored to be neutral in regard to historical cost versus competing valuation schemes. However, we would be remiss if we did not point out that over two-thirds of the respondents selected a market value in the barter case while only 2 percent did so in the no-exchange case. Thus, there is a strong "exchange effect" operating in the conventional theory. That is, an exchange seems to be both a necessary and sufficient condition for valuing at market in one version of the conventional theory. We do not understand why an exchange is considered to be a sufficient condition. Consider this:

Case 1: Firm A holds stock and Firm B holds land. Neither firm can revalue at market because the market value is not objective and verifiable, the market value is not trustworthy because it may go down in the future and the increment is not in a distributable form to pay taxes or dividends. When a barter occurs the result is:

Case 2: Firm A holds land and Firm B holds stock. Since Case 2 is identical to Case 1 in all respects except one, it would seem that all the arguments would apply with equal force. That is, the only difference between Case 1 and Case 2 is the *firm* that holds the particular assets. Thus, insofar as consistency within the conventional theory is concerned, we do not think that an exchange should be considered to be a sufficient condition for valuing at market. Of course, one could argue for a market value on the grounds of relevance or fairness of presentation, but this would raise the question of why an exchange is a necessary condition. That is, if the market value is relevant or fair at the event of an exchange, why is it not relevant or not fair in the absence of an exchange?

STATEMENTS IN QUOTES

"ACCOUNTING POWER"

Excerpts from a talk by Robert R. Sterling, CPA, Arthur Young Distinguished Professor at the University of Kansas, prepared for the Distinguished Lecture Series at Oklahoma State University, March 16, 1972, and published in the July 1972 issue of The Oklahoma CPA

• • •

Accountants were not much more than specialized craftsmen, i.e., bookkeepers, when an almost overwhelming responsibility was rather suddenly thrust upon them. They switched from bookkeeper to independent auditor. As auditors they were required to make public what had been previously jealously guarded private information. They were asked to make independent judgments about the affairs of persons who had previously directed their activities. They were asked to provide information via a device that had previously been used to misinform or conceal. They were required to have integrity when deceit was not uncommon.

As an independent auditor, the accountant needed a strong defense against the always optimistic, sometimes dishonest, financiers and entrepreneurs. Unfortunately, he was not given this defense. Instead, he was placed in the precarious position of being the employee of the person he was obliged to keep honest. In the absence of a cohesive theory, in the absence of police power, in the presence of ignorance and apathy of the community, his only defense was precedent and persuasion. Precedent soon became rule and the rigid application of rules was his primary weapon. It is much easier and more diplomatic to accuse someone of breaking a rule than to accuse him of telling a lie.

INDEPENDENCE

I originally expressed the above thoughts about ten years ago.[1] At that time they raised the hackles of a great many people. My critics said that I was casting doubt upon the independence of auditors and that independence is the keystone of the profession. By casting doubt upon the keystone, I was, according to my critics, casting doubt upon the professional status of accountants. My critics stated that the independence of accountants was beyond question and that my criticism was, therefore, irresponsible. The only result that could come from such criticism, they said, would be detrimental to the profession.

• • •

Accountants have defined independence to be a state of mind. Then, within the community of accountants, we have reassured ourselves that our minds are independent and that, therefore, there is no problem. However, my reading of *The Wall Street Journal, The New York Times, Business Week, Forbes*, etc., has convinced me that although we have persuaded ourselves, we have not persuaded the rest of the world.

• • •

Consider the most famous accountant in English literature—Bob Cratchit. As Scrooge's bookkeeper, there is no question about the lack of independence of Bob Cratchit. Scrooge was the boss, he had all the power and Bob Cratchit did as he was told. I expect that if Scrooge had directed Cratchit to record some cash receipts as debits and others as credits, Cratchit would have complied without a murmur. You will recall that *A Christmas Carol* was published in 1843 and that, although Dickens probably exercised literary license, his depiction of Cratchit in a subservient role is an accurate one. Now compare the date of the publication of *A Christmas Carol*—1843—to the date of the rise of auditing in England. Sir Harold Howitt[2] tells us that the professional public practice of accounting in England changed from being concerned primarily with bookkeeping to a preoccupation with auditing in about the middle of the nineteenth century. Given this information, we can write a sequel to *A Christmas Carol*. It was on Christmas Eve of 1843 when Cratchit was Scrooge's bookkeeper. It is now Christmas Eve of 1850 and Cratchit has switched from bookkeeper to "independent" and "professional" public accountant. Cratchit has completed his examination and approaches Scrooge.

Cratchit: Good day to you, Mr. Scrooge.

Scrooge: Bah! Humbug!

Cratchit: I notice here that you have been capitalizing development costs. I believe that those should be expensed.

Scrooge: Bah! Humbug!

Cratchit: I note that your parent company has been lending money to affiliates and that these affiliates have been in turn lending money to you. Unless you are willing to guarantee the loans, it seems clear that the affiliates cannot repay their loans to the parent company. In those circumstances, I don't think we could show these receivables as assets.

Scrooge: Bah! Humbug!

Cratchit: I have here a number of other adjustments on my worksheet. Consider adjustment number three.

Scrooge: Bah! Humbug!

Cratchit: Consider adjustment number four.

Scrooge: Bah! Humbug!

Later that night . . .

Cratchit: Consider adjustment number n.

Scrooge: Bah! Humbug!

---

[1] See Robert R. Sterling, *Theory of the Measurement of Enterprise Income* (University Press of Kansas: Lawrence, 1970), pp. 255-56.

[2] Sir Harold Howitt, ed., *The History of the Institute of Chartered Accountants in England and Wales 1870-1965* (London: Heinemann, 1966), p. 4.

At some point Cratchit will have to consider the options open to him. Those options are clear. Cratchit can:

1. Swallow his convictions and give Scrooge a clean opinion,
2. Refuse to express an opinion, or
3. Resign.

Usually, the refusal to express an opinion is equivalent to resignation. You will have to tune in next week to find out which course of action Cratchit selected. In the meantime, however, you might consider the following factors: Cratchit has four mouths to feed at home and his wife is pregnant. His son, Tiny Tim, is a cripple and is in desperate need of an operation. Will Cratchit swallow his convictions and grant a clean certificate or will he stand on principle? Will he let his economic straits and his love for his family affect his professional judgment?

Conflict of Interests—1850

Now, you and I know what Cratchit will decide. We know that independence is a state of mind and that Cratchit is mentally independent. Even though cynical sociologists would cite this as a classic case of conflict of interests, we know that Cratchit is an accountant and, therefore, he cannot feel any such conflicts. On this basis, Cratchit will decide to deny an opinion to Scrooge.

Let me now give you a preview of next week's episode. After Cratchit has decided to disclaim an opinion, but before Cratchit has told Scrooge of his decision, Cratchit learns that Joe Softnose, CPA, has been invited to make a presentation to Scrooge. Softnose has never denied a clean opinion to a client. Cratchit is now faced with the following problem: if Cratchit denies Scrooge a clean opinion, Softnose will issue him a clean opinion. The net result of Cratchit's standing on principle will be that Scrooge will get the opinion and Softnose will get the engagement.

Again, you and I know what Cratchit will decide. The literature keeps telling us that independence is a state of mind and that Cratchit is mentally independent. Therefore, it is clear that Cratchit will decide that virtue is its own reward. The fact that Scrooge will get an opinion anyway does not affect his judgment. Thus, Cratchit is fired, Softnose gets the engagement, Scrooge gets the clean opinion and Cratchit gets a feeling of virtue.

All fairy tales must have a happy ending. This is no exception. The textbooks tell us that Cratchit's reputation will be built by this incident and that, although he loses this engagement, he will get many bigger and better engagements in the future. However, since I am the author of this particular fairy tale, my happy ending is different. As Cratchit is walking home, dejected, and wondering what he is going to tell his wife and Tiny Tim, the Great Bookkeeper in the Sky swoops down and crossfoots all of Cratchit's working papers and inducts him into the accounting hall of fame.

Research Topics

Of course, my critics will immediately point out that the above is a fairy tale and that, although this may have been true in 1850, it is not true in 1970. In order to meet this anticipated criticism, I would like to share with you a letter that I recently received. Prior to discussing that letter, however, let me give some background.

Lanny Chasteen recently published a piece[3] in which he demonstrated that the revered notion of "differences in circumstances" as a justification for using different accounting techniques is pure hokum. That is, as you know, when we accountants discuss the existence of alternative accounting techniques, we have argued that like events ought to be accounted for in the same way and that unlike events ought to be accounted for in different ways. Thus, the existence of differing circumstances calls for the existence of different accounting techniques. Now Lanny went out and proved that this is hokum. He examined a bunch of different firms that used different accounting techniques and tried to correlate them with the differing circumstances in those firms. He found that there was no correlation. I think that is a very significant piece of research. Rich Flaherty recently took a look at the role of liquidity in exchange valuation.[4] I thought Rich's paper was excellent. (My evaluation of Rich's paper—the fact that I think that it is excellent—is based upon an *independent* judgment of mine. That is, whenever I made the evaluation of Rich's paper, I was mentally independent and, therefore, I was completely unaffected by the fact that I was a coauthor of that paper.)

The point that I wish to contrast here is that although I think such subjects as differing circumstances and liquidity are interesting and significant, my practitioner friends have a different idea. Many of them chide me about my research interests. They say that the issues that I research are of the wrong kind. There is a gulf between academics and practitioners because practitioners believe that academics should research an entirely different type of problem than that which we actually study. This difference has come to light in regard to the colloquies that have been held at the University of Kansas. Practitioners have attended these colloquies and the reaction of several of them has been that the papers presented were addressed to the wrong kinds of issues. This has resulted in some lengthy correspondence between me and several practitioners. I have attempted to find out what kinds of issues practitioners think that we academics ought to investigate. There has been a general theme followed by a number of these letters. This theme is most succinctly summed up in a letter from a particularly thoughtful practitioner.

Conflict of Interests—1972

In his letter he describes a company "that is diversifying and quite obviously is interested in making a name for itself as well as showing continued growth and continued earnings." He describes the chief executive as "a volatile individual whose chemistry has frequently reacted adversely to our representatives." This chief executive "had published preliminary operating results and in effect had established an earnings amount that put pressure on the company accountants . . . to seek to attain the operating results which he had forecast."

In short, the auditor is faced with a very ambitious, perhaps dishonest, Scrooge who is trying to build his fame and fortune.

The letter from the practitioner continues: "As we approached the wind-up of this engagement we found

[3] Lanny G. Chasteen, "An Empirical Study of Differences in Economic Circumstances as a Justification for Alternative Inventory Pricing Methods," *Accounting Review* (July 1971), pp. 504-08.

[4] Robert R. Sterling and Richard E. Flaherty, "The Role of Liquidity in Exchange Valuation," *Accounting Review* (July 1971), pp. 441-56.

ourselves confronted with three very significant problems, namely:

"1. In starting up new businesses the company has sought to defer development costs. . . .

"2. A significant number of audit adjustments which the company should make were developed during the course of the work, but the . . . [chief executive] was very adamant about considering recording these adjustments.

"3. Substantial advances had been made to certain affiliated companies which were owned by the chief executive. These companies had in turn made rather substantial advances to the chief executive for his personal use. These companies were also in a development stage and consequently did not have the financial substance to repay the advances to the lending company unless the chief executive who had financial substance would guarantee the amounts."

These are the *kinds* of issues that my practitioner friends would like us academics to consider. All right, let us consider them. It seems clear to me that the development costs should not have been capitalized. Everyone that I have talked to agrees with me on this issue. The practitioner also agreed that the development costs should not have been capitalized as is indicated by the fact that he thought that this was a problem. The practitioner also managed to convince the chief executive that these development costs should be expensed and the entries were in fact reversed.

That would seem to settle the case. Unfortunately, it did not. The result of expensing the development costs was that the company showed a net loss instead of a net income. Now the chief executive argued that this net loss ought to be capitalized as a start-up cost. As you know, this is sometimes done in accounting. The practitioner notes this in his letter. He states: "In seeking to find a solution to these problems, illustrations in actual practice were found where companies in the development stage had deferred start-up costs including initial operating losses until such time as the businesses became profitable. . . ." Insofar as I am concerned there is even less justification for capitalizing these losses than there was for capitalizing the development costs. The whole thing appears to me to be a sham.

• • •

The chief executive of this firm is saying, in effect: "I have lost money this year, but I expect to make money next year and now what I want to do is to defer my loss of this year so that I can show a gain for both years." . . . It seems to me that the theoretical issue is clear cut: the loss should not be capitalized.

The particular adjustments mentioned in (2) were not described by the practitioner so there is no way for us to consider the theoretical issues there. In regard to (3) the issue is cut and dried. The chief executive is causing the parent company to loan money to affiliates and these affiliates in turn are advancing money to the chief executive for his personal use. This situation borders on fraud. Neglecting the fraudulent aspects, we can just look at the notes themselves. As my practitioner friend states delicately, "These affiliates do not have the financial substance to repay the notes." In plain English, these notes are worthless. What does one do with worthless notes? Obviously, one writes them off. Then, what is the problem? What is the theoretical issue involved here that this practitioner wants us to examine?

The answer seems to be that, despite the fact that his letter was written this year instead of in 1850, this practitioner faces the same problem that Bob Cratchit faced. I noted above what Cratchit's options were. I am now ready to confess that I stole that statement of options from another practitioner—namely, Leonard Spacek. Spacek writes, ". . . which courses are open to the public accountant in certifying the statements, assuming the difference is material? He can (1) swallow his convictions, or (2) he can qualify his opinion on the basis of his own convictions or (3) he can resign. Usually the latter two courses are one and the same."[5]

Competition

In the same way that Cratchit had to consider the possibility of Joe Softnose taking over the account, this practitioner must consider the same problem. Although we accountants keep reassuring each other that there is no competition among accounting firms and that particularly there is no competition regarding standards, I present for your consideration an excerpt from *The Wall Street Journal*:

"Companies of course, can change CPAs for a variety of reasons and sometimes changes can be frequent. In 1958, the accounting firm of Arthur Andersen & Co. handled the accounts of Alaska Juneau Gold Mining Co. and . . . included many qualifications in its certification of the annual report. The next year the company had a new auditor, Arthur Young & Co. . . . Arthur Young handled Alaska Juneau until 1961, when it listed at length two major qualifications in its certification of the annual report. The next year the company . . . changed again, this time to Haskins & Sells. That firm saw no need for qualifications in the 1962 report."[6]

If you like, you can continue to believe that practicing accountants are supermen and do not consider such things whenever they make their decisions. However, I am afraid, since I am a mere mortal, that if I were to make such decisions, I would consider my competition. If I knew that I was going to lose an engagement by qualifying a report and that my competition would not qualify the report so that the net result would be that the company gets an unqualified opinion and my competition gets the fee, I must confess that I would weigh that fact whenever I made my decision.

THE PROBLEM

A prerequisite to the solution of a problem is the recognition of the existence of that problem. My purpose in going through the previous discussion is to try to demonstrate that a problem exists. Most of the literature that I read is in the nature of a fairy tale. In this literature we continue to reassure ourselves that no problem exists. Although we believe these fairy tales, it appears that nonaccountants do not believe them. There is, in fact, a problem and the reason this problem has existed for over one hundred years is that we have failed to recognize or admit that it is a problem.

Specifically, the problem is that the accountant has been given a responsibility without concomitant author-

[5] Leonard Spacek, "The Need for an Accounting Court," *Accounting Review* (July 1958), p. 371.

[6] *Wall Street Journal*, November 15, 1966, p. 1.

ity. His responsibility far outweighs his authority. Let us consider the responsibility and authority in turn.

Responsibility

I expect that there will be little disagreement in regard to the overwhelming responsibility of the accountant. The dean of the Harvard Law School [Erwin N. Griswold] has compared the accountant to a judge in these words: "In performing this [audit] function, the accountant acts in a very real sense *judicially*. He must decide questions, and he must be wholly free to decide questions against his client's interest if his investigation and judgment lead him to that conclusion."[7] If anything, Griswold has understated the case. The judicial system has divided responsibilities. Codified laws are provided by legislatures, the jury decides questions of fact, and the judge decides questions of law and equity. All of these functions are rolled into one in the accounting case. The auditor must first decide on questions of fact such as the number of units of inventory and the costing of those units. Analogous to deciding on questions of law, the accountant must decide which principles are applicable or acceptable. Analogous to questions of equity, the accountant must present the information so that it is fair to all segments of society. It has also been traditional for theory to come from practice and, thus, the practitioner has the burden of developing the theory—he does not have a legally constituted legislature to help him draft authoritative principles. Finally, the accountant realizes that his is the ultimate decision; he has no system of appellate courts to correct his errors. Worse, when a lower court judge errs, he is simply reversed by an appellate court. The lower court judge is not held liable for his errors. By contrast, when the court finds that an accountant has erred, the accountant has been held liable for those errors.

Authority

In the history of law Maine tells us: "Whenever in the records of very ancient societies, . . . we come upon a personage resembling him who we call the King, he is almost always associated with the administration of justice. . . ."[8] Maine goes on to tell us that judge and king are almost synonymous in many early societies. The authority of a king is unquestioned, and judges have either been kings or representatives of kings and, therefore, the authority of a judge from the earliest time has been equivalent to that of a king. The authority of judges in today's society is equivalent to the authority of the state. When necessary, judges can call upon the police or even the militia to enforce their rulings.

Compare the authority of accountants. Their main weapon is precedent and persuasion. Wise writes that senior partners of accounting firms ". . . devote most of their time to what might be called 'diplomacy'—e.g., persuading clients that furniture cannot be written off in two years. . . ."[9] Evidence that diplomacy or persuasion is their primary weapon also comes from the language that practitioners use. They often speak of the difficulty of "selling a troublesome adjustment." That is, when the auditor finds an error in the books or a misapplied principle that requires an adjustment, he must sell the management on the idea of making the adjustment. Can you imagine a judge in a criminal case being required to sell the defendant on the idea of going to jail? Can you imagine a judge in a civil case being required to persuade the loser to pay off? Judicial opinions end with the words, "So ordered," and there is a vast difference between ordering someone to do something and persuading him to do it.

Persuasion or diplomacy is not the accountant's ultimate weapon. Whenever things really get rough he can pull out his heavy guns. If a client refuses to go along with what the accountant has decided, the accountant can resign. His ultimate weapon is resignation and, hence, silence. That is, note that despite the fact that we have in recent years instituted the possibility of an adverse opinion, when things get really bad the accountant does not issue an adverse opinion. Instead, he resigns from the engagement. The result of a resignation from an engagement is that the accountant does not issue any opinion at all—i.e., he is silent. Now, again, compare this to a judge. Can you imagine a judge, failing to persuade the defendant to go to jail, resigning?

• • •

Whenever we examine the situation in this light, and recognize the precarious position that the practitioner has been put in, I hope you will join with me in admiration of the practitioner. There are two ways of looking at the state of accounting: logically and sociologically. When I logically examine the structure of accounting theory, I am depressed by how bad things are. By contrast, when I sociologically examine the structure of the accounting profession, particularly the balance of responsibility and authority, I am impressed by how well the practitioner has done. Whenever we consider the accountant's overwhelming responsibility and his almost compete lack of authority, I applaud the practitioner for the number of times that he does stand on principle. I do not condemn him for those occasions when he rationalizes his way to issuing a clean certificate.

The Profession's Response

There is some evidence that the profession has recognized the imbalance of responsibility and authority. I have not been able to find any direct evidence of this recognition in a search of the literature. Instead, the evidence is indirect. If we put someone in a position in which his responsibility outweighs his authority, we could expect him to try to move toward a proper balance. There are two ways of trying to move toward a proper balance: (1) increase the authority or (2) decrease the responsibility. Many of the things that the profession has tried to do in recent years can be interpreted as the second course of action, i.e., a decrease of responsibility.

As a minor example, consider the substitution of the word "examination" for the word "verification" in the auditing literature. Statement on Auditing Procedure No. 33 says that we ought to substitute "examination" for "verification,"[10] and since examination is obviously a weaker term, this could be interpreted as an at-

[7] Erwin N. Griswold, "The Tax Practice Problem I," JofA, Dec.55, p. 31, emphasis added.

[8] Sir Henry Maine, *Early Law and Custom*, 1886, Ch. 6, p. 160.

[9] T. A. Wise, "Part I: The Auditors Have Arrived," *Fortune* (November 1960), p. 157.

[10] Committee on Auditing Procedure, AICPA, "Auditing Standards and Procedures," Statement on Auditing Procedure No. 33 (AICPA, 1963), p. 94.

tempt to lessen the responsibility of the auditor. As another example, consider the change in the wording of the opinion. It used to be that the opinion stated that financial statements presented a "true and correct view of the financial condition of the company." We have now substituted the weaker statement that the statements are presented in accordance with generally accepted accounting principles. Legal scholars have noted the attempt to avoid responsibility for the truth of the statements by changing these words and have openly questioned whether or not the courts will allow it. The accepted dictum that the statements belong to management and are the responsibility of management is another bit of indirect evidence that accountants have been trying to lessen their responsibility by placing the responsibility upon management. Whether it is management or the public accountant that is ultimately responsible for the financial statements has been questioned in the legal literature, as well as in the accounting literature.[11] Finally, Alexander, an economist, states the proposition directly:

"Another very powerful factor operating on the development of accounting methods has been the attempt to reduce the accountant's responsibility for the human judgments which must be made in passing from a consideration of the accounts to the conduct of business affairs. This attempted avoidance of responsibility has led accountants to. . . ."[12]

These examples are included in an attempt to demonstrate that accountants have recognized the imbalance of responsibility and authority, not to criticize the profession. It seems to me that if a person is put in a position where his responsibility outweighs his authority, it is quite legitimate for him to try to reduce that responsibility. However, it is also clear that the courts are not going to allow us to take this course of action. The decisions that have been handed down in recent years have had the effect of assigning more responsibility to the accountants. No case that I am aware of has lessened the accountant's responsibility. Two recent cases—*Continental Vending* [*U.S.* v. *Simon*] and *Pacific Acceptance* [*Pacific Acceptance Corporation Ltd.* v. *Forsythe and Others*]—have added significantly to the accountant's responsibilities. As I read these cases, the courts are telling us that we can no longer defend ourselves on the basis of accepted accounting theory and practice. Instead, we must assure ourselves that the statements are true, correct and understandable by nonaccountants.

If this interpretation is valid, it seems clear that there is only one other course of action open to us. Since we cannot lessen the responsibility and since the responsibility outweighs the authority, we must increase the accountant's authority.

Interpreting the History of Accounting

Many people have wondered why it is so difficult to agree upon a set of accounting principles. They cannot understand why we cannot reform accounting in the sense of establishing a fairly clear-cut theory or set of principles. Moonitz has examined this question in a very important, but unfortunately neglected, article by the name, "Why Is It So Difficult to Agree Upon a Set of Accounting Principles?"[13] A logical examination of this question will fail to yield an answer. However, a sociological examination —an examination of the power structure—will yield an answer.

Consider the following bit of history. At the turn of this century several famous names in accounting were writing texts and monographs. On several fundamental issues Hatfield, Dickinson, Montgomery, Esquerré and others were in agreement at least in regard to the essentials. These people wrote at the turn of the century. Moving up to the 1930's, we can examine the writings of several other famous names in accounting, such as Canning, Gilman, Sweeney and MacNeal. Concentrating on MacNeal, we find him arguing the same points that Dickinson, Esquerré, Montgomery and Hatfield had argued. Since then, there have been a number of other people who have made similar points. Despite this list of illuminaries, we find that the situation in regard to accounting principles in 1972 is much the same as it was in 1902.

• • •

Several principles, such as "diversity among entities" will not stand up to logical scrutiny and there is plenty of evidence that the application of this principle has led people astray. The continued general acceptance of these false principles cannot be explained on the grounds of logic. However, if we view the situation as a power struggle between the accountant and management, the explanation seems obvious.

Moonitz hits the nail on the head when, in this context, he notes that "management as a class has sought to consolidate its power."[14] He views the problem as a power struggle between management and accountants. Managements want such things as diversity and flexibility, and accountants want to tell it like it is. Given the relative power of the two groups, you could predict who won. As Grady says, diversity is a fact of life.[15] He might have said that the reason why diversity is a fact of life is that management wants to apply diverse accounting principles and management has more power than the accountant has.

In short, the lack of progress in agreement upon accounting principles and the lack of ability to institute accounting reforms cannot be explained on the grounds of logic. However, whenever we look at the progress of accounting in the context of a power struggle, the explanation is obvious. The accountant could not reform a deficient theory because the dominant institution opposed that reform.

The corollary of this is that management and accountants have opposing interests. We keep kidding ourselves to the effect that we and management are on the same side. This is a myth. Management wants to win; it wants to show increased earnings; it wants to have a good report card. The objective of the public accountant is, or ought to be, to tell it like it is. Given these opposing in-

[11] See, e.g., Herbert E. Miller, "Audited Statements—Are They Really Management's?" JofA, Oct.64, pp. 43-46.

[12] Sidney S. Alexander, "Income Measurement in a Dynamic Economy," in *Five Monographs on Business Income* (New York: Study Group on Business Income of the American Institute of Accountants [now the AICPA], July 1, 1950), p. 2.

[13] Maurice Moonitz, "Why Is It So Difficult to Agree Upon a Set of Accounting Principles?" *The Australian Accountant* (Nov. 1968), pp. 621-31.

[14] *Ibid.*, p. 629.

[15] Paul Grady, *Inventory of Generally Accepted Accounting Principles for Business Enterprises*, Accounting Research Study No. 7 (AICPA, 1965), p. 33.

terests, it seems clear to me that we ought to get management out of the business of establishing accounting principles, especially when the main principle that they want to establish is one of diversity or flexibility. As noted above, the accountant must act judicially. When one acts judicially, one is judging an event rather than being a participant in that event.

• • •

Managerial accountants and public accountants are adversaries in the same way that the opposing lawyers in a trial are adversaries. We have already seen from Chasteen's investigation[16] that managerial accountants do not select their accounting techniques on the basis of differing circumstances. Since we know that they do not select them upon that basis, we might ask the question, Upon what basis do they select them? If you think that they select accounting techniques on the basis of which one presents most fairly or accurately, you have a more lively imagination than I.

I don't have empirical evidence in support of my hypothesis, as did Chasteen and Cadenhead, but I do have several personal experiences and a rather telling quotation. We all know about the recent debacle in regard to the Penn Central. The vice president and controller was a man by the name of William S. Cook who, on October 5, 1967, wrote a "personal and confidential" memo to David C. Bevan, the chief financial officer of Penn Central. The subject of this memo was another accountant, Charles S. Hill, who was manager of general accounting. The memo recommended that Hill's salary be raised by $2,000. As justification for this raise, Cook said: "His imaginative accounting is adding millions of dollars annually to our reported income."[17] This memo does not refer to the imaginative production, or imaginative marketing, that contributed millions to Penn Central's income. Instead, it refers to the imaginative accounting that contributed millions to the income of Penn Central. Further, note that this memo was from one accountant to another referring to a third accountant. These other accountants not only approved of these practices, they encouraged it by giving this man a raise. As long as managements, including managerial accountants, have the flexibility to do this sort of thing and as long as we permit them to do it, I expect that they will continue to use accounting to show what it is that they want to show.

SUMMARY AND CONCLUSION

The major problem facing public accounting today is its lack of power. First, in comparing the power or authority to the responsibility, we find that the responsibility far outweighs the authority. The public accountant must act judicially but he has not been given the power to enforce his rulings. His ultimate weapon is resignation and silence, which puts him in a conflict-of-interest position. No other profession that I know of is put in a position where it must make economic sacrifices in order to enforce the judgments for which it is responsible. The authority is lessened further by the existence of competition among accounting firms. Resignation from an engagement might be an effective means of enforcement if it were not for the fact that other firms may take the engagement and issue an opinion.

Second, in comparing the power of the public accountant to that of management, we find that management's power far outweighs the accountant's. This imbalance is not undesirable per se. When one considers the fact that accountants must judge managements, however, it is not only undesirable, it is intolerable. It would wreck the legal system if litigants were able to hire and fire judges. It would be equally damaging to the legal system if litigants were able to select from diverse or flexible laws as they saw fit. The same is true in regard to accounting: if accountants are to judge managements, then we must deny managements the power to hire and fire accountants and the power to select from diverse accounting principles as they see fit.

Thus, my practitioner friends were right. I have been researching the wrong kinds of problems. The major problem facing accounting is institutional, not theoretical. Of course, there are defects in the theory of accounting, but these defects cannot be corrected by logic and evidence alone. A prerequisite to theoretical reform is obtaining the power to institute those reforms.

When viewed in this way, we can explain several things in the history of accounting that were previously unexplainable. The lack of progress in establishing principles is due to the relative lack of power, not to inherently unresolvable theoretical problems. Moonitz makes a strong case for this point of view by comparing progress in establishing auditing standards to establishing accounting principles. I suspect that there are many other anomalies in the history of accounting that could be explained in the same way. Another example is the profession's attempt to reduce its responsibility. It seems to me that this attempt is evidence of a tacit recognition of the imbalance of authority and responsibility. The attempt to reduce responsibility was an attempt to bring about a balance. However, the courts have not allowed us to use this means of obtaining a balance; instead, they have thrust more responsibility upon us.

Since the problem is a lack of power and since the reduction of responsibility is not available to us, the conclusion is inescapable: the power of the accountant must be increased.

The question that remains is how to increase the power. It seems to me that there are two major alternatives: (1) by law, i.e., seek power from the government, or (2) by organization, i.e., solidify the profession.

The former alternative doesn't seem to be compatible with the profession's views. Quite the contrary, we often scare ourselves by holding up the specter of "government intervention." One of the common themes in the literature is the threat that if we don't reform, the government will intervene. This threat assumes that all government intervention is bad per se. I believe that assumption to be erroneous and offer the judiciary as a counter example. The judiciary has not been ruined by government intervention. Indeed, it is difficult to imagine the judiciary functioning in the absence of government intervention. Of course, I am referring to the government intervention that resulted in the power of the judiciary to enforce its rulings. On most occasions when we speak of government intervention in accounting, we seem to be thinking of the government's writing a rule book of individual detailed

[16] Chasteen, *op. cit.*; see also Gary M. Cadenhead, "'Differences in Circumstances': Fact or Fantasy?" *Abacus* (September 1970), pp. 71-80.

[17] Peter Binzen and Joseph Daughen, *The Wreck of the Penn Central* (Boston: Little, Brown and Company, 1971), p. 244.

practices. That need not be the form of government intervention. The government could grant power to the CPA to enforce his decisions without specifying the particular decision. This is the way that a judge operates. The government doesn't tell the judge what decisions to make. Instead, it sets him free from conflicts and competition and then gives him the power to enforce his decisions. It is possible for the government to do the same for the CPA.

The second alternative requires that CPAs give up part of their individual independence in order to obtain professional independence. By solidarity they could give the power to their organization, say, the AICPA. The AICPA would then police its ranks and sanction its members. Note that other organizations do this. If a teamster crosses a picket line, two things happen: first he is called a "scab" and second he gets his head busted. A CPA who competes by the flexibility of his accounting principles needs to be called a "bookkeeper" and be sanctioned in some fashion. If you find it unflattering to be compared to the Teamsters Union, perhaps we should compare ourselves to the strongest labor union in the world, namely, the American Medical Association. A surgeon, for example, is subjected to postoperative reviews and, if those reviews reveal too many errors in the application of medical principles, then that surgeon is called a "butcher" and is barred from practicing. If we are going to strengthen public accounting, we need a postaudit review and, if that review reveals too much flexibility in accounting principles, then we need to bar that firm or CPA from future audit engagements.

Which of these alternatives is preferable is an open question. The purpose of this paper has been to attempt to establish the existence of a problem. Once we recognize the existence of the problem, then collectively we can set about deciding on the best course of action for its solution.

Accounting in the 1980's

Robert R. Sterling
Rice University

Introduction

> "To confess ignorance in the face of the future is the tragic duty of all scientific philosophy."
>
> (Reichenbach,[18] p. 404.)

I must begin with what Hans Reichenbach called a tragic duty. I cannot say that I am happy to perform my tragic duty, but I can say that I do so freely. I freely confess ignorance in the face of the future of the accounting profession. I need not tell this audience about the many forces impinging on accounting today. We are buffeted about by the courts, by the disarray of our theory, by new and fragile institutions, by internecine strife, and by a host of other factors. Many of these forces are conflicting, and their strengths are unknown. Forecasting the future of accounting under these conditions is like asking a mathematician to calculate the resultant of a large number of vectors with unknown strengths. It simply cannot be done.*

Thus, we cannot accurately forecast the future. Conversely, if we are to guide our destiny, we cannot avoid forecasting the future. We must conjure up the future

The author thanks Joel Demski, Ted J. Fiflis, and Stephen A. Zeff for their helpful discussions. Professor Zeff also read the entire manuscript and provided valuable comments.

* For this reason, I don't need rule 2.04 to prohibit me from using my name in conjunction with a forecast which may lead to the belief that I vouch for the accuracy of that forecast. It seems to me that that rule gives me two choices: to refuse to vouch for the accuracy of my forecasts or to give this talk anonymously. I choose the latter, and that is the reason I am in disguise.

outcomes or consequences of the various alternative courses of action that are available to us. Then, we must select an alternative on the basis of our preferences for the forecasted consequences (see Sterling[24] for an elementary outline of the decision process). Unless we want to just drift aimlessly, as I sometimes think we have in the past, we must conjure up the consequences of various alternative courses of action and then select the preferred consequence.

In my view, we accountants don't have a very good record in this regard. It seems to me that, for the most part, we have not deliberately and consciously selected one of our alternative courses of action. We don't have a history of guiding our destiny through thoughtful forecasting; instead, the profession as a whole, like the APB, has been engaged in putting out brush fires. We have failed to act until a crisis occurs—such as the Great Depression, a McKesson-Robbins-type financial scandal, or a runaway merger movement—and then we react. We are reactionaries in the technical sense of that term. It is my preference that we accountants begin to *act* rather than *react*. This preference caused me to overcome my trepidations about forecasting and to present this paper about our future—a paper which I expect to be wrong in many details and which I hope to be wrong in its major thrust.

At the outset, I must also confess the method that I have used in thinking about the future of accounting. There are many theories of history—great man, economic determinism, technological determinism, etc.—which could be applied to the problem at hand. Without further justification for my selection, I will simply reveal that I believe that the course of history is primarily determined by the ideology of the participants. That is, I think that the greatest, but not the sole, force in shaping the course of history is ideology or, to use a less rebarbative term, habitual thought patterns. Therefore, my projection of the future of accounting is based on an attempt to trace, understand, and explain the extant habitual thought patterns.

The second method that I employ in forecasting our future is even less sophisticated. I assume that the future will be a continuation of the present. In turn, what we are doing in the present is a continuation of what we have done in the past. Moreover, I believe the historians' argument that we cannot fully understand the present without a knowledge of the past. "[History's function is] to master and understand it [the past] as the key to understanding the present" (Carr,[7] p. 29). For both of these reasons, I feel it necessary to begin with an interpretive history of accounting.*

In short, I assume that the past is prologue. The limitation of this assumption has been clearly stated by Russell[20] (p. 63):

> "The mere fact that something has happened a certain number of times causes animals and men to expect that it will happen again. Thus our instincts certainly cause us to believe that the sun will rise tomorrow, but we may be in no better a position than the chicken which unexpectedly has its neck wrung. We have therefore to distinguish the fact that past uniformities *cause* expectations as to the future, from the question whether there is any reasonable ground for giving weight to such expectations after the question of their validity has been raised."

* By "interpretive history," I mean an attempt to find a framework (or perhaps to impose a framework) for the purpose of trying to understand how or why we moved from point A to point B. An interpretive history may be contrasted to the chronicling of a disconnected set of past events.

Just as the chicken was surprised when it unexpectedly had its neck wrung, we accountants may be similarly surprised. Nonetheless, I cannot forecast such surprises, so I will explicitly recognize my psychological propensity toward thinking that past uniformities will continue in the future. I am certain that my critics will raise the question of the validity of this propensity and point out that I have no reasonable ground for giving weight to such expectations.

By way of a final introductory remark, I must warn you that I will not talk about leases or deferred taxes or other specific accounting procedures. The first reason for this avoidance is that I am unable to forecast the outcome of our current specific controversies.*

The second and more important reason is that I believe that the method utilized to try to resolve these

---

* I have previously forecasted the outcome of specific controversies by the methodology that I am utilizing in this paper. In 1969, for example, I argued that, in general, accountants view accounting as exclusively a calculational process as opposed to an empirical process. I said that the calculational habit of thought would permit some forecasts (Sterling,[25] p. 47):

> "If this conjecture is true—that accounting is viewed as a calculational process with the factors supplied by somebody else —it would partially explain why some suggestions have become accepted accounting practices and others have not. It would also permit some predictions as to which suggestions will become accepted and which will not. For example, price-level adjusted historical costs will become an accepted accounting practice because one can calculate those figures and the index used for the calculation is supplied by somebody else."

When the FASB issued its exposure draft, I thought that my forecast had come true. But this merely indicates the difficulty of forecasting anything in accounting. I failed to take account of such things as the SEC's view, the extent of management opposition, and the lowering of the inflation rate which, as it did in the postwar period, removed the problem from the crisis category. Given this environment, I cannot forecast what is going to happen to the price level adjustment proposal at this time.

specific issues will greatly influence, if not determine, the substance of their resolution. My analogy is science, where the methodology utilized in investigating an area often determines the substantive findings (or lack of findings) of the investigation. Another analogy is provided by the law; it has been cogently argued that the procedure of law-making determines to a large extent the substance of the law (see Fiflis,[8] p. 122). For both reasons, I will be more concerned with the methodological outlook of the accounting profession than with the current controversial topics on the FASB's agenda.

Historical Development of the Habits of Thought

> "The problem of ideology is central to historical—as to all social—understanding. If men govern the rest of nature in virtue of their reason and technological power, they are themselves governed by their beliefs." (Leff,[15] p. 155.)

Accounting has always been a highly practical discipline. It was developed to meet a specific need—the need to "keep track of" one's possessions and activities. It is not unique in the fact that it is practical; the same is true of our most abstract, theoretical academic discipline—mathematics. Kline[14] points out that early mathematics—particularly arithmetic, algebra, and geometry—was developed to meet specific practical, economic problems. Kline writes (p. 11) that early mathematics was used

> ". . . to express lengths and weights, to exchange money and merchandise, to compute simple and compound interest, to calculate taxes, and to apportion shares of a harvest to the farmer, church, and state. The division of fields and inheritances led to algebraic problems. The majority of the cuneiform texts involving mathematics (exclusive of the tables and problem texts) were concerned with economic prob-

> lems. There is no doubt as to the influence of economics on the development of arithmetic in the older period."

Similarly, there is no doubt as to the influence of economics on the development of accounting in both the older period and the recent period. Thus, accounting is not unique in regard to its development to meet specific, practical, economic problems. However, it does seem to be unique in the manner in which it was developed. The process of development seems to have been a major factor in determining its content. Let us consider its development in three stages.

First Stage. Undoubtedly, the first accountant was also the owner and manager of the things that he accounted for. As already mentioned, there was a specific, practical need for accounting. The owner-manager needed a record of his possessions and activities. He needed to be able to explain to himself the changes in his possessions and to predict the quantity and kinds of possessions on hand from his record. The word "account" in ordinary usage still retains this meaning. The owner-manager wanted to "account for" his objects of wealth and the changes therein or to provide an "account of" his economic activities. In order to accomplish this goal, the owner-manager became an accountant—he devised his own individualistic system of record-keeping.

A major purpose of this record was to permit the owner-manager-accountant to communicate with his own past. It was *not* to communicate with other people. Quite the contrary, accounting records from ancient to modern times have contained jealously guarded secret information. Census takers have reported, with great surprise, that it is easier to get people to answer questions about their sexual activities than it is to get them to answer questions about their financial affairs. This finding is not surprising to accountants. We have long known that information concerning the financial affairs of an individual is considered by that individual to be almost sacrosanct. It seems to be a natural tendency, at least in the Western World, to consider financial information to be of a private, confidential nature.

Since the accounting records were not designed to be interpersonal communication devices, there was no need to standardize terms or concepts or practices. In addition to the lack of need, there was resistance to standardization. Even today, we would consider it an invasion of our privacy if someone were to try to tell us to standardize our personal accounts. We can keep them by double entry, single entry, or on the back of an envelope, and we would guard our freedom to continue to make this choice. Each person feels the need for the "flexibility" to specify his own system.

Since each owner-manager-accountant designed his own accounting system and since there was no interpersonal communication regarding the contents of that system, there came into existence different terms for the same referent and different practices for the same phenomenon. This diversity was unrecognized, since the records and their contents were secret. In the absence of attempts to compare entities, diversity would not have been considered a problem even if it were recognized that it existed.

It was, however, recognized that there needed to be standardization or consistency within a particular set of records, else there would be no way for the owner-manager-accountant to communicate with his past. Since one of the purposes of the records was to enable the owner-manager-accountant to compare his objects of wealth at one point in time with those at another point in time and his activities of one time period with those of another time period, there needed to be consistency in recording over time in order for those comparisons to be made.

From this brief account, we can note several important and continuing habits of thought:

(1) Accounting was thought to be a practical discipline as opposed to a theoretical discipline.

(2) The accounts were for the purpose of providing information to the owner-manager-accountant. The owner-manager-accountant felt the need for flexibility in designing his accounting system and in specifying the information to be recorded and reported.

(3) The contents of the accounts were private and confidential.

(4) Diversity among entities came about naturally, since each owner-manager-accountant designed his own accounting system.

(5) Consistency over time was recognized to be a requisite to comparisons over time.

Second Stage. With larger accumulations of individual wealth and larger business entities, there came both the ability and the need for the specialization of labor. Various duties were assigned to different people, and they became specialists in performing that duty. One of those specialized duties was assigned to a scribe or a clerk or a bookkeeper, and the function eventually became known as accounting. In this stage, the owners and managers were still the same person (albeit there were some early steward-bookkeepers), and the bookkeepers were then, as now, rather low-level employees. Indeed, in some societies, the early bookkeepers were slaves.

The owner-manager maintained his prerogative of designing his accounts to meet his individual, private needs. He still felt the need for flexibility in order to meet these needs. The contents were still considered to be secret information, and the bookkeeper was required to keep those secrets.

The prerogative of the owner-managers to design individualistic systems and the secrecy of the accounts resulted in the continuation of the development of diverse practices. For the same reasons, consistency over time within an entity continued.*

The major change in this stage was the need for the accounting records to be interpersonal communication devices between the owner-manager and the bookkeeper. The owner-manager was both the supplier of the inputs to the accounting system and the receiver of the outputs of the system. In the terms of communication theory, the system was a closed loop; that is, there was provision for direct and immediate feedback from the owner-manager to the bookkeeper.**

---

* The juxtaposition of the notions of "consistency over time" with "diversity among entities" always puzzled me. Since consistency per se is not an end, but rather a means, of achieving comparability, I could not understand how we accountants could recognize the need for consistency over time and fail to recognize the same need for consistency among entities. It finally occurred to me that it was the owner-managers who desired comparability over time, but did not desire comparability among entities.

** This second stage continues today as internal reporting. There are many difficult problems regarding internal reporting, but these problems are fundamentally different from those of external reporting. External reporting is an open communication system. Internal reporting is a closed communication system in the sense that there is a provision for direct and immediate feedback from the receivers—managers—to the transmitters—managerial accountants—if there are misunderstandings or if additional or different data are needed.

In this situation, the bookkeeper is clearly subservient to the owner-manager. The bookkeeper is a hired hand —the question of the relative power of the two does not arise in this stage, since it is obvious where that power resides. Thus, the bookkeeper became accustomed to being the servant of the owner-manager. The bookkeeper also became accustomed to relying upon the owner-manager to specify the terms, concepts, and practices to be used. The information emanating from the accounts was determined by the owner-manager. Thus, there developed the habit of thought that it was the owner-manager, not the bookkeeper, who was to specify the kind of information that was to be recorded and reported. In all probability, the seeds of the habit of thought of relying upon users to specify informational needs were planted very early in the development of accounting. The same is true of the notion of "management's statements." In this stage, there is no doubt that they are, in fact, the statements of the owner-managers. The bookkeeper had no control over the statements and no responsibility for them beyond following the instructions of the owner-manager.

There was one exception to this assignation of responsibility and authority. Very early in this stage, the bookkeeper was given full responsibility and authority for maintaining the arithmetical accuracy of the accounts. Our history shows little indication that the bookkeeper ever left his high stool to directly examine the objects of wealth or to observe the exchanges; instead, he made his entries and calculations on the basis of instructions from the owner-manager. The entries—inputs to the accounts—were supposed to reflect exchanges, but the bookkeeper did not observe exchanges; instead, he observed written documents from the owner-manager. The balances of the accounts were supposed to represent objects of wealth. But the bookkeeper did not observe these objects of wealth and make comparisons of his balances to those observations. Instead, he calculated those balances on the basis of instructions received from the owner-manager. Originally, these calculations were simple totals and differences. Later, the bookkeeper began to calculate averages of various kinds. These averages were (and are) used to allocate costs between activities and time periods. He was instructed to find the average unit cost of the inventory by taking the purchase price of an inventory lot and dividing by the quantity purchased. Then, he allocated between the expense and asset by using these averages. Later, the bookkeeper was instructed to calculate averages per time period by taking the total cost of a long-life asset and dividing by the number of years of life. The bookkeeper had neither the responsibility nor the authority to supply the figures to be used in these calculations, nor did he have the responsibility or authority for determining the method of calculation to be used. Instead, it was the responsibility of the owner-manager to supply the inputs to the accounts and to supply the method of calculation—it was the responsibility of the bookkeeper to make the entries and do the calculations. Hence, the bookkeeper was a human calculator, not an empiricist: he made entries, footed columns, balanced accounts, calculated averages, made allocations, and took trial balances, but he did not measure economic objects and events.

In the second stage, all of the habits of thought formed in the first stage were carried forward, and some were reinforced and strengthened.

(1) Accounting continued to be considered a practical, as opposed to a theoretical, discipline. The bookkeepers were hired hands with neither the time nor the inclination for reflection or theorizing.

(2) The prerogative of the owner-manager to design the accounting system and specify its inputs and outputs could not be challenged by the hired-hand bookkeeper. On the contrary, it seemed natural to provide the owner-manager with the "flexibility"

to meet his informational needs. In addition, the seeds of the notion of "management's statements" were planted at this stage, since it was so clear that the owner-manager had both the responsibility and the authority for the financial statements.

(3) The natural tendency to view the contents of the accounts as private, confidential information was continued.

(4) The natural tendency for diversity among entities was not changed by the specialization in labor.

(5) Consistency over time remained a desideratum of the owner-manager because of the need to make comparisons over time.

In addition, a new habit of thought was developed:

(6) The bookkeeper came to think of accounting as a calculational, nonempirical activity. His duties were to record and calculate, not to observe or measure or count.

Third Stage. In the first stage, one person was the owner-manager-accountant. In the second stage, one person was the owner-manager, and a separate person performed the accounting function. The thing that characterizes the third stage is the separation of management from ownership. At some point, a part of the capital for the entity was supplied by a separate person or persons. Sometimes a single owner supplied part of the capital, and the remainder was supplied by a large creditor. At other times, a consortium of owners supplied the capital, with a subset of them acting as managers. More recently, the ownership and management functions have become almost completely separated. The managerial class now supplies a negligible amount of the capital—almost all of the capital is supplied by investors and creditors who are not engaged in the management function.

The managers were charged with the responsibility of husbanding the wealth of the owners. They were stewards. In addition, the managers were also charged with the responsibility of increasing that wealth—owners desired a return on their investment, an income from their capital. The differences in the motivations of owners and managers have been well documented. The problem became known as "the separation of ownership and control." In regard to accounting, the separation resulted in the need for the managers to report to the owners. The financial statements were the primary device utilized for reporting.

The problem was that managers could not be expected to objectively report on their own activities. This caused the need for the development of auditors—independent professional accountants. Auditors were needed to provide assurance to the owners and creditors that the financial statements were "true and correct."

Originally, there was close contact among the owners, managers, and auditors. It was a closed loop communication system, in that large owners and creditors could provide immediate feedback to managers regarding the financial statements. These large owners and managers also engaged the auditors directly. When that occurred, there was no question in the auditor's mind to whom he owed allegiance and responsibility. Eventually, however, businesses became large, and ownership became dispersed. The communication system was open-ended: the financial reports went to a vast, heterogenous audience with no effective means of feedback. De jure, the auditors were engaged by the owners, but de facto, they were engaged by the managers.

All of the habits of thought developed in the first two stages were carried forward into the third stage. Auditors had formerly been bookkeepers. The habits of thought they had developed as bookkeepers became the habits of thought of auditors.

Owner-managers considered theory and practice to be in opposition to one another. Since accounting had been developed to meet a practical need, it was considered to be atheoretical. Bookkeepers had adopted management's view of the opposition of theory and practice. When bookkeepers became auditors, they carried this habit of thought forward. It continues today. Theories have little meaning to auditors, as they see it, because they are engaged in a practical activity. As a consequence, auditors approach their problems without an overall theory to guide them. This has resulted in ad hoc solutions to specific problems. In turn, this resulted in a collection of practices which, at best, lacked logical cohesion and, at worst, were contradictory.

This view that accounting was atheoretical also resulted in a conflict between practitioners and academics. Training of accountants gradually shifted from apprenticeship to the classroom. The early professors of accounting were practitioners or former practitioners. As a result, much of the classroom teaching was a continuation of the apprenticeship method—the students were taught to emulate practitioners. Later, academics began to develop a penchant for logic and theory. Some practitioners were bemused; others were alarmed. Auditors, as had bookkeepers before them, adopted the businessmen's anti-theoretical attitude. As soon as academics started to become theoretical, a cleavage developed. There always seemed to be an undercurrent of uneasiness in the relations of the academic and the practitioner, and sometimes it came to the surface. It surfaced most often when academics made proposals that would impact practice. For example, when the American Accounting Association issued the 1936 "Tentative Statement," the general practitioner's reaction was to dismiss it as an impractical, theoretical product of the academic mind. The same attitude prevailed when Sprouse and Moonitz[23] issued their postulates and principles. Perhaps the best, or worst, example of this was Marple's[16] reaction to accounting for current values. Not only did he mount a broadside attack on logic, claiming in effect that logic was irrelevant to accounting, he also attacked the academic community. He openly impugned the motives of academics (p. 479), saying that their publications were for the purpose of getting promoted rather than for the purpose of improving accounting. Most practitioners are more circumspect than this, but it is not difficult to detect hostility toward theory in their pronouncements. This resulted in a conflict that has not yet been fully resolved.

The prerogative of the owner-managers to design the system and supply the inputs was transferred to the management. Without a theory to guide them, there was no possibility of auditors engaging in the process of designing the system and specifying the inputs. Moreover, there was no impetus for auditors to take on this responsibility. The idea was that even when managements are separated from owners, managements still need the flexibility to design the accounting system to meet their needs of managing. The lack of power of auditors also prohibited them from taking responsibility. In the previous stage, the statements had been those of the owner-manager; in this stage, they were "management's statements." All of this sowed the seeds of conflict. The statements were prepared to be used by third parties, and the auditors were supposed to provide assurance as to the truth of those statements; yet the auditors had no authority to control the contents of the statements.

Financial affairs of individuals had been considered to be private and confidential. When the financial statements referred to business entities instead of individuals, the tendency to keep the contents secret was continued and reinforced. There came to be a fear that disclosure of financial information would redound to the benefit of competitors and to the detriment of the entity disclosing the information. Even to this day, almost all proposals for additional disclosure are met with resistance by managements, and the reason given is the benefit to competitors. Disclosure was, and is, anathema to management. But it was the duty of auditors to disclose financial information to owners. Thus, a conflict developed which has not yet been fully resolved.*

---

* The conflict is much more complex and subtle than is indicated in the text. At first glance, it appears to be a conflict between managers who want to be secretive and auditors who want to disclose. But it turns out to be a conflict in the minds of the auditors. Bookkeepers had been required to keep financial information secret. When the bookkeepers were transformed to auditors, they carried forward the habit of thought that the financial information was private and confidential. In addition, as fledgling professionals, they looked longingly at the notion of "privileged communication" which had been granted to the professions of medicine and law. Although in general they were not granted a legal right of privileged communication, auditors voluntarily accepted the notion that communications from their clients were confidential. Rule 301 prohibited a member from disclosing any confidential information obtained in the course of a professional engagement. But the voluntary adoption of this rule vitiates the auditors' raison d'etre.

The conflict was recognized by auditors, and they attempted to restrict it by permitting disclosure of confidential information if it was required for a "fair presentation."

> "It is fundamental that the CPA hold in strict confidence all information concerning a client's affairs which he acquires in the course of his engagement. This does not mean, however, that he should acquiesce in a client's unwillingness to make disclosures in financial reports which are necessary to fair presentation." (AICPA,[1] p. 12.)

The juxtaposition of the two sentences clearly reveals a conflict. I, among others, have pointed out that conflict repeatedly. No changes

The increase in the number of business entities brought an increase in the diversity of accounting practices. Since the auditors were engaged by more than one entity, they must have become aware of this diversity. However, it probably appeared to be a natural thing to the early auditors. Since managements knew better than anyone else what information they needed in order to manage, the early auditors probably considered diversity to be nothing more than an indication that different managements needed different information. However, owners needed to compare entities. Comparisons were needed in order to decide between alternative investments. Comparisons were also needed in order to be able to judge managements' effectiveness and ability. In short, managements felt the need for flexibility which resulted in diversity, whereas owners needed consistency. The auditor was caught in the middle. Thus, a conflict developed which has not yet been fully resolved.

Since intertemporal comparisons had been desired by owner-managers, the notion of consistency over time had been developed in the first two stages. However, in the third stage, consistency became a problem. In the first two stages, the financial information was kept secret. Owner-managers could make their intertemporal comparisons without publicizing the information. Managements were now required to publicize their historical record. Such publicity resulted in a motivation to report a good historical record. If a good historical record required inconsistency, then managements were inclined to become inconsistent. Owners still needed consistency over time in order to make intertemporal comparisons. The auditor

---

were made, because there was no crisis. Recently, the conflict has reached crisis proportions. *The Wall Street Journal* has reported:

"What an auditor should do if he discovers or suspects wrongdoing is an unresolved quandary for the public-accounting profession these days." (Hill,[11] p. 1.)

was caught in the middle. Thus, a conflict developed which has not yet been fully resolved.

The habit of thought that accounting is a calculational-nonempirical activity carried over to auditors. They perceived their duty to tick and cast, not to measure economic objects and events. The auditors came on the scene after the exchanges had occurred, so they could not directly observe the correspondence (or lack of correspondence) of the exchanges to the entries. Instead, they, as the bookkeepers before them, relied on the "basic business documents" supplied by managements. In the beginning, it was possible for auditors to compare the balances of the accounts to the objects of wealth that they were supposed to represent, but the calculational habit of thought had been so ingrained that it did not occur to them. At least it did not occur to them prior to McKesson-Robbins. Prior to that case, empirical verification of the quantity of inventory was not a generally accepted auditing procedure. Instead, the auditors relied upon management to supply the inputs regarding quantities purchased and quantities sold. The quantity balances were calculated from those supplied inputs without comparing those calculated balances to the physical inventories. In reaction to the crisis of McKesson-Robbins, auditing was partially transformed into an empirical activity—quantities were empirically tested. However, the calculational-nonempirical habit of thought prevailed in regard to the dollar figures. Accounting was still thought to be calculational-nonempirical, in that the dollar balances were not compared to empirical phenomena. Indeed, the balances eventually were defined in such a way that they could not, in principle, be compared to empirical phenomena.

In the absence of empirical tests of alternative methods of calculation, any method appears to be equally as good or bad as any other. This situation is not unique to accounting. For example, in the early development of geometry, there were alternative methods of calculating area. Kline[14] (p. 19) reports that one method was:

$$(1)\ [(a + b)/2]\ [(c + d)/2] = A_1$$

where a, b, c and d are the lengths of the sides and A_1 is area. A competing method of calculation was:

$$(2)\ ab \neq A_2$$

Since $A_1 = A_2$, we know from logic that either equation (1) or (2) is necessarily false. That is, for a rectangle with sides of 8 and 4 feet:

$$(1)\ [(8 + 4)/2]\ [(8 + 4)/2] = 36$$

$$(2)\ 8(4) = 32$$

and, since the rectangle cannot have an area of both 36 and 32 square feet, one figure is necessarily false. The two equations are contradictory.* But they are contradictory only if one conceives of A_1 and A_2 as referring to an empirical phenomenon. Otherwise, they are merely different calculations. If they are conceived of as referring to an empirical phenomenon, then one can decide which is true by performing an empirical test, that is, by comparing the results of a separate measurement to A_1 and A_2.

Since accounting was a calculational-nonempirical discipline, it could not decide which calculational method was true. For example, a LIFO calculation was equally as

* The contradiction in accounting is confounded by using the same symbols for different equations. For example, both straight-line and accelerated are referred to as "depreciation," without differentiating subscripts. Following this custom would result in using A for both equations (1) and (2). Hence, by elementary logic, $A = A$; $A = 36$; $A = 32$; therefore, $36 = 32$. Alternatively, $36 \neq 32$; therefore, $A \neq A$.

good (or bad) as a FIFO calculation. Since the auditor had no way to separately measure the "unexpired cost" of the inventory, he could not prove that LIFO was true and FIFO was false or vice versa. From this inability to determine empirically truth or falsity, came the notion that there is no such thing as truth in accounting.* Accountants and auditors began to deny that accounting was concerned with truth; instead, it came to be thought of as concerned with "conventions." They began to talk about the principles of accounting being "conventional" and to contrast them to the principles of the sciences. Thus, different methods of calculation became known as different "conventions." By their very nature, conventions cannot be deemed to be true or false; instead, they are agreements which are reached informally by custom and usage or formally by the vote of a legislature. For example, wearing black to a funeral is a convention derived from custom; driving on the right side of the road in the U.S. and the left in England are conventions derived from legislative agreement. Truth is irrelevant to selecting a convention, since the choice is arbitrary. But it was the auditor's duty to certify that the statements were "true and correct." Thus, a conflict developed which has not yet been fully resolved.

The attempt to resolve the conflict was most ingenious. The long-standing habit of thought of diversity among entities, coupled with the denial of truth, brought forth the idea of "entity relativism." The similarity to "cultural relativism" in anthropology is striking. Anthropologists observe and report the practices of various cultures, but they refuse to make judgments about the superiority or inferiority of any of these practices. For example, they will observe and report that polygamy is

* The habit of thought continues today. The word "truth" in regard to accounting brings forth amusement or hostility or both. For an example of a reaction of amusement, see Jensen.[13]

practiced by some cultures and that monogamy is practiced by other cultures. However, they refuse to make judgments about whether polygamy or monogamy is better. Instead, they just note that such differences are relative to the culture. In a similar fashion, accountants and auditors began to think about how a particular calculational technique was relative to a particular entity, while refusing to make a judgment about the truthfulness of that calculational technique across entities. Although I am sure that it is accidental, even the language is strikingly similar. Grady[10] (pp. 32-35) listed "diversity among entities" as a "basic concept" of accounting. Benedict,[3] in a famous book on anthropology, entitles her second chapter "The Diversity of Cultures" and this is a "basic concept" of anthropology. Thus, we borrowed a notion from anthropology which enabled us to explain and justify diversity among entities. This provided further reinforcement for the continuation of the habit of thought of diversity among entities.

Several other habits of thought also carried over. The subservience of bookkeepers to owner-managers carried over as the subservience of auditors to managers. In the same way that blacks continued to act as slaves after they had been freed, auditors continued to act as employees after they became independent. One problem was (and is) that the client was not clearly identified. Prior to the development of auditing, there was no question about who was the client; in the third stage, a question arose that has not been fully resolved to this date. Some say that the "third party" is the client. Others say that management is the client and that if they serve management well, then the third party will be served well. Although there was confusion in the abstract about who the client was, there was no confusion about who paid the fee. The previous habit of thought of accountants being employees, coupled with management's power of the purse, provides an apparent explanation of the subservient role that auditors assumed.

In spite of their heritage, and to their great credit, auditors developed a sense of social responsibility. This boggles the mind. When one considers the manner in which auditing developed and its institutional setting, the development of a sense of responsibility to third parties seems almost impossible. Nevertheless, it occurred. The auditors recognized that managements were always optimistic and sometimes dishonest. They also recognized that managements possessed the human propensity to put their best foot forward. To meet their responsibility to third parties, the auditors needed a strong defense against such managements. But their heritage had not provided them with a defense, the state had not given them police power, they had no theory to guide them, and they had no tradition of empirical testing. Even today, auditors' main source of power is their ability to persuade diplomatically. Hill[12] (p. 97) of Price Waterhouse recently (1972) said: "What I do for a living is spend my time convincing people they ought to do some things they don't want to do." Wise[29] (p. 157) has reported that "senior partners . . . in general devote most of their time to what might be called diplomacy." Although auditors had the responsibility to certify that the financial statements were "true and correct," the only power that they had was the power of persuasion.

From this lack of direct power and from the lack of a concept of truth, the auditors came to rely upon rules. Without a concept of truth, it was impossible to prove that one accounting procedure was right and another one wrong. Without the power to impose their will on managements, it was impossible to force the selection of a particular convention. On the contrary, the auditors were subservient to managements—they were apparent employees—so they couldn't force anything. They could only persuade. Without truths or proofs, about the only way the auditor could persuade was to look wise, nod sagely, and say, "But the accounting rule is . . . ." In addition, it is much more diplomatic to accuse your employer—fee payer—of breaking a rule than it is to accuse him of being overly optimistic or dishonest. So auditors began to rely upon rules in their discussions (and confrontations) with managements. When they could point to an impersonal rule, they could avoid a personal battle of wills with managements. They could even sympathize with managements about the existence of the rule while insisting upon compliance with that rule. Reliance upon rigid rules became the primary weapon in the auditor's arsenal.

Most of these rules came from previous practices. The notion developed that if one could find another auditor who had accepted a given practice in a previous case then that practice could be accepted in a current case. In the absence of a theory, such precedents were the only source of rules. Soon, such rules became "generally accepted." The habit of thought soon developed that accounting is a collection of rigid rules derived from precedents. Since the precedents were from practice, not theory, these rules were not connected one to another by logic, and the results of their application were not connected to empirical phenomena.

The difficulty was that auditors were confronted with new types of transactions, whereas precedents referred to old types of transactions. Thus, reliance upon precedents did not supply sufficient rules for the auditor to meet his responsibilities. This presented an immense problem. The auditor could recognize bad practices, and in at least the most flagrant abuses, all could agree that they were bad practices. Yet even though we could recognize bad practices, we felt powerless to correct them in the absence of some specific rule covering the case. To use an example that is recent enough to be familiar, consider the merger era. During that era, "funny money" was a term commonly used to describe the "consideration" given when one firm was acquiring another firm. We knew that the money was funny, and we also knew that the accounting was bad, but we felt powerless to stop those bad practices because we had no specific rule to cover that type of case. We thought we had to wait for some rule to be established before we could stand up to the high-flying acquirers and tell them that their money was funny and that their accounting was rotten. In the absence of a rule, we felt that we could do nothing.

The reliance upon rules can be updated even further. At the present time, AcSEC is considering a specific problem that was brought to it because some members of that group have clients who are engaging in practices which the auditors know are bad. Yet, these auditors feel that they can neither change the accounting practices nor refuse to give a clean opinion in the absence of a specific rule to cover the case. Instead of relying on their own good judgment, they are asking for a specific rule to be written. By citing these recent cases, I am getting ahead of my story, but I am trying to drive home the point that reliance upon rigid rules became an entrenched habit of thought in accounting.

In the third stage, all of the habits of thought formed in the prior two stages were carried forward and were reinforced.

(1) Accounting continued to be considered a practical, atheoretical discipline. Auditors adopted this habit of thought in regard to both accounting and auditing. They disdained theory, thinking that it was, at best, irrelevant to their practical problems and, at worst, a hindrance. Some were tolerant of what they considered to be irrelevant theory, and others were openly antitheoretical. This resulted in

accounting becoming a collection of contradictory practices. It also resulted in a conflict between practitioners and academics.

(2) The prerogative of the owner-manager to design the accounting system and specify its inputs and outputs was transferred to the management. The problem was that the auditor had been given responsibility for the contents of the financial statements, but he had not been given the authority to control those contents. A conflict developed.

(3) The contents of the accounts were still considered to be private and confidential. The fear of competition reinforced the notion. Auditors, as bookkeepers before them, needed to be discreet about the financial affairs of the firm. Auditors conceived of the financial information as "confidential" and tried to obtain a "privileged communication" protection for themselves and their clients. At the same time, the auditor was required to disclose this private, confidential information. A conflict developed.

(4) Diverse practices continued to be developed as business activity expanded. But owners needed to be able to compare entities and managements. This required consistency among entities. A conflict developed.

(5) Consistency over time became a problem. Managements sometimes wanted to change their accounting procedures in order to report a better historical record. A conflict developed.

(6) The calculational-nonempirical nature of accounting was adopted by the auditor. Since accounting was calculational in nature, auditing was thought to be a process or recalculation. The auditor's function

was to reexamine the basic business documents, retrace the entries, and recalculate the balances.

In addition, new habits of thought were developed:

(7) The lack of ability to empirically test the alternative calculational methods resulted in accountants denying that there was such a thing as truth in accounting. Instead, accounting was defined as being conventional in nature, and the choice of conventions was considered the prerogative of management. From this came the notion which I call "entity relativism."

(8) The auditors' lack of power and lack of a concept of truth caused them to develop the habit of thought of relying upon rules. Precedent was the source of rules, and the reliance upon those rules became the auditors' primary weapon when they perceived the third party's interests to be different from management's interests.

Legislative History. It had become an established habit of thought that there is no such thing as truth in accounting. The perceived alternative to determining truth was the adoption of rules. Auditors needed rules to provide a defense against the always optimistic, sometimes dishonest, managements. They had come to rely on past practices—precedents—as the source of these rules. There were two problems with relying on precedents: (1) By their very nature, precedents refer to yesterday's problems. They do not provide guidance for new types of problems encountered today. Thus, precedents did not supply sufficient rules to solve all of the practitioner's problems. (2) The ad hoc development of accounting rules in each entity had resulted in a number of different rules applicable to the same problem. In regard to yesterday's problems, there were too many accounting rules. Storey[26]

(p. 32) referred to it as "a superabundance of accepted alternative practices."

In short, precedent-following was deficient in that it did not supply a sufficient number of rules and in that it supplied too many rules. There were not enough rules for new problems and there were too many rules for old problems.

There were several nonreactionary efforts to come to grips with the problem. As early as 1909, a committee on accounting terminology was established for the purpose of legislating standardized terminology. After an initial spurt of activity, however, this committee ceased its efforts. Most such nonreactionary attempts met with a similar fate. Reaction to crises had more results. For example, in 1916, the Federal Trade Commission wrote a letter indicating its dissatisfaction with the lack of uniformity in accounting. This was perceived to be a crisis of major proportions. Carey[6] (pp. 129-130) described the letter as "ominous" and as one which "had the effect of a bombshell." To an outsider, the letter would appear to be rather innocuous. Why did accountants perceive it to be ominous? The answer is found in a more general habit of thought: the fear of government intervention. There is nothing that will elicit a more rapid, intense, negative reaction from the U.S. business community than the possibility of government intervention. It was accountants' fear of government intervention more than the contents of the letter that caused them to perceive the letter to be a crisis.

The final result of the FTC's suggestion was the issuance of a document called "Uniform Accounting" by the Federal Reserve Board. That accountants could not have voluntarily issued such a document—that it was a reaction to a perceived crisis—is evidenced by the fact that the original manuscript had been prepared by Price

Waterhouse and had been in existence for some time prior to the issuance of the FTC's letter. The document had not been voluntarily adopted by accountants and probably would not have been adopted by them had it not been for the outside pressure of the FTC.

Several other nonreactionary efforts were made. The most notable was George O. May's attempt to cooperate with the stock exchanges and the banks. (Whether or not this was entirely nonreactionary is debatable. It could be argued that it was in reaction to Ripley's criticism of accounting, since May's suggestion came in reply to an article by Ripley.) Little progress was made in regard to this effort until another crisis occurred—the Great Depression. In reaction to that crisis, the New York Stock Exchange lent support to May's proposal. Even with this support, the deliberations were long and protracted. It was not until 1934 that "Audits of Corporate Accounts" was issued.*

The committee on cooperation with stock exchanges was both an immense success and a dismal failure. In regard to the influence on accounting thought, it was most successful. The Committee succeeded in succinctly expressing the collective conventional wisdom of accountants. As a result, the Committee's ideas struck a responsive chord in the accounting community. Its influence has continued. Storey[26] (p. 9) refers to the Committee's efforts as "the most important single event in the early efforts to formulate principles of accounting." He goes on to note that it continues to influence our thinking: "Most of the structure of accounting principles is dependent in one way or another on the report of this committee."

* May's suggestion was made in 1926 in a speech before the annual meeting of the AIA (see Carey, [6] pp. 162-163). It took four years, and the Great Depression, for the New York Stock Exchange to lend support to the suggestion. That support came in 1930. Then it took four more years before the Committee issued its document.

What were the Committee's ideas? They were those habits of thought that are enumerated supra. The Committee confirmed that accounting is a practical-atheoretical, calculational-nonempirical discipline. It confirmed that accounting is "necessarily conventional," and therefore its propositions have no truth value. It reaffirmed the notions of consistency over time and diversity among entities. It said that "it is relatively unimportant to the investor which precise rules or conventions are adopted by a corporation in representing its earnings if he knows what method is being followed and is assured that it is followed consistently from year to year." (*Audits of Corporate Accounts*, p. 9.) Thus, in one sentence it institutionalized both diversity and consistency—it said that consistency among entities is unimportant, whereas consistency over time is essential.

It fully accepted the prerogative of management to design their reporting system.

> "The fundamental framework of accounting which the committee established has guided the development of accounting for thirty years. The recommendations were not fully implemented, but the basic concept which permitted each corporation to choose those methods and procedures which were most appropriate for its own financial statements within the basic framework of 'accepted accounting principles' became the focal point of the development of principles in the United States." (Storey,[26] p. 12)

The committee also recognized the need for disclosure in order to temper the effects of diversity. It endorsed the notion of fully disclosing the accounting conventions employed by each corporation.

All of these ideas were accepted by accountants. They still are. Thus, in regard to its influence on accounting thought, the Committee must be deemed an immense success. However, in regard to its primary proposal, the Committee failed. That proposal was the disclosure of the methods utilized by each corporation. This conflicted with management's habits of thought, and therefore, it was not accepted. The final result was the untenable position of allowing diverse accounting procedures to be selected by each management, but not disclosing the procedures that had been selected.

The public, via the Congress, had also reacted to the Great Depression. Among other things, it established the Securities and Exchange Commission, with a clear mandate to legislate accounting rules and the indubitable authority to write the legislation and enforce it. If the letter from the FTC had been a "bombshell," then the establishment of the SEC was a "nuclear holocaust."

The threat of government regulation was immediate and direct. The accounting profession reacted with fear. Almost every writer pointed to the spectre of government regulation. The articles and editorials of this period almost invariably contained the phrase: "If we don't do something, then we will be regulated by the government." That spectre has been a continuing theme in the literature ever since the establishment of the SEC. It was in almost every article in the middle 1930's, and it has continued right up to press time.*

Thus, a spectre was haunting accounting. A crisis was at hand. There was no doubt about the need of accountants to react to that crisis, but there was considerable doubt about how they ought to react.

---

* For example, as late as February 1976:

> "The FASB can be successful in accomplishing its mission only by doing an outstanding job in the public interest and thereby not permitting a void to be created that would need to be filled by government intervention." (Arthur Andersen & Co.,[2] p. 1.)

It was clear that accountants had to do something different from what they had done before. There was a felt need to establish accounting principles but, as Carey[6] (p. 183) pointed out, "the profession's record in developing standards of financial reporting was not impressive." The fear of government intervention provided a powerful stimulus to improve on that record, but the question remained how.

The way in which the question of how to reform was answered requires an examination of conflicting habits of thought. First, recall the habit of thought that accounting propositions had no truth value and that, therefore, accountants relied on a collection of rules. However, accountants resisted the notion of legislating rules of accounting. The Committee on Cooperation with the New York Stock Exchange had considered two alternatives: (1) allowing a "competent authority" to legislate rules of accounting; or (2) officially recognizing the prerogative of management to select rules while requiring disclosure and consistent application over time. As we have already seen, the second alternative was recommended by the Committee and, with omission of the disclosure requirement, it became generally accepted. The first alternative was firmly rejected. Accountants did not want to establish a "competent authority" to legislate accounting rules. The Institute preferred "the 'common-law' approach of settling each case on its merits" (Carey,[5] p. 9) to the legislative approach.

But accounting was now faced with the very real possibility of governmental legislation of accounting rules. The only perceived alternative was to establish private legislative bodies. Thus, the alternatives were perceived to be government legislation versus private legislation. The threats in the literature changed from "if we don't do something, then we will be regulated by the government" to "if we don't establish private regulatory bodies, then we will be regulated by the government."

These two perceived alternatives became the subject of much discussion and debate. Many articles and editorials were devoted to the choice between government regulation and private regulation. It continues today. The Wheat Committee devoted an entire chapter to the issue. The chapter is entitled "A Threshold Question: Should the Board Be Public or Private?" (Wheat Committee,[28] p. 21):

> "One question overshadows all others when considering the best way to set accounting standards. Should the task remain a responsibility of the private sector, or should it be taken over by a governmental body?"

Thus, the choice between government legislation and private legislation is a threshold question and a question which overshadows all others. No other alternative was perceived by the Wheat Committee or in the main theme of the literature which had preceded it. The question is still being debated at press time. Arthur Andersen & Co.[2] (p. 1) stated:

> "... [The] issue is whether the establishment of accounting standards will move from the private sector to the public sector."

But these questions were, and are, rhetorical. The purpose of raising the question is to frighten ourselves with the spectre of government regulation. Everyone who raises the question is well aware of our abhorrence of governmental intervention. Given only two alternatives, and given a consensual abhorrence of one of the alternatives, the choice is a foregone conclusion. The debate is ritual.

The history can be stated rather concisely:

(1) Upon the establishment of the SEC, the perceived alternatives were government versus private legislation of accounting rules. A committee recommended the establishment of a private legislative body—the Committee on Accounting Procedure. The Committee was immediately subjected to criticism. The volume and intensity of the criticism increased over time. After 21 years of operation, the Committee was declared a failure.

(2) Upon the failure of the CAP, the perceived alternatives were government versus private legislation of accounting rules. A committee recommended another private legislative body with an increased staff and budget—the Accounting Principles Board. The Board was immediately subjected to criticism. The volume and intensity of that criticism increased over time. After 13 years of operation, the Board was declared a failure.

(3) Upon the failure of the APB, the perceived alternatives were government versus private legislation of accounting rules. A committee recommended another private legislative body with a further increased staff and budget—the Financial Accounting Standards Board.

The reasons for the failure of the CAP and APB are many and complex. Perhaps they can be summed up by noting that the CAP and APB became the focal points of conflicting habits of thought. Some of the habits of thought, such as managements' prerogative to select accounting practices, clearly were anti-legislation. One does not need a rule in order to allow management to select. Other habits of thought, such as the reliance upon precedents to keep management within bounds, clearly reflected a need for rules. Thus, there was both an aversion to rules and a need for rules. This put the CAP and the APB in a position where they couldn't win.

(1) If they issued rules, they were criticized. Some auditors openly announced that they would not follow the rules of the CAP or APB; instead, they would allow management the prerogative of selecting the rules, and then apply their "professional judgment."

(2) If they didn't issue rules, they were criticized. They were prodded by the SEC to issue more rules. The literature contains many criticism for not writing legislation on this or that problem. Auditors felt the need for specific rules before they could correct abuses.

Further, they were criticized for not legislating an overall conceptual framework—a theory—in a discipline that was avowed to be atheoretical. They were criticized for not reducing the number of alternatives of accounting practices and criticized for not allowing enough alternatives to permit flexibility in designing accounting systems.*

The point that I am trying to make is that the CAP and APB failed because they issued regulations and because they didn't issue regulations. Accounting reformers and the SEC wanted more and more regulations, but every time a regulation was issued which gored someone's ox, it resulted in an attack on the legislative body. Thus, the legislative body was attacked for not issuing regulations *and* for issuing regulations.

* Some wanted the Committee to be more flexible and proceed at a more cautious pace. Others pressed the Committee to make faster progress in "narrowing the areas of difference" in accounting practice. Some wanted the Committee to formulate a comprehensive statement of basic accounting principles, a task the Committee on several occasions preferred not to undertake. (Zeff,[30] p. 167.)

The above sketch of legislative history is linear. It shows the CAP being replaced by the APB being replaced by the FASB. This is not the whole story. There were, and are, multiple bodies—both governmental and private—engaged in accounting legislation of one kind or another. The FTC and Federal Reserve Board were engaged in accounting legislation prior to the SEC. The CAP and APB were not the only legislative arms of the AICPA. There were Auditing Standards and Industry Audit guides, among other things, issued by the AICPA which have the effect of regulating accounting. One of the avowed purposes of establishing the FASB was to get the AICPA out of the regulatory business. It didn't work that way. The AICPA continued to issue accounting regulations in the form of statements of position and industry audit guides. Both AcSEC and AudSEC are legislative bodies. Thus, the FASB was an *additional* private legislative body, not a replacement for the AICPA.

Government legislation didn't stand still during this period. The FASB was supposed to be concerned with financial accounting standards; some perceived that this left a void in regard to cost accounting standards. So the government stepped in and established the Cost Accounting Standards Board. The scope of the applicability of the regulations of this board was supposed to be very narrow. Of course, it didn't work that way. The CASB soon broadened its scope. The FTC got back in the act with its "line of business" proposal. The SEC became increasingly active in issuing Accounting Series Releases. In addition, we have the continuing regulations of the IRS, ICC, CAB, and other specific regulatory agencies. The Congress got in the act with the investment credit and threatened to get in the act on several other occasions. The Moss amendment, for example, threatened to establish uniform accounting procedures for the oil industry.

Perhaps the point that I am trying to make can be summed up by asking the reader to refer to the latest issue of the *Journal of Accountancy*. At press time, the latest issue was dated February 1976, and pages 7 through 24 were required to just provide an abbreviated report of new accounting legislation. The reported legislation emanated from the SEC, AISG, FASB, ASD, AcSEC, AudSEC, and MOFA.

In short, our history shows an increasing number of regulatory bodies. The number seems to be increasing at an increasing rate. Each regulatory body also seems to be inclined to become more and more active. The number of regulations per regulatory body seems to be increasing at an increasing rate. In addition, the length and complexity of each regulation tends to increase. We have already seen the need for issuing "interpretations" of previously issued regulations. Such interpretations are, in effect, an addition to the length and complexity of the previous regulation. Thus, the length and complexity of each regulation is increasing at an increasing rate.

This completes our survey of the development of the habits of thought and the resulting legislative history. We will now turn to forecasting the future.

Forecast: An Emerging Legalistic Profession

> "As formerly we suffered from crimes, so now we suffer from laws." (Tacitus,[27] p. 755.)

As I confessed in the introduction, the method that I utilize to forecast the future is to try to understand habitual thought patterns. It seems to me that all of the previously described habits of thought point inexorably toward an emerging legalistic profession. Auditors' lack of power and their consequent reliance upon rules is an especially telling habit of thought pointing toward legalism. The early development of the habits of thought that accounting is a practical-atheoretical, calculational-nonempirical discipline prohibited these rules from being derived from either theory or empirical test, also pointing toward a legalistic method of adopting rules. The many conflicts that have developed cannot be resolved by appealing to the facts, since accounting has been defined as being necessarily conventional, and this points toward legalism. When taken singly, and especially when taken in combination, it seems to me that these habitual thought patterns make a legalistic profession almost inevitable.

My first and most general forecast, therefore, is that accounting will become more and more legalistic. I assign a high probability to this forecast; indeed, we are so far along toward being a legalistic discipline that it may be that I am describing the present instead of forecasting the future. If so, this description of the present coincides with my second method of forecasting. I confessed in the introduction that I think the future will be a continuation of the present. I think that accounting is now legalistic and that it will become even more legalistic in the future. It will eventually become exclusively a politico-legal profession.

Precedents and Statutes. Evidence for our present status as a legalistic discipline may be adduced from the source of our rules. In the legal profession, there are two sources of law: precedents and statutes. In the accounting profession, there are two sources of rules: precedents and statutes. Our history is similar. In the law, the original precedents were customs. Eventually, precedents became formalized in the doctrine of *stare decisis*. In accounting, our original precedents were taken from customary practices. We have now formalized the method of "surveying practices" in the doctrine of "substantial authoritative support." We have also become much more efficient in the retrieval of precedents. Originally, the retrieval of precedents was a rather haphazard procedure of gathering published financial statements from various sources. Then, the AICPA began a more formal compilation of precedents in *Accounting Trends and Techniques.* The most recent advance has been the computerization of precedents. We can now sit at a remote outlet and access a very large number of published financial statements. In short, precedent-following in accounting has become both more formal and more efficient.

In the legal profession, statutory law became more and more important. Eventually, the notion of "parliamentary supremacy" was adopted (see Sarkesian and Nanda,[22] p. 323). A similar development occurred in accounting. Opinions of the Accounting Principles Board were formally declared to be preferential "substantial authoritative support" by the council of the AICPA. We have followed the law by adopting the notion of "legislative supremacy." In addition, as has the law, we have become more efficient at retrieving the legislation. It has now been classified and cross-indexed. Commerce Clearing House treats our accounting regulations in exactly the same way as they treat any other legal regulations. We even have looseleaf services to update changes in the law. These publications have all the trappings of any other set of laws and regulations. I find it difficult to discern the difference between financial accounting statutes and, say, tax statutes. In short, legislation of accounting rules has become more formal, and retrieval of the rules has become more efficient.

We accountants have been reluctant to recognize the similarity of accounting and law. Lawyers have not shared our reluctance. In 1932, prior to the SEC and prior to the establishment of our private legislative bodies, Berle and Fisher[4] (pp. 573-574) wrote:

> "The Columbia Law School has for several years been experimenting with the subject of accounting as a part of its legal curriculum; it has given a course in accounting since 1929. The technique of treating accountancy as a field of law has been a matter of serious consideration .... This has led to an attempt to compare the recognized principles of accounting with that part of the decided case law ... with the view determining how far . . . , in a word, rules of accounting have become rules of law. The preliminary conclusions appear in this essay. The interweaving process seems to have gone so far that in some measure rules of accounting and rules of law are almost indistinguishable. The tentative conclusion seems warranted that the subject of accounting can be handled in large measure, not as an outside technique of incidental advantage to the lawyer, but as an actual body of law, susceptible of being systematized, digested and taught as in any other field of law. . . ."

Thus, to a lawyer, accounting looked like a specialized field of law in 1932. Given the subsequent developments, especially the legislative history, I am sure that if a lawyer were to examine it today he would find that it looks even more like a specialized field of law.*

Perhaps accountants' reluctance to recognize accounting as a specialized field of law comes from a fear of the consequences of such a recognition. In a paper presented to the 1933 annual meeting of the AICPA, Berle drew some conclusions from his view that accounting is a

---

* I have entertained the idea of treating accounting as a specialized field of law for several years. I had thought that the idea was original with me. It turns out, however, that almost all of my "original ideas" can be traced back to the literature. Often they can be traced back as far as Adam Smith, and sometimes they can be traced back as far as Aristotle. Therefore, when doing the reading for the preparation of this paper, I was not surprised to find that Berle and Fisher[4] had suggested my original idea over 40 years ago.

specialized field of law. There is the general principle that law is not a private matter—it is a public, that is, governmental, matter. Berle drew the parallel by saying: " 'It becomes plain that accounting is rapidly ceasing to be in any sense of the word a private matter.' " (Quoted in Carey,[6] p. 173.)* Since accounting is a public matter, Berle rather naturally drew the conclusion that it should be standardized by a governmental bureau. In what must certainly be the understatement of the decade, Carey[6] (p. 173) reported the reaction of accountants: "The speech was something of a shock to the Institute audience."

I fear that my thoughts on this matter will also come as a shock to this audience. I regret the shock. For what small comfort it may be, I was also shocked. I, too, have been reluctant to recognize our politico-legalistic nature. My reluctance has been because of a fear of the consequences. But, if I am right about our politico-legalistic nature, then the consequences will come whether or not we recognize it. So, let us examine some of the consequences.**

Legislative Forecast

A. In the short run, we can expect a continued tinkering with the institutional structure of our private legislative bodies. The FASB has already undergone two

* To fully understand the lawyer's meaning of "private matter," compare the following:

> "A court's decision is not a mere private affair. It culminates in a court order which is one of the most solemn of governmental acts. Not only is a court an agency of government, but remember that its order, if not voluntarily obeyed, will bring into action the police, the sheriff, even the army. What a court orders, then, is no light matter. The court represents the government, organized society, in action." (Frank,[9] p. 746.)

** The remainder of the paper is outlined, because illness prohibited me from completing the paper in time for the publication deadline.

major staff reorganizations, and it will probably do more restructuring in an effort to cope with its task. Perhaps the Council or the SEC, or both, will recognize that AcSEC is a junior APB and officially designate its output as "substantial authoritative support." Such tinkering is likely to continue without fully meeting the problem.

B. In the intermediate run (less than 10 years), we can expect the demise of the FASB. It will be perceived to be a failure for the same reasons that the CAP and APB were perceived to be failures. In addition, there will come the recognition that the FASB is making laws, and the government will insist upon maintaining its monopoly of the law.

C. In the long run, we can expect the legislation of accounting rules to become exclusively a governmental function. My forecast is that the CASB, not the SEC, will take over the legislation.

Precedent Forecast

A. The current precedent-making function in accounting is unsatisfactory. It is a star chamber process with no record and, hence, no way of analogizing one case to another. Also, the statutes will cover more areas in more detail. For both reasons, reliance upon precedents will become less and less important.

B. A court will eventually be established which will take over the precedent-making function. The court will serve the function of adjudicating disputes about alternative interpretations of the statutes.

CPA Function Forecast

A. The above will relieve the CPA of some of his multiple legalistic functions. However, even with the above changes, the auditor will be both an enforcer of laws and an adviser-advocate. No other law enforcers that I know of are private citizens; all others are government agents. I forecast that the government will maintain its monopoly of the law here also. Some sort of super-GAO will take over the audit function.

B. If he were given the option to be either an enforcer or adviser-advocate, the CPA would choose to be an adviser-advocate, as has been done in the tax area. Thus, when given the choice, the CPA will concur that the government should take over the audit function, so that the CPA can maintain close relations with the client.

References

1. American Institute of Certified Public Accountants: *Restatement of the Code of Professional Ethics.* AICPA, New York (1972).

2. Arthur Andersen & Co.: Pressures Involved in Establishing Accounting Standards ... Leadership for What is Needed More Important than Consensus for What is Wanted. *Executive News Briefs* (February, 1976): 1-2.

3. Benedict, Ruth: *Patterns of Culture.* Houghton Mifflin Company, Boston (1934).

4. Berle, A. A., Jr., and Fisher, Frederic K. S., Jr.: Elements of the Law of Business Accounting. *Columbia Law Review* (April, 1932): 573-622.

5. Carey, John L.: *The Rise of the Accounting Profession: To Responsibility and Authority, 1937-1969.* AICPA, New York (1970).

6. Carey, John L.: *The Rise of the Accounting Profession: From Technician to Professional, 1896-1936.* AICPA, New York (1969).

7. Carr, Edward Hallett: *What is History?* Alfred A. Knopf, New York (1961).

8. Fiflis, Ted J.: The Meaning and Implications of *U.S. vs. Simon* as to the Legal Role of Accountants. In *Institutional Issues in Public Accounting*, edited by Robert R. Sterling. Scholars Book Co., Lawrence, Kan. (1974): 122-136.

9. Frank, Jerome: On Lawsuits as Inquiries Into the Truth. In *The World of Law*, Vol. 2, edited by Ephraim London. Simon and Schuster, New York (1960).

10. Grady, Paul: *Inventory of Generally Accepted Accounting Principles for Business Enterprises.* Accounting Research Study #7. AICPA, New York (1965).

11. Hill, G. Christian: Accountants Brought Equity Funding Fraud Almost to Surface in '71. *The Wall Street Journal* (February 20, 1976): 1; 16.

12. Hill, Henry P.: Discussant's Response to "Toward a Philosophy of Accounting." In *Auditing Looks Ahead*, edited by Howard F. Stettler. School of Business, University of Kansas, Lawrence (1972): 96-99.

13. Jensen, Robert E.: Truth versus Fiction versus Something. *Accounting Review* (October, 1975): 871-873.

14. Kline, Morris: *Mathematical Thought from Ancient to Modern Times.* Oxford University Press, New York (1972).

15. Leff, Gordon: *History and Social Theory.* University of Alabama Press, University (1969).

16. Marple, Raymond P.: Value-itis. *Accounting Review* (July, 1963): 478-482.

17. Moonitz, Maurice: *The Basic Postulates of Accounting.* Accounting Research Study #1. AICPA, New York (1961).

18. Reichenbach, Hans: *Experience and Prediction: An Analysis of the Foundations and the Structure of Knowledge.* The University of Chicago Press, Chicago (1938).

19. Ripley, William E.: Stop, Look, Listen!: The Shareholder's Right to Adequate Information. *Atlantic Monthly* (September, 1926): 380-399.

20. Russell, Bertrand R.: *The Problems of Philosophy.* Oxford University Press, London (1967).

21. Sanders, Thomas Henry, Hatfield, Henry Rand, and Moore, Underhill: *A Statement of Accounting Principles.* American Institute of Accountants, New York (1938).

22. Sarkesian, Sam C., and Nanda, Krish: *Politics and Power: Introduction to American Government.* Alfred Publishing Co., New York (1976).

23. Sprouse, Robert T., and Moonitz, Maurice: *A Tentative Set of Broad Accounting Principles for Business Enterprises.* Accounting Research Study #3. AICPA, New York (1962).

24. Sterling, Robert R.: Decision Oriented Financial Accounting. *Accounting and Business Research* (Summer, 1972): 198-208.

25. Sterling, Robert R.: A Test of the Uniformity Hypothesis. *Abacus* (September, 1969): 37-47.

26. Storey, Reed K.: *The Search for Accounting Principles: Today's Problems in Perspective.* AICPA, New York (1964).

27. Tacitus: Quoted by Montaigne in Form of Experience. In *The World of Law.* Vol. 2, edited by Ephraim London. Simon and Schuster, New York (1960).

28. Wheat Committee (Study Group on Establishment of Accounting Principles): *Establishing Financial Accounting Standards.* AICPA, New York (1972).

29. Wise, T.A.: The Auditors Have Arrived. *Fortune* (November, 1960): 151-157; 186; 191-192; 196; 198.

30. Zeff, Stephen A.: *Forging Accounting Principles in Five Countries: A History and An Analysis of Trends.* Stipes Publishing Co., Champaign, Ill. (1972).

R. J. CHAMBERS RESEARCH LECTURE

1985

AN ESSAY ON RECOGNITION

Robert R. Sterling
Garff Distinguished Professor

Graduate School of Business
University of Utah
Salt Lake City, Utah, USA

The University of Sydney
Accounting Research Centre

R. J. CHAMBERS RESEARCH LECTURE

delivered on

23rd October 1985

ISSN 0158-1945
ISBN 0 908269 76 5

A TRIBUTE TO
EMERITUS PROFESSOR RAYMOND J. CHAMBERS

This monograph is for presentation as the inaugural R. J. Chambers Research Lecture. It is presented to honour Ray, to recognize his unsurpassed contributions to accounting thought, to mark the occasion of his retirement, and to witness the establishment of the ACCOUNTING AND FINANCE FOUNDATION within the UNIVERSITY OF SYDNEY, which provides support for the University's Accounting Research Centre. The establishment of a Research Lecture series in Ray's name seems to me to be singularly appropriate because his name has become synonymous with research in accounting, and because it provides a means for continuing the search for improved accounting which he began here many years ago, and because research centres and research lectures in accounting are almost as rare as men of Ray's calibre in accounting.

TABLE OF CONTENTS

FIGURES

PREFACE

This monograph began as one of many versions of a proposed Concepts Statement that I drafted while on a two year secondment to the Financial Accounting Standards Board (FASB). My main assignment at the FASB was to develop concepts to guide decisions on recognition and to propose those concepts to the FASB for adoption as Concepts Statement 5. Countless versions of numerous fragments were prepared and presented which finally resulted in several versions of the entire Concepts Statement. This monograph is based on one of the versions plus several of the more salient and controversial fragments.

When I wrote a paper or gave a talk while employed by the FASB I was required to include the following standard disclaimer:

> The proposals expressed are the personal views of the author and do not necessarily reflect the views of the FASB or any member of the FASB. Official positions of the FASB on accounting matters are determined only after extensive due process and deliberation.

I do not need to include that disclaimer here, not only because I am no longer employed by the FASB, but also because after extensive due process and deliberation the FASB decided that this monograph does *not* reflect its views.

A number of people who were aware that I have previously endorsed current values--that I happily sup Professor Chambers' proffered cocoa--have said that they expected that outcome from the beginning: my proposals would necessarily be rejected by the FASB because current values are too radically different from current practice to permit their acceptance by the FASB. Although they correctly forecasted my failure,[1] they based their forecast on the incorrect assumption that I proposed the adoption of current values. My objective was much more modest than persuading the FASB to accept current values.

My modest objective was, at least, to clearly express the views of the FASB and, at most, to add a modicum of logical coherence to the concepts and standards. To put it

[1] The current Director of Research, Jim Leisenring, kindly objects to me calling this my failure but that is in fact what it is: I set myself a modest objective and failed to achieve it. Everybody *deserves* one major failure in a lifetime. This is mine and I will not let it be taken from me.

negatively, my modest objective was to avoid the turgid language[2] that is sometimes deliberately used to conceal disagreement, and to avert adopting vacuous and contradictory concepts. Of course, a prerequisite to a clear and coherent expression of views was to discover what those views were. I discussed (in somewhat more tactful terms) this objective and its prerequisite at some length with the then Director of Research, Mike Alexander, and others, before I accepted the assignment. In those discussions I used the phrase "inching the Board along" to express my modest objective.[3] In expressing the prerequisite I used the phrase "discovering the intersection of seven sets of ideas."[4] I reiterate those phrases here to emphasize that I did not adopt the radical objective of persuading the FASB to accept current values.

I do, however, confess to adopting the apparently equally radical objective of persuading the FASB to accept the concept of representational faithfulness. I *know* that representational faithfulness is in Concepts Statement 2 and that the FASB has already unanimously adopted that Concepts Statement. Nonetheless, the question of whether some word or numeral faithfully represents something in the real world is, if asked at all, the last question to be asked. The failure to accept representational faithfulness is revealed at the very beginning in the way the questions are asked. The question "Should we *recognize* x *as* an asset?" is quite different from "*Is* x an asset?" because the former admits the possibility of recognizing or not recognizing x as an asset without regard to whether it is an asset. If x is an asset (verifiably satisfies the definition of an asset) but is not recognized as such, then the financial statements are verifiably not representationally faithful. And the same is true if x is not an asset but is recognized as such. My view of course presupposes that the definition of an asset

---

2 In a misguided attempt to amuse myself, I termed this language "fast bees", from "FASBese", because it sometimes seems to be designed to allow one to flit from place to place, extracting whatever words and phrases one desires, and then putting the extractions together to support whatever preconceived position one had. Some staff members were known for their ability to state a position with such subtle ambiguity that it would be accepted by two or more FASB members who held diametrically opposed positions. My feeble joke went around until it reached some who were definitely not amused.

3 Later, in an unguarded moment, I confessed that I had lowered my sights to "millimetering the Board along" which resulted in a minor flap when I was quoted in the press.

4 I later changed that expression to "discovering the common ground among seven Board Members" when Sandy Burton reminded me that the intersection of sets was not only unfamiliar to most FASB members and constituents but also likely to be offensive to them because it is a logical, academic expression.

refers to something in the real world. If it does not, then there can be no representational faithfulness because there is nothing to represent.

The concept of representational faithfulness is put in the forefront because I think its acceptance is more important than the acceptance of *any* valuation scheme. In addition, I think its consideration is a logical prerequisite to the consideration of the valuation schemes that have been put forward. A third reason is purely political: I agree with those that say that wholesale adoption of current values is impossible at the present time. It was the political reason that caused me *not* to propose a current value system to the FASB and, as the reader can easily verify, not to propose such a system in this monograph. It is not that I have changed my mind nor that I betrayed my convictions but rather that I thought it better to propose some small improvement that had some chance of adoption than to propose a large improvement that had no chance.

Paradoxically, the rejection of current values by some FASB members resulted in their rejection of my proposals not to adopt current values. The obstacle became clear to me when in a formal, public FASB meeting one member said to another: "Just as I see a communist beneath every bush, I see current values beneath his every word." That brought back memories of McCarthy's logic that one's denial of being a communist spy was taken as evidence that one was a communist spy because a communist spy would deny that he is a communist spy. It was then that I realized that my denials were to no avail, that no matter how many times I said I was not proposing current values, some would see my efforts as attempts to lead them down a primrose path. It was then that I also realized that I was part of the problem and I willingly let other, less tainted staff members make the proposals. Unfortunately, they had no more success than I.

The careful reader will correctly discern a controversy beneath every word. Prepublication readers, especially members of the task force, have commented that many sections appear to be a reply to some criticism or competing position. They are correct. Often a challenged word turned into a paragraph of explanation, a disputed paragraph turned into a page of clarification, and so on. Most of these have been left intact to explain my position as well as to allow readers to get an idea of the extent, kind and heat of the controversies at the FASB. Readers are invited to join in the controversy in any way they see fit. Although I can no longer officially issue a request for comment, I can issue such a request unofficially. Any comments that I receive will be shared with the FASB members and staff, thereby at least advancing the dialogue, perhaps even contributing to progress.

ACKNOWLEDGEMENTS

More people have read drafts of this monograph before publication than have read many of my other works after publication. Space prevents me from naming all who helped and the span of time prevents me from remembering all who made significant contributions, but I will happily acknowledge my debt to those who I recall made one or more such contributions.

First, all FASB members read it and critiqued or cursed it. The curses did not hurt and the critiques helped. Don Kirk made his usual extraordinarily perspicacious comments in his usual extraordinarily illegible hand; David Mosso gave it his usual careful study and made his usual thoughtful, gentle comments; Ralph Walters made his usual leap to the heart of the matter and made his usual picturesque, no-nonsense comments.

Second, a number of FASB staff read it and made helpful conceptual or political suggestions, or both. Mike Alexander got it started and Jim Leisenring kept it going. Reed Storey showed me that old dogs can learn new tricks--I know I learned from him and I think he learned one or two things from me. J. T. Ball made a number of insightful comments with one hand while putting out a number of brush fires with the other. Jules Cassel argued cogently and endlessly. And then there were the people with the Rice connection--Todd Johnson, Tim Lucas, and Paul Miller--one of whom was always available and always of great help. Had I heeded Dianna Kahn's initial advice, I would have saved myself two years of effort. June Etes cheerfully provided secretarial services.

Third, several members of the Recognition Task Force criticized and commented. I no longer have access to the files and my memory for names is notoriously bad so I hope they will forgive me for acknowledgement in the following way. Bob, then the CFO at Aetna, now retired, made sensible conceptual and sensitive political comments. Irwin, a local practitioner from Iowa, commented on everything from my epistemological predispositions to my verb tenses.

Fourth, there were five friends who served as my unofficial task force--two senior practitioners, one senior manager, one senior and one junior academic--who were promised anonymity and have not released me from that promise. They read all of the early versions and made many helpful comments, but they gave up when the FASB split 4-3 on the barter case.

Fifth, the members of the brown bag seminar at the University of Utah criticized and commented. Barry Cushing and Paul Dorsey read the entire manuscript and made many helpful and some entertaining suggestions.

To all of the above, my warm thanks and the usual absolution.

1. INTRODUCTION

This monograph proposes a set of recognition tests and discusses the fundamental concepts from which those tests are derived. The discussion of the concepts is considerably more important than the proposed tests because the concepts are the premises and the tests merely the conclusions. The difficult task is to explicate the concepts, not to set forth the recognition tests. Indeed, once the concepts are explicated, setting forth the recognition tests is trivial.

In addition to explicating the concepts, agreement on the explication (or an alternative explication) needs to be obtained. It has become clear that the Concepts Statements issued by the Financial Accounting Standards Board in the United States have failed to serve their intended role of providing coherence to standards setting. It is becoming increasingly clear that the reason for that failure is that there are fundamental disagreements about the meaning of the concepts.[1] A prerequisite to deriving coherent standards from concepts is obtaining some minimum agreement on what those concepts mean.

1.1. SCOPE AND BACKGROUND

Recognition is an ancient accounting notion, almost invariably coupled with the notion of revenue, and meant to provide guidance to the question of when revenues should be displayed on the income statement. In that context the question is usually couched as a choice between the cash basis and the accrual basis. The cash basis required the receipt of cash from a sale while the accrual basis extended revenue recognition to the receipt of claims to cash (liquid, short term receivables and the like) from a sale. Couching the question in this fashion presupposes answers to a large set of other questions, many of which are in dispute. The other questions are also recognition questions: the questions of the recognition of assets, liabilities, expenses, and so forth that are entwined with the question of revenue recognition. Becoming cognizant that the questions are entwined has resulted in broadening the notion of

---

[1] I previously ["Rating"] speculated that the reason the FASB was able to adopt Concepts Statements 1, 2 and 3 is that they contained concepts that are quite abstract and sometimes ambiguously stated, and that increasing disagreement and resistance would be encountered as concrete applications began to be made. Since recognition and measurement are concrete applications, I forecast that those topics, particularly measurement, would encounter much difficulty. As subsequent events have shown, the degree of difficulty was vastly understated in that forecast.

recognition to encompass all the elements of all the financial statements. This monograph employs the broad meaning of the term.

Thus, this monograph is concerned with the fundamental question of which words and numerals should appear on *all* financial statements and what those words and numerals should represent. However, it is not concerned with how those words and numerals should be displayed -- what groups, subcategories, or subtotals should be presented. The concepts to guide decisions about the reporting and display of comprehensive income, cash flows, and financial position of business enterprises are being developed in other documents.[2]

1.1.1. DEFINITION OF RECOGNITION

"Recognition" as used herein means the display of words and numerals on financial statements. Recognition tests are for the purpose of deciding which words and numerals should be displayed and which should not be displayed. Because financial statements are dated, the tests also serve the purpose of deciding when the words and numerals are displayed. Some words and numerals will satisfy the tests at one date and not satisfy them at another date, thereby deciding the question of when certain words and numerals, such as revenues and expenses, will be displayed.

The tests are applicable to the display of both the words and the numerals. The words are all of the terms that describe the individual members or subcategories of the elements of financial statements. Those elements are assets, liabilities, equity, comprehensive income, revenues, expenses, gains, losses, investments by owners, distributions to owners, and others that may be defined in the future. The subcategories of assets include the familiar cash, inventory, buildings, and so forth, and similarly for all the other elements. The numerals are those that are on the face, as opposed to those in the notes, of financial statements and are those that are included in the calculations for arriving at totals and differences, as opposed to parenthetical numerals.

---

[2] The exposure draft on display was issued by the FASB [*Reporting Income*] in 1981 but as of the time of this writing it has not gained sufficient agreement to be adopted despite the fact that it does not address anything controversial.

1.1.2. REPRESENTATIONS

Although the word "recognition" is defined in reference to the words and numerals that are displayed on financial statements, the recognition *tests* are applied to the things and events, and their magnitudes, that the words and numerals represent. Thus, the question as to whether a word is to be recognized--displayed on a financial statement--immediately reduces to the question whether the thing or event that the word is intended to represent qualifies for representation. That question requires testing the thing or event. The definitions of the elements specify certain essential characteristics and determining the existence of those characteristics constitute the tests.[3] It should be obvious that one cannot decide whether the word "building" should appear on a position statement without testing the thing to see if it qualifies as a building and testing further to see if it satisfies the definition of assets as given in Concepts Statement 3.

Just as the question as to whether a word is to be recognized immediately reduces to the questions about the thing or event, the question of whether a numeral should be recognized immediately reduces to the question of the magnitude of some attribute. Unfortunately, the attribute has not yet been identified and defined and it is clearly impossible to know whether a numeral faithfully represents a magnitude of an attribute without knowing the attribute. The problem is that just as there are many things and events and only some of them qualify for recognition, there are many attributes and only some of them should qualify for recognition. It should be obvious that one cannot decide whether the numeral "100" should appear on a financial statement without testing the magnitude of the thing to see if it qualifies as 100 units of x, and that an essential part of that test is to know what x stands for. Thus, the recognition of numerals requires the prior selection and definition of the attribute to be recognized just as the recognition of words requires the prior definition of the things and events to be recognized.

The fact that the attribute has not been selected and defined severely restricts the scope of this monograph. Although it is possible to specify verbal depiction tests for some elements without defining the attribute, there are some cases in which the event is defined exclusively by reference to the attribute. For example, price changes of assets would not be recognized if historical cost were the selected attribute while such price changes would be recognized if current cost were the selected attribute. Not

---

[3] Although Concepts Statement 3 is entitled *Elements of Financial Statements of Business Enterprises* the definitions specify the characteristics of phenomena, not of the words and numerals that appear on financial statements.

only do the different attributes result in different recognized magnitudes of the assets, they either prohibit or require the recognition of holding gains and losses. Thus, whether holding gains and losses are recognized depends on which attribute is selected.[4] Accordingly, this monograph cannot avoid some consideration of the question of which attribute is to be recognized. It does not, however, attempt to provide anything approaching a definitive analysis of that long-standing dispute.

1.2. PURPOSE

The purpose of this monograph is to contribute to accounting thought and thereby contribute to the deliberations of the FASB. The immediate goal is to stimulate research on and thinking about the subject of recognition. The long run purpose is to establish concepts to assist scholars and practitioners in making recognition decisions, and to guide the FASB in setting standards for recognition of the elements and magnitudes to be displayed on financial statements.

General concepts to guide those decisions were previously adopted in Concepts Statements 1, 2, & 3. The recognition tests proposed herein are contained in or follow from the previously adopted concepts, and this monograph casts them in more concrete form for the ultimate purpose of providing more specific guidance where recognition is at issue.

The proposed recognition tests are intended to establish a consistent and coherent conceptual process for making recognition decisions. Those tests identify the questions to be asked when deciding whether a particular thing or event should be recognized. The tests identify the things that should be recognized as assets and liabilities and the effects of events that should be recognized as revenues, expenses, investments by owners, and so on.

1.2.1. CONCEPTS AND THE EVOLUTION OF PRACTICE

The long run purpose of this monograph is to develop concepts and the reason for developing concepts is to improve practice. Improvement of practice cannot occur without changing practice, and the manner and pace in which the change is effected is of concern to preparers and users as well as the FASB and the author. Although I am convinced that the concepts proposed in this monograph would, if implemented,

---

4 Similarly, holding losses but not holding gains would be recognized if lower of cost or market were the mixed attributes to be recognized.

result in improvements in practice, I am equally convinced that the implementation should be evolutionary. In my view, a revolution in practice is entirely inappropriate, as well as impossible. The FASB has stated that the adoption of a Concepts Statement will not herald abrupt changes; instead any future changes will occur at the same slow, deliberate speed that has characterized past changes.

This monograph is at the stage of stimulating research and discussion; there is a vast distance between this monograph and the adoption of a Concepts Statement. There is also quite a distance between the adoption of a Concepts Statement and changes in practice.

The primary purpose of Concepts Statements is to guide decisions by the FASB in setting standards. The standards that are set by the FASB immediately affect practice by prescribing certain methods of accounting; the Concepts Statements subsequently affect practice by guiding the FASB in its deliberations when setting standards. Thus the rate of change in practice is determined by the pace of standard setting, not by the adoption of Concepts Statements.

The FASB has stated that its goal is to bring about improvements in practice as needed in an orderly fashion, to change practice with minimal disruption. Even if adopted concepts lead to conclusions that conflict with existing practice, they will not change practice until the FASB so uses them to reach those conclusions and also decides that the timing is right for incorporating those conclusions in standards.

Concepts Statements also provide direct guidance to practice when new situations arise. If a new type of transaction is encountered, decisions about how to account for that transaction should be based on the concepts contained in the various Concepts Statements. For new situations there is no existing practice and therefore there can be no disruption; instead, the Concepts Statements guide preparers in developing practices in the same way they guide the FASB in developing standards. However, the accounting for familiar types of transactions that are covered either by authoritative literature or by well-established tradition are not affected by the adoption of a Concepts Statement.

The goal of improving practice with minimal disruption may result in the adopted recognition tests being used initially to set standards for disclosure or for recognition in supplementary financial statements. This procedure would leave the primary financial statements undisturbed. After experience is gained and evidence is gathered, a more informed decision can be made about whether to apply those same standards to the primary financial statements. This procedure further assures minimal disruption by adding another intervening step between Concepts Statements and changes in the primary financial statements.

1.3. ORGANIZATION

The following five chapters are concerned with two connected but distinct subjects and may be divided into two main parts: (1) concepts and (2) recognition tests. The concepts are logically prior to the tests, constituting the broad base from which the tests are derived. The tests are much more specific, being little more than elaboration of the previously adopted definitions.

The first part (concepts) consists of Chapters 2 and 3. Chapter 2 is an elaboration and refinement of the concepts contained in Concepts Statements 1, 2 and 3, with emphasis on Concepts Statement 2, *Qualitative Characteristics*. Chapter 3 discusses some additional concepts that should come prior to the derivation of the recognition tests.

The second part (recognition tests) consists of Chapters 4, 5 and 6. Chapter 4 sets forth the tests for recognizing the primitive elements of assets and liabilities. They are "primitive" in that the other elements are defined by reference to them in Concepts Statement 3. Equity, the subject of Chapter 5, is defined as the difference of assets minus liabilities and thus its recognition depends entirely upon the prior recognition of assets and liabilities. The recognition tests for financial change elements are given in Chapter 6. Those elements consist of (a) comprehensive income (composed of revenues, expenses, gains, and losses), which is defined as the net change in equity (assets minus liabilities) from all sources, events and circumstances other than transactions with owners, and (b) investments by and distributions to owners, which is defined as changes in equity (assets minus liabilities) that resulted from transactions with owners.[5] In addition, there is some discussion of recognition of other elements that have not yet been adopted by the FASB.

The appendix is intended to serve as an overview of the process and an easily understandable analogy. Those looking for an "executive summary" might find the appendix an acceptable approximation.

---

5 This awkward phrasing was left intact to give the reader some insight into the reason for FASBese. There is a split between FASB members who hold the asset-liability view and those who hold the revenue-expense view. Although Concepts Statement 3 clearly defines revenues by referencing assets, those who hold the revenue-expense view will not accept a document which says that directly. Thus, the circumlocution.

2. PREVIOUSLY DEVELOPED RECOGNITION CRITERIA

This monograph follows, builds upon, and extends three completed Concepts Statements. Those Concepts Statements contain general criteria for recognition decisions. This chapter reviews the contents of Concepts Statements 1, 2, & 3 and extracts the recognition criteria contained in them.

2.1. OBJECTIVES OF FINANCIAL REPORTING

Financial reporting is not an end in itself but is intended to meet certain objectives. Concepts Statement 1 identifies the goals and purposes of general purpose external financial reporting.

2.1.1. OVERALL CRITERION FOR RECOGNITION

The overall objective of accounting is that financial reporting should provide information that is useful to investors, creditors, and others in making rational investment, credit and similar decisions. Although the primary focus is on investors and creditors, the information provided to meet their needs is likely to be generally useful to a variety of other users.

In addition to specifying the objective of decision usefulness and the users to be served, Concepts Statement 1 also indicated some general types of information that are useful:

a. Information to help investors, creditors and others assess the amounts, timing, and uncertainty of prospective cash flows of the enterprise. (Further elaborated in Concepts Statement 2, and infra, as predictive ability.)

b. Information about the economic resources of an enterprise, the claims to those resources, and the effects of events that change those resources and claims. (Further elaborated in Concepts Statement 2, and infra, as feedback value.)

Concepts Statement 1 also indicated more specific types of information that would be useful by, in effect, specifying the contents of three financial statements. Financial reporting should provide information about the enterprise's (1) economic resources, obligations, and owners' equity, (2) performance of the enterprise as shown by earnings and comprehensive income, (3) acquisition and disbursement of cash and other factors that may affect its liquidity or solvency. It also specified provision of information about how management had discharged its stewardship responsibilities.

Decision usefulness is the foundation of the entire conceptual framework; all of the other concepts are intended to contribute to that objective, to build on that foundation. Concepts Statement 2 states the qualitative characteristics that make accounting information decision useful. Concepts Statement 3 defines elements that are decision useful. This monograph proposes the necessary and sufficient conditions for recognition of things and events, and the attribute of those things and events, that are decision useful. Thus, decision usefulness is the overall objective of accounting and is also the overall criterion for recognition.

2.2. QUALITATIVE CHARACTERISTICS

To achieve the objective of decision usefulness, accounting information must possess certain qualities, which are described in Concepts Statement 2. The qualitative characteristics constitute the ingredients of useful information. As such, they are general criteria that are utilized in making accounting choices: they are the primary means of determining what kinds of information are decision useful. Thus, they contribute to achieving the overall objective of financial reporting and they are also criteria for recognition.

Concepts Statement 2 identifies a hierarchy of qualitative characteristics. The overall objective of decision usefulness is reiterated as the most general and most important qualitative characteristic. An overview of the qualitative characteristics and their relationships is presented in Figure 1.

2.2.1. UNDERSTANDABILITY

For financial statements to be useful, users must be able to understand what financial statements mean, what the words and numerals represent. There is ample evidence that many users do not understand financial statements. Thus it is clear that understandability is a problem but the source of that problem is not so clear.

FIGURE 1

A HIERARCHY OF ACCOUNTING QUALITIES

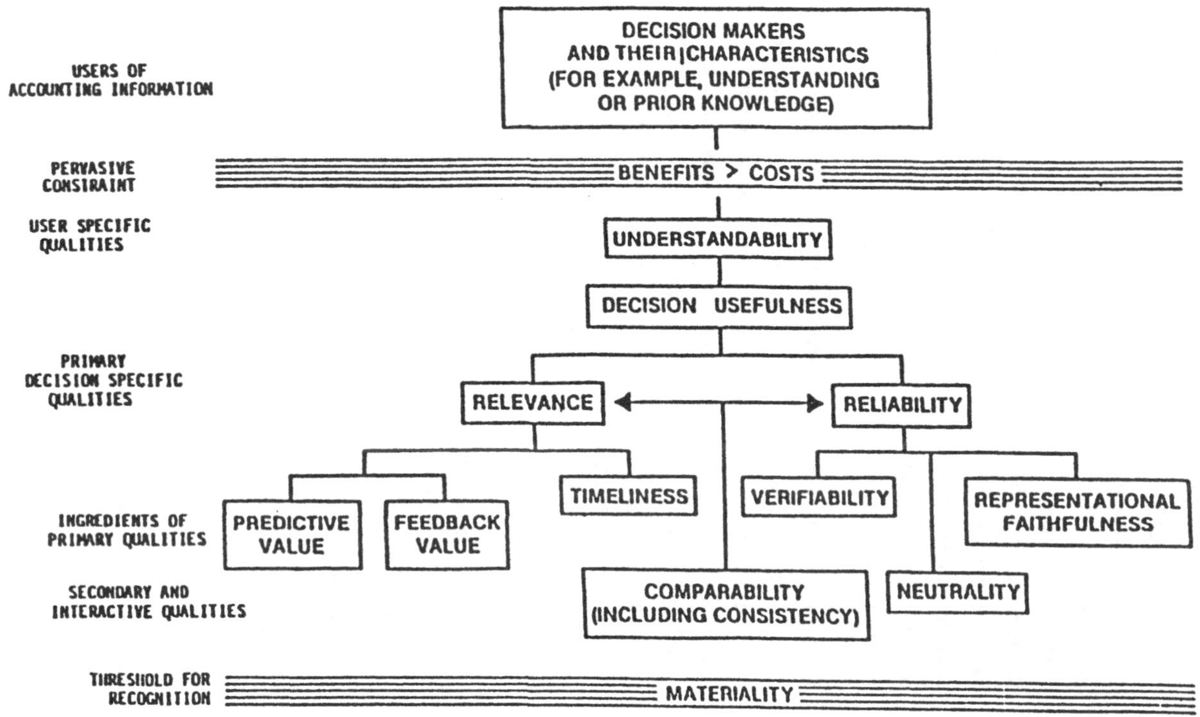

Figure 1. The Qualitative Characteristics

2.2.1.1. Two Possible Sources of the Problem

Understandability has been characterized as a "user-specific quality". That is, the ability to understand financial statements depends on the intelligence, diligence, education, and other such characteristics that are specific to users. Concepts Statement 2 [paragraph 40] observes that understandability is a combination of user characteristics and characteristics inherent in the information. However, others have taken the user-specific phrase as a premise and concluded that not understanding or misunderstanding financial statements is due to the deficiencies of users, not to the deficiencies of financial statements. The view that understandability depends solely on the characteristics of users is mistaken and pernicious.

The reason that the view is mistaken is that there is no *a priori* way to assign blame for not understanding or misunderstanding from observing that it exists. The failure of a French listener to understand a German speaker cannot be blamed on either. Even when using the same language, it is equally likely that a misunderstanding was caused by the writer miswriting as by the reader misreading or by the transmitter erring in encoding as by the receiver erring in decoding. The blame may be determined *a posteriori* and then it may be assigned to one or the other or both. The intended parallel is that accountants begin with information about certain aspects of the entity and encode it, via definitions, in words and numerals on financial statements. The users decode the words and numerals, via definitions, and thereby attempt to garner information about certain aspects of the entity. If that cannot be done or if there are errors in the process, it may be due to deficiencies in the ability and diligence of users or to deficiencies in the financial statements or both.

The reason that the view is pernicious is that it may inhibit improving understandability because it obscures one avenue of possible improvement. If accountants believe that lack of understandability is due solely to deficiencies in users, they are likely to overlook deficiencies in financial statements. The need to educate users about accounting is often noted by accountants and is undoubtedly pressing but it is not clear that the need to educate accountants about users and their decisions is any less pressing, albeit that need is seldom noted. The oft repeated suggestion to "educate the users" would probably improve understandability if it were implemented but there is no way for accountants to effectively implement that suggestion. Accountants could effectively implement a suggestion to educate themselves--and their increased education might permit them to improve the understandability of financial statements--but the view that understandability is user-specific seems to have resulted in overlooking that approach to improving understandability. The suggestion to educate users sometimes means to persuade users to accept accounting as it is rather than expecting it to be improved. The frequent comment that "users need to understand the limitations of accounting" is an example of that meaning. Although that comment is undoubtedly true, the tight focus on educating users about limitations seems to have obscured the alternative of reducing the number of limitations. Achieving the objective of reducing misunderstanding stemming from limitations may be better achieved by reducing the limitations than by explaining them.

In summary, deficiencies in users and deficiencies in financial statements are two possible sources of the problem of lack of understandability. Both sources will be addressed.

2.2.1.2. Users

Understandability of a given message will vary from user to user depending on their intelligence, education, experience, and other such characteristics that are peculiar to each user.[1] A message--financial statement--that contains such technical terms as "debenture" and "allowance for doubtful accounts" cannot be understood by someone who has no education or experience in accounting. Potential users may overcome their inability to understand the financial statements by learning about accounting and its technical terms. However, that learning requires that the potential user put forth a substantial effort--incur a substantial cost--and each potential user needs to compare that cost to the benefits expected to be gained from learning how to understand the financial statements. Alternatively they may incur the costs of hiring an advisor if they think that this route would be more cost-beneficial.

---

1 Users are probably less able and less diligent than they should be and there is no doubt that they are less able and less diligent than many accountants say they ought to be. Their lack of ability and diligence is the source of some of the lack of understandability of financial statements. However, there is little that accountants in general or the FASB in particular can do about this source of the problem. The jurisdiction of the FASB is restricted to the improvement of financial statements, not extending to the improvement of users of financial statements. For this reason, this monograph is restricted to a consideration of the improvement of financial statements.

2.2.1.2.1. Ordinary vs Specialized Languages

A way to avoid the costs of users having to learn technical terms is to eliminate them and express the financial statements in ordinary language. Some users suggest the "elimination of the jargon" and the expression of financial statements in "plain English". Apparently the basis for this suggestion is the mistaken belief that jargon is wholly detrimental and that ordinary language is wholly beneficial. It is true that messages in ordinary language increase the size of the audience that can understand the message and in that sense it enhances understanding. However, ordinary language messages fail to reveal some commonalities and fail to make some distinctions and in that sense it diminishes understanding.

Every specialized occupation has need for a specialized language. The purpose of such a language is to allow clearer, more precise communications (and thought processes) than would be possible by using ordinary language. Thus the benefit of using a well designed specialized language is that it enriches the understanding of those who know the specialized language. The detriment is that it decreases the size of the audience to those who have incurred the cost of learning that language. In general, messages in ordinary language increase the size of the audience who understand the message but they decrease the depth of understanding of the smaller audience who understand the specialized language.

Financial statements are a means by which the specialized occupation of accounting attempts to communicate to general users. It would be desirable to increase the size of the audience and it would be desirable to further enrich their understanding. However, those desiderata are in conflict, requiring a choice between using ordinary language to increase the size of the audience and using a specialized language to enrich the understanding of a smaller audience. That is a hard choice because neither the costs nor the benefits are apparent.

2.2.1.2.2. New Terms vs Redefinitions

Rather than inventing a new term and defining it, sometimes a term from ordinary language is given a new, specialized definition. This is likely to increase the size of the audience who *think* they understand the term because it is familiar but it in fact increases the number of people who misunderstand the term because the specialized definition is unfamiliar. It is also likely to impose additional costs on users because they must learn an additional definition for the same term and then learn when to employ which definition. The term "depreciation" provides an accounting example.

The widespread use of the term in ordinary language increases the size of the audience who misunderstand it when they see it on financial statements. Despite efforts to explain the specialized definition of that term, it has been quite difficult to get the general public to learn that in accounting the ordinary language definition does not apply. For these reasons, inventing a new term would have better achieved understandability than redefining a term from ordinary language.

For these kinds of reasons, a specialized language should be expressed in specialized terms. This requires inventing new terms rather than redefining pre-existing terms. Users are likely to resist the introduction of new terms because it will be apparent that jargon is being introduced and the meaning of the new terms must be learned. That is, they will resist because the unfamiliarity of a new term will make it apparent that they do not understand. They will not resist the redefinition of an extant term because it will not be apparent that they do not understand and for that reason they are likely to *mis*understand. Thus the trade-off between a new term and a redefinition is not between more or less understanding, but between not understanding and being aware of it and misunderstanding and not being aware of it.

The FASB should decide whether additional technical terms are needed on a case-by-case basis, weighing the FASB's assessment of benefits from enriched understanding against its assessment of the costs from learning the new terms plus the detriment of the size of the audience being decreased from some users choosing not to learn the new terms. Obviously if new technical terms are adopted, the FASB will need to provide definitions for those terms. The types of definitions that should be provided are discussed infra [2.2.1.3.1].

In addition to the FASB weighing its assessment of the costs and benefits to users (and accountants) as a group, each user will need to weigh his assessment of his particular costs and benefits and thereby decide whether to learn the definitions of the new terms. Rather than exhorting users to learn the new terms, this monograph will endeavor to improve the financial statements so that users will voluntarily decide that the benefits of the information outweigh the costs of garnering that information.

2.2.1.3. Financial Statements

Financial statements are messages, containing words and numerals, that are intended to convey information to users. Understandability requires that *both* the accountant and the user know the meaning of those words and numerals; knowing the meaning requires that the words and numerals be *defined.* Some types of definitions contribute to understanding and others do not.

2.2.1.3.1. Types of Definitions

Understandability will vary from message to message depending on the words and numerals that are used in those messages and the way in which those words and numerals have been defined. A message that is intended to convey information must utilize a language system that contains words and numerals that are defined by reference to things or events that can be experienced or perceived. These are sometimes called *external definitions* because they refer to something outside the language system. Types of external definitions include ostensive and operational definitions.

If all words and numerals are defined only by reference to other words and numerals, then the messages will not be understandable to users. This point can be illustrated by considering internal definitions as exemplified by common dictionary definitions. Suppose someone who did not speak English sought the meaning of the word "parent". The dictionary might define "parent" as "mother or father", then define "mother" as "female parent", then define "female" as "not male", and so forth. At the end of such a necessarily circular search, the non-English speaker might be able to substitute some words for others but he would not know the meaning of those words and therefore would not be able to understand a message containing those words. Although more easily recognizable for someone who does not speak English, the same is true of someone who does speak English: if "parent" and the other terms used above were the *only* definitions available to us, then we English speakers would not understand messages containing those words because we also would not know the meaning of those words.

In general, although it is possible to define one term by reference to other terms, it is not possible to define all terms in that way because eventually such definitional chains become syntactically *circular*. Avoiding that circularity requires external definitions. Those definitions connect terms with things or events in the real world and such definitions are required for the language system to mean anything, that is, for messages expressed in that language to be understandable. In cases where all the definitions are internal, the source of the problem is a deficiency in the definitions, not a deficiency of the users.

A term may be defined by previously understood terms, and therefore avoid circularity, but understandability also requires that chains of definitions eventually lead back to a term that refers to the real world, that such chains not be syntactically *peninsular*. It is not sufficient for a term to be defined by invoking terms that refer to the real world; the term so defined must also refer to the real world or lead to other terms that refer to the real world. That is, a term may be semantically connected to an object or event by ostensive or operational definition or it may be syntactically connected to such terms and then further syntactically connected to different terms which are semantically connected. Mythology provides familiar examples of peninsular chains. Such terms as "fire" and "breathing" are individually understandable because they are within our experience but the combination "fire breathing" is beyond our experience although not beyond our imagination. Thus "fire breathing" is not circular because it is defined by using terms that refer to the real world; instead it is peninsular because it does not lead back to the real world. Now "fire breathing" may be used in conjunction with other terms to define "dragon", which in turn may be used to define additional terms, and so on. Eventually, however, it will be recognized that these terms form a peninsula, leading only to other terms, not to experience, and therefore they are devoid of meaning, albeit not of entertainment.

The definitions of numerals that are circular or peninsular also suffer from lack of understandability. The numerals obtained from using the Pythagorean theorem to represent hypotenuses are understandable because they are not circular or peninsular. For example, for a right angle with sides of 3 and 4 feet, the calculated hypotenuse of 5 feet is externally (operationally) defined as being equal to the magnitude of the hypotenuse of that right angle. That calculated numeral is said to faithfully represent that magnitude because it corresponds to the numeral obtained from a measurement of that magnitude. It is that correspondence to the measured magnitude that provides meaning to the calculated amount. The discovery of correspondence by such a comparison is a verification. The discovery of a lack of correspondence is a falsification. For example, if someone put forth the proposition that the sum of the sides is equal to the magnitude of the hypotenuse, the fact that the calculated amount of 7 (obtained by summing the sides of 3 and 4) does not equal the measured magnitude of 5 would be sufficient to reject that proposition as being false.

A common example of a numeral that is not understandable because it is peninsular is "hage" which is defined as the product of a person's height and age. "Hage" is peninsular because there are no real world examples that one can point to and there are no known ways to use it to obtain other words or numerals that have real world examples. Thus "hage" is not understandable; at best it is a curiosity.

For a child who is 3 years old and 4 feet in height, the hage amount of 12, obtained by multiplying 3 and 4, is not externally defined, cannot be said to faithfully represent the magnitude of hage because there is no measurement that it is known to correspond to, and cannot be verified by others because there is nothing to compare it with. Of course others can verify the height and age of the child but that is a verification of the inputs to the calculation, not a verification of the hage. Also others can recalculate the amount of hage and obtain the numeral 12 but that is a corroboration that 3 times 4 equals 12, not a corroboration that the hage is 12. Just as such procedures do not verify hage, they also do not falsify it. Therefore if someone were to put forth the proposition that the hage is the sum of height and age, yielding the calculated amount of 7, there is nothing to measure that would falsify the proposition.

In contrast to the discussion of hypotenuse where the numerals were *either* true or false, in the discussion of hage the numerals are *neither* true nor false. There is widespread agreement among epistemologists[2] that such numerals belong to one of only three categories: (1) true, (2) false, or (3) meaningless. Being neither true nor false, the term "hage" and its calculated amounts are meaningless.

2.2.1.3.2. Accounting Definitions

There are several accounting words and numerals that suffer from being circular or peninsular. A few examples will be briefly considered here for the purpose of demonstrating that deficient accounting definitions are a major source of the lack of understandability of financial statements.

An example of an internal definition is provided by the AIA [Terminology Bulletin, paragraph 26]: "...the term *asset*, as used in balance sheets, may be defined as follows: Something represented by a debit balance that is or would be properly carried forward upon a closing of books of account according to the rules or

---

2 This is the legacy of three major schools of thought--logical positivism, operationalism, and pragmatism. For a brief, easily understandable discussion of the almost universally accepted, ancient view that all knowing comes from experience (epistemic empiricism) and the widely held, more recent view that the meaning of a proposition is given by its ability to be tested against experience (semantic empiricism) see Kaplan [*Methodology*, pp. 36-46]. Caws [*Philosophy*, p.184] states this widely-held view in one pithy sentence: "If we rule out ignorance, then meaninglessness is the only alternative to truth and falsity for the truth-value of a sentence."

principles of accounting...." Fortunately, this definition was recognized as deficient and it has been replaced. Unfortunately, the reasons it was deficient have not been fully recognized and therefore there are other internal definitions that have not been replaced and some are still being spawned. Perhaps those who think that the above definition is so obviously deficient that we could never make that mistake again should ponder the definition of "pension goodwill" being proposed by the FASB [Pensions, paragraph 34]. That definition, if adopted, will suffer from the same deficiencies as the earlier definition of an asset as a debit balance. Namely, it will (a) require users (and preparers) to engage in extensive, costly study, (b) not be understandable after the study is undertaken because it does not refer to the real world, and (c) cause confusion because it does not distinguish the characteristics of an account from what the account represents. Worse, it is not an economic resource and therefore it contradicts the previous Concepts Statements where they specified that a characteristic of assets is that they are economic resources.

Definitions of assets as "unexpired costs" or "recoverable costs" are examples of peninsular terms. Although both "unexpired" and "cost" are within our experience, the combination is beyond our experience and it does not lead to other terms within our experience. In that respect "unexpired cost" is similar to "fire breathing" because although we know what the terms mean separately, we do not know what they mean when combined.[3] Adding such phrases as "a cost that will benefit the future" adds to the length of the peninsula but it does not add to understanding for the same reason.

The amount of inventory is an example of a peninsular calculation. The debate over whether inventory should be calculated by LIFO or FIFO is exactly the same in

---

[3] Gombrich [*Art*, p.269] notes that in regard to art the reason for the ease of depiction of such nonexistent things is precisely because they are nonexistent:

> There is an old Chinese treatise about art which throws light on this difference: "Everyone is acquainted with dogs and horses since they are seen daily. To reproduce their likeness is very difficult. On the other hand, since demons and spiritual beings have no definite form and since no one has ever seen them they are easy to execute." The passage of course refers to the painter who can indulge in all kinds of improbabilities where he represents things no human eye ever saw.

It may be that one reason for circular and peninsular definitions in accounting is the ease of depiction of the nonexistent things they define. It would be much more difficult to depict real things. And the same is true of numerals. It is infinitely easier to calculate than it is to find the numeral that represents some magnitude. The problem with that approach is also noted by Gombrich:

> In our context we are more interested in the corollary that what would make art easy for the painter would make it impossible for the beholder.

In our context we are interested in what makes accounting easy for the accountant makes financial statements impossible for the user.

structure as the debate over whether hage should be calculated by multiplying or adding. The conclusion is also the same. Since the numerals derived from both LIFO and FIFO cannot be judged to be true or false by observing anything in the real world, the question of whether they are meaningless must be faced.

These examples of deficient definitions of accounting terms were given in the expectation that a consideration of errors will assist in avoiding making further errors. Knowing what is wrong does not necessarily lead to knowing what is right but it should permit eschewing what is wrong. It is hoped that a study of definitions of accounting terms that did not aid understandability will assist in providing future definitions that will aid understandability.

2.2.2. PRIMARY CRITERIA FOR RECOGNITION

Relevance and reliability are the primary qualities that make accounting information useful for decision making. Accordingly, relevance and reliability are the primary criteria for recognition.

2.2.2.1. Relevance

Relevance is the capacity of information to assist investors, creditors, and others to (a) form predictions about the outcomes of past, present, and future events or (b) confirm or correct expectations. The former is referred to as "predictive value" and the latter as "feedback value."

2.2.2.1.1. Feedback and Predictive Value

Predictive value means value as an input into a predictive process, not value directly as a prediction. Measurements of the effects of past events and present positions are indispensable inputs into most, perhaps all, predictive processes. Information comes from measurements of the past and present: decision makers utilize present measurements and records of past measurements to construct various scenarios of the future. When the future becomes the present, the constructed scenarios can be compared with measurements of what are now past events and present positions. That comparison is one aspect of feedback value. In turn, the more recent measurements become inputs into predictive processes either to update previous predictions or to construct entirely new scenarios of what is now the future. Those measurements have predictive value because they aid in the construction of scenarios of the future. The process is repeated indefinitely as time passes, as what was the future becomes the present and as what is the present becomes the past.

Investment Illustration. The meaning of both predictive and feedback value, and their interrelationship, can be clarified by the simple example of investing cash at interest. The magnitude of cash in bank is one input to the predictive process; the expected interest rate is another input. It takes *both* inputs to predict the future cash flows. Assume that at 31 December 1981 the magnitude of cash in bank is $100,000, the present daily (demand deposit) rate is 12 percent, and the present yearly (certificate of deposit) rate is 15 percent. Some expect the daily rate to increase significantly so that it averages 17 percent in 1982 while others expect it to remain at 12 percent. Regardless of which expectation is held, the $100,000 cash in bank is an indispensable input[4] to the prediction of future cash flows. That magnitude is needed by *both* those who expect the maximizing rate to be 17 percent and those who expect it to be 15 percent. Thus, the $100,000 has predictive value because it is an input into a predictive process, not because it is a prediction per se.

Feedback value, as the name implies, is backward looking. If those who invested in daily demand deposits actually have $116,000 cash in bank at 31 December 1982, they can compare that amount with the (a) $100,000 cash in bank at 31 December 1981, showing $16,000 of comprehensive income; (b) $115,000 they would have had if they had invested at the 15 percent rate; (c) $117,000 they would have had if their expected average rate had been earned; (d) any other target or standard, such as 2 percent above prime, that has been established; and (e) amount of cash or amount (or rate) of comprehensive income of others. Such comparisons provide feedback value.

The $116,000 cash in bank at 31 December 1982 (and the $16,000 comprehensive income) can now be used as inputs to predictive processes for 1983, which can be compared with measurements at 31 December 1983 providing additional feedback value. Since predictive value is forward looking and feedback value is backward looking, measurement of the present magnitude is essential to both. The present

---

4 The interest rate should be applied to the amount of cash available for investment if it differs from the cash in bank. However, the amount of cash available for investment is likely to be a function of the cash in bank. For example, if a cash reserve is needed, the amount of cash in bank less the amount of the reserve is the cash available for investment. Alternatively, the cash available for investment may be the sum of the cash in bank and the cash to be borrowed. Further, the maximum amount of cash that can be borrowed is likely to be a function of the cash in bank plus other assets. The point is that the amount of cash in bank is *one* needed input, not that it is the *only* needed input.

magnitude separates the past from the future and therefore is an indispensable input for both predictive and feedback processes.

The importance of present measurements can be easily seen in this simple example. If the future amount expected by management ($117,000) in 1982 is reported on the 31 December 1981 Statement of Financial Position, it would not assist others in making independent predictions for 1982. The $117,000 *is* a prediction, not an input to predictive processes. It also destroys feedback value because it prohibits those types of comparisons mentioned above. Also if the past amount of $100,000 is reported on the 31 December 1982 Statement of Financial Position, it inhibits independent predictions for 1983 as well as not providing feedback value for 1982. Thus, it is the measurement of a present magnitude that is relevant, that provides predictive and feedback value.

There are a number of suggested alternatives to reporting present measurements. One popular suggestion is to report managements' predictions instead of measurements of present magnitudes because investors are not capable of making independent predictions and because it will provide the appropriate bench-mark for investors to judge managements' performance. Whether managements' predictions should be reported will not be addressed here but note that if they are reported, they must be in addition to, not instead of, present magnitudes to permit the comparisons to be made. If the 31 December 1981 financial statements contain only managements' predictions of what will happen in 1982 and the 31 December 1982 financial statements contain only managements' predictions of what will happen in 1983, how is it possible to judge their performance in 1982? The only available comparison is the prediction of the 31 December 1982 magnitude to the prediction of the 31 December 1983 magnitude when the desired comparison is the prediction of the 31 December 1982 magnitude to the actual the 31 December 1982 magnitude.

Another suggestion is to report a measurement of a past magnitude instead of measurements of present magnitudes because that will provide the appropriate bench-mark for investors to judge managements' performance. Whether a measurement of a past magnitude should be reported on the present financial statements will not be addressed here but note that if they are reported, they must be in addition to, not instead of, present magnitudes to permit the comparisons to be made. If the 31 December 1982 financial statements report the amount of cash that was in bank at 31 December 1981, how is it possible to judge their performance in 1982? The only available data is the actual 31 December 1981 magnitude and that cannot serve as a bench-mark until there is something to compare it with. It is sometimes argued that such past magnitudes should continue to be reported until some critical event, such as an exchange, occurs. Of course no one argues that a past magnitude of cash in bank should continue to be reported on subsequent statements of financial position until that cash is exchanged but they do argue that a past magnitude of cash expended for, say, land should continue to be reported until that land is exchanged.

These and similar suggestions seem to be the result of forgetting that financial statements are issued periodically, that they form a times series. Some have looked at an isolated point in time and (correctly) observed that a decision requires a prediction of the future and (incorrectly) concluded that predictions are the only relevant figures and that the financial statements should report nothing but predictions. Generalizing from this conclusion results in reporting nothing but predictions at all points in time and therefore we can never know whether any of the predictions were right because we never know the present.

Others have looked at an isolated point in time and (correctly) observed that knowledge of history would be helpful and (incorrectly) concluded that some particular historical amount should continue to be reported until some critical event occurs. Generalizing from this conclusion results in reporting nothing but that particular historical amount at all interim points in time and therefore we can never know whether interim changes have occurred because interim changes are never reported. Only the net changes are reported at the critical event.

Decision-making is forward looking and requires comparing a measurement of the present relevant magnitude to a prediction of the future relevant magnitude. Information required for that decision--measurement of present magnitude and prediction of future magnitude--is relevant. Information that aids in making the prediction of the future magnitude has predictive ability and therefore is also relevant, albeit a little less directly. The present magnitude is usually an input to the prediction of a future magnitude. Thus the present magnitude is relevant both because it is compared to the future magnitude and because it has predictive ability.

Evaluation of decisions is backward looking and requires comparing a measurement of the present relevant magnitude to a measurement of the past relevant magnitude. Information required for that evaluation is relevant. Measurements of the present magnitude become measurements of the past magnitude as time passes. Thus the present magnitude is relevant both because it is compared to the past magnitude and because it becomes the past magnitude.

Some will make decisions about others (e.g., investors about the performance of managers) on the basis of evaluating the past decisions of others. Some will make decisions about others (e.g., a potential large creditor about managers) on the basis of comparing the present magnitude to an independent prediction of a future magnitude. Many will make decisions about which decision process to use in the future on the basis of evaluating their past decisions. For all such decisions the present magnitude is relevant.

In summary, in all decisions a prediction of a future magnitude is needed to compare to the present magnitude and in all evaluations a record of past magnitudes is needed to compare to the present magnitude. Suggestions to report only the future or only the past are therefore mistaken.

Navigation Illustration. The necessity of measuring the present magnitude to provide predictive and feedback value extends to more complex accounting situations as well as to non-accounting situations. It can be further illustrated by an analogy with navigation. The present spatial position (the elements of which are latitude and longitude) is an indispensable input to predictions of future spatial positions. Among other things, the present spatial position defines available alternatives: one cannot choose the optimal route to get to the desired destination without knowing the present spatial position since the available alternative routes are limited to those that connect the present spatial position to the desired destination. In turn, the present spatial position is a result of past distances traveled. Some of those past distances traveled may have been in the right or wrong direction--may have been gains or losses--in regard to the desired destination. Spatial positions and distances traveled articulate: the present spatial position is the sum of all past distances traveled from the initial spatial position; net distance traveled is the difference between the initial and present spatial positions. The past distances traveled per time period may be used as inputs to predictions of distances to be traveled and future spatial positions. Those past distances traveled may simply be extrapolated on the basis that future conditions will be identical to past conditions or they may be adjusted for expected differences in future conditions. As the future becomes the present, the spatial positions and distances traveled are measured and recorded. Those present measurements are compared with past measurements and with past predictions of spatial positions and distances to be traveled; they have feedback value. In turn, the more recent measurements are utilized as inputs into predictive processes; they have predictive value.

The analogy is intended to illustrate parallels of spatial position to financial position and distances traveled to comprehensive income. The present financial position and past comprehensive income are inputs to predictions of future financial positions and future comprehensive income, which provides predictive value. As the future becomes the present, the past measurements and past predictions can be compared with measurements of what is now the present financial position and the now past comprehensive income, which provides feedback value.

2.2.2.1.2. Timeliness

Timeliness is an ancillary aspect of relevance and is defined as having information available to decision makers before it loses its capacity to influence decisions. Timeliness may refer to the elapsed time from the date of the financial statements until the date they are issued, or it may refer to the elapsed time from the date of the observation or measurement until the date of the financial statements, or both. Just as an observation or measurement reported on a financial statement dated 31 December that is not issued until the following July may have lost its capacity to influence decisions, an observation or measurement made in July that is reported on financial statements issued the following 31 December may have lost its capacity to influence decisions. Thus, timeliness is not a quality of information per se but rather a function of the time lag between date of the information and its receipt by users. Timeliness alone cannot make information relevant, but a lack of timeliness can rob information of relevance.

2.2.2.1.3. Comparability

Comparability (including consistency) is another aspect of relevance. The very purpose of measurement is to permit comparisons: if no one found it useful to be able to compare the spatial position of one object with that of different objects or the spatial position of the same object at different points in time, measurements of spatial position would not be made. The same is true for the comparison of the financial position of one entity with that of different entities or the financial position of the same entity at different points in time. If the method of measuring the financial position of one entity is peculiar to that entity, that measurement is robbed of relevance because it cannot be compared with other entities. If the method of measuring the financial position at a point in time is peculiar to that point in time, that measurement is robbed of relevance because it cannot be compared at different points in time. If both peculiarities are present, relevance is absent. Thus, comparability is not a quality of information per se but rather a function of the relationship of one piece of information to other pieces of information. Comparability alone cannot make information relevant, but a lack of comparability can rob information of relevance.

2.2.2.2. Reliability

The reliability component of decision usefulness concerns the faithfulness with which information represents what it purports to represent, coupled with an assurance for the user, which comes through verification, that it has that representational quality. Thus, representational faithfulness and verifiability are components of reliability.

2.2.2.2.1. Representational Faithfulness

Representational faithfulness is correspondence or agreement between a verbal or numerical depiction and the phenomenon it purports to represent. Financial statements purport to represent things and events as well as the magnitudes of the things and the magnitudes of the effects of the events, and representational faithfulness applies to both the verbal and the numerical depiction. For example, if the word "building" appears on the Statement of Financial Position, there must be an existing structure to which that verbal depiction corresponds; if no structure exists, the representation is not faithful. By contrast, if a structure exists but the word "building" (or a cognate) does not appear on the statement, the representation is not faithful due to the absence of depiction. The same is true for the verbal depiction of events; the event must have occurred in order for it to be faithfully represented. Thus, there is a straight-forward existence or occurrence test for the representational faithfulness of verbal depictions. Numerical depictions are similar; for example, if the financial statements contain the depiction "cash $1,000,000" when the magnitude of cash is materially different from $1,000,000, the representation is not faithful. The goal is to achieve correspondence between the numerical depiction and the magnitude. Thus, there is a measurement test for numerical depictions. The point of the examples is to clarify the connection of representational faithfulness to decision usefulness: faithful representation is necessary for decision usefulness; unfaithful representations are not decision useful.

2.2.2.2.2. Verifiability

Verification is the process by which independent observers achieve consensus about the faithfulness of the representation. The goal is to provide assurance that there is correspondence between the depiction and the phenomenon it purports to rèpresent. "Phenomena" refers to things and events that exist outside the mind and knowledge of them is obtainable from experience via the senses, as opposed to "noumena", which refers to thoughts or intuitions. Accounting depictions must be representations of phenomena because noumena are impossible to verify. The phenomena that are depicted on financial statements must be detectable by all qualified observers who exert sufficient effort to detect them. Otherwise consensus about existence or occurrence and magnitude cannot be achieved, and without that consensus there can be no assurance of representational faithfulness.

Verifiability requires that there be empirical evidence regarding the existence and magnitude of things and events. The methods of obtaining that evidence and deciding that it is sufficient in a given instance are the province of auditing standards. The purpose of this discussion is to clarify the related concepts of representational faithfulness and verifiability: representational faithfulness is a necessary condition for decision usefulness; verification is a necessary and sufficient condition for assurance of the faithfulness of the representation; empirical evidence of the existence or occurrence and magnitude of a thing or event is necessary for verification.

The words and numerals on financial statements are presumably intended to represent things and events. Verification requires the comparison of the things and events, and their magnitudes, with the words and numerals on the financial statements. It is not sufficient merely to examine the documents and records and to recalculate the numerals in those records. That aspect of verifiability may be clarified by contrasting sophisticated auditing with primitive auditing. In primitive auditing the purpose is to assure that the financial statements faithfully represent the account titles and balances in the ledger with no regard to whether those titles and balances faithfully represent things or events and their magnitudes.

Problems have appeared that demonstrated the insufficiency of that kind of assurance. Not only were there occasional frauds due to deliberate misrepresentation, there were also balances of accounts based on noumena; that is, some account balances were based on nothing more than intentions, expectations, calculations, and other thoughts and intuitions. For example, sometimes economic resources were concealed (secret reserves were created) by calculating excessive expenses based on expectations of future unfavorable business conditions or on the intention to use those concealed resources to carry out plans for the future, such as replacement or expansion. Another example was the recording and reporting of an asset by capitalizing an operating loss on the basis of expectations of future operating income. Both examples resulted in unfaithful representations: in the first, economic resources existed that were not depicted as assets and, in the second, no economic resources existed to correspond to the depiction. Since there is no empirical evidence regarding intentions, expectations, calculations, and the like, primitive auditing was restricted to determining that the adopted procedure was applied consistently and to recalculation of the account balances. The progress of accounting and auditing has been marked by responses to such problems by development of increasingly rigorous requirements for empirical evidence and increasingly sophisticated techniques of measurement and estimation. At the present time, mere assurance of consistent application of procedures and recalculation of balances is not sufficient for verification.

Recalculating the effects of past events is not sufficient for verification. The following examples from current practice indicate the insufficiency of recalculation and the type of empirical evidence that is required. Recalculating the present amount of the cash account by summing the past receipts and expenditures is not sufficient; the existence and magnitude of the cash are verified by a separate count. Recalculating the present amount of the receivables account by summing past credit sales and collections is not sufficient; the existence and magnitude of the promises are verified by a separate confirmation. Recalculating the present amount of the inventory account by summing past purchases and sales of the units is not sufficient to assure faithful representation of inventory; the existence and quantity of the units are verified by a separate count and the existence and maximum amount of book value are verified by a separate determination of market values to ensure that cost is not greater than market. Verification often reveals differences between the calculated amounts and the magnitudes determined by the empirical evidence. Detection of such differences is the purpose of the verification and the fact that such differences are often detected is proof that recalculation of the effects of past events is not sufficient to assure faithful representation.

Recalculating the effects of expected future events also does not qualify as verification. Forecasts cannot be verified because the things do not yet exist or the events have not yet occurred. The lack of existence or occurrence prohibits obtaining empirical evidence; it precludes the comparison of things and events to depictions. A forecaster may use various procedures for deriving expectations of future things or events, including sophisticated mathematical techniques, but those calculations are not representations of things or events; instead they are representations of the forecaster's expectations, the outcome of the forecaster's mental processes or noumena. Others are likely to have different expectations of the things that will exist or the events that will occur. Recalculation of those expectations does not constitute verification because recalculation will reveal only arithmetical or procedural error. Enterprises may disclose plans for the future and expectations of the outcomes of those plans, but those disclosures must be segregated from the financial statements and clearly labeled as forecasts or pro forma statements since they are not representations of phenomena and cannot be verified.

In short, neither recalculation of the effect of past events nor recalculation of the effects of expected future events is sufficient for verification. The Statement of Financial Position lists assets and liabilities as representations of things and their magnitudes that exist at the date of the statement. If there is *no* empirical evidence of the existence and magnitude of the thing at the date of the Statement of Financial Position, if calculation and recalculation of the effects of past or expected future events is all that is available, the absence of evidence of existence should be taken as an indication of nonexistence or a zero magnitude, or both. A verbal depiction of a thing for which there is no empirical evidence of existence or a numerical depiction of a magnitude for which there is no empirical evidence of the amount does not provide the needed assurance of representational faithfulness. As a consequence, that kind of a depiction should be omitted from financial statements because it is not likely to be decision useful.

Verifiability is also required for events. The financial change statements list revenues, expenses, distributions to owners, and so on that are representations of the effects of events that occurred during the time period covered by those statements. Both the occurrence and magnitude of those events must be verifiable. Those representations must reflect phenomena rather than noumena, and their verification requires empirical evidence. However, practical limitations prohibit separate recognition and verification of the effects of some events and therefore they must be inferred from the differences in the things at the beginning and end of the fiscal period. If those practical limitations apply, the required empirical evidence pertains to the existence and magnitude of the things at the beginning and end of the fiscal period rather than to the occurrence of the events.

2.2.2.2.3. Neutrality

Neutrality is an ancillary aspect of reliability. It means that the primary concern should be the relevance and reliability of the information that results, not the effect that it may have on a particular interest. Neutrality is related to bias in that it is possible to use accounting methods that bias the information to achieve a predetermined goal. Bias results in information that is not representationally faithful and therefore not reliable. Also, as noted above, unfaithful representations are not decision useful. Thus, non-neutral information violates the overall objective of decision usefulness.

2.2.2.2.4. Precision

Although correspondence between the numerical depiction and the magnitude of the thing or the effects of the event is the goal, *perfect* correspondence cannot be achieved. There is no way to be certain of the exact magnitude of any phenomenon and therefore all measures are imprecise to some degree.

More precision can be obtained by incurring additional costs, but absolute precision is beyond reach. Even in the physical sciences under conditions of elaborately controlled experiments--and the attendant exorbitant costs--absolute precision cannot be achieved. The impossibility of achieving absolute precision is wellknown and often discussed in the sciences. Accountants who continue to seek more precision are to be admired and encouraged. However, those who seek absolute precision might be instructed by considering what has been learned in the so-called "exact" sciences. Einstein [Sidelights on Relativity, p.28] drew a sharp and clear distinction between the certainty of calculation and the uncertainty of representations of phenomena: "As far as the laws of mathematics refer to reality, they are not certain; and as far as they are certain, they do not refer to reality." The same is true for accounting: as far as the mathematical methods used in accounting refer to reality, they are not certain; as far as they are certain, they do not refer to reality.

The various deferral, accrual, and amortization methods used in accounting are mathematical constructs. The certainty of the numerals obtained by calculation from those methods is often confused with the certainty of the magnitude of the phenomena represented by those numerals.[5] The numerals obtained from employing a given method can be made indefinitely precise (carried to as many decimal places as desired) but the numerals obtained from measuring or estimating the magnitude of phenomena cannot be made indefinitely precise. Numerals obtained from repetitions of the measurement or estimation of the same phenomenon will be imprecise (have a nonzero range or variance) to some degree. It is exceptionally rare for two numerals obtained by measurement to be exactly equal, whether those measurements were

---

5 Part of the reason for confusion in accounting is that the question of whether the numerals obtained by using mathematical methods refer to reality remains unanswered because the previous question of whether those numerals are *intended* to refer to reality remains unanswered. The question whether the application of the mathematical methods of, e.g., LIFO or FIFO, yields numerals that in fact refer to reality is seldom broached because it is not settled as to whether the objective is for those numerals to refer to reality. One reason for the allure of not referring to reality is that it provides the security of certainty.

made by the same person or made by one person and verified by another.[6] Of course, in the absence of arithmetical or procedural error, calculation and recalculation will result in exactly equal numerals; however, this is the precision of mathematics, not the precision of correspondence of the numeral to the phenomenon.

In regard to precision of correspondence in the "exact" sciences, Ziman [*Reliable Knowledge*, pp. 26-7, emphasis supplied] introduces his discussion with the same terms that are used herein: "Grant that we can make quite *reliable* quantitative *measurements* ... [but] we still cannot assert that scientific knowledge, embodied in well-*articulated* theoretical models, is a [perfectly] *faithful representation* of the real world ... [because] statements about the real world are always subject to uncertainty." After a discussion of the simple example of measuring the distance between two cities he concludes: "The point is that this sort of statement--or any other empirical statement--could not be made indefinitely *precise*." If financial statements are representations of the real world, if they contain empirical statements, they will be subject to uncertainty, they cannot be made indefinitely precise.

The penchant for precision in accounting is often based on the mistaken idea that it is necessary for verifiability or representational faithfulness, and therefore for reliability, or that imprecise representations are ipso facto irrelevant. Verification is agreement between independent, qualified observers that a numerical depiction corresponds to the phenomenon it purports to represent. The requirement is that the observers agree on a numeral or a range of numerals, not that the numerals obtained from repetitive measurements of the phenomenon be equal. The requirement is that there *be* correspondence, not that there be *perfect* correspondence. Relevance is the connection of the type of decision to the phenomena depicted. The requirement is that the depiction be a representation of the magnitude of the relevant attribute, not that the magnitude be exact. Decision usefulness requires relevance and reliability but it cannot require precision because absolute precision is beyond our ken.

The amount of imprecision may be lessened by incurring additional costs and the ill effects of imprecision may be mitigated by stating ranges or variances, but imprecision cannot be eliminated. Therefore, precision is not a necessary condition for recognition.

---

6 The counting and recounting of discrete units results in numerals that are exactly equal. Except for a few instances, such as petty cash, however, the numerical depictions in accounting require measurement or estimation rather than counting.

2.2.2.3. Relationship of Relevance and Reliability

Decision usefulness is the overall objective; relevance and reliability are the qualities that make information decision useful. If one kind of information were both more relevant and more reliable than another kind of information, there would be no difficulty in choosing the kind of information that best achieves the objective of decision usefulness. However, if one kind of information were more reliable but less relevant (or vice versa) than another kind of information, trade-offs would be required. Fear has been expressed about the possibility of such situations arising and the need for deciding the relative importance of relevance and reliability in order to make the trade-offs. Clarification of the concepts reveals that the fear is unfounded. Decision usefulness requires both relevance and reliability. Neither can be traded for the other because they perform different roles in the decision process. Relevance refers to the connection of the *phenomena* to the *decision*. Reliability refers to the connection of the *phenomena* to the *representation*. They refer to *different* connections and therefore it is difficult to understand the allegation that more of one can be traded for less of the other.

2.2.2.3.1. The Three Stages

The decision process as it relates to relevance and reliability is diagrammed in Figure 2. There are three required stages:

a. *Specification of the Decision*. The type of decisions to be served must be specified before the concept of relevance can be applied because different phenomena are relevant to different types of decisions. In extreme cases the differences are clear: for example, phenomena relevant to investment decisions are vastly different from phenomena relevant to navigation decisions. The word "relevance" is too abstract to stand alone. The concept of relevance requires the phrase "relevant *to* x decision" to make the concept concrete enough to provide guidance about the phenomena that should be represented.

b. *Identification of the Relevant Phenomena*. The specification of the type of decisions to be served permits the partitioning of phenomena into the broad categories of relevant and irrelevant. Of course, phenomena that are irrelevant to the specified decisions are relevant to other decisions--spatial position is relevant to navigation decisions but irrelevant to rational investment, credit and similar decisions. Thus, the concept of relevance is concerned solely with the connection of phenomena to specified decisions. Its role is to identify the phenomena that are specified by a particular type of decision.

c. *Representation of the Relevant Phenomena.* Reliability refers to the connection of the phenomena to the representation. The concept is concerned solely with the correspondence or lack of correspondence of the phenomena to the representations and, on that basis, it partitions all representations into the two broad categories of faithful and unfaithful. It is possible to faithfully represent irrelevant phenomena or relevant phenomena: unfaithful representations refer only to those representations that do not correspond to the phenomena that they purport to represent. However, the word "representation" is too abstract to permit verification; it requires a phrase specifying the phenomena that it purports to represent to make it concrete enough to permit verifiers to make judgments about the faithfulness of the representation. Qualified, independent observers must know that it purports to be a representation *of* financial position or a representation *of* spatial position before they can reach a consensus that the representation is or is not faithful. Thus, reliability is concerned solely with the correspondence of the phenomena to the representation.

Decision Useful. It is the *combination* of relevance and reliability that provides decision usefulness. The representation must be (1) faithful and (2) of the relevant phenomena to be decision useful. Neither a faithful representation of irrelevant phenomena nor an unfaithful representation of relevant phenomena is decision useful. A representation of spatial position is not useful for investment decisions regardless of its reliability and vice versa for the usefulness of the representation of financial position. Similarly, a representation that is not a faithful representation (such as the word "building" when there is no corresponding structure) is not decision useful even though buildings are phenomena that are relevant to rational investment, credit and similar decisions. Thus, *either* irrelevance (phenomena not connected with the decision to be made) or unreliability (representation not faithful) is sufficient to destroy decision usefulness. Each is necessary and together they are sufficient for decision usefulness.

Forecasts. Although sufficient for decision usefulness, any particular representation is not likely to be sufficient to make a decision. All decisions require forecasts of the outcomes of various courses of action and the faithful representation of the relevant phenomena will not provide forecasts although it often provides an input to those forecasts.

FIGURE 2

The Role of Relevance and Reliability

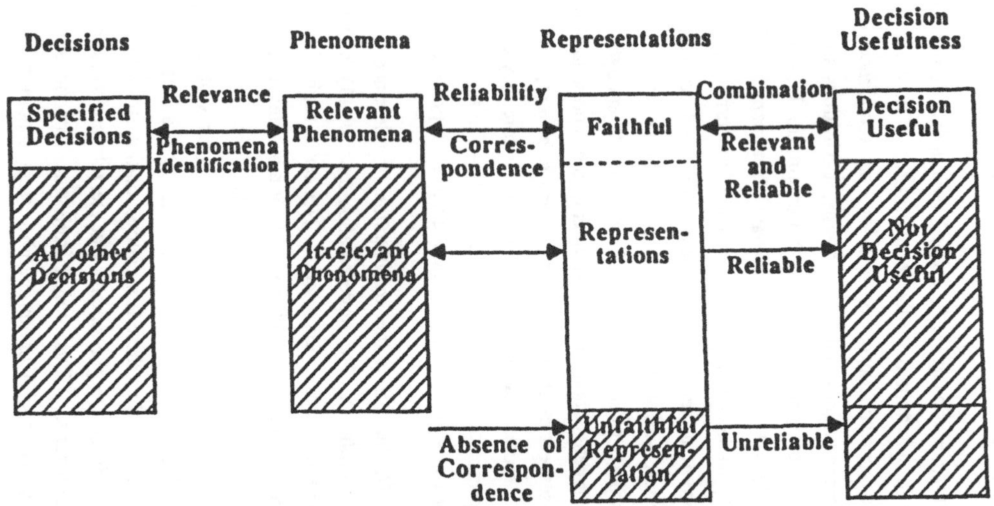

Figure 2. Relevance and Reliability

*2.2.2.3.2. **Precision vs Reliability***

Many of the expressions of concern regarding the need for trade-offs have failed to distinguish reliability from precision. In regard to accounting it is often said that if one does not know the exact amount of a given magnitude, then it is not reliable because one cannot rely on it when making decisions. Although this idea is appealing--evidently in part because its phraseology uses "rely" to deny "reliability"--and therefore often invoked when considering accounting issues, it is never used in other pursuits, not even by accountants. Consider for example an accountant whose bathroom scale reads 200 pounds when he steps on it. Since it is almost certain that his weight is something different from exactly 200 pounds, he should conclude that the figure is not reliable because he cannot rely on it when deciding whether to go to breakfast or to go jogging. Of course accountants do in fact rely on imprecise figures in nonaccounting pursuits but they impose the impossible criterion of absolute precision in accounting pursuits. Because the distinction is apparently easier to understand outside of accounting, it will be explained by using a nonaccounting illustration.

Navigation Illustration. A continuation of the analogy with navigation will illustrate the need for a clear distinction between reliability and precision as well as further illustrating the relationship of relevance and reliability. In the previous navigation illustration the relevance--feedback and predictive value--of the present spatial position was demonstrated. Prior to the development of modern techniques, measurements of spatial position made at sea were highly imprecise. Such extensive imprecision was clearly material to the decisions of seafarers but regardless of the efforts or costs expended the extant measurement techniques were such that the imprecision could not be reduced. A precise measure could be obtained only when the ship was proximate to a known landmark; for example, the spatial position of the ship while in harbour could be measured with precision.

The problem is to decide what spatial position to report when the ship is at sea, for example, when it is approximately midway between its Sydney origin and its Los Angeles destination. The choices are to report the ship's position as (1) precisely in the Sydney harbour or (2) approximately (plus or minus 250 miles) at the midpoint. The criterion of decision usefulness makes the choice abundantly clear. First, relevance to rational navigation decisions requires reporting the present spatial position. Second, reliability requires reporting a faithful representation (assured by verification) of the relevant phenomenon--the present spatial position. Thus, decision usefulness requires reporting that the ship is approximately at the midpoint.

If precision is not distinguished from reliability, it could be argued that a report of the present, approximate spatial position is less reliable but more relevant than a report of the past, precise spatial position and therefore a trade-off of relevance for reliability is necessary. That such trade-offs are not only unnecessary but also inappropriate can be demonstrated by considering the decision usefulness of a report of the past, precise position.

First, a report that the ship *was* in the Sydney harbour is not relevant to the captain in making his navigation decisions when the ship is at sea nor is it relevant to others who evaluate the outcomes of the captain's decisions. The precision of the measure in such a report does not contribute to feedback value (such as the distance traveled from Sydney) nor to predictive value (such as the distance to be traveled to Los Angeles or the date of arrival) and therefore the precision of the measure does not contribute to the relevance of the report. Rational navigation decisions require a measure or estimate of the present spatial position, and all navigators would agree that the report contains a measure of the wrong phenomenon. Thus, it is a verifiably *ir*relevant report.

Second, a report that the ship *is* in the Sydney harbour is not reliable. The precision of the measure in such a report does not contribute to the faithfulness of the representation and therefore the precision of the measure does not contribute to the reliability of the report. Instead, the report contains an unfaithful representation of what it purports to represent, and all qualified observers would agree that the ship is not in the Sydney harbour; that is, they would verify that it is an unfaithful representation. Thus, it is a verifiably *un*reliable report.

Since a report that the ship is or was in the Sydney harbour is verifiably irrelevant or unreliable, it is verifiably not decision useful. On the other hand, a report of the approximate midpoint is a faithful representation of the relevant phenomenon. Moreover, the faithfulness of that representation can be assured by verification--independent, qualified observers would agree that the ship is at the midpoint plus or minus 250 miles. The problem with the report of the approximate midpoint is that the representation is imprecise, not that it is unreliable by being unfaithful or unverifiable. Thus, no trade-off of relevance for reliability is necessary because the report of the approximate midpoint is *both* relevant and reliable. More important, no trade-off is appropriate because decision usefulness requires both--the faithful representation (assured by verification) of the relevant phenomena.

Accounting Illustration. The analogy is intended to apply directly to accounting.[7] The single most contentious issue in accounting is whether to report historical costs or current values. It is often said that historical costs are more reliable and current values are more relevant, necessitating a trade-off of relevance for reliability. This results in some people lining up on the side of reliability and others on the side of relevance in exactly the same way they previously lined up on the sides of historical costs and current values, with no improvement in understanding nor progress toward agreement. The following accounting illustration is presented in the hope of improving understanding about the relationship of relevance and reliability, not to engage in the argument about historical costs versus current values.

Although there is a difference between historical costs and past prices, historical costs are usually interpreted as (unadjusted) past prices when considering reliability and precision. In this interpretation the mutually exclusive alternatives are usually seen to be more reliable, less relevant past prices versus less reliable, more relevant present prices, necessitating a trade-off of relevance for reliability. That is an incorrect characterization of the problem. Decision usefulness requires both relevance and reliability: the first task is to determine which phenomena (past versus present prices in this instance) are relevant to rational investment, credit, and similar decisions; the second task is to find ways to estimate or measure and verify the relevant phenomena.

The incorrect characterization of the problem stems from the failure to distinguish reliability from precision. Past prices that were measured at the event of past cash exchanges are likely to be more precise than present prices that must be estimated in the absence of cash exchanges. However, past prices are not a faithful representation of present prices and present prices are not a faithful representation of past prices. Thus, whether past or present prices are more reliable cannot be answered in the abstract; it depends on what phenomena the numerals purport to represent. What the numerals purport to represent depends on what phenomena are relevant to the decision.

---

[7] The analogy is also based on fact. The response to imprecision by seafarers was to use whatever evidence was available to estimate their present spatial position. They often erred in their estimates but they never made the mistake of substituting a precise measure of irrelevant phenomena for an imprecise estimate of relevant phenomena. The outcome of continued attempts to estimate the relevant phenomena (and the attendant costs including offering large cash prizes for innovations) was continued improvement of measurement techniques accompanied by continued improvement in precision. Today the imprecision is "negligible" in navigation terminology or "immaterial" in accounting terminology. See Kline [*Mathematical Thought*, pp. 336-37] for a brief history upon which the analogy is based.

The accounting illustration parallels the navigation illustration in all significant respects. Consider land which in present practice is reported at its (unadjusted) past price because that figure was measured precisely when it was acquired in a cash exchange just as the past spatial location of the ship could be measured precisely when it was in the Sydney harbour. The present price of the land cannot be measured precisely just as the present spatial position of the ship at sea could not be measured precisely. The future price of the land will be able to be measured precisely when it is sold for cash just as the future spatial position of the ship will be measured precisely when it reaches another harbour. Thus the above comments about the navigation illustration apply to the accounting illustration.

Substituting accounting terms for navigation terms yields the following:

a. At the present time measurements or estimations of present prices made between exchanges are highly imprecise. Such extensive imprecision is clearly material to the decisions of investors, creditors and others but the extant measurement techniques are such that the imprecision cannot be reduced. A precise measure can be obtained only when the land is exchanged for cash.

b. The problem is to decide what price to report when the land is between exchanges. The choices are to report the land's price as (1) precisely what it was when acquired or (2) approximately (plus or minus x dollars) what it is now. The criterion of decision usefulness is used to make the choice. First, relevance to rational investment decisions requires reporting the present price. Second, reliability requires reporting a faithful representation (assured by verification) of the relevant phenomenon--the present price. Thus, decision usefulness requires reporting the present price of the land.

Alternatively, the above conclusion can be stated as: First, relevance to rational investment decisions requires reporting the past price. Second, reliability requires reporting a faithful representation (assured by verification) of the relevant phenomenon--the past price. Thus, decision usefulness requires reporting the past price of the land.

The reason for stating the two alternatives is to make the point that if relevance requires reporting a past price, then reporting a present price destroys the usefulness of that report regardless of the precision of that present price. And the same is true if relevance requires reporting a present price. Thus the first question is which price is relevant and the second question is whether the relevant price is faithfully represented. One cannot trade-off the relevance of a present (past) price for the reliability of a past (present) price.

The above discussion is an attempt to explain the relationship of the concepts of relevance and reliability, the distinction between reliability and precision, and how to apply those concepts. It is not an attempt to decide between past and present prices. That decision should be subsequent to and follow from the specification and explanation of the qualitative characteristics rather than being concurrent with (and therefore perhaps confused with) that specification and explanation.

Relative Precision. Obviously, other things equal, more precision is preferred to less and therefore precision is persistently put forth as a recognition criterion. Sometimes this is based on the chimera of having achieved precision by confusing the precision of calculation with the imprecision of measurement. Other times it is based on the mistaken belief that one attribute is always more precise than another.

If land (or another asset) is acquired in a cash exchange, the cost may be known with precision to the penny. However, that does not necessarily settle the issue. In some cases the cost will be different from the price, i.e. it will be a fortunate or unfortunate purchase, and then the question arises whether the price or the cost should be recognized at acquisition. Some are of the view that cost is the relevant attribute and therefore the magnitude of that attribute should be recognized without regard to the characteristics of the price attribute. Others hold the view that price is the relevant attribute and therefore the magnitude of that attribute should be recognized without regard to the characteristics of the cost attribute. Still others, under the influence of conservatism, hold the view that the lesser magnitude be recognized, that the rule of lower of cost or market be applied. Thus, under this view, if the price is less than the cost (an unfortunate purchase), then the price of the asset should be recognized and the difference recognized as a loss.

Which of these views is correct is not at issue here; instead the issue is how to go about deciding which attribute to recognize in general and in particular whether precision should have a bearing on that decision. Those who have a greater appreciation of conservatism are also those that have a smaller tolerance for imprecision and they may need to ponder the trade-off of a more conservative, less precise price for a less conservative, more precise cost but there is no trade-off between relevance and reliability. If the land or other asset is initially recognized at its price because of conservatism or other reasons, then the relative precision of the initial price and a subsequent price is an open question. It seems to be easy to forget that *the* cost is sometimes nothing more than *a* past price that was *recorded* at acquisition and then to endow that past price with greater precision than a present price because its recording was carried to the penny.

Moreover, if the land (or other assets) is acquired by some means other than a cash exchange--such as a credit purchase, barter, or investment by owners--the amount to be recognized is usually defined as the price of the acquisition or sacrifice, whichever is more easily determinable. At the date of acquisition that is a present price and at subsequent financial reporting dates it becomes a past price, albeit often referred to as "the cost". From the viewpoint of subsequent financial reporting dates, whether the estimate of the past price is more or less precise than an estimate of the present price cannot be answered in the abstract. It depends on the availability and quality of the evidence at the time of the estimation. Thus, even if precision were adopted as a recognition test, it would not provide a general answer to the question of whether to recognize past or present prices.

Historical costs are not the same as past prices in most instances. Almost all assets that are described as being depicted at "historical cost" are past prices that have been subjected to one or more deferral, accrual, or amortization methods. The research that has been done to date indicates that current values are more precise (less disperse) than historical costs.[8] Since that research did not cover all types of assets or all types of firms, it is not conclusive. Whether representations of current values are in general more or less precise than historical costs is not known at this time. However, if precision were to be adopted as a recognition test, the presently available evidence would indicate a preference for current values. Whether future evidence would support this preference is an open question that must await future research.

The above discussion concerns the relative precision of different attributes and attempts to show that the comparison is often between imprecise prices rather than between imprecise prices and precise costs. However the answer to the question of relative precision comes out, it should not affect the choice of what phenomena to report. Imprecision in representations of phenomena is inevitable. If the history of other fields is a guide, continued efforts (and the attendant costs) to estimate or measure the relevant phenomena will reveal techniques that are unknown at this time, and those techniques will result in increased precision. In the meantime, the quest for increased precision should not interfere with the quest for increased decision usefulness.

---

8 See, for example, McDonald ["Test Application"], McKeown ["Empirical Test"], Parker ["Testing Comparability and Objectivity"], and Sterling ["Uniformity Hypothesis"].

2.2.3. CONSTRAINTS ON RECOGNITION

Concepts Statement 2 establishes two pervasive constraints on all financial information. Accordingly, they are constraints on recognition. First, the benefits of recognition must exceed the costs of recognition. The benefits of information are determined by its decision usefulness; the costs of information include those incurred by both preparers and users of financial statements. The second constraint is materiality. If the magnitude of a thing or the effects of an event are judged to be too small to affect users' decisions, it is not decision useful and therefore recognition is not required.

Materiality and cost-benefit are additional criteria for recognition. However, they are presented as constraints instead of criteria because most often they will play a negative rather than a positive role in the recognition process. Another reason for presenting them as constraints is that they are applicable at all stages of the recognition process. In general, the constraints are designed to avoid endeavors that are not worthwhile or that are concerned with trifles. All recognition tests presented in this monograph are understood to be subject to the cost-benefit and materiality constraints.

2.3. ELEMENTS OF FINANCIAL STATEMENTS

The elements of financial statements are defined in Concepts Statement 3. Elements are the building blocks with which financial statements are constructed. The definitions serve to identify the things and events that qualify for verbal depiction on the financial statements. Those definitions followed Concepts Statements 1 & 2 and were framed in such a fashion to implement the overall objective of decision usefulness, the qualitative characteristics of which are relevance and reliability.

2.3.1. CRITERIA FOR DEPICTION IN WORDS

The definitions given specify certain characteristics that things or the effects of events must possess to qualify as an element. If any of those specified characteristics are missing, the thing or the effects of the event in question does not qualify for verbal depiction as an element. Accordingly, the characteristics specified in the definition of elements are criteria for recognition.

The essential characteristics of an asset are:

a. It embodies a probable future benefit that involves a capacity, singly or in combination with other assets, to contribute directly or indirectly to future net cash inflows.

b. A particular enterprise can obtain the benefit and control others' access to it.

c. The transaction or other event giving rise to the enterprise's right to or control of the benefit has already occurred.

The essential characteristics of a liability are:

a. It embodies a present duty or responsibility to one or more other entities that entails settlement by probable future transfer or use of assets at a specified or determinable date, on occurrence of a specified event, or on demand.

b. The duty or responsibility obligates a particular enterprise, leaving it little or no discretion to avoid the future sacrifice.

c. The transaction or other event obligating the enterprise has already happened.

Financial change elements--comprehensive income (composed of revenues, expenses, gains and losses) and investments by and distributions to owners--are defined by reference to assets and liabilities and therefore require the prior definition of assets and liabilities. The essential characteristics that are common to the financial change elements are:

a. They are changes in assets or liabilities.

b. They affect the assets or liabilities of a particular entity.

c. The change has already occurred.

All of the above characteristics are essential for recognition and are included in the proposed recognition tests.

The FASB has stated that it may find it desirable to define additional elements in the future. Although this monograph focuses on the elements defined in Concepts Statement 3, the intention is to state the recognition tests in a sufficiently general form to be applicable to additional elements that may be defined.

2.4. CONCLUDING REMARKS

The previous Concepts Statements were developed in a sequence. That sequence begins with more general, more abstract concepts and moves to the more specific, more concrete concepts. The sequence is rational insofar as each concept follows from, builds upon, extends, and elaborates the previous concepts. The definition of the elements are identifications of things and events that are relevant, and thus is an application of the qualitative characteristics. In turn, the specification of the qualitative characteristics that make information decision useful is an extension of the objective of decision usefulness. Thus, the pyramid is from broad based, general objective to more narrowly focused, elaborative qualitative characteristics to specific application by identifying and defining elements.

One reason for developing the concepts sequentially is that not enough was known to do it all at once. Knowledge often progresses by conceiving a broad outline and then filling in the details. Then the filling in of details results in conceptual learning and that requires refinement or modification of the outline. The process is iterative with the outline guiding the search for details and the details guiding the way the outline is refined and modified. Thus, insofar as developing subsequent Concepts Statements contributes to learning, previous concepts may need to be modified or refined. It is hoped and expected that the refinements and modification will be concerned with minor points and that the general thrust will remain unaltered.

Some are opposed to all refinements and modifications of previous Concepts Statements. A prominent reason for this opposition is the fear of losing some hard fought gains. There is the fear of sliding down the slippery slope of revision: the reason for refusing to reconsider a tiny point is because if a slight refinement were made it might lead to a small modification elsewhere, then to a more substantial modification, and so on to perhaps eventually changing the entire contents of all of the previous Concepts Statements. Even if the slippery slope of revision can be avoided, a reason for averting reconsideration is that the original agreement was so tenuous that it might evaporate on reconsideration and thus there would not be enough votes to readopt the unrevised Concepts Statements. Although seeing the force of that view, I think that the alternative is worse. Restricting subsequent Concepts Statements to an exegesis of the previous Concepts Statements is likely to lead to stagnation. Progress requires learning and to shut off avenues toward learning has worse consequences than failure to obtain or maintain agreement.

The discussion of the previous Concepts Statements was intended primarily to elaborate and clarify, and in some places to merely remind by repeating. A secondary, minor intention of that discussion was to extend and to propose minor but important modifications. Although my intentions were modest, some thought that I accomplished a major revision. Almost every line was disputed. Some merely thought it to be an erroneous interpretation while others thought it dangerously heretical and wanted to restrict this monograph to a rechauffe of Concepts Statements 1, 2, & 3.

Regardless of whether the discussion is judged to be extension, elaboration, modification, or whatever, it should be evaluated on its merits. If the conclusion that, say, one cannot trade-off relevance for reliability is valid, then the choice is the modification of a previous Concepts Statement or permitting a known invalidity to continue to guide the FASB in developing other concepts and in setting standards. Of course, if it is invalid, that choice is not presented. Avoidance of error requires that the validity be evaluated and the choice made.

3. YET-TO-BE-DEVELOPED RECOGNITION CONCEPTS

Recognition is the depiction of things and events in words and numerals. The previous Concepts Statements identified and defined the things and events the words are to depict but the question of what attribute the numerals are to depict was not addressed. Thus, the next step is the identification and definition of the attribute(s) to be depicted.

The sequencing of the Concepts Statements is outlined in Figure 3. Concepts Statement 1 established the objective of providing information that is decision useful. Concepts Statement 2 established the qualitative characteristics that make accounting information decision useful. Concepts Statement 3 identified things and events that are decision useful, that are relevant to rational investment, credit, and similar decisions. As Figure 3 indicates, what is now needed is to identify the attribute(s) that is (are) decision useful, the attribute(s)[1] that is (are) relevant to rational investment, credit and similar decisions.

By identifying the things and events that are relevant to rational investment, credit and similar decisions, Concepts Statement 3 established the necessary and sufficient conditions for those things and events to be depicted in words. The identification of the attribute that is relevant to rational investment, credit and similar decisions is a prerequisite to establishing the necessary and sufficient conditions for depiction in numerals.

When the necessary and sufficient conditions for verbal depiction are combined with those for numerical depiction, the result is establishment of the necessary and sufficient conditions for depiction in words *and* numerals. That is, the combination establishes the necessary and sufficient conditions for recognition.

3.1. PRIMACY OF DEFINITION

At base recognition is nothing more than the intelligent application of definition. A well formed definition connects a symbol (word or numeral) with phenomena. It provides criteria that allow one to decide whether a particular phenomenon is or is not within the ambit of the definition. It partitions phenomena into two classes: those that satisfy the criteria and those that do not. Just as a well formed definition of

---

[1] Henceforth, for ease of exposition, it will be attribute rather than attribute(s). However, it should be understood that multiple attributes is a possible decision and therefore the exposition is intended to apply to either the singular or plural.

"animal" allows one to examine phenomena and decide that this is an animal and that is not, a well formed definition of "asset" allows one to examine phenomena and decide that this is an asset and that is not.[2] The same is true of the definition of an attribute. A well formed definition of "weight" will allow one to examine phenomena and say this is weight and that is not just as a well formed definition of, say, "acquisition cost" will allow one to say this is acquisition cost and that is not. Thus, well formed definitions allow one to recognize (in the ordinary language sense) an animal or asset, a weight or cost. For that reason they also provide criteria for recognizing (in the accounting language sense) an asset or cost.

A system of well formed definitions will permit progressively finer partitioning. Animals can be narrowed to mammals, then to canines, and so forth down to the unique "my dog Rover" just as assets can be narrowed to plant, then to buildings, down to the unique "this entity's building at 123 Main Street". Attributes are similar: "Rover now weighs 50 lbs plus or minus 100%" is quite broad while "Rover now weighs 50 lbs plus or minus .001%" is quite narrow. The ability to narrow the weight attribute depends in part on the definition of weight, and the history of weight reveals that refining the definition permits more precision and more precision permits further refining of the definition, and that the process began with gross imprecision and has progressed to exquisite precision.[3] "The present (past) price of the building at 123 Main Street is $50,000 plus or minus x%" is structurally identical to the statements about Rover's weight. The attribute needs to be defined, the definition applied, the knowledge gained from application used to refine the definition, that refined definition applied, and so forth. It is the definition of the attribute that allows one to recognize (in the ordinary language sense) the magnitude of the attribute and it is also that definition that provides criteria for recognition (in the accounting language sense).

---

2 This does not mean that it is always easy, especially at the boundaries. Even after all the previous work in biology, a few things still seem to be right on the boundary between plant and animal. And the seemingly sharp boundary around mammals becomes a little blurred when classifying monotremes. The point is not that having a well formed definition answers all of one's questions but rather that in the absence of a definition, one does not know the question much less the answer.

3 Hypothetically the weight of Rover is unique so that there is only one magnitude of weight in the world that corresponds to the numeral depicting Rover's weight just as there is only one dog in the world that corresponds to the words "my dog Rover". However, despite the many extraordinary advancements in science, weight cannot be determined with sufficient precision to know Rover's unique weight. *All* measures are imprecise to some degree.

FIGURE 3

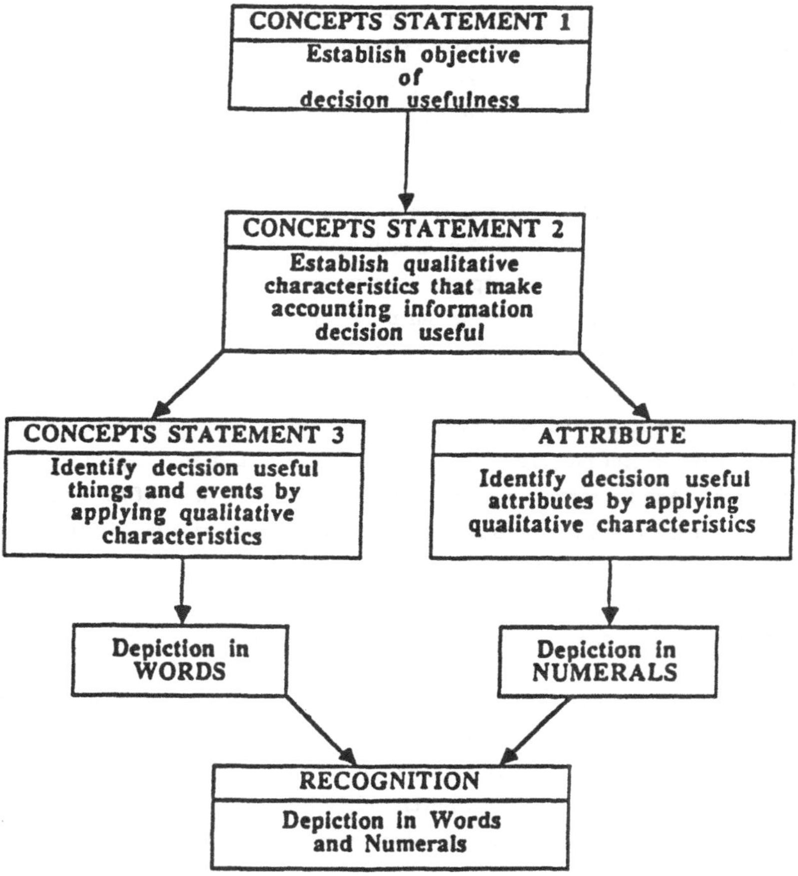

Figure 3. Recognition in the Conceptual Framework

It is possible to separate the definitions of animals and assets from the definitions of weight and cost and therefore it is possible to separate some questions about verbal depiction from those of numerical depiction. Sometimes this is erroneously expressed as the ability to separate recognition of elements from the recognition of attributes or even to separate all recognition questions from all measurement questions. The reason the view is erroneous is that there are several key elements that are defined as totals of or differences between some magnitudes and therefore the recognition of those elements depends on the prior recognition of the magnitude. Comprehensive income and its components (revenues, expenses, gains and losses) are such elements. Whether there is a gain, for example, to be recognized depends on what attribute is measured.

The notion of gain and similar elements is equally as applicable to animals as to assets. Without specifying whether animal-gain refers to weight, height, girth, temperature or whatever, it is impossible to recognize a gain. One can state the obvious, abstract definition that $x-y=z$ and $z>0$ is a gain and $z<0$ is a loss but until the magnitude represented by x and y is specified, that definition will remain too abstract to provide meaning to users or preparers, much less guidance to the FASB in standard setting. What appears to be an unresolvable conceptual problem is reduced to a mere difficult measurement problem once it has been decided that animal-gain refers to, say, weight. And the same is true for asset-gain. The recognition of asset-gain is a problem that has vexed accountants for so long that some have decided that it is an unresolvable conceptual problem. A major, perhaps the only, reason that the problem appears unresolvable is the erroneous view that the concepts that guide the recognition of a gain can be separated from the attribute to be recognized.

The need to specify the attribute prior to recognition does not presuppose the adoption of current values. Both asset and animal attributes can be measured at given dates, such as 31 December every year, or at given events, such as exchanges. A steer could be weighed at acquisition and then never weighed again. Subsequently that steer could be given in exchange for a cow which could also be weighed at acquisition. Then the weight of the cow at acquisition minus the weight of the steer at acquisition is the weight gain from acquisition of steer to acquisition of cow.[4] Note however that without specifying that it is weight that is to be measured, the notion of gain at exchange is equally as ambiguous as the notion of gain at 31 December. Thus the decision to measure a given attribute is crucial to determining gain; the decision to

---

4 Since it *is* the gain, it could be *recognized* as the gain. We often say "it could be *recognized* as a gain" as if the recognition process did not depend on whether it *is* a gain.

measure that attribute at a date versus an event is a separate issue. The extension to a barter in accounting should be apparent. One can hold the view that an asset acquired in a barter be measured at, say, its current cost at that event without necessarily holding the view that the current cost of that or other assets be measured every 31 December. Thus the requirement of specification of the attribute prior to developing recognition concepts is not an attempt to surreptitiously obtain agreement to recognize current values.

To reach the conclusion that the relevant attribute needs to be identified and defined before establishing the recognition concepts is likely to be a disappointment to FASB members and many others. Some want to avoid addressing the selection of the attribute because the question will be very controversial and they want to avoid controversy.[5] Others want to avoid addressing the selection because it will permit raising critical questions about historical costs and they want to avoid that criticism and the resulting possibility of changing or adding to the attributes to be recognized. Some have said that the viability of the FASB depends on avoiding this issue. Granting that these may be good and sufficient reasons for avoiding or deferring addressing attribute selection, it does not follow that one can reasonably address recognition before addressing attribute selection. In my view, if attribute questions must be deferred, then recognition questions must also be deferred.

3.2. ALTERNATIVE ATTRIBUTES

A number of alternative attributes and calculations have been proposed as candidates for recognition. The proposed candidates are or are based on one or more prices. There are six varieties of proposed prices that differ by (1) the two markets--purchasing or selling--in which the entity exchanges resources and obligations and (2) the three temporal locations--past, present and future--at which they are or could be exchanged. The purchasing market prices are usually called costs: Past or Historical Costs, Present or Current Costs, Future or Expected Costs. The selling market prices

---

5 The avoidance of controversy is apparently the only reason for the decision to consider recognition and display prior to attribute selection. At an early stage, evidently when the subject was less controversial and decisions could be made more on the basis of ratiocination than politics, the FASB [*Issues*, Part 1, p.1] planned the sequence to be (1) objectives, (2) qualitative characteristics, (3) elements definition, and (4) attribute selection. Because attribute selection--historical costs versus current values--is the single most controversial topic in accounting today, the FASB decided to change the sequence, to defer addressing attribute selection until recognition and display had been addressed. The problem is that what may make good political sense does not necessarily make good conceptual sense.

are sometimes called exit values: Past Exit Values, Present or Current Exit Values, Future or Expected Exit Values.

Some propose that one or the other of the present prices be recognized initially and subsequently. Others agree for initial recognition but propose that for subsequent recognition the past or future prices be adjusted by calculation and then the adjusted amounts recognized. There are a number of different methods of adjusting the past or future prices: just as LIFO and FIFO are alternative ways to adjust the past price of an inventory lot, discounting at the historical or current rate are alternative ways of adjusting the future forecasted price of receivables. When taking account of the various methods of adjustment and their possible combinations, the total number of alternatives is astronomical.

The above is a very general description of the proposed alternatives from which the FASB could select. (Or the FASB could generate additional alternatives.) That selection will undoubtedly be very difficult, politically and conceptually. A prerequisite to a rational selection is a careful definition of each of the major alternatives--one needs to know *what* one is considering before one can accept it or reject it. Thus, the next step is the provision of rather complete definitions of the various attributes.

Provision of a reasonably complete definition of any one of the alternatives is a rather laborious and lengthy process and therefore beyond the scope of this monograph. (More detailed attempts to provide neutral definitions of the major alternatives, as opposed to advocating one of the alternatives, can be found in FASB [Issues, Part III] and Sterling [*Costs vs Values*, Section 1].) Instead of considering the various attributes and thereby risking the charge of fomenting a revolutionary change to current values, this monograph will suggest some slight, evolutionary refinements of the historical cost attribute.

3.2.1. REFINING THE DEFINITION OF HISTORICAL COSTS

Most readers will readily see the need to provide definitions of the unfamiliar attributes but few will see the need to provide a definition of historical costs because it is widely believed that "everybody knows that definition". Nonetheless, this monograph will briefly consider the definition of historical costs for two reasons: (1) Perhaps the need for the careful definition of the alternative attributes can be best demonstrated by giving an example of some unknown characteristic in a definition that "everybody knows". (2) Perhaps the demonstrated need for some non-cost attribute within the historical cost system will permit both supporter and detractor to reason together.

3.2.1.1. The Need for a Non-Cost Attribute

One of the obstacles to improving the historical cost system is the tenacity of demonstrably erroneous ideas about costs. The careless comment that "all assets are valued at cost" is often uttered and seldom challenged. When it is challenged the speaker will usually grant that there are a few, rare exceptions, such as lower of cost or market, and then offer the amendment that "all assets are almost always valued at cost", overlooking cash and claims to cash that are almost always valued at non-cost. The fact is that the structure of the historical cost system requires the use of a non-cost attribute in several instances.

3.2.1.1.1. Cost vs Non-Cost Attributes

The cost of acquiring an economic resource is the magnitude of other resources (or obligations) sacrificed to acquire (by exchange, production, etc.) that economic resource. (See Concepts Statement 3, paragraphs 20n and 110-114 for further discussion of the definition of cost.) The procedure for measuring the magnitude of the cost of an acquired resource is to (1) associate the acquired resource(s) with the sacrificed resource(s) and (2) measure or estimate the magnitude of the selected attribute of the sacrificed resource(s). That is, the amount of the credit is determined and the debit is set equal to the credit. This procedure precludes the recognition of comprehensive income at exchange because the resource acquired is *set equal* to the resource sacrificed and therefore the difference is *zero* by definition of the term "cost".

Given that a major objective of historical cost accounting is to report comprehensive income, it *requires* that some economic resources be depicted at something other than cost. If all economic resources were depicted at cost, no comprehensive income would ever be reported. To illustrate, consider an exchange in which a receivable is acquired and, say, land is sacrificed. In regard to the possibility of recognizing comprehensive income, the first question is whether the receivable is to be depicted at cost or non-cost. The fact that this is a "sale" may permit recognition of a non-cost attribute in present practice but sales do not require non-cost attributes. The installment sale method is an example of depicting the receivable at cost--setting the net amount of the receivable equal to the sacrifice--and thereby precluding the possibility of recognizing a gain at the event of the exchange. It is selecting a non-cost attribute for the receivable that permits the recognition of comprehensive income, not the fact that it is a sale.

Obtaining agreement that there is need for a non-cost attribute exposes a second question: which non-cost attribute should be selected to measure the receivable? As long as that question remains unanswered the question of the proceeds or revenue or gain from the sacrificed resource will remain unanswered.

3.2.1.1.2. Cost from Non-Cost Attributes

When cash is received in exchange for a payable the amount of the payable is set equal to the cash. This procedure is well understood and the term "historical proceeds" has begun to be used to describe it. However, when, say, land is received in exchange for a payable, the usual procedure is to determine the amount of the payable and set the amount of land equal. The amount of cost of the land is defined to be the amount of the payable. The question is: which non-cost attribute should be selected to measure the payable? As long as that question remains unanswered the question of the cost of the acquired resource will remain unanswered.

The question extends to all non-cash exchanges. In barters, for example, the acquisition may be set equal to the book value or to the current value of the sacrifice and either of those defined as the cost of the acquisition. Although some argue that the "real" cost of the acquisition must be the current value of the sacrifice because book values cannot possibly measure the cost of acquisitions, they are willing to accept that the cost of, say, a building is equal to the sum of the book values of the assets sacrificed to construct that building. It is not the purpose of this monograph to debate the merits of such issues but rather to merely point out that "the cost" depends upon "the amount of the sacrifice" and that the attribute of the sacrifice is in dispute. The general question is: which non-cost attribute should be selected to measure the sacrifice? As long as that question remains unanswered the question of the cost of the acquired resource will remain unanswered.

3.2.1.1.3. Non-Cost from Non-Sacrifice

The question of attribute selection also arises in non-cash investments by and distributions to owners and in non-cash grants and gifts. The FASB has defined investments by owners as non-reciprocal transfers as opposed to exchanges requiring sacrifices. Grants and gifts are by definition without direct sacrifice. In cases where there is no sacrifice there is no cost incurred and therefore the magnitude of the cost is zero. Relevance probably requires depicting the resources so acquired at something other than zero. The question is: which non-cost attribute should be selected in such instances?

3.2.1.1.4. Initial vs Subsequent Recognition

Note that the mentioned instances where the question of attribute selection was raised are concerned only with *initial* recognition, not with *subsequent* recognition. Thus, consideration of non-cost attributes is not the sole province of periodic *re*valuation in current value systems, it extends to the *first* valuation in historical cost systems. Note also that the mentioned instances covers all the ordinary ways in which economic resources are acquired. Thus, the question of which non-cost attribute should be selected is a part of the mainstream, routine activities in present accounting practice and therefore deserves priority consideration in a conceptual framework.

3.2.1.2. Cash Equivalents

The preoccupation with cost has inhibited widespread awareness of the need to decide which non-cost attribute should be used in the historical cost system of accounting.[6] As a consequence there has been little consideration of the various non-cost attributes among historical cost supporters. A notable exception is Paton & Littleton [Accounting Standards] who, in their classic explanation and defense of the historical cost system, suggested an attribute called "cash equivalent".[7] That term and its

6 Indeed, some apparently think it inappropriate to consider the issue because it is contradictory to depict at non-cost when a cost system is being used. Such is the power of words. The term "historical cost" seems to blind both supporter and detractor to the fact that a major objective of the system is to report income and that the reporting of non-zero income requires the use of some non-cost attribute.

7 For a discussion of the term "cash equivalent" and its definition see Paton & Littleton [*Accounting Standards*, pp. 24, 26ff]. They also use "current cash value", "bargained price", "money-equivalent", and a number of other terms that are synonymous. Chambers [*Accounting, Evaluation*] has proposed a type of current value accounting and named his attribute "current cash equivalent". Despite his flawless logic and felicitous phraseology, his proposed system is too radically different from current practice to permit it to be examined, much less adopted. The attributes "cash equivalent" and "current cash equivalent" are identical except for temporal location (and except for rigour in development and definition). Paton & Littleton propose measuring the attribute at the event of exchange but not at balancing dates, thus depicting *past* cash equivalents as time passes, while Chambers proposes measuring the attribute at every balancing date, thus depicting *current* cash equivalents. As a consequence, current cash equivalents may be viewed as an

referenced attribute has been selected for discussion in this monograph because of its apparent relevance, as well as to emphasize that measurement is the establishment of the equality or equivalency of the resource or obligation to a specific amount of cash.

3.2.1.2.1. Credit Instruments

Credit transactions illustrate the frequent need for and meaning of cash equivalents. In such transactions the receipt or payment of cash is delayed and therefore the contracted amount of cash is likely to be greater than the amount that would be received or paid if final settlement were effected at once. The cash equivalent of the credit instrument is the estimated amount of cash that would immediately effect final settlement; the amount of cash that would be required to be paid to immediately discharge a payable or the amount of cash that would be received from an immediate sale of a receivable. Thus, the cash equivalent of the credit instrument is an estimate of the immediate cash price of that instrument.

There are several extant alternatives in current practice. For receivables there are the usual alternatives of net realizable value and the amortized (either by the straight line or compound interest method) amounts, as well as the unusual alternatives of cost (as in installment sales) and the rare unadjusted face amount. Payables are not symmetrical. There are the same amortized amounts but unadjusted face amounts are common and the counterpart of net realizable value is unknown. There is little authoritative guidance about which attribute is to be used when measuring credit instruments and the guidance that does exist is highly detailed with no apparent conceptual cohesion.

The definition of cash equivalents would provide that conceptual cohesion. It would establish what attribute is to be measured and leave it up to the measurer to apply that definition in the vast variety of instances in which it arises. Thus it is proposed that credit instruments be numerically depicted at their estimated cash equivalents at the event of exchange.

3.2.1.2.2. Costs and Proceeds

If it were accepted that the cash equivalent is the attribute of credit instruments to be measured and recognized, it would provide a more definite meaning of "cost" and "proceeds" in exchanges involving such instruments. When an economic resource is

---

extension of cash equivalents and Chambers as a disciple of the venerable Paton & Littleton rather than a heretic whose proposal does not deserve examination.

acquired by giving a payable, the cost of that economic resource in that exchange is the cash equivalent of the payable in that exchange. When a receivable is acquired by giving an economic resource, the proceeds from that economic resource is the cash equivalent of the receivable in that exchange. (A sub-category of proceeds is "revenue", being that fraction of proceeds arising from central or on-going operations.)

The process is a chain of equalities. What is unknown is the number of monetary units that is equal in exchange to an economic resource, E=?. What is observed is the equality in exchange of the economic resource and a credit instrument, E=C. What is estimated is the number of monetary units that is equal in exchange to the credit instrument, C=$. From that it is inferred that E=$.

The suggestion is that costs and proceeds be *defined* as equal to the cash equivalents of credit instruments given or received in exchange, not necessarily that acquisitions and dispositions be depicted at their costs or proceeds. The distinction is made because of the conviction that a clear definition of the object of discourse is a prerequisite to rational discourse. The need for the distinction can be clearly illustrated by the ancient accounting problem that goes under the name of "fortunate and unfortunate purchases".

The price of an economic resource may be defined to be equal to the cash equivalent of the credit instrument given in *that* exchange. However, the particular price in that exchange may be different from the generally available price for that economic resource. The generally available price of the economic resource is probably equal or almost equal to the cash equivalent of the payable in almost all credit transactions. However, the possibility of nonarm's length transactions or the ignorance or error of one of the transactors suggests that the cash equivalent sacrificed for the economic resource be compared with other exchanges of the same or similar economic resources for the purpose of ensuring that the equality in fact holds. If the equality does not hold, it presents the question of whether it is the cost or the generally available price that is the attribute to be recognized.

Consider the unfortunate purchase of gold bullion for $400 per ounce when the generally available price on the gold exchange is $300 per ounce. Which attribute, price or cost, should be used to depict the gold? Practice varies but in this particular case most would probably recognize the price of the gold and the difference as a loss. More variation in practice might be observed if it were a fortunate purchase--the cost and price were reversed--but probably a majority would still recognize the price and the difference as a gain. Still more variation in practice might be observed if it were an unfortunate purchase of land instead of gold but most would probably recognize the price of the land and the difference as a loss. If it were a fortunate purchase of land, the variation in practice would likely be lessened with most recognizing the cost.

It is not the purpose of this discussion to try to resolve such issues but rather to point out that the way to resolve them is to select the attribute to be recognized. The alternatives are to depict non-cash resources at the generally available prices and recognize differences as gains or losses or to depict non-cash resources at costs where there is no difference and therefore no gain or loss to be recognized.

No recommendation is made in this monograph regarding the choice between cost and price of non-cash economic resources acquired in credit transactions. Instead, the recommendation is merely that the FASB select the attribute on the basis of achieving the objective of decision usefulness, the primary characteristics of which are relevance and reliability. The only recommendation in this monograph regarding attributes is that credit instruments be depicted at their cash equivalents. The political sensitivity of the issue is such that henceforth the yet to be selected attribute of other economic resources and obligations will be referred to as the "yet-to-be-selected attribute".

Although no recommendation is made as to which attribute should be selected, the author is convinced that the proper application of the qualitative characteristics will lead to the selection of either cost or price, or both, but not to lower of cost or market, because there is no evidence that the relative magnitudes of attributes affect their relevance or reliability. If cost is relevant and price is not when it is a fortunate purchase, then cost will continue to be relevant when it is an unfortunate purchase. If price is too unreliable to be selected when it is a fortunate purchase, then it will also be too unreliable when it is an unfortunate purchase. Prudence may require selecting the lower end of a range of a given attribute, as discussed below, but it cannot require substituting an irrelevant attribute for a relevant one or an unreliable attribute for a reliable one.

3.2.1.2.3. Estimation, Imprecision and Prudence

In a non-cash exchange the amount of the cash equivalent of a receivable or payable is not observable: it requires estimation. Most accountants loathe estimation and the accompanying imprecision. Which attribute to choose is not the primary point in this context. If it were decided that, say, discounted value is preferred to cash equivalent, estimation would not be avoided. The point is that the historical cost system requires estimation in *all* non-cash exchanges: being clear that estimation is required should direct attention and effort toward how to estimate and how to deal with the accompanying imprecision. The cost of an economic resource acquired by giving a credit instrument is no more precise than the estimate of the cash equivalent of that instrument and since the vast majority of economic resources owned by businesses are acquired in credit transactions, the vast majority of initially recognized costs are imprecise. Perhaps awareness of that will assist in avoiding invidious comparisons of "reliable [precise] costs" to "unreliable [imprecise] prices" and thereby assist in making a selection on the basis of the merits of the alternatives.

The meaning of imprecision is that the estimation of the magnitude of the cash equivalent of a credit instrument will usually result in a range of numerals rather than a single numeral. When some numeral within that range is judged to be a better representation of the magnitude than any other numeral within that range, that numeral should be selected for depiction. When no numeral within the range is a better representation of the magnitude than any other numeral, prudence may require the selection of the minimum numeral within the range for the depiction of receivables, and the maximum numeral for the depiction of payables. If zero is the best representation of the magnitude or if zero is the minimum of a range that contains no best representation, recognition is not permitted, although disclosure is not prohibited.

Consider, for example, a receivable from a bankrupt firm. If it is judged that zero is the best estimation of the cash equivalent of that receivable (which means that the receivable is not an economic resource because it is not desirable enough to anyone else for them to pay a price), then it does not qualify for recognition. If zero and 2 cents on the dollar are judged to be equally good estimations of the amount of cash it would fetch in the market, prudence may require the selection of zero and therefore nonrecognition. Note that what is sought is the present price of the receivable--the amount of cash received if factored without recourse--as opposed to a discounted or otherwise adjusted forecast of the amount that will be collected. Similarly for the numerical depiction of an obligation arising from a lawsuit in the process of being adjudicated, a "contingent liability", where zero and 2 percent of the contested amount are judged to be equally good estimations, prudence may require the selection of the larger amount. Again what is sought is the present price of that obligation--the premium that would be charged by Lloyd's to indemnify the entity--not a discounted or otherwise adjusted forecast of the payment at the conclusion of the trial.

In summary, the best or most prudent estimate of the magnitude of the cash equivalent of a credit instrument is the amount to be recognized. If zero is the best or most prudent estimate, recognition is not permitted.

3.3. FINANCIAL STATEMENTS: MODELS OF PHENOMENA

In a literal and superficial sense, financial statements are pieces of paper marked with ink--they contain mere words and numerals. The significance and usefulness of financial statements comes from the things and events that the words and numerals represent. Such representations are often called *models*. The recognition tests are applicable to the things and events. If a thing or event satisfies the recognition tests, it qualifies for representation on the financial statements. If a thing or event does not satisfy the tests, it does not qualify for representation on financial statements.

Financial statements constitute a model of things and events and the relationship between things and events. Individually they represent the financial position of an enterprise at a given date or the financial changes of an enterprise during a given period. Collectively, via articulation, they represent the relationship between the financial position and the financial changes of an enterprise.

3.3.1. FINANCIAL POSITION

The Statement of Financial Position displays the assets, liabilities, and equity of an entity at a given moment in time. Those elements are representations of things--economic resources, obligations and owners' interest--and the magnitude of an attribute of those things that exist at that moment in time.[8] The recognition process is concerned with which things and which attribute of those things are to be so represented.

3.3.2. FINANCIAL CHANGES

The Statements of Income, Cash Flows, Owners' Investments and Distribution, and others as needed display the revenues, expenses, gains, losses, sources of cash, uses of

---

[8] The requirement that the things and magnitude of the things exist at the date of the Statement of Financial Position does not presuppose current values. Supporters of depicting assets at their unexpired cost use adjusting entries for the purpose of reducing the unexpired cost by the amount that has expired during the period thus depicting the present unexpired cost.

cash, investments by owners, and distributions to owners of an entity over a given period of time. Those elements are representations of the effects of events--exchange transactions, nonreciprocal transfers, transformations, and so on--that have occurred during that period of time. The recognition process is concerned with which events and which attribute of those events are to be so represented.

3.3.3. ARTICULATION

The articulation of the financial statements describes a particular relationship between things and events. The extant things are the result of past events, and a difference in things at two points in time is proof that one or more events occurred in the interim. The financial change elements represent the effects of the events that occurred which changed the things. The financial position elements represent the things that are the cumulative effects of past events. The articulation of the financial change elements and the financial position elements represents the relationship between the things and events.

3.3.3.1. Articulation vs Non-Articulation

Articulation versus non-articulation of financial statements is an ancient issue that has been widely debated but never resolved. Its perceived importance is indicated by it being listed as "issue one" by the FASB [*Issues*, paragraph 25]. The issue is stated there (and elsewhere) as if the FASB were free to decide whether financial statements should articulate. That is an erroneous conception of the problem and that conceptual error is the main reason that it remains unresolved. Faithful representation requires that if the phenomena articulate, then financial statements must articulate, and vice versa if the phenomena do not articulate. Stating the problem in this fashion makes it a matter of evidence about how phenomena behave rather than a matter of free choice by the FASB.

In essence, articulation is a matter of the additivity of the selected attribute. The quantity of cash, for example, is additive and therefore a cash flow statement *must* articulate with a cash position statement if *both* statements are faithful representations. If the cash flow statement shows a net cash increase of $x while the cash position shows a difference between the beginning and ending amount that is different from $x, then at least one of the statements is not a faithful representation. Articulation of the statements is not a convention to be decided by the FASB but rather a factual question about the behaviour of the phenomena. The cash flow statement must articulate with the cash position statement for the straightforward reason that the phenomena articulate.

Contrast the quantity of cash with an attribute that is not additive, e.g., temperature. If the temperature of the coins and currency at every receipt and disbursement were measured and debited and credited to the cash account, then faithful representation would result in non-articulation (except by coincidence) because temperature is not additive. That is, if the sum of the temperature debits less the sum of the temperature credits were x degrees, and the difference between the beginning and ending temperature were different from x degrees, *both* statements could be a faithful representation of the temperature. The statements should not articulate because the phenomena do not articulate.

3.3.3.1.1. Data Expansion

Some are opposed to articulation because it is thought that it does not permit reporting relevant but non-additive attributes. Quality of management, for example, is arguably something accountants should report. The fact that quality of management is not additive does not mean that accountants cannot or should not prepare statements about it, but it does mean that accountants cannot cast it in statements that articulate. There is no conflict between reporting cash flows *and* quality of management. The desire to prepare statements about phenomena that do not articulate does not require abolishing articulated statements for phenomena that do articulate. Thus the data that is to be reported by accountants can be expanded without deciding or even addressing the question of articulation versus non-articulation.

3.3.3.2. Asset-Liability vs Revenue-Expense

A part of the long-standing articulation debate is the conflict between those who hold the revenue-expense view and those who hold the asset-liability view. This conflict has also been expressed by contrasting the income to the position statement, events to objects, and dynamics to statics. See FASB [*Issues*, paragraphs 24ff] for an extended discussion. In brief, the idea is that one needs to choose whether to focus on revenues-expenses or assets-liabilities because different answers are obtained from different focuses. One needs to decide the relative importance of the income and position statements because a good income statement results in a bad position statement and vice versa.

Consider again the cash flow and the cash position statements. One need not choose between the cash flow (or the source-use) view and the cash position view because the attribute is additive. When the attribute is additive, the statements are complementary, not conflicting. The difference between the amount of cash at the beginning and ending of the period is an aggregate change, which is disaggregated on the cash flow statement. Thus there is no conflict between aggregation and disaggregation because of articulation, although the question of the level of aggregation is always present and always difficult in this and many other contexts. There is no conflict between events and amounts for the same reason. Those who propose listing the events without regard to the amounts have set a very difficult task for themselves. The list of *all* the events that could affect cash would include, for example, the amount of petty cash that might be accidentally burned as well as the possibility of a conscience stricken employee surreptitiously returning cash to the box after it had been written off. The objective of the cash flow statement is to explain all events that affected cash and the way to check on the completeness of that explanation is to compare the sum of the events to the difference in the position.

Of course, the debaters say that they are concerned with the "complicated" revenue-expense versus asset-liability question, not the "simple" source-use versus cash position question. The LIFO-FIFO question is often cited as the most telling example of the conflict because it is said that LIFO results in a good income statement and a bad position statement, and vice versa for FIFO, so that one is forced to choose. Those who do not want to choose, who want both good income and position statements, suggest abolishing articulation.

Consider an analogous physical process in which goods come in one gram blocks. The volume of the first block acquired was 1 cc so the inventory account was debited for that amount. By the time the second block was acquired the temperature had risen so that its volume was 1.1 cc and the inventory account was debited for that amount, now showing a balance of 2.1 cc. Later when 1 block was shipped, one person proposed the FANG (first acquired now gone) method so that the measurement of the VGS (volume of goods shipped) would be 1 cc and the balance of the inventory account would be 1.1 cc. Another person proposed the SANG (second acquired now gone) method so that the measure of VGS would be 1.1 cc leaving a balance in the inventory account of 1 cc.

The problem starts before the need to decide between SANG and FANG: although the sum of 1 and 1.1 is 2.1, there is nothing in the warehouse that corresponds to that sum. Volume is not additive under these conditions. This means that 2.1 is nothing but a numeral and as soon as that is recognized, it follows that SANG-FANG is a dispute over how to divide numerals. The *subject matter* is numerals, not volume. The problem is not a rubber yardstick: the cc's per gram vary with the ambient weather conditions just as the dollars per gram vary with the ambient economic conditions. The problem is that no one has bothered to try to measure the volume. The reason no one has tried to measure the volume is that measurement is confused with calculation,[9] symbols are confused with what they are intended to represent.

If the volume in the warehouse were measured, it would be noticed that the volume of both blocks had changed and then eventually someone would discover that the change was due to a change in the ambient temperature. That is how discoveries are made in science. If the volume were calculated, the difference between the measured magnitude and the 2.1 obtained from calculation could not be noticed, precluding the question of what caused the difference, precluding the possibility of the discovery. If the difference between the measured amount and the calculated amount were noticed, the amount in the account could be adjusted (by a familiar adjusting entry) so that it faithfully represented the volume, thereby avoiding the need to consider articulation versus non-articulation, revenue-expense versus asset-liability, and other similar false issues.

3.4. DISTINGUISHING REPRESENTATIONS FROM PHENOMENA

Surprising as it may seem, there is a tendency for people who work closely with models to begin to confuse the symbols in models with the phenomena that those symbols represent. Such confusion is both ancient and pervasive. That it is ancient is evidenced by it being discussed by Francis Bacon [*Advancement*, book 1, section IV, paragraph 3] in the 17th century: "Here therefore is the first distemper of learning, when men study words and not matter...." That it is pervasive is evidenced by it being discussed by Whitehead [*Science*, p. 58] in regard to all sciences. He termed it the "fallacy of misplaced concreteness" because the abstract symbols are sometimes taken to be concrete phenomena. Boulding [*Economics*, p. 75] makes the same point by contrasting abstraction with reality:

---

9 ***Measured***, an empirical procedure, not *calculated*, a logical procedure. In the preceding paragraphs the words "measure" and "measurement" were deliberately misused as an experiment to see if the reader would catch it. So far all prepublication readers who were accountants passed over the paragraph without comment because it is standard usage in accounting to equate measure and calculate. The one non-accountant reader questioned the choice of words. The point is not a pedantic nicety about correct usage but rather a problem in communication (and thinking). When accountants talk about "*measuring* cost of goods sold by the LIFO (FIFO) method" it inhibits their recognition of the distinction between measurement and calculation.

> What all this involves is not a case against abstraction, which is essential, but a warning against mistaking abstraction for reality. We would be foolish to try to go for a walk across a map, but a map may be very helpful if we are going for a real walk.

The map analogy is apt because it is unlikely that anyone would confuse the symbols on a map with the things those symbols are intended to represent, and therefore it makes the distinction clear. But the reason for employing the analogy is to explain the distinction, and the explanation is needed because the distinction is often blurred.

Model builders have a tendency to become so familiar with their mental constructs and abstract symbols that they mistake them for phenomena and incorporate them in their models. (See the discussion of the definition of an asset, supra [2.2.1.3.2], for an example of this confusion in accounting.) When that happens some of the symbols in a model do not represent phenomena: the symbols correspond only to other symbols or noumena, not to phenomena. The usefulness of a model comes from its symbols faithfully representing relevant phenomena: the usefulness of a model is destroyed when the symbols no longer faithfully represent the relevant phenomena because the symbols are confused with phenomena.

Accountants are not immune to this confusion. The words and numerals generated by accounting concepts and methods are sometimes taken to *be* phenomena rather than representations *of* phenomena. For example, no one would confuse "building" with the structure that it represents, but there does seem to be considerable confusion about what phenomena the "book value" or the "depreciation" of building represents. The AIA [Terminology Bulletin, paragraph 54] wrote: "Definitions are unacceptable which imply that *depreciation for the year* is a measurement ... of anything that actually occurs within the year." That definition means that "depreciation" does not represent phenomena--it is a symbol that does not correspond to any phenomena and therefore it cannot faithfully represent any phenomena. Since the absence of representational faithfulness destroys decision usefulness, the definition must be changed. The FASB must decide what phenomena are to be represented by that word (and others) or else strike them from the lexicon of accounting.

The example of depreciation is intended to show that the need for the clear distinction of representations and phenomena is equally as applicable to accounting as to other fields. More important is the need to be clear that the intention is to represent phenomena. The suggestion that the FASB endorse the ancient accounting tradition of faithfully representing "worksheet calculations" on financial statements merely transfers the question to what phenomena the worksheet calculations represent. The observation that the definition of faithful representation includes the phrase "purports to represent" is true but that does not allow one to conclude that if one numeral faithfully represents another numeral, then the former numeral faithfully represents phenomena.

3.4.1. TERMINOLOGY THAT MAKES THE DISTINCTION

Part of the confusion in accounting, as in other fields, is caused by using the same terms to refer to both the representation and to the phenomenon. For example, "asset" may refer to an economic resource or it may refer to the words or numerals representing the economic resource. The terms "real-world assets" and "assets" have begun to be used to make the distinction in FASB publications. In previous accounting literature (including previous FASB publications) it is not always clear whether "asset" refers to the representation or the phenomenon. Another example is that assets are often defined as "costs that are expected to benefit the future", which confuses the manner of numerically depicting an economic resource with the resource. Obviously, it is the economic resource that is expected to benefit the future, not the cost of that resource.

The reason for using relatively unfamiliar terminology in this monograph is to try to clearly distinguish the phenomena from the representation and therefore avoid the confusion. For example, "things" refer to phenomena in general and "economic resources" and "obligations" refer to specific kinds of things. "Assets" and "liabilities" are more specific: those terms refer to economic resources and obligations, respectively, that satisfy the recognition tests for a specific entity. "Depictions" or "representations", by contrast, refer to the ink marks on financial statements that correspond to things and events. The "recognition of an asset" means the representation (ink marks) of an economic resource that satisfies the recognition tests. The attempt is to communicate clearly by sharply segregating the symbols from the phenomena by using different terms for each. When the context makes the referent clear the short-hand, familiar terms will continue to be used.

3.5. SUMMARY

The dictionary defines "recognition" as the "identification of some person or thing as having been known before or as being of a certain kind". It seems clear that a prerequisite to recognizing a thing as being of a certain kind is that the kind of thing be identified and defined. It boggles the mind to think about how one would recognize a, say, monotreme without having previously identified monotremes as the kind of thing one wants to recognize and having previously defined what one means by monotreme. It is equally boggling to think about how to recognize the magnitude of a monotreme without having previously identified and defined the attribute. Thus, definition of what one wants to recognize comes prior to recognition.

Considerable work has gone into identifying and defining the elements of financial statements but political considerations have delayed work on identifying and defining the attribute. Until that work has been undertaken there is little that can be said about recognition of magnitudes. *A fortiori*, there is even less that can be said about differences (gains or losses) in magnitudes.

One obstacle to rational consideration of the attribute is the erroneous view that the current system is based exclusively on cost. The title "historical cost-realization system" was used at one time and it better described the requirement to measure a non-cost attribute under some conditions. This monograph restricts its scope to considering non-cost attributes at initial recognition and a modest refinement of the historical cost system is proposed, namely, the adoption of cash equivalents for credit instruments.

Another obstacle to progress is the confusion between calculation and measurement, between operations on numerals and discovering the numeral that represents a magnitude of a given attribute. The objective of representing phenomena provides a clear avenue toward obtaining answers to several long-standing controversies. Articulation is an example: if the phenomena articulate, then the financial statements must articulate, and vice versa. That objective also reveals that some other long-standing controversies are false issues. Revenue-expense versus asset-liability is an example: if the phenomena articulate, then there cannot be a conflict between these views.

A part of the reason for the latter obstacle is the tendency to mistake symbols for what the symbols represent. Although we think it amusing to be warned against mistaking a map for the landscape, we regularly meander through the symbols without recognizing that they are symbols. Thus a prerequisite to solving some "recognition" problems is the ability to "recognize" the distinction between symbols and what those symbols represent.

4. RECOGNIZING THINGS AS ASSETS AND LIABILITIES

Assets and liabilities are certain kinds of things and the magnitude of a certain attribute of those things that exist at a point in time. The recognition process is concerned with determining which things qualify for verbal depiction as assets and liabilities and which attribute qualifies for numerical depiction of the magnitude of those assets and liabilities. The outcome of the process is either to depict a thing and its magnitude as an asset or liability on the Statement of Financial Position if it satisfies the tests for recognition or to omit the depiction if it fails those tests. The recognition tests incorporate and extend the general recognition criteria discussed supra, especially Chapter 2, serving the purpose of providing more specific, concrete guidance in determining which things, and which attribute of those things, are or are not decision useful and therefore should or should not be recognized as assets and liabilities.

4.1 APPLICATION OF THE TESTS

Either the occurrence of an event, such as an exchange, or reaching a specified point in time, such as the end of a fiscal period, may trigger the application of the recognition tests. The tests *must* be applied at or near the date of the issuance of financial statements; they *may also* be applied at the occurrence of events. The perpetual and periodic inventory systems provide an example of the distinction: in the perpetual system the effects of sales on inventory are recognized in individual amounts at the occurrence of each sale event; in the periodic system the effects of all sales of the period (and other events that reduced inventory) are recognized as a single amount at the date of the issuance of the financial statements. However, the possibility of error or failure to detect some events, such as spoilage or pilferage, necessitates the application of the recognition tests to perpetual inventories at or near the date of financial reporting as well as at the occurrence of events. Thus, application of the recognition tests is *required* at or near the date of financial reporting; application of those tests is *permitted* at the occurrence of events.

The example is intended to illustrate the general principle that the application of the recognition tests at the date of financial reporting is necessary and sufficient for the recognition of assets and liabilities on the Statement of Financial Position. Whether the tests are applied at the occurrence of events in addition to being applied at the date of financial reporting depends on cost-benefit considerations specific to enterprises and therefore cannot be stated as a general concept. Thus, at a minimum, the recognition tests are to be applied at or near each financial reporting date. The recognition process must be completed, the decision reached to recognize or not to recognize, prior to the issuance of the financial statements.

4.2 THE TESTS

The recognition process consists of six interrelated tests that must be satisfied for a thing to be recognized as an asset or liability on the Statement of Financial Position. The tests constitute the necessary and sufficient conditions for recognition. Each test is necessary because all must be satisfied for a thing to be recognized as an asset or liability; that is, if a thing fails to satisfy one of the tests, it does not qualify for recognition as an asset or liability. Collectively, the tests are sufficient because no other test is required for recognition; that is, if a thing satisfies all of the specified tests, it qualifies for recognition as an asset or liability without further testing. The sequence in which the tests are applied is of little importance. Often two or more of the tests can be efficiently applied simultaneously.

4.2.1. DETECTION OF EXISTENCE

The first test for recognition is the detection of the existence of a thing (tangible or intangible) that may be a candidate for recognition. Detection of the existence of a thing is essential to initiate the recognition process as well as being a necessary but not a sufficient condition for recognition.

4.2.2. ECONOMIC RESOURCES AND OBLIGATIONS

The second test for recognition identifies the kind of things that are to be recognized. It was previously decided (Concepts Statements 1, 2 & 3) that the kind of things that are to be recognized are economic resources and obligations because they are relevant to rational investment, credit and similar decisions. This provides a general screen for recognizing things: all things that are not economic resources or obligations are excluded from recognition. The goal of this test is to include all things that have the characteristics of an economic resource, and thus are eligible for recognition as assets, or the characteristics of an economic obligation, and thus are eligible for recognition as liabilities. Alternatively, the goal is to exclude all things that do not have those characteristics and thus are not eligible for recognition as assets or liabilities. Therefore, having the characteristics of an economic resource or obligation is a necessary but not sufficient condition for recognition as an asset or liability.

The essential characteristics of an economic resource are that the thing be (1) scarce and (2) desirable. When a thing has both of those characteristics it will command a price. The major distinction between economic resources and noneconomic resources is that economic resources can only be obtained for a price if not owned or that they can be sold for a price if owned. Noneconomic resources do not command a price because they lack either scarcity or desirability. For example, air is desirable, indeed indispensable, but it is not sufficiently scarce to command a price; smallpox virus is exceptionally scarce but is not desirable and therefore does not command a price. Since air and smallpox virus do not command a price, they are not economic resources[1] and therefore do not qualify for recognition as assets.

The existence of a price is conclusive evidence that a thing is an economic resource. It is also a necessary and sufficient evidence of a future economic benefit. The ability of a thing to command a price means that more than one person or enterprise expects it to yield future economic benefits. If only one person or enterprise expects a thing to yield future economic benefits, no one else would sacrifice other resources to acquire it or accept it as settlement of an obligation--it would not command a price. Such idiosyncratic expectations are not subject to verification and therefore are not sufficient for classifying a thing as an economic resource.

Many things are frequently exchanged and therefore the magnitude of their prices can be easily estimated. Other things are rarely exchanged and therefore the magnitude of their prices is difficult to estimate. The ease or difficulty of estimating the magnitude of the price of a thing is not pertinent to the determination of whether it is an economic resource; that a thing commands a price is sufficient to satisfy this test.

Economic obligations are the converse of economic resources. An economic obligation to one entity must be an economic resource of a different entity. An economic resource is a benefit while an economic obligation is a burden. The resource is desirable and the obligation is undesirable. Both command a price: it requires the outflow of cash or other resources to settle an obligation and the amount of the outflow required is the price of the obligation; the amount of the inflow of cash or other resources to the holder of the obligation is the price of that resource. Thus, the requirement of a price to settle is conclusive evidence that a thing is an economic obligation.

---

[1] Of course bottled air or oxygen and laboratory specimens of smallpox virus do command a price and therefore would qualify as economic resources when in that form. However, in their usual state they will not command a price and will not qualify.

All things that command a price are economic resources. Some economic resources of one entity are economic obligations of another entity and also require a price from the obligor. Things that command or require a price define the class of all assets and liabilities in general--the things that are eligible for recognition on all Statements of Financial Position. Things that do not command or require a price are not economic resources or obligations and are not eligible for recognition.

4.2.3. ENTITY ASSOCIATION

The third test for recognition identifies a necessary relationship of the economic resource or obligation to the entity under consideration. That entity must control the resource or the obligation must be owed by that entity. The benefits obtained as a result of controlling the resource must accrue to that entity; the duty or responsibility must be such that it leaves the entity little or no discretion in whether to fulfill the obligation. The goal of this test is to include all economic resources that are controlled by the entity and all obligations that are owed by the entity. All controlled economic resources and owed obligations are eligible for recognition as assets and liabilities by the entity. Alternatively, the goal is to exclude all economic resources and obligations that are controlled or owed by other entities. Thus, an entity's control or owing of economic resources and obligations is a necessary but not a sufficient condition for recognition of them as assets and liabilities on the Statement of Financial Position of that entity.

The purpose of the entity association test is to identify *which* entity has control of the economic resource and therefore must recognize that resource as an asset on *its* Statement of Financial Position. Control permits the entity wide latitude in its decisions regarding the resource--the entity can exchange it for other resources, use it to produce other resources, extract a price for others' use of it, transfer it to settle liabilities, distribute it to owners, or let it lie idle. If the entity is restricted from receiving the benefits from the economic resource, that resource does not qualify for recognition as an asset on that entity's Statement of Financial Position.

The purpose of the entity association test is also to identify *which* entity is obligated and therefore must recognize an economic obligation on *its* Statement of Financial Position. Obligation requires the entity to transfer economic resources to the obligee to settle the obligation. The obligor entity has little latitude in its decisions regarding the obligation--the entity must settle the obligation by transferring cash or other economic resources acceptable to the obligee at or before a specified or determinable date or event in a specified or determinable amount. If the entity is not so restricted, if it can avoid transferring cash or other economic resources to the obligee, there is no obligation that qualifies for recognition as a liability.

4.2.4. NON-ZERO MAGNITUDE

The fourth test for recognition establishes a magnitude of the yet-to-be-selected attribute. To be recognized a thing must have a non-zero magnitude of the yet-to-be-selected attribute. The yet-to-be-selected attribute must be non-zero rather than positive because negative amounts of some elements will qualify for recognition. A loss or deficit, for example, is a negative but non-zero amount that will qualify for recognition.

One reason for this test is parsimony of display. It would be possible to faithfully represent a receivable from a bankrupt limited liability company that had wound up it affairs by displaying the word "receivable" accompanied by the numeral zero but parsimony suggests the omission of that representation and the adoption of the convention that the absence of that display is intended to represent a zero magnitude of the yet-to-be-selected attribute. Thus, if "receivable" does not appear on the Statement of Financial Position, it indicates either the absence of an obligation by another entity or a zero magnitude of the yet-to-be-selected attribute, or both.

Beyond the non-zero magnitude requirement, there is little that can be said about this test until the relevant attribute is identified and defined.

4.2.5. TEMPORAL ASSOCIATION

The fifth test for recognition identifies the date at which the tests must be satisfied. To be recognized a thing must satisfy all tests on the date that they are applied. The fact that a thing satisfied the tests at a past date or that it is expected to satisfy the tests at a future date is not pertinent to its recognition at the date the tests are applied. If any test is not satisfied on the date of application, the thing under consideration does not qualify for recognition as an asset or liability at that date.

As explained previously, the tests may be applied at the occurrence of events (or at interim dates), but they must be applied at or near the date of financial reporting. The decision as to whether the tests are satisfied at the date of the financial statements must be reached prior to the issuance of the financial statements, else they will not be issued. Thus, satisfaction of all the tests at the date of the Statement of Financial

Position is a necessary and a sufficient condition for the recognition of a thing as an asset or liability on that Statement of Financial Position.

The goal of the temporal association test is to include all things that satisfy the tests at the date of the Statement of Financial Position as assets and liabilities on *that* Statement of Financial Position. Alternatively, the goal is to exclude all things that do not satisfy the tests at that date, to prohibit the recognition of things as assets and liabilities on the Statement of Financial Position if they do not satisfy the tests on the date of that Statement of Financial Position. The temporal association test often requires the derecognition of things as assets or liabilities that were properly recognized on a past Statement of Financial Position but that no longer satisfy one or more of the recognition tests. It also often requires delaying the recognition of things as assets or liabilities that are expected to satisfy all the tests in the future but do not yet satisfy one or more of the tests. At each financial reporting date the temporal association test separates the past from the future by identifying the things and magnitudes that qualify for recognition in the present. The present or current Statement of Financial Position is intended to depict those economic resources and obligations, and the magnitudes of their yet-to-be-selected attribute, that qualify for recognition as assets and liabilities presently or currently. Temporal association is applicable to all of the tests:

a. *Existence and Detection.* Both current existence and current detection of existence are required for present recognition. Sometimes existence and detection are separated in time. An example is the discovery of an oil deposit. It is clear that the oil deposit existed prior to its discovery but it is also clear that it was not detectable prior to its discovery. The deposit does not qualify for recognition prior to its detection because it is not an economic resource prior to its detection. Undetected oil will not command a price although the right to explore for oil may command a price and therefore be eligible for recognition. "Mineral interests" is an asset that represents the right to explore and produce oil that is discovered, and its yet-to-be-selected attribute may be estimated in several ways, including accumulating past costs. However, oil deposits and mineral interests are different kinds of economic resources and they must be sharply segregated. The subsequent discovery of an oil deposit does not in any way validate the prior recognition of mineral interests nor does it validate the prior estimation of its yet-to-be-selected attribute by accumulation of costs or by any other technique. The present ability to detect the oil deposit and the conclusive evidence that it existed prior to discovery does not permit prior recognition of that oil deposit by correction of prior financial statements. For the same reasons, the detection of nonexistence (discovery of a dry hole) does not invalidate the prior recognition of mineral interests nor is the derecognition of that resource by a correction of prior financial statements permitted when a dry hole is discovered. Instead the discovery of a dry hole that results in a zero price for mineral interests requires the present derecognition of mineral interests as an asset and the present recognition of an expense.

b. *Economic Resources and Obligations.* Only current economic resources and obligations qualify for present recognition. Some things qualify as an economic resource or obligation at one point in time but do not qualify at other points in time. A receivable, for example, qualifies as an economic resource if it can command a price--if it can be factored or otherwise sold without recourse. If it does not command a price at a later time, it no longer qualifies as an economic resource. The discovery that it does not command a price requires the present derecognition of the receivable as an asset and its recognition as an expense, not a correction of the prior recognition. The enterprise that issued the receivable may have become insolvent subsequently or it may have been insolvent at the date of issuance and its insolvency may have been detected subsequently. Neither event should result in a correction of a prior recognition; a thing *is* an economic resource or obligation at the date it can command a price without regard to subsequent events that cause it to gain or lose its ability to command a price.

c. *Control or Obligation.* Current control or obligation is required for present recognition. Change in control or obligation is often accomplished by exchange. An enterprise normally gains control of an economic resource and loses control of another resource (or incurs an obligation) at the event of exchange. The intention to engage in a future exchange does not result in gaining control of the intended acquisition nor in losing control of the intended sacrifice. Thus, neither recognition of the acquisition nor derecognition of the sacrifice is permitted by intended future exchanges.

d. *Yet-to-be-selected Attribute.* Only present magnitudes of the yet-to-be-selected attribute qualify for present recognition. The magnitude of a past yet-to-be-selected attribute should have been recognized in the past and the magnitude of a future yet-to-be-selected attribute must await future recognition. It is the recognition of the present yet-to-be-selected attribute that separates the past magnitude from the future magnitude. The fact that the magnitude of the yet-to-be-selected attribute changes over time does not invalidate past or present yet-to-be-selected attributes nor allow corrections of previously recognized magnitudes of the yet-to-be-selected attribute.

4.2.6. VERIFIABILITY

All of the previous tests are concerned with identifying things, and the magnitude of the yet-to-be-selected attribute, that should be recognized because they are relevant to investment, credit and similar decisions. To achieve the overall objective of decision usefulness, depictions must also be reliable--representationally faithful and verifiable. The sixth test is verifiability, the ability to provide assurance that the depictions are representationally faithful. The words and numerals must represent the phenomena that they purport to represent, and qualified observers must be able to achieve consensus that they do so. Verifiability applies to all of the above tests. There must be assurance of the representational faithfulness of (a) the existence of the thing, (b) that it is an economic resource or obligation, (c) that it is under the control of or obligates the entity under consideration, (d) that the magnitude of the yet-to-be-selected attribute has been reasonably measured or estimated, and (e) that all of those tests are satisfied at the date of the Statement of Financial Position. The goal of this test is to include all depictions that are representationally faithful, and verification is the process of providing assurance that they are. Alternatively, it is to exclude all depictions that do not faithfully represent the things and magnitudes identified by the previous tests. Thus, verifiability[2] is a necessary but not a sufficient condition for recognition.

4.3. SUMMARY AND RESTATEMENT

The process of recognizing things may be restated and summarized as a series of tests that partition things into successively narrower categories:

a. *Detection of Existence*. The process is initiated by the detection of the existence of a thing; hypothetically, all things that exist and are detected are candidates for recognition.

---

[2] Although all things that are depicted as assets and liabilities must be verifiable, not all are required to be verified. The verification of the representational faithfulness of a sample of assets and liabilities often permits the inference that the population of assets and liabilities is representationally faithful. Similarly, the tests must be satisfied at the date of the Statement of Financial Position but they need not be applied at exactly that date. Often the application of the tests at other dates permits the inference that they are satisfied at the financial reporting date.

b. *Economic Resources and Obligations*. The things are partitioned into two broad categories: economic resources and obligations versus all other things. Only economic resources and obligations are candidates for recognition; all other things are excluded from further consideration.

c. *Entity Association*. The economic resources and obligations are partitioned by entity. Only economic resources that are under the control of a particular entity are eligible for recognition as assets by that entity. Similarly, only obligations that are owed by a particular entity are eligible for recognition as liabilities by that entity. This test identifies the economic resources and obligations eligible for recognition as assets and liabilities by a particular entity; it excludes all economic resources and obligations that are to be recognized as assets and liabilities by all other entities.

d. *Yet-to-be-selected Attribute*. The attributes of the economic resources and obligations are partitioned into two broad categories: the yet-to-be-selected attribute versus all other attributes. Only magnitudes of the yet-to-be-selected attribute of economic resources and obligations are candidates for recognition; all other attributes are excluded from further consideration. Only nonzero magnitudes of the yet-to-be-selected attribute are eligible for recognition; all zero magnitudes are excluded from further consideration.

e. *Temporal Association*. All things and magnitudes that are a candidate for recognition by satisfying the first four tests are partitioned by time. All of the previous tests must be satisfied at the date of the Statement of Financial Position to qualify for recognition on that Statement of Financial Position. This test excludes all things and magnitudes that satisfied the tests in the past but no longer satisfy the tests as well as all things and magnitudes that are expected to satisfy the tests in the future but do not yet satisfy these tests. The test separates the past from the future by requiring that things and magnitudes satisfy the tests in the present to qualify for present recognition.

f. *Verifiability*. Independent, qualified observers must be able to reach consensus that all of the previous tests are satisfied. This test excludes all things and magnitudes for which there is inadequate empirical evidence to permit verifiers to agree that the representation is faithful. It assures the faithfulness of the representations by requiring sufficient empirical evidence regarding each of the previous tests to permit qualified observers to reach consensus.

Purpose. The purpose of the tests is to identify the things, and the attribute of those things, that are relevant to rational investment, credit and similar decisions and to assure that they are faithfully represented. The assurance of faithful representation provides reliability. The combination of relevance and reliability provides decision usefulness.

4.4. DISPLAY

The way in which assets and liabilities are displayed on the Statement of Financial Position is beyond the scope of this monograph. The above tests are not intended to specify either the order in which they should be displayed or the level of aggregation at which groups of similar assets or liabilities should be displayed. The previous discussion of buildings, receivables, payables, and so on was for illustrative purposes only. A building, for example, may be displayed separately or the magnitude of its yet-to-be-selected attribute may be aggregated with those of other resources and displayed under the category of Plant and Equipment.

5. EQUITY RECOGNITION

Equity is defined as the residual interest in the assets of an entity that remains after deducting its liabilities. The tests outlined above are not applicable to equity because it is a calculated residual. Equity exists only if economic resources exist from which extant obligations can be deducted, and therefore no separate existence test for equity is required. Equity must pertain to a particular entity, the entity association test, but that test is satisfied by association of the economic resources and obligations with an entity. Equity also pertains to a particular point in time, but the temporal association test is satisfied by associating the economic resources and obligations with that point in time. The numerical depiction of equity is not a magnitude of the yet-to-be-selected attribute but rather an amount derived from the magnitudes of the yet-to-be-selected attributes by summation and subtraction, and therefore measurement does not apply to equity. The numerical depiction of equity is a dependent variable; the numerical depictions of economic resources and obligations are independent variables from which the equity is calculated.

Equity is similar to liabilities in that it represents a claim on the economic resources of the entity. In that sense it is an obligation of the entity and, as such, it is an economic resource of those persons or entities that control those claims. Since shares of ownership rights are often traded in active markets, it might be possible to measure or estimate the yet-to-be-selected attribute of those rights and then use that magnitude as the numerical depiction of equity. This is not done, however, for reasons of decision usefulness. The residual equity is one input to rational investment decisions, and it is those decisions that establish the price of the shares. Another input to rational investment decisions is the various expectations of the decision makers. To measure the equity claim independently would combine the two inputs to the decision process; recognizing equity as a residual properly separates the inputs and requires that decision makers supply their own expectations.

Equity has one essential characteristic: ownership rights. The distinction between obligations and ownership rights serves to partition the broad category of claims on economic resources into the narrower categories of liabilities and equity. The characteristic of ownership rights is a necessary and sufficient condition for recognition of equity as the representation of a separate claim on economic resources.

The way in which equity is to be displayed on the Statement of Financial Position is beyond the scope of this monograph. The recognition of equity is concerned with its

total, residual amount. The disaggregation of equity is not encompassed in its recognition.

6. RECOGNIZING THE EFFECTS OF EVENTS

As explained, supra [4.1], the occurrence of an event may trigger the application of the recognition tests. The tests for recognizing the effects of events are quite similar to those for recognizing things. Articulation of the financial statements requires that the tests be similar: the recognition of things and events are inextricable because the events of interest are those that change the things and the things of interest are those that are changed by events. This relationship is indicated by the fact that the financial change elements are defined by reference to assets and liabilities in Concepts Statement 3 and therefore they presuppose and depend on the definition of assets and liabilities. Thus, the tests applicable to the recognition of things are, with minor modifications, also applicable to the recognition of the effects of events. For this reason, the tests are presented in summary form.

6.1. TESTS FOR RECOGNIZING THE EFFECTS OF EVENTS

a. *Detection of Occurrence.* The process is initiated by the detection of events; hypothetically, all events that occur and are detected are candidates for recognition.

b. *Changes in the Substance of Economic Resources and Obligations.* All events that change the substance of economic resources and obligations that are controlled or owed by an entity must be recognized by that entity. Production, for example, is an event that changes the substance of economic resources. Production requires changing the verbal depiction from "raw materials" to "work in process" or "finished goods" so that the words correspond to the underlying phenomena. It may or may not require changing the numerical depiction depending on whether it changes the magnitude of the yet-to-be-selected attribute, for example, depending on whether value was or was not added (or subtracted).

c. *Changes in Entity Association.* All events that change the entity that controls or owes economic resources or obligations must be recognized by the entity that acquires or sacrifices control of economic resources or incurs or settles obligations. Exchanges, for example, change the entity that controls economic resources without changing the substance of those resources. An exchange of one economic resource for another requires the recognition of the acquired resource as an asset and the derecognition (deletion of the depiction) of the sacrificed resource.

d. *Changes in the Magnitude of the Yet-to-be-selected Attribute of Economic Resources and Obligations.* All events that change the magnitude of the yet-to-be-selected attribute of economic resources and obligations that are controlled or owed by an entity must be recognized by that entity. Price changes and interest rate changes are examples of events that may change the magnitude of the yet-to-be-selected attribute of economic resources and obligations without changing their substance. These events require changing the numerical depiction so that it corresponds to the underlying phenomena.

e. *Temporal Association.* The events that change the economic resources and obligations of an entity are partitioned by time. Only the events that changed the substance or magnitude of economic resources and obligations that were controlled or owed by the entity, or changed the entity that controlled or owed the resources and obligations, during the fiscal period covered by the financial change statements can be recognized during that time period. This excludes all past events that occurred prior to the beginning of the fiscal period as well as all future events that have not yet occurred.

f. Verifiability. Independent, qualified observers must be able to reach a consensus that the previous tests have been satisfied. This test requires that all effects of events be verifiable, not that all be verified.

6.2. RECOGNITION BY CHANGING FINANCIAL POSITION ELEMENTS

Events may change the substance or magnitude of the yet-to-be-selected attribute of economic resources and obligations under the control of or owed by an entity, or they may change the entity that controls or owes economic resources and obligations, or a combination. The effects of *all* such events must be recognized by changing the words or numerals, or both, of financial position elements. Whether the effects of events qualify for recognition as financial change elements depends on the outcome of additional tests, which are presented infra.

The effects of events that change the substance or magnitude of economic resources and obligations that are controlled or owed by an entity, or change the entity that controls or owes the resources or obligations, are depicted on the sequential Statements of Financial Position of that entity. The application of the recognition tests at the date of each Statement of Financial Position results in changing the verbal or numerical depictions, or both, to correspond to the effects of such events. Thus, sequential Statements of Financial Position of an entity recognize the effects of *all* such events by changing the verbal or numerical depictions of economic resources and obligations. Since equity is the residual of assets and liabilities, the sequential Statements of Financial Position also recognize the effects of all events that change the equity of an entity. Comparative Statements of Financial Position permit users to discern the net effects of all such events.

Changing the financial position elements is the only type of recognition required for the effects of some events. For example, the barter of some economic resources (such as buildings for land) with equal magnitudes of the yet-to-be-selected attributes does not satisfy any of the tests for recognition as a financial change element. The effects of that event are not displayed on the Statement of Cash Flows since cash is not exchanged, nor on the Statement of Comprehensive Income since it does not change residual equity nor is it a transaction with customers, nor on the Statement of Owner Investments and Distributions since it is not a transaction with owners. Thus, the effects of that event are recognized only by changing the verbal depiction of the sacrificed resource to that of the acquired resource. The only way that the user can discern the effects of the event is by comparing the sequential Statements of Financial Position.

Recognition on sequential Statements of Financial Position, albeit all inclusive, is not an adequate recognition of the effects of many events for two reasons: (1) the difference in the amount of a given asset or liability at two points in time usually represents the net effects of several events; (2) the effects of events are not classified in ways that are relevant to rational investment, credit and similar decisions. Relevance requires the recognition of the separate effects, as opposed to the net effects, of certain events, and it also requires the classification of the effects in various ways. Recognizing the separate effects and their classification is the function of the financial change elements.

6.3. TESTS FOR FINANCIAL CHANGE ELEMENTS

Financial change elements--comprehensive income (composed of revenues, expenses, gains and losses), investments by owners, distributions to owners, sources of cash and uses of cash--are representations of the separate effects of certain kinds of events that have occurred during a fiscal period. The following additional recognition tests are for the purpose of determining which events qualify for recognition as financial change elements. The outcome of the tests is either to depict the effects of an event as a financial change element on one or more of the financial change statements (Statements of Comprehensive Income, Owner Investments and Distributions, and

Sources and Uses of Funds) if it satisfies the tests or to omit the depiction if it fails those tests.

6.3.1. RESOURCE OR OBLIGATION ASSOCIATION

The events that change any particular economic resource or obligation, or particular group of resources or obligations, may be used to separately recognize the effects of events as financial change elements or to subclassify financial change elements. This is the primary test used in the preparation of Statements of Sources and Uses of Funds. All events that affected "funds" (however defined) are separately recognized for no other reason than that they affected funds.

This test partitions events into two categories: (1) those that affected the designated resources and obligations; (2) those that did not affect the designated resources and obligations. Thus, for example, in the preparation of a Statement of Cash Flows, all events that affected cash are partitioned from events that did not affect cash. The increases of cash are then segregated from the decreases of cash, given the titles of sources and uses respectively, subclassified as needed, and displayed on the Statement of Cash Flows for the purpose of explaining all events that affected cash during the fiscal period covered by that statement.

The FASB [*Reporting Income*, paragraph 45] reached the conclusion at exposure draft stage that a Statement of Cash Flows is more useful than other funds statements but it has not yet issued an authoritative document expressing that conclusion, nor did it define sources and uses as elements in Concepts Statement 3. However, the resource or obligation association test is applicable to the net amount of monetary resources and obligations, "net working capital", or to any other subset of resources and obligations controlled by or owed by an entity. Thus, it is applicable to all funds statements regardless of how "funds" may be defined.[12] Indeed, it is applicable to any group of resources and obligations for which an explanation of the separate effects of events on those resources and obligations is deemed sufficiently beneficial to exceed the costs of recognition.

---

1 This test is also applied when providing what is often called "the analysis of an account". The term "analysis" is apt because the purpose is to display the separate effects of all events that affected the resource of obligation represented by the account. It is applicable to any account or any group of accounts for which an analysis is desired.

6.3.2. TRANSACTOR ASSOCIATION

The events that change economic resources and obligations that result from transactions with a particular group of people or entities may be used to separately recognize the effects of events as financial change elements or to subclassify financial change elements. This is the primary test used in the preparation of the Statement of Owner Investments and Distributions. The effects of transactions with owners are separately recognized for no other reason than that the resources or obligations came from or went to owners in their capacity as owners. It may also be used to recognize the separate effects of transactions with any other designated transactors.

This test partitions all events that affected economic resources and obligations into two categories: (1) those that resulted from transactions with the designated transactors; (2) those that resulted from all other transactions and other events and circumstances. Thus, in regard to owners, the effects of transactions with owners are partitioned from the effects of all other events, the increases in resources (decreases in obligations) are segregated from the decreases in resources (increases in obligations), given the titles of investments and distributions respectively, subclassified as needed, and displayed on the Statement of Owner Investments and Distributions for the purpose of explaining all transactions with owners during the fiscal period covered by that statement.

The transactor association test may be combined with the resource or obligation association test to provide information about the effects of events that satisfy *both* tests. The combination of these two tests may be used to subclassify financial change elements or provide components of any financial change statement. For example, investments by and distributions to owners are often subclasssified on the basis of whether they affected cash. The investments by and distributions to owners displayed on the Statement of Cash Flows are restricted to cash investments and cash distributions. The Statement of Owner Investments and Distributions displays both cash and noncash investments and distributions. Thus, the cash investments and distributions are displayed on two financial change statements because they satisfy both tests while the noncash investments and distributions are displayed on only one statement because they satisfy only one test.

The transactor association test is applicable to any other group of people or entities. Transactions with creditors, debtors, suppliers, taxing authorities, customers, and others may be used to subclassify financial change elements. Transactions with customers, for example, is often used to provide a component on the Statement of Comprehensive Income. The transactor association test may be combined with the resource association test to also provide a component of the Statement of Cash Flows. The Statement of Comprehensive Income displays both cash and noncash inflows and outflows resulting from transactions with customers while the Statement of Cash Flows displays only the cash inflows and outflows resulting from transactions with customers. The inflows of cash from customers displayed on the Statement of Cash Flows are also known as "realized revenues" while those displayed on the Statement of Comprehensive Income are both realized (in cash) and unrealized. Similarly, outflows to taxing authorities is often an important component of expenses displayed on the Statement of Comprehensive Income. The cash outflows to taxing authorities are displayed on the Statement of Cash Flows because they satisfy both tests while all outflows (cash and noncash resources or the incurrence of obligations) to taxing authorities are displayed on the Statement of Comprehensive Income.

6.3.3. ACTIVITY ASSOCIATION

The effects of events that result from certain activities may be used to separately recognize the effects of events as financial change elements or to subclassify financial change elements. This is the primary test used in segment reporting, for example. The events that affected a given segment of the entity are separately recognized for no other reason than that they affected that segment. Another major use of this test is to segregate the changes in economic resources and obligations resulting from the ongoing central or major operations of the entity, and therefore are revenues or expenses, from the changes in economic resources and obligations resulting from other activities, and therefore are not revenues or expenses.

This test partitions all events that affected economic resources and obligations into two categories: (1) those that resulted from the designated activities; (2) those that resulted from all other activities. In regard to revenues and expenses, the test requires that the effects of the events that result from ongoing central or major operations be partitioned from the effects of all other events. Revenues are the inflows or other enhancements of economic resources of an entity or settlements of its obligations (or a combination of both) during a period from activities that constitute the entity's ongoing major or central operations. Expenses are the outflows or other using up of economic resources of an entity or its incurrences of obligations (or a combination of both) during a period from activities that constitute the entity's ongoing major or central operations. Thus, the events that constitute the ongoing major or central operations of an entity are partitioned from all other activities; those that increase residual equity (revenues) are segregated from those that decrease residual equity (expenses), subclassified as needed, and displayed on the Statement of Comprehensive Income.

Gains and losses may also be recognized by applying this test. The effects of events that are the result of peripheral or incidental activities are partitioned from all other activities; those that result in increases in residual equity (gains) are segregated from those that result in decreases in residual equity (losses), subclassified as needed, and displayed on the Statement of Comprehensive Income.

6.3.4. ARTICULATION TEST

Articulation requires that the sum of the separate effects of all events during a fiscal period equal the change in the magnitude of the pertinent economic resources and obligations from the beginning to the end of that period. If the sum of the separate effects recognized do not equal the change in magnitude, it is conclusive evidence that there were additional events that occurred during the period that have not yet been recognized. The difference between the sum of the separate effects recognized and the change in magnitude is the combined effects of the additional, previously unrecognized events. That difference must be recognized prior to the issuance of financial statements.

This test is applicable to all economic resources and obligations controlled or owed by the entity during the fiscal period. The sources and uses of cash, for example, are displayed on the Statement of Cash Flows for the purpose of explaining the effects of events that changed cash during the fiscal period covered by that statement, and the difference between sources and uses must equal the difference between the magnitude of cash at the beginning of the fiscal period and at the end of that period. That is, the Statement of Cash Flows must articulate with the change in the magnitude of cash. The articulation test assures that the effects of *all* events that affected cash during a fiscal period are recognized on the Statement of Cash Flows covering that period. Often there will be a difference between the sum of the recognized separate effects and the change in the magnitude of cash. That difference is the combined effect of additional, previously undetected events. "Cash over and short" is a common account title that depicts such differences and the balance in that account must be recognized as an element of comprehensive income to satisfy the articulation test.[2]

---

2 Sources and uses of cash normally represent the inflows and outflows of the quantity of cash without regard to the price of cash. Changes in the price of cash (foreign exchange rates) may also be deemed to affect the magnitude of cash. If so, the articulation test would require that the effects of price changes as well as cash

The same comments also apply to all other economic resources and obligations. The amount of difference in inventory, for example, due to pilferage, spoilage, and error is recognized on the basis of the articulation test. All other economic resources and obligations must articulate with the changes in economic resources and obligations in the same way.

The net change in all economic resources and obligations controlled or owed by the entity during a period is the change in the residual equity of that period. The change in residual equity must articulate with the sum of the comprehensive income and investments by and distributions to owners. If the sum of the separate effects of events recognized on those two statements does not equal the change in residual equity, then the difference is presumed to be due to the combined effects of some previously unrecognized events that must be recognized as a gain or loss[3] on the Statement of Comprehensive Income because comprehensive income is defined to include all such changes.

flows be recognized in the Statements of Cash Flows. In addition, articulation would require that the effects of changes in the price of cash be recognized on the Statements of Income. However, this depends on the yet-to-be-selected attribute because it is possible to initially and subsequently recognize cash at its price at acquisition and wait for it to be realized in domestic cash before recognizing changes. Similar comments are applicable to changes in purchasing power.

3 Concepts Statement 3 [paragraphs 67-68] provides a clear definition: "Gains [losses] are increases [decreases] in equity (net assets) from peripheral or incidental transactions of an entity and from all other transactions and other events and circumstances affecting the entity during a period except those that result from revenues [expenses] or investments by [distributions to] owners."

7. APPENDIX: AN OVERVIEW AND ANALOGY

Recognition is often considered to be a process that is not only difficult but also one that is unique to accounting. Recognition is in fact difficult but is not unique to accounting. It is a decision process that is shared by all model builders, albeit it is not called recognition in other areas.

For reasons that remain unclear, recognition in accounting is also thought to be mysterious and almost magical. It seems to be the view that as soon as the recognition mystery is solved all of the hard decisions will go away. The fact is that recognition is neither mysterious nor magical. Recognition specifies and clarifies the decisions that need to be made but it does not make them go away.

The purpose of this appendix is to remove the mystery of the recognition process by presenting an overview of that process as it is performed in both accounting and cartography. The difficulty of apprehending the recognition process may be alleviated by paralleling it with the familiar process of map making.

7.1. RECOGNITION PROCESS

Recognition addresses the fundamental accounting question: which phenomena should be represented on financial statements? Certain phenomena are represented on, and others are omitted from, financial statements. It is the recognition process that segregates the phenomena that are represented from those that are omitted. Although the subject matter differs, the process is the same as that employed by cartographers (and others who construct models of phenomena).

7.1.1. DECISION USEFULNESS

There is a wide variety of models in current use. They differ mainly in which phenomena they represent. A map, for example, represents phenomena that are vastly different from those represented on financial statements. Aside from that difference, however, maps are quite similar to financial statements. The first and most important similarity is the objective. Both maps and financial statements are intended to be decision useful, the characteristics of which are relevance and reliability.

7.1.1.1. Relevance and Reliability

The problem of deciding which phenomena to represent is shared by cartographers and accountants. The root of the problem is the need to represent the relevant phenomena and to omit the irrelevant phenomena. The omission of irrelevant phenomena is imperative for two major reasons. First, it is likely to be impossible, and almost certain not to be cost-beneficial, to represent *all* phenomena or even *all* aspects of any phenomenon. Second, the representation of irrelevant phenomena may obscure the relevant phenomena, rendering the model less useful. All models are abstractions in the sense that more phenomena are omitted than represented. A map of the floor plan of a building, for example, is quite abstract. Its abstraction of the relevant phenomena is a major factor in its usefulness; the omission of the irrelevant phenomena permits the user to focus on the relevant phenomena. Too many representations are likely to cause confusion, sometimes called "information overload", since the user is required to sort the relevant from the irrelevant representations. Thus, deciding which phenomena are to be represented and which are to be omitted is the first problem faced by both cartographers and accountants.

Relevance is the concept that guides the decision about which phenomena to represent and which to omit. However, it is first necessary to identify the types of decisions that are to be made when using the model. A road map, for example, is not relevant to a ship captain in his capacity as a captain but it is relevant to him in his capacity as a motorist. Which phenomena are relevant is decision specific: relevance depends on the type of decisions that are to be made. Therefore, the cartographer must first identify the types of decisions for which the map will be used and then select the phenomena that are relevant to those types of decisions.

Since relevance depends on the kinds of decisions that are to be made, the first reference is to the FASB specification of the kinds of decisions that financial statements are designed to serve, namely, rational investment, credit, and similar decisions. Thus, the first task of recognition is to select the phenomena that are relevant to rational investment, credit and similar decisions.

The second task of recognition is to faithfully represent the relevant phenomena and to provide assurance, via verification, that they are faithfully represented. Just as the cartographer must be sure that the lines on maps do in fact correspond to roads and their lengths, accountants must be sure that the words and numerals on financial statements do in fact correspond to economic resources and obligations, the magnitudes of their selected attribute(s), and the changes in them. These two tasks have been divided into six interrelated recognition tests.

7.2. RECOGNITION TESTS

The first, and most general, recognition test is the detection of existence of a thing or the occurrence of an event that may be a candidate for recognition. Cartographers must first detect the existence of candidates for representation before they can decide whether or not to represent them on maps. Similarly accountants must first detect the existence or occurrence of candidates for recognition before they can decide whether or not to represent them on financial statements.

The second test is to determine whether or not the candidate for recognition is the kind of thing or event that is relevant to the type of decisions previously identified. Waterways and water depths, for example, would not satisfy this test if the cartographer had previously decided to represent things relevant to a motorist; roads and highways are the kind of things relevant to that type of decision. Similarly, accountants must identify the kind of things that are relevant to rational investment, credit and similar decisions. It has been decided previously that the relevant kinds of things are economic resources and obligations and the relevant kinds of events are those that change economic resources and obligations.

Third, the scope of the model must be specified on the basis of the prior identification of the type of decisions. In cartography, whether the region to be mapped is a city, state, or continent depends on the type of decisions to be served. A road map of a given state, for example, will include representations of roads and highways within that state and exclude representations of roads and highways of all other states. Similarly, the scope of financial statements depends on the type of decisions to be served. It has been decided that relevance to rational investment, credit and similar decisions restricts the scope to a given entity. Hence, a given entity is the "region" to be modelled; economic resources and obligations controlled or owed by a given entity, and events that change them, are to be represented on the financial statements, while those of all other entities are to be omitted.

Fourth, the attribute of things and events depends on the relevance to the identified decisions. In cartography, possible choices of attributes are elevations of the terrain, ground distances, and air distances, to name a few. Air distances are relevant to the decisions of an airplane pilot while ground distances are relevant to the decisions of a motorist. Thus, the selection of the attribute depends on the type of decisions to be served. In the same manner, the selection of the attribute to be represented on financial statements depends on relevance to rational investment, credit and similar decisions.

Fifth, models represent phenomena that exist at a particular point in time, usually the present. Roads, and their distances, that existed in the past may be relevant to some decisions (such as those made by historians) and expected future roads may be relevant to other decisions (such as those made by land speculators), but present roads and distances are relevant to the decisions of a motorist. Similarly, the economic resources and obligations that presently exist, are presently under the control of or are owed by the entity, and the present magnitude of the yet-to-be-selected attribute of those resources and obligations are relevant to rational investment, credit and similar decisions.

Verifiability is the sixth test. This provides assurance for the user that the model faithfully represents the phenomena that it purports to represent. Several cartographers should be able to reach consensus that the representations on a map are faithful, and each should be able to derive the same representations independently, albeit with some degree of imprecision. Similarly, several accountants should be able to reach consensus that the representations on financial statements are faithful, and each should be able to derive the same representations independently, albeit with some degree of imprecision.

7.2.1. CONSTRAINTS

Costs constrain all model building. The eventual benefit from representing something must exceed the cost of the representation. In cartography, this constraint is applicable to selecting what is to be represented on a map as well as the precision of measurements. As the detail and precision of a map increases, its cost increases also; a point will be reached where an increase in the detail and precision of the map is not accompanied by a proportionate increase in usefulness. Similarly, costs constrain the detail and precision of measurements of representations on financial statements.

Materiality is also a constraint in all model building. Representations of things or events with magnitudes that are too small to be relevant to the identified decisions are not decision useful and they may even detract from the usefulness of the model. In a map of the continental United States, side roads and city streets are not represented because they are immaterial to the decisions intended to be served. In financial statements, economic resources and obligations, or events that change them, whose magnitude of the yet-to-be-selected attribute is too small to be relevant, need not be recognized, or the amounts may be combined with similar economic resources and obligations or with the effects of similar events.

8. WORKS CITED

American Institute of [Certified Public] Accountants, Committee on Terminology [AIA]. *Accounting Terminology Bulletin No. 1: Review and Resume.* New York: formerly AIA now AICPA, August 1953.

American Institute of Certified Public Accountants, Accounting Principles Board [APB]. *Opinion No. 29: Accounting for Nonmonetary Transactions.* New York: AICPA, May 1973.

Bacon, Francis. *Advancement of Learning.*

Braithwaite, Richard Bevan. *Scientific Explanation: A Study of the Function of Theory, Probability and Law in Science.* Cambridge: The Cambridge University Press, 1953.

Boulding, Kenneth E. *Economics as a Science.* New York: McGraw-Hill Book Co. Inc., 1970.

Caws, Peter. *The Philosophy of Science: A Systematic Account.* Princeton, New Jersey: D. Van Nostrand Company Inc., 1965.

Chambers, Raymond J. *Accounting, Evaluation and Economic Behavior.* Englewood Cliffs, New Jersey: Prentice-Hall, Inc., 1966. Reprinted Houston: Scholars Book Co.

Einstein, Albert. *Sidelights on Relativity.* New York: E.P. Dutton and Company, n.d.

Financial Accounting Standards Board [FASB]. *Discussion Memorandum; An Analysis of the Issues Related to Conceptual Framework for Financial Accounting and Reporting: Elements of Financial Statements and Their Measurement.* Stamford, Conn.: FASB, December 1976.

Financial Accounting Standards Board [FASB]. *Statement of Financial Accounting Concepts No. 1: Objectives of Financial Reporting by Business Enterprises.* Stamford, Conn.: FASB, November 1978.

Financial Accounting Standards Board [FASB]. *Statement of Financial Accounting Concepts No. 2: Qualitative Characteristics of Accounting Information.* Stamford, Conn.: FASB, May 1980.

Financial Accounting Standards Board [FASB]. *Statement of Financial Accounting Concepts No. 3: Elements of Financial Statements of Business Enterprises.* Stamford, Conn.: FASB, December 1980.

Financial Accounting Standards Board [FASB]. *Proposed Statement of Financial Accounting Concepts (Exposure Draft): Reporting Income, Cash Flows, and Financial Position of Business Enterprises.* Stamford, Conn.: FASB, November 16, 1981.

Financial Accounting Standards Board [FASB]. *Statement of Financial Accounting Concepts No. 5: Recognition and Measurement in Financial Statements of Business Enterprises.* Stamford, Conn.: FASB, December 1984.

Financial Accounting Standards Board [FASB]. *Proposed Statement of Financial Accounting Standards (Exposure Draft): Employers' Accounting for Pensions.* Stamford, Conn.: FASB, March 1985.

Gombrich, E.H. *Art and Illusion: A Study in the Psychology of Pictorial Representation.* Princeton, New Jersey: Princeton University Press, 1960.

Kaplan, Abraham. *The Conduct of Inquiry: Methodology for Behavioral Science.* San Francisco, Calif.: Chandler Publishing Company, 1964.

Kline, Morris. *Mathematical Thought from Ancient to Modern Times.* New York: Oxford University Press, 1972.

McDonald, Daniel L. "A Test Application of the Feasibility of Market Based Measures in Accounting." *Journal of Accounting Research*, Spring 1968, pp. 38-49.

McKeown, James C. "An Empirical Test of a Model Proposed by Chambers." *The Accounting Review*, January 1971, pp. 12-29.

Parker, James E. "Testing Comparability and Objectivity of Exit Value Accounting." *The Accounting Review*, July 1975, pp. 512-524.

Paton, W.A., and Littleton, A.C. *An Introduction to Corporate Accounting Standards.* Chicago: American Accounting Association, 1940.

Sterling, Robert R. "A Test of the Uniformity Hypothesis." *Abacus*, September 1969, pp. 37-47.

Sterling, Robert R. "10: A Rating of the Conceptual Framework." *Proceedings of the Symposium on the Conceptual Framework for Financial Accounting and Reporting,*

June 24, 1980, Financial Accounting Standards Board. Abridgment reprinted as "The Conceptual Framework: An Assessment", *Journal of Accounting*, November 1982, pp. 104-107.

Sterling, Robert R. "Costs (Historical versus Current) versus Exit Values." *Abacus*, December 1981, pp. 93-129.

Whitehead, Alfred N. *Science and the Modern World.* New York: Macmillan Publishing Co., The Free Press, 1967.

Ziman, John. *Reliable Knowledge: An Exploration of the Grounds for Belief in Science*. Cambridge: At the University Press, 1978.

CONFESSIONS OF A FAILED EMPIRICIST

Robert R. Sterling

1. INTRODUCTION

> The aim of writing is not simply to make oneself understood but to make it impossible to be *mis*understood.—Cicero

Contrary to those writers who think that being understood is incompatible with being scholarly or scientific, I try very hard to make myself understood. Despite my best efforts, however, I have spent about 25 years struggling to explain a rather simple point. One of the more intense efforts to explain that point and one of the more visible failures occurred during my two year secondment as the Senior Fellow at FASB.

Until fairly recently I have blamed my failure on my lack of communication skills. As a consequence, I kept searching for ways to make my explanations

Advances in Accounting, Volume 6, pages 3–35.

ISBN: 0-89232-892-4

understood by using more straightforward prose, shorter sentences, simpler words, more telling examples, more apposite analogies, and funnier jokes. Continued failure eventually caused me to entertain the alternate explanation that it was the inability of accountants to understand rather than my inability to communicate.

I think I first began to seriously entertain the alternate explanation after I made a formal presentation to FASB members one day and then the next day I made an informal presentation to some former colleagues at The Sloan Physics Lab. The almost total absence of understanding by FASB members was in sharp contrast to the almost total presence of understanding by Lab members. The same preliminary point was presented to both groups but the reaction was truculent rejection by several FASB members contrasted to affable acceptance by most Lab members. The only observable commonality of members of the two groups was impatience: several FASB members were impatient to get on to the concrete accounting material because they couldn't understand the "abstruse" preliminary point whereas most Lab members were impatient to get on to the interesting material because the preliminary point was "too elementary" to require more than brief mention. It was this contrast that set me to thinking about the difference between accountants and physicists and the reasons therefor.

1.1. Purpose

The purpose of this paper is to explain the preliminary point that I have previously failed to explain to my accounting colleagues and to FASB, namely, that with rare exceptions accounting numerals do not represent phenomena, *any* phenomena, and that making numerals represent or not represent phenomena is a matter of choice.

1.2. Organization

Previous failures to explain the point have caused me to try to explain it in this paper by the indirect method of employing an analogy as the basis for the explanation and as the basis for a behavioral test. I will begin (§ 2.1) by discussing the analogy and then turn (§ 2.2) to a presentation of the test and some results from the test. Relying on the test and the results, I will assert (§ 3) that representing phenomena is a free choice and, after having recanted my previous attempts to convince accountants that they could choose to represent phenomena, I will attempt to convince physicists that they can choose *not* to represent phenomena. If physicists accept my suggestion, it will permit physics to be converted from a science to an art (§ 3.1) which will lead to a social science of physics (§ 3.2) and finally to a politico-legal system of physics (§ 3.3).

2. THE TEST

Human kind cannot stand very much reality. —T. S. Eliot

Usually one designs an empirical test for the purpose of finding out if a proposition is *either* true or false; that is, whether some set of symbols does or does not correspond to phenomena. This case is different: although the initial purpose is to discover whether physicists differ from accountants in regard to their ability to recognize the correspondence of numerals to phenomena, the ultimate purpose is to try to explain that accounting numerals are *neither* true nor false because there are no phenomena to examine to determine whether there is or is not a correspondence. Accountants tend to think of accounting as dealing with the most concrete reality but I think they suffer from what is called "maya" in Eastern philosophy[1]—the illusion that numerals *are* reality as opposed to numerals *corresponding* to or *representing* reality. Despite the widespread belief to the contrary among accountants, it is fairly easy to demonstrate that there are no phenomena that correspond to most of the numerals that appear on financial statements. (The commonplace as well as the scientific test of whether numerals correspond to phenomena is to ask whether other independent, qualified observers can detect or observe those phenomena.)

2.1. An Analogy

A common reaction to such comments, especially my assertion that accounting numerals do not represent phenomena, *any* phenomena, is surprise and dismay, which often elicits bizarre criticism. A recent example was an accounting colleague who sternly accused me of "wanting to tell the truth" to which I unthinkingly confessed, having momentarily forgotten that in accounting it is a crime to want to tell the truth. A frequent interpretation of my attempts to persuade colleagues to make accounting an empirical science by requiring that accounting numerals have empirical referents is to charge that I am an apriorist opposed to empiricism.[2] Evidently because of my reputation for endorsing current values, many take the assertion "accounting numerals have no empirical referents" to refer exclusively to the historic cost versus current value debate, and then they assess the assertion on the basis of their convictions about that debate rather than assessing it on the basis of evidence and argument about the existence of and need for empirical referents. FASB members were particularly inclined to see that assertion (and many others) as pertaining to the historic cost versus current value controversy.

The point is that instead of addressing the arguments and evidence for the assertion, listeners and readers often just react negatively, and this inhibits further communication. In an effort to avoid the problem, I began to employ analogies[3] to explain the point, thinking that the neutrality of the subject matter in the analogy would permit communications to continue. This has helped but it has not been entirely successful because there is opposition to employing analogies in accounting, especially analogies from the physical sciences.

Nonetheless, I persist because I believe, following Ziman [*Reliable* p 25], that "we can scarcely avoid the conclusion that most of our thinking is analogical and metaphorical" and because it is clear that analogies have played an important role in science in the creation of theories. (Their role in the justification of theories, however, is less clear.) As Nagel [*Structure* p 108–9] puts it:

> [T]he history of theoretical science supplies plentiful examples of the influence of analogies upon the formation of theoretical ideas; . . . [They have] served both as a guide for setting up the fundamental assumptions of a theory, as well as a source of suggestions for extending the range of their application.

It is their important role and widespread use that causes me to want to persuade you to seriously consider the analogy discussed infra and that was the basis for the questionnaires in Appendices 1 and 2. I know that many of you think that all analogies are frivolous and most of you think that analogies drawn from the physical sciences are not applicable to accounting, even dangerously misleading to accountants. You may be more willing to seriously consider the analogy if I assure you that I will not use it to urge the adoption of scientific concepts in accounting.

2.1.1. Cost and Volume

Compare the variability of costs or prices to the variability of volume. The cost or price of materials expands and contracts with economic changes: the volume of materials expands and contracts with temperature changes. Thus, all of those comments about variable units, unstable measurements, rubber yardsticks, and the like apply to physics and chemistry as well as to economics and accounting.

Keeping track of volume per unit of weight seems to be an obvious extension of double-entry. When that extension is made, a comparison will reveal that the journal entries are structurally identical. The following two entries differ only in regard to content.

1/1	Oil Inventory in Tank 1	$400	
	Accounts Payable (Union Pacific)		$400
	To record the purchase of $400 of oil (100 tons @ 4.00 dollars/ton) from the Union Pacific Railroad.		
1/1	Oil Inventory in Tank 1	฿400	
	Union Pacific		฿400

To record the receipt of Ƀ400 of oil (100 tons @ 4.00 barrels/ton) from the Union Pacific Railroad.

Although the isomorphism should be apparent, there are some differences. In addition to dollars versus barrels per ton, there is the difference between a transfer and an exchange. The exchange (purchase in this instance) obligates the recipient to make a reciprocal transfer (dollars in this instance) whereas in the physical system there is no such obligation. We often refer to liabilities as sources of assets as well as claims on assets whereas in the physical system the credit balances would be sources but not claims. This difference results in our saying purchase *from* Union Pacific and accounts payable *to* Union Pacific in accounting whereas we would say only receipts *from* Union Pacific in physics. However, such differences are not pertinent to the purpose of accounting for either the cost or volume of oil.

At March 1 when the dollars/ton and barrels/ton have increased, the following entries could be used to record another purchase or receipt.

3/1	Oil Inventory in Tank 1	\$440	
	Accounts Payable (Long Island)		\$440
	To record the purchase of \$440 of oil (100 tons @ 4.40 dollars/ton) from the Long Island Railroad.		
3/1	Oil Inventory in Tank 1	Ƀ440	
	Long Island		Ƀ440
	To record the receipt of Ƀ440 of oil (100 tons @ 4.40 barrels/ton) from the Long Island Railroad.		

The receipt of two lots of oil at different dollars/ton or barrels/ton presents several problems, one of which is determining the cost or volume of oil shipped. As in the questionnaire, if 60 tons were sold or shipped, how do we go about determining the cost of goods sold or the equivalent volume of goods shipped?

2.1.2. *Flow Assumptions*

The accounting method is to measure the volume of goods shipped by making a flow assumption. (Or, if possible, a flow determination because specific identification is thought to be better.) If 60 tons were shipped, the three common flow assumptions yield the three amounts of volume of goods shipped in the credit row of the following table. The amounts in the credit row were determined by applying the lifo, fifo and average inventory methods. The problem of determining the volume of goods shipped (equivalent to cost of goods sold) may be stated generally as the selection of one of the three amounts in the credit row of the table or some other amount.

Table 1. Cost or Volume of Oil in Tank 1

	FIFO	LIFO	AVG
Debits:			
(from Union Pacific) at Jan 1	400	400	400
(from Long Island) at March 1	440	440	440
Balance at March 1	840	840	840
Credit:			
(to Roadway) at June 30	240	264	252
Balance at July 1	600	576	588

2.2. A Conjecture

The similarities of volumes and costs caused me to wonder about the similarities of physicists and accountants in the way they would go about accounting for volumes. I conjectured that the two groups would differ markedly and I further conjectured that it would be difficult for each of them to learn from the other because they are well trained in their respective disciplines. As Kaplan [*Conduct* p 29] observed:

> The price of training is always a certain "trained incapacity": the more we know how to do something, the harder it is to learn to do it differently (children learn to speak a foreign language with less of an accent than adults do only because they did not know their own language so well to start with).

Thus, we could expect both accountants and physicists to exhibit trained incapacity. This is a common idea that goes by different names, for example, Ziman [*Reliable* p 8] discusses the "brainwashing implicit in the long process of becoming technically expert" and Kuhn [*Revolutions* p 193] talks about people being "in part conditioned by education."[4] I will call it "trained incapacity" in this article to continue my long-standing theme that accountants seem to have learned accounting so well that they find it exceptionally hard to learn to do it differently. Accountants seem to find scientific concepts and scientific norms[5] so foreign that not only do they speak science with a heavy accent, they often reverse the meanings of scientific terms. Indeed, they find it difficult to even think about how accounting might adopt scientific concepts and scientific norms. The only addition to my long-standing theme in this article is the conjecture that the reverse is also true: scientists will find it difficult to even think about how science might adopt accounting concepts.

The difference, in brief, is that accountants are trained to calculate whereas physicists are trained to observe. Calculations are the end product of accounting whereas in physics calculations are an intermediate product, the numerical output of which must be compared to observations. Accountants often refer to methods of calculations as "conventions" and they "test" them by examining documents and recalculating: they seldom concern themselves with whether the calculated numerals represent anything or not. Physicists refer to methods of calculation as "hypotheses" and they "test" them by comparing the calculated numerals to direct observations: they almost always concern themselves with whether the numerals represent something and are disdainful of numerals that do not represent anything. After repeated confirmations they change the name from "hypotheses" to "laws" and only then do they rely on the outputs of those calculations without testing them by an observation.

As a result of this difference in outlook[6] we should expect accountants and physicists to be skeptical of the others' concepts and methods. Both would tend to extend their concepts and methods to similar problems in the other's domain but both would resist such extension of the other's concepts and methods.

2.2.1. *Testing the Conjecture*

The questionnaires in Appendices 1 and 2 were designed to partially test the conjecture. For the reasons given above, I expected accountants and physicists to give different answers to question 1. Specifically I expected:

> Accountants would select one of the flow assumptions (lifo, fifo or average) or specific identification and be content to report the accompanying numeral without requiring observations of the volume shipped or in the tank. Thus, a majority of accountants was expected to answer A, B, C, or D to question 1.
>
> Physicists would disavow flow assumptions or specific identification and require a measurement (observation) of the volume of oil shipped or in the tank or both. Thus, a majority of physicists was expected to answer E to question 1.

A test was run by giving the questionnaire to 28 third year accounting students and to 32 third year physics students who had never studied accounting, not even high school bookkeeping.[7] The answers to question 1 are given in Table 2. The

Table 2. Responses to Question 1

Answer	*Physicists*		*Accountants*	
A (Fifo)	1	3%	0	0%
B (Lifo)	0	0%	3	11%
C (Avg)	2	6%	18	64%
D (Spec. Id.)	2	6%	3	11%
E (None)	27	84%	4	14%
SUM	32	100%	28	100%

disparity of results is most clearly shown by comparing the 84% of the physicist-subjects to the 14% of accountant-subjects who answered E. Thus, 86% of the accountant-subjects[8] accepted answers based on accounting concepts whereas only 16% of the physicist-subjects accepted answers based on accounting concepts.

The disparity was even more apparent in the post-test interviews. The accountant-subjects were quite content with the way the question was structured and the range of the answers. They did not volunteer any suspicions, nor did they voice any when asked. By contrast, the physicist-subjects were annoyed with the question and thought that the choices of answers were foolish. Several attempted to leave before they had answered the questions and had to be persuaded to continue. The typical physicist-subject volunteered that they were suspicious of the test. They thought there was a hidden purpose (e.g., "one of those wierd psychology experiments") that had something to do with assessing their personality or sanity because the answers were so obviously wrong.

The four accountant-subjects who answered E expressed the view that volume was so much different from cost that the accounting conventions would not be applicable. In effect, they did not accept the analogy as was evidenced by them continuing to talk about the problem of variable units and uncertainty in accounting and contrasting that to the constancy and certainty in the physical sciences. I did not anticipate this response so the interviewer (Kwang) was unprepared for it. A subsequent interview was arranged to try to persuade the four accountant-subjects that the problems were structurally identical. This was not successful: they were of the view that the problems of accounting for costs are unique and that there are no counterparts or analogues in science and the attempts to convince them otherwise met continued resistance.

All of the accountant-subjects were aware of the requirement to measure (observe) the quantity of the final inventory which resulted in some confusion about the questionnaire. Several accountant-subjects seemed to vacillate between interpreting volume as a quantity to be observed and interpreting it as the intended analogue for cost. However, none expressed a desire to measure (observe) the volume of goods shipped even when interpreting volume as a quantity that was required to be observed for inventory. This conceptual chasm is apparently the result of GAAS requiring observations of the quantity of inventory but not requiring observations of the quantity of goods sold. Several accountant-subjects (including the four who answered E) mentioned the need to "measure the volume shipped" but further queries soon revealed that they were using "measure" in its accounting sense of calculate[9] rather than in the physics sense of observe and discover.

The one physicist-subject who answered A (fifo) explained that he just checked the first answer because the question "obviously" had a hidden purpose and therefore was not worth expending effort answering it. The two who answered C (average) did so on the basis that if the times of the receipts and issues were random, then the average would be nearer the actual volume over a long series of trials but they volunteered that such an average might be far wrong for any particular shipment. The two physicist-subjects who answered D (specific identification) misinterpreted the answer by equating the ability to identify with the ability to measure (observe) the oil that was shipped.

In short the answers to the questionnaire support my conjecture that there is a vast difference between accountants and physicists.[10] The post-test interviews indicate that the difference is greater than what was revealed by the answers to the questionnaire. All of the physicists would have required a measurement (observation) of the volume shipped while apparently all of the accountants would have been satisfied with a calculation.[11]

Although the test clearly demonstrates a difference between these two groups of subjects, it doesn't demonstrate anything about the cause of that difference. We must infer the cause.[12] I infer that it is due to the education they receive in school and the further education they receive on the job. Thus, rather than looking for the cause in others, we teachers should start by looking in the mirror.

2.2.2. The Distinction Summarized

The difference can be summarized as accountants' tendency to use conventional calculations versus physicists' tendency to disdain proffered conventions. In accounting for volume under conditions of changing temperature:

> Physicists, in the absence of a well-confirmed law that would allow them to predict (by calculation) the volume, would measure the volume and would consider conventional calculations to be unthinkable. Under the best interpretation, physicists would treat lifo and fifo as competing hypotheses and measure (observe) the oil shipped and in the tank to see which of those hypotheses resulted in a faithful representation of the volume. If neither lifo nor fifo resulted in a faithful representation of the volume, they would discard both and rely on direct measurements while proposing and testing other hypotheses.
>
> Accountants see no need to measure (observe) the oil shipped and in the tank for the purpose of comparing it to the lifo or fifo calculations. They view the selection of lifo or fifo to be a matter of convention rather than a matter of empirical testing. Reformers might argue for uniformity of conventions among firms or consistency of conventions over time but no one (other than the misguided Sterling) would propose that accountants begin to measure (observe) instead of calculate and most accountants would not understand such a proposal when it was made. Some reformers would also argue for the need to establish a regulatory body such as the CAP, APB or FASB to achieve the desired uniformity or consistency.

Thus, the role of calculation methods, such as lifo and fifo, is antithetical in the two disciplines.

But the difference is even more fundamental, going to the basic issue of what is an acceptable subject matter. Physicists reject subject matters that are not amenable to empirical test. If one explains to them that there is a subject matter, such as the expired cost of goods sold and unexpired cost of inventory, that is calculable but is not measurable (not even in principle), they suggest the selection of another subject matter, one that is measurable (at least in principle). Accountants, on the other hand, are puzzled by a subject matter that is amenable to empirical test. Practitioners have no idea what it means because they are accustomed to calculating and they know that it is impossible to measure the expired cost of goods sold or unexpired cost of inventory, and academics think that empirical testing is to be done exclusively on subjects (people) rather than on calculations. If one explains to practitioners or academics that there is a subject matter, such as volume, that is measurable so that various calculations can be treated as hypotheses to be empirically tested, they suggest the selection of a realistic analogy, one that has an "attribute" like unexpired and expired cost which is in principle unmeasurable.

In short, physicists reject the subject matter and accountants reject the analogy. The rejections are based on diametrically opposed views of what is a proper subject matter.

3. A MATTER OF CHOICE

My way of joking is to tell the truth. It's the funniest joke in the world.—George Bernard Shaw

It seemed clear to me that representing or not representing phenomena is a free choice and therefore that accountants could represent phenomena, *some* kind of phenomena, by doing nothing more then adopting and enforcing the requirement to do so. However, I was very lonely in that position: the opposite seems equally clear to almost all accountants. Although there is considerable disagreement among accountants about what accounting *is*, there seems to be unanimity about what it is *not*, namely that it is not a device capable of representing phenomena. Many accountants begin their response to my arguments with remarks to the effect that there is something inherent in the theory or practice of accounting that prohibits it from representing phenomena.[13] I have been told this so often, for so many years, that I have finally decided to recant. Therefore, I want to disavow my previous attempts to explain to accountants that:

- it is possible to represent phenomena by deciding to do so,
- accounting could move toward being a science (and away from the present self-professed art) by deciding to represent phenomena,
- accounting could have a subject matter that is not composed exclusively of subjects (people) if it represented phenomena, and
- it is not necessary to regulate accounting, at least not as it is done at the present time, if it represented phenomena.

Those positions must be wrong and I confess my error in having previously expressed them.

However, I think that my error pertains only to accounting. I still believe that other disciplines have a free choice. Physicists are not inclined to talk about "the intrinsic nature of physics" and they regularly profess willingness to change physics if the arguments and evidence indicate such a change is needed. For that reason, instead of continuing to attempt to show accountants how they can convert the accounting art to a science, I will try to show physicists how they can convert the physics science to an art. After that it is fairly easy to establish a cluster of social sciences of physics and to demonstrate the need for establishing a regulatory agency to issue a flood of regulations.

3.1. Toward an Art of Physics

Converting physics from a science to an art requires nothing more than the definition of two terms: define an unmeasurable "attribute" and define "physicking" as the art of recording, classifying, summarizing, and interpreting that attribute. That seems simple enough but it is indispensible because if physicists allow the possibility of physicking for a measurable attribute, such as volume, there would be the constant danger that someone would measure the volume and thereby arrest the conversion from a science to an art. Thus, physicists must both define an unmeasurable attribute and restrict the scope of physicking to that attribute. I suggest that the "attribute" be called "conventional-volume" which would be defined as the sum of the volume receipts less the sum of the permissible conventional (lifo, fifo, average) calculations, and the balance of the Oil Inventory account would be called the "unexpired volume" as contrasted to the "expired volume" in the Volume of Goods Shipped account. To complete the modifications of volume, I will call the magnitude of the measurable volume the "unconventional-volume."

Note that once such an unmeasurable attribute has been defined, physicists are forever freed from the nuisance of measuring unconventional-volume. The measured amount of unconventional-volume in the tank at the statement date is not pertinent to the calculated amount of the conventional-volume at that date because, as any fool can plainly see[14], they are "different attributes." Indeed, there is no measurement whatsoever that would allow one to determine the magnitude of the unexpired volume in the tank or the expired volume of the amount shipped. What has been accomplished here is the conversion from physicking for phenomena to physicking for nonphenomena. Instead of the subject matter of physics being *oil in tanks* it has become *numerals in accounts.*

To understand this point more fully, note that the problem in Table One starts *before* the selection of lifo or fifo. All three columns in Table 1 show a March 1 balance of 840 barrels in the Tank 1 account[15] but it would be easy to empirically demonstrate that the amount of oil in the tank is different from 840 barrels. Thus, the lifo versus fifo choice cannot be based on faithfully representing the division of the volume of oil between that shipped and that remaining because such choices are restricted to dividing the numeral 840 between two accounts[16] and the 840 does not represent the volume of oil. The account would need to be adjusted to faithfully represent the amount of oil on hand before the shipment at June 30 to make it possible to divide the numeral to faithfully represent the amount shipped and the amount remaining.[17]

After taking the crucial step of adopting an unmeasurable attribute, all else is defensive. Physicists need to do whatever is necessary to protect the sanctity of conventional-volume. The first thing to do is to repeatedly *assert* that physics is *necessarily* an art. An effective defensive strategy is to reshape the English language, such as referring to conventional-volume as "objective" when it depends on the subject because there is no object that it refers to and "verifiable" when it can be recalculated but cannot be independently verified. After this usage is established, physicists can reject proposals to measure and report unconventional-volume because such measurements would be "subjective and unverifiable", thereby completely reversing the meaning of the terms. Making "measure" synonymous with "calculate" should be done early on because it deflects all proposals to measure in the original sense of observe.

Another effective defensive strategy is to make sweeping allegations, unencumbered by reason or evidence, about the usefulness or relevance of conventional-volume. If someone challenges these assertions, physicists should point out that physicking is historical, not prophetic, and that measuring and recording the present unconventional-volume would spoil the historical record, but since history is useful it follows that conventional-volume is useful. If the challenger doesn't comprehend the advanced logic in that argument, physicists should remember that some people are less gifted than they and try not to be too condescending.

After sufficient defenses have been built, physicists can begin to seek sympathy for the peculiarly difficult problems that artists face. They could say that "trying to transform physics into a science is impossible", and therefore we deserve your pity because our problems cannot be solved easily as they are in science. They can complain that physics "principles cannot be established, as they are in the realm of natural sciences, by experimentation" and therefore the only thing they can do is rely on conventions, such as lifo and fifo. They could point out that "it is important to remember that physics principles are man-made, in contrast to natural law" after enough time has elapsed so that everyone has forgotten it was they who man-changed those principles so that they have nothing to do with nature and therefore could not be in accord with natural law.[18]

3.2. Toward a Social Science of Physics

The sequencing of the conversion process is critical. Physics must first be converted from a science to an art before it can be moved toward a social science. The reason is the need to obfuscate the subject matter. When physics was a science, it was clear that the subject matter was unconventional-volume but many will be confused about what the subject matter is when physicking becomes a process of recording, classifying, summarizing, and interpreting conventional-volume. It seems clear to me that the subject matter has become

numerals but most physicists, like most accountants, will bridle at the suggestion that the only thing they are studying and arguing about is blobs of ink on paper.

It is the rejection of numerals as the subject matter, and the search for a more acceptable subject matter, that will result in some physicists deciding to redefine their subject matter to be people. After the scope of physicking has been restricted to an attribute that is not observable, then the *only* observables (other than numerals) are people.[19] It is this process of eliminating other possible subject matters that will lead physics on an irresistible march toward a social science.

Thus, becoming a social science is a direct consequence of adopting an unmeasurable attribute. After repeatedly *asserting* that physics is *necessarily* a social science, all else is defensive. If someone proposes the selection of a measurable attribute, such as unconventional-volume, physicists should explain that they cannot do that because physics is a *social* science. If someone expresses puzzlement about what the calculation of conventional-volume has to do with being a social science—with the type of investigations common in anthropology, psychology, economics, and the like—physicists ought to invoke the as-any-fool-can-plainly-see proof. If the proof does not work, physicists should establish a squad to shout "normative", "a priori," "antiempirical," "impossibility theorem," "social welfare effects", "positive theories" and other slogans at recalcitrant offenders who continue to suggest adopting a nonsocial empirical domain, such as unconventional-volume.

After physicists are secure in being a social science, they can seek sympathy because problems in the social sciences are much more difficult than those in the natural sciences. They can deplore that physics "unlike natural science, deals with a system created by people, hence its fundamental characteristics are constantly changing and evolving," as contrasted with dealing with a system of oil in tanks evidently created by non-people, hence its fundamental characteristics, such as unconventional-volume, remain stable even when the temperature changes. They can plead for pity because physics, being a "human creation" is "prone to many influences of a nondeterministic nature" and "whose subject matter is of such diversity and changing complexity that attempts to" forecast the future are impossible and therefore this precludes measuring the present unconventional-volume. The general problem has been well-stated by Stamp ["Accounting" p 21]:

> Nevertheless, they [accountants] might be able to adopt the pure scientific method, and perhaps enjoy . . . much success if . . . they only had to deal with the behavior of inhuman molecules. But in contrast, the accountant's 'molecules' think and feel, they have traditions and cultures, they are governed by laws, act sometimes rationally and often irrationally, and are susceptible to an enormous variety of psychological, social, economic, cultural and political influences.

If you will study that passage carefully, substituting "physics" for "accounting," you will eventually come to understand that oil producers, explorers, refiners, users, etc. and their agents and employees, Department of Energy and other governors and regulators, receivers of reports of conventional volume, as well as the physicists who calculate conventional-volume, are *people*. As soon as you are clear that these people are people, you will be able to plainly see that physicists must study them, even though it would be much easier to study molecules or unconventional-volume. Once everyone understands the difficult life of physicists as social scientists, they will sympathize with them because the social sciences are more difficult than the physical sciences.

Eventually it will occur to some physicists that they ought to imitate social scientists (if for no other reason than to secure their license to peddle in the market for excuses) rather than just continuing to seek sympathy for being a social science. The problem of selecting which social science to imitate will then replace the problem of selecting which conventional calculation (lifo versus fifo) to use.

3.2.1. *Anthropology*

Some physicists will imitate anthropologists and advocate the establishment of Generally Accepted Physics Principles (GAPP) by observing the actions of a primitive tribe of practicing calculators called physicists. GAPP will come to include lifo, fifo, and average (because they will be generally accepted) but will exclude the sum-of-the-tons-digit method (because it will not be generally accepted), as well as excluding the measurement of unconventional-volume, and this will be called the *inductive* method of theory construction. If someone questions whether "generally accepted" is an appropriate criterion, questions whether such a criterion is, in effect, deriving "ought" from "is" by concluding that physicists ought to be doing what they are in fact doing, proponents can reply that practicing physicists are reasonable and honorable men and therefore their practices must be the best that they can be—that no proposal can make them better because if they could have become better they would have become better.

Someone may chide them for, in effect, becoming Darwinists, for accepting without evidence that only the fittest practices survive, but they will miss the point of the chiding and adopt the name. Such Darwinism in physics can be borrowed intact from accounting, having been originated (but not named) by Littleton, criticized (and named) by Sterling, and then resurrected by Butterworth et al. ["Accounting Theory"] because it is essential to agency theory. The very fact that numerals representing unconventional-volume are not now extant will be taken as proof that they did not survive and this will be sufficient reason for concluding they are not fit. Questions about whether such mutant numerals existed and became extinct or never existed must be deflected because one cannot deduce not-fit-enough-to-survive from never-existed.

Eventually the theory developed by these anthropologists will be called the "inductive theory of *physics*," although it seems clear that it is a theory of *physicists* rather than a theory of physics. But physicists, if they continue to emulate accountants, will resist calling it a theory of physicists, and explain that there is no need to observe the outputs of calculations if one can observe the calculators because sufficient observations of calculators proves that the outputs of the calculations are useful, else so many people wouldn't calculate them.

The anthropological branch of the social science of physics can be extended to other tribes. One group of anthropologists will say that "the objective of physicking theory is to explain and predict physicking practices" and start building a positive theory of physics by observing sophisticated tribes of cunning agents manipulating the calculations of conventional-volume. If someone points out that it is funny (or perhaps even silly) to say that the purpose of a theory is to explain and predict the practices (i.e., the actions of practitioners) rather than the phenomena that those practitioners deal with, they can be silenced by saying that it would be *normative* to explain and predict such phenomena and that we must establish a *positive* theory in order to be *scientific*, and the purpose of a positive theory is to explain and predict the practices.

Eventually this will come to be called the "positive theory of *physics*" when it seems clear that it is a positive theory of numeral *manipulators*. But physicists will resist calling it a theory of numeral manipulators, and explain that there is no need to observe the outputs of calculations if one can observe the manipulators because sufficient observations of manipulators proves that the outputs of the calculations are important, else so many people wouldn't manipulate them.

After establishing the legitimacy of explaining and predicting the physicking practices, these anthropologists will hypothesize that if the income or bonus of an agent depends on the conventional-volume numerals, or if any other contract (such as a debt contract) is defined by reference to those numerals, then the agents will tend to switch reported numerals from 240 to 264 (fifo to lifo) or from 264 to 240 (lifo to fifo) depending upon which contractual outcome they desire. After they have observed the cunning agents manipulate such calculations for a while, the world will be able to watch with awed admiration as these anthropologists make the breathtakingly bold conjecture that the purpose of such manipulations is to maximize the agents' self-interest.[20]

3.2.2. *Psychology*

Other physicists will imitate psychologists (from the stimulus-response school), establishing some important properties of conventional-volume by observing the responses of an aberrant group called volume market agents.[21] They will discover that volume market agents respond to the stimulus of the numerals 240, 264, and 242 and that they respond to a switch from 240 to 264 (fifo to lifo) but not to a switch from 264 to 240 (lifo to fifo). These psychologic-physicists will be able to conclude that all three of the numerals have "information content" because the volume market agents responded to all of those numerals. From that they will be able to deduce that the market cannot be fooled by cosmetic changes and predict a nonresponse to cosmetic changes. If someone concludes that a switch from fifo to lifo is not cosmetic (because the agents responded) whereas the switch from lifo to fifo is cosmetic (because the agents did not respond), he can be dismissed as being antiempirical, the proof of which is that he used logic to draw that conclusion.

If someone imitates scientists from other fields by suggesting that we ought to consider the possibility that such a response is conditioned or habituated, or even pathological, rather than taking it as incontrovertible proof of the usefulness of the numerals, he can be referred to the assumption that volume market agents are *rational* and the *empirically observed* responses prove that they *use* the numerals in *rational* decisions and therefore both fifo and lifo—both 240 and 264—reflect real world phenomena. If someone points out that the same real world phenomena cannot be *both* 240 and 264, and that claiming such is a contradiction, he can be dismissed as an apriorist who has demonstrated that he is not a volume market empiricist by the very act of drawing a valid logical conclusion. If someone suggests that the coupling of an untested, counter-intuitive assumption with some observations of people's reactions is not the best or most direct way to empirically prove that numerals reflect real world phenomena, he can be ignored because he doesn't believe that volume markets instantaneously and unbiasedly impound all publicly available information.

3.2.3. *Economics*

The possibility of viewing conventional-volume numerals as economic goods provides a means for making physics a branch of economics. Since it is possible for there to be a market for almost anything, one can look at the market for conventional-volume numerals and analyze the different costs of producing 240, 264, and 252, and compare those costs to the different benefits derived from each numeral. If someone suggests that there might be more benefit from numerals that have empirical referents, such as unconventional-volume, economic-physicists can reply that supplying such numerals would violate consumer sovereignty.

If someone proposes that instead of or in addition to viewing conventional-volume numerals as economic goods, one could, with at least equal justification, view unconventional-volume numerals as economic goods, physicists can resist switching to reporting the unconventional-volume on the grounds that such a switch has not been shown to be Pareto optimal, may redistribute wealth or have other social welfare effects, violates the proof of the impossibility of normative standards, must mesh with formal concepts of welfare economics if it is to be accorded scientific status, among other reasons. Timing is the crucial factor in the establishment of such economic prohibitions: economic-physicists must be careful to wait until after they have started producing conventional-volume numerals because the prohibitions against switching from conventional-volume to unconventional-volume numerals also apply to switching from unconventional-volume to conventional-volume numerals.

3.3. Toward a Politico-Legal System of Physics

Physics will reach its pinnacle when it is recognized that it is *by its very nature* a politico-legal system, requiring the establishment of a solemn regulatory body with an elaborate due process which operates democratically in sunshine, as opposed to smoke-filled rooms. The regulatory body might be called the "Physicking Principles Board" or the "Physicking Standards Board."

You will undoubtedly be surprised to learn that there is no extant Board in physics. Indeed, physics is in such an underdeveloped state that at the present time there is no *need* for such a Board! Up to this point physics has limped along by relying on the individual efforts of each physicist (including the individual efforts of the likes of Galileo, Newton and Einstein), not realizing just what they are missing but not having a regulatory body to issue an unending flow of regulations.

The reason for the primitive state is that physics has not yet been converted to an art. As long as the subject matter is unconventional-volume, individual effort is all that is needed. One can rely on individuals to measure and verify unconventional-volume. It is also more productive to rely on individuals (rather than mandating a committee) to get bright ideas about the ability of various formulae (such as tables of expansion coefficients) to predict (by calculation) the unconventional-volume. Then all the individuals who are interested can check those formulae (test those hypotheses) by measuring (observing) the unconventional-volume.

The ability to rely on individuals vanishes as soon as the unmeasurable conventional-volume is defined and the scope of physicking is restricted to that "attribute." Since it has been decided to "measure" (calculate) conventional-volume, one cannot choose between "measurement" (calculational) methods, such as fifo and sum-of-the-tons-digits, by measuring (observing) unconventional-volume, and since the giga-bytes of empirical findings about people (from the social sciences of physics) provide no help, the only thing left is to establish a Physicking Standards Board.

Thus, the need to establish a Physicking Standards Board is a direct consequence of adopting an unmeasurable attribute. As soon as the Board is established, all else is defensive. The first thing to do is to repeatedly *assert* that physics is *necessarily* politico-legal and therefore a standards board is *essential.* If someone were to suggest adopting a measurable attribute, such as unconventional-volume, physicists should explain that we live in a democracy where such things are decided in a democratic manner and, therefore, physics cannot be left to the whims of individual physicists testing such things. If that someone were so bold as to suggest that physics did fairly well without such a Board for hundreds of years, physicists should explain that the unconventional-volume of oil is an item of wealth, and that the reporting of the conventional-volume of oil results in wealth transfers, and changing the way we calculate conventional-volume would result in changing those wealth transfers (the distributive welfare effects), which decisions cannot be made because of the impossibility of comparing interpersonal utilities, and therefore we need the Standards Board to make those undecidable decisions but we can't switch to measuring unconventional-volume because of its distributive welfare effects. If you don't follow that, keep it quiet because it proves that there is something wrong with you, not something wrong with the argument.

Another effective defensive strategy is to raise the specter of governmental regulation and urge private sector regulation because this results in regulation winning by default by diverting attention from the question of the *desirability* of regulation to the question of the desirable *source* of the regulations.

After the Physicking Standards Board is securely established, physicists can begin to seek sympathy because physics "by its very nature" is a political process and physicists would have a much easier life if physics were a science. Members of the Physics Standards Board can at first express surprise and then remorse at the "political pressure" from the various "constituents" that forces them to "make political decisions" instead of "rational decisions" including keeping the lifo versus fifo "hot potato" off the agenda. Then all physicists (inexplicably) will become incensed when Congress legislates certain physicking methods. Perhaps the reason for being incensed is that Congress is more adept at the political process. Once everyone understands the untold difficulties of being a politico-legal system, everyone will sympathize with physicists because their job is much harder than that of scientists.

One group that will be openly happy about the conversion to an art then to a politico-legal process will be the political scientists. They could not join the first wave rushing toward a social science of physics because there was little for them to study prior to the establishment of the Physicking Standards Board. After its establishment there will be ample opportunity to study voting patterns, lobbying efforts, coalition formations, and the like. Another happy group will be the historians because the intrigue of politics makes much more interesting history than the mundane measurement and verification of unconventional-volume. One historian can make a career by showing that, contrary to the wide-spread belief that standards are set in concrete, they must be iron-clad because they were all forged.

Although no particular time lapse is needed to establish the Physicking Standards Board, assurance of the continuation of the Physicking Standards Board requires that about 40 years (at least two generations) have elapsed from the conversion from a science to art. This time lapse will ensure that no member of the Board, nor any of his cohorts, will have had any exposure to outmoded, measurable (observable) attributes, such as unconventional-volume. As a consequence of total unfamiliarity with such attributes, Board members will find them to be so foreign as to be unthinkable.

The two generation requirement is crucial. If members of the Board were familiar with measurable attributes, they might find them thinkable and thinking about them might lead to the fatal error of adopting one. That this error is truly fatal can be seen by projecting its consequences: there would be little left for the Board to do and they might be forced to go earn an honest living. Although the possibility of such a fatal mistake is remote, the FASB came close enough to making such an error for it to be advisable for members of the Physicking Standards Board to study the case to help it avoid the same near-miss.

A brief outline of the case follows:

The FASB unanimously adopted a
•conceptual framework
which began with the objective of providing
•decision useful information
and specified that the two primary qualitative characteristics of useful information are
•relevance and reliability
and specified that the two components of reliability are
•representational faithfulness and verifiability
and defined representational faithfulness as
•correspondence or agreement between a measure and the phenomenon it purports to represent.

The problem is that a careful reading of this compels one to the conclusion that the faithful representation of *phenomena* is necessary (but not sufficient) to achieve reliability and reliability is necessary (but not sufficient) to achieve decision usefulness.

This came perilously close to forcing the FASB to deal with representing phenomena. An attempted escape came when one Board member found a passage in the Conceptual Framework which read "the reliability of a measure rests on the faithfulness with which it represents what it purports to represent" as opposed to the dangerous phrasing of "the phenomenon it purports to represent." Although this attempted escape was not entirely successful, it did seem to give heart to the other members so that they finally resolved the issue by defining "phenomena" broadly enough to include "worksheet calculations."[22] Thus, when it appeared that FASB was cornered by its unanimously adopted concepts, it adroitly escaped by requiring that one blob of ink faithfully represent another blob of ink. Members of the Physicking Standards Board would do well to emulate such shrewd maneuvers if they want to assure that their Board is a permanent institution.

4. SUMMARY AND CONCLUSIONS

Norms of validation can be grouped according to the three major philosophical conceptions of truth: correspondence or semantical norms, coherence or syntactical norms, and pragmatic or functional norms. The first set is the basic one somehow; the others must be regarded as analyses or interpretations of correspondence. Science is governed by the reality principle, its thought checked and controlled by the characteristics of the things it thinks about.—Abraham Kaplan

The purpose of this paper was to explain that with rare exceptions accounting numerals do not represent phenomena, *any* phenomena, and that making numerals represent or not represent phenomena is a matter of choice.

The explanation was first attempted by presenting the results of a simple behavioral test in which physicists and accountants were asked to solve a problem and noting the vast difference in the way in which two groups reached a solution. In general the accountants were content to calculate but the physicists insisted on comparing the calculations to observations. This result was interpreted as having been caused by the way that we teach accounting both in school and in practice. Such teaching causes accountants to be unable to distinguish numerals from reality.

The explanation was also attempted by projecting the history of physics if it decided to adopt the accounting method of calculation without observation. Physics could define an unmeasurable, conventional "attribute" identical to the expired and unexpired cost "attribute" that we now account for and this would allow physics to first be converted from a science to an art, then to a social science and finally to a politico-legal discipline with the need for a Board to set essentially arbitrary standards. After this had been accomplished and after several generations had passed, physicists would be unable to understand papers that tried to show them that it was possible to represent phenomena.

Thus, this paper took on the Herculean task (perhaps more akin to cleansing the Augean stables than slaying the Cithaeron lion) of explaining

1. the need for a norm of correspondence in a field whose members denigrate anything normative and
2. the possibility of numerals corresponding to reality in a field whose members are under the illusion that numerals are reality.

Providing such correspondence is a necessary (but not a sufficient) condition for converting accounting into an empirical science. Convincing my colleagues that providing such correspondence is both possible and desirable has been my failure as an empiricist. However, hope springs eternal.

APPENDIX 1

(For Accountants)

TO THE PARTICIPANT

Thank you for agreeing to participate in this experiment. The experiment consists of asking you about a problem and comparing your answers to the answers of others. The objective is to see how different people go about solving such problems, *not* to grade your answers.

There are no tricks or hidden data in the problem. However, we cannot answer questions about the problem because what we tell you might influence your answers. We want *your* answers, not answers which are partially yours and partially ours.

THE PROBLEM

Background Information

The Oklahoma Company (OKACO) receives oil from various Railroads (in railcars), holds the oil in its tanks until needed, and then issues it to various Trucklines (in semitrailers). OKACO needs to know the volume (number of barrels) of oil in each tank as well as where the oil came from when received and where it goes when issued.

Both the railroads and trucklines weigh their tank cars before and after a receipt or issue and can thereby easily determine the weight of the oil received or issued. However, determining volume (number of barrels) is more difficult and only the railroads have a gauge that will measure the volume pumped. The trucklines do not have such a gauge. Despite the difficulty, OKACO needs to know the volume for reasons that are not pertinent here.

Although weight is not affected by temperature changes, volume expands and contracts with temperature increases and decreases. OKACO is located in Oklahoma where the normal temperature is lowest in January, higher in March, and still higher in June and July. The oil is never refrigerated or heated so that its volume varies with the ambient temperature. The tanks and tank cars are sealed so that evaporation does not occur. There were no leaks in the pipelines, tanks or tank cars, nor were there any thefts. There is no oil left in the pipelines after pumping. There are no tables or ratios of volume to weight of oil because there are many different kinds of oil.

Data

At December 31 all of OKACO's tanks were empty. The following is a complete listing of all transfers that occurred from January 1 to July 1:

January 1	A Union Pacific railcar pumped 100 tons or 400 barrels into Tank 1.
March 1	A Long Island railcar pumped 100 tons or 440 barrels into Tank 1.
June 30	Pumped 60 tons (and an unknown number of barrels) from Tank 1 to a Roadway Express semitrailer.

All figures given about are true or correct, that is, they are faithful representations (within plus or minus .01%) of the respective volumes and weights indicated.

Objective

The objective is to establish a system of accounting for the oil that will faithfully represent the number of barrels of oil that was

1. received from the railroads and the dates of those receipts,
2. on hand and available to be issued from March 1 to June 29,
3. issued to trucklines and the date of that issue, and
4. remaining on hand at July 1.

As a means of achieving the objective OKACO has adopted a double-entry system to keep track of the oil and the following journal entries were made on the dates indicated.

January 1 Tank 1 400
Union Pacific 400
To record the receipt of 400 barrels (100 tons @ 4 barrels per ton) in Tank 1 from the Union Pacific Railroad.

March 1 Tank 1 440
Long Island 440
To record the receipt of 440 barrels (100 tons @ 4.4 barrels per ton) in Tank 1 from the Long Island Railroad.

Although all accept the objective stated above, there are questions about how to achieve that objective. Many of these questions concern the amount of the issue to Roadway Express at June 30. That questionable amount is indicated as z in the following entry.

June 30 Roadway z
Tank 1 z
To record the issue of z barrels (60 tons @ x barrels per ton) to the Roadway Express Truckline from Tank 1.

Three proposals for the amount of the June 30 credit and the balance at July 1 are contained in Columns A, B, and C of the following table. (This table is also pertinent to Question 2.)

Question 1

Which, if any, of the figures in the Credit row in Table One faithfully represent the volume of oil issued at June 30? The first three of the following possible

Table 1. Proposals for Tank 1 (All amounts are in barrels.)

	A	*B*	*C*
Debits:			
(from Union Pacific) at Jan 1	400	400	400
(from Long Island) at March 1	440	440	440
Total Debits at March 1	840	840	840
Credit:			
(to Roadway) at June 30	240	264	252
Balance at July 1	600	576	588

answers correspond to the columns in Table One and each answer explains how the credit in the column was obtained.

A. The 240 barrel figure in Column A. That figure was obtained as follows: (60 tons × 4.0) = 240. The proposal for reporting that figure is made on the basis of the assumption that the first receipt is likely to be the source of the first issue (that is, "FIFO").
B. The 264 barrel-figure in Column B. That figure was obtained as follows: (60 tons × 4.4) = 264. The proposal for reporting that figure is made on the basis of the assumption that the last receipt is likely to be the source of the first issue, (that is, "LIFO").
C. The 252 barrel figure in Column C. That figure was obtained as follows: (60 tons × 4.2) = 252. The proposal for reporting that figure is made on the basis of the assumption that the receipts would combine and therefore the issue would be at the average barrels per ton of both receipts (that is, "average").
D. Making proposals on the basis of associating the issue with receipts is on the right track but it should be based on knowledge of the association rather than on an assumption about the association. If one knew which receipt or receipts was the source of the issue (that is, if the issue were specifically identified as coming from a particular receipt), then one could derive the figure that is a faithful representation of the volume of oil issued on June 30. Thus, any of the figures in the credit row of Table One could be a faithful representation if the assumption about the association happens to be the actual association.
E. Making proposals on the basis of associating the issue with receipts is on the wrong track. Even if one knew which receipt or receipts was the

source of the issue, it would not be of help in deriving the figure that is a faithful representation of the volume of oil issued at June 30. Thus, none of the figures in the credit row of Table One is a faithful representation of the issue regardless of the actual or assumed association of receipts and issues.

APPENDIX 2

(For Non-Accountants)

TO THE PARTICIPANT

Thank you for agreeing to participate in this experiment. The experiment consists of asking you about a problem and comparing your answers to the answers of others. The objective is to see how different people go about solving such problems, *not* to grade your answers.

There are no tricks or hidden data in the problem. However, we cannot answer questions about the problem because what we tell you might influence your answers. We want *your* answers, not answers which are partially yours and partially ours.

THE PROBLEM

Background Information

The Oklahoma Company (OKACO) receives oil from various Railroads (in railcars), holds the oil in its tanks until needed, and then issues it to various Trucklines (in semitrailers). OKACO needs to know the volume (number of barrels) of oil in each tank as well as where the oil came from when received and where it goes when issued.

Both the railroads and trucklines weigh their tank cars before and after a receipt or issue and can thereby easily determine the weight of the oil received or issued. However, determining volume (number of barrels) is more difficult and only the railroads have a gauge that will measure the volume pumped. The trucklines do not have such a gauge. Despite the difficulty, OKACO needs to know the volume for reasons that are not pertinent here.

Although weight is not affected by temperature changes, volume expands and contracts with temperature increases and decreases. OKACO is located in Oklahoma where the normal temperature is lowest in January, higher in March, and still higher in June and July. The oil is never refrigerated or heated so that its volume varies with the ambient temperature. The tanks and tank cars are sealed so that evaporation does not occur. There were no leaks in the pipelines, tanks or tank cars nor were there any thefts. There is no oil left in the pipelines after pumping. There are no tables of ratios of volume to weight of oil because there are many different kinds of oil.

Data

At December 31 all of OKACO's tanks were empty. The following is a complete listing of all transfers that occurred from January 1 to July 1:

January 1	A Union Pacific railcar pumped 100 tons or 400 barrels into Tank 1.
March 1	A Long Island railcar pumped 100 tons or 440 barrels into Tank 1.
June 30	Pumped 60 tons (and an unknown number of barrels) from Tank 1 to a Roadway Express semitrailer.

All figures given above are true or correct, that is, they are faithful representations (within plus or minus .01%), of the respective volumes and weights indicated.

Objective

The objective is to establish a system of keeping track of the oil that will faithfully represent the number of barrels of oil that was

1. received from the railroads and the dates of those receipts,
2. on hand and available to be issued from March 1 to June 29,
3. issued to trucklines and the date of that issue, and
4. remaining on hand at July 1.

As a means of achieving the objective OKACO has designed a simple system of recording the receipts and issues in the following way:

January 1 Tank 1 received 400 barrels from Union Pacific.
To record the receipt of 400 barrels (100 tons @ 4 barrels per ton) in Tank 1 from the Union Pacific Railroad.

March 1 Tank 1 received 440 barrels from Long Island.
To record the receipt of 440 barrels (100 tons @ 4.4 barrels per ton) in Tank 1 from the Long Island Railroad.

June 30 Tank 1 issued z barrels to Roadway.
To record the issue of z barrels (60 tons @ x barrels per ton) to the Roadway Express Truckline from Tank 1.

Although all accept the objective stated above, there are questions about how to achieve that objective. Many of these questions concern the amount of the

Table 1. Proposals for Tank 1 (All amounts are in barrels.)

	A	B	C
Receipts:			
(from Union Pacific) at Jan 1	400	400	400
(from Long Island) at March 1	440	440	440
Total Receipts at March 1	840	840	840
Issue:			
(to Roadway) at June 30	240	264	252
Stock at July 1	600	576	588

issue to Roadway Express at June 30. That questionable amount is indicated as z in the above recording.

Three proposals for the amount of the June 30 issue and the stock at July 1 are contained in Columns A, B, and C of the above table. (This table is also pertinent to Question 2.)

Question 1

Which, if any, of the figures in the Issue row in Table One faithfully represent the volume of oil issued at June 30? The first three of the following possible answers correspond to the columns in Table One and each answer explains how the issue in the column was obtained.

A. The 240 barrel figure in Column A. That figure was obtained as follows: (60 tons × 4.0) = 240. The proposal for reporting that figure is made on the basis of the assumption that the first receipt is likely to be the source of the first issue.
B. The 264 barrel figure in Column B. That figure was obtained as follows: (60 tons × 4.4) = 264. The proposal for reporting that figure is made on the basis of the assumption that the last receipt is likely to be the source of the first issue.
C. The 252 barrel figure in Column C. That figure was obtained as follows: (60 tons × 4.2) = 252. The proposal for reporting that figure is made on the basis of the assumption that the receipts would combine and therefore the issue would be at the average barrels per ton of both receipts.
D. Making proposals on the basis of associating the issue with receipts is on the right track but it should be based on knowledge of the association

rather than on an assumption about the association. If one knew which receipt or receipts was the source of the issue (that is, if the issue were specifically identified as coming from a particular receipt), then one could derive the figure that is a faithful representation of the volume of oil issued on June 30. Thus, any of the figures in the issue row of Table One could be a faithful representation if the assumption about the association happens to be the actual association.

E. Making proposals on the basis of associating the issue with receipts is on the wrong track. Even if one knew which receipt or receipts was the source of the issue, it would not be of help in deriving the figure that is a faithful representation of the volume of oil issued at June 30. Thus, none of the figures in the issue row of Table One is a faithful representation of the issue regardless of the actual or assumed association of receipts and issues.

ACKNOWLEDGMENTS

Earlier versions, fragments, and outlined extensions of this paper have been presented at the Lee Kuan Yew Distinguished Lecture, National University of Singapore; Raymond J. Chambers Distinguished Lecture, University of Sydney; Israel Conference of Accountants; Deloittes Distinguished Lecture, University of Edinburgh; Lowden Distinguished Lecture, TCU; Annual Distinguished Speaker Series, Long Beach State University; Meeting of the Arizona Society of CPAs, University of Arizona; Andersen Distinguished Lecture, University of New Mexico; Colorado Consortium of Accounting Professors, Colorado Society of CPAs and FEI; Eccles Distinguished Lecture, Weber State University; Faculty from Louisiana Universities, University of New Orleans; Faculty-Phd Seminar, Temple University; Mid-Atlantic Regional AAA Meeting, Atlantic City; and Brown Bag Seminar, University of Utah. I am grateful for interesting discussion and helpful comments from many members of those audiences. Additional thanks are due to the members of the audiences who returned questionnaires and thereby became subjects of the experiment as well as discussants of the report of the experiment. Hospitality or comment or both was provided by Lim Pin, Ronald Ma, Han Kang Hong, Tan Teck Meng, Murray Wells, Moshe Levin, Mike Horowitz, Tom Lee, Jack Shaw, Don Nichols, Carl Allen, Mohamed Moustafa, Russ Barefield, Joan Norvelle, Alan Porter, Ray Radesovich, Todd Johnson, Bob Zimmer, Allen Simkins, Herman Brasseaux, Gordon Hosch, Bill Schwartz, Stephen Fogg, and Ron Bagley. Paul Dorsey, Peter Wolnizer, Flemming Ruud, Rolland Munro, and Kevin McBeth served ably as research associates or assistants at various times during the preparation of the paper. To all of the above my warm thanks and the usual absolution.

NOTES

1. Some accountants do not believe that it is possible to make such an "obvious" error and sometimes they are insulted at my "accusation" that they confuse numerals with reality. Perhaps my suggestion can be made less insulting by pointing out that the malady is not restricted to accountants.

The map metaphor that is often used in accounting to explain representational faithfulness is also often used in science to explain maya. Ziman [*Reliable*, p. 85] writes of the "vulgar [common] fallacy—the tendency to conflate scientific knowledge with the material reality that it purports to describe. No sane person would suppose a map to be identical with the land that it represents." Capra [*Tao of Physics*, p. 78] succinctly defines it as follows: "*Maya* is the illusion of taking these concepts for reality, of confusing the map with the territory." Boulding [*Economics as a Science*, p. 75] employs the same metaphor: "What all this involves is not a case against abstraction, which is essential, but a warning against mistaking abstraction for reality. We would be foolish to try to go for a walk across a map, but a map may be very helpful if we are going for a real walk."

See also Whitehead [*Science*, p. 58] for a discussion of "the fallacy of misplaced concreteness" and Radhakrishnan and Moore [*Indian Philosophy*] for a general review of maya.

2. A conference, for example, with the stated purpose of providing an even-handed assessment of accounting research, assigned Sterling [*Enterprise Income*] to the class of works that relied exclusively on the "a priori" method, overlooking that the first proposition listed in that book is that messages are required to "faithfully describe the world" [p. 41], a clear empirical tenet. An AAA monograph, for another example, with the stated purpose of explaining research, uses Sterling ["Theory Construction"] as the exemplar of anti-empirical works when the major purpose of that article was to explain the structure of empirical theories and to critically note that current accounting outputs are not empirically verifiable. Such classifications illustrate what I think is a general, unfortunate tendency for some empiricists to confuse proposals to access a *different* empirical domain with *anti*-empiricism.

3. In fact I have employed the analogy used in the questionnaire and others like it ever since having noticed the similarity of the logical structure of double entry to that of the conservation laws in physics when I was a postdoctoral fellow at The Sloan Physics Lab. I extended it in Sterling ["Explication"] and worked it out in more detail in Sterling [*Mathematical and Empirical*].

4. In psychology a similar effect, called *einstellung* or habituation, has been experimentally demonstrated by Luchins [*Mechanization*] and described as follows: "The successive, repetitious use of the same method mechanized many of the subjects—blinded them to the possibility of a more direct and simpler procedure [p 1]."

What is meant by "successive, repetitious use of the same method" in this experiment is that the subjects (graduate students, college instructors and research workers, many possessing Ph.D. or MD degrees) were presented with the solution to six simple (about fifth grade level) problems at intervals of 2½ minutes and then were asked to solve two similar but more directly solvable problems. The results were: "Not one subject used the more direct method in Problems Seven and Eight. Having become habituated to the mode of solution [presented], they used it in the succeeding similar problems."

Those who are skeptical about the trained incapacity of accountants might want to ponder the relative effects of the few minutes of training given to subjects in the described experiment to the many years of training given to accountants in the classroom and on the job.

Luchins' subjects, after the experiment was complete and the direct method of solution revealed, "were excited about how foolish and blind they had been [p 14]" and "spontaneously said, more or less passionately, 'How dumb I was;' 'How stupid of me;' 'How blind I was;' or made other similar comments [p 2]." By contrast, many accountants in the audiences listed in the acknowledgements expressed the view that it was the test, not they, that was foolish or dumb. Instead of accepting that they had overlooked the possibility of measuring (as opposed to calculating) the volume, accountants tended to attempt to discredit the experiment. Thus, in addition to accountants and non-accountants giving strikingly different answers to the question, there was also a marked difference in their post-test reactions.

I am indebted to Rolland Munro for the reference to Luchins and discussion of this literature.

5. Yes, despite all those admonitions against being "normative" emanating from "scientific" accountants, the primary purpose of treatises on scientific methodology is to set forth the norms of

scientific inquiry and the reasons for them. Indeed, the primary purpose of this paper is to try to explain what Kaplan [*Conduct*, p. 312] calls the "norm of correspondence". I don't want to offend refined accountants by using four letter words but coarse philosophers of science regularly use the snicker-generating "true" as well as the prohibited "norm" in their writings. Kaplan neatly summarizes the critical points in the three sentences quoted following the heading at §4. My primary point is that accounting numerals violate the basic norm of correspondence, they are not governed by the reality principle. My secondary point has been flagrantly normative: those numerals ought to be governed by the norm of correspondence, by the reality principle.

6. I think the difference in outlook is caused by a difference in training but another possible explanation is the difference in personality: certain personality types chose to be accountants and others choose to be physicists. Aranya and Wheeler [p. 187, citing Holland] write "People do not become conventional in order to be accountants, they choose to be accountants because they are conventional." In regard to this paper that sentence could be changed to "People do not become calculators in order to be accountants, they choose to be accountants because they are calculators" and "People do not become observers in order to be physicists, they choose to be physicists because they are observers". But this raises a question of the origins of disciplines. How did a discipline become what it is so that compatible personality types could select it? For my views on how accounting became what it is, see Sterling, ["1980's"].

7. I am grateful to Mary Teresa Kwang, an apprentice psychometrician, for vetting the questionnaire, administering it to the subjects, conducting the post-test interviews, and reviewing the presentation of the results in this article.

8. Various versions of this questionnaire have also been given to several audiences mentioned in the acknowledgments. The proportion of respondents in those audiences who answered E was significantly more than the proportion of accountant-subjects in the test who gave that answer. This may be due to the increased sophistication of the faculty and Phd students in those audiences, the desire of the third-year students to demonstrate their knowledge of accounting, to the variation in the way the questions were phrased or administered, or to some other factor(s). The results reported in the text are from only one test and are therefore accompanied by even more than the usual caveats about the results. More extensive testing and the reporting of such tests' results awaits a student who needs a dissertation topic.

9. The use of "measure" as a synonym for "calculate" is not peculiar to these subjects. That the usage is prevalent among accountants is evidenced by its frequent appearance in the literature. Two recent, widely used and highly regarded accounting texts, one at the elementary level and the other at the advanced undergraduate or graduate level, provide examples of that usage.

> . . . expenses are *measured* by the costs of assets consumed or services used during an accounting period. Depreciation on equipment [and other] expenses . . . are determined by *measuring* the amount of assets or services consumed (or expired) during an accounting period. Walgenbach et al. [*Principles*, p. 17, emphasis altered].
>
> Ending inventory is *measured* by first determining the quantity on hand, then multiplying this quantity times the unit acquisition cost. A choice must be arbitrarily made on the assumed unit cost, and this depends on the flow assumptions made. The attribute being *measured* is historical cost in all methods. Wolk et al. [*Accounting Theory*, p. 268, emphasis supplied].

Students learn two lessons from such texts: (1) how to calculate expenses such as depreciation and inventory, and (2) to think that they have "measured" something by those calculations. From this comes the idea that measurements do not involve observations and this contributes to the trained incapacity to observe. Several accountant-subjects spoke of "measuring volume by the lifo or fifo method" thereby demonstrating that they had learned their lesson well. If you think you are immune to such usage, think back over your reading of this paper and see if the use of "measure" as a synonym for "calculate" gave you pause. Previous experience leads me to believe that not one accountant would notice that in introducing the section on flow assumptions I wrote: "The accounting method is to *measure* the volume of goods shipped by making a flow assumption." If you are an accountant and you noticed that peculiar usage, please write and inform me.

10. Indeed, my concern is that this test provides too much support for my conjecture: such tests are usually not very tidy unless the investigator inadvertently influences the subjects. I fear that may have happened here. Although I have not been able to identify any sources of bias, I remain suspicious for the sole reason that the test results are too consistent. We should expect some contrary findings even if they are just noise.

11. I say "apparently" in regard to accountants because their propensity to assign unique meanings to words, such as the above mentioned use of "measure" to mean "calculate", made it difficult for the interviewer (Kwang) to interpret the comments.

12. I stress the distinction between the observation and inference because the failure to make that distinction has been a continuing source of misunderstanding about my views on the role of empirical research, especially efficient market research. I have frequently expressed the view that one can *observe* market reactions to accounting numerals but one must *infer* what such reactions mean. To say that reactions to changes in accounting numerals prove that there were changes in real world phenomena confuses observations with inferences drawn from observations. To say that my disagreement with such inferences shows that I don't "believe" in efficient markets evidently stems from the same confusion. The most startling confusion, however, is to classify me as an anti-empiricist on the basis of my suggestion that there are more direct *empirical* tests for detecting changes in real world phenomena.

13. Perhaps the clearest statement of this view is Stamp's ["Accounting," p. 20] reliance on his idea of "the intrinsic nature of accounting" to reject the possibility of representing phenomena. This is evidently a widely held view. By contrast, I am puzzled by the very concept of the "nature" of accounting: I think that accounting should *represent* some aspect of nature rather than *having* a nature.

14. It is at this point that we must introduce physicists to a new form of logical proof originated by Mammy Yokum and refined to its present advanced state by accountants. As you may recall, Mammy Yokum could always prove a point by raising her forefinger and saying "As any fool can plainly see," leaving it deliciously ambiguous as to whether the point was so obvious that *even* fools could see it or that it was so preposterous that *only* fools could see it. The accounting refinement has been to allow one to invoke the proof tacitly. At the present time the only thing needed to invoke the proof is to raise the finger. Although originally one had a choice of several fingers, there now seems to be convergence on one generally accepted accounting finger.

15. Many accountants think that the analogy is transparent. If you think so, ask yourself whether you had any concern with the balance figure prior to reading the text questioning it. To date none of the accountant-subjects or members of previous audiences have volunteered any concern about the balance nor expressed any about it when asked. Several accountants have disagreed with my claim that the problem with inventory accounting begins with the addition (calculation) of the numerals to get the March 1 balance rather than at the selection of the flow assumption to calculate expired cost and the addition (calculation) of the negative numeral to get the July 1 balance.

16. The problem with adding the debits to get the balance is exactly the same problem as adding the balance to the (negative) credit, and the amount of the credit is determined by the lifo-fifo selection. This is called the "additivity" problem and has been discussed by several people in the accounting literature. Larson ["Descriptive Validity"] provides a particularly lucid discussion and Vickrey ["Measurement Discipline"] provides a more technical treatment.

In brief, the test for whether an attribute is additive can be stated generally as follows: if m(A) is the numeral derived from the measurement of object or event A and & is some physical method of combining objects or events A and B, then the attribute is additive if

$$m(A) + m(B) = m(A \& B)$$

and it is not additive if that expression is not an equality. Thus, length is additive because if we measure the length of rod A, rod B and then rod A and B joined end to end, we will find that the above expression is an equality. By contrast, if we measure the temperature of fluid A, fluid B, and then fluid A and B poured together, we will find that the above expression is *not* an equality, and thus temperature is not additive.

The additivity of volume requires more specification of the circumstances. We know that volume poured together is not additive if the fluids are at different temperatures and we know that certain different kinds of fluid are not additive. For example, the volumes of alcohol and water are not additive. Note that one cannot determine whether something is or is not additive by reasoning. The only test is the empirical one of measuring the combination and seeing if that measurement corresponds to the numerals obtained from addition. Some of the accounting discussions of additivity have overlooked that elementary point.

More generally, the requirement of additivity is simply one example of the overall requirement that goes by the name "norm of correspondence." That is, the requirement that numerals correspond to phenomena (and can be empirically shown to do so by independent observations) rather than a special requirement of additivity.

In this case, we know (more accurately, we can confidently predict) that the magnitude of the volume is not 840 because the ambient temperature has varied. For this reason, even if we were certain that the volume shipped was (say) 300 barrels, then the remaining oil would not be 540 because the initial oil was not 840. That is, the original lack of additivity of the debits causes the subsequent lack of additivity of the debit and (negative) credit.

17. Such (upward) adjustments to make the balance faithfully represent the oil should be prohibited in physics because they are *not* reliable, realized, conservative, factual, measurements, objective, verifiable, an accurate history, and many other *equally* valid reasons.

18. The sources of these slightly altered quotations are given in Sterling [*Toward a Science*, p. 10]. The main alteration is to change "accounting" to "physics."

19. When the only observables become people it will cause even the more thoughtful authors to think that being a social science is self-evident. For example, Cooper and Zeff ["Kinney's"] assert that accounting is "an area of social science research" without further explanation or justification. Their approving citation of Stamp ["Accounting"] may be an indication that they agree with him that it is "the intrinsic nature of accounting" that makes it a social science.

20. It was Popper who said that the essence of science is to make bold conjectures and then make severe attempts to refute them but I'll bet he never imagined that anyone would be so bold as to conjecture that people seek their own self interest! Indeed Popper [*Realism*, p. xx] presented the idea of seeking self-interest as a clear example of a statement that is not scientific because it cannot be refuted. He said "Clearly this [self-interest] theory, with all its variants, is not falsifiable: no example of an altruistic action can refute the view that there was an egotistic motive hidden behind it." But this assertion can be safely ignored because it is clear that Popper was seeking his self-interest when writing it.

21. I previously made the error of claiming that observing the actions of accountants might result in a theory of accountants but not a theory of accounting, and that observing the reactions of capital market agents to accounting signals might tell one something about reactions but it would not tell one anything about the truth value of the signal. The error became clear to everyone when I employed analogies such as claiming that one can neither derive nor test a theory of psychology from observing psychologists shocking rats nor a theory of electricity from observing the reactions of rats being shocked.

It further occurred to me that if one observed the reaction of rats being shocked, and if one defined "reaction by rats" to be the same as "information content," then one could prove that electricity has information content. My error was compounded when I extended the procedure by noting that if one equated "reaction by rats" to "pneumonia", then one could also prove that electricity has pneumonia. I am not sure of the nature of my error but its existence can be demonstrated empirically: expose efficient market researchers to the above rat-electricity-pneumonia analogy, equate "acrimonious reaction" to "error content", and you will have ample *empirical* evidence that my analogy has error content.

22. This is a true story. In an attempt to anchor the recognition-measurement phase of the Conceptual Framework to the previously adopted phases, I tried to draw out the implications of the previously adopted concepts, especially relevance and reliability, and present those implications to FASB. All phases were difficult but representational faithfulness was a disaster, resulting in the decision to faithfully represent worksheet calculations.

As I pointed out to FASB at the time, this means that "12" on a financial statement would not be a faithful representation of "twelve" on a worksheet, but it would permit "Sterling is 12 feet tall" on a financial statement to be considered to be a faithful representation if "Sterling is 12 feet tall" appeared on a worksheet. I suggested that representational faithfulness should address the question of the correspondence of "12 feet" to my height rather than correspondence to a blob of ink on a worksheet. This suggestion was rejected by FASB because height is measurable and unexpired costs are not in much the same way that the accountant-subjects rejected the analogy because volume is measurable and unexpired costs are not.

This was my failure at FASB. Contrary to popular belief, I did not attempt to convince FASB to adopt current values and therefore I don't consider the fact that they didn't adopt current values to be a failure. However, I did try to convince them to represent phenomena, in accord with their previously adopted concepts, and I failed in that attempt.

REFERENCES

Aranya, Nissim, and John T. Wheeler, "Accountants' Personality Types and Their Commitment to Organization and Profession," *Contemporary Accounting Research* (1986), pp. 184–99.

Boulding, Kenneth E., *Economics as a Science*, (New York: McGraw-Hill, 1970).

Butterworth, John E., Michael Gibbins, and Raymond D. King, "The Structure of Accounting Theory: Some Basic Conceptual and Methodological Issues," In *Research to Support Standard Setting in Financial Accounting: A Canadian Perspective*. Proceedings of the 1981 Clarkson Gordon Foundation Research Symposium, edited by Sanjoy Basu and J. Alex Milburn (Toronto: The Clarkson Gordon Foundation, 1982).

Capra, F. *The Tao of Physics*, (London: Fontana/Collins, 1975).

Cooper, William W. and Stephen A. Zeff, "Kinney's Design for Accounting Research," unpublished, 1987.

Kaplan, Abraham, *The Conduct of Inquiry: Methodology for Behavioral Science* (San Francisco: Chandler Publishing Company, 1964).

Kuhn, Thomas S., *The Structure of Scientific Revolutions*, 2d ed. enl. (Chicago: University of Chicago Press, 1970).

Larson, Kermit D., "Descriptive Validity of Accounting Calculations," *The Accounting Review*, (1967) pp. 480–488.

Luchins, Abraham S., "Mechanization in Problem Solving," In *Psychological Monographs*, John F. Dashiell, editor (Evanston: The American Psychological Association, Inc., 1942).

Nagel, Ernest, *The Structure of Science: Problems in the Logic of Scientific Explanation* (New York: Harcourt, Brace & World, 1961).

Popper, Karl R., *Realism and the Aim of Science*, Edited by W. W. Bartley III. (Totowa, N.J.: Rowman and Littlefield, 1983).

Radhakrishnan, Sarvepalli and Charles A. Moore, *Indian Philosophy*, (Princeton: Princeton University Press, 1957).

Stamp, Edward, "Why Can Accounting Not Become a Science Like Physics," *Abacus* (1981), pp. 13–27.

Sterling, Robert R., *Theory of the Measurement of Enterprise Income* (Lawrence: University Press of Kansas, 1970. Reprint, Scholars Book Co.).

Sterling, Robert R., "On Theory Construction and Verification," *The Accounting Review* (1970), pp. 444–57.

Sterling, Robert R., "An Explication and Analysis of the Structure of Accounting Part One," *Abacus* (1971), pp 137–52.

Sterling, Robert R., "An Explication and Analysis of the Structure of Accounting Part Two," *Abacus* (1972), pp. 145–62.

Sterling, Robert R., *Accounting: A Mathematical and Empirical Investigation, Vol. 1, Quantity Accounting*, (Houston: Scholars Book Company, 1975).

Sterling, Robert R., "Accounting in the 1980's," in *Accountancy in the 1980's—Some Issues*, Proceedings of The Arthur Young Professors Roundtable, edited by N. M. Bedford (Reston, Va.: The Council of Arthur Young Professors, 1977).

Sterling, Robert R., *Toward A Science of Accounting* (Houston: Scholars Book Co., 1979).

Vickrey, Don W., "Is Accounting a Measurement Discipline?", *The Accounting Review*, (1970) pp. 731–742.

Walgenbach, Paul H., Norman E. Dittrich and Ernest I. Hanson, *Principles of Accounting* (San Diego: Harcourt, Brace, Javonovich, 1984).

Wolk, Harry I., Jere R. Francis and Michael G. Tearney, *Accounting Theory* (Boston: Kent Publishing, 1984).

Ziman, John, *Reliable Knowledge: An Exploration of the Grounds for Belief in Science* (Cambridge: Cambridge University Press, 1978).

6 The subject matters of accounting

Robert R. Sterling

A TRIBUTE TO EDDIE STAMP

> We are concerned here with some deep philosophical questions that I believe are of profound importance to accountants. . . . Practitioners as well as academics need to think carefully about these matters.
>
> (Stamp 1981)

This chapter was prepared to celebrate the life of Eddie Stamp rather than to mourn his death. More specifically, it was prepared to celebrate his professional life because the professional side of Eddie Stamp is the only side that I ever saw.

The Eddie Stamp that I knew was a consummate professional, totally dedicated to the improvement of accounting. His dedication was a major reason that I came to know only his professional side: all of our conversations, even on ostensible social occasions, focused exclusively on accounting or related topics, never on personal matters. He was a principled man, passionately committed to what he considered right and proper. His passion was a major reason that our exchanges are accurately characterized as zesty arguments, as opposed to bland discussions. His principles were a major reason that those exchanges are accurately characterized as arguments, as opposed to quarrels.

Since Eddie's many contributions to accounting will be recognized elsewhere in this volume, there is no need for me to repeat them here, but I must mention one contribution because it is likely to be overlooked by others and because it is one for which I am particularly grateful: he somehow managed to get a philosopher, Lyas, to write a paper about accounting (Lyas 1984). I have been privileged to have had many philosopher friends and acquaintances over the years but I have never been able to convince any of them that accounting is sufficiently interesting or important to warrant the effort of writing a paper. Indeed, I sometimes find it difficult to convince them that the subject is sufficiently interesting to warrant a ten-minute conversation. My failure in such attempts should explain why I am impressed enough to single out that particular, rather obscure, achievement when there are many other achievements that could be mentioned.

I have been informed that the audience for this volume will include scientists and philosophers, in additon to accountants. I will attempt to tailor[1] my remarks to make them more interesting and more easily understandable to the expanded audience in the hope that it will result in a further extension of Eddie's achievement. My fondest hope is that scientists' and philosophers' contributions to accounting will continue and multiply, eventually constituting a perpetual bequest to accounting from Eddie Stamp.

PURPOSE

> There is a method which might be described as 'the one method of philosophy'. But it is not characteristic of philosophy alone; it is, rather, the one method of all *rational discussion*, and therefore of the natural sciences as well as of philosophy. The method I have in mind is that of stating one's problem clearly and of examining its various proposed solutions *critically*.
>
> (Karl Popper)

The first purpose of this chapter is to stimulate (or provoke) scientists and philosophers to begin (and Lyas to continue) a critical examination of accounting. Toward that end I will attempt to describe the subject matter of accounting practice and accounting research clearly enough to permit interested scientists and philosophers to understand it and convincingly enough to permit them to believe it. My goal is to entice scientists and philosophers to make contributions to accounting thought by examining the fascinating problems that are the direct result of the unique subject matters of accounting.

The second purpose of this chapter is to stimulate (or provoke) other accountants to begin a critical examination of accounting. Toward that end I will attempt to explain how the subject matter of accounting differs crucially from the subject matter of scientific disciplines clearly enough to permit them to understand it and convincingly enough to permit them to believe it. My goal is to try to entice accountants to begin to critically examine accounting, and accounting research, rather than just doing it. I have no objection to doing accounting or doing accounting research but I do object to it being done mechanically, that is, without being clear about what one is doing and why one is doing it.

These two purposes present two formidable problems that seem to be completely separate but are in fact peculiarly related: scientists and philosophers find it difficult to believe that it is possible that accountants do what they in fact do and accountants find it difficult to believe that it is possible to do anything different.[2] Both are incredulous and the object of the incredulity of both is the subject matter of accounting. Thus, the heroic task of this chapter is to convince one sceptical audience that the subject matter *is* the way it is described and to convince another sceptical audience that the subject matter *could be different from* the way it is described.

THE SUBJECT MATTER OF ACCOUNTING PRACTICE

> If controversies were to arise, there would be no more need of disputation between two philosophers than between two accountants. For it would suffice to take their pencils in their hands, to sit down to their slates, and to say to each other (with a friend as witness, if they liked): let us calculate.
>
> (Gottfried Wilhelm von Leibniz)

Although differing in wording and in detail, statements of purpose or definitions of accounting practice invariably include something about the *recording* and *reporting* of economic resources (assets) and obligations (liabilities) and the changes in them. Briefly, it is the recording and reporting of *wealth* and wealth *changes*, including *profit*. A typical statement is provided by FASB:

> In accounting, the phenomena to be represented are economic resources and obligations and the transactions and events that change those resources and obligations.
>
> (FASB 1983: para. 63)

Although at the boundaries there are problems in deciding exactly which objects qualify as economic resources and obligations, it is quite clear that the subject matter of accounting practice includes such things as cash, claims to cash, stock-in-trade, machines, buildings, land, and the like. Unfortunately, that is the end of clarity: as soon as we move to a consideration of the *amount* of those things or events, we face a maze of murky ideas.

Reporting an amount paid

For reasons that are not pertinent here, accountants long ago decided to record and report the *historical costs* of assets (economic resources) and liabilities (obligations). Some academic accountants have proposed the recording and reporting of *current values* (current costs or exit values) instead of or in addition to historical costs. The discussion of the alternatives has been highly confused, in large part due to the multiple meanings of 'historical cost'.

In ordinary usage the 'historical cost of *x*' means the 'amount previously paid for *x*'. In accounting usage it sometimes means that, but it usually means 'a calculated amount based on the amount previously paid for *x*', and sometimes it just means 'a calculated amount assigned to *x*' without regard to what was paid for *x*. Thus, 'historical cost' is a term-of-art in accounting and non-accountants are often misled by interpreting it in its ordinary usage sense.

Surprisingly, accountants are also often misled by the term. They vacillate among the meanings which frequently results in the presentation of arguments that commit the informal fallacy of equivocation. For example:

> The criterion of, say, ease of determination should be used to decide what to report.
>
> Historical costs (amounts paid) are more easily determined than current values.
>
> Therefore, historical costs (calculated amounts) should be reported.

Lyas provides an illustration of both the multiple meanings of the term in accounting and how non-accountants usually interpret it. Since he is not an accountant, it is reasonable to assume that he relied on accountants' descriptions of alternative valuation proposals, and that such descriptions used the term-of-art 'historical costs' to describe current practice, when he wrote:

> Consider here, by way of elementary example, the problem of determining the present value for accounting purposes of a piece of machinery and the difference between making the value what was paid for it (in 'real' terms?) as opposed to (i) what one *might* get for it *if* one were to sell it and (ii) what it might cost to replace, *if* an exact replacement could be found.
>
> (Lyas 1984: 101)

Lyas' presentation of this typical accounting argument fails because he substituted 'what was paid' for 'historical cost' and thereby avoided the equivocation. Although there is no reason for a philosopher to know what accountants do, the fact is that accountants almost never report what was paid for anything. Thus, the implied conclusion that it is better to report 'what was paid' is irrelevant to those who are trying to assess the relative merits of 'historical costs' and 'current values'.

Philosophers' propensity to use clear, simple terms is a major reason that I welcome their examination of accounting. Lyas' statement of the argument is just one example of the benefit that would be derived from that propensity: using the clear 'what was paid' instead of the equivocal 'historical cost' is all that is needed to avoid a long-standing, pernicious error. More generally, philosophers' appreciation of the connection of clarity of language to clarity of thought (and communication) is the reason for welcoming them to accounting. Accountants seem to lack such appreciation and the result is the perpetuation of a number of errors and fallacies that can be traced directly to linguistic turbidity.

Reporting a calculated amount

Instead of reporting the amount paid, accountants usually report a calculated amount. One form of calculation, accurately described by Lyas (1984: 101) as 'ubiquitous in accounting', is the *allocation* (also called *apportionment*, *amortization*, and sometimes *accrual*) of the amount paid among various activities, products, time periods and the like. That is, the particular form of calculation called *averaging* or *dividing*[3] in ordinary language. Although subject to several unessential qualifications, the process is simply the calculation of an average unit cost (u) by dividing the amount paid for, or cost (C) of, an item by some observed, estimated or forecasted quantity (q) of that item.

$$u = C/q$$

Then the 'historical cost' is said to 'expire' as q declines (is used or sold or otherwise disappears) and the 'unexpired' amount of the 'historical cost' is the product of u and the amount of q remaining on hand. The 'expired' amount is an 'expense' to be deducted from revenues to get one's profit, and the 'unexpired' amount is an 'asset' to be added to other assets to get one's wealth.

A well-worn example in the economics literature is the apportionment of the amount paid for a steer between the carcass and the hide.

If the cost of the steer was £100, it weighed 500 pounds (and the accountant selected weight as the basis for apportionment), then the average unit cost per pound would be £0.20.

$$0.20 = \frac{100}{500}$$

Given that the carcass and hide weighed 450 and 50 pounds, respectively, the accountant would report the 'historical cost' of £90 and £10 for the carcass and hide, respectively.

A number of objections have been raised to this particular method of apportioning costs and a number of different methods have been proposed. A common objection is that the disparity of the 'value per pound' of the carcass and hide will result in reports that are 'unfair' or 'misleading' or some similar criticism. If, for example, the carcass were expected to sell for £135 and the hide for £5, then reporting the hide at £10 is thought to result in an 'overstatement' of the hide since its 'historical cost' is twice its expected selling price. Other objections are raised from considerations of reports of profits such as the following:

	Carcass	*Hide*	*Total*
Selling price	135	5	140
Cost (expired)	90	10	100
Profit	45	−5	40

One objection to such reports is that it is 'unfair' to report a loss for the hide department or activity since without the sale of the hide the total profit would be decreased by £5. Thus, the paradox of the elimination of an unprofitable activity causing profits to decrease. Another objection is that if the carcass were sold in different years, it would be 'misleading' to report a £45 profit in year 1 and £5 loss in year 2, or vice versa, when the profit over both years is expected to total £40.

The response to criticism of a given method of dividing costs has been to propose another method of division, for example, make it proportional to the forecasted total selling price rather than proportional to the weight. This selling price method has been subjected to similar criticism, which has resulted in proposals to employ other methods, which have been subjected to similar criticism, which. . . .

Perhaps as much as 90 per cent of the accounting literature in this century has, in one way or another, been concerned with discussing such cost allocations. Many accountants begin by explaining the reasons for allocating and almost all such explanations involve an argument to the effect that accountants *must* allocate because *the* alternative would result in reports that are, at best, indisputably inferior and, at worst, dangerously misleading. Thus, allocations are thought to be *unavoidable* or *indispensable*. Lyas (apparently echoing the accountants who have explained accounting to him) provides another example of this line of thinking when he writes (Lyas 1984: 101) 'The accountant sometimes has to allocate a value' which in the context seems to mean that he accepts the typical accountant's view that accountants *must* allocate, that allocations are unavoidable or indispensable.[4]

If the question were regarding the amount of the machinery to report in Lyas' comparison, for example, the argument would run to the effect that although the amount paid could be reported at the moment of purchase (when it is new), it would be 'unfair' or 'misleading' to report the amount paid at the end of years 1, 2, 3, and 4 (when it is used), and it would be 'unthinkable' to report the amount paid at the end of year 10 (when it is worn out or obsolete and ready to be discarded). Therefore, so the argument goes, we must use the familiar procedure of figuring an average (u) unit cost by dividing the amount paid for, or (C) cost of, an item by some observed, estimated or forecasted (q) quantity of that item ($u = C/q$). If the cost of the machinery was £100 and it was expected to provide 500 hours of operation (and the accountant selected machine-hours as the basis for division), then the average unit cost per machine-hour would be £0.20.

$$0.20 = \frac{100}{500}$$

At year end, when the machine has been used for, say, 50 hours the accountant will apportion £90 to unused machine hours, report it as the 'historical cost of the machine' and apportion £10 to the used machine-hours and, in the simplest case, report it as 'depreciation expense'. The interested reader will have noticed that this is exactly the same procedure as that used to apportion the cost of the steer to the carcass and the hide. It is also subject to the same sort of criticism and the same sort of proposals of different methods of dividing the costs.

The intriguing thing about such arguments is that they contrast the alternatives of reporting the amount paid to reporting a calculated amount. It should be apparent that this commits the fallacy of posing a false dilemma: the reporting alternatives under consideration have been restricted to the amount paid versus a calculated amount, overlooking all other alternatives including the proposal to report current values which was previously rejected in favour of reporting an amount paid.

An example of the combined arguments

The combination of the two arguments presented above is intended to replicate combinations found in the accounting literature. It is not the case that the two arguments are made by different authors or even by the same author in different works, but rather that both are usually found in the same work. The sequencing in the literature is also the same as above: (1) conclude (by equivocation) to report the amount paid and (2) conclude (by posing a false dilemma) to report a calculated amount.[5] Although I think these fallacies are sufficiently common to be easily found in the accounting literature after readers have had them brought to their attention, those who feel the need for a specific case to examine[6] could consult Butterworth *et al.* (1982).

The stated purpose of that work is to provide a theory of accounting choices, that is, a theory that explains why accountants elect to record and report one thing and not another. They are particularly concerned with *differences* between the choices of the *practitioner* and the *academic*, which they refer to as the 'paradox' of the 'extraordinary' 'consistency of practice' as contrasted to the 'disarray at the level of theory' (Butterworth *et al.* 1982: 3). It is the 'consistent application of specific reporting rules based almost exclusively on acquisition [historical] cost' that is of particular interest. Indeed, it seems that the major purpose of that work devolves to an explanation of why 'historical costs' have survived in the face of sustained attacks and suggested alternatives, as indicated by the 'major point' that 'all attempts to introduce changes in valuation methods that depart radically from historical costs have been resisted . . .' (Butterworth *et al.* 1982: 8) and eventually rejected. Thus, their purpose is not just to provide one more comparison of the merits of historical costs and current values but rather to provide a grand historical overview of those relative merits by explaining why accountants have continued to choose to report historical costs for 'six hundred years' (Butterworth *et al.* 1982: 3).

The cornerstone of their explanation is the *objectivity* of 'historical costs' which they equate to transactions or exchanges as, for example, when they explain that 'objectivity dictates the choice of transactions as the basis for accounting information' and that 'market exchanges that are not consummated cannot be verified, and therefore do not meet the objectivity criterion' (Butterworth *et al.* 1982: 25). In short, current values lack objectivity and verifiability because they are not based on transactions or consummated exchanges and therefore historical costs (amounts paid in consummated exchanges) have been and continue to be selected to be reported.

Later, however, they reject 'the exclusive use of cash exchanges [because it] does not satisfy the risk-constraint criterion' and they also reject 'the exchange value of all transactions of the period' because 'it is affected by the random (or deliberately chosen) occurrence of large transactions' (Butterworth *et al.* 1982: 27). Examples of 'large transactions' are the purchase of the steer and machine discussed above, and the problem with reporting those amounts is also the ancient one discussed above, although Butterworth *et al.* state it differently:

> So, faced with this dilemma, and insisting on reports that satisfy our six criteria, we are driven *inexorably* toward an aggregation method that eliminates the problem of moral hazard by *averaging* major expenditures over the periods that benefit from them.
>
> (Butterworth *et al.* 1982: 27–8, emphasis added)

The problem, of course, is that they posed the false dilemma of reporting the amount paid versus averaging or allocating, and they are driven inexorably toward averaging only because they overlooked other alternatives.

In summary, Butterworth *et al.* began by comparing amounts paid to current values and concluded that amounts paid are preferable because they are objective. Then they decided to report calculations because reporting the amounts paid did not yield satisfactory results. Thus, in essence, the argument is: one should report historical costs (amounts paid) because they are more objective than current values but reporting historical costs (amounts paid) yield unsatisfactory results so that one should report historical costs (calculated amounts).

The explanation for the survival of historical costs is similar: the primary reason that historical costs (calculated amounts) have been reported for six hundred years is that historical costs (amounts paid) are more objective than current values. In my view, a better explanation for the survival of historical costs is the survival of fallacious arguments that they are objective, not that they *are* objective.

Accounting numerology

Arguments similar in form and in conclusion to those discussed above have existed for many years. The outcome of the ancient arguments was that numerals became the subject matter of accounting practice. The outcome of the continuation of the arguments is the continuation of the subject matter of numerals.

The amounts reported by accountants, with few exceptions, are free-floating arithmetical constructs. Although characterized as 'objective' in the accounting literature, they are not objective in the sense of existing independently of a knowing subject; rather an accounting numeral is, within very broad bounds, nothing but an idiosyncratic product of a subject. They are not objective in the sense of conforming to fact without being influenced by personal feeling or prejudice; on the contrary, they are heavily influenced by personal feeling and there are no facts to which the reported amounts conform. They are not objective in the sense of depending on scientific test implications because there are no test implications that bear on them. In short, accounting numerals are not objective in any of the senses that are commonly found in the non-accounting literature.

None the less, accountants continue to characterize the numerals they report as 'objective' and they continue to reject suggested alternatives because they are 'subjective'. It seems that this characterization is due to a definition of 'objectivity' that is unique to accounting, a definition which has more to do with the certainty of the outcome of calculation than with referring to magnitudes of objects and events.[7]

In a few places accountants state quite clearly that their numerals do not and are not intended to refer to magnitudes of objects and events. The most lucid statement is the 'official' or 'authoritative' definition of 'depreciation' (the name for the particular allocation method applied to the machine discussed above) which is said to be a 'process of allocation' (calculation) in 'a rational and systematic manner' and 'is not intended to be a measurement' of the effect of such events as 'the physical deterioration . . . or of the decline in monetary value, or indeed, of anything that actual occurs during the year' (*Accounting Research and Terminology Bulletins* 1961: paras 56, 54).[8] Although there are many bits of evidence scattered throughout the accounting literature that would support the view that accountants embrace a radical rationalism, the above depreciation definition is one place where it is stated with such clarity that there can be no doubt of the position: depreciation is a rational and systematic calculation that is not intended to be a representation of any kind of phenomenon.[9]

In short, the subject matter of accounting practice is numerals, not magnitudes of wealth and profit. Although almost all accountants deny that, claiming that the numerals represent historical costs, the fact that historical costs are not in any sense observable or measurable[10] negates their argument. Indeed, accounting numerals do not yield any test implications whatsoever.[11] The questions that accountants ask are how to calculate, not how to represent or to test representations. Thus, Leibniz once again showed his perspicacity by selecting accountants to exemplify calculators.[12] Being one of the architects of rationalism, no one comes to mind who would be more appropriate as the intellectual patron of accounting and his 'let us calculate' would be an apposite motto.

THE SUBJECT MATTER OF ACCOUNTING RESEARCH

> Anthropology, the study of the origin of myth, legend and cult . . ., tells us how men have thought and what have been the purposes and consequences of different kinds of thinking. . . . Especially does the record of the growth of the various sciences afford instruction in those concrete ways of inquiry and testing which have led men astray and which have proved efficacious.
>
> (Dewey 1963)

That accounting is a social science is unquestioned by almost all accounting academics. For some time I was perplexed by accounting academics claiming that accounting *is not*[13] a science *and* that accounting *is* a social science. Originally I thought this was an ordinary, if obvious, howler but the persistent, earnest urging of the position caused me to begin to think that perhaps I was meant to conclude that a social science is not a science. The root of the problem is, once again, equivocation: the meaning of 'accounting' when it refers to accounting practice is quite different from when it refers to accounting research. Distinguishing the two allows the position to be stated without inconsistency: accounting research is (and ought to be) a science (social) whereas accounting practice is not (and cannot be) a science.[14]

The emphasis on *social* science provides the first clue as to the subject matter of accounting theory: it is the study of the behaviour of people, often people who are accountants or managers making accounting decisions.

Recording practitioner behaviour

The recommendation that we observe and codify practitioner behaviour is not new. Over twenty years ago I ventured (Sterling 1970: 449) that 'the most ancient and pervasive method of accounting theory construction is to observe accountants' actions and then rationalize those actions by subsuming them under generalized principles'. This method was so popular that the meaning of 'inductive' in accounting was narrowed to 'derived from observations of accountants' behavior'. The view seemed to be that there was no reason to retain the usual, broader meaning of 'derived from observations' because there was nothing to observe other than practitioner behaviour.[15]

At one time my claim that the dominant subject matter of accounting research is observations of practitioner behaviour was met with strong, concerted resistance. Non-inductivists did not believe that inductivists derived accounting theory from observing accountants and inductivists did not believe they could do anything else.[16] In more recent years the words have come closer to matching actions as neo-inductivists have become increasingly clear about what they are doing. Demski's description was selected to exemplify the neo-inductivists position because it is stated with admirable clarity.

According to Demski (1987: 89–90) 'an injection of the social science perspective' has resulted in a realization that the old questions about wealth and profit would not yield to attempts to 'sharpen our measurement instruments' so, except for vestiges in textbooks, we abandoned our search for how 'accounting ought to be done' and began to seek knowledge about the 'end user' but this 'remained an illusive goal' so we abandoned that search also. We have now entered the 'age of agnosticism wherein we [researchers] claim no ability to identify the best accounting system'. I wonder why he didn't call it the *golden* age of agnosticism because he concludes that 'this change is welcome, healthy and productive'.

I also wonder why he didn't call it the age of ignorance (absence of knowledge) rather than agnosticism (doubting the existence of knowledge) because he expresses the belief that the practitioner has knowledge. The agnosticism title comes from researchers' doubts about *their* ability to judge accounting or accounting systems.

> Note well that the agnostic's position is that the practitioner can, with error, identify the best accounting system but the researcher has no comparative advantage in this regard. Rather, the researcher assumes the role of *social recorder* of behavior. Here, with error, we observe, we document, we codify behavior. (Demski 1987: 90)

In this and other places Demski's argument appears to run along the lines that researcher ignorance and practitioner knowledge allows one to conclude that researchers should record the behaviour of practitioners in order to obtain knowledge.

Practitioners know best

It is admirably honest and becomingly modest for researchers to admit ignorance of what is best when they are in fact ignorant of what is best, but a moment's reflection reveals that such ignorance also prevents them from asserting that practitioners know what is best. It seems clear that if A identifies X as best and B identifies Y as best, then for C to claim that A knows best (or knows better than B), then C must know that X is best (or better than Y). It seems that Demski and other social-recorders[17] fall into that trap: when faced with practitioners who think that X is best and, say, non-social-recorders who think that Y is best, social-recorders apparently conclude that practitioners know best on the basis of the fact that social-recorders' are ignorant of which is best.[18]

It is difficult to know why Demski believes that practitioners know what is best because he presents neither argument nor evidence to that effect. One might think he is appealing to authority (*argumentum ad verecundiam*) were it not for the fact that he makes no attempt to qualify practitioners as authorities or experts. (Perhaps we need to invent a cynic's maxim to counter anticipated naive attempts at such qualification: experts are people who continue to repeat the same errors.) After looking carefully for argument or evidence and failing to find it, I am forced to conclude that 'practitioners know best' is an unsupported, tacit assumption. After coupling that to researchers' ignorance and supplying it as a premise, it appears that the argument is:

> Practitioners know what is best and researchers are ignorant of what is best.

Therefore, researchers should record the behaviour of practitioners in order to discover what is best.

The argument is still enthymematic: we need to supply another premise to the effect that the best way to obtain knowledge is to record the actions of those who have knowledge. But that premise is also suspect: it is likely to be better (more efficient, more productive of knowledge, less productive of error, or some similar sense of better) to record the behaviour of the material rather than to record the behaviour of the people who record the behaviour of the material. Ornithologists, for example, who want to learn about the behaviour of birds find it better to record the behaviour of birds than to record the behaviour of ornithologists who are recording the behaviour of birds.[19]

In short, 'practitioners know best' is unsupported, indeed essentially unexamined, by those who apparently rely on it and there are several lines of criticism that render it lame if not dead. If 'practitioners know best' cannot be supported, there is no conspicuous reason to record practitioner behaviour save unadorned curiosity. Since the scientific community invariably requires a research programme to be supported by reasons beyond curiosity, the social-recorder-of-practitioner-behaviour programme would be rejected although, of course, such rejection would not prohibit individuals from researching whatever they want.

I suspect that the reason that 'practitioners know best' is unexamined is that it is not a fundamental tenet of those who are or want to be social-recorders. If one pays careful attention to what the social-recorders say, especially what they say about social science, and what they don't say, especially what they don't say about accounting, one is likely to come away with the view that the underlying reason is nothing more than a desire to be social scientists. My conjecture is that the desire is based on the feeling that being a social scientist is honorific and being an accountant-researcher is ignominious. To the Hatfield hounds!

Accounting anthropology

Arguments similar in form and in conclusion to those discussed above have existed for many years. The outcome of the ancient arguments was that the behaviour of accountants became the subject matter of accounting research. The outcome of the continuation of the arguments is the continuation of the subject matter of the behaviour of accountants.

The predominant subject matter currently being studied by accountant-researchers is the behaviour of accountant-practitioners, broadly conceived to include auditors and managers when they are making accounting decisions, and often called 'positive accounting theory' as well as 'social-recorder', both of which are offsprings of the old 'inductivist' theories. Although such studies and the associated theories are characterized as 'scientific' or 'social scientific' in the accounting literature, the study of the practitioners of one's own discipline is, to my knowledge, unique in the history of science. There are instances in the history of science where researchers *began* by observing skilled craftsmen but there are no instances to my knowledge where they *ended* with such observations.[20] The distinction is crucial: scientists take knowledge from wherever they can obtain it, including from skilled craftsmen, but then they try to extend, correct, and refine that knowledge by the research process, which improved knowledge they then pass back to the craftsmen for the purpose of improving the craft. They do not make the study of skilled craftsmen an end but rather a means to knowledge about what the craftsmen deal with. Nor do they prohibit trying to extend, correct and refine the knowledge of the craftsmen on some mistaken belief that accumulation of such knowledge is normative while accumulation of knowledge of the behaviour of the craftsmen is positive.

Of course, there are some scientists, notably anthropologists and sociologists, who make the study of people an end rather than a means. It was the striking similarity of 'inductivists' to anthropologists that caused me to describe their activities as the 'anthropological approach' to accounting theory construction. Assignment of that name was not for the purpose of prohibiting or discouraging such studies but rather an attempt to clearly distinguish the study of accountants from the study of wealth and profit. It was over twenty years ago (in 1970) when I naively thought that introducing the term 'anthropology' and drawing analogies to other disciplines would make the distinction abundantly clear:

> The theory of accounting ought to be concerned with accounting phenomena, not practicing accountants, in the same way that theories of physics are concerned with physical phenomena, not practicing physicists.
>
> (Sterling 1970: 450)

The distinction was repeated (in 1979) in response to efficient market researchers' belief that their subject matter (behaviour of capital market agents as exhibited by stock market responses) was the only appropriate subject to be studied, which belief they used as the basis for strong criticism of all other research that studied different subject matters:

> If a chemist rejected the research of a psychologist because the psychologist did not examine the atomic composition of chemical elements, we would easily recognize it to be inappropriate.
>
> (Sterling 1979: 53)

And made again in regard to 'positive theorists' by Christenson in 1983:

> Chemical theory consists of propositions about the behavior of chemical entities (molecules and atoms), not about the behavior of chemists.
>
> (Christenson 1983: 6)

And reinforced by Whittington (1987: 334) when he refers to it as 'the fundamental criticism' of Watts and Zimmerman (1986). Despite these repeated attempts to make this elementary distinction clear, most accountant-researchers continue to fail to make it, some from ignorance of the distinction and others from ignorance of the benefits of being clear about what one is talking about.

Failing to make the distinction between wealth and the behaviour of accountants is harmful because it perpetuates needless confusion and pointless strife. Prohibiting assessment of accountants' practices is fatal because it perpetuates ignorance. Had we prohibited scientific assessment of Greek medical practices, we would be ignorant of Galenian medicine as well as all subsequent work that built on it. Had we prohibited scientific assessment of Babylonian and Egyptian earth measurements, we would be ignorant of Euclidian geometry as well as all subsequent work that built on it. The perpetuation of such ignorance in accounting, paradoxically, is done in the name of science.

All of this was anticipated by John Dewey (1963) who characterized anthropology as telling us 'how men have thought' but goes on without pause to a consideration of 'the consequences of different kinds of thinking', noting that some kinds 'have led men astray' and other kinds 'have proved efficacious'. The possibility of being led astray was emphasized by mentioning that anthropology is the study of myth, legend and cult. The possibility of finding something efficacious was illustrated with a discussion of the development of empirical sciences and of mathematics and logic. Discovering what men think is relatively easy. Deciding whether what they think is myth or science is much more difficult but also infinitely more productive.[21]

SUMMARY AND CONCLUSION

> Eighteenth century [science] was a triumph of organized common sense. It had got rid of medieval phantasies. . . . It grounded itself upon what every plain man could see with his own eyes, or with a microscope of moderate power. It measured the obvious things to be measured, and it generalized the obvious things to be generalized. For example, it generalized the ordinary notions of weight and massiveness.
>
> (Whitehead 1967)

My summary in regard to accounting practice is that it is numerology. Although putatively a measurement of wealth and profit, accounting practice is in fact a calculational activity and the results of those calculations have no empirical referents. My conclusion is that such a state is a problem in need of correction. The most serious problem is that accounting practice numerals are *meaningless* in the logical positivist[22] sense of not being either analytic or verifiable, in the pragmatist sense of not being decision-useful, and in the operationist sense of not being operationally defined. Accounting practice numerals need to be made meaningful by making them empirically verifiable, demonstrating that they are decision-useful (not merely used), and defining them operationally.

My summary in regard to accounting research is that it is anthropology. Although ostensibly about accounting – that is, having something to do with the measurement and communication of wealth and profit – accounting research is in fact about accountants, broadly defined. My conclusion is that this state is also a problem that needs correction. The first problem is the confusion that has resulted. Just as referring to the study of biologists as 'biological research' would result in vast confusion, referring to the study of accountants as 'accounting research' has in fact resulted in vast confusion, even among accounting researchers. This problem is easily rectified by providing a descriptive title (such as 'accounting anthropology' or 'sociology of accountants') for such work. A second problem is that I don't see how studies of accountants can ever bear fruit, especially in view of the fact that proscribing the assessment of practitioner behaviour makes such study an end rather than a means. I think that courtship rituals of aborigines is a more interesting and potentially more fruitful topic than calculation rituals of accountants. Although I wouldn't want to deny anyone the right to study anything they want, including the rituals of accountants, I do want to title such studies descriptively, primarily to avoid confusion and secondarily in the hope that eventually they could be placed in anthropology or sociology journals where those with similar interests could more easily find them.

My summary in regard to the combination of accounting research and accounting practice is that they are divorced. My conclusion is that this state is also a problem that needs correction. I (and several others) have worried for some years about the growing estrangement of accounting practice and accounting research and have proposed various means of reconciliation. I failed. The divorce is now complete, as is evident when one compares the accepted purposes and consequent subject matters:[23] the customary, mutually beneficial ties between research and practice have been severed. In other professions or applied sciences, such as medicine or engineering, there is a fairly clear division of duties but also a fairly clear confluence of purposes. The purpose of medical practitioners is to provide good health and the purpose of medical researchers is to provide knowledge about health, including how to attain good or better health. In civil engineering the purpose of engineering practitioners is to provide good bridges and the purpose of physics and engineering researchers is to provide knowledge about bridges, including how to attain good or better bridges. In accounting the purposes do not join, which permits the subject matters to remain divergent. At the present time the stated purpose of accounting practice is to record and report wealth and profit whereas the stated purpose of accounting theory is to record and report the behaviour of accountants.

These summaries and conclusions can be restated as objectives. The first objective is to move accounting practice up to the eighteenth century state of science as described by Whitehead. This would require two steps: (1) getting rid of accounting fantasies, that is, those things that are said to be 'measured' but are in fact calculated because they cannot be observed or otherwise detected; and (2) measuring the obvious things to be measured[24] and (eventually) generalizing the obvious things to be generalized. In this way accounting practice would move toward a science.[25]

The second objective is to reconnect accounting practice and accounting research, to redirect accounting research to the study of the same subjects as that which is dealt with in practice. Then the purpose of accounting practice would be to provide good information and the purpose of accounting research would be to provide knowledge about information, including how to attain good or better information. When so redirected accounting research would soon discover that the prime characteristic of good information is that it should refer to something in the real world, that informative numerals have empirical referents.

ACKNOWLEDGEMENTS

David Bennett (Philosophy, University of Utah) provided many instructive and enjoyable general discussions and detailed discussions of commonly overlooked points regarding the analytic—synthetic and a priori—a posteriori distinctions, Carl G. Hempel (Philosophy, Princeton) provided discussion of logical positivism in general and the error of studying practitioner behaviour in particular, Clifton D. McIntosh (Philosophy, University of Utah) read and commented on arguments that had been challenged by others, K.V. Peasnell (Accounting, University of Lancaster) provided valuable editorial comment as well as thought-provoking argument, Michael Power (Accounting, London School of Economics) presented a general critique as well as specific criticism of an earlier title, C. Wade Savage (Philosophy, University of Minnesota) helped me to clarify several philosophical arguments especially some subtleties in the argument from design, and Ralph Walters (California Society of CPAs) was wickedly witty in response to several points. Kevin McBeth provided general research assistance as well as calling my attention to the Leibniz quotation. To all the above my warm thanks and the usual absolution.

NOTES

1 One tailoring device is to put much more material in 'Notes' than usual so that it can be easily ignored while still being available for those who desire it. Some of this material will be in the nature of background, sometimes background for scientists and philosophers about accounting, and sometimes vice versa.

2 It is my contention that accountants have been brainwashed in the sense used by Ziman (1978: 8) when he writes of the 'brainwashing implicit in the long process of becoming technically expert'. In psychology this brainwashing, called *einstellung* or habituation, has been experimentally demonstrated by Luchins (1942: 1) and described as follows: 'The successive, repetitious use of the same method mechanized many of the

subjects – blinded them to the possibility of a more direct and simpler procedure'.

I have experimentally demonstrated such habituation among accountants in the sense that they attempted to calculate where observation was obviously possible, and obviously appropriate. Specifically, they attempted to calculate the volume of liquids, which were expanding under conditions of increasing temperature, by the application LIFO–FIFO rather than by measuring (observing) the volume. The control group were scientists who insisted on measuring and rejected LIFO–FIFO calculations out-of-hand. The results of that experiment are reported in Sterling (1988).

It is this habituation that accounts for the difficulty in explaining the subject matter to both groups. Those who have been calculating all of their lives find it almost impossible to think about measuring – and vice versa.

3 It is the absence of an empirical referent for the result of the calculation, not the particular type of calculation, that leads to the problem. Many discussions of allocations of cost leave the impression that it is the division that causes problems, overlooking the fact that addition, multiplication, and subtraction cause problems of exactly the same kind. For example, 'the additivity problem' is that the sum does not have an empirical referent whereas 'the allocation problem' is that the quotient does not have an empirical referent.

4 In 1848 John Stuart Mill (1909: book 3, chapter 16) announced that a 'principle is wanting to apportion' joint costs. He did *not* announce that such apportionments are unavoidable or indispensable. On the contrary, his purpose was to advise others not to apportion because a principle was wanting. None the less, accountants continued to make such apportionments, continued to allege that they are indispensable, and continued to seek an acceptable or defensible method of making them. More than 150 years later, Arthur L. Thomas (1969) announced that 'all allocations are arbitrary'. He did *not* announce that such allocations are unavoidable or indispensable. On the contrary, he concluded that allocations produce nonsense and suggested that the least dangerous way to stop reporting nonsense is just to stop reporting nonsense (Thomas 1974: 114–15). None the less, to this day accountants continue to make such allocations, continue to allege that they are indispensable, and some continue to seek an acceptable or defensible method of making them.

Why have accountants continued to allocate in the face of the ancient, undisputed findings by Mill and the more recent, unrefuted findings of Thomas? Why do accountants say that they accept those findings, adopting 'all allocations are arbitrary' as a slogan, and then continue to argue that one allocation is 'better' than another? I agree with Butterworth *et al.* (1982) that such questions are interesting and important, but my answer is the exact opposite of theirs. Rather than accepting their explanation that it is the 'objectivity' of 'historical costs' that causes accountants to continue to report and defend them, my view is that it is the failure to recognize the reason for the arbitrariness of the allocations.

Compare the allocation of the weight of the steer to the allocation of its cost. If I were to suggest that the weight of the steer could be divided

80 per cent carcass and 20 per cent hide, my suggestion would be interpreted as a crude prediction. In the event where after slaughter the actual weights were discovered to be 450 and 50 pounds, I would be said to have been *wrong*. On the other hand, if I made the same suggestion about the cost, there is no way to discover whether I am *either* right or wrong, and it is the inability to discover rightness *or* wrongness that makes the allocation *arbitrary*. There is a world of difference between being wrong (or right) and being arbitrary. The major difference is that the weight of the carcass and hide can be measured but the cost can only be calculated. That is, the prediction of the relative weights refers to reality (can be empirically tested) whereas the calculation of the cost does not refer to anything.

Accountants have a tendency to reply to this by pointing out that weight and cost are different. I agree. It is the conclusion drawn from that difference where we disagree. My conclusion is that we abandon 'historical costs' because they don't refer to reality and find some other attribute that can be empirically tested. Their conclusion is that we continue to account for 'historical costs' and continue to lament the fact that they are arbitrary.

Compare the contrast of meaningless to true *or* false in Note 22 to the contrast of arbitrary to right *or* wrong in this Note.

5 One of the interesting characteristics of this line of reasoning is that the sequencing influences the ultimate conclusion. If the first argument were to chose to report a calculated amount and reject the amount paid, then the second argument would be forced into a comparison of a calculated amount and a current value, and current values usually satisfy the proposed criteria better than the calculated amount. Thus, the sequencing presented in the text is essential to the conclusion to report a calculated amount.

Lyas (1984: 101) is the only exception that I know of to this sequencing. He discusses the need for allocations prior to comparing the ease of determination of amounts paid to current values. The problem is that he seems to be unaware that allocations are calculations, usually divisions of amounts paid, as opposed to amounts paid. Again, there is no reason for a philosopher to know what accountants do but the fact is that an allocation is a calculation.

6 One of Stamp's major criticisms (Stamp 1981: 15) of my work was that 'when Sterling criticizes the work of others he frequently fails to give references to their writing. . . . Omissions of this kind make it very difficult (and in many cases impossible) for serious readers to refer back to the material that Sterling is criticizing or attempting to refute'. I thought I had provided sufficient justification for that omission by explaining that 'my purpose is to expose an error, not to expose those who have committed an error' and that I had avoided the problem of the serious reader by offering to 'supply the citations upon request' (Sterling 1979: 48, note). I still believe that my offer avoids the immediate problem but Stamp's criticism caused me to think that there might be a long-run problem – the slim chance that a future historian or student would want to examine a typical source – and therefore I decided to supply a citation in this paper. I selected Butterworth *et al.* for consideration and citation

because they make an argument, rather than an allegation, as well as because I was the assigned discussant (Sterling 1982) when it was first presented and therefore my more lengthy assessment of both its strengths and weaknesses is already on record.

7 Some years ago I became so puzzled by accountants' reversal of the meanings of 'objective' and 'subjective' that I began to entertain far-fetched speculations, such as a connection between Scotland being the birthplace of modern accounting and also of Duns Scotus. Perhaps ancient Scottish accountants had been influenced by Duns Scotus' usage of 'objective' as an idea in the mind without independent existence. (It was that Scotistic usage that previously caused me to suggest that accountants abandon the term because I thought it would be easier to replace the term than to change inherited, ingrained usage.)

Less far-fetched is that accountants have confused objectivity with certainty. Their abhorrence of uncertainty is long-standing and apparently universal, evidently because it makes them vulnerable to criticism and, more recently, to lawsuits. In the accounting literature certainty is thought to be achieved by consensus and, thus, consensus is equated with objectivity. For example, obtaining consensus that a particular cost allocation (calculation) is acceptable results in the numeral from that calculation being characterized as 'objective' without regard to questions about representation.

Eventually it occurred to me that accountants had substituted the certainty of calculation for the uncertainty of objectively representing reality. I don't recall whether that occurred to me before or after reading Einstein's remark that 'as far as the propositions of mathematics refer to reality, they are not certain; and as far as they are certain, they do not refer to reality' (Einstein 1954: 233), but his clear, succinct distinction cemented the thought if it didn't originate it.

The thought was reinforced by my experience at FASB where Board members seemed to be of the view that *the* solution to accounting problems is to achieve consensus among Board members about what accountants are required to calculate. It didn't seem to be of concern whether the numeral from the calculation 'faithfully represented' the 'phenomena it purports to represent' (as required by FASB Concepts Statement 2 (1983, para 63)) but it did seem to be of overwhelming concern that the Board reach agreement about the method of calculation. The Staff's adopted objective was to 'get some paper on the street' which expressed the Board's consensus, not to get the numeral to represent some phenomena.

I am indebted to Professor Tom Lee for discussions regarding the apparent universal interpretation of auditing as providing assurance that a numeral is calculated in conformance with the appropriate regulations (GAAP), without regard to whether the numeral corresponds to anything. I am indebted to Professor Bart Ward for a spirited defence of that (to me, indefensible) interpretation, and for pointing out its extension to the auditor's concept of 'materiality' so that an 'immaterial amount' (that is, a negligible amount or an amount within acceptable tolerance limits) is judged by how far the accountant has deviated from a strict application of the regulations rather than how far the numeral deviates from a faithful representation.

8 Staubus (1987: 11–12), in reviewing the harmful miscues in accounting history, says of the depreciation definition: 'No one seems to be able to say anything good about it, but no authoritative body has been willing to change it'. Staubus rhetorically asks why '*numbers representing no economic phenomena* should be of interest to users' which raises the question why accountants continue to report numerals that are of no interest to users and why authoritative bodies refuse to change the definition despite sustained attack. That is, it rephrases the question posed by Butterworth *et al.* in such a way that it demands an answer different from the objectivity of the numerals.

9 Perhaps this definition and my opposition to it will allow me to make my position clear enough for it to be understood by non-accountants. Lyas (1984: 103) interprets my position as 'the flight from judgement to calculation' whereas the fact is that my position is the flight from calculation to measurement. I am not trying to *eliminate* judgements and decisions made by people but rather trying to *redirect* them toward measurements and away from calculations. I have no disagreement with those who seek 'standards which, while not circumscribing judgement by some inflexible book of rules, none the less allow the quality of accounting judgements to be assessed' but I do disagree with those who want to make judgements about the way to calculate and then assess those types of judgements. I want to assess the judgements made about observations, including measurements, not about calculations. The distinction is between 'the kind of judgement that does not lend itself to verification by measurement' (Lyas 1984; 104) and the kind that does, not between judgement and no judgement.

Thus, Lyas (1984: 105) is correct when he says that 'Sterling's hypothesis . . . does not do away with the need for judgement' but is incorrect when he adds 'in the way that Sterling hopes'. In the discussion (Sterling 1979: 77) I made it explicit that such a hypothesis would 'increase the use of his professional judgment . . . not reduce it' and contrasted it to the current state where judgement is not required because it is a calculation and there is nothing 'to do but check the accuracy of the arithmetic'. I regret that my views were not sufficiently clear to permit Lyas to focus on where we disagree rather than using his valuable time and effort criticizing me for taking positions which I explicitly denied.

10 Previous experience convinces me that this sentence will be misunderstood by accountant readers because they have been taught to use 'measure' as a synonym for 'calculate', as is evidenced by the following 'official' or 'authoritative' pronouncement by FASB (1984, No. 5, para. 67, emphasis added):

> Items currently reported in financial statements are *measured* by different attributes. . . . Property, plant, and equipment and most inventories are reported at their historical cost, which is the amount of cash, or its equivalent, paid to acquire an asset, commonly adjusted after acquisition for amortization or other allocations.

That is, one 'measures' by making a calculation (allocation) based on the amount paid. Then this calculation is called 'historical cost'.

Textbooks imitate the 'authoritative' literature. Even the best texts are not immune to substituting logic for empirics – the logical operation of calculating for the empirical operation of measuring:

> Ending inventory is *measured* by first determining the quantity on hand, then *multiplying* this quantity times the unit acquisition cost [which was obtained by *dividing*]. A choice must be arbitrarily made on the assumed unit cost, and this depends on the flow assumptions made. The attribute being *measured* is historical cost in all methods.
> Wolk *et al.* 1984: 268, emphasis added)

Students learn two lessons from such texts: (1) how to obtain amounts by calculation, and (2) to think that they have 'measured' something by those calculations. From this comes the inability to distinguish and the misunderstanding of the sentence in the text.

11 For some years I have been trying to convince colleagues that the fact that calculations start with empirical inputs does not have any bearing on whether the output has an empirical referent. Borrowing from Kline's description (1972: 19) of an ancient error in geometry, I posed the case of area, A, being calculated as:

$$A = \frac{(a + b)}{2} \times \frac{(c + d)}{2}$$

where a, b, c, d are the length of the adjacent sides of a rectangle. Since the right formula for area is the product of length and width (i.e. a×b or c×d) this formula yields a false area (except for squares and accidents) despite the accuracy of the length of the sides. None the less, accountants have continued to insist that if they checked the accuracy of the inputs of the various cost allocations (such as for the steer and machine discussed previously), and they ensured that the calculation was arithmetically correct, then they would be faithfully representing historical cost. The fact that another method of allocation was equally as acceptable, and indeed used by other firms with identical assets, did not alter their belief that both represented the historical cost. In accounting, it is not considered a contradiction or an inconsistency to say that the 'historical cost of x is £y and it is £z' where y is significantly different from z.

To illustrate the point I have tried to find cases so extreme as to be manifestly absurd. For example, I have asked if 'hage' (the product of a person's height and age as described by Hempel (1967: 46) does represent some kind of reality. This absurdity hasn't worked. Instead of 'hage' and other such calculations causing accountants to rethink the numerals they calculate, they have embraced hage and defended it. The argument seems to be as follows:

> Numerals derived from accounting calculations represent the phenomena that they purport to represent.
>
> The numerals derived from calculating 'hage' are identical in relevant respects to the numerals derived from accounting calculations.
>
> Therefore, 'hage' represents the phenomena that it purports to represent.

Of course this begs the question but more importantly it illustrates accountants' confidence in accounting and their self-imposed isolation. If one listens carefully, one can almost hear: if science differs from accounting, then so much the worse for science, or as Boulding (1958: 95) put it: 'Accounting for the most part, remains a legalistic and traditional practice, almost immune to self-criticism by scientific methods'.

I am indebted to Professor James Loebbecke for reaffirmation of the (to me, wrong) view that both 'historical cost' and 'hage' represent some kind of phenomena.

12 When Japan imported western accounting they translated 'accounting' as *kaikei* which means 'calculate' and thus indicates that they fully understood what they were importing. I am indebted to Professor Gisuke Murase for informing me of this interesting titbit.

13 And, in rebuttal to my arguments, that it is impossible to convert it to a science, that it is inherently unscientific. Most of these rebuttals misunderstand my proposal, taking it to be that accounting should become a kind of physics. By contrast, Lyas (1984: 106) understood what I had tried to say:

> When Sterling argued that accounting could be a science, he did not wish to suggest that it should become a kind of physics but that scientific methodology has as much a place in the study by accountants of their material as it has in the study by physicists of their material.

It is the adoption of scientific methodology in accounting and the application of that methodology in the study by accountants of their *materials* that I have proposed, not the adoption of the materials of physics. I am grateful to Lyas for understanding that much misunderstood point and for stating it so clearly. I hasten to add, however, that the adoption of scientific methodology limits the kinds of materials to those that can in fact be studied as opposed to those that can only be calculated.

14 Perhaps this could be called the 'informal *non*-fallacy of equivocation' since it is the opposite of the informal fallacy of equivocation. That is, the compound sentence 'X is Y and X is not-Y' is true if the atomic sentences are both true and in this instance both are true because the meaning of X is different in each. When restated as 'X_1 is Y and X_2 is not-Y' it is obvious that it can be true.

15 The comments I made about accounting anthropology (Sterling 1970: 449) are reproduced beginning in the next paragraph in their entirety with only slight modifications and the elimination of footnotes. I think they are still appropriate. Indeed, the serious consideration of these remarks is probably more appropriate today since the current fad is 'positive accounting theory' whereas at the time I wrote the fad was 'efficient markets'. That is, the previous fad was the study of that collection of people known as capital market agents whereas it has now changed back to the 'inductivists' tradition of studying people who are accountants.

Probably the most ancient and pervasive method of accounting theory construction is to observe accountants' actions and then rationalize those actions by subsuming them under generalized principles. The result is not a theory about accounting or a theory about the things to be accounted for: instead it is a theory about accountants. The 'principles of accounting' then is a theory that says that under such and such conditions the accountant will act in such and such a way. The input is the condition and the output is the accountants' action.

This is quite similar to various anthropological theories which allow to predict that under certain conditions, primitive man will act in a certain way. The test of the theory is the observations of the actions of primitive man. In the same fashion, the test of an anthropological theory of accounting is the observations of the actions of accounting man. For example, if the accounting anthropologist has observed that accounting man normally records a 'conservative' figure and generalizes this as the 'principle of conservatism', then we can test this principle by observing whether or not accounting man does in fact record a conservative figure. If the accounting anthropologist sets forth the 'principle of diversity', then we can test this principle by observing whether or not accounting man does in fact record similar occurrences in different ways – and so forth.

There are several difficulties with this kind of theorizing. First, it is not necessarily true that accounting man acts in the manner in which he ought to act. It is an error to conclude that because *x is* the case, then *x ought* to be the case. There is no way to arrive at the way accounting man ought to act from observing and generalizing how he in fact does act. Thus, this kind of theorizing may provide us with an explanation of why accountants act in a certain way and it may provide us with the ability to predict their actions, but it does not yield a judgement about the goodness of their actions. To judge the goodness of their actions requires other criteria. Second, the process does not permit change. By requiring the present generation of accountants to act in accordance with generally accepted principles of accounting – which principles were derived by observing the actions of the previous generation of accountants – change has been prohibited. If the requirement were strictly enforced, each generation would act just like the previous generation and this could be traced back to the first generation. Of course, changes have been made in accounting theory, but these changes are not explained or provided for by the anthropological interpretation. Third, subsequent to the first generation, the process is circular. We observe accountants' actions to discover what to teach, then we teach them how to act, then we observe accountants actions to discover what to teach, etc. Fourth, and most importantly, is my judgement that the theory of accounting ought to be concerned with accounting phenomena, not practising accountants, in the same way that theories of physics are concerned with physical phenomena, not practising physicists. The anthropological investigations may provide useful information. It may turn out to be important for us to know how practising accountants act and why they act that way. Comprehension of those actions is aided if they can be generalized under a few 'principles' but to avoid confusion they should be called 'principles of the behaviour of accountants' rather than 'principles of accounting'. However, such knowledge of principles does not provide a basis for a theory of accounting, as opposed to a theory of accountants' actions, and it would be wholly beneficial to call them by descriptive names.

16 To illustrate the controversy consider the *brouhaha* that resulted from the issuance of Accounting Research Studies No. 1 and No. 3 and the

pacification from the issuance of Accounting Research Study No. 7. I commented at the time that the chief error of No. 1 (Moonitz 1961) and No. 3 (Sprouse and Moonitz 1962) was that they had strayed from anthropology and that the primary appeal of No. 7 (Grady 1965) was that it returned to anthropology. I was surprised that there was disagreement about that comment because the title of No. 7 – *Inventory of Generally Accepted Principles* – clearly revealed that its purpose was to record practitioner behaviour by recording an inventory of their practices in the same way one would record an inventory of stock-in-trade. None the less, a large number (perhaps a majority) of accountant practitioners denied that Grady was being an accounting anthropologist and defended him on the basis of the 'sound accounting' he espoused, not recognizing that the reason they thought his accounting was sound was that it reflected what they were doing.

The controversy, as I saw it, was whether Grady did a good job because his *product* was 'sound accounting' or because his *process* was anthropology. I opted for the process. If one included human flesh on the inventory of victuals for cannibals, it is likely that cannibals would think that one had proposed a 'sound diet' because it reflected what they were doing. If one recommended that they become vegetarians for health reasons, they would probably reject it as being too 'radically different' from current generally accepted dietetic practices.

Such disagreement continues to the present time albeit in a slightly different form. The 'positive accounting theorists' *define* accounting theory as that which explains and predicts accounting practices. They deny that it is possible to judge 'sound accounting' because such judgements are normative and therefore the *only* question is what accountants do, not whether what they do is sound.

Everyone would also agree that, by including human flesh on the inventory of victuals for cannibals, one had compiled an accurate inventory because it reflected what cannibals do. After that agreement, however, there is a chasm. Positive cannibal theorists would prohibit one from recommending the addition or substitution of vegetables in the diet because such recommendations are normative and therefore unscientific, regardless of the amount of scientific evidence regarding the nutritional qualities of vegetables. This 'normative theorist' would say that the positive theorists are studying what cannibals eat as contrasted to nutritionists who are studying nutritional effects of what one eats. Thus, the distinction is the subject matter one has selected for study, not scientific positivism versus non-scientific normativism.

If we make that distinction, it would alleviate, perhaps eliminate, the continuing conflict of normative versus positive, a priori versus empirical, social recorder versus asset recorder, and so forth.

17 It seems that 'social-recorder' differs from 'inductivist' in several ways, including Demski being critical of textbooks that have a 'tendency to tell the student how the accounting ought to be done' whereas Littleton, an early inductivist and leading proponent of the method, supplemented observations of practice with justifications for the purpose of teaching students how accounting ought to be done:

> [Accounting] methods devised by many different people were used [and became] generally accepted accounting principles. Teachers of bookkeeping and later accounting and auditing found it necessary to supplement the accumulated rules and descriptions of procedure by explanations and justifications. This was done in order that study should be something more than the memorizing of rules. Hence it is appropriate to say that both the methods of practice and the explanations of theory were inductively derived out of experience.
>
> (Littleton 1953: 185)

Ijiri (1975: 28), a leading modern inductivist, is even more direct, saying that 'the purpose of such an [inductive] exercise is to highlight where changes are most needed and where they are feasible'.

18 Instead of the usual form of *argumentum ad ignorantiam* (*N* is *X* because no one has proved that *N* is not-*X*) the form of this argument is: A knows *N* is *X* because we are ignorant of whether *N* is *X* or *N* is not-*X*. This is an especially noxious error when it is extended to claim that B does not know that *N* is not-*X* because we are ignorant of whether *N* is *X* or not-*X*. In the absence of even attempting to qualify or disqualify A or B as authorities, the choice of A over B is groundless.

19 An appropriate name for one who studies ornithologists would be 'ornithologist-ologist'. For that reason, I have previously suggested that accounting be renamed 'plutology' (from Plutus, god of wealth, hence the study of wealth and wealth changes including profit) because the study of plutologists would become plutologist-ology, the structure and repetitiveness of which might cause plutologist-ologists to pause long enough to think about what they are doing. Then when Watts and Zimmerman (1979) present the case that self-interest motivates plutologist-ologists (and Peasnell and Williams (1986) present a rebuttal) they would be called 'plutologist-ologist-ologists'. A planned paper of mine will present the case that Watts and Zimmerman were seeking their self-interest when they wrote 'The demand for and supply of accounting theories: the market for excuses'; so my paper ('The demand and supply of accounting papers: the market for hubris') will be plutologist-ologist-ologist-ology. We may be on to an all-day sucker here.

An equally important reason for the name change is that it would allow my next book to be *Principia Plutometrica* which title would befit the exalted plutometrician I expect to become, leaving behind my present, ignoble status as a normativist and my former, equally ignoble status as an apriorist.

20 There are also instances of arguments that a full or deep understanding of a discipline cannot be obtained without including practitioners of that discipline in the many things to be studied. For example, it is argued that one will not have a full understanding of geometry without studying practitioners of geometry (surveyors and other earth measurers) *in addition* to studying the earth, the rules of thumb used by Babylonians and Egyptians, the idealized concepts and the life and times of Euclid, as well as Descartes, Gauss, Lobachevsky, and others, topology, history, and other related topics. However, to the best of my knowledge no one has ever suggested that the study of geometry be *restricted* to the observation of the practices of surveyors and other geometricians. Nor

has anyone ever alleged that it would be normative to improve or correct the then current earth measurement methods.

21 Dewey illustrates the productivity of winnowing the good from the bad practices with the history of mathematics:

> Men began with counting and measuring things just as they began with pounding and burning them. One thing, as common speech profoundly has it, led to another. Certain ways were successful – not merely in the immediately practical sense, but in the sense of being interesting, of arousing attention, of exciting attempts at improvement. The present-day mathematical logician may present the structure of mathematics as if it had sprung all at once from the brain of a Zeus whose anatomy is that of pure logic. But, nevertheless, this very structure is a product of long historic growth, in which all kinds of experiments have been tried, in which some men have struck out in this direction and some in that, and in which some exercises and operations have resulted in confusion and others in triumphant clarifications and fruitful growths; a history in which matter and methods have been constantly selected and worked over on the basis of empirical success and failure.
>
> (Dewey 1963: 93)

Had there been a 'social recorder perspective' or a 'positive theory' of counting and measuring, the assessment of the practices would have been proscribed – it would have been considered 'normative' to decide success and failure of matter and method. The prescription of a 'positive-scientific' description would, in essence, prescribe the status quo ante.

Dewey's assessment of the distinction follows:

> The parrot-like repetition of the distinction between an empirical description of what is and a normative account of what should be merely neglects the most striking fact about thinking as it empirically is – namely, its flagrant exhibition of cases of failure and success – that is, of good thinking and bad thinking.

I agree. It is not the simple-minded distinction between the descriptive and prescriptive for the purpose of sanctioning one and censuring the other that is important but rather the cogency of the argument for the prescriptions and the adequacy of the evidence for the descriptions.

22 Hempel recognized early on that the analytic–synthetic distinction presents some formidable difficulties, even contributing to the explication of those difficulties (1965: 101ff), which weaken the verifiability theory of meaning but he maintains that 'the empiricist criterion of meaning is basically sound' and that its 'application has been, on the whole, enlightening and salutary'. I agree, and I think its application would be particularly enlightening and salutary in accounting.

Compare the contrast of arbitrary to right *or* wrong in Note 4 to the contrast of meaningless to true *or* false in Hempel and others in the philosophy of science literature.

23 There is now little dispute about the fact of divorce but there remains dispute about whether the effect of the divorce is good or bad. Hall, an eminent practitioner, and Demski, a well-known theorist, describe the divorce in a remarkably similar manner. Hall (1987: 31–2) writes about

the growing gap between practice and the 'theory as advanced in articles' and notes that it would be reasonable to 'question whether the subject matter [of those articles] was accounting'. Demski (1987: 89) contrasts the contents of a journal at two dates, saying that the 'first [1964] list of articles speaks to how to do the accounting or how to analyze some particular (investment) decision' whereas the 'second [1986] list speaks to something else, perhaps asteroids'. The second level of humour in Demski's joke is that many practitioners would take it seriously, agreeing that current accounting research is in outer space, being conducted by space cadets, and needs to be brought down to earth. Equally intense, if less colourful, disdain for practice is expressed by many academics.

Many practitioners who are concerned about the divorce plead for more applied or practical research. Many academics are pleased with the divorce, seeing it as a triumph of pure research. I agree that there is a problem but I don't see it stemming from the tension between pure and applied research. Instead I see it as the direct result of the complete divorce of subject matters.

Hall (1987: 35) is not one of the practitioners who expresses disdain for theory although he does plead for clearer expression of theory. I join in that plea. Perhaps we accountants could adopt what Chalmers (1976: xi) called a 'noteworthy feature of the Popperian school' namely 'the pressure it put on one to be clear about the problem one was interested in and to express one's views on it in a simple and straightforward way'. It seems to me that some accountants think that being understood is incompatible with being scientific or scholarly and therefore they are deliberately obscure. Is it possible to be *that* obscure accidentally?

24 Michael Power (personal communication) kindly pointed out that 'it is simply not clear from the paper that such an ontology of accounting phenomena is obvious'. I agree. I hasten to rectify that omission by noting that a central purpose of this chapter is to show the absence of ontology of 'historical costs' and therefore that they are modern fantasies to be shed in the same way that our ancestors shed medieval fantasies. In place of such fantasies we should ground accounting in what every plain man can see, measuring and generalizing the obvious things to be measured and generalized.

In other works I have suggested that we account for one of the 'ordinary notions' of economics, namely prices. In economics there is no question about the ontology of prices, although of course there might be many questions about the amount of a particular price, as was made clear by Leontief:

> As an empirical science, economics dealt from the outset with phenomena of common experience. Producing and consuming goods, buying and selling, and receiving income and spending it are activities engaging everyone's attention practically all the time. Even the application of the scientific principle of quantification did not have to be initiated by the analyst himself – measuring and pricing constitute an integral part of the phenomena that he sets out to explain.
>
> (Leontief 1982)

Conspicuous by its absence from this list of the 'phenomena of common experience' is historical costs. Since prices are inevitably included and historical costs are inevitably omitted when economists make such lists, I find it odd to require argument for the ontology of the ordinary notion of price and not to require argument for the ontology of the extraordinary notion of historical costs.

I suspect that the reason for this oddity is another instance of equivocation regarding 'historical costs' similar to that discussed on p. 126. A clue supporting that suspicion can be found when Power accepts the traditional way of framing the question of valuing cars and buildings as a choice of 'either selling price, replacement cost or *actual* historic cost' (Power 1986: 391, emphasis added) thereby apparently questioning the ontology of current purchase and selling prices by contrasting them to the actual, granting the ontology of historic costs (amounts paid) by characterizing it as actual, and then extending that grant, via equivocation, to historic costs (calculated amounts).

25 Peasnell distinguishes science from a 'service activity' when he writes:

> Accounting is not a science, it is a service activity [and] . . . should be equated with fields like medicine, technology and the law [that] . . . make use of scientific (i.e. empirical) knowledge – they often contribute to it – but their principal concern is with doing a particular job of work, fulfilling a social need.
>
> (Peasnell 1978: 220–1)

I fully agree and, except for the name 'service activity', I have drawn similar comparisons and suggested that we pattern ourselves after such service activities, especially medicine and engineering. What I mean when I suggest that accounting move toward a science is simply that it take the first step by switching from calculating numerals to measuring (observing) and reporting some kind of verifiable magnitude, such as prices. If we do this, perhaps we can play the role of a Tycho Brahe to an accounting Johannes Kepler. Although we cannot be sure that an accounting Kepler will appear if we do measure, we can be sure that one will not appear if we continue to calculate. If Tycho had calculated the 'historical positions' of the planets instead of measuring them, Kepler would not have had a data base to use to compare to his conjectured calculations, which comparison were necessary to convert some of the conjectures to the famous laws.

REFERENCES

Accounting Research and Terminology Bulletins (1961) final edition, New York: American Institute of Certified Public Accountants.

Boulding, K.E. (1958) *The Skills of the Economist*, Cleveland: Howard Allen.

Butterworth, J.E., Gibbins, M. and King, R.D. (1982) 'The structure of accounting theory: some basic conceptual and methodological issues'. in S. Basu and J.A. Milburn (eds) *Research to Support Standard Setting in Financial Accounting: A Canadian Perspective*, proceedings of the 1981 Clarkson Gordon Foundation Research Symposium. Toronto: Clarkson Gordon Foundation.

Chalmers, A.F. (1976) *What is this Thing called Science? An Assessment of the Nature and Status of Science and its Methods*, St Lucia: University of Queensland Press, second edition.

Christenson, C. (1983) 'The methodology of positive accounting', *Accounting Review*, January.

Demski, J.S. (1987) '(Theoretical) research in (managerial) accounting', in B.E. Cushing (ed.) *Accounting and Culture: Plenary Session Papers and Discussants' Comments from the 1986 Annual Meeting of the American Accounting Association*, Sarasota, Florida: American Accounting Association.

Dewey, J. (1963) 'The significance of logical reconstruction', in R. Jager (ed.) *Essays in Logic: From Aristotle to Russell*, Englewood Cliffs: Prentice-Hall.

Einstein, A. (1954) *Ideas and Opinions*, New York: Crown Publishers.

FASB (Financial Accounting Standards Board) (1983) *Accounting Standards: Statement of Financial Accounting Concepts 1–4*, Stamford, Connecticut: FASB.

—— (1984) *Statement of Financial Accounting Concepts No. 5*, Stamford, Connecticut: FASB.

Grady, P. (1965) *Inventory of Generally Accepted Accounting Principles for Business Enterprises*. Accounting Research Study No. 7, New York: American Institute of Certified Public Accountants.

Hall, W.D. (1987) *Accounting and Auditing: Thoughts on Forty Years in Practice and Education*, Chicago: Arthur Andersen & Co.

Hatfield, H.R. (1924) 'An historical defense of bookkeeping', *Journal of Accountancy*, April.

Hempel, C.G. (1965) *Aspects of Scientific Explanation and Other Essays in the Philosophy of Science*, New York: Free Press.

—— (1967) *Fundamentals of Concept Formation in Empirical Science*, Chicago: University of Chicago Press.

Ijiri, Y. (1975) *Theory of Accounting Measurement*. Studies in Accounting Research No. 10, Sarasota, Florida: American Accounting Association.

Kline, M. (1972) *Mathematical Thought from Ancient to Modern Times*, New York: Oxford University Press.

Leontief, W. (1982) Letter to the Editor, *Science*, 9 July.

Littleton, A.C. (1953) *Structure of Accounting Theory*, Monograph No. 5, Sarasota, Florida: American Accounting Association.

Luchins, A.S. (1942) 'Mechanization in problem solving', in J.F. Dashiell (ed.) *Psychological Monographs: The Effect of Einstellung*, 54 (6), Evanston: American Psychological Assoc.

Lyas, C. (1984) 'Philosophers and accountants', *Philosophy*, 59 (227): 99–110.

Mill, J.S. (1909) *Principles of Political Economy: With Some of Their Applications to Social Philosophy*, New York: Colonial Press.

Moonitz, M. (1961) *The Basic Postulates of Accounting*. Accounting Research Study No. 1, New York: American Institute of Certified Public Accountants.

Peasnell, K.V. (1978) 'Statement of accounting theory and theory acceptance: a review article', *Accounting and Business Research*, 8(31): 217–25.

Peasnell, K.V. and Williams, D.J. (1986) 'Ersatz academics and scholar-saints: the supply of financial accounting research', *Abacus*, 22(2): 121–35.

Power, M. (1986) 'Taking stock: philosophy and accountancy'. *Philosophy*, 61 (237), 387–94.

Sprouse, R.T. and Moonitz, M. (1962) *A Tentative Set of Broad Accounting Principles for Business Enterprises*. Accounting Research Study No. 3. New York: American Institute of Certified Public Accountants.

Stamp, E. (1981) 'Why can accounting not become a science like physics?' *Abacus*, Spring 17(1): 13–22.

Staubus, G.J. (1987) 'The Dark Ages of cost accounting: the role of miscues in the literature'. *Accounting Historians Journal*, Fall: 1–18.

Sterling, R.R. (1970) 'On theory construction and verification', *Accounting Review*, July.

—— (1979) *Toward a Science of Accounting*, Houston: Scholars Book Co.

—— (1982) 'Discussant's comments', in S. Basu and J.A. Milburn (eds) *Research to Support Standard Setting in Financial Accounting: A Canadian Perspective*, proceedings of the 1981 Clarkson Gordon Foundation Research Symposium, Toronto: Clarkson Gordon Foundation.

—— (1988) 'Confessions of a failed empiricist', *Advances in Accounting*, Vol. 6. JAI Press.

Thomas, A.L. (1969) *The Allocation Problem in Financial Accounting Theory*, Studies in Accounting Research No. 3, Sarasota, Florida: American Accounting Association.

—— (1974) *The Allocation Problem in Financial Accounting Theory, Part Two*, Studies in Accounting Research No. 9, Sarasota, Florida: American Accounting Association.

Watts, R.L. and Zimmerman, J.L. (1979) 'The demand for and supply of accounting theories: the market for excuses', *Accounting Review*, 54(2): 273–305.

—— (1986) *Positive Accounting Theory*, Englewood Cliffs: Prentice-Hall.

Whitehead, A.N. (1967) *Science and the Modern World*, New York: The Free Press.

Whittington, G. (1987) 'Positive accounting: a review article', *Accounting and Business Research*, Autumn issue.

Wolk, H.I., Francis, J.R., and Tearney, M.G. (1984) *Accounting Theory: A Conceptual and Institutional Approach*, Boston: Kent Publishing Co.

Ziman, J. (1978) *Reliable Knowledge: An Exploration of the Grounds for Belief in Science*, Cambridge: Cambridge University Press.

ACCOUNTING EDUCATION AND RESEARCH

INTRODUCTION

Sterling on Accounting Education and Research

P. W. Wolnizer

The disjunction between research and education in accounting, and the consequent maintenance of the status quo in accounting practice, is a recurrent theme in Bob Sterling's writings. Though discussed in many papers, the matter was directly at issue in Sterling (1973, 1975 and 1982). In his judgment, the contact between accounting research and practice "... is so nebulous that it can be disregarded ... [whereas] education and practice seem to be complementary in that educators teach accepted practice and practitioners accept and practice what they are taught. This complementary relationship excludes research from the chain of events that determine what is taught and what is practiced" (1973, pp.46, 49). Consequently, "The results of research [in accounting] have very little impact on teaching or practice" (1975, p.58). His suggestion, at that time, was "... that educators teach research results as *the desired state* and teach accepted practices as *the current state*" (1973, p.52).

In addressing this matter, Sterling contrasts the training of engineers (in 1975) and medical practitioners (in 1982) with that of accountants. He argues that when medical theory and practice were connected, "... medical practice improved dramatically. New students were taught new techniques as they were discovered and they implemented those new techniques when they went into practice. They did not have to unlearn old techniques, they did not suffer from trained incapacity, and therefore at the date of graduation there was no dichotomy between theory and practice" (1982, p.70). They were not taught reverence for dogma. However, "teaching generally accepted accounting principles means ... that the new generation of students is taught to do what previous generations are now doing. This is reinforced when the new generation is hired by the previous generations and required to emulate them to achieve success" (1982, p.71). From his earliest writings, Sterling has been concerned that accounting students be taught theory rather than "the intricacies of arithmetic" (1962), and warned that in accounting we teach tolerance of "cognitive dissonance" (1967).

Sterling is vitally concerned with the quality of accounting education, for it is his "... settled view that the betterment of accounting must begin in the classroom. Today's students are tomorrow's practitioners and the ideas we impart to them will determine, in significant measure, the future course of accounting practice" (1989, p.82). His experiences as Senior Fellow at the Financial Accounting Standards Board convinced him "... of the significant influence of teachers on standard setters and thence on standards" (1989, p.82).

For this reason, Sterling proposes "... that we begin to teach ... the need for correspondence of a calculated numeral to an independent observation (measurement) of the phenomena that the numeral purports to represent. This is a commonsense idea as well as a criterion [and practice] common to *all* sciences, and a little used, less understood qualitative characteristic [representational faithfulness] in FASB's conceptual framework" (1989, p.85). To investigate the relative understandings of the "correspondence concept" by accountants and scientists, Sterling devised a simple set of questions based on the difference between the calculation and measurement of the attributes "cost" and "volume." The test results are reported, in varying contexts, in Sterling (1988, 1989 and 1990). He found that accountants generally do not understand the correspondence concept - a "fatal error," he declares - whereas scientists fully comprehend it and consider it to be "crucial" (1989). Later, by use of the same test, Sterling (1990) found that accountants, unlike scientists, did not understand the essential element of the notion of additivity.

Though urging teachers to teach the correspondence concept, Sterling observes that those who do so "... will be disappointed if they expect to find support or guidance in the accounting research literature" (1989, p.92). Remembering his suggestion in 1973, that accounting research results be taught to accounting students, Sterling now writes "That lacuna requires that I rescind my previous [1973] recommendation ... [However] that recommendation [was made] at a time when most researchers asked questions about what to record and report or how to improve the reporting, but accounting research has become increasingly distant from questions of that kind" (1989, p.92).

In a devastating - and hitherto unanswered - critique of positive accounting theory, Sterling (1990) describes the vastness of that distance. "For decades, the 'fundamental question of accounting' has been *which objects and events* and *which attribute(s) of them* should be represented in accounts and on financial statements? ... At base, that question concerned the states and activities of the firm, especially in regard to wealth and income, and how best to account for them. ... Positive accounting theorists assert that ... the question should be changed to 'What *are* accounting practices?'" (1990, pp.97-8) This, he explains, is a "radical alteration of the fundamental question of accounting" (1990, p.98). Having critically examined positive accounting theory (1990), and its "empirical" forerunner (with Harrison, 1974), Sterling (1990, p. 131) concludes that the errors of positive accounting theory are "egregious" (because it confuses "disparate subject matters"), "pernicious" (because it restricts inquiry to the "positive study of practices and practitioners"), and "untutored" (because it claims to be "in accord with economics and science"). Having already argued that "The ultimate test of any research programme is whether or not it bears fruit" (1982, p.67), Sterling concludes that "The accomplishments of [positive accounting theory] are nonexistent. Instead of bringing forth interesting or unexpected or edifying results, [positive accounting theory] has presented us with findings that are empty and commonplace" (1990, p.131). Later, he describes positive accounting research as "anthropology," and declares "... I don't see how studies of accountants can ever bear fruit, especially in view of the fact that proscribing the assessment of practitioner behaviour makes such study an end rather than a means" (1993, p.139).

Seeking only the advancement of accounting knowledge, the solution of accounting problems, and the improvement of accounting practice, Sterling recommends "... that we carefully assess proposed research programs *before* accepting or rejecting them" (1990, p.132); and advises that "One of the ways to avoid being swept up by fads is to demand simplicity and clarity, and refuse to be intimidated by jargon, mathematical symbols, equations and highly stylized methods of expression that tend (intentionally or inadvertently) to cloud rather than clarify". (1990, p.132). And, after a conscientious reading of Sterling's work, no one could conclude other than that simplicity, clarity and intelligibility are distinctive hallmarks of his published discourses.

THE TEACHERS' CLINIC

Glen G. Yankee

Editor's Note: This section of The Accounting Review is devoted to matters of particular interest to accounting instructors. The contribution of articles bearing on the nature and purpose of various types of accounting education, or dealing with techniques of accounting instruction, is invited. Address all correspondence to Glen G. Yankee, School of Business, Western Reserve University, Cleveland 6, Ohio.

DETERMINATION OF GOODWILL AND BONUS ON THE ADMISSION OF A PARTNER

Robert R. Sterling, *University of Florida*

The comment is often heard that accounting for the admission of a partner is relatively simple, but that it is one of the more difficult areas to teach. This paradox appears to be a result of a lack of delineation as to what is a problem in accounting theory and what is a problem in arithmetic. It is apparent that most textbook and CPA problems concerning the admission of a partner are essentially problems in arithmetic. Thus, it would appear that the short-hand notation and method of the mathmetician could be used advantageously in the solution thereof. For this reason, the author has reduced problems of this nature to three basic formulae in the hope that the students would become more facile with the intricacies of the arithmetic and thus, permit more concentration on the theory. Obviously, any calculations of this sort are subordinate to any agreement among the partners. That is, the formulae are applicable only when the goodwill or bonus is *implied* by the statement of the problem.

The formulae are presented below in the belief that other teachers may find this approach both time-saving and less frustrating.

Definition of Symbols:

C = total capital in the ex-post partnership

f = fractional share of the total capital in the ex-ante partnership of the incoming partner.

I = total assets given up by the incoming partner

B = Bonus

G = Goodwill

Bonus Problems. The kernel of the Bonus problem is to determine the capital credit to the incoming partner.

Where an interest is purchased the total capital is not changed, hence, C times f yields the capital credit. The difference between the capital credit and the amount paid is the "bonus" Thus

$$Cf - I = B.$$

Note that if the capital credit exceeds the payment then the bonus is to the incoming partner. If the payment exceeds the capital credit then the bonus goes to the selling partners. That is, a positive or negative sign on B indicates the partners to receive the bonus. Of course, a zero answer indicates the payment is equal to book value of the capital credit.

Basically this same formula is used when the incoming partner contributes assets to the *partnership* versus the partners (Investment for an Interest). The difference is that the total capital changes by the amount of the investment. Thus, the above formula is modified to:

$$(C+I)f-I=B.$$

The signs are the same—positive is bonus to incoming, negative to ex-post partners and zero when the contribution equals book value.

Goodwill and Asset Revaluation Problems. The essence of the goodwill problem is to determine the total capital of the ex-ante partnership. In the case of the purchase of an interest, the payment by the incoming partner may be used to make this determination. If the payment is a given fraction of the total then the capital of the ex-ante partnership (equals x, the unknown) may be expressed as

$$fx=I$$

$$x=\frac{I}{f}$$

This division, I/f, yields the ex ante total capital and the difference between that and the capital of the ex-post partnership is the amount of the asset revaluation or goodwill. Thus

$$\frac{I}{f}-C=G.$$

A positive answer requires either the write-up of undervalued assets or the recognition of goodwill by the amount of the answer. Likewise, a negative answer requires the write-down of the assets, or, if the particular assets that are overvalued are undeterminable then the account "allowance for overvaluation" may be used. Again, a zero solution indicates equality with book value.

In the case of an investment for an interest the same formula holds except the net tangible assets are changed by the amount of the investment. Thus

$$\frac{I}{f}-(C+I)=G_1.$$

Again, a positive answer indicates asset undervaluation or the existence of goodwill in the ex-post partnership. A negative answer indicates asset overvaluation. However, the problem may be complicated in this case by having the goodwill credit going to the incoming partner and the capital of the ex-post partnership used as a basis for valuation. Thus

$$\frac{C}{1-f}-(C+I)=G_2.$$

A positive answer here indicates that the credit for goodwill goes exclusively to the incoming partner.

Students many times find it difficult to differentiate between goodwill to ex-post and incoming partners; i.e., which base—the ex-post capital or the investment—to use in determining ex-ante total capital. This problem is automatically solved in the preceeding two formuli. G_1 and G_2 will always have opposite signs and a negative answer should be construed as irrational. (As noted above a negative G is rational if the object is to write-down assets.) Hence, either of the formulae may be chosen and if positive it can be safely assumed to be the correct one and vice-versa.

Allocation of Goodwill, Bonus or Asset Increment. It is quite clear in accounting theory that asset increments and decrements are *partnership* (as opposed to partners) gains and losses. Therefore, any asset revaluation above should be allocated in the profit and loss ratio. Note that if goodwill is conceived as the "master valuation account" it is included in the above statement and should be allocated in the profit and loss ratio. Or, if goodwill is conceived as the "present worth of expected future income in excess of the normal return," the definition indicates "income", thus, the allocation is in the profit and loss ratio.

Likewise, in the case of an investment it is clear that the bonus is a *partnership* transaction and the profit and loss ratio should be used. However, in the purchase of an interest case, ***personal property*** of the partner (s) is sold and the division of the bonus is indeterminate in the absence of a specific agreement. None-the-less, the commonly accepted solution is in the profit and ratio.

In short, the profit and loss ratio is used in all cases. Obviously, the partners may agree to do otherwise.

Summary.

Bonus:

Purchase of an interest:
$Cf-I=B$ (+B to incoming) (−B to ex-post)

Investment for an interest:
$(C+I)\,f-I=B$ (+B to incoming) (−B to ex-post)

Goodwill:

Purchase of an interest:
$\frac{I}{f}-C=G$ (+G to ex-post) (−G is asset over-valuation)

Investment for an interest:
$\frac{I}{f}-(C+I)=G_1$ ($+G_1$ to ex-post) ($-G_1$ is asset over-valuation)

$\frac{C}{1-f}-(C+I)=G_2$ (to incoming)

The allocation of B or G in all the formuli should be in the profit and loss ratio.

In some problems the data are not presented in exactly the same terms as that employed in the formulae. This should present no problem if the formulae are well understood. For example, some problems state the total capital desired by the partners and ask for the amount of the goodwill. This is readily solved by the realization that the first term in the Goodwill formula is the calculation of the new total capital. Thus, the desired capital is substituted for I/f or C/(1-f), whichever is applicable.

A Case of Valuation and Learned Cognitive Dissonance

Robert R. Sterling
Yale University

In "A Case of Valuation,"[1] Howard W. Wright presented an array of different values of the Nickel Smelting Company and drew the following conclusions:

> In summary, at least eight different values, ranging from zero to $15 million, were involved. These different values may make it easier to understand why many accountants consistently adhere to recorded cost, with all its weaknesses, and to verifiable, objective evidence.

The eight different values referred to were:

1. Reproduction cost less depreciation	$11,921,233
2. Number 1 less 10% for risk factors	10,730,000
3. Fair market value	9,440,000
4. Company's appraisal presented to tax commission	11,723,593
5. Negotiated tax appraisal	15,113,240
6. Unamortized cost on Company's books	-0-
7. Unamortized cost by IRS guidelines	11,500,000
8. Formula-computed purchase price	1,700,000

My examination of these figures leads me to the opposite conclusion. Note that the figures in 1 through 5 are appraisals. Wright excluded from his conclusions the appraisals by the State Tax Commission and the amount the plant was insured for. I think this is proper but I would go further. Figures (4) and (5) are a haggle over the amount of taxes to be paid and have little if anything to do with the value of the

[1] Howard W. Wright, "A Case of Valuation," The Accounting Review, July 1966, pp. 559–60.

plant. If this is granted, then there are three appraisals to be considered. They range from $9.4 to $11.9 million and the $2.5 million deviation is unfortunate and sufficient cause for concern. Inclusion of figure (5) increases the deviation to $5.7 million and is worse.

Compare these to the possibilities for recorded cost. The Company used an amortization method that resulted in a zero book value. If it had used IRS guidelines it would have $11.5 million book value, and if it purchases the plant as agreed it will have $1.7 million book value. The deviation of $11.5 million is about five times as large or twice as large as the appraisal deviations. In fact, by any variation measure that one chooses, the recorded cost figures come out a poor second.

Second, there is the concern over the number of different appraisals with the implication, I presume, that there is a single cost figured. Mr. Drebin states it directly: "If ten skilled appraisers are called . . . it is likely that they will provide ten different estimates. Accountants would rather rely upon a single cost figure . . . ."[2] Everyone would agree with the "ten different appraisals" proposition but the "single cost" proposition is rather odd in view of the commonplace complaints about different depreciation methods, different life estimates, and different salvage estimates. Certainly in the case of Nickel Smelting there is no single cost.

We all know that initial construction costs ($21.0 million) are subject to various methods of allocation (e.g., overhead) which are subject to various methods of accumulation (e.g., depreciation of equipment included in overhead) which are subject to various methods of cost collection (e.g., amount capitalized and attached to the equipment), and so forth until we get back to the cash expended or a fair market value at some past time or some other value. Thus, the initial cost is subject to (perhaps wide) variation. Then the additions and replacements ($1.8 million) are subject to variations of the same kind. After all of this we are ready to apply different life estimates, etc. and depreciate "the" cost by various methods.

Finally, there is the objective and verifiable notion. This is even more puzzling. The accountant takes a set of figures (dollars expended, allocations of previous dollars expended, years of life, salvage value) which he freely admits are subjective, arranges them in an equation, and then calculates a figure (depreciation, book value) that he considers to be objective. Exactly how one can get objectivity by manipulating subjectivity is not clear to me. The auditor then "verifies" this figure. This must mean that he verifies the physical existence of the object and checks the arithmetical accuracy of the figure.

In summary, I find:

(1) A wider variation in the recorded costs than in appraisal values.

(2) Equally as many recorded costs as appraisal values.

(3) Equally as much subjectivity in recorded costs as in appraisal values.

That is, all the arguments against appraisal values can be applied to recorded costs with at least equal force. Accountants seem to be aware of this situation when they lament the lack of uniformity and the subjective estimates in recorded costs. Yet when appraisal values (or other alternatives) are suggested they reject them *because* they are subjective and diverge. They often imply and sometimes state

[2] Allan R. Drebin, "Accounting for Proprietary Research," The Accounting Review, July 1966, p. 419. Mr. Drebin is arguing that market values provide more realistic and more important information and says "Accountants are generally reluctant to utilize market values because subjective estimates are usually required . . . ," and then continues with the different appraisals-single cost propositions. He may be reporting an argument that he doesn't support.

that costs are objective and univocal. They almost always argue that costs are more objective and subject to less variation than appraisals.

Sometimes this is called cognitive dissonance. In accounting I think it is learned; I think we *teach* cognitive dissonance. The typical text devotes a chapter to "theory" in which cost is characterized as objective, verifiable, and univocal. Alternative values are dismissed as subjective, conjectures, and divergent. The remainder of the text considers the assets seriatim and laboriously explains the different methods, comments on subjective estimates, and gives examples of variations in costs. The advanced students have assimilated this compartmentalization so well that they can parrot the pejoratives on a theory question and practice them on a problem question without ever making a connection. It takes about a semester of graduate work to unlearn them. Perhaps we shouldn't teach it in the first place.

I. INTRODUCTION

A glance at the accounting literature reveals that there has been a broadening of what accountants perceive to be appropriate research questions. Previously, the predominant view seemed to be that the research questions of accounting should be severely circumscribed. Primary emphasis was placed on the questions of the proper method of cost allocation and the appropriate timing of revenue realization. Currently, the predominant view seems to be that anything which is affected by accounting and anything which affects accounting is an appropriate research question. Thus, the number of questions considered to be appropriate for accounting research has been greatly expanded in recent years.

Concurrent with the expansion of research questions has been an expansion of the research methods utilized by accounting researchers. Many of these new methods are borrowed from other disciplines and applied to the problems of accounting. This has come about in two ways:

> First, there have been some attempts to redefine the purpose and the subject matter of accounting. For example, a previous definition of accounting included the terms "recording" and "reporting." A current definition replaces these terms with "measuring" and "communicating." Although it can be argued that the terms have the same meaning, the point in regard to research methods is that the new terms suggest that the concepts and methods of measurement and communication theory are pertinent to accounting, and there has been research in this direction. Another example is the view that accounting should supply "relevant information" instead of "matching costs and revenues." This has resulted in the application of the concepts and methods of decision and information theory to the problems of accounting.
>
> Second, there have been attempts to broaden the analysis of the accounting function. Previously, the analysis of the accounting function stopped with the issuance of financial statements. The current view is that the effects of financial statements is an appropriate research question. There have been investigations of the market effects of their issuance, and these investigations have utilized the concepts, methods, and previous findings of the disciplines of economics and finance. Othere have investigated the effects of financial statements in laboratory settings, utilizing the concepts, methods, and previous findings of the behavioral sciences.

These two categories are not mutually exclusive but we may refer to them broadly as research *in* accounting as opposed to research *about* accounting. The former are efforts to establish what the subject matter of accounting ought to be and to discover attributes of that subject matter. The latter are efforts to discover how accounting fits into the total scheme of things. The investigators are attempting to find out how accounting inputs and outputs mesh, or clash, with the inputs and outputs of other disciplines.

Given these goals, there is an almost limitless number of other disciplines whose concepts, methods, and previous findings are pertinent to research in accounting. Since accounting provides information to management as well as information about managment's performance, management science is pertinent. Since technology is a crucial factor in the establishment of a communication system, in addition to the fact that the computer is a powerful research tool, computer science is pertinent. Since the act of measuring is likely to affect the behavior of those receiving the results of the measurements, as well as the behavior of those being measured, the behavioral sciences are pertinent. And so forth.

The listed disciplines are intended to be suggestive, not exhaustive. The point that I want to make is that the expansion of research *questions* has resulted in an expansion of research *methods*. It is evident that if one wants to explore the behavioral effects of accounting, then the methods of the behavioral sciences are appropriate; if one wants to explore the mathematical characteristics of accounting, then the methods of mathematics are appropriate; etc. Thus, the appropriateness of a research method depends upon the research question to be investigated. One cannot judge the appropriateness of a research method without placing it in the context of the research question that is being explored.

Since the selection of a research method depends upon the research question, the basis for the selection of methods reduces to the basis for selection of questions. Ultimately, the criterion for selecting a research question is the importance of the answer to that question. But, we are unable to know the importance of the answer until that answer has been obtained, i.e., until after the research has been performed. Indeed, we cannot know that we will be able to obtain an answer until after the research has been performed. Thus, one must address a research question because he *believes* that he can obtain an answer and that the answer is likely to be important. Since one cannot demonstrate the importance of the research results prior to performing the research, the selection of a research question requires a leap of faith. As Polanyi [7, p. 123] puts it, a scientific discovery requires the jumping of a "logical gap" and one can never be sure of his ability to make the jump until he has tried. Of course, the length of the leap will vary, since some research questions are more routine than others. Usually, but not always, the more routine the research question, the greater the chance of being able to answer the question but the smaller the chance that the answer to that particular research question will be important. The cumulative effect of routine research may result in an important break-through, but it is unlikely that the results of any single project will result in that break-through. Therefore, the length of the leap of faith and the importance of the results probably vary directly. Unfortunately, it is likely that the length of the leap of faith also varies directly with the probability of failure.

In discussing the advancement of science, Bernal distinguishes between "tactics" and "strategy." He defines "tactics" as the method of attacking a problem or question. By contrast,

> The essential feature of a strategy of discovery lies in determining the sequence of choice of problems to solve. Now it is in fact very much more difficult to see a problem than to find a solution for it. The former requires imagination, the latter only ingenuity. (Bernal [2, p. 39])

Bernal's purpose is not to denigrate the solving of problems (by saying that they require "only" ingenuity), but, instead, to make the contrast between working within a well defined area and breaking new ground. The latter is much more difficult and risky but, if successful, the payoffs are much greater. He cites the cases of Newton, Darwin and Faraday as examples of researchers who "set themselves to find and solve problems of their own" [2, p. 39]. Cohen and Nagel [3, p. 392] make the same point when they write: "The ability to formulate problems whose solution may also help solve other problems is a rare gift, requiring extraordinary genius."

There is no reason to believe that accounting is different from science in general in this regard. How are we to know beforehand that research question X will yield more fruitful results than research question Y? The answer is that we cannot, and therefore, *each* researcher must select his research question on the basis of his belief about the importance of the answer to the question.[1]

[1] Of course, we are speaking here of an idealized researcher. In actuality, there are a good many other factors involved in the selection of the research question. These include the interests, skills and perhaps prejudices of the researcher, as well as the overriding criterion of the availability of funds to support the research.

Given the requirement of extraordinary genius for the selection of research questions, it would be most presumptuous if I were to attempt to argue that some questions are appropriate for research by accountants and that others are inappropriate. My view is quite the opposite. I think that the broadening of accounting research questions has been wholly beneficial and that any attempt to restrict the scope of the questions would be detrimental. In fact, I could list a number of questions which I think we should investigate. However, since these questions are based upon *my* interests and beliefs, the only way for me to demonstrate to you that these are fruitful lines of inquiry is for me to do at least some of the necessary research. Therefore, I will not importune you to do something that interests me nor will I attempt to restrain you from doing something that interests you.

Since the research methods depend upon the questions and since I am unwilling to place restrictions on questions, it follows that I am unwilling to place restrictions on methods. I conclude, therefore, that all of the research methods from all of these other disciplines are appropriate for accounting. To put it another way, the goal of research is to obtain results which will contribute to our knowledge. The danger of excluding a research method is that, in so doing, we will be excluding some research results which may contribute to our knowledge. To avoid this danger, I am unwilling to *ex*clude any research method, and therefore, I must *in*clude *all* research methods.

This rather sweeping conclusion is likely to be disappointing to those who had expected me to label some research methods as "unscientific" and to endorse others. I am sorry to disappoint, but that is precisely the attitude to which I am opposed.[2] I do not believe that it is possible to define "the scientific method" and thereby to delimit the set of research methods that are appropriate to accounting. Although the research methods of all of the scientific disciplines have some general properties in common, the more striking feature is their diversity. Kaplan [5, p. 27] has observed that any definition of the scientific method which is specific enough to be of use in methodology is not general enough to embrace all of the methods which scientists use or may come to use. I would only add that any definition which is general enough to embrace all of the methods is not specific enough to be of any use.

There have been a number of attempts over the years to provide a concise definition of "the scientific method." All of these attempts have failed. They have failed because, as the historians of science have shown, sometimes science progresses in one way and sometimes in another.[3] This is the basis for Kaplan's observation that no definition is general enough to embrace all useful procedures. Since there are a variety of methods and since an attempt to restrict methods is likely to be harmful, he concludes (citing Conant) that it is "a public service" to emphasize "that there is no such thing as *the* scientific method." [5, p. 27] Another reason for failure is that if the procedures of science were reduced to rules so that one could systematically create knowledge, then we would not consider the results of the procedures to be scientific discoveries.

[2] In particular, I am opposed to those who provide a definition of the scientific method for the apparent purpose of criticizing the work of others as "unscientific." The definition that they provide is unbearably narrow and naive in the first place, and more importantly, it violates the basic tenet of science that *nothing* is indubitable and final, including the methods of science. "The canons of inquiry are themselves discovered in the process of reflection, and may themselves become modified in the course of study." (Cohen and Nagel [3, pp. 395–6])

[3] "Such an absolute conception of it [method of science] is belied by the whole history of science, with its continual development of a multiplicity of new methods. The method of science is not a fixed thing, it is a growing process. . . . Consequently scientific method, like science itself, defies definition. It is made up of a number of operations, some mental, some manual. Each of these, in its time, has been found useful, first in the formulation of questions that seem urgent at any stage and then in the finding, testing and using the answers to them." (Bernal [2, p. 35])

As Polanyi [7, p. 123] puts it, "no solution of a problem can be accredited as a discovery if it is achieved by a procedure following definite rules." A major part of the scientific process is the scientist's creation of the method[4] which allows him to carry out his investigation. If discoveries could be made by following a routine procedure, such that any fool or machine could grind them out, then they would not be considered discoveries.

Of course, much of scientific enterprise is not concerned with making discoveries in the sense that Polanyi is using the term. Kuhn [6, p. 35] contrasts "normal science" with the making of discoveries and points out that "the most striking feature" of "normal research" is that it does not "aim to produce novelties, conceptual or phenomenal." He notes (p. 24) that practitioners of "normal science" spend most of their lives in "mopping-up operations." He likens mopping-up operations to "puzzle-solving" and argues that the framework of the normal science, or "paradigm," provides assurance that the puzzle has a solution (p. 37). As the terms suggest, these activities are much more routine than the activities required for making discoveries. In some cases, the method of a normal science can, at least in principle, be completely systematized. However, even in these more routine activities, the systematic method is too inefficient to use. Consider, for example, the common children's puzzle consisting of a box with 15 sequentially numbered squares and one empty position. Turing [8, p. 9] calculated the total number of positions and found it to be finite but rather large, viz., 20,922,789,888,000. If one attempted to solve this puzzle by systematically surveying all of these positions, it would take over a million years, yet many children have solved it in a few minutes. The puzzles of normal science are much more complex, and therefore, the systematic method of solution is simply too inefficient to be used. Instead, as Kuhn says [6, p. 36], the solutions require "ingenuity" and "skill," and these two terms are clearly antonyms for "systematic solution."[5]

Thus, it is not possible or not efficient to use a systematic method for either making discoveries in science or for solving the puzzles of normal science. Perhaps considerations of this kind caused P. W. Bridgman to make his widely quoted remark: "The scientist has no other method than doing his damnedest." Doing one's damnedest neither restricts the scope of the questions to be investigated nor does it restrict the method of investigation to be utilized.

My quarrel, then, is only with those who attempt to make such restrictions. We can now begin to identify several separate schools of accounting by the way in which they attempt to make such restrictions. Representatives of each school have a tendency to claim that *their* particular research questions are the only important ones and that *their* methods are the only scientific ones and that the subject matter that *they* examine is the only pertinent evidence. To use only two broad categories, we can note that some empirists disparage analytical methods, and vice versa. This is a false issue. There are empirical questions and there are analytical questions, and it makes little sense to try to answer an empirical question with analytical methods, or vice versa. For

[4] A prime example of this is Glaser's invention of a device (bubble chamber) for measuring the paths of particles, i.e., the creation of a method of doing research on particles. Since its invention, the bubble chamber has been used in experiments which produced important results. However, it was Glaser who received the Nobel Prize, not the subsequent experimenters. The reason for this is that the process of using a bubble chamber is much more systematic or routine than the process of inventing it. Glaser, by his own account, got the idea while gazing at the bubbles rising in his beer.

[5] Turing [8, p. 23] makes the same point in different words in his concluding remarks. "These, and some other results of mathematical logic may be regarded as going some way towards a demonstration, within mathematics itself, of the inadequacy of 'reason' unsupported by common sense."

example, a paper by Ijiri, Jaedicke and Livingstone [4] addressed itself to the question of the effect of different inventory methods on full and direct costing. An analytical (mathematical) solution was presented. An empirical test of this question would have been entirely inappropriate, because, among other reasons, the empirical test would not have been able to provide a conclusive and general answer. On the other hand, a paper by Beaver [1] addressed itself to the question of investor reaction to earnings' announcements. Analytical methods would have been entirely inappropriate for much the same reasons, e.g., lack of conclusiveness, because there are *a priori* arguments that lead to contradictory conclusions.

Unfortunately, such internal strife seems to be one of those properties which is common to all disciplines. Kaplan [5, p. 30] has complained of the same thing in regard to the behavioral sciences. He notes that there are two tactics: (1) "defensive incorporation," in which each school says "everybody ought to work on ———," and (2) "exclusion," in which each school says "nobody ought to ———." He concludes:

> These tactics lend themselves to rationalization by their identifying some particular phase or other of the complex process of inquiry as the core of "scientific method." For the experimentalist science progresses only in the laboratory; the theoretician views experiments rather as guides and tests for his models and theories; others see as the most important task making counts and measures, or arriving at predictions, or formulating explanations; the field worker and clinician have still other viewpoints. *All of them are right; what is wrong is only what they deny, not what they affirm.* [5, p. 30] (italics supplied)

The point can be stated in terms of the specialization of labor. Dividing science into disciplines by the subject matter which is examined is one form of specialization. Dividing the tasks within a particular discipline is another form of specialization. There are experiments to be performed, mathematical relations to be discovered, and concepts to be clarified. It is impossible for any one person to do all there is to be done, and it is likely that the productivity will be greater if individuals are permitted to specialize. Of course, an imbalance may result in the same way that bottlenecks develop in manufacturing. However, as in manufacturing, the solution is to try to maintain the proper balance, not to denigrate the importance of one of the specialties. Thus, the "data grubbing" of the empiricist, the "abstract meanderings" of the mathematician or logician, and the "idle dreaming" of the theorist are all appropriate methods. The only thing that is inappropriate is the pejorative terms used to describe them.

These observations are even more germane to accounting than to science in general. Accounting is currently in a state of flux; it does not have the paradigm necessary for it to be classified as a normal science in which only puzzle-solving is needed. We have not yet even decided what should be the subject matter of accounting. Many of the disputes in the current literature are, in essence, disagreements over what the subject matter of accounting ought to be.[6] For example, should the subject matter be costs or values or information? Should we focus on decision makers or on decision models? Should we study the reactions of individuals or their reactions aggregated by the market? Should we supply information relevant to decisions or confine ourselves to the stewardship function? Since we do not know how such questions will be resolved or which research methods will contribute to their resolution, we must tolerate, if not encourage, a

[6] My critics unwittingly provided me with some empirical evidence for this assertion. Several of them denied that the subject matter of accounting was in dispute and then informed me of the nature of that subject matter. However, each critic had a different opinion of the nature of that subject matter. For example, one asserted that the economics of information is the basic subject matter of accounting, while another asserted that "accounting must be, in the final analysis, a behavioral science."

variety of research questions from a variety of disciplines utilizing a variety of methods by a variety of specialists.

For this reason, my answer to the charge of identifying the methods appropriate for research in accounting can be stated quite simply: All methods are appropriate. Unfortunately, my answer to this part of the charge prohibits the fulfillment of the remainder of the charge. In addition to identifying the methods, the charge also specifies that the appropriate methods be explained and illustrated. Obviously, it is impossible to explain and illustrate all research methods. Therefore, the Committee was forced to select only a small subset of research issues for examination.

Given the views expressed above, a nondirective approach to the organization of the Committee seemed reasonable, and this approach was adopted. Each member of the Committee selected a topic on research methodology on the basis of his interests and his belief in the importance of that topic. Thus, the particular research methods and issues which are discussed in the following set of papers are a reflection of the interests of the members of the Committee, and the set is not intended to contain an exhaustive list of all methods that are appropriate for research in accounting nor even, necessarily, the methods that are most preferred for research in accounting. Had there been different members of the Committee with different interests, different research methods and research issues would have been selected for examination.

The result of this selection process is a rather diverse set of topics. Given the diversity of the members of the Committee, this is to be expected. About the only thing common to all the authors is that they have made significant research contributions. In making these contributions, their diversity of interests is evidenced by the diversity of research questions which they address and the concomitant diversity of research methods which they utilize. Such diversity would have made it difficult, if not impossible, for the Committee to prepare a useful common report. We would have had to try to discover the (probably null) intersection of eight different sets of ideas or else express the report in such general language that it said nothing or everything. I preferred to try to make use of each person's special skills by asking them to explore an issue which they believed to be important.

The Committee met three times. The first meeting was organizational, and the nondirective approach was adopted. The second meeting was for the purpose of discussing the preliminary drafts of the papers. This discussion was devoted to constructive criticism, not to an attempt to get agreement. The spirit of cooperation was such that members of the Committee offered suggestions for strengthening positions which they opposed. Thus, the ideas expressed in each paper are those of the author, not the Committee. There are disagreements, including, I am sure, disagreements with these introductory remarks. This is intentional. I prefer to expose and examine disagreements rather than to conceal them with delicate phraseology.

The third meeting was devoted to a presentation and discussion of the final drafts of the papers. This final meeting was combined with Accounting Colloquium II. This allowed us to invite nonmembers to author additional papers and discussion remarks, as well as to get immediate feedback from all of the conferees.

The Accounting Colloquia series of the University of Kansas is sponsored by the Arthur Young Foundation. The Committee instructed me to express their gratitude to the Foundation. It is a pleasure to carry out those instructions and to add my personal thanks, especially to Stanley P. Porter and Robert S. Mueller.

References

1. Beaver, William H., "The Information Content of Annual Earnings Announcements," *Empirical Research in Accounting: Selected Studies, 1968,* supplement to the *Journal of Accounting Research,* University of Chicago, 1968, pp. 67–92.

2. Bernal, J. D., *Science in History, Volume I: The Emergence of Science,* The M.I.T. Press, 1971.

3. Cohen, Morris R., and Nagel, Ernest, *An Introduction to Logic and Scientific Method,* Harcourt, Brace & World, Inc., 1934.

4. Ijiri, Yuji, Jaedicke, Robert K., and Livingstone, John L., "The Effect of Inventory Costing Methods on Full and Direct Costing," *Journal of Accounting Research* (Spring, 1965), pp. 63–74.

5. Kaplan, Abraham, *The Conduct of Inquiry: Methodology for Behavioral Science,* Chandler Publishing Company, 1964.

6. Kuhn, Thomas S., *The Structure of Scientific Revolutions,* The University of Chicago Press, 1962.

7. Polanyi, Michael, *Personal Knowledge: Towards a Post-Critical Philosophy,* Harper & Row, Publishers, 1964.

8. Turing, A. M., "Solvable and Unsolvable Problems," in A. W. Haslett (ed.), *Science News,* Penguin Books, 1954, pp. 7–23.

accounting research, education and practice

by Robert R. Sterling

Any practitioner or teacher in the field of accounting would find it difficult to assert that there is a congruence between research in his field and actual education and professional practice. Can this absence of harmony be termed a conflict? I have been searching for conflicts, and this search has led me to some conclusions I want to share. In looking for instances of conflict I systematically compared research findings (i.e., articles in research journals) with education (i.e., contents of textbooks) and with practice (i.e., Accounting Principles Board pronouncements and *Accounting Trends and Techniques*). This comparison resulted in a rather lengthy list of differences.

My first inclination was to classify these differences as conflicts. Two things bothered me about this classification. First, I noticed that some of these differences had existed for over 30 years and both sides had been unwilling to compromise. How could this be? In political science we would expect such a situation to lead to open warfare. The absence of open warfare between research and education–practice caused me to hesitate in classifying the differences as conflicts.

Second, I noticed that these differences did not seem to concern my friends and colleagues. This lack of concern was vividly illustrated when, while visiting another university, I sat in on a friend's class. I heard him vigorously defend a position that was contrary to a position that he had earlier taken in the literature. When queried about this apparent conflict, he replied that he was preparing his students for practice, not research. Had it been a Ph.D.

Robert R. Sterling, *Ph.D., is currently Arthur Young Distinguished Professor of business administration at the University of Kansas in Lawrence. Among the numerous academic honors he has received is the gold medal, awarded by the AICPA, for "Most Notable Contribution to Research in Accounting During 1968." He has been involved in much committee work for the AAA, and has been a prolific contributor of books, articles and papers to the field of accounting. This article has been adapted from a speech before the Seventh Annual Meeting of the Western Region of the AAA.*

If accounting educators teach research results as the desired state of the art, and accepted practices as the current state, the resistance to reform within the accounting profession might be somewhat lessened.

seminar, he said, he would have taken the contrary position.

In searching for an explanation for this behavior, schizophrenia occurred to me. However, that seemed overly harsh, as well as not providing an explanation for the prolonged presence of uncompromised differences without open warfare. Finally another explanation occurred to me; it is drawn from the field of political science and requires an initial digression. Consider the model in Figure 1, page 46, in terms of conflict and isolation.

The solid lines indicate the transportation capabilities of three countries in the 12th century. The transportation curves of England and France indicate the capability of each country for transporting troops and supplies (or diplomats and goods for exchange) to the other. There was a potential for conflict between these two countries *for this reason.* There was also the potential for compromise and complementarity. At various times in history all three occurred: wars, diplomatic arrangements, reciprocal trade and defense agreements.

There was a complete absence of conflict between Japan and England in the 12th century. The reason was isolation, not harmony. There were vast differences in the interests and cultures of the two countries, but since the curves did not intersect, these differences did not, in fact could not, result in conflict. For the same reason there was no need, in fact no possibility, for compromise. Similarly, there was no possibility of complementary relations.

In short, contact is a necessary condition for the occurrence of conflicts, compromises or complementarities. Isolation prohibits all three relations.

In our own field, this isolation attaches to research. Figure 2, page 46, sets forth the situation as I visualize it. Just as the isolation of 12th century Japan and England precluded conflicts despite different interests and cultures, so does the isolation of accounting research and education–practice preclude conflicts despite vast differences between them. There is no relationship. They are isolated.

There are indeed a few textbooks that present research results, but usually only to dismiss them with some offhand comment about being contrary to acceptable practice. There is even less contact

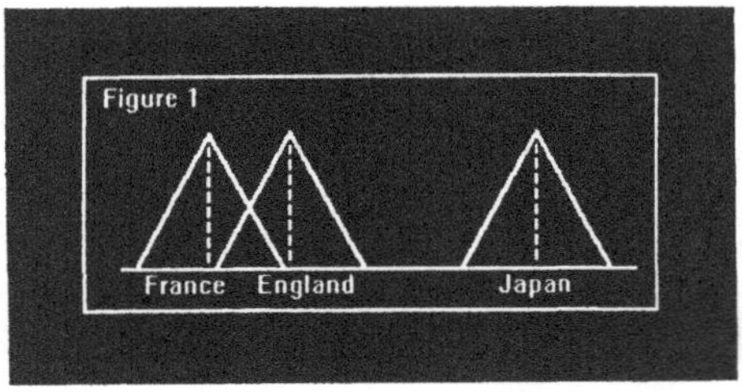

between research and practice. Consider, for example, the vast amount of research time and effort devoted to price levels. This research resulted in the APB's permitting supplementary statements adjusted for price level change, but the 1971 *Accounting Trends and Techniques* (p. 49) reports that "none of the survey companies presented financial statements adjusted to a common dollar basis."[1] In short, although I recognize the existence of some contact, it is my judgment that this contact is so nebulous that it can be disregarded.

The relation of education to practice

On the other hand, the absence of conflicts between education and practice is due to harmony, not isolation. This also explains the lack of compromises, for two subjects with harmonious interests do not need to make any.

This complementary relation is due mainly to educators' predilection to prepare students for practice; we educators teach our students acceptable practices so that they can get jobs. Practice complements education in that it provides educators with information on what are the acceptable practices and practitioners practice what educators teach them. The process is summarized in Figure 3, page 47.

Strictly interpreted, Figure 3 would prohibit change. Since changes do, in fact, occur, we know that there are exogenous inputs to the circle. The source of these inputs is practice, not education or research. That is, practitioners add to (they rarely subtract from) their store of accepted practices and then educators observe, codify and teach these additional accepted practices.

An example

The conclusions presented above can be illustrated, albeit not proved, by an example, the problem of valuing marketable securities. I selected this because (1) the APB has been considering the problem and issuing exposure drafts, (2) the problems encountered in accounting for marketable securities are more tractable than those encountered in accounting for other kinds of assets and (3) there is some clear evidence that there are nonaccounting forces at work on this problem.

Research. The research on marketable securities per se has been sparse. The index to the *Accounting Review* magazine does not contain a subject matter classification for "marketable securities" or for "investments" or for any cognate. Despite the paucity of specific articles on the subject, a number of authors have discussed marketable securities as an illustrative problem or as a subcategory of their main topic.

Going only as far back as 1939, I find that Kenneth MacNeal was concerned with the valuation problem in general but that he used marketable securities as one easily understandable example. One of the fables with which he begins his book, *Truth in Accounting*, concerns investment trusts holding marketable securities. MacNeal explains how the managements of these trusts could manipulate income by the timing of their sales. One of the trusts reported a large net income in Year 1 by selling its securities, thereby "realizing" a profit, and then it reinvested the cash in the same securities. The other trust did not sell any securities and, therefore, did not "realize" a profit. In this way the reported income of the two trusts went up and down at the discretion of the management. MacNeal showed how unscrupulous managements could bilk the shareholders by this device. He also showed that valuing marketable securities at their current market value both eliminated the possibility of such manipulations and gave investors and potential investors relevant information.

In the subsequent literature there were sporadic comments about the desirability of valuing marketable securities at current market price. However, most of the postwar literature was concerned with price levels, as opposed to price relatives, and these two issues became confused. The beginning of the

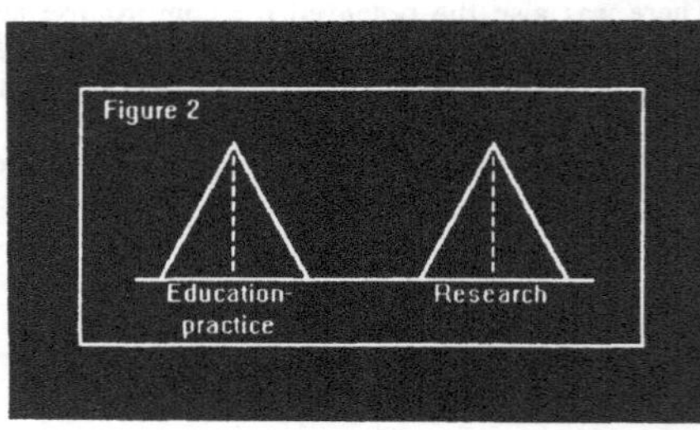

[1] Woolsey Carmalt, ed., *Accounting Trends and Techniques: Annual Survey of Accounting Practices Followed in 600 Stockholders' Reports* (New York, N.Y.: AICPA, 1971).

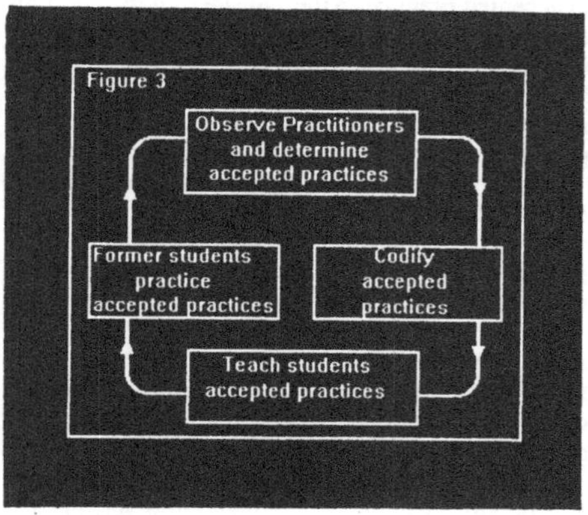

1960's saw a renewed interest in the formulation of accounting principles and in looking specifically at the valuation problem. It was then that Moonitz (Accounting Research Study No. 1) and Sprouse and Moonitz (ARS No. 3) appeared. The postulates contained in the former were criticized as being "self-evident observations" by Spacek; the general attitude seemed to be that Moonitz had simply made a collection of truisms and labeled them postulates of accounting. Utilizing these truisms as postulates or premises, Sprouse and Moonitz drew some conclusions, one of which was that marketable securities "should be measured by their current market price." In addition to the deduction, they pointed out that this practice would reveal good and bad decisions of the management in respect to holding these securities as well as eliminate the anomaly of valuing identical and interchangeable securities at different magnitudes. Shortly thereafter Sprouse's "Historical Costs of Current Assets–Traditional and Treacherous"[2] expanded upon the conclusion that he and Moonitz had reached in ARS No. 3. With admirable patience and good humor, he once again explained the absurdities that could result if marketable securities were valued at historical cost (including an actual case, à la MacNeal, in which the management had manipulated its income by timing its sales of marketable securities) and the advantages that would result if marketable securities were valued at market price.

Insofar as I know, no one has challenged Sprouse's and Moonitz's conclusion. In my opinion their logic was flawless. We noted above that their postulates were criticized for being truistic. This is a logician's Valhalla. To have unchallenged, truistic postulates and unchallengened, flawless logic is a state to which all logicians aspire but few achieve. In such a situation the conclusions are not only valid (because of the flawless logic) but they are also likely to be sound (because of the true premises).

Several other research reports have appeared, such as Edwards and Bell, and Chambers.[3] Although there have been some criticisms of the general valuation schemes of these authors, I have not seen any criticisms in regard to marketable securities in particular. I also wrote a book which used a trader in securities as a vehicle for discussion,[4] hoping that by narrowing the discussion we could reach agreement on a particular issue even if we couldn't solve the global problems of accounting. My work received some critical comments by Mattessich,[5] but he did not disagree with my conclusion: Marketable securities ought to be valued at market.

The last research report to which I will refer is contained in a recent article by Beaver. Utilizing the findings of empirical research on stock prices, he concludes as follows:

"A constant lament in accounting is that we do not have sufficient evidence upon which to base policy decisions regarding appropriate reporting rules for financial statement preparation. The area of the valuation of marketable securities is rare in the sense that extensive evidence exists, supporting the current market value rule with remarkable consistency."[6]

...different people from different schools of thought using different postulates and...research methods have[concluded that] marketable securities ought to be valued at market.

Note that this statement comes from considerations different from those of, say, Sprouse and Moonitz. Beaver utilizes concepts and evidence from finance in order to arrive at his conclusion. It is not simply a reiteration of what has gone before but comes from an entirely new direction. This being so, we should have even more confidence in the validity and soundness of that conclusion.

[2] Robert T. Sprouse, "Historical Costs of Current Assets—Traditional and Treacherous," *Accounting Review*, October 1963, pp. 687-95.

[3] E. O. Edwards and P. W. Bell, *The Theory of Measurement of Business Income* (Berkeley: U. of California Press, 1964); R. J. Chambers, *Accounting Evaluation and Economic Behavior* (Englewood Cliffs, N.J.: Prentice Hall, 1966).

[4] R. Sterling, *The Theory of the Measurement of Enterprise Income* (Lawrence: The University Press of Kansas, 1970).

[5] Richard Mattessich, "The Market Value Method According to Sterling: A Review Article," *Abacus*, Dec. 1971, pp. 176-93.

[6] William H. Beaver, "Reporting Rules for Marketable Equity Securities," JofA, Oct.71, p.61.

Practice. The 1971 edition of *Accounting Trends and Techniques* reveals that for marketable securities in the current asset section the most frequently reported valuation method is unqualified "cost." Adding the qualifications "plus accrued interest" and "amortized" runs the total of cost valuations up to 92%. The breakdown of those companies reporting their valuation method is given in Table 1, below.

Table 1

Marketable securities valuation
Current asset section

Cost	75%	
Cost plus accrued interest	14	
Amortized cost	3	
Total cost		92%
Lower of cost or market		5
Market		2
Other		1
Total reporting valuation method		100%

Source: *Accounting Trends and Techniques*, 1971, Table 2-4, p. 53.

As expected, almost all (97%) of practice is on the basis of cost and lower of cost or market. Securities were valued at market in only 2% of the cases. Identical findings are reported in Sterling, Tollefson and Flaherty.[7] A random sample of 168 CPAs revealed that only 2% of the respondents would value marketable securities at market in the absence of an exchange.

Education. Naturally, textbooks furnished the main source of my evidence in regard to education. I restricted my examination of these to the respective "intermediate theory" volume in the popular elementary-intermediate-advanced series. The reason for this restriction, as supported by publishers' representatives and my personal observations, is that the intermediate theory volume is the only book containing theory that is widely used in undergraduate curriculums. Since over 95% of accounting students do not go past the baccalaureate degree, these intermediate texts are the sole source of theory education in perhaps 90% of the cases. (This figure is a guess. I tried to get a better estimate by asking various publishers' representatives to state their share of the market as a percentage. Unfortunately, the various individual estimates summed to 183%. On this basis I should conclude that 183% of our students use these intermediate texts.)

In regard to marketable securities held as temporary investments, the typical intermediate text presents the valuation of marketable securities as a question and then answers that question by referring to accepted practice. After considering the question of the "informative quality" of different valuation methods, Finney and Miller conclude: ". . . because such an alternative [market value] method could result in writing up an asset above cost, it is not generally accepted."[8] Another popular text says, "Whether realization should be limited to the period of sale when applied to marketable securities is a question worth considering" and after a half a page of consideration it concludes: "The question which must be answered is, 'What event in the life of the enterprise gives rise to the recognition of gains and losses from holding securities in lieu of cash?' Practicing accountants have generally applied the lower of cost or market rule to the valuation of marketable securities."[9]

A text published last year listed market valuation as a possible accounting method. However, the authors' reason for the listing was that "The APB is drafting an Opinion that would require fair value accounting for marketable securities."[10] In other words, the basis of this listing is the *authors' prediction of future accepted practice*, not research results. It has turned out, as we shall see later, that their prediction was wrong.

My secondary source of information was our former students. In the previous section, I stated that *Accounting Trends and Techniques* reported how our former students value marketable securities in practice. In addition, in connection with another activity, I recently asked 246 seniors in public practice to indicate the valuation method for marketable securities held as temporary investments

...intermediate texts raise the question of valuing marketable securities but... do not present the results of the research [which are thus] contradicted in education and practice.

that is (a) in accordance with GAAP and (b) theoretically correct. Of the usable 239 responses, 229 (96%) checked "cost" or "lower of cost or market" as the answer to (a) and 220 (92%) checked the

[7] Robert R. Sterling, John O. Tollefson and Richard E. Flaherty, "Exchange Valuation: An Empirical Test," *Accounting Review*, October 1972, pp. 709-21.

[8] H. A. Finney and Herbert E. Miller, *Principles of Accounting Intermediate*, 6th ed., Prentice-Hall Accounting Series (Englewood Cliffs, N.J.: Prentice-Hall, Inc., 1965), p. 256.

[9] Walter B. Meigs, Charles E. Johnson and Thomas F. Keller, *Intermediate Accounting* (New York, N.Y.: McGraw-Hill Book Co., 1963), pp. 221-22.

[10] Glenn A. Welsch, Charles T. Zlatkovich and John A. White, *Intermediate Accounting*, 3rd ed., Williard J. Graham Series in Accounting (Homewood, Ill.: Richard D. Irwin, Inc., 1972), p. 240.

same answers to (b). Ten (4%) checked "net realizable value" or "market value" as the answer to (a), and 19 (8%) checked the same answers to (b).

In another test Sterling, Tollefson and Flaherty found that 82% of a random sample of CPAs agreed with the cost method of valuing marketable securities even though the market value was 3750% of the cost.

Conclusions from the example

In research different people from different schools of thought using different postulates and different research methods have drawn the same conclusion: Marketable securities ought to be valued at market. That conclusion has not been challenged in the research literature.

In practice the predominant method of valuation is cost, with lower of cost or market a distant second. Combined, the two valuation methods amount to about 97% of practice.

In education the intermediate texts raise the question of valuing marketable securities, but they "answer" this question by stating the accepted practice. These texts do not present the results of the research that has been done in this area. Over 80% of our former students believe that the present accepted practice is the theoretically correct method. Students tend to identify theoretically correct with accepted practice. I would conjecture that the manner of presentation in the texts (and in the lectures) is the reason for this identification.

Thus, the research results regarding marketable securities are contradicted in education and practice. Education and practice seem to be complementary in that educators teach accepted practice and practitioners accept and practice what they are taught. This complementary relationship excludes research from the chain of events that determine what is taught and what is practiced. Research is an isolated activity in accounting, as in Figure 2.

Normative relationships

Turning from the *is* to the *ought*, I now consider the prescribing of relationships, the normative function of research in the educational process.

In the first half of the 19th century research as an organized activity was an unknown and alien notion. At that time universities concentrated on the teaching function, under the assumption that there was nothing new to discover. It was thought that the function of a university was to pass along the received dogma. In the second half of the 19th century British universities began to think of research as an activity complementary to teaching. Along about 1875 the relationship of the three activities became

1 R(x)→ E(x)→ P(x)—that is, if researchers found that x is the case, then students were taught that x is the case and then, upon graduation, students implemented x in practice.

The chain in (1) is now common to almost all disciplines. In medicine, for example, researchers discovered that phenoxymethylpenicillin has a powerful bacteriostatic effect against pneumococci and certain other malevolent bacteria. Subsequent to this discovery they educated their students in terms of this discovery.

They also educated their former students to this effect by publishing less technical articles in practitioners' magazines and inserting entries in the *Physician's Handbook* and *Physician's Desk Reference* that say, in effect, "If your patient has pneumonia, give him a shot of penicillin." The reader is invited to examine the various accounting and auditing handbooks and compare their pronouncements on marketable securities to the research results presented earlier.

> Except for some theologies, I don't know of any other disciplin that perceives its duty to be the passing along of accepted practices.

By contrast, the chain in accounting is

2 P(x)→E(x)→P(x)—that is, if x is practiced, then students are taught that x is practiced and then, upon graduation, students implement x in practice. Note what would have happened in medicine had this procedure been followed. A survey of practicing physicians would have revealed that the accepted practice for treating pneumonia was the administration of sulfa drugs. Then medical professors would have taught their students to administer sulfa drugs in pneumonia cases. Upon graduation, their students would have implemented that treatment in practice. Then the teachers would have surveyed their former students and repeated the process. As is immediately apparent, the problem with (2) is that it prohibits progress. Had medical teachers adopted this procedure in the 18th century, they would still be teaching their students how to let blood between haircuts.

The solution is also immediately apparent: adopt chain (1), i.e., teach research results. I know that that is a revolutionary idea in accounting and that we accountants tend to be conservative. However, since that idea was adopted by all other disciplines in 1875, perhaps it is safe for us to adopt it in 1975. Except for some theologies, I don't know of any other discipline that perceives its duty to be the passing along of accepted practices. Many accountants have complained about the lack of respect accorded our discipline. You will recall that Hatfield complains about the "contempt of our colleagues."[11] Some, including Hatfield, have offered a defense of accounting. Perhaps it would be more productive to change accounting than to complain about the lack of respect. Perhaps if we changed we wouldn't need to defend our discipline.

The objection to teaching research results is that students need jobs, and, in order to get jobs, they need to know accepted practices, not research results. This is true, but to teach accepted practices to the exclusion of research results creates more problems than it solves. Perhaps we can teach both. In my undergraduate theory class I try to teach both by distinguishing between theory and GAAP. The theory part is taught like other theory courses in economics, management science, etc. The GAAP part is taught like a law or tax course. In regard to marketable securities, for example, a typical problem assignment would require (1) valuation in accordance with research results and (2) valuation in accordance with GAAP. For the GAAP part of the assignment the students are required to cite "substantial authoritative support" for the method that they use. Thus, in the same way that the students must find and follow the tax laws and precedents in order to determine taxable income, they must find and follow the APB laws and precedents in order to determine GAAP income. As far as I am concerned, the analogy is perfect. The fact that it is the law doesn't necessarily mean that it is right. It simply means that it is the law and one must know what the law is in order to obey it.

I believe the careful drawing of this distinction is vital to the progress of accounting. We educators have not been making this distinction clear in the past. The result is a rather subtle but particularly nefarious effect on our students.

If we teach research results, there will be a complimentary relationship between research and education. If this course is adopted, conflict is inevitable, but it is preferable to isolation.

The typical text collects accepted practices and tries to rationalize them by fitting them into a theory. Since the practices are inconsistent, the texts necessarily contain contradictions. For example, they characterize market values as indeterminable and too subjective to be used in one place, and in another they present the lower of cost or market rule which requires that market values be determined and used. Our students learn these contradictions: worse, it appears that they learn to reason by contradiction. Consider the following bit of evidence.

The questionnaire mentioned earlier (administered to the 246 seniors) included the following questions:

"1 Application of the current market price method of valuing inventories can best be described as (check one word on each line)

__feasible __infeasible
and
__objective __subjective

"2 Application of the lower of cost or market rule to inventories when market is below cost can best be described as (check one word on each line.)

__feasible __infeasible
and
__objective __subjective"

(The two questions were separated by a number of other questions on the questionnaire.) The results were: 3% checked "feasible" and 6% checked "objective" in answer to question 1. In answer to question 2, 99% checked "feasible" and 62% checked "objective."

I was startled and dismayed by these results: some variation in the answers to the two questions was to be expected, but certainly not a difference of 96% and 52%. Although I don't have a control group, I don't believe that a group of nonaccountants would contradict themselves to this extent. I think we have to *teach* our students to make such contradictions. I also think that such teaching is dysfunctional.

If we teach research results, there will be a complementary relationship between research and education. If this course is adopted, conflict is inevitable, but it is preferable to isolation. I opt for conflict for two reasons.

First, I have faith in research. It provides the best chance for us to solve our problems. Admittedly, it does not provide us with a guarantee that the problems will be solved. Recently many accountants, particularly practitioners, have become disenchanted with it. They point out that research has failed to find the answer in many instances. I agree that research often fails us and I, too, sometimes become discouraged. But what is the alternative?

In medicine, research has failed to provide a cure for cancer despite the expenditure of more than a billion dollars. This is discouraging. However, the only two recognized alternatives in medicine are to (1) give up or (2) continue the research. In accounting, research has also failed to find the answer to our problems. But then we have spent practically no money on it: The whole American Accounting Association research budget is less than that for

[11] Henry Rand Hatfield, "An Historical Defense of Bookkeeping," *Significant Accounting Essays*, Maurice Moonitz and A. C. Littleton, ed. (Englewood Cliffs, N.J.: Prentice-Hall, Inc., 1965), p. 4.

undergraduate research in a single science department at a typical university. As in medicine, we can either (1) give up on the problem or (2) continue to do research.

If we choose to continue research, then we must connect it to education and practice. To find the solution to a problem and then fail to teach it or practice it is to fail to solve the problem. Certainly, we would not consider cancer to be cured if a cure was found that was never taught or practiced. A problem is "solved" only after the solution is implemented. This requires that research be in contact with education and practice. If the outcome is conflict, then sobeit.

In short, the APB wanted to issue an Opinion that was in accord with the research results...Management resisted. The Board...finally capitulated.

Second, the conflicts that come out of this contact may be beneficial. Political scientists, particularly those influenced by Hegel, argue that one should expose conflicts or, if there is an embryonic conflict, then one should "exacerbate the cleavage," so that a new and better theory can spring from the conflicting theories. The crisis theory of democracy, with the conflicts that attend crisis, is a similar idea.

Consider another medical analogy. A physician at an accident scene without sterile instruments may be faced with an accident victim in need of a tracheotomy. Medical theory specifies (1) a tracheotomy and (2) sterile techniques. The exigencies of practice force the physician to make a choice. Hence, a conflict arises. The physician recognizes the conflict because he has been taught that he *ought* to use sterile instruments. As a direct result of this kind of conflict, researchers have developed packaging techniques that permit sterile instruments to be portable. In this way practice and research reinforce one another. New research was initiated because of conflicts between the necessary and the possible, and progress was the result.

Contrast an accountant on the job. The exigencies of practice (for example, current generally accepted accounting principles) may require that he account for marketable securities at cost. If he has been taught only accepted practices, and especially if he identifies accepted practices with theoretically correct practices, then he will not recognize a conflict. In the absence of such conflicts research and practice will not reinforce one another and no progress will be made. Therefore, I opt for conflict. Students should be taught what ought to be done even when it conflicts with accepted practice, nay, *especially* when it conflicts with accepted practice.

The relation of management to accounting practice

The influence of management upon accounting practices is too important to be neglected in this discussion. We noted above that practitioners add to their store of practices but that they rarely subtract from that store. If we inquire into the reasons for this, we will find that managements desire additional practices and that managements have the power to get what they want.

Moonitz,[12] in an important but unfortunately neglected article, has compared problems encountered in the establishment of auditing standards to those encountered in the establishment of accounting principles. He finds one major difference: managements. It seems that managements are vitally interested in accounting principles. They would like to have a set of alternative practices from which to select. Further, they have sufficient power to implement their desires,[13] and they are the source of the exogenous inputs to the circle shown in Figure 3.

3 $M(x) \rightarrow P(x) \rightarrow E(x)$—that is, if managements desire x to be an accepted practice, then x will become an accepted practice and educators will teach that x is an accepted practice.

Chain (3) is illustrated by the recent history of the proposed marketable securities Opinion. The Accounting Principles Board issued a draft of an Opinion dated September 1, 1971, which required the valuation of marketable securities at market and the inclusion of the value differences in income. Managements disagreed.[14]

A somewhat weakened draft of the Opinion was issued January 10, 1972. Managements disagreed with that draft also. In fact, "somebody" started a mail campaign to Congress and the SEC. A review of all the possibilities was issued on March 29, 1972, which said, "The Board has not, however, reached a conclusion on the most appropriate recommendation." A recent report from the APB stated that they were going to "start all over" on the question of marketable securities. It now appears that no Opinion will be issued.

In short, the APB wanted to issue an Opinion that was in accord with the research results presented above. Managements resisted. The Board did not have the power to overcome managements' resistance and so it backed off and finally capitulated.

---

12 Maurice Moonitz, "Why Is It So Difficult to Agree Upon a Set of Accounting Principles?" *The Australian Accountant*, November 1968, pp. 621-31.

13 See Robert R. Sterling, "Accounting Power," JofA, Jan.73, pp. 61-67.

14 For an example of this disagreement, see "APB Committee Considers Views on Equity Security Reporting," JofA, July71, p. 10.

There are two things to note about this case. First, if you think that managements' defense of historical cost is based on the belief that it more fairly or accurately presents, you have a livelier imagination than I. It seems to me to be quite clear that managements desire "flexibility." In this case they want enough flexibility to be able to realize and report the amount of income that suits their purposes. Thus some, if not most, accepted practices spring from managements' desire to serve their own ends. For this reason, some accepted practices are bad practices. I would hope that you would agree that it is not the duty of educators to codify and teach bad practices.

Of course, the long-run solution is to give the APB (or the Financial Accounting Standards Board) the power to resist managements' self-serving wishes and to implement research results. The ability of the APB to institute reforms against managements' wishes would have been enhanced if there were agreement among public accountants.

The second thing to note about this case is this very lack of agreement. In addition to managements' resistance, the APB was faced with the resistance of a large number of public accountants. Evidence for this resistance is that the APB felt it necessary to include in their drafts those tired, invalid arguments for historical cost that were demolished by MacNeal in 1939 and by many other scholars since then. The problem is that many of our former students believe in those tired, invalid arguments and, therefore, they joined managements in resisting the APB's Opinion. Had there been solidarity among accountants, we would have had a better chance of issuing the Opinion. Had educators taught research results instead of accepted practices, perhaps we would have had more agreement among accountants and, hence, more solidarity.

Summary

My argument is:

1 Research is isolated from education-practice.

2 Education and practice are complementary in that educators teach accepted practices and practitioners practice what they are taught.

3 Accepted practices are inconsistent and, therefore, the "theory" of accepted practice is contradictory.

4 Students taught the "theory" of accepted practices tend to identify "theoretically correct" with "accepted in practice." Students taught a contradictory theory tend to reason by contradiction. Students taught only accepted practices tend to resist attempts to reform practices by the APB.

5 Managements tend to resist accounting reforms that threaten to inhibit their own flexibility.

6 The resistance by management and by former students (practitioners) has been a major cause of our inability to reform practice.

My suggestion is that educators teach research results as *the desired state* and teach accepted practices as *the current state*. Adoption of this suggestion ought to lessen the resistance to reform within the profession and lessen the tendency to reason by contradiction. It may even endow accounting with sufficient prestige so that we will no longer need to apologize or defend its methods. Obviously, adoption of the suggestion won't solve the problem of managements' resistance to reform practices, but it ought to allow us to present a more solid front and, therefore, to enhance our chances of instituting reforms. ■

Discussion of
Capital Market Equilibrium, Information Production, and Selecting Accounting Techniques: Theoretical Framework and Review of Empirical Work

ROBERT R. STERLING* and WILLIAM HARRISON†

Introduction

The Gonedes-Dopuch (henceforth G-D) paper represents a significant milestone in the efficient market research effort. It is an attempt to provide a theoretical framework for efficient market research. Utilizing this framework, it also critiques the previous efficient market research (with a section devoted to nonprice research) and evaluates the previous interpretations of the findings of that research. The evaluation will be particularly welcomed by nonefficient market researchers because G-D have begun to seriously question the validity of the previous interpretations. Since only mature research areas engage in self-criticism, this paper is an indication that the efficient market research area has come of age.

Before discussing section 9—our primary responsibility—we will present some background comments and an overview of the paper.

Background

A PRIORI RESEARCH

G-D begin with a historical perspective which includes a statement to the effect that previous a priori research efforts have not permitted us to draw univocal conclusions regarding the desirability of various accounting procedures. Obviously they are right in this observation. We could not adjudicate the disputes regarding alternative procedures within the historical cost system (e.g., LIFO vs. FIFO), let alone adjudicate the disputes

* Rice University; † Oregon State University

regarding alternative valuation systems. Apparently it was this failure of a priori research that caused efficient market researchers in general and members of the Chicago school in particular to disdain a priori research.

G-D state two things as being wrong with a priori research: (1) theoretical [logical] deficiencies and (2) the possibility of drawing different [valid] conclusions from different a priori models. Since G-D are correctly, albeit too briefly, making an important point about a priori research we will expand upon what we think they mean.

There are two kinds of scientific tests: logical and empirical. A theory consists of a set of concepts logically connected by certain inference rules. If intended to be an empirical theory, as opposed to a nonempirical theory such as pure mathematics or logic, some of these concepts must be operationally defined as observation terms. The purpose of an empirical theory is to permit one to make observations and then to conceptually move, via the logically connected concepts, to the anticipation of some unobserved phenomena. An empirical test is a comparison of the anticipations to observations. Thus, it is possible to (1) logically test the connections of the concepts and (2) empirically test the congruence of the anticipated phenomena to the subsequently observed phenomena. This is, in very abbreviated form, the essence of logical-empiricism, which is the basis of modern philosophy of science.[1]

Theoretical deficiencies. From this brief summary we can note that there are several possible logical deficiencies in any theory:

(1) Ambiguity. The theory is not sufficiently precise to permit logical testing of the connections of the concepts.
(2) Contradiction. The concepts are inherently contradictory. This condition permits any conclusion to be drawn, including contradictory conclusions.
(3) Incompletion. Concepts necessary to draw the kind of conclusions desired are missing or are suppressed (enthymemes).
(4) Invalidities. Conclusions drawn from the theory are demonstrably invalid.

If these are what G-D mean by theoretical deficiencies then we fully agree that the historical cost a priori model contained all of these deficiencies.[2]

Although we agree with G-D in regard to the historical cost model, we do not understand why they tar the a priori works of Chambers and Edwards and Bell with the same brush. We are not aware of a demonstration that these particular works have been found to be theoretically defi-

[1] See, e.g., Pap for a general discussion and Sterling, "Theory Construction," for an application to accounting.

[2] For an attempt to demonstrate that all of these deficiencies are found in the historical cost system see Sterling, *Theory of the Measurement of Enterprise Income,* Chapter XI. For a detailed analysis of particular concepts see, e.g., Sterling and Flaherty, as well as Sterling, "Going Concern" and "Conservatism."

cient in the sense described above. We must assume, therefore, that the existence of these theoretical deficiencies is a discovery of G-D. Unfortunately, we cannot corroborate that discovery since they do not exhibit any support for their assertion. Instead of simply asserting the existence of theoretical deficiencies in these works, it is incumbent upon G-D to demonstrate those deficiencies or to provide citations of such demonstrations.[3]

Different conclusions from different models. G-D's second point about a priori research is well taken, although it is not clear that they recognize its universal applicability. The problem is that one's conclusion depends upon one's axiom system. Since there are alternative axiom systems, there are alternative valid conclusions. This means that validity can be used as the sole criterion for judging conclusions only if everyone accepts a particular axiom system. This expands the problem to the selection of a particular axiom system from the set of alternative axiom systems. But the selection of a particular axiom system is a conclusion to be drawn from a meta-axiom system. Since there are alternative meta-axiom systems, there are alternative valid conclusions regarding which particular axiom system should be selected. This expands the problem of a priori research to the selection of a meta-axiom system—which selection requires the use of a higher order axiom system and, since there are alternative higher order systems, it requires a still higher order axiom system. And so forth to an infinite regress.

In regard to accounting, this means that since they employ different axiom systems, Chambers may draw a valid conclusion (current cash equivalents) which is different from the valid conclusion (current costs) drawn by Edwards and Bell. Thus, one cannot choose between current cash equivalents and current costs on the basis of validity. Instead, the problem is expanded to a selection of one of the axiom systems which, in the absence of the community of accounting researchers' accepting one of the systems, leads to the infinite regress mentioned above.

This is a serious shortcoming of a priori research and if this is what G-D mean then they are to be commended for reminding us of it. We would like to return the favor by reminding them that this shortcoming also applies to their paper. The specifics of this application will be presented below.

EMPIRICAL RESEARCH AND ITS INTERPRETATION

G-D state: "Such criticism [of a priori research] *led to* an increased emphasis on the use of empirical analyses . . ." (p. 50; italics supplied). Even though this may be true, it is an empirical generalization about the motiva-

[3] Incidentally, I was happy to note that they did not include *Theory of the Measurement of Enterprise Income* in their list of theoretically deficient a priori works. I assume its omission means that they think it does not contain theoretical deficiencies. Of course, I realize that there are other implications that could be drawn from the omission but I prefer to interpret it as an implicit compliment. On the basis of that assumption, I congratulate G-D for their perspicacity and thank them for the compliment. RRS

tions of accounting researchers without any cited empirical evidence in support of that generalization. The reason for making this point is that it often happens in the reverse order. In science the appearance of a significant piece of a priori research often causes a flurry of empirical research. A case for similar ordering could be made in regard to empirical research in accounting. For example, the empirical research by Corbin was undoubtedly prompted by previous a priori research on price levels; the empirical work by McDonald and McKeown was undoubtedly prompted by the previous a priori research on alternative valuation systems, etc. Thus, it is not at all clear that the general impetus for empirical research in accounting was a dissatisfaction with a priori research. Instead, the empirical research may have been prompted by previous a priori research.

G-D are probably projecting their own motivation to the entire population of empirical researchers. That is, the emphasis on empirical research in the efficient market vein probably was motivated by a disdain for a priori research. However, other empirical researchers seem to have been motivated by the appearance of a priori research. The point is that in this context G-D seem to think of a priori and empirical research as being mutually exclusive and therefore in order for empirical research to be performed one must reject or be dissatisfied with a priori research. The reason for stressing the reverse order is to point out that it is possible for the two to be complementary. Moreover, it is mutually beneficial for a priori and empirical researchers to view their respective efforts as complementary activities.[4]

Regardless of the reason, it is true that empirical research in accounting has expanded greatly in the last decade. The G-D paper mentions the establishment of the Empirical Research Conferences at Chicago and correctly imply their contribution to this expansion. Accounting theorists, particularly logical-empiricists, eagerly looked forward to receiving the empirical findings resulting from this expanded effort. Soon, however, many theorists began to have serious reservations about efficient market research.

The first reservation was occasioned by efficient market researchers' restricting the empirical domain of accounting to observations of the actions of the aggregated capital market. For example, observations of the behavior of individuals were excluded because they were not thought to be relevant to market efficiency. In addition to a disdain for a priori research, efficient market researchers came to have a disdain for empirical research that did not bear directly on the capital market. As we shall see in our review of section 9, some remnants of this disdain still exist. In our view, this was (and is) a much too narrow definition of accounting's empirical domain.

The second reservation was caused by the exaggerated claims of the efficacy of efficient market research and the interpretations of the findings.

[4] See Sterling, "Introduction," for additional comments.

The view from Chicago seemed to be that efficient market research would solve all of our problems; it would provide a method of adjudicating disputes regarding alternative procedures within the historical cost system as well as disputes about alternative valuation systems. Given that view as a premise, it is easy to see how one might conclude that all other (a priori and nonprice empirical) kinds of research were not worth doing and, if they were done, not worth serious consideration. Instead, the thing to do was to closely examine a stock market price tape, for that was where all the answers were to be found.[5]

In terms of the G-D paper, it is claimed that one can assess "the *desirability* of alternative accounting procedures" by observing the actions of the market.[6] This is a puzzling claim. In its most general form, the problem is one of getting "ought" from "is." How can one conclude that the market ought to react to an accounting number from an observation that the market does react? It may be that capital market agents react to accounting numbers simply because they observe that other agents react and they know that the market price depends upon the combined reactions of the agents. Thus, it is not irrational for capital market agents to react to an accounting number because the price may in fact depend on that number. However, the fact that they do react does not imply anything at all about whether accountants ought to report that particular number. To put it another way, how can one conclude that an accounting number is useful from an observation that it is used? It can be observed that heroin is used but this does not permit one to validly conclude that it is useful.[7]

This is not to deny the significance of efficient market research. That

[5] On the basis of these early claims, it seemed that the price tapes would not only provide all of the accounting answers, but that they would also provide a conclusive ontological argument for the existence of God and, when taken internally, would revitalize tired blood, remove warts, and cure hemorrhoids.

[6] Gonedes [1972] and Dopuch [1971] provided two examples of this claim.

> . . . observations of the *market reactions of recipients* of accounting output should govern evaluations of the actual information content of accounting numbers produced via a given set of procedures and the informational content of accounting numbers produced via an alternative set of accounting procedures (Gonedes, p. 12; italics supplied).

Dopuch (pp. 33–34) summarized the claim by arguing that the "utility of present accounting information" can be validly deduced from the observation of the market because "the existence of various sources of information provides the market with a means by which it can verify or refute the validity of accounting numbers." He says he does not believe that users will continue to react to accounting numbers if these numbers result in dysfunctional decisions. This allows him to conclude that "if accounting information bears a correlation to market price behavior then this is consistent with the notion that accounting information also reflects real world phenomena." Although Dopuch doesn't state Gonedes' conclusion directly, it would seem to readily follow that if user reaction is an indicant of real world phenomena then user reaction could be used to assess the ability of alternative accounting procedures to reflect real world phenomena.

[7] See Sterling, "Decision Oriented," for additional comments on the distinction between used and useful.

capital market agents react to or use accounting numbers is an important finding. However, the fact that they react should be taken as data by accounting theorists, not as a justification for a particular procedure or valuation method. Instead, it is up to the theorists to decide whether or not the observed reactions are pathological. Consider the following analogy. One can go to a Las Vegas crap table and observe that many people think the odds on making a pass change when several sequential passes have been made. People react (make bets) on the basis of information about the number of passes made. They use the information. However, instead of statisticians' taking the observation of these reactions as a justification for reporting the number of passes, they refer to it as the "gambler's fallacy" and judge the reaction to be pathological. They do not conclude that the information is useful from the observation that it is used. As has been previously suggested,[8] accounting theorists ought to make similar judgments about the reactions of capital market agents.

Another puzzling aspect of efficient market interpretations is the oft-repeated assertion that the market cannot be "fooled" by accounting reports.[9] First, if this is true then the financial accounting function is in jeopardy. Instead of relying on the competing sources of information to verify or refute the validity of accounting numbers, why not rely on them for the initial data? Second, if the market cannot be fooled, then what happened in, e.g., the McKesson-Robbins, the Penn Central, and the Equity Funding cases? It seems clear that the market was fooled in those cases in the fundamental sense that the market was led to believe that assets and revenues existed when they did not in fact exist. The accounting numbers did not reflect real world phenomena. An empirical finding that the market unbiasedly and instantaneously impounded the false information in those reports does not provide a justification for the reporting of that false information. It seems too obvious to require explicit statement that one ought not to report false figures regardless of whether or not capital market agents react to or adjust or do not react to or do not adjust those figures. If one grants this then it is but a small logical step to also grant that one ought not to report arbitrarily allocated sunk costs regardless of whether or not capital market agents react to or adjust those figures. In short, efficient market research findings are not directly pertinent to such questions as whether or not one ought to report false figures or ought to report arbitrarily allocated sunk costs. Finally, even if the aggregated market is not fooled, it may be that some individuals are fooled (and the nonprice studies indicate that some are in fact fooled).[10] It doesn't follow from

[8] See Sterling, "Theory Construction," for the suggestion and an expanded discussion.

[9] See, e.g., Dopuch, p. 34.

[10] Since it is often asserted that the nonprice studies are not pertinent evidence because they are not based on actual economic decisions by actual capital market agents, we will present additional empirical evidence for our belief that some individuals are fooled. We have observed one capital market agent (who is alleged to be more knowledgeable

any logic that we know of that one can justify fooling some individuals by observing that the aggregated market is not fooled.

Additional criticisms of the interpretations being drawn from the efficient market research findings have been made in other places. There is little comfort in being told that there are competing sources of information so that regardless of what accountants report these other sources of information will correct the errors. We are interested in the usefulness of accounting numbers, not in the ability to correct those numbers by using competitive sources of information. The fact that someone else may tell you the truth does not give us license to tell you a lie. The fact that competitive sources of information allow capital market agents to correct misleading accounting numbers does not give accountants license to report those misleading numbers. The finding that the market can use these competing sources of information to adjust for different accounting procedures used by different firms does not imply anything at all about whether or not we ought to allow those different procedures to be used. The finding that the market is a "fair game," in the sense that no one can specify a trading policy that permits an abnormal rate of return, does not imply anything at all about what one ought to report. As an information supplier to participants in a yacht race one could report the latitude and longitude of their present location by consulting a table of random numbers. The fact that this would still be a fair game—not allowing anyone an advantage over anyone else—would not provide justification for using the table of random numbers.

The above comments about the interpretations of efficient market research findings should not be taken as a denigration of the efficient market research effort. On the contrary, we believe that efficient market research is a worthwhile activity. However, we also believe that the early claims for the efficacy of such research were grossly exaggerated and that many of the interpretations contained egregious errors.

Overview

G-D'S AXIOM SYSTEM

Given the fact that G-D cite the failures and shortcomings of a priori research, it is surprising to find their paper to be a pure a priori exercise. No data are to be found in their paper. Instead, they attempt to "assess the logical validity of assertions" (p. 114). The fact that they are here engaging in a priori research makes it difficult to interpret their general

than the average investor or financial analyst in matters of accounting) make one actual economic decision on the basis of some actual accounting numbers without realizing that those accounting numbers did not accurately reflect real world phenomena. Personal interviews with this capital market agent reveal that he was in fact fooled by the accounting numbers. On September 7, 1971, Sterling bought 400 shares of Boise Cascade at 27¾ after having read the annual report. The underlying data for this study will be supplied on request.

criticism of a priori research. We suspect the appropriate interpretation is that they did not intend to criticize a priori research in general but rather to criticize particular pieces of previous a priori research. If so then they should make the point explicit instead of making disparaging remarks about a priori research in general. Such disparaging remarks undoubtedly have contributed to the view held by an increasing number of accounting researchers that "a priori" is a dirty word. We believe that G-D understand that both a priori and empirical research are needed and we take the existence of this paper as evidence of their high regard for a priori research. The fact that a priori is being used pejoratively in accounting makes it particularly important for influential researchers, such as G-D, to clearly state their view on this matter so that we avoid future misinterpretations and, hopefully, contribute to the resolution of the current internal strife regarding research methods.[11]

Since the G-D paper is a priori research, their conclusions depend upon their chosen axiom system. Unless other researchers agree to accept their axiom system we will remain in the position of having alternative valid conclusions and no way to choose between them. This is a distinct possibility since G-D's selected axiom system is rather restricted, as will be shown in the outline of their system that follows.

The axiom system provided by G-D clearly allows one to conclude, in the tradition of Blackwell and Marschak, that more information is better than less information up to the point of information processing overload. The expectation of utility maximization on the part of investors is a nondecreasing function as long as the investor is supplied with more information. More information in this particular case is defined as a completely reliable signal from nature which restricts the true or underlying distribution to increasingly refined partitions.

We certainly agree that more information as defined will lead to the claimed results for expected utility maximization on the part of the investor. However, the definition of refinement includes the restriction that the partitions of the $k + 1^{st}$ partitioning are contained in the partitions of the kth partitioning. The results claimed for expected utility maximization depend upon this definition. Partitionings for which this condition does not hold are not comparable in general, and we cannot make claims about expected utility maximization when comparing two partitionings where the refinement condition is not met.

For example, let us assume that our current information is that the true distribution (F^*) is a member of some set $F = \{F_1, F_2, \ldots F^*, \ldots, F_{n-1}, F_n\}$. We will be at least as well off with respect to expected utility maximization if we costlessly acquire a completely reliable signal which identifies any proper subset of F as containing F^*. That is, any subset

[11] See Sterling, "Introduction" (p. 5), for further discussion of the current internal strife in accounting.

containing F^* is a partition which meets the refinement criterion, and we are at least as well off with the finer partition as we were with the information that F^* is contained in the original set F (again with respect to expected utility maximization). But we can continue to make this claim only for subsets which are contained in subsets of a previous partition. We cannot compare the subset $\{F_2, F_6, F^*, F_{27}\}$ with the subset $\{F_8, F_{10}, F^*, F_{19}\}$ or even with $\{F_2, F_6, F^*, F_{28}\}$ unless we know the distributions themselves.

Therefore, if we are to use the axiom system provided by G-D then we must restrict our investigations to accounting techniques which satisfy the refinement criterion. Unless the information disclosed in accounting alternative A is contained in or can be transformed to the information disclosed in accounting alternative B (or vice versa) then we can say nothing under this theoretical framework about investor expected utility maximization without placing very restrictive assumptions on investor utility functions. It is not at all clear that contemporary arguments about the superiority of alternative accounting techniques are concerned with the refinement of partitions. Thus, it is not clear that the G-D axiom system will contribute to the resolution of our disputes. That is, it may suffer the same fate as the previous a priori research efforts.

This is not to say that the axiom system is useless. On the contrary, the lab/field studies seem to us to be interpretable in this framework and to provide empirical support for it. Dyckman in his study of conventional versus price-level adjusted statements gave his subjects insufficient information to do the transformation from one to the other. The result was that the functional fixation hypothesis was confirmed. The (admittedly very limited) market was fooled. On the other hand, Barrett and McIntyre gave their subjects sufficient information to do the transformation and the functional fixation hypothesis was not supported. Both sets of results seem consistent with the partitioning argument presented above.

The results claimed for more information in the sense of increasingly refined partitions say that if we can restrict the possible attribute distributions to increasingly smaller subsets then we can achieve a state at least as good as the prior state. The results seem to say nothing about whether conventional statements or price-level adjusted statements allow us to achieve the finer partition except that if we costlessly have both statements we can be assured of being at least as well off as with either statement alone.

G-D'S CONCLUSIONS

G-D address two important questions:

(1) Does efficient market research permit an assessment of the desirability of alternative accounting procedures?

(2) Does efficient market research permit an assessment of the effects of alternative accounting procedures?

After a very lengthy, careful piece of a priori research they present their two main conclusions:

(1) No.
(2) Yes.

We fully agree with conclusion (1). We would have agreed without the research in the G-D paper. Indeed, we previously reached the same conclusion by a different route.[12] We welcome G-D's corroboration of that conclusion.

We are less confident about conclusion (2). Although we cannot fault G-D's logic and therefore we agree that conclusion (2) is valid (follows from the axioms), we have some reservations about the ability to empirically test accounting effects. There may be more separation problems than are presently recognized. Since there are competing sources of information, since there are market-wide factors which must be controlled for, since risk adjustments are required, etc., it would be very difficult and maybe impossible to precisely separate the accounting effects. However, efficient market researchers have shown great ingenuity in refining their techniques. Therefore, it may be that such separation problems can be solved and that our reservations will prove to be unfounded.

The above are the two main conclusions drawn by G-D. They also draw some implications from those conclusions. First, on the basis of conclusion (1) they state that "we should neither expect nor want such bodies [e.g., APB and SEC] to rely exclusively on the kinds of evidence reviewed in this paper" (p. 115). We agree. If regulatory bodies are trying to decide on the desirability of alternative accounting procedures and if efficient market research will not allow one to assess the desirability of those procedures then the regulatory bodies should not rely on that research. A second implication is that if a given accounting procedure produces a number which can be costlessly transformed to another procedure then we should not debate which procedure to use. We agree, but we do not understand why it took all of that careful reasoning to reach that obvious implication. G-D state a third implication to the effect that if a firm can produce two sets of numbers with insignificant incremental costs then it should do so. That seems somewhat less than controversial.

G-D then move to some observations about the political nature of establishing accounting principles. Although this is an important topic and although their observations are interesting, their discussion does not seem to be closely connected to the rest of their paper.

In summary, our overview of the G-D paper is:

(1) It criticizes a priori research in general and then proceeds to engage in a lengthy a priori exercise.

[12] See section 2, as well as, e.g., Sterling, "Theory Construction" and "Decision Oriented."

(2) It notes (in our explication) that different axiom systems result in different valid conclusions, which shifts the problem to a selection of a particular axiom system. It then selects a rather restricted axiom system.

(3) It draws the conclusion that efficient market research cannot assess the desirability of alternative accounting procedures. This is a welcome corroboration of the more concise, more straightforward, and more cogent arguments that previously have reached the same conclusion.

(4) It draws some implications from the above conclusion which seem obvious, if not trivial.

(5) It draws the conclusion that efficient market research can assess the effects of alternative accounting procedures. Although the conclusion is valid, there are some unresolved empirical problems in assessing effects.

It may appear that this summary is a contradiction of our introduction in which we characterized the G-D paper as "a significant milestone." We don't believe it is contradictory. The significance of the paper is not in what conclusions were drawn but rather in who drew them. The same conclusions that were drawn earlier by nonefficient market researchers either have been ignored or misunderstood by efficient market researchers. Since G-D are in the mainstream of efficient market research, their conclusions are likely to have much more impact on their fellow researchers. We hope that this is true because we can then look forward to a more balanced view of the place of efficient market research in accounting. If G-D's paper results in a more balanced view of efficient market research then it will be a most significant contribution.

Review of Section 9

G-D have reviewed and criticized selected nonprice empirical studies. We have no quarrel with their selection of studies or, in general, with the representation of the findings of the studies. However, the criticisms that G-D have leveled at these studies are, in many cases, inappropriate. We believe G-D have erred in their criticisms in three main ways:

(1) They have imposed an efficient market framework on nonefficient market studies.

(2) They have criticized explorations or investigations because they were not experiments.

(3) They have misunderstood the nature and purpose of controlled experiments.

IMPOSING AN EFFICIENT MARKET FRAMEWORK

Given their interests and the subject matter of their paper, it is not surprising for G-D to have looked at these nonefficient market studies from the viewpoint of an efficient market framework. However, it is inappropriate for them to have criticized a study that was explicitly concerned with something else for not having been concerned with market equilibrium. For example, in their discussion of lab/field studies they state that "... studies of the behavior of particular types of investors (e.g., 'average' investors or 'financial analysts') are not likely to lead to reliable generalizations about the relationship between the production of accounting information and capital market equilibrium" (p. 106).

Even if we were convinced of the validity of this conclusion—and we are not—it is still an inappropriate criticism of lab/field studies simply because those studies were not concerned with capital market equilibrium. Instead, they were concerned with individual behavior. As far as we can tell, the authors criticized made no attempt to extend their results to capital market equilibrium. Barrett (p. 60) claims only that "footnote disclosure ... appears to be acted upon by professional financial analysts." Dyckman spends six or seven pages describing the limitations of his research design. Dickhaut deals only with individual behavior and does not claim the extrapolation. McIntyre (p. 584) states: "Further research is needed to determine if the advantages claimed for current-cost financial statements are large enough to be of value in actual investment situations."

The point can be made by reversing the criticism. Surely no one would criticize efficient market research because it did not lead to reliable generalizations about individual behavior. If one is doing a research on x then it is inappropriate to criticize that research because it does not shed light on y. One may appropriately lament the fact that other researchers' findings do not apply to one's problems but it is inappropriate to criticize on that basis.

G-D have made the same error in several other places. For example, both the smoothing and objectivity studies have been criticized by invoking efficient market criteria. We interpret the smoothing studies to be an attempt to find out whether or not smoothing existed, not whether or not the market was fooled by the existence of smoothing. We interpret the objectivity studies as simply an empirical test of the frequently heard assertion that historical costs are objective and market values are not. (Since Sterling was one of the authors of one of the objectivity studies, we are fairly certain of one interpretation of one of these studies.) Admittedly, the test results do not have much significance because they pertain to an assertion rather than to a theory. However, a vast number of people have argued that objectivity ought to be an important criterion in assessing alternative techniques. Viewed from the historical cost framework, objectivity is of great use in assessing alternative techniques. However, G-D clearly impose another framework when they write: "... [objectivity's] pertinence to capital market agents' behavior would have to be established before it could be of much use in assessing alternative techniques" (p. 113).

EXPERIMENTS VERSUS EXPLORATIONS

The second error is that G-D have criticized explorations or investigations because they were not experiments. In this context, experiment refers to the testing of a theory. By contrast, exploration and investigation are merely attempts to find out something about the world or to test some singular concept or assertion rather than to test a logically connected collection of concepts, i.e., rather than to test a theory.[13]

Section 9 (paragraph 2) states the following criticism: "The main reason for this is that they [nonprice studies] are not based upon a strong theoretical foundation. . . ." The statement is true. In the absence of such strong theoretical foundations one cannot experiment. Instead, one can only explore or investigate.

In the following statement G-D criticize lab/field studies because they were explorations: "If these kinds of factors really do have systematic effects on the observed results then they should have been identified as important factors by some body of theory. In the absence of such a theory, we do not know what variables must be controlled in the invented decision settings of the lab/field studies" (p. 105). We fully agree that it would have been better had there been some extant theory that could have been tested by an appropriately designed experiment. But in the absence of such a theory what should the researchers do? Should they refuse to do research until such a theory is formulated? Instead of waiting for the formulation of such a theory, the lab/field study researchers began to make tentative explorations and investigations. In the Demski sense, they have been forced to research simplifications of the complete model because the complete model cannot be specified. They came up with what are, to our minds, significant and interesting findings. Although we, too, would have preferred that these findings fit neatly into some overall theory, we are not willing to discard them because they don't. Instead, we prefer to store these findings and hope they will contribute to the formulation of the overall theory that we all desire.

G-D continue: "Typically, the importance ascribed to accounting income numbers is never deduced from theoretical considerations; it is simply asserted." As we read the referenced lab/field studies, the importance of income numbers was not asserted; it was tested. The researchers focused on one variable, e.g., an income number, and then attempted to determine its effects. Again, this can be put in the efficient market research context. Beaver investigated the price and volume reaction to earnings announcements. His study is not to be interpreted as being an assertion that income numbers are important, but rather a test of whether or not the market reacted to those numbers. The same is true for the lab/field studies—they were explorations about whether or not income numbers were important, not assertions about their importance.

---

[13] See Mackenzie (pp. 93–94) for a discussion of the distinction.

CONTROLLED EXPERIMENTS

The third error that G-D seem to have made in assessing the nonprice studies concerns the nature and purpose of controlled experiments. They are interested in studying "... the workings of the system as a whole, or *aggregate* market behavior ..." (p. 106); and it is this working of the system as a whole that results in "the attainment of equilibrium." It is perfectly legitimate for someone to study a part of the forces that operate on the market to keep it in equilibrium. The notion of equilibrium in economics was originally taken from physics. In physics equilibrium is defined as a set of forces with a zero resultant. That is, if a body has several opposing forces working on it so that it either moves steadily or stays at rest steadily then that body is said to be "in equilibrium."

A physicist can study that body in its equilibrium state. Alternatively, a physicist can control the forces so that he can determine what will happen to that body when only a fraction of the forces is operating. No physicist would claim that the fraction of the forces completely describes the state of the body in its equilibrium condition, but he would not criticize the controlled experiment for that reason. Instead, physicists welcome a controlled experiment as providing knowledge to them about the operation of partial forces.

It would seem to us that the same is true in economics. We do in fact describe market equilibrium by first appealing to individual preference orderings, indifference curves, and supply and demand curves. As G-D point out, market equilibrium is a function of the "interactions among rivalrous price-takers." That is, "rivalry" is a set of opposing forces, a set of investors with different utility functions and subjective probability assessments. What is wrong with studying a fraction of those opposing forces? To put the question more directly, what is wrong with studying individual behavior? As previously stated, none of the nonprice researchers claim that their research on individual behavior, being only a partial force operating on the market in equilibrium, does provide us with insights into how the market operates.

G-D state "equilibrium ... is induced by the workings of the system as a whole ... not by the actions of particular individuals" (p. 106). It seems to us that the capital market is in fact made up of individuals whose behavior in the aggregate leads to market equilibrium. Therefore, individual behavior seems quite pertinent to the actions of a market. It is not clear why the authors seem to insist that studies of individual behavior are not pertinent to accounting research in general and not pertinent to the operations of markets in particular. It seems to us that studies of individual behavior are simply controlled experiments in which the researcher is looking at one aspect or one force instead of looking at the system as a whole.

The failure to understand the nature of controlled experiments also arises in regard to the issue of competitive information. G-D complain that

". . . available lab/field studies fail to simulate competition among sources of information. Indeed, the information available to subjects is usually *deliberately limited* to accounting information. This limitation makes the settings of these studies even further removed from the setting within which the equilibrium prices of firms' ownership shares appear to be established" (p. 106; italics supplied). We do not deny that there are competing sources of information and, insofar as we know, none of the nonprice researchers have denied it. Instead, the nonprice researchers were trying to perform a controlled experiment. The idea of deliberately limiting the source of information to accounting reports was so that they could determine the effect of accounting reports upon individuals, not the total effects of all sources of information. Since accountants have no control over competing sources of information but they do have some control over accounting reports, it would seem that the determination of the isolated effects of accounting reports would be more pertinent to accountants than the total effects of all information.

REFERENCES

BARRETT, M. EDGAR. "Accounting for Intercorporate Investments: A Behavior Field Study," *Empirical Research in Accounting: Selected Studies, 1971*. Supplement to *Journal of Accounting Research* 9: 50–65.

BEAVER, WILLIAM H. "The Information Content of Annual Earnings Announcements," *Empirical Research in Accounting: Selected Studies, 1968*. Supplement to *Journal of Accounting Research* 6: 67–92.

BLACKWELL, D., and GIRSHICK, M. A. *Theory of Games and Statistical Decisions*. New York: John Wiley & Sons, 1954.

CHAMBERS, R. J. *Accounting, Evaluation and Economic Behavior*. Englewood Cliffs, N.J.: Prentice-Hall, 1966.

CORBIN, D. "A Case Study of Price-Level Adjustments," *The Accounting Review* 30 (April 1955): 268–81.

DEMSKI, JOEL. *Information Analysis*. Menlo Park, California: Addison-Wesley Publishing Co., 1972.

DICKHAUT, JOHN W. "Alternative Information Structures and Probability Revisions," *The Accounting Review* 48 (January 1973): 61–79.

DOPUCH, NICHOLAS. "Discussion of An Empirical Test of the Relevance of Accounting Information for Investment Decisions," *Empirical Research in Accounting: Selected Studies, 1971*. Supplement to *Journal of Accounting Research* 9: 32–40.

DYCKMAN, THOMAS R. *Investment Analysis and General Price-Level Adjustments*. New York: American Accounting Association, 1969.

EDWARDS, EDGAR O., and BELL, PHILIP W. *The Theory and Measurement of Business Income*. Berkeley: University of California Press, 1965.

GONEDES, NICHOLAS J. "Efficient Capital Markets and External Accounting," *The Accounting Review* (January 1972): 11–21.

MACKENZIE, KENNETH D. "A Datum Are a System," *Research Methodology*. Edited by Robert R. Sterling. Lawrence, Kansas: Scholars Book Co., 1972.

MARSCHAK, J. "Information Economics Reconsidered." Working paper No. 149, Revised November 1970, Western Management Science Institute.

MC DONALD, DANIEL L. "A Test Application of the Feasibility of Market-Based Measures in Accounting," *Journal of Accounting Research* 6 (Spring 1968): 38–49.

MC INTYRE, EDWARD V. "Current Cost Statements and Investment Decisions," *The Accounting Review* 48 (July 1973): 575–85.

MC KEOWN, JAMES C. "An Empirical Test of a Model Proposed by Chambers," *The Accounting Review* 46 (January 1971): 12–29.

PAP, ARTHUR. *An Introduction to the Philosophy of Science*. New York: The Free Press of Glencoe, 1962.

STERLING, ROBERT R. "Conservatism: The Fundamental Principle of Valuation in Traditional Accounting," *Abacus* 3 (June 1967): 109–32.

———. "The Going Concern: An Examination," *The Accounting Review* 43 (July 1968): 481–502.

———. "Theory Construction and Verification," *The Accounting Review* 45 (July 1970): 444–57.

———. *Theory of the Measurement of Enterprise Income*. Lawrence, Kansas: The University Press of Kansas, 1970.

———. "Decision Oriented Financial Accounting," *Accounting and Business Research* 7 (Summer 1972): 198–208.

———. "Introduction," *Research Methodology*. Edited by Robert R. Sterling. Lawrence, Kansas: Scholars Book Co., 1972.

———, and FLAHERTY, RICHARD E. "The Role of Liquidity in Exchange Valuation," *The Accounting Review* 46 (July 1971): 441–56.

Professional Schools of Accounting: Some Academic Questions

By Robert R. Sterling, Jesse Jones Professor, Rice University

Introduction

It is a distinct pleasure for me to be here today to consider this important and timely topic. I must apologize for giving this talk off the top of my head. I did have a speech prepared, but when I was visiting Sandy [John C. Burton] in Washington, D.C. last week, I ran into Rosemary Woods. She stepped on my foot and my whole speech disappeared.

I was flattered when Kerm [Larson] and Ed [Summers] called with the invitation to make this presentation. Originally, I declined their kind invitation for the very simple reason that I had no knowledge of the topic. I was even more flattered when they persisted. As they put it, my lack of knowledge would allow me to approach the topic with a completely open mind, with no preconceived notions. Thus, they said, I could be completely objective. I found this to be an intriguing criterion. My main qualification is my ignorance of the subject. This allows me to honestly, if somewhat immodestly, claim to be the most highly qualified person here. You are lucky to have me here. I could have gone down to Acapulco today to read a paper to the obstetricians convention since I know even less about obstetrics.

My high qualifications—that is, my abject ignorance—did allow me to discover one advantage of a school of accounting that has been completely overlooked by the previous speakers: the initials of a school of accounting are much better than those of a school of business. Perhaps if I taught in a school of accounting, people will begin to refer to me as an SOA instead of an SOB.

Need for More and Better Accounting Education

Educators in general and especially accounting educators perform two separate but related functions: education and screening. We both teach our students the subject matter and we do some preliminary screening for potential employers. Presumably, the students who get through college are a little more intellectually able and a little more motivated than those who don't. Thus, for some professions and occupations a college degree is a predictor of success and the lack of a college degree is a predictor of failure. These two functions are interrelated because if a student does not comprehend the subject matter, he fails and is thereby screened out of those job markets that require a college degree.

If we ask how well we accounting teachers have succeeded in performing these two functions, I think that we would have to give ourselves rather poor marks. We have not done as good a job of educating our students as we should, nor have we done a very good job of weeding out the students who are not likely to succeed in the profession.

Evidence of our poor job can be had by simply looking at our graduates. This evidence is easiest to come by in regard to our graduates who go with national accounting firms. To an educator, the most striking feature of the national accounting firms is their extensive educational program. When a student joins a national firm the first thing he does is to go to school. Think about that. After four years of school our students find that the only thing they are qualified to do is to go to school. Our students' first experience in public accounting is in a classroom setting. Then our students are periodically returned to the classroom for further education. However, instead of these classrooms being in a university, they are in a firm. As you know, some national firms have gone so far as to purchase their own universities in order to meet the educational needs of their professional staffs. There is no other profession or occupation which even approaches the quantity of education that is currently being offered in the national accounting firms. Theirs is a most extensive and expensive program. One firm reports a cost of education, exclusive of faculty salaries, of $10 million for fiscal 1973. Compare that to Rice University's budget. With thirty-two hundred full-time students, Rice University's budget, exclusive of faculty salaries, was only $8 million. Thus, one firm has a more extensive education program, by $2 million, than one entire university. If we added faculty salaries to that firm's budget, at the average rate, we would have a budget for their educational efforts that exceeds any school of business in the country and very nearly equals the budget for the University of Kansas which has twenty thousand full-time students.

The national firms' education program is clear evidence that more education is needed. Of course, there will always be a need for continuing education beyond college. Therefore, the initial degree can never fulfill all of the educational needs of the profession. However, I do believe that we educators could and should expand our educational efforts so that it would be less of a burden to the firms.

Our performance of the screening function is even worse than that of education. Consider the attrition rate in public accounting. Although we don't have reliable statistics on attrition in the profession as a whole, we do have some statistics for individual firms. One firm recently reported a 70 percent attrition rate in the first five years. The problem with this statistic is that we don't know how many of the people who left the firm went with another firm instead of moving out of public accounting into industrial accounting or into another occupation. Nonetheless, such figures are shocking. In dollar terms, it means that if a firm hires 100 people and spends x dollars per person on education, then loses 70 of these people, the remaining 30 people have been educated at a cost of 333 percent of x dollars. That is, if one were to average the education cost of the firm only over those people who remain with the firm, then the education cost per person would be 333 percent of the reported figure.

The attrition rate is clear evidence that we accounting educators have not been performing our screening function in a satisfactory manner. We are attracting the wrong kind of people to accounting education or we are not being tough enough in weeding them out or both. I don't believe that it is possible for us to ever reach the point of being perfect screeners, but I do believe that we can do a much better job than we have done heretofore.

These shortcomings in education and screening lead me to the conclusion that we need more and better education for accounting students. First, our students need more education to be able to better cope with the increased complexities and expansion of the function of accounting, as well as to alleviate the burden of the education now being performed by the firms. In addition, the students need a broader, more liberal education than they have had heretofore. I am not suggesting a broader, more liberal education for its own sake (although I think that such a position is defensible) but instead I am recommending it because it would be of direct benefit to future practitioners. Let me cite four examples that will illustrate what I mean.

Auditors have devised methods of determining the quantity of bulk goods, such as lumber, by the use of photography. By use of a planimeter they determine the area covered by the lumber in the photograph and then convert it to the quantity of lumber in the inventory. A planimeter is a mechanical device for determining an integral. Now one might argue that students need a course in integral calculus in order to be broadly or liberally educated. Although that argument is defensible, consider the fact that in this case the principles of integral calculus are a necessary tool of auditing. Similarly, one could legitimately argue that a course in the principles of physics is necessary for anyone to be broadly or liberally educated. In addition to that argument, the principle of physics known as the "ideal gas law" is indispensable to the proper accounting for the quantity of oil or gas in a well. If an accountant or auditor does not know the principle of physics that relates pressure, temperature, and volume, then there is no way for him to properly account for or audit an inventory of gas or oil. In such cases, this principle of physics is a necessary tool of accounting as well as being a part of a broad or liberal education.

Consider the following quotation:

> This process charges high-purity ethylene (99.9 percent). At moderate temperatures (200° to 400°F) and pressures (100 to 500 psi), in the presence of a catalyst, the ethylene, whose molecular weight is 28, is polymerized to a product having a molecular weight as high as 30,000.

That quotation appears to come from a chemistry text but in fact it comes from an accounting text entitled *Petroleum Accounting Practices* (p. 435) authored by Stan Porter, a partner in a national firm. It would be possible to mechanically account for such a chemical process, one could "cookbook" Porter's text, but in order to intelligently account for or audit this process, an elementary course in chemistry would be certainly highly desirable and may be indispensable. Finally, consider the many social programs which we are required to account for and audit. The Health, Education, and Welfare program in Detroit is a well-known case in point. A knowledge of the principles of sociology is a highly desirable, if not indispensable, prerequisite to intelligent accounting for or auditing of such programs.

These four courses—calculus, physics, chemistry, and sociology—would be required for a liberal education. However, we don't need to rely upon that criterion as a justification for including them in an accounting curriculum. They should be included in an accounting curriculum because they are of direct benefit to an accountant or auditor in performing the many and varied tasks that he is called upon to perform.

In addition to needing a broader, more liberal education, today's accountant also needs a more intensified specialized professional education. The accounting curriculum has been shrinking steadily for the last twenty years. Given the mechanical kinds of courses that we used to teach and the changing needs of the profession, there is ample justification for cutting back on those kinds of courses. However, instead of shrinking the accounting curriculum, I believe it would have been better had we revamped it. That is, instead of teaching fewer courses, what we needed to do was to teach approximately the same number of courses but to substitute different subject matter. I think the kinds of courses that we have taught in the past provide a partial explanation for the high attrition rate in accounting firms. When we teach the mechanics of accounting, we at least implicitly lead our students to believe that the problems of accounting are well structured and that closure is obtainable. Many, perhaps most, students are attracted to accounting because closure is psychologically satisfying. The students can work a problem and get their balance sheet or work sheet to balance. This is a satisfying experience. However, it is a gross disservice to the students because when they go into practice they find the problems to be ill structured, ill defined, and open-ended. Thus, the practice of accounting does not yield the same kind of satisfaction that attracted them to the study of accounting. Many of them never overcome this initial shock and move off into other occupations. To put it another way, instead of performing the screening function, we accounting teachers seduce the students by making them believe that accounting problems are well structured, well defined, and have an easily recognizable solution. They go into practice and find that this is not true. This is at least a partial explanation for the high attrition rate.

We made a mistake when we cut back on the number of courses in the accounting curriculum. I fully agree that we should have eliminated the overemphasis on mechanics, but we made an error when we cut the courses out altogether instead of substituting more relevant subject matter. For example, I think we rather desperately need a course in what might be called Cases in Auditing Practice. By this I mean that we should gather actual cases from the research departments of the firms and present them to our students. One major benefit of such a course would be to let the students know just how ill-structured, ill-defined, and open-ended actual practical problems are. I am talking about a judicious selection of the problems that audit partners call in to their research departments. That these problems are not trivial is evidenced by the fact that the audit partner feels he needs help from the research department in solving them. That they are interesting to accountants is evidenced by the fact that the morning cases are often the subject of the luncheon conversation when I visit my friends in these research departments.

As another example, I think that we ought to include the problem of determining quantities in some accounting course. Textbook problems always specify the quantity of units in the inventory, the quantity of years of service life, etc., as a datum. Our accounting curriculum completely overlooks the fact that someone must determine those quantities and that this is no trivial task. Defining what is included in the inventory or what is obsolete is a practical problem that the students should be exposed to before they go into practice. The efficient determination of quantities, such as the method of using photography and a planimeter mentioned above, is also an important part of accounting, as well as an interesting subject.

These two examples came to mind rather readily although I must admit that I caged them a little. I deliberately avoided making the usual suggestion to add courses in accounting for social costs, human resources, computerized accounting, etc., in order to make the point that we don't need to go very far afield to see the inadequacies of our present curriculum. I am sure that you could think of many better examples.

In summary, our students need more education in the liberal arts as well as more intensified education in accounting. When we count up the needed courses we see that they easily exceed the four-year bachelor's degree. This point is important to me. I object to the argument that accounting is a profession and that, since other professions require postbaccalaureate education, then accounting ought to also require postbaccalaureate education. That argument is based upon status seeking. The argument ought to be made on its merits instead of being made on invidious comparisons to other professions. Moreover, I think the argument for postbaccalaureate education is a sound one when examined solely on its merits.

Educational Advantages of an SOA

In the previous section I argued that we need more and better education for accounting students. I did not make an argument regarding the particular institutional structure which is best suited to achieve that goal. It does not necessarily follow that we need a school of accounting from the fact, if you accept it as a fact, that we need more and better education. The goal of more and better education could, at least in principle, be achieved in a school of business. Despite the fact that the goal could, in principle, be achieved, I don't believe that it can in fact be achieved in a school of business.

The major curricular problem that the accounting faculty has to contend with in a school of business is that they are in the minority. Curriculum decisions are made by the faculty as a whole and, since the accounting faculty is in the minority, the curriculum decisions are dominated by nonaccountants. The problem is that nonaccounting faculty members seem to be rather insensitive to the peculiar curricular needs of accountants. Sometimes they seem to be hostile to the curricular needs of accountants. Part of the difficulty is that nonaccounting people in general, as well as nonaccounting faculty in particular, regard the accounting system as, at best, a necessary evil. The annual audit is regarded with even more disdain as is evidenced by its being commonly referred to as the annual nuisance. We also have a history to live down. In the early days, accounting dominated the curriculum of business schools. Many of the earlier schools were named something like the school of commerce and accounts. In those times the accounting faculty was the largest and most powerful group in the business schools and its curriculum attracted the cream of the student crop. In those days we accountants did not hesitate to wield this power, and we were not always as sensitive as we might have been to the needs of other disciplines. As a consequence, there is some residual hostility from nonaccountants with long memories.

Regardless of the reason, the fact is that decisions about the *accounting* curriculum are dominated by *nonaccounting* faculty. If the accounting faculty wants to add a course in, say, psychology as a prerequisite for accounting students, it usually cannot be done unless all of the nonaccounting faculty agree that such a prerequisite would also be appropriate for nonaccounting students. The number of accounting courses is also constrained by the nonaccounting faculty, as well as by American Assembly of Collegiate Schools of Business restrictions. Thus, the course structure is determined by nonaccountants.

In addition, the course content is heavily influenced by nonaccountants. The introductory courses in accounting are dominated by nonaccounting students. These nonaccounting students, as well as their nonaccounting faculty, want the introductory courses to be a survey. They want a course that should be entitled "accounting appreciation" in much the same fashion as high schools have courses called "music appreciation." On the face of it there is nothing wrong with offering a course on accounting appreciation since we accountants generally believe that we would be better off if more people understood what accounting is all about. However, let us compare the student contact hours in the introductory courses to those in the advanced courses. Last year, at the University of Kansas, the introductory courses generated a total of about 1,800 student contact, or student credit, hours. By contrast, the advanced courses in accounting, with their lower enrollments, generated approximately 750 student contact hours. In percentage terms, about 71 percent of the student contact hours were spent in teaching "accounting appreciation" and 29 percent in teaching accounting. Insofar as I can determine, this is a unique phenomenon. No other profession spends that much time teaching others about the subject, as opposed to teaching the subject per se. For example, the law school, if it offers a course in legal appreciation at all, spends less than one percent of its time on that kind of thing.

This situation has a debilitating effect on the accounting faculty. Accounting is a difficult subject to teach even when one is trying to teach it to accounting majors. It is much more difficult to teach accounting appreciation to nonaccounting majors. A large amount of the accounting faculty's time and energy is spent thinking about how to teach accounting appreciation instead of thinking about accounting.

The point is that the content of the introductory courses is determined to a large extent by nonaccounting faculty and students. The nonaccounting faculty determines the prerequisites and total number of accounting courses, and the nonaccounting students and faculty determine the content of almost three-quarters of the student contact hours taught.

These are the two situations that could be rectified in a school of accounting. I believe that they are two strong points in favor of a school of accounting. It would be quite an advantage for an accounting faculty to be able to determine the content and extent of its curriculum.

Need for More and Better Accounting Research

Research is classified as basic or applied. Of course, these are related, since it is impossible to apply something in the absence of a previous discovery and it is useless to make a discovery without carrying it through to application. Although we normally think of research being sequential—going from basic to applied research and then to practice—it would be more accurate to describe its parts as interactive. Sometimes a basic discovery is made that requires applied research before it can be implemented in practice. At other times, however, applied research or practice leads to basic discoveries. Thus, basic research, applied research, and practice complement one another. For this reason, we should not assign higher status to any one of them.

In addition to a research result's being put into practice, it is also put into the curriculum. In most disciplines, research results appear in the teaching materials soon after they are published. The teachers read of the research in the journals and add those results to their teaching materials. Then, upon graduation, their former students implement those results in practice. Thus, there are two routes to the implementation of research results: teaching and practice.

The problem with research in accounting is that it appears to be an isolated activity. The results of research have very little impact on teaching or practice. Accounting educators concentrate, in the main, on teaching the present set of accepted practices. That is, they teach the *existing* Generally Accepted Accounting Principles to the exclusion of proposed modifications in GAAP arising from research discoveries. Today's students become tomorrow's practitioners and, thus, most practitioners start their careers without even having been exposed to accounting research in either its basic or applied form.

As a consequence, we witness a communication gap between researchers and practitioners as well as between researchers and teachers. There is precious little professional interaction between researchers and practitioners. Both suffer from the absence of interaction. Researchers do not receive the benefit of feedback from attempted implementation of their results. Practitioners do not receive the benefit of knowing about the results so that they can attempt to implement them. To a researcher it seems that each time practitioners undertake to do research they reinvent the wheel. To a practitioner it seems that research is, at best, of no practical value and, at worst, unintelligible gobbledygook.

The situation is growing worse instead of better. The communication gap is getting wider and wider. We are in the happy situation of having a virtual explosion of research in accounting. We are in the unhappy situation of not having much, if any, of that research implemented. Evidence for the gap between practice and research abounds. The great hopes that were raised by the establishment of a research department at the AICPA were never realized. Mautz and Gray concluded that the APB "acted contrary to research recommendations as often as it moved to implement research results." Despite the APB's explicit objective of reducing accounting alternatives, there were more alternatives available at its demise than at its inception. Despite the great hopes accompanying the establishment of the FASB, it is hampered by the absence of a unified theory to guide it. So far, the FASB appears to be operating on the same case-by-case, ad hoc basis for which the APB received so much criticism. The FASB has announced that it will establish a unified theory but, then, the APB made a similar announcement. More accurately, they made several similar announcements. Recall that the APB went through Moonitz's *Postulates*, Sprouse and Moonitz's *Principles*, Grady's *Inventory* and Statement No. 4 without acquiring the desired unified theory. I don't want to be a prophet of doom, but it does seem to me that there is ample evidence of a communication gap and that it is growing wider and wider.

I believe that many of our troubles can be traced to this gap. Instead of research and practice reinforcing one another, interacting with one another, or helping one another, they are going in separate directions. The current journal articles seem to have no thought of implementing their results in practice, and the current practice seems to be completely unaware of the research literature.

Research Advantages of an SOA

Many of my friends want to attach the blame for the existence of the communication gap on either the researchers or the practitioners. My practitioner friends say that the researchers ought to be concerned with the implementation of their research results. At least, the practitioners say, the researchers ought to write in such a fashion that their findings could be easily read and understood by practitioners. My researcher friends complain that practitioners ignore research results. They say that practitioners should at least review the literature prior to taking a position. I think that both of these views are in error. The two views are correct in trying to close the gap, but they are in error in trying to get either the researcher or the practitioner to move closer to the other. The two views are concentrating on each side of the gap and asking each side to move toward the other. I believe that we should focus on the gap instead of focusing on the two sides. Instead of trying to move the sides, let us find some way of *filling* the gap. I believe that a school of accounting could go a long way toward filling that gap.

I take an engineering school as my model for filling the gap. Practicing engineers, like practicing accountants, don't have the time or inclination to keep up with the latest research results in physics. Theoretical physicists, like accounting researchers, are consumed by the task of doing their research. They don't have the time or the inclination to translate their research findings into practical applications. Thus, there is a gap between a practicing engineer and a theoretical physicist in the same way that there is a gap between accounting researchers and practitioners. It would be an error to ask either one of them to move closer to the other. If they did so it would reduce the total productivity. Both the practicing engineer and the theoretical physicist would suffer substantial opportunity costs if they tried to move toward the other. The net result would be a greater total cost to society. Instead of the two moving toward each other, the engineering school has come into being with the primary purpose of filling the gap between them.

A comparison of physics textbooks to engineering textbooks will illustrate the point. In a physics textbook the principle of the conservation of mass is presented with elaborate theoretical and empirical support. The empirical support for the law comes from controlled or "artificial" laboratory experiments, not from practice. By contrast, an engineering textbook will normally devote only the first paragraph to the principle of the conservation of mass. It provides neither theoretical nor experimental support for this principle; it simply asserts it. After asserting the principle, the remainder of the engineering text is devoted to explaining how that principle can be implemented in various practical situations. In the engineering text these applications are called "materials balances," a concept that is never mentioned in a physics text. Often the engineering textbook will explain that a particular theoretical refinement can be ignored because it will not affect the outcome. The engineering term for this is "negligible"; the accounting term is "immaterial." The discovery of what is negligible (immaterial) usually comes from applied engineering research, not from basic research in physics.

The same contrast can be drawn between the physics and engineering journals. Physics journals cannot be easily understood by practicing engineers. Engineering journals are specifically designed so that they can be easily understood by practicing engineers. The physics journals concentrate on the discovery of the principles, their theoretical and empirical support. Engineering journals concentrate on how these principles can be implemented.

In regard to research I would model a school of accounting after the engineering schools. We need much more applied research in accounting. Most of the academic research that has been done to date has been more basic than applied. Unlike some critics of basic research, I don't mean to imply that we need less basic research in accounting. On the contrary, I think we need more basic research, but I also think that we have an urgent need to balance the basic research with much more applied research. The communications gap exists, in large measure, because of the absence of applied research. A school of accounting could be devoted to filling that need for applied research, to filling the communication gap.

To be able to do this, the school of accounting faculty must be fluid. For an applied researcher to be effective he must have a working knowledge of practice. Applied researchers must have access to practical problems. This would require that the applied researchers on the faculty of a school of accounting be able to rather freely move in and out of the research departments of the firms. I would hope that this fluidity would also apply to practitioners. In addition to applied researchers taking temporary positions with firms, I think it would be of great benefit for practitioners to take temporary positions with a school of accounting. From my own personal experience I know that I learn a great deal by spending time in the research departments of the firms. I think that practitioners could also benefit from spending time in a school of accounting.

In summary, a school of accounting, like a school of engineering, could fill in the gap between accounting researchers and practitioners. The majority of the faculty of the school could concentrate on applied research. They would be the connecting link between the exigencies of practice and the discoveries of basic research. The school could improve communications between practitioners and researchers to the benefit of both.

Synergistic Effects

In the previous remarks, I separated the curriculum from the research. I'll now say only a few words about the synergistic effects.

First, if the accounting faculty could get control of the content and extent of its curriculum, and if the accounting faculty could have a close working relationship with practitioners, then we would have both the time and the ability to begin to teach research as well as to teach current GAAP. A school of accounting would allow us to add a few more courses in accounting. This would give us a little more time so that we could teach proposed practices arising from research discoveries in addition to teaching GAAP. The faculty's familiarity with practical problems arising from a closer relationship with practice would enhance their ability to provide the text and cases for such a curricular revision.

This curricular revision would make the teaching of accounting more realistic. The students would be exposed to accounting as it actually is rather than as a set of well-defined problems with an easily recognizable solution. This ought to result in a higher attrition rate in school and a lower attrition rate in the firms. The more realistic approach to accounting ought to reduce the firm's educational burden. Of course, the firms will still have to teach their own work-sheet techniques and other things that are peculiar to the firm, but the graduates of a school of accounting, as I envision it, ought to need less education in the firm than do our current graduates.

The fluidity of the faculty in a school of accounting and their concentration on applied research should enable such a school to offer more and better continuing education courses than has been possible up to this time. Instead of each firm's creating its own teaching materials for its continuing education courses, a school of accounting could create those teaching materials for all firms. If this could be accomplished, the cost of continuing education to each individual firm could be considerably reduced.

The teaching of research should benefit research as well as benefit the curriculum. As all teachers discover very early, the teacher learns more than the students. A teacher must prepare for the subject and then articulate that subject in such a fashion that other people can understand it. In both the preparation and the articulation the teacher learns a great deal. The learning of research results by teachers will almost inevitably result in the refinement and the improvement of research.

The teaching of research results to tomorrow's practitioners ought to enhance our chances of improving tomorrow's practices. The practitioners' attempts to implement the research results could be used as data for the applied researchers and thereby improve the research as well as improve practice.

Some Problems With Establishing an SOA

Up to this point, I have made the argument that an SOA would be beneficial to teaching, research, and practice. I will now turn to a consideration of the problems of establishing an SOA. I will discuss the more minor problems before considering what is, to my mind, the major and fundamental problem.

I do see a problem in recruiting students to an SOA. In contrast to law or medicine, we seldom find students who come to school with the idea of becoming accountants. I expect that most accounting majors are recruited in the required introductory courses. They would never have become majors without having taken the introductory courses, and they would never have taken the introductory courses without having been required to do so.

One problem with recruiting students is our anonymity and, worse, the confusion about what we do. As the studies show, almost everyone recognizes the professions of law and medicine, while the converse holds for the recognition of accounting. We are the least-recognized profession. Worse, while no one would confuse a nurse's aide with a physician, almost no one can distinguish a bookkeeping machine operator from a CPA since both are called "accountants." The way that high school "accounting" classes are taught and the fact that they are classified as vocational, as opposed to college preparatory, perpetuate this confusion.

I do not have any suggestions for solving this problem, but it is one that we must recognize and solve when establishing an SOA.

The next problem is the recruiting of graduates by firms. The need for professional staff has been so great that many firms have not been willing to wait for postbaccalaureate education. Many firms have recruited nonmajors and others have recruited majors that had intended to go on to postbaccalaureate education. For example, the University of Kansas established a five-year program a long time prior to the Beamer report. The faculty and students knew that we had a five-year program, but the recruiters didn't. Although the University of Kansas eliminated the undergraduate accounting major and moved most accounting courses to the fifth year, the recruiters couldn't wait; they recruited the nonmajors at the end of four years. As a consequence, the five-year program never got off the ground. The net result of the faculty's efforts was an elimination of the accounting major at the University of Kansas, not an establishment of a five-year major.

A similar fate may be in store for an SOA. The establishment of an SOA will completely eliminate recruits in the first year of operation. All of those graduating students who would have otherwise gone with the firm will now go to the SOA. Given the high demand for accountants, the firms may not be able to tolerate a dry year.

Even if they could tolerate a dry year, they may not be willing to do so for fear of competition. At the University of Kansas each of the firms said that they would be willing to wait until the end of the fifth year if all of the firms would do the same. However, no single firm would wait for fear other firms would drain off the best students at the end of four years. Thus, the problem is that the firms may recruit all of the potential entrants to an SOA and, in effect, reduce it to a four-year program.

A related problem must be blamed on the academics. We teach our students cost-benefit analysis, opportunity costing and to adjust (discount) for the time value of money. Perhaps if we didn't teach this, then our students wouldn't realize that the cost of the fifth year is their lost salary plus their out-of-pocket costs of staying in school. Perhaps they couldn't compare that total cost to the extra $600 to $1,000 per year salary that they get for staying for the fifth year. Perhaps they wouldn't discount that $600 to $1,000 per year at 9 percent and see that this benefit is much less than their cost. The point is that at the present time there is too little distinction to permit a rational student to enter and stay. If an SOA is to succeed, there must be a sufficient distinction to permit a rational student to enter and stay.

The foremost problem that I see in the establishment of an SOA is the usual one: money. Professional schools are expensive. No matter how you figure it, cost per student or cost per faculty or cost per contact hour, it simply costs more to run a professional school.

I don't know how we would go about getting the funds to establish a school of accounting. State support is not a likely source. Unfortunately, we are talking about establishing a new, expensive school at the very time when budgets are being cut back as a reaction to the student activism of a few years ago, the present leveling off and the predicted decline of student enrollment, and the general economic slowdown. It seems clear that the golden age of education is over. We had a sputnik a few years ago which caused our political leaders to become concerned about the gap between us and the Soviet Union. This was coupled with a general economic expansion and an increase in enrollment. The expanded educational budgets were needed to meet the increased enrollment and they were relatively easy to come by because of the added tax revenues occasioned by the economic expansion. This situation is now reversed. I don't know of a single university that has managed to escape the budget crunch. I would hesitate to approach a university president or a legislative committee at the present time with a proposal to establish a school of accounting. I fear I would be tossed out on my ear.

Of course, we could change the name of the Department of Accounting to the School of Accounting without any additional costs. However, if we want to accomplish our objectives, if we want to be a true professional school, then we must be cognizant of the fact that law school budgets per student or per faculty member are about double the budgets of the ordinary department of accounting. It is necessary to get this increase in the budget in order to eliminate those huge lecture sections, to get the class sizes down to manageable proportions, to get the released time and equipment necessary to do the applied research, and to get the ancillary help that the faculty so desperately needs.

We have a budgetary problem, and the availability of state funds makes it unlikely that we would be able to meet and solve that problem. I think the picture in regard to foundation funds is equally bleak. None of the huge foundations is interested in supporting accounting education. Many of them, such as the National Science Foundation, specifically exclude accounting from the programs that they support. One accountant, namely, Bill Cooper of Carnegie-Mellon University, recently obtained an endowment of $10 million to set up a separate school. However, he set up a School of Urban and Public Affairs, not a school of accounting. The fault lies with you practitioners. You have been derelict in not getting rich enough to be able to establish a foundation for the support of accounting. Until you figure out some way to avoid paying ordinary income taxes so that you can accumulate enough wealth to establish such a foundation, I don't think that we can expect a foundation to provide the endowment for a school of accounting.

It may be that we could get the accounting firms to collectively make the necessary contributions. An endowment of $10 million would probably do the trick. By itself, $10 million sounds like an unattainable goal; it is a very large figure. However, when one realizes that just one firm spent $10 million on education in just one year, the figure seems a little more attainable.

You know better than I about the possibility of obtaining such funds. Until we face up to the high costs, until we have reasonable probability of getting the funds, musings such as this and symposia such as this are little more than wishful thinking.

Discussant's Comments
Robert R. Sterling

Description

If we could banish all preconceptions when we read, that would be an admirable beginning. Do not dictate to your author; try to become him. Be his fellow-worker and accomplice.

—Virginia Woolf

On the first several readings of this paper I followed Virginia Woolf's advice. My objective was to learn from this paper by becoming a fellow-worker to Butterworth, Gibbins and King (henceforth, BGK). In this part of my discussion remarks, I will attempt to banish my preconceptions and describe what I found. I will delay evaluation until subsequent sections.

The most general thing that I found is that there are four separate sub-papers, a violation of the rule that the number of sub-papers equals the number of co-authors. In this case there were only three authors but there were four separate sub-papers.[1] All four sub-papers employ an agency theory perspective. A perspective or framework will allow one to classify the phenomena in such a fashion that it will help one to understand that phenomena and to perceive the problems. BGK devote much space to such classification and problem perception.

Paper 1. In accounting there are two kingdoms: research and practice. It can be observed that in practice there is no rational basis for principles and there is resistance to change; practice follows its own course regardless of theoretical considerations, and is consistent with the entity theory rather than the proprietorship theory. The problem is that there is a dichotomy between research and practice; there seems to be no connection between the theory of accounting and the practice of accounting.

Paper 2. In the kingdom of practice there are three phyla of information uses: predictive, contractual, and retrospective. There are classes of uses in each phylum, which BGK spell out for us. The problem here is that most theoreticians have concentrated on the predictive uses and have not recognized that accounting information is also useful if it aids in contracting or in making sense out of the past.

The contractual phylum has a family of characteristics consisting of

---

Robert Sterling PhD was the Francis G. Winspear Distinguished Professor of Accounting, Faculty of Business Administration and Commerce, The University of Alberta during 1980-1981. Previously he was the Jesse H.Jones Distinguished Professor of Management and Dean of the Graduate School of Administration at Rice University. He is a two-time winner of the AICPA Award for Notable Contributions to Accounting Literature. At present he is a Senior Fellow at the Financial Accounting Standards Board, Stamford, Connecticut.

objectivity, time additivity, enterprise additivity, irrevocability, risk constraint, and cash convergence. It may be that this family of characteristics applies to all phyla – predictive and retrospective as well as contractual – but it seems that BGK intend it to apply primarily to contractual uses.

Paper 3. In research methodologies there are two kingdoms: theoretical and empirical. In the kingdom of the theoretical there are two phyla: normative and positive. I am not entirely clear what BGK perceived to be the primary problem here except for the need to distinguish the various kinds of methodologies. Perhaps their primary problem is the necessity for normative decisions in accounting and the difficulty of making those normative decisions.

Paper 4. In one or both of the phyla of research there are two genera: pre-response and user response. The genus of user response consists of the species of individual, market, firm, and second-order responses. Again, it was not clear exactly what BGK perceived the problem to be here. Perhaps it was merely a desire to understand previous research better by providing a framework of classification.

Overall, the paper is essentially a prolegomenon of a research effort to be undertaken rather than a report on research that has been done. The authors have become convinced that such a research programme is promising and they are here trying to explain their programme to us. In effect, they are saying that if we employ the agency theory perspective and the classification scheme outlined above, then it will yield research results which will contribute to the solution of our problems.

First stage evaluation

Ye shall know them by their fruits. Do men gather grapes of thorns, or figs of thistles? . . . Every tree that bringeth not forth good fruit is hewn down, and cast into the fire.

—Matthew 7:16,19

The ultimate test of any research programme is whether or not it bears fruit. Both Matthew and economic methodologists, e.g., Lionel Robbins [1932], are agreed that economic theories must eventually bear fruit and that the ultimate test of a theory is what kind of fruit it bears. The problem with evaluating a prolegomenon is that we cannot observe the fruit. The only thing available to observe is the seed. Whether that seed will grow into a tree depends upon the efforts of BGK and others. Whether that tree will bear figs or thistles cannot be determined until the future crops are gathered.

Thus, we cannot fully evaluate the paper at this time because the results are not yet in. If the results are good, this will be referred to as a "seminal [seed-like] paper." If not, it will be forgotten. At the present time, only the "aha" test can be employed. If after reading the paper one says, "aha, I understand that better now," then it has passed the aha test. Unfortunately, the paper only partially passed my aha test. I was certainly instructed by the paper, but I was also frustrated by it. I was instructed by what BGK had to tell me about agency theory and I found their enthusiasm contagious. I was frustrated by the level of abstractness, which prevented me from seeing how it could be applied.

It seemed to me that many of the things that were said in this paper have been said previously in various parts of the literature. Perhaps the major contribution is in synthesizing the fragmented concepts in a single paper. Another contribution may be the recasting of familiar concepts in an agency theory perspective. That perspective, and the associated language, may provide insights and relationships that we now overlook. In regard to recasting, I was particularly impressed by BGK's ability to separate the future from the past – the predictive from the retrospective uses of accounting information – and their recognition of the contributions that different kinds of research efforts can make. In this day of methodological disputes, it is refreshing to find BGK discussing "normative," "positive," "theoretical," and "empirical" in a dispassionate and insightful fashion. I was also impressed by the even-handed treatment of previous research efforts. Past prolegomena in accounting have too often been characterized by exaggerated claims and egregious errors as well as out-of-hand rejection of all previous research that did not fit into the mould prescribed by the proponents. To their credit, BGK do not make such exaggerated claims or commit such egregious errors.

Second stage evaluation

The problem of ideology is central to historical – as to all social – understanding. If men govern the rest of nature in virtue of their reason and technological power, they are themselves governed by their beliefs.

– Gorden Leff

We can go a bit further in evaluating this paper if you will allow me to use other criteria. In an attempt to illustrate what I mean by other criteria, I will start by relating a recent experience at a dinner party. The pre-dinner entertainment consisted of five people participating in a water witching experiment. We took some coat hangers, straightened them out to make a pair of divining rods, and then took turns trying to divine water. We found that four of the five could in fact divine the water. Much to my surprise, and despite my scepticism, I was one of the four that could do it – you are looking at a water witch. The host knew where the water (a cistern) was, so that we had, in effect, a controlled experiment. As might be expected in a group of academics and theoreticians, these unusual phenomena became the subject of a lively conversation over dinner. There was a thing to be explained and the object of the dinner conversation was to explain it. One of the participants was a distinguished physician whose primary research interest is genetics. He explained it by imposing a genetic framework: the deviations in various genetic characteristics of those who could water witch and those who could not provided the basis for his explanation. Another participant was a well-known physicist and he explained the phenomena by imposing a physicist's framework regarding magnetic forces. As an accountant I had no pertinent framework to impose so I did a little anthropological research by noting that each of the people who attempted to explain the phenomena imposed the framework of their own discipline to do so.

Thus, there was a thing to be explained. The general definition of "explanation" is showing discursively that a phenomenon obeys or can be subsumed under a law. The law that each used came from the discipline that each practised. My point is that the mind-set of the person determines how he looks at things, how the problems are to be explained, how the phenomena are to be classified, and what analytical and empirical techniques are to be applied. In his letter to participants, Alex Milburn mentioned that we would be bringing different mind-sets to this Symposium. BGK mentioned a similar phenomenon in regard to retrospective uses by decision makers, as well as in regard to researchers' outlooks. In addition to its having been mentioned by Alex and BGK, it is a well-known phenomenon in other disciplines. Sometimes it is called learned behaviour in psychology, the law of the instrument or trained incapacity in the philosophy of science, ideology in sociology and history, aculturization in anthropology, structuring in linguistics and logic, paradigm commitment in the history of science, and so forth.

Whatever it is called, BGK do it. They use the economic framework of agency theory to structure the problems and subsume the things to be explained under this pre-learned theory or mind-set. This is *not* a criticism. I will now do it also. You will also do it both in evaluating BGK as well as in evaluating my evaluation. We all do it. My plea is that we recognize that we are doing it. To put it negatively, I have noticed that a number of people in accounting employ their own mind-set or paradigm to criticize the works of others who are using a different mind-set or paradigm. When this is done without recognition that a different paradigm is the root cause of the difference, it results in internecine strife which is not productive because it has no hope of reaching resolution.

Paper 1

The perceived problem in Paper 1 is the dichotomy between research and practice. BGK explain that dichotomy by imposing agency theory. I agree with the statement of the problem, but I imposed a different framework when I attempted to explain it [Sterling, 1973]. In essence, I laid the blame at the door of us teachers because we teach "generally accepted accounting principles" instead of research results. Our former students practise what we taught them, become successful, and then train the subsequent generation to do the same thing. The result is what Kaplan [1964, p. 29] calls "trained incapacity"; he notes that "the more we know-how to do something, the harder it is to learn to do it differently (children learn to speak a foreign language with less of an accent than adults do only because they did not know their own language so well to start with)."

Kaplan's notion of trained incapacity is intended to apply to scientists in general. I imposed that general notion to the specific case of accounting practitioners when I looked at the problem of the dichotomy between research and practice. By contrast, BGK impose agency theory. Now the question is which one provides the best explanation. One test of such different ways to explain things is their relative generality: we prefer more general to less general explanations. I think that my explanation is more general since it is applicable to other disciplines. Medicine is one discipline that has faced similar problems. For example, Sir John Pringle, in the 1750s, introduced antiseptic surgical techniques in British military hospitals, which reduced gangrene incidence dramatically and hence also reduced post-operative mortality rates. US Civil War surgical handbooks, however, considered sepsis to be normal and the gangrene rate remained alarmingly high. Thus, there was a theoretical advance that had not been generally adopted in practice over 100 years later, a clear dichotomy between medical theory and medical practice. Is agency theory sufficiently general to explain that dichotomy? The fact that surgeons were trained to be skilful with the knife and were not trained in antiseptic techniques does explain it. That trained incapacity also explains practising surgeons' resistance to adopting the new technique. I think the same notion provides an accurate description of the dichotomy between accounting theory and practice.

The history of medical education also provides parallels to accounting education. Early education was apprenticeship – the emulation of successful practitioners – in both disciplines. Eventually education was taken over by schools, but the apprenticeship method of instruction was continued in the schools. That is, the professors were practitioners or former practitioners who taught what they did in practice. Although Boerhaave had established systematic clinical instruction at the Leiden School by about 1700, it was not until the Flexner Report in 1910 that research was *combined* with clinical bedside teaching. That is, the Flexner Report required that theory and practice be connected, and the locus of that connection was in the medical schools, with Johns Hopkins providing the template. Once that connection was made, medical practice improved dramatically. New students were taught new techniques as they were discovered and they implemented those new techniques when they went into practice. They did not have to unlearn the old techniques, they did not suffer from trained incapacity, and therefore at the date of graduation there was no dichotomy between theory and practice.

It seems to me that accounting education is in about the same place that medical education was at the time of Boerhaave. Teaching generally accepted accounting principles means, by definition, that the new generation of students is taught to do what previous generations are now doing. This is reinforced when the new generation is hired by the previous generations and required to emulate them to achieve success. By the time they become successful enough to be influential, their trained incapacity is in such an advanced state that Kaplan's example of learning a foreign language pales by comparison.

The above is a brief outline of my explanation of the dichotomy between theory and practice. As is obvious, the mind-set or framework that I impose on the problem comes from my avocational interest in the philosophy and history of science. BGK have imposed an agency theory framework on the same problem. Which provides the best explanation depends initially on your aha test and depends ultimately on in-depth research into the problem.

A related disputatious issue is BGK's view that accountants should respond to the market by supplying the kind of information demanded. This again depends upon what framework or paradigm one imposes. Obviously, a pure economic framework will view information as a commodity and then look to the market forces for explanations of what kind of commodity is now and has been supplied. Just as producers of ice cream respond to the wants of consumers by supplying vanilla instead of pistachio, BGK see accountants responding to the wants of consumers by supplying historical costs instead of current costs. Thus, the explanation of the persistence of historical cost reporting is found by simply looking at the market demand. Moreover, the research programme proposed by BGK is to find out why this is so and use that as a basis for a theory of accounting. On one level of inquiry, this is indisputable. However, that level of inquiry is so general that it serves to define a problem instead of providing a means to solve it. Just as surgical patients demand good care, not antiseptic techniques, users demand good information, not a particular valuation technique, and the burden of the surgeon and the accountant is to decide what is "good" in order to respond to that demand. The outcome of relying upon the demand for antiseptic techniques by Civil War surgical patients was to not supply such techniques because the patients were not aware of them. The same is true of supplying current costs to the previous generations of users of accounting information. The fact that surgeons introduced antiseptic techniques *caused* subsequent generations of patients to demand such techniques. If we now rely upon patient demand to justify supplying antiseptic techniques, we have completed a vicious circle. Moreover, if we rely upon the demand of patients for antiseptic techniques, we will prohibit the introduction of aseptic techniques. And so forth as each new technique is discovered. To put it in economic terms, we have something analogous to Say's Law – the supply of particular techniques creates its own demand. I think the same thing happens in accounting. Prior to the introduction of depreciation techniques by accountants in about 1913 there was no demand for them. There is now a demand for depreciation techniques that was *caused* by accountants introducing those techniques. It is viciously circular to justify depreciation now by reference to market demand. Moreover, if we now find a new technique that is better, reliance upon the demand for depreciation prohibits introduction of that better technique. It is for these reasons that I have fundamental reservations about BGK's suggestion that accounting should respond to market demand for information.

BGK put a good deal of emphasis on accounting practice following its own course and "being unaccountably resistant to innovation and experiment." I think that the notion of trained incapacity of both practitioners and users accounts for that "unaccountable resistance." BGK are also concerned about the failure to observe the impact of such innovations and experiments in the marketplace and are puzzled by a profession that "has taken pains to encourage the consistent application of specific reporting rules." It seems to me that they have overlooked the obvious: the need for comparability requires rules. Some see the problem as exactly opposite to BGK – that it is the existence of too much innovation and experiment in practice that caused the demand for the tightly written rules in an effort to achieve comparability.

When we combine the two notions of trained incapacity and comparability it reveals (at least to me) a rather urgent need for research to support standard setting, the overall topic of this Symposium. Note that in regard to comparability the medical analogy does not fit. Research in medicine has shown that different generations of physicians practise different brands of medicine – physicians who graduated in 1980 practise slightly differently from those who graduated in 1979 but vastly differently from those who graduated in 1940. In effect, the medical profession relies upon new generations of students to introduce new techniques in practice. The need for comparability in accounting requires that new techniques be introduced by all generations simultaneously. But this requirement runs squarely into the resistance mentioned by BGK, which I think is due to trained incapacity. I think this is an urgent research question. Not only must we decide *when* to introduce new techniques, we also must learn *how* to introduce those techniques to practitioners and users who have been trained in previous techniques. I fear there are no easy answers to either question. To rely upon market demand to tell us when to introduce new techniques will not work in accounting any more than it will work in medicine. To rely upon continuing education to overcome trained incapacity also will not work in accounting as has already been evidenced by its modest results in medicine.

Paper 2

As indicated above, I am delighted that BGK were able to distinguish between the past and the future, between retrospective and predictive uses of accounting information. I had a little difficulty with their wording on the first several readings since they seemed to me to be deliberately avoiding the word "explanation" by substituting more indirect locutions such as "sense making." Since they use "explanation" in Paper 1 to describe what they are doing in regard to the history of accounting but go to great lengths to avoid using "explanation" in Paper 2, I originally thought they had something different in mind. I could not discern that difference and therefore I have a minor quibble. It seems to me that "explanation" is a perfectly good term to use to describe the purpose of income measures. Just as I can use caloric intake and output to explain my past weight gains and losses even though that does not allow me to predict (forecast) future weight gains and losses, it seems that we should be able to use similar explanations of wealth gains and losses without regard to their aid or lack thereof in forecasting future income.

If we can obtain an accurate explanation of the past, we have identified the causal factors that will aid us in *controlling* the future. Surely controlling the future makes information useful even if it does not permit it to be forecasted. Gravity cannot be controlled but having an accurate explanation of its effects allowed us to know how much force would be required to overcome its effects. In years past it was universally forecasted that we would never be able to generate enough force to overcome the gravitational pull of the earth. The inability to forecast accurately putting a man on the moon does not in any way negate the usefulness of the past explanations of gravity. The error stemmed from an inability to forecast one of the inputs – generation of force – not from the past explanation. In the same way, you cannot forecast my future weight because you cannot forecast my caloric intake and output, but that does not negate the usefulness of the past explanations of my weight gains and losses. Income statements are also explanations of past wealth changes that provide very little aid in forecasting the future because the revenues and expenses cannot be forecasted, but that does not negate the usefulness of the past explanations.

In accounting we have overlooked the relationship of explanations and forecasting. We have focused narrowly on forecasting to the point where it has become a synonym for "usefulness." Indeed, it seems to me that temporal confusion, not aggregation as BGK would have it, is the most pervasive and pernicious fallacy in accounting. In previous times we were told that we had to report past costs because it was impossible to measure the present and that the reason we presented past costs was that they would benefit the future. Now we are told that we can measure the present but that any measure is deficient since only the future is of interest. Accountants seem to have overlooked the present altogether. It seems to me that BGK also skip the present. They use the three phyla of predictive, contractual, and retrospective. It is clear that *predictive* is a synonym for the *future* and *retrospective* is a synonym for the *past*. It seems to me that *contractual* is, or should be, a synonym for the *present*. I tried to think of contractual uses that do not require measurement of present magnitudes Of course, one can contract to do anything that one wants and agree to measure or forecast anything that one wants in that contract, but rational contracts of an economic nature almost invariably require a measurement of the present. I don't want to anticipate the Atkinson and Feltham paper [this volume], but in going through all of the examples of share-cropping that I am familiar with, the one thing that continues to recur is the need to measure present prices and quantities in order to decide how to make the contract in regard to the future division of the production. Thus it seems to me that present measurements (of prices and quantities) are necessary but not sufficient for efficient contracting.[2] If that is true, then the three phyla of BGK are future, present, and past. I encourage them to continue to pursue this, since the language of agency theory may permit other people to distinguish those three temporal locations, whereas the particular language that I and others have used to try to make the distinctions has been for the most part unsuccessful.

When I go on to consider BGK's deduced characteristics of information I am less sanguine. I must say that I admire their knowledge of agency theory a good deal more than I admire their knowledge of financial accounting. I find their ability to deduce objectivity from agency theory to be mildly interesting but entirely irrelevant since objectivity is much more important and pervasive than its use in contracting by agents. Indeed, it is an essential requirement of all scientific endeavours. The discussion about time additivity eludes me completely. I do not know which current values are not time additive. I can think of some rather elementary errors that have been made in the past in regard to the inability to add changes in current values because those current values could go either up or down, but surely BGK do not mean that current values are not time additive in that sense. I would simply ask them to spell out precisely what they mean by time additivity and would point them in the direction of a substantial body of literature in regard to the additivity question. The same is true of enterprise additivity. Except for using different terms to eliminate intercompany holdings, I don't know what they mean by enterprise additivity. Again, there is a substantial body of literature on additivity that would raise serious questions about adding the historical costs of one enterprise to those of another enterprise.

Irrevocability of income is a most puzzling characteristic. I don't know what BGK mean by this but I do know that past accounting theorists have continued to seek something that was irrevocable, but they have always failed to find it since even realized (cash) income of any given year can be offset by a loss when that cash is reinvested in a subsequent year. Perhaps this ties back to the same elementary question in regard to time additivity. It seems to me to be particularly ironic for BGK to talk about how agency theory and traditional accounting go hand in hand in Paper 1 and then to talk about a characteristic of agency theory, income being irrevocable, in Paper 2; one of the major problems of traditional accounting has been the fact that income is not irrevocable, as is evidenced by the continuing argument about corrections of prior periods, dirty surplus, big bath accounting, and so forth. I guess I would need further explanation of what is meant by risk-constraining before I could evaluate it. The way that it is stated seems to me to be old wine in new bottles. The notion of income being cash convergent also raises some questions. For example, price-level adjusted income is not cash convergent. Do they mean to exclude price-level adjustments for that reason?

In short, in Paper 2, I am in full agreement with their distinction between predictive and retrospective. I hope that what they mean by contractual is that there is also a need to measure the present, but that is not clear from their remarks. I would also say that it seems to me that concern with all types of contractual information is another way of stating that information should be useful for decision making. That is, whether or not to enter into a contract *is* a decision, and the information that is relevant to that decision falls under the general rubric of the decision usefulness school. How does this differ from contractual information? The characteristics of income are even more troublesome since it seems that BGK have overlooked an entire body of financial accounting literature in regard to each of the characteristics.

Paper 3

I was delighted with the distinction between and even-handed treatment of theoretical and empirical research. The reason for my delight was that it appeared for a while in accounting that "a priori" was a dirty word. A priori is not a dirty word in BGK's lexicon. My mind-set would have caused me to prefer BGK to present a few words about the difference between necessary truth and contingent truth because that is the basic distinction between theoretical or a priori and empirical efforts.

I also appreciate the insightful discussion of normative and positive. My reasons are similar: "normative" has become a dirty word in accounting circles. My mind-set would have caused me to prefer that they more clearly state the fact that *all* propositions can be stated in normative form or in positive form. The only difference between a normative proposition and a positive proposition is the statement of a goal or objective. For example, the Pythagorean theorem can be stated either positively or normatively. In its positive or descriptive form it merely says that the length of a hypotenuse is equal to the square root of the sum of the squares of the sides. In its normative form it says, if you want a brace that will fit on a given diagonal, then you ought to use the Pythagorean theorem to calculate the length of that brace. If you don't care whether or not the brace will fit, then you can use Sterling's theorem instead. If you want to avoid gangrene, then you ought to use antiseptic surgery. If you want to contact gangrene, then you ought not to use antiseptic surgery. Scientific propositions are intended to tell us something about the world so that we can pursue goals. The more we know about the world the more efficient our normative propositions can be. The continued insistence upon avoiding normative propositions in accounting borders on the absurd. In medicine, for example, we would have been laughed out of court had we continued to insist upon avoiding normative propositions, since all medical propositions are normative in the sense that they assume that you want to achieve good health. Indeed, *all* scientific propositions are normative in the sense that you can use them to achieve objectives. If you cannot use them to achieve objectives, then they are useless. But the original statement of such propositions are positive. They merely tell you how two or more empirical phenomena are related. Once you know how the empirical phenomena are related then you can utilize that knowledge to achieve an objective.

In short, I am in full agreement with everything that the authors say in regard to the distinction between theoretical and empirical and between normative and positive. My only criticism would be that they did not go far enough in making the distinctions crystal clear as has been done in much of the philosophy of science literature and in some of the past accounting literature.

Paper 4

It seems that the objective of Paper 4 is to classify research in accordance with an agency theory perspective. My problem with the classification scheme is that it is at once too broad and too narrow. It is too broad in that it classifies all research as either pre-response or user response. The pre-response group contains a heterogeneous collection of a great many different kinds of research that a good classification scheme would distinguish. I am in full accord with BGK's classification of the genus of user response and the inclusion of each of the species therein. I might warn them that they are likely to encounter a rather dramatic negative response by putting individual and market response in the same genus. I agree with BGK that they are measures of user response and that they should be in the same genus, but when I put them in the same group on a previous occasion [Sterling, 1970] the people who studied aggregate markets considered it an entirely inappropriate classification. The point in regard to the paper, however, is that BGK have gone to some lengths to make fine distinctions between various categories of user responses, while they have lumped together all sorts of different research efforts in the pre-response group.

My mind-set would cause me to prefer some other classification scheme, such as Dewhirst's [1974], since it is more inclusive of the various research efforts and a more natural classification of the kinds of problems that the various researchers addressed. The classification scheme that I have found most useful is to divide research efforts by the empirical domain that the researchers have examined. For example, at one time I suggested an anthropological classification because some researchers examine accountants' activities rather than user responses. BGK's classification scheme does not permit an anthropological species.[3]

The empirical domain type of classification will allow us to see clearly a vast difference between the agency theory approach to accounting theory formation and the approach that Skinner [this volume] calls economic reality, which is similar, if not identical, to what I have previously called empirical testability and to what the FASB calls representational faithfulness. An example from the history of mathematics will make the distinction crystal clear. Kline [1972, p. 19] tells us that the priests of the Temples of Edfu utilized the following equation to determine the area of a rectangle.

$$\text{Area} = \left(\frac{a+b}{2}\right)\left(\frac{c+d}{2}\right).$$

where a, b, c, and d are the lengths of the adjacent sides of a rectangle. As we now know, that equation is wrong. The area of a rectangle is the product of its length and width. The agency theory approach is to look at the sign "area" and to study it as any other economic good, including the demand for that sign, while being attuned to the social welfare effects of changing the method of calculating that sign, especially its redistributional effects. By contrast, the economic reality approach is to worry about how well the sign "area" reflects the underlying phenomena. In other works I have borrowed the terms "pragmatic informational content" versus "semantic informational content" from other disciplines to distinguish the two empirical domains. For example, if I yell "fire" and all of you run to the exits, then the sign "fire" has pragmatic informational content because you have responded to that sign. Thus, we can study the user response to the sign "fire." On the other hand, we can study the semantic informational content of the sign "fire" by examining whether or not there are flames in this room. If there are flames, then it also has semantic informational content but, if there are no flames, then it has semantic misinformational content. The same is true of the sign "area" in the above equation. It contains semantic misinformation, but it is also clear that it had pragmatic informational content because people did in fact react to the sign "area" as it was calculated by the priests of the Temples of Edfu. Indeed, there was probably homogeneity of beliefs about that sign and that is the way BGK define objectivity in their approach to accounting theory formation. But those who take the economic reality approach would consider objectivity to be the inter-observer agreement of independent measurers of the area of the rectangle.

If we put ourselves back to the time when that equation was being used, and if we imagine how the theory might have developed, I think you would agree that, if we had applied an agency theory approach, it would have resulted in an entirely different theory than the one that we now call Euclidean geometry. One of the first problems that we would encounter is that the priests of the Temples of Edfu used such calculations to reallocate the lands after the flooded Nile had receded. If we change the equation for the calculation of area to length times width, this would have had redistributional effects and some accountants would tell us that we could not change it because we could not compare interpersonal utilities. We would be in a position of what BGK call Pareto non-comparability. Since we could not change it, the basis for the development would have been on the use of this equation to derive other equations that also had social welfare effects. That is, in fact, what happened. The priests of the Temples of Edfu decided that when they were calculating the area of a triangle they should use the same equation as above except that, since a triangle had only three sides, then d is equal to zero. That seems plausible but, of course, it is also wrong. But once that method had been put into effect we could not change that either for the same reasons as given above. Of course, the way that geometry developed was tantamount to the economic reality approach. At some point it was discovered that the above formula was wrong and it was changed to length times width.

When that change was made, it was also discovered that the formula for a triangle was wrong and it was also changed. And so forth, to the point where we had a sufficient number of such individual equations and rules of thumb, empirically derived, that allowed Euclid to subsume all of them in one general, elegant, system that has proved to be vastly useful and therefore, one would assume, has had tremendous social welfare benefits.

The analogy seems to me to fit rather well. What we are currently faced with is a continued insistence that we cannot utilize "normative" propositions even if they contain semantic information, because of their pragmatic effects, because there is no demand for such information, or because they will have redistributional effects. Of course, there are a number of people who deny that there is an economic reality and therefore they deny the applicability of the analogy. If that is the case, then I suggest that we have been perpetrating a gigantic hoax on the world for a very long time. Surely there must be *some* kind of economic reality and we are supposed to be measuring something. If not, then I suggest that we close up shop and try to find some way to make an honest living. To put it bluntly, I don't think that voting schemes or other social choice mechanisms have anything to do with how we ought to calculate the area of a rectangle. Similarly I don't think that voting schemes or other social choice mechanisms have anything to do with how we measure the price and quantity of corn produced or the price and quantity of seed planted. I think that what we ought to do is to concentrate on accurate measures of relevant variables and if they have redistributional effects, then recognize that those redistributional effects are based upon the reality of the measures instead of worrying about interpersonal comparisons of utilities.

Third stage evaluation

The application of logic decides what elementary propositions there are. What belongs to its application, logic cannot anticipate. It is clear that logic must not clash with its application. But logic has to be in contact with its application.

—Ludwig Wittgenstein

My final evaluation stems from unsuccessful attempts to apply agency theory to particular accounting problems. I took what I learned from BGK and ran through a list of particular problems to see if it would help in solving those problems. One such problem that I considered was pensions. It is clear that a pension plan *is* a contract between the management and the employees, that management is the agent of the owners and that such contracts will alter the riskiness of the creditors. The problem is to design an information system that will facilitate efficient contracting. After extended reflection I found that I could not say anything about how to design the information system. BGK evidently view the problem as a change in the *accounting rule* for reporting pensions that will make someone better or worse off, which makes it a normative question analogous to the size of the minimum wage. By contrast, I view the problem as the *pension plan* already having made someone better or worse off and the question is what accounting rule best reports how much better or worse off they are. I view it as a measurement (positive) question analogous to the area of a rectangle. Perhaps my inability to apply the concepts of agency theory is due to limitations in my understanding, rather than to a deficiency in the theory, so I shall not conclude that it cannot be applied. Instead, I shall ask BGK to apply it. Given all you know about agency theory, what does it tell you about how to account for pensions?

I do not mean to restrict the question to pensions. I would be happy to see the theory applied to any accounting problem and therefore I will encourage BGK to take a problem of their choosing and work out the implications of agency theory for the benefit of those of us with lesser understanding. Until that is done, I shall remain frustrated by a level of abstractness that prevents me from seeing how it can be applied to our many pressing problems.

Notes

1. Like the omniscient aggregate market, I cannot be fooled. Not only did I see through the single title to the fact that there are four sub-papers, I was also able to discern that the fourth author is an undercover *agent* of the KGB (King, Gibbins and Butterworth) whose actions can undoubtedly only be explained by *agency* theory.

2. I find it particularly puzzling when *accountants* who employ an *economic perspective*, of the agency theory variety or any other variety, insist that the relevancy of present prices has not been proven or that the demand for historical cost information provides evidence of the relevance of historical costs. *Economists* who employ an *economic perspective* reach opposite conclusions. Samuelson [1966] is particularly pertinent to this Symposium since he discusses share-cropping in speculative (contracting, risk-sharing) markets. The entire analysis concerns present and future prices and quantities [p. 184 ff.]. Nowhere does he conclude that past prices are relevant. He also concludes that no one knows how future prices will move [p. 205]. This leaves only present prices and quantities as relevant and knowable. Why is it that a Nobel Laureate economist sees that so clearly when accountant-economists do not? Perhaps mind-sets provide the answer here as elsewhere.
3. Incidentally, one of the prime anthropologists was Littleton who seemed to have a very optimistic outlook on the accounting principles that existed at any given moment in time. I have used the phrase "accounting Darwinism" to describe Littleton's outlook. I was surprised to find BGK using accounting Darwinism explicitly. When they say that only the fittest practices survive, I wonder how they would go about testing that proposition.

References

Atkinson, A.A. and G.A. Feltham. "Agency Theory Research and Financial Accounting Standards," (this volume, pp. 257-289).

Dewhirst, John F. "The Financial Accounting Theory Course in a Changing Environment," *CAmagazine* (November 1974), pp. 67-70.

Kaplan, Abraham. *The Conduct of Inquiry: Methodology for Behavioral Science* (San Francisco: Chandler Publishing Company, 1964).

Kline, Morris. *Mathematical Thought from Ancient to Modern Times* (New York: Oxford University Press, 1972).

Robbins, Lionel. *An Essay on the Nature & Significance of Economic Science* (1932. Reprint. Darby, Penn.: Darby Books, 1981).

Samuelson, Paul A. "Intertemporal Price Equilibrium: A Prologue to the Theory of Speculation," in *Collected Scientific Papers of Paul Samuelson*, vol. 2, ed. Joseph E. Stiglitz (Cambridge, Mass.: MIT Press, 1966).

Skinner, Ross M. "Research and Standard Setting in Financial Accounting – An Illustrative Case," (this volume, pp. 153-202).

Sterling, Robert R. "Accounting Research, Education and Practice – Conflicts, Compromises or Complements," *Journal of Business Administration* (Spring 1973), pp. 15-30.

——. "On Theory Construction and Verification," *The Accounting Review* (July 1970), pp. 444-457.

Issues in Accounting Education
Vol. 4 No. 1
Spring 1989

Teaching the Correspondence Concept

Robert R. Sterling

THIS paper is addressed to accounting faculty. It is intended primarily for consideration by accounting faculty in their role as teachers, although teaching presupposes previous learning and my view is that the learning (self-teaching) function is identical to the research function in many important respects. There is also some overlap with the role of administration, particularly administering curriculum. However, the main purpose of this paper is to propose a means to improve the teaching of accounting.

THE IMPORTANCE OF THE TEACHING FUNCTION

The reason for focusing on the teaching function is my settled view that the betterment of accounting must begin in the classroom. Today's students are tomorrow's practitioners and the ideas we impart to them will determine, in significant measure, the future course of accounting practice. Also a small fraction of today's students are tomorrow's faculty and the ideas we impart to them will influence the future course of accounting education and accounting research. The impact of teachers is certainly much greater than usually recognized, and in regard to long-term impact I would venture that it is greater than that of researchers, administrators and, yes, even standard setters.

The effect of ideas was declared greater than vested interests in Keynes' [1935, p. 383–384] famous passage:

> . . .there are not many who are influenced by new theories after they are twenty-five or thirty years of age, so that the ideas which civil servants and politicians and even agitators apply to current events are not likely to be the newest. But, soon or late, it is ideas, not vested interests, which are dangerous for good or evil.

Robert R. Sterling is Kendall D. Garff Professor of Business Enterprise at the University of Utah.

This is an abridgement of a paper presented to the American Accounting Association New Faculty Consortium at Spacek University, St. Charles, Illinois on February 13, 1988. The deletions, suggested by the editor, consisted mainly of notes that compared accounting to science. Anyone interested in an unabridged version can obtain a copy from the author.

Most readers remember this passage for its forceful statement of the power and tenacity of ideas but overlook the age at which those ideas are obtained. The part that is overlooked implicitly burdens teachers with a heavy responsibility: the age after which new theories are no longer influential is near the usual age of receipt of a university degree and thus the influential theories are undoubtedly those that were imparted by university teachers. This makes teachers responsible for ideas that, for good or evil, will continue their influence for the remainder of the students' working lives.

Such considerations should also put to rest the perennial proposal that teachers teach GAAP and standard setters formulate GAAP, with the implication that the two functions are entirely unrelated. My experience at FASB convinced me of the significant influence of teachers on standard setters and thence on standards. I am not convinced that teachers' influence on standards is greater than the influence that comes from concerted pressure by corporate managers, but I am convinced that it is vastly greater than the vested interests of standard setters. I also believe that it is greater than those factors (such as firm affiliation or client interests) whose influence has been subjected to repeated testing.

A PROPOSAL TO IMPROVE TEACHING

My view of the dominant influence of teaching on the future development of accounting has led me to consider ways to improve teaching and to make a proposal. Instead of the usual entreaty to "teach concepts instead of mechanics" (leaving the concepts to teach unspecified), I will propose teaching one specific, elementary, commonsense concept. The similarity of accounting for volume to accounting for costs is a convenient vehicle to explain and illustrate the elementary concept to be proposed.

Similarity of Volume and Cost

By just substituting "transfer" for "transaction" we can account for volume in the same way that we now account for costs. Instead of debiting and crediting the dual effects of transactions, we can debit and credit the dual effects of transfers—receipts and issues at two different locations.

We often hear of the "unique" or "peculiarly difficult" problems in accounting, especially those caused by changing prices, including the dreaded "rubber yardstick" problem, but notice that an identical situation exists when accounting for volume. The cost or price of materials expands and contracts with economic changes; the volume of materials expands and contracts with temperature changes. Recording the receipt of volume per unit of weight can be done in exactly the same way that we now record cost per unit of weight.

1/1	Oil Inventory in Tank 1	$400	
	Accounts Payable (Union Pacific)		$400

To record the purchase of $400 of oil (100 tons @ 4.00 dollars/ton) from the Union Pacific Railroad.

1/1	Oil Inventory in Tank 1	฿400	
	Union Pacific		฿400

To record the receipt of ฿400 of oil (100 tons @ 4.00 barrels/ton) from the Union Pacific Railroad.

TABLE 1
Volume of Oil

	A FIFO	B LIFO	C Average
Debits:			
(from Union Pacific) at January 1	400	400	400
(from Long Island) at March 1	440	440	440
Balance at March 2	840	840	840
Credit:			
(to Roadway) at June 30	240	264	252
Balance at July 1	600	576	588

The structure of the two entries is identical (they are "isomorphic"), differing only in content.

At March 1 when the barrels/ton have increased (due to ambient temperature increases from January to March) and the dollars/ton have increased (due to ambient economic changes), the following entries could be used to record another purchase or receipt.

3/1	Oil Inventory in Tank 1	$440	
	Accounts Payable (Long Island)		$440

To record the purchase of $440 of oil (100 tons @ 4.40 dollars/ton) from the Union Pacific Railroad.

3/1	Oil Inventory in Tank 1	₿440	
	Long Island		₿440

To record the receipt of ₿440 of oil (100 tons @ 4.40 barrels/ton) from the Long Island Railroad.

The receipt of two lots of oil at different barrels/ton presents the same problem in accounting for volume as different dollars/ton presents for costs.

Since the same problem is presented, the same solution can be offered, namely choosing LIFO, FIFO, average, or specific identification to determine the cost of goods sold or the volume of goods shipped. If 60 tons were sold or shipped to Roadway Express at July 1 and FIFO were selected, the entries would be:

7/1	Cost of Goods Sold	$240	
	Oil Inventory in Tank 1		$240

To record the sale of $240 of oil at FIFO (60 tons @ 4.00 dollars/ton) to Roadway Express.

7/1	Volume of Goods Shipped	₿240	
	Oil Inventory in Tank 1		₿240

To record the shipment of ₿240 of oil at FIFO (60 tons @ 4.00 barrels/ton) to Roadway Express.

And similar entries could be made if the LIFO, specific identification, or average method were selected.

The results of LIFO, FIFO, and average entries are compared in Table 1. As will be familiar from accounting for costs, there is no disagreement about the first three rows in the table but there is a long-standing controversy about the fourth and fifth rows. The problem arises in the measurement of the Volume of Goods Shipped. That measurement requires a flow assumption or, if possible, a flow determination because that would permit measurement by specific identification and avoid the necessity of making an assumption. The flow assumption (or determination) used for the Volume of Goods Shipped affects the amount of volume on hand at July 1 (the ending inventory) and this sparks the debate about the relative importance of the balance sheet and income statement. It is argued that the more important statement should display the more current volumes (current costs) and the less important statement the more out-of-date volumes. In an attempt to avoid that choice, some suggest abandoning articulation and that leads to another controversy. And so on for most of the long-standing controversies in accounting.

The Correspondence Concept

The specific, elementary, commonsense concept that I propose that we begin to teach is the need for correspondence of a calculated numeral to an independent observation (measurement) of the phenomena that the numeral purports to represent. This is a commonsense idea as well as a criterion common to *all* sciences, and a little used, less understood qualitative characteristic in FASB's conceptual framework [FASB, 1980, par. 63]. Although there is confusion about how this concept could be applied to cost, it should be obvious how it could be applied to volume. Under this concept, LIFO, FIFO, average, and other calculation methods would be considered to be hypotheses to be tested, and calculated figures such as 240, 264, and 252 would be compared to observations (measurements) of the volume to find out which, if any, of those figures correspond to, or faithfully represent, the measured amount. If, over a series of trials under varying conditions, some calculation method were found to yield numerals that closely corresponded to the measured amount, that method would be selected for continued use and the others would be discarded. If no such correspondence were found, all calculation methods would be discarded and measurements would be made and their results reported.[1]

COMPREHENSION OF THE CONCEPT

There are a number of indications that accountants do not or only partially comprehend the correspondence concept. Previously I thought that accountants did not understand the importance of the concept—the crucial role it plays in science—but subsequently I have come to believe that they do not comprehend the concept. By contrast, there are a number of in-

[1] Perhaps I can motivate teachers to more carefully consider this too obvious, too elementary concept by calling attention to Einstein's [1950, p. 66] extraordinary declaration:

> Everything depends on the degree to which words and word combinations correspond to the world of impression....What science strives for is an utmost acuteness and clarity of concepts as regards their mutual relation and their correspondence to sensory data....The connection between concepts and statements on the one hand and the sensory data on the other hand is established through acts of counting and measuring whose performance is sufficiently well determined.

It rivets my attention when a deep thinker, especially one not given to exaggeration or to careless use of all inclusive terms, says *everything depends*.

dications that nonaccountants, particularly scientists, fully comprehend the concept as well as the importance of applying it. My conjectures about the difference in comprehension of the concept and its importance caused me to seek evidence by designing and conducting the test described in the following paragraphs.

A Test of Relative Comprehension

A questionnaire was prepared that described accounting for volume in the same way it was described earlier and then the following question was asked:[2]

> Which, if any, of the figures in the credit row in Table 1 faithfully represents the volume of oil issued at June 30? The first three of the following possible answers correspond to the columns in Table 1 and each answer explains how the credit in the column was obtained.
>
> A. The 240 barrel figure in column A. That figure was obtained as follows: 60 tons × (400 barrels ÷ 100 tons) = 240. The proposal for reporting that figure is made on the basis of the assumption that the first receipt is likely to be the source of the first issue (that is, FIFO).
>
> B. The 264 barrel figure in column B. That figure was obtained as follows: 60 tons × (440 barrels ÷ 100 tons) = 264. The proposal for reporting that figure is made on the basis of the assumption that the last receipt is likely to be the source of the first issue (that is, LIFO).
>
> C. The 252 barrel figure in column C. That figure was obtained as follows: 60 tons × (840 barrels ÷ 200 tons) = 252. The proposal for reporting that figure is made on the basis of the assumption that the receipts would combine and therefore the issue would be at the average barrels per ton of both receipts (that is, average).
>
> D. Making proposals on the basis of associating the issue with receipts is on the right track but it should be based on knowledge of the association rather than on an assumption about the association. If one knew which receipt or receipts was the source of the issue (that is, if the issue were specifically identified as coming from a particular receipt), then one could derive the figure that is a faithful representation of the volume of oil issued on June 30. Thus, any of the figures in the credit row of Table 1 could be a faithful representation if the assumption about the association happens to be the actual association.
>
> E. Making proposals on the basis of associating the issue with receipts is on the wrong track. Even if one knew which receipt or receipts was the source of the issue, it would not be of help in deriving the figure that is a faithful representation of the

[2] I am grateful to Mary Teresa Kwang, an apprentice psychometrician, for vetting the questionnaire, administering it to the subjects, conducting the posttest interviews, and reviewing the presentation of the results. The test vis-á-vis accounting as a social science is discussed in Sterling [1988].

TABLE 2
Physics vs. Accounting Subjects
Responses to the Question

Answer	Physicists		Accountants	
A (FIFO)	1	3%	0	0%
B (LIFO)	0	0%	3	11%
C (Average)	2	6%	18	64%
D (Specific Identification)	2	6%	3	11%
E (None)	27	84%	4	14%
SUM	32	100%	28	100%

volume of oil issued at June 30. Thus, none of the figures in the credit row of Table 1 is a faithful representation of the issue regardless of the actual or assumed association of receipts and issues.

The above question was given to 28 third-year accounting students. The same question (altered slightly to make it understandable to nonaccountants by, for example, substituting "receipts" and "issues" for "debits" and "credits") was given to 32 third-year physics students who had never taken an accounting course. Answers to the question from the two groups are compared in Table 2.

The disparity of results is most clearly shown by comparing the 84 percent of the physicist-subjects to the 14 percent of accountant-subjects who answered E. Thus, 86 percent of the accountant-subjects selected answers based on accounting methods whereas only 16 percent of the physicist-subjects selected answers based on accounting methods. The disparity became more apparent during the posttest interviews. Correcting for the misunderstandings that were revealed in those interviews would alter the results to all of the physicists and virtually none of the accountants giving E as their answer.[3]

Inferences From the Test

Although the test clearly reveals a difference between these two groups of subjects, it doesn't reveal anything about the cause of that difference. We must infer the cause. I infer that the reason the accountant-subjects didn't apply the correspondence concept is that they don't understand it and are not aware of

[3] The test results support my conjecture that there is a vast difference between accountants and physicists in regard to their understanding of this concept. My worry is that it provides too much support. Such tests are usually not very tidy unless the investigator inadvertently influences the subjects. I fear that may have happened here. Although neither Kwang nor I have been able to identify any sources of bias, I remain suspicious for the sole reason that the test results are too consistent. We should expect some contrary findings even if they are just noise.

its importance. I further infer that the reason for lack of understanding and awareness is due to not being taught about it. That inference is strengthened by the comparison to physicist-subjects who are in fact taught about testing numerals by such measurements (observations) and the importance of such testing is instilled in them from the first day of class in elementary physics.[4]

Confidence in the inference is augmented by the fact that accountant-subjects did sanction answers obtained from applying the methods that they were taught even though this particular application of those methods is far outside the context in which they were taught. Physicist-subjects, by contrast, were annoyed by answers obtained from those methods and insisted on measuring the volume. This divergence became even more apparent in the post-test interviews which revealed that the accountant-subjects were content with the choice of answers presented and they did not volunteer any suspicions about the test nor did they voice any when asked. By contrast, the physicist-subjects thought that the choices of answers were foolish and several attempted to leave before they had answered the questions and had to be persuaded to continue. The typical physicist-subject volunteered that they were suspicious of the test. They thought there was a hidden purpose (e.g., "one of those weird psychology experiments") that had something to do with assessing their personality or sanity because the answers were so obviously wrong.

When pressed to explain why they objected to LIFO—FIFO type calculations, all but one[5] of the physicist-subjects presented an explanation to the effect that the resulting numerals would be shown to be "wrong" or "false" (or a cognate) if compared to a measurement of the volume. By contrast, when accountant-subjects were pressed to explain why they thought it was appropriate to use a LIFO-FIFO type calculation, none of them suggested a comparison to a measurement of the volume nor did any of them use the world "right" or "true" (or a cognate) to describe the numerals emanating from their endorsed calculation. Instead they presented reasons concerned with flow assumptions and consistency (e.g., the particular flow assumption wouldn't make any difference if it were applied consistently) which were incomprehensible to the nonaccountant interviewer (Kwang) and, therefore, the recording of these explanations was less effective than that of the physics explanations.

---

[4] The textbook recently used in elementary physics at the University of Utah is typical in this regard. The first chapter of Serway [1986, p. 3] is titled "Introduction: Physics and Measurement" and the first two sentences of that chapter introduce the concept:

> Physics is a fundamental science concerned with understanding the natural phenomena that occur in our universe. It is a science based on experimental observations and quantitative measurements.

In addition to establishing the concept by precept in texts, it is established by example in physics laboratories where students measure and observe. By contrast, accounting texts use "calculation" as a synonym for "measurement" and accounting laboratories are rooms where students calculate but where they do not measure and observe.

[5] The one who didn't present that particular explanation couldn't present any explanation at all. He seemed to be dumfounded by being asked to explain something that he thought was "too simple" to require explanation. Repeated questioning did not elicit any response other than that it is "too simple" to be explained.

In short, it is inferred that accountants in general do not understand the correspondence concept and are not aware of its importance. This inference was drawn from test results from a small sample of accounting students who did not apply the correspondence concept to the task of accounting for volume nor did they mention it in post-test interviews. It is further inferred that the reason they did not apply it or mention it is that it was not taught to them, and that this explanation extends to the population of accountants.

Additional Evidence

Testing the correspondence concept has been the subject of 15 recent lectures[6] at which members of the audiences kindly consented to answering various preliminary versions of the above described questionnaire prior to the beginning of the lecture. The proportion of respondents in those audiences who answered E ranged from 43 percent to 55 percent which is significantly more than the 14 percent response rate reported in Table 2. This may be due to the increased sophistication of the faculty and Ph.D. students in those audiences, to the desire of the third-year students to demonstrate their knowledge of accounting methods, to the variation in the way the questions were phrased or administered, or to some other factor(s). The questionnaire was administered to these audiences to illustrate the point of the lecture rather than to formally gather data, and the lack of controls renders that data suspect. Nonetheless, the fact that about 50 percent of *each* audience tested answered E strikes me as significant. In addition, similar results were obtained by Professor W. T. Baxter [personal communication]. He administered the questionnaire to a group of accounting students from The London School of Economics and informed me that 18 of 32 (56 percent) of the students answered E with eight (25 percent) answering C (average) and six (19 percent) answering D (specific identification).

Half Full or Half Empty

Most members of the audiences expressed great satisfaction from their higher proportion of E answers, using it as the basis for arguing that the students in my sample were not representative or as the basis for the conclusion that the problem is not serious, or both. Professor Baxter expressed similar sentiments about the results he obtained:

> This is quite encouraging (though a cynic might suggest that it shows our teaching of accounts is not very thorough).

[6] I am grateful to the sponsors of the Lee Kuan Yew Distinguished Lecture, National University of Singapore; Raymond J. Chambers Distinguished Lecture, University of Sydney; Israel Conference of Accountants; Deloitte's Distinguished Lecture, University of Edinburgh; Lowden Distinguished Lecture, TCU; Annual Distinguished Speaker Series, Long Beach State University; Meeting of the Arizona Society of CPAs, University of Arizona; Andersen Distinguished Lecture, University of New Mexico; Colorado Consortium of Accounting Professors, Colorado Society of CPAs and Colorado Chapter of FEI; Eccles Distinguished Lecture, Weber State University; Faculty from Louisiana Universities, University of New Orleans; Faculty-Ph.D. Seminar, Temple University; Mid-Atlantic Regional AAA Meeting, Atlantic City; and Brown Bag Seminar, University of Utah. In addition I am grateful to the Accounting Faculty of the University of Alberta for allowing me to tape the discussion following the lecture. In that case I requested permission to give the lecture without payment of expenses or honorarium because I wanted to use the taped discussion as data for further testing, and I thought that purpose would be more appropriate at an uninvited, unfunded presentation.

I fear that I am such a cynic. Rather than being encouraged by this glass being half full, I am disheartened by it being half empty. I receive no satisfaction from discovering that half of all accounting faculty respondents do not make the error because that means that half do make the error. I think whether we are encouraged or disheartened is due to the difference in our assessment of the problem. I view the failure to apply the correspondence concept to be a fatal error whereas many accountants see it as a trifling technicality.

Scientists, by contrast, consider the correspondence concept to be crucial. Whether a thought (or symbol for the thought) corresponds with its object is the very essence of the scientific method. The independent observation of the object to discover whether correspondence is present or absent is the process of verifying or falsifying scientific statements and, therefore, the correspondence concept is indispensable to science.

APPLICABILITY OF THE CONCEPT

The results reported in Table 2 have been presented to about 2,000 people who comprised the audiences mentioned in footnote 6. A significant number of the members of these audiences asked questions and made comments about the findings and inferences. Despite the diversity of geography (six different countries), education (ranging from practitioners with no university education to teachers with doctorates), experience, culture, business practices, etc., all of these audiences voiced a common theme:

> The correspondence concept may be applicable to volume but it is not applicable to historical cost and, therefore, it is not applicable to accounting.

Reasons given in support of that common theme started from various places but they all reached the conclusion that historical cost is based on *conventions*, not on *measurements*. Since historical cost is in a class by itself, so the argument goes, we cannot learn by drawing analogies to other attributes nor can we apply standards or criteria that are applied to attributes in other disciplines.[7]

The Alternatives

Those who believe that historical cost is completely different from volume and other measurable attributes are right. One can say that the differ-

[7] The isolation of accounting that springs from the belief that its problems are unique is troublesome because it results in developing idiosyncratic criteria and standards rather than importing well-tested criteria and standards from other disciplines. Kaplan [1964, p. 3] warns about such isolation:

> There is no doctrine of states' rights, as it were, in accord with which the sovereignty of a particular discipline can be interposed between a parochial creed and the stern judgment of the scientific community as a whole. It will not do to say, "You people simply don't understand our problems!" or, "We have our own logic, our sources and standards of truth." There are indeed differences among the various disciplines, and these differences are important to the conduct of inquiry in each case. But they do not serve to cut the sciences off from one another.

Expressions of my worry about the isolation of accounting usually bring forth the reply that accounting is not a science and, therefore, it must develop its own standards because it cannot use scientific standards, which reply serves to increase my worry about the isolation of accounting.

ence makes the correspondence concept *not applicable* to historical cost or that the difference is the result of the *failure to apply* the correspondence concept to historical cost. The alternatives are: (1) accept the correspondence concept and use it as a criterion for designing and assessing attributes and thereby reject historical cost or (2) accept historical cost and use it as a criterion for designing and assessing concepts and thereby reject the correspondence concept.

The alternatives, and the educational influence on the choice, can be illustrated by continuing the consideration of accounting for volume. Suppose that for many generations there has existed an attribute called "historical volume" which is defined to be different from "ordinary volume" and an example of which is presented in Table 1. The defining difference is that historical volume is restricted to the selection of LIFO, FIFO, average, or some similar way of calculating a numeral whereas ordinary volume is determined by the empirical operation of measurement. Now suppose that each generation has been taught how to calculate historical volume (and not taught how to measure ordinary volume) and then has spent a lifetime practicing what they were taught. If someone then comes along to suggest that the criterion for accepting a calculation method for historical volume should be the correspondence of the calculated numerals to measurements, the automatic reply would be that the criterion is not applicable because historical volume is not measurable. The fact that none of the historical volume numerals corresponds to measures of ordinary volume would be taken as proof that ordinary volume is different from historical volume, not as proof that those methods of calculation should be abandoned in favor of measurements.

This line of thinking makes historical volume inviolate. The attribute has become the criterion by which concepts are judged: instead of searching for attributes that satisfy the criterion, we search for concepts that are satisfied by the attribute. For example, we could devise the concepts or standards of realization, conservatism, going concern, periodicity, entity, recognition, matching and attaching, and so forth, all of which *must* be applicable to historical volume for the forthright reason that they were designed to be applicable to that particular attribute. Then we could teach those concepts as criteria or standards and show how historical volume satisfies them, thereby further reinforcing the strength of belief in that attribute by the subsequent generation.

After being taught and practiced for several generations, the attribute of historical volume would become so familiar that it would be, as common speech profoundly has it, "second nature," whereas ordinary volume would remain foreign and unfathomable because it was not taught and practiced. Historical volume would have become, in the words of Tolstoy (cited by Gleick [1987, p. 38]), an idea "which they have delighted in explaining to colleagues, which they have proudly taught to others, and which they have woven, thread by thread, into the very fabric of their lives."

The analogy should illuminate two important points: (1) historical volume doesn't make sense to those who haven't been subjected to prolonged teaching and practicing of historical volume because they implicitly apply the correspondence concept to volume and (2) it would make sense to members of an occupation that had a long history of teaching and practicing historical volume and they would reject the correspondence concept because it is not applicable to historical volume rather than altering the attribute so that it corresponds to something. I think that is precisely what has happened in accounting: we have conditioned our students so that they (1) think that historical cost makes sense even though it doesn't make sense to those in the population that haven't been subjected to accounting education and practice and (2) would reject the correspondence concept because it is not applicable to historical cost rather than altering the attribute so that it corresponds to something.

TEACHER'S CHOICE

Each teacher is free to choose to include the correspondence concept in the topics covered or to omit it. Each teacher is compelled, however, to make the choice because the refusal to choose is, in fact, the choice to maintain the status quo. Teachers will influence their students one way or the other—to not influence them is not an option—and, thus, the teacher must decide which way to influence them. My recommendation is to include the correspondence concept and to omit one of the myriad cryptic calculation methods, such as the nth method of inventory valuation, that require so much incremental effort to learn and provide so little incremental benefit.

Research Support and Guidance

Teachers who decide to teach the correspondence concept will be disappointed if they expect to find support or guidance in the accounting research literature. That lacuna requires that I rescind my previous recommendation to teach research results in addition to teaching GAAP. I made that recommendation [Sterling, 1973] at a time when most researchers asked questions about what to record and report or how to improve the reporting, but accounting research has become increasingly distant from questions of that kind. Instead of investigating what to represent on financial statements or how to improve the representation, it is now fashionable to investigate the market's reaction to financial statements, the social welfare effects of changing the statements, the motivation of managers for manipulating the statements, and similar subjects. Thus, teachers will not be able to find guidance for what to record and report in the accounting research literature for the straightforward reason that the subject is rarely discussed in that literature. We also will not be able to find support for the correspondence concept because it is irrelevant to the topics being examined. The question of whether the numerals correspond to something is irrelevant to the question of whether the market reacts to those numerals, for example.

Almost unanimous support, as well as an abundance of examples that provide contextual guidance, can be found in the scientific literature, however. Although some philosophers hold opposing views, the daily procedures of scientific inquiry virtually compels practicing scientists to accept some sort of realist position, at least during their working hours. An idealist would find it difficult to earn a living in science because the norms of scientific communication and corroboration require that the terms and sentences of science refer to an observable reality. Beyond the examples within the specific science, however, little guidance can be found in the scientific literature because application of the correspondence concept is so widely accepted and well understood that it is seldom discussed after the introductory chapter of the elementary text. For guidance beyond examples one must look to the philosophical literature where realism is subjected to close examination and contrasted to other schools of thought. However, *all* of the various schools of thought—scientific realism, logical positivism, constructive empiricism, operationism, etc.—in the philosophy of science (but not in general philosophy) accept the correspondence concept, albeit with varying degrees of explicitness, enthusiasm, emphasis, and discomfiture. Additional guidance, albeit less direct, can be found in the cognitive psychology literature where "cognitive maps," "schemata," or "mental models" are said to "fit" the external world in certain respects, that is, correspond to the external world.

Teachers who find the prospect of understanding the philosophy of science to be daunting should find it comforting to know that, in general, it is much more easily understood than most of the recent accounting research literature. One reason is that being understood is given high priority by acknowledged scholars. A second reason is that science, and its elucidation by philosophers of science, is *commonsense*, or, as Einstein [1950, p. 17] put it: "The whole of science is nothing more than a refinement of everyday thinking."

REFERENCES

Einstein, A., *Essays in Physics* (New York: Philosophical Library, 1950).

Financial Accounting Standards Board (FASB), *Statement of Financial Accounting Concepts No. 2* (Stamford: Financial Accounting Standards Board, 1980).

Gleick, J., *Chaos: Making a New Science* (New York: Viking, 1987).

Kaplan, A., *The Conduct of Inquiry—Methodology for Behavioral Science* (San Francisco: Chandler, 1964).

Keynes, J. M., *The General Theory of Employment Interest and Money* (New York: Harcourt, Brace and Company, 1935).

Serway, R. A., *Physics for Scientists & Engineers with Modern Physics*, Second Edition (Philadelphia: Saunders College Publishing, 1986).

Sterling, R. R., "Confessions of a Failed Empiricist," *Advances in Accounting* (Spring 1988), pp. 3–35.

——, "Accounting Research, Education and Practice," *The Journal of Accountancy* (September 1973), pp. 44–52.

Journal of Accounting Education, Vol. 8, pp. 1-16, 1990
Printed in the USA.

0748-5751/90 $3.00 + .00

TEACHER, EDUCATE THYSELF

Robert R. Sterling
UNIVERSITY OF UTAH

Abstract: A test of the willingness of subjects to apply accounting calculations (LIFO, FIFO, average, specific identification) to nonaccounting phenomena was conducted. A majority of nonaccountant subjects were unwilling while a majority of accountant subjects were willing to apply accounting calculations to nonaccounting phenomena. A second "unobtrusive" and a third "quasi-obtrusive" test was conducted on subjects' willingness to accept the addition of numerals and the same difference between accountants and nonaccountants was observed. The basis of the difference in all tests was nonaccountants' requirement that numerals derived from calculations correspond to an independent measurement while accountants were unaware that such a requirement existed. The difference in subjects was inferred to be the result of nonaccountants having been taught about the correspondence concept and accountants not having been so taught. A recommendation that the accounting curriculum include the correspondence concept is offered.

In (Sterling, 1989) I proposed the teaching of the correspondence concept (explained in the next section) on the grounds that it would improve accounting as students learned it and implemented it in their practice or incorporated it in their research after graduation. That proposal was accompanied by a report of the responses to a questionnaire about an application of the correspondence concept. Those responses showed a vast difference between accountant-subjects and physicist-subjects in their application of the concept, which I took as evidence that accounting students don't understand the concept and from which I inferred that the reason they don't understand it is that it is not taught in accounting. A subsequent test revealed that accounting teachers do not understand the concept and therefore cannot teach it until they have educated themselves about it. Hence, the name of this article.

The test was designed to explore two[1] applications of the correspondence concept, one obtained from subjects' responses to an overt question and the other from voluntary responses to a covert question, that is, one obtrusive test and the other unobtrusive. The obtrusive test was presented in the previous article. The

This paper was prepared for presentation to the members of the AAA New Faculty Consortium at Spaeck University, St. Charles, IL, February 1990. It is a follow-up of the paper presented February 13, 1989 and published as (Sterling, 1989).

purpose of this article is to present the results of the unobtrusive test and a follow-up "quasi-obtrusive" test, as well as to discuss the implications of those tests.

This paper is structured as follows: (a) an explanation of the correspondence concept, (b) a discussion of what I mean by "obtrusive" and "unobtrusive" tests, (c) a brief review of the results of the previous obtrusive tests and the presentation of some additional results obtained by others, the presentation of the results of the (d) unobtrusive tests and (e) quasi-obtrusive tests, and (f) some conclusions regarding teaching.

THE CORRESPONDENCE CONCEPT

The correspondence concept was developed by the ancient philosophers and is currently in use by almost all humans.[2] Aristotle expressed it clearly in several of his works, for example, in *Metaphysics* (IX, 10; 1051 b) he writes:

> ... when is what is called truth or falsity present, and when is it not? We must consider what we mean by these terms. It is not because we think truly that you are pale, that you *are* pale, but because you *are* pale that we who say this have the truth.

That is, correspondence is the agreement of the thought, or sentence that expresses the thought, to the state of the world. If you are pale, then the sentence "you are pale" is said to correspond to the state of your complexion. If you are ruddy or black, then the sentence "you are pale" does not correspond to the state of your complexion. It is the *observation* of the state of your complexion that is said to verify or falsify the sentence.

The philosophical position adopted by Aristotle is now called "common sense realism" by, e.g., Popper (1972), Putnam (1987), and others. It certainly is common to the senses of accountants in our personal lives: we expect the butcher's sentence "this package contains 3 pounds of hamburger" (which is often shortened to "hamburger 3 pounds" when placed on a label) to correspond to the type and weight of the object in the package. By contrast, it is completely foreign to accountants in our professional lives: we do not understand what it *means* to require that the accountant's sentence "this warehouse contains $3 of inventory" (which is often shortened to "inventory $3" when placed on a financial statement) correspond to some state of the world.

The meaning of correspondence for accounting sentences is the same as the meaning for "you are pale" or "hamburger 3 pounds" and other ordinary sentences. Observations (which includes measurements but does *not* include calculations) allow us to determine whether or not they correspond to the state of the world. It is as simple as that. It is also as profound as that, as evidenced by the use of the correspondence concept by virtually all scientists. This view, sometimes called "scientific realism," has been clearly and repeatedly explained by Einstein (1954, p. 336):

> What science strives for is an utmost acuteness and clarity of concepts as regards their mutual relation and their correspondence to sensory data.

He goes on (p. 336) to say that correspondence "...is established through acts of counting and measuring..." and from this we come to understand that the esoteric sentences found in the theory of relativity are subjected to the same tests as the mundane sentences found in the butcher shop.

The tests described below were designed to (a) discover the degree of understanding of the correspondence concept among accountants (and compare it to nonaccountants), and (b) illustrate the meaning of the correspondence concept by applying it to the common problem of accounting for inventory.

OBTRUSIVE VERSUS UNOBTRUSIVE TESTS

Although teachers might not be familiar with the term "obtrusive" as it is applied to tests or observations, all have probably employed "unobtrusive" tests in their classroom in the same way that they were employed in the test reported herein. A teacher of the elementary course, for example, might explain the equality of debits and credits and also explain the bookkeeping cycle, then ask a direct question about the effect of that equality on the trial balance. In addition, the teacher might display a balance sheet that does not balance and observe which of the students mention the error. The first is obtrusive in that the overt question focuses the students' attention on the subject of the question and therefore directs the students to the type of answer expected by the teacher. The second is unobtrusive in that it does not focus the students' attention on a question (no question is overtly asked) and does not direct the students to the expectations of the teacher.

The unobtrusive test puts a much heavier burden on students, requiring that they (a) understand the bookkeeping cycle well enough to see that the equality of debits and credits entails that the balance sheet balance, (b) notice that the displayed balance sheet does not balance, and (c) be confident or aggressive enough to mention it. For that reason, the scores on unobtrusive are generally lower than on obtrusive tests. And that ordering of scores was expected to be the same for the tests reported herein.

The primary focus of this paper is the report of the latter type of test. Instead of asking another direct question, the subjects were given multiple opportunities to volunteer that they noticed that something was wrong. In later tests they were told that something (unspecified) is wrong with Table 1 and then asked to explain what is wrong, a "quasi-obtrusive" test.

Table 1. Volume of oil

	A FIFO	B LIFO	C Avg
Receipts:			
January 1 (100 tons @ 4 bbls/ton)	400	400	400
March 1 (100 tons @ 4.4 bbls/ton)	440	440	440
Amount at March 2	840	840	840
Issue:			
June 30 (60 tons @ ? bbls/ton)	240	264	252
Amount at July 1	600	576	588

THE OBTRUSIVE TEST

This section contains (a) a brief review of the previously reported results, and (b) new results obtained by others. Readers of Sterling (1988 or 1989) may skip the review but some recollection of the obtrusive question is necessary for the understanding of the report of the unobtrusive test.

The sequencing of the topics in this paper presents the interested reader with the opportunity to conduct a self-test. If desired, the following review of the results of the obtrusive test can be used by readers to see if they can determine what is wrong with Table 1 before reading the discussion of the unobtrusive tests in the next section. There is considerable evidence that subjects who have been told about the test beforehand tend to think that they would have discovered the error when the fact is that those that were not told did not discover the error. Thus, a self-test might allow readers to avoid misleading themselves.

Review of Previous Results

The previous test presented the problem of accounting for volume when the number of barrels per ton (analogous to dollars per ton) of oil varied with the ambient temperature. After describing two receipts at two different values of barrels per ton, the subjects were asked to account for the issue of 60 tons. The information and three of the five multiple choice answers are displayed in Table 1.

The other two of the five multiple choice answers were (D) specific identification and (E) all the previously offered answers are on the wrong track. The responses of the subjects are contained in Table 2.

The difference in the two groups is most clearly shown by comparing the percentage of E responses: 86% of the accountant-subjects selected answers based on accounting methods, whereas 84% of the physicist-subjects thought those answers to be on the wrong track. Correcting for the misunderstandings that were revealed in the post-test interviews would alter the results to all of the physicists and virtually none of the accountants giving E as their answer.[3]

Table 2. Physics vs. accounting subjects' responses to question 1

Answer	Physicists		Accountants	
A (FIFO)	1	3%	0	0%
B (LIFO)	0	0%	3	11%
C (Average)	2	6%	18	64%
D (Specific Identification)	2	6%	3	11%
E (Wrong Track)	27	84%	4	14%
SUM	32	100%	28	100%

In addition to the above evidence, there is less formal evidence that was gathered by presenting the questionnaire (in various preliminary versions) to more than 2,000 members of audiences (accountants) where the test was discussed. (See Sterling [1989] for a list of those audiences.) The results of those informal tests were that the responses to E clustered around 50%, staying within the narrow range of 43% to 55%.

More discussion of the above tests with reference to teaching can be found in Sterling (1989) and discussion with reference to accounting as a social science can be found in Sterling (1988). More detail about the results can also be found in both and the questionnaires are reproduced in the latter.

Additional Results

The questionnaire was also administered by Professors W. T. Baxter (London School of Economics), Daniel McDonald (Simon Fraser), and George J. Murphy (Saskatchewan) to their classes and the responses they generously shared with me are reproduced in Table 3.

Table 3. Additional accounting subjects — responses to question 1

	Baxter	McDonald	Murphy	Total
A (FIFO)	0%	8%	7%	5%
B (LIFO)	0%	0%	0%	0%
C (Average)	25%	23%	27%	26%
D (Specific Identification)	19%	4%	19%	15%
E (Wrong Track)	56%	65%	47%	54%
Number of subjects	32	26	59	117

Both Baxter and Murphy obtained response rates close to the 50% rate that I obtained from audiences at lectures. McDonald's letter accompanying his report contained the conjecture that his 65% response rate to E was due to the particular reading material that he had assigned shortly before the tests. When all three are combined the 54% falls within the range of 43% to 55% found in my audiences. Instead of taking that as support, however, I take it as an illustration that large samples are equally as dangerous as small samples, that we risk overlooking information about diversity when testing too many subjects and risk the information being unrepresentative when testing too few.

What remains most puzzling is that the E answers from their subjects (and from my audiences) is as high as 50% while only 14% of my accountant-subjects answered E. That is, the E answers from accountant-subjects displayed in Table 2 are significantly lower than those in Table 3 and, as reported infra, response rates similar to those reported in Table 2 have been subsequently obtained from the same subject pool.

An informal administration of the test by George Slater (Case Western) yielded intriguing longitudinal results: 100% of his first-accounting-course students answered E whereas 50% of his second-accounting-course students answered E. This is consistent with the results obtained by Tweedie (1977) and Lee (1984). Their tests were designed to detect the effects of traditional accounting teaching on the subjects' ideas about wealth and profit, and both authors report that subjects with no education in accounting have views ("intuitive concepts") that are radically different from those with accounting education. Lee compared pre- and post-tests of students who took just one course in accounting (p. 126) and concluded (p. 136):

> The teaching process, perhaps not surprisingly, was sufficiently persuasive to override these [previously held] intuitions and replace them with what was being taught.

Slater's informal finding of a change from 100% to 50% in just one course is consistent with that conclusion.

Additional longitudinal results were obtained from students at the University of Utah. I gave the questionnaire to 62 undergraduates at a Beta Alpha Psi meeting and obtained about the same response as reported in Table 2. (Nine students or 15% answered E.) Then I spent almost one hour at that meeting explaining how one could measure volume instead of or in addition to calculating, the importance of calculated numerals corresponding to numerals obtained from measurements, how physicist-subjects had answered the question, and so forth. Almost one year later, five of the students who had answered the questionnaire at that meeting registered for my Masters level accounting theory course where I administered the same questionnaire. Only one (20%) of the students answered E, essentially the same rate as when they were part of the Beta Alpha Psi group. Thus, the explanation at the Beta Alpha Psi meeting had no discernable effect on these students.[4]

The purpose of administering the questionnaire to my class was to initiate a discussion of the distinction, not to compare the consistency of responses over time. The almost identical response rate came as a complete surprise because I had expected the students to have been so influenced by the Beta Alpha Psi lecture that all would answer E.

I had invited two research associates, Kevin McBeth and Kiyotaka Ueno, to attend the class to observe the contaminated subjects and compare them to previous observations of uncontaminated subjects, especially as it extended to the unobtrusive test. The consistency of the results caused the discussion after the class to focus on the question of how subjects who had previously answered the questionnaire and listened (even inattentively) to a one hour explanation of the answer *not* be contaminated by that experience. Instead of worrying about the inadvertent introduction of subtle clues that might influence the subjects, my worry switched to how a lengthy explanation of the questionnaire could fail to influence the subjects. I offer the following conjecture: one hour of explaining the distinction between measurement and calculation is not enough to overcome the intervening hundreds of hours of accounting instruction where measurement is taken to be synonymous with calculation.

Readers who want to take the self-test by determining what is wrong with Table 1 should do so before reading further.

THE UNOBTRUSIVE TEST

The first unobtrusive test was conducted in the post-test interviews of the obtrusive test. Both sets of subjects were given every opportunity to volunteer comments about any part of the test. At that stage the tests were truly unobtrusive in that the interviewer (Kwang) was scrupulously careful not to give any clues about the problem for fear of biasing the responses.

The obtrusive test concerned determining the amount of the *shipment* by applying one of the many generally accepted methods (LIFO, FIFO, etc.) of calculation. The unobtrusive test concerned determining the amount of the *inventory* by applying another generally accepted method (addition) of calculation. The numerals assigned to both the shipment and the inventory arise from calculations and therefore, the correspondence question arises in both instances. In this case the increase in the ambient temperature would have caused the volume of the oil received atJanuary 1 to expand so it would also be about 4.4 bbls/ton at March 1 and 2. Thus, the first three rows of Table 1 should have been changed to the amounts shown in Table 4 in order for the "Amount at March 2" figure to more closely correspond to the amount of oil in the tank at March 2.

Table 4. Adjusted volume of oil

	A FIFO	B LIFO	C Avg
Receipts:			
January 1 (100 tons @ 4 bbls/ton)	400	400	400
Expansion from January 1 to March 1	40	40	40
Adjusted January 1 receipt	440	440	440
March 1 (100 tons @ 4.4 bbls/ton)	440	440	440
Amount at March 2	880	880	880

None of the accountant-subjects mentioned anything about the 840 sum labeled "Amount at March 2" in Table 1. By contrast, *all* (save one[5]) of the physicist-subjects mentioned this "additivity problem" and explained it to the interviewer (Kwang) in tones that ranged from incredulous to avuncular. Thus, a vast difference in responses which I infer to be caused by a difference in understanding of the correspondence concept stemming from a difference in education.

Confirming, albeit less formal, evidence was obtained at lectures where I administered various preliminary versions of the questionnaire to the members of the audiences: *None* of the approximately 2,000 accountants who comprised those audiences mentioned the additivity problem despite the fact that over time I became increasingly open about there being a problem with Table 1 and increasingly free with hints.

Although this seems conclusive, my lack of confidence in the results of the unobtrusive test caused me to delay reporting them until Kwang and I had a chance to review the tests in more depth and to conduct the quasi-obtrusive tests reported in the next section. The problem was (and to some extent still is) that neither Kwang nor I are accustomed to obtaining results in which *all* subjects do (or fail to do) *anything* and we were skeptical of the results for that reason.

THE QUASI-OBTRUSIVE TEST

I call the last test "quasi-obtrusive" because it is designed to get the subjects to focus on something that contains an error and inform them that it contains an error without identifying the kind of error or asking a specific question about the error. The plan was to skip administering the questionnaire (thereby lessening the chance that the subjects were fixated on LIFO-FIFO to the exclusion of additivity), go directly to the unobtrusive test via a discussion of the results of the obtrusive test (thereby allowing the subjects to disassociate themselves from the previous subjects who had answered the question), and, if the above did not elicit a response about additivity, switch to the quasi-obtrusive test by announcing "something is wrong with Table 1" to see if that broad hint elicited comments about additivity.

Results From Interviews

The interview test was planned as a comparison of the responses of 25 physicians (who were residents at a medical center) to 25 accountants (who were employees of a large financial institution attending a training session). A random sample was selected from each group. All of the medical residents had more than one year and less than five years of experience working at a hospital and all had received MD degrees. None of the physicians had a course in accounting, not even high school bookkeeping. All of the accountants had more than one year and less than three years experience working at the corporation and 18 had bachelors degrees in accounting, six had masters degrees in accounting, and one had an MBA. None had an education in science.

Kwang scheduled each subject for a 50 minute interview at which the plan was to:

1. Explain the correspondence concept by referring to determining the amount of oil shipped (without mentioning the addition of the receipts) by placing a copy of Table 1 in front of the subject and pointing to the pertinent words and figures with her pen as she went through the explanation.
2. Explain how volume expands and contracts with temperature increases and decreases.
3. Explain the difference in results obtained from the physicists and accountants tants by placing a copy of Table 2 in front of the subject and pointing to the figures with her pen as she went through the explanation.
4. Ask them what they thought about the differences in responses by replacing Table 1 in front of the subject and reviewing the figures by pointing at them with her pen as she went though the review.

Instead of trying to avoid leading the subjects as in the previous tests, in this test the plan was for Kwang to intentionally lead the subjects to focus on Table 1 by taking every opportunity to point at a pertinent word or figure on that Table as the interview proceeded. In addition, if the subject began to talk about correspondence (or lack of) the plan was to encourage them with smiles, nods, murmurs, gestures, and body language. She did not intend to lead them to the specific subject of additivity but she did intend to lead them to the general subject of correspondence. And she planned to try to overcome any reluctance they might have in pointing out errors by using the same type of smiles, nods, etc. to encourage them to continue if they broached the subject.

If the additivity problem had not been mentioned by the subject before the 30 minute mark in the interview, Kwang planned to announce "Something is wrong with Table 1 which I would like for you to tell me about if you notice it" and then return to the discussion of the responses to the obtrusive test. This allowed ample time (20 minutes) for the subjects to respond to the announcement.

Of the 19 responses by physicians, *all* mentioned the additivity problem. (There were five no-shows and one who had been without sleep for 24 hours and was excused after he dozed during the interview.) Although they had a variety of ways of expressing it, 16 of the physicians mentioned the additivity problem prior to the planned announcement at the 30 minute mark and the other three mentioned it after the announcement.

Of the 24 accountants (one no-show), *none* mentioned it. The protocol was changed for the last nine accountant-subjects after the first 15 had not mentioned additivity. At the 45 minute mark, Kwang asked, "Do you see anything wrong with the addition in this Table?" while pointing at the heading of Table 1. All nine looked at Table 1 and more or less obviously footed the columns before responding "no" without mentioning a problem with additivity.

Results From Audiences

I was particularly anxious to conduct the test at the New Faculty Consortium so I could obtain results from the créme de la créme of the new entrants into teaching and research. That test was conducted essentially as described above. The pre-publication typescript of Sterling (1989) was distributed to all consortium participants several weeks prior to the meeting. At my one-hour presentation at the Consortium, I spent about 10 minutes summarizing the paper with the help of transparencies of journal entries recording the receipts and shipment of the oil, as well as transparencies of Tables 1 and 2. After the summary, I left Table 1 on the screen, announced that something was wrong with the Table that I would ask about at the end of the hour, and proceeded to discuss correspondence in some detail and respond to questions. All the while Table 1 remained on the screen, a total time of almost one hour.

Despite being notified that something was wrong with Table 1 near the beginning of the hour, lengthy discussion of correspondence during the hour, and being subjected to repeated questions about Table 1 at the end of the hour, *none* of the participants at the consortium mentioned anything about a problem with additivity. One participant ventured that the error had to do with my facetious comments about how I could report my weight at a svelte calculated 160 pounds instead of the corpulent measured 210 pounds, another thought that the 10% variation might be excessive, a resident faculty questioned why I would continue to talk about such an old fashioned topic as correspondence, and so forth, but *none* questioned whether 400 + 440 = 840 was likely to be a faithful representation of the oil on hand at March 2.

Almost identical results were obtained from about 500 members of other audiences where I conducted identical tests following the identical procedure.[6] Discussants were assigned at three of these lectures. Neither the assigned discussants nor any (save one) of the members of the audiences mentioned anything about additivity despite a manifest eagerness to critically discuss the paper.

The one exception was Assistant Professor Teresa Gordon (Idaho) who responded to my "something is wrong with Table 1" announcement with a full explanation of the problem with the sum at the conclusion of my session at the Western Regional AAA meeting.

Results From Readers

Similar results were obtained from about 70 readers.

There were 36 pre-publication readers who read the paper carefully enough to send extensive written comments. Those readers were acknowledged in the pre-publication version but the list was cut from Sterling (1989) by the editor to conserve space. All but three — Professors Richard Mattessich (British Columbia), Arthur L. Thomas (Kansas), and Harry I. Wolk (Drake) — of those 36 readers failed to mention the additivity problem, and two of those who mentioned it (Thomas and Wolk) explained that previous exposure to my work caused them to suspect what I was doing.

There have been 22 post-publication readers (18 telephone calls and four letters) who read it carefully enough to seek me out to discuss it. None mentioned additivity.

The most careful readers are reputed to be referees of journals because they must decide to publish or not publish submitted articles. The referees and editor of *Issues in Accounting Education* read it carefully enough to decide to publish it and to suggest a number of deletions, yet they did not mention additivity.[7] After it was accepted by *Issues in Accounting Education*, I submitted it to *Abacus* to see if the referees and editor of that journal would mention the error. They didn't.[8]

I also asked three doctoral students to read and critique it. They had a number of things to say about several topics but nothing about a problem with additivity.

CONCLUSIONS

The results reveal a vast difference between accountants and nonaccountants in their application of the correspondence concept. I attribute accountants' failure to apply the concept to their lack of knowledge of it which, in turn, I attribute to it not being included in the accounting curriculum. The application of the concept by physicists and physicians is attributed to their knowledge of it (albeit they are often ignorant of its name) which is, in turn, attributed to it being included in the physics and medical (including pre-medical) curriculum.

Curricular Recommendations

I think the absence of the correspondence concept is a serious deficiency in the accounting curriculum that should be rectified. Unfortunately, it is a deficiency that is not likely to be easily rectified because in accounting each generation depends heavily on the previous generation for its knowledge. The subjects in the first test were third year students, and they were unaware of the correspondence concept because it is not included in the undergraduate curriculum. The subjects in the second test included beginning teachers at the Consortium and they were unaware of the correspondence concept because it is also not included in the graduate curriculum. The reason it is not included in the *present* accounting curriculum is that it was not included in the *past* curriculum: the senior faculty in the audiences did not include it in the curricula that they had designed during their careers because they were not aware of the concept and they were not aware because it had not been included in the curriculum when they were students. The reason it is not likely to be included in *future* curricula is that it is not included in the *present* curriculum: the new teachers are unlikely to include it in the curricula they design during their careers because they are not aware of it and they are not aware because it was not included in the curriculum when they were students.

Although all disciplines depend on the teachers of the current generation to pass on previously accumulated knowledge to future generations of practitioners and teachers, other disciplines also inject recently acquired knowledge (research results) in the curriculum. Accountants have been reluctant to do that which, in my view, is the primary reason for accounting having become nearly immune to improvement. Research designed to improve accounting has not been implemented because it has not been taught to future practitioners nor future professors (students) and the outcome has been the stagnation of both accounting practice and teaching.

An additional outcome has been the increasing estrangement of accounting research. Recently it has become popular to say that accounting research ought to "positively" describe what managers and practitioners do instead of "normatively" prescribing what they ought to do. In regard to this case, this means that we ought to describe the fact that accountants added the volume receipts of 400 and 440 but we ought not to describe the fact that the volume expanded so that the calculated 840 does not correspond to a measurement of the volume on hand. That comparison of descriptions is intended to show that the difference between "positive accounting theory" and "normative accounting theory" is the subject matter being studied, not that the former is positive-scientific and the latter is normative-unscientific.

Of course it *is* normative to say that accountants ought to make their numerals correspond to some phenomena, but it is *not* unscientific. On the contrary, the correspondence concept is often described as the *basic scientific norm* since it is indispensable to the requirement that scientific research be verifiable. One behavioral science methodologist of high repute (Kaplan, 1964, p. 312) explains its function in science as follows:

> Norms of validation can be grouped according to the three major philosophical conceptions of truth: correspondence or semantical norms, coherence or syntactical norms, and pragmatic or functional norms. The first set is the basic one somehow; the others must be regarded as analyses or interpretations of correspondence.

Thus, it is an error to claim that the correspondence concept is unscientific because it is in fact the basic norm for the validation of scientific claims.

Teacher, Educate Thyself

The problem facing accounting teachers is that they were not taught about the correspondence concept and therefore if they are to teach it to subsequent generations, they must first teach it to themselves. Unfortunately, most current accounting research (such as the "positive" research described above) is of no help so the teacher must look elsewhere.[9] My recommendation is to start with the slim volume by Ziman (1978, p. 11) because he takes a communication perspective to explain how science achieves reliable knowledge. He starts by saying "since science is more than personal knowledge, it can consist only of what can be communicated from person to person" and then proceeds to discuss the requirements and problems of what can be so communicated. Since accounting is supposed to be a communication system, since financial statements are supposed to be messages that are more than personal knowledge, the lessons learned in science could be applied directly, and with great benefit, to accounting. Therefore, I urge that teachers educate themselves about the correspondence concept and then teach it to their students.

Acknowledgements — I am indebted to Alan Barton (Australian National), Will Baxter (London School), Paul Dorsey (Penn State), Thomas Lee (Edinburgh), Kevin McBeth (Weber), George Murphy (Saskatchewan), Paul Rosenfield (AICPA), David Solomons (Penn), Kent St. Pierre (James Madison), Daniel Thorton (Calgary), David Tweedie (Peat Marwick-London), Murray Wells (Sydney), and Peter Wolnizer (Deakin) for comment and criticism. My greatest debt is to Mary Teresa Kwang, an apprentice psychometrician visiting from the University of Beijing, for vetting the questionnaire, administering it to the subjects, conducting the interviews, and reviewing the presentation of the results.

ENDNOTES

1. Originally it was designed to explore more than two issues. Another issue was motivated by the recently-renewed suggestions to abandon articulation so that LIFO could be used for the income statement and FIFO for the balance sheet, thereby showing costs that are more current on both statements. Although I wrote another obtrusive question designed to determine support for that sug

gestion in the initial test, the post-test interviews raised questions about whether the results were usable and therefore the results will not be reported until further testing is complete. In the meantime, I solicit the readers' help in designing a question that will elicit interpretable responses about the comparative support for using LIFO for calculating the shipments and FIFO for the remaining inventory (or vise versa) in contexts other than cost.

2. I must restrict the scope to *almost* all humans because there are a few exceptions such as nihilists, solipsists, most sophomore philosophy students, and a few accountants who, for one reason or another, have decided to deny that anything exists or that if it does exist we cannot know anything about it. I must respect their views, of course, but I do wonder why they bother to press those views on you and me. Since the proposition that nothing exists means that you and I don't exist, it does seem to be a waste of their time, it not a contradiction, for them to try to communicate with those of us that don't exist.

3. I am forced to say "virtually" because the nonaccountant interviewer (Kwang) could not understand what the four accountant-subjects who answered E were saying and therefore could not effectively pursue the questioning to determine what answer they would give without running the risk of leading them.

4. Subsequently a research associate (McBeth) discovered that the one student who had answered E did so because he vaguely remembered that I had endorsed that answer at the Beta Alpha Psi lecture, not because he believed it to be the best answer. Thus, the effect was that had I not given the lecture, *all* the subjects would have given a non-E answer.

5. The exception was a subject who could not explain what was wrong with LIFO-FIFO, who seemed to be dumfounded by being asked to explain something that he thought was "too simple" to require explanation as reported in Sterling (1989). Kwang conjectured that embarrassment about being unable to explain what he thought was wrong with LIFO-FIFO caused him to be reticent about volunteering that something was wrong with the sum for fear of being further embarrassed.

6. Audiences were at the Drake Alumni Day Lectures, University of Nebraska-Lincoln Distinguished Lecture Series, University of Nebraska-Omaha Faculty Lecture, Agency for International Development Lectures, FASB Joint Staff and Board Educational Meeting, and my session at the 1989 Western Regional AAA annual meeting. I am grateful to Michael J. Barrett, Kung H. Chen, T. P. Howard, Timothy S. Lucas, Ronald Ma, Ronald E. Milne, Gary J. Previts, and Harry I. Wolk for making the presentations possible.

7. Indirect editorial evidence comes from one of the reasons for rejection of Wells and Wolnizer's (1988) discussion of additivity. In his rejection letter, the editor of the *Accounting Review* said, "...the fact that the 'problem' has not seemed to cause either scholars or practitioners any grief over at least the last decade seems to argue against..." publication. The evidence presented in this article confirms that the problem has not caused accountants any grief but it also indicates that the reason for the lack of grief is the lack of understanding of the

correspondence concept. If accountants do not recognize that it is even possible, much less desirable, for a sum to correspond to a measurement, then it is not likely for accountants to grieve over the lack of such correspondence.

I am grateful to Murray Wells (personal communication) for responding to my query about what happened to Wells and Wolnizer (1988) by sharing the letters with me and to William Kinney (personal communication) for clarifying and further explaining his and the referees' views.

8. I selected *Abacus* because my long association with the editor led me to believe that he wouldn't be upset by a test disguised as a submission, and he wasn't. On the contrary, unlike most other readers who expressed embarrassment about not noticing the absence of additivity or found reasons (excuses?) for not noticing, the editor expressed surprise at how his accounting habits had become so ingrained that he didn't notice the absence of additivity despite the fact that he had previously discussed the problem of additivity of volume when the temperature varied (Wells, 1971, p. 175).

9. The older, so-called "a priori" or "normative" accounting literature contains discussions of the concept. In regard to correspondence or representational faithfulness, for example, I wrote that the first requirement for a message to be deemed "information" is that it "describe the real world faithfully" but I did not go into sufficient depth because of my then-erroneous belief that such a requirement is "clear and obvious" (Sterling, 1970, p. 40). That I have spent the subsequent 20 years trying to explain that requirement is ample evidence that my statement that is "clear and obvious" is an egregious error.

Larson (1967, p. 487) made the same point in different words in regard to additivity:

> ...calculations such as addition and subtraction are acceptable only upon empirical verification. That is, the additivity of the property under examination must be empirically verified before similar calculations can be attributed any descriptive validity. The general character of such empirical verification involves an independent measurement of the quantity of property exhibited by the combination of systems which possess that property.

And the topic of additivity has been discussed in several works [e.g. Sterling (1970, pp. 100-105) and Vickrey (1970)] since then.

Incidently, for accounting "empiricists" to have classified the works that made or were based on that fundamental empirical tenet as "a priori" would be amusingly ironic if the results had not been so pernicious.

REFERENCES

Einstein, A. (1954). The common language of science. In *Ideas and Opinions* (p. 336). New York: Crown Publishers, Inc.

Kaplan, A. (1964). *The conduct of inquiry: Methodology for behavioral science.* San Francisco, CA: Chandler Publishing Company.

Larson, K. (1967, July). Descriptive validity of accounting calculations. *The Accounting Review.*

Lee, T. A. (1984, Fall). Cash flows and net realizable values: Further evidence of the intuitive concepts. *Abacus.*

Putnam, H. (1987). *The many faces of realism: The Paul Carus lectures.* LaSalle, IL: Open Court Publishing Co.

Popper, K. R. (1972). *Objective knowledge: An evolutionary approach.* Oxford: The Clarendon Press.

Sterling, R. R. (1970). *Theory of the measurement of enterprise income.* Houston: Scholars Book Co.

Sterling, R. R. (1988). Confessions of a failed empiricist. *Advances in Accounting, 6.*

Sterling, R. R. (1989, Spring). Teaching the correspondence concept. *Issues in Accounting Education.*

Tweedie, D. P. (1977, Winter). Cash flows and realizable values: The intuitive accounting concepts? An empirical test. *Accounting and Business Research.*

Vickrey, D. W. (1970, October). Is accounting a measurement discipline? *The Accounting Review.*

Wells, M. C. (1971, Spring). Axioms for historical cost valuation. *Journal of Accounting Research.*

Wells, M. C., & Wolnizer, P. W. "Additivity Revisited." Unpublished Photocopy, 1988.

Ziman, J. (1978). *Reliable knowledge: An exploration of the grounds for belief in science.* Cambridge, MA: Cambridge University Press.

ABACUS, Vol. 26, No. 2, 1990

ROBERT R. STERLING

Positive Accounting: An Assessment

Positive accounting theory, using the book of the same name by Watts and Zimmerman (1986) as the primary source of information about that theory, is subjected to scrutiny. The two pillars — (a) value-free study of (b) accounting practices — upon which the legitimacy of that theory are said to rest (and the absence of which is said to make other theories illegitimate) are found to be insubstantial. The claim that authorities — economic and scientific — support the type of theory espoused is found to be mistaken. The accomplishments — actual and potential — of positive theory are found to have been nil, and are projected to continue to be nil. Based on these findings, the recommendation is to classify positive accounting theory as a 'cottage industry' at the periphery of accounting thought and reject its attempt to take centre stage by radically redefining the fundamental question of accounting.

Key words: Accounting theory; Scientific method; Theory.

INTRODUCTION

What ought accounting practices be? More fully, *which objects and events*, and *which attribute(s) of them*, should be represented in accounts and on financial statements? That ancient question was examined by all of the past contributors to accounting thought,[1] and by consensus of those contributors, it was the fundamental question of accounting. At base, that question concerned the states

[1] Contributors who examined the ancient question comprise an honour roll of names in accounting: Pacioli, Dicksee, Sprague, Hatfield, Paton, Edwards and Bell, Littleton, May, Baxter, Moonitz, Chambers, Scott, Sweeney, and Esquerré to name but a few.

ROBERT R. STERLING is Kendall D. Garff Professor of Business Enterprise, Graduate School of Business, University of Utah.

The author is indebted to W.T. Baxter (London School), Philip Bell (Boston), John W. Buckley (UCLA), Raymond J. Chambers (Sydney), Barry Cushing (Penn State), W. W. Cooper (Texas-Austin), James M. Fremgen (Naval Postgraduate), James C. Gaa (McMaster), James B. Heian (Wellington), Richard Laughlin (Sheffield), Richard Mattessich (British Columbia), Alan MacGregor (Otago), Kevin McBeth (Weber), Maurice Moonitz (Cal), Roland Munro (Edinburgh), George Murphy (Saskatchewan), K. V. Peasnell (Lancaster), Paul Rosenfield (AICPA), Ross M. Skinner (Toronto), David Solomons (Penn), Paul Weilenmann (Zurich), Harry I. Wolk (Drake), Stephen A. Zeff (Rice) and the anonymous referees for reading the entire manuscript and offering comments and suggestions, many of which were mutually exclusive but all of which were helpful and stimulating. Thanks also to the late Richard Feynman (Cal Tech), Carl Hempel (Princeton), Melvin W. Reder (Chicago), Kenneth C. Warner (Toledo Scale Corporation), John Watkins (London School), and Frederick Wegner (Congregation Kol Ami) for comments on particulars. The author is also grateful to Thomas R. Dyckman (Cornell), Keith Duncan (Bond), Wiliam R. Kinney (Texas-Austin), Paul Montagna (Brooklyn) and D. J. Williams (ANZ Macaghan, Melbourne) for responding to my request to all people cited to check the accuracy of my interpretation of their work.

and activities of the firm, especially in regard to wealth and income, and how best to account for them. Now comes 'positive accounting theory' (hereinafter PAT) with the message that questions about what ought to be the contents of accounts are unscientific. Positive theorists assert that, for reasons to be discussed, the question should be changed from 'What *ought* accounting practices be?' to 'What *are* accounting practices?'

This is a radical alteration of the fundamental question of accounting: instead of trying to determine how to improve the present state of accounting we are told to try to determine the present state of accounting. Radically altering the fundamental question of a discipline is a matter of utmost import to that discipline and therefore proposals for such alterations require in-depth consideration prior to their adoption. The purpose of this article is to contribute to that consideration.[2]

Although *Positive Accounting Theory* (hereinafter *Positive*), by Watts and Zimmerman (hereinafter W&Z; 1986), will serve as the primary (but not exclusive) source of information about PAT, this article is not intended to be a thoroughgoing review of that book. Instead, it will concentrate on the foundations of and justifications for PAT to the neglect of consideration of the details of its superstructure. In general it is efficient to sequence examination of a theory to, first, the foundation, and second, the superstructure, because any theory that does not withstand examination of its foundation is almost certain not to withstand examination of its superstructure. To put it another way, this article is concerned primarily with positive accounting *theory*, and positive accounting *research* is considered only in regard to accomplishments, not in regard to techniques employed. (Those interested in the superstructure will find Whittington, 1987, a particularly insightful and thorough critique of such topics as disclosure regulation and efficient markets, as well as more basic topics.)

Overview of Positive

The first chapter of *Positive* is titled 'The Role of Accounting Theory', the first sentence of that chapter says 'This book is about accounting theory', and 'Nature of Theory' is the title of the first section heading. Such an introduction makes it clear that the topic of theory is of fundamental importance to W&Z and therefore it leads the reader to expect a rather thorough discussion of the basic ideas of theory construction and verification and how they are applied in accounting. That expectation is immediately dashed. The 'Role of Accounting Theory' chapter occupies only 14 of the 362 pages of text and the section on the nature of theory is only one-half of one of those 14 pages. Such brevity is puzzling in light of the introduction and even more so in light of the fact that the justification of PAT rests entirely on the claim that it *is* a scientific theory whereas other accounting literature is composed of unscientific musings.

[2] Other considerations include Christenson (1983), Lowe, Puxty and Laughlin (1983), Peasnell and Williams (1986), Schreuder (1984; 1985) which were critiques of positive theory in general or 'Excuses' (W&Z, 1979) in particular prior to the publication of *Positive Accounting Theory* (W&Z, 1986). Review articles of that book include Demski (1988), Whittington (1987), and Whitley (1988). Solomons (1986, pp. 239-41) provides a brief yet incisive critique of PAT in regard to the positive theory of standard setting.

Based on the space occupied, it would have been more accurate for W&Z (1986, p. ix) to have said that the book is a réchauffé of the 'economics-based empirical literature' in accounting, not a book about theory or accounting theory. The review and reinterpretation of that literature occupy chapters three to thirteen. The topics in those chapters are ordered chronologically, spanning the time period from 1968 (the date of the earliest *Journal of Accounting Research* cited) to 1985 (the date of the latest *Journal of Accounting and Economics* cited), and run from efficient markets (described on p. 71 as 'in the positive tradition') through disclosure regulation (called a 'prelude' to PAT on p. 156) to the more recognizable PAT topics such as the effect of management compensation plans on accounting. The penultimate chapter, titled 'The Role of Accounting Research', is an edited abridgment of their 'Excuses' paper (W&Z, 1979) and the ultimate chapter is called 'Summary, Evaluation and Prospects'.

Although scant space (somewhat less than 5 per cent) is devoted to the role of theory, it is crucial space because it contains the basic ideas that guide the remainder of the book. W&Z (1986) draw attention to the importance of Chapter 1 in the last sentence of the book: 'However, we have confidence that the methodology outlined in Chapter 1 *and used throughout this book* will produce a useful positive accounting theory' (p. 362, emphasis added). Thus, Chapter 1 is the foundation upon which the other 95 per cent of the book is built. That chapter describes the fundamentals of PAT and the remaining chapters describe the details, or, to paraphrase Hillel (*Talmud*, Sabbath), Chapter 1 is the whole theory; all the rest is mere commentary. For that reason, Chapter 1 demands careful scrutiny.

FOUNDATIONS

The first task that W&Z (1986, p. 1) set for themselves is to distinguish their view of theory from the different views found in the accounting literature. The importance they place on that distinction is indicated by the fact that it is the first topic addressed in *Positive*, as well as having been the topic addressed in the first sentence of the 'Excuses' paper (W&Z, 1979, p. 273). The importance is further indicated from their frequent assertion that their view of theory is the same as that in economics and science, with the obvious implication that since other accounting theories are different from PAT then they are different from those in economics and science. From this springs the justification of PAT that it *is* a theory whereas others are pseudo-theories, although ignorant usage of the term has resulted in pseudo-theories being erroneously *called* theories. (That position is most clearly stated in 'Excuses' (W&Z, 1979, p. 273) but is also espoused throughout *Positive*.)

The previous paragraph describes the dual process of attempting to convince readers that (a) PAT is worthy of acceptance and emulation, perhaps adulation, whereas (b) other accounting pseudo-theories are worthy of rejection and neglect, perhaps contempt. They refer to the second process as 'the *natural desire* of proponents of a new set of theories and methodology (of a new paradigm) to *demolish* the existing paradigm's theories' (1986, p. 16, emphasis altered). Although they were describing researchers who preceded them 'in the positive tradition' (1986, p. 71) when they discovered that natural desire, the reader will easily recognize that in the process of adopting and augmenting the positive tradition, W&Z have also adopted and augmented the desire to demolish all theories other than PAT. (See also W&Z, 1986, p. 6, for the statement of their belief that their predecessors in the positive tradition had succeeded in demolishing the old explanations.)

Thus, the foundation of PAT is said to be its congruence with economics in particular and science in general. Their demarcation between science and non-science (or between theory and pseudo-theory) rests on two pillars:

1. Phenomena studied. Studying accounting practices is scientific whereas studying other phenomena is not scientific. PAT is scientific because it studies accounting practices whereas other accounting 'theories' are not scientific, indeed only pseudo-theories.
2. Value-free. Avoiding questions of value (being positive or descriptive) is scientific whereas addressing questions of value (being normative or prescriptive) is unscientific. PAT is positive and therefore scientific whereas other accounting 'theories' are normative and therefore not scientific, indeed only pseudo-theories.

These two pillars will be considered seriatim.

Phenomena Studied

To their credit W&Z (1986) are quite clear about their view of theory, stating it boldly and placing it prominently: 'The objective of accounting theory is to *explain* and *predict* accounting practice' (p. 2). As I read *Positive*, this is the fundamental sentence of the book because it clearly and concisely defines PAT, thereby differentiating it from all other accounting literature.

Studying Practices. Specification of the study of *accounting practice* is the major difference between PAT and other accounting theories. The elaboration that follows the fundamental sentence leaves no doubt about what W&Z (1986) believe ought to be explained and predicted:

> *Explanation* means providing reasons for observed practice. For example, an accounting theory should explain *why* certain firms use the last-in, first-out (lifo) method of inventory rather than the first-in, first-out (fifo) method. *Prediction* of accounting practice means that the theory predicts unobserved accounting phenomena . . . For example, an accounting theory can provide hypotheses about the attributes of firms that use lifo versus the attributes of firms using fifo. (p. 2)

This passage defines 'accounting phenomena' as the various mathematical constructions (for example, lifo and fifo) used to derive accounting figures. Instead of the phenomena being the widgets that are represented on the financial statements, the 'accounting phenomena' of PAT are the set of formulae that are available for selection when preparing the financial statements.

This is analogous to cartographers defining 'cartographical phenomena' as the map instead of the territory. That the analogy fits can be seen by the fact that the substitution of cartographic terms in the quotation produces a perfectly parallel 'positive cartography theory':

> *Explanation* means providing reasons for observed practice. For example, a cartography theory should explain *why* certain firms use the Mercator method of projection rather than the conical method. *Prediction* of cartographic practice means that the theory predicts unobserved cartographical phenomena . . . For example, a cartography theory can provide hypotheses about the attributes of cartographic firms that use Mercator versus the attributes of firms using conical.

This passage defines 'cartographical phenomena' as the various mathematical constructions (for example, Mercator and conical) used to derive cartographic figures. Instead of the phenomena being the continents and oceans that are represented on the maps, the cartographical phenomena of positive cartography theory are the set of formulae that are available for selection when preparing the maps.

The mistake of confusing the map with the territory is well known in economics and science, being called 'maya' in some circles. For example, a scientific methodologist (Ziman, 1978) asserts that 'no sane person would suppose a map to be identical with the land that it represents' (p. 85) and a respected economist (Boulding, 1970) advises against attempting to traverse maps:

> What all this involves is not a case against abstraction, which is essential, but a warning against mistaking abstraction for reality. We would be foolish to try to go for a walk across a map, but a map may be very helpful if we are going for a real walk. (p. 75)

Instead of confusing the accounting map[3] (financial statements) with the accounting territory (economic goods), PAT fails to recognize (or at least acknowledge) the existence of an accounting territory. Apparently W&Z think of financial statements as free-floating collections of words and numerals instead of as representations of things and events.[4]

'The study of words and not matter', cautioned Francis Bacon (1605, I, IV, 3), is 'the first distemper of learning' because 'words are but the images of matter' and 'to fall in love with them is all one as to fall in love with a picture'. That observation provides a discerning diagnosis of W&Z's error: they have proposed a research program with the objective of explaining and predicting words and numerals without mentioning their correspondence (or lack) to things and events, thereby leading me to believe that they have fallen in love with pictures (financial statements) without recognizing that they need be images of matter (economic goods).

3 See Solomons (1978, p. 70) for perhaps the first and certainly a lucid discussion employing the map analogy in an accounting context.

4 For evidence of the extent of this error see Sterling (1989), which reports a test of the difference between accountants and scientists in apprehending and appreciating the need for correspondence of numerals to an independent measurement of the phenomena.

Studying Practitioners. In extension the 'accounting phenomena' of PAT are the decisions as to which formula to use (for example, lifo not fifo), not the fact that it is being used. The 'observed practice' of PAT refers to observing which formula was selected by the process of observing which formula is being used. One cannot observe the decision process but one can observe its result, and the formula being used is its result.[5] The first question addressed by PAT is *which* formulae were selected. The second question is *why* the formulae were selected — what causes *practitioners* to select various *practices*. In this extension 'accounting practitioner' is broadly construed to include all people who select accounting methods but with the primary focus on managers.

Utility Maximization. Since PAT studies practitioners and since practitioners are people, in this extension PAT may be thought of as a behavioural science. It differs from behavioural science, however, in several significant ways, one of which is what may be assumed and what is required to be investigated. Instead of trying to *discover* what motivates practitioners, as we would expect from behaviourists, W&Z *assume* that everybody is a utility maximizer and then they look for evidence to support that assumption.

After mentioning a number of different people whose welfare is affected by the selection of accounting methods, they present their blanket assumption (W&Z, 1986):

> We assume that all of these various parties in selecting or recommending accounting and auditing procedures act so as to maximize their own welfare (i.e., their expected utility). To make a decision on accounting reports, individuals want to know how the alternative reporting methods affect their welfare. For example, in choosing among alternative depreciation methods, corporate managers want to know how straight-line depreciation affects their welfare vis-à-vis accelerated depreciation. (p. 3)

Although there is some question about why they place the statement of this assumption under the heading 'Why Accounting Theory is Important', there is no question about its overweening importance in PAT: it is the keystone behavioural assumption, serving as the sole explanation of the motivation of *all* the various parties that select accounting practices as well as the basis for the research program.[6]

[5] Professor William Cooper (personal communication) offers the additional criticism that there are better techniques for determining decision processes than those employed by positive researchers. I agree. If one wants to know something about the decision process employed by practitioners, it would be better to use the methods of behavioural science that are designed to allow researchers to *discover* the features of such processes, including the motivation, rather than *assuming* utility maximization and then using predetermined methods and predetermined data to seek evidence to support that assumption.

That positive research has often yielded disappointing results indicates the need to expand the methods used and the data examined. That positive researchers have not expanded their methods and data may indicate that they are not aware of them, as Cooper suggests, but I suspect it is because they are more committed to their predetermined methods and data than to obtaining knowledge about practitioners. That is, instead of being knowledge-driven or problem-driven, PAT is methods-driven and data-driven research.

[6] Discussions with Kevin McBeth, especially his perceptive question 'What does it mean to say that x per cent of the variance is explained on the basis of examining certain methods of maximizing utility when the rest of the variance *must* be explained by other methods of maximizing utility?' helped to clarify my ideas on this topic.

The way the assumption is employed may be illustrated as follows:

Why does a firm use lifo?
Because it maximizes the utility of the practitioner that made the selection, for example, the owner or the manager acting as the owner's agent.
How does one know that?
Because *everybody* maximizes their utility.
Of what use is it?
It guides the positive researcher when looking for evidence to support the assumption, for example, see if lifo maximizes cash flows by minimizing taxes thereby maximizing the owner's utility.

If the firm switched from lifo to fifo, the explanation would be the same, namely, fifo maximizes the utility of the practitioner who made the selection, for example, the manager or the managerial accountant acting as the manager's agent, because everybody maximizes their utility. The basis for research would also be the same. It would guide the positive researcher to look for ways in which fifo maximizes the practitioner's utility, for example, see if fifo maximizes reported earnings and if the manager's earnings are tied to reported earnings thereby maximizing the manager's utility.

To accept observations of income as supporting evidence one must have reason to believe that income (or cash flows, wealth, or a similar financial variable) is positively correlated with utility. However, although income changes continue to be used as evidence of utility changes, it cannot always be so used, as becomes abundantly clear when one discovers that philanthropy is explained as maximizing the utility, but *not* the income, of the philanthropist. Explaining it as altruism must be rejected because everybody maximizes their utility and therefore positive researchers must look for the subtle ways in which utility is being maximized in situations that appear to be altruistic.

The assumption with its surrounding reasoning contains a number of errors, any one of which is sufficient to disqualify it as the basis for a research program and as an explanation of behaviour.

It cannot be used as an explanation because it explains too much. Since *all* behaviour is explained by utility maximization — the fireman will be said to have maximized his utility by his heroic charge into the inferno to save the child and by his cowardly refusal to enter the inferno — it in fact explains *no* behaviour. In that respect, it is similar to explanations that invoke fate, destiny, God's will, and the like. Since fate may be invoked to explain why *x* occurred (when it occurred) and also invoked to explain why *x* did not occur (when it did not occur), it explains both *x* and not-*x* and therefore explains neither. For the same reasons, utility maximization is not an acceptable explanation. Undoubtedly it has some truth to it and therefore it would probably be worthwhile to define it more precisely, that is, delimit the term so it could be used to explain some behaviour by preventing it from explaining all behaviour.

It cannot be used as the basis for a research program because it is non-nullifiable, or in Bayesian terms, the investigators' priors are too strong to be affected by evidence. When the miser's maximized utility is confirmed by his increased income and the philanthropist's maximized utility is confirmed by non-pecuniary evidence (but not disconfirmed by decreased income), one begins to suspect that utility maximization is being used to test the acceptability of evidence rather than the other way around. For reasons of this kind, Popper (1983) selected it to illustrate a concept that is not scientific because it is not falsifiable: '[That] all human actions are egotistic, motivated by self-interest . . . is widely held . . . [but it] is not falsifiable: no example of an altruistic action can refute the view that there was an egotistic motive hidden behind it' (p. xx). W&Z justify PAT by asserting that it qualifies as a scientific theory, presenting Popper's putative agreement with PAT as support for it being scientific, when in fact Popper singles out PAT's keystone behavioural assumption as an exemplary case of a concept that is unscientific because it is not falsifiable. It is difficult to imagine a more conspicuously fatal flaw in an appeal to authority.

Although it is tempting to explore what I suspect are strong barriers to disconfirming evidence in the way that positive tests are *conducted*, space precludes more than passing mention.[7] Suffice it to say that the way that positive researchers look for evidence may be an instance of what is called the 'confirmation bias' in the philosophy of science (stemming from work in psychology on the favourable evidence reported for parapsychology), from decisions about type I versus type II errors which introduce a value judgement in statistics as described by Nagel (1961, p. 497), and from absence of rules about when propositions or theories are disconfirmed as outlined by Hines (1988, p. 661). In addition to space limitations, such exploration would lead to an evaluation of positive research, most of which would duplicate the criticism cited in footnote 1.[8] Since I want to concentrate on theory to the neglect of research, and since earlier commentators have effectively evaluated the research, I will go directly to the more theoretical question of how empirical evidence is *interpreted* by members of the Chicago School, because PAT is a direct application of the tenets of that school.

The way that evidence is interpreted is explained in a sympathetic, candid and quite illuminating description of the Chicago School by Reder (1982), who informs us that:

> Any apparent inconsistency of empirical findings with implications of the theory, or report of behavior not implied by the theory . . . [requires] one of the following actions: (i) re-examination of the data . . . (ii) redefinition . . . of the variables . . . *(iii) alteration of the theory* . . . (iv) placing the finding on the research agenda as researchable anomaly.

[7] McKee, Bell and Boatsman (1984, pp. 647, 658, emphasis added) replicated and extended W&Z's (1978) tests with a larger sample and found the positive theory to be 'unimpressive' because 'a model which predicts that *all* submissions will be unfavorable' outperforms the positive theory. Nonetheless, although W&Z (1986) refer the reader to McKee *et al.* 'for a critique of the Watts and Zimmerman tests' (p. 274), there is no further discussion. Antithetical findings are usually subjected to intense scrutiny in science.

[8] Another work that came to my attention too late to be incorporated herein is Williams (forthcoming), which makes the nice logical point that if the data produced by managers are too unreliable to be used to assess the value of the firm they are also likely to be too unreliable to assess managements' motivations.

> TP [tight prior or Chicago School] implies shunning (iii): i.e., the subject matter of the tight prior [Chicago School] is the adequacy of this approach to theory as an explanation of whatever behavior is considered as economic. (p. 13, emphasis added)

Reder goes on to say that it is not appropriate to characterize this way of interpreting evidence as dogmatic. I agree that it *need not* be dogmatic but I also note that the interpretation often *is* dogmatic, especially in the hands of those in the flush of enthusiasm for a new program. Its dogmatic application is due not only to 'shunning alteration of the theory' but also to the way in which the subject matter is defined: 'whatever behavior is considered as economic' is a defining characteristic of the subject matter *as well* as the question being tested. To state 'all birds can fly' as an ornithological principle and then to make ability to fly a defining characteristic of birds prohibits falsification of the principle. Observations of penguins are not falsifications because their inability to fly makes them non-birds and therefore not part of the subject matter of ornithology. In this case the principle to be tested is 'all people maximize their utility' but the subject matter is limited to 'economic behaviour' which is another name for utility-maximizing behaviour. When taken literally this means that the observation of non-maximizing behaviour does not disconfirm the principle because such behaviour is excluded from the subject matter being examined.

Reder (1982) goes on to say that

> TP [Chicago School] adherents — with variation among individuals — focus attention upon (i) and (ii) and, failing a quick resolution of the anomaly, move to (iv) but pay little attention to (iii). By contrast, DP [diverse prior or non-Chicago School] adherents consider all possibilities, varying research strategy with circumstances, but showing no strong pre-disposition to neglect (iii). (p. 13)

One can rightly say that this is just a disagreement between two camps, with W&Z in the TP camp and me in the DP camp,[9] but the reader needs to be aware that the camps are fundamentally different: those of us with 'no strong pre-disposition to neglect alteration of the theory' tend to be more accepting of different kinds of research methods and this leads to acceptance of more kinds of evidence to bring to bear on the question which leads further to scepticism about the theory. And vice versa for those, such as W&Z, in the TP camp.

This is not a question that can be decided by 'empirical research' until it has been decided what *ought* to *count as empirical evidence*. Reder (1982) is well aware that what *is* 'the evidence' depends on that decision and he draws the distinction quite clearly:

> TP [Chicago School] adherents tend to give little weight to self-reports of participants in the economic process describing their motives, decision making processes, objectives, sources of information, etc. . . . if the behavior supports TP, and is inconsistent with

[9] Although I have no objection to my Chicago School friends criticizing me for being in the DP camp, they might want to reconsider their criticism that I am the leader of that camp because it makes followers of the likes of Paul Samuelson, Herbert Simon and James Tobin.

> the self-reports, the self reports will be ignored. DP [non-Chicago School] theorists urge the contrary procedure: i.e., use whatever information we can get about decision maker's behavior regardless of its lack of consistency with TP. (p. 21, note)

That is, some are persuaded that utility maximization ought to stand *or* fall on the basis of a *broad* definition of evidence obtained from *various* research strategies. From that (DP) perspective the problem with PAT is that it has an unacceptably *narrow* definition of evidence, *restricts* the research methods employed, and *ignores* evidence that is not in accord with the tight priors of the researchers.

The greater error, however, is not that W&Z make the decision on the restrictive-narrow side but that they do not realize (or at least acknowledge) that such a decision must be made. All of those strident claims that 'a priori' or 'normative' work must be *replaced* by 'empirical' or 'positive' research are shown to be misguided by this example.[10] Obviously one cannot empirically decide what ought to count as empirical evidence because one does not know what ought to count as empirical evidence for that decision.[11] And doing positive research would not help because all that would do is show that TP adherents do not count self reports as evidence while DP adherents do count self reports as evidence, which is wasted effort because we already know that from Reder's (and others') description. For W&Z and others in 'the positive tradition' to dismiss discussions about decisions about what ought to count as evidence by labelling them 'a priori' or 'normative' must mean that they have normatively decided *a priori* what ought to count as evidence without realizing that they have done so.

Perhaps the best way to summarize these considerations of utility maximization is to note that from my DP perspective the putative studies of utility maximization are in fact studies of the ingenuity of the researcher. Contrary to common belief, R^2 is an Investigator Ingenuity Index because if the TP conviction that all behaviour is utility maximizing is in fact true, then a particularly clever researcher will be able to explain 100 per cent of the variance by finding all the ways in which utility is being maximized in a given situation. Any data that explains less than 100 per cent of the variance reveals a lack of investigator ingenuity, not a lack of explanatory power. Thus, the positive studies do not help us judge the motivation of the actors but they do allow us to judge the ingenuity of the positive researchers who investigate the motivation of actors but they do allow us to judge the ingenuity of the positive researchers who investigate the motivation of actors. [12]

[10] The conceptual work needed here is what ought to count as evidence so that one can *initiate* the empirical research. It is often said in science that we cannot know what all these new empirical results mean until after some armchair theorist has figured it out. The import of that remark is that conceptual work is also needed to *conclude* the empirical research. In fact, empirics and reasoning iterate at all stages of inquiry and thus both are needed — neither can replace the other — so the claims that imply that they are mutually exclusive are mistaken.

[11] One of the ancients, perhaps it was Socrates, is reported to have been confronted by students with 'Prove to us that we should study logic'. The reply 'How would you know it is a good proof?' not only silenced the students but revealed a fundamental problem about using a method to justify itself, which problem is similar to the paradoxes arising from self-referential statements. The same kind of fundamental problem is encountered today by those who are so enamoured with empiricism that they demand empirical evidence for everything, including propositions about empiricism, to which I reply (with apologies to Socrates): How would you know it is good evidence?

Anthropology and/or Accounting. Accountants' affinity for the study of practitioners — or practices that are generally accepted and implemented by practitioners — caused me to address the general question of the subject-matter of accounting some twenty years ago. In that rather ancient discussion (Sterling, 1970) I termed the study of accountants the 'anthropological approach' to accounting theory construction to draw attention to the fact that the research was focused on people's (accountants') actions rather than on what they were acting on (accounting for), and tried to distinguish the two by analogy to physics: 'the theory of accounting ought to be concerned with accounting phenomena, not practicing accountants, in the same way that theories of physics are concerned with physical phenomena, not practicing physicists' (p. 450). Referring to the 'sociology of accounting', Christenson (1983, p. 6) drew the same distinction by analogy to chemistry when criticizing the 'Rochester School of Accounting' in general and W&Z's prior work in particular: 'Chemical theory consists of propositions about the behavior of chemical entities (molecules and atoms), not about the behavior of chemists' (p. 6). Since Christenson is listed in the bibliography of *Positive* we can assume that W&Z are aware of the distinction and of the errors that ensue when it is neglected. Despite the citation, they do not mention the distinction, let alone present a reasoned reply or even an explanation for ignoring it, an omission not in the best tradition of science.

Drawing the distinction between anthropology or sociology and accounting is not an attempt to prescribe research on one subject and proscribe research on another. On the contrary, my view is that there should be virtually no restrictions on research questions for the plain reason that we cannot know the benefits of knowledge until we obtain the knowledge, and we cannot obtain the knowledge until we have done the research. It was my fear of depriving ourselves of knowledge by the escalating propensity to prescribe efficient market research and proscribe 'a priori' (the pejorative term that preceded the pejorative 'normative') research by predecessors of W&Z 'in the positive tradition' that previously prompted me (1972) to distinguish 'research *about* accounting' from 'research *in* accounting' (p. 1) and argue the routine, albeit crucial, scientific point that both should be at least tolerated, preferably encouraged.[13]

[12] This can be illustrated by examining Table 11.3 and the surrounding discussion (W&Z, 1986, pp. 255–7). It is said that the data in that table provide 'strong evidence' for the hypotheses that managers maximize their utility but the 'model's low [9%] R^2' is an indication that there is 'plenty of room for improvement in the model' and it 'suggests that researchers should derive more powerful hypotheses from it'. That is, researchers should seek more ingenious ways to run the test to get their Investigator Ingenuity Index above the unacceptably low 9 per cent. There is no suggestion that the evidence might cast doubt on utility maximization.

[13] Since it is essential to understanding, I am pleased that Kinney (1989, p. 121) drew the same distinction ('theories *of* accounting' versus 'theories *about* accounting'), but I am dismayed that, to the best of my knowledge, he is the only positive researcher who has done so, and disappointed that he did not take the next step of explicitly recognizing that theorizing about accounting in no way requires one to demolish or disparage theories of accounting, and vice versa, because they are theories about different subject matters. Indeed, he seems to imply the opposite — that positive research is the only kind of research worth doing.

That both make contributions is illustrated by the sociological excursions into the sciences and professions. A thriving sub-field of sociology, the sociology of science associated with the sociologist Robert Merton (1973), has made significant contributions to our understanding of how the scientific enterprise works. It has not, however, made any direct contributions to science. It did not, for example, tell us anything about the characteristics of NASA rockets but it did tell us something about the characteristics of the NASA scientists who determined the characteristics of NASA rockets. A nascent sub-field of sociology, the sociology of accounting associated with the sociologist Paul Montagna (1974), has made contributions to our understanding of how accounting practice works but has not made any direct contributions to accounting. Specifically directed to PAT is the explanation of accounting research provided by a sociologist of science (Whitley, 1988, pp. 640–3) which contributes to our understanding of how accounting research works but does not contribute directly to accounting.

The differences between such sociological studies and PAT are so vast that they appear to be from different worlds. Instead of a broad, open sociological study that lets the evidence lead where it will, PAT constricts the study to a search for evidence that will support a monolithic motivation. As a result, the sociological findings describe interesting multi-faceted humans whereas PAT findings describe monotonous single-purpose automata. (See Lowe *et al.*, 1983, for an astute analysis of 'Excuses' in general and further comments about the problems of oversimplification in particular.) No sociologist claims that studying sociological subject matter, such as scientists or accountants, is scientific and that studying the phenomena of the underlying discipline is not. They do not feel it necessary to demolish theories of science or accounting to establish their sociological theories of scientists or accountants. Instead of contentious comparisons to pseudo-theories based on the patently false belief that science dictates subject matter, the sociologists recognize that theories about incommensurable subject matters do not provide criteria for non-trivial 'normative' comparisons. They realize, for example, that a test of how ornithologists or accountants maximize their utility says nothing whatsoever about the scientific status of a theory of birds or economic goods.

Thus, the criticism is not that PAT is sociology *rather* than accounting, the criticism is that PAT is *neither* sociology *nor* accounting. Instead it is a search for evidence to confirm the non-nullifiable assumption that people maximize their utility when selecting accounting practices. Worse, it tries to demolish studies of other phenomena, thereby depriving us of knowledge of those phenomena, on the basis of the grotesquely misguided view that science restricts knowledge instead of expanding it.

An Analogy. Perhaps further insight into the distinction and its consequences can be garnered by considering an analogous situation in the measurement of weight. Not too long ago merchants could purchase either a spring or a counter-balanced scale to measure the weight of the merchandise they sold. Had there been 'positive weighing theory' its researchers may have noticed an unusual pattern of purchases by butchers: the greater the mass of the usual sale the greater the tendency to purchase spring scales. Shops that sold beef by the quarter or side had a much higher incidence of selecting spring scales than those that sold it by the roast or steak. Slaughterhouses that sold beef by the carcase had an even higher incidence and the delicatessens that sold it by the slice had an even lower incidence.

Although such a finding might contribute to a theory about the behaviour of butchers it would not contribute to a theory about weight and its measurement. For that reason, it would be an error if this were called a theory of weigh*ing* when it is in fact a theory of weigh*ers*, and if the collection of articles on this topic were published in a journal with the title 'Economics and Weigh*ing*' instead of 'Economics and Weigh*ers*'. And the same is true of the theory of account*ants* versus account*ing* and the journal of 'Economics and Account*ants*' instead of 'Economics and Account*ing*'. The purpose of insisting on that distinction is to be clear about a crucial point, not to correct a linguistic punctilio. Being clear about the subject being studied is of highest priority because a muddle about that — the starting place of the inquiry — is almost certain to result in an even greater muddle at all subsequent places in that inquiry.

Of at least equal concern is the attempt to displace research about accounting with research about accountants. In addition to such displacement violating the general scientific norm of not hampering the acquisition of knowledge by equating one's research program with the only research program of merit, there is the likelihood that successful displacement will cause a failure to find knowledge pertinent to the positive research. The butcher analogy makes the problem apparent. Restricting research to the positive subject matter would result in restricting the study to butchers' selections of scales, which would result in restricting the finding to the correlation of the incidence of selecting spring scales to the bulk of beef sold. By such restriction positive researchers would deny themselves an explanation for that correlation. Positive theorists would undoubtedly *assume* that butchers were maximizing their utility by this pattern of purchases, but this line of research would not allow them to discover *how* it was being maximized.

In a previous draft of this paper I explained the reason for that correlation at the beginning of the presentation of the analogy. That this 'contaminated' several prepublication readers was revealed when they questioned why a restriction to a positive research program would preclude knowledge of the reason for the correlation. I have changed the order of presentation in this draft to give the interested reader the opportunity to pause and ponder before reading further. How could anyone know the reason for the correlation if the subject matter were restricted to the behaviour of butchers? Indeed, other than serendipity, how would anyone discover the correlation?

The reason is that the spring scale had the characteristic that the amount of the error increased with the distance from the point of calibration. To simplify, suppose that if spring scales were calibrated at the usual zero point (the scale set to read 'precisely' zero when nothing is on it), then at 1 pound it would overstate the weight by 0.1 per cent, at 10 pounds by 1 per cent, at 100 pounds by 10 per cent, and so forth. The existence of counter-balanced scales (which had different flaws) provided the opportunity for a positive study of the selection of scales by butchers. However, positive researchers would have precluded attaining knowledge about the pattern of errors in the stated weight resulting from using spring scales, and thus the reason for the correlation would remain a perpetual puzzlement. By contrast, researchers who worked on measurement of weight could discover the described characteristic of spring scales and that knowledge, coupled with even the crudest folk psychology, would provide them with an explanation of the correlation. Their puzzle would be why positive theorists would deliberately perpetuate their ignorance of weight measurement, and why perpetuating ignorance would be done in the name of science.

A further problem can be illustrated by considering the biblical question (Micah vi. 10–11): 'Shall I acquit the man with wicked scales and with a bag of deceitful weights?' The PAT prescription is to describe the actions of that man: instead of being normative by acquitting or convicting him, we should positively study him and others like him. If we had followed that prescription for research in the years subsequent to that ancient question, we would have accumulated tonnes of descriptive studies about the behaviour of weighers but we would have not made any progress toward eliminating wicked scales and deceitful weights. In short, by limiting itself to descriptions, by prohibiting problem solving, the positive research program does not contribute to what many of us would (perhaps normatively) think of as the ultimate purpose of research: improvement of the human condition.

Justification. After a very brief discussion in *Positive* (less than one-half page, almost all of which is quoted supra) of 'The Nature of Theory', the study of practices (and therefore practitioners in extension) is justified as follows (W&Z, 1986): 'The preceding view of theory, explicitly or implicitly, underlies most empirical studies in economics. It is also the view of theory in science (e.g., Poincaré, 1905; Popper, 1959; Hempel, 1965)' (p. 2). This is the fundamental justification of PAT. It succinctly and explicitly asserts that W&Z's view of theory — explaining and predicting accounting practices — is scientific, being the same as that in empirical economics, as well as in accord with the views of Poincaré, Popper and Hempel, who are put forth as authorities on science. It also differentiates W&Z's view from others with the implicit but clear claim that other views should be repudiated because they do not satisfy the canons of science.

It is difficult to know what that passage means. A charitable interpretation is that theories of science explain and predict phenomena and that PAT is scientific because it explains and predicts accounting practices, which *are* phenomena. That broad interpretation of W&Z's meaning, however, fails to differentiate PAT from a number of other theories of accounting, which prohibits them from using that interpretation to justify PAT or to discredit the other theories. A theory to explain and predict something about wealth and profit, for example, would qualify as scientific because economic goods *are* phenomena, albeit of a different type. Their desire to discredit theories about other phenomena, such as economic goods, implies that they think that it is the particular phenomena that make PAT scientific and the others unscientific.

I would be tempted to interpret such claims as careless writing that resulted in a misstatement of their position were it not for the fact that repeated readings of the relevant passages leave me with the conviction that it is an accurate expression of their views. Apparently they intend to convey that PAT is a legitimate, scientific theory *because* it specifies the *study of accounting practices*.

That extraordinary position is stated in several places. For example, they introduce the book (W&Z, 1986) by contrasting not-theory with theory evidently on the basis that theory is what explains practice: 'Theory does not present a rule for choosing among alternative accounting procedures (e.g., choose the one that better matches revenue and expense). Rather, theory provides an explanation for accounting and auditing practice' (p. ix). And then they summarize what they have done throughout the book as falling under science's concept of theory, which entails the objective to explain and predict accounting practice: 'Throughout this book, we use science's concept of theory (positive theory). Under that concept, the objective of accounting theory is to explain and predict accounting practice (broadly defined)' (p. 338). There seems to be only one interpretation of such passages: if one uses science's concept of theory, then one will adopt the objective of explaining and predicting accounting practice. The failure of others to adopt that objective is used as the basis for the conclusion that other theories are not scientific.

Interpreted literally, their position means that anthropology, botany, chemistry, . . . , and zoology do not use science's concept of theory because none of them explains and predicts accounting practices. Interpreted as probably intended, it means that anthropology is not scientific because it does not explain and predict anthropological practices, botany is not scientific because it does not explain and predict botanical practices, and so forth through zoology where we reach the absurd conclusion that *all* of the *sciences* are *unscientific* because *none* of them explains and predicts the practices of the respective disciplines. The fact that none of the sciences use what W&Z allege is 'science's concept of theory' should be sufficient to cause us to reject the allegation.

As these counter-examples show, and as is manifest from the very fact that the empirical sciences are segregated by the phenomena studied, many kinds of phenomena can be studied scientifically (or unscientifically) and therefore one cannot use the kind of phenomena studied to distinguish between science and non-science. That 'science is characterized by its method of formulating and testing propositions, not by its subject matter' is made explicit by Blaug (1980, p. 12; the authority on economic methodology cited by W&Z) as well as by almost all others who write on the topic. Thus, W&Z err when they attempt to justify PAT on the basis that it studies accounting practices and when they attempt to demolish other accounting theories on the basis that they do not study accounting practices.

Value-Free

The second pillar of W&Z's demarcation is the belief that science is value-free or positive and non-science is value-laden or normative. Their choice of 'positive' as a modifier of 'accounting theory' when naming their theory is a clear signal of its importance to them as well as an indication that they think that other accounting theories are normative and therefore ought to be rejected as pseudo-theories or as unscientific musings.

Problems with the Distinction. Despite its pivotal role in PAT, one of the more conspicuous lacunae in *Positive* is a discussion of the positive–normative distinction or a discussion of the importance of being positive. The failure to demonstrate an understanding of even the frequently discussed complexities and pitfalls, let alone the subtle problems, of the distinction is itself a serious shortcoming for a work that invariably recurs to being positive when claiming certification as scientific. Schreuder (1984) provides an intelligent discussion of this vast subject in an accounting context.

One example of that shortcoming is the terse discussion under the heading 'Positive and Normative Propositions' that indicates that W&Z think that they can easily divide all propositions (and all theories) into those two categories. Adler and Van Doren (1972, p. 69), by contrast, conclude their discussion of the signs of the distinction by cautioning the reader 'to learn to mistrust' those signs. Reliance on the imperative versus the indicative mood as a sign is a sufficiently common error to warrant specific warnings. Blaug (1980) is one who offers such counsel:

> But how do we tell whether a given utterance is an is-statement or an ought-statement? It is clearly not to be decided by whether the sentence containing the statement is or is not grammatically formulated in the indicative mood, because there are sentences in the indicative mood, like 'murder is a sin,' which are thinly disguised ought-statements dressed up as is-statements. (p. 129)

The problem can be illustrated by W&Z's fundamental sentence: 'The objective of accounting theory *is* to explain and predict accounting practice'. Being in the indicative mood might lead the unwary to classify it as positive or descriptive, but a moment's reflection will reveal a lethal flaw in that classification: no-one other than W&Z and their disciples define accounting theory that way, so if it is classified as descriptive it must be ruled a *false* description. W&Z's undoubted cognizance of its falsity must mean that they did not intend it to be descriptive. Is it a thinly disguised ought-statement, like 'murder is sin'? Since 'The objective of accounting theory *ought* to be to explain and predict accounting practice' accurately reflects the fact that they are presenting a proposal, this would make it seem so. But the sentence cannot be normative or prescriptive because it would require W&Z to repudiate it since they repudiate everything normative.

This apparent dilemma illustrates that the dichotomy is simplistic — a reasonable interpretation of the sentence requires a third[14] classification — as well as the difficulty

[14] Christenson (1983, p. 14), following Popper, suggested the addition of a third classification of 'technological prediction', but W&Z did not accept that suggestion, thereby restricting themselves to the dichotomy. That presents a genuine case of being hoisted by one's own petard because their retention of the dichotomy means that their fundamental sentence must either be rejected as a false description or repudiated as an unscientific prescription. Once the fundamental sentence goes, the whole theory goes.

Sometimes the third class is called the 'can' so we wind up with is-statements, ought-statements and can-statements, or as Schreuder (1984) says, 'if positive theory means anything, it refers not to "what is" but to "what can be". Normative theory does tell us "what ought to be" but in a specific sense' (p. 214). See Bell (1987) for an expression of a similar view.

of making the distinction. Moreover, it illustrates just how irresponsible it is to make 'normative' a dyslogistic modifier and use it as shot for a blunderbuss trained at everything different from PAT.

Requiring nothing more than stating a proposal as a conditional is another example of this shortcoming. Evidently W&Z (1986, p. 7) believe that the conversion of the normative-bad 'you ought to do *x*' to the positive-good requires nothing more than supplying 'if you want *y*' as an antecedent. This raises two questions, one linguistic and the other scientific.

The linguistic question is whether the omission of such antecedents as 'if you want a good (or better) bridge' before saying 'you ought to use steel' is likely to result in confusion. If so, that is sufficient reason to require that they be supplied. If not, if it is a case of the common linguistic practice of dropping 'understood clauses' when they are in fact understood, there is no reason to require them. Thus, this is an empirical question about the change in the degree of understanding when antecedents are changed from implicit to explicit, and therefore it is an error to conclude that authors who do not supply antecedents are being normative-bad.

A similar linguistic requirement is to change explanations (or arguments) to conditionals. Although left tacit by positive theorists, the requirement is revealed by the way they arrive at the classification of propositions as normative. The reasons in explanations (or arguments) are often ignored while the propositions being explained (or conclusions) are characterized as premises or assumptions. To say that 'some theories of accounting *posit* that current cost . . . should be used . . .' (Kinney 1989, p. 121, emphasis added), for example, overlooks the many reasons supplied by current costers. Edwards and Bell (1961), Revsine (1973), and others present long explanations in the form 'You ought to use current cost because it will accomplish such and such (desirable) ends'. One is free to agree or disagree with the desirability of the ends and whether current costs will accomplish those ends (including but not restricted to the empirical evidence for the accomplishment), but it is a grievous error to characterize current costs as a premise or assumption that was posited. W&Z's comments about conditionals make it clear that they think it is legitimate to employ the conditional 'If you want to accomplish *y*, you ought to do *x*' but they are silent about the linguistically equivalent explanation 'You ought to do *x* because it will accomplish *y*', which silence evidently leads some to the error of classifying explanations as normative-bad.

The scientific question is whether the ought-statement is warranted — whether there is sufficient (scientific) evidence to say 'you ought to use' steel for bridges, penicillin for pneumonia, current values for financial statements, and so forth. It seems that the positive-normative distinction is not worth making if the only thing needed to make those statements legitimate is to add the understood antecedent 'if you want good (or better)' bridges, health, information, and so forth. To require that such an antecedent be supplied by all those naughtily normative accounting theorists would be equally as silly as requiring all physicians to supply the antecedent 'if you want to get well' before they say 'you ought to take this medicine' when they write a *prescription*. In my view we ought to redirect our attention from that linguistic triviality to the important scientific questions.

This is not to say that the distinction is unimportant but rather to say that it is too important to receive the cavalier treatment accorded it in PAT. Making 'positive' so central that it is included in the name of the theory, and exerting every effort to make 'normative' the eighth deadly sin, without demonstrating that they have investigated the distinction, and without attempting to educate the rest of us by presenting what that investigation revealed, is not in the best tradition of scholarship.

Positive Practice. The concentration on the study of practice or practitioners is continued after a repeat of the dubious historical claim[15] that 'after the securities acts the accounting literature became normative in the sense that it sought to prescribe the contents of accounting reports', which is contrasted to the PAT position (W&Z, 1986):

> By itself, theory, as we describe it, yields no prescriptions for accounting practice. It is concerned with explaining accounting practice. It is designed to explain and predict which firms will and which firms will not use a particular method of valuing assets, but it says nothing as to which method a firm should use. (p. 7)

This passage is equally as concerned with reinforcing the subject matter — accounting practices — that they think ought to be studied as with proclaiming their positive stance, despite the fact that it was placed under the positive/normative heading.

The invariable coupling of the study of practices with being positive causes me to suspect that they are inseparable in the minds of W&Z. That is, it appears that they intend to convey that PAT is a legitimate, scientific theory *because* it specifies the *positive study* of accounting *practices*. That is the exact opposite of the situation found in science. Most studies of practices or practitioners in other disciplines are normative in the sense that they attempt to find out whether the practices meet standards, which standards are almost invariably theory dependent. Examples abound, three of which will be briefly described.

First, consider the studies of surgical practices, many of which are familiar because they have been reported in the press: the researchers who have studied surgical

[15] My severely limited reading of the history of accounting practice and somewhat less limited reading of the history of accounting thought leads me to believe that fifteenth-century merchants and subsequent owner-manager-practitioners, as well as academics from Pacioli this way, were deliberately normative and therefore I am sceptical of the claim that there was a shift from positive to normative literature around 1933. Although there were 'inductivists' who studied practices, they were normative in that their purpose was to winnow the good practices from the bad. To the best of my knowledge, a research program that imposes a prohibition on the evaluation of practices is unique in the history of accounting thought, indeed in the history of scientific thought, and I invite historians to test that conjecture. (See Moonitz, 1970, for some general counter-examples.)

Evidence contrary to that adduced by W&Z (1979) has been presented by Lowe *et al.* (1983), along with the incisive observation that PAT is a provincial theory because nothing like the SEC exists in Great Britain; and Peasnell and Williams (1986), along with astute questions about the incentives for non-U.S. citizens to 'supply' excuses 'demanded' in the U.S. by the SEC, mentioning Chambers as a prominent example. Despite their professed affection for empirical evidence, *Positive* repeats the dubious claim without citing, let alone discussing, the contrary evidence, an omission not in the best tradition of empiricism.

practices have usually done so for the purpose of determining whether surgery was warranted in the cases in which it was performed, and vice versa. The researchers have sometimes found that 'excessive surgery' has been performed, which is equivalent to my saying that the practice was 'wrong' or that the surgeons '*ought* not to have performed surgery' in those instances. When excessive surgery is thought to be the result of honest mistakes, the practice has been deplored and the suggested remedy has usually been additional or more effective education of surgeons. When it is suspected to be motivated by income (utility) enhancement, the practice has been condemned and the suggested remedy has been harsh, sometimes extending to incarceration. In no instances have the researchers pursued the misguided goal of establishing surgical or medical theory by observing surgical practices, nor have they laboured under the erroneous idea that science prohibits them from normatively assessing surgical practices by comparing them to medical theory that concerns itself with the health of the patients instead of the utility of the surgeons.

Second, W&Z (1986, p. 7) present the example (quoting Passmore) of physics not telling us whether we ought to build a bridge or a ferry. I agree. However, the reason is not the desire to be positive but rather that such decisions are beyond the scope of physicists' expertise or, equivalently, beyond the scope of the theories of physics. By contrast, if we have decided to build a bridge, a physicist would likely have no hesitation in telling us we ought to drive the pile to bedrock, ought to put the rivets no more than x centimetres apart, ought to use diagonal braces, and a myriad of other ought-statements that are within the scope of his expertise. The likelihood of his willingness to utter such ought-statements would increase dramatically if we were either students of physics or practising physicists (i.e., civil engineers). The investigation of the Challenger disaster provides ample evidence of the willingness of researchers to apply ought-statements to physics practitioners. Physics Nobel laureate Richard Feynman (personal communication), who served on the Presidential Commission, repeatedly said words to the effect that there was no question about whether theory *ought* to have been applied, but there were a number of questions about whether it *was* applied or was *properly* applied. Feynman held the universal scientific view that the objective of theories of physics is to explain and predict physical phenomena (such as O-rings), not the practices of the engineers at NASA or Morton-Thiokol (and especially not the utility-maximizing practices of the management thereof), and he did not withhold judgment about those practices out of some mistaken notion that being scientific required him to restrict himself to a description of practices.

Third, the willingness to be normative includes those disciplines that make permissiveness an integral part of their theories. Even the strictly non-directive psychoanalysts were non-directive only in regard to their patients, not in regard to current students (future practitioners) or past students (current practitioners). Non-directive psychoanalytic teachers told their students that they ought not fall asleep while listening non-directively to their patients, that they ought to avoid becoming emotionally or sexually involved with patients, and a host of other directives. The studies, some of which have been reported in the press, that revealed that a significant percentage of psychotherapists have been sexually involved with their patients have been quite normative, with suggested sanctions running from reprimands through revoking licences to practice, a vast distance from a positive study of their sexual activities. In no event did anyone suggest the incorporation of sex with patients in the theory because of some mistaken notion that theory is a description of what utility-maximizing practitioners do instead of being a guide to what they ought to do.[16]

As such examples show, one function of a theory of a discipline is to provide guidelines to the practitioners of that discipline, and practitioners are sometimes studied to see if they are properly following the dictates of the appropriate theory. Far from such studies being positive, those who are found to violate the dictates of the theory may be subject to sanctions. Others who are found to be ignorant of the appropriate theory may be required to remedy their deficiency by further or 'continuing' education. Thus, claims that theory should be a positive *reflection* of practice instead of a normative *guide* for practice show a profound misunderstanding of the functioning of the scientific enterprise and the use of its theories.

Positive Education. We are told (W&Z, 1986, pp. 340, 350) that there is a 'pedagogic demand' for 'accounting literature' which is one of two 'demands for a theory that explains and predicts accounting practice (positive theory)'. They explain the educational benefit from positive theory in one sentence: 'If there is a developed positive accounting theory teachers use it to structure the variation found in practice and thereby assist learning' (1986, p. 341). But this is exactly the same justification used by previous inductivists who were quite normative.[17] Thus, the codification and subsumption of practices under principles for the purpose of assisting learning may be done either positively or normatively so the distinction is irrelevant to that purpose. Nonetheless, proposals to educate positively persist. Those proposals come in two forms: (a) teach PAT to students and (b) teach positively or avoid being normative when teaching.

[16] If the reader finds that comparison too far-fetched, consider W&Z's (1986, p. 185) attitude about managerial theft: 'Stealing by the owner-manager is analogous to the owner-manager's over-consumption of perks [perquisites]' (p. 185). If they think that being scientific requires them to positively incorporate the crime of theft in PAT, the incorporation of sex with patients in a positive psychoanalytic theory seems assured. It is for that reason that I have not made the obvious *reductio ad absurdum* move by asking whether the observation of the utility-maximizing practice of embezzlement by accountants is incorporated in PAT. Although that was the first question that occurred to me when positive theory was proposed, there is no point in asking because the answer will be affirmative and I will consider that absurd but W&Z will not, so I pass it by. I will, however, hasten to cancel my life insurance before my utility-maximizing beneficiaries read the next instalment of PAT and learn that 'murder by beneficiaries is analogous to beneficiaries' early-consumption of insurance proceeds'.

[17] Littleton (1953, p. 185) supplemented observations of practice with 'explanations and [normative] justifications' of that practice 'in order that study should be something more than the memorizing of rules' and thus taught students how accounting ought to be done. Ijiri (1975) makes the point of inductive research the identification of what changes are (normatively) needed in practice, writing that 'the purpose of such an [inductive] exercise is to highlight where changes are most needed' and where they are feasible' (p. 28).

Teaching PAT. One purpose of *Positive* is said to be 'to train students' (W&Z, 1986, p. 352) by using it as a textbook and therefore we know that PAT is intended to be taught, but W&Z do not provide us with reasons for teaching it. The reason given by Kinney (1989) is that it is a subject 'that doesn't go out of date for an entire professional career!' (p. 122). That is, the belief that utility maximization remains constant over time is thought to justify teaching PAT, as confirmed and explained further by Duncan (1987) in his syllabus:

> By understanding [of accounting] we do *not* mean a knowledge of accounting methods (i.e., how to account for particular transactions). Such knowledge is subject to rapid obsolescence as accounting standards change. Instead, we [want] . . . the student to understand why different firms chose different accounting procedures. (p. 15)

Of course it would not take the student long to understand *why* the firms choose since utility maximiazation is *always* the answer according to the assumption of W&Z, but it would take the student a long time to learn the contents of *Positive* because it contains an onerous amount of detail about the tests designed to demonstrate how utility is being maximized.

It is instructive to compare the felt need for additional or continuing education for practitioners of other disciplines, such as surgeons, to the proposal for positive education of accountants. Perhaps the best way to make the comparison is to substitute surgical terms in the previous quotation:

> By understanding [of surgery] we do *not* mean a knowledge of surgical methods (i.e., how to perform particular operations). Such knowledge is subject to rapid obsolescence as surgical techniques change. Instead, we [want] . . . the student to understand why different surgeons chose different surgical procedures.

And then one could teach the students to expect, for example, more than medically indicated Caesarian sections, and fewer than medically indicated vaginal deliveries, because the price of the former is higher than the latter, hence utility maximizing for surgeons. Since surgeons have allegedly practised this form of utility maximization from the time of Caesar, as the name implies, we can reasonably expect it not to go out of date for the present students' entire professional careers. Therefore, so the argument goes, we should teach the abiding principle of utility maximization instead of the transient surgical techniques.[18]

[18] This footnote is being added at publication stage because of recently received, rather heated, rejections of the point on the grounds that surgery is a physical science whereas accounting is a social or behavioural science. To accommodate those critics the point is recast in regard to psychology as follows:

> By understanding [of psychology] we do *not* mean a knowledge of psychological methods (i.e., how to treat particular neuroses or psychoses). Such knowledge is subject to rapid obsolescence as psychological techniques change. Instead, we [want] . . . the student to understand why different psychologists chose different psychological procedures.

And then one could teach the students to expect, for example, to observe more long-term psychoanalytic techniques than short-term behavioural modification techniques because the fees received for the proverbial 'ten years on the couch' are much more than for a few sessions of directive therapy, hence utility maximizing for the psychologist.

In fact the exact opposite occurs. In surgery, as in science in general, there is a chain of interrelated activities: (a) researchers search for and sometimes discover improved techniques, (b) teachers teach those improved techniques, and (c) practitioners implement those improved techniques. The goal common to all three activities is to *make* present techniques *obsolete* by discovering, teaching and implementing *improved* techniques. A curriculum that does not teach improved techniques would cut the chain and freeze surgical techniques at the state they were in at the time such a positive curriculum was inaugurated. Indeed, if the curriculum were restricted to such positive topics, surgery would be destroyed because no one would be taught how to perform any surgical techniques, even obsolete ones. Surgical students would be taught about an extinct profession whose members maximized their utility by performing surgical techniques that are no longer performed because they are no longer taught.

The description of the chain from research to teaching to practice and the loss occasioned by missing links has been confronted with the assertion by W&Z (1979, p. 285) that accounting theorists 'bemoan the fact' that they are not 'allow[ed] to determine accounting standards' and echoed by Kinney (1989, p. 121) that theorists are 'bemoaning the fact' that they 'have had little visible impact' on practice. The wording and tone, especially Kinney's likening such bemoaning to the trauma he suffered when teenage girls refused his invitations to dance, seems to belittle the description of the consequences of missing links in the chain. Evidently the authors think that normative theorists are making indecorous complaints about their personal loss from lack of appreciation of their work by it not being taught and practised.

It seems clear to me that Dyckman (1989), the direct object of Kinney's criticism, was talking about the loss to accounting and to society from breaking the chain from research to teaching to practice, not a personal loss to him or any other individual. I know that Sterling (1973), cited disapprovingly in this connection by both W&Z (1979) and Kinney, was talking about the societal loss from the failure of accounting to provide better information, not a personal loss. Just as a flower that 'is born to blush unseen, and waste its sweetness on the desert air' (Gray's 'Elegy') is much more a loss to us from being deprived of the beauty and fragrance than it is a loss to the flower, a neglected scientific discovery that wastes its benefits on the library shelf is much more a loss to us than to the discoverer who goes unappreciated.

By contrast, a handy textbook on psychotherapy (normatively) advises the student to

> . . . seek to learn as much as possible about *technique* . . . and psychological *theory* . . . [so that] you will best be able to understand and answer for yourself the question of which method is likely to be most successful. Then, if the method you select isn't working, you will be free to change your theory and techniques to adapt to the special needs of the unique client before you. (Ivey, 1980, p. 165)

The attitude of the Ivey text is that the practitioner ought to learn the techniques and then select those that have the most beneficial effect on the welfare (health) of patients, not on the welfare (income) of therapists. The research discussed in that book focuses exclusively on explaining and predicting the effect of the techniques on the behaviour of patients, not on the behaviour of therapists. Thus, the physical versus social or behavioural distinction does not alter the point that PAT is radically different from other sciences in regard to both subject matter and the prohibition to assess practices.

W&Z and Kinney fail to see the point of the loss to the discipline and to society from cutting the chain. Or perhaps they deny the point because of their suspicions that societal justifications are rationalizations for seeking self-interest. They probably apply their all-embracing utility-maximization assumption: the researcher's utility is maximized by her research being appreciated by being taught and therefore is disappointed when it is not taught. Given that assumption we can determine that descriptions of societal losses are in reality the bemoaning of a personal loss. Thus, these descriptions are *excuses* and we know that (W&Z, 1986), 'it is optimal for individuals to claim . . . [that chains are] required for public interest reasons when in fact they are demanded for self-interest reasons' (p. 350). Observe that the utility maximization *assumption* stated on p. 3 has been transformed to what is *in fact* the case on p. 350.

This provides an idea for a paper in the education journals: the real reason for proposals of curriculum reform is to maximize the utility of the teacher who makes the proposal and all of the stated public interest reasons are just excuses. But this invites a reply of the *tu quoque* type. Somebody could say that the real reason I wrote the education paper was to maximize my utility and my stated reasons were just excuses. And the same reply is applicable to positive theorists. The real reason they propose to teach PAT is self-aggrandizement and all their stated reasons are just excuses. As the reader can easily see, this does not lead anywhere: after determining that the real reason for *all* actions is that it maximizes the utility of the actor, we must decide the original question. In this case the original question was whether to teach PAT or not, and my answer is that we should not for the same reasons that surgeons do not teach positive surgical theory.

Teaching Positively. W&Z add the complaint that 'financial accounting texts also tend to adopt normative (i.e., prescriptive) positions' (1986, p. 7), thereby including textbooks within the ambit of the normative criticism with the clear implication that only positive (i.e., descriptive) textbooks are acceptable. Unfortunately, they do not tell us what that means and there are two likely meanings.

First, it could mean that textbooks (and teachers) ought not to be normative in regard to students. That is, they should not prescribe what students learn and should not assess how well the students have learned it. But this violates the very nature of education as we presently understand it. All education is normative in the sense that it is concerned with how something ought to be done or understood. The very first textbook, in conjunction with the teacher, tells students how 'See Jane run' *ought* to be read, and that the answer to 'What is two plus two?' *ought* to be 'Four', not 'What number do you have in mind?' as given in the embarrassingly accurate satire of accountants. Even the assignment of grades is normative in that it is an assessment of how well the student has learned how such things ought to be done or understood.

For such reasons I find W&Z's criticism of textbooks because they are normative to be perplexing. Perhaps they share former Governor of Arizona Mecham's (apparently positive) view that 'teachers have no business telling a student the Earth is round if the student believes it's flat' (Goudinoff and Tobias, 1987, p. A-17), which view destroys the *raison d'être* of education. If at the end of the day students can believe what they want, if teachers and textbooks have no superior knowledge to impart, what is the purpose of education?

Second, it could mean that textbooks (and teachers) ought to describe practices instead of describing means for assessing practices. But this is an argument about the content of the curriculum: it is the opposition of two normative views about what ought to be taught, not the opposition of the positive-good and the normative-bad. The argument about the content reverts to the previous discussion of teaching PAT but it also leads to a number of logical traps, two of which will be sketched here.

One, requiring the students to learn the described present practices, and prohibiting teachers and texts from presenting means to normatively assess such practices, will almost ineluctably lead the students to implement those practices when they graduate. This has the same effect as normatively approving of the described practices and disapproving of alternatives. Similar to the fact that not making a decision *is* a decision, not assessing practices *is* an assessment of practices. Both not making a decision and not assessing practices have the effect of continuing the *status quo ante*. W&Z need to recognize this effect and explain why they prefer present practices, as well as why they want normatively to prohibit others from expressing preferences for alternative practices.

Two, requiring textbook authors and teachers to write and teach positively is an instance of being normative, a violation of the positive position. Critically assessing textbooks for being normative *is being* normative, a commission of the putative error that W&Z are accusing others of committing. It is apparent that W&Z are not cognizant of the problem because of their normative prescription for textbook authors to positively describe practices and practitioners. Thus, W&Z violate their own positive principles.

Is PAT Positive? As just shown, W&Z are normative about being positive when teaching. They *prescribe* that textbook authors and teachers *describe* practices. They are also normative about being positive when researching and theorizing. They *prescribe* that theorists and researchers *describe* practices. Thus, the positive pillar of their foundation is applied selectively, but they never explain why they think they can normatively say that the rest of us ought to be positive. A parallel is grandparents who are convinced that permissive child rearing is good (and directive is bad) but who direct their children to raise the grandchildren permissively, thereby contradicting their own convictions. The fact that their children are directive to the grandchildren does not provide sufficient reason for the grandparents to violate their *own self-imposed* permissiveness by directing the children to *be* permissive. And the same is true of positive theorists. Why do they feel the need to become normative about being positive? Why do not they just describe the actions of all of us normative theorists, researchers and teachers?

It sometimes seems that W&Z are saying 'nobody ought to say ought', which edict is violated by uttering the edict, but at other times they seem to be saying 'nobody but us ought to say ought', thereby proclaiming themselves the sole arbiters of all that ought to be. In tone and design, as well as in the use of the imperative mood (starting with what 'an accounting theory *should* explain' and ending with what 'accounting researchers *should* continue to develop'; W&Z, 1986, pp. 2, 358), but especially in their condemnation of everything non-PAT, *Positive* goes beyond the mere normative to the imperiously dictatorial.

It was a previous member of the Chicago School of economics (Simons, 1938), who warned of those who 'maintain a pretense of rigorous, objective analysis untinctured by mere ethical considerations' (p. 1) but in fact do the opposite:

> Having been told that sentiments are contraband in the realm of science, they religiously eschew a few proscribed phrases, clutter up title-pages and introductory chapters with pious references to the science of public finance, and then write monumental discourses upon their own prejudices and preconceptions. (p. 2)

If I had not known that Simons' comments were written many years ago, I would have suspected that they were specifically directed at *Positive*.

APPEALS TO AUTHORITIES

W&Z allege that authorities in economics and science agree with and therefore provide support for their views. Appeals to authority are legitimate (technically known as *argumentum ad verecundiam*) provided that the appellate is in fact an authority on the subject of the appeal and that the appellant accurately represents the appellate's views.

Economics

Positive begins (W&Z, 1986) with the assertion that 'the preceding view of theory, explicitly or implicitly, underlies most empirical studies in economics' (p. 2) and it ends with the assertion that 'the development of a positive accounting theory will place accounting in the mainstream of economics and finance research' (p. 358), with many similar comments in between. The use of *most* and *mainstream* in those assertions indicates that one could pick up almost any work in economics and find theories and research programs similar, if not identical, to PAT.

It is fortunate that economists also conduct research on and practise accounting — national income accounting — so we have an almost identical activity as a basis for comparison. In addition, the development of the national income accounts is generally regarded as one of the most important and far reaching empirical developments in the history of economics. For both reasons, if W&Z are right about the view of theory of most mainstream economists, then we should expect to find the application of 'positive economic theory' to national income accounting with the resulting parallels of:

1. redefining national income accounting theory as the explanation and prediction of national income accounting practices and calling it 'positive national income accounting theory';
2. studies attempting to demonstrate that national income accountants and others act in their self-interest when selecting national income accounting methods;

3. charges that Kuznets, Stone, Meade, Ruggles and others were being unscientific-normative when they wrote papers arguing which was the better way to account for national income; and
4. allegations that Kuznets, Stone *et al.* were merely responding to some market demand, such as the demand for excuses, in contrast to their claim to be researching and theorizing about national income accounting.

The fact is that despite the congruence of national income accounting and business accounting, no such parallels are to be found in economics. The absence of such parallels should be sufficient to disprove the assertions that the positive view of theory underlies *most* empirical studies in economics and that positive accounting theory would be in the *mainstream* of economics.

In addition, I gathered some empirical evidence pertinent to those assertions: a brief outline of an earlier version of PAT, plus the above four points, was presented to the members of the Board of Directors of the National Bureau of Economic Research, a mainstream economics organization. (It had to be presented at coffee breaks because my fellow board members deemed the question too frivolous to be put on the agenda of the formal meeting.) The points were rejected out of hand by all ($N = 11$) of those mainstream economists.

That W&Z inaccurately represent[19] the views of mainstream economics is of less concern to me than the difference between economists' and accountants' reactions to such presentations: all economists that I queried looked at the *points* being made and judged them absurd whereas most accountants have looked for the *source* of the points and judged them acceptable because the source is acceptable. That is, accountants have responded to queries about the points by mentioning that the authors are well-known; that the points have been published in refereed journals; that previous papers on similar points have won prizes; and, especially pertinent in this context, that they are applying generally accepted *economic* principles. It seems to me that this goes beyond a particular instance of the genetic fallacy to a general tendency of accountants to look to authority, such as searching for 'substantial authoritative support' for accounting techniques instead of examining the techniques in question, or to accept figures on financial statements on the basis of management's representation rather than on the basis of evidence about those figures. Scientists, by contrast, look for evidence, not the source. That Linus Pauling has won the Nobel Prize, for example, does not cause scientists to accept his views about vitamin C curing the common cold. When they found no evidence for that cure, they rejected those particular views without withdrawing their acceptance of his other views or their esteem for him as a person. I urge that we accountants do the same in general as well as in this particular: that we separate PAT from W&Z because I am convinced that PAT is fatally flawed although, insofar as I know, W&Z are totally free from flaws.

[19] It is undoubtedly an error rather than a deliberate misrepresentation, probably stemming from the fact that W&Z identify so closely with the Chicago School that they are not aware that it is not the mainstream of economics, that a majority of economists hold opposing views. Incidentally, PAT may not be mainstream Chicago School economics because the divergence of views between Friedman and Stigler has created two branches of that school, and positive theory is compatible with only one of those branches.

This is not to suggest that we not rely on any authority, for that is impossible. Our inability to investigate everything requires us to rely on authorities in other disciplines but not in our own. We *are* the authorities in accounting, and that authority is based on the expertise obtained from careful investigation of the subject matter, not on the authority of other accountants. In this instance we may need to rely on the authority of economists since that is outside our scope of expertise.

The problem with economics *vis à vis* PAT is two-layered. Accountants (a) tend to accept PAT on the basis of the authority of W&Z and (b) they tend to accept W&Z as authorities on the basis of the authority of economists. That is, it is believed that economists endorse W&Z's views, W&Z endorse PAT, which produces the belief that economists endorse PAT. Not only is the assumed transitivity tenuous (that Al loves Betty and Betty loves Chuck does not imply that Al loves Chuck), it also contains a factual error: the vast majority of economists do not endorse W&Z's views.

A comparison of the views of Blaug (1980) — the only work on economic methodology (other than Friedman's essay) cited in *Positive* — to the views expressed in *Positive* will reveal that they are antithetical at the very basic point of Pareto optimality. Reder (1982, p. 11), a retired Chicago economist, says that the 'essence [of] the Chicago view' is the same as 'a definition of Pareto optimality' and Pareto optimality is another name for economic efficiency,[20] which is where W&Z (1986, p. 8) start by claiming: 'Choosing an objective, other than economic efficiency, amounts to choosing among individuals and, therefore, necessarily entails a value judgment' (p. 8). Blaug (1980) expresses an antithetical view:

> Pareto optimality, so patently shot through with value judgments . . . *should* not be confused with the theorems of positive economics. If this implies that economists must give up the notion that there are purely technical, value-free efficiency arguments for certain economic changes, and indeed that the very terms 'efficient' and 'inefficient' are terms of normative and not positive economics, so much the better: immense confusion has been sown by the pretense that we can pronounce 'scientifically' on matters of 'efficiency' without committing ourselves to any value judgments. (pp. 146–8)

Such antithetical views require that if we accountants are to rely on the authority of economists, we must look directly to economists rather than to the positive theorists who erroneously claim that they have the support of economists.

Science

W&Z frequently claim that support for PAT can be found in science as, for example, when they write: 'It is also the view of theory in science (e.g., Poincaré, 1905;

[20] Koopmans (1957) states the case as a choice between equity and efficiency:

> A competitive equilibrium, even if it is also a Pareto optimum, may involved a more unequal distribution of income than is regarded as desirable from a social point of view. The concept of a Pareto optimum is insensitive to this consideration, and in that respect the term 'optimum' a misnomer. A term like 'allocative efficiency' would have been more accurately descriptive of the concept. (p. 49)

Positive theorists, by contrast, make the value judgment that a Pareto optimum is a desirable state, and criticize those who question the desirability of that state for being normative because such questioning requires a value judgment.

Popper, 1959; Hempel, 1965)' (1986, p. 3). In addition to seeking support for PAT from authorities on science they seek support for demolishing other theories from the same authorities. Such attempted demolition extends beyond accounting pseudo-theories to logical positivism.

The concept of theory used in logical positivsm is distinguished from the concept of theory 'used in science' which W&Z claim is the same concept they espouse:

> the concept of theory used in science (the concept we describe) has traditionally been called *positive theory* . . . This terminology . . . often leads to the concept of positive theory (the concept used in science) being confused with another, different view of the philosophy of science, logical positivism. (1986, p. 8)

The footnote that follows continues by distinguishing the concept of facts found in logical positivism from that found 'in positive or scientific theory' with the 'or' serving to equate their brand of positive theory with scientific theory and to differentiate it from, thereby discrediting, logical positivism.

Thus, they claim that logical positivism differs from science whereas PAT is the same as science. The investigation of such claims, however, is forestalled by the fact that *all* the scientific authorities cited by W&Z *are* logical positivists or are closely related thereto. The four authorities on science W&Z cite are Hempel, Passmore, Poincaré, and Popper. Poincaré is credited with (or blamed for) being an ancestor of logical positivism. Hempel is an avowed logical positivist, having been heavily influenced by Schlick and Carnap, and being well-known for his contributions to logical positivist theories such as the verifiability theory of meaning and the covering law theory of explanation (which is also known as the Popper-Hempel theory of explanation). Similarly, although Popper does not classify himself as a logical positivist, he was influenced by them (and had considerable influence on Carnap), and his *Logic of Scientific Discovery* was published (in German) by the Vienna Circle, the birthplace and long-time home of logical positivism. The article by Passmore (1953) from which W&Z extracted a quotation is a defence of logical positivism.[21]

This puts logical positivists in the odd position of being the authorities on science cited to prove that the views of logical positivism are unscientific! W&Z claim support for PAT being scientific from logical positivists and then claim that logical positivism is unscientific, thereby destroying the support claimed. Thus, W&Z contradict themselves when they seek support from these authorities.[22]

[21] The only works listed in the References section of *Positive* that are not in accounting or economics are by the four authors mentioned in the text, plus Kockelmans. The piece by Kockelmans (1968) is a description of the views of Ernst Mach contained in an introduction to an article by Mach, and Mach was the inspiration of the logical positivism movement. Thus, *all* of the non-accounting, non-economics authorities that are submitted as support for the claim that PAT is scientific are either logical positivists or have a close relation to logical positivism, yet PAT discredits logical positivism, thereby impeaching its own witnesses.

[22] My view is that W&Z are correct when they disassociate their position from logical positivism, and that those, for example Christenson (1983), who classify them as logical positivists are in error. Although Chicago School positivism (developed, but not originated, by Milton Friedman and adopted,

Worse, the cited authorities take positions that are in direct opposition to the positions espoused by W&Z. A major section of Hempel (1965, the work cited by W&Z), for example, is devoted to the verifiability theory of meaning which if applied to such notions as lifo and fifo would result in them being discarded as meaningless rather than their selection being studied. Even clearer is the discussion of 'hage' (Hempel 1967, p. 46), which was expressly invented to demonstrate that such notions do not qualify as scientific concepts. Similarly, as mentioned above, Popper (1983, p. xx) uses the seeking-self-interest or utility-maximization concept as an example of a proposition that is not falsifiable and therefore not scientific. Indeed, it seems to me that the whole tenor of Popper's belief that the appraisal of a theory is coterminous with the appraisal of its critical discussion, as well as his insistence upon the requirement of severe attempts to falsify theories, is at variance with W&Z's failure to respond to criticism of PAT, as well as their focus on verification instead of falsification.

The same is true of Passmore's views about social science. If one reads the entire article (or even the entire paragraph) from which W&Z take the quotation, one would realize that the application of its views would discredit PAT instead of providing support for it. Passmore is explicitly opposed to the avoidance of issues of central importance which leads to triviality in social science, the wrong belief that science is the collection of information, mistaking cowardice for positivism , social advocacy disguised as science, simple-minded views about morality, and the like, all of which are contrary to PAT. The sentence immediately preceding the passage quoted by W&Z is instructive: 'A positive social science must be value-free in the sense that it is not social advocacy in disguise, but not in the sense that it has nothing to say about values' (Passmore, 1953, p. 676). W&Z, in contrast, evidently believe that being scientific precludes one from saying anything about values, as is evidenced when they 'positively' describe managerial theft (W&Z, 1986, p. 285).

I have not studied Poincaré so I cannot comment about the compatibility of his views with those of W&Z, but I can say that the views of Hempel, Passmore and Popper are frequently antipodal to those of W&Z. Therefore, we must reject W&Z's contention that those authorities provide support for PAT.

Since support might be found elsewhere I launched a 'positive study' designed to determine the degree of support for the basic ideas of PAT from scientific disciplines. Specifically, I asked a PhD candidate (who, not incidentally, is enamoured of PAT and also enamoured of needless empiricism) to gather empirical evidence by surveying the chairmen of all science departments at the University of Utah to see how many of them would accept a positive redefinition of their discipline. For example, would

- historians be willing to redefine 'history' so that its objective would be the explanation and prediction of historians' practices (selection of historiographic

often simplistically, by almost all graduate students who study related disciplines at the University of Chicago) and logical positivism may have the same ancestry, they have grown so far apart that it is now an error to say that they are identical or even similar.

techniques by practising historians) instead of an explanation of the events of the past?

- anthropologists be willing to begin studying the practices of anthropologists studying Samoans and abandon the study of Samoans, and, if so, what would anthropologists study when there were no more anthropologists studying Samoans to study?[23]
- mathematicians be willing to call articles about the utility-maximizing behaviour of mathematicians 'mathematics' and publish them in mathematics journals?
- clinical psychologists agree to begin trying to explain and predict the utility-maximizing behaviour of clinical psychologists instead of explaining and predicting behaviour of patients?

And so forth.

I assured the student that he would have publishable results if he could find just *one* department chairman who would accept a positive redefinition of his or her discipline, and I promised to reward him personally for such a finding by refraining from asking further Socratic questions about PAT. Despite the assured publication, the proffered reward, and a two-year time lapse, the student has not yet reported his findings. Although it would not be proper for me to infer anything from zero data, I must confess the suspicion that the absence of a report is due to failure to find even one instance of support for PAT. Until something beyond W&Z's *ipse dixit* is forthcoming, I will remain massively sceptical that such support exists.

If we look for support of various views about PAT, I recommend John Dewey, who is generally regarded to be the foremost philosopher ever produced in the American hemisphere, and a former professor at Chicago, who wrote:

> Anthropology, the study of the origin of myth, legend and cult . . . all tell us how men have thought and what have been the purposes and consequences of different kinds of thinking . . . The parrot-like repetition of the distinction between an empirical description of what is and a normative account of what should be merely neglects the most striking fact about thinking as it empirically is — namely, its flagrant exhibition of cases of failure and success — that is, of good thinking and bad thinking. (1920, pp. 135–6)

Although written many years ago, it explicitly and critically addresses both the study of people — their myths and legends — and the parroting of the positive/normative distinction, the two pillars of PAT.

[23] Such questions would be much easier to state and read (albeit less fun) if we had a name for the study of anthropologists. I suggest anthropologists-ology so that we could refer to those who study Samoans as anthropologists and those who study anthropologists as anthropologists-ologists. This avoids the apparent paradox of the positive redefinition of anthropology doing away with a subject matter to study by making it clear that the subject matter of anthropology is quite distinct from that of anthropologists-ology. The achievement of such clarity is the reason that I have suggested, not entirely facetiously, that we rename accounting 'plutology' (from Plutus, god of wealth, hence the study of wealth and wealth changes) so that those who want to study accountants could be called plutologists-ologists, the structure and repetitiveness of which might help them understand what they are studying, and that their study of plutologists does not require prohibition of studying wealth or other aspects of the firm.

ACCOMPLISHMENTS

In addition to their foundations, the assessment of the past, actual, and the future, potential, accomplishments of theories is helpful. They will be discussed in turn.

Actual

What have been the accomplishments of PAT? The final chapter (W&Z, 1986, pp. 352, 354, emphasis supplied) '. . . begins by summarizing the evolution of the theory and its *major empirical findings*' (p. 352, emphasis added). Those summarized findings are:

> (1) managers of firms with earnings-based compensation plans are more likely to choose procedures that increase current earnings (bonus hypothesis); (2) the larger a firm's debt/equity ratio the more likely the firm's manager is to select procedures that increase current earnings (debt/equity hypothesis); and (3) the larger the firm the more likely the manager selects procedures that decrease current earnings (size hypothesis). (p. 354)

That is, one can expect to observe managers manipulating accounting numerals when it is to their advantage to do so.[24] For example, according to the first (bonus) hypothesis, if a manager's compensation is based on an accounting numeral, he is more likely to manipulate that numeral than if he is not paid on that basis. And if compensation is a percentage of the accounting numeral, we can expect managers to manipulate the numeral to make it larger, not smaller.

W&Z then turn to an evaluation of the theory and discuss it under two headings: explanation and prediction. In regard to explanation they write:

> We think the theory is strong in this dimension in both accounting and auditing. To most, accounting is a confusing mixture of methods. We think the theory has the potential to give order to the confusion. The lower of cost or market rule becomes more understandable when cast in light of the manager's debt contract and compensation plan

[24] I believe that managers tend to manipulate accounting numerals when they perceive it to be to their advantage, but my belief is based on personal observations and reports of personal observations of others ('anecdotal evidence'), not on the positive tests of the three hypotheses. I think those tests are so flawed that if they were the only evidence, I doubt I would be persuaded that managers manipulate. First, the bonus hypothesis is concerned only with the *existence* of compensation plans — using a zero-one variable — which leaves out the characteristics of those plans. My limited experience on compensation committees causes me to believe that such plans vary so widely that the mere existence of a plan does not reveal enough to be the basis for a test. Second, my experience with giant corporations leads me to believe that they are not concerned about debt covenants for the simple reason that they are not governed by covenants. On the contrary, when observing several meetings of managers and lenders it became clear to me that the managers dictated the terms to the lenders rather than the other way around. I do not know the extent of this, but it does cause me to wonder about tests in which selection of accounting methods is interpreted as the result of managerial incentives to manipulate the debt/equity ratio because debt covenants specify some boundaries on that ratio, when the sample includes giant corporations that do not have such covenants. Third, the size hypothesis reminds me of the days when we had to go to the Agronomy Department to find courses in what was then advanced (now elementary) statistics, and my agronomy professor regularly brought the class back down to earth by calling attention to the fact that the size of the farms explained more than anything else that we had been discussing. Having learned that lesson, there are not many correlations with size that would surprise me.

> incentives to increase current earnings. . . . Choices between depreciation methods no longer appear arbitrary. (1986, p. 355)

Thus, confusion about accounting methods is dispelled by explaining that managers manipulate accounting numerals when they think it is to their advantage. For example, a manager's choice of one accounting numeral (depreciation) is easily understandable (not arbitrary) if it affects another accounting numeral (earnings) and her compensation is based on that (earnings) numeral.

The theory also:

> provides some predictions that should be useful to accounting users . . . but its potential in providing useful predictions is much greater . . . Using the theory, investors or analysts do not interpret balance sheet and earnings numbers as unbiased estimates of firm value and changes in firm value. Instead, they recognize the effect of the contracting and political process on the calculation of earnings and balance sheet numbers. For example, the manager's incentive to choose earnings increasing/decreasing accounting methods depend on the existing compensation and debt contracts. (W&Z, 1986, p. 356)

Thus, if accounting users recognize that managers are apt to manipulate the accounting numerals when it is to their advantage, they will not take the numerals to be unbiased estimates of value. If users could determine what the existing compensation and debt contracts are, they could predict which way, or maybe even by how much, managers will manipulate the accounting numerals. That is, 'an investor or analyst could adjust the earnings number for expected management manipulations . . .' (1986, p. 356).

In short, W&Z start with the *assumption* that all people act to maximize their utility when selecting accounting methods and after 350 pages they conclude with the *major empirical finding* that managers act to maximize their utility when selecting accounting methods.

That conclusion is underwhelming, being neither unexpected nor beneficial. It is not unexpected because we have a huge backlog of experience with some owners' and managers' tendency to seek their self-interest by manipulating accounting numerals (and by selling shoddy or impure merchandise, false labelling and misleading advertising, and short-changing their customers, among other things). That experience resulted in establishing the auditing function (and establishing various regulatory commissions, passage of laws requiring pure food and drugs, truth in labelling and advertising, and the habit of counting one's change, among other things). It is not beneficial because it is stated as a conclusion, as a solution to a problem and the end of the research path resulting in a theory, whereas I take it to be an uninformative restatement of a well-known problem, the place to begin research into ways to solve the problem.

For these reasons, I assess PAT's addition to knowledge to be nil, because such problems have been pointed out by normative theorists and others for decades.[25]

[25] Or for centuries if we go beyond accounting to measurement in general. The need for normatively correcting abuses in measurement was widely recognized, appearing in such unexpected places as the Magna Charta. One historian (Klein, 1974) explains that the reform attempted in the Magna

To cite just one normative theorist, MacNeal (1939) describes 'three fables' for the purpose of illustrating how utility-maximizing managers can manipulate accounting figures to their advantage and to the disadvantage of others. The difference is that MacNeal *begins* his book with that as a *statement of a problem* whereas W&Z *conclude* their book with that as a *major empirical finding*. Instead of following Popper's (1972, p. 44) advice to try to 'discover the most urgent problems' and then try to 'solve them', they have presented us with a well-known problem and prohibited us from solving it by requiring that we be positive, that we stop after providing descriptions of such events.

That we are not solving problems is evidenced by the increasing frequency of questions about the importance or significance of empirical findings being 'answered' with the comment that the researcher is providing a 'scientific description' and does not want to be normative or, like Joe Friday, wants to deal with 'just the facts ma'am' and not deal with 'policy issues'. The infamous bathtub counting of former sociologists was discredited because the number of bathtubs had no importance or significance (Brodbeck, 1968, pp. 6, 8) even though empirically, positively determined. (See Schreuder, 1985, for a delightful yet painful parody of PAT that makes the same point.) In accounting the crucial deficiency of insignificance is cloaked by irrelevant, often condescending, comments about being positive–good instead of normative–bad. Perhaps ridding ourselves of that terminology would jettison that cloak and expose the naked insignificance of the findings.[26]

The 'explanations' of PAT are equally unhelpful. To be told that the choice of an accounting method 'becomes more understandable when cast in light of the manager's debt contract and compensation plan incentives to increase current earnings' is the same as being told that the choice of surgical techniques, for example, Caesarian sections versus vaginal delivery, is understandable in light of surgeons' incentives to increase their income. Patients (or other surgeons) want a *medical* explanation and if surgical researchers supplied a positive explanation, it would be considered non-responsive, if not a travesty. To be told that accounting choices 'no longer appear arbitrary' when we understand managers' motivation to maximize their utility by maximizing earnings is the same as being told that the choice of a particular rotl (a Near Eastern unit of weight ranging from about one to six

Charta was not successful: 'The record of units of weight and measure used in England is, notwithstanding the Magna Charta, contradictory, complex and racy, replete with deviations, devices and dodges, most of them tending to enrich cheating merchants' (p. 29). Almost every housewife and schoolboy knew of the merchants' tendency to cheat, and of their need to guard against it, so there was no need for positive tests to establish that they were maximizing their utility by cheating, but there was considerable need to establish normatively 'uniform units, recognized, reproducible, and reproduced, on which buyers as well as sellers could rely'.

26 Another example of the perfidious effects of this language is the recent AAA document that speaks of the 'normative recommendations of the Bedford committee' as if 'positive recommendations' were an available alternative when in fact 'recommendation' *means* a suggestion presumably based on an evaluation, not a mere description of the extant state. At best such phrases contain redundancies and at worst they are vacuous slogans that may hinder something being said by veiling the fact that nothing is being said.

pounds) does not appear arbitrary when we understand Near Eastern butchers' motivation to maximize utility or earnings by maximizing reported weight.

Although W&Z claim 'predictive ability' for their theory, I doubt that investors and financial analysts will take much comfort in learning that they can improve their predictions by adjusting for expected management manipulation. In effect this says that if positive research can tell us about the incentives that butchers have to put a thumb on the scale, it will help us predict how often or how hard they will put it on the scale in the future. Is it better to improve predictions of future misleading financial statements by positively determining the kinds of incentives that managers have to mislead, or to try normatively to improve the truth content of financial statements?

One of the authorities on science cited by W&Z spoke of the fear that the 'actual effect of positivism in the social sciences is to lead to the production of a vast quantity of work that boasts of being scientific but is empty and commonplace' (Passmore, 1953, p. 675). In my view that fear has been realized in PAT.

Potential

What are the potential accomplishments? I forecast more of the same: twenty years from now we will have been inundated with research reports that managers and others tend to manipulate accounting numerals when it is to their advantage to do so. Given the positive-proscription of doing anything other than describing the often greedy, sometimes corrupt, utility-maximizing actions of management — because it would be normative to try to prevent such actions — we can expect the greedy and corrupt actions to continue, perhaps increase, so the same amount of, perhaps more, research will be needed in the future.

Boulding (1970) reminds us that 'just as no stream can rise above its source, no science can rise above its original data collection' (p. 185) and I would extend that principle to no science can rise above the questions it asks. PAT cannot rise above giving the same answers because it restricts itself to the descriptive questions. If it ever asked how to solve a problem or correct an error (both of which require going beyond a description to an evaluation of the situation), then it might go on to different questions and obtain different answers after the previous problem was solved. If we had restricted the medical question to the description of the smallpox virus, for example, precluding prescriptions to be vaccinated, we would need more and more descriptive studies as the virus population increased and mutations appeared. Luckily Edward Jenner was naughtily normative, which allowed him to discover how cowpox could be used as a vaccine so smallpox was eventually eliminated, which made room for different questions on the medical research agenda.

SUMMARY AND CONCLUSIONS

The first and most egregious error of PAT is its confusion of disparate subject matters. Initially it confuses the map (financial statements) with the territory (economic goods) and in extension it confuses accountants with accounting. Although it purports to be a study of accounting, it is in fact a study of accountants (and other people who select accounting methods). It should be abundantly obvious that accountant is to accounting as biologist is to biology, cartographer is to cartography, . . . , zoologist is to zoology, and that distinguishing the practitioner from the subject matter in all these disciplines is as crucial as it is obvious.

The second and most pernicious error of PAT is the restriction to the positive study of practices and practitioners. First, restriction to the study of practices and practitioners deprives us of knowledge of other things, and deprivation of knowledge is pernicious. Second, progress occurs only when research allows the (normative) judgment that *x* is in some sense better than *y* and therefore *x* ought to be used or implemented. To prohibit assessment of practices is to preclude progress, and thus restriction to being positive is pernicious.

The third and most untutored error of PAT is the allegation that it is in accord with economics and science. Although there is the parallel situation of national income accounting in economics, there is no parallel 'positive national income theory' in economics and mainstream economists consider the proposal to establish such a theory to be absurd. The only authority on economic methodology cited (other than Friedman's essay) contradicts W&Z on the basic point of Pareto optimality; other leading economic theorists (such as Paul Samuelson, 1963, and Herbert Simon, 1963) disagree with the type of theory employed in PAT; and others disagree with what type of data is admissible (as explained by Reder, 1982). Thus, the claim that PAT is in accord with mainstream economics is an error evidently resulting from viewing the whole of economics from the big end of a telescope.

And the situation is worse in regard to science. Instead of PAT applying the norms of science, it flagrantly violates those norms, even to the extent of disavowing all norms. Instead of PAT garnering support by applying the teachings of the scientific authorities cited, it contradicts those teachings. Claiming that PAT is in accord with science by citing logical positivists as authorities and then disassociating PAT from logical positivism leads me to conjecture that they had predetermined what they wanted to do and that they were looking for *excuses* to do that, which, like those who use accounting theories to bolster preconceived ideas, allowed them to look for the odd statement that, out of context, could be interpreted as support. Although that procedure might be acceptable in positive accounting, it is not acceptable in normative science.

The accomplishments of PAT are nonexistent. Instead of bringing forth interesting or unexpected or edifying results, PAT has presented us with findings that are empty and commonplace. When one *dis*proves the commonplace it is called a 'scientific discovery' and further tests are called 'confirmations' or 'replications' or similar names. After a sufficient number of confirmations, and a sufficient amount of time has passed, the discovery *becomes* the commonplace, and then further confirming tests are called 'wasted effort'. The putative accomplishments of PAT are in the category of wasted effort, and prohibiting the solving of problems, the prescription to stop at describing, presage more of the same.

POSTSCRIPT FOR THE GENERAL READER

This article is directed to the general reader, not to positive researchers, because I expect that positive researchers have gone too far to be redirected by argument or evidence. My hope is that the general reader has not become so swept up by the mistaken claims for PAT that it is too late for them to assess it. We accountants have a tendency to allow our course to be influenced by the fickle winds of fashion. Instead of examining the foundations of efficient market research, for example, many just jumped on the bandwagon and participated in the 'most concerted and ambitious research in accounting history' (Lev and Ohlson, 1982, p. 249) with, at best, paltry accomplishments. Most of those who in the beginning were so eager to embrace efficient markets subsequently became equally eager to distance themselves from them, and they are now even more eager to embrace PAT, a sequence more appropriate to the products of couturiers than of scientists.

Instead of flitting from one fad to the other, my recommendation is that we carefully assess proposed research programs *before* accepting or rejecting them. Those programs that are too undeveloped to be assessed should be set aside until they become sufficiently developed to permit assessment. In this way we will encourage innovation and new research directions but we will designate each novel research program a 'cottage industry' (as it is called in science) until it has proved itself. All will be free to work on any subject they like, to join the mainstream or create a new cottage industry, to establish a journal, and so forth, but judicious application of scientific standards will prevent any cottage industry from becoming the latest fad that dominates the journals, the agenda, the terminology, and so forth, to the virtual exclusion of all other research programs. Specifically, I recommend that we welcome PAT as a cottage industry and hope that it will surprise us someday by supplying us with some interesting, perhaps even significant, findings. But in no way should we accept it as the new fashion and condemn everything else as old-fashioned.

One of the ways to avoid being swept up by fads is to demand simplicity and clarity, and refuse to be intimidated by jargon, mathematical symbols, equations and highly stylized methods of expression that tend (intentionally or inadvertently) to cloud rather than clarify. A similar aid is to demand comprehensible overviews in plain language and refuse to be inundated with masses of data, repetitious studies, and unsupported assertions that tend (deliberately or accidentally) to conceal instead of reveal. Foundations of quicksand and empty findings should not be accepted because they are surrounded by such trappings because no amount of mathematical notation or statistical testing will bring a significant answer from a trivial question. In other disciplines leading scholars often explain difficult concepts to themselves as well as to others in 'pre-scientific terms' by employing simple analogies, such as Einstein's walking on a moving tram to explain relative motion, Leontief's cake recipe to explain production functions, Boyle's billiard balls to explain gas molecules, and so forth. If positive researchers do not offer such analogies (or otherwise make themselves clear), it may be an indication of the lack of understanding by the researchers because, as all teachers know, it is often the case that the reason a teacher cannot explain clearly is that the teacher does not understand clearly.

Clarity is a scientific norm[27] and the obscurity of an idea is reason for its rejection, not for its acceptance. In contrast, most accountants who have shared their thoughts with me about PAT have admitted, sooner or later, one way or another, that they do not understand it, *yet they are inclined to accept it.* I fear that in accounting we tend to err by equating the obscure with the profound, to believe that if we do not understand an idea, the fault lies with us instead of with the idea or the explanation of the idea. To believe that incomprehensibility is evidence of profundity has vast deleterious consequences, not the least of which is to foster obscurantism for, as Nietzsche cautioned, some may deliberately muddy the water to make it appear deep.

The contrapositive — equating the lucid with the superficial — is equally deleterious and probably more common. I suggest that it be named 'Groucho's guillotine' (in the tradition of Hume's guillotine, God's hatchet, and Ockham's razor) to indicate that it is similar to the way Groucho Marx gauged social clubs: he said he would never join a club that had standards low enough to permit him to join. As a referee or editor Groucho would probably have said that he would never accept an article that was stated simply and clearly enough to permit him to understand it. Several young friends have shared letters from editors (accompanied by referees' reports) that come very close to saying that the evidence for the rejected article's failure to contribute to knowledge is that it states its case clearly enough for the referees to understand it. Dyckman's (1989) perceptive remarks about the typical 'researcher [who] cleverly hides the results under bales of academic jargon *designed to secure publication* in an erudite academic journal' (p. 115, emphasis added) is, I fear, a description of a common response to Groucho's guillotine.

Diametrically opposed to Groucho's guillotine is 'Samuelson's razor' which is that all economic concepts 'that have no common-sense core that you can explain to your wife will soon fail' (Samuelson, 1963, p. 235) and therefore should be discarded. Having first-hand evidence that PAT fails that test, I recommend that accountants adopt the weaker, shamelessly stolen, 'Sterling's scalpel' which is that any accounting concept that does not have a common-sense core that you can explain to *yourself* should be discarded. I am confident that a careful application of that criterion in accounting will result in PAT becoming a cottage industry and displace it as the current dominant fad, as well as provide protection from future fads.

[27] As expressed by Popper (1972): 'aiming at simplicity and lucidity is a moral duty of all intellectuals: lack of clarity is a sin, and pretentiousness is a crime' (p. 44). Whether *Positive* is sinful or criminal (or neither or both) will be left to the judgment of the reader.

REFERENCES

Adler, J., and C. Van Doren, *How to Read a Book*, Simon and Schuster, 1972.

Bacon, F. *Advancement of Learning*, 1605.

Bell, P., 'Accounting as a Discipline for Study and Practice: 1986', *Contemporary Accounting Research*, Spring 1987.

Blaug, M., *The Methodology of Economics or How Economists Explain*, Cambridge University Press, 1980.

Boulding, K. E., *Economics as a Science*, McGraw-Hill, 1970.

Brodbeck, M., 'General Introduction', in M. Brodbeck (ed.), *Readings in the Philosophy of the Social Sciences*, Macmillan, 1968.

Christenson, C., 'The Methodology of Positive Accounting', *The Accounting Review*, January 1983.

Demski, J. S., 'Positive Accounting Theory: A Review', *Accounting Organizations and Society*, Vol. 13, No. 6, 1988.

Dewey, J., *Reconstruction in Philosophy* (enlarged edn), Beacon Press, 1920.

Duncan, K., 'Positive Theories of Accounting', in T. J. Burns (ed.), *Accounting Trends 21: Innovative Accounting and Information Systems: Course Outlines from Twenty-four Universities*, McGraw-Hill, 1987.

Dyckman, T. R., 'Commentary on Practice to Research — What Have You Done for Me Lately?', *Accounting Horizons*, March 1989.

Edwards, E. O., and P. W. Bell, *The Theory and Measurement of Business Income*, University of California Press, 1961.

Goudinoff, P., and S. Tobias, 'Mecham Is a Joke, But Voters May Have Last Laugh', *The Salt Lake Tribune*, 18 October 1987.

Hempel, C. G., *Aspects of Scientific Explanation and Other Essays in the Philosophy of Science*, The Free Press, 1965.

——, *Fundamentals of Concept Formation in Empirical Science*, The University of Chicago Press, 1967.

Hines, R. D., 'Popper's Methodology of Falsificationism and Accounting Research', *The Accounting Review*, October 1988.

Ijiri, Y., *Theory of Accounting Measurement*, Studies in Accounting Research No. 10, American Accounting Association, 1975.

Ivey, A. E., with L. Simek-Downing, *Counseling and Psychotherapy: Skills, Theories, and Practice*, Prentice-Hall, 1980.

Kinney, W. R., Jr, 'Commentary on The Relation of Accounting Research to Teaching and Practice: A "Positive" View', *Accounting Horizons*, March 1989.

Klein, H. A., *The Science of Measurement: A Historical Survey*, Dover Publications, 1974.

Kockelmans, J. H., 'Introduction [to Ernst Mach]', in J. H. Kockelmans (ed.), *The Philosophy of Science: The Historical Background*, The Free Press, 1968.

Koopmans, T. C., *Three Essays on The State of Economic Science*, McGraw-Hill, 1957.

Lev, B., and J. A. Ohlson, 'Market-Based Empirical Research in Accounting: A Review, Interpretation, and Extension', *Journal of Accounting Research*, Supplement, 1982.

Littleton, A. C., *Structure of Accounting Theory*, American Accounting Association Monograph No. 5, American Accounting Association, 1953.

Lowe, E. A., A. G. Puxty and R. C. Laughlin, 'Simple Theories for Complex Processes: Accounting Policy and the Market for Myopia', *Journal of Accounting and Public Policy*, Spring 1983.

MacNeal, Kenneth, *Truth in Accounting*, 1939; reprinted by Scholars Book Co., 1970.

McKee, A. James, Jr, T. B. Bell and J. R. Boatsman, 'Management Preferences Over Accounting Standards: A Replication and Additional Tests', *The Accounting Review*, October 1984.

Merton, R. K., *The Sociology of Science: Theoretical and Empirical Investigations*, Norman W. Storer (ed.), The University of Chicago Press, 1973.

Montagna, P. D., *Certified Public Accounting: A Sociological View of a Profession in Change*, Scholars Book Co., 1974.

Moonitz, M., 'Three Contributions to the Development of Accounting Principles Prior to 1900', *Journal of Accounting Research*, Spring 1970.

Nagel, E., *The Structure of Science*, Harcourt, Brace & World, 1961.

Passmore, J. A., 'Can the Social Sciences Be Value-Free?', in H. Feigl and M. Brodbeck (eds), *Readings in the Philosophy of Science*, Appleton-Century-Crofts, 1953.

Peasnell, K. V., and D. J. Williams, 'Ersatz Academics and Scholar-saints: The Supply of Financial Accounting Research', *Abacus*, September 1986.

Poincaré, H., *Science and Hypothesis*, Walter Scott, 1905.

Popper, K. R., *Objective Knowledge: An Evolutionary Approach*, The Clarendon Press, 1972.

——, *Realism and the Aim of Science*, Rowman and Littlefield, 1956, 1983.

——, *The Logic of Scientific Discovery*, Harper & Row, 1959.

Reder, M. W., 'Chicago Economics: Permanence and Change', *Journal of Economic Literature*, March 1982.

Revsine, L., *Replacement Cost Accounting*, Prentice-Hall, 1973.

Samuelson, P. A., 'Problems of Methodology — Discussion', *The American Economic Review*, May 1963.

Schreuder, H., 'Positively Normative (Accounting) Theories', in A. Hopwood and H. Schreuder (eds), *European Contributions to Accounting Research*, Free University of Amsterdam, 1984.

——, 'Suitable Research: On the Development of a Positive Theory of the Business Suit', *Accounting Organizations and Society*, Vol. 10, No. 1, 1985.

Simon, H. A., 'Problems of Methodology — Discussion', *The American Economic Review*, May 1963.

Simons, H., *Personal Income Taxation*, The University of Chicago Press, 1938.

Solomons, D., 'The Politicization of Accounting', *The Journal of Accountancy*, November 1978.

——, *Making Accounting Policy*, Oxford University Press, 1986.

Sterling, R. R., 'On Theory Construction and Verification', *The Accounting Review*, July 1970.

——, 'Introduction', in R. R. Sterling (ed.), *Research Methodology in Accounting*, Scholars Book Co., 1972.

——, 'Accounting Research, Education and Practice', *Journal of Accountancy*, September 1973.

——, 'Teaching the Correspondence Concept', *Issues in Accounting Education*, Spring 1989.

Watts, R. L., and J. L. Zimmerman, 'Toward a Positive Theory of the Determination of Accounting Standards', *The Accounting Review*, January 1978.

——, 'The Demand for and Supply of Accounting Theories: The Market for Excuses', *The Accounting Review*, April 1979.

——, *Positive Accounting Theory*, Prentice-Hall, 1986.

Whitley, R. D., 'The Possibility and Utility of Positive Accounting Theory', *Accounting, Organizations and Society*, Vol. 13, No. 6, 1988.

Whittington, G., 'Positive Accounting: A Review Article', *Accounting and Business Research*, Autumn 1987.

Williams, P. F., 'The Logic of Positive Accounting Research', *Accounting, Organizations and Society*, forthcoming.

Ziman, J., *Reliable Knowledge: An Exploration of the Grounds for Belief in Science*. Cambridge University Press, 1978.

OTHER PUBLICATIONS OF ROBERT R. STERLING

Books and Monographs

These publications have not been reproduced in this volume. The numerical sequence follows that started in the *Contents* section.

46. *Theory of the Measurement of Enterprise Income*, University Press of Kansas, 1970.

47. (With W. F. Bentz) (eds.), *Accounting in Perspective*, South-Western Publishing Co. 1971.

48. (ed.), *Asset Valuation and Income Determination: A Consideration of the Alternatives*, Scholars Book Co., 1971.

49. (ed.), *Research Methodology in Accounting*, Scholars Book Co., 1972.

50. (ed.), *Institutional Issues in Public Accounting*, Scholars Book Co., 1972.

51. (contributor), *A Statement of Accounting Theory and Theory Acceptance*, American Accounting Association, 1977.

52. (contributor), *Book-Reserving Pension Fund Contributions*, George B. Buck Consulting Actuaries Inc., 1978.

53. (with A. L. Thomas) (eds.), *Accounting for a Simplified Firm Owning Depreciable Assets: Seventeen Essays and a Synthesis Based on a Common Case*, Scholars Book Co., 1979.

54. *Toward a Science of Accounting*, Scholars Book Co., 1979.

55. *A Critique of Physical Capital*, University of Waikato Press, 1981.

56. (with K. Lemke) (eds.), *Maintenance of Capital: Financial Versus Physical*, Scholars Book Co., 1982.

Articles and Other Contributions

57. 'Advanced Accounting Theory' and 'Seminar for Contemporary Accounting Theory,' in T. J. Burns (ed.), *Accounting Trends II*, McGraw Hill, 1968.

58. 'An Abstract of Accounting Theory,' *Annuals of Economics and Management Science*, 1968.

59. 'An Explication of the Structure of Accounting,' in K. Larson (ed.), *The Accounting Colloquium*, University of Texas, 1969-70.

60. 'Costs Versus Values: An Empirical Test,' *The Australian Accountant*, June 1971.

61. (contributor), 'Report of the Committee on Accounting Theory Construction and Verification,' *The Accounting Review*, Supplement, 1971.

62. 'Liquidity and Assigned Values,' *DR Scott Memorial Lectures in Accountancy*, Volume III, University of Missouri, 1971.

63. 'Conflicts in Income Measurement,' *Accounting Papers of the Twenty-Fifth Annual Conference of Accountants*, University of Tulsa, 1971.

64. 'Accounting Power,' *Oklahoma CPA*, July 1972.

65. 'Decision-Orientated Financial Accounting,' *Accounting and Business Research*, Summer 1972.

66. 'Research Methods Appropriate for Accounting,' in R. R. Sterling (ed.), *Research Methodology in Accounting*, Scholars Book Co., 1972.

67. 'Accounting Research, Education and Practice: Conflicts, Compromises or Complements,' *Journal of Business Administration*, Spring 1973.

68. 'BAAD: Board to Adjudicate Accounting Disputes,' *Proceedings of Ernst & Ernst Symposium for Educators*, Ernst & Ernst, July 1973.

69. *Current Value Accounting in the Extrastive Industries*, Southwest Legal Foundation, 1974.

70. *Accounting for Changes in Prices and Price Levels*, University of California, 1974.

71. 'Legislating Accounting Principles: Synergism or Dissidence,' *Proceedings of the Ross Institute Symposium*, 1974.

72. 'Are Oil Profits Obscene?,' *Petroleum Independent*, January-February 1975.

73. 'The Coming Revolution in Accounting,' *Presidential Lecture*, Rice University, February 1975.

74. 'The Future of the Accounting Profession: An Academic Perspective,' *Proceedings of the Arthur M. Sargent Symposium on Public Accounting and Futurism*, October 1975.

75. 'A Difference of Opinion,' *Fortune*, January 14, 1980.

76. A Rating of the Conceptual Framework,' *Proceedings of a Symposium: Conceptual Framework for Financial Accounting and Reporting*, Financial Accounting Standard Board, June 1980.

77. 'Physical Capital: An Examination,' *Emmanuel Saxe Distinguished Lecture*, CUNY Press, January 1981.

78. 'An Evaluation of the Structure of Accounting Theory,' *Proceedings of the Clarkson Gordon Foundation Research Symposium*, May 1981.

79. 'After 8 Years Is the End in Sight,' *FASB Viewpoints*, Financial Accounting Standards Board, June 2, 1982.

80. 'Status of Conceptual Framework Projects,' *Status Report*, Financial Accounting Standards Board, March 3, 1983.

81. 'The Conceptual Framework,' *Journal of Accountancy*, July 1983.

82. 'Establishing GASB,' *Research in Governmental and Non-Profit Accounting*, Volume 1, 1985.

83. 'The Stuff and Nonsense of Setting Standards,' *Business Review Weekly*, November 1, 1985.

REPRODUCTIONS OF THE PUBLICATIONS OF ROBERT R. STERLING

The numbers relate to the numerical sequence used in the *Contents* section of this volume, and in the *Other Publications* section.

1. In R. N. Anthony, A. D. Barton, *et al* (eds.), *Readings in Advanced Financial Accounting*, Butterworths, 1979.

4. In *Price Waterhouse Distinguished Lecture Series*, Stamford University, 1975.

   In *The Week in Review*, Haskins & Sells, October 1975 (abridged).

   The Arthur Andersen Chronicle, January 1976.

   In J. J. Staunton (ed.), *Theory Construction and Verification in Accounting*, University of New England, 1976.

   In *National Investor Relations Institute Notes*, January 1976.

   In R. N. Anthony, A. D. Barton, *et al* (eds.), *Readings in Advanced Financial Accounting*, Butterworths, 1979.

6. In *World*, Spring 1976.

   In *Transactions*, Michigan State University, 1976.

10. In E. S. Hendricksen and B. P. Budge (eds.), *Contemporary Accounting Theory*, Dickenson Publishing Company, 1974.

12. In J. J. Staunton (ed.), *Theory Construction and Verification in Accounting*, University of New England, 1976.

15. In J. J. Staunton, (ed.), *Theory Construction and Verification in Accounting*, University of New England, 1976.

16. In Harvard case studies, American Management Association readings, University of Washington accounting readings, Dalhousie University accounting readings, University of Wyoming College of Commerce case studies, IPADE Mexico case studies, and Certified General Accountants' Association of Canada lesson notes.

In B. N. Schwartz (ed.), *Readings in Financial Accounting*, Dickenson Publishing, 1975.

In P. Rosenfield (ed.), *Accounting for Price Levels in Four Countries*, Prentice-Hall, 1975.

In Ohio State University, *Executive Development Program*, August 1975.

In *The Chartered Financial Analyst's Digest*, 1975

In S. Davidson, C. P. Stickney and R. L. Weil (eds.), *Inflation Accounting: A Guide for the Accountant and the Financial Analyst*, McGraw Hill, 1976.

In R. F. Vancil and R. L. Weil (eds.), *Replacement Cost Accounting: Readings on Concepts, Uses and Methods.* Thomas Horton and Daughters, 1976.

In D. Fraser, M. O'Conner and P. Shelluch (eds.), *Issues in External Reporting*, New South Wales University Press, 1979.

22. In T. J. Burns and H. S. Hendricksen (eds.), *The Accounting Sampler*, McGraw Hill, 1972.

In G. J. Staubus, *Making Accounting Decisions*, Scholars Book Co., 1977.

23. In R. G. J. Vangermeersch (ed.), *Accounting: Socially Responsible and Socially Relevant*, Harper & Row, 1972.

In S. A. Zeff and T. F. Keller (eds.), *Financial Accounting Theory: Issues and Controversies*, McGraw Hill, 1973.

30. In University of Western Ontario case studies, and Harvard case studies.

In P. H. Eddey and M. C. Miller (eds.), *Issues in External Reporting*, University of New South Wales, 1975.

In D. Fraser, M. O'Conner and P. Shelluch (eds.), *Issues in External Reporting*, New South Wales University Press, 1979.

37. In G. J. Staubus, *Making Accounting Decisions*, Scholars Book Co., 1977.

39. In W. T. Baxter and S. Davidson (eds.), *Studies in Accounting* Theory, Irwin, 1975.

In W. T. Baxter and S. Davidson (eds.), *Studies in Accounting*, Institute of Chartered Accountants in England and Wales, 1977.

46. Reprinted by Scholars Book Co., 1979.

47. Reprinted by Scholars Book Co. 1978.

64. In G. J. Staubus, *Making Accounting Decisions*, Scholars Book Co., 1977.

In R. H. Parker (ed.), *Readings in Accounting and Business Research: 1970-1977*, Institute of Chartered Accountants in England and Wales, 1978.

In R. N. Anthony, A. D. Barton, *et al* (eds.), *Readings in Advanced Financial Accounting Theory*, Butterworths, 1979.

For Product Safety Concerns and Information please contact our EU representative GPSR@taylorandfrancis.com Taylor & Francis Verlag GmbH, Kaufingerstraße 24, 80331 München, Germany